The OECD's Global Minimum Tax and Its Implementation in the EU

The OECD's Global Minimum Tax and Its Implementation in the EU

A Legal Analysis of Pillar Two in the Light of Tax Treaty and EU Law

Valentin Bendlinger

Wolters Kluwer

Published by:
Kluwer Law International B.V.
PO Box 316
2400 AH Alphen aan den Rijn
The Netherlands
E-mail: lrs-sales@wolterskluwer.com
Website: www.wolterskluwer.com/en/solutions/kluwerlawinternational

Sold and distributed by:
Wolters Kluwer Legal & Regulatory U.S.
920 Links Avenue
Landisville, PA 17538
United States of America
E-mail: customer.service@wolterskluwer.com

ISBN 978-94-035-3287-5

e-Book: ISBN 978-94-035-3297-4
web-PDF: ISBN 978-94-035-3307-0

To my love Ranjana

Table of Contents

List of Figures

List of Tables

List of Abbreviations and Acronyms

General Abbreviations

ACTT	Additional Current Top-up Tax
AOA	Authorized OECD Approach
AT	Austria
BE	Belgium
BEFIT	Business in Europe: Framework for Income Taxation
BG	Bulgaria
Bull.	Bulletin
Can.	Canada/Canadian
CbC	Country-by-Country
CbCR	CbC Reporting
CCCTB	Common Consolidated Corporate Tax Base
CE	Constituent Entity
CEs	Constituent Entities
CFA	Committee of Fiscal Affairs
CFC	Controlled Foreign Company
CFR	Charter of Fundamental Rights of the European Union
CIL	Customary International Law
CIT	Corporate Income Tax
CJEU	Court of Justice of the European Union
CY	Cyprus
CZ	Czech Republic
DE	Germany
DK	Denmark
DST	Digital Services Tax
DTC	Double Tax Convention

e.g.	exempli gratia (for example)
ECJ	European Court of Justice
E-Commerce	Electronic Commerce
ed.	Editor/edition
eds	editors
EE	Estonia
ES	Spain
et. seq.	et sequens (and the following)
ETR	Effective Tax Rate
EU	European Union
EUR	Euro
FI	Finland
Fla.	Florida
FR	France
GAAP	General Accepted Accounting Principles
GloBE	Global Anti-Base-Erosion
GR	Greece
HR	Croatia
HU	Hungary
i.a.	*inter alia* (among others)
ibid.	ibidem (repetition of the preceding citation)
i.e.	in example
IAS	International Accounting Standards
IBFD	International Bureau of Fiscal Documentation
IE	Ireland
IF	Inclusive Framework
IFRS	International Financial Reporting Standards
IIR	Income Inclusion Rule
Intl.	International
IPE	Intermediate Parent Entity
IRD	Interest and Royalties Directive
IT	Italy
J.	journal
JV	Joint Venture(s)
LT	Lithuania
LTCE	Low-Taxed Constituent Entity
LU	Luxembourg
LV	Latvia
MLC	Multilateral Convention
MLI	Multilateral Instrument

MNE	Multinational Enterprise
MOCE	Minority-Owned Constituent Entity
MOPE	Minority-Owned Parent Entity
MT	Malta
n.	note/footnote
NL	Netherlands
OCI	Other Comprehensive Income
OECD	Organisation for Economic Co-operation and Development
OECD MC	OECD Model Tax Convention
OECD TPG	OECD Transfer Pricing Guidelines
p.	page
Pac.	Pacific
para.	paragraph
paras	paragraphs
PE	permanent establishment
PEs	permanent establishments
PL	Poland
POPE	Partially Owned Parent Entity
PoW	Programme of Work to Develop a Consensus Solution to the Tax Challenges Arising from the Digitalisation of the Economy (OECD Report, 31 May 2019)
pp.	pages
PSD	Parent-Subsidiary Directive
PT	Portugal
QDMTT	Qualified Domestic Top-up Tax
RO	Romania
SBIE	Substance-Based Income Exclusion
SE	Sweden
s.	section
SI	Slovenia
SK	Slovakia
SOR	Switch-Over Rule
STTR	Subject-To-Tax-Rule
TAG	Technical Advisory Group
Taxn.	Taxation
TEU	Treaty of the EU
TFEU	Treaty of the Functioning of the EU
UN	United Nations
UPE	Ultimate Parent Entity
US	United States

USA	United States of America
USD	United States Dollar
UTPR	Undertaxed Profits Rule
v.	versus
VAT	Value-Added Tax
VCLT	Vienna Convention on the Law of Treaties

Abbreviations of Cited Journals

Asia-Pac. Tax Bull.	Asia-Pacific Tax Bulletin (IBFD)
BTR	British Tax Review
Bull. Intl. Taxn.	Bulletin for International Taxation (IBFD)
Can. Tax J.	Canadian Tax Journal
Col. L. Rev.	Columbia Law Review
digitax	beck.digitax
Dea. L. Rev.	Deakin Law Review
EJIL	European Journal of International Law
EuR	Europarecht (Journal)
EuZW	Europäische Zeitschrift für Wirtschaftsrecht
Eur. Taxn.	European Taxation
Fla. Tax Review	Florida Tax Review
Fla. J. Int'l L.	Florida Journal of International Law
Harv. Int'l. Law. J.	Harvard International Law Journal
IStR	Internationales Steuerrecht (Beck)
ITPJ	International Transfer Pricing Journal
Nat. Tax J.	National Tax Journal
StAW	Spektrum der Steuerwissenschaften und des Außenwirtschaftsrechts
StuW	Steuern und Wirtschaft
Syracuse J. Int'l L.	Syracuse Journal of International Law and Commerce
SWI	Steuer- und Wirtschaft International
SWK	Steuer- und Wirtschafts Kartei
Tax Mgt. Int'l J.	Tax Management International Journal
Tax Notes Int'l	Tax Notes International
Tul. Eur. & Civ. Law. F.	Tulane European and Civil Law Forum
Tul. Law Rev.	Tulane Law Review
TPI	Transfer Pricing International
Va. Tax Rev.	Virginia Tax Review
WTJ	World Tax Journal (IBFD)

Preface and Acknowledgements

The OECD's Pillar Two project has shaped the global tax community in recent years: hardly any other topic has been discussed and debated as intensively and emotionally as the global minimum tax. When the author of this book began to examine the global minimum tax from the perspective of a PhD student in May 2019, the OECD published a policy note and a work programme. Even the authors of these reports probably did not believe that the global minimum tax would become a hard reality within less than the following five years. Now, in July 2023, the OECD has already published thousands of pages on Pillar Two and has recently released its second update of the Commentary to the OECD Model Rules, which the EU has already converted into a binding directive that will come into force in early 2024. The fast-moving nature of the subject soon proved to be a particular challenge for a PhD project. However, it was the excitement of these tax policy developments that attracted the author and motivated him to complete this book, which is based on the doctoral thesis of the author that had been accepted at the Vienna University of Economics and Business Administration in March 2023 and successfully defended in 2023. This book takes into account all developments up to and including August 2023.

However, it would be presumptuous to believe that this book would have been possible without the generous support of many people. First of all, I would like to thank my main supervisor, supporter and mentor, Prof. *Georg Kofler*. When the global minimum tax was still unknown to most people, even in the global tax community, he advised me with incredible foresight to devote myself to what was called Pillar Two. His support, however, went far beyond a topic suggestion: he not only taught me the craft of academic work but also guided me through the jungle of international tax policy and European tax law; finally, I followed him to the Institute for Austrian and International Tax Law at the Vienna University of Economics and Business (WU), when he left Johannes Kepler University of Linz (JKU) in 2020.

This brings me to the Institute for Austrian and International Tax Law, to which I also owe a great deal. First of all, I would like to thank Prof. *Alexander Rust* and Prof. *Daniela Hohenwarter-Mayr* (now at the University of Vienna), both of whom took on the arduous task of co-supervising and reviewing my dissertation and were always available for advice and assistance. I would also like to acknowledge the generous support of Prof. *Michael Lang* and Prof. *Claus Staringer*, who were not only great academic role models but also gave me the freedom to pursue my research at the Institute. Their legal writings have influenced this book at various points. Special thanks also go to Dr *Christoph Marchgraber* and Prof. *Kasper Dziurdz*, who gave me extremely valuable input on the content of this book. I would also like to thank Prof. *Daniel Blum*, Prof. *Karoline Spies*, and Prof. *Rita Szudoczky*, who have been instrumental in helping me to improve my legal writing and academic methodology. In addition, there were many other colleagues and friends, including *Rainer Borns, Eric Coenen, Valentina Emanuele, Florian Fiala, Thomas Frenkenberger, Michael Gleiss, Stefanie Gombotz, Vera Hellebrandt, Michael Hubmann*, Dr *Andreas Langer, Yasmin Lawson*, Dr *Martin Klokar, Christian Knotzer, Bence Péter Komár, Yasmin Lawson*, Dr *Matthias Mayer, Markus Mittendorfer, Katharina Moldaschl, Marcelo Moura, Theres Neumüller, Nicholas Pacher*, Dr *Christina Pollak, Kilian Posch, Mario Riedl, Jürgen Romstorfer, Philipp Scharizer, Severin Schragl, Stefanie Stöcklinger*, Dr *Annika Streicher*, Dr *Selina Siller, Iris Tschatsch, Andreas Ullmann* and *Franz Wallig*, and many others who have accompanied me during my time at the Institute for Austrian and International Tax Law. In view of the size of our Institute, I hope that if I have forgotten to mention anyone, you will forgive me.

The support I received at the Johannes Kepler University of Linz should also not go unmentioned. I am very grateful for the training I received from Prof. *Markus Achatz*, Prof. *Michael Tumpel* and Prof. *Thomas Bieber*, whose mentorship also inspired me in many ways and encouraged me to write a dissertation. In addition, I would also like to mention *Michael Denk*, Dr *Daniel Leonov*, Dr *Martin Greifeneder*, and Dr *Manuel Neusiedler*, who were all very influential in the early stages of my career as a legal researcher.

But what would professional support be without family? Of course, this book would not exist without my beloved mother, *Elisabeth Bendlinger*, who will always be in my heart. Furthermore, it is difficult to find the right words to thank my parents, Prof. *Stefan Bendlinger* and *Sabine Bendlinger*, as well as my dear aunt *Maria Schenk-Neumann*, who have been there for me even in the most difficult situations of my life. Most importantly, I would like to thank the love of my life, Dr *Ranjana Andrea Achleitner*. She was not just another academic role model. Rather, she gave me love and support and motivated me to carry on when I would have given up, even at times when I must have been unbearable. Dear Ranjana, I cannot tell you how grateful I am to have you in my life. May this book be dedicated to you!

CHAPTER 1
Introduction

Rarely in the history of international tax law have there been so many evolutions in such a short space of time: The fight against aggressive tax planning and artificial profit shifting is one of the top priorities for policymakers, especially in the Organisation for Economic Co-operation and Development (OECD) and the EU, both of which are increasingly vying to be the leaders in global tax policy. While bilateral double tax conventions (DTCs) once dominated the international tax world, the OECD's BEPS project has unleashed a wave of multilateralization that dwarfs previous developments in international tax law. In a dizzying array of reports, work programs, consultations and announcements, the OECD, with active support from the EU, has created a framework for a global minimum tax that is unprecedented even in the traditionally complex field of tax law. But even more impressively, this wave of multilateralism has also overcome previously insurmountable hurdles: The OECD's GloBE Model Rules[1] and Commentary[2] are now supported by more than 140 Inclusive Framework (IF) member countries.[3] A significant number of jurisdictions have already decided to fully implement the complex regulatory framework of Pillar Two,[4] and even jurisdictions

1. OECD/G20 Inclusive Framework on BEPS, *Tax Challenges Arising from Digitalisation – The Global Anti-Base Erosion Model Rules (Pillar Two)* (OECD 20 Dec. 2021), https://www.oecd.org/tax/beps/tax-challenges-arising-from-the-digitalisation-of-the-economy-global-anti-base-erosion-model-rules-pillar-two.pdf (last visited 22 Mar. 2022).
2. OECD/G20 Inclusive Framework on BEPS, *Tax Challenges Arising from Digitalisation – Commentary to the Global Anti-Base Erosion Model Rules (Pillar Two)* (OECD 14 Mar. 2022), https://www.oecd.org/tax/beps/tax-challenges-arising-from-the-digitalisation-of-the-economy-global-anti-base-erosion-model-rules-pillar-two-commentary.pdf (last visited 22 Mar. 2022).
3. *See* the regularly updated list of IF Member States as of 1 Dec. 2022 OECD, *Members of the OECD/G20 Inclusive Framework on BEPS (Updated: December 2022)* (1 Dec. 2022), https://www.oecd.org/tax/beps/inclusive-framework-on-beps-composition.pdf (last visited 25 Mar. 2023).
4. *See*, e.g., UK, the Netherlands, Germany, Liechtenstein, South Korea and Switzerland having already published draft legislation to implement the global minimum tax, *see* for the UK https://assets.publishing.service.gov.uk/government/uploads/system/uploads/attachment_data/file/1092586/Draft_legislation.pdf (accessed 6 Feb. 2023); for the Netherlands Ministerie van Financiën, nieuwsbericht, *Netherlands Launches Online Consultation on Draft Bill for the Proposed Minimum Tax Rate Act 2024 – News Item – Government.Nl*, https://www.government.nl

once known to be tax havens have announced plans to increase their domestic corporate tax rates or have even decided to introduce unprecedented comprehensive systems of corporate income tax.[5] It can already be argued that the OECD's Pillar Two objective of curbing tax competition is starting to materialize. The 'critical mass' of jurisdictions to implement a global tax cartel in the form of a minimum tax rate of 15% for multinational groups with a revenue of EUR 750 million seems to be forming. Even within the EU, where the development of tax law has often been accused of being at a standstill, it has not been possible to stop the wave of multilateralism. Despite prolonged resistance from several Member States, the EU-wide adoption of Pillar Two has finally achieved the long unthinkable and overcome the hurdle of unanimity. In December 2022, the EU Commission solemnly announced that the GloBE-Directive[6] had successfully been approved by the Council, despite the fact that harmonization of tax rates for direct taxes has previously been an absolute taboo in the EU.

The more quickly a major wave of regulatory changes happens, the more traces it leaves. And now that the waters around the Pillar Two project are calming down for the first time, these traces are becoming visible. The real challenges of this implementation are becoming apparent: The various IF Member States face the challenge of incorporating an incredibly complex set of rules into their national legal systems. Various normative conflicts and systemic weaknesses are becoming apparent that simply had not been considered or had been ignored during the rapid evolution of the global minimum tax debate. The once underestimated relationship between the minimum tax and the existing division of tax sovereignty is coming to light, and within the EU, for the first time, the Member States have to face the dilemma that they run the risk of having to break their existing tax treaties due to EU law requirements. The debate on how far EU tax harmonization can go and where its limits lie is resurfacing. The question arises as to how the OECD and the EU influence each other and what influence developments at the OECD level can have on the interpretation of EU law.

/latest/news/2022/10/24/netherlands-launches-online-consultation-on-draft-bill-for-the-proposed-minimum-tax-rate-act-2024 (last visited 9 Feb. 2023); for Germany German Ministry of Finance, *Entwurf eines Gesetzes für die Umsetzung der Richtlinie zur Gewährleistung einer globalen Mindestbesteuerung für multinationale Unternehmensgruppen und große inländische Gruppen in der Union (Mindestbesteuerungsrichtlinie-Umsetzungsgesetz – MinBestRL-UmsG)* (17 Mar. 2023); for Liechtenstein Administration of Liechtenstein, *Press Release – Regierung verabschiedet Vernehmlassungsbericht zur Einführung der globalen Mindestbesteuerung in Liechtenstein*,/de/medienmitteilungen/regierung-verabschiedet-vernehmlassungsbericht-zur-einfuehrung-der-globalen-mindestbesteuerung-in-liechtenstein (last visited 19 Apr. 2023); on the South Korean draft legislation, *see 'First Domestic Pillar Two Global Minimum Tax Law Enacted'* (9 Jan. 2023), https://oecdpillars.com/first-domestic-pillar-two-global-minimum-tax-law-enacted-2/ (last visited 9 Feb. 2023); and for Switzerland, *see* the Swiss draft legislation available at https://www.newsd.admin.ch/newsd/message/attachments/72626.pdf (accessed 6 Feb. 2023).

5. *See*, e.g., the Cayman Islands and the Bahamas, well known for establishing a very comfortable tax environment for corporations, have announced to implement Pillar Two, *see* Lee Hadnum, *The Bahamas & Cayman Islands Approach To The Global Minimum Tax*, oecdpillars.com, https://oecdpillars.com/the-bahamas-seychelles-approach-to-the-global-minimum-tax/ (last visited 19 Apr. 2023).
6. Council Directive (EU) 2022/2523 of 14 Dec. 2022 on ensuring a global minimum level of taxation for multinational enterprise groups and large-scale domestic groups in the Union, OJ (2523).

Above all, the EU faces unique challenges but, at the same time, opportunities: The external competence of the EU in direct tax law is becoming an issue, and the harmonization of tax bases is no longer a utopia.

All of these questions await answers. For this reason, the following thesis aims to address fundamental and technical issues regarding the global minimum tax (in the following global anti-base erosion (GloBE)). The thesis aims to shed light on the complex ramifications of the technical framework of GloBE and intends to explore the complex relationship between OECD's soft-law materials, including the GloBE Model Rules and the GloBE Commentary, DTCs and the EU's recently adopted GloBE-Directive.

CHAPTER 2
Procedure of the Examination and Methods Applied

2.1 RESEARCH QUESTIONS, STRUCTURE AND SCOPE OF THE THESIS

The goal of this thesis is to deeply analyse the OECD's GloBE Model Rules[7] as well as the EU's GloBE-Directive[8] and to explore how a minimum taxation system could be appropriately implemented in the current framework of bilateral tax treaties and EU law. The scope of this thesis, however, is limited to the *substantive* issues of the global minimum tax. Questions of procedural and administrative law have been deliberately excluded for reasons of scope and will, therefore, only be dealt with in passing.

The formulation of a clear research question is an essential part of the development of a thesis. The central research question of the proposed thesis reads as follows:

How does the global minimum tax pursuant to the OECD's GloBE Model Rules work, in which way has it been adopted within the GloBE-Directive (Directive 2022/2523), what effects can a minimum taxation system achieve, how does GloBE relate to tax treaty and customary international law, how can potential conflicts between GloBE and tax treaties or potential customary international law be solved and what is the impact of the EU's GloBE-Directive on the EU's legal order and on the domestic legal spheres of EU Member States?

7. *GloBE Model Rules*.
8. GloBE-Directive (2022/2523).

As can be seen, the question is broad and can be divided into several sub-questions that must be addressed within this thesis. In an overview, the study will be divided into four substantive sections:

Section 3 of the thesis deals with the background of discussion about minimum taxation. This chapter will comprehensively review the background of the OECD GloBE Proposal. It will first discuss the emergence of the E-Commerce discussion in international tax law and will, thus, start with the OECD's Ottawa taxation framework in 1998[9] and will further discuss the evolution of the debate on the taxation of the Digital Economy in the course of the OECD BEPS project.[10] Finally, the section will analyse the development of the OECD's global tax reform in the form of the two-pillar solution to further elaborate on the background of the global minimum tax[11] and eventually give an overview of the status quo of the current Pillar Two implementation.[12]

Section 4 will focus on the technical design of the global minimum tax pursuant to the OECD's GloBE Model Rules and the GloBE-Directive. The current design of the global minimum tax regime will be comprehensively reviewed in this section. The whole section will discuss both the OECD's GloBE Model Rules as well as the GloBE-Directive. For this reason, this section will first contain a short note on the relevance of the OECD materials for the interpretation of the GloBE-Directive.[13] The structure of section 4 will follow that of the GloBE Model Rules and the GloBE-Directive as closely as possible. Both the GloBE Model Rules and their implementation within the GloBE-Directive will be discussed in parallel. This approach aims to identify and investigate deviations between the GloBE Model Rules and their implementation within the EU. The thesis will first move into the technical framework of GloBE and will begin by exploring the scope of GloBE.[14] This is followed by extensive sections on the calculation of the ETR[15] on the one hand and on the calculation of the 'Top-up Tax' on the other.[16] These parts mainly explore the technical details for the actual calculation and collection of the minimum tax. The actual tax policy consequences of the complex framework ultimately emerge only from the analysis of the technical functioning of GloBE's system. For this reason, the last subsection of section 4 will form eight policy-related theses resulting from the technical analysis of GloBE.[17]

Section 5 will then focus on the relation of GloBE to existing international tax law. The purpose of section 5 is to examine how GloBE fits into the decades-old framework of international tax law and will identify whether there are potential conflicts between GloBE and how such conflicts could be solved. First, section 5 will give an overview of the issue and the state of the debate.[18] It will define the sources of

9. *See* s. 3.1.
10. *See* s. 3.2.
11. *See* s. 3.3.
12. *See* s. 3.4.
13. *See* s. 4.1.
14. *See* s. 4.2.
15. *See* s. 4.3.
16. *See* s. 4.4.
17. *See* s. 4.5.
18. *See* s. 5.1.

international tax law that might be relevant for analysing GloBE's compatibility with the existing international tax landscape. For this reason, section 5 will start with the analysis of potential conflicts between tax treaties and the regulatory framework of GloBE.[19] This analysis will primarily be based on the OECD Model Tax Convention (OECD MC) and common deviations among the international network of bilateral tax treaties. Once the thesis has identified whether and what potential normative conflicts might arise, it will explore the question of how such conflicts are to be solved. Separate subsections are devoted to the resolution of normative conflicts between domestic GloBE implementation[20] and the resolution of normative conflicts between the EU's GloBE-Directive and tax treaties concluded by the Member States.[21] Finally, another subsection is devoted to the question of whether GloBE might conflict with sources of customary international (tax) law[22] and eventually, section 5 will end with a conclusion on the relation of GloBE and international tax law.[23]

Section 6 will discuss the legal issues GloBE raises within the legal framework of the EU. The section will start with a short overview of the recent developments in EU tax policy and the EU's involvement in the development of Pillar Two.[24] The section will elaborate on the emergence of the GloBE-Directive and will first address constitutional issues around the GloBE-Directive. First of all, the division of internal competences between the EU and the Member States with respect to direct taxation will be analysed to answer the question of whether the enactment of the GloBE-Directive was in line with the division of competence within the Treaty of the Functioning of the EU (TFEU).[25] Once the question of internal competence has been addressed, the thesis will explore the question of whether the EU gains external competence with respect to the regulatory content of the GloBE-Directive.[26] After that, the thesis moves on to the question of how the GloBE-Directive fits into the EU's internal market. In particular, the relationship of the GloBE-Directive to fundamental freedoms[27] and the prohibition of state aid[28] will be examined. As a consequence, the question of the relationship to other secondary legal acts of the Union also arises.[29] Finally, an interim conclusion will outline the expected impact of the GloBE-Directive on the legal order of the EU.[30]

Section Chapter 7 of this thesis will finally draw the conclusions of this examination. This section aims to finally summarize the research findings of the previous sections to finally answer the research question(s) presented at the beginning of this section.

19. *See* s. 5.2.
20. *See* s. 5.3.
21. *See* s. 5.4.
22. *See* s. 5.5.
23. *See* s. 5.6.
24. *See* s. 6.1.1.
25. *See* s. 6.1.2.
26. *See* s. 6.1.3.
27. *See* s. 6.2.2.1.
28. *See* s. 6.2.2.2.
29. *See* s. 6.3.
30. *See* s. 6.4.

2.2 THE THESIS' AXIOMs

In order to answer the research question(s) properly, it is of particular relevance to determine the methodology which is applied to the respective study. Since this thesis is in the field of law (theory of law or science of law),[31] the traditional methods of legal dogmatic research are applied. According to *Kelsen* and his *'pure theory of law'*,[32] the term law thereby refers to a *'norm, or, more exactly, a set of norms, a normative order'*. The validity of this set of norms, or this normative order, according to *Kelsen*, is based on a so-called *basic norm*, which is *'only presupposed in juristic thinking'*. This basic norm *'may be presupposed with reference to every coercive order established by acts of human beings* [...], *whatever its content may be, that is to say, without regard to its justice or injustice'*.[33] This study primarily deals with normative provisions of tax treaty law as well as EU law and will also examine the relation of both legal spheres. Tax treaties are sources of public international law,[34] while the EU sets its own legal framework within the sphere of public international law. The binding nature of tax treaties under the *pacta sunt servanda* principle, as well as the sources of EU primary law, are therefore presupposed as *'basic norms'* and thus the axioms for the purposes of this thesis, which are not questioned but are assumed for the purposes of this examination.

2.3 LEGAL METHODS OF INTERPRETATION

In principle, traditional legal research consists of a two-step process, including the compilation of relevant norms based on the axioms of the *'basic norms'* and the subsequent interpretation and analysis of these.[35] According to *Gassner*,[36] the application of an abstractly formulated norm to a specific factual situation requires a conclusion. The applicability of a certain norm in the form of a legal provision presupposes that a certain factual situation falls within the scope of this legal provision. In this context, the scope of a provision must be determined by means of interpretation. By way of interpretation, jurisprudence attempts to determine the substantive content of a norm.[37] Hence, jurisprudence has developed the so-called *classical canon of interpretation*, which is composed of four basically equilibrated methods of interpretation:[38]

31. *See* H. Kelsen, *What Is the Pure Theory of Law?*, 34 Tul. Law Rev. 269 et seq. (1959–1960).
32. H. Kelsen, *Reine Rechtslehre – 5. Neudruck der 2. Auflage aus 1960* (Verlag Österreich 2020).
33. Hans Kelsen, *supra* note 31, at 276.
34. To the theoretical nature of public international law, *see* Hans Kelsen, *supra* note 32, at 333 et seq.
35. T. Hutchinson & N. Duncan, *Defining and Describing What We Do: Doctrinal Legal Research*, 17 Dea. L. Rev. 110 (2012) DOI: 10.21153/dlr2012vol17no1art70.
36. W. Gassner, *Interpretation und Anwendung der Steuergesetze: kritische Analyse der wirtschaftlichen Betrachtungsweise des Steuerrechts* 5 (Orac 1972).
37. Hans Kelsen, *supra* note 32, at 359.
38. Providing for fundamental considerations, *see* W. Brugger, *Concretization of Law and Statutory Interpretation*, 11 Tul. Eur. & Civ. Law. F. 231 et seq. (1996).

- **Textual interpretation** is the most fundamental method (also referred to as textual or semantic), which examines the wording of a provision (‘*what is literally said?*’).[39] In any case, it is necessarily the starting point of any legal interpretation.
- **Contextual interpretation** (also systematical or structural) attempts to explain the meaning of a certain legal provision through contextual connections with other legal provisions. According to *Brugger*, in a contextual interpretation, ‘*ambiguous words are eliminated by reference to other related provisions or concepts in which the same word or term appears*’.[40]
- **Historical interpretation** attempts to determine the meaning of a norm by the will of previous lawmakers.[41] This method of interpretation tries to examine the intention and the backgrounds for the creation of a particular provision.
- **Teleological interpretation** (also purposive) supports the textual, contextual and historical interpretation by examining the purpose of a certain provision (*ratio legis*). Since it is related to all other methods of interpretation, teleological interpretation is mainly useful when textual, contextual and historical interpretation leads to different or contradictory results. Although historical interpretation is also obviously concerned with determining the purpose of a norm as well, teleological interpretation must be considered separately from historical interpretation. In contrast to historical interpretation, the focus is not on the ‘will of previous lawmakers’ but on the current goals of the norm, taking into account the entire normative system.[42]

All of the aforementioned methods are of relevance to this thesis. However, since the interpretation of tax treaties and EU law are of particular relevance for this study, existing peculiarities for these areas of law must be taken into account. For the interpretation of tax treaties as a source of international law, the Vienna Convention on the Law of Treaties (VCLT) is of particular relevance.[43] A general rule on the interpretation of international treaties is laid down in Article 31 (1) VCLT, which reads as follows: ‘*A treaty shall be interpreted in good faith in accordance with the ordinary meaning to be given to the terms of the treaty in their context and in the light of its object and purpose.*’ Articles 32 and 33 VCLT contain further details on the interpretation of treaties. However, the VCLT’s rules on the interpretation of international treaties are very much based on the ‘*classical canon of interpretation*’. Thus, the text of a tax treaty remains the starting point for interpretation.[44]

The ‘*classical canon of interpretation*’ is also of relevance for the interpretation of EU law. Nevertheless, certain special features must be observed with regard to Union law. First, one should emphasize that EU law forms an autonomous constitutional

39. *Ibid.*
40. *Ibid.*, at 237 et seq.
41. *Ibid.*, at 240.
42. Comprehensively, *Ibid.*, at 242–246.
43. F. Engelen, *Interpretation of Tax Treaties under International Law* 426–427 (IBFD 2004).
44. Explicitly *Ibid.*, at 427.

order of states,[45] which prevails over domestic law of its Member States (supremacy of EU law).[46] Given the multilateralism of the EU, the texts of EU law are, according to Article 55 Treaty of the EU (TEU), equally authentic and binding in all 24 national languages. Linguistic conflicts of interpretation are, therefore, not always avoidable. According to the case law of the European Court of Justice (ECJ), teleological and contextual interpretation, therefore, take precedence over textual interpretation.[47] The ECJ furthermore held that in the case of several possible ways to interpret a provision of EU law, '*the most liberal interpretation must prevail*'[48] and that preference shall be given to that kind of interpretation which better '*ensure*[s] *that the provision retains its effectiveness*'.[49] With regard to the historical interpretation of EU legal acts, it should be emphasized that only the will of the EU and its institutions are to be taken into account. EU legal acts are often based on political compromises. If the intention of every Member State was examined separately, it would never be possible to draw conclusions without contradictions.[50] Therefore, focusing on the individual intentions of the Member States for the purpose of historical interpretation would distort the result of the interpretation and would hardly lead to comprehensible outcomes.[51]

However, also the drafting history of legislative acts, according to the ECJ, is only of limited use for the interpretation of EU law.[52] This particularly becomes evident in the AG Opinion in *Milac*, where AG *Warner* elaborated on the question of whether the *travaux préparatoires* were an appropriate means for the interpretation of treaties and expressed his doubt that this is the case: '*The Members of the Council may agree on a text without necessarily having the same views as to its meaning.*'[53]

45. I. Govaere & G. Sacha, *Introduction: The Interface Between EU and International Law*, in *The Interface between EU and International Law* 14–15 (I. Govaere & G. Sacha eds, Hart Publishing 2019).
46. *See* the ECJs landmark decisions in Case C-6/64, *Flamanio Costa v. ENEL*; and Case C-26/62, *NV Algemene Transport – en Expeditie Onerdneming van Gend & Loos v. Netherlands Inland Revenue Administration*.
47. *See, i.a.*, Case C-283/81, *Srl CILFIT and Lanificio di Gavardo SpA v. Ministry of Health*, paras 18–20. In detail also *see* K. Lenaerts & J. A. Gutiérrez-Fons, *To Say What the Law of the EU Is: Methods of Interpretation and the European Court of Justice*, European University Institute 10 (2012), (last visited 28 Sep. 2021).
48. *See, i.a.*, Case C-29/69, *Erich Stauder v. City of Ulm, Sozialamt*, para. 4.
49. *See, i.a.*, Case C-187/87, *Saarland and Others and Ministre de l'Industrie, des Postes et Télécommunications et du Tourisme and Others*. In detail on this judgment and providing for further reference, *see* K. Lenaerts & J.A. Gutiérrez-Fons, *supra* note 47, at 16.
50. On the issue of political consensus within the EU and its impact on interpretation of EU law, *see* M. P. Maduro, *Interpreting of European Law: Judicial Adjudication in a Context of Constitutional Pluralism*, 1 European Journal of Legal Studies (2007) DOI: 10.2139/ssrn.1134503.
51. For a comprehensive analysis, *see* Lenaerts & Gutiérrez-Fons, *supra* note 47, at 22.
52. *See*, in particular, Case C-443/03, *Götz Leffler v. Berlin Chemie AG*, para. 48.
53. Case C-28/76, *Milac GmbH Groß- und Außenhandel v. Hauptzollamt Freiburg*, para. 1664. Also *see* Lenaerts & Gutiérrez-Fons, *supra* note 47, at 22.

CHAPTER 3

Background of Discussion Around a Minimum Tax Regime: From E-Commerce Via BEPS to the Pillars

3.1 E-COMMERCE AND INTERNATIONAL TAXATION: OTTAWA TAXATION FRAMEWORK CONDITIONS AND EARLY DISCUSSION OF E-COMMERCE

Digitization does not pose very new challenges for the international tax system but at least exacerbates them fundamentally.[54] This insight is already older than one would assume: as early as the mid-1990s, the international tax community was concerned with the taxation problems associated with digitalization.[55] In 1996, the US Department of the

---

54. *See, i.a.*, L. Hinnekens, *New Age International Taxation in the Digital Economy of the Global Society*, 25 Intertax 116 et seq. (1997) DOI: 10.54648/taxi1997027; D.L. Forst, *The Continuing Vitality of Source-Based Taxation in the Electronic Age*, 15 Tax Notes Intl. 1455 and 1472 (1997); J. Owens, *Progress Report: Taxation and Electronic Commerce*, 39 Eur. Taxn. 422 (1999); L. Hinnekens, *Income Taxation of Electronic Commerce and Other Cross-Border Business Coordinated by the OECD Also Involves the European Community*, 41 Eur. Taxn. 299 (2001).
55. *See* only a few of countless examples in literature in the mid-1990s, *i.a.*, D.R. Tillinghast, *The Impact of the Internet on the Taxation of International Transactions*, 50 Bull. Intl. Taxn. 524–526 (1996); P.J. Bourgeois & L. Blanchette, *Income_taxes.ca.Com: The Internet, Electronic, Commerce, and Taxes – Some Reflections: Part 1*, 45 Can. Tax J. 1127–1149 (1997); P.J. Bourgeois & L. Blanchette, *Income_taxes.ca.Com: The Internet, Electronic, Commerce, and Taxes – Some Reflections: Part 2*, 45 Can. Tax J. 1378–1415 (1997); H.E. Abrams & R.L. Doernberg, *How Electronic Commerce Works*, 14 Tax Notes Intl. 1573 et seq. (1997); J.P. Powers, *International Tax Issues in Cyberspace: Taxation of Cross-Border Electronic Commerce*, 25 Intertax 120–142 (1997); G. Strunk, *Grenzüberschreitende Geschäftsaktivität durch das Internet als weißer Fleck der Besteuerung*, 6 ISTR 257 et seq. (1997); D.L. Forst, *supra* note 54, at 1455 et seq.; L. Hinnekens, *New Age International Taxation in the Digital Economy of the Global Society*, *supra* note 54, at 116–119; I. Lejeune et al., *Does Cyber-Commerce Necessitate a Revision of International Tax Concepts? – Part I*, 38 Eur. Taxn. 2–13 (1998); I. Lejeune et al., *Does Cyber-Commerce Necessitate a Revision of International Tax Concepts? – Part II*, 38 Eur. Taxn. 50–58 (1998); L. Hinnekens, *The Challenges of Applying VAT and Income Tax Territoriality Concepts and Rules to*

Treasury published a first policy paper[56] in which initial tax policy approaches to digitalization were discussed.[57] The US called for the principle of '*neutrality*'[58] to be followed. Commercial activities over the internet (generally referred to as 'E-Commerce'[59]) should be treated equally to conventional channels of commerce.[60] In particular, the digitized world should be spared from '*quixotic*', specially created taxes.[61] According to Pinkernell, the demand for this kind of 'tax neutrality' has been directed at both (i) US states and (ii) OECD Member States, as well as emerging economies:[62] In the mid-1990s, several US States discussed or even introduced taxes on the usage of the internet. The Federal Government tried to counteract these developments, which in 1998 led to the congress' decision to enact the so-called *Internet Tax freedom act*.[63] The '*Internet Tax freedom act*' (US-ITFA)[64] prohibited the introduction of taxes on Internet access, '*bit taxes*'[65] and multiple or discriminatory taxation of E-Commerce through individual

International Electronic Commerce, 26 Intertax 52–70 (1998) DOI: 10.54648/taxi1998009; R.L. Doernberg, *Electronic Commerce and International Tax Sharing*, 16 Tax Notes Intl. 1013–1022 (1998); L. Hinnekens, *Looking for an Appropriate Jurisdictional Framework for Source-State Taxation of International Electronic Commerce in the Twenty-First Century*, 26 Intertax 192–200 (1998) DOI: 10.54648/taxi1998036; M. Geurts, *How to Tax Electronic Commerce Transactions?*, 26 Intertax 301–303 (1998) DOI: 10.54648/taxi1998059; X. Oberson & L. Piaget, *Electronic Commerce and Taxation: A Swiss Perspective*, 52 Bull. Intl. Taxn. 535–540 (1998); R. Weninger, *http://www.e-commerce.xy/no-tax/anonymous?! Verändert der elektronische Geschäftsverkehr die Besteuerung?*, 73 SWK 69–78 (1998); R.L. Doernberg & L. Hinnekens, *Electronic Commerce and International Taxation* (Kluwer Law International 1999); J.S. Schwarz, *Transfer Pricing and Electronic Commerce*, 53 Bull. Intl. Taxn. 286–290 (1999); S. Bendlinger, *Internet und E-Commerce im internationalen Steuerrecht*, 9 SWI 306–312 (1999).

56. US Department of the Treasury, *Selected Tax Policy Implications of Global Electronic Commerce* (1996), https://www.treasury.gov/resource-center/tax-policy/Documents/Report-Global-Electronic-Commerce-1996.pdf (last visited 9 Jul. 2021).
57. Powers, *supra* note 55, at 121; Bourgeois & Blanchette, *Income_taxes.ca.Com: The Internet, Electronic, Commerce, and Taxes – Some Reflections: Part 1*, *supra* note 55, at 1128; P. Fernandez et al., *Tax Policy and Electronic Commerce*, 56 Bull. Intl. Taxn. 30 (2002); R. Pinkernell, *Internationale Steuergestaltung im Electronic Commerce* 18 et seq. (IFST 2014); V. Bendlinger, *Die Besteuerung der Digital Economy – Eine kritische Würdigung*, 3 StAW 116 (2018).
58. '*Neutrality requires that the tax system treat economically similar income equally, regardless of whether earned through electronic means or through more conventional channels of commerce*', *Selected Tax Policy Implications of Global Electronic Commerce*, at 19.
59. In general to the meaning and common understanding of the expression 'E-Commerce' and questions raised at that time, *see*, e.g., Abrams & Doernberg, *supra* note 55, at 1573 et seq.; Bourgeois & Blanchette, *Income_taxes.ca.Com: The Internet, Electronic, Commerce, and Taxes – Some Reflections: Part 1*, *supra* note 55, at 132 et seq.; Doernberg & Hinnekens, *supra* note 55, at 45 et seq. and 72 et seq.; R. Krever, *Electronic Commerce and Taxation – A Summary of the Emerging Issues*, 6 Asia-Pac. Tax Bull. 151 et seq. (2000).
60. *Selected Tax Policy Implications of Global Electronic Commerce*, at 19.
61. *Ibid.*, at 1; also referring to the policy paper Reimar Pinkernell, *supra* note 57, at 18.
62. Reimar Pinkernell, *supra* note 57, at 18.
63. Further information, *see* P. Fernandez et al., *Tax Policy and Electronic Commerce*, 56 Bull. Intl. Taxn., *supra* note 57, at 31; Reimar Pinkernell, *supra* note 57, at 18.
64. Internet Tax freedom act, H.R. 3529, 105th Cong. (1998).
65. A '*Bit tax*' can be defined as an excise duty on the traffic of data. The bit tax should tax information sent over the Internet and comparable networks based on the volume of data moved through those channels, *see*, *i.a.*, Prafula Fernandez et al., *supra* note 57, at 31; The essential limitation of a Bit Tax has always been seen in the fact that it is levied on the amount of information transmitted and not on the extrinsic value of the 'data transaction', *see* in detail about the criticism of bit taxes P.J. Bourgeois & L. Blanchette, *Income_taxes.ca.Com: The Internet, Electronic, Commerce, and Taxes – Some Reflections: Part 2*, 45 Can. Tax J., *supra* note

states.[66] The act primarily intended to protect '*the free flow of commerce via the internet*'. However, the US also had to defend the international tax landscape, especially against the development of taxing rights for source states.[67] The experts of the US Department of the Treasury assumed that the US IT industry, which at this time was a leading power,[68] would in the future be able to offer its services without a physical presence on the global market.[69] Obviously, this statement was politically motivated. A strengthening of the taxation rights for the states of residence should ensure that the huge profits of the US IT industry could still be taxed in the US.[70]

It is obvious that the US position was contrary to the interests of developing countries:[71] the rising US IT industry was increasingly able to access international markets without being subject to taxation in source states.[72] The United Nations (UN), which has traditionally represented developing countries, therefore called for the tax revenues of the source states to be safeguarded by means of their own digital services taxes or additional taxing rights to apply withholding taxes.[73] As the representative of the Western economic powers, the OECD, as well as the EU,[74] in contrast to the UN, supported the US position.

55, at 1382; as well as L. Hinnekens, *The Challenges of Applying VAT and Income Tax Territoriality Concepts and Rules to International Electronic Commerce*, 26 Intertax, *supra* note 55, at 69; L. Hinnekens, *Looking for an Appropriate Jurisdictional Framework for Source-State Taxation of International Electronic Commerce in the Twenty-First Century*, 26 Intertax, *supra* note 55, at 193; A. Uricchio, *Some Thoughts for E-Reforming the Tax System: Beyond the Bit Tax*, 34 Intertax 618 (2006) DOI: 10.54648/taxi2006087.

66. In detail on the origin of the US-IFTA and its content, *see* M. Butler et al., *Taxation of Global E-Commerce*, 6 Asia-Pac. Tax Bull. 201–202 (2000).
67. The US Department of the Treasury strongly forced residence based taxation. The US argued that in a digitalized world it would be '*difficult, if not impossible, to apply traditional source concepts to link an item of income with a specific geographical location*', *see Selected Tax Policy Implications of Global Electronic Commerce*, s. 7.1.5.
68. In literature, it was estimated that in 1997, 90% of all websites were American, *see* D.L. Forst, *supra* note 54, at 1472 in particular n. 27 (1997).
69. Reimar Pinkernell, *Internationale Steuergestaltung im Electronic Commerce*, *supra* note 57, at 18.
70. In detail, P.J. Bourgeois & L. Blanchette, *Income_taxes.ca.Com: The Internet, Electronic, Commerce, and Taxes – Some Reflections: Part 2*, *supra* note 55, at 1393 et seq.; *see also* M. Butler et al., *supra* note 66, at 200–201; and D.L. Forst, *supra* note 54, at 1458–1459; Reimar Pinkernell, *supra* note 57, at 18.
71. *See, i.a.*, P.J. Bourgeois & L. Blanchette, *Income_taxes.ca.Com: The Internet, Electronic, Commerce, and Taxes – Some Reflections: Part 2*, *supra* note 55, at 1394; C.E. McLure, *Globalization, Tax Rules and National Sovereignty*, 55 Bull. Intl. Taxn. 335 (2001).
72. Reimar Pinkernell, *supra* note 57, at 19.
73. *Ibid.*, at 19–20.
74. The EU's tax policy perspective largely coincided with the US position. Already in April 1997 the EU released a paper titled 'A European Initiative in Electronic Commerce' in which the EU also clarified its tax policy position. Like the US, the EU called for the principle of tax neutrality and explicitly rejected the imposition of 'bit taxes', *see* EC Commission, *A European Initiative in Electronic Commerce*, COM(97) 157 final, paras 56–59 (16 Apr. 1997); On 5 December 1997, the US and EU also published a joint statement with regard to their policy on electronic commerce and agreed that taxation of electronic commerce should be clear, consistent, neutral and non-discriminatory, *see* Joint Statement released in conjunction with the US – EU Summit on 5 Dec. 1997, *see Electronic Commerce – Joint Statement Released in Conjunction with the U.S.-EU Summit* (5 Dec. 1997), https://1997-2001.state.gov/www/regions/eur/eu/971205_useu_js_electronic.html (last visited 10 Jul. 2021). For further details to the early EU-position on the taxation of Electronic Commerce, *see* P. Fernandez et al., *Tax Policy and Electronic Commerce*,

Like the US Department of the Treasury, the OECD's Committee on Fiscal Affairs (CFA) also started to deal with tax issues related to E-Commerce in 1996.[75] A milestone in international tax policy was finally reached at the OECD Ministerial Conference in Ottawa in October 1998.[76] The OECD CFA, therefore, prepared a report titled 'Electronic Commerce: Taxation Framework Conditions',[77] which was endorsed by the ministers.[78] The OECD members agreed that the taxation of E-Commerce should be based on the following five principles: (i) neutrality, (ii) efficiency, (iii) certainty and simplicity, (iv) effectiveness and fairness, as well as (v) flexibility.[79] Although these principles have only been defined vaguely,[80] the Ottawa Conference 1998 should set the framework for the international tax policy in the following years.[81]

However, the OECD's position was clear. No special taxes should be levied,[82] but the conventional rules should, as far as possible, also be applied to E-Commerce.[83] To further discuss the taxation of E-Commerce, in January 1999, the OECD CFA set up five so-called Technical Advisory Groups (TAGs), each of which was assigned a certain subject area.[84] The TAGs were given a period of two years to consider tax policy and

---

56 Bull. Intl. Taxn., *supra* note 57, at 31; as well as L. Hinnekens, *Income Taxation of Electronic Commerce and Other Cross-Border Business Coordinated by the OECD Also Involves the European Community*, 41 Eur. Taxn., *supra* note 54, at 306.

75. Rosemarie Portner, *Ertragsteuerliche Aspekte des E-Commerce* 13 (IFST 2001).
76. *See also* D. Fehling & M. Valta, *Aktionpunkt 1: Besteuerung der digitalen Wirtschaft*, in *BEPS-Handbuch* 34 (G. Kofler & A. Schnitger eds, C.H.Beck 2019).
77. OECD CFA, *Electronic Commerce: Taxation Framework Conditions* (1998), https://www.oecd.org/ctp/consumption/1923256.pdf (last visited 9 Jul. 2021).
78. M. Butler et al., *Taxation of Global E-Commerce*, 6 Asia-Pac. Tax Bull., *supra* note 66, at 203–204; C. Lau & A. Halkyard, *From E-Commerce to E-Business Taxation*, 9 Asia-Pac. Tax Bull. 4 (2003); R. Anthony, *Electronic Commerce and Transfer Pricing*, 12 Asia-Pac. Tax Bull. 68 (2006).
79. *Electronic Commerce: Taxation Framework Conditions*, para. 9; in detail to the principles, *i.a.* L. Hinnekens, *International Taxation of Electronic Commerce: An Emerging Framework*, 27 Intertax 440–441 (1999) DOI: 10.54648/taxi1999074; J. Owens, *Taxation and E-Commerce: Progress Report*, 29 Intertax 10–11 (2000); Professor R. Anthony, *supra* note 78, at 68; Collin Lau & Andrew Halkyard, *supra* note 78, at 3–4.
80. *See* as well L. Hinnekens, *Looking for an Appropriate Jurisdictional Framework for Source-State Taxation of International Electronic Commerce in the Twenty-First Century*, 26 Intertax, *supra* note 55, at 192.
81. Reimar Pinkernell, *Internationale Steuergestaltung im Electronic Commerce*, *supra* note 57, at 20; Rosemarie Portner, *Ertragsteuerliche Aspekte des E-Commerce*, *supra* note 75, at 13.
82. *See*, *i.a.*, S.O. Lodin, *What Ought to Be Taxed and What Can Be Taxed: A New International Dilemma*, 54 Bull. Intl. Taxn. 216 (2000).
83. P.G. Végh, *Facing the Challenges of Electronic Commerce (Direct Taxation)*, 41 Eur. Taxn. 155 (2001); R. Adhikari, *Tax Policy and Administration in Asian Countries: A Review of Key Issues and Options*, 56 Bull. Intl. Taxn. 51 (2002); N. Tadmore, *Source Taxation of Cross-Border Intellectual Supplies – Concepts, History and Evolution into the Digital Age*, 61 Bull. Intl. Taxn. 10 (2007).
84. In detail, OECD, *Taxation and Electronic Commerce: Implementing the Ottawa Taxation Framework Conditions*, para. 12 (OECD 2001), https://www.oecd.org/tax/consumption/Taxation%20and%20eCommerce%202001.pdf (last visited 9 Jul. 2021); J. Owens, *Progress Report: Taxation and Electronic Commerce*, 39 Eur. Taxn., *supra* note 54, at 423; M. Butler et al., *Taxation of Global E-Commerce*, 6 Asia-Pac. Tax Bull., *supra* note 66, at 204; J. Owens, *supra* note 79, at 11; Collin Lau & Andrew Halkyard, *supra* note 78, at 4; D. Fehling & M. Valta, *Aktionpunkt 1: Besteuerung der digitalen Wirtschaft*, *in BEPS-Handbuch*, *supra* note 76, at 35.

practice options.[85] In terms of content, the focus of the TAGs work was divided into three broader areas:[86] (i) consumption tax issues, (ii) international direct tax issues, and (iii) tax administration issues. In February 2001, the separate TAGs[87] published their conclusions in several topic-related reports.[88] Additionally, the OECD published a final report in 2001 entitled 'Taxation and Electronic Commerce - Implementing the Ottawa Taxation Framework Conditions' summarizing the progress of work, including the conclusions of the TAGs' work.[89] Since the OECD considered, as already mentioned, the existing regulations being, in principle, sufficient to meet the tax challenges related to E-Commerce,[90] the discussion in the fields of direct taxation focused on the application of existing tax treaty law.[91] Especially two of the TAGs, the so-called Treaty Characterization TAG,[92] as well as the 'Business Profits TAG',[93] had been concerned with topics of direct taxation and focused on the interpretation and the future adaption of existing provisions of the OECD MC. The results with regard to direct taxation presented in the 2001 reports can be summarized in three thematic areas:[94]

- **Concept of permanent establishment:** Both the definition of PE and the attribution of profits to PEs were examined in detail by the 'Business Profits TAG'. With regard to the definition of permanent establishment, the report stressed that the CFA had been able to reach a consensus, which included that a website could not '*in itself, constitute a permanent establishment*'.[95] The substantive work focused more on the question of whether computer equipment ('servers') could constitute PEs[96] and how profits could be attributed[97] to such 'server PEs'.[98]

85. *Taxation and Electronic Commerce: Implementing the Ottawa Taxation Framework Conditions*, para. 12; Jeffrey Owens, *supra* note 79, at 11.
86. Jeffrey Owens, *supra* note 79, at 11; referring to Owens, *see* Collin Lau & Andrew Halkyard, *supra* note 78, at 4.
87. For detailed information on the work of the individual TAGs *see* M. Lambooij et al., *Recent OECD Initiatives With E-Commerce Taxation*, 22 Tax Notes Intl. 2091–2114 (2001).
88. *See*, e.g., OECD TAG on Treaty Characterization of Electronic Commerce Payments, *Tax Treaty Characterization Issues Arising from E-Commerce, Report to Working Party No. 1 of the OECD Committee on Fiscal Affairs* (2001), http://www.oecd.org/tax/consumption/1923396.pdf (last visited 9 Jul. 2021); OECD TAG on Monitoring the Application of Existing Treaty Norms for the Taxation of Business Profits, *The Impact of the Communications Revolution on the Application of 'Place of Effective Management' as a Tie Breaker Rule – February 2001* (2001), http://www.oecd.org/tax/treaties/1923328.pdf (last visited 9 Jul. 2021).
89. *Taxation and Electronic Commerce: Implementing the Ottawa Taxation Framework Conditions*.
90. This is also evident in the 2001 report, which states: '*The CFA believes that existing taxation rules can implement these principles*', *see Ibid.*, at 11.
91. Explicitly *ibid.*, at 14.
92. In detail J. Owens, *Taxation and E-Commerce: Progress Report*, 29 Intertax, *supra* note 79, at 11.
93. *Ibid.*, at 12.
94. In detail, *see* P.G. Végh, *Facing the Challenges of Electronic Commerce (Direct Taxation)*, 41 Eur. Taxn., *supra* note 83, at 155 et seq.; *see also* Reimar Pinkernell, *Internationale Steuergestaltung im Electronic Commerce*, *supra* note 57, at 21.
95. *Taxation and Electronic Commerce: Implementing the Ottawa Taxation Framework Conditions*, at 80.
96. *Ibid.*
97. *Tax Treaty Characterization Issues Arising from E-Commerce, Report to Working Party No. 1 of the OECD Committee on Fiscal Affairs*; *see also Taxation and Electronic Commerce: Implementing the Ottawa Taxation Framework Conditions*, at 102.

- **Definition of royalties in the OECD MC:** The 'Treaty Characterization TAG' tried to clarify the characterization of electronic commerce payments under tax conventions. In particular, demarcation problems in connection with the definition of royalties under Article 12 OECD MC were discussed.[99] The 'Treaty Characterization TAG' finally recommended amendments to the Commentary on Article 12 OECD MC in order to clarify a clear distinction between royalties under Article 12 OECD MC and business profits under Article 7 OECD MC.[100]
- **Place of effective management as a tiebreaker rule:** The 'Business Profits TAG' was also concerned with the question of how potentially upcoming limitations of the application of the 'place of effective management' could be handled.[101]

The isolated discussion of questions of interpretation of existing tax treaty law once more makes it clear that, at that time, the OECD was still assuming that most emerging challenges of E-Commerce could be met by the application of existing tax treaty law.[102]

In the following years, the OECD continued this approach. In 2003, another summary report was released on the 'Implementation of the Ottawa Taxation Framework Conditions'.[103] The 2003 report referred to the 2001 report and only summarized the advanced results of the TAGs, which at that time had just been incorporated into the OECD MC being published in the 2003 Update[104] to the OECD MC.[105] Although the merits of the revised 2003 Commentary were mainly seen in the amendments to the

98. A good overview of the issues discussed at that time concerning the concept of and the attribution of profits to permanent establishments is provided by M. Lambooij et al., *Recent OECD Initiatives With E-Commerce Taxation*, 22 Tax Notes Intl., *supra* note 87, at 2092–2103.
99. *Taxation and Electronic Commerce: Implementing the Ottawa Taxation Framework Conditions*, at 85; *see also* C. Lau & Andrew Halkyard, *From E-Commerce to E-Business Taxation*, 9 Asia-Pac. Tax Bull., *supra* note 78, at 4.
100. On 1 February 2001, the 'Treaty Characterization TAG' published the results in a separate report, *see Tax Treaty Characterization Issues Arising from E-Commerce, Report to Working Party No. 1 of the OECD Committee on Fiscal Affairs*; in detail to the report and its conclusions, *see* W. Schickli, *Characterization of E-Commerce Revenue – The Final OECD Report Revealed*, 22 Tax Notes Intl. 1671 et seq. (2001); and G.D. Sprague & O.A. Schindler, *Another Step Towards Uniformity – Relative Consensus of the OECD TAG on Income Characterization of E-Commerce Transactions*, 30 Tax Mgt. Int'l. J. 267 et seq (2001).
101. *The Impact of the Communications Revolution on the Application of 'Place of Effective Management' as a Tie Breaker Rule – February 2001*; *see also Taxation and Electronic Commerce: Implementing the Ottawa Taxation Framework Conditions*, at 143.
102. *See*, *i.a.*, Lodin in 2001 regarding income taxes and E-Commerce: '*It should, however, be possible to resolve the income tax problems without too great difficulties because they concern mainly an agreement on the common principles for how to divide the tax base between tax jurisdictions*'. *See* S.O. Lodin, *International Tax Issues in a Rapidly Changing World*, 55 Bull. Intl. Taxn. 5 (2001); From today's perspective, this statement seems to be an overly optimistic approach.
103. OECD, *Implementation of the Ottawa Taxation Framework Conditions – The 2003 Report* (2003), https://www.oecd.org/tax/administration/20499630.pdf (last visited 9 Jul. 2021).
104. *OECD Model Tax Convention on Income and on Capital – Condensed Version January 2003* (OECD ed., OECD 28 Jan. 2003).
105. *Implementation of the Ottawa Taxation Framework Conditions – The 2003 Report*, para. 23 et seq.

Commentary on Article 1 OECD MC,[106] the 2003 revision also brought significant adaptations of the commentaries on Articles 5 and 12 OECD MC with regard to E-Commerce.[107] The 2003 revision, namely, implemented the proposed changes by the 'Business Profits TAG' and the 'Treaty Characterization TAG.[108] Particularly noteworthy are the Commentary changes proposed by the 'Business Profits TAG' on the definition of PE, which became subject of extensive literary discussion at that time.[109] As a result, the adjustments led to a lowering of the 'PE-threshold' and therefore reinforced source state taxing rights.[110] However, the Commentary also made it clear that a website, due to lack of physical presence, cannot in itself constitute a PE. An enterprise carrying on business through a website could only constitute a PE if it 'has the server at its own disposal, for example, it owns (or leases) and operates the server on which the website is stored and used'.[111] Apart from the PE definition, the 2003 revision also brought certain clarifications related to E-Commerce for the application and interpretation of Article 12 OECD MC.[112] Several new paragraphs were added to the Commentary on Article 12 OECD MC, especially related to the demarcation of business profits and royalties[113] as well as the treaty characterization of 'software payments'.[114]

106. A.M. Jimenez, *The 2003 Revision of the OECD Commentaries on the Improper Use of Tax Treaties: A Case for the Declining Effect of the OECD Commentaries?*, 58 Bull. Intl. Taxn. 17 et seq. (2004) DOI: 10.2139/ssrn.2392517; and B.J. Arnold, *Tax Treaties and Tax Avoidance: The 2003 Revisions to the Commentary to the OECD Model*, 58 Bull. Intl. Taxn. 244 et seq. (2004).
107. N. Tadmore, *Source Taxation of Cross-Border Intellectual Supplies – Concepts, History and Evolution into the Digital Age*, 61 Bull. Intl. Taxn., *supra* note 83, at 10.
108. The finally implemented changes to the Commentary on Arts 5 and 12 had already been suggested in the 2001 final report, *see Taxation and Electronic Commerce: Implementing the Ottawa Taxation Framework Conditions*, at 82 et seq. and 89 et seq. OECD, Taxation and Electronic Commerce – Implementing the Ottawa Taxation Framework Conditions (2001), at 82 et seq. and 89 et seq.
109. *See*, *i.a.*, H. Pijl, *The Concept of Permanent Establishment and the Proposed Changes to the OECD Commentary with Special Reference to Dutch Case Law*, 56 Bull. Intl. Taxn. 554–562 (2002); B.J. Arnold, *Threshold Requirements for Taxing Business Profits under Tax Treaties*, 57 Bull. Intl. Taxn. 476–492 (2003); A. Caridi, *Proposed Changes to the OECD Commentary on Article 5: Part I – The Physical PE Notion*, 43 Eur. Taxn. 8–19 (2003); Professor R. Anthony, *Electronic Commerce and Transfer Pricing*, 12 Asia-Pac. Tax Bull., *supra* note 78, at 70 et seq.
110. Pijl, *supra* note 109, at 561; generally to the understanding of the PE-threshold at that time, *see* Arnold, *supra* note 109, at 478 et seq. and 492 et seq.
111. *OECD Model Tax Convention on Income and on Capital: Commentary on Article 5*, para. 42.3 (28 Jan. 2003); in detail, *see* Professor R. Anthony, *supra* note 78, at 70 et seq. In the latest 2017 version of the commentary, the same wording is found in *OECD Model Tax Convention on Income and on Capital: Commentary on Article 5*, para. 124 (21 Nov. 2017); Niv Tadmore, *supra* note 83, at 10.
112. A.M. Jimenez, *The 2003 Revision of the OECD Commentaries on the Improper Use of Tax Treaties: A Case for the Declining Effect of the OECD Commentaries?*, 58 Bull. Intl. Taxn., *supra* note 106, at 17 and 26; C. Brokelind, *Royalty Payments: Unresolved Issues in the Interest and Royalties Directive*, 44 Eur. Taxn. 253 et seq. (2004); A. G. Heredia, *Software Royalties in Tax Treaties: Should Copyright Rights Be Reconsidered in the OECD Commentary on Article 12?*, 59 Bull. Intl. Taxn. 225 et seq. (2005).
113. *See OECD Model Tax Convention on Income and on Capital: Commentary on Article 12*, para. 11.1 to 11.6 (28 Jan. 2003); same in *OECD Model Tax Convention on Income and on Capital: Commentary on Article 12* 11.1 to 11.6 (21 Nov. 2017); These paragraphs relate to the concept of 'know-how', which is subject to Art. 12 (2) OECD MC. This concept distinguishes royalties from business profits. While business profits result from customary skills (para. 11.1), royalties

While the 2003 revision brought significant adjustments with regard to the definition of PEs and demarcation problems of Business Profits and royalties, the OECD Member States could neither reach an agreement on the attribution of profits to PEs[115] nor on a refinement of the place of effective management concept.[116] Although the OECD worked intensively on both issues and published separate reports[117] relating to those topics in the following years, no agreement was reached even within the framework of the 2005 update of the OECD MC.[118] In December 2005, the OECD also released an overall report entitled 'Are the Current Treaty Rules for Taxing Business Profits Appropriate for E-commerce? Final Report' prepared by the 'Treaty Characterization TAG'.[119] The report more or less summarized the progress made in recent years,

result from special knowledge and experience (para. 11.2.). In detail to the mentioned paragraphs of the commentary, *see* Cécile Brokelind, *supra* note 112, at 253 et seq.

114. *See OECD Model 2003: Commentary on Article 12, supra* note 113, para. 17.1 to 17.4. The corresponding paragraphs are still in the 2017 version (*see OECD Model 2017: Commentary on Article 12, supra* note 113, para. 17.1 to 17.4) and specify Art. 17 and the treaty qualification of digital products, downloads and the use of copyrights in digital products. Paragraph 17 had already been introduced in 1992 in response to a separate OECD report entitled 'the tax treatment of software payments', *see* OECD, *The Tax Treatment of Software* (1992), https://www.oecd-ilibrary.org/docserver/690f0e4a-en.pdf?expires = 1625867446&id = id&accname = ocid177428&checksum = 94DB83A48D3E1C1119B5830F2DC61307 (last visited 9 Jul. 2021); and clarifies that such payments result from so-called 'mixed contracts'. 'Mixed contracts' are contracts that lead to income covered by different distributive rules and were addressed by a separately implemented para. 11.6 added in the course of the 2003 update. Paragraph 17 states that software payments must therefore be 'broken down on the basis of the information contained' in the contract and the relevant distributive rule (Art. 7 or Art. 12) must be applied to each part of the divided payment. In detail to the mentioned paragraphs of the Commentary, *see* Cécile Brokelind, *supra* note 112, at 253 et seq.; Heredia, *supra* note 112, at 226 et seq. and 234 et seq.; Niv Tadmore, *supra* note 83, at 10.

115. A.J. Bakker, *Attribution of Profit to a Permanent Establishment of a Global Trading Company*, 11 ITPJ 255 and 262 (2004); Professor R. Anthony, *supra* note 78, at 72; H. Pijl, *Interpretation of Article 7 of the OECD Model, Permanent Establishment Financing and Other Dealings*, 65 Bull. Intl. Taxn. 303 (2011).

116. In detail to the background of discussion and the lack of consensus regarding the place of effective management concept at this time, *see* OECD, *Draft Contents of the 2008 Update to the Model Tax Convention*, para. 1 et seq. (2008), https://www.oecd.org/tax/treaties/40489100.pdf (last visited 9 Jul. 2021); in detail to the place of effective management and its development, *see* J.F. Avery Jones, *2008 OECD Model: Place of Effective Management – What One Can Learn from the History*, 63 Bull. Intl. Taxn. 183 et seq. (2009).

117. Regarding the Attribution of Profits to permanent establishments, *see* OECD, *Discussion Draft on the Attribution of Profits to Permanent Establishment – Part I (General Consideration)* (2 Aug. 2004), https://www.oecd.org/ctp/transfer-pricing/33637685.pdf (last visited 9 Jul. 2021). Regarding the Place of effective management, *see, i.a.*, OECD, *Discussion Draft 27 May 2003 – Place of Effective Management Concept: Suggestions for Changes to the OECD Model Tax Convention*, https://www.oecd.org/tax/treaties/2956428.pdf (last visited 9 Jul. 2021); in detail to this report, *see* J.F. Avery Jones, *Place of Effective Management as a Residence Tie-Breaker*, 59 Bull. Intl. Taxn. 20–24 (2005).

118. The 2005 OECD Model brought minor amendments in several areas. However, no noteworthy adjustments were made with regard to E-Commerce. *See* at a glance, R. Russo, *The 2005 OECD Model Convention and Commentary: An Overview*, 45 Eur. Taxn. 560–565 (2005).

119. OECD TAG on Treaty Characterization of Electronic Commerce Payments, *Are the Current Treaty Rules for Taxing Business Profits Appropriate for E-Commerce?* (2005), http://www.oecd.org/ctp/treaties/35869032.pdf (last visited 9 Jul. 2021).

which, in part, had already been implemented through the 2003 revision of the OECD MC. However, the OECD's position has hardly changed over the years. Thus, the conclusion of the report states: '*Indeed, at this stage, E-commerce and other business models resulting from new communication technologies would not, by themselves, justify a dramatic departure from the current rules.*'[120] Once again, the OECD made clear that the existing tax treaty network was considered sufficient to meet the challenges posed by the advent of E-Commerce.[121]

In the following years, the work of the OECD did not specifically focus on E-Commerce and digitization. Relevant changes, however, have to be mentioned in relation to E-Commerce concerning profit attribution to PEs and the place of effective management concept, as these issues were significantly influenced by the TAGs' work on tax challenges of E-Commerce. Both issues were finally reflected in the 2008 OECD Model and the revised Commentary.[122] Especially regarding the attribution of profits to PEs, the OECD tried to reach a consensus among the Member States. While the previous discussion draft on the attribution of profits to PEs from 2004 failed to achieve consensus, the OECD members finally agreed on a revised draft[123] released in the year of 2006.[124] In 2008, the CFA finally agreed upon a report[125] which could build on a broad consensus.[126] The findings of the report should be implemented through the 2008 Revision of the Model and the Commentary. The so-called Authorized OECD Approach (AOA) should be implemented. The AOA can be described as a completely new approach to attribute profits to a PE and consists of a two-step process:[127] in the first step, it is hypothesized that the PE is a legally independent enterprise. In the second step, the OECD Transfer Pricing Guidelines (OECD TPG) are applied by analogy.[128] The AOA thus uses a legal fiction to apply existing transfer pricing regulations on the attribution of profits to PEs. Although certain aspects of the AOA

120. *Ibid.*, para. 358.
121. N. Tadmore, *Source Taxation of Cross-Border Intellectual Supplies – Concepts, History and Evolution into the Digital Age*, 61 Bull. Intl. Taxn., *supra* note 83, at 10 et seq.
122. At a glance, R. Russo, *The 2008 OECD Model: An Overview*, 48 Eur. Taxn. 459–466 (2008); B.J. Arnold, *The 2008 Update of the OECD Model: An Introduction*, 63 Bull. Intl. Taxn. 178–182 (2009) DOI: 10.1787/9789264044395-3-en.
123. OECD, *Report on the Attribution of Profits to Permanent Establishments, Parts I (General Considerations), II (Banks) and III (Global Trading)*, para. 7 et seq. (2006), https://www.oecd.org/tax/transfer-pricing/37861293.pdf (last visited 9 Jul. 2021).
124. A. Wintsch, *Attribution of Profits to Permanent Establishments: The 2008 Article 7 versus the 2010 Article 7 of the OECD Model Tax Convention*, 71 Bull. Intl. Taxn. 343 (2017).
125. OECD, *Report on the Attribution of Profits to Permanent Establishments* (17 Jul. 2008), https://www.oecd.org/tax/transfer-pricing/41031455.pdf (last visited 9 Jul. 2021).
126. M. Bennett, *The Attribution of Profits to Permanent Establishments: The 2008 Commentary on Art. 7 of the OECD Model Convention*, 48 Eur. Taxn. 476 (2008).
127. At a glance Russo, *supra* note 122, at 461, in more detail *see, i.a.*, Bennett, *supra* note 126, at 467–471.
128. *Report on the Attribution of Profits to Permanent Establishments*, para. 10.

were apparently in direct contradiction to the wording of Article 7 OECD MC, only the Commentary to Article 7 OECD MC has been changed for the time being. However, it was obvious that Article 7 OECD MC also needed to be amended.[129] The 2008 Report, therefore, already announced that Article 7 OECD MC would be revised in a 2010 update of the OECD MC (*see* below).[130] Although the amendments with regard to profit attribution to PEs were not specifically addressed to E-Commerce, the 2008 report also referred to certain related issues. The report states, e.g., that '[an] *interesting issue can arise in an E-commerce operation in circumstances, where it is accepted that the location of a server of itself constitutes a PE, as functions may be performed at that location without personnel*'.[131] In the same paragraph, the report also refers to the groundwork of the 'Business Profits TAG'. Ultimately, however, the reference to E-Commerce is limited to the findings that although a server could possibly constitute a PE, it is unlikely that profits could be attributed to it[132] and that physical capital would become less significant due to the advent of E-Commerce.[133]

Regarding the place of effective management, the OECD members were not able to reach a final consensus. Nevertheless, the 2008 revision of the Commentary also brought a change in the meaning of place of effective management by deleting a sentence in the Commentary,[134] which previously gave rise to disputes. The mentioned paragraph stated that the place of effective management '*will ordinarily be the place where the most senior person or group of persons (for example a board of directors) makes its decisions*'.[135] Many countries had expressed that '*undue priority*' was given '*to the place where the board of directors of a company would meet over the place where the senior executives of that company would make key management decisions*'.[136] According to Avery Jones J. F., the deletion was not proof of consensus but rather a demonstration of a 'lack of agreement' on the interpretation of the term place of effective management.[137] However, no further discussion was held in connection with E-Commerce.

---

129. P. Baker & R. Collier, *2008 OECD Model: Changes to the Commentary on Article 7 and the Attribution of Profits to Permanent Establishments*, 63 Bull. Intl. Taxn. 199 (2009); B. J. Arnold, *The 2008 Update of the OECD Model: An Introduction*, 63 Bull. Intl. Taxn., *supra* note 122, at 179; Alexandra Wintsch, *supra* note 124, at 342.
130. *See* already in the preface, *Report on the Attribution of Profits to Permanent Establishments*, para. 18.
131. *Ibid.*, para. 95.
132. *Ibid.*
133. *Ibid.*, para. 105.
134. Last sentence of *OECD Model Tax Convention on Income and on Capital: Commentary on Article 4*, para. 24 (29 Apr. 2000).
135. In detail J.F. Avery Jones, *2008 OECD Model: Place of Effective Management – What One Can Learn from the History*, 63 Bull. Intl. Taxn., *supra* note 116, at 185 et seq.
136. *Draft Contents of the 2008 Update to the Model Tax Convention*, para. 3. Referring to this statements, *see* G. Bizioli, *The Evolution of the Concept of the Place of Management in Italian Case Law and Legislation: Interaction with Tax Treaties and EC Law*, 48 Eur. Taxn. 528 in particular n. 9 and 25 (2008).
137. J.F. Avery Jones, *supra* note 116, at 186.

As already announced in the draft of the 2008 model revision,[138] another update of the OECD MC and Commentary was released in July 2010,[139] but E-Commerce also played a very minor role in the 2010 update. By far, the most significant amendments concerned those related to Article 7 OECD MC. The wording of Article 7(2) OECD MC has now been directly aligned with the AOA.[140] In addition, the Commentary was adapted again, and a new report[141] was released.[142] Other amendments of the 2010 revision, besides those on Article 7 OECD MC that are related to E-Commerce in the broadest sense, included Telecommunications Transactions.[143] Several paragraphs were added to the Commentary on Article 5, which clarified, e.g., that neither a satellite in geostationary orbit[144] nor a roaming agreement with a local operator[145] could constitute a permanent establishment of the foreign enterprise. Besides those, no other E-Commerce issues have been addressed by the 2010 revision.

As a result of this historical analysis, it can be concluded that the OECD has maintained its position already set by the Ottawa Conference 1998 for the following decade and beyond. The traditional distribution of taxation rights pursuant to the OECD MC was, in principle, considered to be sufficient to address the rising tax challenges due to the advent of E-Commerce and digitalization. Several updates of the Commentary have brought clarifications on the demarcation between business profits and royalties and brought a broader understanding of the PE definition. Finally, the rules for the attribution of profits to PEs were also comprehensively amended by the 2008 and 2010 revisions to the Model and the Commentary. These amendments were laid on the groundwork of the TAGs, which originally had been set up to discuss issues arising due to the advent of E-Commerce. However, in the following years, the challenges associated with digitization were pushed by the main agenda and the focus on E-Commerce-related issues of taxation was lost. Anyway, the introduction of a minimum tax level had not yet been on the agenda of OECD's tax policy at that time.

---

138. *Report on the Attribution of Profits to Permanent Establishments*, para. 18.
139. A. Wintsch, *Attribution of Profits to Permanent Establishments: The 2008 Article 7 versus the 2010 Article 7 of the OECD Model Tax Convention*, 71 Bull. Intl. Taxn., *supra* note 124, at 342.
140. The 2010 revision also supplied a new para. 3, *see OECD Model Tax Convention on Income and on Capital: Commentary on Article 7*, para. 3 (22 Jul. 2010), but also deleted paras 3 to 6 of the previous 2008 Model, *see OECD Model Tax Convention on Income and on Capital: Commentary on Article 7*, para. 3 to 6 (17 Jul. 2008). Paragraph 7 of the *OECD Model 2008: Commentary on Article 7, supra* therefore moved forward and was incorporated into para. 4 of the *OECD Model 2010: Commentary on Article 7, supra*. Further details, *see* Alexandra Wintsch, *supra* note 124, at 346 et seq.
141. OECD, *Report on the Attribution of Profits to Permanent Establishments* (22 Jul. 2010), https://www.oecd.org/ctp/transfer-pricing/45689524.pdf (last visited 9 Jul. 2021).
142. Alexandra Wintsch, *supra* note 124, at 342.
143. At a glance E. Barret, *Aspects of the 2010 Update Other than Those Relating to Article 7 of the OECD Model Tax Convention*, 65 Bull. Intl. Taxn. 16 et seq. (2011).
144. *OECD Model Tax Convention on Income and on Capital: Commentary on Article 5*, para. 5.5 (22 Jul. 2010); in the latest version *OECD Model Tax Convention on Income and on Capital: Commentary on Article 5*, *supra* note 111, para. 27; in detail Barret, *supra* note 143, at 16 et seq.
145. *OECD Model 2010: Commentary on Article 5, supra* note 144, para. 9.1; in the latest version *OECD Model 2017: Commentary on Article 5, supra* note 111, para. 38; in detail Barret, *supra* note 143, at 17.

3.2 THE OECD/G20 AND THE BEPS-PROJECT

It was not until 2010 that the digital revolution would be back on the agenda of international tax policy discussions. More than ten years after the Ottawa Ministerial Conference, more and more critical media reports on tax planning strategies of various US IT giants became public. In particular, a critical article[146] by investigative reporter *Jesse Drucker* published by Bloomberg caused a broad outcry in the US, which has not been overheard even in Europe.[147] In his article, *Drucker* stated that *Google* had managed to keep the effective tax rate at 2.4 % in 2010 despite profits in the billions and a nominal tax burden of approximately 41 % in the state of California, where *Google's* headquarters was located.[148]

The intense media coverage and emotional debate about the low taxation of various large US corporations was the reason for the OECD, supported by the G20, to put the framework of international tax law on a new footing: On 12 February 2013, the OECD and the G20 published a report titled '*Addressing Base Erosion and Profit Shifting*'[149] leading to a paradigm shift in the international tax debate. The famous OECD/G20 BEPS project was born. The report contained a detailed analysis of artificial profit shifting and announced the development of an action plan to address the various challenges of '*Base Erosion and Profit Shifting*'. The report also concluded '*that current international tax standards may not have kept pace with changes in global business practices, in particular in the era of* [...] *the digital economy*'.[150] Just a few months later, the OECD finally published its '*Action Plan on Base Erosion and Profit Shifting*'.[151] From today's perspective, one of the most interesting statements of the 'Action Plan – Report' is the following:

> No or low taxation is not per se a cause of concern, but it becomes so when it is associated with practices that artificially segregate taxable income from the

146. Jesse Drucker, *Google 2.4% Rate Shows How $60 Billion Is Lost to Tax Loopholes*, Bloomberg.com (21 Oct. 2010), https://www.bloomberg.com/news/articles/2010-10-21/google-2-4-rate-shows-how-60-billion-u-s-revenue-lost-to-tax-loopholes (last visited 9 Jul. 2021).
147. Many consider Drucker's article as being the starting point of the discussion about taxation of the Digital Economy and the OECD-BEPS-Project, *see, i.a.*, E.D. Kleinbard, *The Lessons of Stateless Income*, 11 Fla. Tax Review 707 in particular n. 11 (2011); R. Pinkernell, *Ein Musterfall zur internationalen Steuerminimierung durch US-Konzerne*, 89 StuW 369 in particular n. 3 (2012); H.J. Ault et al., *OECD Base Erosion and Profit Shifting: A Roadmap for Reform*, 68 Bull. Intl. Taxn. 275 in particular n. 6 (2014); G. Mayr & C. Schlager, *Digitale Geschäftsmodelle und Betriebsstättenkonzept, in Digitalisierung im Konzernsteuerrecht* 23 in particular n. 5 (S. Kirchmayr et al., eds, Linde 2018); M. Mitterlehner, *Die Digital Economy im internationalen Steuerrecht, in Die österreichischen DBA nach BEPS – SWI-Spezial* 157 et seq. in particular n. 2 and 41 (S. Bendlinger et al., eds, Linde 2018); V. Bendlinger, *Die Besteuerung der Digital Economy – Eine kritische Würdigung*, 3 StAW, *supra* note 57, at 118; D. Fehling & M. Valta, *Aktionpunkt 1: Besteuerung der digitalen Wirtschaft, in BEPS-Handbuch, supra* note 76, at 36 in particular n. 13.
148. Siehe R. Pinkernell, *supra* note 147, at 369.
149. OECD, *Addressing Base Erosion and Profit Shifting* (12 Feb. 2013), https://read.oecd-ilibrary.org/taxation/addressing-base-erosion-and-profit-shifting_9789264192744-en (last visited 3 Feb. 2023).
150. *Ibid.*, at 7.
151. OECD, *Action Plan on Base Erosion and Profit Shifting* (19 Jul. 2013), https://www.oecd.org/ctp/BEPSActionPlan.pdf (last visited 23 Mar. 2023).

> activities that generate it. In other words, what creates tax policy concerns is that, due to gaps in the interaction of different tax systems, and in some cases because of the application of bilateral tax treaties, income from cross-border activities may go untaxed anywhere, or be only unduly lowly taxed.[152]

At the time, the OECD apparently did not see tax competition as a real harm to be addressed by BEPS but rather saw artificial profit shifting as a problem that needed to be addressed by the BEPS project. In any case, the 'Action Plan - Report' finally identified the need for '[f]*undamental changes [...] to effectively prevent double non-taxation, as well as cases of no or low taxation associated with practices that artificially segregate taxable income from the activities that generate it*'.[153] For the implementation of these 'fundamental changes', 15 actions have been defined, covering almost all areas of cross-border taxation. The very first of these actions was entitled 'Addressing the tax challenges of the digital economy'. Digitization was finally back on the OECD tax agenda, and as a consequence, also the EU Commission soon published a separate Report[154] addressing the challenges of the Digital Economy.

In the following years, the OECD published comprehensive reports on each of the 15 BEPS Actions, including a Final Report on Action 1 that was finally published on 5 October 2015. It contained a comprehensive analysis of the tax challenges posed by the so-called Digital Economy.[155] The report consisted of around 290 pages and tried to identify the characteristics of digitization. However, the Action 1 Final Report already famously anticipated in its Executive Summary that '[b]*ecause the digital economy is increasingly becoming the economy itself, it would be difficult, if not impossible to ring-fence the digital economy from the rest of the economy for tax purposes*'.[156] This anticipation already prophesied the conclusion of the report: Although the so-called TFDE ('Task Force on the Digital Economy') considered several solutions, such as the creation of a significant digital presence (digital PE), own withholding taxes or so-called equalization levies (now commonly referred to as 'digital services taxes')[157,158] the report ultimately did not consider any of them to be suitable options for solving the problems of the Digital Economy in international tax law and did not

152. *Ibid.*, at 10.
153. *Ibid.*, at 13.
154. European Commission, *Report of the Commission Expert Group on Taxation of the Digital Economy* (28 May 2014), https://www.diplomacy.edu/wp-content/uploads/2021/10/COMMISSION-EXPERT-GROUP-ON-TAXATION-OF-THE-DIGITAL.pdf.
155. OECD, *Addressing the Tax Challenges of the Digital Economy, Action 1 – 2015 Final Report* (OECD 5 Oct. 2015), https://www.oecd-ilibrary.org/taxation/addressing-the-tax-challenges-of-the-digital-economy-action-1-2015-final-report_9789264241046-en (last visited 3 Feb. 2023).
156. *Ibid.*, at 11.
157. In detail on the various proposed concepts presented in the Action 1 Final Report, *see* V. Bendlinger, *Die Besteuerung der Digital Economy – Eine kritische Würdigung*, 3 StAW, *supra* note 57, at 137 et seq.
158. On the debate on potential measures to tackle the tax challenges of the digital economy at that time, *see* exemplary Georg Kofler et al., *Taxation of the Digital Economy: 'Quick Fixes' or Long-Term Solution?*, 59 Eur. Taxn. 523–532 (2017); Georg Kofler et al., *Taxation of the Digital Economy: A Pragmatic Approach to Short-Term Measures*, 58 Eur. Taxn. 123–129 (2018); Wolfgang Schön, *Ten Questions About Why and How to Tax the Digitalized Economy*, 72 Bull. Intl. Taxn. 278–292 (2018).

make any recommendations.[159] Rather, the OECD promised to work towards a Final Report ('final consensus') to be presented in 2020.[160]

It took until March 2018 for the OECD to publish another comprehensive report on the Digital Economy.[161] The so-called Interim Report followed on from the Final Report on Action 1 and already considered the first effects of BEPS implementations[162] and unilateral national initiatives with regard to the taxation of the Digital Economy.[163] However, the 'Interim Report' did not provide any recommendation either. The quintessence of the report was ultimately that taxation should take place where value is created, but that within a digitized economic environment, it would be disputed how and where the creation of value takes place.[164] The 'Interim Report', thus, ended essentially with no significant results, but the OECD still promised that a final consensus would be presented in 2020.[165] Immediately after the publication of the Interim Report, the Commission published two proposals for directives, one for the introduction of a significant digital presence[166] (including a recommendation for the Member States to implement such a 'significant digital presence' within their DTCs)[167] and one for a common EU-wide digital services tax.[168] Both directive proposals ultimately failed to achieve unanimous agreement in the Council.[169] The results of BEPS in relation to the tax challenges of the Digital Economy have, therefore, been

159. '*None of the other options analysed by the TFDE were recommended at this stage*', *see* *Addressing the Tax Challenges of the Digital Economy, Action 1 – 2015 Final Report*, para. 357.
160. *Ibid.*, para. 361.
161. OECD, *Tax Challenges Arising from Digitalisation – Interim Report 2018: Inclusive Framework on BEPS* (OECD 16 Mar. 2018), https://www.oecd-ilibrary.org/taxation/tax-challenges-arising-from-digitalisation-interim-report_9789264293083-en (last visited 3 Feb. 2023).
162. *See* the separate chapter on the impact of BEPS implementation in *ibid.*, at 89–131.
163. The TFDE discussed several different unilateral measures that had been introduced, or at least announced, by several countries in response to the OECD's BEPS Action 1 report at the time of the publication of the 'Interim Report', *see Ibid.*, at 133–164.
164. *See* the chapter on value creation, provided for in *ibid.*, at 23–59. In particular para. 160 of the latter report draws the following interim conclusion: '*Differences in views over whether and the extent to which data and user participation contribute to value creation will have an impact on whether there are considered to be tax challenges arising from changing business models, or whether those are unique to the application of international tax rules to digitalised firms, or whether any challenges apply to the international tax rules more broadly. Additionally, tax challenges may not arise for some digitalised businesses if such challenges are defined by purely referring to the reliance on data and user participation. Not all digitalised businesses rely upon data and user participation to the same degree*'.
165. *Ibid.*, paras 510 and 513.
166. Proposal for a Council Directive laying down rules relating to the corporate taxation of a significant digital presence, COM(2018) 147 final.
167. Commission Recommendation of 21.3.2018 relating to the corporate taxation of a significant digital presence, C(2018) 1650 final.
168. Proposal for a Council Directive on the common system of a digital services tax on revenues resulting from the provision of certain digital services, COM(2018) 148 final.
169. The proposal on the 'significant digital presence' was last discussed in Council in mid-2018 and has not been reintroduced by the Commission since, *see* Opinion of the European Economic and Social Committee on COM(2018) 147 final and COM(2018) 148 final, 2018/0072(CNS). The proposal for the EU DST was at the agenda of the Council at 8th of March 2019 and had not been further discussed since then, *see* Note from the Council Presidency to the Permanent Representatives Committee/Council, 2018/0073(CNS). In any case, it is also unlikely that the proposals will ever be voted on again.

modest. BEPS has not led to any significant progress on the taxation of the Digital Economy, neither at the OECD nor at the EU level.

3.3 FROM BEPS TO THE PILLARS: THE OECD'S TWO PILLAR APPROACH TO ADDRESS THE DIGITAL ECONOMY THAT RATHER ADDRESSES ALL

Given the sparse progress and the pressing deadline for the promised consensus for 2020, the OECD, on 23 January 2019, together with the G20, finally published a Policy Note[170] on the way forward for taxing the Digital Economy. The policy note can be seen as the birth of the OECD's two-pillar solution:

> Consistent with the analytical framework of both the Action 1 Report and the Interim Report, there is agreement to examine proposals involving two pillars which could form the basis for consensus. One pillar addresses the broader challenges of the digitalised economy and focuses on the allocation of taxing rights, and a second pillar *addresses remaining BEPS issues*[171] (emphasis added).

With respect to these 'remaining BEPS issues', the policy note further added:

> 'Under the second pillar, the Inclusive Framework agreed to explore on a 'without prejudice' basis taxing rights that *would strengthen the ability of jurisdictions to tax profits where the other jurisdiction with taxing rights applies a low effective rate of tax to those profits*. These proposals recognise that in part the tax challenges of the digitalisation of the economy form part of the larger landscape relating to remaining BEPS challenge [...]. *The proposal under this pillar does not change the fact that countries or jurisdictions remain free to set their own tax rates or not to have a corporate income tax system at all*. Instead, the proposal considers that in the *absence of multilateral action there is a risk of un-coordinated, unilateral action*, both to attract more tax base and to protect the existing tax base, with adverse consequences for all countries, large and small, developed and developing'[172] (emphasis added).

Even if the policy note did not yet give any indication of how comprehensive this 'second pillar' would become, the statements of the note are exciting from several points of view. First of all, the last quoted paragraph reflects the division among the IF Member States: The second pillar should, on the one hand, allow '*to tax profits where the other jurisdiction with taxing rights applies a low effective rate of tax to those profits*' and on the other hand, the states should '*remain free to set their own tax rates or not to have a corporate income tax system at all*'.[173] These contrasting statements are representative of the divergent positions of Western industrialized nations and developing countries. The OECD was, thus, visibly attempting a balancing act to reconcile all

170. OECD/G20 Base Erosion and Profit Shifting Project, *Addressing the Tax Challenges of the Digitalisation of the Economy – Policy Note – As Approved by the Inclusive Framework on BEPS on 23 January 2019* (23 Jan. 2019), https://www.oecd.org/tax/beps/policy-note-beps-inclusive-framework-addressing-tax-challenges-digitalisation.pdf.
171. *Ibid.*, at 1.
172. *Ibid.*, at 2–3.
173. *Ibid.*

positions within the IF. But the last sentence of the passage is particularly interesting. Recognizing the need for a multilateral solution, the OECD quietly revealed in the Policy Note the specific purpose of the second pillar: The second pillar aimed to bring together states with differing fiscal interests to form a cartel of taxing jurisdictions to the benefit of all states involved.

In response to the Policy Note, the OECD released a programme of work (in the following PoW) in May 2019 that first included some technical considerations on both pillars.[174] Indeed, the PoW is the first document that dealt with potential design features of a global minimum tax. Chapter 3 of the PoW was dedicated to the second pillar and was titled '*Global anti-base erosion proposal (pillar II)*' which ultimately gave rise to the abbreviation GloBE, which is regularly used as a synonym for the second pillar of the OECD's 'global tax deal'. For this reason, the term will also be used by this book as a general reference to the global minimum tax.

The content of Chapter 3 was aptly summarized in the Introduction of the document: '*Chapter III focuses on remaining BEPS issues (Pillar Two), and describes the work to be undertaken in the development of a global anti-base erosion (GloBE) proposal that would, through changes to domestic law and tax treaties, provide jurisdictions with a right to 'tax back' where other jurisdictions have not exercised their primary taxing rights or the payment is otherwise subject to low levels of effective taxation*'.[175] Although the PoW, from today's point of view, was short on details, the PoW is still the basis for many ideas that are ultimately reflected in the final consensus of the GloBE Model Rules. For example, the PoW outlines for the first time the essential elements of the Income Inclusion Rule (IIR)[176] and the Undertaxed Profits Rule (UTPR).[177] It already elaborated on the use of a commonly defined minimum tax rate[178] and, for the first time, considered the use of financial accounts to determine a common tax base for the global minimum tax.[179] The relevance of the considerations set out in the PoW for the final design of the GloBE Model Rules will become particularly clear in section 4.3.2.1.

But what is particularly noteworthy with respect to the discussion of GloBE's background is its context with BEPS Action 1 on the tax challenges of the Digital Economy. In this respect, the PoW held the following:

> Recognising, as stated in the Action 1 Report, that it would be difficult, if not impossible, to ring-fence the digital economy from the rest of the economy for tax purposes, *the scope of the anti-base erosion proposal is not limited to highly digitalised businesses*. By focusing on the remaining BEPS challenges, it proposes a systematic solution designed to ensure that all internationally operating businesses pay a minimum level of tax. *In so doing, it helps to address the remaining BEPS challenges linked to the digitalising economy, where the relative importance of*

174. OECD/G20 Inclusive Framework on BEPS, *Programme of Work to Develop a Consensus Solution to the Tax Challenges Arising from the Digitalisation of the Economy* (29 May 2019), https://www.oecd.org/tax/beps/programme-of-work-to-develop-a-consensus-solution-to-the-tax-challenges-arising-from-the-digitalisation-of-the-economy.pdf.
175. *Ibid.*, para. 19.
176. *Ibid.*, paras 59 et seq.
177. *Ibid.*, paras 73 et seq.
178. *Ibid.*, paras 61–67.
179. *Ibid.*, para. 71.

intangible assets as profit drivers makes highly digitalised business often ideally placed to avail themselves of profit shifting planning structures'[180] (emphasis added).

As can be seen, the PoW sort of draws the final conclusion from the BEPS Action 1 discussion: It assumed that what today is called the 'global tax deal' could not be limited to digitalized businesses but should rather be applicable to all business models, whether digitized or not. Nevertheless, it is interesting that every GloBE-related document published by the OECD still bears the title '*Tax Challenges Arising from the Digitalisation of the Economy*'. This is also the case with the recently published GloBE Administrative Guidances 2023, which also include this phrase in their full title.[181] This can probably only be explained from a marketing point of view. In reality, the slogan '*Tax Challenges Arising from the Digitalisation of the Economy*' is only a proxy for the IF's overall recognition that the existing framework of international tax law is outdated. However, the title is unfortunately misleading and has no remaining connection with global tax reform, including Pillar Two.

In any case, the OECD made a lot of progress within the following months and finally published a Public Consultation Document in November 2019 already, including very sophisticated tax policy considerations with respect to the final design of Pillar Two. The document made evident the OECD's progress, in particular, with the detailed elaborations on the determination of the tax base, including the use of consolidated financial statements of the UPE[182] and necessary adjustments for permanent and temporary differences,[183] that had been raised for discussion for the first time. Furthermore, the document emphasized the need for a uniform determination of profits based on a limited number of 'Acceptable Financial Accounting Standards'[184] and finally raised the issue of how much blending of low- and high-taxed income should be permissible for the purposes of a global minimum tax.[185] Above all, the Public Consultation Document discussed the need for carve-outs.[186] Again, many of the considerations in the Public Consultation Document of November 2019 will be discussed with respect to the technical evolution of the ETR computation in section 4.3.2.1.

180. *Ibid.*, para. 55.
181. OECD/G20 Base Erosion and Profit Shifting Project, *Tax Challenges Arising from Digitalisation – Administrative Guidance on the Global Anti-Base Erosion Model Rules (Pillar Two)* (OECD 2 Feb. 2023), https://www.oecd.org/tax/beps/agreed-administrative-guidance-for-the-pillar-two-globe-rules.pdf (last visited 4 Feb. 2023) and OECD/G20 Base Erosion and Profit Shifting Project, *Tax Challenges Arising from Digitalisation – Administrative Guidance on the Global Anti-Base Erosion Model Rules (Pillar Two)* (OECD 17 July 2023), https://www.oecd.org/tax/beps/administrative-guidance-global-anti-base-erosion-rules-pillar-two-july-2023.pdf (last visided 26 Aug. 2023).
182. OECD/G20 Inclusive Framework on BEPS, *Public Consultation Document – Global Anti-Base Erosion Proposal ('GloBE') – Pillar Two 8 November 2019 – 2 December 2019*, para. 18 et seq. (8 Nov. 2019), https://www.oecd.org/tax/beps/public-consultation-document-global-anti-base-erosion-proposal-pillar-two.pdf.pdf.
183. *Ibid.*, paras 24–52.
184. *Ibid.*, paras 17 and 22.
185. *Ibid.*, para. 53.
186. *Ibid.*, paras 73 et seq.

The OECD received feedback from 186 different respondents, including international Multinational Enterprise (MNE) Groups, governments, NGOs and other institutions exceeding a total of 2,000 pages, demonstrating the strong political momentum of the minimum tax discussion at that time,[187] and since the global consensus was announced in 2020, the OECD was under pressure to work out a technical design for the two pillars. Meanwhile, the two-pillar approach had become the focus of international tax policy. This held particularly true for the EU and its institutions. For example, the Commission expressed its support for global corporate tax reform as early as June 2021, but at the same time held that it '*stands ready to act if no global agreement is reached*'[188] and announced to publish an '*Action Plan for Business Taxation for the 21st century*'. The EU Parliament also followed suit and expressed its support in a motion for a resolution, calling on the Commission to implement the two-pillar approach across the Union if no global solution is found by the end of 2021.[189]

In October 2020, the OECD finally published a series of documents,[190] including the report entitled '*Report on the Pillar Two Blueprint*'[191] (hereafter Pillar Two Blueprint), which is considered one of the most important milestones of the entire Pillar Two/GloBE project. The document consists of 250 pages and contains explanations on almost all topics of the global minimum tax. Fundamental tax policy decisions have already been made, such as the decision in favour of jurisdictional blending,[192] the focus on the consolidated financial statements, the entire calculation of the effective tax rate,[193] and the basic design of the 'formulaic substance-base carve-out'[194]

187. In detail on the responses to the Public Consultation Document of November 2019, *see* V. Bendlinger, *Minimum Taxation – Ergebnisse der Konsultationen zum GloBE Proposal der OECD*, 32 SWI 16–31 (2020).
188. European Commission, *Communication from the Commission to European Parliament and the Council – An Action Plan for Fair and Simple Taxation Supporting the Recovery Strategy*, COM(2020) 312 final 2 (15 Jul. 2020).
189. The EU Parliament held that it '[s]trongly encourages the Commission and the Member States to achieve a deal at international level which would then be transposed at EU level through relevant EU and national legislation; *likewise supports the commitment of the Commission President to propose an EU solution should an international deal not be reached by the end of 2020*, on the condition that this EU solution is not limited to digital businesses; understands that such a solution would strengthen the single market by establishing a minimum level of tax that would prevent unilateral measures', *see* European Parliament, *Motion for a Resolution – European Parliament Resolution of Fair Taxation in a Digitalised and Globalised Economy: BEPS 2.0, B9-0238/2019*, para. 39 (12 Dec. 2019).
190. OECD/G20 Inclusive Framework on BEPS, *Tax Challenges Arising from Digitalisation – Report on Pillar One Blueprint* (OECD 14 Oct. 2020), https://www.oecd-ilibrary.org/docserver/beba0634-en.pdf?expires=1640550469&id=id&accname=ocid177428&checksum=BEFF379130D2B3BC8092A2CAE00CBF5B (last visited 12 Jul. 2021); OECD/G20 Inclusive Framework on BEPS, *Tax Challenges Arising from Digitalisation – Report on Pillar Two Blueprint* (OECD 14 Oct. 2020), https://www.oecd-ilibrary.org/taxation/tax-challenges-arising-from-digitalisation-report-on-pillar-two-blueprint_abb4c3d1-en (last visited 12 Jul. 2021); OECD, *Tax Challenges Arising from Digitalisation – Economic Impact Assessment* (OECD 14 Oct. 2020), https://www.oecd-ilibrary.org/docserver/0e3cc2d4-en.pdf?expires=1639166673&id=id&accname=guest&checksum=2B3F1C7C5DA81212491BC040081EC41E (last visited 10 Dec. 2021).
191. *Tax Challenges Arising from Digitalisation – Report on Pillar Two Blueprint*.
192. *Ibid.*, para. 128.
193. *See* Chapter 3 of the *Ibid.*, paras 45–82.
194. *Ibid.*, para. 332 et seq.

that finally was implemented into the GloBE Model Rules as the 'substance-based income exclusion' (SBIE). The Pillar Two Blueprint can, thus, be described as the foundation of GloBE's architecture. Both the GloBE Model Rules and the GloBE Commentary are largely based on the considerations in the Pillar Two Blueprint. Moreover, the GloBE Commentary, as will be revealed in section 4, has even adopted entire paragraphs that had been included in the Pillar Two Blueprint. As will be seen, however, the design of the UTPR has changed significantly from the Blueprint to the GloBE Model Rules, one of the few fundamental design elements discarded from the Pillar Two Blueprint.

However, the Blueprints for both Pillar One and Pillar Two still did not achieve the promised final consensus. Rather, the OECD postponed and held '*to swiftly address the remaining issues with a view to bringing the process to a successful conclusion by mid-2021 and to resolve technical issues, develop model draft legislation, guidelines, and international rules and processes as necessary to enable jurisdictions to implement a consensus based solution*'.[195]

3.4 FINAL CONSENSUS: THE GloBE MODEL RULES AND STATUS QUO OF PILLAR TWO IMPLEMENTATION

In the absence of the promised 2020 consensus, the OECD continued its work on the technical frameworks of the two pillars, in particular Pillar Two, the latter visibly outpacing the developments in Pillar One. When it became obvious that the OECD would not meet the mid-2021 deadline either, the EU renewed its commitment in May 2021 to the two pillars and announced in its famous Communication '*Business Taxation for the 21st Century*' that it was considering implementing the two pillars by means of directives.[196] Indeed, in a Policy Note released on 1 July 2021 (hereafter July Statement), the OECD, together with the G20, announced that the key components of both pillars had been agreed upon, but the detailed implementation plan could only be finalized by October 2021.[197] Nevertheless, the July Statement already included some interesting details on the final consensus on Pillar Two: First of all, it stated that GloBE should have the status of a 'common approach', meaning that IF Member States should not be '*required to adopt the GloBE rules, but, if they choose to do so, they will implement and administer the rules in a way that is consistent with the outcomes provided for under Pillar Two*'[198] and that IF Member States '*accept the application of the GloBE rules applied by other IF members including agreement as to rule order and the application of any agreed safe harbours*'[199].[200] The document furthermore held, for the first time, that

195. *Ibid.*, at 12.
196. European Commission, *Communication from the Commission to the European Parliament and the Council – Business Taxation for the 21st Century* 8 (18 May 2021).
197. OECD/G20 Inclusive Framework on BEPS, *Statement on a Two-Pillar Solution to Address the Tax Challenges Arising From the Digitalisation of the Economy – 1 July 2021* 1 (1 Jul. 2021).
198. *See Ibid.*, at 3.
199. *See Ibid.*
200. The 'common approach' will be extensively discussed with respect to the relation of GloBE to public international law in s. 5.3.

the minimum rate would be set at a percentage of '*at least 15%*'.[201] In addition, the July Statement outlined the basic design features of Pillar Two, widely matching the design as set out in the Pillar Two Blueprint already. Only with respect to the UTPR, the document held that its '*methodology* [still had] *to be agreed*'.[202] Accordingly, the global minimum tax '*should be brought into law in 2022, to be effective in 2023*'.[203]

On 8 October 2021, the OECD finally presented its so-called October Statement. It closely followed the July Statement but finally announced that the IF had agreed on the main components of Pillar Two.[204] There was little new information in the October Statement that had not already been included in the July Statement. However, it was stated that the minimum tax rate used should be equal to 15%[205] (not 'at least' 15%), and the October Statement teased some details on the UTPR, which was obviously different from the design presented in the Blueprint.[206] With respect to the implementation timeline, the October Statement kept the plan to bring Pillar Two into law in 2022, coming into effect in 2023, but further added that the UTPR should only come into effect in 2024.[207]

Nevertheless, the Annex of the document contained an implementation plan:

> *Model rules to give effect to the GloBE rules will be developed by the end of November 2021.* These model rules will define the scope and set out the mechanics of the GloBE rules. They will include the rules for determining the ETR on a jurisdictional basis and the relevant exclusions, such as the formulaic substance-based carve-out. The model rules will also cover administrative provisions that address an MNE's filing obligations and the use of any administrative safe-harbours. The model rules will further include transition rules. The model rules are supplemented by commentary that explains the purpose and operation of the rules and addresses the need for a switch-over rule in certain treaties and in circumstances that otherwise commit the contracting parties to the use of the exemption method.[208]

Furthermore, the document announced that the OECD would develop (i) a model treaty provision including a Commentary on a Subject-To-Tax-Rule (STTR) until the end of November 2021, (ii) a multilateral instrument to be presented by mid-2022 '*to facilitate the swift and consistent implementation of the STTR in relevant bilateral treaties*'[209] and, (iii) at latest by the end of 2022, a so-called implementation framework

201. *See* OECD/G20 Inclusive Framework on BEPS, *supra* note 197, at 4.
202. *See Ibid.*
203. *See Ibid.*, at 5.
204. OECD/G20 Inclusive Framework on BEPS, *Statement on a Two-Pillar Solution to Address the Tax Challenges Arising From the Digitalisation of the Economy – 8 October 2021* (8 Oct. 2021), https://www.oecd.org/tax/beps/statement-on-a-two-pillar-solution-to-address-the-tax-challenges-arising-from-the-digitalisation-of-the-economy-october-2021.pdf.
205. *Ibid.*, at 4.
206. While the allocation of the 'Top-up Tax' according to the Blueprint was still to be carried out on the basis of deductible payments, *see Tax Challenges Arising from Digitalisation – Report on Pillar Two Blueprint*, at 123 et seq., the October Statement merely stated that '[t]*he UTPR allocates top-up tax from low-tax constituent entities including those located in the UPE jurisdiction*', *see OECD/G20 Statement 8 October*, at 4.
207. *OECD/G20 Statement 8 October*, at 5.
208. *Ibid.*, at 7.
209. *Ibid.*

to set out administrative procedures and safe-harbours '*to facilitate both compliance by MNEs and administration by tax authorities*'.[210] Above all, the OECD stated that it would consider the development of a Multilateral Convention (MLC) to coordinate the implementation of GloBE.[211]

After a slight delay, the 55-page GloBE Model Rules[212] were proudly published on 20 December 2021, representing a consensus of 135 IF Member States at that time and including a note that its '*implementation* [...] *is envisaged by 2023*'.[213] Only two days later, the EU Commission published a proposal for a GloBE-Directive[214] '*reflect*[ing] *the global OECD agreement, with some necessary adjustments, to guarantee conformity with EU law*'[215] including 57 articles. The proposal originally aimed to follow the timeline of the October Statement and was to be implemented before the end of 2022 and take effect from 2023 (with the exception of the UTPR, which will take effect from 1 January 2024).[216] In the legislative process, the compromise texts negotiated in Council should amend the transposition article to require domestic implementation until 31 December 2023, which effectively meant that the proposal would come into effect from 1 January 2024, as some Member States argued that '*implementation as of 1 January 2023 would cause them significant practical or institutional difficulties*'.[217]

When the OECD published the Commentary on the GloBE Model Rules (in the following GloBE Commentary) in March 2022, the EU had already struggled to find a political consensus for achieving unanimity in the Council to finally pass the GloBE-Directive Proposal. The unanimity requirement of Article 115 TFEU proved to be a hurdle for the planned GloBE-Directive: Although the French Council Presidency placed a strong focus on global tax reform in the first half of 2022 and brought the GloBE-Directive proposal to a vote several times, the proposal failed several times due to the veto of individual Member States. Initially, concerns were raised with respect to (i) the missing link between Pillar One and Pillar Two, as some Member States argued that both Pillars were to be seen as a package, (ii) the strict deadline for implementation at the beginning of 2023 and furthermore (iii) some Member States argued that the application of the IIR should not be mandatory but optional.[218]

While the latter two issues were to some extent addressed in the compromise text soon, by shifting the implementation to the end of 2023 and by adding an option for Member State in which no more than 10 UPEs are 'located' to not apply the GloBE Rules,[219] the missing link to Pillar One was further invoked by some Member States. In

210. *Ibid.*
211. *Ibid.*
212. *GloBE Model Rules.*
213. *See* the foreword of *ibid.*, at 3.
214. Proposal for a Council Directive on ensuring a global minimum level of taxation for multinational groups in the Union, COM(2021) 823 final.
215. *See* the Explanatory Memorandum of *ibid.* 1.
216. *See* Art. 55 *Ibid.* 71.
217. Note from the Permanent Representatives Committee (Part 2) to Council on the Directive on ensuring a global minimum level of taxation for multinational groups in the Union, 2021/0433(CNS) 5.
218. *See Ibid.*, 4–5.
219. The article had initially been implemented as Art. 47a of a compromise text dated 12th March 2023, *see* Draft Council Directive on ensuring a global minimum level of taxation for

particular, Poland held up the claim that Pillar Two should not be adopted without Pillar One and voted against the adoption of the revised compromise text[220] at the ECOFIN meeting on 5 April 2022. When the French Presidency put the proposal to the vote again in the ECOFIN meeting of 17 June 2022,[221] things became dramatic: Poland, at first, again opposed the proposal. Later, however, it lifted its reservations and signalled its approval. Meanwhile, Hungary, which had previously voted in favour of the proposal on 5 April 2022, prevented a unanimous decision with little warning.[222] Finally, the French Presidency in Council ended in mid-2022 without any successful enactment of the GloBE-Directive, leading to a joint declaration of Germany, France, Spain, Italy and the Netherlands to implement GloBE unilaterally if no consensus could be achieved at the EU level.[223] Initially, there had been speculation that the end of the French Presidency might also mean the end of the GloBE-Directive. Nevertheless, the Czech Presidency, following the French term, soon expressed further support the global tax deal and announced that it would continue to work towards an agreement for an EU-wide implementation of Pillar Two.[224] After tough negotiations, Hungary dropped its veto in December 2022,[225] and the Council took a valid unanimous decision to adopt the GloBE-Directive,[226] and the EU announced the successful unanimous decision of the Council in a press release[227] dated 12 December 2022. On 22 December

multinational groups in the Union – Compromise Text 12 Mar. 2022, 2021/0433(CNS). Today, the provision is found in Art. 50 of the adopted GloBE-Directive (2022/2523). In detail on this provision, *see* s. 4.4.2.8.4.

220. Draft Council Directive on ensuring a global minimum level of taxation for multinational groups in the Union – Compromise Text 28 Mar. 2022, 2021/0433(CNS).

221. *See* the compromise text discussed on 17 June 2022, Draft Council Directive on ensuring a global minimum level of taxation for multinational groups in the Union—Compromise Text 21 June 2022, 2021/0433(CNS).

222. *See* the audio transcripts available at https://video.consilium.europa.eu/event/en/25923 (accessed 6 Feb. 2023).

223. *See* the *Joint Statement by France, Germany, Italy, Netherlands and Spain* (9 Sep. 2022), (last visited 9 Feb. 2023), where it was held: '*At the June 2022 Ecofin, 26 out of 27 EU member states expressed their willingness to implement this important step towards tax justice, and our first goal remains to gather a consensus. Should unanimity not be reached in the next weeks, our governments are fully determined to follow through on our commitment. We stand ready to implement the global minimum effective taxation in 2023 and by any possible legal means. We are also fully committed to complete the work on the better reallocation of taxing rights from huge global multinationals' profits with the objective of signing a multilateral convention by mid-2023*'.

224. In the media, *see*, e.g., Aneta Zachová, *Czech EU Presidency Aims for 15% Corporate Tax Deal by End of October*, www.euractiv.com, https://www.euractiv.com/section/politics/short_news/czech-eu-presidency-aims-for-15-corporate-tax-deal-by-end-of-october/ (last visited 6 Feb. 2023).

225. In the media, *see*, e.g., János Allenbach-Ammann, *Orbán Backs down: EU Agrees on Ukraine Aid and Minimum Tax*, www.euractiv.com, https://www.euractiv.com/section/economy-jobs/news/orban-backs-down-eu-agrees-on-ukraine-aid-and-minimum-tax/ (last visited 6 Feb. 2023).

226. Note from the Presidency to Council on the Council Directive ensuring a global minimum level of taxation for multinational enterprise groups and large-scale domestic groups in the Union, 2021/0433(COD).

227. European Council, *Press Release 12 December 2022 – International Taxation: Council Reaches Agreement on a Minimum Level of Taxation for Largest Corporations*, https://www.consilium.europa.eu/en/press/press-releases/2022/12/12/international-taxation-council-reaches-agreement-on-a-minimum-level-of-taxation-for-largest-corporations/ (last visited 6 Feb. 2023).

2022, the GloBE-Directive was published in the Official Journal of the EU.[228] Pursuant to Article 56 GloBE-Directive, the Member States shall transpose the directive by 31 December 2023 and shall apply the rules of the directive for 'Fiscal Years' beginning from 31 December 2023. In addition to the EU, many jurisdictions, including the UK,[229] the Netherlands,[230] Germany,[231] Liechtenstein,[232] South Korea[233] and Switzerland,[234] have now also published or are working on draft legislation for the implementation of Pillar Two. Others have at least publicly committed to Pillar Two and have announced to plan to implement Pillar Two into their domestic laws.[235] However, in particular, the US position will be significant for the successful implementation of Pillar Two, but as yet, it is far from clear whether the US Congress will agree to a major shift in the international tax landscape, including the global minimum tax.[236] So, what is the status quo on the OECD level?

The OECD is still behind schedule. What is still missing from the October statement 2021[237] is (i) a guidance on as to whether and how the once proposed Switch-Over Rule (SOR) will ever be implemented to ensure that the GloBE Rules can be applied with respect to exempted PE income[238] and furthermore, it seems that (ii) the MLC for Pillar Two, which had been considered by the IF, is, at least for the time being, off the table.[239] It remains to be seen, however, whether or not it will come back with regard to the debate on the treaty compatibility of GloBE (in detail, *see* section 5.6.).

In any case, within the last year, the OECD has made considerable progress on the remaining topics of Pillar Two. Beginning from the end of 2022, the OECD published a

228. GloBE-Directive (2022/2523).
229. *See* the UK's draft legislation available at https://assets.publishing.service.gov.uk/government/uploads/system/uploads/attachment_data/file/1092586/Draft_legislation.pdf (accessed 6 Feb. 2023).
230. Ministerie van Financiën, nieuwsbericht, *Netherlands Launches Online Consultation on Draft Bill for the Proposed Minimum Tax Rate Act 2024 – News Item – Government.Nl, supra* note 4.
231. *See* German Ministry of Finance, *Entwurf eines Gesetzes für die Umsetzung der Richtlinie zur Gewährleistung einer globalen Mindestbesteuerung für multinationale Unternehmensgruppen und große inländische Gruppen in der Union (Mindestbesteuerungsrichtlinie-Umsetzungsgesetz – MinBestRL-UmsG), supra* note 4.
232. *See* Administration of Liechtenstein, *Press Release – Regierung verabschiedet Vernehmlassungsbericht zur Einführung der globalen Mindestbesteuerung in Liechtenstein, supra* note 4.
233. *See First Domestic Pillar Two Global Minimum Tax Law Enacted», supra* note 4.
234. *See* the Swiss draft legislation available at https://www.newsd.admin.ch/newsd/message/attachments/72626.pdf (accessed 6. Feb 2023).
235. For an overview, *see* John Vella, *The Two Pillar Solution One Year On*, 67 BTR 504 et seq. (2022).
236. For a broad perspective on the US position to the international tax reform, *see* Mindy Herzfeld, *How to Think About How the US Congress Thinks About International Tax Reforms*, 67 BTR 550 et seq. (in particular 571–572) (2022).
237. *OECD/G20 Statement 8 October*, at 7.
238. Although the October Statement still mentioned the SOR in its Annex, *see OECD/G20 Statement 8 October*, at 7, it did not contain any further details on the SOR, and finally, any guidance on a possible implementation of the SOR is still missing. The GloBE Commentary only shortly addresses the possibility to secure treaty compatibility of the IIR by way of including the SOR in treaties, *see GloBE Commentary on Article 2 GloBE Model Rules (2022)*, para. 2.
239. Also *see* C. Noonan & V. Plekhanova, *Compliance Challenges of the BEPS Two-Pillar Solution*, 67 BTR 524 (2022).

series of new documents on Pillar Two. The first of these documents was published on 6 October 2022, addressing the impact of GloBE on tax incentives.[240] This document was followed by another report released on 15 December 2022, which addresses the design of safe harbour regulations for the first time.[241] Furthermore, just a few days later, the OECD published a public consultation document on the GloBE Information Return, which was supplemented with a further document on 13 July 2023.[242] On the same day, the OECD also published a document providing extensive information on the design of a treaty-based and Pillar Two-related STTR.[243] Since both the administrative issues and the STTR as a separate treaty provision are beyond the scope of this book, which focuses on the substantive issues of the global minimum tax (for details on the scope of this book, *see* section 2.1.), these documents are of limited relevance to this examination.

However, on 2 February 2023, as well as on 13 July 2023,[244] the OECD released the first so-called GloBE Administrative Guidances, two documents that contain the first clarifications to the GloBE Model Rules alongside the GloBE Commentary and provide for first amendments and additions to the GloBE Commentary. In particular, those clarifications provided in the GloBE Administrative Guidance released in February 2023 are highly relevant to this thesis and have already been fully taken into consideration. The GloBE Administrative Guidance published in July 2023 has been taken into account as far as possible at the time of going to press.

---

240. OECD, *Tax Incentives and the Global Minimum Corporate Tax: Reconsidering Tax Incentives after the GloBE Rules* (6 Oct. 2022), https://www.oecd-ilibrary.org/taxation/tax-incentives-and-the-global-minimum-corporate-tax_25d30b96-en (last visited 9 Feb. 2023).
241. OECD/G20 Base Erosion and Profit Shifting Project, *Safe Harbours and Penalty Relief: Global Anti-Base Erosion Rules (Pillar Two)* (15 Dec. 2022).
242. OECD, *Public Consultation Document – Pillar Two – GloBE Information Return* (20 Dec. 2022), https://www.oecd.org/tax/beps/public-consultation-document-pillar-two-globe-information-return.pdf (last visited 6 Feb. 2023). Also see OECD/G20 Base Erosion and Profit Shifting Project, *Tax Challenges Arising from Digitalisation – GloBE Information Return (Pillar Two)* (13 July 2023), https://www.oecd.org/tax/beps/globe-information-return-pillar-two.pdf (last visited 26 Aug. 2023).
243. OECD/G20 Base Erosion and Profit Shifting Project, *Tax Challenges Arising from Digitalsiation – Subject to Tax Rule (Pillar Two)* (13 July 2023), https://www.oecd-ilibrary.org/docserver/9afd6856-en.pdf?expires=1693084252&id=id&accname=ocid177380&checksum=2B01FD16DB458C2BBED34A309350FE1A (last visited 26 Aug. 2023). On the delay of the STTR and the corresponding Commentary, *see* Vella, *supra* note 235, at 507., https://www.oecd.org/tax/beps/safe-harbours-and-penalty-relief-global-anti-base-erosion-rules-pillar-two.pdf (last visited 6 Feb. 2023).
244. OECD/G20 Base Erosion and Profit Shifting Project, *Tax Challenges Arising from Digitalisation – Administrative Guidance on the Global Anti-Base Erosion Model Rules (Pillar Two)* (OECD 2 Feb. 2023), https://www.oecd.org/tax/beps/agreed-administrative-guidance-for-the-pillar-two-globe-rules.pdf (last visited 4 Feb. 2023) and OECD/G20 Base Erosion and Profit Shifting Project, *Tax Challenges Arising from Digitalisation – Administrative Guidance on the Global Anti-Base Erosion Model Rules (Pillar Two)* (OECD 13 July 2023), https://www.oecd.org/tax/beps/administrative-guidance-global-anti-base-erosion-rules-pillar-two-july-2023.pdf (last visited 26 Aug. 2023).

CHAPTER 4

The Technical Design of the GloBE Model Rules and Their Implementation in the GloBE-Directive

4.1 AN OVERVIEW AND AN ASSUMPTION WITH REGARD TO THE INTERPRETATION OF THE GLOBE-DIRECTIVE

The GloBE Model Rules represent the final consensus of more than 130 jurisdictions of the IF and provide for a comprehensive set of rules: they include 60 pages of model legislation, supplemented by a definition chapter of more than ten pages and a Commentary exceeding 300 pages. Furthermore, the OECD provides an Example catalogue that aims to further clarify the operation of specific provisions. The EU's GloBE-Directive is strongly based on the GloBE Model Rules and only deviates from them in very exceptional cases. Most of the contents have been adopted by the EU and, in some cases, even word for word. The GloBE-Directive also adopted the basic structure of the GloBE Model Rules.

The following section is dedicated to the technical framework of both the GloBE Model Rules and the GloBE-Directive. Correspondingly, the following section is structured similarly to both frameworks: section 4.2. will examine the scope of GloBE that includes the ambit of an 'MNE Group' and the application of the famous EUR 750 million threshold. The subsequent section 4.3. will deal with the computation of the ETR being the division between 'Covered Taxes' paid within a specific jurisdiction and the 'GloBE Income' received in that jurisdiction. Section 4.4. is devoted to the actual computation and the charging of the 'Top-up Tax'. Finally, section 4.5. points out eight theses resulting from the technical analysis of GloBE.

The whole section is based on the assumption that those provisions of the GloBE-Directive that are modelled in accordance with the GloBE Model Rules are to be interpreted in the same way as the latter and the interpretations set out in the OECD's GloBE Commentary and the Examples can also be invoked for the GloBE-Directive.

This assumption is first based on recital 6, where the GloBE-Directive notes the following: '*It is necessary to implement the OECD Model Rules agreed by the Member States in a way that remains as close as possible to the global agreement, in order to ensure that the rules implemented by the Member States pursuant to this Directive are qualified within the meaning of the OECD Model Rules.*'[245] Second, recital 24 of the GloBE-Directive also refers to the OECD materials mentioned above with respect to the GloBE-Directive's interpretation: '*In implementing this Directive, Member States should use the OECD Model Rules and the explanations and examples in the Tax Challenges Arising from the Digitalisation of the Economy – Commentary to the Global Anti-Base Erosion Model Rules (Pillar Two) released by the OECD/G20 Inclusive Framework on BEPS, as well as the GloBE Implementation Framework, including its safe harbour rules, as a source of illustration or interpretation in order to ensure consistency in application across Member States to the extent that those sources are consistent with this Directive and Union law. Such safe harbour rules should be of relevance as regards MNE groups as well as large-scale domestic groups.*'[246] The assumption that provisions of the GloBE-Directive merely reflect the GloBE Model Rules are to be interpreted along the lines of the latter and will, therefore, not be questioned in the following section. However, this assumption should not obscure the fact that the OECD materials mentioned are neither a source of law nor of any other binding nature for the EU, its Member States, IF Member States or any other states. It is not doubted by the author that the provisions of the GloBE-Directive are, in principle, to be interpreted autonomously. Furthermore, the assumption is only applied in the respect that the GloBE-Directive reflects an equivalent provision in the GloBE Model Rules. The assumption is neither applied if the GloBE-Directive deviates from the GloBE Model Rules nor if it implements any content that is not reflected in the GloBE Model Rules at all. Above all, the assumption also fails with respect to OECD materials that had been released after the GloBE-Directive had been enacted and notified on 23 December 2022. For this reason, the changes proposed by the February and July 2023 GloBE Administrative Guidances,[247] published on 2 February 2022, cannot be readily applied to the interpretation of the GloBE-Directive. Particular caution is therefore required with regard to subsequent amendments to the OECD materials on which the GloBE-Directive is based: An interpretation of the GloBE-Directive on the basis of the GloBE Administrative Guidances or any further clarifications that might be released in the future is only possible if the result of the interpretation can also be supported in view of the wording of the GloBE-Directive and if the reasoning put forward is convincing.

Due to the fact that both the GloBE Model Rules as well as the GloBE-Directive make extensive use of legal definitions, any expression that is separately defined either in the GloBE Model Rules or the GloBE-Directive will be put in between question marks to disclose that the respective term is subject to an individual definition within the GloBE Model Rules (e.g., 'Excluded Entity'). They are, as in the GloBE Model Rules (but different from the GloBE-Directive), written with capital letters. If the definitions

245. Recital 6 GloBE-Directive (2022/2523).
246. Recital 24 *Ibid.*
247. *GloBE Administrative Guidance February 2023* and *GloBE Administrative Guidance July 2023.*

within the GloBE Model Rules and the GloBE-Directive deviate from each other, the respective differences will be addressed separately.

4.2 THE SCOPE OF GLOBE

4.2.1 The 'MNE Group' as a Taxable Subject: Membership in an 'MNE Group' as a Prerequisite for Minimum Tax Liability

Corporate Income Taxes (CITs) typically tax individual corporations. Most jurisdictions, thus, consider each individual legal entity as a taxable person ('separate entity approach'). This international practice is particularly evident in Articles 1 and 4(1) OECD MC, where the applicability of a tax treaty to corporations is explicitly linked to the term 'person'. In contrast, Article 1.1.1. GloBE Model Rules states that *'the GloBE Rules apply to Constituent Entities that are members of an MNE Group that has annual revenue of EUR 750 million or more in the Consolidated Financial Statements of the Ultimate Parent Entity (UPE)'*.[248] Although this wording clearly subjects individual so-called Constituent Entities (hereinafter 'CEs') to the minimum tax, it only applies to them if the combined so-called MNE Group meets the revenue threshold of EUR 750 million. One is therefore tempted to compare GloBE with national group taxation schemes that allow offsetting profits and losses of different taxpayers, which are linked to each other through 'Ownership Interest'. In contrast to national group taxation schemes, however, the individual CEs are only subject to tax if they are part of an 'MNE Group'. Within the framework of GloBE, the group membership decides whether an entity is liable to the minimum tax or not. In other words, as the Commentary states, *'the Constituent Entities of a Group will not be subject to the GloBE Rules unless they are members of an MNE Group'*.[249]

4.2.2 Requirement of Multinationality of an 'MNE Group' and EU Extension to 'Large-Scale Domestic Groups'

Pursuant to Article 1.2.1. GloBE Model Rules an 'MNE Group' *'means any Group that includes at least one Entity or Permanent Establishment that is not located in the jurisdiction of the Ultimate Parent Entity'*.[250] GloBE, thus, is only applicable from the outset if an entity has at least one subsidiary or branch in a different tax jurisdiction. However, a single foreign entity or foreign PE is sufficient to fulfil the scope of GloBE.[251] Only purely domestic groups are exempted from the GloBE Model Rules, even if the EUR 750 million threshold is exceeded. Consequently, tax jurisdictions are free to tax purely domestic groups below the minimum tax level of 15%,[252] as defined by GloBE. The policy rationale for excluding purely domestic groups is simple: the application of

248. Article 1.1.1. *GloBE Model Rules*. Also *see* Art. 2(1) GloBE-Directive (2022/2523).
249. *GloBE Commentary on Article 1 GloBE Model Rules (2022)*, para. 18.
250. Article 1.2.1. *GloBE Model Rules*.
251. *See GloBE Commentary on Article 1*, *supra* note 249, para. 20.
252. *See* Art. 10.1. *GloBE Model Rules*, at 60.

GloBE to domestic groups simply makes no sense, as purely domestic groups do not give rise to profit shifting. Furthermore, the OECD regularly emphasizes that GloBE is a 'common approach'[253] and even IF Member States are, thus, free to decide whether to adopt GloBE or not. If purely domestic groups were to be covered, this would be tantamount to imposing a 15% corporate income tax on groups exceeding the EUR 750 million threshold. Such an obligation would not be politically enforceable even within the IF and would directly restrict jurisdictions' tax sovereignty. Apart from this, groups of cooperations operating solely within a single jurisdiction and exceeding EUR 750 million in revenues are likely to be a rare phenomenon.

As theoretical as this discussion may be, the limitation of the scope of application to 'multinational' groups has relevance, especially for the EU: The EU internal market is characterized by prohibitions of discrimination,[254] first and foremost those of the fundamental freedoms which are intended to curb discrimination of cross-border compared to domestic situations.[255] Consequently, it does not require a deeper analysis to conclude that the multinationality requirement in Article 1.2.1 GloBE Model Rules contains a discriminatory element that is in tension with fundamental freedoms. In this respect, it is not surprising that the EU Commission deliberately extended the scope in Article 2 GloBE-Directive to so-called large-scale domestic groups[256] consisting solely of entities which are located within a single Member State.[257] Capturing these 'large-scale domestic groups' serves two functions for the GloBE-Directive:[258] first, the extension of the GloBE-Directive to domestic groups enables the EU to base its competence to issue the GloBE-Directive on the argument that the GloBE-Directive ensured the implementation of GloBE in compatibility with the fundamental freedoms,[259] and second, capturing domestic groups ensures that the GloBE-Directive itself complies with the fundamental freedoms. Finally, secondary law must also meet the requirements of primary law.[260] Furthermore, the GloBE-Directive, contrary to the GloBE Model

253. *OECD/G20 Statement 8 October*, at 3.
254. Article 18 TFEU.
255. Article 26(2) TFEU.
256. *See* the definition of 'large-scale domestic groups' in Art. 3(5) GloBE-Directive (2022/2523).
257. *See* Recital 6 of the *Ibid.*, where it is held: '*To ensure compatibility with primary Union law, and more precisely with the freedom of establishment, the rules of this Directive should apply to entities resident in a Member State as well as non-resident entities of a parent entity located in that Member State. This Directive should also apply to very large-scale, purely domestic groups. In this way, the legal framework would be designed to avoid any risk of discrimination between cross-border and domestic situations*'.
258. *See* V. Bendlinger, *Die OECD Model Rules für ein globales Mindestbesteuerungsregime*, 32 SWI 14 (2022).
259. In detail, *see* s. 6.1.2.3.3.
260. *See, i.a.*, R. Szudoczky, *The Relationship Between Primary, Secondary and National Law*, in *Research Handbook on European Union Taxation Law* 93 et seq. (C. Panayi et al., eds, Edward Elgar Publishing 2020); R.A. Achleitner, *Die sekundärrechtliche Ausformung der Grundfreiheiten des Binnenmarktes*, in *Autoritäres vs Liberales Europa* 89 et seq. (M. Kopetzki et al., eds, Jan Sramek 2019). In detail, also *see* s. 6.2.1.

Rules,[261] is also obliged to collect 'Top-up Tax' arising at the level of domestic subsidiaries of 'MNE Groups'.[262]

4.2.3 The 'Group' and Its Scope: The Relevance of 'Consolidated Financial Statements' and the 'Acceptable Financial Accounting Standards'

4.2.3.1 Structure of the Definition of the Term 'Group'

The term 'MNE Group' contains not only the criterion of multinationality but, above all, the requirement of a 'Group'. The term 'Group' is determined in Article 1.2.2. GloBE Model Rules (Article 3[3][a] GloBE-Directive) and '*means a collection of Entities that are related through ownership or control such that the assets, liabilities, expenses and cash flows of those Entities: (a) are included in the Consolidated Financial Statements of the Ultimate Parent Entity; or (b) are excluded from the Consolidated Financial Statements of the Ultimate Parent Entity solely on size or materiality ground, or on the grounds that the Entity is held for sale*'.[263] Furthermore, according to Article 1.2.3. GloBE Model Rules (Article 3[3][b] GloBE-Directive), a 'Group' also '*means an Entity that is located in one jurisdiction and has one or more*' PEs in other jurisdictions without having any foreign subsidiaries. A separate sub-chapter is devoted to each of these three scenarios below.

4.2.3.2 Group Membership Due to Inclusion in the 'Consolidated Financial Statements' of the UPE

According to Article 1.2.2.(a) GloBE Model Rules and Article 3(3)(a) GloBE-Directive a 'Group' '*means a collection of Entities that are related through ownership or control such that the assets, liabilities, expenses and cash flows of those Entities: (a) are included in the Consolidated Financial Statements of the Ultimate Parent Entity*'.[264] A 'Group' consequently consists of all legal entities that are consolidated on a line-by-line basis within the 'Consolidated Financial Statements' of the UPE (so-called accounting consolidation test[265]). The GloBE Model Rules, as well as the GloBE-Directive, define the term 'Consolidated Financial Statements' as '*the financial statements prepared by an Entity in accordance with an Acceptable Financial Accounting Standard, in which the assets, liabilities, income, expenses and cash flows of that Entity and the Entities in which it has a Controlling Interest are presented as those of a single economic unit*'.[266]

---

261. Pursuant to Art. 2.1.6. *GloBE Model Rules* a 'Parent Entity' shall only apply the IIR with respect to a 'Low-Taxed Constituent Entity that is *not* located' (emphasis added) in the same jurisdiction as the 'Parent Entity'.
262. *See* Arts 5(2), 6(2), 7(2) and 8(2) GloBE-Directive (2022/2523).
263. Article 1.2.2. *GloBE Model Rules*.
264. Article 1.2.2.(a) *Ibid*.
265. *See GloBE Commentary on Article 1 GloBE Model Rules (2022)*, *supra* note 249, para. 20.
266. *See* letter a of the definition of 'Consolidated Financial Statements' in Art. 10.1. *GloBE Model Rules*, at 53. Also *see* the corresponding definition with marginal textual differences in Art. 3(6)(a) GloBE-Directive (2022/2523).

Thus, the scope of the 'Group' depends on the scope of consolidation (in German '*Konsolidierungskreis*') of the accounting standard applied by the UPE.

The use of consolidation standards to define the scope of GloBE was intensively discussed in the Pillar Two Blueprint published in October 2020, where the OECD concluded that relying on existing standards first brings the scope of GloBE in line with definitions used for purposes of CbC Reporting (CbCR)[267] in BEPS Action 13[268] and second, '*has a number of* [further] *advantages*'.[269] It was stated that consolidation rules are '*robust, comprehensive and relatively consistent*' across different accounting standards, that these standards are regularly reviewed '*by independent financial accounting auditors*' and that the definition of the term 'Group', by simply referring to the consolidated standard applied, could even '*reduce the incentive for* ['Groups'] [...] *to adopt structures designed to artificially exclude or include subsidiaries from the group*'.[270] The starting point for these considerations was probably the fact that the largest global companies consolidate primarily in International Financial Reporting Standards (IFRS) or US-GAAP and other comparable internationally 'accepted' accounting standards. Finally, the OECD stated, albeit not on the scope but on income determination, that the '*International Financial Reporting Standards (IFRS) and the generally accepted accounting principles (GAAP) of many Inclusive Framework jurisdictions have far more commonalities than differences.*'[271]

Nevertheless, the definition of Group in Article 1.2.2.(a) GloBE Model Rules and Article 3(3)(a) GloBE-Directive reveals that the accounting standard is of paramount importance for the scope of GloBE, and it would probably have been peculiar to leave the scope of the global minimum tax exclusively to domestic corporate laws: Since the GloBE Model Rules (as well as the GloBE-Directive) by relying on the 'Consolidated Financial Statements' define the scope of minimum taxation by a mere reference to national accounting standards, it would be up to the state of residence of the UPE to reduce the scope of application of GloBE for resident 'MNE Groups' by simply implementing particularly lax consolidation rules in domestic corporate law. Low-Tax Jurisdictions could simply protect resident MNE corporations from the GloBE Rules by lowering consolidation requirements. Despite this conceptual risk, it was also clear from the outset that a political consensus for the exclusive use of a single accounting standard (exclusive use of IFRS was under discussion in this regard)[272] could neither be achieved with political consensus nor would it have been reasonable to oblige all

267. *See Tax Challenges Arising from Digitalisation – Report on Pillar Two Blueprint*, paras 43 and 45.
268. OECD/G20, *Transfer Pricing Documentation and Country-by-Country Reporting, Action 13: 2015 Final Report* (OECD 5 Oct. 2015), https://read.oecd-ilibrary.org/taxation/transfer-pricing-documentation-and-country-by-country-reporting-action-13-2015-final-report_9789264241480-en#page1 (last visited 23 May 2022).
269. *See Tax Challenges Arising from Digitalisation – Report on Pillar Two Blueprint*, para. 44. In the same vein on the use of financial accounts for the purpose of GloBE's tax base determination, also *see Ibid.*, para. 157.
270. *See Tax Challenges Arising from Digitalisation – Report on Pillar Two Blueprint*, para. 44.
271. *Ibid.*, para. 158.
272. Comprehensively on this discussion and the responses to the public consultation process on Pillar Two in 2020, *see* V. Bendlinger, *Minimum Taxation – Ergebnisse der Konsultationen zum GloBE Proposal der OECD*, 32 SWI, *supra* note 187, at 21 and 27 et seq.

in-scope MNEs used to prepare their financial statements in local GAAP to suddenly be forced to switch to the IFRS. Consequently, the OECD had to acknowledge several accounting standards but, at the same time, had to define a certain benchmark for the accounting standards to be 'accepted' for purposes of GloBE to combat circumvention by domestic corporate laws.[273]

Within GloBE, this benchmark is called the 'Acceptable Financial Accounting Standard'.[274] The IFRS[275] and various other accounting standards of IF Member States, in particular also all accounting standards of '*Member States of the European Union*', are considered as an 'Acceptable Financial Accounting Standard'.[276] The primary mention of IFRS is implicitly intended to give IFRS a certain guiding effect:[277] the global minimum tax should, of course, also cover 'MNE Groups' that either (i) do not prepare their accounts in accordance with an 'Acceptable Financial Accounting Standard' or (ii) do not even have to prepare a 'Consolidated Financial Statement' according to Article 1.2.2.(a) GloBE Model Rules or Article 3(3)(a) GloBE-Directive (also *see* Articles 3[27] and 15[3] GloBE-Directive) in their state of residence at all. In these cases, the 'Consolidated Financial Statements' are those financial statements which either (i) '*have been prepared subject to adjustments to prevent any Material Competitive Distortions*'[278] or (ii) '*would have been prepared if such Entity were required to prepare such statements in accordance with an Authorised Financial Accounting Standard that is either an Acceptable Financial Accounting Standard or another financial accounting standard that is adjusted to prevent Material Competitive Distortions*'.[279] The policy rationale behind this 'Material Competitive Distortion' test is aptly set out in the Commentary, where it is held that the '*Material Competitive Distortions limitation serves as a normalising rule to limit the benefit that MNE Groups might otherwise achieve from unique accounting principles and standards permitted under an Authorised Financial Accounting Standard that are not available under an agreed Acceptable Financial Accounting Standard.*'[280] The so-called Material Competitive Distortion Test

273. In detail on the question whether GloBE might lead to a competition of accounting standards, *see* s. 4.5.7.
274. *See* Art. 10.1. *GloBE Model Rules*, at 52. Also *see* Art. 3(22) GloBE-Directive (2022/2523).
275. In this context, Art. 3(22) GloBE-Directive (2022/2523) refers to Regulation (EC) No 1606/2002 of the European Parliament and of the Council of 19 July 2002 on the application of International Accounting Standards, OJ (1).
276. *See* Art. 10.1. *GloBE Model Rules*, at 52, listing the following 'Acceptable Financial Accounting Standards': '*International Financial Reporting Standards (IFRS) and the generally accepted accounting principles of Australia, Brazil, Canada, Member States of the European Union, Member States of the European Economic Area, Hong Kong (China), Japan, Mexico, New Zealand, the People's Republic of China, the Republic of India, the Republic of Korea, Russia, Singapore, Switzerland, the United Kingdom, and the United States of America*'.
277. In this vein, also *see* V. Bendlinger, *Die OECD Model Rules für ein globales Mindestbesteuerungsregime*, 32 SWI, *supra* note 258, at 5.
278. *See* letter c of the definition of 'Consolidated Financial Statements' in Art. 10.1. *GloBE Model Rules*, at 54. Also *see* the corresponding definition with marginal textual differences in Art. 3(6)(c) GloBE-Directive (2022/2523).
279. *See* letter d of the definition of 'Consolidated Financial Statements' in Art. 10.1. *GloBE Model Rules*, at 54. Also *see* the corresponding definition with marginal textual differences in Art. 3(6)(d) GloBE-Directive (2022/2523).
280. *GloBE Commentary on Article 10 GloBE Model Rules (2022)*, para. 59.

is, therefore, precisely intended to counteract the aforementioned problem: The aim is to prevent MNE Groups from falling out of the GloBE regime due to particularly lax consolidation rules in their state of residence. For this reason, the definition of 'Material Competitive Distortion' in the GloBE regime is of fundamental importance: the term is a yardstick for the accounting standard applied that is not listed under the 'Acceptable Financial Accounting Standards' and ensures a consistent application of the scope of GloBE even if an 'MNE Group' is subject either to very generous financial accounting rules or is not even obliged to file financial statements in its state of residence.[281]

What is meant by 'Material Competitive Distortions' is again set out by the GloBE Model Rules in a separate definition:

> Material Competitive Distortion in respect of the application of a specific principle or procedure under a set of generally accepted accounting principles means an application that results in an aggregate variation greater than EUR 75 million in a Fiscal Year as compared to the amount that would have been determined by applying the corresponding IFRS principle or procedure. Where the application of a specific principle or procedure results in a Material Competitive Distortion, the accounting treatment of any item or transaction subject to that principle or procedure must be adjusted to conform to the treatment required for the item or transaction under IFRS in accordance with any Agreed Administrative Guidance.[282]

Within the GloBE-Directive, the corresponding definition is laid down in Article 3(27) GloBE-Directive.[283] What is remarkable, however, is not so much the numerical thresholds but the definition of IFRS as a benchmark for 'reliable' accounting and obviously also consolidation (the phrase '*applying the corresponding IFRS* [...] *procedure*'[284] is likely to allude to the consolidation process). In a sense, GloBE requires the preparation of some form of 'IFRS equivalent' consolidated financial statements. For the scope of this discussion, this means that if an 'MNE Group' does not prepare consolidated financial statements in an 'Acceptable Financial Accounting Standard' and a variation arises, e.g., due to non-consolidation of certain controlled entities, which leads to a variation exceeding the specified threshold of EUR 75 million, the (i) financial statements prepared in local GAAP must to be adjusted to IFRS principles[285] or (ii) if the MNE is not even obliged to file consolidated financial accounts, the MNE

281. In literature on the 'Material Competitive Distortion Test', *see*, e.g., E. Eberhartinger & G. Winkler, *Pillar Two and the Accounting Standards*, 51 Intertax 141 et seq. (2023) DOI: 10.54648/taxi2023010.
282. *See* Art. 10.1. *GloBE Model Rules*, at 60.
283. The GloBE-Directive Proposal did include the definition of 'Material Competitive Distortion' in Art. 14(3) COM(2021)823 final (predecessor of Art. 15[3] GloBE-Directive). Interestingly, contrary to the GloBE Model Rules, it also included a 10% revenue threshold for the purpose of the 'Material Competitive Distortion' Test, also *see* Eva Eberhartinger & Georg Winkler, *supra* note 281, at 141.
284. *See* Art. 10.1. *GloBE Model Rules*, at 60.
285. *See* letter c of the definition of 'Consolidated Financial Statements' in conjunction with the definition of 'Material Competitive Distortion' in Art. 10.1. *Ibid.*, at 54 and 60. Also *see* Art. 3(6)(c) in conjunction with Art. 3(27) GloBE-Directive (2022/2523).

is de facto required to prepare financial statements in IFRS or at least any other 'Acceptable Financial Accounting Standard'.[286]

As illustrated, the scope of the 'Group' is formed by an extremely complex set of rules consisting of a chain of various linked definitions. The interesting conclusion derived from an analysis of these definitions is that the scope of GloBE is very directly linked to the accounting standard used by an in-scope MNE, and in doing so, GloBE has defined a set of 'safe harbour' for a definitive list of 'Acceptable Financial Accounting Standards'. If an MNE prepares its 'Consolidated Financial Statements' in accordance with an 'Acceptable Financial Accounting Standard', the consolidation requirements of that standard define the scope of the 'Group' for GloBE purposes without objection. However, if there are no consolidated financial statements prepared in accordance with such a standard, GloBE either requires (i) an adjustment to the consolidated financial statement prepared if the variation exceeds a EUR 75 million threshold in order to comply with IFRS 'principles and procedures' (elimination of so-called Material Competitive Distortions), or (ii) de facto requires the (re)preparation of 'Consolidated Financial Statements' in accordance with an 'Acceptable Financial Accounting Standard' or any other standard again adjusted to correct 'Material Competitive Distortions'. In other words, there are two situations to distinguish: First (i), if a company prepares 'Consolidated Financial Statements' that are not listed as an 'Acceptable Financial Accounting Standard', this accounting standard nevertheless determines the size of the 'Group' subject to GloBE (e.g., determination of EUR 750 million threshold), but this accounting standard is measured against IFRS and may have to be adjusted to IFRS in the event of deviations exceeding EUR 75 million. Second (ii), if an MNE does not prepare a 'Consolidated Financial Statement' at all, GloBE requires the preparation of such a statement either according to an 'Acceptable Financial Accounting Standard' or any other standard adjusted to IFRS in the event of deviations exceeding EUR 75 million. As it turns out, GloBE promotes IFRS enforcement: For all accounting standards that are not listed as 'Acceptable Financial Accounting Standard', the IFRS are established as a kind of stand-alone benchmark. If a specific set of consolidated financial statements does not meet this benchmark, appropriate adjustments are required. An adjustment to an 'Acceptable Financial Accounting Standard' other than the IFRS is permitted neither under the GloBE Model Rules nor under the GloBE-Directive.[287] Consequently, from a global perspective, GloBE seems to promote the enforcement of IFRS.[288]

---

286. *See* letter d of the definition of 'Consolidated Financial Statements' in conjunction with the definition of 'Material Competitive Distortion' in Art. 10.1. *GloBE Model Rules*, at 54 and 60. Also *see* Art. 3(6)(d) in conjunction with Art. 3(27) GloBE-Directive (2022/2523).
287. *See* Art. 3(27) GloBE-Directive (2022/2523) also explicitly referring to IFRS.
288. Also on this argument, *see* s. 4.5.7.

4.2.3.3 *Group Membership Despite Exclusion from the 'Consolidated Financial Statements' of the UPE*

From a reverse conclusion from Article 1.2.2.(a) GloBE Model Rules and the first limb of Article 3(3)(a) GloBE-Directive, it can be deduced that entities which are not included in the 'Consolidated Financial Statements' of the UPE are not within the scope of a 'Group'. However, since even the 'Acceptable Financial Accounting Standards' do not prescribe consolidation of controlled entities without exception, the GloBE regime could not cover all entities part of an MNE. For this reason, Article 1.2.2.(b) GloBE Model Rules states that the Group also covers entities that *'are excluded from the Consolidated Financial Statements of the Ultimate Parent Entity solely on size or materiality grounds, or on the ground that the Entity is held for sale'*,[289] for the determination of GloBE's scope. This means, for example, that for the purposes of determining the EUR 750 million threshold, non-consolidated entities are also to be taken into account. According to the Commentary, this should apply *'as long as* [the controlled entity] *remains sufficiently within the control of the UPE to fall within the general consolidation requirements of the relevant Acceptable Financial Accounting Standard'*.[290] Consequently, an entity that is not consolidated in the financial statement is nevertheless part of the 'Group' if it would have been consolidated under the *'general consolidation requirements'* but isn't due to the grounds mentioned in Article 1.2.2.(b) GloBE Model Rules (and second limb of Article 3[3][a] GloBE-Directive). The additional inclusion of such entities obviously creates additional administrative burdens due to the fact that the financial statements must be adjusted solely for the purpose of GloBE. Nevertheless, the rationale of this extension to the general scope is obvious: the scope of GloBE should not be deliberately circumvented by using exceptions from consolidation, e.g., by splitting business operations into several small-sized entities.

4.2.3.4 *Extension of Scope to So-called Consolidated Entities or 'Partnership Groups: MNE Groups Consisting Exclusively of PEs*

In Article 1.2.3. GloBE Model Rules (also *see* Article 3[3][b] GloBE-Directive) the definition of 'Group' is further expanded to include corporations which do not have any foreign subsidiaries, but only PEs ('consolidated entities' or 'partnership groups').[291] Such corporations would not be covered by the Group definition in Article 1.2.2. GloBE Model Rules simply due to the fact that in such a structure, there are no ownership or control relations between different entities. After all, such 'Groups' only consist of one legal entity, which does not consolidate any other subsidiaries in its financial statements. Rather, it only prepares its own financial statements. In these cases, the

289. Article 1.2.2.(b) *GloBE Model Rules* and the second limb of Art. 3(3)(a) GloBE-Directive (2022/2523).
290. *See GloBE Commentary on Article 1 GloBE Model Rules (2022), supra* note 249, para. 24.
291. *'In order to ensure MNE Groups that meet the consolidated revenue threshold and engage in cross-border operations through PEs rather than subsidiaries are also subject to the GloBE Rules, Article 1.2.3 provides a supplementary definition of "Group"', see ibid.*, paras 25–26.

financial statements prepared in accordance with an 'Acceptable Financial Accounting Standard' are considered as the 'Consolidated Financial Statements' for the purposes of GloBE (letter b of the definition of 'Consolidated Financial Statement' in Article 10.1. GloBE Model Rules and Article 3[6][b] GloBE-Directive); if there are no financial statements prepared in accordance with an 'Acceptable Financial Accounting Standard', the respective corporation is required to adjust its financial statements to prevent 'Material Competitive Distortions',[292] or to prepare financial statements in an *'Authorised Financial Accounting Standard that is either an Acceptable Financial Accounting Standard or another financial accounting standard that is adjusted to prevent Material Competitive Distortions'*[293] (already *see* section 4.2.3.2.).

4.2.4 Membership Within an 'MNE Group'

4.2.4.1 The 'Constituent Entities'

4.2.4.1.1 The Individual 'Entities' Forming the 'Group'

Pursuant to Article 1.1.1. GloBE Model Rules,[294] the *'GloBE Rules apply to Constituent Entities that are members of an MNE Group'*.[295] It has already been discussed that only 'MNE Groups' are subject to the minimum tax regime. However, for this purpose, the determination of the so-called Adjusted Covered Tax, as well as the determination of the 'GloBE Income or Loss'[296] received, and the charging of the minimum tax liability take place at the level of individual entities included within the 'Group'. While section 4.2.3. has dealt with the 'Group' as a *'collection of Entities'*,[297] this section is dedicated to the actual members of the group, which are called 'Constituent Entities' (CEs) within GloBE's regulatory framework.

What is to be understood as a Constituent Entity (CE) is defined in Article 1.3. GloBE Model Rules and correspondingly in Article 3(2) GloBE-Directive, which distinguish between two different kinds of CEs: first, CEs are 'Entities' that are included in a 'Group' (within the GloBE-Directive this also includes 'large-scale domestic groups'). The term covers any legal persons (non-individuals) as well as any *'arrangements that* [prepare] *separate financial accounts, such as a partnership or trust'*.[298] The definition

292. Letter c of the definition of 'Consolidated Financial Statements' in Art. 10.1. *GloBE Model Rules*, at 54. Also *see* Art. 3(6)(c) GloBE-Directive (2022/2523).
293. Letter d of the definition of 'Consolidated Financial Statements' in Art. 10.1. *GloBE Model Rules*, at 54. Also *see* Art. 3(6)(d) GloBE-Directive (2022/2523).
294. Also *see* nearly the same phrase in Art. 2(1) GloBE-Directive (2022/2523). However, the scope of Art. 2(1) GloBE-Directive is explicitly restricted to *'constituent entities located in the Union'*. Finally, the GloBE-Directive can only impose the 'Top-up Tax' on CEs established within the borders of the EU.
295. Article 1.1.1. *GloBE Model Rules*.
296. *See* explicitly referring to the 'Constituent Entities', Art. 3.1.1. *Ibid.* and Art. 14(1) GloBE-Directive (2022/2523).
297. Article 1.2.2. *GloBE Model Rules* and Art. 3(3)(a) GloBE-Directive (2022/2523).
298. *See* the definition of 'Entity' in Art. 10.1. *GloBE Model Rules*, at 56. Correspondingly, *see* Art. 3(1) GloBE-Directive (2022/2523).

of CE is, therefore, directly linked to legal personality. Any other arrangements not qualifying as a legal person nevertheless may constitute a CE if such an arrangement is under an obligation to prepare separate financial statements. Therefore, fiscally transparent vehicles are to be considered CEs as long as they are required to prepare financial statements. Second, the definition of CE also covers any PE of a 'Main Entity', that is, the Entity including the PE income in its financial statements,[299] qualifying as a CE. PEs are, therefore, considered separate CEs and must also be considered separate entities for the purpose of GloBE.

4.2.4.1.2 *Permanent Establishments Are 'Constituent Entities'*

The recording of PEs as separate CEs can only be grasped by examining the overall concept of GloBE: GloBE aims to establish a minimum taxation system whereby, as will be shown in detail, the 'Effective Tax Rate' (ETR) and, therefore, also the calculation of the minimum tax due ('Top-up Tax') is to be determined on a country-by-country basis (*'jurisdictional blending'*[300]).[301] However, due to the fact that the consolidated financial statements are used as a starting point not only for scope but also for tax base determination, a breakdown into individual jurisdictions is necessary (in detail, *see* section 4.3.2.1.3.). Nevertheless, this is not an easy task: the consolidated financial statements do not support such a jurisdictional perspective. Rather, within the framework of consolidated financial statements, all separate legal entities connected by means of ownership interests are presented as if the entire group were a single company. The consolidation process is ultimately carried out by including all assets and liabilities of controlled companies in the financial statements of the UPE. However, this still requires the preparation of individual financial statements in the accounting standard applied by the UPE of each single entity. For basic determination purposes, GloBE uses these individual financial statements prepared by the individual entities in preparation for consolidation[302] to finally aggregate the 'GloBE Income or Losses' jurisdiction-wise.[303] Nevertheless, this results in an incompatibility between the consolidated financial statements and international tax principles: while from the perspective of the consolidated financial statements, the consolidated legal entities are merely individual business units. International tax practice requires legal entities to split among various tax jurisdictions for the purpose of allocation of tax rights under the PE concept established in the comprehensive global networks of bilateral tax treaties. Thus, the jurisdictional calculation of the ETR and the 'Top-up Tax' requires the statements of every separate entity to split into its 'Main Entities' and foreign PEs. For this reason, as will be seen, the income of an entity that is a CE needs to be allocated

299. *See* the definition of 'Main Entity' in Art. 10.1. *GloBE Model Rules*, at 60 and Art. 3(40) GloBE-Directive (2022/2523).
300. *See* s. 4.3.2.1.3.
301. At a glance on the jurisdictional perspective of GloBE, *see Introduction to the GloBE Commentary on the GloBE Model Rules (2022)*, paras 7–9.
302. *See* Art. 3.1.2. *GloBE Model Rules* and Art. 15(1) GloBE-Directive (2022/2523).
303. *See* Art. 5.1.1. *GloBE Model Rules* and Art. 26(1) GloBE-Directive (2022/2523).

to its PE constituting separate CEs (in detail, *see* section 4.3.3.5.).[304] Consequently, within the framework of GloBE, any PEs of CEs must be recorded as separate CEs.[305]

However, filtering PEs within an 'MNE Group' is again a tricky issue: GloBE is applied to 'MNE Groups' that are formed by a wide variety of legal entities operating in different jurisdictions. Each of the entities within the group can establish various PEs in different jurisdictions, being subject to different tax treaties and, thus, different understandings of the term PE. Consequently, it was necessary to establish a separate PE definition for the purpose of GloBE in the abstract. Article 10.1. GloBE Model Rules (*see* correspondingly Article 3[13] GloBE-Directive) distinguishes four different types of places of business to be considered as PEs for the purpose of GloBE[306] (the corresponding descriptions in italics come from the author and can neither be found in the GloBE Model Rules nor in the GloBE-Directive):

- *PEs under an applicable tax treaty*: A PE for purposes of GloBE occurs if a place of business is situated in a jurisdiction and is treated as a PE in accordance with an applicable and enforceable tax treaty, which provides for a distributive rule for business profits similar to Article 7 OECD MC.[307] For this reason, GloBE allocates income among the 'MNE Group' broadly in line with the existing network of tax treaties.[308]
- *PEs under domestic laws*: In the absence of a tax treaty, a place of business is to be treated as a PE if the income attributable to such an operation is taxed on a net basis under the domestic laws similar to residents of the state where the place of business is established.[309]
- *PEs not being subject to CIT at their place of establishment:* A place of business established in a jurisdiction that has no corporate income tax system is to be considered as a PE if the respective place of business would be treated as a PE under the OECD MC and the respective state had the right to tax the income attributable to it according to Article 7 OECD MC.[310]
- *Exterritorial PEs*: A place of business which operates outside the jurisdiction where the 'Entity' is located is to be considered as a PE if the residence state of the entity exempts the income attributable to that place of business.[311]

---

304. *See* Art. 3.4. *GloBE Model Rules* and Art. 18 GloBE-Directive (2022/2523).
305. Comprehensively on PEs within the system of GloBE, *see* V. Bendlinger & G. Kofler, *Computation of the Effective Tax Rate and the 'Top-up Tax'*, in *Pillar 2 Global Minimum Tax* (Werner Haslehner et al., eds, 2022) forthcoming.
306. In detail on the four different GloBE PEs, *see* S. Bendlinger, *Betriebsstätten im Rahmen der globalen Mindestbesteuerung*, 33 SWI 7–9 (2023).
307. Letter a of the PE definition in Art. 10.1. *GloBE Model Rules*, at 60. Also *see* Art. 3(13)(a) GloBE-Directive (2022/2523).
308. In detail on this issue, *see* s. 5.2.3.
309. Letter b of the PE definition in Art. 10.1. *GloBE Model Rules*, at 60 Also *see* Art. 3(13)(b) GloBE-Directive (2022/2523).
310. Letter c of the PE definition in Art. 10.1. *GloBE Model Rules*, at 60 Also *see* Art. 3(13)(c) GloBE-Directive (2022/2523).
311. Letter d of the PE definition in Art. 10.1. *GloBE Model Rules*, at 60 Also *see* Art. 3(13)(d) GloBE-Directive (2022/2523).

From this list of four scenarios, a certain order of tests can be derived: in determining a 'Group's' PEs, it is first necessary to filter out in which states the respective CE has PEs under a tax treaty in force. In the absence of a treaty, it is to be determined whether there is a place of business which is taxable under domestic laws of the state where it is established. *PEs not being subject to CIT at their place of establishment,* as well as *exterritorial PEs*, can only occur if there is a certain place of business which is, however, not subject to CIT at all. Both of the latter scenarios are likely to be rare phenomena. With respect to *exterritorial PEs,* it is noteworthy that such PEs are to be considered as 'Stateless Constituent Entities', which GloBE considers to be 'located' in separate tax jurisdictions.[312]

The complex PE definition provided for in Article 10.1 GloBE Model Rules and Article 3(13) GloBE-Directive is comprehensively discussed in the Commentary[313] and shows the delicate balancing act of GloBE, trying, on the one hand, to establish a global framework for a minimum corporate tax, while, at the same time, trying to acknowledge tax sovereignty interests and international agreements (tax treaties) on the distribution of taxing rights among the jurisdictions. The technical complexity of the CE definition in Article 1.3. GloBE Model Rules and Article 3(2) GloBE-Directive is merely an expression of the complex interrelationship of GloBE and the traditional international tax landscape.

4.2.4.1.3 Being Subject to the GloBE Rules Without Being a 'Constituent Entity'?: The Special Status of Joint Ventures

Since the scope of a 'Group' depends on the line-by-line inclusion in the UPE's 'Consolidated Financial Statements', 'Joint Ventures' would generally fall outside the scope of GloBE: 'Joint Ventures' are characterized by the fact that they are under some form of joint control, and neither person involved has sole control over the arrangement. For this reason, they are usually not accounted for line-by-line in many accounting standards but according to the equity method.[314] This is particularly true for IFRS.[315]

For this reason, Article 6.4. GloBE Model Rules and Article 36 GloBE-Directive extend '*the scope of the GloBE Rules to Entities in which the UPE of an MNE Group owns 50% or more of the Ownership Interests*'.[316] According to Article 10.1 GloBE Model Rules (Article 36[1][a] GloBE-Directive), a 'Joint Venture' for the purposes of GloBE means an 'Entity' that is included in the 'Consolidated Financial Statements' under the equity

312. *See* the definition of 'Stateless Constituent Entity' referring to Art. 10.3.3.(d) in Art. 10.1. *GloBE Model Rules*, at 66. Within the GloBE-Directive, there is not a separate definition. However, the term is used in several provisions, *see*, e.g., Art. 3(19)(b) GloBE-Directive (2022/2523).
313. *OECD Model Tax Convention on Income and on Capital: Commentary on Article 10*, paras 96–114 (21 Nov. 2017).
314. *See GloBE Commentary on Article 6 GloBE Model Rules (2022)*, para. 83.
315. *See* IAS 28.11 and IFRS 11.24 and 11.25 (*Joint Arrangements*).
316. *See GloBE Commentary on Article 6, supra* note 314, para. 84.

method and does neither qualify as a UPE nor as an 'Excluded Entity'.[317] For such 'Joint Ventures', Article 6.4.1 GloBE Model Rules (Article 36[3] GloBE-Directive) creates a special regime: the ETR and the 'Top-up Tax' shall be computed as if '*the Joint Venture and its JV Subsidiaries [...] were Constituent Entities of a separate MNE Group and as if the Joint Venture was the Ultimate Parent Entity of the Group*'.[318] 'JV Subsidiaries'[319] (the GloBE-Directive uses the term 'joint venture affiliates')[320] are those entities that are or would have to be consolidated on a line-by-line basis by the 'Joint Venture' under an 'Acceptable Financial Accounting Standard' or PEs of the 'Joint Venture' or its 'JV Subsidiaries'. As a result, a 'Joint Venture', contrary to existing accounting practice,[321] is recognized as part of the 'Group' for GloBE purposes; however, with the special feature that the 'Joint Venture' and its 'JV Subsidiaries' ('joint venture affiliates') are considered a separate group for GloBE purposes. For example, options in the calculation of the 'GloBE Income or Loss' or the 'Adjusted Covered Taxes' are not exercised together with the entire 'MNE Group' but only within the 'JV Group'[322].[323] In addition, the individual members of the 'JV Group' are excluded from the jurisdictional blending of the actual 'MNE Groups' involved in the 'Joint Venture'.[324] Although the 'Joint Venture' and its 'JV Subsidiaries' are not CEs of either 'MNE Group' involved. The 'Top-up Tax' calculated at the level of the 'JV Group's' members is allocated to the participating 'MNE Groups' according to their allocable shares by way of IIR[325] or, in the case of remaining 'Top-up Tax', by way of UTPR.[326] As a result, a 'Joint Venture' and all its subsidiaries and PEs are captured by GloBE without qualifying as CEs in any 'MNE Group'.[327]

4.2.4.2 The 'Ultimate Parent Entity'

4.2.4.2.1 Prerequisites for the Existence of an 'Ultimate Parent Entity'

The 'Ultimate Parent Entity' (UPE) is of significant importance for the entire GloBE regime. The very definition of 'MNE Group' in Article 1.2.1 GloBE Model Rules (Article

317. *See* the negative conditions in letters a to e of the 'Joint Venture' definition in Art. 10.1. *GloBE Model Rules*, at 59 and Art. 36(1)(a) GloBE-Directive (2022/2523).
318. Article 6.4.1.(a) *GloBE Model Rules* and, using a slightly different wording, Art. 36(3) GloBE-Directive (2022/2523).
319. *See* the definition of 'JV Subsidiary' in Art. 10.1. *GloBE Model Rules*, at 59.
320. *See* Art. 36(1)(b) GloBE-Directive (2022/2523).
321. Again *see*, e.g., IAS 28.11 and IFRS 11.24 and 11.25.
322. According to Art. 10.1. *GloBE Model Rules*, at 59 a 'JV Group' includes the 'Joint Venture' and its 'JV Subsidiaries'. Art. 36 GloBE-Directive (2022/2523) does not provide for a corresponding definition.
323. This follows from the general reference in Art. 6.4.1.(a) *GloBE Model Rules* and Art. 36(3) GloBE-Directive (2022/2523) to the computation of the 'GloBE Income', the 'Adjusted Covered Taxes' and the computation of the 'Top-up Tax'.
324. According to Art. 6.4.1.(a) *GloBE Model Rules* and Art. 36(3) GloBE-Directive (2022/2523) state that 'Joint Ventures' and its 'JV Subsidiaries' ('joint venture affiliates') are to be treated '*as if they were Constituent Entities of a separate*' 'MNE Group'. The individual members of the 'JV Group' are therefore not part of any 'MNE Group' for the purposes of GloBE.
325. Article 6.4.1.(b) *GloBE Model Rules* and Art. 36(2) GloBE-Directive (2022/2523).
326. Article 6.4.1.(c) *GloBE Model Rules* and Art. 36(4) GloBE-Directive (2022/2523).
327. Also *see GloBE Commentary on Article 2 GloBE Model Rules (2022)*, *supra* note 238, para. 11 referring to CEs as follows: '*Constituent Entity (or treated as such in the case of JVs)*'.

3[3][a] GloBE-Directive) presupposes the existence of a UPE. Furthermore, the UPE defines the financial accounting standard to be used within the 'Group', and as will be seen, the UPE has priority in the application of the GloBE Rules (in detail, *see* section 4.4.2.8).[328] The Commentary thus correctly states that the definition of UPE is *'the starting point for identifying all the Entities that comprise the MNE Group'*.[329]

It can be stated at the outset that the UPE is a special form of CE: the UPE is always the top 'Entity' of a 'Group's' structure and is usually obliged to prepare 'Consolidated Financial Statements'. Since these 'Consolidated Financial Statements' also include the assets and liabilities of the UPE, the UPE always fulfils the definition of a CE requiring the inclusion in a 'Group'.[330] This is particularly evident in Article 2.1.1. GloBE Model Rules, referring to a *'Constituent Entity, that is the Ultimate Parent Entity'*.[331] Only 'Excluded Entities' have a special status in that regard: They can qualify as UPEs without simultaneously qualifying as CEs (in detail on 'Excluded Entities', *see* section 4.2.4.3.).[332]

Since a UPE regularly also qualifies as a CE, the definition of UPE is essentially a chain of tests designed to clearly distinguish the UPE from other CEs within the same 'Group'. The definition of UPE is found in both Article 1.4. GloBE Model Rules and Article 3(14) GloBE-Directive, and is divided into two letters, respectively. In letter b (Article 1.4.[b] GloBE Model Rules and Article 3[14][b] GloBE-Directive), the UPE definition is extended to the 'Main Entity' of a Group to clarify the UPE character of the 'Main Entity' in the exceptional cases of 'consolidated entities' or 'partnership groups'. This element has already been discussed and needs no further explanation (already *see* section 4.2.3.4.). The most relevant and equally interesting definition can be found in Article 1.4.(a) GloBE Model Rules and Article 3(14)(a) GloBE-Directive: Both define three cumulative prerequisites for a vehicle to qualify as a UPE. First (i), only 'Entities' can qualify as a UPE (*Entity Test*). Second (ii), the respective 'Entity' needs to own directly or indirectly a 'Controlling Interest' in any other 'Entity' (*Controlling Interest Test*) and third (iii) the respective 'Entity' may not be owned, with a 'Controlling Interest', directly or indirectly by another 'Entity' (*Ultimativity Test*).

4.2.4.2.2 Which Vehicles Do Qualify as an 'Entity'?: The Entity Test

In order to grasp the first prerequisite of the UPE definition, it is again necessary to refer to the term 'Entity': As already mentioned (*see* section 4.2.4.1.), the term 'Entity' (Article 10.1. GloBE Model Rules and Article 3[1] GloBE-Directive) covers *'any legal person'* or *'an arrangement that prepares separate financial accounts* [Art 10.1. GloBE Model Rules adds the phrase "*such as partnerships or trusts*"]'. From this, it becomes clear that a UPE can be a legal person but does not necessarily have to be. The UPE can

328. At a glance on the crucial role of UPE for the GloBE regime, *see GloBE Commentary on Article 1 GloBE Model Rules (2022)*, *supra* note 249, para. 32.
329. *See Ibid.*
330. *See* Art. 1.2.2. and 1.3.1.(a) *GloBE Model Rules*.
331. Article 2.1.1. *Ibid.*
332. *See* Art. 1.3.3. *Ibid.*

also be a transparent vehicle such as a partnership, foundation, fund or any other legal entity lacking legal personality under the domestic law of their state of domicile. However, as a prerequisite, such vehicles or 'arrangements' only qualify as UPE if they need to prepare separate financial accounts. This extremely broad concept of 'Entity' is interesting in that such vehicles are treated as fiscally transparent, are thus not subject to corporate income tax in many jurisdictions, and usually are not entitled to tax treaties.[333] Nevertheless, for purposes of GloBE, it was necessary to also cover such 'arrangements' because otherwise, the scope of GloBE could be circumvented by using a fiscally transparent entity as a group's holding. Only arrangements that do not prepare any financial statements at all would fall outside the 'Entity' definition and would, thus, not qualify as a UPE. This would possibly be conceivable in the case of civil partnerships in which two individuals join forces and decide to jointly manage shareholdings. If such a civil partnership does not prepare separate financial accounts, it would therefore not qualify as an 'Entity' and thus could not constitute a UPE.

In any case, the broad term 'Entity' also implies that fiscally transparent vehicles are eligible as UPE. However, considering fiscally transparent vehicles as distinct 'Entities' can lead to issues with regard to the computation of the ETR: the 'Effective Tax Rate' (ETR) of fiscally transparent entities (in the GloBE regime, such 'Entities' are referred to as 'Flow-through Entities'),[334] will regularly amount to zero, since the income received by the 'Entity' as such is not taxed at the level of this 'Entity', but in the hands of its shareholders.[335] For this reason, Article 7.1. GloBE Model Rules (Article 38 GloBE-Directive) contains a separate provision for such entities, which essentially provides that the 'GloBE Income' of such 'Flow-through Entities' may be reduced in certain circumstances if the respective income is taxed in respect of the shareholder's 'Ownership Interest' at a nominal rate equal to, or in excess of the minimum rate. Consequently, for GloBE purposes, the ETR of such UPEs is measured by the taxes paid by its shareholders. An equivalent regime is provided for in Article 7.2. GloBE Model Rules (Article 39 GloBE-Directive) addressing UPEs that are subject to a 'Deductible Dividend Regime'. Such regimes allow an entity, which is, in principle, considered non-transparent for tax purposes, to deduct dividends paid to its shareholders as business expenses in order to achieve a single level of taxation.[336] Here, too, the ETR is measured by the taxes levied at the shareholder's level by reducing the 'GloBE Income' accordingly by the amounts distributed as a 'Deductible Dividend'.[337]

333. *See* Art. 1(2) OECD MC.
334. *See* the definition of the term 'Flow-through Entity' in Art. 10.2. *GloBE Model Rules* and the synonymous, albeit less comprehensive, definition provided for in Art. 3(12) GloBE-Directive (2022/2523).
335. *See GloBE Commentary on Article 7 GloBE Model Rules (2022)*, para. 3.
336. *See* the definition of the term 'Deductible Dividend Regime' in Art. 10.1. *GloBE Model Rules*, at 54. Also *see* Art. 39(1)(a) GloBE-Directive (2022/2523).
337. *See* the definition provided for 'Deductible Dividend' in Art. 10.1. *GloBE Model Rules*, at 54. Art. 39(1)(b) GloBE-Directive (2022/2523).

4.2.4.2.3 *Does the Vehicle Control Other Entities?: The Controlling Interest Test*

Once it has been determined whether an 'Entity' exists, the determination of the UPE requires a *Controlling Interest Test*: As the very term 'Ultimate Parent Entity' anticipates, only a parent entity holding ownership interest can actually qualify as a UPE. However, as already explained in detail, GloBE's scope is directly linked to the inclusion of entities in the consolidated financial statements. Thus, according to Article 1.4.1.(a)(i) GloBE Model Rules and Article 3(14)(a) GloBE-Directive a direct or indirect 'Controlling Interest' in any other 'Entity' is required. A 'Controlling Interest' (Article 3[21] GloBE-Directive) is defined as an 'Ownership Interest' (Article 3[23] GloBE-Directive) – that is, any equity interest carrying the right to the profits, capitals or reserves (including profits, capitals or reserves of PEs) – in an 'Entity' such that the interest holder either (i) '*is required to consolidate the assets, liabilities, income, expenses and cash flows of the Entity on a line-by-line basis in an Acceptable Financial Accounting Standard*'[338] or (ii) '*would have been required* [to do so] *if the interest holder had prepared Consolidated Financial Statements*'[339] (using slightly different wording, *see* Article 3[21] GloBE-Directive). Again, the close interconnectedness of GloBE and the consolidated financial statements becomes apparent here.

As a result, one can conclude that an entity can only constitute a UPE if it consolidates at least one other 'Entity' (or includes a PE within its financial statements, according to Article 1.4.[b] GloBE Model Rules and Article 3(14)(b) GloBE-Directive). This is also true with respect to the GloBE-Directive and its extension of scope to 'large-scale domestic groups'. 'Large-scale domestic groups' are 'Groups', which are characterized by the fact that according to Article 3(5) GloBE-Directive, all CEs are located in the same Member State. For this reason, a single 'Entity' could also qualify as a 'large-scale domestic group'.[340] A 'large-scale domestic group' must, therefore, according to Article 49 GloBE-Directive, also have a UPE, whereby the term UPE in Article 3(14) GloBE-Directive is defined identical to that of 'MNE Groups'.

4.2.4.2.4 *Is the 'Entity' the Last One in the Ownership Chain?: The Ulimativity Test*

'Entity' and 'Controlling Interest' in another 'Entity' are not unique characteristics of the UPE. Rather, every other CE within the 'MNE Group' could potentially fulfil these criteria. To distinguish the UPE from common CEs, a third test is necessary, and that is the *Ultimativity Test*: According to Article 1.4(a)(ii) GloBE Model Rules and Article 3(14)(a) GloBE-Directive an 'Entity' is to be considered as the UPE if it is not owned, with a 'Controlling Interest', directly or indirectly by any another 'Entity'. As a result, under the *Ultimativity Test*, an 'Entity' can only qualify as UPE if its shareholders are

338. Letter a of the definition of 'Controlling Interest' in Art. 10.1. *GloBE Model Rules*, at 54.
339. Letter b of the definition of 'Controlling Interest' in Art. 10.1. *Ibid.*
340. Finally, the wording '*all constituent entities are located in the same Member State*' as used in Art. 3(5) GloBE-Directive (2022/2523) says nothing about the number of 'entities' that have to be 'located' in this Member State to qualify is a 'large-scale domestic group'.

either individuals or such 'Entities' that are not required or would not be required to consolidate the respective 'Entity' or do fail the 'Entity Test'[341] themselves.[342] The UPE must therefore be the *ultimate* legal entity in the chain of 'Controlling Interests'. An exception to this rule only exists for 'Excluded Entities' if they are required to consolidate the corresponding 'Entity', as 'Excluded Entities' cannot form part of the 'Group' as they cannot qualify as CEs (in detail on this issue, *see* section 4.2.4.3.).

4.2.4.2.5 Multiple UPEs Within a Single 'Group'?: The Special Case of 'Multi-Parented MNE Groups'

In principle, there can only be one UPE in a 'Group'. This would allow to circumvent the scope of GloBE by deliberately splitting a 'Group' into several Sub-Groups simply to not exceed the EUR 750 million threshold. However, this presupposes that these sub-groups are not connected by the same 'Entity'; and as already mentioned, the term 'Entity' covers various forms of companies and does not presuppose legal personality. Nevertheless, business activities can also be combined by contractual agreement without having to establish a separate parent 'Entity'. The top entities of several groups could, for example, decide to bind each other's businesses by other contractual agreements without being bound to each other by means of 'Ownership Interests'. In such structures, it would also be possible to divide the shares of subsidiaries among several UPEs in such a way that none of the UPEs would have a 'Controlling Interest' in the respective entity, leading to the result that the respective subsidiary would not be part of either 'Group'.

In order to '*ensure that the GloBE Rules apply to these structures in the same way they would apply to a Group with single UPE*'[343] and to '*extend the definition of Constituent Entity to those Entities that would not meet the definition if each Group were tested separately*',[344] Article 6.5. GloBE Model Rules and Article 37 GloBE-Directive provide for special rules for so-called Multi-Parented MNE Groups, which intend to tackle artificial fragmentation of 'MNE Groups'.[345] A 'Multi-Parented MNE Group' can arise in two scenarios: The first scenario concerns so-called Stapled Structures, which are characterized by the fact that at least 50% or more of the 'Ownership Interests' in the UPEs of the separate 'Groups' are combined in such a way that they cannot be transferred or traded independently of each other[346] and one of the UPE prepares

341. *See* s. 4.2.4.2.2.
342. *Argumentum e contrario* to the definition of 'Controlling Interest' in Art. 10.1. *GloBE Model Rules*, at 54 and Art. 3(21) GloBE-Directive (2022/2523).
343. *See GloBE Commentary on Article 6 GloBE Model Rules (2022)*, *supra* note 314, para. 95.
344. *See Ibid.*, para. 102.
345. This issue had already been addressed in the Pillar Two Blueprint, where the OECD held that further '*work could be undertaken to consider whether the consolidation threshold should be supplemented with a targeted anti-avoidance rule to avoid the fragmentation of a single MNE Group into different subgroups in order to avoid the EUR 750 M threshold*', *see Tax Challenges Arising from Digitalisation – Report on Pillar Two Blueprint*, para. 126. Art. 6.5. GloBE Model Rules (2021), *supra* note 120 is the result of the announced work.
346. *See* letter a of the definition of 'Stapled Structure' in Art. 10.1. *GloBE Model Rules*, at 66. Also *see* Art. 37(1)(b)(i) GloBE-Directive (2022/2523).

'Consolidated Financial Statements' in which all 'Groups' are included.[347] The second scenario concerns 'Dual-listed Arrangements', where the listed UPEs '*agree to combine their business by contract alone*',[348] only make distributions to their shareholders on a fixed ratio,[349] combine their business management[350] while their shares nevertheless being traded separately,[351] and one of the UPEs prepare 'Consolidated Financial Statements'.[352]

One of the special features of such 'Multi-parented MNE Groups', however, is that one might assume that there will be no single 'Consolidated Financial Statements' for all 'Groups'. With respect to the 'Consolidated Financial Statements' of 'Multi-Parented MNE Groups' Article 6.5.1.(c) GloBE Model Rules (similar Article 37[3] GloBE-Directive) states that '*the Consolidated Financial Statements of the Multi-Parented MNE Group shall be the Consolidated Financial Statements referred to in the definition of Stapled Structure or Dual-listed arrangement (as relevant) prepared under an Acceptable Financial Accounting Standard, which is deemed to be the accounting standard of the Ultimate Parent Entity*'. Interestingly, the definitions of 'Stapled Structures' and 'Dual-listed Arrangements' differ with regard to the 'Consolidated Financial Statements': According to letter b of the definition of 'Stapled Structure' in Article 10.1. (correspondingly Article 37[1][b][ii] GloBE-Directive) a 'Stapled Structure' requires that '*one of the*' UPEs prepares 'Consolidated Financial Statements in which 'the assets, liabilities, income, expenses and cash flows of *all the Entities of the Groups* are presented together as those of a single economic unit' (emphasis added).[353] Consequently, a 'Stapled Structure' can only exist if the structure has to prepare at least one joint 'Consolidated Financial Statement'. Conversely, letter e of the definition of 'Dual-listed Arrangements' in Article 10.1. GloBE Model Rules (correspondingly Article 37[1][c][v] GloBE-Directive) states that 'the *Ultimate Parent Entities* [not one of the UPEs as stated with regard to 'Stapled Structures'] prepare Consolidated Financial Statements in which the assets, liabilities, income, expenses and cash flows of *all the Entities of the Groups* are presented together as those of a single economic unit' (emphasis added).[354] Does this mean that a 'Dual-listed Arrangement' might also occur if there is not a single 'Consolidated Financial Statement' but several ones within the same 'Multi-Parented MNE Group'? Unfortunately, also the Commentary is not helpful in that regard, as it merely notes that '*whenever there is a reference to the accounting standard of the UPE, then it should be deemed to be the accounting standard that has been used by the Multi-Parented MNE Group*'. Interestingly, only Article 37(3) GloBE-Directive states that the 'Consolidated Financial Statements' of a 'Multi-Parented MNE

347. *See* letter b *GloBE Model Rules*, at 66. Also *see* Art. 37(1)(b)(ii) GloBE-Directive (2022/2523).
348. *See* letter a of the definition of 'Dual-listed Arrangement' in Art. 10.1. *GloBE Model Rules*, at 55. Also *see* Art. 37(1)(c)(i) GloBE-Directive (2022/2523).
349. *See* letter b Art. 10.1. *GloBE Model Rules*, at 55. Although missing in the initial proposal, this scenario is now defined as a 'dual-listed arrangement' in Art. 37(1)(c)(ii) GloBE-Directive (2022/2523).
350. *See* letter c *GloBE Model Rules*, at 55. Art. 37(1)(c)(iii) GloBE-Directive (2022/2523).
351. *See* letter d *GloBE Model Rules*, at 55. Art. 37(1)(c)(iv) GloBE-Directive (2022/2523).
352. *See* letter e *GloBE Model Rules*, at 55. Art. 37(1)(c)(v) GloBE-Directive (2022/2523).
353. Article 10.1. *GloBE Model Rules*, at 66. Also *see* Art. 37(1)(b)(ii) GloBE-Directive (2022/2523).
354. Article 10.1. *GloBE Model Rules*, at 55.

Group' '*shall be the combined consolidated financial statements*'. The GloBE-Directive, thus, seems to assume that there will always be a single 'Consolidated Financial Statement' of the 'Multi-Parented MNE Group'.

With regard to the application of the IIR and the UTPR, Article 6.5. GloBE Model Rules and Article 37 GloBE-Directive merely refer to the provisions provided for in Article 2 GloBE Model Rules and Articles 5–10 and 12–14 GloBE-Directive, respectively.[355] In principle, there are no special exceptions when it comes to the application of the GloBE Rules. In this sense, the only peculiarity of 'Multi-Parented MNE Groups' is the fact that a UPE might be obliged to apply the IIR with respect to 'Entities' that it does not control but which are controlled by or together with another UPE within the same 'Multi-Parented MNE Group'. In any case, the specific provisions on 'Multi-Parented MNE Groups' seem to be intended to ensure that the scope of GloBE cannot be circumvented by artificially splitting a single corporate structure into several 'Groups', whose business activities are nevertheless linked on a contractual basis. The Commentary is particularly clear in that respect, noting that the provisions for 'Multi-Parented MNE Groups' are '*important for applying the consolidated revenue threshold in Article 1.1, which takes into account the revenue of Entities that are members of the combined Group*'.[356] Furthermore, the provisions of Article 6.5.1.(b) GloBE Model Rules and Article 37(2) GloBE-Directive ensure that entities are treated as CEs of the 'Multi-Parented MNE Group' (within the GloBE-Directive also for 'large-scale domestic groups'),[357] even in cases where the single UPEs would not have a 'Controlling Interest' in the respective entity.[358]

4.2.4.3 *'Excluded Entities'*

4.2.4.3.1 Conceptual Thoughts on 'Excluded Entities'

The previous chapters have now dealt intensively with the individual entities forming the 'MNE Group': while CEs define the scope of the 'Group', the UPE is a special CE essentially characterized by the fact that it is the top 'Entity' of a 'Group'. This is relevant as Article 1.1.1 GloBE Model Rules states that '*the GloBE Rules apply to Constituent Entities*' (in a similar manner to Article 1 GloBE-Directive, which also refers to the single 'Constituent Entities').

For a variety of tax policy considerations, however, certain types of companies are excluded from the scope of GloBE. These types of entities are referred to as 'Excluded Entities' and are given special treatment in two respects: first, Article 1.1.3. GloBE Model Rules states that 'Excluded Entities' are not subject to the GloBE Rules (IIR and UTPR). Second, Article 1.3.3. GloBE Model Rules states that the term

355. *See* Art. 6.5.1.(e) and (f) *GloBE Model Rules* and Art. 37(5) and (6) GloBE-Directive (2022/2523).
356. *See GloBE Commentary on Article 6 GloBE Model Rules (2022), supra* note 314, para. 101.
357. *See* explicitly Art. 37(2) GloBE-Directive (2022/2523).
358. *See* Art. 6.5.1.(b) *GloBE Model Rules*, Art. 37(2) GloBE-Directive (2022/2523) and *GloBE Commentary on Article 6, supra* note 314, paras 102 and 105–108.

'Constituent Entity' does not include 'Excluded Entities' (which, however, does not mean that they cannot qualify as UPE, *see* section 4.2.4.3.3.). The GloBE-Directive adopts this special status with a slightly different regulatory technique in Article 2(3) GloBE-Directive, where it states that the Directive *'does not apply'* to 'Excluded Entities'. In this respect, the term 'Excluded Entity' feeds the misconception that the alleged 'exclusion' of these 'Entities' means that they completely fall outside the GloBE regime. As will be seen shown shortly, this is not the case.

4.2.4.3.2 The Numerus Clausus *of 'Excluded Entities'*

While, as already mentioned, the role of 'Excluded Entities' is recurrent in specific material provisions throughout both the GloBE Model Rules and the GloBE-Directive, the definition of the term 'Excluded Entity' is found in Article 1.5. of the GloBE Model Rules and Article 2(3) of the GloBE-Directive. Both provisions exhaustively enumerate various types of entities that are considered 'Excluded Entities' (*numerus clausus* of 'Excluded Entities'), which can essentially be divided into two categories:[359]

- The first category (Article 1.5.(a) to (d) GloBE Model Rules) captures 'Governmental Entities',[360] 'International Organisations',[361] 'Non-profit Organisations'[362] as well as 'Pension Funds'[363] (*entities serving general interests*). All of the terms are specifically defined in Article 10.1. GloBE Model Rules and the GloBE-Directive, respectively, and are further explained in the Commentary. The exclusion of these entities is comprehensive and independent of their status in a 'Group': Entities which are covered by one of these four terms are considered 'Excluded Entities' even if they are included in the 'Consolidated Financial Statements' of any other legal entity. Of course, this will hardly be the case with regard to 'Governmental Entities' or 'International Organisations'.
- The second category of 'Excluded Entities' (Article 1.5.(e) to (f) GloBE Model Rules) covers 'Investment Funds'[364] and 'Real Estate Investment Vehicles'[365] (*collective investment vehicles*). Again, both Article 10.1. GloBE Model Rules and the GloBE-Directive provide a legal definition of both terms. The essential difference to the excluded *entities serving general interests*, however, is that

359. The two categories are also reflected in the Commentary, *see GloBE Commentary on Article 1 GloBE Model Rules (2022)*, *supra* note 249, paras 41–42.
360. *See* the definition provided for in Art. 10.1. *GloBE Model Rules*, at 57. Also *see* Art. 3(9) GloBE-Directive (2022/2523).
361. *See* the definition provided for in Art. 10.1. *GloBE Model Rules*, at 58. Also *see* Art. 3(10) GloBE-Directive (2022/2523).
362. *See* the definition provided for in Art. 10.1. *GloBE Model Rules*, at 61. Also *see* Art. 3(11) GloBE-Directive (2022/2523).
363. *See* the definition provided for in Art. 10.1. *GloBE Model Rules*, at 63 and Art. 3(33) GloBE-Directive (2022/2523)
364. *See* the definition provided for in Art. 10.1. *GloBE Model Rules*, at 59 and Art. 3(31) GloBE-Directive (2022/2523).
365. *See* the definition provided for in Art. 10.1. *GloBE Model Rules*, at 65 and Art. 3(32) GloBE-Directive (2022/2523).

> the exclusion only applies to 'Investment Funds' and 'Real Estate Investment Vehicles' that qualify as UPEs. If such entities are included within the 'Consolidated Financial Statements', they are not excluded and thus qualify very well as CEs and are subject to the GloBE Rules. 'Investment Funds' and 'Real Estate Investment Vehicles', which are included within the 'Consolidated Financial Statements' of a UPE that are not an 'Excluded Entity', qualify as so-called Investment Entities.[366] For these 'Investment Entities', special rules are provided in Articles 7.4. to 7.6. GloBE Model Rules, and correspondingly in Articles 41 to 43 GloBE-Directive relating to the computation of the 'Top-up Tax' with respect to such 'Entities'. These provisions are addressed in section 4.4.2.8.

The policy rationale for the exclusion of *entities serving general interests*, on the one hand, and *collective investment vehicles*, on the other hand, reflected in Article 1.5. GloBE Model Rules and Article 2(3) GloBE-Directive, can be traced back to discussions made in the Pillar Two Blueprint published in October 2020.[367] With respect to *entities serving general interests*, the OECD concluded that such entities usually pursue purposes of '*general interest*'[368] and are usually exempt from CIT in the state where they are established. Thus, the ETR would regularly fall below the minimum tax rate, and a 'Top-up Tax' would arise with respect to such entities. However, it would be odd to collect such a 'Top-up Tax' by means of the UTPR, especially in the case of 'Governmental Entities' or 'International Organizations' being formed by sovereign jurisdictions. With regard to the IIR, it is difficult to even see how the IIR could be applied to 'Governmental Entities' or 'International Organisations', as it can be assumed that in most cases, no other entity could own a stake in such entities. Furthermore, applying the GloBE Rules (irrespective of whether the IIR or the UTPR) to such entities would allow each jurisdiction to tax the other.[369] In any case, the exclusion of *entities serving general interests* intends to '*protect* [their] *specific interests*'[370] and to preserve '*domestic tax policy goals*'.[371]

With respect to *collective investment vehicles*, the OECD considered that it was necessary to preserve tax neutrality regimes applicable to such entities in many

366. *See* the definition provided for in Art. 10.1. *GloBE Model Rules* and Art. 3(30) GloBE-Directive (2022/2523).
367. *Tax Challenges Arising from Digitalisation – Report on Pillar Two Blueprint*, at 31–37.
368. Also *see* this justification put forward in Recital 7 GloBE-Directive (2022/2523).
369. *See* in particular the considerations made with respect to 'Governmental Entities' in *Tax Challenges Arising from Digitalisation – Report on Pillar Two Blueprint*, para. 90: '*Where a Governmental Entity such as a sovereign wealth fund has a low ETR under the GloBE this is likely to reflect the specific tax treatment granted to that entity because of the exercise of its government functions. In such a case, it would seem counter-intuitive to require a top-up tax. If it were otherwise, the GloBE rules could have the effect that the government in the residence jurisdiction would be incentivised to impose taxation on itself in order to prevent its own revenue being exposed to a top-up tax by other governments*'. Also *see Ibid.*, para. 92 with respect to 'International Organisations', where the OECD noted that '[t]*axing these organisations on their low tax profit would undo the benefit of the tax exemptions granted to these organisations by agreement under international law*'.
370. Recital 7 GloBE-Directive (2022/2523).
371. *Tax Challenges Arising from Digitalisation – Report on Pillar Two Blueprint*, para. 86.

IF-Member States. The Blueprint noted that '*the tax treatment of the investment fund is not driven by a need or desire to attract investment from one jurisdiction to another, but rather to allow collective investments to be made through the fund without imposing any additional tax burden on the investment return*'[372] and that '*tax neutrality of the fund does not mean that the investment returns earned by the fund go untaxed* [but rather that] *a further layer of taxation may be imposed in the hands of the ultimate investor*'.[373] This led the OECD to the conclusion that '*GloBE rules should not distort*'[374] the policy goal of tax neutrality regimes applied to collective investment vehicles. The recitals of the GloBE-Directive have also taken up this reasoning.[375]

4.2.4.3.3 Extension of the Definition of 'Excluded Entities' to Entities Directly Owned by an 'Excluded Entity'

Article 1.5.2. GloBE Model Rules and Article 2(3)(b) and (c) GloBE-Directive extend the definition of 'Excluded Entities' to entities owned by an 'Excluded Entity'.[376] The provision is primarily intended to recognize the fact that the 'Excluded Entities' listed in Article 1.5.1 GloBE Model Rules and Article 2(3)(a) GloBE-Directive cannot always act directly due to legal limitations but can only act through private legal entities which would otherwise not be covered by the catalogue of 'Excluded Entities'. In this context, the Commentary refers in particular to 'Investment Funds', noting that '*commercial or regulatory requirements may prevent an Investment Fund* [...] *from investing directly in an asset and may require the investment to be made through a separate vehicle to limit the Investment Fund's liability*'.[377] Especially for 'Investment Funds' and 'Real Estate Investment Vehicles' Article 1.5.2. GloBE Model Rules and Article 2(3)(b) and (c) GloBE-Directive lead to a significant extension since such entities are actually only excluded if they qualify as UPE. However, Article 1.5.2 GloBE Model Rules and Article 2(3)(b) and (c) GloBE-Directive also exclude entities directly held by such collective investment vehicles.[378] At the election of the 'Filing Constituent Entity', the application of Article 1.5.2 GloBE Model Rules and Article 2(3)(b) and (c) GloBE-Directive can be waived (in detail, *see* below in section 4.2.4.3.4.).[379]

Technically, the extension of the 'Excluded Entity' definition in Article 1.5.2. GloBE Model Rules and Article 2(3)(b) and (c) GloBE-Directive is divided into two different types of excluded subsidiaries:

- First, an 'Entity' according to Article 1.5.2.(a) GloBE Model Rules (and identical in content Article 2[3][b] GloBE-Directive) qualifies as an 'Excluded

372. *Ibid.*, para. 77.
373. *Ibid.*, para. 78.
374. *Ibid.*, para. 77.
375. *See* Recital 7 GloBE-Directive (2022/2523), where it is held that collective investment vehicles '*should also be excluded* [...] *when they are at the top of the ownership chain, since* [...] *the*[ir] *income earned is taxed at the level of the owners*'.
376. *See GloBE Commentary on Article 1 GloBE Model Rules (2022)*, *supra* note 249, para. 43.
377. *See Ibid.*
378. *See Ibid.*, para. 45.
379. Article 1.5.3. *GloBE Model Rules* and Art. 2(3) GloBE-Directive (2022/2523).

Entity' '*where at least 95% of the value of the Entity is owned (directly or through a chain of Excluded Entities) by one or more Excluded Entities* [...] *(other than a Pension Services Entity*[[380]]*)*'[381] (so-called Ownership Test)[382] and the respective 'Entity' either '*operates exclusively or almost exclusively to hold assets or invest funds for the benefit of the Excluded Entity*'[383] or '*only carries out activities that are ancillary to those carried out by the Excluded Entity or Entities*'[384] (so-called Activities Test).[385] It is obvious that especially the 'Activity Test' might give rise to difficult interpretation issues. Especially the phrases '*almost exclusively*', '*for the benefit*' and '*activities that are ancillary*' are highly indeterminate, and even the Commentary only comments superficially on these issues.[386] It is not surprising that the GloBE Administrative Guidance February 2023 added some clarifications on the 'Activities Test'.[387] However, it is doubtful whether the additions can contribute significantly to the interpretation of Article 1.5.2. GloBE Model Rules.

- Second, an 'Entity' according to Article 1.5.2.(b) GloBE Model Rules (and identical in content Article 2[3][c] GloBE-Directive) qualifies as an 'Exclusive Entity' '*where at least 85% of the value of the Entity is owned (directly or through a chain of Excluded Entities), by one or more Excluded Entities [...] (other than a Pension Services Entity) provided that substantially all of the Entity's income is Excluded Dividends or Excluded Equity Gain or Loss that is excluded from the computation of GloBE Income or Loss in accordance with Articles 3.2.1(b) or (c)*'.[388] Unlike the vehicles listed in Article 1.5.2(a) GloBE Model Rules, this exception does not relate to the activity of an 'Entity' held by an 'Excluded Entity' but to the fact that it only receives income that is excluded from the 'Top-up Tax' computation anyway. Article 1.5.2.(b) GloBE Model Rules is obviously intended to pursue a kind of simplification purpose. According to the Commentary, the wording '*substantially all of its income*' is intended to create leeway in order to avoid the exclusion being inapplicable for the sole reason that the respective 'Entity' '*receives a small amount of income*

380. Article 1.5.2. *GloBE Model Rules* and Art. 2(3)(b) and (c) GloBE-Directive (2022/2523) explicitly exclude so-called Pension Services Entities (*see* the definition of the term in Art. 3[34] GloBE-Directive). 'Pension Services Entities' meet the definition of a 'Pension Fund' and are therefore considered as 'Excluded Entities' according to Art. 1.5.1.(d) GloBE Model Rules and Art. 2(3)(a) GloBE-Directive. Such entities are established and operated exclusively or almost exclusively to invest funds or to carry out activities that are ancillary to those of a 'Pension Fund', *see* Art. 10.1. *GloBE Model Rules*, at 63 and Art. 3(33) GloBE-Directive (2022/2523).The recognition of sub-entities of such 'Pension Services Entities' would, according to the Commentary, '*dilute the intended effect*' of Art. 1.5.2. GloBE Model Rules, *see GloBE Commentary on Article 1*, *supra* note 249, para. 44.
381. Article 1.5.2.(a) *GloBE Model Rules* and Art. 2(3)(b) GloBE-Directive (2022/2523).
382. *See GloBE Commentary on Article 1*, *supra* note 249, paras 47–51.
383. Article 1.5.2.(a)(i) *GloBE Model Rules* and Art. 2(3)(b)(i) GloBE-Directive (2022/2523).
384. Article 1.5.2.(a)(ii) *GloBE Model Rules* and Art. 2(3)(b)(ii) GloBE-Directive (2022/2523).
385. *See GloBE Commentary on Article 1*, *supra* note 249, paras 52–54.
386. *See Ibid.*, paras 53–54.
387. *See* the newly added paras 43.1 and 54.1 and the addition made in para. 53 on the Commentary on Art. 1, *see GloBE Administrative Guidance February 2023*, at 25–26.
388. Article 1.5.2.(b) *GloBE Model Rules*.

other than dividend and other equity returns on controlled companies [...] [f]*or example, the interest received from a bank on money that passes through the Entity's bank account*'.[389] Again, one can doubt whether this statement is helpful with regard to the application of this rule.

4.2.4.3.4 Scope and Legal Consequence of Classification as an 'Excluded Entity'

But what is the consequence of the classification as an 'Excluded Entity'? Does this mean that the corresponding 'Entity' falls out of the GloBE regime altogether? It has already been pointed out that this precisely is not the case: As already follows from the definition of 'Group' in Article 1.2.2. GloBE Model Rules and Article 3(3)(a) GloBE-Directive, respectively, a 'Group' consists of '*a collection of entities that are related by ownership and control*' and that are '*included in the consolidated financial statements of the Ultimate Parent Entity*'. Even if Article 1.3.3 GloBE Model Rules explicitly exclude the 'Excluded Entities' from the concept of CE, this does not mean that 'Excluded Entities' are out of the scope of the 'Group'. Rather, an 'Excluded Entity' remains part of the 'Group' as long as its assets and liabilities are consolidated within its 'Consolidated Financial Statements' or within those of a different UPE. This is precisely why the revenues of 'Excluded Entities' are still included in the calculation of the EUR 750 million revenue threshold in the same way as those revenues generated by CEs (in detail, *see* section 4.2.5).[390] But what, then, is the impact of the special status of 'Excluded Entities' within the 'Group'?

According to the Commentary, there are three special features that apply to 'Excluded Entities': first, any profits or losses, as well as taxes paid, are removed from the calculation of the jurisdictional 'GloBE Income or Loss' and the 'Adjusted Covered Taxes'. 'Excluded Entities' are therefore not taken into account at all in the calculation of the jurisdictional ETR. This also applies to tangible assets and payroll expenses for the computation of the 'Substance-based Income Exclusion' (SBIE).[391] Second, neither of the GloBE Rules is applied at the level of the 'Excluded Entity'. Rather, the IIR is applied at the level of the next 'Entity' in the ownership chain, not being excluded.[392] With regard to the UTPR, no 'Top-up Tax' can be attributed to an 'Excluded Entity'.[393] Third, as a consequence, 'Excluded Entities' are exempt from any administrative obligations.[394] There is also no need to report any information on 'Excluded Entities' with regard to the 'GloBE Information Return'. However, the Commentary only names one exception to this: According to Article 8.1.4.(b) GloBE Model Rules the 'MNE Group' is obliged to report '*Information on the overall corporate structure of the MNE*

389. *See GloBE Commentary on Article 1, supra* note 249, para. 56.
390. *See Ibid.*, paras 12 and letter b of 37.
391. *See* letter b of *Ibid.*, para. 37.
392. With respect to the IIR, *see GloBE Commentary on Article 2 GloBE Model Rules (2022), supra* note 238, paras 3 and 18.
393. *See* letter a of *GloBE Commentary on Article 1, supra* note 249, para. 37.
394. *See* letter c of *Ibid.*

Group'.[395] Since the 'MNE Group' also includes 'Excluded Entities', the 'Excluded Entities' of the group are to be named in the 'GloBE Information Return'.

According to Article 1.5.3. GloBE Model Rules and Article 2(3) GloBE-Directive a 'Filing Constituent Entity' may elect not to treat an 'Entity' as an 'Excluded Entity' according to Article 1.5.2 GloBE Model Rules and Article 2(3)(b) and (c) GloBE-Directive. Thus, the election is not available for the original 'Excluded Entities' but only for those entities qualifying as 'Excluded Entities' because they are owned by an 'Excluded Entity'. The election binds the 'MNE Group' for five years. But why should an 'MNE Group' forgo the exclusion? Indeed, there may be situations where the inclusion of the potentially 'Excluded Entity' can be beneficial. Such a situation could occur, for example, if the respective 'Entity' receives losses that might reduce the 'Net GloBE Income' ('GloBE Income' received in a specific jurisdiction) or owns tangible assets and has payroll expenses in a 'Low-Tax Jurisdiction' and consequently the SBIE for that jurisdiction can be increased. Furthermore, it is also conceivable that the taxes paid by the entity raise the ETR of a jurisdiction above the minimum tax rate. The Commentary, on the other hand, sees the purpose of the regulation as avoiding the UTPR:[396] If an 'Investment Fund' has to consolidate various subsidiaries but is itself considered an 'Excluded Entity', a 'Top-up Tax' incurred at the level of one of the CEs could not be collected by way of IIR. However, since the UTPR requires an allocation of the top-up tax to all substantial CEs, the application of the IIR at the level of the 'Investment Fund' may be more advantageous than a complex allocation by means of the UTPR.[397]

In summary, the essence of the 'Excluded Entity' concept is the following: 'Excluded Entities' remain part of the 'Group' without qualifying as CEs, which is why their revenues are to be included in the calculation of the revenue threshold, and can also qualify as UPEs. However, they are made completely invisible for GloBE with respect to the calculation of the ETR and the 'Top-up Tax' for levying the 'Top-up Tax' by means of the IIR and UTPR and are exempt from any administrative burdens created by the GloBE regime. If an 'Excluded Entity' is at the top of a 'group' as UPE, this does not mean that the 'Group' is not covered by GloBE. Rather, the 'group' continues to fall under GloBE, but the obligations arising from GloBE must be fulfilled *'by the next Entity in the ownership chain (that is not itself an Excluded Entity)'*.[398]

4.2.4.4 The Territorial Allocation of Constituent Entities

4.2.4.4.1 The Fundamental Role of the Concept of 'Location' Within GloBE's Framework

GloBE establishes a global minimum taxation system that compares the ETR of an 'MNE Group' against the minimum tax rate of 15%. For this purpose, the ETR is

395. Article 8.1.4.(b) *GloBE Model Rules*.
396. *See GloBE Commentary on Article 1, supra* note 249, para. 57.
397. *See Ibid.*
398. *See* letter a of *Ibid.*, para. 37.

calculated on a jurisdictional level. It has already been discussed that the calculation of the jurisdictional ETRs is ultimately based on the financial reports prepared by individual CEs within the 'Group' and that the jurisdictional perspective of GloBE, therefore, requires that the 'Group' be split up into its entities to finally aggregate their income received and taxes paid jurisdiction-wise. This presupposes, of course, that each CE (on the character of the CE definition, see already section 4.2.4.1.) is assigned to a specific jurisdiction or, as the Commentary puts it: '*Determining the location of an Entity and PE is important for jurisdictional blending and for determining where the Top-up Tax has to be paid.*'[399]

For this reason, GloBE provides its own rules for determining the 'location' of CEs. At first glance, GloBE's choice to use the term 'location' seems odd. The term 'residency' has established itself in international tax practice as an overarching concept, which is not only enshrined in Articles 1 and 4 OECD MC but has also become established in various domestic tax laws for defining domestic tax liability of individuals as well as legal entities. GloBE, however, consciously breaks away from the term '*residence*': As will be shown, GloBE does indeed rely on the concept of tax residency '*whenever possible*'[400] to determine to which jurisdiction an 'Entity' should be assigned, but the 'location' of an 'Entity' for purposes of GloBE does not necessarily reflect its residency under domestic law or a tax treaty. Even though GloBE makes extensive use of the concept of 'residency' to determine 'location', a separate set of rules for the delimitation of tax jurisdictions was necessary.[401] Finally, the term 'Entity' used by GloBE (as already pointed out in section 4.2.4.2.2.) clearly goes beyond the concept of covered persons in Article 1 OECD MC. This is also reflected in the fact that GloBE determines the 'location' of 'Flow-through Entities'[402] as well as PEs,[403] which are not at all considered 'resident persons' in international tax practice. Furthermore, as will be shown, there are CEs that cannot be assigned to any jurisdiction at all ('Stateless Constituent Entities'[404]), resulting in a situation where any 'Top-up Tax' calculated must be levied at the level of the individual 'stateless' CE.

The GloBE Model Rules refer to the 'location' in various places. The first reference is already made in the definition of the 'MNE Group' in Article 1.2.1 GloBE Model Rules stating that the 'Group' at least includes one 'Entity' or PE '*that is not located in the jurisdiction of the Ultimate Parent Entity*'.[405] In addition, 'location' is referenced in countless other places within the GloBE Model Rules[406] and the GloBE-Directive.[407] Finally, the term 'location' is of fundamental importance within the framework of GloBE. It is, therefore, all the more surprising that Article 10.3. GloBE Model Rules entitled '*Location of an Entity and a Permanent Establishment*' is found on

399. *See GloBE Commentary on Article 10 GloBE Model Rules (2022)*, *supra* note 280, para. 170.
400. *See Ibid.*, para. 172.
401. V. Bendlinger & Georg Kofler, *Computation of the Effective Tax Rate and the 'Top-up Tax,' in Pillar 2 Global Minimum Tax*, *supra* note 305.
402. *See* Art. 10.3.2. *GloBE Model Rules*.
403. *See* Art. 10.3.3. *Ibid.*
404. *See* the definition provided for in Art. 10.1. *Ibid.*, at 66.
405. Article 1.2.1. *GloBE Model Rules*.
406. *See*, e.g., Arts 2.1., 2.4., 5.1.2 *ibid.*, and many other places.
407. *See*, e.g., Art. 5-14 GloBE-Directive (2022/2523) and many other places.

the last two pages of the GloBE Model Rules. In the author's opinion, the definition of 'location' should have been included in Article 1 GloBE Model Rules. In this respect, it is to be appreciated that the GloBE-Directive regulates the 'location' in 'Chapter I' entitled 'General Provisions' in a separate Article 4 GloBE-Directive, immediately following the definition article and before the GloBE Rules. In terms of content, the concept of 'location' as defined in Article 4 GloBE-Directive does not differ from that provided for in Article 10.3. GloBE Model Rules. Both separately define the location of 'Entities' on the one hand and PEs on the other. For this reason, both are discussed separately below.

4.2.4.4.2 The 'Location' of 'Entities'

With respect to the 'location' of 'Entities' (in detail on the term 'Entity', see already section 4.2.4.2.2.), GloBE distinguishes between 'Entities' not qualifying as 'Flow-through Entities' (Article 10.3.1. GloBE Model Rules and Article 4(1) GloBE-Directive) and those that do (Article 10.3.2. GloBE Model Rules and Article 4(2) GloBE-Directive): while the 'location' of the former can be determined on their residency for tax purposes, the latter are usually not considered resident for tax purposes, which is why GloBE creates fictions to determine the 'location' of such 'Flow-through Entities'. Conversely, non-'Flow-through Entities' might even be resident in more than one jurisdiction. Accordingly, Article 10.3.4. GloBE Model Rules and Article 4(4) to (6) GloBE-Directive provide a set of 'tie-breaker rules' for such 'Entities' along the lines of Article 4(2) OECD MC for individuals.

The examination of the location of an 'Entity' for the purposes of GloBE, thus, starts with the determination of whether the respective 'Entity' is a 'Flow-through Entity' (either a 'Tax Transparent Entity' or a 'Reverse Hybrid Entity', according to Article 10.1. GloBE Model Rules).[408] In case the 'Entity' at issue is not a 'Flow-through Entity', Article 10.3.1. GloBE Model Rules (Article 4[1] GloBE-Directive using a similar wording) applies, which determines the 'location' in two steps: If the 'Entity' is a '*tax resident in a jurisdiction based on its place of management, place of creation or similar criteria,* [it] *is located in that jurisdiction*'.[409] For this test, residency under a tax treaty is irrelevant. Rather, this provision links the location of an 'Entity' to tax liability under domestic law;[410] and if an 'Entity' is tax resident in neither jurisdiction, GloBE deems the 'Entity' to be located in the jurisdiction '*where it was created*'.[411] The latter fiction

408. *See* the corresponding definitions of the term 'Flow-through Entity' including those of 'Tax Transparent Entity' and 'Reverse Hybrid Entity' in Art. 10.2. *GloBE Model Rules*. The GloBE-Directive also distinguishes between 'Tax Transparent Entity' and 'Reverse Hybrid Entity', but nevertheless covers both within the definition of the term 'flow-through entity' as defined in Art. 3(12) GloBE-Directive (2022/2523).

409. Article 10.3.1.(a) *GloBE Model Rules*. Also *see* the first sentence of Art. 4(1) GloBE-Directive (2022/2523).

410. *See GloBE Commentary on Article 10 GloBE Model Rules (2022)*, *supra* note 280, paras 172 and 179.

411. Article 10.3.1.(b) *GloBE Model Rules*. Also *see* the second sentence of Art. 4(1) GloBE-Directive (2022/2523).

will, therefore, only apply if the jurisdiction in which the entity was created does not levy CIT at all.[412]

Much more relevant is the reverse case, in which an 'Entity' is considered a tax resident under the domestic law of more than one state. In this case, the examination of Article 10.3.1 GloBE Model Rules is followed by another chain of tests according to Article 10.3.4. GloBE Model Rules, which ultimately filter the 'location' of an 'Entity' depending on whether a Tax Treaty in force is applicable to the respective 'Entity' (Article 10.3.4.(a) GloBE Model Rules and Article 4(4) GloBE-Directive): Thus, it is first necessary to check whether the respective 'Entity' is covered by a tax treaty. If this is the case, the 'Entity' is deemed to be located where it is resident for the purposes of the tax treaty. The same applies if more than two jurisdictions and, thus, more than one tax treaty is involved.[413] This rule alone is likely to solve most dual-residency cases.

If, however, the tax treaty either fails to define the residency of an 'Entity' (e.g., because the competent authorities fail to find a mutual agreement),[414] or does not provide for relief for dual resident entities,[415] or if no Tax Treaty applies between the jurisdictions at all, the 'location' is notionally determined by Article 10.3.4.(b) GloBE Model Rules: The 'Entity' is deemed to be 'located' in the jurisdiction in which the higher 'Covered Taxes' (not including taxes paid due to Controlled Foreign Company (CFC) regimes) were incurred,[416] and if these are also not determinative, the higher SBIE is decisive;[417] and if there is still no jurisdiction winning the 'tie-break', the entity is deemed to be stateless or – if it is the UPE of the 'MNE Group' – deemed to be located where it was created.[418] Admittedly, it is unlikely that a stateless entity will actually emerge after this cascade of tests. In practice, such a result is only conceivable in the case of dual resident entities lacking any substance that are, nevertheless, considered tax residents in more than one state but are subject to personal tax exemptions in either state. After all, it is otherwise hardly conceivable that exactly the same amount of 'Covered Taxes' was paid in more than one state.[419]

The GloBE tie-breaker in Article 10.3.4. GloBE Model Rules, as well as Article 4(4) and 4(5) GloBE-Directive, are also supplemented by Article 10.3.5. GloBE Model Rules and Article 4(6) GloBE-Directive that allows the loser state of the tie-breaker to apply the IIR if the winner state does not apply an IIR and if the loser state is not restricted by a treaty. In this way, GloBE avoids a situation wherein the tie-breaker locates a 'Parent

412. *See GloBE Commentary on Article 10, supra* note 280, para. 184.
413. *See Ibid.*, para. 207.
414. Article 10.3.4.(a)(ii) *GloBE Model Rules* and the second sentence of Art. 4(4) GloBE-Directive (2022/2523).
415. Article 10.3.4.(a)(iii) *GloBE Model Rules* and the third sentence of Art. 4(4) GloBE-Directive (2022/2523).
416. Article 10.3.4.(b)(i) *GloBE Model Rules* and the first and second sentence of Art. 4(5) GloBE-Directive (2022/2523).
417. Article 10.3.4.(b)(ii) *GloBE Model Rules* and the third sentence of Art. 4(5) GloBE-Directive (2022/2523).
418. Article 10.3.4.(b)(iii) *GloBE Model Rules* and the last sentence of Art. 4(5) GloBE-Directive (2022/2523).
419. In the same vein V. Bendlinger & Georg Kofler, *Computation of the Effective Tax Rate and the 'Top-up Tax'*, in *Pillar 2 Global Minimum Tax, supra* note 305.

Entity', where it is not subject to a 'Qualified IIR'.[420] The Commentary adds that the dual resident CE, however, may not be made subject to the IIR by the loser state if the residence of the CE is '*the result of the application of the tiebreaker rule in a Tax Treaty*'.[421] Furthermore, the Commentary specifically refers to tax treaties following Article 4(3) OECD MC 2017, according to which the two contracting states determine the residency of dual resident entities by means of an agreement by the competent authorities: if the competent authorities succeed in finding an agreement, the loser state may not apply the IIR to the respective CE because it would be restricted as the CE would be considered as a resident of the other contracting state. However, if the authorities fail to reach an agreement, the loser state may indeed apply its IIR to the dual resident entity because Article 4(3) OECD MC 2017, in this case, explicitly denies any treaty benefits to the respective entity.[422]

If a 'Flow-through Entity' is at issue, Article 10.3.2. GloBE Model Rules (Article 4(2) GloBE-Directive) fictitiously determines the 'location': as such entities are generally not considered tax resident in any jurisdiction, they are considered stateless (so-called 'Stateless Constituent Entity') for purposes of GloBE. Such a CE is then considered to be the only CE located in a fictitious separate jurisdiction for the purpose of 'Top-up Tax' computation (on the treatment of 'Stateless Constituent Entities', *see* below section 4.2.4.4.4.).[423] Nevertheless, there are two exceptions to this rule: According to Article 10.3.2.(a) GloBE Model Rules (Article 4(2) GloBE-Directive) a 'Flow-through Entity' is considered 'located' where it was created, either (i) if the 'Flow-through Entity' is the UPE of the 'MNE Group' or (ii) if it is required to apply an IIR. The purpose of the refusal to assign such 'Entities' to a specific jurisdiction is probably to avoid the deliberate use of fiscally transparent vehicles to avoid the minimum tax: 'MNE Groups' could make use of fiscally transparent vehicles, to deliberately undermine income and tax allocation principles of GloBE, e.g., by using an intermediate fiscally transparent entity to allocate certain Covered Taxes paid in high-tax jurisdictions by a parent entity to a low-taxed subsidiary in a 'Low-tax Jurisdiction' to increase the ETR of this 'Low-tax Jurisdiction' where the low-taxed subsidiary is located, although the tax would not be allocable to that jurisdiction at all. GloBE simply solves this issue by denying the assignment to a specific jurisdiction and considering the respective 'Entity' as being stateless. In this way, a kind of steering effect can be achieved: as will become clear, the status of 'Stateless Constituent Entity' is associated with negative consequences within the framework of GloBE, as such entities are completely excluded from jurisdictional blending ('*stand-alone top-up tax calculation*'[424]). However, since 'Flow-through Entities' are not residents anywhere either, there is usually no 'Covered Tax', which means that the ETR of such a CE will regularly be zero. In case the 'Entity' is the UPE or it is subject to an IIR anyway, however, there is no need to protect the allocation of income or tax payments since, in

420. *See GloBE Commentary on Article 10 GloBE Model Rules (2022)*, *supra* note 280, para. 208.
421. *See Ibid.*, para. 209.
422. Also *see Ibid.*
423. Last sentence of Art. 5.1.1. *GloBE Model Rules* and Art. 26(4) GloBE-Directive (2022/2523).
424. *See GloBE Commentary on Article 10*, *supra* note 280, para. 174.

these cases, the structure could not benefit from shifting 'Covered Taxes' to a lower CE anyway: There is no CE above the UPE[425] and if the transparent CE is not the UPE but subject to an IIR in its state of creation, the full collection of 'Top-up Tax' arising from subsidiary CEs is ensured anyway.

Finally, both Article 10.3.6. GloBE Model Rules and Article 4(7) GloBE-Directive provide for a special clarification in cases where a CE changes its 'location' within a 'Fiscal Year'. In this case, the 'location' of the CE shall be deemed to be 'located' in the jurisdiction where it was 'located' at the beginning of the 'Fiscal Year'.[426]

4.2.4.4.3 The 'Location' of Permanent Establishments

As with 'Flow-through Entities', the 'location' also needs to be determined for PEs by means of fiction. Finally, in international practice, PEs are also not considered taxable persons. Rather, a PE is merely a taxable nexus for non-resident taxpayers in the state where they operate a place of business. As already explained, GloBE has its own definition of PE and includes four different types of PEs that are considered as CEs within GloBE's systematic (already *see* section 4.2.4.1.2.). The location of PEs is linked to the PE definition in Article 10.1 GloBE Model Rules and Article 3(13) GloBE-Directive and differs for each of the four PE types:[427]

- *PEs under an applicable tax treaty* are located in the jurisdiction where they are treated as a PE and are taxed under the applicable Tax Treaty in force (Article 10.3.3.[a] GloBE Model Rules and the first sentence of Article 4[3] GloBE-Directive).
- *PEs under domestic laws* are located where they are taxed on a net basis (Article 10.3.3.[b] GloBE Model Rules and the second sentence of Article 4[3] GloBE-Directive).
- *PEs not being subject to CIT at their place of establishment* are located where they are situated (Article 10.3.3.[c] GloBE Model Rules and third sentence of Article 4[3] GloBE-Directive).
- *Exterritorial PEs* are considered stateless (Article 10.3.3.[d] GloBE Model Rules and the fourth sentence of Article 4[3] GloBE-Directive).

4.2.4.4.4 Group Members Not Assigned to a Specific Jurisdiction: The Phenomenon of 'Stateless Constituent Entities'

So far, several references have been made to 'Entities' and PEs that cannot be assigned to a jurisdiction and are therefore considered stateless for the purposes of GloBE

425. On the special case of 'Flow-through Entities' forming the UPE of an 'MNE Group' (Art. 7.1. GloBE Model Rules and Art. 38 GloBE-Directive), *see* s. 4.2.4.2.2.
426. *See GloBE Commentary on Article 10*, *supra* note 280, para. 210.
427. Also *see* in detail *Ibid.*, paras 189–194.

(so-called Stateless Constitute Entities[428]). But how can it be that no allocation is made at all? How are 'Stateless Constituent Entities' treated within the framework of GloBE?

These so-called Stateless Constituent Entities are treated by GloBE as if they were the only corporation of an 'MNE Group' that is located in a fictitious tax jurisdiction. This is particularly evident in the last sentence of Article 5.1.1 GloBE Model Rules (Article 26[4] GloBE-Directive), where it is stated for the purposes of calculating the 'Top-up Tax' that a '*Stateless Constituent Entity shall be treated as a single Constituent Entity located in a separate jurisdiction*'.[429] Thus, 'Stateless Constituent Entities' fall outside of jurisdictional blending and are, as the Commentary puts it, '*subject to a standalone top-up tax calculation*'.[430] All parameters for the calculation of the 'Top-up Tax', e.g., the 'GloBE Income or Losses', 'Adjusted Covered Taxes' as well as the SBIE, are therefore calculated at the level of this individual 'Stateless Constituent Entity'. Such a 'Stateless Constituent Entity' can arise in three situations:

- An 'Entity' that is neither a 'Flow-through Entity' nor a UPE can qualify as a 'Stateless Constituent Entity' if it is located in more than one jurisdiction and the location can be determined neither by a Tax Treaty by the amount of Covered Taxes paid nor by the amount of SBIE (Article 10.3.4[b][iii] GloBE Model Rules and last sentence of Article 4[5] GloBE-Directive). As stated above, CEs that are neither 'Flow-through Entities' nor PEs will only occur to be stateless in very exceptional cases.[431]
- A 'Flow-through Entity' is to be treated as a 'Stateless Constituent Entity' if it neither qualifies as a UPE nor is required to apply an IIR (Article 10.3.2.[b] GloBE Model Rules and Article 4[2] GloBE Model Rules). Compared to 'Entities' not qualifying as 'Flow-through Entity', the emergence of a 'Stateless Constituent Entity' is much more likely: Any vehicle treated as fiscally transparent within the jurisdiction it was created is considered stateless if it is not the UPE or if it is not subject to an IIR in that jurisdiction. As most jurisdictions do not treat such entities as taxable persons, many jurisdictions will not apply IIR to them.[432] Since transparent vehicles, such as partnerships, regularly establish a PE in the state of their creation, income from 'Flow-through Entities' is generally allocated to the jurisdiction where the PE is located anyway (*see* in detail section 4.2.4.4.3.). The Commentary, thus, assumes that 'Reverse Hybrid Entities' will be the only practical use case of stateless CEs: Such entities are characterized by the fact that they are treated as tax transparent in the jurisdiction where they have been created but are

428. *See* the definition of the term 'Stateless Constituent Entity' in Art. 10.1 *GloBE Model Rules*, at 66.
429. Article 5.1.1. *GloBE Model Rules*. *See* the similar wording provided for in Art. 26(4) GloBE-Directive (2022/2523).
430. *See GloBE Commentary on Article 10*, *supra* note 280, para. 174.
431. Interestingly, this situation is not mentioned in the definition of 'Stateless Constituent Entity' in Art. 10.1 *GloBE Model Rules*, at 66. Apparently, the OECD also assumes that 'Entities' (not 'Flow-through Entities') can be assigned to a specific jurisdiction in most cases under the 'tie-breaker' rules provided for in Art. 10.3.4. *GloBE Model Rules* as well as Art. 4(4) and Art. 4(5) GloBE-Directive (2022/2523).
432. *See GloBE Commentary on Article 10*, *supra* note 280, para. 187.

treated as a taxable person in the state of its shareholders so that the income is not considered as income of a resident person in any state.[433]

- An *exterritorial PE* might qualify as a 'Stateless Constituent Entity' if it is involved in operations conducted outside the jurisdiction where the 'Main Entity' is located, provided that such jurisdiction exempts income attributable to such operations (Article 10.3.4.[d] in conjunction with letter d of the PE definition in Article 10.1. GloBE Model Rules and Article 4[3], in conjunction with Article 3[13][d] GloBE-Directive, already *see* 4.2.4.1.2.).[434]

Indeed, as shown, there can be CEs that cannot be assigned to any jurisdiction; however, stateless CEs are likely to be rare phenomena. The most common cases of stateless CEs are likely to be 'Flow-through Entities', i.e., partnerships or other fiscally transparent vehicles, which are neither UPE nor subject to the IIR in the jurisdiction where they have been created.

4.2.5 Revenue Threshold of EUR 750 Million

4.2.5.1 Background and Connex to CbCR (BEPS Action 13)

The analysis of the scope of GloBE so far has mainly dealt with the notion of the 'MNE Group',[435] the scope of this 'Group'[436] and its members.[437] The EUR 750 million revenue threshold, however, has not yet been dealt with in depth, and for a good reason: As Article 1.1.1. GloBE Model Rules (also *see* Article 2[1] GloBE-Directive) states, GloBE shall apply to 'MNE Groups' that have an '*annual revenue of EUR 750 million or more in the Consolidated Financial Statements of the Ultimate Parent Entity (UPE) in at least two of the four Fiscal Years immediately preceding the tested Fiscal Year*'.[438] The EUR 750 million threshold is, therefore, a threshold derived from the 'Consolidated Financial Statements'. The scope of the 'Group', thus, consequently also impacts the computation of the EUR 750 million threshold.

The restriction of the scope of Pillar Two to 'MNE Groups' with revenues of at least EUR 750 million was first discussed in the Pillar Two Blueprint. There it is stated that the threshold of EUR 750 million was adopted from the BEPS Action 13 report on CbCR, as were the terms 'MNE Group', 'Constituent Entity' or 'Ultimate Parent Entity'.[439] This should allow synergies with CbCR to be exploited: '*MNEs that are not subject to CbCR have no independent financial reporting reason to separately report the income of the branch and head office of the same entity as they are required to under the GloBE rules. The use of the same threshold may also facilitate the use of simplification*

433. *See Ibid.*, para. 176.
434. On the issue of stateless PEs, *see* Stefan Bendlinger, *Betriebsstätten im Rahmen der globalen Mindestbesteuerung*, 33 SWI, *supra* note 306, at 8–9.
435. *See* s. 4.2.2.
436. *See* s. 4.2.3.
437. *See* s. 4.2.4.
438. Article 1.1.1. *GloBE Model Rules* and similar Art. 2(1) GloBE-Directive (2022/2523).
439. *Tax Challenges Arising from Digitalisation – Report on Pillar Two Blueprint*, paras 41–42.

options.'[440] Thus, the idea was that the GloBE framework could be linked to the CbCR already being implemented in many jurisdictions. Although GloBE, as will become apparent, has emerged to be very autonomous in this respect, a connection with data from the CbCR is not yet off the table with respect to future simplifications of GloBE. In any case, the above-cited statement sheds light onto the purpose and the background of the restriction of scope to 'MNE Groups' exceeding revenues of EUR 750 million: as early as 2020, the OECD considered the GloBE framework too complex to impose on smaller multinationals and had in mind above all the splitting of the 'Consolidated Financial Statements' into individual jurisdictions: '*The use of the CbCR reporting threshold will exclude small and medium enterprises (SMEs) operating in more than one jurisdiction, where the application of these rules could be a significantly greater burden. A EUR 750 million revenue threshold will mean that between 85% and 90% of MNE Groups will be outside the scope of the rules. This, in turn, reduces the pressure on Inclusive Framework on BEPS members to provide carve-outs from the GloBE rules for SMEs that benefit from targeted domestic tax incentives.'*[441] The Blueprint furthermore assumed that, however, the in-scope 'MNE Groups' '*earn over 90% of global corporate revenues*' and that the threshold would accordingly '*preserve* [...] *the impact of GloBE rules*'[442].[443]

4.2.5.2 *Significance of Consolidated Revenues*

The revenue threshold in Article 1.1.1. GloBE Model Rules and Article 2(1) GloBE-Directive explicitly refers to the revenues in the 'Consolidated Financial Statements'. Conversely, this already predicts that all revenues of members of the 'Group', which are not included in the 'Consolidated Financial Statements', will not be included in the calculation of the revenue threshold. Consequently, although not explicitly addressed in the Commentary, for example, the revenues of 'Entities' being excluded from the 'Consolidated Financial Statements' of the UPE solely on size or materiality grounds (Article 1.2.2.[b] GloBE Model Rules and Article 3[3][a] GloBE-Directive) are taken into account in the computation of the revenue threshold. The same is true for 'Joint Ventures', for example, which are included in the group for the purposes of the GloBE Rules, but are generally not consolidated on a line-by-line basis (*see* section 4.2.4.1.3.).

However, once an 'Entity' is consolidated on a line-by-line basis, the revenue threshold includes the revenues reflected in the 'Consolidated Financial Statements' of the UPE and, thus, also includes revenues that could be allocated to minority interests of third parties.[444] GloBE, therefore, relies, probably for reasons of simplification, directly on the reported group turnover, without any adjustments. The Commentary also clarifies this: '*The threshold applies based on the consolidated revenue of the MNE*

440. *Ibid.*, para. 115.
441. *Ibid.*, para. 117.
442. *Ibid.*, para. 118.
443. Also *see* the justification of the EUR 750 million threshold for CbCR in *BEPS Action 13: 2015 Final Report*, paras 52–53.
444. *See GloBE Commentary on Article 1 GloBE Model Rules (2022)*, *supra* note 249, para. 11.

Group, not the aggregate of the revenues of each Group Entity' which is why '*revenues from transactions with other Group Entities that are eliminated in the consolidation process are excluded from the revenue threshold test*'.[445] Intra-group sales that have to be eliminated in the consolidation process are, therefore, not added back for the purposes of the revenue threshold.

An interesting note with respect to the significance of the 'Consolidated Financial Statement' for the purpose of the revenue threshold can be found in the Pillar Two Blueprint, where it is held that those revenues of two or more 'MNE Groups' not being part of the same 'Consolidated Financial Statement' '*should not be aggregated even if they are controlled by the same person (e.g., an individual)*'.[446] The Commentary does not contain further comments on these situations. Nevertheless, GloBE still strictly focuses on the 'Consolidated Financial Statements'. If the shareholder owning a controlling interest in several 'MNE Groups' is not required to prepare a 'Consolidated Financial Statement', e.g., because the shareholder is an individual or the shareholder prepares a comprehensive 'Consolidated Financial Statement' under an 'Acceptable Financial Accounting Standard' which, however, does not need to include those 'Groups' within its 'Consolidated Financial Statements', the revenues of the respective controlled 'MNE Groups' are not to be aggregated. Rather, the consolidated revenue threshold is examined for each 'MNE Group' separately. Similar situations can arise with respect to 'Investment Funds' and 'Real Estate Investment Vehicles' that control several 'MNE Groups', which, however, are not required to consolidate such participations within its 'Consolidated Financial Statements'. Due to the fact that such entities are excluded, the respective issue is discussed in the following section (*see* section 4.2.5.3).

The problem of several 'MNE Groups' in the hands of the same shareholder or shareholders discussed here is, to a certain extent, related to the special regime for 'Multi-Parented MNE Groups' already discussed (*see* section 4.2.4.2.5.). 'Multi-Parented MNE Groups' are also characterized by the fact that several 'Groups' are involved in a special relationship. Such structures are, however, according to Article 6.5.1. GloBE Model Rules and Article 37 GloBE-Directive, to be treated as members of a single 'MNE Group'. Consequently, the revenue threshold is also to be calculated as if all 'Groups' were members of a single 'MNE Group'.[447]

However, this exception again confirms the rule that only the revenues reported in the 'Consolidated Financial Statement' can be decisive for the purposes of the revenue threshold. If a sub-group is, for whatever reason, not included in the 'Consolidated Financial Statements' of another 'Group', its revenues are not part of this other 'Group'.

445. *Ibid.*
446. *Tax Challenges Arising from Digitalisation – Report on Pillar Two Blueprint*, para. 121.
447. *See GloBE Commentary on Article 6 GloBE Model Rules (2022)*, *supra* note 314, para. 101.

4.2.5.3 Revenues of 'Excluded Entities' Remain in the Revenue Threshold

As already discussed, excluded entities are not CEs, but are, if included within the 'Consolidated Financial Statements', nevertheless part of the 'Group' (*see* already section 4.2.4.3.). While the income and Covered Taxes of 'Excluded Entities' fall outside the GloBE regime, the revenues of 'Excluded Entities' remain in the calculation of the consolidated revenue threshold.[448] According to the Commentary, this shall ensure '*consistency with the threshold for reporting under CbCR and avoids requiring additional rules to address the treatment of revenues attributable to transactions between the Excluded Entity and the rest of the Group (including anti-avoidance rules to protect against fragmentation)*'.[449] This contrasts with the Blueprint, where it had been suggested to still exclude the revenues of 'Excluded Entities' from the calculation of the consolidated revenue threshold.[450]

An interesting question arises in this context in relation to very common group structures where the UPE is either an 'Investment Fund' or a 'Real Estate Investment Vehicle'. As already discussed in detail, such vehicles qualify as 'Excluded Entities' according to Article 1.5.(e) and (f) GloBE Model Rules (Article 2[3][a] GloBE-Directive). While such vehicles are not required to apply the GloBE Rules, the revenue of all sub-groups controlled by the vehicle would have to be aggregated for the purposes of GloBE. While the GloBE Model Rules and Commentary, and the GloBE-Directive, do not provide any guidance on this issue, the Blueprint gives insightful information in that respect: The Blueprint recognized that: '[a]*ccording to IFRS 10, investment entities are not required to consolidate an investment in a subsidiary, unless the main purposes and activities of the subsidiary is to provide services related to the investment entity's activities. Thus, an investment entity that is the controlling shareholder of two or more MNE Groups would typically not consolidate these groups into its financial statements and would not be considered as the Ultimate Parent Entity of these groups*'.[451] Indeed, IFRS 10.31 to 10.33 foresee an exception to consolidation for investment entities. Thus, based on IFRS, 'Investment Funds' and 'Real Estate Investment Vehicles', which generally also meet the definition of 'investment entities' in IFRS 10, would not be required to consolidate their investments, even if they had control over the respective investment. Rather, as the Blueprint further notes,'[i]*n these cases, each MNE Group would typically have separate consolidated financial statements, and these groups would be considered as separate MNE Groups*'.[452] Thus, as investment entities are not required to consolidate controlled sub-groups under IFRS, each sub-group must separately determine whether or not the consolidated revenue threshold is met.

Although most 'Acceptable Financial Accounting Standards' do not require investment entities to consolidate their investments, there might be 'Acceptable

448. *See GloBE Commentary on Article 1*, *supra* note 249, para. 12.
449. *See Ibid.*
450. *Tax Challenges Arising from Digitalisation – Report on Pillar Two Blueprint*, para. 125.
451. *Ibid.*, para. 122.
452. *Ibid.*, para. 123.

Financial Accounting Standards' which do not exempt such vehicles from consolidating their controlled sub-groups. In these cases, the consolidated revenue threshold, therefore, refers to the excluded UPE, including all controlled subgroups.

4.2.5.4 *Timing Issues: Four-Year Perspective, the Relevance of 'Fiscal Years' and Currency Conversion*

Pursuant to Article 1.1.1. GloBE Model Rules (Article 2[1] GloBE-Directive), an 'MNE Group' is within the scope of GloBE if it exceeds the EUR 750 million threshold *'in at least two of the four Fiscal Years immediately preceding the tested Fiscal Year'*[453] (*two-out-of-four-years test*[454]). The 'Fiscal Year' in which the 'MNE Group' is assessed to GloBE is therefore not taken into account, simply due to the fact that every 'MNE Group' needs to know in advance whether it is subject to GloBE.[455] Thereby, the term 'Fiscal Year' relates to the period with respect to which the UPE prepares its 'Consolidated Financial Statements'. The 'Fiscal Year' is, however, deemed to be the calendar year if the UPE does not prepare 'Consolidated Financial Statements' at all.[456] If the 'Fiscal Year' is a period other than 12 months (e.g., due to a reorganization), the EUR 750 million threshold is to be adjusted proportionally to the respective period.[457] The Commentary proposes to divide the respective period into months when calculating the adjusted revenue threshold with respect to periods other than 12 months.[458]

Another timing issue relates to currency issues. Many jurisdictions will not set the revenue threshold in euros but in their domestic currencies other than EUR. Thus, the Commentary states that if the amount *'changes on a yearly basis, the applicable revenue threshold* [for the four-year perspective] *is the last revenue threshold in effect as of the beginning of the Fiscal Year'*.[459] The OECD obviously seems to assume that all jurisdictions implementing GloBE but not using euros will regularly adjust the revenue threshold to equal the EUR 750 million threshold. Interestingly, the currency issue in relation to the revenue threshold is not directly addressed either in the GloBE Model Rules or the GloBE-Directive (not every EU Member State is using the Euro).

4.2.5.5 *Special Issues with Regard to Group Mergers and Demergers*

Within the four-year observation period, a 'Group' may change: one 'Group' can merge with another, individual 'Entities' outside the group can merge onto CEs of the 'Group', and, in the same way, the 'Group' can demerge. In the case of such reorganizations, questions of temporal allocation arise: From which 'Fiscal Year' onwards are the

453. Article 1.1.1. *GloBE Model Rules.*
454. *See GloBE Commentary on Article 1, supra* note 249, para. 6.
455. *See Ibid.*
456. *See* the definition of 'Fiscal Year' in Art. 10.1. *GloBE Model Rules*, para. 56.
457. Article 1.1.2. *GloBE Model Rules* and Art. 3(7) GloBE-Directive (2022/2523).
458. *See GloBE Commentary on Article 1, supra* note 249, paras 14–15.
459. *See Ibid.*, para. 13.

revenues of the merged entities to be taken into account for the consolidated revenue threshold and from which year onwards is it reduced for the demerged entities?

Both Article 6.1. GloBE Model Rules and Article 33 GloBE-Directive complement the two-out-of-four-year revenue test with respect to such timing issues and provide specific rules for three different scenarios:[460]

- The first scenario is addressed in Article 6.1.1.(a) GloBE Model Rules and Article 33(2) GloBE-Directive and concerns the merger,[461] concerns two or more different 'Groups'. Due to the fact that those 'Groups' do not have a single 'Consolidated Financial Statement', the consolidated revenue threshold of the 'MNE Group' for any four preceding years is deemed to be met for the tested year if the sum of the revenue included in each of their 'Consolidated Financial Statements' for that year is equal or greater than EUR 750 million.[462] It should be noted that the time of the merger should not be relevant: The revenues of the two groups are to be aggregated for 'any' 'Fiscal Year', meaning that the revenues are to be also combined for the years before the merger took place.[463]
- The second scenario relates to single 'Entities' either acquiring another single 'Entity' or a 'Group' or being either acquired by a single 'Entity' or a Group (Article 6.1.1.[b] GloBE Model Rules and Article 33[3] GloBE-Directive). In this case, it might occur that either the acquirer or the acquired 'Entity' does not prepare 'Consolidated Financial Statements' at all, which is the reason that these types of mergers[464] are not included within the first scenario. The legal consequence, however, equals the first scenario: GloBE deems the consolidated revenue threshold to be met for any of the four tested 'Fiscal Years' if the sum of the revenues included in each of their Financial Statements or 'Consolidated Financial Statements for the year is equal or greater than EUR 750 million.[465]
- The third scenario covers demergers,[466] where a single 'MNE Group' that once met the scope of GloBE is split into at least two separate Groups (Article 6.1.1.[c] GloBE Model Rules and Article 33[4] GloBE-Directive). In this case, the consolidated revenue threshold is deemed to be met for the first Fiscal Year ending after the demerger. For the second to fourth 'Fiscal Years' ending after the demerger, each separate 'MNE Group' needs to determine whether it has annual revenues of at least EUR 750 million.[467]

460. *See GloBE Commentary on Article 6 GloBE Model Rules (2022), supra* note 314, paras 19–20.
461. Separately defined in Art. 6.1.2.(a) *GloBE Model Rules* and Art. 33(1)(a)(i) GloBE-Directive (2022/2523).
462. In detail, *see GloBE Commentary on Article 6, supra* note 314, paras 21–23.
463. *See Ibid.*, para. 23.
464. Separately defined in Art. 6.1.2.(b) *GloBE Model Rules* and Art. 33(1)(a)(ii) GloBE-Directive (2022/2523).
465. In detail, *see GloBE Commentary on Article 6, supra* note 314, paras 24–30.
466. Separately defined in Art. 6.1.3. *GloBE Model Rules* and Art. 33(1)(b) GloBE-Directive (2022/2523).
467. In detail, *see GloBE Commentary on Article 6, supra* note 314, paras 31–36.

4.3 THE COMPUTATION OF THE 'EFFECTIVE TAX RATE'

4.3.1 The Fundamental Role of the 'Effective Tax Rate' Computation Within GloBE's Framework

After an analysis of the scope of GloBE, this section is dedicated to the calculation of the ETR. GloBE clearly intends to implement a system of minimum taxation, ensuring that (excess)[468] profits of an in-scope 'MNE Group' are taxed at least at the minimum tax rate of 15%. A minimum tax system can only achieve this goal by means of a comparison: The taxes actually paid on income (within GloBE, this is the ETR) are to be compared with the minimum tax level (within GloBE 15%), and if the taxes actually paid do not reach the minimum tax level, the difference (within GloBE this is the amount of 'Top-up Tax', *see* section 4.4.) is to be collected as the minimum tax due (within GloBE by means of the Qualified Domestic Minimum Top-up Tax (QDMTT), IIR or UTPR, *see* section 4.4.2.8). In essence, like every minimum tax system, GloBE is, thus, characterized by a comparison of the actual tax level with a politically determined target tax level that is, as *Becker* and *Englisch* aptly put it, deemed to be '*acceptable*'[469].[470] As simple as this observation may be, it is all the more important for a deeper understanding of GloBE, and as will be seen shortly, the implementation of the comparison just mentioned was not a simple undertaking, neither from a political nor a technical perspective.

In any case, not only the choice of the minimum tax rate but also the calculation of the ETR is a political issue. During the technical development of GloBE, very fundamental tax policy choices had to be made with respect to the computation of the ETR: Should the minimum tax rate be compared with the nominal tax level or with a percentage relation between taxes paid and income received? And if the latter, which taxes should be covered, and what is the tax basis against which the taxes paid could be put into relation? And even if a uniform understanding of the parameters of taxes paid and income received could be found, there remained the question of whether the ETR should be determined on a worldwide, country-by-country or entity-by-entity basis.[471]

In creating the GloBE Model Rules, the IF had to take a clear position on each of these issues, and, naturally, each has its pros and cons. It is all the more impressive that the OECD has succeeded in creating a common framework, currently supported by 142 jurisdictions (December 2022),[472] including a uniform understanding of an '*accepted*' minimum tax rate and, above all, a uniform framework to calculate the ETR that can be

468. On this issue, *see* s. 4.4.2.5. and 4.5.2.
469. Johannes Becker & Joachim Englisch, *International Effective Minimum Taxation – The GLOBE Proposal*, 11 WTJ 496 (2019) DOI: 10.2139/ssrn.3370532.
470. For very fundamental thoughts on minimum tax systems, *see* Daniel Shaviro, *What Are Minimum Taxes, and Why Might One Favor or Disfavor Them?*, 40 Va. Tax Rev. (2021) DOI: 10.2139/ssrn.3604328. Also *see* V. Bendlinger & Georg Kofler, *Computation of the Effective Tax Rate and the 'Top-up Tax,'* in *Pillar 2 Global Minimum Tax*, *supra* note 305.
471. Also *see* V. Bendlinger & Georg Kofler, *supra* note 305.
472. *Members of the OECD/G20 Inclusive Framework on BEPS (Updated: December 2022)*.

compared to the minimum tax rate.[473] In any case, it is even an understatement when the Commentary refers to the ETR computation as *'a central element of the GloBE Rules'*;[474] in fact, *'the ETR computation is the central element of the GloBE Rules'*.[475]

Finally, within the GloBE Model Rules, the ETR computation is enshrined in the second sentence of Article 5.1.1 GloBE Model Rules, which reads as follows: *'The Effective Tax Rate of the MNE Group for a jurisdiction is equal to the sum of the Adjusted Covered Taxes of each Constituent Entity located in the jurisdiction divided by the Net GloBE Income of the jurisdiction for the Fiscal Year.'*[476] The same principle is laid down in Article 26(1) GloBE-Directive. Essentially, under the author's opinion,[477] three main tax policy decisions have been made by the OECD with regard to the ETR calculation: first, (i) the ETR is a fraction of taxes paid ('Adjusted Covered Taxes') and income received ('Net GloBE Income'). Second, (ii) both parameters of the fraction are to be determined on an entity level, and third, (iii) the ETR is aggregated jurisdiction-wise. All three of these tax policy choices are more or less interrelated but not necessarily dependent on each other. The following section 4.3.2. aims to explore and critically assess these tax policy choices and their interrelation, to finally discuss their implementation within the GloBE Model Rules and the GloBE-Directive. Subsequently, sections 4.3.3 and 4.3.4. will analyse the determination of the two parameters of the ETR fraction and will analyse the determination of both the 'GloBE Income or Loss' and the 'Adjusted Covered Taxes'. The computation of the final minimum tax liability, the so-called Top-up Tax, will be addressed in section 4.4.

4.3.2 Conceptual Thoughts on the ETR Computation

4.3.2.1 Development of and Tax Policy Considerations on the Computation of the ETR Within GloBE: A Bundle of Three Fundamental Tax Policy Decisions

4.3.2.1.1 First Decision: The ETR as a Fraction of Taxes Paid on Income Received

From the very beginning of the development of GloBE, it was clear, for obvious reasons, that an effective global minimum taxation system would need a common yardstick for measuring the ETR: The nominal corporate tax rate of a tax jurisdiction does not in itself indicate the actual tax liability or tax expense. Rather, the actual tax liability depends on the nominal tax rate and the underlying tax base. Thus, a global minimum tax is needed to measure the actual corporate taxes paid against a uniformly

473. V. Bendlinger & Georg Kofler, *supra* note 305.
474. *See GloBE Commentary on Article 5 GloBE Model Rules (2022)*, para. 2.
475. V. Bendlinger & Georg Kofler, *supra* note 305. Also emphasising the key role of the ETR computation in the system of GloBE, *see* H.V. Dam et al., *Taxing the Digitalized Economy: Key Takeaways from the OECD Public Consultation on the Pillar One and Pillar Two Blueprints*, 28 ITPJ 170 (2017).
476. Article 5.1.1. *GloBE Model Rules*.
477. The categorization into exactly three decisions is admittedly not compulsory but seems appropriate to the author.

determined tax base. However, taxes on income are at the core interest of state sovereignty and are not only important fiscal instruments but political pivots for national governments. There is not a single concept of income; rather, national concepts of income reflect the values and objectives of a particular society, and moreover, as those values and objectives might change over time, the concept of income might change as well.[478]

Although the PoW published in May 2019 only referred to the fact that the '*effective tax rate that is below a minimum rate*'[479] without going into the details of what the ETR might be, it took note of the underlying issue: '*The programme of work starts from the proposition that in principle the tax base would be determined by reference to the rules that jurisdictions already use for calculating the income of a foreign subsidiary under their CFC rules, or in the absence of CFC rules, for domestic CIT purposes.*'[480] The PoW, therefore, already recognized that the nominal tax rate or the tax base in the CFC's state of residence could not be relied upon. However, the PoW did not provide any further information in that respect.

Finally, the OECD's first comprehensive statement on the possible calculation of the ETR can be found in the Public Consultation Document published in November 2019.[481] For the first time, the document provided thorough details as to how a global minimum tax regime could look like and did very much focus on the determination of the ETR: the document mainly asked for comments on the use of financial accounts as a starting point for tax base determination and on the blending of high and low taxed corporate income. In this respect, the OECD, for the first time, suggested that for reasons of simplification, financial accounting rules should be used to determine the income which '*could be used in the denominator of the effective tax rate fraction*' while the numerator of the respective fraction '*could be based on the actual tax liability or the tax expense accrued for accounting purposes*' (on that issue *see* below at section 4.3.2.1.2.).[482] With this statement, it was clear that the ETR must be the ratio between tax paid and income received to be determined according to uniform rules. The further development of GloBE has built on this simple but nonetheless fundamental tax policy decision.

4.3.2.1.2 Second Decision: Tax Base and Tax Liability Determination at an Entity Level Based on the Financial Statements Prepared for Consolidation

The decision to move away from nominal tax rates towards a uniform ETR that measures actual tax liability against a uniform income definition implies the inherent requirement of a uniform income definition or at least a common framework for the

478. Comprehensively on the concept of 'income', *see* K. Holmes, *The Concept of Income: A Multi-Disciplinary Analysis* 576 (IBFD 2001).
479. *Programme of Work*, para. 56.
480. *Ibid.*, para. 68.
481. *Public Consultation Pillar Two 2019*. For a comprehensive discussion of the content of this document and the public comments, *see* V. Bendlinger, *Minimum Taxation – Ergebnisse der Konsultationen zum GloBE Proposal der OECD*, 32 SWI, *supra* note 187, at 16 et seq.
482. *Public Consultation Pillar Two 2019*, para. 16.

determination of income. As already pointed out, the PoW indeed took note of the issue and considered determining the tax base by reference to domestic rules on CFC legislation already in use to determine the income of low-taxed foreign subsidiaries.[483] However, the PoW also recognized that this approach would have its drawbacks: Each subsidiary of an 'MNE Group' would be required '*to recalculate its income in accordance with the tax base calculations in the parent jurisdiction*'.[484] This would also result in '*significant compliance costs*' and could '*lead to situations where technical and structural differences between the calculation of the tax base in the parent and subsidiary jurisdiction*',[485] like the carry-forward of losses or other temporary differences, trigger the minimum tax, although they do not give '*rise to the policy concerns*'[486] that GloBE intends to address. The PoW finally concluded that the use of financial accounts '*prepared under the laws and relevant accounting standards of the jurisdiction of incorporation or establishment*'[487] could be considered as an option to simplify the determination of the tax base.

The Public Consultation Document of November 2019 built on the considerations provided for in the PoW and, for the first time, went into detail on possible ways to determine GloBE's tax base. An entire chapter was devoted to the issues of determining the tax base, and it was soon emphasized that a simple solution was needed for the purposes of a global minimum tax. In this context, the document once again noted that the '*income calculated for accounting purposes* [could] *then be subject to agreed adjustments in order to align accounting income with a proper measure of taxable income*' and that the '*income so determined* [could] *be used in the denominator of the effective tax rate fraction*'.[488] The numerator '*could be based on the actual tax liability or the tax expense accrued for accounting purposes, which may need to be further adjusted to remove accruals of tax related to a different period*'.[489] However, the insight that financial accounts should be used for the purpose of tax base determination is not in itself a solution but merely opens up numerous follow-up questions: If the tax base determination should be carried out on the basis of accounting rules, which accounting standard should be used? That of the potentially low-taxed subsidiary or that of the parent entity? How should differences in national accounting standards be dealt with? Wouldn't GloBE need a uniform accounting standard? How to avoid that an entity is required to recalculate its income in accordance with a different accounting standard used by another entity within the same 'Group'?

The first considerations of these questions in the course of the public consultation process in November 2019 have been extremely guiding for the development of GloBE and are ultimately the basis for the final design of GloBE. The OECD's elaboration starts with the obvious premise that '[t]*he simplest financial accounting standard for an MNE*

483. *Programme of Work*, para. 68.
484. *Ibid.*
485. *Ibid.*
486. *Ibid.*, para. 69.
487. *Ibid.*, para. 71.
488. *Public Consultation Pillar Two 2019*, para. 16.
489. *Ibid.*

to use is one that it already used for other purposes'.[490] Within an 'MNE Group', however, nearly every entity will be obliged to prepare financial statements according to local GAAPs. Thus, even within a single 'MNE Group', there might be several accounting standards in use. So which accounting standard could be the basis to determine the GloBE base? The OECD convincingly argued that using the local GAAPs applicable to the respective group members would '*present a number of challenges for tax administrations*' running '*counter some of the GloBE policies*':[491] the use of different standards would (i) challenge tax administrations usually being '*unfamiliar with some or all of the accounting standards applied by the various subsidiaries*', (ii) would '*produce different results for otherwise similarly situated enterprises*', and (iii) would lead to distortive effects with regard to transactions between subsidiaries using different accounting standards.[492] But are there financial accounts prepared by all entities according to the same standard across a whole 'MNE Group'?

From a purely legal perspective, there are none. However, from a factual perspective, the answer is different: The Public Consultation Document recognized that the UPEs of 'MNE Groups' are regularly required to prepare consolidated financial accounts presenting the assets and liabilities of all its controlled entities. Thus, 'MNE Groups' preparing such consolidated financial statements '*compute the income of their subsidiaries using the financial accounting standard applicable to the ultimate parent entity of the group as part of the consolidation process*'.[493] It is true that controlled entities are not obliged to prepare financial statements according to the standard used by the UPE. However, UPE needs to recalculate the financial accounts of its subsidiaries anyway for the preparation of line-by-line consolidation.

From today's perspective, the suggestion to use consolidated financial accounts to determine a uniform tax base might seem obvious. Nevertheless, when the OECD made this suggestion, the use of consolidated financial accounts was indeed a novelty in the international tax landscape and can be seen as an extremely significant development in the course of the minimum tax debate. The reactions in the public consultation process were also predominantly positive on the idea of using consolidated financial statements for profit determination.[494] Although this seems to be a clever move at first glance, the OECD entered the unknown territory in between consolidated financial statements and tax base determination, which, until today, as will be seen, is still to be discovered.

Nevertheless, when using consolidated accounts, the question remained open as to which accounting standard should be used for the purposes of GloBE. Should there be a single 'gold standard' or a list of acceptable financial accounting standards, or should every local GAAP be accepted? And what if an MNE is not even obliged to prepare consolidated financial statements under domestic corporate laws? The Public Consultation Document finally also raised these questions concluding that the IFRS are

490. *Ibid.*, para. 18.
491. *Ibid.*, para. 20.
492. *Ibid.*
493. *Ibid.*, para. 19.
494. V. Bendlinger, *Minimum Taxation – Ergebnisse der Konsultationen zum GloBE Proposal der OECD*, 32 SWI, *supra* note 187, at 27.

widely used but that there are numerous other standards, like the US or Japanese GAAP, that might be acceptable for the purpose of calculating the minimum tax.[495] In relation to situations where the UPE does not prepare consolidated accounting standards, the Public Consultation Document noted that further consideration would be required to address this issue.[496] Both the question of whether a single standard should be used and the question of how to deal with 'MNE Groups' that do not prepare consolidated financial statements were therefore put out for consultation,[497] and interestingly, both questions were answered very controversially. Company representatives argued for the creation of a comprehensive catalogue of acceptable financial accounting standards to also avoid additional burdens to MNEs not preparing consolidated financial statements, while, above all, representatives of academia and government-related institutions argued for a uniform benchmark. However, the feedback during the consultation was at least unanimous in the respect that, if one were to provide a uniform standard, IFRS should clearly be the benchmark.[498]

However, it was doubted from the very beginning that it would be possible at the political level to agree on IFRS as the only permissible standard;[499] and finally, that was proven true. But how should any variations in the individual accounting standards be dealt with? Finally, the Blueprint on Pillar Two stated that '[a]*lthough there are variations in financial accounting standards among jurisdictions, International Financial Reporting Standard (IFRS) and the generally accepted accounting principles (GAAP) of many Inclusive Framework jurisdictions have far more commonalities than differences*' and furthermore held that it would not be '*feasible to create, from the ground up, a new international accounting standard for computing profit (or loss) before tax under the GloBE rules*'.[500] The Blueprint, thus, stipulated that while IFRS, as the most commonly used accounting standard, should certainly be the benchmark for GloBE,[501] nevertheless GloBE should also accept '*any financial accounting standard that is equivalent to IFRS*'.[502] With regard to those MNE Groups that prepare their consolidated financial statements according to other unacceptable accounting standards and those that do not prepare any at all, the Blueprint concluded that it would neither be '*proportionate*' nor '*reasonable*' to require such MNEs to prepare such statements '*solely for purposes of complying with the GloBE rules*'.[503] GloBE should, thus, permit the use of any accounting standard '*provided that the use of that standard would not result in a material competitive distortion*',[504] which the Blueprint understood as an

495. *Public Consultation Pillar Two 2019*, para. 22.
496. *Ibid.*, para. 23.
497. *See* the question-box *ibid.*, at 11.
498. Comprehensively on the responses, *see* V. Bendlinger, *supra* note 187, at 28.
499. *See, i.a.*, J. Becker & J. Englisch, *International Effective Minimum Taxation – The GLOBE Proposal*, 11 WTJ, *supra* note 469, at 503–604. Also *see* V. Bendlinger, *supra* note 187, at 28.
500. *Tax Challenges Arising from Digitalisation – Report on Pillar Two Blueprint*, para. 158.
501. *Ibid.*, para. 168.
502. *Ibid.*, para. 169.
503. *Ibid.*, para. 173.
504. *Ibid.*

outcome significantly departing from IFRS principles.[505] These considerations have already indicated the final implementation of the GloBE Model Rules.[506]

As we have just seen, it was a rocky road to the final decision on the tax base determination of GloBE, which included courageous decisions made by the IF. In the end, the use of the 'Consolidated Financial Statements' prepared by the UPE was the only possible way to fix a uniform accounting standard, at least within an 'MNE Group' without requiring individual CEs to prepare accounts that do not already exist for accounting purposes. Thus, the OECD has made the second tax policy decision that the income is to be determined according to those financial accounts prepared for the consolidation within the financial statements of the UPE.[507]

4.3.2.1.3 Third Decision: The Choice of Jurisdictional Blending – Merits and Flaws of Blending Income Jurisdiction-Wise

As has just been shown, the first two fundamental tax policy decisions regarding the calculation of the ETR were already fixed in 2019 with the Public Consultation Document: Both the reliance on a calculated ratio between tax liability and taxable income and the use of consolidated financial statements prepared in preparation for consolidation were already proposed in this document and are, albeit further developed, reflected in the GloBE Model Rules and the GloBE-Directive. Differently, however, the third tax policy decision concerns the scope of the ETR determination: although the issue of 'blending' had already been mentioned in the PoW[508] and had been intensively discussed in the Public Consultation Document of November 2019,[509] the fundamental decision in favour of a jurisdictional blending approach was only taken with the Pillar Two Blueprint published in October 2020.[510]

505. *Ibid.*, para. 174.
506. The concepts of the 'Consolidated Financial Statements' and the 'Acceptable Financial Accounting Standards' have already been discussed in the course of the examination of GloBE's scope in s. 4.2.3.2.: Both, Art. 1.2.2. *GloBE Model Rules* and Art. 2(1) GloBE-Directive (2022/2523) rely on the 'Consolidated Financial Statements' (defined in Art. 10.1 GloBE Model Rules and Art. 3[6] GloBE-Directive) to determine whether a MNE is within the scope of GloBE and which entities form part of the respective 'MNE Group'. Such 'Consolidated Financial Statements' can either be prepared under an 'Acceptable Financial Accounting Standard' or any other standard, provided that any 'Material Competitive Distortion' is prevented, whereby the latter is understood as an aggregate variation greater than EUR 75 million per year. In the case that an 'MNE Group' does not prepare any consolidated financial accounts, GloBE deems as 'Consolidated Financial Statements' those statements that would have been prepared if the UPE were required to prepare such statements either under an 'Acceptable Financial Accounting Standard' or any other standard adjusted to prevent 'Material Competitive Distortions'. In detail *see* s. 4.2.3.2.
507. *See* Art. 3.2.1. *GloBE Model Rules* and Art. 15(1) GloBE-Directive (2022/2523). *See* also the Commentary emphasizing the advantages of '*using the information used to prepare the Consolidated Financial Statements*', *see GloBE Commentary on Article 3 GloBE Model Rules (2022)*, para. 7.
508. *Programme of Work*, at 29.
509. *See Public Consultation Pillar Two 2019*, at 17–22.
510. *Tax Challenges Arising from Digitalisation – Report on Pillar Two Blueprint*, paras 128 and 248–285.

The term 'blending' was first mentioned in the PoW and was defined in a footnote: '*Blending refers to the ability of taxpayers to mix high-tax and low-tax income to arrive at a blended rate of tax on income that is above the minimum rate.*'[511] In any case, 'blending' has become the catchword for the allowed degree of mixing high and low-taxed income within GloBE:[512] In the end, it makes a paramount difference whether one relates the ETR to the entire 'MNE Group', to individual jurisdictions, individual entities or even specific categories of income within individual entities.[513] The smaller the frame of the ETR calculation, the more likely low-taxed profits will be taxable under a minimum tax system. Above all, the consideration of losses is also inextricably linked to the very conceptual question of blending: The broader the perspective for determining the ratio of taxes paid and income received, the more likely it is that losses incurred will reduce the GloBE Income in the denominator, causing the ETR to soar.[514]

The decisive tax policy considerations are finally found in the Public Consultation Document 2019, which discusses and weighs up three different blending approaches:

- Under the **worldwide blending** approach (synonymous with '*overall approach*'), the ETR would be established for the whole 'MNE Group'. The minimum tax would only be triggered if the profits of the whole MNE were taxed below the minimum rate. Worldwide blending, thus, can mitigate volatility in the ETR calculation caused by temporary differences,[515] is best suited to the consolidated financial statements[516] and avoids complex allocation of income between branch and head office[517] as well as allocation of income from transparent entities,[518] at least with respect to income in the foreign context. Furthermore, there would also be no need to allocate taxes paid to a specific jurisdiction or a specific entity,[519] which might raise complex issues with respect to taxes paid due to CFC legislation[520] or withholding taxes which are not collected from the taxable person who actually owes the tax.[521]

511. *Programme of Work*, at 29.
512. Also in detail on the discussion of the different blending approaches, *see* V. Bendlinger, *Minimum Taxation – Ergebnisse der Konsultationen zum GloBE Proposal der OECD*, 32 SWI, *supra* note 187, at 23–24; V. Bendlinger & Georg Kofler, *Computation of the Effective Tax Rate and the 'Top-up Tax'*, *in Pillar 2 Global Minimum Tax*, *supra* note 305.
513. For a comprehensive analysis of the different blending approaches, *see* Johannes Becker & Joachim Englisch, *International Effective Minimum Taxation – The GLOBE Proposal*, 11 WTJ, *supra* note 469, at 501–503. Also *see* the US perspective to the different approaches before the OECD developed the GloBE Proposal, *see* H. Grubert & R. Altshuler, *Fixing the System: An Analysis of Alternative Proposals for the Reform of International Tax*, 66 Nat. Tax J. 697–701.
514. *See Public Consultation Pillar Two 2019*, paras 53–54.
515. *See Ibid.*, paras 60–61.
516. *See Ibid.*, para. 62.
517. *See Ibid.*, para. 64.
518. *See Ibid.*, para. 67.
519. In the same vein, *see* H. Grubert & R. Altshuler, *Fixing the System: An Analysis of Alternative Proposals for the Reform of International Tax*, 66 Nat. Tax J., *supra* note 513, at 697; V. Bendlinger, *Minimum Taxation – Ergebnisse der Konsultationen zum GloBE Proposal der OECD*, 32 SWI, *supra* note 187, at 23–24.
520. *See Public Consultation Pillar Two 2019*, para. 68.
521. *See Ibid.*, para. 72.

The conclusion from the OECD's deliberations in the public consultation document was that the merits of the worldwide blending approach lie primarily in its simplicity. It is not surprising that, in the course of the public consultation process, especially corporate representatives expressed their preference for the worldwide blending approach: This group of representatives argued that the worldwide blending approach was the one causing the lowest administrative tax burden and only this approach was compatible with the use of consolidated financial statements to determine the GloBE base.[522] The worldwide approach also finds partial support in the literature.[523] However, the advantage of simplicity is countered by the fact that the worldwide blending approach would significantly reduce the effectiveness of a minimum taxation system.[524] Many representatives of the academic community, therefore, have quite rightly argued that such an approach would undermine the effects of a global minimum tax and leave almost no scope for GloBE:[525] Various 'MNE Groups' with low corporate tax rates have their headquarters and various branches in high-tax countries. Under a worldwide blending approach, it would be easy for them to control the ETR by deliberately blending low-taxed and high-taxed income in such a way that it is just above the required minimum tax rate.

- **Entity blending** is the most granular approach considered by the Public Consultation Document. This approach would require the determination of taxes paid, and income received on an entity level. Blending among several entities would be denied. Rather, the ETR would be determined on the level of a single entity. An advantage of entity blending would be that no aggregation with the earnings and taxes paid by other companies would be required. Consequently, it would be possible to simply refer to the individual financial statements of the individual company prepared in preparation for consolidation to determine the ETR of the respective entity. Furthermore, it has been argued in the literature that entity blending could take into account international juridical double taxation[526] and that entity blending would better fit into the environment of CFC legislation and switchover clauses.[527] Nevertheless, the Public Consultation Document seemed to be sceptical about the concept of entity blending, especially because of national group taxation regimes: many tax jurisdictions allow the aggregation of income and losses within a group of

522. With comprehensive references to the individual responses in the course of the public consultation process, *see* V. Bendlinger, *supra* note 187, at 29.
523. Harry Grubert & Rosanne Altshuler, *supra* note 513, at 701. The authors also bring up a very interesting argument in favour of the worldwide blending approach, arguing that worldwide blending might '*provoke fewer attempts by foreign jurisdictions to soak up*' the tax collected by the jurisdiction that levies a minimum tax.
524. *Public Consultation Pillar Two 2019*, para. 56.
525. *See, i.a.*, J. Becker & J. Englisch, *International Effective Minimum Taxation – The GLOBE Proposal*, 11 WTJ, *supra* note 469, at 501.
526. *See, i.a., ibid.*, at 502.
527. *Ibid.*, at 503.

controlled entities leading to the effect that the tax liability of a single entity would not reflect the amount of tax that would be due on a standalone basis.[528]

- In contrast, **jurisdictional blending** (synonymous with *'per-country approach'*) takes a country-by-country perspective. Jurisdictional blending allows an 'MNE Group' to mix low and high-taxed income at least within one jurisdiction. The minimum tax would only be triggered if the ETR of the respective jurisdiction is exceeded. Contrary to worldwide blending, this requires an 'MNE Group' to split its foreign income received and the respective taxes paid to specific jurisdictions. Every amount of taxes paid and income received needs to be allocated to a specific jurisdiction. To determine both the taxes paid and the income received per jurisdiction, the Public Consultation Document noted that it would be necessary to aggregate all amounts of tax and income by all group members resident within the same jurisdiction.[529] Thus, jurisdictional blending stands in between the entity and worldwide blending approach. 'MNE Groups' would be prevented from mixing low-taxed profits received in tax havens with high-taxed profits received in other jurisdictions. Nevertheless, an 'MNE Group' could still profit from certain preferential regimes as long as the same 'MNE Group' receives enough high-taxed profits within the same jurisdiction.[530] Obviously, jurisdictional blending is more effective than worldwide blending but still more flexible than entity blending and would still ensure that the 'MNE Groups' could not take advantage of very low CIT rates in tax havens. Thus, some authors from the US expressed their preference for a per-country perspective in the context of minimum taxes even before the OECD's GloBE project came into existence.[531]

As has been shown, all of the three proposed approaches have their merits and drawbacks and as the OECD also recognized, '[a]*ll three different approaches to blending raise different challenges*'.[532] The more granular the perspective, the more effective the minimum tax; however, the broader, the more efficient the system from an administrability perspective. Thus, e.g., *Becker* and *Englisch* convincingly described the choice of blending as *'a trade-off between effectiveness and efficiency'*.[533]

The final decision in favour of jurisdictional blending was revealed with the publication of the Pillar Two Blueprint in October 2020, which already held in its executive summary that '[t]*he effective tax rate (ETR) is determined by applying the tax base and covered taxes on a jurisdictional basis*'.[534]

528. *Public Consultation Pillar Two 2019*, para. 57. Also discussing this issue, *see* V. Bendlinger, *Minimum Taxation – Ergebnisse der Konsultationen zum GloBE Proposal der OECD*, 32 SWI, *supra* note 187, at 24.
529. *See* letter b of *Public Consultation Pillar Two 2019*, para. 55.
530. On that argument, *see* Johannes Becker & Joachim Englisch, *supra* note 469, at 501.
531. S.E. Shay et al., *Designing a 21st Century Corporate Tax – An Advance U.S. Minimum Tax on Foreign Income and Other Measures to Protect the Base*, 17 Fla. Tax Review 706 (2015).
532. *Public Consultation Pillar Two 2019*, para. 57.
533. Johannes Becker & Joachim Englisch, *supra* note 469, at 503.
534. *Tax Challenges Arising from Digitalisation – Report on Pillar Two Blueprint*, para. 16.

Although the specific reasons for the political success of jurisdictional blending can only be speculated and are, of course, not explicitly revealed in the Blueprint, the trade-off between effectiveness and efficiency just mentioned was probably the decisive factor: Although the worldwide blending approach would undoubtedly have been much simpler than jurisdictional blending, it would not have been possible to reach consensus within the IF on a global minimum tax using a worldwide blending approach. In the early development of Pillar Two, the political discourse mainly discussed the level of the minimum tax rate, whereby the proposed minimum tax rates have always ranged between 10% and 15%. According to the third edition of OECD corporate tax statistics, which was published in mid-2021, the average corporate tax rate in 109 countries was around 20%.[535] Moreover, most of the most powerful and, above all, most assertive tax jurisdictions within the IF were above this average. Worldwide blending would have made it possible for the largest 'MNE Groups' to get close to the minimum tax rate by cleverly blending income in order to avoid any minimum taxes levied in the course of GloBE altogether. Against this background, it was foreseeable that worldwide blending would hardly have been consensual within the IF. Entity blending, on the other hand, had probably been ruled out for reasons of efficiency and would have disregarded the sovereignty interests of certain countries and entrepreneurial interests too much: focusing on individual entities would have triggered undesirable tax policy consequences and would have nullified certain harmless tax regimes from the outset. One only needs to think of loss-making situations of individual entities that could not prevent the levying of a minimum tax on another entity belonging to the same 'Group' although both entities were taxable within the same jurisdiction.

The compromised character of jurisdictional blending and the comparatively simple link with CbCR may therefore have favoured the jurisdictional blending approach. The following statement can be taken from the Blueprint: '*The starting point for determining the jurisdictional ETR is the assignment of income to jurisdictions. The rules for assigning income among jurisdictions build on the rules applicable to country by country reporting.*'[536] The passage just quoted shows that the pre-existing technical basis of the CbCR could also have been decisive for the fact that the jurisdictional blending approach made the race. Since the OECD relies on the interoperability of GloBE with the CbCR in many areas (e.g., revenue threshold and simplifications such as safe harbour rules), it made sense to rely on jurisdictional blending; naturally including all the conceptual disadvantages that jurisdictional blending entails, which will be addressed immediately (*see* section 4.3.2.3.).

535. OECD, *Corporate Tax Statistics: Third Edition* 9 (OECD 29 Jul. 2021), https://www.oecd.org/tax/tax-policy/corporate-tax-statistics-third-edition.pdf (last visited 9 Jun. 2022).
536. *Tax Challenges Arising from Digitalisation – Report on Pillar Two Blueprint*, para. 271.

4.3.2.2 The Technical Implementation of the ETR Computation Within GloBE

4.3.2.2.1 Structure of the Rules on the ETR Computation

The three tax policy decisions just discussed are each reflected in Article 5.1.1. GloBE Model Rules and Article 26(1) GloBE-Directive. The second sentence of Article 5.1.1. GloBE Model Rules reads as follows: '*The Effective Tax Rate of the MNE Group for a jurisdiction is equal to the sum of the Adjusted Covered Taxes of each Constituent Entity located in the jurisdiction divided by the Net GloBE Income of the jurisdiction for the Fiscal Year.*'[537] In contrast, Article 26(1) of the GloBE-Directive states that '[t]*he effective tax rate of an MNE group shall be computed, for each fiscal year and for each jurisdiction provided that there is net qualifying income*'[538] in accordance with a formula that is directly provided in the text of Article 26(1) GloBE-Directive:

$$Effective\ Tax\ Rate = \frac{adjusted\ covered\ taxes\ of\ the\ constituent\ entities\ in\ the\ jurisdiction}{net\ qualifying\ income\ of\ the\ constituent\ entities\ in\ the\ jurisdiction}$$

Furthermore, Article 26(1) GloBE-Directive states that '*the adjusted covered taxes of the constituent entities is the sum of the adjusted covered taxes of all the constituent entities located in the jurisdiction determined in accordance with Chapter VI*'.[539]

Although the regulatory technique of Article 5.1.1 GloBE Model Rules and Article 26(1) GloBE-Directive differ, there are no differences in substance: both provisions indicate that (i) the ETR is the ratio of taxes paid ('Adjusted Covered Taxes'), and income received ('Net GloBE Income'[540] in the GloBE Model Rules and 'net qualifying income'[541] in the GloBE-Directive), that (ii) both parameters of this ratio are computed at the level of the individual CEs of the 'MNE Group',[542] and that (iii) both are to be aggregated among CEs 'located' in the same jurisdiction.[543] The GloBE-Directive only differs from the GloBE Model Rules by using the term 'net qualifying income' instead of 'Net GloBE Income'. As will be shown, this does not result in any material differences.

Both of the respective provisions are of fundamental importance in their respective frameworks. Thus, both provisions introduce the chapters on computation of the ETR and the 'Top-up Tax', each with almost the same title.[544] This is interesting because the actual calculation of the tax base and the covered tax are anchored in

537. Article 5.1.1. *GloBE Model Rules*.
538. Article 26(1) GloBE-Directive (2022/2523).
539. Article 26(1) *Ibid*.
540. Article 5.1.2. *GloBE Model Rules*.
541. Article 26(2) GloBE-Directive (2022/2523).
542. *See* explicitly Art. 3.1.1., 3.1.2. and 4.1.1. *GloBE Model Rules* as well as Arts 15(1) and 21(1) GloBE-Directive (2022/2523).
543. Article 5.1.2. *GloBE Model Rules* and Art. 26(2) GloBE-Directive (2022/2523).
544. Chapter 5 of the *GloBE Model Rules* is titled '*Computation of Effective Tax Rate and Top-up Tax*', whereas in the GloBE-Directive (2022/2523) Chapter V is titled '*Computation of the effective tax rate and the top-up tax*'.

separate chapters of both sets of rules. The third chapter is devoted to the calculation of 'GloBE Income or Loss' (GloBE Model Rules) and 'qualifying income or loss' (GloBE-Directive), while the fourth chapters deal with the calculation of 'Adjusted Covered Taxes'. From a practical perspective, it made sense to outsource the tax base determination and the calculation of covered taxes to separate chapters. From a systematical perspective, however, both calculations are actually part of the ETR fraction. In this respect, it would have made sense to regulate the respective provisions for the calculation of the ETR in Article 5.1.1 GloBE Model Rules and Article 26(1) GloBE-Directive even before the actual tax base determination and the covered taxes. Instead, the ETR is found in Chapter 5 of the GloBE Model Rules and Chapter V of the GloBE-Directive, including the rules on the calculation of the 'Top-up Tax'. Finally, as will be shown in section 4.4., the ETR calculation itself is part of the 'Top-up Tax' computation. But why is the regulatory structure of GloBE in relation to the ETR relevant at all?

The separation of the calculation of 'GloBE Income or Loss' (qualifying income or loss') and the 'Adjusted Covered Taxes' from the actual calculation of the 'Top-up Tax' tempts to consider these elements as separate building blocks of GloBE. From a systematic perspective, however, income and covered taxes are inextricably linked to the ETR computation. For this reason, and in contrast to the GloBE Model Rules and the GloBE-Directive, the calculation of the 'GloBE Income or Loss' ('qualifying income or loss') and 'Adjusted Covered Taxes' is presented here in sections 4.3.3 and 4.3.4. as part of the ETR computation. Before that, however, the analysis of the ETR calculation requires a closer look at the individual elements of Article 5.1.1 GloBE Model Rules or Article 26(1) GloBE-Directive, in particular, the jurisdictional aggregation of the CEs 'GloBE Income' ('net qualifying income') and 'Adjusted Covered Taxes'.

4.3.2.2.2 The Technical Implementation of Jurisdictional ETR Calculation

Both 'Adjusted Covered Taxes'[545] and 'GloBE Income'[546] ('net qualifying income'[547]) are to be determined at the level of each individual CE. The jurisdictional calculation of the ETR, therefore, requires to aggregate 'Adjusted Covered Taxes' and 'GloBE Income' ('qualifying income') of all CEs 'located'[548] in the same jurisdiction. In this respect, it is important to emphasize that both the income and the taxes in relation to each group member are included in the ETR calculation, irrespective of the 'Ownership Interests' held by the UPE. Those parts of taxes and income that are attributable to 'Ownership Interests' of non-group members are, therefore, also part of the ETR calculation.[549] Furthermore, for purposes of the ETR computation, it is irrelevant at which CE the

545. Article 4.1.1. *GloBE Model Rules* and Art. 21(1) GloBE-Directive (2022/2523).
546. Article 3.1.1. *GloBE Model Rules*.
547. Article 15(1) GloBE-Directive (2022/2523).
548. Once again, this underlines the fundamental role of the 'location' concept within GloBE. In detail on the term 'location' *see* s. 4.2.4.4.
549. *See* the last sentence of *GloBE Commentary on Article 5 GloBE Model Rules (2022)*, *supra* note 474, para. 3.

'Top-up Tax' is ultimately levied.[550] Rather, as the Commentary states, *'the ETR is computed by reference to all the Constituent Entities of the MNE Group located in that jurisdiction'*[551] regardless of whether the respective 'Entity' that has to apply the IIR, for example, actually holds shares in all entities located in the jurisdiction at issue. Jurisdictional blending, therefore, means that all income and taxes are to be included by each CE regardless of the ownership structure of the 'MNE Group'. In principle, only income and taxes of 'Excluded Entities', although qualifying as members of the 'Group', are excluded from the ETR calculation[552] because they do not qualify as CEs.[553] However, exceptions exist for 'Investment Entities',[554] 'Stateless Constituent Entities',[555] 'Minority-Owned Constituent Entities'[556] and 'Joint Ventures'[557] which, each for specific reasons, fall outside the jurisdictional blending and are, for the purposes of GloBE, either considered as single CEs within a separate jurisdiction or as CEs being part of a separate 'MNE Group' (in detail on these exceptions, see the following section 4.3.2.2.3.).

In any case, Article 5.1.1. GloBE Model Rules and Article 26(1) GloBE-Directive first require calculating the 'sum of the Adjusted Covered Taxes', which is the numerator of the ETR fraction. In this respect, both provisions refer to the 'Adjusted Covered Taxes' to be calculated according to the fourth chapter and only require the jurisdictional aggregation of the respective amounts.[558] While the numerator requires a simple aggregation of the amounts of 'Adjusted Covered Taxes', separate terms are used for the aggregated sum of the income that forms the denominator of the ETR fraction: the 'sum of the Adjusted Covered Taxes' is to be divided by the 'Net GloBE Income' according to Article 5.1.1. GloBE Model Rules and the 'net qualifying income' according to Article 26(1) GloBE-Directive. The terms are synonymous and are defined specifically in Article 5.1.2. GloBE Model Rules and Article 26(2) GloBE-Directive, respectively: the 'Net GloBE Income' ('net qualifying income) is the difference between the sum of income of all CEs within the same jurisdiction[559] and the sum of CE-losses within the same jurisdiction in a 'Fiscal Year' (*see* Figure 1).[560] Consequently, before the ETR calculation is conducted, the losses can be offset against profits within the same jurisdiction. In the case of losses, the denominator of the ETR fraction is thus reduced, thereby increasing the ETR. Losses in one jurisdiction can thus prevent the minimum tax from being levied on low-taxed profits received within the same jurisdiction.

550. On this insight, *see* V. Bendlinger & G. Kofler, *Computation of the Effective Tax Rate and the 'Top-up Tax,' in Pillar 2 Global Minimum Tax, supra* note 305.
551. *See GloBE Commentary on Article 5, supra* note 474, para. 4.
552. *See* letter b of *GloBE Commentary on Article 1 GloBE Model Rules (2022), supra* note 249, para. 37. In detail already *see* s. 4.2.4.3.4.
553. *See* explicitly Art. 1.3.3 *GloBE Model Rules* and Art. 2(3) GloBE-Directive (2022/2523).
554. Article 5.1.3. *GloBE Model Rules* and Art. 26(3) GloBE-Directive (2022/2523).
555. Last sentence of Art. 5.1.1. *GloBE Model Rules* and Art. 26(4) GloBE-Directive (2022/2523).
556. Article 5.6.1. *GloBE Model Rules* and Art. 31(2) GloBE-Directive (2022/2523).
557. Article 6.4.1 *GloBE Model Rules* and Art. 36(3) GloBE-Directive (2022/2523).
558. *See GloBE Commentary on Article 5 GloBE Model Rules (2022), supra* note 474, para. 3.
559. Article 5.1.2(a) *GloBE Model Rules* and Art. 26(2)(a) GloBE-Directive (2022/2523).
560. Article 5.1.2(b) *GloBE Model Rules* and Art. 26(2)(b) GloBE-Directive (2022/2523).

Figure 1 Conducting Jurisdictional Blending According to Article 5.1.2. GloBE Model Rules and Article 26(2) GloBE-Directive

Art 5.1.2. GloBE Model Rules:

Net GloBE Income = GloBE Income of all CEs – GloBE Losses of all CEs

Art 26(2) GloBE-Directive:

net qualifying income or loss = qualifying income of the CEs – qualifying losses of the CEs

If the 'GloBE Losses' ('net qualifying losses') are equal to or higher than the 'GloBE Income' ('net qualifying income'), the ETR would either not be calculable or negative. Thus, Article 5.1.2. GloBE Model Rules clarifies that 'Net GloBE Income' can only be a '*positive amount*',[561] while according to Article 26(1) GloBE-Directive, the ETR is only to be calculated '*provided that there is net qualifying income*'.[562] Consequently, the denominator of the ETR fraction is always a positive value and the ETR, as a rule, is a positive percentage[563].[564] As will be seen in section 4.4.2.3., however, the ETR could become negative if the amount of 'Adjusted Covered Taxes' is negative. This might occur, e.g., if the 'MNE Group' receives tax credits that exceed the actual tax liability in a specific jurisdiction, which will, however, only materialize in exceptional situations. As a consequence, the 'Top-up Tax Percentage' can indeed exceed 15 %.

If the loss equals or exceeds the income of a specific jurisdiction, the ETR has no value, which in principle also means that no 'Top-up Tax' can arise.[565] However, as will become clear in section 4.3.4.7., a 'Top-up Tax' may also arise for a jurisdiction if the domestic losses exceed the 'GloBE Losses' in a specific 'Fiscal Year'. Furthermore, a 'Top-up Tax' might also arise in a loss year if a recalculation of a previous 'Fiscal Year' is due in subsequent years; an 'Additional Current Top-up Tax'[566] (within the GloBE-Directive 'Additional Top-up Tax')[567] may occur even if there is no or negative income in a particular jurisdiction.[568]

561. Article 5.1.2. *GloBE Model Rules*.
562. Article 26(1) GloBE-Directive (2022/2523).
563. According to the Commentary to be rounded to the fourth decimal place, *see GloBE Commentary on Article 5, supra* note 474, para. 3.
564. Also in detail on this issue, *see* V. Bendlinger & G. Kofler, *Computation of the Effective Tax Rate and the 'Top-up Tax', in Pillar 2 Global Minimum Tax, supra* note 305.
565. *See GloBE Commentary on Article 5, supra* note 474, para. 11.
566. Article 5.4. *GloBE Model Rules*.
567. Article 28 GloBE-Directive (2022/2523).
568. Article 4.1.5. *GloBE Model Rules* and Art. 21(5) GloBE-Directive (2022/2523). In detail on these issues, *see* s. 4.4.2.6.

4.3.2.2.3 *Exceptions to Jurisdictional ETR Computation*

It has already been anticipated that GloBE provides for exceptions,[569] albeit few, to jurisdictional blending. All these exceptions have in common that they concern special CEs for which an allocation to a specific jurisdiction is either not possible, or the inclusion in the jurisdictional blending was considered to be inappropriate by the OECD for different reasons. Thus, there is no catalogue of exceptions to jurisdictional blending in either the GloBE Model Rules or the GloBE-Directive. Rather, these result from special provisions in the respective frameworks. Only the Commentary to Article 5 GloBE Model Rules deals with exceptions to jurisdictional blending and states that there are only three such special exceptions:[570]

- **'Investment Entities' and 'Insurance Investment Entities':** According to Article 5.1.3. GloBE Model Rules, reflected in Article 26(3) GloBE-Directive, the '*Adjusted Covered Taxes and GloBE Income or Loss of Constituent Entities that are Investment Entities are excluded from the determination of the [ETR]*'[571] and the jurisdictional aggregation of the income received. The special nature of 'Investment Entities' has already been anticipated in sections 4.2.4.3.2 and 4.2.5.3.: due to the special treatment of 'Investment Entities', both in accounting rules as well as domestic tax laws, Articles 7.4 to 7.6 and 41 to 43 GloBE-Directive provide for specific rules on the computation of the ETR and the 'Top-up Tax' with respect to such entities: with regard to the special features in accounting rules, it is worth taking a look at the IFRS. The term 'Investment Entity' was obviously adopted from the IFRS 10,[572] providing for specific consolidation rules for such entities. According to IFRS 10.31, '*an investment entity shall not consolidate its subsidiaries*'. Consequently, within the IFRS, 'Investment Entities' do not have to consolidate their investments.[573] However, according to IFRS 10.33, a '*parent of an investment entity shall consolidate all entities that it controls, including those controlled through an investment entity subsidiary, unless the parent itself is an investment entity*'. Thus, within an 'MNE Group', at least under the IFRS, the UPE is obliged to consolidate its controlled 'Investment Entities'. GloBE has adhered to these rules and uses the term 'Investment Entities',[574] including both 'Investment

569. *See* s. 4.2.4.4.4. and 4.3.2.2.2.

570. *See GloBE Commentary on Article 5*, *supra* note 474, paras 5–9. For a detailed examination of these exceptions, also *see* V. Bendlinger & Georg Kofler, *Computation of the Effective Tax Rate and the 'Top-up Tax', in Pillar 2 Global Minimum Tax, supra* note 305.

571. Article 5.1.3. *GloBE Model Rules*.

572. Explicitly on the close connection of the definition of 'Investment Fund' (which are considered as 'Investment Entities') to the rules provided for in IFRS 10, *see GloBE Commentary on Article 10 GloBE Model Rules (2022)*, *supra* note 280, para. 36. Also *see* the provisions of IFRS 10.27 to 10.30 providing for rules how to determine whether an entity is an 'Investment Entity'.

573. Only in exceptional cases does IFRS 10.32 prescribes 'Investment Entities' to consolidate subsidiaries '*whose main purpose and activities are providing services that relate to the investment entity's investment activities*'.

574. *See* the definition of 'Investment Entity' provided for in Art. 10.1. *GloBE Model Rules*, at 58 and Art. 3(30) GloBE-Directive (2022/2523).

Funds'[575] and 'Real Estate Investment Vehicles'[576] that qualify as CEs due to their inclusion in the 'Consolidated Financial Statements' of the UPE. However, both 'Investment Funds' and 'Real Estate Investment Vehicles' and their directly held sub-vehicles[577] are considered 'Excluded Entities' if they qualify as UPEs of the respective 'MNE Group'; this is not least due to the fact that 'investment entities', as just described, are not required to consolidate their investments under IFRS 10.31. It follows that the term 'Investment Entities' only covers those 'Investment Funds' or 'Real Estate Investment Vehicles' that are not themselves qualified as UPEs or directly held through a chain of other 'Investment Funds' or 'Real Estate Investment Vehicles' that qualify as UPEs. The Commentary, thus, notes that the specific provisions on 'Investment Entities' only refer to '*controlled Investment Entities*'.[578] However, not only do accounting rules provide for special regulations for 'Investment Entities' but also do many domestic tax systems: many jurisdictions, including most of the IF Member States, either provide for tax neutrality regimes or deductible dividend regimes to secure a single level of taxation for collective investment vehicles. When calculating the minimum tax, this can lead to situations where, due to the lack of tax subjectivity of such entities under domestic CIT, such entities regularly do not bear any tax burden at all within their jurisdiction. This means that the ETR for such 'Investment Entities' will regularly be 0%, obviously triggering a 'Top-up Tax'. The Commentary on Article 7 GloBE Model Rules states in this regard: 'The income of Investment Entities and Insurance Investment Entities *is often subject to little or no tax at the entity level. Article 7.4 calculates the ETR and Top-up Tax of these Entities on a standalone basis to prevent an MNE Group from blending this low-taxed income with income of other Constituent Entities. Article 7.4 also seeks to ensure that minority investors are not subject to Top-up Tax on their interest in a low-taxed Investment Entity controlled by an MNE Group.* It does so by calculating the ETR and Top-up Tax of a controlled Investment Entity only to the extent that the income is attributable to the MNE Group'[579] (emphasis added). The essential technical provision with regard to 'Investment Entities' can be found in Article 7.4.2. GloBE Model Rules (correspondingly Article 41[1] and [2] GloBE-Directive), which reads as follows: 'The *Effective Tax Rate for an Investment Entity that is a Constituent Entity shall be calculated separately from the Effective Tax Rate of the jurisdiction in which it is located.* The [ETR] for each such Investment Entity is *equal to the Investment Entity's Adjusted Covered Taxes divided by the MNE Group's Allocable Share of the Investment Entity's GloBE Income* determined under Chapter 3. If there is more than one Investment Entity located in the jurisdiction, the Adjusted Covered

575. Article 10.1. *GloBE Model Rules*, at 59 and Art. 3(31) GloBE-Directive (2022/2523).
576. Article 10.1. *GloBE Model Rules*, at 65 and Art. 3(32) GloBE-Directive (2022/2523).
577. *See* s. 4.2.4.3.3.
578. *See GloBE Commentary on Article 7 GloBE Model Rules (2022)*, *supra* note 335, para. 73.
579. *See Ibid.*, para. 74.

Taxes and the MNE Group's Allocable Share of each Investment Entity's GloBE Income or Loss determined for each such Investment Entity are combined to compute the Effective Tax Rate of all such Investment Entities'[580] (emphasis added). The peculiarity of the ETR calculation with respect to 'Investment Entities' is therefore twofold: First, the 'Adjusted Covered Taxes' and the 'GloBE Income' ('net qualifying income') of 'Investment Entities' are excluded from the jurisdictional blending of the remaining group. Rather, jurisdictional blending only takes place among the controlled 'Investment Entities' of the 'MNE Group' located within the same jurisdiction. Second, their ETR is only calculated with respect to the 'Allocable Share' of the 'MNE Group'. Those amounts of 'Adjusted Covered Taxes' and 'GloBE Income' ('net qualifying income') attributable to minority shareholders are not included in the ETR and 'Top-up Tax' computation. Rather, these parts of the income of the 'Investment Entities' fall completely outside the minimum tax regime. This results in special features, especially for the calculation of the 'Top-up Tax' and the application of the IIR, which are still to be discussed. However, it is important to note that, according to Article 7.4.1. GloBE Model Rules (Article 41[1] GloBE-Directive), the respective rules provided for in Article 7.4. GloBE Model Rules (Article 41 GloBE-Directive) do not apply to 'Investment Entities' that are (i) either tax transparent or that have made an election according to (ii) Article 7.5. (Article 42 GloBE-Directive) or (iii) Article 7.6. GloBE Model Rules (Article 42 GloBE-Directive) provide for special regimes to avoid low-tax outcomes for 'Investment Entities'. If an 'Investment Entity' is treated as tax transparent, there is no need for a special regime to avoid low-tax outcomes. The income of the respective 'Investment Entity' would be attributed to the controlling CE anyway. The otherwise threatening low taxation could not occur at all because then the controlling CE would have to pay tax on the income attributed to it anyway. This idea also justifies the election provided for in Article 7.5 GloBE Model Rules (Article 42 GloBE-Directive) to treat an otherwise non-transparent controlled 'Investment Entity' as fiscally transparent for GloBE purposes '*if the Constituent Entity-owner is subject to tax in its location under a mark-to market or similar regime based on the annual changes in the fair value of its Ownership Interest in the Entity and the tax rate applicable to the Constituent Entity-owner [...] equals or exceed the Minimum Rate*'.[581] If the 'Filing Constituent Entity' makes this election, the share of the income of the controlled 'Investment Entity' '*results as income of the Constituent Entity-owner for GloBE purposes*'.[582] In this case, Article 7.4 GloBE Model Rules (Article 41 GloBE-Directive) does not apply. The income of the controlled investment entity attributable to the CE-owner falls within the jurisdictional blending of the CE-owner. Another election is finally provided for in Article 7.6. GloBE Model Rules (Article 43 GloBE-Directive), which also aims

580. Article 7.4.2. *GloBE Model Rules*.
581. *See* Art. 7.5.1. *Ibid.* and correspondingly Art. 42(2) GloBE-Directive (2022/2523).
582. *See GloBE Commentary on Article 7, supra* note 335, para. 92.

to avoid the outcome of Article 7.4. GloBE Model Rules (Article 41 GloBe-Directive): differently to Article 7.5. GloBE Model Rules (Article 42 GloBE-Directive), however, under the so-called Taxable Distribution Method Election, the controlled 'Investment Entity' is not treated as tax transparent, but rather the CE-owner may include distributions and deemed distributions within its 'GloBE Income' ('net qualifying income') *'if the Constituent Entity-owner can be reasonably expected to be subject to tax on distributions from the Investment Entity at a tax rate that equals or exceeds the Minimum Rate'*.[583] But for what reason is it advantageous to choose either the tax transparency or the deemed taxable distribution method? Both elections make sure that the allocable share of the income attributable to the 'MNE Group' falls within the normal jurisdictional blending of the CE-owner. In many cases, those elections reduce the risk that the income would be considered as lowly taxed when considering all 'Investment Entities' in the same jurisdiction in isolation. Furthermore, both elections enable the CE-owner to apply its SBIE with regard to its share of income. As the Commentary aptly notes, the *'Eligible Payroll Expenses and Eligible Tangible Assets related to managing the Investment Entity's or Insurance Investment Entity's activities will not arise in the Investment Entity or Insurance Investment Entity itself, but instead will be those of the Constituent Entity-owners'*.[584] As a result, the elections provided for in Article 7.5. and 7.6. GloBE Model Rules and Articles 42 and 43 GloBE-Directive can prevent the incurrence of 'Top-up Tax' with respect to an 'MNE Group's' share of income from controlled 'Investment Entities'. As a result, one can assume that due to these elections and the fact that many jurisdictions treat 'Investment Funds' and 'Real Estate Investment Vehicles' as tax transparent anyway, the exception from jurisdictional blending for 'Investment Entities' is likely to be a rare phenomenon.[585]

- **'Minority-Owned Constituent Entities' (in the following MOCEs):** The membership of entities in an 'MNE Group' is determined, as already examined in detail,[586] on the basis of the accounting rules applied by the UPE:[587] an 'Entity' is part of the 'MNE Group' if it is consolidated on a line-by-line basis within the 'Consolidated Financial Statements' of the UPE holding a 'Controlling Interest'[588] in the controlled 'Entity'. But when does a UPE have a

583. *See* Art. 7.6.1. *GloBE Model Rules* and correspondingly Art. 43(1) GloBE-Directive (2022/2523).
584. *See GloBE Commentary on Article 7, supra* note 335, para. 97.
585. In the same vein V. Bendlinger & G. Kofler, *Computation of the Effective Tax Rate and the 'Top-up Tax', in Pillar 2 Global Minimum Tax, supra* note 305.
586. *See* s. 4.2.3.
587. Article 1.2.2. *GloBE Model Rules* and Art. 3(3)(a) GloBE-Directive (2022/2523).
588. *See* the definition of 'Controlling Interest' provided for in Art. 10.1. *GloBE Model Rules*, at 54. Also *see* in particular the compact definition in Art. 3(21) GloBE-Directive (2022/2523) where it is held that '"controlling interest" means an ownership interest in an entity *whereby the interest holder is required*, or would have been required, *to consolidate the assets, liabilities, income, expenses and cash flows of the entity on a line-by-line basis, in accordance with an acceptable financial accounting standard; a main entity is deemed to hold the controlling interests in its permanent establishment*' (emphasis added).

'Controlling Interest' in an 'Entity'? This depends on the respective accounting standard applied, and in many accounting standards, in particular, those listed as 'Acceptable Financial Accounting Standard', control does not solely depend on the 'Ownership Interest' held by the controlling entity. Rather, a shareholder might control an 'Entity' even if the respective shareholder only owns a minority of the shares, while the majority of shares are held by other parties. Finally, a shareholder may have control and can significantly affect the returns[589] of an investment due to de facto situations, e.g., if the majority of shares are free float and those shareholders do not exercise their voting rights uniformly,[590] or if the shareholder owns contractual rights like a contractual privilege to appoint the board of directors.[591] Most accounting standards, including first and foremost the IFRS,[592] therefore provide for so-called de facto *control*[593] concepts, which require line-by-line consolidation even if the 'Entity' preparing the statements does not own the majority of shares in the respective investment but does control an 'Entity' for different reasons. Since GloBE determines the characteristics of a CE solely on the basis of the line-by-line inclusion in the 'Consolidated Financial Statements', such entities also undoubtedly qualify as CEs. Both their income and taxes would, thus, be included in the jurisdictional blending as well, within the remaining CEs of the same 'MNE Group' located within the same jurisdiction. Nevertheless, Article 5.6. GloBE Model Rules and Article 31 GloBE-Directive provide for specific provisions on so-called MOCEs, excluding certain entities from jurisdictional blending below a certain threshold: According to GloBE, a CE qualifies as a MOCE if the UPE holds, either directly or indirectly, 30% or less of the

589. *See* the criteria provided for in IFRS 10.7 and 10.17-18. In particular, *see* IFRS 10.17 where it is stated that '[a]n investor controls an investee if the investor not only has power over the investee and exposure or rights to variable returns from its involvement with the investee, *but also has the ability to use its power to affect the investor's returns from its involvement with the investee*' (emphasis added). Also *see* in that respect, IFRS 10.B41 where it is held that '[a]n investor with less than a majority of the voting rights has rights that are sufficient to give it power when the investor has *the practical ability to direct the relevant activities unilaterally*' (emphasis added).
590. *See* Example 4 provided for directly below IFRS 10.B43.
591. Also *see* IFRS 10.11 where the obligation for line-by-line consolidation does not solely depend on a mere majority of shares or voting rights: 'Power arises from rights. Sometimes assessing power is straightforward, such as when power over an investee is obtained directly and solely from the voting rights granted by equity instruments such as shares, and can be assessed by considering the voting rights from those shareholdings. *In other cases, the assessment will be more complex and require more than one factor to be considered, for example when power results from one or more contractual arrangements*' (emphasis added).
592. *See* the provisions on 'control' in IFRS 10.5 to 10.18 and IFRS 10.B41 to 10.B46 and the examples provided there.
593. On the concept of '*de-facto control*', *see, i.a.*, L. Anker-Sørensen, *Financial Engineering as an Alternative Veil for the Corporate Group*, 13 European Company Law 159 (1 Oct. 2016); S. Leitner-Hanetseder & D. Schausberger, *Änderung der Einbezugskriterien gem. IFRS 10*, 6 IRZ 383 (2011). On tax related issues in connection with the 'de facto control' concept, in particular with regard to Art. 9 OECD MC, *see* S.J. Ramon Dwarkasing, *The Concept of Associated Enterprises*, 41 Intertax (2013).

'Ownership Interests'.[594] If such a MOCE itself holds 'Controlling Interests' in other so-called Minority-Owned Subsidiaries,[595] the former qualifies as a 'Minority-Owned Parent Entity'[596] (in the following MOPE) and forms a 'Minority-Owned Subgroup'[597] including its 'Minority-Owned Subsidiaries'. In this respect, Article 5.6.1. GloBE Model Rules (Article 31[2] GloBE-Directive) states that the '*computation of the Effective Tax Rate and the Top-up Tax for a jurisdiction* [...] *with respect to members of a Minority-Owned Subgroup shall apply as if they were a separate group. The Adjusted Covered Taxes and GloBE Income or Loss of members of a Minority-Owned Subgroup are excluded from the determination of the remainder of the MNE Group*'.[598] Although the chain of legal definitions seems confusing, the provisions of Article 5.6.1. GloBE Model Rules, reflected in Article 31(2) GloBE-Directive, simply aim to peel the entire MOCEs of a 'Minority-Owned Subgroup' out of the jurisdictional blending of the remaining 'MNE Group'. Jurisdictional blending then only takes place within the 'Minority-Owned Subgroup'. For those MOCEs that are not part of a 'Minority-Owned Subgroup', the ETR, according to Article 5.6.2. GloBE Model Rules and Article 31(3) GloBE-Directive, is to be computed on an entity basis. These rules, therefore, address individual MOCEs which themselves do not hold 'controlling interests' in other CEs. In this regard, it is also important to note that the exception for MOCEs does not apply to controlled 'Investment Entities'.[599] The 'Investment Entity' exception, thus, prevails over the special regime for MOCEs.[600] The order of precedence is relevant insofar as 'Investment Entities' by their very nature will regularly be collective investment vehicles and, thus, even if they are controlled by an 'MNE Group', many shares will regularly be held by non-group minority shareholders. Consequently, overlaps are not only conceivable but are also likely to occur frequently.The special provision for MOCEs in Article 5.6. GloBE Model Rules and Article 31 GloBE-Directive represent an interesting break within GloBE's regulatory framework: although MOCEs within the consolidated group are characterized by the fact that the UPE does not hold a majority of the 'Ownership Interests', this does not change the fact that they, due to kind of 'de facto' control, are consolidated within the 'Consolidated Financial Statements' of the UPE on a line-by-line basis. So what is the justification for this break in the system? In this regard, the Commentary notes the following: '*If the*

594. *See* the definition of 'Minority-Owned Constituent Entity' provided for in Art. 10.1. *GloBE Model Rules*, at 60 and Art. 31(1)(a) GloBE-Directive (2022/2523).
595. *See* the definition of 'Minority-Owned Subsidiary' provided for in Art. 10.1. *GloBE Model Rules*, at 60 and Art. 31(1)(d) GloBE-Directive (2022/2523).
596. *See* the definition of 'Minority-Owned Parent Entity' provided for in Art. 10.1. *GloBE Model Rules*, at 60 and Art. 31(1)(b) GloBE-Directive (2022/2523).
597. *See* the definition of 'Minority-Owned Subgroup' provided for in Art. 10.1. *GloBE Model Rules*, at 60 and Art. 31(1)(c) GloBE-Directive (2022/2523).
598. Article 5.6.1. *GloBE Commentary on Article 7 GloBE Model Rules (2022)*, *supra* note 335.
599. *See* the last sentence of Art. 5.6.2. *GloBE Model Rules* and the last sentence of Art. 31 GloBE-Directive (2022/2523).
600. *See GloBE Commentary on Article 5 GloBE Model Rules (2022)*, *supra* note 474, para. 107.

income and taxes of these different [MOCEs] *were blended in the jurisdictional ETR computations, low-tax outcomes in one Entity could result in a Top-up Tax for the jurisdiction, some of which would be borne by non-Group Entity owners of a different Constituent Entity. While this can occur to some extent under the normal jurisdictional blending rules, the magnitude of the effect in the context of* [MOCEs] *and the potential detrimental impact on these investment structures justifies a different rule.'*[601] However, this justification is not at all convincing. First, jurisdictional blending could, for example, if a MOCE is itself an Low-Taxed Constituent Entity (LTCE) but other CEs within the same jurisdiction are highly taxed, also prevent the non-group shareholders from a 'Top-up Tax' that would otherwise be levied.[602] Second, the Commentary itself admits that the jurisdictional ETR computation in every other case does not take into account third-party shareholders. Rather, as will be seen, the UTPR, in specific situations, obliges to collect 'Top-up Tax' attributable to 'Ownership Interests' held by non-group shareholders, irrespective of whether those 'Ownership Interests' exceed 70% or not.[603] This also applies to the 'Top-up Tax' allocated to a MOCE. Thus, the tax policy reasoning behind the special regime for MOCEs is questionable. It harms consistency and unnecessarily increases complexity.

- **'Stateless Constituent Entities':** 'Stateless Constituent Entities' can only arise with respect to 'Flow-through Entities',[604] PEs[605] and 'dual-located Entities'[606] and are characterized by the fact that they cannot be assigned to a specific jurisdiction.[607] This is why Article 5.1.1. GloBE Model Rules states that for the purpose of 'Top-up Tax' computation, '*each Stateless Constituent Entity shall be treated as a single Constituent Entity located in a separate jurisdiction*'.[608] In the same vein, Article 26(4) GloBE-Directive notes that the ETR of '*stateless constituent entities located in a jurisdiction shall be computed* [...] *separately from the* [ETR] *of all other* [CEs]'.[609] The exception is self-evident: In the absence of an allocation to a specific jurisdiction, GloBE deems a separate jurisdiction and requires an entity-by-entity calculation of the ETR and thus also of the 'Top-up Tax'.

The Commentary assumes that the mentioned exceptions are likely to arise '*only in a minority of cases*'[610] and adds that there was no need to specifically address those exceptions within the Commentary on Article 5 GloBE Model Rules. Nevertheless, as

601. *See Ibid.*, para. 97.
602. On this argument, also *see* V. Bendlinger & G. Kofler, *Computation of the Effective Tax Rate and the 'Top-up Tax,' in Pillar 2 Global Minimum Tax, supra* note 305.
603. *See* s. 4.4.2.8.3.
604. Article 10.3.2.(b) *GloBE Model Rules.*
605. *See* para. (d) of the PE definition in Art. 10.1. and Art. 10.3.3.(d) *ibid.*
606. Article 10.3.4.(b)(iii) *ibid.*
607. In detail on the phenomenon of 'Stateless Constituent Entities' and their emergence, *see* s. 4.2.4.4.4.
608. Article 5.1.1. *GloBE Model Rules.*
609. Article 26(4) GloBE-Directive (2022/2523).
610. *See GloBE Commentary on Article 5 GloBE Model Rules (2022), supra* note 474, para. 9.

will be seen, the exceptions for 'Investment Entities', MOCEs and 'Stateless Constituent Entities' influence various detailed questions regarding the calculation of the 'Top-up Tax'. Thus, the Commentary adds that whenever one of the exceptions applies, '*the Commentary should be interpreted in light of and consistent with the exception*'.[611] Nevertheless, it can be anticipated that this statement will not be able to contribute to the solution of various questions of interpretation in connection with the exceptions just discussed.

While the Commentary only explicitly mentions these three exceptions, a closer look at the provisions for 'Joint Ventures' also reveals an exception to jurisdictional blending. Finally, Article 6.4.1(a) GloBE Model Rules and Article 36(3) GloBE-Directive state that, for the purposes of computing the 'Top-up Tax', the 'Joint Venture' and its 'JV Subsidiaries' (within the GloBE-Directive 'joint venture affiliates'[612]) shall be made as if they were CEs of a separate 'MNE Group' and the 'Joint Venture' was the UPE of the respective 'MNE Group'. The bottom line is that the calculation of 'Top-up Tax' for individual 'Joint Ventures' and 'JV Groups' is comparable to that of 'Investment Entities': first, the jurisdictional blend only takes place among the 'JV Subsidiaries' located within the same jurisdiction. Second, the ETR and 'Top-up Tax' are only calculated with respect to the allocable share of the income allocable to the 'MNE Group'. The difference between 'Joint Ventures' and the other exceptions to jurisdictional blending is, however, that 'Joint Ventures' and their 'JV Subsidiaries' do usually not qualify as CEs: Within many accounting standards, including the IFRS, 'Joint Ventures' are accounted by using the equity method.[613] 'Joint Ventures', thus, regularly do not form part of an 'MNE Group' requiring line-by-line consolidation within the 'Consolidated Financial Statements' of the UPE. Thus, the special provisions on 'Joint Ventures' merely aim to '*extend*[...] *the application of the GloBE Rules*'[614] without including those entities within the scope of either 'MNE Group' (on the special status of 'Joint Ventures' already *see* section 4.2.4.1.3.). This is likely to be the reason why 'Joint Ventures' are not explicitly mentioned in the Commentary under the exceptions to jurisdictional blending.

In an overall view of the exceptions to jurisdictional blending, it can be stated that the only exception for 'Stateless Constituent Entities' results from GloBE's system itself. For 'Stateless Constituent Entities', jurisdictional blending simply cannot occur because there is no state to which this CE can be assigned. Contrarily, the exceptions for 'Investment Entities', MOCEs and 'Joint Ventures' lead to systematic breaks within GloBE: Their special treatment ultimately results from special features in accounting rules and/or tax regimes. All three of these systematic breaks have in common that the justification for their existence provided by the OECD is related to the fact that such 'Entities' are, by their very nature, largely held by non-group shareholders.[615] With

611. *See Ibid.*
612. *See* Art. 36(1)(b) GloBE-Directive (2022/2523).
613. *See* IFRS 11.24.
614. *See GloBE Commentary on Article 6 GloBE Model Rules (2022), supra* note 314, para. 84.
615. *See* on 'Investment Entities', *GloBE Commentary on Article 7 GloBE Model Rules (2022), supra* note 335, para. 74. On MOCEs *GloBE Commentary on Article 5, supra* note 474, para. 97. and on 'Joint Ventures' *GloBE Commentary on Article 6, supra* note 314, para. 83.

regard to 'Investment Entities' and 'Joint Ventures', GloBE solves this by calculating the ETR and levying the 'Top-up Tax' from the outset only with respect to the allocable share held by the 'MNE Group', excluding them from jurisdictional blending with other CEs (that are not 'Investment Entities' or 'JV Subsidiaries' of the same subgroup) of the respective 'MNE Group' located within the same jurisdiction. In the author's opinion, the special tax and corporate law treatment of such entities in many jurisdictions justifies these unsystematic exceptions.

The concept of MOCEs differs from the other exceptions in that respect. Although the 'Adjusted Covered Taxes' and the 'GloBE Income or Losses' ('net qualifying income or losses') of 'Minority-Owned Subgroups' or single MOCEs are excluded from jurisdictional blending, both taxes and income attributable to the third party shareholders holding 70% or more are still included within the ETR and 'Top-up Tax' computation. The UTPR may even lead to the imposition of the 'Top-up Tax' attributable to the 'Ownership Interests' held by such third parties. In this respect, the exception for MOCEs should be viewed critically: It complicates the already complex ETR calculation and has no real tax policy justification: If GloBE already relies on 'Acceptable Financial Accounting Standards' and uses their rules and regulations for the purposes of both the scope of application and the tax base determination, it is incomprehensible to deviate from the consolidation requirements of those standards, including the requirement of line-by-line consolidation also in cases of 'de facto' although the controlling 'Entity' does not hold the majority of the 'Ownership Interest'. The Commentary's rationale for justifying the special rules for MOCEs is also circular: While the Commentary states that jurisdictional blending in these cases would lead to a '*potential detrimental impact*',[616] the question remains why the OECD seems to not be worried about levying a 'Top-up Tax' allocable to non-group shareholders at all in several other situations. Why should jurisdictional blending be abandoned equal or below a participation level of 30% if the 'Top-up Tax' attributable to the third-party shareholders can also be levied in these cases anyway?

In summary, it can be stated that the exceptions to jurisdictional blending are extremely complex, raise a number of technical issues and seem to constitute systematic breaks within the system of GloBE. The Commentary reassures by stating that the exceptions will only arise '*in a minority of cases*'.[617] Considering that concepts such as 'de facto' control are very widespread for good reasons and that CIVs are also an integral part of economic life, the Commentary's statement is cold comfort for the legal practitioner; and, as will become apparent in the examination of the 'Top-up Tax'[618] computation and the GloBE Rules,[619] the exceptions are not only relevant for the calculation of the ETR.

616. *See GloBE Commentary on Article 5*, *supra* note 474, para. 97.
617. *See Ibid.*, para. 9.
618. *See* s. 4.4.
619. *See* s. 4.4.2.8.

4.3.2.3 *Interim Conclusions: The Drawbacks of Jurisdictional ETR Determination*

As has been shown, the reliance on the 'Consolidated Financial Statements' was originally intended as a simplification. From today's perspective, it is, however, obvious that the use of 'Consolidated Financial Statements' is anything but simple. In a one-paragraph summary, the computation of the minimum tax according to GloBE can be described as follows: the 'Consolidated Financial Statements' of an 'MNE Group' must first be split into the individual financial statements of the individual CEs. When such individual financial statements are available for each CE, the results are aggregated jurisdiction-wise in order to be able to calculate the jurisdictional ETR and the 'Jurisdictional Top-up Tax'. As will be shown, however, the collection of the 'Top-up Tax' again requires an allocation to the individual CEs 'located within the same jurisdiction'.[620] But why are the 'Consolidated Financial Statements' of the UPE used as a basis if this basis must be fragmented and reassembled all over again?

Basically, there was no alternative to using the 'Consolidated Financial Statements': any other option would have required a completely new set of rules and could hardly have been based on existing foundations. Own rules for the determination of profits would have been necessary, but above all, a definition of the term 'group' to define the scope of such a system would have been needed, and if a group definition had been waived, the minimum tax would still rely on a strict separate entity perspective and would hardly differ from the existing CFC legislation as promoted by BEPS Action 3. In contrast, the use of 'Consolidated Financial Statements' has numerous merits: first, (i) there are already accounting rules that are widely used in global corporate laws. There are hardly any jurisdictions that have no legal obligation to prepare consolidated financial statements at all. Second, (ii) 'Consolidated Financial Statements' summarize the individual results of the legal entities of a group as if the sum of all legal entities were a single company. Third, (iii) consequently, the profit of the individual entities is already determined according to the same principles among the whole group, irrespective of where the separate entities are registered or tax resident.

If the OECD had opted for worldwide blending, the use of 'Consolidated Financial Statements' would be straightforward: most accounting standards require that the income tax burden of a consolidated group must be reported separately.[621] The ETR could thus be easily determined, apart from a few technical adjustments, by simply dividing the reported tax amount by the reported group result. Yet, for reasons already explained, a minimum tax system based on worldwide blending would be ineffective and would leave the door wide open for tax planning. 'MNE Groups' subject to the minimum tax regime would be incentivized to establish undertakings in low-tax jurisdictions to keep the group's ETR just above the minimum tax level. The worldwide blending approach was, therefore, hardly likely to limit tax competition and might even

620. *See* s. 4.4.2.7.

621. *See*, e.g., IAS 12 providing on detailed rules on the financial reporting of current and deferred taxes. In detail on the presentation of tax assets and liabilities *see* IAS 12.71 et seq.

have encouraged the *'race to the bottom'* so denounced by the OECD. This only left entity and jurisdictional blending as viable policy choices.[622] While the former seemed to be a too granular perspective, the latter compromised the separate entity and the worldwide blending approach and seemed perfectly suited to achieve the initial purpose of GloBE: If the purpose of GloBE is to reduce the incentive for countries to create a low-tax environment and for 'multinationals' to benefit from such an environment, it makes sense to separately calculate the ETR for each respective jurisdiction.

As can be seen, there are good arguments in favour of both the decision to use 'Consolidated Financial Statements' and the decision to adopt the jurisdictional blending approach. However, the complexity of GloBE lies in the technical incompatibility of both decisions. It is a matter of fact that financial accounts do not support a jurisdictional perspective. Rather, it is the very purpose of 'Consolidated Financial Statements' to present the whole 'MNE Group' as if it were a single entity to prevent assets and liabilities from being hidden behind investment positions. So how can the accounts' worldwide perspective be reconciled with GloBE's jurisdictional perspective?

In fact, they can only be reconciled with mutual adjustments. As is well known, the OECD tried to solve this issue by relying on those separate financial statements of individual group members that had to be prepared *'as part of the consolidation process'*[623] anyway. By simply aggregating the profits reported in those statements jurisdiction-wise, the jurisdictional blending approach seemed easy to implement. It was clear from the beginning, however, that this is only a part of the truth. Especially the case of PEs shows that in many situations, a separate statement prepared for consolidation does not even exist: A PE is not a separate legal entity but part of a legal entity. PEs simply do not exist from an accounting perspective. The attribution of assets, liabilities and profits to PEs is, therefore, completely alien to accounting rules. However, it is settled international tax practice that a PE defines the border between taxing rights of source and residence state, which is why GloBE could not simply ignore the PE principle within its regulatory framework.[624] As a consequence, GloBE had to establish rules on how to allocate both income[625] and taxes[626] to PEs within the same 'MNE Group' in line with the 'Consolidated Financial Statements' prepared by the UPE. As a result, each PE within an 'MNE Group' must keep its own account solely for purposes of GloBE: while accounting rules do not even see the PE at all, the PE's accounts for tax purposes are not at all related to the group's accounting standard. A PE does not prepare accounts in line with the UPE's accounting standard *'as part of the consolidation process'*.[627] Thus, the case of PEs within the framework of GloBE is most representative of the complex interrelationship between accounting and tax rules as created by GloBE. Nevertheless, this does not mean that the same problems could not also arise with respect to separate legal entities: On the contrary, there are also group members that do not prepare preparatory financial statements, for example, if the

622. *See* s. 4.3.2.1.3.
623. *Public Consultation Pillar Two 2019*, para. 19.
624. *See* s. 4.2.4.1.2.
625. Art. 3.4. *GloBE Model Rules* and Art. 18 GloBE-Directive (2022/2523).
626. Art. 4.3.2.(a) *GloBE Model Rules* and Art. 24(1) GloBE-Directive (2022/2523).
627. *Public Consultation Pillar Two 2019*, para. 19.

respective accounting standard exempts certain entities from consolidation while GloBE nevertheless obliges to include them.[628]

Ultimately, GloBE tries to square the circle by compromising 'Consolidated Financial Accounts' with jurisdictional blending. Corporate Laws, including accounting rules, are simply incompatible with a jurisdictional perspective. Corporate Law is influenced by civil law and, thus, is based on the concept of legal persons. Whether and to what extent such a legal person is active across borders is simply irrelevant for accounting purposes. The financial accounts are supposed to picture the financial situation of an enterprise, regardless of where the enterprise operates its businesses. However, the place where entrepreneurial activity is carried out (irrespective of where this place is supposed to be under domestic law or under tax treaties) is certainly relevant for tax laws, simply due to the fact that cross-border activity always raises the question of which state should be permitted to tax the respective profits. Although GloBE, at least pursuant to the OECD, is not about redistributing taxing rights, it very well impacts tax allocation. Since GloBE enables the collection of additional tax revenue, it also needs to determine which state is allowed to tap this revenue. This need to allocate minimum tax revenues to specific jurisdictions probably is another argument in favour of the jurisdictional blending concept. If a jurisdiction fails to tax the profits of a specific 'MNE Group' falling within its tax jurisdiction at least at the minimum rate of 15%, the difference may be skimmed off by others. GloBE simply reallocates specific amounts of tax revenues if a jurisdiction does not claim them for itself. Finally, by combining the 'Consolidated Financial Statements' with a jurisdictional tax perspective, GloBE allows two worlds to collide and merge into a completely new, largely unexplored tax universe.[629] The following sections aim to shed light on this universe and attempt to trace GloBE's link between 'Consolidated Financial Statements' and the determination of taxable profits, which is the computation of the 'GloBE Income or Loss'.

4.3.3 The GloBE Base: Computation of 'GloBE Income or Loss'

4.3.3.1 Preliminary Considerations on the GloBE Base and Structure of the Rules on Base Determination

Both in the GloBE Model Rules as well as in the GloBE-Directive, separate chapters[630] are dedicated to the tax base determination. First of all, it should be noted that the two sets of rules use different terminology in relation to the tax base: While the GloBE-Directive refers to the tax base as 'qualifying income or loss',[631] whereas the GloBE

628. *See* the case of CEs that are excluded from the UPE's 'Consolidated Financial Statements' on size or materiality grounds, *see* Art. 1.2.2.(b) *GloBE Model Rules* and the second limb of Art. 3(3)(a) GloBE-Directive (2022/2523).
629. Also *see* V. Bendlinger, *Die OECD Model Rules für ein globales Mindestbesteuerungsregime*, 32 SWI, *supra* note 258, at 16.
630. Article 3 *GloBE Model Rules* and Chapter III (Arts 15 to 19) GloBE-Directive (2022/2523).
631. *See* the headline of Chapter 3 *GloBE Model Rules*.

Model Rules refer to 'GloBE Income or Loss'.[632] Nevertheless, linguistic differentiation does not result in any differences in content. On the contrary, as far as can be seen, there are neither structural nor substantive differences between the GloBE-Directive and the GloBE Model Rules with regard to the determination of the tax base and for good reason: if the tax base determination in the GloBE-Directive were to deviate in any way from the OECD model legislation, conflicts of qualification with third states also implementing GloBE would be inevitable.

The role of the chapter on tax base determination is aptly summed up in the Commentary, where it is held that it operates '*to convert Financial Accounting Net Income or Loss to the GloBE Income or Loss, which is then utilised in subsequent Chapters to determine the ETR and Excess Profits for purposes of determining whether Top-up Tax is payable with respect to a particular jurisdiction*'.[633] The Commentary addresses the double relevance of the GloBE base for the final calculation of the 'Top-up Tax': First, the GloBE base is relevant to determine the denominator of the ETR fraction. For a given tax liability, the rule is: the higher the income, the lower the ETR and vice versa. The tax base is, therefore, a decisive factor for the question of whether a particular jurisdiction can be subject to a 'Top-up Tax' at all by virtue of falling below the minimum tax rate. Second, if the ETR actually falls below the minimum tax rate, the tax base also determines the amount of the 'Top-up Tax' liability: the 'Top-up Tax' liability is finally calculated by multiplying the 'Top-up Tax Percentage'[634] (difference between 15% and the ETR) and the 'Excess Profits'[635] (GloBE base minus SBIE).[636] Once again,[637] it reveals that the GloBE base determination is merely a preliminary step for the actual 'Top-up Tax' calculation. Accordingly, the third and fifth chapters of the GloBE Model Rules and the GloBE-Directive are closely intertwined. The following sections, however, will focus exclusively on the actual determination of the 'GloBE Income or Loss' ('qualifying income or loss').

As extensively discussed in the previous sections,[638] GloBE's base determination, according to Article 3.1.1. and 3.1.2. GloBE Model Rules starts from the '*Financial Accounting Net Income or Loss determined for the Constituent Entity for the Fiscal Year*',[639] whereby the '*Financial Accounting Net Income or Loss is the net income or loss determined for a Constituent Entity (before any consolidation adjustments eliminating intra-group transactions) in preparing Consolidated Financial Statements of the Ultimate Parent Entity.*'[640] Nearly the same phrases are used in Article 15(1) GloBE-Directive Proposal. The significance of the statements made in Article 3.1.1. and 3.1.2. GloBE Model Rules and Article 15(1) GloBE-Directive is that the income or loss is to be calculated for each individual CE and not for the entire 'MNE Group'. For the base

632. *See* the headline of Chapter III GloBE-Directive (2022/2523).
633. *See GloBE Commentary on Article 3 GloBE Model Rules (2022)*, *supra* note 507, para. 1.
634. Article 5.2.1. *GloBE Model Rules* and Art. 26(2) GloBE-Directive (2022/2523).
635. Article 5.2.2. *GloBE Model Rules* and Art. 26(4) GloBE-Directive (2022/2523).
636. In detail on these issues, *see* s. 4.4.
637. Already *see* 4.3.2.2.1.
638. *See* s. 4.3.2.
639. Article 3.1.1. *GloBE Model Rules.*
640. Article 3.1.2. *Ibid.*

determination, it is therefore also irrelevant in which jurisdiction the respective CE is 'located'. The GloBE base determination takes place in complete isolation from the jurisdictional perspective of the ETR calculation. Finally, jurisdictional blending to calculate the denominator of the ETR fraction takes place after the income determination at the level of the individual CEs.[641]

From the very beginning, it was clear, however, that the 'Financial Accounting Net Income or Loss' could not be suitable as a common base for a minimum tax without adjustments.[642] In many jurisdictions, accounting profits are not related to the determination of CIT bases at all; and even in jurisdictions that link the determination of taxable profits to accounting rules (*see*, e.g., the so-called Maßgeblichkeit in the German legal tradition), tax laws regularly require significant adjustments. The reasons for the need for adjustments can be manifold: Certain business expenses may be included as expenses in the profit and loss statement but may be excluded from deduction for tax policy reasons (e.g., bribes, penalties and interest payments and other so-called Policy Disallowed Expenses[643]). Contrary to this, certain profits might be included in the profit and loss statement under accounting rules but are tax exempt under tax rules (e.g., dividends).[644] Furthermore, tax laws may only allow the deduction of certain items over several fiscal years. Nevertheless, one could ask, why are adjustments even necessary if only accounting rules are to be relevant for the determination of the GloBE tax base?

In this context, it is important to remember that the 'Consolidated Financial Statements' were intended to create a uniform benchmark for the calculation of the ETR. As a result, the covered taxes are measured against the accounting income received. If the differences mentioned were ignored simply for the purposes of the GloBE base determination, the ETR calculation would lead to completely inappropriate results. The clearest example of such distortions is dividend income:[645] Most jurisdictions provide for specific exemptions (or other mechanisms of relief) for dividend income at the recipient's level (e.g., so-called participation exemptions) in order to

641. *See* s. 4.4.2.2.
642. The necessity to address differences between accounting rules and domestic tax schemes had already been intensively discussed in the Public Consultation Document published in November 2019, when it was not even clear which accounts would really be used for the purposes of GloBE. The document devotes an entire section (2.3) to the adjustments to be considered when using financial accounts to determine the ETR. Right in the introduction to this section it states: '*The most straightforward approach to determining the net amount of low-taxed profits would be to take income and expense figures directly from an entity's financial statements without adjustment. [...] However, relying on the unadjusted figures in the accounts could mean that an entity's net profits for accounting purposes may be overstated or understated when compared to the amount reported for tax purposes*', *see Public Consultation Pillar Two 2019*, para. 24. Thus, in the very next paragraph the document further held that '[t]*he accounting profit reflected in an entity's financial statements could be adjusted to take account certain permanent and temporary differences between the income computed under financial accounting standards and under the income tax rules*', *see Ibid.*, para. 25.
643. Article 10.1. *GloBE Model Rules*, at 64.
644. Also *see* the introduction of the Commentary to Art. 3 GloBE Model Rules, using the example of dividends, *see GloBE Commentary on Article 3 GloBE Model Rules (2022)*, *supra* note 507, para. 1.
645. Also *see Ibid.*

avoid economic double taxation of the distributed profits that usually had already been taxed at the level of the distributing corporation.[646] However, the exemption does not, in principle, lead to non-taxation but rather avoids (economic) double taxation of dividends (at least if the distributing corporation had been taxed on its profits). If GloBE did not provide for a special regime for dividends, each exempt dividend would be associated with a fall in the ETR: the tax paid on the dividend being in the numerator of the ETR fraction would be zero; nevertheless, the dividend income would be fully included in the tax base according to accounting rules in the denominator. Every holding company solely receiving dividend income for which it is granted a participation exemption within its residence state would have an ETR of zero, although the underlying profits might have been taxed well above the minimum tax rate of 15%. This example shows that GloBE could not simply ignore settled state practice in tax law. Therefore, Article 3.2. GloBE Model Rules, mirrored in Article 16 GloBE-Directive, provides for an extremely comprehensive set of rules dealing with adjustments of the 'GloBE Income or Loss' ('qualifying income or loss') that *'are common in Inclusive Framework jurisdictions'*.[647] The adjustments of Article 3.2. GloBE Model Rules and Article 16 GloBE-Directive, therefore, foresee a minimum link of the GloBE tax base to common principles of common domestic CIT bases. While those provisions address common permanent differences between domestic tax laws and common accounting standards, GloBE considers temporary differences at the level of the 'Adjusted Covered Taxes' in the numerator of the ETR fraction (Article 4.4. GloBE Model Rules and Article 21 GloBE-Directive).[648] These rules are, therefore, the complementary piece to the income adjustment rules within GloBE's system.

It is important to note that certain adjustments in the GloBE base need to be reflected in both the amount of the 'GloBE Income or Loss' ('qualifying income or loss') and the amount of 'Adjusted Covered Taxes'. Finally, the adjustments provided for in Article 3.2. of the GloBE Model Rules and Article 15 of the GloBE-Directive reveal an interconnection of the numerator and denominator of the ETR fraction: If GloBE, for example, excludes certain items of income from its base, the tax on the respective item is to be excluded as well.[649] Otherwise, the ETR would be distorted because the undiminished amount of tax in the numerator and the diminished income in the denominator would lead to an inflated estimate of the ETR. Article 4.1.3.(a) GloBE Model Rules and Article 21(3)(a) GloBE-Directive take note of these issues and shall *'ensure that the ETR calculation for the relevant Constituent Entity reflects only taxes that arise in respect of GloBE Income or Loss'*. This topic is dealt with primarily in section 4.3.4 and is addressed here only selectively in connection with the GloBE base.

It can be anticipated already that by far the most comprehensive and complex part of the corresponding (third) chapters on tax base determination within the GloBE Model Rules and the GloBE-Directive consist of rules on the use of financial accounts

646. Also *see Ibid.*, para. 35.
647. Also *see Ibid.*, para. 17.
648. In detail *see* s. 4.3.4.
649. *See* explicitly Art. 4.1.3.(a) *GloBE Model Rules* and Art. 21(3)(a) GloBE-Directive (2022/2523). Also *see GloBE Commentary on Article 3, supra* note 507, para. 19.

(Article 3.1. GloBE Model Rules and Article 15 GloBE-Directive) as well as the necessary adjustments to those accounts (Article 3.2. GloBE Model Rules and Article 16 GloBE-Directive) as already briefly touched upon. The other provisions provided for in the third chapters deal, on the one hand, with the exception of 'International Shipping Income' (Article 3.3. GloBE Model Rules and Article 17 GloBE-Directive), and on the other hand, with the allocation of income to CEs that are PEs (Article 3.4. GloBE Model Rules and Article 18 GloBE-Directive) or 'Flow-through Entities' (Article 3.5. GloBE Model Rules and Article 19 GloBE-Directive). While the 'International Shipping Income' exclusion, as will be seen, is merely an unsystematic industry-specific carve-out from the minimum tax, the allocation rules of Article 3.4. and 3.5. GloBE Model Rules and Articles 18 and 19 GloBE-Directive form an extremely essential part of GloBE as well: the allocation of income to specific CEs within the 'MNE Group' is necessary to finally determine the income jurisdiction-wise for jurisdictional blending. Since PEs do not form separate taxpayers and are part of a legal entity while the income of 'Flow-through Entities' naturally is allocated to its partners, GloBE had to define its own rules on how to separate the tax base between different CEs, to finally determine to which jurisdiction-specific income belongs. Eventually, the allocation of income in the ETR calculation makes a significant difference: depending on which state the income is assigned to, the income must be measured against the taxes incurred in that state. The allocation of income to CEs is, therefore, of decisive importance for the question of whether a minimum tax is due at all and, if so, in what amount.

The following sub-sections are dedicated to the topics briefly mentioned in the order prescribed by the GloBE Model Rules and the GloBE-Directive. First and foremost, therefore, the relevance of determining income according to accounting rules must be examined.

4.3.3.2 Significance of Financial Accounts in the Determination of 'GloBE Income or Loss'

4.3.3.2.1 Financial Accounting Net Income or Loss Determined for Each Individual CE Before the Start of the Consolidation Process

The determination of the 'GloBE Income or Loss' ('qualifying income or loss') starts with the 'Net Accounting Income or Loss' of each individual CE adjusted for the items provided for in the corresponding sets of rules of Article 3.1. to 3.5. GloBE Model Rules and Articles 15 to 19 GloBE-Directive as '*determined for a Constituent Entity (before any consolidation adjustments eliminating intra-group transactions) in preparing Consolidated Financial Statements of the Ultimate Parent Entity*'.[650] Thus, when GloBE refers to the relevance of the 'Consolidated Financial Statements', this does not mean that the GloBE base determination is actually carried out on the basis of the 'Consolidated Financial Statements'. Unlike, for example, the turnover threshold, which is

650. Article 3.1.2. *GloBE Model Rules*. Also, *see* Art. 15(1) GloBE-Directive (2022/2523) merely using a slightly different syntax.

calculated directly from the 'Consolidated Financial Statement'[651] prepared by the UPE, the base determination is made based on the separate financial statements of the individual CEs prepared in advance of the actual consolidation process. The GloBE base, therefore, does not make use of the 'Consolidated Financial Statements' of the 'MNE Group' as such but merely uses the CEs' separate financial accounts uniformly prepared in line with the accounting standard of the UPE. For the purposes of the base determination, it is therefore also irrelevant in which ownership relationships the individual CEs stand to each other. Each CE determines the income attributable to it according to GloBE separately and in complete isolation from the other group members. As a consequence, also intra-group transactions stay within the calculations of a CEs income; or as the Commentary puts it: '[T]*he starting point for calculating GloBE income or loss, is the bottom-line net income or loss of the Group Entity before making any consolidation adjustments that would eliminate income or expense attributable to intra-group transactions.*'[652]

Furthermore, for the purpose of base determination, it is also irrelevant whether all shares in a CE are actually held by the 'MNE Group' or not. Thus, income that could be attributed to minority shareholders is also included in the GloBE base determination.[653] This is entirely consistent: The 'Top-up Tax' calculation also includes taxes and income attributable to minority interests, and in certain cases, such 'Top-up Tax' is actually skimmed off by the UTPR. Only the IIR excludes the 'Top-up Tax' allocable to minority shareholders because it is only levied with respect to the '*Parent Entity's Allocable Share of the Top-up Tax*'[654].[655] Special rules in that regard (that will be discussed below in detail)[656] only exist for PEs[657] and 'Flow-through Entities':[658] the income of such CEs is by their very nature reflected within the financial statements of a different CE; with respect to PEs this is the 'Main Entity'[659] and with respect to 'Flow-through Entity'[660] the CE owning shares in the respective 'Flow-through Entity'. In these cases, a split of the respective financial statements is therefore inevitable. However, this is not an exception to the rule that the GloBE base is to be determined separately for each CE; rather, these rules ensure that CEs that are PEs and 'Flow-through Entities' also determine their 'GloBE Income or Loss' ('qualifying income or loss') separately.

651. Already *see* s. 4.2.5.2.
652. *See GloBE Commentary on Article 3, supra* note 507, para. 3.
653. *See Ibid.*, para. 7.
654. *See Ibid.*
655. In detail on the application of the GloBE Rules with respect to non-group minority shareholders, *see* s. 4.4.2.8.
656. *See* s. 4.3.3.5 and 4.3.3.6.
657. Article 3.4. *GloBE Model Rules*. Also, *see* Art. 18 GloBE-Directive (2022/2523).
658. Article 3.5. *GloBE Model Rules*. Also, *see* Art. 19 GloBE-Directive (2022/2523).
659. Remember the definition of 'Main Entity' provided for in Art. 10.1. *GloBE Model Rules*, at 60 and Art. 3(40) GloBE-Directive (2022/2523).
660. *See* the definition of 'Flow-through Entity' provided for in Art. 10.2. *GloBE Model Rules* and Art. 3(12) GloBE-Directive (2022/2523).

4.3.3.2.2 *Financial Accounting Standard Used to Determine CE's Income*

The 'GloBE Income or Loss' ('qualifying income or loss') is generally to be determined in accordance with the 'Acceptable Financial Accounting Standard' applied by the UPE of the 'MNE Group'. This is accompanied by the same problems that have already been discussed in connection with the scope of an 'MNE Group':[661] What if the 'MNE Group' does prepare its 'Consolidated Financial Statements' according to accounting rules that do not qualify as 'Acceptable Financial Accounting Standards' and what if the UPE of an 'MNE Group' is not even obliged under the rules of its state of incorporation to prepare financial statements at all? Both sets of rules solve this in the basic provisions for the GloBE base determination in Article 3.1.1 GloBE Model Rules as well as Article 15(1) GloBE-Directive by referring to the term 'Consolidated Financial Statements' specifically defined in Article 10.1 GloBE Model Rules and Article 3(6) GloBE-Directive, respectively. The definitions of 'Consolidated Financial Statements' include those cases in which the UPE does not (i) use an 'Acceptable Financial Accounting Standard' or (ii) does not prepare 'Consolidated Financial Statements' at all. In the former case, the applied standard can be maintained but must be adjusted for 'Material Competitive Distortions' ('*greater than EUR 75 million*'[662]);[663] in the latter case, financial statements must be prepared specifically as they would have been prepared if the UPE had been required to prepare them.[664] With regard to the definitions of 'Consolidated Financial Statements' and 'Material Competitive Distortions', reference can be made to section 4.2.3.2.

The definition of the 'Group' in GloBE is extremely comprehensive and, as has already been shown, in part even goes beyond the scope of consolidation of the respective accounting standard applied: GloBE also includes 'Entities' in the group which, although they would have to be included in the 'Consolidated Financial Statements' on the basis of control, are excluded from being consolidated '*solely on size or materiality grounds, or on the grounds that the entity is held for sale*'.[665] Such CEs, therefore, basically never prepare a financial statement in preparation for consolidation in line with the UPE's accounting standard, simply because they do not have to be consolidated at all according to the accounting standard of UPE. Nevertheless, such CEs are explicitly included in the 'MNE Group'. The question, therefore, arises as to how the income or loss of these CEs must be determined. Interestingly, neither the GloBE Model Rules nor the GloBE-Directive gives guidance in that respect. In principle, both sets of rules very well provide an exemption to the obligation to apply the accounting standard of the UPE in Article 3.1.3 GloBE Model Rules and Article 15(2)

661. *See* s. 4.2.3.2.
662. *See* Art. 10.1. *GloBE Model Rules*, at 60.
663. Letter c of the definition of 'Consolidated Financial Statements' provided for in Art. 10.1. *Ibid.*, and Art. 3(6)(c) GloBE-Directive (2022/2523).
664. Letter d of the definition of 'Consolidated Financial Statements' provided for in Art. 10.1. *GloBE Model Rules*, at 60 and Art. 3(6)(d) GloBE-Directive (2022/2523).
665. Article 1.2.2.(b) *GloBE Model Rules* and, merely using a slightly different wording, second limb of Art. 3(3)(a) GloBE-Directive (2022/2523).

GloBE-Directive (to these provisions immediately below); however, this is not applicable if the accounting standard itself does not require consolidation. But how, then, one could ask, is the income of such CEs to be determined? The Commentary makes the following statement in that regard:

> Because the accounting standards used to prepare the Consolidated Financial Statements include a materiality threshold, minor or inconsequential deviations from a strict application of the UPE's accounting standard in the computation of a particular Constituent Entity's Financial Accounting Net Income or Loss for purposes of preparing the Consolidated Financial Statements do not need to be adjusted when such threshold is not exceeded. The financial accounting auditor's acceptance of a deviation in the Consolidated Financial Statements without a qualification to the auditor's opinion is good evidence that the difference is immaterial. [...] In addition, if a UPE uses an accounting standard permitted by the Authorised Accounting Body in the UPE Jurisdiction and the Authorised Accounting Body permits the UPE to apply a different accounting standard to compute the Financial Accounting Net Income or Loss of foreign Constituent Entities (for purposes of preparing the Consolidated Financial Statements), the Financial Accounting Net Income or Loss computed for those foreign Constituent Entities using the different accounting standard need not be adjusted to strictly conform to the UPE's accounting standard.[666]

The Commentary's statement is of limited help and, unfortunately, uses extremely vague phrases. On the one hand, only the accounting standard is relevant, and if it allows an exclusion, the exclusion should be accepted for purposes of GloBE; on the other hand, the Commentary keeps the door open for possible objections: According to the Commentary, '*minor or inconsequential deviations from a strict application*' may be ignored. This phrase alone raises more questions than it can answer. What does 'minor' or 'inconsequential' mean, and what is a 'strict application'? The Commentary, therefore, expresses its confidence in the financial accounting auditor (finally, the auditor's acceptance might be 'good evidence') and the 'Authorised Accounting Body' without actually binding itself to the opinions of those bodies. Even if this is only a problem that mainly concerns immaterial CEs, its practical relevance should not be underestimated: If an 'MNE Group' has only one CE in a jurisdiction, which is immaterial from the 'MNE Group's' point of view, but which may give rise to a 'Top-up Tax' revenue for the jurisdiction in question, e.g., by means of the UTPR, tax administrations might very well be interested in the financial statements of this respective CE and could, e.g., object to the application of the materiality threshold or argue that a specific deviation is not minor. Further clarification on the question of base determination for CEs below a certain materiality threshold is therefore desirable.

Apart from the cases of CEs excluded from consolidation, there is no doubt that in the process of consolidation, separate financial statements are not actually prepared for each individual entity in accordance with the accounting standard applied by the UPE, but converting the individual financial statement from local GAAP would often involve a disproportionate effort. In any case, it is an illusion that all CEs of 'MNE

666. *See GloBE Commentary on Article 3 GloBE Model Rules (2022)*, *supra* note 507, para. 12.

Groups' actually prepare their own profit or loss statements according to the accounting standard of UPE. GloBE attempts to honour this circumstance with a special exception. According to Article 3.1.3. GloBE Model Rules (reflected in Article 15[2] GloBE-Directive), a CE can, '[i]*f it is not reasonably practicable to determine the Financial Accounting Net Income or Loss for a Constituent Entity based on the accounting standard used in preparation of Consolidated Financial Statements of the*' UPE, determine its income '*using another Acceptable Financial Accounting Standard or an Authorised Financial Accounting standard*'[667] under the following three cumulative conditions: (i) the financial accounts of the CE are maintained based on that accounting standard, (ii) the information contained in the financial accounts is reliable, and (iii) permanent differences in excess of EUR 1 million arising from the application of a particular principle or standard to items of income or expense or transactions that differ from the standard applied by the UPE are '*conformed to the treatment required under the accounting standard used in the Consolidated Financial Statements*'.

In the author's opinion, it is to be expected that the provision will have significant practical relevance. Finally, it allows each consolidated CE to use its individual accounts for the determination of the GloBE base, which will usually be more readily available than those accounts prepared during the consolidation process. However, the provision is not only of particular practical importance but also very much in need of interpretation: first of all, the question arises when it is not 'reasonably practicable' to determine the 'Financial Accounting Net Income or Loss' on the basis of the accounting standard used for the 'Consolidated Financial Statements'. At first sight, 'reasonably practicable' could apply to various situations. As already pointed out several times, many CEs, e.g., also PEs, will, in very few cases, actually have prepared a separate statement in preparation for consolidation. It is interesting that the Commentary takes the opposite view, where it is held that the '*rule is not expected to apply in many cases because an MNE Group will typically have mechanisms in place to convert a subsidiary's entity-level accounts to the UPE's accounting standard in connection with the preparation of the Consolidated Financial Statements*'[668] since, in those cases, it would be '*reasonably practicable to accurately calculate*'[669] the CEs' 'Financial Accounting Net Income or Loss'. Rather, the Commentary assumes that '*the rule could apply, for example, when the MNE Group has undertaken a recent acquisition of a group of Entities that have historically used a different accounting standard* [...]'.[670] The Commentary's restrictive interpretation is not apparent – neither from the GloBE Model Rules nor the GloBE-Directive. In the author's opinion, it is odd to interpret such a vague formulation in such a restrictive way. It is a matter of fact that the very purpose of 'Consolidated Financial Statements' is to present the financial situation of a 'Group' exactly as if the 'Group' were a single company, which is why many CEs do not prepare separate financial statements applying the accounting standard used by the UPE. It is difficult to see why it is 'reasonably practical' to convert a CE's financial statements to the

667. Article 3.1.3. *GloBE Model Rules*.
668. *See GloBE Commentary on Article 3, supra* note 507, para. 13.
669. *See Ibid.*
670. *See Ibid.*

accounting standard of the UPE if certain CEs do not prepare such statements at all and the consolidation process regularly only takes place at the level of the UPE.

In any case, if the 'reasonably practicable' test is fulfilled, there are three tests remaining to make use of the exceptions provided for in Article 3.1.3. GloBE Model Rules and Article 15(2) GloBE-Directive. The first test consists of two sub-elements and requires first, (i) that the respective CE determines its income according to an 'Acceptable Financial Accounting Standard' or an 'Authorised Financial Accounting Standard' and second, (ii) that the financial accounts of the respective CE are maintained based on that standard. By referring to the so-called Authorised Financial Accounting Standard, GloBE also allows to use accounting standards that are not listed within the 'Acceptable Financial Accounting Standard'.[671] 'Authorised Financial Accounting Standard' is defined as a '*set of generally acceptable accounting principles permitted by an Authorised Accounting Body in the jurisdiction where that entity is located*',[672] where an 'Authorised Accounting Body' is to be understood as a '*body with legal authority in a jurisdiction to prescribe, establish, or accept accounting standard for financial reporting purposes*'[673] (the OECD clearly had the IASB in mind here). The second sub-element clarifies that an 'MNE Group' cannot freely decide which accounting standard it may use for the respective CE at issue. Rather, the respective CE must maintain to prepare its financial statements pursuant to the local standard of the jurisdiction where it is 'located' for purposes of GloBE.[674] In the case a CE does not maintain to use the respective standard, '*it must compute its financial accounting income using the UPE's financial accounting standard, notwithstanding any practical difficulties*'.[675] This is convincing because if a CE chooses to use a different standard, its respective financial statements need to be prepared from scratch anyway. There would not be any need for simplification under Article 3.1.3. GloBE Model Rules and Article 15(2) GloBE-Directive.

The second test requires that the information provided in the CE's statements is 'reliable'. Although this term is very common in the context of accounting rules, it is difficult to grasp as well. The Commentary seems to assume reliability if the statements are '*tested and deemed acceptable to the financial accounting auditor pursuant to generally accepted auditing standard applicable in the location of the UPE or the Constituent Entity*'.[676]

Finally, the third test provides for a monetary threshold of EUR 1 million: the CE may only use its maintained and reliable accounts if permanent differences arising from the use of a deviating accounting standard exceeds EUR 1 million and if the respective differences are adjusted in such a way that they '*conform to the treatment*

671. The term has already been briefly addressed in the chapters on GloBE's definition of the term 'Group', *see* s. 4.2.3.2.
672. *See* the definition of 'Authorised Financial Accounting Standard' in Art. 10.1. *GloBE Model Rules*, at 53. Also, *see* Art. 3(26) GloBE-Directive (2022/2523).
673. *See* the definition of 'Authorised Financial Body' in Art. 10.1. *GloBE Model Rules*, at 53. Also, *see* Art. 3(26) GloBE-Directive (2022/2523).
674. *See GloBE Commentary on Article 3*, *supra* note 507, para. 14.
675. *See* the last sentence of *ibid.*
676. *See Ibid.*, para. 15.

that would apply under the UPE's financial accounting standard'.[677] Temporary differences are excluded from this threshold.[678] The relatively low threshold requires that adjustments to the accounting rules of the UPE are made, at least for the most important permanent differences. However, the EUR 1 million threshold is also likely to lead to considerable uncertainties: if it subsequently transpires that a necessary adjustment was not made, the question arises as to whether the exemption from preparing financial statements in accordance with the accounting standard of the UPE ceases to apply retroactively. However, the Commentary does not directly address this issue with respect to these provisions.

4.3.3.2.3 What Is the Scope of Financial Accounting Net Income or Loss?

Various accounting standards exclude certain items of income or expenses from the actual profit or loss statement but provide for a separate statement of so-called Other Comprehensive Income[679] (in the following OCI), which is considered an adjustment to the equity of an entity. Regularly, the OCI includes gains or losses which have not yet been realized but occur due to the revaluation of an asset or liability.[680] With regard to GloBE's base determination, however, a further question arises as to what is to be the 'Financial Accounting Net Income or Loss'. Although neither the GloBE Model Rules nor the GloBE-Directive provides any guidance in this respect, the issue is addressed in the Commentary on Article 3 GloBE Model Rules, which states that only the 'Financial Accounting Net Income or Loss' only covers those income and losses '*reflected in the profit and loss statement*'[681] excluding items of income or expenses that are reported as OCI or elsewhere.[682] The scope of the 'GloBE Income or Loss' ('qualifying income or loss') is, therefore, directly connected to the scope of the profit and loss statement to be reported in accordance with the accounting standard applied by the UPE. Does this leave jurisdictions room to avoid the application of GloBE to its resident 'MNE Groups' by narrowing the scope of the profit and loss statements to be reported under its local GAAP? As far as the respective GAAP is covered within the list of 'Acceptable Financial Accounting Standards', this is conceivable. With respect to all other accounting standards, there is still the 'Material Competitive Distortion' Test preventing that deliberately liberating accounting rules could prevent the emergence of a 'Top-up Tax'.[683]

---

677. *See Ibid.*, para. 16.
678. *See Ibid.*
679. *See* the definition of 'Other Comprehensive Income' for the purposes of GloBE, *see* Art. 10.1. *GloBE Model Rules*, at 62.
680. The Commentary also names, e.g., foreign currency exchange gains and losses, gains and losses of debt or equity instruments as well as changes in liabilities under pension plans, *see GloBE Commentary on Article 3, supra* note 507, para. 9.
681. *Ibid.*
682. In detail on items reported in the OCI, *see Ibid.*, paras 9–11.
683. In detail already *see* s. 4.2.3.2

4.3.3.3 *Adjustments to the GloBE Base*

4.3.3.3.1 The Crux of Considering Permanent Differences Within the Framework of GloBE

It has already been mentioned[684] that national tax bases are almost never entirely congruent to the profit or loss determined according to accounting rules. This already results from the diverging purposes of tax base determination and financial reporting: the former are basically aimed at determining the ability to pay of a particular taxpayer (whatever the policy may define as the ability to pay), while the latter serves to provide stakeholders with information on the financial situation of the entrepreneur. Both interests do not necessarily run in the same direction but can also be directed against each other, necessarily leading to differences. Thus, it may be that national tax law does not tax an item of income but that the same item of income must be considered under accounting rules. Conversely, it may be that national tax law taxes an item of income that is not considered income under accounting rules. Similarly, differences can also arise from the different treatment of expenses. Since the ETR fraction compares the actual amount of taxes paid ('Adjusted Covered Taxes') with an income figure calculated according to accounting principles, differences between financial accounting results and taxable income results could not simply be ignored by the regulatory framework of GloBE.

Based on the ETR fraction, the question arises as to whether the necessary adjustment must be made to the 'Adjusted Covered Taxes' in the numerator or to the 'GloBE Income or Loss' ('net qualifying income') in the denominator or whether an adjustment in the denominator also requires an adjustment in the numerator. Shall the financial accounting results be adjusted to the tax accounting results or vice versa, and when does one adjustment imply another? How should GloBE connect the domestic tax bases to the profit and loss determination under accounting rules?

GloBE solves these conceptual issues by distinguishing between permanent differences on the one hand and temporary differences on the other.[685] Temporary differences differ from the former in that these differences between financial accounting and tax accounting reverse over time. On the contrary, permanent differences remain and never reverse. Thus, it is obvious that the technical consideration of temporary differences is easier compared to permanent ones: In the case of temporary differences, both accounting rules and tax laws start from an identical base but treat this base differently over time. Such a base might, e.g., be the costs of an asset, which usually do not differ in tax and accounting rules. However, if, for example, the accounting rules provide for a shorter period of amortization compared to tax laws, the ETR fraction could either consider this temporary difference in the numerator by increasing the amount of covered taxes in the numerator to align the covered taxes to the GloBE base, or by decreasing the income in the denominator to align the GloBE base to the covered taxes. Since GloBE starts from the financial accounts of a CE, the IF

684. *See* s. 4.3.3.1.

685. *See GloBE Commentary on Article 3, supra* note 507, para. 17.

agreed on considering temporary differences by adjusting the 'Adjusted Covered Taxes' in the numerator.[686] Since, in the case of temporary differences, there is still a link between the 'Adjusted Covered Taxes' and the GloBE base, there is no need to adjust the latter. Temporary differences are solely addressed in the fourth chapter[687] of the GloBE Model Rules and the GloBE-Directive, respectively.[688]

Obviously, the consideration of permanent differences within the ETR fraction is much trickier because a link between the accounting income and taxable income is completely missing: if, for example, a specific jurisdiction provides for a participation exemption for certain kinds of dividends, those dividends would be tax exempt but would very well be considered as profits under accounting rules. The different treatment would never reverse, as the exemption granted under domestic tax laws will not reverse over time. Simply adjusting the amount of 'Adjusted Covered Taxes' in the numerator would not be feasible, simply due to the fact that the amount of 'Covered Taxes' needed to be increased by an amount of fictitious taxes levied on the respective dividend. For this reason, GloBE takes a different path with respect to permanent differences compared to temporary ones: Permanent differences are taken into account by increasing or decreasing the GloBE base in the denominator of the ETR fraction. This, however, also requires that any tax levied on the respective income that is excluded from the GloBE base needs to be adjusted as well. If, for example, a jurisdiction taxes a dividend which is to be excluded from the GloBE base in the denominator, the amount of 'Covered Taxes' would still include the tax on the dividend, resulting in an overestimation of the ETR.[689] The adjustment of the GloBE base to consider a permanent difference in the denominator of the ETR fraction, thus, necessarily also requires an adjustment of the 'Adjusted Covered Taxes' in the numerator.[690]

4.3.3.3.2 Final Catalogue of Permanent Differences

In the development of GloBE, the question was not only how but, above all, which permanent differences should be taken into account at all. Finally, the IF Member States' definitions of taxable income, as well as the various accounting standards in use by 'MNE Groups', differ in various ways. The difficult process of finding a definition for permanent differences to be considered for purposes of GloBE is aptly summarized in paragraph 21 of the Commentary on Article 3 GloBE Model Rules:

686. Now reflected in Art. 4.4. *GloBE Model Rules* and Art. 21 GloBE-Directive (2022/2523). On these provisions *see* s. 4.3.4.5.
687. Chapter 4 titled 'Computation of Adjusted Covered Taxes' *GloBE Model Rules* and the corresponding Chapter IV of the GloBE-Directive (2022/2523) bearing the same title.
688. *See GloBE Commentary on Article 3*, *supra* note 507, para. 17.
689. If the denominator is decreased while the nominator stays the same, the ETR necessarily rises.
690. *See GloBE Commentary on Article 3*, *supra* note 507, para. 19: '*To the extent an adjustment required by Article 3.2 excludes an amount of income from the GloBE Income or Loss computation, any Covered Taxes associated with that income must also be excluded from Adjusted Covered Taxes pursuant to Article 4.1.3(a).*'

> Each Inclusive Framework jurisdiction has its own unique combination of additions to and exclusions from financial accounting net income or loss to arrive at taxable income under its domestic tax law. Because financial accounts are utilised as the starting point for determining the GloBE Income or Loss for all Constituent Entities wherever located, certain permanent differences will arise between the taxable income and the GloBE Income or Loss computed for some Constituent Entities [...] and it would not be possible or desirable [...] to develop a comprehensive set of adjustments to bring the GloBE Income or Loss fully into line with the taxable income calculation rules of all Inclusive Framework members. Indeed, many permanent differences, such as the exclusion of income from the tax base, will give rise to the types of low-tax outcomes that the GloBE Rules are intended to address. Nevertheless, some adjustments to financial accounts are appropriately based on the policies of the GloBE Rules and tax policy more generally, such as the treatment of bribes and fines. While the number of adjustments have been kept at a minimum to minimise complexity, the adjustments set out in Article 3.2 reflect cases that are sufficiently material and widely accepted in Inclusive Framework jurisdictions.[691]

The passage just quoted sums up the dilemma of adjustments to the 'Financial Accounting Net Income or Loss': GloBE had to strike a balance between the consideration of legitimate tax policy interests, systemic simplicity, and expediency of a minimum tax. Finally, the provisions on adjustments to the GloBE base in Article 3.2. GloBE Model Rules and Article 16 GloBE-Directive represent a trade-off between these factors. The IF Member States agreed on an exhaustive list of permanent differences to increase or decrease the 'Financial Accounting Net Income or Loss', which is reflected in Article 3.2.1. GloBE Model Rules and Article 16(2) GloBE-Directive.[692] Both provisions list nine different permanent differences. The corresponding permanent differences are then specifically defined in Article 10.1 GloBE Model Rules and Article 16(1) GloBE-Directive. In the following, all of these will be briefly discussed:

- **'Net Taxes Expense'**: The first adjustment to the 'Financial Accounting Net Income or Loss' is the current tax expense of the respective CE. As a rule, current tax expenses reduce the profit or increase the loss reported in the profit and loss statements according to accounting rules, whereas domestic CIT systems commonly do not allow the deduction of income tax due. Thus, the 'Net Taxes Expenses' of a CE are listed in Article 3.2.1.(a) GloBE Model Rules and Article 16(2)(a) GloBE-Directive, respectively, and '*must be added-back to income in order to accurately calculate the tax on total income*'.[693] Consequently, the Commentary also concludes that the '*adjustment for Net Tax Expense will typically be a positive amount (i.e. an increase to GloBE income) because it adds back taxes in respect of net income*'[694] but also recognizes that it could also be '*a negative amount where the Constituent Entity incurs a net*

691. *See Ibid.*, para. 21.
692. For a discussion in literature, *see* F. Brugger et al., *Globale Mindestbesteuerung: Ermittlung des GloBE-Einkommens*, 97 SWK 600 (2022).
693. *See GloBE Commentary on Article 3*, *supra* note 507, para. 22.
694. *See Ibid.*, para. 23.

loss that results in the creation of a deferred tax asset'.[695] The meaning of the term 'Net Taxes Expenses' is specifically defined in Article 10.1 GloBE Model Rules and Article 16(1)(a) GloBE-Directive: The term includes (i) '*any Covered taxes accrued as an expense*' including deferred Covered Taxes,[696] (ii) '*any deferred tax asset attributable to a loss*'[697] for the respective 'Fiscal Year', (iii) QDMTT levied by 'low-tax jurisdictions',[698] as well as (iv) 'Top-up Tax' levied by means of the IIR or UTPR[699] and (v) any so-called Disqualified Refundable Imputation Tax[700] accrued as an expense.[701] The latter includes taxes levied on income that are excluded from the definition of 'Covered Taxes' simply due to the fact that the respective tax might be refunded upon the distribution of a dividend. Consequently, such an amount of tax that initially reduced accounting income is to be added back to the GloBE base.[702]

- **'Excluded Dividends':** The exclusion of dividends has already been used to explain the necessity to adjust permanent differences[703] and not without reason: The adjustment of permanent differences arising through dividends probably is the most important of the adjustments listed in Article 3.2.1. GloBE Model Rules and Article 16(2) GloBE-Directive. Regarding the background of the provision, the Commentary states that the taxation of dividends '*varies from one jurisdiction to the next*' while a '*significant number of Inclusive Framework jurisdictions provide for a credit, exemption or some other form of tax relief*'.[704] To simplify the recognition of dividends, regularly subject to tax relief in the recipient's state of residence, the IF Member States agreed '*to apply a consistently bright-line test that builds on components found in the participation exemptions applied*'[705] by several IF jurisdictions. For this reason, Article 3.2.1. GloBE Model Rules and Article 16(2) GloBE-Directive list 'Excluded Dividends' that need to be adjusted during GloBE's base determination. Unfortunately, the GloBE Model Rules use an extremely complex chain of definitions to define the scope of the term 'Excluded Dividend': according to

695. *See Ibid.*
696. *See* letter a of the definition of 'Net Taxes Expense' in Art. 10.1. *GloBE Model Rules*, at 61 and the corresponding provision in Art. 16(1)(a)(i) GloBE-Directive (2022/2523).
697. *See* letter b of the definition of 'Net Taxes Expense' in Art. 10.1. *GloBE Model Rules*, at 61 and the corresponding provision in Art. 16(1)(a)(ii) GloBE-Directive (2022/2523).
698. *See* letter c of the definition of 'Net Taxes Expense' Art. 10.1. *GloBE Model Rules*, at 61 and the corresponding provision in Art. 16(1)(a)(iii) GloBE-Directive (2022/2523).
699. *See* letter d of the definition of 'Net Taxes Expense' Art. 10.1. *GloBE Model Rules*, at 61 and the corresponding provision using the phrase '*taxes arising pursuant to the rules of this Directive*' in Art. 16(1)(a)(iv) GloBE-Directive (2022/2523).
700. *See* the definition of 'Disqualified Refundable Imputation Tax' in Art. 10.1. *GloBE Model Rules*, at 55 and the corresponding definition in Art. 3(37) GloBE-Directive (2022/2523).
701. *See* letter e of the definition of 'Net Taxes Expense' Art. 10.1. *GloBE Model Rules*, at 61 and the corresponding provision in Art. 16(1)(a)(v) GloBE-Directive (2022/2523).
702. In detail on the permanent differences arising from 'Disqualified Refundable Imputation Taxes', *see GloBE Commentary on Article 3 GloBE Model Rules (2022)*, *supra* note 507, paras 25 and 33.
703. *See* s. 4.3.3.1 and 4.3.3.3.1.
704. *See GloBE Commentary on Article 3*, *supra* note 507, para. 35.
705. *See Ibid.*

Article 10.1. GloBE Model Rules an 'Excluded Dividend'[706] is a dividend or other distribution received in respect of an 'Ownership Interest', except for so-called Short-term Portfolio Shareholdings (or an 'Ownership Interest' in an 'Investment Entity' subject to an election[707] under Article 7.6. GloBE Model Rules[708]). The term 'Short-term Portfolio Shareholding'[709] is again defined separately, also referring to another separate definition of 'Portfolio Shareholding'. In summary, according to this chain of definitions (except for the very specific case of a CE subject to the election of Article 7.6. GloBE Model Rules), an 'Excluded Dividend' is a dividend received by a CE from a shareholding that is either held for at least one year at the date of the distribution or in which the participation exceeds 10 %.[710] Fortunately, the corresponding definitions in the GloBE-Directive have been summarized in a separate letter b within Article 16(1) GloBE-Directive. Consequently, if a monetary transaction qualifies as an 'Excluded Dividend' as defined in Article 3.1.2.(b) GloBE Model Rules or Article 16(2)(b) GloBE-Directive, the 'Financial Accounting Net Income or Loss' is to be adjusted by '*reducing that Net Income (or by increasing the Loss) by the amount of any Excluded Dividends received during the Fiscal Year*'.[711] Dividends received from 'Short-term Portfolio Shareholdings' (holding period less than a year *and* participation below 10%) are to be included within GloBE's tax base; and, correspondingly, also taxes levied on them remain within the computation of the amount of 'Adjusted Covered Taxes'.[712] CEs, therefore, have to treat dividends received from 'Short-term Portfolio Shareholdings' differently from all other dividends, which might raise complex issues, in particular when the one-year period needs to be tested. In this context, the examples published by the OECD give a taste of this complexity, showing how to calculate the one-year holding period.[713] Meanwhile, the OECD addressed the issue and provided a specific election to include all

706. *See* the definition of 'Excluded Dividend' in Art. 10.1. *GloBE Model Rules*, at 56.
707. So-called deemed taxable distribution method, in detail *see* s. 4.3.2.2.3.
708. The reason for the exception from the 'Excluded Dividend' definition is simple: If the election of Art. 7.6. GloBE Model Rules (Art. 43 GloBE-Directive, *see* the reference in Art. 16[1][b][ii] GloBE-Directive) is applied, the 'Investment Entities' income as well as the taxes due on this income is to be allocated to the 'Constituent-Entity Owner' (the parent entity). If the dividend were now excluded from the GloBE base determination, the taxes to be collected from the 'Investment Entity' would still be in the numerator of the ETR fraction. The ETR would thus be overestimated. However, the Commentary only comments on this very briefly, *see GloBE Commentary on Article 3, supra* note 507, paras 25 and 33.
709. *See* the definition of 'Short-term Portfolio Shareholding' in Art. 10.1. *GloBE Model Rules*, at 65.
710. In detail on the determination of the holding period and the 10% ownership threshold, *see GloBE Commentary on Article 3, supra* note 507, paras 38–44.
711. *See Ibid.*, para. 46
712. *See Ibid.*, para. 45 Note that para. 45 has been extended by the *GloBE Administrative Guidance February 2023*, at 77.
713. *See* Example 3.2.1(b) in OECD/G20 Inclusive Framework on BEPS, *Tax Challenges Arising from Digitalisation –Global Anti-Base Erosion Examples (Pillar Two)* 23–24 (OECD 14 Mar. 2022), https://www.oecd.org/tax/beps/tax-challenges-arising-from-the-digitalisation-of-the-economy-global-anti-base-erosion-model-rules-pillar-two-commentary.pdf (last visited 22 Mar. 2022).

Portfolio Shareholdings (whether short- or long-term) in a CE's 'GloBE Income or Loss'. Of course, the election is not necessarily advantageous for an 'MNE Group'. Pursuant to the OECD, it aims to provide an option for simplification, in particular, for insurance companies, as it eliminates the need to separately account for short- and long-term shareholdings.[714] In any case, if domestic tax systems apply their participation exemption regimes to 'Short-term Portfolio Shareholdings' as well, such dividends consequently lead to a reduction of the ETR.[715] By excluding dividend income from the denominator of the ETR fraction, the ETR increases. However, if, contrary to GloBE's assumption, taxes are levied on these 'Excluded Dividends', these must also be removed from the numerator of the ETR fraction according to Article 4.1.3.(a) GloBE Model Rules and Article 21(3)(a) GloBE-Directive. Otherwise, the ETR would be overestimated.

- **Excluded Equity Gains or Loss:** The adjustment of equity gains and losses is rooted in the usual permanent differences that arise, on the one hand, (i) from different valuation rules between accounting rules and tax rules and, on the other hand, (ii) from exemptions for the disposition of shareholdings, commonly provided for in domestic tax laws, which regularly complement participation exemption schemes. The first group of situations includes gains and losses from changes in fair value, which are often not reflected in the tax accounts,[716] or profits or losses resulting from the application of the equity method (usually for participations between 20% and 50%)[717] in relation to 'Ownership Interest' held by the parent entity, which is not tax effective either.[718] Revaluation gains and losses are usually only recognized for tax purposes in most tax systems when they are actually realized, whereas accounting rules require a regular adjustment of book values. Consequently, according to Article 3.2.1.(c) GloBE Model Rules and Article 16(2)(c) GloBE-Directive, such changes in fair value as well as profits or losses resulting from the application of the equity method are to be adjusted in such a way that the GloBE base needs to be reduced by gains or profits and increased by losses suffered in the course of such revaluations.[719] The second group is addressed to the sale or disposition of 'Ownership Interests' held in participations.[720] Correspondingly to dividends, in '*many Inclusive Framework jurisdictions,*

714. *GloBE Administrative Guidance February 2023*, at 77.
715. Finally, such dividends are fully included in the GloBE base in the denominator, whereas no tax is payable on the corresponding dividends in the numerator.
716. *See* letter a of the definition of 'Excluded Equity Gain or Loss' provided for in Art. 10.1. *GloBE Model Rules*, at 56 and the corresponding definition provided for in Art. 16(1)(c)(i) GloBE-Directive (2022/2523).
717. *See GloBE Commentary on Article 3*, *supra* note 507, para. 50.
718. *See* letter b of the definition of 'Excluded Equity Gain or Loss' provided for in Art. 10.1. *GloBE Model Rules*, at 56 and the corresponding definition provided for in Art. 16(1)(c)(ii) GloBE-Directive (2022/2523).
719. *See GloBE Commentary on Article 3*, *supra* note 507, paras 49 and 51.
720. *See* letter c of the definition of 'Excluded Equity Gain or Loss' provided for in Art. 10.1. *GloBE Model Rules*, at 56 and the corresponding definition provided for in Art. 16(1)(c)(iii) GloBE-Directive (2022/2523).

gains arising from the disposition of Ownership Interests are wholly or partially exempt from tax [...] *and losses arising* [...] *may not be deductible*'.[721] Thus, GloBE also eliminates gains and losses from the disposition of shareholdings, except for 'Portfolio Shareholdings' ('Ownership Interest' below 10%),[722] from the GloBE base.[723] Again, gains lead to a negative adjustment, while losses need to be added back to the GloBE base. In turn, any taxes levied need to be removed from the 'Adjusted Covered Taxes' in the numerator of the ETR fraction.[724] In the meanwhile, the OECD added some notes on the application of Article 3.2.1.(c) GloBE Model Rules with respect to hedges of investments in foreign operations in the Commentary on Article 3 GloBE Model Rules in the GloBE Administrative Guidance February 2023.[725]

- **Included Revaluation Method Gain or Loss:** Many 'Acceptable Financial Accounting Standards', including the IFRS,[726] allow to account for property, plant and equipment either under the cost model or the revaluation model.[727] While the former method is usually consistent with the determination of profit for tax purposes, fair value accounting regularly results in permanent differences: If the revaluation model is in use, most accounting standards, first and foremost the IFRS,[728] treat increases and decreases of the fair value differently. While decreases (impairment losses) are usually recognized in the profit and loss statement,[729] increases in value are regularly recognized in OCI.[730] This takes into account the fact that uncertain increases in value do not distort the profit or loss, whereas impairments are immediately taken into account in the sense of prudent accounting. However, since the GloBE base starts from the 'Financial Accounting Net Income or Loss', revaluation gains would generally be excluded from the base determination (*see* already section 4.3.3.2.3), leading to an increase of the ETR while impairment losses would also be recognized resulting in a reduction of the ETR. By including all 'Included Revaluation Method Gains and Losses' according to Article 3.2.1.(d) GloBE Model Rules and Article 16(2)(d) GloBE-Directive, this effect is eliminated across all 'Acceptable Financial Accounting Standards'. Technically, GloBE implements the adjustment of 'Included Revaluation Method Gain or Loss' via the respective definitions of the term in Article 10.1 GloBE Model Rules and Article 16(1)(d) GloBE-Directive: The term includes any gains or losses,

721. *See GloBE Commentary on Article 3*, *supra* note 507, para. 54.
722. In detail on the prerequisites for the exclusion of a shareholding, *see Ibid.*, paras 55–57.
723. *See Ibid.*, para. 54
724. Article 4.1.3.(a) *GloBE Model Rules* and Art. 21(3)(a) GloBE-Directive (2022/2523).
725. *See* the newly added paras 57.1 to 57.3 and the new Example 3.2.1.(c)-1, in *GloBE Administrative Guidance February 2023*, at 31–34.
726. *See* IAS 16.29 on the measurement of property, plant and equipment after recognition: '*An entity shall choose either the cost model* [...] *or the revaluation model* [...] *as its accounting policy and shall apply that policy to an entire class of property, plant and equipment.*'
727. *See GloBE Commentary on Article 3*, *supra* note 507, para. 58.
728. *See*, e.g., IAS 16.31 to 16.42.
729. *See*, e.g., IAS 16.40.
730. *See*, e.g., IAS 16.39.

increased or decreased by any associated 'Covered Taxes' in respect of all property,[731] plant and equipment that arises under accounting rules where the CE cumulatively (i) adjusts the carrying value of such property periodically to the fair value,[732] (ii) records the changes in OCI[733] and (iii) does not subsequently report the gains or losses recorded in OCI through profit and loss.[734] Consequently, an adjustment of the 'Financial Accounting Net Income or Loss' is only required if the revaluation gain or loss is not recognized in the profit or loss statement but in the OCI of the respective CE. If the accounting standard in use obliges to reflect such revaluations in the profit or loss anyway, there is no need to adjust the 'Financial Accounting Net Income or Loss'. Furthermore, Article 3.2.5. GloBE Model Rules and Article 16(6) GloBE-Directive provide for an election to exclude gains and losses resulting from the use of the revaluation model, although such gains or losses are reflected in the OCI.[735] For more detail on this election, *see* section 4.3.3.3.5.

- **Gain or loss from disposition of assets and liabilities excluded under Article 6.3. GloBE Model Rules and Article 35 GloBE-Directive: Article** 6.3. GloBE Model Rules and Article 35 GloBE-Directive provide specific rules on the transfer of assets and liabilities. The basic rule for gains and losses, both gains and losses from the disposition or acquisition of assets and liabilities, is in Article 6.3.1. GloBE Model Rules and Article 35(2) GloBE-Directive states that such gains and losses must be included in the GloBE base. In principle, this does not result in any difference to accounting rules: Since GloBE does not use the 'Consolidated Financial Statements' but the separate financial statements of the individual CEs for the base determination, dispositions and acquisitions of assets are shown in the profit or loss anyway.[736] However, GloBE (according to Article 3.2.1.(e) GloBE Model Rules and Article 16(2)(e) GloBE-Directive) grants an exception to the recognition of gains or losses from the disposition of assets or liabilities in the course of reorganizations (Article 6.3. GloBE Model Rules and Article 35 GloBE-Directive): In many jurisdictions, gains or losses arising from the transfer of assets or liabilities during mergers, demergers,

731. As the Commentary clarifies, this is supposed to mean that any associated tax shall be taken into account if the respective gain or loss 'was recorded net of Covered Taxes'. In any case, the tax associated with 'Included Revaluation Gains or Losses' are recognized in the amount of 'Adjusted Covered Taxes' in the nominator of the ETR fraction, *see GloBE Commentary on Article 3, supra* note 507, paras 60 and 61.
732. Letter a of the definition of 'Included Revaluation Method Gain or Loss' in Art. 10.1. *GloBE Model Rules*, at 58 and Art. 16(1)(d)(i) GloBE-Directive (2022/2523).
733. Letter b of the definition of 'Included Revaluation Method Gain or Loss' in Art. 10.1. *GloBE Model Rules*, at 58 and Art. 16(1)(d)(ii) GloBE-Directive (2022/2523).
734. Letter c of the definition of 'Included Revaluation Method Gain or Loss' in Art. 10.1. *GloBE Model Rules*, at 58 and Art. 16(1)(d)(iii) GloBE-Directive (2022/2523).
735. On the relation of Art. 3.2.1.(d) GloBE Model Rules (Art. 16[2][d] GloBE-Directive) and Art. 3.2.5. GloBE Model Rules and Art. 16(6) GloBE-Directive, *see GloBE Commentary on Article 3, supra* note 507, para. 62.
736. In the same vein, *see Ibid.*, para. 64.

liquidations or other similar transactions are exempt from tax.[737] Instead, the acquiring entity takes over the assets and liabilities at the carrying values of the disposing/transferring entity using the historical values of the transferred assets and liabilities. In order to take this common legal practice into account when calculating the ETR, Article 6.3.2 GloBE Model Rules and Article 35(3) GloBE-Directive provide for an exception to the respective basic rules and allow the exclusion of gains or losses from the GloBE base. While the '*disposing*' CE (within the GloBE-Directive, the 'transferring entity'[738]) may exclude the respective profit or loss from its income or loss, the acquiring CE may determine the GloBE base using the disposing or transferring CEs carrying values. Consequently, a gain leads to a negative adjustment of the 'GloBE Income or Loss' ('net qualifying income or loss'), while a loss leads to a positive adjustment.[739] Both the GloBE Model Rules and the GloBE-Directive use different definitions of the term 'reorganization' (the GloBE Model Rules use 'GloBE Reorganisation'[740]). The deviation of Article 35(1) GloBE-Directive is due to the facts that first, the term 'GloBE Reorganization' heavily relies on domestic legal systems[741] and second, that the EU has already implemented its own secondary legislation on reorganizations, which is the Merger Directive.[742] Although an explicit reference is missing, the definition of Article 35(1) GloBE-Directive is evidently based on the scope of the Merger Directive.[743] The specific scope of 'reorganisations' in the GloBE Model Rules as well as the GloBE-Directive, is extremely complex and will not be discussed in depth here for reasons of scope.[744]

- **Asymmetric Foreign Currency Gains or Losses:** In many situations, the currency in use for determining a CE's taxable income (so-called tax functional currency) will be different to the currency used for accounting purposes to prepare the 'Consolidated Financial Statements' of the UPE. This is inevitably accompanied by permanent differences '*that do*[...], *and should, affect the ETR of the jurisdiction*'.[745] The definition of 'Asymmetric Foreign Currency Gains and Losses' distinguishes between four different situations in which GloBE

737. On this fact, *see* explicitly *GloBE Commentary on Article 10 GloBE Model Rules (2022), supra* note 280, para. 21.
738. *See* Art. 35(3)(a) GloBE-Directive (2022/2523).
739. *See GloBE Commentary on Article 3, supra* note 507, para. 65.
740. *See* the definition of 'GloBE Reorganisation' in Art. 10.1. *GloBE Model Rules*, at 57.
741. *See* in particular letter c of the definition of 'GloBE Reorganisation' in Art. 10.1. *Ibid.*
742. Council Directive 2009/133/EC of 19 October 2009 on the common system of taxation applicable to mergers, divisions, partial divisions, transfers of assets and exchanges of shares concerning companies of different Member States and to the transfer of the registered office of an SE or SCE between Member States, OJ (133). On the relation of GloBE and the Merger Directive, also *see* s. 6.3.
743. *See*, in particular, Art. 2 *ibid.*, which obviously is the origin of the 10% payment threshold in Art. 35(1) GloBE-Directive (2022/2523).
744. In detail on the scope of the term 'GloBE Reorganisation' used by the GloBE Model Rules, *see GloBE Commentary on Article 10 GloBE Model Rules (2022), supra* note 280, paras 21–25.
745. *See GloBE Commentary on Article 3 GloBE Model Rules (2022), supra* note 507, para. 67.

requires an adjustment.[746] The underlying problem is the same with respect to all four situations and can best be described by means of an example: If, for example, a US-based CE owes a certain amount in EUR, which is also reflected in euros within the financial statement in preparation for consolidation, there may be a significant impact on the ETR due to exchange rate changes: If the United States Dollar (USD) loses against the EUR, this loss is not reflected in the financial statements because the liability is reported in euros anyway. However, the currency loss reduces the US tax burden because the liability in euros is shown in the tax accounts in USD, having lost value compared to EUR. The loss, therefore, reduces the US tax burden but is not reflected in the GloBE base. In this example, the ETR would be too low because the GloBE base does not take into account the currency effect in the denominator of the ETR fraction but includes the resulting lower US tax burden in the numerator. In the case shown here, a negative adjustment of the GloBE base would have to be made according to the Commentary[747] and the Examples[748] provided by OECD. The reduction of the GloBE base in the denominator of the ETR fraction increases the ETR calculated for the US.

- **Policy Disallowed Expenses:** Although the term 'Policy Disallowed Expenses' might indicate that it could cover all deductions denied under domestic laws, the term is specifically defined for the purposes of GloBE. According to GloBE, 'Policy Disallowed Expenses' include expenses accrued by a CE for '*illegal payments, including bribes and kickbacks*'[749] as well as '*expenses accrued by the Constituent Entity for fines and penalties that equal or exceed EUR 50 000 (or an equivalent in the functional currency in which the Constituent Entity's Financial Accounting Net Income or Loss was calculated)*'.[750] Hence, the way this adjustment works is simple: According to accounting principles, such expenses would have to be recognized in the profit and loss statement and would therefore reduce the amount in the denominator of the ETR fraction and thus increase the ETR. By making a positive adjustment by adding those expenses to the 'GloBE Income or Loss' ('net qualifying income or loss'), the 'Policy Disallowed Expense' does not reduce the denominator of the ETR fraction, and the ETR decreases. While bribes and kickbacks must be corrected irrespective of their amount, GloBE foresees a *de minims* threshold for fines and penalties of EUR 50,000. The threshold applies for accrued fines and penalties of every single CE and works like a free amount: If the accrued fines of a CE exceed this EUR 50,000 threshold, the EUR 50,000 remain deductible for the purposes of GloBE. Only those expenses exceeding EUR 50,000 have to

746. *See* the definition of 'Asymmetric Foreign Currency Gains or Losses' in Art. 10.1. *GloBE Model Rules*, at 53 and Art. 16(1)(e) GloBE-Directive (2022/2523).
747. *See GloBE Commentary on Article 3, supra* note 507, para. 69.
748. *See* the illustrative OECD examples on Art. 3.2.1(f) *GloBE Examples*, at 25–28.
749. *See* letter a of the definition of 'Policy Disallowed Expenses' in Art. 10.1. *GloBE Model Rules*, at 64 and Art. 16(1)(f)(i) GloBE-Directive (2022/2523).
750. *See* letter b of the definition of 'Policy Disallowed Expenses' in Art. 10.1. *GloBE Model Rules*, at 64 and Art. 16(1)(f)(ii) GloBE-Directive (2022/2523).

be added back to the GloBE base. According to the Commentary, the threshold's purpose is '*to continue to allow deductions for smaller fines that may not be specifically recorded as separate items in the accounts of the Constituent Entity. This approach avoids the complexity of tracking small fines and penalties for GloBE purposes while at the same time preventing MNEs from escaping a Top-up Tax because of a few large, non-deductible fines or penalties*'.[751] A corresponding adjustment of the 'Adjusted Covered Taxes' is not necessary: if such payment were deductible under domestic law, this would reduce the numerator of the ETR fraction and, thus, the ETR as well, anyway. This is also explicitly stated in Article 4.1.3.(b) GloBE Model Rules and Article 21(3)(a) GloBE-Directive, where a reduction of the Adjusted Covered Taxes is only to be made '*with respect to income excluded*' and not also for expenses excluded.

- **Prior Period Errors and Changes in Accounting Principles:** It often turns out that financial statements from previous years have to be corrected, also affecting the financial statements of the 'Fiscal Year' at the point of issue. Since such corrections can have a significant impact on the ETR, GloBE dedicates a separate Article 4.6. GloBE Model Rules (reflected in Article 25 GloBE-Directive) to such 'post-filing adjustments', according to which the ETR and the 'Top-up Tax' must be recalculated retrospectively if the respective adjustment leads to a decrease in the 'Covered Taxes' included in a CE's amount of 'Adjusted Covered Taxes' for a previous 'Fiscal Year'. In this case, no permanent adjustment would occur because the respective error would be recorded in the previous 'Fiscal Year' anyway.[752] However, in the case of subsequent increases or so-called immaterial decreases of the 'Covered Taxes' (less than EUR 1 million), GloBE assumes that a complete recalculation of the ETR and the 'Top-up Tax' for the previous period at issue would be disproportionate. For this reason, such changes in 'Covered Taxes' are to be included in the amount of 'Adjusted Covered Taxes' of the current 'Fiscal Year'. In this case, Article 3.2.1.(h) GloBE Model Rules and Article 16(2)(h) GloBE-Directive make sure that any changes in income or losses stemming from previous 'Fiscal Years' in the current 'Fiscal Year' are corrected as permanent differences because otherwise, the intended effect of including the 'Adjusted Covered Taxes' from previous years would be reversed (*see* in further detail section 4.3.4.9.).[753] The connection of these adjustments with the provisions of Article 4.6. GloBE Model Rules and Article 25 GloBE-Directive is laid down in the respective definitions of the term 'Prior Period Errors and Changes in Accounting Principles', according to which the term is defined as a change in the opening equity at the beginning of the Fiscal Year of a Constituent Entity attributable either to a correction of an error from previous Fiscal Years '*except to the extent such error correction resulted in a material decrease to a liability for*

751. *See GloBE Commentary on Article 3*, *supra* note 507, para. 78.
752. *See Ibid.*, para. 81.
753. *See Ibid.*, paras 80 and 81.

Covered Taxes subject to Article 4.6.'.[754] Furthermore, according to the definitions of 'Prior Period Errors and Changes in Accounting Principles', such an adjustment can also arise due to '*a change in accounting principle or policy*'.[755] Such situations occur, for example, if a CE makes use of an accounting election that has not been used in previous years. If such '*change in accounting principle or policy*' requires the re-determination of the opening equity (because the financial statements need to be prepared as if the respective accounting principle or policy, like an election, had already been applied in previous years),[756] GloBE requires to make a respective adjustment by increasing or reducing the GloBE base according to the respective accounting adjustment.

- **Accrued Pension Expense:** An 'Accrued Pension Expense' is the difference between the amount of pension liability and the contributions made to a 'Pension Fund' by a specific CE.[757] But why is there a need to account for a permanent difference for such 'Accrued Pension Expenses'? Both Article 3.2.1.(i) GloBE Model Rules and Article 16(2)(i) GloBE-Directive had the following problem in mind: Many companies finance pension liabilities against their employees by regularly contributing to 'Pension Funds'. These 'Pension Funds' again invest the contributions made by the company, and if the money is successfully invested, the earnings of the pension fund will reduce '*the contributions that the company must make to fund its employee's retirement benefits*'[758] or, in the case of a loss, might even increase the contributions. For the purpose of GloBE, only the contributions made to the 'Pension Fund' (irrespective of the earnings or losses of the respective fund) should be deductible. But why is there an issue with respect to the ETR computation? Pursuant to the OECD, the earnings of the 'Pension Fund' will regularly be recognized within the OCI and not within profit and loss statements. So, as a rule, the earnings or losses of the 'Pension Fund' that might impact a company's net contributions will not be within the GloBE base anyway (as long as any surplus is not distributed to the CE and will be 'recycled' into the profit and loss statement),[759] as the GloBE base does not take into account any item shown in the OCI (already *see* section 4.3.3.2.1). However, some financial accounting standards do not distinguish between a profit and loss statement and a separate OCI. For this reason, Article 3.2.1.(i)

754. *See* letter a of the definition of 'Prior Period Errors and Changes in Accounting Principles' in Art. 10.1. *GloBE Model Rules*, at 64 and correspondingly in Art. 16(1)(g)(i) GloBE-Directive (2022/2523).
755. *See* letter b of the definition of 'Prior Period Errors and Changes in Accounting Principles' in Art. 10.1. *GloBE Model Rules*, at 64 and correspondingly in Art. 16(1)(g)(ii) GloBE-Directive (2022/2523).
756. *See GloBE Commentary on Article 3*, *supra* note 507, para. 82.
757. *See* the definition of 'Accrued Pension Expense' provided for in Art. 10.1. *GloBE Model Rules*, at 52 and Art. 16(1)(h) GloBE-Directive (2022/2523).
758. *See* para. 3 at *GloBE Administrative Guidance February 2023*, at 42.
759. *See* the newly added para. 86 of the Commentary on Art. 3 GloBE Model Rules, *see Ibid.*, at 43–44.

GloBE Model Rules and Article 16(2)(i) GloBE-Directive aim to avoid distortions between different accounting standards[760] by excluding the difference between the amount of pension liability and the contributions made to a 'Pension Fund' if the respective amount is included in the GloBE base of a CE. So, if the profit and loss statement of a CE includes retained earnings or losses of a 'Pension Fund', the respective amount of 'Accrued Pension Expense' will be removed from the GloBE base. If the respective amounts are recognized in the OCI anyway, there is no need to make an adjustment pursuant to Article 3.2.1.(i) GloBE Model Rules and Article 16(2)(i) GloBE-Directive. Thus, it seems that the purpose of excluding 'Accrued Pension Expenses' in Article 3.2.1.(i) GloBE Model Rules and Article 16(2)(i) GloBE-Directive is to ensure that pension expenses, which regularly constitute a significant item within the financial accounts of an entity, are included in the ETR calculation in a reasonably uniform manner among the different accounting standards in use. Following extensive feedback from various stakeholders on the application of Article 3.2.1.(i) GloBE Model Rules, the OECD has provided comprehensive clarifications in its GloBE Administrative Guidance February 2023 and added an example on the 'Accrued Pension Expenses' to the Example Catalogue.[761] The adjustment of 'Accrued Pension Expenses' only addresses structures in which pension liabilities are financed via contributions to a 'Pension Fund'. However, this special adjustment should not be understood to mean that direct pension payments to employees would not be deductible for GloBE purposes.[762] Rather, Article 3.2.1.(i) GloBE Model Rules and Article 16(2)(i) GloBE-Directive solely aim to eliminate distortions among accounting standards with respect to gains and losses of 'Pension Funds' that invest the contributions to ensure that the company can ultimately pay its pension liabilities.

The analysis of the catalogue of adjustments provided in Article 3.2.1. GloBE Model Rules and Article 16(2) GloBE-Directive shows a picture of extremely heterogeneous problems resulting from differences between tax and financial accounts. The common feature of the adjustments provided in the GloBE Model Rules and the GloBE-Directive, respectively, however, is that without the respective adjustments, undesirable positive and negative distortion effects would arise with respect to the ETR calculation. By means of a final catalogue of adjustments, GloBE attempts to establish a uniform determination of profits on the one hand, which, on the other hand, considers the common tax law practice of the IF Member States. The practical implementation, however, is likely to pose major challenges for 'MNE Groups': the determination of the GloBE base requires the correction of various items of income and expenses. Finally, the calculation of the 'GloBE Income or Loss' ('qualifying income or

760. *See GloBE Commentary on Article 3*, *supra* note 507, para. 85.
761. *See* the elaborations and revised and newly added paras 85–86.1 for the Commentary on Art. 3 GloBE Model Rules as well as the Example 3.2.1.(i) – 1 in *GloBE Administrative Guidance February 2023*, at 42–47.
762. *See* para. 7 *Ibid.*, at 43.

loss') will also influence the accounting policy of 'MNE Groups'. If, for example, the accounting standard used by a CE provides for certain elections or allows for different accounting policies, GloBE might influence whether the CE makes use of the election and accounting policy leeways or not: Some accounting elections or policies might trigger or avoid adjustments to the GloBE base and might influence the calculation of the ETR. The best example of such an election is the measurement of property, plant and equipment after recognition, which does not result in an adjustment if the cost model is used but does very well require an adjustment of 'Included Revaluation Method Gains or Losses' if an entity uses the revaluation method.[763]

4.3.3.3.3 Special Additional Adjustments Besides the Catalogue of Permanent Differences

Apart from the catalogues provided in Article 3.2.1. GloBE Model Rules and Article 16(2) GloBE-Directive, both frameworks foresee additional mandatory adjustments to the GloBE base. The special nature of these differences is probably the reason why they were not explicitly included in the catalogue of permanent differences provided for in Article 3.2.1. GloBE Model Rules and Article 16(2) GloBE-Directive. The respective adjustments can only be touched very briefly here:

- **Qualified Refundable Tax Credits:** According to Article 3.2.4. GloBE Model Rules and Article 16(5) GloBE-Directive so-called Qualified Refundable Tax Credits '*shall be treated as income*'[764] for the computation of the 'GloBE Income or Loss' ('net qualifying income or loss'). According to Article 10.1. GloBE Model Rules (reflected in Article 3[38] GloBE-Directive) the term covers '*refundable tax credit*[s] *designed in a way such that it must be paid as cash or available as cash equivalents within four years from when a Constituent Entity satisfies the conditions for receiving the credit under the laws of the jurisdiction granting the credit*'.[765] In other words, 'Qualified Refundable Tax Credits'[766] are monetary government incentives paid by a jurisdiction to a CE via the underlying tax system to attract certain business activities, e.g., research or development and foreign direct investments.[767] Instead of treating such tax credits as a reduction of 'Adjusted Covered Taxes', such 'Qualified Refundable Tax Credits' increase the GloBE base in the denominator of the ETR fraction in order to treat such incentives in the same way as government grants which, contrary to such tax credits, usually '*form part of income*'.[768] This broadly

763. *See* the respective election provided for in IAS 16.29.
764. Article 3.2.4. *GloBE Model Rules* and Art. 16(5) GloBE-Directive (2022/2523).
765. Article 10.1. *GloBE Model Rules*, at 65 and Art. 3(38) GloBE-Directive (2022/2523).
766. *See* the definition of 'Qualified Refundable Tax Credit' provided for in Art. 10.1. *GloBE Model Rules*, at 65 and Art. 3(32) GloBE-Directive (2022/2523). In detail on the interpretation of the term, *see GloBE Commentary on Article 10 GloBE Model Rules (2022)*, *supra* note 280, paras 134–138. Furthermore, *see* s. 4.3.4.3.4.
767. *See* the description provided for in *GloBE Commentary on Article 3 GloBE Model Rules (2022)*, *supra* note 507, para. 110.
768. *See Ibid.*, para. 111.

conforms to the accounting treatment according to IAS 12 and IAS 20[769] of such incentives, which tend to record investment tax credits same as government grants (in further detail, *see* section 4.3.4.3.4.). Consequently, such 'Qualified Refundable Tax Credits' result in a positive adjustment of the 'GloBE Income or Loss' ('net qualifying income or loss'). In order to avoid double counting of such tax benefits within the ETR fraction, the tax benefit resulting from the respective 'Qualified Refundable Tax Credits' is to be added back to the amount of 'Adjusted Covered Taxes' according to Article 4.1.2.(d) GloBE Model Rules and Article 21(2)(d) GloBE-Directive, provided the credit has actually reduced the tax expenses (in detail, *see* section 4.3.4.3.4.).[770] This does not apply to so-called Non-Qualified Refundable Tax Credits,[771] which do not meet the definitions of 'Qualified Refundable Tax Credits' in the respective definitions provided for in Article 10.1. GloBE Model Rules and Article 3(32) GloBE-Directive. Such tax credits are to be considered as reductions of the 'Adjusted Covered Taxes' according to Article 4.1.3.(b) GloBE Model Rules and Article 20(3)(b) GloBE-Directive.[772] The treatment of 'Qualified Refundable Tax Credits', thus, is highly beneficial compared to the treatment of 'Non-qualified Refundable Tax Credits' because the impact on the ETR is relatively moderate.[773] The easiest way to describe this effect is to use a simple example: Assume a CE receives 'GloBE Income' of 1000, while the 'Adjusted Covered Taxes' amount to 200. This results in an ETR of 20%. Now suppose that the CE receives a tax credit of 100 in the jurisdiction where it is located. If the respective tax credit qualifies as a 'Qualified Refundable Tax Credit', the GloBE Income is increased by 100, resulting in an ETR of 18.18% (200/[1000 + 100]). However, if the tax credit is qualified as a 'Non-Qualified Refundable Tax Credit', it reduces the amount of 'Adjusted Covered Taxes', resulting in an ETR of 10.00% ([200-100]/1000).[774] Thus, low-tax jurisdictions, in particular, should pay special attention to the rules for 'Qualified Refundable Tax Credits' to design future tax incentives in a way that they do qualify as 'Qualified Refundable Tax Credits' under the GloBE regime to protect the incentive from being nullified by the global minimum tax.[775] However, as Devereux, Vella & Wardell-Burrus note, any 'Qualified Refundable Tax Credit' could also be unfavourable if it interacts with the SBIE. Since 'Qualified Refundable Tax

769. In the same vein, Joachim Englisch, *GloBE Rules and Tax Competition*, 50 Intertax (2022).
770. In detail on the corresponding addition to the amount of 'Adjusted Covered Taxes', *see GloBE Commentary on Article 3*, *supra* note 507, para. 112.
771. *See* the definition of 'Non-Qualified Refundable Tax Credits' provided for in Art. 10.1. *GloBE Model Rules*, at 62. Also *see* Art. 3(39) GloBE-Directive (2022/2523).
772. *See GloBE Commentary on Article 3*, *supra* note 507, para. 113. In the meanwhile, the GloBE Administrative Guidance published in July 2023 brought additional clarifications on tax credits, particularly including the treatment of 'Transferable tax credits'. See the additions made to the Commentary in *GloBE Administrative Guidance July 2023*, at 40 et seq.
773. Also *see* Joachim Englisch, *supra* note 769, at 3.d.
774. A similar example is provided by M. Devereux et al., *Pillar 2's Impact on Tax Competition*, SSRN 33 (Oxford University Centre of Business Taxation 26 Aug. 2022).
775. In the same vein, *see* Joachim Englisch, *supra* note 769, at 3.d.

Credits' increase the GloBE Income, there may be situations where the tax credit increases income above the SBIE, whereas, if the same credit were to qualify as a 'Non-Qualified Refundable Tax Credit', no 'Top-up Tax' would occur at all due to the lack of 'Excess Profits'.[776]

- **Intragroup Financing Arrangements:** Article 3.2.7. GloBE Model Rules, reflected in Article 16(8) GloBE-Directive, provides for a special rule addressing so-called Intragroup Financing Arrangements. The underlying problem of such 'Intragroup Financing Arrangements'[777] is the fact that in the course of a transaction between CEs, which are members of the same 'MNE Group', an expense of a 'Low-Tax Entity'[778] does not lead to an increase of the taxable income of the 'High-tax Counterparty'[779] (which is a CE of the same 'MNE Group') within the duration of such an arrangement. According to the Commentary, the rule thus aims to prevent '*MNE Groups from engaging in transactions that are intended to increase the ETR in a jurisdiction that is below the Minimum Rate by reducing the GloBE Income or Loss in such jurisdiction without increasing the taxable income of the counterparty to the arrangement. A payment should not be treated as increasing the taxable income of a High-tax Counterparty if it is eligible for an exclusion, exemption, deduction or credit or other tax benefit under local law and the amount of that benefit is calculated by reference to the amount of payment received.*'[780] The rule is, therefore, reminiscent of Article 9(2) ATAD on the avoidance of hybrid mismatches in relation to so-called deduction non-inclusion cases. According to the Commentary on Article 3 GloBE Model Rules, such an 'Intragroup Financing Arrangement' might occur where a CE located in a high-tax jurisdiction subject to a domestic interest limitation rule lends money to a low-taxed CE:[781] If, for example, the high-tax jurisdiction has excess interest capacity from previous years (carry-forward of non-deductible interest expenses) which is not expected to be used, the interest payments received from the low-taxed CE would not increase the taxable income of the high-taxed CE, because the latter could offset the interest income received with the excess interest expenses from previous years. The consequence announced by Article 3.2.7. GloBE Model Rules and Article 16(8) GloBE-Directive is that the deduction of the expense at the 'Low-tax Entity' is to be denied by making a positive adjustment to the GloBE base. As it turns out, the provision is extremely complex, raises

776. *See*, in detail, M. Devereux et al., *supra* note 774, at 33–34.
777. *See* the definition of the term 'Intragroup Financing Arrangements' provided for in Art. 10.1. *GloBE Model Rules*, at 58. Within the GloBE-Directive the term is not defined separately, but is directly implemented in Art. 16(8) GloBE-Directive (2022/2523).
778. *See* the definition of 'Low-tax Entity' in Art. 10.1. *GloBE Model Rules*, at 60. Within the GloBE-Directive the term is not defined separately, but is directly implemented in Art. 16(8) GloBE-Directive (2022/2523).
779. *See* the definition of 'High-tax Counterparty' in Art. 10.1. *GloBE Model Rules*, at 58. Within the GloBE-Directive the term is not defined separately, but is directly implemented in Art. 16(8) GloBE-Directive (2022/2523).
780. *See GloBE Commentary on Article 3 GloBE Model Rules (2022)*, *supra* note 507, para. 127.
781. *Ibid.*

numerous questions[782] of interpretation and is unlikely to materialize, at least within the EU, especially since such situations are to be adjusted at the level of taxable income already due to the ATAD's hybrid mismatch rules. The Examples provide two specific cases on 'Intragroup Financing Arrangements'.[783]

- **Exclusion of certain insurance company income:** According to Article 3.2.9. GloBE Model Rules (Article 16[10] GloBE-Directive) an '*insurance company shall exclude from the computation of the GloBE Income of Loss amounts charged to policyholders for Taxes paid by the insurance company in respect of returns to policy holders*'.[784] Furthermore, such insurance companies shall include '*any returns to policyholders that are not reflected in the Financial Accounting Net Income or Loss to the extent the corresponding increase or decrease in liability to the policyholders is reflected in its Financial Accounting Net Income or Loss*'.[785] The Commentary attempts to explain the purpose of the provision in a somewhat unfortunate passage.[786] The essence of this passage can be summarized as follows: In many jurisdictions, insurance companies are subject to taxes levied on returns paid to policyholders (this refers, e.g., to interest from life insurance policies). Usually, such taxes are to be collected by the insurance company, which passes it on to the policyholder. In principle, there is no influence on the ETR: most accounting standards treat the returns as income of the insurance company leading to a corresponding expense due to the fact that the return is to be paid to the policyholder. With respect to the tax, this means that the tax expenses reduce the income of the insurance company but, at the same time, reduce the liability of the insurance company to pay the return to the policyholder, increasing the income of the insurance company, resulting in a '*net zero effect*'.[787] Some accounting standards, however, treat such taxes as income taxes leading to a tax expense without considering the reduction in policy liabilities. For the ETR, this means that the amount of 'Adjusted Covered Taxes' in the numerator increases and the GloBE base decreases, although the latter should, in fact, be increased by a reduction in the policy liability resulting in a profit of the insurance company. The Commentary thus notes that '*instead of offsetting the reduction in the policyholder liability with no effect on the ETR computation, the tax would effectively provide shelter from Top-up Tax to other low-taxed income earned by the insurance company*'.[788] GloBE solves this by excluding the charge of tax from

782. Unfortunately the Commentary is of limited help and merely replicates the relevant definitions of the GloBE Model Rules, *see Ibid.*, paras 128–132.
783. *See* Examples 3.2.7. - 1 and 3.2.7. - 2 *GloBE Examples*, at 30–31.
784. Art. 3.2.9. *GloBE Model Rules* and the corresponding provision of Art. 16(10) GloBE-Directive (2022/2523).
785. Art. 3.2.9. *GloBE Model Rules* and the corresponding provision of Art. 16(10) GloBE-Directive (2022/2523).
786. *See GloBE Commentary on Article 3*, *supra* note 507, paras 138–141.
787. *See Ibid.*, para. 139.
788. *See Ibid.*, para. 140.

the GloBE base as well as from the amount of the 'Adjusted Covered Taxes', whereby the effect just described cannot arise.[789]

- **Additional Tier One Capital:** Article 3.2.10. GloBE Model Rules (reflected in Article 16[11] GloBE-Directive) addresses a certain permanent difference arising with respect to specific prudential regulations in the banking[790] as well as the insurance[791] sector: 'Additional Tier One Capital' means an instrument issued by a CE, which is convertible to equity or written down if, for example, losses occur. Such 'Additional Tier One Capital' generally serves to ensure the liquidity of banks, e.g., in financial crises. But how could permanent differences materialize in such cases? According to the Commentary, 'Additional Tier One Capital' can lead to permanent differences due to the fact that many financial accounting standards treat such amounts as equity, whereas tax laws treat it as debt which enables the issuer to deduct interest expenses.[792] Thus, Article 3.2.10. GloBE Model Rules and Article 16(11) GloBE-Directive state that decreases in 'Additional Tier One Capital' shall be treated as an expense while increases are to be included in the computation of the GloBE Income or Loss ('net qualifying income or loss').
- **Adjustments with regard to Corporate Restructuring and Holding Structures and Tax neutrality and distribution regimes:** Both the GloBE Model Rules as well as the GloBE-Directive provide for separate chapters (Chapters 6 and 7 GloBE Model Rules and Chapters VI and VII GloBE-Directive) on corporate structurings and holding structures as well as tax neutrality and distribution regimes requiring specific adjustments[793] to the GloBE base determination.[794] However, those adjustments are specifically addressed in the respective chapters anyway. Consequently, the provision of Article 3.2.11. GloBE Model Rules is obsolete, which might be the reason for the fact that Article 16 GloBE-Directive does not contain a corresponding provision to Article 3.2.11. GloBE Model Rules. Rather, the individual adjustments are regulated in Articles 33 to 43 GloBE-Directive.

4.3.3.3.4 Adjustments to Ensure Consistency with the Arm's Length Principle

According to Article 3.2.3. GloBE Model Rules (reflected in Article 15(4) GloBE-Directive) '[a]*ny transaction between Constituent Entities located in different jurisdictions that is not recorded in the same amount in the financial accounts of both*

789. *See Ibid.*, para. 141.
790. *See Ibid.*, para. 142.
791. *See* the addition made with respect to insurance companies in para. 142 of the Commentary on Art. 3 GloBE Model Rules by the *GloBE Administrative Guidance February 2023*, at 74.
792. *GloBE Commentary on Article 3, supra* note 507, para. 143.
793. *See*, e.g., the adjustments to the GloBE Income or Loss foreseen in Art. 6.2.1.(c), Arts 7.1.1., 7.1.2., 7.2.1., 7.2.2. and 7.6. GloBE Model Rules and the corresponding provisions in Arts 34(3), 38(1), 38(2), 39(2), 39(3) and 43 GloBE-Directive. The list of provisions mentioned here is not exhaustive.
794. *See GloBE Commentary on Article 3, supra* note 507, para. 145.

Constituent Entities or that is not consistent with the Arm's Length Principle must be adjusted so as to be in the same amount consistent with the Arm's Length Principle'.[795] Furthermore, in the second sentence, it is added that *'a loss from a sale or other transfer of an asset between two Constituent Entities located in the same jurisdiction that is not recorded consistent with the Arm's Length Principle shall be recomputed based on the Arm's Length Principle if that loss is included in the computation of GloBE Income or Loss'*.[796] At first sight, the relation between the Arm's Length Principle and GloBE seems to be odd. Why is it necessary to apply the Arm's Length Principle between two CEs of the same 'MNE Group' if GloBE is applied to the whole Group anyway? Furthermore, profits or losses resulting from transactions between members of the same group are eliminated in the 'Consolidated Financial Statement' from the outset (so-called *intercompany eliminations*). So why does the determination of the GloBE base require the observance of the Arm's Length Principle?

First, the 'GloBE Income or Loss' ('net qualifying income or loss') of a CE is to be determined according to the financial statements prepared before consolidation or as Article 3.1.2. GloBE Model Rules (also *see* Article 15[1] GloBE-Directive) the GloBE base is to be determined *'before any consolidation adjustments eliminating intra-group transactions'*.[797] The separate statements of the CEs in preparation for consolidation, therefore, still include intra-group transactions. Second, jurisdictional blending alone requires an allocation of income among the CEs that is in line with the Arm's Length Principle: the jurisdiction-wise computation of the ETR requires that each income received by an 'MNE Group' is attributed to a specific jurisdiction. Since within the system of GloBE the income or loss is to be determined on the level of each individual CE, such attribution is to be carried out among CEs in accordance with the Arm's Length Principle. But how does GloBE achieve safe alignment with the Arm's Length Principle?

Article 3.2.3. GloBE Model Rules (Article 16[4] GloBE-Directives) requires adjusting the GloBE base if transactions between different CEs are either not recorded in the same amount in the financial statements of all involved CEs or are not consistent with the Arm's Length Principle. By doing so, the provision serves to prevent double taxation and double non-taxation: If a certain transfer price of a transaction is adjusted at the level of a single CE, the respective amount needs to be adjusted correspondingly at the level of the other involved CE as well; otherwise, intra-group transactions would distort the computation of the ETR: assume that a CE located in a low-tax jurisdiction (State A) delivers goods to a CE located in high-tax jurisdiction (State B) at a price of 100. The CE located in State A, thus, receives an income of 100, while the CE located in State B has an expense of 100. If, however, the Arm's Length Price would only amount to 50, State B would only allow the deduction of 50, which raises the amount of tax paid in State B. However, since GloBE solely relies on the financial accounts to

795. First sentence of Art. 3.2.3. *GloBE Model Rules*. Also *see* the first sentence of Art. 16(4) GloBE-Directive (2022/2523).
796. Second sentence of Art. 3.2.3. *GloBE Model Rules* Also *see* the second sentence of Art. 16(4) GloBE-Directive (2022/2523).
797. Article 3.1.2. *GloBE Model Rules* and Art. 15(1) GloBE-Directive (2022/2523).

determine GloBE Income, this would mean that the CE in State A would still have a GloBE Income of 100, potentially leading to a 'Top-up Tax' calculated from the full amount of 100. In this case, the 'Top-up Tax' would be levied on 100, although 50 has indeed been taxed in State B, leading to a double taxation caused by GloBE.[798] How does Article 3.2.3 GloBE Model Rules (Article 16[4] GloBE-Directive) solve the issue? The GloBE Income ('qualifying income') of the CE in State B would be increased for an amount of 50, while the CE located in State A would be permitted to reduce its income by an amount of 50. In this way, Article 3.2.3. GloBE Model Rules (Article 16[4] GloBE-Directive) prevents that the amount of 50 already being subject to tax in State B would be exposed to 'Top-up Tax' in State A again. As the Commentary aptly notes: '*Without this adjustment, the income included in the high-tax jurisdiction under local law would be subject to double taxation – once in the high-tax jurisdiction and again under the GloBE Rules.*'[799] However, vice versa to the example just given, transfer pricing adjustments may also result in double non-taxation, where certain income is neither included within the 'GloBE Income' of a CE nor exposed to potential 'Top-up Tax'.[800] Also, in these cases, Article 3.2.3. GloBE Model Rules (Article 16[4] GloBE-Directive) kick in to prevent the undesired impacts on the GloBE base determination. The functioning of the adjustments with respect to intra-group transactions in the various situations of potential double taxation and double non-taxation is clearly illustrated in the OECD Examples.[801] An adjustment must not be made if the adjustment itself causes double taxation or double non-taxation.[802]

Only between CEs 'located' within the same jurisdiction, the application of the Arm's Length Principle is usually not required for the purposes of GloBE because the income of CEs located within the same jurisdiction is aggregated in the course of the ETR computation anyway[803] and '*the shifting of income from one taxpayer to another within the same jurisdiction will* [thus] *generally not impact on the overall amount of income subject to tax in that jurisdiction*'.[804] Nevertheless, compliance with the arm's length principle also in between CEs located in the same jurisdiction is required according to the second sentence of Article 3.2.3. GloBE Model Rules and Article 16(4) GloBE-Directive, if losses '*from a sale or other transfer*'[805] of assets are included in the computation of the GloBE Income or Loss ('net qualifying income or loss') that are not recorded in line with the Arm's Length Principle. The purpose of the provision is not obvious. The Commentary merely notes: '*The rule is intended to prevent MNE Group's from manufacturing losses through sales or other transfers between Group members at*

798. *See* the similar example provided for in Example 3.2.3 – 2 *GloBE Examples*, at 28–29.
799. *See GloBE Commentary on Article 3*, *supra* note 507, para. 102.
800. *See Ibid.*, and Example 3.2.3 – 1 *GloBE Examples*, at 28–29.
801. Examples 3.2.3 – 1 to 3.2.3. – 2 *GloBE Examples*, at 28–29.
802. For the description of such situations *see GloBE Commentary on Article 3*, *supra* note 507, para. 103 and Example 3.2.3 – 3 *GloBE Examples*, at 28–29.
803. Article 5.1.2. *GloBE Model Rules* and Art. 26(2) GloBE-Directive (2022/2523).
804. *See GloBE Commentary on Article 3*, *supra* note 507, para. 106.
805. Second sentence of Art. 3.2.3. *GloBE Model Rules* and, very similar, Art. 16(4) GloBE-Directive (2022/2523).

prices that are not consistent with the Arm's Length Principle.'[806] It is unclear what the OECD had in mind in that respect.

Although neither Article 3.2.3. GloBE Model Rules nor Article 16(4) GloBE-Directive explicitly indicate that the Arm's Length Principle needs to be respected between CEs located in the same jurisdiction, besides the cases of transferred assets, the Arm's Length Principle, as the Commentary notes, must also be respected between MOCEs or 'Investment Entities' and other CEs of the same Group located in the same jurisdiction.[807] This is because the ETR of such entities is calculated as if they were located in a separate jurisdiction. Since both Article 3.2.3. GloBE Model Rules and Article 16(4) GloBE-Directive explicitly oblige to respect the Arm's Length Principle between CEs '*located in different jurisdictions*', it was not necessary to explicitly refer to those kinds of entities directly in Article 3.2.4. GloBE Model Rules and Article 16(4) GloBE-Directive; for GloBE purposes, MOCEs[808] and 'Investment Entities'[809] are considered to be located in 'different jurisdictions' anyway. Although not explicitly addressed in the Commentary, the same is true for 'Stateless Entities', which are considered to be located in a separate jurisdiction[810] as well and for 'Joint Ventures' for which the 'Top-up Tax' is calculated as '*if they were Constituent Entities of a separate MNE Group*'.[811]

4.3.3.3.5 Elections with Respect to Adjustments of Permanent Differences

All adjustments to permanent differences now under discussion have in common that they are mandatory. This is true for the final catalogue of permanent differences in Article 3.2.1. GloBE Model Rules (Article 16[2] GloBE-Directive), the specific adjustments in Article 3.2.4., 3.2.7., 3.2.9., 3.2.10, 3.2.11 GloBE Model Rules (Article 16[5], [8], [10], [11] GloBE-Directive) and for the inter-company transaction adjustments according to Article 3.2.3. GloBE Model Rules (Article 16[4] GloBE-Directive). In the meantime, however, Article 3.2. GloBE Model Rules (Article 16 GloBE-Directive) also provides for adjustments that are available at the election of certain CEs (Article 3.2.2., 3.2.5., 3.2.6. and 3.2.8 GloBE Model Rules and Article 16[3], [6], [7] and [9] GloBE-Directive). The elections apply to very specific situations but nevertheless have their commonalities: first, all elections, if exercised, are binding to all CEs within the same jurisdiction. This is a consequence of jurisdictional blending: Since GloBE takes a strict jurisdictional perspective, it would be odd if individual CEs in the same jurisdiction could exercise their elective rights differently. Although not explicitly addressed either by the GloBE Model Rules or the GloBE-Directive nor by the Commentary, under a systematic interpretation, the elections may very well be made separately in the case of exceptions from jurisdictional blending. Consequently, the

806. *See GloBE Commentary on Article 3, supra* note 507, para. 107.
807. *See Ibid.*, para. 108
808. Article 5.6.1 and Art. 5.6.2. *GloBE Model Rules* and Art. 31(2) and Art. 31(3) GloBE-Directive (2022/2523).
809. Article 5.1.3. *GloBE Model Rules* and Art. 26(3) GloBE-Directive (2022/2523).
810. Article 5.1.1. *GloBE Model Rules* and Art. 26(4) GloBE-Directive (2022/2523).
811. Article 6.4. *GloBE Model Rules* and Art. 36 GloBE-Directive (2022/2523).

elections can be made separately for MOCEs (or 'Minority Owned Subgroups') or 'Investment Entities' that are located in the same jurisdiction as other CEs of the same 'MNE Group' and for 'Stateless Entities' as well as 'Joint Ventures' that are also separated from jurisdictional blending. Second, all elections are made by specific CEs, either by a separate 'Filing Constituent Entity', which is a CE determined to file the so-called GloBE Information Return[812] for an MNE Group, or, in the case of the election provided for in Article 3.2.8. GloBE Model Rules and Article 16(9) GloBE-Directive, by the UPE. Third, all the elections impact the GloBE base determination over several 'Fiscal Years', which is why the elections are, apart from the election of Article 3.2.6. GloBE Model Rules (Article 16[7] GloBE-Directive), binding for five years (in the GloBE terminology, so-called Five-Year Elections[813]). The GloBE-Directive furthermore dedicates a separate Article 45 GloBE-Directive to the modalities of the elections provided for in Article 16 GloBE-Directive (besides the one provided for in Article 16[7] GloBE-Directive). In any case, these similarities should not obscure the fact that all elections have specific prerequisites, which are discussed below:

- **Election to correct permanent differences regarding stock-based compensations:** The first election is laid down in Article 3.2.2. GloBE Model Rules, as well as Article 16(3) GloBE-Directive, and applies to so-called Stock-based Compensations. The Commentary paraphrases the rationale of this election as follows: '*In many jurisdictions, a corporation is entitled to deduct for tax purposes the value of stock-based compensation that it paid based on the market value of the stock when it is exercised.*'[814] '*For financial accounting purposes, companies generally account for stock-based compensation based on the present value of the stock option at the time of issuance and amortise that amount over the exercise period. [...] If the market value of the stock increases* [...], *the corporation will deduct an amount for tax purposes that is higher than the amount of expenses for financial accounting purposes, which is a permanent difference.*'[815] The Commentary, thus, fears that '[t]*his disparity* [...] *would often depress the GloBE ETR, in some cases below the Minimum Rate*'.[816] To eliminate the negative impact of deductibility of stock-based compensation under domestic laws, Article 3.2.2. GloBE Model Rules reflected in Article 16(3) GloBE-Directive allow to elect that the deduction of stock-based compensation is also considered in the GloBE base as a reduction of the 'GloBE Income or Loss' ('net qualifying income or loss'). Interestingly, the term 'Stock-based compensation' is not further defined either in the GloBE Model Rules or the GloBE-Directive. In any case, the scope of the provision is

812. This is a standardised return, which is still to be developed by OECD in the course of the GloBE Implementation Framework, *see* the definition of 'GloBE Information Return' in Art. 10.1. *GloBE Model Rules*, at 57. Also *see* the definition of 'filing constituent entity' in Art. 3(8) and the provisions on 'Filing obligations' in Art. 44 GloBE-Directive (2022/2523).
813. A 'Five-Year Election' is defined as an election 'that cannot be revoked with respect to the election year or the four succeeding Fiscal Years', *see* Art. 10.1. *GloBE Model Rules*, at 56.
814. *See GloBE Commentary on Article 3 GloBE Model Rules (2022)*, *supra* note 507, para. 87.
815. *See Ibid.*, para. 88.
816. *See Ibid.*, para. 89.

circumscribed in the Commentary where it is held that '[t]*he scope of the election is limited to compensation expenditures in the form of stock, stock options, stock warrants (or an equivalent) where the amount allowed as an expense is computed differently for local tax purposes than for financial accounting purposes*'.[817] The election is binding for five 'Fiscal Years' and applies to all CEs located within the same jurisdiction.

- **Election to use realization method in lieu of fair value accounting:** Much less specific is the option in Article 3.2.5 GloBE Model Rules and Article 16(6) GloBE-Directive, which allows MNE groups to apply the realization method for assets and liabilities for GloBE purposes, although the fair value method or impairment method is applied for those assets in the financial accounts. This election is likely to be the most important of the elections provided for in Article 3.2. GloBE Model Rules and Article 15 GloBE-Directive: Many tax jurisdictions do not valuate assets and liabilities according to their fair values but rather apply the realization method leading to significant permanent differences: If a CE buys an investment property at a price of 100, both financial accounting rules as well as tax laws usually require that the asset be reported at its cost of 100. Under national tax law, the asset is depreciated over a certain useful life in subsequent years. Changes in value in subsequent years are generally only recognized for tax purposes upon realization. Under common 'Acceptable Financial Accounting Standards' including the IFRS, the fair value method may be applied with respect to such assets obliging to report any changes in value with respect to the underlying assets. If, for example, the value of the investment property rises to 120 in the following year, the 20 in value increase would be reflected in the GloBE base as well, whereas the 20 are not taxed under domestic tax laws. By increasing 'GloBE Income', the ETR would be significantly depressed. In this case, the fair value election of Article 3.2.5 GloBE Model Rules and Article 16(6) GloBE-Directive provide for a solution: The value change of 20 would, by means of an adjustment, be removed from the financial accounts so that the increase in fair value is not reflected in the ETR fraction anymore. Only if the asset is realized the respective gain would directly flow into the ETR calculation.[818] In any case, as the Commentary clearly states, the purpose of the provision is '*to reduce volatility by allowing the taxpayer to crystallise the gain for GloBE purposes as the actual date of disposition rather than from one period to the next in line with the accounting treatment*'.[819] It can be assumed that many MNE Groups applying the fair value method will consider taking the GloBE fair value election to mitigate the temporal effects of fair value and impairment accounting.With respect to the scope of the election, it is important to note again that this election also applies to all CEs within the same jurisdiction (besides the exceptions listed above), so it is not possible to carve-out individual CEs from

817. *See Ibid.*, para. 90.
818. On this principle *see Ibid.*, para. 116.
819. *See Ibid.*, para. 117.

its effects. Furthermore, the election '*generally applies with respect to all assets and liabilities*'[820] that are subject to fair value or impairment accounting. Both Article 3.2.5 GloBE Model Rules and Article 16(6) GloBE-Directive, however, allow for a limitation to apply the election only to tangible assets or to 'Investment Entities'.[821] The election can only be revoked after five years. In such a case, the respective CEs 'GloBE Income or Loss needs to be adjusted by the difference between the fair value of the asset or liability in the year the election was made and the carrying value of the asset or liability determined pursuant to the election.[822]

- **Election to spread gains arising from the disposal of immovable property over five years:** If a CE sells immovable property within a single fiscal year, this may have a significant impact on the amount of 'GloBE Income or Loss' ('net qualifying income or loss'). To mitigate the effects of increasing values that accumulated over several 'Fiscal Years', Article 3.2.6. GloBE Model Rules and Article 16(7) GloBE-Directive provide for an election to offset such gains against losses from the sale of immovable property (within the GloBE Model Rules, the so-called Local Tangible Asset[823]) from previous years.[824] If a certain amount of gains that cannot be offset against previous losses[825] remains, the respective gains may be spread pro-rated over a 'Look-back Period'[826] of the election year and the previous four 'Fiscal Years'.[827] Since the 'Top-up Tax' allocation requires allocating the 'Top-up Tax' to specific entities (*see* section 4.4.2.8), both Article 3.2.6. GloBE Model Rules and Article 16(7) GloBE-Directive provide for a formula to allocate the gains among the CEs of the same jurisdiction to which the election applies.[828] The policy justification for the election is simple: By allowing to net and spread high gains from the disposal of immovable property over several 'Fiscal years', the GloBE base determination '*provides* [for] *a better measure of whether the MNE Group has been subject to a minimum level of tax in the jurisdiction over that period*'.[829] It is obvious

820. *See Ibid.*, para. 115.
821. *See Ibid.*
822. *See* explicitly Art. 3.2.5. *GloBE Model Rules* and the last sentence of Art. 16(6) GloBE-Directive (2022/2523). For further explanation *see GloBE Commentary on Article 3, supra* note 507, para. 118.
823. The term 'Local Tangible Asset' is defined as '*immovable property located in the same jurisdiction as the Constituent Entity*', *see* Art. 10.1. *GloBE Model Rules*, at 60. The Commission did well not to adopt this unnecessarily complex interweaving of different legal definitions. Art. 16(7) of the GloBE-Directive simply refers to 'immovable property'.
824. Article 3.2.6.(b) and (c) *GloBE Model Rules* and second subparagraph of Article 16(7) GloBE-Directive (2022/2523). *See* the explanation provided for in *GloBE Commentary on Article 3, supra* note 507, paras 122–123.
825. Article 3.2.6.(d) *GloBE Model Rules* and for further details on the 'spread' of the remaining net gains, *see GloBE Commentary on Article 3, supra* note 507, para. 124.
826. *See* the definition of 'Look-back Period' in Art. 10.1. *GloBE Model Rules*, at 60.
827. *See* Example 3.2.6 – 1 in *GloBE Examples*, at 29–30.
828. *See* the formula provided for in Art. 3.2.6.(d) *GloBE Model Rules*. Within the GloBE-Directive the same formula is verbalized in the last sentence of the third subparagraph of Art. 16(7) GloBE-Directive (2022/2523).
829. *See GloBE Commentary on Article 3, supra* note 507, para. 119.

that this election is closely related to the fair value election provided for in Article 3.2.5. GloBE Model Rules and Article 16(6) GloBE-Directive: If fair value or impairment accounting is used within the financial statements of a CE, the 'Filing Constituent Entity' can elect to use the realization method for the purposes of GloBE and may then make use of the election to offset the gain against losses from previous years and spread the remaining gains among the current and the previous four 'Fiscal Years'. The Commentary also explicitly states that the options in Article 3.2.5 and 3.2.6 GloBE Model Rules (Article 16[6] and [7] GloBE-Directive) may be combined.[830] For the purpose of the immovable property gain election, the respective gains or losses ('Net Asset Gain'[831] or 'Net Asset Loss'[832]) are aggregated among all CEs located within the same jurisdiction ('Aggregated Asset Gain'[833]) and the 'Fiscal Year' in which the election is made. The reduction of the 'GloBE Income or Loss' ('qualifying income or loss') by spreading the gains over several years necessarily requires a mirror adjustment of the amount of 'Adjusted Covered Taxes' by excluding the amount of 'Covered Taxes' in the numerator of the ETR fraction.[834] Otherwise, the election would overestimate the ETR. Technically, this is explicitly regulated in Article 3.2.6.(a). GloBE Model Rules, requiring the exclusion of any current tax expense with respect to excluded income. Within the GloBE-Directive, the corresponding provision, in deviation from the GloBE Model Rules, can be found within the rules on the computation of the 'Covered Taxes' in Article 20(3) GloBE-Directive directly referring to the election of Article 16(7) GloBE-Directive.[835] As a result, any 'Covered Taxes' on the gains for which the option is exercised will not be reflected in the ETR fraction. The Commentary justifies this approach on the one hand by the need for simplification and, on the other, by the preferential effects of the carry-back allowance: '*Determining the amount of Covered Taxes to apportion to each year would be unduly cumbersome and the allowance of a carry-back tailored to match losses in prior years is a substantial benefit.*'[836] In any case, this reveals that the option provided for in Article 3.2.6. GloBE Model Rules and Article 16(7) GloBE-Directive has a major drawback: any 'Covered Taxes' levied on the gains of immovable property get lost as a consequence of the election. The election is, therefore, particularly advantageous in jurisdictions that tax gains from immovable property more favourably than other income or where losses have been realised in the past from the disposition of such assets. Conversely, it is not advisable to make use of this option if the gains are taxed at a higher rate than other streams of income.The scope of the election provided for in Article 3.2.6. GloBE Model Rules and Article 16(7) GloBE-Directive is limited to

830. *See Ibid.*, para. 120.
831. *See* the definition of 'Net Asset Gain' in Art. 10.1. *GloBE Model Rules*, at 61.
832. *See* the definition of 'Net Asset Loss' in Art. 10.1. *Ibid.*
833. *See* the definition of 'Aggregate Asset Gain' in Art. 10.1. *Ibid.*, at 52.
834. *See GloBE Commentary on Article 3*, *supra* note 507, para. 125.
835. Further on this issue, *see* s. 4.3.4.2.
836. *See GloBE Commentary on Article 3*, *supra* note 507, para. 125

gains from immovable property located in the same jurisdiction as the CE. Consequently, the election is neither applicable to gains from immovable property of a CE located in a different jurisdiction nor to gains from movable assets.[837] Furthermore, the election is explicitly limited to transfer of immovable property between Group Members and third parties, excluding intra-group transfers of immovable property.[838] This is '*because the spread period includes all years in which Constituent Entities held the property*'.[839] If intra-group transfers of real estate between companies located in the same country were permitted, the same gains or losses would be recognized more than once. It is interesting that the scope of the term 'disposal of immovable property' is not further defined. This leaves the question of whether the election also applies, e.g., to the disposal of housing and building rights or long-term leasing agreements. Does it depend on domestic law to define the scope of 'disposal of immovable property'? Since the Commentary is silent on that issue, the question can be affirmed with regard to non-EU jurisdictions. Within the scope of the GloBE-Directive, the term is to be interpreted autonomously from the GloBE-Directive and cannot be understood as a reference to domestic law. Finally, as with all interpretative issues regarding the GloBE-Directive, the Court of Justice of the European Union (CJEU) has jurisdiction to define the scope of this election. Contrary to the other elections provided for in Article 3.2. GloBE Model Rules and Article 16 GloBE-Directive, the immovable property gain election is an 'Annual Election' and is not binding for subsequent fiscal years. Consequently, the 'Filing Constituent Entity' can decide each year whether the election should be taken or not. However, what truly distinguishes the immovable property gain election from the other elections provided for in Article 3.2. GloBE Model Rules and Article 16 GloBE-Directive is the fact that the usage of the election requires a re-calculation of the ETR for the 'Look-back period' leading to an 'Additional Current Top-up Tax' (within the GloBE-Directive 'additional top-up tax') according to Articles 5.4.1. and 29 GloBE-Directive (*see* section 4.4.2.6.) if the election leads to a fall of the ETR below the minimum tax rate in one of the 'Fiscal Years' in the respective 'Look-back Period'.[840]

- **Election to apply consolidation accounting treatment with respect to domestic tax consolidation group:** According to Article 3.2.8 GloBE Model Rules and Article 16(9) GloBE-Directive, a UPE '*may elect to apply its consolidated accounting treatment to eliminate to eliminate income, expense, gains,*

837. This is revealed in the definition of the term 'Local Tangible Asset', *see* Art. 10.1. *GloBE Model Rules*, at 60. Within the GloBE-Directive this is clarified directly within the first sentence of Art. 16(7) GloBE-Directive (2022/2523). On the purpose of this limitation, *see GloBE Commentary on Article 3*, *supra* note 507, para. 120.
838. This is revealed in the definition of the term 'Aggregate Asset Gain', *see* Art. 10.1. *GloBE Model Rules*, at 52. Within the GloBE-Directive this is clarified directly within the first sentence of Art. 16(7) GloBE-Directive (2022/2523).
839. *See GloBE Commentary on Article 3*, *supra* note 507, para. 120.
840. *See Ibid.*, para. 124.

and losses from transactions between Constituent Entities that are located, and included in a tax consolidation group, in the same jurisdiction for purposes of computing each such Constituent Entity's Net GloBE Income or Loss'.[841] The election clearly aims to simplify the ETR computation in jurisdictions that apply a consolidation or group tax relief regime.[842] Once the option is taken, there is no need for adjustments with respect to transactions between the CEs covered by the election. Only when the election is made or revoked are adjustments necessary to '*ensure that there is no duplication or omission of items of the GloBE Income or Loss*'.[843] Again, the election is limited to transactions between CEs located within the same jurisdiction, excluding those CEs that are excluded from jurisdictional blending for which the election can be made separately. Transactions between CEs and third parties[844] or other CEs located in different jurisdictions still need to be in line with the Arm's Length Principle (Article 3.2.3. GloBE Model Rules and Article 16[4] GloBE-Directive).[845] Although the election is to be made by the UPE, this does not mean that the election is limited to those CEs that are located in the same jurisdiction as the UPE. Rather, the UPE of an 'MNE Group' may take the election with respect to every jurisdiction where the CEs of the 'Group' are located. It is not clear why only the UPE and not another 'Filing Constituent Entity' is permitted to exercise the election.

4.3.3.4 Industry-Specific Carve-Out for Ship Operators: The Shipping Income Exclusion

Are there industries or specific sectors that should not be subject to the global minimum tax? This issue was already discussed when GloBE came into existence and was promptly included as a major point of discussion in the November 2019 Public Consultation Document, which even dedicated a separate chapter to carve-outs.[846] Not surprisingly, strong business representatives from a wide range of industries have jumped on the bandwagon, lobbying for various exemptions with a variety of alleged justifications and putting them up for discussion. Industries that requested an industry-specific carve-out included the financial services sector, gambling, the non-profit sector, and shipping, just to name a few of them.[847]

However, it was evident that every exemption of specific sectors is clearly at odds with the object and purpose of a global minimum tax. What is the point of a global minimum tax if individual sectors are exempted again anyway? In addition, before

841. Article 3.2.8. *GloBE Model Rules* and Art. 16(9) GloBE-Directive (2022/2523).
842. *See GloBE Commentary on Article 3, supra* note 507, para. 133.
843. *See Ibid.*, para. 137.
844. *See Ibid.*, para. 134.
845. *See Ibid.*, para. 136.
846. *See* Chapter 4 in *Public Consultation Pillar Two 2019*, at 23–24.
847. For further reference, *see* V. Bendlinger, *Minimum Taxation – Ergebnisse der Konsultationen zum GloBE Proposal der OECD*, 32 SWI, *supra* note 187, at 30.

plans to implement GloBE in the framework of a directive became known,[848] the EU's prohibition of state aid[849] was seen as a hurdle for industry-specific carve-outs within the EU.[850] The OECD soon acknowledged these arguments from the consultation feedback and literature and did indeed address those within the Pillar Two Blueprint of October 2020: '*The GloBE rules are designed to apply to all operating businesses. The exclusion of any specific sector could raise additional BEPS risks and fairness issues among different business sectors and jurisdictions. This could undermine the effectiveness of the GloBE rules. However, the unique features of the international shipping industry will require further work on whether, and to what extent, the GloBE rules should apply to this industry.*'[851] But what are the 'unique features' that justify special treatment for the shipping industry? The Blueprint identified the following: first, the shipping industry is subject to special tax rules. This probably refers, on the one hand, to the fact that the Article 8 OECD MC contains a distinct distributive rule for 'International Shipping and Air Transport' and, on the other hand, to the fact that many IF Member States levy specific taxes to the shipping industry (e.g., tonnage taxes and other widespread alternative tax regimes) and exclude it from the scope of domestic CIT systems. Second, the Blueprint adds that also the '*capital intensive nature, the level of profitability and* [the] *long economic cycle*'[852] might be a justification for a specific carve-out. Third, the Blueprint argued '*that the revenue effect may be limited given the design includes an unlimited loss carry-forward, a formulaic substance-based carve-out and tonnage taxes would constitute covered taxes*'.[853] The Commentary to the GloBE Model Rules has adopted the Blueprint's arguments almost word for word.[854] Nevertheless, from a scientific point of view, one can doubt whether these so-called unique features are convincing justifications for an industry-specific carve-out.

In any case, what the Blueprint did not reveal was the design of the carve-out for the shipping industry. Finally, some of the sectors initially discussed as potential industry-specific carve-outs have been implemented by way of the catalogue of 'Excluded Entities' in Article 1.3. GloBE Model Rules (Article 2[3] GloBE-Directive), e.g., 'Non-profit Organisations' and the financial services industry with respect to 'Pension Funds', 'Investment Funds' and 'Real Estate Investment Vehicles' (in detail on 'Excluded Entities', *see* section 4.2.4.3). However, with respect to a particular income schedule, such as shipping income, an exemption by way of excluding certain legal entities would not make sense: a single legal entity may be involved in all kinds of business activities and may derive a wide variety of income streams. But how, then, should such an industry-specific carve-out be implemented?

848. According to Art. 107 TFEU '*any aid granted by a Member State or through State*' is incompatible with the internal market. Article 107 TFEU, thus, does not pose any limits to EU secondary law, because the EU is not a 'Member State', in detail *see* s. 6.2.2.2.
849. Article 107 TFEU.
850. V. Bendlinger, *supra* note 187, at 24.
851. *Tax Challenges Arising from Digitalisation – Report on Pillar Two Blueprint*, para. 110.
852. *Ibid.*, para. 111.
853. *Ibid.*, para. 112.
854. *See GloBE Commentary on Article 3 GloBE Model Rules (2022)*, *supra* note 507, para. 146.

GloBE has solved this problem through a specific 'International Shipping Income Exclusion' laid down in Article 3.3. GloBE Model Rules and Article 17 GloBE-Directive. Instead of excluding the legal entity itself, 'International Shipping Income' and the so-called Qualified Ancillary International Shipping Income are excluded from the GloBE base according to Article 3.3.1. GloBE Model Rules (Article 17[2] GloBE-Directive). Correspondingly, according to Article 4.1.3.(a) GloBE Model Rules (Article 21[3] GloBE-Directive), related taxes are also excluded from the amount of 'Adjusted Covered Taxes'. The numerator of the ETR fraction is thus reduced by taxes attributable to 'International Shipping Income', and the denominator is either reduced by the amount of positive 'International Shipping Income'[855] (or increased in case it is negative)[856].[857] In other words, GloBE simply ignores 'International Shipping Income' and the taxes levied on it for purposes of the ETR computation; but notably, just for these purposes, revenues from international shipping activity are very well included in the total revenue threshold as long as they are reported within the 'Consolidated Financial Statements' of the UPE. This confirms that the 'International Shipping Income Exclusion' is merely an adjustment to the 'GloBE Income or Loss' ('net qualifying income or loss') and works in the same way as adjustments of permanent differences listed in Article 3.2. GloBE Model Rules and Article 16 GloBE Model Rules, such as excluded dividends under Article 3.2.1.(b) GloBE Model Rules and Article 16(2)(b) GloBE-Directive. The 'International Shipping Income Exclusion' could just as well have been regulated in Article 3.2 GloBE Model Rules or Article 16 GloBE-Directive; perhaps the need for a comprehensive definition of 'International Shipping Income' and 'Qualified Ancillary Shipping Income' is the reason why a separate article was dedicated to GloBE's only industry-specific carve-out.

Finally, Article 3.3.2. GloBE Model Rules, reflected in Article 17(1)(a) GloBE-Directive, provides for an exhaustive catalogue of activities giving rise to 'International Shipping Income' obtained by a CE. The list heavily borrows from Article 8(1) OECD MC, the definition of 'international traffic' provided for in Article 3(1)(e) OECD MC and the Commentary on Article 8 OECD MC.[858] However, it is important to note that the ambits of GloBE's 'International Shipping Income Exclusion' and Article 8(1) OECD MC are not quite identical: Most importantly, the latter covers income from *shipping and air transportation* while GloBE only excludes income arising from international *shipping*. Income from air transportation very well is to be included in the computation of the 'GloBE Income or Loss'. Other nuances are revealed in the GloBE Commentary and will shortly be addressed below.

855. The operation of the shipping income exclusion is explained quite clearly in Example 3.3.1. – 1, *see GloBE Examples*, at 32.
856. *See* the last sentence of Art. 3.1.1. *GloBE Model Rules* and Art. 16(3) GloBE-Directive (2022/2523). Specifically on loss situations, *see GloBE Commentary on Article 3*, *supra* note 507, para. 150. Furthermore, the operation of the shipping income exclusion in loss situations is illustrated in Example 3.3.1. – 2 in *GloBE Examples*, at 33.
857. *See GloBE Commentary on Article 3*, *supra* note 507, para. 147.
858. *OECD Model Tax Convention on Income and on Capital: Commentary on Article 8* (21 Nov. 2017).

In any case, the following sources of income are listed to fall within the scope of 'International Shipping Income': (i) the transportation of passengers and cargo by ships that are operated in 'international traffic', whether the ship is owned leased or otherwise at the disposal of a CE;[859] (ii) or whether it is operated under so-called slot-chartering arrangements (this subtle, however, is missing within the GloBE-Directive);[860] (iii) the leasing of a ship on charter fully equipped, crewed and supplied;[861] (iv) the leasing of a ship to another CE;[862] (v) participation in a pool, a joint business or an international operating agency;[863] (v) the sale of a ship, provided that the ship has been held by the CE for at least one year[864] and the respective ship is used each for the transportation of passengers or cargo in 'international traffic'. All activities listed in Article 3.3.2. GloBE Model Rules and Article 17(1) GloBE-Directive, thus, have in common that they only give rise to excluded 'International Shipping Income' if they are not (i) '*obtained from the transportation of passengers or cargo by ships via inland waterways within the same jurisdiction*'[865] but (ii) are obtained in the course of 'international traffic'.[866] The latter term 'international traffic' is clearly drafted in line with Article 3(1)(e) OECD MC and, according to the GloBE Commentary, '*means any transport by a ship, except when the ship is operated solely between places within a single jurisdiction (regardless of whether such jurisdiction is the same jurisdiction as the one in which the Constituent Entity is located)*'.[867] The GloBE Commentary, however, also adds that this interpretation of 'international traffic' for purposes of GloBE slightly deviates from the definition provided for in Article 3(1)(e) OECD MC: According to the latter provision, the exception only applies if the operator of the ship is not a resident of the same jurisdiction. This difference in scope between Article 8(1) OECD MC and GloBE is best illustrated by means of an example: if a corporation resident in state A operates a ship between two harbours within state A, the respective income would not be covered by Article 8(1) OECD MC, due to the fact that 'international traffic' defined in Article 3(1)(e) OECD MC covers all shipping, except for income from transportation by ships (i) operated solely between places within a single jurisdiction and (ii) the enterprise operating the ship is not an enterprise of that state. Since the latter requirement is not fulfilled in the example just mentioned, the respective income

859. Article 3.3.2.(a) *GloBE Model Rules* and Art. 17(1)(a)(i) GloBE-Directive (2022/2523). In detail, *see GloBE Commentary on Article 3, supra* note 507, para. 156.
860. Article 3.3.2.(b) *GloBE Model Rules*. On the scope and understanding of 'slot-chartering agreements', *see GloBE Commentary on Article 3, supra* note 507, para. 155. Also *see* Art. 17(1)(a)(ii) GloBE-Directive (2022/2523).
861. Article 3.3.2.(c) *GloBE Model Rules* and Art. 17(1)(a)(iii) GloBE-Directive (2022/2523). In detail, *see GloBE Commentary on Article 3, supra* note 507, para. 156.
862. Article 3.3.2.(d) *GloBE Model Rules* and Art. 17(1)(a)(iv) GloBE-Directive (2022/2523). In detail, *see GloBE Commentary on Article 3, supra* note 507, para. 157.
863. Article 3.3.2.(e) *GloBE Model Rules* and Art. 17(1)(a)(v) GloBE-Directive (2022/2523). In detail, *see GloBE Commentary on Article 3, supra* note 507, para. 158.
864. Article 3.3.2.(f) *GloBE Model Rules* and Art. 17(1)(a)(vi) GloBE-Directive (2022/2523). In detail, *see GloBE Commentary on Article 3, supra* note 507, para. 159.
865. Explicitly *see* the last sentence of Art. 3.3.3. *GloBE Model Rules* and Art. 17(1)(a)(i) GloBE-Directive (2022/2523). Also *see GloBE Commentary on Article 3, supra* note 507, para. 151.
866. Every subtitle of Art. 3.3.3. *GloBE Model Rules* and Art. 17(1)(a) GloBE-Directive (2022/2523) explicitly requires that the respective income is obtained in the course of 'international traffic'.
867. *See GloBE Commentary on Article 3, supra* note 507, para. 152.

would still fall within the scope of 'international traffic' for the purposes of the OECD MC and would, thus, fall within the ambit of Article 8(1) OECD MC. Within GloBE, however, the respective income would not qualify as excluded 'International Shipping Income' because GloBE does not consider income from transportation solely between places within a jurisdiction to qualify as income related to 'international traffic'.

Finally, the question there remains, how the scope of the phrase '*operated solely between places within a single jurisdiction*' should be interpreted? Interestingly, the GloBE Commentary does not go into the details with respect to the scope of the inland waterway exception; only the Commentary on Article 3 OECD MC reveals details about its interpretation. Accordingly, shipping income does not arise from 'international traffic' '*when a ship* [...] *is operated in between two places* [...] *even if part of the transport takes place outside the State*'.[868] For the purposes of GloBE, this would mean that if, for example, a CE located in Germany operates a vessel cruising from New York to Los Angeles via the Panama Channel without a stop[869] in a non-US harbour, the income received from the transportation of passengers or cargo would not be excluded either by Article 3.3. Model Rules or by Article 17 GloBE-Directive. Since there are differences regarding the understanding of the term 'international traffic', one could doubt whether one can interpret the term 'international traffic' along the lines of the Commentary on the OECD MC. However, since the GloBE Commentary explicitly states that it '*adopts a qualified income approach based on the scope of Article 8 of the OECD Model Tax Convention*', one can indeed assume that the drafters of GloBE had the Commentary on Articles 3 and 8 OECD MC in mind. For this reason, one can argue that the scope of the international shipping exclusion should be interpreted along the lines of the Commentary on the OECD MC unless the GloBE Model Rules and the GloBE Commentary make clear that they deliberately decided to deviate from Article 3(1)(e) and Article 8 OECD MC.

Operating ships requires much more than solely cruising a ship from one harbour to the next: a container ship needs to be loaded and unloaded, ships must be repaired, tickets have to be sold, etc. Thus, it would be odd to only exclude 'International Shipping Income' from sources listed in Article 3.3.2 GloBE Model Rules and Article 17(1)(a) GloBE-Directive without also excluding income that is closely connected to such streams of income. In line with the Commentary on Article 8 OECD MC, Article 3.3.3. GloBE Model Rules and Article 17(1)(b) GloBE-Directive also exclude so-called Qualified Ancillary International Shipping Income, which covers income from listed activities '*that are performed primarily in connection with the transportation of passengers or cargo by ships in international traffic*',[870] including income from (i) leasing of a ship on a bareboat charter basis to another shipping enterprise that is not a CE, provided that the charter does not exceed three years,[871] (ii) sales of tickets issued

868. *OECD Model Tax Convention on Income and on Capital: Commentary on Article 3*, para. 6.4 (21 Nov. 2017).
869. *Ibid.*
870. First sentence of Art. 3.3.3. *GloBE Model Rules* and correspondingly in Art. 17(1)(a) GloBE-Directive (2022/2523).
871. Article 3.3.3.(a) *GloBE Model Rules* and Art. 17(1)(b)(i) GloBE-Directive (2022/2523). In detail, *see GloBE Commentary on Article 3*, *supra* note 507, paras 163–164.

by other shipping enterprises for the domestic leg of an international voyage,[872] (iii) leasing or short-term storage of containers or detention charges for the late return of containers,[873] (iv) provision of services to other shipping enterprises (e.g., by engineers, maintenance staff, cargo handlers, catering staff and customer services personal)[874] and (v) investment income where the investment is made as an integral part of the continued operation of the ships in international traffic.[875] Like the list provided in Article 3.3.2. GloBE Model Rules (Article 17[1][a] GloBE-Directive), the list of ancillary shipping activities is exhaustive. Other sources of income, even if it would be conceivable to consider them as 'ancillary', are not excluded according to Article 3.3.3. GloBE Model Rules and Article 17(1)(b) GloBE-Directive. This is, for example, true for ancillary inland transportation related to international shipping income, which would be covered by Article 8 OECD MC according to the Commentary on Article 8 OECD MC (so-called Pick-up/drop-off services).[876] However, the GloBE Commentary explicitly notes that such income shall, in deviation to Article 8 OECD MC, not be excluded according to Article 3.3. GloBE Model Rules to avoid unintended distortive effects.[877]

Furthermore, according to Article 3.3.4. GloBE Model Rules and Article 17(4) GloBE-Directive, the aggregated 'Qualified Ancillary International Shipping Income' '*shall not exceed 50% of those Constituent Entities' International Shipping Income*'. The purpose of the 50% limitation is obvious: the shipping income exclusion should primarily protect activity in genuine international shipping operations[878] and should not enable income to be deliberately declared from non-shipping sources as excluded income to artificially provide shelter for low-taxed income. Due to this limitation, it indeed matters whether income is qualified as 'International Shipping Income' or as 'Qualified Ancillary International Shipping Income'. To finally determine the monetary limit of 50% of 'International Shipping Income', it is also necessary to compute the net income covered by Article 3.3.2. GloBE Model Rules (Article 17[1][a] GloBE-Directive) and Article 3.3.3. GloBE Model Rules (Article 17[1][b] GloBE-Directive) separately from each other.[879] Thus, costs also need to be allocated to either genuine or ancillary shipping income.[880] Furthermore, the wording of Article 3.3.4. GloBE Model Rules and Article 17(4) GloBE-Directive clarify that the limitation is to be applied jurisdiction-wise.[881] If a 'MNE Group' has more than one CE in a jurisdiction that receives 'International Shipping Income', ancillary income sources may be blended among the

872. Article 3.3.3.(b) *GloBE Model Rules* and Art. 17(1)(b)(ii) GloBE-Directive (2022/2523). In detail, *see GloBE Commentary on Article 3, supra* note 507, para. 165.
873. Article 3.3.3.(c) *GloBE Model Rules* and Art. 17(1)(b)(iii) GloBE-Directive (2022/2523). In detail, *see GloBE Commentary on Article 3, supra* note 507, para. 166.
874. Article 3.3.3.(d) *GloBE Model Rules* and Art. 17(1)(b)(iv) GloBE-Directive (2022/2523). In detail, *see GloBE Commentary on Article 3, supra* note 507, para. 167.
875. Article 3.3.3.(e) *GloBE Model Rules* and Art. 17(1)(b)(v) GloBE-Directive (2022/2523). In detail, *see GloBE Commentary on Article 3, supra* note 507, paras 168–170.
876. *See OECD Model Tax Convention on Income and on Capital: Commentary on Article 8, supra* note 858, para. 7.
877. *See GloBE Commentary on Article 3, supra* note 507, para. 171.
878. *See Ibid.*, para. 172
879. *See Ibid.*, para. 173.
880. Article 3.3.5. *GloBE Model Rules* and Article 17(5) GloBE-Directive (2022/2523).
881. *See GloBE Commentary on Article 3, supra* note 507, para. 173.

CEs for purposes of this limitation. Indeed, it makes sense to apply the limitation from a jurisdictional perspective: if a CE engaged in international shipping outsources any ancillary activities to a different legal entity, the latter would almost always exceed the 50% limitation, although, from a jurisdictional perspective, the ancillary income would be less than 50% of the 'International Shipping Income' received in that jurisdiction. Should the 'Qualified Ancillary International Shipping Income' exceed the thresholds of Article 3.3.4. GloBE Model Rules and Article 17(4) GloBE-Directive, the excess amount remains within the GloBE base.[882] Also, the 'Covered Taxes' with respect to this excess amount of 'Qualified Ancillary International Shipping Income' (that would otherwise be excluded from the amount of 'Covered Taxes' as well)[883] remains within the amount of 'Covered Taxes'.[884] If there are more than one CEs in a jurisdiction receiving shipping income, the excess amount is to be allocated among the respective CEs in proportion to their 'Qualified Ancillary International Shipping Income'.[885]

Both terms 'International Shipping Income' and 'Qualified Ancillary International Shipping Income' are to be understood as net income, which is why costs are also to be excluded from the GloBE base.[886] Thus, according to Article 3.3.5. GloBE Model Rules and Article 17(5) GloBE-Directive any direct costs[887] incurred by a CE that are attributable to such income are deductible for the purposes of GloBE. Any indirect costs that are attributable to either 'International Shipping Income' or 'Qualified Ancillary International Shipping Income' may be deducted as well; however, such costs '*shall be allocated on the basis of a Constituent Entity's revenues from such activities in proportion to its total revenues*'.[888] The Commentary provides several numerical examples that illustrate the allocation of direct and indirect costs for the purpose of Article 3.3. GloBE Model Rules (Article 17 GloBE-Directive) in general and, more specifically, also for the computation of the 50% limit provided for in Article 3.3.5. GloBE Model Rules (Article 17[5] GloBE-Directive).[889]

Furthermore, both terms 'International Shipping Income' and 'Qualified Ancillary International Shipping Income', although exhaustively defined in Article 3.3.2. and 3.3.3. GloBE Model Rules (Article 17[1][a] and [b] GloBE-Directive) leave certain room for interpretation, and there is no need to provide evidence that the exclusion of a specific category of income necessarily entails risks of abuse. For this reason, both Article 3.3.6. GloBE Model Rules and Article 17(2) GloBE-Directive provide for the exclusion of shipping income only on condition that the CE '*demonstrate*[s] *that the strategic or commercial management of all ships concerned is effectively carried on from*

882. The operation of the 50% limitation for 'Qualified Ancillary International Shipping Income' is further illustrated in Example 3.3.1. – 2 in *GloBE Examples*, at 32–33.
883. Article 4.1.3.(a) *GloBE Model Rules* and Art. 21(3)(a) GloBE-Directive (2022/2523). In detail on this provision, *see* s. 4.3.4.4.1.
884. *See GloBE Commentary on Article 4 GloBE Model Rules (2022)*, para. 9.
885. *See GloBE Commentary on Article 3, supra* note 507, para. 173
886. *See* the last sentence of Art. 3.3.5. *GloBE Model Rules* and Art. 17(6) GloBE-Directive (2022/2523).
887. For an illustration of directly attributable costs, *see GloBE Commentary on Article 3, supra* note 507, paras 174–175.
888. Second sentences of Art. 3.3.5. *GloBE Model Rules* and Art. 17(5) GloBE-Directive (2022/2523).
889. *See GloBE Commentary on Article 3, supra* note 507, paras 176–179.

within the jurisdiction where the Constituent Entity is located'.[890] According to the Commentary, this requirement is called a '*substance criterion*' that aims to '*establish an economic link*' between the shipping company and the respective jurisdiction.[891] The Commentary also tries to define the scope of the term '*strategic or commercial management*', which, nevertheless, remains difficult to grasp.[892] It seems that the quintessence of this '*substance criterion*' is that '[t]*he mere fact that a vessel is flagged in a particular jurisdiction* [should] *not* [be] *a relevant factor in the determination of whether strategic or commercial management is effectively carried on from within that jurisdiction*'.[893] Nevertheless, the ambivalence of the exclusion for shipping income becomes evident here: every industry-specific carve-out might leave tax planning leeways. Article 3.3.6. GloBE Model Rules and Article 17(2) GloBE-Directive are supposed to close these leeways, probably with limited success. The scope of '*strategic or commercial management*' remains vague and still leaves interpretative loopholes. In the author's opinion, this so-called *substance criterion* is emblematic of the tax policy inconsistency of the industry-specific carve-out for shipping income.

4.3.3.5 Allocation of Income or Loss Between a Main Entity and a PE

According to Article 3.1. GloBE Model Rules and Article 15 GloBE-Directive the GloBE Income or Loss (within the GloBE-Directive the 'qualifying income or loss') is the 'Financial Accounting Net Income or Loss' determined for the CE in preparation for consolidation within the 'Consolidated Financial Statement' of the UPE. While Article 3.2. and 3.3. GloBE Model Rules (Articles 16 are 17 GloBE-Directive) are dedicated to the adjustments necessary to eliminate permanent differences and to compute the 'GloBE Income or Loss' for GloBE's ETR computation, jurisdictional blending also results in the need for territorial delimitability of income. What income and costs are attributable to which CEs? While it is true that GloBE, by its very purpose, does not primarily care about the distribution of taxing powers, the ETR still needs to be computed per jurisdiction, which is why every income also needs to be clearly allocated to a specific jurisdiction. In principle, GloBE solves this issue by referring to the Arm's Length Principle: any transactions between CEs of the same 'MNE Group' are to be processed according to the Arm's Length Principle as required by Article 3.2.3 GloBE Model Rules and Article 16(4) GloBE-Directive. The Arm's Length Principle, thus, serves to correctly allocate income or losses among jurisdictions to exactly calculate the ETR on a jurisdictional basis.

However, as already extensively discussed in section 4.2.4.1.2., GloBE also considers PEs to be separate CEs. For this reason, like when applying Article 7 OECD MC, the application of GloBE requires the allocation of the income of legal entities qualifying as CEs between their 'Main Entities' and their PEs 'located' in different jurisdictions. With respect to the allocation of income between the 'Main Entity' and its

890. Article 3.3.6. *GloBE Model Rules* and correspondingly Art. 17(2) GloBE-Directive (2022/2523).
891. *See GloBE Commentary on Article 3, supra* note 507, para. 180.
892. *See Ibid.*, paras 181–185.
893. *See Ibid.*, para. 182.

foreign PEs, the Arm's Length Principle is of little help. Rather, the PE concept fictitiously divides the taxable income of a corporate taxpayer between the jurisdictions in which the corporate taxpayer conducts its business. This, however, is at odds with GloBE's reliance on financial accounts: financial accounts are prepared for legal entities, which means that, as the Commentary well recognizes, '*financial accounting information may not always be separately maintained in respect of the PE*'.[894] For this reason, the case of PEs within the framework of GloBE has already been identified as the most representative example of the complex interrelationship between accounting and tax rules as created by GloBE in section 4.3.2.3. But how does GloBE resolve the allocation of income between the 'Main Entity' and foreign PEs of a CE? What is the 'Financial Accounting Net Income or Loss' to be determined according to Article 3.1.1. GloBE Model Rules and Article 15(1) GloBE-Directive for a CE that is not a legal entity but a PE?

The territorial delimitation of the GloBE Income or Loss ('qualified net income or loss') is governed by Article 3.4. GloBE Model Rules and Article 18 GloBE-Directive, which are aimed at following '*the accounting treatment* [...] *as far as possible*',[895] however, making the accounting treatment '*subject to the income and expense allocation rules under a Tax Treaty or domestic tax law*'.[896] The reference to both tax treaties as well as domestic laws relates to the type of PE at issue and, finally, the allocation of income to PEs, according to Article 3.4. GloBE Model Rules and Article 18 GloBE-Directive, is also linked to the respective type of PE. Although GloBE's definition of the term PE[897] and the 'location' of PEs has extensively been discussed above,[898] it is, thus, necessary to once again distinguish the different types of PEs that are considered separate CEs under GloBE. GloBE distinguishes (i) *PEs under an applicable tax treaty* which are places of businesses that are situated in a jurisdiction and are treated as a PE in accordance with an applicable tax treaty in force which provides for a distributive rule for business profits similar to Article 7 OECD MC,[899] (ii) *PEs under domestic laws* that are places of businesses considered as and taxed like a PE under domestic law, although no tax treaty is in force,[900] (iii) *PEs not being subject to CIT at their place of establishment* that are places of businesses established in a jurisdiction having no corporate income tax system at all and if the respective place of business would be treated as a PE under Article 7 OECD MC[901] and (iv) *exterritorial PEs* that are places of businesses which operate outside the jurisdiction where the Entity is located but are

894. *See Ibid.*, para. 186.
895. *See Ibid.*, para. 187.
896. *See Ibid.*
897. In detail on the definitions of 'Main Entity' and PEs for the purposes of GloBE, *see* s. 4.2.4.1.2.
898. *See* s. 4.2.4.4.3.
899. Letter a of the PE definition in Art. 10.1. *GloBE Model Rules*, at 60. Also *see* letter a of Art. 3(13) GloBE-Directive (2022/2523).
900. Letter b of the PE definition in Art. 10.1. *GloBE Model Rules*, at 60 Also *see* letter b of Art. 3(13) GloBE-Directive (2022/2523).
901. Letter c of the PE definition in Art. 10.1. *GloBE Model Rules*, at 60 Also *see* letter c of Art. 3(13) GloBE-Directive (2022/2523).

exempt by this jurisdiction from CIT.[902] The respective category of the PE then determines according to which rules the profits are to be attributed to the PE.

Regarding (i) *PEs under an applicable tax treaty,* (ii) *PEs under domestic laws* and (iii) *PEs not being subject to CIT at their place of establishment,* the 'Financial Accounting Net Income or Losses', according to Article 3.4.1. GloBE Model Rules and Article 18(1) GloBE-Directive, is the *'net income of loss reflected in the separate financial accounts of the* [PE]. *If the* [PE] *does not have separate financial accounts, then the amount that would have been reflected in its separate financial accounts if prepared on a stand alone basis and in accordance with the accounting standard used in the preparation of the Consolidated Financial Accounts of the* [UPE]'.[903] Thus, both Article 3.4.1. GloBE Model Rules and Article 18(1) GloBE-Directive require the preparation of separate accounts along the lines of the accounting standard[904] used by the UPEs for every PE of all CEs within the MNE Group.[905] It is worth remembering here that the use of financial accounts was once touted as *'simplification'*.[906] From today's perspective, this seems like a mockery: the income allocation between the 'Main Entity' and the PE for GloBE purposes is not based on tax accounts but on the financial accounts prepared in advance of the consolidation of the 'Main Entity'. Even if a profit allocation has already been performed by a legal entity for tax purposes, this is not sufficient for GloBE because GloBE solely accepts accounts prepared in the accounting standard applied by the UPE. It can therefore be anticipated that such separate financial accounts of a PE, as indicated by the first sentences of Article 3.4.1. GloBE Model Rules and Article 18(1) GloBE-Directive, will practically never exist. The fact that separate accounts must be prepared for PEs is one thing. The other is how the income is to be allocated between the 'Main Entity' and the PE. Finally, as the Commentary notes, *'given that a PE is a tax concept, there are no specific accounting rules for determining which items and amounts of income and expenses'*[907] by the 'Main Entity' or the PE. This issue is handled in Article 3.4.2. GloBE Model Rules and Article 18(2) GloBE-Directive, which again distinguish between (i) *PEs under an applicable tax treaty,* (ii) *PEs under domestic laws,* and (iii) *PEs not being subject to CIT at their place of establishment*:

- In the case of (i) *PEs under an applicable tax treaty,* a tax treaty is in force between the jurisdiction of the 'Main Entity' and the jurisdiction where the PE is located anyway. In this case, according to Article 3.4.2.(a) GloBE Model Rules and the first sentence of Article 18(2) GloBE-Directive, GloBE simply

902. Letter d of the PE definition in Art. 10.1. *GloBE Model Rules*, at 60 Also *see* letter d of Art. 3(13) GloBE-Directive (2022/2523).
903. Article 3.4.1. *GloBE Model Rules* and, only slightly rephrased, Art. 18(1) GloBE-Directive (2022/2523).
904. That either is and 'Acceptable Financial Accounting Standard' or another standard (so-called Authorised Financial Accounting Standards) amended to prevent 'Material Competitive Distortions', *see GloBE Commentary on Article 3 GloBE Model Rules (2022), supra* note 507, para. 189. In detail on the scope of 'Acceptable Financial Accounting Standard' and 'Authorised Financial Accounting Standards', *see* already s. 4.2.3.2.
905. *See Ibid.*, para. 190.
906. *Public Consultation Pillar Two 2019*, para. 18. *See* in detail s. 4.3.2.1.2.
907. *See GloBE Commentary on Article 3, supra* note 507, para. 191.

relies on the allocation rules for business profits as provided for in the respective treaty applicable to the respective CE. It should be mentioned here that a *PE under an applicable tax treaty* does not occur if a treaty does not contain a provision '*similar to Article 7*'[908] OECD MC. If, for example, a treaty exists, which is, however, structured like the Andean Model Convention that does not follow the PE principle, there would not be any rules which GloBE could rely on with respect to income allocation. In this case, a PE would only occur as a *PE under domestic law*.

- In the case of (ii) *PEs under domestic law*, there is no tax treaty applicable between the jurisdiction of the 'Main Entity' and the PE (or the tax treaty does not contain a provision similar to Article 7 OECD MC). In this case, any items of income and expenses are attributed to the PE in accordance with the jurisdiction where the PE is located '*regardless of the amount of income subject to tax and the amount of deductible expenses in that jurisdiction*'.[909] This clarifies that the income and expenses are to be allocated according to domestic rules, but not with respect to the domestic tax base but rather in line with the accounting standard applied by the UPE.[910] GloBE simply ignores the domestic tax base and only refers to the allocation principles of the domestic law of the jurisdiction where the PE is 'located'[911].[912]
- Regarding (iii) *PEs not being subject to CIT at their place of establishment*, the allocation of income is a tricky issue: such PEs only occur if there is neither a tax treaty nor domestic law defining how income and expenses are to be allocated among 'Main Entity' and the PE. In this case, Article 3.4.2.(b) GloBE Model Rules and the second sentence of Article 18(2) GloBE-Directive require that the PEs 'Financial Accounting Net Income or Loss' needs to be adjusted '*to reflect only the amounts and items of income and expense that would have been attributed to it in accordance with Art 7 of the OECD Model Tax Convention*'.[913] Thus, in the absence of any other available set of rules, a fictitious tax treaty in the form of the OECD MC is used as a set of rules for the attribution of income to the PE. The result seems truly odd: income and expenses must be allocated according to the AOA, although there is neither a tax treaty between the jurisdiction of the 'Main Entity' and the PE nor national law for the implementation of the AOA in national law.

As can be seen, Article 3.4. GloBE Model Rules and Article 18 GloBE-Directive do not provide for their own allocation rules. Rather, GloBE initially relies on applicable

908. Letter a of the PE definition in Art. 10.1. *GloBE Model Rules*, at 60. Also *see* Art. 3(13)(a) GloBE-Directive (2022/2523).
909. Article 3.4.2.(a) *GloBE Model Rules* and the first sentence of Art. 18(2) GloBE-Directive (2022/2523).
910. *See GloBE Commentary on Article 3*, *supra* note 507, para. 192.
911. In detail on the location of PEs, *see* s. 4.2.4.4.3.
912. *See* the examples provided for in *GloBE Commentary on Article 3*, *supra* note 507, paras 193–195.
913. Article 3.4.2.(b) *GloBE Model Rules* and the second sentence of Art. 18(2) GloBE-Directive (2022/2523). Also *see GloBE Commentary on Article 3*, *supra* note 507, para. 196.

tax treaties. Only if no treaty exists is domestic law used to determine the income attributable to the PE, and only if neither a treaty nor domestic law is available a notional application of the OECD MC is required. For the last category of (iv) *exterritorial PEs*, however, there is no legal framework available to allocate items of income and expenses between the 'Main Entity' and the PE. Also, a notional application of the OECD MC would not make any sense: *Exterritorial PEs* do qualify as separate CEs solely because of specific exemptions for exterritorial income in the jurisdiction where the 'Main Entity' is 'located'. For this reason, Article 3.4.3. GloBE Model Rules and Article 18(3) GloBE-Directive state that the income used for computing its 'Financial Accounting Net Income or Loss' shall be the income that is exempt in the jurisdiction where the Main Entity is located and which is attributable to the PE. Costs that are not deductible in the jurisdiction of the 'Main Entity' and that are attributable to the *exterritorial PE* may be deducted at the level of the *exterritorial PE*.[914] In deviation from Article 3.4.2. GloBE Model Rules and Article 18(2) GloBE-Directive, the income of *exterritorial PEs* is to be determined along the lines of the domestic tax base exemption and does not necessarily require the preparation of a separate financial account for the PE: rather, every income that is not taxable but attributable to the operation conducted outside the jurisdiction of the 'Main Entity' is to be allocated to the *exterritorial PE*.

Finally, Article 3.4.4. GloBE Model Rules and Article 18(4) GloBE-Directive make clear that any income attributed to the PE is to be excluded in determining the GloBE tax base of the 'Main Entity'. Otherwise, the same income or loss would be reflected in the ETR calculation of two jurisdictions, once in the jurisdiction where the 'Main Entity' is 'located' and once where the PE is located. The 'Main Entities' 'Financial Accounting Net Income or Loss' is, thus, to be reduced by any GloBE Income and increased by any GloBE Loss attributed to a PE 'located' in a different jurisdiction.[915]

However, excluding losses from the 'Financial Accounting Net Income or Loss' might lead to unfavourable results: many jurisdictions allow the deduction of PE losses, if such losses cannot be deducted in the PE state and the worldwide income of the respective entity simply includes the losses suffered in a different state. As the Commentary aptly notes, '[a]*bsent a special rule, the ETR of the Main Entity may be understated in a Fiscal Year when a PE loss is taken into account for domestic tax purposes but not for GloBE Income or Loss purposes*'.[916] For this reason, Article 3.4.5. GloBE Model Rules and Article 18(5) GloBE-Directive provide for a 'special rule' that allows offsetting foreign PE losses from the 'Financial Accounting Net Income or Loss' if and to the extent (i) domestic law permits treating foreign PE losses as expense in the computation of the domestic tax base and if (ii) the respective loss cannot be set off against income under domestic tax bases of both the 'Main Entity's' jurisdiction and the PE jurisdiction.

The first prerequisite of Article 3.4.5. GloBE Model Rules and Article 18(5) GloBE-Directive clarifies that the 'Main Entity' may only deduct the foreign PE losses if this is explicitly permitted under the domestic law of the jurisdiction where it is located.

914. *See GloBE Commentary on Article 3, supra* note 507, para. 197.
915. *See Ibid.*, para. 198.
916. *See Ibid.*, para. 199.

If the jurisdiction of the 'Main Entity' does not allow offsetting losses attributable to foreign PEs, there would not be any risk that the ETR is understated: rather, the respective jurisdiction would tax the profits of the 'Main Entity' without considering the foreign losses anyway, which is why the respective loss would not reduce the 'Adjusted Covered Taxes' in the numerator of the ETR fraction. Furthermore, the extent to which the deduction of foreign PE losses is also permissible under domestic law is significant for the purpose of Article 3.4.5. GloBE Model Rules and Article 18(5) GloBE-Directive: if, for example, the jurisdiction of the 'Main Entity' limits the deduction of foreign PE losses to 50% of those losses, GloBE would only permit the 'Main Entity' to set off those 50%. According to the Commentary, however, any time limits to the carry-forward of losses under domestic laws are not significant for the purpose of Article 3.4.5. GloBE Model Rules and Article 18(5) GloBE-Directive. Thus, the 'Main Entity' may still deduct the loss, even if the carry-forward expired under domestic law.[917]

The second prerequisite of Article 3.4.5. GloBE Model Rules and Article 18(5) GloBE-Directive shall prevent the use of the same loss twice, once in the jurisdiction of the 'Main Entity' and once in the jurisdiction of the PE. Such situations might occur, e.g., if the same CE has a loss-making PE and a profitable PE within the same jurisdiction, and the income of both PEs may be offset against each other in the PE jurisdiction, whereas the jurisdiction of the 'Main Entity' also allows the deduction of the PE losses or if both jurisdictions allow sharing losses among different legal entities and PEs under common control in the course of a group consolidation regime.[918] In simple terms: the 'Main Entity' cannot deduct the foreign PE losses if they can also be used in the PE state, even if the domestic law of the 'Main Entity' would grant the deduction in principle.

Furthermore, the second sentences of Article 3.4.5. GloBE Model Rules and Article 18(5) GloBE-Directive require recapturing the previously deducted PE losses, in the case the PE subsequently receives 'GloBE Income' ('qualifying income'): '*GloBE Income arising in the* [PE] *shall be treated as GloBE income of the Main Entity (and not the* [PE]*) up to the amount of the GloBE Loss that previously was treated as an expense for purposes of computing the GloBE Income or Loss of the Main Entity.*'[919] This aims to prevent the multiple use of the same loss over several periods. Finally, if a PE becomes profitable again, the losses might be deducted in the PE state, although they did previously reduce the 'GloBE Income' ('qualifying income') of the 'Main Entity' in a different jurisdiction. For this reason, the amount of losses previously deducted by the 'Main Entity' must be added back to the 'Main Entity's' 'GloBE Income or Loss' ('qualifying income or loss') in the subsequent fiscal year to the extent that the previously deducted losses are covered within the PEs subsequent profits. However, according to the Commentary, recapture is even required if the 'Main Entity' failed to use the losses due to a loss carry-forward time limit according to domestic law of the

917. *See Ibid.*, para. 200.
918. The latter example is given in *Ibid.*, paras 201–202.
919. *See* the second sentence of Art. 3.4.5. *GloBE Model Rules* and, using a slightly different wording, the second sentence Art. 18(5) GloBE-Directive (2022/2523).

'Main Entity'.[920] Moreover, both Article 3.4.5. GloBE Model Rules and Article 18(5) GloBE-Directive also seem to require recapture at the level of the 'Main Entity', even if the domestic law of the PE jurisdiction does not allow to carry-forward losses, and the PE loss cannot subsequently be used in the PE jurisdiction at all. However, this does not harm MNE Groups since the lack of loss utilization would be reflected in the amount of 'Adjusted Covered Taxes' in the PE state and would, thus, not lead to an understatement of the ETR. In this respect, it is important to note that Article 3.4.5. GloBE Model Rules and Article 18(5) GloBE-Directive do not have any impact on the 'Financial Accounting Net Income or Loss' of the PE itself; rather, both provisions are exclusively addressed to the 'Main Entity'.

4.3.3.6 Allocation of Income or Loss from a Flow-Through Entity

Similar to PEs, 'Flow-through Entities' also face the problem of territorial delimitation of income or losses. The definition of 'Flow-through Entities' (Article 10.2.1. GloBE Model Rules and Article 3[12] GloBE-Directive) and their 'location' (Article 10.3.2. GloBE Model Rules and Article 4[2] GloBE-Directive) has already been examined in detail in sections 4.2.4.2.2. and 4.2.4.4.2.: although the definitions of 'Flow-through Entities' in Article 10.2.1 GloBE Model Rules and Article 3(12) GloBE-Directive slightly deviate from each other,[921] their scopes are nearly identical and simply cover any 'Entities' that are treated as fiscally transparent in the jurisdiction where they were created and are not subject to tax on their income or profit in another jurisdiction. Consequently, any income or losses of the respective 'Flow-through Entity' are always allocated to the owners of the 'Flow-through Entity'. In principle, any income or losses of a 'Flow-through Entity' are thus included within the ETR of the jurisdiction where the CE-owners are 'located'.

However, things are not that simple: contrary to PEs, 'Flow-through Entities' are regularly obliged to prepare separate financial accounts according to accounting rules '*showing their Financial Accounting Net Income or Loss regardless of the fact that they have no taxable net income or loss because it has been allocated to its owners under the tax rules*'.[922] Different from the allocation issues of PEs, where the financial statements of a CE need to be split into a statement of the 'Main Entity' and PEs, with respect to 'Flow-through Entities' (which do, like PEs, qualify as separate CEs but only under the condition that they are obliged to prepare for separate financial statements),[923] it is to be determined whether and to which extent the 'Flow-through Entity's' income or loss in its financial statements is to be allocated to other CEs. Such a CE could either be another 'Entity' holding 'Ownership Interest' in the 'Flow-through Entity' or a PE. Eventually, fiscally transparent arrangements regularly create PEs for their owners

920. *See GloBE Commentary on Article 3*, *supra* note 507, para. 203.
921. Already *see* s. 4.2.4.4.2., in particular *supra* note 408.
922. *See GloBE Commentary on Article 3*, *supra* note 507, para. 204.
923. *See* the definition of 'Entity' in Art. 10.1. *GloBE Model Rules*, at 56. Correspondingly *see* Art. 3(1) GloBE-Directive (2022/2523). In detail on the scope of the term 'Entity', *see* s. 4.2.4.1.1.

according to international treaty practice.[924] Put differently, the 'Financial Accounting Net Income or Loss' is to be allocated '*among PEs, CE-owners and the* [Flow-through] Entity *itself*'.[925] It can already be anticipated here that the allocation of income or losses of 'Flow-through Entities' is a tricky issue that could not have been solved simply by relying on the rules provided for the allocation of income and losses between the 'Main Entity' and PEs. For this reason, Article 3.5. GloBE Model Rules and Article 19 GloBE-Directive provide for specific provisions determining how the income or losses of 'Flow-through Entities' are to be allocated between the jurisdiction where the 'Flow-through Entity' was created and the jurisdictions where the owners of the respective entity are 'located' or conduct a PE via the respective 'Flow-through Entity'. To finally allocate the 'Financial Accounting Net Income or Loss among those jurisdictions, both Article 3.5. GloBE Model Rules and Article 19 GloBE-Directive provide for a fixed scheme containing five steps:

- **Step 1[926] – Separation of income attributable to non-Group shareholders:** First of all, Article 3.5.3 GloBE Model Rules and Article 19(1) GloBE-Directive require the reduction of the 'Financial Accounting Net Income or Loss of the 'Flow-through Entity' '*by the amount allocable to its owners that are not Group Entities and that hold their Ownership Interest in the Flow-through Entity directly or through a Tax Transparent Structure*'.[927] Any 'Ownership Interest' held by non-Group shareholders would, according to domestic tax laws, be attributable to those shareholders. For this reason, such income should not be included in the ETR computation of any CEs of the MNE Group, which is why such amounts are subtracted from the 'Flow-through Entity's' 'Financial Accounting Net Income or Loss' first.[928] Otherwise, such income would be included within the denominator of the ETR fraction, although any taxes paid by the non-Group shareholder would not be included within the 'Covered Taxes' in the numerator, which would lead to an understatement of the ETR. Consequently, only the amount of income or loss that is attributable to members of the 'MNE Group' will be allocated among PEs, CE-owners and the 'Flow-through Entity' itself.[929] Although tax transparent entities as such are characterized by the fact that they are not subject to tax themselves in the jurisdiction where they are created, the Commentary notes that there could nevertheless occur 'Covered Taxes' if, for example, a third jurisdiction imposes taxes that are reflected within the financial statements of the 'Flow-through Entity'. In this case, any taxes attributable to the income that is allocated to non-group shareholders is to be correspondingly excluded from the amount of 'Adjusted Covered Taxes' according to Article 4.1.3.(a) GloBE

924. *See, i.a., OECD Model Tax Convention on Income and on Capital: Commentary on Article 5, supra* note 111, para. 43.
925. *See GloBE Commentary on Article 3, supra* note 507, para. 209.
926. *See Ibid.*, paras 206 and 227.
927. Article 3.5.3. *GloBE Model Rules* and, using a slightly different wording, Art. 19(1) GloBE-Directive (2022/2523).
928. *See GloBE Commentary on Article 3, supra* note 507, para. 226.
929. *See Ibid.*, paras 227–229.

Model Rules and Article 21(3)(a) GloBE-Directive.[930] As a result, the total ETR fraction must be adjusted for income (or losses) and the related 'Covered Taxes' attributable to non-group shareholders.The exclusion of income or losses attributable to non-group shareholders must, however, be prevented if the 'Flow-through Entity' is itself the UPE of an MNE Group. Otherwise, the whole MNE Group's income would fall out of the GloBE regime: If an 'MNE Group' established a tax transparent entity as the UPE, its income would be reduced by Article 3.5.3 GloBE Model Rules and Article 19(1) GloBE-Directive leaving no income at the level of the UPE, since no shareholder of the UPE can ever qualify as a group member. For this reason, according to Article 3.5.4. GloBE-Directive and Article 19(1)(a) and (b) GloBE-Directive, the 'Financial Accounting Net Income or Loss' of a 'Flow-through Entity' is not reduced by the amount of income or loss allocable to non-group shareholders, if the 'Flow-through Entity' is the UPE of the 'MNE Group' itself, or is directly or indirectly owned by another 'Flow-through Entity' that qualifies as the UPE of an MNE Group.[931] Finally, the allocation of income or losses to such tax transparent UPEs is operated in step 4. In detail on 'Flow-through Entities' forming the UPE of a 'MNE Group', *see* section 4.2.4.2.2.

- **Step 2 – Identification of CE-owners for the purpose of allocating group's share of income:** When the non-group member's share is removed from the 'Financial Accounting Net Income or Loss' of the 'Flow-through Entity', the remaining income or loss is to be allocated *'among PEs, CE-owners and the* [Flow-through}*Entity itself*'.[932] The actual allocation is determined in Article 3.5.1. GloBE Model Rules and Article 19(3) to (5) GloBE-Directive. But even before an allocation can be made, the CE-owner of the 'Flow-through Entity' and their respective 'Ownership Interests' must be identified: according to Article 3.5.2. GloBE Model Rules and Article 19(6) GloBE-Directive, the allocation of income or losses as provided for in Article 3.5.1. GloBE Model Rules and Article 19(3) to (5) GloBE-Directive *'shall be applied separately with respect to each Ownership Interest in the Flow-through Entity'*.[933] For this reason, all of the following steps must be applied separately for each CE-owner of the 'Flow-through Entity'.[934] If, for example, two CEs hold 50% of a 'Flow-through Entity', the following Steps 3 to 6 need to be applied twice – once for each CE-owner. Finally, any income or loss that is reallocated from the 'Flow-through Entity' to another CE again reduces its 'Financial Accounting Net Income or Loss'.[935]
- **Step 3 – Allocation of income and losses to PEs of the 'Flow-through Entity':'** First, Article 3.5.1.(a) GloBE Model Rules and Article 19(3) GloBE-Directive require that any income or loss that can be attributed to one or more

930. *See Ibid.*, para. 230.
931. *See Ibid.*, para. 231.
932. *See Ibid.*, para. 209.
933. *See* Art. 3.5.2. *GloBE Model Rules* and Art. 19(6) GloBE-Directive (2022/2523).
934. In detail, *see GloBE Commentary on Article 3, supra* note 507, para. 225.
935. *See* Art. 3.5.5. *GloBE Model Rules* and Art. 19(2) GloBE-Directive (2022/2523).

PEs (irrespective of where those PEs are 'located') through which the 'Flow-through Entity' carries out its business is allocated to those PEs according to the rules provided for in Article 3.4. GloBE Model Rules and Article 19 GloBE-Directive.[936] Any income or loss allocated to those PEs is finally again removed from the 'Financial Accounting Net Income or Loss' of the 'Flow-through Entity'.[937] Therefore, the income or loss attributable to the Group is first allocated to all jurisdictions in which the 'Flow-through Entity' has PEs. Such PEs can exist either in the jurisdiction where the 'Flow-through Entity' was created, where its owners are located or in any other third jurisdiction. If the respective PE jurisdictions levy 'Covered Taxes' on PE income, the 'Covered Taxes' are to be allocated pursuant to Article 4.3.2.(a) GloBE Model Rules and Article 24(1) GloBE-Directive to the jurisdiction where the PE is (the PEs are) 'located'. The primary allocation to PEs ensures that the allocation of taxing rights between jurisdictions remains balanced and consistent with tax treaties concluded between jurisdictions.

- **Step 4 – Residual allocation to the direct CE-owners according to the 'Ownership Interests' held in the 'Flow-through Entity':** The residual amount of the 'Flow-through Entity's' 'Financial Accounting Net Income or Loss' allocable to other members of the 'Group' is to be allocated to the CE-owners '*in accordance with their Ownership Interests*'[938] pursuant to Article 3.5.1.(b) GloBE Model Rules and Article 19(4) GloBE-Directive. In this way, GloBE ensures that the allocation is made along the '*tax treatment in both the Entity's and owner's jurisdiction*'.[939] In case the CE-owner is another 'Flow-through Entity' or a chain of such entities, the income or loss is allocated to the next CE that is a fiscally non-transparent legal entity or, if all remaining 'Entities' upwards in the ownership chain are tax transparent entities, to the UPE of the 'MNE Group'. Finally, neither Article 3.5.1.(b) GloBE Model Rules nor Article 19(4) GloBE-Directive apply if the 'Flow-through Entity' is the UPE of the group. In this case, step 5 is to be applied.
- **Step 5 – Residual amount of 'Financial Accounting Net Income or Loss' remains at the 'Flow-through Entity' that is either the UPE of the 'MNE Group' or a 'Reverse Hybrid Entity':** Any remaining amount of income or loss that can neither be allocated to PEs or to CE-owners of the 'Flow-through Entity' remain at this entity according to Article 3.5.1.(c) GloBE Model Rules and Article 19(5) GloBE-Directive. As both to Article 3.5.1.(c) GloBE Model Rules and Article 19(5) GloBE-Directive make clear, an income or loss can only remain with the 'Flow-through Entity' if it is either (i) the UPE of its 'MNE Group' itself or (ii) if it is a so-called Reverse Hybrid Entity. In the former case, there is no other solution but to allocate the remaining income or loss to the 'Flow-through Entity' due to the fact that '*the owners are not Constituent*

936. On these provisions, *see* s. 4.3.4.8.
937. *See* Art. 3.5.5. *GloBE Model Rules* and Art. 19(2) GloBE-Directive (2022/2523).
938. *See* Art. 3.5.1.(b) *GloBE Model Rules* and Art. 19(4) GloBE-Directive (2022/2523).
939. *See GloBE Commentary on Article 3, supra* note 507, para. 213.

Entities of the MNE Group required to apply the GloBE Rules'.[940] If GloBE were to allocate the income or loss to the owners of the UPE, the 'Top-up Tax' attributable to it could not be levied. For this reason, Article 7.1. GloBE Model Rules and Article 39 GloBE-Directive provide specific rules for 'Flow-through Entity' that are the UPE of an MNE Group.[941] In principle, they allow the tax transparent UPE to further reduce its income if the respective income is taxed in the hands of the owner within 12 months of the end of the MNEs Group 'Fiscal Year' at a rate that equals or exceeds 15 %.[942] This is necessary because otherwise, '*the ETR of the UPE itself will be nil (or very low)*'[943] due to the fact that the UPE, being fiscally transparent, is not subject to tax in the jurisdiction where it is 'located'. If a 'Flow-through Entity' entity is not a UPE, income or loss can usually not remain with the 'Flow-through Entity' due to the fact that any income could, in principle, be allocated to a CE-owner or the UPE anyway.[944] However, in the case of 'Reverse Hybrid Entities', the jurisdiction of the CE-owner considers the 'Entity', contrary to the law of the jurisdiction where it was created, to be non-transparent. For this reason, the former jurisdiction prevents the income from being allocated to the CE-owners.[945] For this reason, Article 3.5.1.(c) GloBE Model Rules and Article 19(5) GloBE-Directive, as with respect to tax transparent UPEs, allocate the remaining income or loss to the respective 'Reverse Hybrid Entities' (which is included within the term 'Flow-through Entity').[946] But which jurisdiction is the tax transparent UPE's or the 'Reverse Hybrid Entity's' income or loss finally assigned to? The respective income or loss falls within the jurisdiction where the 'Flow-through Entity' is 'located'. In the case of tax transparent UPEs, that is the jurisdiction where the 'Entity' was created.[947] In the case of 'Reverse Hybrid Entities', it depends: if the 'Reverse Hybrid Entity' is required to apply an IIR in the jurisdiction where it was created, its income is to be assigned to this jurisdiction.[948] In any other case, the respective 'Reverse Hybrid Entities' would be considered 'stateless', meaning that the ETR would be calculated on an entity basis.[949] In the latter case, the ETR is to be computed separately on a stand-alone basis for the respective 'Flow-through Entity', which will regularly be nil[950] and, thus, give rise to 'Top-up Tax'.[951]

940. *See Ibid.*, para. 222.
941. Already *see* s. 4.2.4.2.2.
942. Article 7.1.1. *GloBE Model Rules* and Art. 36(1) GloBE-Directive (2022/2523).
943. *See GloBE Commentary on Article 7 GloBE Model Rules (2022)*, *supra* note 335, para. 3.
944. *See* Art. 3.5.1.(b) *GloBE Model Rules* and Art. 19(5) GloBE-Directive (2022/2523).
945. *See GloBE Commentary on Article 10 GloBE Model Rules (2022)*, *supra* note 280, para. 176.
946. *See* Art. 10.2.1.(b) *GloBE Model Rules*. Also *see* Art. 3(12)(b) GloBE-Directive (2022/2523).
947. First limb of Art. 10.3.2.(a) *GloBE Model Rules* and the first exception in Art. 4(2) GloBE-Directive (2022/2523).
948. Second limb of Art. 10.3.2.(a) *GloBE Model Rules* and the second exception in Art. 4(2) GloBE-Directive (2022/2523).
949. Article 10.3.2.(b) *GloBE Model Rules* and Art. 4(2) GloBE-Directive (2022/2523).
950. Nevertheless, there might be situations where an amount of 'Covered Tax' remains at the level of the 'Reverse Hybrid Entity', *see* s. 4.3.4.8.3.
951. In detail on the location of 'Flow-through Entities', *see* s. 4.2.4.4.2. and 4.2.4.4.4.

As has just been shown, fiscally transparent 'Entities' obliged to prepare separate financial accounts ('Flow-through Entities') drive the complexity of GloBE's jurisdictional blending to the extreme. Every piece of 'Financial Accounting Net Income or Loss' needs to be allocated to either a PE, a CE-owner and, in the worst case, to the 'Entity' itself. For reasons of administrability, each 'MNE Group' is well advised to replace fiscally transparent structures with separate legal entities in the same jurisdiction. It is advisable to only make use of transparent vehicles if their 'Ownership Interests' are held via a legal entity located within the same jurisdiction.

4.3.4 The Taxes Actually Paid: Computation of 'Adjusted Covered Taxes'

4.3.4.1 Preliminary Considerations on the Covered Taxes and the Structure of the 'Adjusted Covered Taxes' Computation

Complementary to the rules for determining the 'GloBE Income or Loss' ('qualifying income or lost') discussed in the previous sections, the respective fourth chapters of the GloBE Model Rules and the GloBE-Directive contain the rules for calculating the amount of the 'Adjusted Covered Taxes' to determine the numerator of the ETR fraction.[952] As with the 'GloBE Income or Loss' ('qualifying income or loss'), the amount of 'Adjusted Covered Taxes' is to be determined at the level of each separate CE. Again, the determination of 'Covered Taxes' starts from the financial accounts of the respective CE:[953] According to Article 4.1.1. GloBE Model Rules (Article 21[1] GloBE-Directive) the amount of '*Adjusted Covered Taxes of a Constituent Entity for the Fiscal Year shall be equal to the current tax expense accrued in its Financial Accounting Net Income or Loss with respect to Covered Taxes* […].'[954] Consequently, like the GloBE base, the 'Covered Taxes' are determined from the current tax expense reported in the financial accounts of a CE prepared for consolidation in line with the accounting standard applied by the UPE. What is to be considered a 'Covered Tax' is separately defined in Article 4.2. GloBE Model Rules (Article 20 GloBE-Directive). Any taxes that do not qualify as a 'Covered Tax' under Article 4.2. GloBE Model Rules (Article 20 GloBE-Directive) are to be removed from the amount of current tax expenses according to the first sentence of Article 4.1.1. GloBE Model Rules (first sentence of Article 21[1] GloBE-Directive).[955]

However, GloBE requires several adjustments to convert the amount of current tax expense reported in the financial accounts into the 'Adjusted Covered Taxes'. The structure of the computation of 'Adjusted Covered Taxes' is defined in Article 4.1. GloBE Model Rules and Article 21 GloBE-Directive:

952. *See GloBE Commentary on Article 4 GloBE Model Rules (2022)*, *supra* note 884, para. 1.
953. Also *see Ibid.*, para. 4.
954. First sentence of Art. 4.1.1. *GloBE Model Rules* and correspondingly the first sentence of Art. 21(1) GloBE-Directive (2022/2523).
955. As the Commentary notes, this is not an adjustment but rather follows directly from the first sentence of Art. 4.1.1. *GloBE Model Rules, see GloBE Commentary on Article 4, supra* note 884, para. 4.

- First of all, Article 4.1.1.(a) GloBE Model Rules and Article 21(1)(a) GloBE-Directive require certain additions and reductions to 'Covered Taxes'. Finally, the current tax expenses reported in the financial accounts might not give a full picture of the taxes paid in a specific 'Fiscal Year': there might be, for example, taxes paid that are considered expenses under the accounting rules of the UPE and are not included within the position of the current tax expenses, even though they fall within the definition of 'Covered Taxes'[956] or there might occur uncertain tax expenses that had to be considered as current tax expense under accounting rules, although the respective CE is, in the end, not obliged to pay them.[957] If GloBE simply used the current tax expenses from the CE's financial statements, distortive effects would be inevitable. On the other hand, there might be positions within the amount of current tax expenses that need to be removed, for example, 'Covered Taxes' that are attributable to items which are excluded according to Article 3.2 GloBE Model Rules (Article 15 GloBE-Directive).[958] For this reason, Article 4.1.2. GloBE Model Rules (Article 21[2] GloBE-Directive) includes an exhaustive list of additions to the 'Covered Taxes' followed by a list of reductions in Article 4.1.3. GloBE Model Rules (Article 21[3] GloBE-Directive). By way of additions and reductions to 'Covered Taxes', as the Commentary sums up, GloBE '*take*[s] *into account Taxes of a Constituent Entity that are not recorded in the tax line of the profit and loss statement and* [...] *exclude*[s] *Taxes that are not related to GloBE Income or Loss*'.[959]
- Second, Article 4.1.1.(b) GloBE Model Rules and Article 21(1)(b) GloBE-Directive state that the current tax expense shall be adjusted by the so-called Total Deferred Tax Adjustment Amount (within the GloBE-Directive the so-called total deferred tax adjustment amount). Specifically defined in Article 4.4 GloBE Model Rules and Article 22 GloBE-Directive, this is GloBE's mechanism for addressing temporary differences between tax rules and accounting rules: while permanent differences are persistent and consequently require adjustment at the income level (and sometimes additionally at the covered tax level), temporary differences can be accounted for by adjusting the 'Covered Taxes' alone.[960] In the case of temporary differences, the difference between the tax balance and the financial accounts is reversed over a defined period of time. GloBE, therefore, leaves the GloBE Income or Loss unaffected but simply accounts for such differences by recognizing deferred tax assets or liabilities already known from financial accounting principles: deferred tax assets and liabilities are items that must be recognized in an entity's financial statements in order to allocate to each period for which financial statements are prepared the tax expense actually incurred in that period, even if the tax expense has

956. *See* Art. 4.1.2.(a) *GloBE Model Rules* and Art. 21(2)(a) GloBE-Directive (2022/2523).
957. *See* Art. 4.1.2.(c) *GloBE Model Rules* and Art. 21(2)(c) GloBE-Directive (2022/2523).
958. *See* Art. 4.1.3.(a) *GloBE Model Rules* and Art. 21(3)(a) GloBE-Directive (2022/2523).
959. *See GloBE Commentary on Article 4, supra* note 884, para. 3.
960. Already *see* s. 4.3.3.3.1.

already been paid (in this case a deferred tax asset) or will have to be paid in a future period (in this case a deferred tax asset). Accounting for deferred taxes is a fundamental principle in almost all current accounting standards to address temporary differences between financial and tax accounts, which is why it also has been adopted for the purposes of GloBE.[961] However, this should not obscure the fact that GloBE prescribes an entirely separate deferred tax mechanism, which is based on accounting rules but nevertheless requires extensive adjustments. The mechanism for adjusting temporary differences is at the core of the calculation of 'Adjusted Covered Taxes' and is of the highest practical relevance: the most frequent differences between tax regulations and accounting rules are of a temporary nature. Such differences often relate to different depreciation values due to diverging useful lifetimes or differences in carrying amounts that are reversed over the useful life of an asset or a liability. Finally, the 'Total Deferred Tax Adjustment Amount' either increases or decreases the amount of 'Adjusted Covered Taxes' depending on whether the 'Total Deferred Tax Adjustment Amount' is either a deferred tax asset or a deferred tax liability in the respective 'Fiscal Year'. The detailed computation of the 'Total Deferred Tax Adjustment Amount' according to Article 4.4 GloBE Model Rules and Article 22 GloBE-Directive will be examined below.[962]
- Third, according to Article 4.1.1.(c) GloBE Model Rules and Article 21(1)(c) GloBE-Directive, the current tax expense is adjusted for either an increase or decrease in 'Covered Taxes' if the respective tax is not recorded within the current tax expense but in equity or OCI. Otherwise, taxes that are offset against equity and not recorded in the income or loss statement would not be included in the amount of adjusted covered taxes.[963]

The purpose of the complex scheme provided for in Article 4.1. GloBE Model Rules (Article 21 GloBE-Directive) is to set up a solid system that, on the one hand, includes all 'Covered Taxes' within the ETR computation and, on the other hand, avoids any amount of 'Covered Taxes' that are included within the numerator of the ETR fraction more than once.[964] Eventually, the 'Adjusted Covered Taxes' in the nominator of the ETR fraction increase the ETR. The higher the amount of 'Covered Taxes', the lower the probability that a different jurisdiction will be in a position to levy 'Top-up Tax'. Since the adjustments provided for in Article 4.1. GloBE Model Rules (Article 21 GloBE-Directive) overlap, GloBE explicitly states that any amount of 'Covered Tax' may only be considered once[965].[966]

The precise calculation scheme for deriving the amount of 'Adjusted Covered Taxes' from the current tax expense as reported in the CE's financial statements is presented in Table 1, which also reflects the structure of the following sections.

961. For further background, *see* s. 4.3.4.5.1.
962. In detail, *see* s. 5.3.4.5.
963. In detail, *see* s. 4.3.4.6.
964. *See* Art. 4.1.4. *GloBE Model Rules* and Art. 21(4) GloBE-Directive (2022/2523).
965. Article 4.1.4. *GloBE Model Rules* and Art. 21(4) GloBE-Directive (2022/2523).
966. *See GloBE Commentary on Article 4 GloBE Model Rules (2022), supra* note 884, para. 18.

Table 1 Overview of the Structure of the Computation of the Amount of 'Adjusted Covered Taxes'

	Computation of the 'Adjusted Covered Taxes' – Overview			
	From Current Tax Expenses to the 'Adjusted Covered Taxes'	*Model Rules*	*GloBE-Directive*	*Reference*
	Current tax expense with respect to 'Covered Taxes' accrued in a CEs 'Financial Accounting Net Income or Loss'	Articles 4.1.1. and 4.2.	Articles 21(1) and 20	section 4.3.4.2.
+	**Additions to Covered Taxes for the 'Fiscal Year'**	Article 4.1.1.(a)	Article 21(1)(a)	section 4.3.4.3.
	+ Covered Tax accrued as an expense in profit before taxation	Article 4.1.2.(a)	Article 21(2)(a)	section 4.3.4.3.1.
	+ GloBE Loss Deferred Tax Adjustment Amount	Articles 4.1.2.(b) and 4.5.3.	Articles 21(2)(b) and 23(3)	section 4.3.4.3.2.
	+ Covered Taxes related to uncertain tax positions	Article 4.1.2.(c)	Article 21(2)(c)	section 4.3.4.3.3.
	+ Credit or refund in respect of 'Qualified Refundable Tax Credits'	Article 4.1.2.(d)	Article 21(2)(d)	section 4.3.4.3.4.
–	**Reductions to Covered Taxes**	Article 4.1.1.(a)	Article 21(1)(a)	section 4.3.4.4.
	– Covered Taxes with respect to excluded income	Article 4.1.3.(a)	Article 21(3)(a)	section 4.3.4.4.1.
	– Credit or refund due to Non-Qualified Refundable Tax Credits	Article 4.1.3.(b)	Article 21(3)(b)	section 4.3.4.4.2.
	– Credited or refunded Covered Taxes not included within financial accounts	Article 4.1.3.(c)	Article 21(3)(c)	section 4.3.4.4.3.
	– Amount of current tax expense related to uncertain tax position	Article 4.1.3.(d)	Article 21(3)(d)	section 4.3.4.4.4.
	– Current tax expense that is not expected to be paid within three years	Article 4.1.3.(e)	Article 21(3)(e)	section 4.3.4.4.4.
+/–	**'Total Deferred Tax Adjustment Amount'**	Articles 4.1.1.(b) and 4.4.	Articles 21(1)(b) and 22	section 4.3.4.5.
+/–	**Increase or Decrease of Covered Taxes recorded in equity or OCI**	Article 4.1.1.(c)	Article 21(1)(c)	section 4.3.4.6.
	Amount of 'Adjusted Covered Taxes' of a CE	Article 5.1.1.	Article 26(1)	section 4.4.2.2.

As just shown, the 'Adjusted Covered Taxes' is to be determined for each CE individually to finally aggregate the taxes of all CEs jurisdiction-wise to generate the numerator of the ETR fraction. For this reason, the question arises as to which CE 'located' in which jurisdiction a specific amount of 'Covered Taxes' is assigned. At first glance, this might seem to be an easy task: one could simply argue that every tax is allocated to the CE, which has to pay the tax.[967] However, the reality is not that simple: a jurisdiction might, for example, tax non-resident corporations if they have a PE within their territory and, as already discussed,[968] a PE is to be considered as a separate CE and does not necessarily have separate accounts from which its current tax expenses could be deduced.[969] However, tax allocation issues go far beyond the issue of allocating tax between a PE and the 'Main Entity': what about the case of tax transparent entities whose profits are only taxed in the hands of the CE-owner?[970] To which CE is a withholding tax on payments in between the same 'MNE Group' assigned? Is it the CE that is obliged to withhold and pay the tax to local tax authorities, or is it the CE receiving the respective income that is supposed to be taxed by means of the withholding tax?[971] What if jurisdictions tax profits of foreign CEs by way of CFC rules at the level of the CE parent, although GloBE, in principle, assigns profits to the CE that reports the income or loss in their financial accounts?[972] All these issues make it clear that questions of territorial delimitation arise not only in relation to the tax base of GloBE but in the same way in relation to the 'Adjusted Covered Taxes'.[973] For this reason, Article 4.3. GloBE Model Rules and Article 24 GloBE-Directive contain complex rules on the allocation of 'Covered Taxes' among the different CEs within the same MNE Group. The allocation of 'Covered Taxes' will be further discussed in section 4.3.4.8.

The exact amount of taxes finally paid to fiscal authorities might deviate from the current tax expense previously reported in the financial statements and initially reported in a 'GloBE Information Return' for a specific 'Fiscal Year': taxpayers might be involved in tax litigation having significant impact on the amounts of 'Covered Taxes' paid. Errors may occur, and estimates may turn out to be wrong. As the Commentary is aware, such '*changes to accrued tax expense may have impacted the MNE Group's Top-up Tax liability with respect to a preceding Fiscal Year*'.[974] However, an effective minimum tax system must account for such subsequent changes in 'Covered Taxes' in some form. Otherwise, MNE Groups could deliberately pay tax amounts not due to simply increase the ETR in order to reclaim them later in provoked tax proceedings, or states could simply refund 'Covered Taxes' in subsequent 'Fiscal Years'. For this reason, the respective fourth chapters of the GloBE Model Rules and the GloBE-Directive also contain rules to adjust 'Covered Taxes' after the 'GloBE Information Return' for a specific 'Fiscal Year' has been filed. The provisions titled 'Post-filing Adjustments and Tax Rate Changes' are found in Article 4.6. GloBE Model Rules and

967. *See Ibid.*, para. 42, where it is held: '*In many cases, Covered Taxes will be paid by the Constituent Entity with respect to its own income and to a tax authority in the jurisdiction in which it is located and no allocation is required.*'
968. *See* s. 4.3.2.3. and 4.3.3.5.
969. *See* Art. 4.3.2.(a) *GloBE Model Rules* and Art. 24(1) GloBE-Directive (2022/2523).
970. *See* Art. 4.3.2.(b) *GloBE Model Rules* and Art. 24(2) GloBE-Directive (2022/2523).
971. For dividends, *see* Art. 4.3.2.(e) *GloBE Model Rules* and Art. 24(5) GloBE-Directive (2022/2523).
972. *See* Art. 4.3.2.(c) *GloBE Model Rules* and Art. 24(3) GloBE-Directive (2022/2523).
973. In the same vein, *see GloBE Commentary on Article 4 GloBE Model Rules (2022)*, *supra* note 884, para. 41.
974. *See Ibid.*, para. 119.

Article 25 GloBE-Directive, respectively. The provisions distinguish between subsequent increases and subsequent decreases in 'Covered Taxes':[975] in the case of an increase, the respective increase shall be treated as a simple addition to the 'Covered Taxes' in the 'Fiscal Year' in which the adjustment is made. However, with respect to decreases in the ETR and 'Top-up Tax', both the ETR and the 'Top-up Tax' of the respective 'Fiscal Year' need to be recalculated. This can give rise to the so-called Additional Current Top-up Tax, according to Article 5.4. GloBE Model Rules (Article 29 GloBE-Directive uses the term 'additional top-up tax') that is to be added to the 'Jurisdictional Top-up Tax' and, thus, might give rise to a minimum tax to be paid by an MNE Group.[976] 'Post-filing Adjustments and Tax Rate Changes' are therefore not simple adjustments to 'Covered Taxes' as provided for in Article 4.1 GloBE Model Rules and Article 21 GloBE-Directive, which is why the GloBE Model Rules and the GloBE-Directive each devote separate Articles (Article 4.6. GloBE Model Rules and Article 25 GloBE-Directive) to them, which will be further examined in section 4.3.4.9.

However, before going into such details of the determination of 'Covered Taxes', it is first necessary to examine what is to be considered a 'Covered Tax' in the first place. The following section, thus, is devoted to GloBE's definition of 'Covered Taxes'.

4.3.4.2 Current Tax Expense with Respect to 'Covered Taxes' in the Financial Accounts: The Definition of 'Covered Taxes' for the Purposes of GloBE

According to Article 4.1.1. GloBE Model Rules reflected in Article 21(1) GloBE-Directive '[t]*he Adjusted Covered Taxes of a Constituent Entity for the Fiscal Year shall be equal to the current tax expense accrued in its Financial Accounting Net Income or Loss with respect to Covered Taxes*'.[977] Consequently, the amount of 'Adjusted Covered Taxes' therefore includes '*only amounts that meet* [the] *definition*'[978] of 'Covered Taxes'. Any amounts of tax that are shown within the position of current tax expenses within the 'Financial Accounting Net Income or Loss' are, thus, not part of the 'Adjusted Covered Taxes' '*without the need for a specified adjustment*'.[979] But what is the scope of 'Covered Taxes'?

It is not surprising that the groundwork of a separate definition for 'Covered Taxes' had already been laid in the Pillar Two Blueprint published in October 2020.[980] Lastly, the ETR calculation depends significantly on the scope of the 'Covered Taxes'. Most importantly, the term influences possible defensive strategies of 'Low-Tax Jurisdictions': 'Low-Tax Jurisdictions' have an incentive to modify their domestic tax systems so that specific taxes are considered as 'Covered Taxes'. Furthermore, those

975. Article 4.6.1. *GloBE Model Rules* and Art. 24(1) GloBE-Directive (2022/2523).
976. In detail on the computation of the 'Additional Current Top-up Tax' and its impact on the 'Jurisdictional Top-up Tax', *see* s. 4.4.2.6.
977. Article 4.1.1. *GloBE Model Rules* and Art. 21(1) GloBE-Directive (2022/2523).
978. *See GloBE Commentary on Article 4*, *supra* note 884, para. 1.
979. *See Ibid.*, para. 4.
980. Comprehensively, *see Tax Challenges Arising from Digitalisation – Report on Pillar Two Blueprint*, paras 129–153.

jurisdictions could try to shift any investment incentives granted by their income tax system to taxes (e.g., payroll or personal income taxes) that are not 'Covered Taxes' to avoid that the incentive reduces the 'Covered Taxes' of the 'MNE Group' in that jurisdiction.[981] But also, MNE Groups will try to bring as much evidence as possible with regard to payments that potentially could be within the ambit of the 'Covered Tax' definition. In any case, the technicality of the definition should not obscure the fact that the scope of 'Covered Taxes' is a significant cornerstone of GloBE and has a significant influence on GloBE's impact on tax competition.[982]

Now both the GloBE Model Rules and the GloBE-Directive incorporate the concept of 'Covered Taxes' in separate articles, specifically Article 4.2. GloBE Model Rules and Article 20 GloBE-Directive reflect the ideas that had been developed in the Blueprint. The Commentary on Article 4.2. GloBE Model Rules is also mainly based on the explanations provided in the Blueprint;[983] entire paragraphs of the Blueprint have been reproduced in the Commentary.[984]

In any case, the technical structure of the definition is simple: it contains an exhaustive list of taxes that are considered 'Covered Taxes' in paragraph 1 and another list of taxes that are explicitly excluded in paragraph 2. Now, one may ask why a negative list is necessary if the list of 'Covered Taxes' is exhaustive. However, this can be explained as follows: the taxes listed in the second paragraph of Article 4.2. GloBE Model Rules and Article 20 GloBE-Directive would indeed qualify as 'Covered Taxes' but are excluded for systematic reasons, which will be revealed below in this section.

First of all, there is the question of what should be considered a 'Tax' for purposes of GloBE; and indeed, the GloBE Model Rules do provide for a definition of the term 'Tax': accordingly, a 'Tax' *'means a compulsory unrequited payment to General Government'*.[985] This is a commonly used definition among several international organizations; however, it is only partly helpful as such but at least excludes any fees or contractual relationships where a corporation merely pays a consideration in proportion to, for example, a specific service or to receive a specific benefit. Furthermore, the definition excludes any fines, penalties and interest paid with respect to tax liabilities.[986] The reference to compulsory payments also excludes any voluntary payments.

Clearly, the distinction between 'Taxes' that are covered and those that are not is more important. As the Commentary indicates, the scope of 'Covered Taxes' is deliberately *'broadly defined to include Taxes imposed on a Constituent Entity's income or profits as well as Taxes that are functionally equivalent to such income taxes and Taxes on retained earnings and corporate equity'*[987] but does not include taxes *'such as indirect taxes, payroll and property taxes, which are not based on a measure of income*

981. In detail on this argument *see* Joachim Englisch, *GloBE Rules and Tax Competition*, 50 Intertax, *supra* note 769.
982. In the same vein, *see Ibid.*
983. *Tax Challenges Arising from Digitalisation – Report on Pillar Two Blueprint*, paras 129–153.
984. Compare, *i.a.*, *Ibid.*, para. 134 and *GloBE Commentary on Article 4*, *supra* note 884, para. 25.
985. Article 10.1. *GloBE Model Rules*, at 66.
986. *See GloBE Commentary on Article 4*, *supra* note 884, para. 24.
987. *See Ibid.*, para. 2.

or Top-up Taxes imposed under the GloBE rules themselves'.[988] But what does '*broadly*' defined really mean? This is clearly an implicit comparison with the material scope of DTCs: already within the Pillar Two Blueprint, it was pointed out that there should be '*no direct interaction with Article 2 (Taxes Covered) of the OECD Model Tax Convention*',[989] which already anticipates that the scope of 'Covered Taxes' for the purposes of GloBE goes beyond Article 2 OECD MC. For the interpretation of the term 'Covered Taxes' as defined in Article 4.2. GloBE Model Rules and Article 20 GloBE-Directive, it is therefore not advisable to refer to any comments made in the Commentary on Article 2 OECD MC.[990] Rather, the term 'Covered Taxes' in Article 4.2. GloBE Model Rules and Article 20 GloBE-Directive form a separate definition.

Whether a 'Tax' qualifies as a 'Covered Tax' for GloBE purposes is closely tied to the characteristics of the respective tax. In this regard, the Commentary emphasizes that neither the (i) name of the tax, (ii) ways to collect the tax, (iii) whether or not the tax is implemented within a specific legal act, (iv) the fact who actually bears the tax have any impact on whether a tax is covered or not[991] nor (v) whether the tax can be deducted from the tax base of another tax[992] plays a role with respect to the determination of whether a certain tax is covered or not. Rather, Article 4.2.1. GloBE Model Rules and Article 20(1) GloBE-Directive provide for an exhaustive list of characteristics that make up a 'Covered Tax'.

- 'Taxes' recorded in the financial accounts of a CE with respect to its income or profits or profits of a CE in which it owns an 'Ownership Interest': Article 4.2.1.(a) GloBE Model Rules and Article 20(1)(a) GloBE-Directive cover all taxes with respect to a CE's income or profits recorded in the financial accounts, irrespective of the fact in which position (profit or loss statement or OCI) the tax is included. However, the decisive element of this characteristic is that the respective 'Tax' is levied on income or profits. What, then, is the term income supposed to mean, one might ask, since there is, obviously, not a common understanding of the term income. The Commentary simply argues that a tax on income is characterized by the fact that it measures '*the taxpayers increase in wealth for the period*',[993] irrespective of whether this is done precisely,[994] and that '*it applies to income calculated on a net (rather than gross) basis*'.[995] Furthermore, it adds that a '*Tax imposed on gross income or revenue without any deductions (i.e. a tax on turnover) would not be considered an income tax.*'[996] This also excludes withholding taxes from the scope of

988. *See Ibid.*
989. *Tax Challenges Arising from Digitalisation – Report on Pillar Two Blueprint*, para. 129. The same formulation is also used in *GloBE Commentary on Article 4*, *supra* note 884, para. 22.
990. *OECD Model Tax Convention on Income and on Capital: Commentary on Article 2* (21 Nov. 2017).
991. *See GloBE Commentary on Article 4*, *supra* note 884, para. 23.
992. *See Ibid.*, para. 22.
993. *See Ibid.*, para. 25.
994. *See Ibid.*, para. 27.
995. *See Ibid.*, para. 25.
996. *See Ibid.*, para. 27.

Article 4.2.1.(a) GloBE Model Rules and Article 20(1)(a) GloBE-Directive, however, GloBE considers withholding taxes to be 'Taxes' imposed *'in lieu of a generally applicable corporate income tax'* covered by Article 4.2.1.(c) GloBE Model Rules and Article 20(1)(c) GloBE-Directive. The addition that 'Taxes' should also be covered if levied on profits of another CE in which the CE at issue owns 'Ownership Interests' is clearly addressed to taxes levied in the course of CFC regimes. The fact that a 'Tax' obliges to tax profits of a different person does not change anything with respect to the respective 'Taxes' characterization that it is levied with respect to income or profits.[997] Additionally, the Commentary notes that also industry-specific taxes for the banking sector and the exploitation of natural resources might be considered as 'Taxes' on income or profits if levied on a net amount.[998]

- 'Taxes' on distributed profits, deemed profit distributions, and non-business expenses imposed under an Eligible Distribution Tax System: such 'Taxes' are listed in Article 4.2.1.(b) GloBE Model Rules and Article 20(1)(b) GloBE-Directive and are closely connected to the definition of 'Eligible Distribution Tax Systems' provided for in Article 10.1. GloBE Model Rules and Article 3(42) GloBE-Directive. GloBE considers a 'Tax' as an 'Eligible Distribution Tax System' if (i) it imposes an income tax on a corporation only when its profits are distributed, are deemed to be distributed, or incurs on certain non-business expenses, (ii) it equals or exceeds the minimum rate of 15% and (iii) was in force already on or before 1 July 2021. The inclusion of distribution taxes should be seen as a concession to a small number of IF Member States: in particular, Estonia is well known for exempting undistributed profits from its corporate tax base but only levies CIT if profits are distributed. With respect to GloBE, this would mean that the ETR of CEs located in Estonia in 'Fiscal Years' where no distributions are made is always zero due to a lack of 'Covered Taxes' paid in the respective year.[999] To consider the legitimate interests of jurisdictions to keep such tax regimes that have been *'continuously in force since or before'*[1000] the IF agreed on the special treatment of 'Eligible Distribution Tax Systems' on 1 July 2021,[1001] to include such 'Taxes' within the definition of 'Covered Taxes' for the purpose of GloBE. This special treatment is implemented within Article 7.3. GloBE Model Rules and Article 40 GloBE-Directive that allow an 'MNE Group' to add an amount of so-called Deemed Distribution Tax to the amount of 'Adjusted Covered Taxes' in the jurisdiction applying an 'Eligible Distribution Tax System' to increase the ETR by including

997. *See Ibid.*, para. 26.
998. *See Ibid.*, para. 28.
999. Also *see GloBE Commentary on Article 7 GloBE Model Rules (2022), supra* note 335, para. 53.
1000. *See* the statement in the Commentary with respect to 1 Jul. 2021, in *GloBE Commentary on Article 10 GloBE Model Rules (2022), supra* note 280, para. 17.
1001. *See* OECD/G20 Inclusive Framework on BEPS, *Statement on a Two-Pillar Solution to Address the Tax Challenges Arising From the Digitalisation of the Economy – 1 July 2021, supra* note 197, at 4, where it was held: '*In respect of existing distribution tax systems, there will be no top-up tax liability if earnings are distributed within 3 to 4 years and taxed at or above the minimum level*'.

'Covered Taxes' that will be levied on subsequently distributed profits. However, any 'Deemed Distribution Tax' considered is to be recaptured by way of 'Additional Current Top-up Tax' ('additional top-up tax')[1002] if the respective profits have not been distributed within four years from when they were earned.[1003] The question of how a tax must be designed in order to qualify as an 'Eligible Distribution Tax System' is discussed in more detail in the Commentary to Article 10 GloBE Model Rules: first, the Commentary makes clear that the definition does not include any withholding taxes on distributed profits (such as withholding tax on dividends to tax the income of the shareholder), but rather only covers taxes that are imposed on the respective CE.[1004] Furthermore, it adds that the definition also needs to cover taxes levied on deemed distributions and non-business expenses to also cover those amounts of taxes that are levied to prevent circumvention of the distribution tax by making deemed or hidden distributions.[1005] The requirement that the 'Eligible Distribution Tax System' needs to equal or exceed the minimum rate is aimed at denying the allowance to consider 'Deemed Distribution Taxes' with respect to income '*that would be low-taxed income in any case*'.[1006]

- 'Taxes' imposed in lieu of a generally applicable corporate income tax: the third characteristic that could qualify a 'Tax' as being covered, according to Article 4.2.1.(c) GloBE Model Rules and Article 20(1)(c) GloBE-Directive is that the respective tax is '*imposed in lieu of a generally applicable corporate income tax*'.[1007] This element is undoubtedly the one that is most difficult to interpret within the definition of 'Covered Taxes'. What is a tax in '*lieu of a generally applicable*' CIT? Could jurisdictions simply argue that they levy consumption taxes '*in lieu*' of a CIT to not being forced to introduce a system of CIT? Finally, one could argue that digital services taxes (DST) are levied '*in lieu*' of a CIT because most states, having introduced a DST, justify it by the need to make up for lack of corporate income due to a missing taxable nexus. However, the Commentary clearly states that taxes on gross revenues, including DSTs, consumption taxes, excise or stamp duties, payroll taxes or property taxes levied on specific items, shall not be considered to fall within the ambit of 'Covered Taxes'.[1008] But where now is the fine line between '*lieu of a generally applicable*' CIT and all other taxes? The Commentary notes on this issue that '[t]*he 'in lieu of' test includes Taxes that are not described in the generally applicable income tax definition but which operate as substitutes for such taxes. This test,* [...] *would generally include withholding taxes on*

1002. Article 5.4.1. *GloBE Model Rules* and Art. 29(1) GloBE-Directive (2022/2523). In detail on the 'Additional Current Top-up Tax', *see* s. 4.4.2.6.
1003. Article 7.3.5. *GloBE Model Rules* and Art. 40(5) GloBE-Directive (2022/2523).
1004. *See GloBE Commentary on Article 10, supra* note 280, para. 14.
1005. *See Ibid.*, para. 15.
1006. *See Ibid.*, para. 16.
1007. Article 4.2.1.(c) *GloBE Model Rules* and Art. 20(1)(c) GloBE-Directive (2022/2523).
1008. *See GloBE Commentary on Article 10, supra* note 280, para. 36.

interest, rents and royalties, and other taxes on other categories of gross payments such as insurance premiums, provided such taxes are imposed in substitution for a generally applicable income tax. [This] [...] *would also include taxes arising from the Subject to Tax Rule*'.[1009] The Commentary further notes that the '*in lieu*' test serves to also include taxes that are levied on basis other than net income. One can doubt whether these statements really provide for sufficient guidance to distinguish 'Covered Taxes' from other monetary payments made to governments. In any case, the vague scope of the '*in lieu*' test seems to leave some tax policy leeway to jurisdictions to create alternative tax systems that might nevertheless be considered as 'Covered Taxes' under GloBE.

- 'Taxes' levied by reference to retained earnings and corporate equity, including a Tax on multiple components based on income and equity: finally, Article 4.2.1.(d) GloBE Model Rules and Article 20(1)(d) GloBE-Directive also include certain taxes levied on corporate equity within the definition of 'Covered Taxes'. It is important to distinguish taxes on equity from property taxes: while the latter are levied on the ownership of specific categories of property, the former are levied with respect to retained earnings or equity of a specific corporation. According to the Commentary, such equity taxes are regularly linked to domestic CIT schemes. A common example includes taxes that are levied within jurisdictions' CIT systems but are levied on equity to generate tax revenues even if the corporate taxpayer in the fiscal year at issue does not receive any profits or suffers losses[1010].[1011] The coverage of 'multiple components' clearly is a reference to Saudi Arabia's corporate Zakat, that is, a tax levied on income and equity at the same time. Also, the corporate Zakat, thus, qualifies as a 'Covered Tax'.[1012]

All separate letters of Article 4.2.1.(a) GloBE Model Rules and Article 20(1) GloBE-Directive obviously overlap. However, a delimitation of the individual letters among themselves is obsolete because the fulfilment of one of the enumerated characteristics leads to the same outcome. If a tax payment is covered, it qualifies as a 'Covered Tax' and can be included in the numerator of the ETR fraction.

As already anticipated above, some sort of taxes are specifically excluded from the catalogue of 'Covered Taxes' according to Article 4.2.2. GloBE Model Rules and Article 20(2) GloBE-Directive, although they would, in principle, qualify as 'Covered Taxes'. First, this concerns 'Top-up Tax' either levied by means of the IIR, QDMTT or

1009. *See GloBE Commentary on Article 4 GloBE Model Rules (2022), supra* note 884, para. 31.

1010. Austria, e.g., levies a so-called *Mindestkörperschaftsteuer* ('minimum CIT') which is calculated from a corporate taxpayer's equity and which is levied and collected, for budgetary reasons, even if a corporate taxpayer suffers losses in the respective fiscal year at issue. If the same corporate taxpayer receives profits in subsequent years, the '*Mindestkörperschaftsteuer*' paid previously may be fully credited against CIT liability arising in years in which the corporation receives profits. The Austrian '*Mindestkörperschaftsteuer*', thus, is an example for a tax covered by Art. 4.2.1.(d) GloBE Model Rules and Art. 20(1)(d) GloBE-Directive.

1011. *See GloBE Commentary on Article 4, supra* note 884, para. 33.

1012. *See Ibid.*, para. 35, which explicitly refers to the corporate Zakat.

UTPR.[1013] The exclusion of the 'Top-up Tax' levied by GloBE is a systematic necessity: if 'Top-up Tax' were to be considered as a 'Covered Tax' this '*would undermine the agreed Minimum Rate because it would reduce the amount of Top-up Tax that would need to be paid for the jurisdiction in the subsequent year*'.[1014] The exclusion of the GloBE Rules from the scope of 'Covered Taxes' is particularly interesting with regard to the QDMTT: the very purpose of the QDMTT is that the jurisdiction where 'Top-up Tax' is arising can soak up any pending 'Top-up Tax' within its jurisdiction, to prevent other jurisdictions from collecting the 'Top-up Tax' by means of IIR or UTPR. So, it could have been considered to leave QDMTTs within the scope of 'Covered Taxes'. However, GloBE took a different path and did not include the QDMTT to the 'Covered Taxes' but rather credits the tax levied by means of QDMTT against the 'Top-up Tax' other states could collect via the IIR and UTPR.[1015] Conversely, however, if a jurisdiction implements a different kind of '*soak up*' tax that does not qualify as QDMTT, such a tax would not necessarily be excluded from the definition of 'Covered Taxes' according to Article 4.2.2.(c) GloBE Model Rules and Article 20(2)(c) GloBE-Directive and could very well be considered a 'Covered Tax'. This could, for example, be relevant for the acknowledgement of foreign taxes that, *i.a.*, determine profits on a worldwide basis and do, thus, not qualify as a QDMTT as defined in the GloBE Model Rules and the GloBE-Directive.[1016] However, as will be seen, exclusion of QDMTT raises difficult issues with regard to GloBE's rule ordering (in detail section 4.4.2.6.3.).

Second, Article 4.2.2.(d) and (e) GloBE Model Rules and Article 20(2)(d) and (e) GloBE-Directive exclude two other kinds of taxes from the 'Covered Tax' definition. The first of these are so-called Disqualified Refundable Imputation Taxes that are taxes which are fully or partly refundable after a certain period of time. To prevent that the consideration of such taxes distorts the ETR of a specific 'Fiscal Year', GloBE carves them out of the 'Covered Taxes' definition.[1017] Furthermore, GloBE also excludes certain kinds of taxes for the insurance industry, which are strongly related to the adjustment of permanent differences with respect to taxes in the insurance industry addressed in Article 3.2.9. GloBE Model Rules and Article 16(10) GloBE-Directive already discussed in section 4.3.3.3.3. In the case and to the extent an adjustment is required, GloBE does not consider taxes paid by the insurance company in respect of returns of the policyholders as being 'Covered Taxes'. Thus, the exclusion of these taxes simply aims to reflect in the numerator the adjustments made in the denominator of the ETR fraction.[1018]

In deviation from Article 4.2. GloBE Model Rules, Article 20(3) GloBE-Directive has a third paragraph addressing the election to spread gains arising from the disposal

---

1013. Article 4.2.2. *GloBE Model Rules* and Art. 20(2) GloBE-Directive (2022/2523).
1014. *See GloBE Commentary on Article 4, supra* note 884, para. 38.
1015. *See Ibid.*
1016. *See* the definition of 'Qualified Domestic Minimum Top-up Tax' in Art. 10.1. *GloBE Model Rules*, at 64. Within the GloBE-Directive the corresponding term 'qualified domestic top-up tax' is defined in Art. 3(28) GloBE-Directive (2022/2523). In detail on the definition of QDMTT, *see* s. 4.4.2.6.3.
1017. *See GloBE Commentary on Article 4, supra* note 884, para. 39.
1018. *See Ibid.*, para. 40.

of immovable property over five years, as provided for in Article 3.2.6. GloBE Model Rules and Article 16(7) GloBE-Directive already discussed in section 4.3.3.3.5. While Article 3.2.6.(a). GloBE Model Rules requires the exclusion of any 'Covered Taxes' with respect to income for which the election is made, the corresponding provision of Article 16(7) GloBE-Directive is silent in this respect. Rather, the exclusion of taxes with respect to the election provided for in Article 16(7) GloBE-Directive has been incorporated in Article 20(3) GloBE-Directive. This is, therefore, not a difference in content but a purely aesthetic adjustment by the EU legislature.

4.3.4.3 Additions to Covered Taxes

4.3.4.3.1 Covered Taxes Accrued as an Expense

As with the GloBE base, simply relying on the values reported in the financial accounts would ignore various factors in determining the amount of 'Covered Taxes'. Consequently, GloBE uses adjustments to arrive at the amount of 'Adjusted Covered Taxes' that is used to compute the ETR. Article 4.1.2. GloBE Model Rules and Article 21(2) GloBE-Directive regulate certain positive adjustments, or in other words, additions to be made with respect to the amount of 'Covered Taxes' determined from the current tax expense reported in the financial accounts of a CE. The first of these additions addresses amounts of 'Covered Taxes' that are not reported as an income tax expense according to the accounting standard applied with respect to a specific 'MNE Group'. Finally, accounting standards may differ with regard to the disclosure of income tax expenses. If, however, a certain accounting standard does not record a tax that is considered as a 'Covered Tax' according to Article 4.1.2. GloBE Model Rules and Article 21(1) GloBE-Directive as an income tax expense but as an expense to be included within the computation of profit and loss before tax, the respective 'Covered Tax' would not be included within the numerator of the ETR fraction.[1019] For this reason, Article 4.1.2.(a) GloBE Model Rules and Article 21(2)(a) GloBE-Directive require to add tax payments qualifying as 'Covered Taxes', which are not included in the disclosed amount of tax expenses to the amount of 'Covered Taxes'. At the same time, the respective amount of tax needs to be correspondingly added back to the 'GloBE Income or Loss' ('net qualifying income or loss') pursuant to Articles 3.2.1.(a) and 15(1)(a)(i) GloBE-Directive (*see* already section 4.3.3.3.2), because the ETR would otherwise eventually be overstated. But what are examples of such 'Covered Taxes' that are regularly considered tax expenses and not as taxes on income under financial accounting rules? This is probably easiest to explain on the basis of IFRS: IAS 12, which is the relevant standard with respect to income taxes, states that '[f]*or the purposes of this Standard, income taxes include all domestic and foreign taxes which are based on taxable profits. Income taxes also include taxes, such as withholding taxes, which are payable by a subsidiary, associate or joint venture on distributions to the reporting*

1019. *See Ibid.*, para. 5a.

entity'.[1020] This rather broad definition not only includes taxes levied on net profits but also withholding taxes that GloBE acknowledges as '*taxes in lieu*' of general income taxes. However, IAS 12 does not cover taxes on equity, which clearly qualify as 'Covered Taxes' under Article 4.1.2.(d) GloBE Model Rules and Article 21(1)(d) GloBE-Directive. The Commentary, therefore, also refers to equity taxes as an example of an addition pursuant to Article 4.1.2.(a) GloBE Model Rules and Article 21(2)(a) GloBE-Directive.[1021] However, based on IFRS, other examples apart from equity taxes that require an adjustment pursuant to Article 4.1.2.(a) GloBE Model Rules and Article 21(2)(a) GloBE-Directive are likely to be a rare phenomenon. Nevertheless, this might be different with respect to other accounting standards.

4.3.4.3.2 GloBE Loss Election

Of much greater practical importance is the second addition to the amount of 'Covered Taxes', incorporated in Article 4.1.2.(b) GloBE Model Rules and Article 21(2)(b) GloBE-Directive, which concerns amounts of 'GloBE Loss Deferred Tax Assets' (within GloBE-Directive 'qualifying loss deferred tax assets'). Understanding this adjustment requires taking a step back: losses pose challenges not only to domestic tax legislatures but also to the incorporation of a framework of a minimum tax. One might think of two issues in this respect: first, no income taxes are due in the year in which the losses occur, and second, losses can usually be carried forward under national tax systems and might reduce 'Covered Taxes' in subsequent periods. The first issue, however, vanishes: if, in a loss year, no taxes are levied on a CE, there will be no income either. For this reason, with respect to the 'Fiscal Year' in which losses are incurred, there is no risk that the ETR will fall below the minimum rate. What, however, remains is the issue of previously occurred losses in subsequent 'Fiscal Years'. Finally, losses carried forward to subsequent 'Fiscal Years' do not reduce 'GloBE Income or Loss' ('net qualifying income or loss') of future years but rather reduce domestic tax liability. Consequently, in years where the losses can finally be used, the ETR plummets. Put to the extreme: if, for example, in one year, all profits under domestic law of a jurisdiction can be offset against past losses, there would be no 'Covered Taxes', which is why the ETR would be zero. But how should carried-forward losses be treated for the purpose of a global minimum tax?

The problem of considering losses carried forward within a system of minimum taxation was already recognized in the PoW from spring 2019, where it was held that '*differences between countries in the treatment of carry forward losses and the timing of recognition of income and expenses could impact on the calculation of the effective rate of tax in different jurisdictions*'.[1022] Both the Public Consultation Document of November 2019 and the Pillar Two Blueprint of October 2020 discussed losses among other temporary differences, and finally, within the GloBE Model Rules, they are to be considered as a temporary difference by way of deferred tax accounting pursuant to

1020. *See* IAS 12.2.
1021. *See GloBE Commentary on Article 4*, *supra* note 884, para. 5a.
1022. *Programme of Work*, at 28.

Article 4.4. GloBE Model Rules (Article 22 GloBE-Directive).[1023] GloBE's deferred tax mechanism to consider temporary differences will, however, in accordance with the computation scheme of the 'Adjusted Covered Taxes', only be discussed in section 4.3.4.5. and will be addressed here only very briefly in this section.

Pursuant to Article 4.4. GloBE Model Rules and Article 22 GloBE-Directive, temporary differences are corrected by increasing or decreasing the amount of 'Covered Taxes'[1024] by the 'Total Deferred Tax Adjustment Amount', which is to be calculated from the deferred tax expenses accrued in the financial accounts of a CE: the respective deferred tax expense needs to be recast at the minimum rate and is to be adjusted with respect to several individual items.

In any case, even before an extensive analysis is made in section 4.3.4.5 one can conclude that Article 4.4. GloBE Model Rules and Article 22 GloBE-Directive provide an extremely sophisticated mechanism to consider temporary adjustments. However, since the 'Total Deferred Tax Adjustment Amount' is to be determined mandatorily for each CE (neither Article 4.4. GloBE Model Rules nor Article 22 GloBE-Directive is optional), the calculation of the 'Total Deferred Tax Adjustment Amount' amount can be tedious and cannot always justify the administrative efforts involved. For simplification purposes, Article 4.5. GloBE Model Rules and Article 23 GloBE-Directive, thus, allow an 'MNE Group' to waive the application of the deferred tax accounting mechanism for a specific jurisdiction by exercising the so-called GloBE Loss Election (within the GloBE-Directive the so-called Qualifying loss election) and still carry forward losses for GloBE purposes. As a consequence of the 'GloBE Loss Election' ('Qualifying loss election'), the provisions of Article 4.5. GloBE Model Rules and Article 23 GloBE-Directive apply 'in lieu'[1025] of Article 4.4. GloBE Model Rules and Article 22 GloBE-Directive. Once the election is made, all other temporary differences not resulting from losses are disregarded for GloBE purposes. For this reason, the Commentary sees the benefit of Article 4.5. GloBE Model Rules (Article 23 GloBE-Directive) in particular with respect to jurisdiction levying low CIT rates: '*Accordingly, Art 4.5 is generally expected to be of greatest utility as a simplification in jurisdictions that do not impose a corporate income tax or impose one at a very low rate given that when the election is made, Art 4.4.* [Art 22 GloBE-Directive] *no longer applies and temporary differences may result in Top-up Tax.*'[1026] However, the 'GloBE Loss Election' ('Qualifying loss election') might also be useful even in small but high-tax market jurisdictions, where temporary differences are not material.

The operation of the 'GloBE Loss Election' ('Qualifying loss election') is very simple: a CE simply adds to its 'Covered Taxes' an amount that equals the 'Net GloBE Loss' ('net qualifying loss') multiplied by the minimum rate of 15%. This amount is specifically referred to as the 'GloBE Loss Deferred Tax Asset' (within the GloBE-Directive, the so-called qualifying loss deferred tax asset) and may be carried

1023. On the development of the consideration of temporary differences within GloBE, *see* s. 4.3.4.5.
1024. Article 4.1.1.(b) *GloBE Model Rules* and Art. 21(1)(b) GloBE-Directive (2022/2523).
1025. Article 4.4.1. *GloBE Model Rules* and Art. 22(2) GloBE-Directive (2022/2523).
1026. *See GloBE Commentary on Article 4, supra* note 884, para. 113.

forward[1027] without a specific time limit.[1028] Once the 'GloBE Loss Deferred Tax Asset' ('qualifying loss deferred tax asset') is used, Article 4.1.2.(b) GloBE Model Rules and Article 21(2)(b) GloBE-Directive require the amount used to be added to the 'Covered Taxes', leading to an increase in the ETR.[1029] In any case, once there are profits within the jurisdiction, the respective 'GloBE Loss Deferred Tax Asset' ('qualifying loss deferred tax asset') is mandatorily to be used as soon as possible.[1030] The used amount then reduces the 'GloBE Loss Deferred Tax Asset' ('qualifying loss deferred tax asset').[1031] Any remaining amounts of 'GloBE Loss Deferred Tax Asset' ('qualifying loss deferred tax asset') remain eligible to be carried forward.[1032]

According to Article 4.5.1. GloBE Model Rules and Article 23(1) GloBE-Directive, the 'GloBE Loss Deferred Tax Asset' ('qualifying loss deferred tax asset') is calculated with respect to a whole jurisdiction and not for single CEs. Both provisions require that there is a 'Net GloBE Loss' (within the GloBE-Directive 'net qualifying loss'), which is the negative sum of all 'GloBE Income or Loss' ('net qualifying income or loss') of all CEs of an 'MNE Group' that are 'located' within the same jurisdiction. However, this seems truly odd due to the fact that Article 4.1. GloBE Model Rules and Article 21(1) GloBE-Directive require that the amount of 'Adjusted Covered Taxes' per CE be calculated. So how to allocate the 'GloBE Loss Deferred Tax Asset' ('qualifying loss deferred tax asset') among CEs within the same jurisdiction? Interestingly, there is no comment on this issue in the Commentary. Admittedly, however, the problem only is of a theoretical nature: the 'Adjusted Covered Taxes' of CEs 'located' within the same jurisdiction are to be aggregated in the course of the ETR computation anyway.[1033] Thus, it seems that used amounts of 'GloBE Loss Deferred Tax Assets' are not added to the 'Adjusted Covered Taxes' of a CE, but finally to the sum of aggregated 'Adjusted Covered Taxes' of all CEs within the same jurisdiction.

The election, pursuant to Article 4.5.5. GloBE Model Rules and Article 23(5) GloBE-Directive, has to be made by the 'Filing Constituent Entity' in the very first year of having a CE in the jurisdiction at issue and may not be made[1034] with respect to jurisdictions that apply an 'Eligible Distribution Tax System'[1035] according to Article 7.3. GloBE Model Rules and Article 40 GloBE-Directive.[1036] Thus, as the Commentary

1027. Article 4.5.2 *GloBE Model Rules* and Art. 23(3) GloBE-Directive (2022/2523).
1028. *See GloBE Commentary on Article 4, supra* note 884, para. 114. The Commentary, however, acknowledges that jurisdictions '*may limit the practical application*' of the 'GloBE Loss Election' by way of introducing time limits or record keeping obligations.
1029. *See Ibid.*, para. 5b.
1030. Explicitly, *see* Art. 4.5.3 *GloBE Model Rules* and Art. 23(2) GloBE-Directive (2022/2523).
1031. Article 4.5.2 *GloBE Model Rules* and Art. 23(3) GloBE-Directive (2022/2523).
1032. Article 4.5.3 *GloBE Model Rules* and Art. 23(2) GloBE-Directive (2022/2523).
1033. *See* Art. 5.1.1. *GloBE Model Rules* and Art. 26(1) GloBE-Directive (2022/2523).
1034. The reason for this exclusion is reasonably explained by the Commentary: '[P]*ermitting a deemed deferred tax asset for losses in jurisdictions with an Eligible Distribution Tax System as defined in Article 7.3* [Art 40 GloBE-Directive] *would result in an overstated ETR in such jurisdictions, giben that distribution tax is only applicable when positive earnings are distributed*', *see* the last sentence in *GloBE Commentary on Article 4, supra* note 884, para. 116.
1035. On 'Eligible Distribution Tax Systems', *see* s. 4.3.4.2.
1036. Article 4.5.5 *GloBE Model Rules* and the last sentence of Art. 23(1) GloBE-Directive (2022/2523).

sums up that the election *'may only be made once'*.[1037] The reason for only accepting elections within the first year aims to limit the use of the 'GloBE Loss Deferred Tax Asset' ('qualifying loss deferred tax asset') to actual necessities and to make the election unavailable for tax planning purposes.[1038] Furthermore, the election does not transfer with a CE, but rather is only binding the 'MNE Group' that has taken the election: so if a CE is subject to an acquisition, the 'MNE Group' that buys the respective entity is not bound to the election but rather can decide to make use of the election, if the respective new CE is the first within this jurisdiction. If the acquiring 'MNE Group' already has a CE within the same jurisdiction but did not take the election within that specific jurisdiction, the option cannot be taken for the new CE either.[1039]

Although the 'GloBE Loss Election' ('qualifying loss deferred tax asset') can only be exercised in the first 'Fiscal Year', it is revocable under Article 4.5.4. GloBE Model Rules and Article 23(4) GloBE-Directive. Thus, MNE Groups may decide to switch back to the 'full' deferred tax mechanism according to Article 4.4. GloBE Model Rules and Article 22 GloBE-Directive. In this case, however, the 'GloBE Loss Deferred Tax Asset' ('qualifying loss deferred tax asset') is to be reduced to zero. This is due to the fact that the transition rules provided in Article 9.1. GloBE Model Rules and Article 47 GloBE-Directive then require computing the deferred taxes as *'if they had been calculated [...] for the prior Fiscal Years'*.[1040] If it were allowed to keep the remaining 'GloBE Loss Deferred Tax Asset' ('qualifying loss deferred tax asset') in the year of revocation, the pending loss carry-forward could be used twice since any loss carry-forwards are to be considered within the 'Total Deferred Tax Adjustment Amount' ('total deferred tax adjustment amount') as well.[1041]

Both, Article 4.5.6. GloBE Model Rules and Article 23(6) GloBE-Directive contain a special supplement for 'Flow-through Entities' that are UPEs: such tax transparent UPEs are permitted to make the election separately from all other CEs 'located' within the same jurisdiction.[1042] Tax transparent UPEs are addressed in Article 7.1. GloBE Model Rules and Article 38 GloBE-Directive and have already shortly been addressed in section 4.2.4.2.2. and 4.3.3.6. The reason for their special treatment is the fact that their ETR needs to be calculated, although they are usually not subject to tax themselves within the jurisdiction they are located, and their income is only taxed in the hands of their shareholders. Since the shareholders of a UPE are not part of the MNE Group, no 'Top-up Tax' could be levied with respect to the 'Flow-through' UPE, which is why the determination of the ETR is made with respect to the taxes levied in the hand of the shareholders. With respect to losses incurred by such UPEs, there is the risk that the respective losses are used twice, once at the level of the UPE and once by the shareholder. Article 7.1.2. GloBE Model Rules and Article 38(3) GloBE-Directive, therefore, only allow tax transparent UPEs to keep their losses to the extent that they did not already reduce the tax burden of its shareholders. With respect to the losses that

1037. *See GloBE Commentary on Article 4, supra* note 884, para. 116.
1038. *See Ibid.*
1039. *See* the example provided for in *Ibid.*, para. 117.
1040. *See Ibid.*, para. 115.
1041. *See Ibid.*
1042. *See Ibid.*, para. 118.

have not already been used by its shareholders, the transparent UPE may make use of the election under Article 4.5. GloBE Model Rules and Article 23 GloBE-Directive. But why exactly is this special exception for transparent UPEs needed? Neither the GloBE Model Rules, the GloBE-Directive, nor the Commentary are clear in this respect. However, the explanation could lie in specifics of financial account rules: in some jurisdictions, 'Flow-through Entities' like partnerships are not obliged to prepare for 'Consolidated Financial Statements'. In these cases, financial statements are only available with respect to legal entities held by the respective 'Flow-through' UPE. For GloBE purposes, the absence of a 'Consolidated Financial Statement' means that the respective UPE needs to prepare statements *'that would have been prepared if such Entity were required to prepare such statements in accordance'*[1043] with either an 'Acceptable Financial Accounting Standard' or an 'Authorised Financial Accounting Standard' (in detail on situations of UPEs not required to prepare financial statements, *see* section 4.2.3.2.). The 'GloBE Loss Election' ('qualifying loss deferred tax asset') may, thus, be very helpful for 'Flow-through' UPEs, because it saves them from tedious computations for the 'Total Deferred Tax Adjustment Amount' ('total deferred tax adjustment amount') pursuant to Article 4.4. GloBE Model Rules and Article 22 GloBE-Directive.

4.3.4.3.3 Uncertain Tax Positions

Financial accounting rules are often more 'cautious' than tax rules: financial accounting rules oblige the disclosure of expenses, even if it is uncertain whether they will occur at all. This might also hold true with respect to taxes: there might be uncertain tax positions included within the financial statements, although they have not really been paid or are not payable at all. In principle, Article 4.1.3.(d) GloBE Model Rules and Article 21(3)(d) GloBE-Directive oblige the reduction of the amount of 'Covered Taxes' with regard to such uncertain tax positions (in detail, also *see* section 4.3.4.4.4.). GloBE, thus, denies the inclusion of uncertain tax liabilities within the amount of 'Adjusted Covered Taxes'. However, if in the following years, the uncertain tax liability finally materializes, Article 4.1.2.(c) GloBE Model Rules and Article 21(3)(c) GloBE-Directive allow adding the respective payments to the amount of 'Adjusted Covered Taxes' in the 'Fiscal Year' in which the tax is finally to be paid. This is because *'once the amount is paid, it is appropriate to include* [it] *in Covered Taxes'*.[1044]

4.3.4.3.4 Credit or Refund of Qualified Refundable Tax Credits

'Qualified Refundable Tax Credits' have already been addressed with regard to the adjustment of permanent differences in section 4.3.3.3.3., where it has been shown that such tax benefits given to taxpayers via the tax system are considered as increases

1043. *See* letter d of the definition of 'Consolidated Financial Statements' in Art. 10.1. *GloBE Model Rules*, at 54 and Art. 3(6)(d) GloBE-Directive (2022/2523).
1044. *See GloBE Commentary on Article 4, supra* note 884, para. 5c.

in income instead of reductions to 'Covered Taxes'.[1045] Thus, according to Article 4.1.2.(d) GloBE Model Rules and Article 21(2)(d) GloBE-Directive, any amount of credit or refund to be paid with respect to 'Qualified Refundable Tax Credits' is to be added back to the amount of 'Covered Taxes' if financial accounting rules treated such credit or refund as a reduction of current tax expenses.[1046] Finally, if the respective tax credit would be treated as an item of 'GloBE Income or Loss' ('net qualifying income or loss') but not be added to the 'Adjusted Covered Taxes', the ETR would be understated.[1047] If a 'Qualified Refundable Tax Credit' is recognized within the financial accounts as a grant (e.g., according to IAS 20[1048]) not reducing the amount of current tax expense, an adjustment pursuant to Article 4.1.2.(d) GloBE Model Rules and Article 21(2)(d) GloBE-Directive is superfluous. For this reason, both provisions require that the respective credit is '*recorded as a reduction to the current tax expense*'[1049].[1050]

For those MNE Groups that apply the IFRS, an addition to 'Covered Taxes' will regularly not be required: although IAS 20 ('Accounting for Government Grants and Disclosure of Government Assistance') explicitly states that it does not deal with '*government assistance that is provided for an entity in the form of benefits that are available in determining taxable profit or tax loss, or are determined or limited on the basis of income tax liability* [...] [including] [...] *income tax holidays, investment tax credits, accelerated depreciation allowances and reduced income tax rates*',[1051] 'Qualified Refundable Tax Credits' are regularly recognized in line with IAS 20. This is also because IAS 12, dealing with income taxes, explicitly excludes '*investment tax credits*' from its scope.[1052] However, according to IAS 8 (Accounting Policies, Changes in Accounting Estimates and Errors), '[i]*n the absence of an IFRS that specifically applies to a transaction* [...]'[1053] the management shall '*refer to, and consider the applicability of [...] the requirements in the IFRSs dealing with similar and related issues*'[1054].[1055]

1045. Also *see GloBE Commentary on Article 10 GloBE Model Rules (2022)*, *supra* note 280, para. 134.

1046. *See GloBE Commentary on Article 4*, *supra* note 884, para. 5d.

1047. *See Ibid.*, para. 16.

1048. It should be added that IAS 20 (Accounting for Government Grants and Disclosure of Government Assistance) explicitly states that it does not deal with '*government assistance that is provided for an entity in the form of benefits that are available in determining taxable profit or tax loss, or are determined or limited on the basis of income tax liability* [...] [including] [...] *income tax holidays, investment tax credits, accelerated depreciation allowances and reduced income tax rates*', *see* IAS 20.2b. However, also IAS 12 (Income Taxes) explicitly excludes '*investment tax credits*' from its scope, *see* IAS 12.4.

1049. Article 4.1.2.(d) *GloBE Model Rules* and correspondingly, using a slightly different wording, *see* Art. 21(2)(d) GloBE-Directive (2022/2523).

1050. For further details on the treatment of 'Qualified Refundable Tax Credits', *see* s. 4.3.3.3.3.

1051. IAS 20.2b.

1052. *See* IAS 12.4.: '*This Standard does not deal with the methods of accounting for government grants (see IAS 20 Accounting for Government Grants and Disclosure of Government Assistance) or investment tax credits*'.

1053. IAS 8.10.

1054. IAS 8.11a.

1055. *See* for one of the rare sources on the question how to account investment tax credits under the IFRS, *see* Katharina Maier, *Investitionsanreize im Spannungsfeld der Bilanzierungsvorschriften von IAS 12 und IAS 20 Zuwendungen*, PWC – IFRS Aktuell (2017).

Consequently, according to the IFRS, investment tax credits such as 'Qualified Refundable Tax Credits' are to be recognized by the standard that better fits the respective tax incentive. In principle, therefore, both IAS 12 and IAS 20 come into question. If one closely examines the definition of 'Qualified Refundable Tax Credits' and the corresponding paragraphs in the Commentary, it becomes clear that such credits do regularly better fit within IAS 20: according to Article 10.1. GloBE Model Rules (reflected in Article 3[38] GloBE-Directive) the term covers 'refundable tax credit[s] designed in a way such that it must be paid *as cash or available as cash equivalents* within *four years* from when a Constituent Entity satisfies the conditions for receiving the credit under the laws of the jurisdiction granting the credit' (emphasis added).[1056] 'Qualified Refundable Tax Credits', thus, as the Commentary notes, need to be '*designed to identify tax credits that are, as a matter of substance and not merely form, likely to be refunded*'[1057] and must be designed in a way '*such that the refund mechanism has practical significance for those taxpayers that will be entitled to the credit*'.[1058] Any tax credits that either '*cannot be refunded in cash or credit against another tax, is not refundable*'[1059] or '*will be of no practical significance to taxpayers*'[1060] are not to be qualified as 'Qualified Refundable Tax Credits'.[1061] Given these specifics, it is obvious that 'Qualified Refundable Tax Credits' much better fit into the accounting concept of IAS 20, according to which government grants are included as profit in the profit and loss statement. For this reason, it is likely that most MNE Groups applying IFRS do not record 'Qualified Refundable Tax Credits' as reductions to the current tax expenses but rather as an increase of income. For this reason, required adjustments to the GloBE base (Article 3.2.4. GloBE Model Rules and Article 15(5) GloBE-Directive) and additions to the 'Covered Taxes' (Article 4.1.2.(d) GloBE Model Rules and Article 21(2)(d) GloBE-Directive) will, in most cases, not be necessary for 'MNE Groups' applying the IFRS.

4.3.4.4 Reductions to Covered Taxes

4.3.4.4.1 Taxes with Respect to Excluded Income or Loss

The first reduction of 'Covered Taxes' forms the counterpart to the adjustments to the 'GloBE Income or Loss' ('net qualifying income or loss') in Article 3.2. GloBE Model Rules and Article 16 GloBE Model Rules: any taxes that would qualify as 'Covered Taxes' but that are attributable to income or losses that had been excluded from the GloBE base, need, pursuant to Article 4.1.3.(a) GloBE Model Rules and Article 21(3)(a) GloBE-Directive, to be removed from the amount of 'Covered Taxes'. If this were not

1056. Article 10.1. *GloBE Model Rules*, at 65 and Art. 3(38) GloBE-Directive (2022/2523).
1057. *See GloBE Commentary on Article 10 GloBE Model Rules (2022)*, *supra* note 280, para. 136.
1058. *See Ibid.*
1059. *See Ibid.*, para. 135.
1060. *See Ibid.*, para. 136.
1061. For an extensive discussion of the definition of 'Qualified Refundable Tax Credits' in literature, *see* J. Englisch, *GloBE Rules and Tax Competition*, 50 Intertax (2022), *supra* note 769.

the case, the ETR calculation would be distorted: if taxes with respect to excluded income, like, e.g., 'Qualified Shipping Income' were included within the 'Covered Taxes', the ETR would be overstated because the numerator of the ETR fraction would include a tax attributable to income that is not taken into account with respect to the denominator: assume a CE is located in a jurisdiction that levies CIT at a flat rate of 15% but does not exempt dividend income. The CE receives 50 in business profits and another 50 from dividends excluded according to Article 3.2.2.(b) GloBE Model Rules (Article 15(2)(b) GloBE-Directive). Consequently, the total amount of tax paid in this jurisdiction is 15. If GloBE would only exclude the dividend, the ETR would amount to 30% for this jurisdiction (15/50 = 30%). By way of reducing the CEs 'Covered Taxes' based on the ratio of excluded and total income (in this example, 50/100 = 50%), the amount of 'Covered Taxes' is 7.5 (15 x 50%). The ETR would, thus, amount to 15% (7.5/50 = 15%).[1062] Consequently, Article 4.1.3.(a) GloBE Model Rules and Article 21(3)(a) GloBE-Directive make sure that the numerator of the ETR fraction only includes taxes with respect to items of income that are included in the denominator as well.

Conversely, the ETR would be understated in the case of losses because losses taken into account regularly reduce the taxes levied in the numerator and at the same time, the income in the denominator would also decrease, resulting in a disproportionate reduction in the ETR: assume a CE incurred losses from excluded shipping activities of 100 but receives other income of 200.[1063] The total amount of income, thus, is 100. The jurisdiction of the CE levies a flat tax of 20% on the total income of 100, which results in a tax paid of 20 (100 x 20%). In this case, the ETR would be 10% (20/[100 + 100]). Interestingly, however, neither the GloBE Model Rules nor the GloBE-Directive provide for a mechanism to correct distortions of the ETR with respect to a reduction in 'Covered Taxes' caused by excluded losses. While 'Covered Taxes' with respect to excluded positive income is removed from the GloBE base, any excluded loss might cause a reduction of 'Covered Taxes' that cannot be reversed by way of an addition to the amount of 'Covered Taxes'. This becomes particularly evident in the wording of Article 4.1.3.(a) GloBE Model Rules, referring to 'the amount of current tax expense with respect to *income excluded* from the computation of GloBE Income or Loss'[1064] (emphasis added). Since the term income is not separately defined, one could question whether the term income[1065] is also supposed to cover negative income, i.e., losses. However, this interpretation is not convincing because the OECD included a distinct provision to reduce the 'Covered Taxes' with respect to excluded income in Article 4.1.3.(a) GloBE Model Rules and Article 21(3)(a) GloBE-Directive, while the

1062. This example is based on Example 4.1.3. - 1 *GloBE Examples*, at 34.
1063. As Example 3.3.1. - 3 in *GloBE Examples* reveals, any losses from excluded shipping activities need to be added back to the amount of 'GloBE Income or Loss' ('net qualifying income or loss').
1064. Article 4.1.3.(a) *GloBE Model Rules*. Also Art. 21(3)(a) GloBE-Directive (2022/2523) solely refers to '*income*'.
1065. Also the Commentary on Art. 4.1.3.(a) GloBE Model Rules exclusively refers to the term 'income': 'Paragraph (a) removes the amount of Covered Taxes with respect to *income* excluded from the computation of GloBE Income or Loss under Chapter 3' (emphasis added), *see GloBE Commentary on Article 3 GloBE Model Rules (2022), supra* note 507, para. 7.

corresponding provision on additions to the 'Covered Taxes' in Article 4.1.2. GloBE Model Rules and Article 21(2) GloBE-Directive does not provide for a corresponding adjustment. The Commentary also seems to accept that there is no addition to 'Covered Taxes' in the case of excluded losses. In paragraph 19 of the Commentary on Article 3 GloBE Model Rules, it is held: 'To the extent an adjustment required by Article 3.2 excludes an amount of *income* from the GloBE Income or Loss computation, any Covered Taxes associated with that income must also be excluded from Adjusted Covered Taxes pursuant to Article 4.1.3(a)'[1066] (emphasis added). From a tax policy perspective, reducing the amount of 'Covered Taxes' by the amount of taxes that are attributable to excluded income is a systematic necessity. Otherwise, the exclusion of income could shield other items of income from the minimum tax. At first glance, it seems odd that the reverse distortive effect occurring in the case of excluded losses is accepted by GloBE. Nevertheless, there might be two tax policy considerations that might justify not adding reductions in 'Covered Taxes' caused by excluded losses: first, if it were permitted to make a positive adjustment to 'Covered Taxes' with respect to such loss situations, this would incentivize domestic tax systems to generously accept deduction of losses with respect to items of income or losses that are excluded under GloBE. Second, an addition to the 'Covered Taxes' would require an addition of deemed tax payments, necessarily including the risk that 'MNE Groups' would abusively overstate such a deemed tax position. Nonetheless, not allowing to increase the amount of 'Covered Taxes' with respect to excluded losses leads to disadvantages, especially with respect to those jurisdictions that levy a flat CIT on all income and, for example, do not grant a special tax regime, e.g., for the shipping industry. Because even if the nominal CIT is well above the minimum tax rate, the ETR may plummet below the minimum rate if domestic law allows offsetting losses excluded under GloBE from profits made with respect to income that is included within the GloBE base. Overall, it seems unsystematic that GloBE does not provide for an adjustment with respect to 'Covered Taxes' in the case of excluded losses.

From the wording '*with respect to income excluded*',[1067] it can also be deduced that a reduction of 'Covered Taxes' is only to be made to the extent that income actually is excluded.[1068] If a particular income stream is only partially excluded, the amount of 'Covered Taxes' also only is to be reduced with respect to that amount of tax that is attributable to the excluded part of income. This, for example, might occur with respect to the excess limitation provided for 'Qualified Ancillary Shipping Income' in Article 3.3.4. GloBE Model Rules and Article 17(5) GloBE-Directive: if the limitation is exceeded, the respective income remains within the GloBE base, and so does the amount of 'Covered Taxes' attributable to the excess amount because the amount of 'Covered Taxes' only is to be reduced '*with respect to income excluded*'.[1069] Furthermore, as the Commentary notes, '*the excluded taxes must be determined on the same*

1066. *See Ibid.*, para. 19.
1067. Article 4.1.3.(a) *GloBE Model Rules* and Art. 21(3)(a) GloBE-Directive (2022/2523).
1068. *See* the last sentence in *GloBE Commentary on Article 4 GloBE Model Rules (2022)*, *supra* note 884, para. 10.
1069. Article 4.1.3.(a) *GloBE Model Rules* and Art. 21(3)(a) GloBE-Directive (2022/2523).

basis without regard to any related expenses'.[1070] If, e.g., a jurisdiction levies a withholding tax on the gross amount of an excluded dividend, the entire amount of withholding tax is to be subtracted from the amount of 'Covered Taxes' even if there might, e.g., be financing costs related to the respective dividend. Furthermore, any taxes paid by a CE that are not attributable to the 'MNE Group' need to be excluded as well. If, for example, a jurisdiction forces a CE-owner to apply a CFC rule also with regard to shareholders that do not belong to the group, the amount of 'Covered Taxes' attributable to the minority interest needs to be excluded from the amount of 'Covered Taxes' of the CE qualifying as CFC.[1071] Finally, that portion of CFC tax is to be considered as an income tax levied for the minority shareholder and cannot be assigned to the MNE Group's share of 'Covered Taxes'.

Eventually, the Commentary also clarifies that income received by other CEs is to be considered as excluded income. For this reason, Article 4.1.3.(a) GloBE Model Rules and Article 21(3)(a) GloBE-Directive also apply with respect to taxes levied on income that is attributable to a different CE. This is particularly relevant with respect to withholding taxes levied on excluded dividends and taxes levied in the course of CFC regimes: according to Article 4.3.2.(e) GloBE Model Rules and Article 24(5) GloBE-Directive any amount of 'Covered Taxes' that is accrued in the financial accounts of the CE-owner is to be allocated to the entity distributing the dividend. GloBE, thus, counts withholding taxes levied on dividends to the amount of 'Covered Taxes' of the distributing entity. One could now argue, however, that this amount of dividend withholding tax is to be removed from the 'Covered Taxes' of the distributing entity because it is related to income received by the CE-owner. However, the Commentary notes that '[a]*lthough dividends received from other Constituent Entities are excluded from the GloBE Income or Loss, taxes on those dividends represent new or additional taxes on the income of the distributing Constituent Entity that has been included in the GloBE Income or Loss*'.[1072] Thus, Article 4.1.3.(a) GloBE Model Rules and Article 21(3)(a) GloBE-Directive shall not apply with respect to taxes assigned to the distributing CE pursuant to Article 4.3.2.(c) GloBE Model Rules and Article 24(5) GloBE-Directive, but only to the CE-owner to which the excluded dividend was distributed.

A similar issue arises, as already anticipated, with respect to taxes levied in connection with CFC regimes: CFC regimes regularly include retained profits of foreign-controlled entities into the tax base of the parent entity, which is obliged to tax the CFCs income at the local tax level of the parent entity. With respect to GloBE, however, the income of the CFC that is taxed at its parent entity is, according to Article 4.3.2.(e) GloBE Model Rules and Article 24(3) GloBE-Directive, to be allocated to the CFC (which is the CE-subsidiary). For this reason, Article 4.1.3.(a) GloBE Model Rules and Article 21(3)(a) GloBE-Directive apply with respect to the parent-CE and reduce its amount of 'Adjusted Covered Taxes'. However, both provisions do not apply with respect to the CE, that is, the CFC: the CFC's income that is taxed by way of a CFC regime at the level of its CE-owner is included within the CFCs GloBE Income or Loss.

1070. *GloBE Commentary on Article 4, supra* note 884, para. 10.
1071. *See Ibid.*
1072. *See Ibid.*, para. 11.

However, the Commentary adds that if, for whatever reason, the CFC reallocation rule of Article 4.3.3. GloBE Model Rules (reflected in Article 24[6] GloBE-Directive) does not apply, and the respective tax stays at the level of the CE-owner; the respective CFC tax is very well to be included within the 'Adjusted Covered Taxes' of the CE-owner.[1073]

4.3.4.4.2 Non-qualified Refundable Tax Credits

Pursuant to Article 4.1.3.(b) GloBE Model Rules and Article 21(3)(b) GloBE-Directive, the amount of 'Covered Taxes' is to be reduced by any tax credits that do not qualify as 'Qualified Refundable Tax Credit' ('Non-Qualified Refundable Tax Credits'). This adjustment, thus, is the complement to the adjustments made with respect to 'Qualified Refundable Tax Credits': whereas such tax credits are treated as increases of income and have to be included within the 'Adjusted Covered Taxes', any tax credits or other refunds that do not meet the definition of 'Qualified Refundable Tax Credit' do indeed reduce the amount of 'Covered Taxes'. In return, however, such tax credits and refunds are to be excluded from the GloBE base according to the respective second sentences of Article 3.2.4. GloBE Model Rules and Article 16(5) GloBE-Directive.[1074] Evidently, a reduction pursuant to Article 4.1.3.(b) GloBE Model Rules and Article 21(3)(b) GloBE-Directive is only required if the tax credit has not already been deducted from the current tax expenses in accordance with financial accounting rules.

4.3.4.4.3 Refunded and Credited Tax Not Included Within Financial Accounts

Apart from 'Non-Qualified Refundable Tax Credits', Article 4.1.3.(c) GloBE Model Rules and Article 21(3)(c) GloBE-Directive also require a reduction of the 'Covered Taxes' if any 'Covered Taxes' are credited or refunded and had not been recorded as a reduction to the current tax expenses.[1075] Both provisions do not address reductions due to 'Qualified Refundable Tax Credits'. This addition, thus, is a complement to Article 4.2.1.(c) GloBE Model Rules and Article 21(2)(c) GloBE-Directive, which cover exactly the opposite situation where a 'Covered Tax' paid is not included within the current tax expense in the financial accounts. The Commentary admits that the scope of Article 4.1.3.(c) GloBE Model Rules and Article 21(3)(c) GloBE-Directive might be very limited: any adjustments to the amount of 'Covered Taxes' with respect to previous 'Fiscal Years' is addressed by Article 4.6. GloBE Model Rules (Article 24 GloBE-Directive), which takes precedence over Article 4.1.3.(c) GloBE Model Rules (Article 21[3][c] GloBE-Directive). What remains within the scope of Article 4.1.3.(c) GloBE Model Rules and Article 21(3)(c) GloBE-Directive, whereby any taxes refunded or credited in the same year in which they were paid or if taxes of previous years are refunded that are not adjusted according to Article 4.6. GloBE Model Rules and Article

1073. *See Ibid.*, para. 12.
1074. *See Ibid.*, para. 13.
1075. *See Ibid.*, para. 14.

24 GloBE-Directive.[1076] Furthermore, Article 4.1.3.(c) GloBE Model Rules and Article 21(3)(c) GloBE-Directive might kick in, where a CE gets a refund or a credit for a 'Covered Tax' that had been paid to a different CE.[1077] This is likely to affect, in particular, withholding taxes on dividends that are attributed to the distributing CE under Article 4.3.2.(e) GloBE Model Rules and Article 24(5) GloBE-Directive, but for which domestic laws regularly grant a refund to the CE-owner.

4.3.4.4.4 Uncertain Tax Positions and Taxes Not Expected to Be Paid Within Three Years

Many financial accounting standards oblige the recognition of expenses before they really occur, or at least oblige building up reserves (provisions or contingent liabilities)[1078] to finally be able to pay an anticipated liability. GloBE, pursuant to Article 4.1.3.(d) GloBE Model Rules and Article 21(3)(d) GloBE-Directive, deny including uncertain tax positions within the 'Adjusted Covered Taxes' '*given the MNE Group's determination (and possibly its explicit or implicit assertion to the relevant tax authority) that the taxes are not owed and the high degree of uncertainty with respect to whether such amounts will be paid in a future period*'.[1079] Thus, any movements with respect to reserves recognized in the financial accounts remain inconsiderable with respect to the amount of 'Adjusted Covered Taxes'.[1080]

Similarly, GloBE, according to Article 4.1.3.(e) GloBE Model Rules and Article 21(3)(e) GloBE-Directive, refuses to take into account future tax expenditures that may even be certain but not expected to be paid within three years of the 'Fiscal Year' in question. The reasoning for the denial to consider such amounts within the amount of 'Adjusted Covered Taxes' is similar to uncertain tax liabilities: such tax positions might also be uncertain and, furthermore, it might be within the MNE Group's disposal when to pay the tax. This could, as the Commentary seems to fear, potentially give rise to abuse: if a CE '*could assert that it does not intend to pay the tax in a year where the Constituent Entity is well over the Minimum Rate, and then subsequently pays the tax liability in a year in which it is below the Minimum Rate, using the rule to escape what would otherwise be Top-up Tax liability*'.[1081]

In any case, once the uncertain or long-term tax liability that had to be excluded from the amount of 'Covered Taxes' finally is to be paid, it may be included within the 'Covered Taxes' in the 'Fiscal Year' in which the payment is made (*see* section 4.3.4.3.3.).

1076. *See Ibid.*, para. 15.
1077. *See Ibid.*
1078. *See, i.a.*, IAS 37.
1079. *See GloBE Commentary on Article 4, supra* note 884, para. 16.
1080. *See Ibid.*
1081. *See Ibid.*, para. 17.

4.3.4.5 *The 'Total Deferred Tax Adjustment Amount' to Address Temporary Differences*

4.3.4.5.1 The Crux of Considering Temporary Differences Within the Framework of GloBE

As early as November 2019, the consideration of temporary differences emerged as one of the core topics to be discussed in the course of the public consultation made between November and December 2019. The Public Consultation Document dealt with the question of how the global minimum tax should deal with temporary differences in general.[1082] The document suggested various alternative mechanisms for discussion, such as (i) allowing a carry-forward for excess taxes paid above the minimum rate,[1083] (ii) deferred tax accounting,[1084] or (iii) multi-year averaging of the GloBE base[1085].[1086] Feedback varied widely but did show a slight preference for deferred tax accounting: many argued that deferred tax accounting is widely used among all different accounting standards and that it would therefore be the most simple and promising approach to consider temporary differences, including loss carry-forwards.[1087]

Interestingly, however, the Blueprint was extremely sceptical of the use of deferred tax accounts and seemed to have a clear preference for a carry-forward mechanism:

> The principal policy risk of deferred tax accounting, however, is that it relies on a taxpayer's estimate of future liability for tax in a subsidiary jurisdiction to determine its current liability under the GloBE rules. The carry-forward approach, in contrast, relies on actual tax liabilities existing at the time tax liability under the GloBE rules is determined.[1088]

Furthermore, the Blueprint stated the following:

> The carry-forward and deferred tax accounting approaches both impose some compliance and administration burdens. On the surface, the deferred tax accounting approach appears to be simpler because taxpayers use deferred tax accounting for financial purposes already. However, differences between the policies of the GloBE rules and financial reporting will likely mean that modifications would need to be made to certain deferred tax accounting outcomes in order to adapt deferred tax accounting to the GloBE rules. These modifications would add a significant amount of additional complexity and may lead to uncertainty. Although maintaining memorandum accounts in respect of carry-forwards is somewhat burdensome, it is a familiar exercise for both taxpayers and tax administrations. Accordingly, while there appear to be some advantages with a deferred tax accounting approach

1082. *See* s. 2.3.2. in *Public Consultation Pillar Two 2019*, paras 31–44.
1083. *Ibid.*, paras 34–39.
1084. *Ibid.*, paras 40–43.
1085. *Ibid.*, para. 44.
1086. For extensive discussion, *see* V. Bendlinger, *Minimum Taxation – Ergebnisse der Konsultationen zum GloBE Proposal der OECD*, 32 SWI, *supra* note 187, at 21–22.
1087. For an analysis of the responses to the public consultation with respect to temporary differences, *see Ibid.*, at 28–29.
1088. *Tax Challenges Arising from Digitalisation – Report on Pillar Two Blueprint*, para. 293.

> the members of the Inclusive Framework do not consider that such an approach would serve as an appropriate mechanism to address timing differences. They do consider, however, that financial information on deferred tax accounting could play a useful role in the development of simplification options [...].[1089]

Against this background, it was quite a surprise when the OECD published the GloBE Model Rules on 20 December 2021, including a comprehensive mechanism based on deferred tax accounting. So why did the IF finally adopt deferred tax accounting to address temporary differences?

One can only speculate about the actual background of this decision. Nevertheless, one can assume that it had not been reasonable to rely heavily on financial accounts with respect to both base and tax determination but deviate from it with regard to temporary differences by adopting a carry-forward mechanism. In this regard, it is interesting that the Blueprint considered '*that financial information on deferred tax accounting could play a useful role in the development of simplification options*'.[1090] As will be shown shortly, the deferred tax accounting regime of GloBE is anything but simple. In fact, the mechanism for considering temporary differences within the ETR fraction is not only the most significant adjustment in terms of the amount of 'Adjusted Covered Taxes' but also the most challenging one. But how does deferred tax accounting work?

In simple terms, the purpose of accounting for deferred taxes is to correctly allocate tax liabilities to the period in which they arose in the case that deviations in tax and accounting laws lead to temporary differences that reverse over time. To understand how deferred taxes work, there is no way around an example: assume a corporation is subject to a CIT of 15% and bought an asset for 100 in year Y1 and is permitted to immediately recognize the asset as an expense for tax purposes. However, according to accounting rules, the asset amortizes over its useful life of five years. Thus, for accounting purposes, the tax liability in Year X1 does not fit the expenses recorded in financial accounts: the CE was able to consider a tax expense of 100 in year Y1, although the financial accounts only record an expense of 20, leading to a remaining carrying value of 80 for the underlying asset. However, in the following years, Y2 to Y5, the financial accounts will, for each year, record expenses of 20, while those book expenses do not reduce CIT liability because the asset had already been fully offset in Y1. Financial accounting rules, thus, oblige corporations to recognize either a deferred tax asset or a deferred tax liability to align the reported profits and losses with tax liability. For this reason, in Y1, the respective corporation will recognize a deferred tax liability of 12 (80 x 15%), because, from an accounting perspective, this amount of tax will increase the tax liabilities of Y2 to Y4 due to the fact that in those years the corporation will not be permitted to offset the 20 expenses it will record in its financial statements. In the following years, the deferred tax liability of 12 will be reduced by 3 for each year.[1091] But what does this have to do with GloBE?

1089. *Ibid.*, para. 294.
1090. *Ibid.*
1091. This example is based on the example provided for in *GloBE Commentary on Article 4 GloBE Model Rules (2022)*, *supra* note 884, para. 67.

Let's stay with the example just given: assume the corporation mentioned is a CE 'located' in a jurisdiction that constantly applies a nominal CIT at a rate of 15% and that the respective CE earns an income of 100 in Y1 to Y6, not including any amortization for the asset at issue. Since GloBE computes the ETR based on financial accounts, it does not matter that domestic law permits offsetting the whole value of the asset in Y1. Rather, from the perspective of GloBE, only the accounting perspective counts. For this reason, the CE will be considered low-taxed in Y1 and will be subject to a 'Top-up Tax' at the amount of 12, even if the difference merely exists temporarily over a period of five years and finally reverses over Y2 to Y5 (*See* Table 2).

Table 2 Computation of the ETR if GloBE Did Not Provide for a Deferred Tax Mechanism

	Covered Taxes	*GloBE Income or Loss*	*ETR (%)*	*Top-Up Tax*
Y1	0	80 (100 – 20)	0.00	12 (80 × 15%)
Y2	15	80 (100 – 20)	18.75	0
Y3	15	80 (100 – 20)	18.75	0
Y4	15	80 (100 – 20)	18.75	0
Y5	15	80 (100 – 20)	18.75	0
Y6	15	100	15.00	0

For this reason, Article 4.1.1.(b) GloBE Model Rules and Article 21(1)(b) GloBE-Directive allow increasing or reducing the amount of 'Adjusted Covered Taxes' with respect to the amount 'Total Deferred Tax Adjustment Amount', which is separately defined in Article 4.4. GloBE Model Rules and Article 22 GloBE-Directive and which is, at least in principle, the amount of deferred tax liabilities or assets as recorded in the financial accounts. While any amount of deferred tax liability increases the amount of 'Covered Taxes', the amount of 'Covered Taxes' is to be reduced with respect to deferred tax assets. Based on the above example, the calculation of ETR and 'Top-up Tax' would be as follows (*See* Table 3).

Table 3 Correction of Temporary Differences by Way of Deferred Tax Accounting

	Covered Taxes			*GloBE Income or Loss*	*ETR (%)*	*Top-Up Tax*
	Tax	*Deferral*	*Total*			
Y1	0	12	**12**	80 (100 – 20)	15.00	0
Y2	15	–3	**12**	80 (100 – 20)	15.00	0
Y3	15	–3	**12**	80 (100 – 20)	15.00	0
Y4	15	–3	**12**	80 (100 – 20)	15.00	0
Y5	15	–3	**12**	80 (100 – 20)	15.00	0
Y6	15	0	**15**	100	15.00	0

As can be seen in this table, the inclusion of the deferred tax item from financial accounting makes it possible to smooth the temporary difference from Y1 to Y6. While in Y1, a deferred tax liability of 12 arises, in Y2 to Y4, the deferred tax expense from the financial accounts is added back to the 'Covered Taxes', and overall five years, the temporary tax benefit from the first year is offset again. The ETR remains constant over the entire period of five years, as if the temporary difference did not exist at all.

Behind this comparatively simple logic lies the technical complexity of GloBE's deferred tax mechanism. As already mentioned, temporary differences are calculated by adding or subtracting the so-called Total Deferred Tax Adjustment Amount from the amount of 'Adjusted Covered Taxes' (Article 4.1.1.[b] GloBE Model Rules and Article 21[1][b] GloBE-Directive). The computation of the 'Total Deferred Tax Adjustment Amount' is separately laid down in Article 4.4. GloBE Model Rules and Article 22 GloBE-Directive. The fact that a 'total' amount is mentioned here already anticipates that the deferred tax mechanism does not make an adjustment for each asset or liability or category thereof. Rather, the calculation of the 'Total Deferred Tax Adjustment Amount' is based on the item of deferred tax liabilities or assets as reported in the financial statements of a specific CE. However, as with all other elements that GloBE takes over from financial accounts, the deferred tax item also requires various adjustments in order to comply with GloBE's policy goals or, as the Commentary puts it, '*to protect the integrity of the GloBE Rules*'.[1092] The following sections are therefore dedicated to the specifics of the calculation of the 'Total Deferred Tax Adjustment Amount' as laid down in Article 4.4. GloBE Model Rules and Article 22 GloBE-Directive.

4.3.4.5.2 Deferred Tax Expense According to Financial Accounts as Starting Point for the 'Total Deferred Tax Adjustment Amount' and Recast to the Minimum Rate

The starting point for computing the 'Total Deferred Tax Adjustment Amount' is the item of deferred tax liabilities or assets '*with respect to Covered Taxes*'[1093] as accrued in the financial statements of a CE in preparation for consolidation. In this way, Article 4.4. GloBE Model Rules and Article 22 GloBE-Directive aim to '*use existing deferred tax accounts maintained by MNE Groups to the greatest extent possible to simplify compliance*'.[1094] However, the phrase '*with respect to Covered Taxes*'[1095] also implies that any deferred taxes included in the financial accounts that are not 'Covered Taxes' need to be removed from the 'Total Deferred Tax Adjustment Amount'. One could now raise the question of whether Article 4.4.1. GloBE Model Rules and Article 22(2) GloBE-Directive also allow the inclusion of deferred taxes with respect to 'Covered Taxes' that are not taken into account in the financial accounts. Nevertheless, due to the fact that both provisions require that the deferred tax expense is '*accrued in its* [the CEs] *financial accounts*', it seems that GloBE only permits to include deferred tax expenses to the extent that they have been recognized in the financial statements.

1092. *See Ibid.*, para. 68.
1093. Article 4.4.1. *GloBE Model Rules* and Art. 22(2) GloBE-Directive (2022/2523).
1094. *See GloBE Commentary on Article 4, supra* note 884, para. 68.
1095. Article 4.4.1. *GloBE Model Rules* and Art. 22(2) GloBE-Directive (2022/2523).

Both Article 4.4.1. GloBE Model Rules and Article 22(2) GloBE-Directive require that the respective amount of deferred tax expense (or tax benefit in the case of negative deferred tax expenses)[1096] reported in the financial statements are recast at the 'Minimum Rate' of 15% if the applicable tax rate in the jurisdiction where the CE is located is above the 'Minimum Rate'. For this reason, the 'Total Deferred Tax Adjustment Amount' is always recomputed as if the CE was subject to a CIT 15% if the CE is subject to a nominal CIT rate of above 15%. Only if the CIT rate of the jurisdiction where the CE is 'located' applies a rate below the 'Minimum Rate' and the respective deferred tax expenses had been calculated on this rate, there is no recast. The reason for this is simple: if GloBE would permit including deferred tax amounts at a higher rate, the respective deferred tax item could '*shelter*[...] *unrelated GloBE Income*'.[1097] Assume a jurisdiction does levy a CIT rate of 30% but provides for a patent box that reduces the tax rates on royalties significantly to 5%. In such a tax system, 'MNE Groups' could use deferred tax assets or liabilities that are calculated at a rate of 30% to 'shelter' the royalties that are not even related to the asset or liability for which the deferred tax asset or liability had been recognized. By requiring a recast at the 'Minimum Rate', GloBE ensures that the deferred tax item only corrects the temporary difference related to the asset or liability that gave rise to this temporary difference and only nullifies 'Top-up Tax' to the extent it is caused by the temporary difference at issue. In any case, it is accepted by the Commentary that the recast can be made with respect to '*all items recorded at the same rate*'.[1098] This is significant in particular for CEs that are subject to a CIT that is levied at a flat rate: the recast can be made simply using the item of deferred taxes from the financial accounts and the nominal tax rate applied without having to make the recast with respect to every asset or liability. If, for example, the financial accounts of a CE show a deferred tax liability of 100 and the CIT rate applied is 25%, the deferred tax expense for GloBE purposes amounts to 60 (100 x 15%/ 25%).[1099]

If the applicable tax rate is below the 'Minimum Rate', GloBE accepts that the deferred tax item is calculated based on the tax rate applied in the respective jurisdiction. Although it would then still be possible to shelter particularly low-taxed income by means of a deferred tax liability or asset calculated on the basis of a higher tax rate that is still below 15%, in these cases, the deferred tax asset could never avoid a 'Top-up Tax' since the ETR would then be below the 'Minimum Rate' anyway. However, according to Article 4.4.3. GloBE Model Rules and Article 22(6) GloBE-Directive, any deferred tax assets that are attributable to a 'GloBE Loss' ('qualifying loss') may be recast at the 'Minimum Rate'. Pursuant to the Commentary, the rule '*preserves the basic tenet that a GloBE Loss of EUR 1 should offset GloBE Income of 1*'.[1100] The purpose of this rule can be explained by means of an example:[1101] If a CE is subject

1096. *See GloBE Commentary on Article 4, supra* note 884, para. 70.
1097. *See Ibid.*, para. 68.
1098. *See Ibid.*, para. 70.
1099. For a discussion of the recast of deferred tax expenses, *see* Florian Brugger et al., *Globale Mindestbesteuerung: Ermittlung des GloBE-Steueraufwands*, 97 SWK 659–662 (2022).
1100. *See GloBE Commentary on Article 4, supra* note 884, para. 87.
1101. *See Ibid.*

to a CIT of 5 and suffered a loss of 100, the financial accounts would record a deferred tax asset of 5. If the same CE receives a profit of 100 in the following year, the deferred tax asset will reverse and increase the amount of 'Adjusted Covered Taxes' by 5. In the second year, the ETR, thus, would be 10 (5 tax plus 5 deferred tax), resulting in an ETR of 10%, causing a 'Top-up Tax' of 5. However, the profit of 100 in the second year is fully covered by the loss of the previous year. From a multi-period perspective, there could not be any 'Top-up Tax' because the overall 'GloBE Income' would be zero. By allowing to recast the deferred tax asset to the 'Minimum Rate' of 15%, GloBE simply allows to eliminate this effect and '*provides that a loss of 100 shelters 100 of income*'.[1102] In the example given above, Article 4.4.3. GloBE Model Rules and Article 22(6) GloBE-Directive would permit recording the deferred tax asset at an amount of 15, providing shelter from 'Top-up Tax' in the second year. It should be added here that the application of both, Article 4.4.3. GloBE Model Rules and Article 22(6) GloBE-Directive, is a mere permission and is, thus, not mandatory. The recast provided in Article 4.4.3. GloBE Model Rules and Article 22(6) GloBE-Directive is optional but can be used without further conditions (e.g., a formal election as sometimes foreseen with regard to certain permanent differences)[1103] if its requirements are met.

Although both Article 4.4.1. GloBE Model Rules and Article 22(2) GloBE-Directive explicitly use the term '*deferred tax expense*', the respective amount can be negative as well if the deferred tax assets exceed the deferred tax liabilities in specific 'Fiscal Years'.[1104] In this case, GloBE recognizes a negative 'Total Deferred Tax Adjustment Amount' as a reduction to the amount of 'Covered Taxes'. The fact that the amount can be a negative value does not change anything with respect to the recast: if the underlying deferred tax asset as accrued in the financial accounts of the CE is calculated at a tax rate of above 15%, the respective tax asset is to be recalculated at the rate of 15%.[1105]

It has been clear from the outset that GloBE could not use the amount of deferred tax expenses from financial accounts without any adjustments. The Blueprint clearly feared the complexity caused by possible needs for adjustments and expressed concerns that '*differences between the policies of the GloBE rules and financial reporting will likely mean that modifications would need to be made to certain deferred tax accounting outcomes in order to adapt deferred tax accounting to the GloBE rules. These modifications would add a significant amount of additional complexity and may lead to uncertainty*'.[1106] These concerns were justified: both, Article 4.4.1. GloBE Model Rules and Article 22(2) GloBE-Directive, require several adjustments to recompute the deferred tax expenses to finally get to the 'Total Deferred Tax Adjustment Amount' to be taken into consideration in the amount of 'Adjusted Covered Taxes'. The necessary adjustments can be divided into four main categories:

1102. *See Ibid.*
1103. Remember the elections provided for with respect to the GloBE base, discussed in s. 4.3.3.3.5.
1104. *See GloBE Commentary on Article 4*, *supra* note 884, para. 70, clarifying that deferred tax assets are to be recorded as '*negative expense*[s]'.
1105. *See Ibid.*, para. 71.
1106. *Tax Challenges Arising from Digitalisation – Report on Pillar Two Blueprint*, para. 294.

- First, the deferred tax expenses from the financial accounts are to be recast at the rate of 15% if the applicable tax rate is above.[1107] If the applicable tax rate is below this, a recast is only required if a deferred tax asset is attributable to a GloBE loss.[1108]
- Second, according to Article 4.4.1.(a) to (e) GloBE Model Rules and Article 22(5) GloBE-Directive, some deferred tax items are excluded from the 'Total Deferred Tax Adjustment Amount' for different reasons. This includes, for example, deferred tax items with respect to excluded income or deferred tax items with respect to so-called Disallowed Accruals[1109] or Unclaimed Accruals.[1110]
- Third, there are certain additions and reductions to be made pursuant to Article 4.4.2.(a) to (c) GloBE Model Rules and Articles 22(3) and (4) GloBE-Directive. The additions and reductions refer to situations requiring correcting differences between financial accounting rules and GloBE.
- Fourth, as will be seen, Article 4.4.4. GloBE Model Rules and Article 22(7) GloBE-Directive only allow to take into account temporary differences that are 'paid' (within the GloBE-Directive 'paid or reversed') within the five subsequent years; otherwise, the amount of deferred tax expenses needs to be added back to the 'Covered Taxes' by way of a recalculation in the fifth subsequent year. To prevent such a subsequent recapture that could give rise to 'Top-up Tax', MNE Groups can elect to adjust the deferred tax expenses according to Article 4.4.7 GloBE Model Rules and Article 22(1)(b) GloBE-Directive so that it only considers amounts that are likely to be 'paid' within five years. However, both provisions exempt certain common differences (so-called Recapture Exception Accruals separately defined in Article 4.4.5. GloBE Model Rules and Article 22[8] GloBE-Directive) from the five-year recapture rule.

The precise calculation scheme for deriving the amount of the 'Total Deferred Tax Adjustment Amount' from the deferred tax expenses as reported in the CE's financial statements is presented in the following table, which also reflects the structure of this and the following sections (*See* Table 4).

1107. Article 4.4.1. *GloBE Model Rules* and Art. 22(2) GloBE-Directive (2022/2523).
1108. Article 4.4.3. *GloBE Model Rules* and Art. 22(6) GloBE-Directive (2022/2523).
1109. Article 4.4.6. *GloBE Model Rules* and Art. 22(1)(a) GloBE-Directive (2022/2523).
1110. Article 4.4.7. *GloBE Model Rules* and Art. 22(1)(b) GloBE-Directive (2022/2523).

Table 4 Overview of the Structure of the Computation of the 'Total Deferred Tax Adjustment Amount'

	Computation of the 'Total Deferred Tax Adjustment Amount' – Overview			
	From Deferred Tax Expenses to the 'Total Deferred Tax Adjustment Amount'	*Model Rules*	*GloBE-Directive*	*Reference*
	Deferred tax expense accrued in a CE's financial accounts at the applicable tax rate below or equal to 15% or recast at 15% if above	Article 4.4.1.	Article 22(2)	Section 4.3.4.5.2.
–	**Exclusions from deferred tax expenses**	Article 4.4.1.	Article 22(5)	Section 4.3.4.5.3.
	+/– Deferred tax expenses with respect to excluded items of income	Article 4.4.1.(a)	Article 22(5)(a)	Section 4.3.4.5.3.
	+/– Deferred tax expenses with respect to 'Disallowed Accruals' and 'Unclaimed Accruals'	Article 4.4.1.(b), 4.4.6. and 4.4.7.	Article 22(5)(b) and 22(1)	Section 4.3.4.5.3.
	+/– Impact of valuation adjustment or accounting recognition adjustment with respect to a deferred tax asset	Article 4.4.1.(c)	Article 22(5)(c)	Section 4.3.4.5.3.
	+/– Amount of deferred tax expense arising from a re-measurement with respect to a change in applicable domestic tax rate	Article 4.4.2.(d)	Article 22(5)(d)	Section 4.3.4.5.3.
	+/– Amount of deferred tax expense with respect to the generation and use of tax credits	Article 4.4.2.(e)	Article 22(5)(e)	Section 4.3.4.5.3.
+/–	**Adjustments to the 'Total Deferred Tax Adjustment Amount'**	Article 4.4.2.	Article 22(3) and (4)	Section 4.3.4.5.4.
	+ Amount of any 'Disallowed Accrual' or 'Unclaimed Accrual' paid during 'Fiscal Year'	Article 4.4.2.(a), 4.4.6. and 4.4.7.	Article 22(3)(a)	Section 4.3.4.5.4.
	+ Amount of any 'Recaptured Deferred Tax Liability' determined in a preceding 'Fiscal Year' which has been paid during the 'Fiscal Year'	Article 4.4.2.(b)	Article 22(3)(b)	Section 4.3.4.5.4.
	– Amount that would be a reduction to the 'Total Deferred Tax Adjustment Amount' due to recognition of a loss deferred tax asset for a current year tax loss, where a loss deferred tax asset has not been recognized because the recognition criteria are not met	Article 4.4.2.(c)	Article 22(4)	Section 4.3.4.5.4.

	Computation of the 'Total Deferred Tax Adjustment Amount' – Overview			
	From Deferred Tax Expenses to the 'Total Deferred Tax Adjustment Amount'	*Model Rules*	*GloBE-Directive*	*Reference*
–	**Deferred tax liabilities that are not paid or do not reverse within five years and do not qualify as 'Recapture Exception Accrual'**	Article 4.4.4. and 4.4.5	Article 22(7) and (8)	Section 4.3.4.5.5.
	'Total Deferred Tax Adjustment Amount' of a CE to be added (liability) to or subtracted (asset) from the amount of 'Covered Taxes'	Article 4.1.1.(b)	Article 21(1)(b)	Table provided in section 4.3.4.1.

4.3.4.5.3 Exclusions from the 'Total Deferred Tax Adjustment Amount'

The 'Total Deferred Tax Adjustment Amount' is computed from the deferred tax items recorded in the financial accounts. However, the deferred tax item, as shown in the financial statements, includes deferred tax liabilities or assets with respect to items that are either excluded from the GloBE base in the denominator of the ETR fraction or must be excluded for other systematic or tax policy reasons. Article 4.4.1. GloBE Model Rules and Article 22(5) GloBE-Directive, therefore, list amounts that are to be excluded from the amount of deferred tax expenses:

- **Deferred tax expenses with respect to income that is excluded from the 'GloBE Income or Loss' ('qualifying income or loss'):** If a certain item of income gives rise to income excluded from the GloBE base, according to Article 4.4.1.(a) GloBE Model Rules and Article 22(5)(a) GloBE-Directive, any deferred tax expenses recorded for such an item need to be excluded from the 'Total Deferred Tax Adjustment Amount' as well. This exclusion is a systematic necessity: if deferred tax assets or liabilities are recorded for a temporary difference in carrying values of an item that is assignable to a source of excluded income, this will distort the ETR: assume that a CE is subject to a CIT of 10% and incurs a loss of 500 and an additional 'Excluded Equity Loss' of 500 (Article 3.2.1.[c] GloBE Model Rules and Article 15[2][c] GloBE-Directive) that is excluded from the tax base. In this case, the financial accounts would record a deferred tax asset of 100 ([500 + 500] x 10%) because the losses will lead to future tax relief. The 'GloBE Loss' in this situation would, however, amount to 500 because the 'Excluded Equity Loss' is not included within the GloBE base.[1111] Assume that, in the next year, the same CE receives a profit of 600 and an additional 'Excluded Equity Gain' of 600. The domestic tax base would be 200 because the whole loss could be carried-forward, resulting in a tax liability of 20. From the perspective of GloBE, however, the income would amount to 600, and the 'Covered Taxes', if no correction to the deferred tax

1111. *See GloBE Commentary on Article 4 GloBE Model Rules (2022), supra* note 884, para. 74.

asset was made, would amount to 110 (tax with respect to included income 10 [20-10 attributable to excluded income][1112] plus deferred tax expense of 100). The ETR would amount to 20% (120/600), which is well above the nominal tax rate of 10%. If GloBE did not require an adjustment, the ETR, thus, would be distorted in subsequent years because the 'Adjusted Covered Taxes' could be increased by the reversing tax asset that is attributable to a loss that had not been taken into consideration by GloBE. As shown in the example, deferred tax expenses related to excluded items of income or loss could provide shelter from the 'Top-up Tax' for included income.[1113] For this reason, the amount of the deferred tax asset that is attributable to the 'Excluded Equity Loss' (in the example above, this would be an amount of 50 [500 x 10%]) is to be added back to the deferred tax asset. Consequently, GloBE would, thus, only allow to recognize a deferred tax expense of 50 in the second year, and this would properly result in an ETR of 10% ([10 + 50]/600).[1114] This example clearly shows that deferred tax items with respect to excluded income or loss could prevent the emergence of 'Top-up Tax', even if the nominal tax rate would well be below the 'Minimum Rate'.

- **Deferred tax expenses with respect to 'Disallowed Accruals' and 'Unclaimed Accruals': Article** 4.4.1.(b) GloBE Model Rules and Article 22(5)(b) GloBE-Directive also require removing any deferred tax expenses arising from so-called Disallowed Accruals and Unclaimed Accruals. Both terms are separately defined and do address different issues: the term 'Disallowed Accrual' is defined in Article 4.4.6.(a) GloBE Model Rules and Article 22(1)(a) GloBE-Directive and include (i) any movements in deferred tax assets that relate to an uncertain tax position and (ii) any movement related to a distribution of a different CE. As already discussed in section 4.3.4.4.4., GloBE does not permit to include uncertain tax positions within the amount of 'Adjusted Covered Taxes'[1115] for obvious reasons:[1116] By reporting uncertain tax positions in the financial statements, a CE could deliberately use accounting policies to increase its tax burden and, thus, also its ETR. Against this background alone, it would be strange to allow deferred tax attributable to uncertain tax positions for the calculation of the 'Adjusted Covered Taxes'. Complementary, it would be odd to allow deferred tax accounting with respect to distributions: the Commentary aptly notes that distributions are regularly taxed when the distribution is made and finally '[g]*iven that the MNE Group generally decides the timing of such distributions between Constituent Entities, it would be inappropriate to provide a current increase to Adjusted Covered Taxes for*

1112. Any 'Covered Taxes' with respect to excluded income need to be removed from the tax base, *see* Art. 4.1.3.(a) *GloBE Model Rules* and Art. 21(3)(a) GloBE-Directive (2022/2523). In detail *see* s. 4.3.4.4.1.
1113. *See GloBE Commentary on Article 4, supra* note 884, para. 72.
1114. A similar but less obvious example is provided for in *Ibid.*, para. 73.
1115. Article 4.1.3.(d) *GloBE Model Rules* and Art. 21(3)(d) GloBE-Directive (2022/2523).
1116. *See GloBE Commentary on Article 4, supra* note 884, paras 109–110.

deferred tax amounts accrued in respect of distribution taxes'.[1117] The term 'Unclaimed Accruals', is defined in Article 4.4.7. GloBE Model Rules and Article 22(1)(b) GloBE-Directive and is closely related to Article 4.4.4. GloBE Model Rules and Article 22(7) GloBE-Directive. As already shortly mentioned in the previous chapter[1118] and as will be further discussed below,[1119] GloBE only allows to consider deferred tax liabilities if they are paid within the five subsequent 'Fiscal Years'. If it subsequently turns out that a specific deferred tax liability had not been paid within this time limit, the ETR and 'Top-up Tax' for the respective 'Fiscal Year' need to be recalculated and may give rise to 'Additional Current Top-up Tax' (within the GloBE-Directive 'additional top-up tax') in the fifth preceding 'Fiscal Year' (Article 5.4.1. GloBE Model Rules and Article 29[1] GloBE-Directive). To avoid that outcome, Article 4.4.7. GloBE Model Rules and Article 22(1)(b) GloBE-Directive provide for an election to exclude 'Unclaimed Accruals' from the 'Total Deferred Tax Adjustment Amount' pursuant to Article 4.4.1.(b) GloBE Model Rules and Article 22(5)(b) GloBE-Directive: any deferred tax liability '*that is not expected to be paid within*'[1120] five subsequent 'Fiscal Years'. According to the Commentary, Article 4.4.7. GloBE Model Rules (Article 22(1)(b) GloBE-Directive) is supposed to provide for a simplification '*allow*[ing] *for the exclusion of deferred tax liabilities that are almost certain to require recapture, which reduces compliance monitoring such liabilities and recalculation Top-up Tax several years later*'.[1121] The election has to be made by the 'Filing Constituent Entity' annually with respect to the relevant 'Fiscal Year'. For a detailed illustration of the operation of Article 4.4.7. GloBE Model Rules and Article 22(1)(b) GloBE-Directive, *see* section 4.3.4.5.5.

- **Impact of valuation adjustment or accounting recognition adjustment with respect to a deferred tax asset:** Accounting rules require regular valuation of every item reported in the financial statements. This is especially true for deferred tax assets: deferred tax assets are regularly caused by losses and are merely fictional assets based on an estimated future tax benefit. For this reason, many accounting standards require a regular review of whether the requirements for recognizing a deferred tax asset are still met. If, for example, a corporation estimates that it will not be able to deduct the losses in the future, financial accounting rules will regularly not permit to record a deferred tax asset (this is the case, e.g., with respect to the IFRS),[1122] due to the fact that

1117. *See Ibid.*, para. 111
1118. *See* s. 4.3.4.5.2.
1119. *See* s. 4.3.4.5.5.
1120. Article 4.4.7. *GloBE Model Rules*. Using a slightly different wording, *see* Art. 22(7) GloBE-Directive (2022/2523).
1121. *See GloBE Commentary on Article 4, supra* note 884, para. 112.
1122. *See*, e.g., IAS 12.24 where it is held that '[a] deferred tax asset shall be recognised for all deductible temporary differences to the extent *that it is probable that taxable profit will be available against which the deductible temporary difference can be utilised* [...]' (emphasis added). On the question when it is '*probable that taxable profit will be available*', *see* IAS 12.28.

there will not be a future tax benefit.[1123] However, for the purposes of GloBE, '*it is necessary to ensure that a deferred tax asset relating to a domestic tax loss is recorded in the same year as the loss for GloBE purposes*'.[1124] For the purposes of GloBE, it is irrelevant whether a CE will ever be able to use a specific item of loss. GloBE simply needs to smooth out temporary differences to avoid distortions of the ETR computation. Thus, pursuant to Article 4.4.1.(c) GloBE Model Rules and Article 22(5)(c) GloBE-Directive, any valuation adjustments to deferred tax assets are to be excluded from the 'Total Deferred Tax Adjustment Amount' to '*ensure*[...] *that the deferred tax asset is recorded for GloBE purposes in the same year as the economic loss which gave rise to such asset*[s]'.[1125] Assume a CE is subject to tax at a rate of 10% and incurs a 'GloBE Loss' ('qualifying loss') of 1000, which, in principle, would give rise to a deferred tax asset of 100. However, financial accounting rules prohibit recognizing the asset due to a negative financial forecast, pretending that the loss will not be usable for the respective entity. In this case, Article 4.4.1.(c) GloBE Model Rules and Article 22(5)(c) GloBE-Directive kick in and exclude the valuation adjustment and would require to recognize the deferred tax asset of 100. As the Commentary notes, the generation of the tax asset might become necessary in subsequent years:[1126] If, for example, the financial forecasts ameliorates in the following year, financial accounts will again oblige to record a deferred tax asset of 100 that initially had not been generated due to a negative financial forecast. If Article 4.4.1.(c) GloBE Model Rules and Article 22(5)(c) GloBE-Directive did not exist and would simply rely on accounting rules, the 'Adjusted Covered Taxes' would be reduced in that second year and would potentially give rise to 'Additional Current Top-up Tax' ('additional top-up tax') because the 'Adjusted Covered Taxes' would then be less than zero according to Article 4.1.5. GloBE Model Rules and Article 21(5) GloBE-Directive (in detail on this issue, *see* section 4.3.4.7.). However, due to the fact that GloBE ignores valuation adjustments with respect to deferred tax assets, GloBE would reduce the generation of the deferred tax asset in the second year because the respective deferred tax asset had already been recognized in the preceding year.

- **Amount of deferred tax expense arising from a re-measurement with respect to a change in applicable domestic tax rate:** After GloBE is implemented by a critical mass of countries, it is likely that several, or at least some, jurisdictions will increase their nominal tax rates. Accounting rules, however, oblige adjusting deferred tax items in advance if domestic tax legislatures announce that they will increase the CIT tax rate. Assume jurisdiction A applies a nominal tax rate of 10% in Year Y1 but announces that it will increase the nominal tax rate to 15% at the beginning of year Y2. Furthermore, assume

1123. *See GloBE Commentary on Article 4, supra* note 884, para. 76.
1124. *See Ibid.*, para. 77.
1125. *See Ibid.*
1126. *See Ibid.*, para. 78.

that a CE 'located' in jurisdiction A receives profits of 200 but purchased an asset for 100 fully deductible in the first year, which, according to accounting rules, is to be written-off over its useful life of five years (depreciation of 20 per year). For this reason, financial accounting rules will require recording a deferred tax liability of 12 (80 x 15%), already taking into account that the tax rate increases in year Y2. Nevertheless, the taxable profits of the CE in year Y1 still amount to 100 and tax liability would be 10. If GloBE would permit to account for the deferred tax liability at a tax rate of 15%, the ETR, in this case, would be 12.22% ([10 + 12]/[200-20]). However, for the purpose of GloBE, it would be inappropriate to accept announcements of future tax increases to overstate the ETR in a 'Fiscal Year' in which a lower tax rate is still applied.[1127] Article 4.4.1.(d) GloBE Model Rules and Article 22(5)(d) GloBE-Directive, thus, oblige reducing the deferred tax liability with respect to the re-measurement of the deferred tax expense required under accounting rules. In the example given here, GloBE would exclude an amount of 4 (80 x [15% – 10%]) from the 'total deferred tax adjustment' so that the deferred tax liability for GloBE purposes would be only 10. In this case, the ETR would finally be 10% ([10 + 8]/[200-20]) and, thus, again reflects the nominal tax rate. The treatment of tax rate changes is finally specifically addressed in Article 4.6. GloBE Model Rules[1128] and Article 25 GloBE-Directive and will be further discussed in section 4.3.4.9.

- **Amount of deferred tax expense with respect to the generation and use of tax credits:** Many IF jurisdictions provide for certain kinds of various tax credits. According to Article 4.4.1.(e) GloBE Model Rules and Article 22(5)(e) GloBE-Directive any deferred tax liabilities or assets generated with respect to tax credits shall be excluded from the 'Total Deferred Tax Adjustment Amount'. The character of such tax credits is aptly summed up in the Commentary: '*A tax credit is an amount that taxpayers can subtract directly from taxes owed to a government* [...] *and differ from deductions, which reduce the amount of taxable income. Instead, they directly reduce the amount of tax owed*'.[1129] Pursuant to the Commentary, the term tax credit as used in Article 4.4.1.(e) GloBE Model Rules (Article 22[5](e) GloBE-Directive) does not only include investment tax credits like R&D credits but also foreign tax credits granted either unilaterally or due to a tax treaty.[1130] But why is there a need to exclude deferred tax assets with respect to tax credits? Assume a CE is located in jurisdiction A and receives profits of 100 in two consecutive years. Jurisdiction A levies a CIT at a rate of 25%. It grants an investment tax credit for 10% of R&D expenses, however, the credit is only available at an amount of 10

1127. Also *see Ibid.*, para. 79
1128. *See* the last sentence of *Ibid.*, which explicitly emphasizes that '*Articles 4.6.2. and 4.6.3.* [equivalent to Article 25(2) and 25(3) GloBE-Directive] *provide for rules that govern how domestic tax rate changes are taken into account for GloBE purposes to ensure appropriate credit is given for tax paid*'.
1129. *See Ibid.*, para. 80.
1130. *See Ibid.*

per year, but any excess credit may be carried-forward without a time limit and can be used in following years.[1131] Assume that, in the first year, the respective CEs income of 100 included qualifying R&D expenses of 20. Domestic law of jurisdiction A would, thus, permit to use a tax credit of 10 in the first year and allows to carry-forward a tax credit of 20, of which 10 can therefore be used in the subsequent year. In this situation, financial accounts would regularly record a deferred tax asset of 2.5 (10 x 25%), which is to be recast for GloBE purposes at an amount of 1.5 (10 x 15%). The deferred tax asset would reduce the 'Covered Taxes' in the first year, so the ETR would be 13.5% ([25-10-1.5]/ 100). In the second year, the deferred tax asset would reverse and be added to the amount of 'Adjusted Covered Taxes', which would level up the ETR in the second year to 16.5% ([25-10 + 1.5]/ 100). Thus, the deferred tax related to the tax credit would give rise to 'Top-up Tax' in the first year on the one hand but, on the other hand, leads to an overstated ETR in the second year. For this reason, both Article 4.4.1.(e) GloBE Model Rules and Article 22(5)(e) GloBE-Directive exclude the consideration of any deferred tax expenses or benefits with respect to tax credits.[1132] In this case, the deferred tax asset in year one would not be taken into consideration, leading to an ETR of 15% ([25-10]/ 100). Complementary, there would not be an increase in the 'Adjusted Covered Taxes' in the second year, also resulting in an ETR of 15% ([25-10]/ 100).[1133]

4.3.4.5.4 Adjustments to the 'Total Deferred Tax Adjustment Amount'

Complementary to the exclusions from the 'Total Deferred Tax Adjustment Amount' provided in Article 4.4.1. GloBE Model Rules and Article 22(5) GloBE-Directive, Article 4.4.2. GloBE Model Rules and Article 22(3) and (4) GloBE-Directive provide certain adjustments to the 'Total Deferred Tax Adjustment Amount'. But what is the difference between an 'exclusion' and an 'adjustment'? While the former only allows ignoring a certain accounting treatment, 'adjustments' require certain additions or reductions to the 'Total Deferred Tax Adjustment Amount' in deviation from accounting treatment. The adjustments provided for in Article 4.4.2. GloBE Model Rules and Article 22(3) and (4) GloBE-Directive are closely intertwined with the exclusions provided for in Article 4.4.1. GloBE Model Rules and Article 22(5) GloBE-Directive, but the 'adjustments' expressly allow not merely to ignore but to correct the deferred tax expenses. Both the GloBE Model Rules and the GloBE-Directive require three adjustments to the 'Total Deferred Tax Adjustment Amount':

- Increase of 'Total Deferred Tax Adjustment Amount' by any amount paid with respect to 'Disallowed Accruals' or 'Unclaimed Accruals': as already discussed

1131. Also *see* Example 4.4.1 – 1 that is based on a domestic tax system that grants limited tax credits but allows for a credit carry-forward, *see GloBE Examples*, at 39–40.
1132. *See GloBE Commentary on Article 4*, *supra* note 884, para. 81.
1133. Also *see* Example 4.4.1 – 1 in *GloBE Examples*, at 39–40.

in the previous section, Article 4.4.1.(b) GloBE Model Rules and Article 22(5)(b) GloBE-Directive prohibit the inclusion of any deferred taxes with respect to 'Disallowed Accruals' or 'Unclaimed Accruals' due to their '*speculative nature*'[1134] and their uncertainty. So, when financial accounting rules oblige accounting for the deferred tax liability, GloBE will ignore the respective adjustment and will not allow increasing the 'Adjusted Covered Taxes' with respect to deferred taxes attributable to such items. However, once the respective tax liability is paid, it should very well be included in the 'Adjusted Covered Taxes' in the numerator of the ETR fraction. Due to the fact that accounting rules already did record such taxes as deferred tax expense in previous years, the financial statements would not include the amount in the 'Fiscal Year' the payment is finally made: '*Although the tax paid will be included in current taxes* [in the financial statements], *this may be offset by the decrease in the deferred tax liability, to the extent the deferred tax liability is included in the Total Deferred Tax Adjustment Amount*'.[1135] For this reason, Article 4.4.2.(a) GloBE Model Rules and Article 22(3)(a) GloBE-Directive to increase the 'Total Deferred Tax Adjustment Amount' with respect to deferred tax liabilities that had been ignored due to being exempt as 'Disallowed Accruals' or 'Unclaimed Accruals' from deferred tax accounting in previous years due to the application of Article 4.4.1.(b) GloBE Model Rules and Article 22(5)(b) GloBE-Directive. Otherwise, the corresponding tax amounts would never qualify as 'Covered Taxes' even if they were eventually paid; neither in the year in which financial accounting rules recorded a deferred tax liability nor in the year in which it is paid. The adjustment provided by Article 4.4.2.(a) GloBE Model Rules and Article 22(3)(a) GloBE-Directive is, thus, a systematic addition to Article 4.4.1.(b) GloBE Model Rules and Article 22(5)(b) GloBE-Directive. For a detailed illustration of the operation of Article 4.4.2.(a) GloBE Model Rules and Article 22(3)(a) GloBE-Directive with respect to 'Unclaimed Accruals', *see* section 4.3.4.5.5.

- Increase of 'Total Deferred Tax Adjustment Amount' by the amount of any 'Recaptured Deferred Tax Liability' determined in a preceding 'Fiscal Year' that has been paid during the 'Fiscal Year': a very similar situation occurs with respect to the time limit to recognize deferred tax liabilities according to Article 4.4.4. GloBE Model Rules and Article 22(7) GloBE-Directive, which will be discussed in further detail below in section 4.3.4.5.5. Amounts of deferred tax expenses that are not likely to be paid within the subsequent five 'Fiscal Years' need to be recaptured from the for GloBE purposes in the fifth preceding year. However, in the 'Fiscal Year' in which the liability is finally paid, the financial accounts would eliminate this expense by way of decreasing a deferred tax liability that had been recorded in previous years. The respective tax expense would neither be taken into account in the 'Fiscal Year' when it is paid nor in any other previous 'Fiscal Year'. Article 4.4.2.(b) GloBE Model Rules and

1134. *See GloBE Commentary on Article 4, supra* note 884, para. 83.
1135. *See Ibid.*

Article 22(3)(b) GloBE-Directive, thus, also permit increasing the 'Total Deferred Tax Adjustment Amount' with respect to 'Recaptured Deferred Tax Liabilities'.[1136] For a detailed illustration of the operation of Article 4.4.2.(b) GloBE Model Rules and Article 22(3)(b) GloBE-Directive, *see* section 4.3.4.5.5.

- Reduction of 'Total Deferred Tax Adjustment Amount' by the amount that would be a reduction to the 'Total Deferred Tax Adjustment Amount' due to recognition of a loss deferred tax asset for a current year tax loss, where a loss deferred tax asset has not been recognized because the recognition criteria are not met: finally, Article 4.4.2.(c) GloBE Model Rules and Article 22(4) GloBE-Directive require a corresponding reduction of the 'Total Deferred Tax Adjustment Amount' if accounting rules deny the generation of a deferred tax asset due to the fact that recognition criteria are not met. As already set out in the previous section,[1137] any revaluation adjustments with respect to deferred tax assets are to be ignored according to Article 4.4.1.(c) GloBE Model Rules and Article 22(5)(c) GloBE-Directive, because *'it is necessary to ensure that a deferred tax asset relating to a domestic tax loss is recorded in the same year as the loss for GloBE purposes'*.[1138] In addition to Article 4.4.1.(c) GloBE Model Rules and Article 22(5)(c) GloBE-Directive, Article 4.4.2.(c) GloBE Model Rules and Article 22(4) GloBE-Directive oblige recording a deferred tax asset, even if financial accounting rules do not record such an asset at all. This adjustment, thus, enables 'MNE Groups' to generate a deferred tax asset for losses, even if financial accounting rules prohibit to recognize such an asset.[1139] Article 4.4.1.(c) GloBE Model Rules and Article 22(5)(c) GloBE-Directive only allow ignoring recognition criteria but not explicitly deviating from accounting rules; thus, Article 4.4.2.(c) GloBE Model Rules and Article 22(4) GloBE-Directive give permission to deviate with respect to the recognition of deferred tax assets in loss situations.

4.3.4.5.5 Need to Recapture Deferred Tax Liability if Tax Is Not Paid Within Five Subsequent 'Fiscal Years' and Exception for 'Recapture Exception Accruals'

As already anticipated previously, GloBE only permits considering temporary differences with respect to a certain time limit and requires recapture if the respective tax liability that has been recorded as a deferred tax liability is not 'paid' within the fifth subsequent 'Fiscal Year'. The provision is laid down in Article 4.4.4. GloBE Model Rules (reflected in Article 22[7] GloBE-Directive) and reads as follows:

> To the extent a deferred tax liability, that is not a Recapture Exception Accrual, is taken into account under this Article and such amount is not paid within the five

1136. *See Ibid.*, para. 84.
1137. *See* s. 4.3.4.5.3.
1138. *See GloBE Commentary on Article 4, supra* note 884, para. 77.
1139. *See Ibid.*, paras 85–86.

> subsequent Fiscal Years, the amount must be recaptured pursuant to this article. The Amount of the Recaptured Deferred Tax Liability determined for the current Fiscal Year shall be treated as a reduction to Covered Taxes in the fifth preceding Fiscal Year and the Effective Tax Rate and Top-up Tax of such Fiscal Year shall be recalculated under the rules of Article 5.4.1. The Recaptured Deferred Tax Liability for the current Fiscal Year is the amount of the increase in a category of deferred tax liability that was included in the Total Deferred Tax Adjustment Amount in the fifth preceding Fiscal Year that has not reversed by the end of the last day of the current Fiscal Year unless such amount relates to a Recapture Exception Accrual as set forth in Article 4.4.5.[1140]

The text of Article 22(7) GloBE-Directive has been slightly adapted, but as will become clear, there are probably no differences in content. In any case, the purpose of the provision seems to be obvious: GloBE intends to avoid that the ETR could be distorted by long-term temporary differences. For this reason, Article 4.4.4. GloBE Model Rules (Article 22[7] GloBE-Directive) shall ensure '*that deferred tax liabilities recorded with respect to categories that do not relate to specific policy allowed categories are actually settled within the required period of time*'.[1141] However, it is also evident that both Article 4.4.4. GloBE Model Rules and Article 22(7) GloBE-Directive are highly complex and leave many open questions with regard to their interpretation. Interestingly, the Commentary only dedicated two paragraphs to Article 4.4.4. GloBE Model Rules.[1142] The Example catalogue[1143] published by OECD does not even include an Example that illustrates the application of the deferred tax recapture rule.

First of all, the provision is only applicable with respect to deferred tax liabilities that do not qualify as 'Recapture Exception Accruals'. Consequently, there is no recapture for any deferred tax assets. This is due to the fact that a deferred tax asset reduces the amount of 'Covered Taxes' and leads to a reduction of the 'Covered Tax'. Thus, there is no risk that 'MNE Groups' use long-time deferred tax assets to lower the ETR in a specific jurisdiction. Furthermore, the provision does not apply with respect to 'Recapture Exception Accruals' that are separately listed in Article 4.4.5. GloBE Model Rules and Article 22(8) GloBE-Directive. The list excludes certain categories of deferred tax liabilities that do not lead to recapture, even if the respective deferred tax liability is not 'paid' within the five subsequent years. According to the Commentary, this is due to the fact that the listed temporary differences '*are typically tied to substantive activities in a jurisdiction or are differences that are not prone to taxpayer manipulation*' but '*that are generally material to MNE Groups*'.[1144] However, the list does not follow an overarching rationale. Rather, the Commentary presents a wide variety of tax policy reasonings for the individual items listed. Both Article 4.4.5. GloBE Model Rules and Article 22(8) GloBE-Directive list the following items that qualify as 'Recapture Exception Accruals': (i) cost recovery allowances on tangible assets (that is essentially everything that is reported as property, plant and equipment in the financial

1140. Article 4.4.4. *GloBE Model Rules*.
1141. *See GloBE Commentary on Article 4, supra* note 884, para. 89.
1142. *See Ibid.*, paras 89–90.
1143. *GloBE Examples*.
1144. *See GloBE Commentary on Article 4, supra* note 884, para. 91.

accounts),[1145] (ii) costs of a license or similar arrangement from the government for the use of immovable property or exploitation of natural resources that entails significant investment in tangible assets (e.g., long-term leasing arrangements or concessions for the exploitation of natural resources),[1146] (iii) research and development expenses,[1147] (iv) de-commissioning and remediation expenses (e.g., obligation to deconstruct a nuclear power plant or a revitalization of a mining site),[1148] (v) fair value accounting on unrealized gains,[1149] (vi) foreign currency exchange net gains,[1150] (vii) insurance reserves,[1151] (viii) gains from the sale of tangible property located in the same jurisdiction as the CE that are reinvested (this nullifies so-called roll-over or deferral benefits granted by tax system with respect to promote replacement investments),[1152] (ix) any additional amounts accrued with respect to changes in accounting principles with respect to the listed expenses (e.g,. change from conventional depreciation to fair value impairment)[1153].

Once it is determined that there is a deferred tax liability, that is not a 'Recapture Exception Accruals', Article 4.4.4. GloBE Model Rules raise the question as to whether the respective deferred tax liability is '*paid*' within the five subsequent 'Fiscal Years'. But what does '*paid*' mean in this context? A deferred tax position is characterized by the fact that it is not '*paid*' as such but rather is solely included for the purpose of financial accounting. It could therefore be assumed that a deferred tax liability is never '*paid*' because it is only created fictitiously to maintain the accrual principle. A deferred tax liability is only 'paid' indirectly through an 'increased' tax liability compared to accounting profits in a subsequent 'Fiscal Year', and this occurs when the temporary differences finally '*reverses*'. Hence, from a systematic point of view, the provision only makes sense if the term '*paid*' is equated with the term '*reversed*'. However, the first sentence of Article 4.4.4. GloBE Model Rules solely uses the term '*paid*'. Nevertheless, both the context of Article 4.4.4. GloBE Model Rules, as well as the Commentary, suggest that the first sentence of the provision is to be interpreted that recapture is only required if a certain deferred tax liability does not 'reverse' within the time limit: first, the last sentence of Article 4.4.4. GloBE Model Rules explicitly states that '[t]he Recaptured Deferred Tax liability for the current Fiscal Year is the amount of the

1145. Article 4.4.5.(a) *GloBE Model Rules* and Art. 22(8)(a) GloBE-Directive (2022/2523). In detail, *see GloBE Commentary on Article 4, supra* note 884, paras 92–95.
1146. Article 4.4.5.(b) *GloBE Model Rules* and Art. 22(8)(b) GloBE-Directive (2022/2523). In detail, *see GloBE Commentary on Article 4, supra* note 884, para. 96.
1147. Article 4.4.5.(c) *GloBE Model Rules* and Art. 22(8)(c) GloBE-Directive (2022/2523). In detail, *see GloBE Commentary on Article 4, supra* note 884, para. 97.
1148. Article 4.4.5.(d) *GloBE Model Rules* and Art. 22(8)(d) GloBE-Directive (2022/2523). In detail, *see GloBE Commentary on Article 4, supra* note 884, paras 98–101.
1149. Article 4.4.5.(e) *GloBE Model Rules* and Art. 22(8)(e) GloBE-Directive (2022/2523). In detail, *see GloBE Commentary on Article 4, supra* note 884, para. 102.
1150. Article 4.4.5.(f) *GloBE Model Rules* and Art. 22(8)(f) GloBE-Directive (2022/2523). In detail, *see GloBE Commentary on Article 4, supra* note 884, para. 103.
1151. Article 4.4.5.(g) *GloBE Model Rules* and Art. 22(8)(g) GloBE-Directive (2022/2523). In detail, *see GloBE Commentary on Article 4, supra* note 884, paras 104–106.
1152. Article 4.4.5.(h) *GloBE Model Rules* and Art. 22(8)(h) GloBE-Directive (2022/2523). In detail, *see GloBE Commentary on Article 4, supra* note 884, para. 107.
1153. Article 4.4.5.(i) *GloBE Model Rules* and Art. 22(8)(i) GloBE-Directive (2022/2523). In detail, *see GloBE Commentary on Article 4, supra* note 884, para. 108.

increase in a category of deferred tax liability [...] *that has not reversed by the end of the last day of the current Fiscal Year*'[1154] (emphasis added) and second, the Commentary explicitly states that Article 4.4.4. GloBE Model Rules requires recapture for deferred tax liabilities '*that do not reverse*'[1155] within the five subsequent 'Fiscal Years'. Although the GloBE Model Rules also use the term '*paid*' in a different manner elsewhere,[1156] there is, therefore, much to suggest that the term '*paid*' in the first sentence of Article 4.4.4. GloBE Model Rules has the meaning of '*reversed*'.[1157] In any case, it is interesting to note in that respect that Article 22(7) of the GloBE-Directive explicitly refers to '*paid or reversed*'.

In any case, it is the first sentence of Article 4.4.4. GloBE Model Rules and Article 22(7) GloBE requires recapture if the temporary difference has not dissolved within the five subsequent 'Fiscal Years'. For this reason, as the Commentary states, '[e]*ach item of deferred tax expense for a Constituent Entity is not in a category that meets the Recapture Exception Accrual definition should be tested in each 'Fiscal Year' for recapture*'.[1158] It is obvious that this is a rather burdensome task. In particular, the question arises as to whether the test should be performed for each individual asset or liability underlying the deferred tax item ('*each item*'). However, a closer look at the wording of Article 4.4.4 GloBE Model Rules reveals that a test might only be necessary for individual categories: the third sentence of Article 4.4.4 GloBE Model Rules uses the phrase '*category of deferred tax liability*',[1159] and the Commentary uses the term '*categories*'.[1160] Thus, it seems reasonable to apply the test only for aggregated items that are separately recorded in the financial statements. An example of this: it is sufficient that the *six-year test* (the current and [!] the five subsequent 'Fiscal Years')[1161] with respect to deferred tax liabilities for property, plant and equipment is only made with respect to the aggregated sum of property, plant and equipment instead of testing every single asset that is included within the item property, plant and equipment. However, a separate test would very well be required with respect to provisions or other contingent liabilities. In this respect, it should be added that Article 22(7) GloBE-Directive does not give any guidance in this respect and does not confirm whether it is allowed to apply the test regarding aggregated items in the balance sheet. Rather, the content of the third sentence in Article 4.4.4. GloBE Model Rules is missing in Article 22(7) GloBE-Directive. In the author's opinion, however, it would not be justified to apply the six-year test in Article 4.4.4. GloBE Model Rules and Article 22(7) GloBE-Directive with respect to every separate asset and liability of a CE. Rather it

1154. *See* the third sentence of Art. 4.4.4. *GloBE Model Rules*.
1155. *See GloBE Commentary on Article 4, supra* note 884, para. 89.
1156. *See*, e.g., Art. 4.4.2.(a) or Art. 4.1.3.(e) GloBE Model Rules where it is clear that '*paid*' must mean the actual payment of the tax amount.
1157. This argumentation originates from an extraordinary fruitful discussion of the author with Priv.-Doz. Dr *Christoph Marchgraber* in August 2022. The author is extremely grateful for his support.
1158. *See GloBE Commentary on Article 4, supra* note 884, para. 90.
1159. *See* the third sentence of Art. 4.4.4. *GloBE Model Rules*.
1160. *See GloBE Commentary on Article 4, supra* note 884, para. 89.
1161. Also *see* the example provided for in *Ibid.*, para. 90.

makes sense to aggregate '*categories*', and as has been shown, there is a strong indication that such an approach is permissible.

But what then is the legal consequence when a category of deferred tax liability turns out to not be 'paid' (in the sense of 'reversed') in the fifth subsequent (which is the sixth) 'Fiscal Year'? The legal consequence is revealed in the respective second sentences of Article 4.4.4. GloBE Model Rules and Article 22(7) GloBE-Directive: '*The Amount of the Recaptured Deferred Tax Liability determined for the current Fiscal Year shall be treated as a reduction to Covered Taxes in the fifth preceding Fiscal Year and the Effective Tax Rate and top-up Tax of such Fiscal Year shall be recalculated under the rules of Art 5.4.1.* [within the GloBE-Directive this is Article 29(1) GloBE-Directive]'.[1162] Consequently, the respective tax liability subsequently reduces the numerator of the ETR fraction for the 'Fiscal Year' in which the respective deferred tax liability was initially included in the 'Total Deferred Tax Adjustment Amount'.[1163] But how does a subsequent adjustment of the ETR and the 'Top-up Tax' work out? Finally, this is done by adding an amount of 'Additional Current Top-up Tax' (within the GloBE-Directive 'Additional Top-up Tax') to the 'Top-up Tax' of the fifth subsequent year. The 'Top-up Tax' arising due to a subsequent recalculation of the first year increases the 'Top-up Tax' liability of an 'MNE Group' in the sixth year. The exact operation of the 'Additional Current Top-up Tax' will further be examined in section 4.4.2.6.

To avoid tedious recapture in subsequent years, Article 4.4.7. GloBE Model Rules and Article 22(1)(b) GloBE-Directive provide an election to exclude amounts of deferred tax liabilities that are not expected to be paid within the subsequent five 'Fiscal Years' from the 'Total Deferred Tax Adjustment Amount' as 'Unclaimed Accruals' under Article 4.4.1.(b) GloBE Model Rules and Article 22(5)(b) GloBE-Directive. In this way, 'MNE Groups' can exclude any amount that will not reverse directly in the respective 'Fiscal Year' at issue in which the amount of deferred tax liability is generated. Both Article 4.4.1.(b) GloBE Model Rules and Article 22(5)(b) GloBE-Directive have already been addressed in section 4.3.4.5.3.

Finally, the third sentence of Article 4.4.4. GloBE Model Rules provides a clarification and states that the amount of recapture is equal to 'the *amount of the increase* in a category of deferred tax liability that was included in the Total Deferred Tax Adjustment Amount in the fifth preceding year that has not reversed by the end of the last day of the current Fiscal Year'[1164] (emphasis added). This statement reveals the obvious fact that the recapture only refers to the amount for which the 'Total Deferred Tax Adjustment Amount' did increase in the 'Fiscal Year' in which the deferred tax liability had been generated. Probably because of this apparentness, these additions were omitted from Article 22(7) GloBE-Directive.

Finally, there is no way around an example: assume a CE bought a business and generated a goodwill of 15,000. According to financial accounting rules, any goodwill is to be offset over a period of 10 years, while tax law only permits to offset goodwill over a period of 15 years. The CE is subject to a CIT of 25%, which is why the deferred

1162. Article 4.4.4. *GloBE Model Rules* and correspondingly Art. 22(7) GloBE-Directive (2022/2523).
1163. *See GloBE Commentary on Article 4, supra* note 884, para. 89.
1164. Article 4.4.4. *GloBE Model Rules*.

tax liability, according to accounting rules, needs to be recast at a rate of 15%.[1165] The following table shows the operation of the recapture required pursuant to Article 4.4.4. GloBE Model Rules and Article 22(7) GloBE-Directive (*See* Table 5).

1165. This example is based on Austrian law: In 2022 the Austrian CIT rate amounts to 25%. Any goodwill must be depreciated over a period of 15 years according to s. 8 para. 3 of the Austrian Income Tax Act. However, Austrian GAAP, which qualify as 'Acceptable Financial Accounting Standard', oblige corporations to set off any goodwill over 10 years, according to s. 203 para. 5 of the Austrian Commercial Code.

Table 5 Operation of the Five-Year Recapture of Deferred Tax Liabilities under Article 4.4.4. GloBE Model Rules and Article 22(7) GloBE-Directive

	Tax		*Accounting/GloBE*		*Deferred*		*Deferred Tax Recapture*				*GloBE Covered Tax*		*GloBE Total Deferred*
	Depreciation	*Book Value*	*Depreciation*	*Book Value*	*Change*	*Total*	*Reference*	*Reversal*	*Recapture*	*Recalc.*	*Reduction*	*Increase*	
Y0		15,000		15,000									
Y1	1,000	14,000	1,500	13,500	75	75	Y6	Y11	75		–75		–
Y2	1,000	13,000	1,500	12,000	75	150	Y7	Y11	75		–75		–
Y3	1,000	12,000	1,500	10,500	75	225	Y8	Y12	75		–75		–
Y4	1,000	11,000	1,500	9,000	75	300	Y9	Y12	75		–75		–
Y5	1,000	10,000	1,500	7,500	75	375	Y10	Y13	75		–75		–
Y6	1,000	9,000	1,500	6,000	75	450	Y11	Y13	75	for Y1	–75		–
Y7	1,000	8,000	1,500	4,500	75	525	Y12	Y14	75	for Y2	–75		–
Y8	1,000	7,000	1,500	3,000	75	600	Y13	Y14	75	for Y3	–75		–
Y9	1,000	6,000	1,500	1,500	75	675	Y14	Y15		for Y4			75
Y10	1,000	5,000	1,500	–	75	750	Y15	Y15		for Y5			75
Y11	1,000	4,000	–		–150	600				for Y6		150	–
Y12	1,000	3,000	–		–150	450				for Y7		150	–
Y13	1,000	2,000	–		–150	300				for Y8		150	–
Y14	1,000	1,000	–		–150	150						150	–
Y15	1,000	–	–		–150	–							–150

The table shows that the depreciation, according to tax rules, amounts to 1,000 per year, whereas, according to accounting rules, an amount of 1,500 may be offset every year. For the first ten years, this gives rise to an increase of deferred tax liability of 75 per year (for the first year [14,000-13,500] x 15%). Within the financial statements, the yearly change in deferred tax liability is cumulated in the total amount of deferred tax. As can be seen, the change in deferred tax liability turns negative in Y11: this is due to the fact that, under accounting rules, the goodwill is fully amortized. Five years of depreciation remain under tax rules, leading to a yearly reduction of the deferred tax liability of 150 in the years Y11 to Y15. So, the first year in which the deferred tax liability is 'paid' is Y11. However, the fifth subsequent 'Fiscal Year' of Y1 is the 'Fiscal Year' of Y6. For this reason, the deferred tax liability of Y1 needs to be recaptured in Y6. In Y6, the ETR of Y1 needs to be recalculated, potentially leading to an 'Additional Current Top-up Tax' in Y6. The same logic applies to the increases in deferred tax liabilities in Y2 to Y8, which need to be recaptured each in Y7 to Y13, respectively. Only the amounts of deferred tax liability generated in Y9 and Y10 are 'paid' in Y15 and, thus, remain within the time limit of Article 4.4.4. GloBE Model Rules and Article 22(7) GloBE-Directive. Finally, in Y11 to Y14, the respective 'Recaptured Deferred Tax Liabilities' are finally paid, as, according to financial accounting rules, deferred tax assets of 150 are generated every year. In this example, the deferred tax liabilities generated in Y1 and Y2 are paid in Y11, Y3 and Y4 are paid in Y12 and so on. However, GloBE would assume a reduction in 'Covered Taxes' of 150 each year. For this reason, Article 4.4.2.(b) GloBE Model Rules and Article 22(3)(b) GloBE-Directive require to increase the 'Total Deferred Tax Adjustment Amount' by the amount of 'Recaptured Deferred Tax Liabilities' from a preceding year which has been paid in the 'Fiscal Year' at issue. For this reason, the 'Total Deferred Tax Adjustment Amount' is to be increased by 150 from Y11 to Y14. Otherwise, GloBE would record a deferred tax benefit in Y11 to Y14 that had already been taken into account by way of recapture in Y1 to Y8.

To avoid necessity of subsequent recalculation, Article 4.4.1. (b) and 4.4.7. GloBE Model Rules, as well as Article 22(1)(b) and Article 22(5)(b) GloBE-Directive, allow excluding the amounts of deferred taxes as recorded in the financial statements if it is not expected that the liability is to be paid within the five subsequent 'Fiscal Years' (so-called Unclaimed Accruals), provided that the 'Filing Constituent Entity' makes an election. In these cases, the calculation of the above example would be as follows (*See* Table 6).[1166]

1166. In detail on the elections provided for in Art. 4.4.7. GloBE Model Rules and Art. 22(1)(b) GloBE-Directive, *see* s. 4.3.4.5.3.

Table 6 Operation of the 'Unclaimed Accrual' Exception Pursuant to Article 4.4.1.(b) and Article 4.4.7. GloBE Model Rules and Article 22(1)(b) and Article 22(5)(b) GloBE-Directive to Avoid Subsequent Recalculation

	Tax		*Accounting/GloBE*		*Deferred*		*Deferred Tax Recapture*			*GloBE Total Deferred Tax*	
	Depreciation	*Book Value*	*Depreciation*	*Book Value*	*Change*	*Total*	*Reference*	*Reversal*	*Unclaimed Accruals*	*Increase*	*Total*
Y0		15,000		15,000							
Y1	1,000	14,000	1,500	13,500	75	75	Y6	Y11	–75		–
Y2	1,000	13,000	1,500	12,000	75	150	Y7	Y11	–75		–
Y3	1,000	12,000	1,500	10,500	75	225	Y8	Y12	–75		–
Y4	1,000	11,000	1,500	9,000	75	300	Y9	Y12	–75		–
Y5	1,000	10,000	1,500	7,500	75	375	Y10	Y13	–75		–
Y6	1,000	9,000	1,500	6,000	75	450	Y11	Y13	–75		–
Y7	1,000	8,000	1,500	4,500	75	525	Y12	Y14	–75		–
Y8	1,000	7,000	1,500	3,000	75	600	Y13	Y14	–75		–
Y9	1,000	6,000	1,500	1,500	75	675	Y14	Y15			75
Y10	1,000	5,000	1,500	–	75	750	Y15	Y15			75
Y11	1,000	4,000	–		–150	600				150	–
Y12	1,000	3,000	–		–150	450				150	–
Y13	1,000	2,000	–		–150	300				150	–
Y14	1,000	1,000	–		–150	150				150	–
Y15	1,000	–	–		–150	–					–150

As can be seen, the respective increase in the financial accounting deferred tax asset in those 'Fiscal Years' that might give rise to subsequent recapture is excluded as 'Unclaimed Accrual' according to Article 4.4.1.(b) GloBE Model Rules and Article 22(5)(b) GloBE-Directive for purposes of the calculation of the GloBE deferred tax expenses. For this reason, the goodwill does not give rise to a GloBE deferred tax expense in the 'Fiscal Years' Y1 to Y8. From the beginning of year Y9, there is no need to make use of the election provided for in Article 4.4.7. GloBE Model Rules and Article 22(1)(b) GloBE-Directive, because the increases in deferred tax liability in Y9 and Y10 both reverse within the five subsequent 'Fiscal Years'. However, what's with the deferred tax assets generated in Y11 to Y14? Finally, Y9 and Y10 both reverse in Y15, whereas the deferred tax assets generated in Y11 to Y14 would not reverse but would reduce the 'Total Deferred Tax Adjustment Amount'. In this case, Article 4.4.2.(a) GloBE Model Rules and Article 22(3)(a) GloBE-Directive kick in:[1167] both provisions state that the 'Total Deferred Tax Adjustment Amount' needs to be increased by the amount of 'Unclaimed Accruals' in the year in which they are paid. In this example, the 'Unclaimed Accruals' of Y1 and Y2 are paid in Y11, Y3 and Y4 are paid in Y12 and so on. Finally, at the beginning of Y15, all 'Unclaimed Accruals' have been reversed, so there is no need for an increase in Y15.

Can a conclusion be drawn from the above example? In the author's opinion, the example raises the question of whether the policy rationale behind Article 4.4.4. GloBE Model Rules and Article 22(7) GloBE-Directive really justifies the complexity of the six-year limitation for the consideration of deferred tax expenses. Finally, the effect of deferred tax expenses on the ETR may be significant in some cases but will regularly only have a minor impact from a multi-period perspective. Because even if the deferred tax expenses are nullified by Article 4.4.4. GloBE Model Rules and Article 22(7) GloBE-Directive, the respective temporary difference finally reverses anyway over the useful life of an asset or liability. It can be assumed that the GloBE Loss Election provided in Article 4.5. GloBE Model Rules and Article 22 GloBE-Directive might be a promising tool to avoid GloBE's tedious deferred tax accounting. However, the use of the latter is limited to situations where 'MNE Groups' expand their businesses to new jurisdictions.[1168]

4.3.4.6 Increase or Decrease in 'Adjusted Covered Taxes'

Once the additions and reductions have been made with respect to the amount of 'Covered Taxes' and the 'Total Deferred Tax Adjustment Amount' has been added or deducted from the 'Covered Taxes' as well, Article 4.1.1.(c) GloBE Model Rules and Article 21(1)(c) GloBE-Directive require a final adjustment to the amount of 'Covered Taxes' to finally reach the amount of 'Adjusted Covered Taxes' for the numerator of the ETR fraction. The provisions require that any increase or decrease in 'Covered Taxes' recorded in equity or OCI relating to amounts included in the computation of the

1167. *See* the last sentence of *GloBE Commentary on Article 4, supra* note 884, para. 83.
1168. *See* s. 4.3.4.3.2.

'GloBE Income or Loss' ('net qualifying income or loss') need to be either added or deducted from the amount of 'Covered Taxes'. The purpose of this addition is evident: it ensures that any change with respect to 'Covered Taxes' is included within the numerator of the ETR fraction, '*even if they are not recorded in current or deferred tax expense and reported in the profit and loss statement*'.[1169] The Commentary convincingly assumes that the provision of Article 4.1.1.(c) GloBE Model Rules (Article 21[1][c] GloBE-Directive) will mostly be relevant with respect to taxes levied on gains and losses when the revaluation method (fair value accounting) is used.[1170] However, there may be various situations in which a certain amount of 'Covered Tax' might be included in the OCI rather than the profit or loss statement.

4.3.4.7 'Top-up Tax' in Loss Situations: The Special Rule for 'Expected Adjusted Covered Taxes'

Finally, Article 4.1. GloBE Model Rules and Article 21 GloBE-Directive provide for a very special provision in 'Fiscal Years' in which there is no 'Net GloBE Income' within a specific jurisdiction, but the domestic tax loss exceeds the 'GloBE Loss' due to a permanent difference. In this case, Article 4.1.5. GloBE Model Rules and Article 21(5) GloBE-Directive require to collect a 'Top-up Tax' in the amount of the deferred tax asset that is generated due to the permanent difference that causes the domestic loss to exceed the 'GloBE Loss' ('net qualifying loss'). The provision reads as follows:

> [i]n a Fiscal Year in which there is no Net GloBE Income for a jurisdiction, if the Adjusted Covered Taxes for a jurisdiction are less than zero and less than the Expected Adjusted Covered Taxes Amount the Constituent Entities in that jurisdiction shall be treated as having Additional Current Top-up Tax for the jurisdiction under Article 5.4 [Art 29 GloBE-Directive] arising in the current Fiscal Year equal to the difference between these amounts. The Expected Adjusted Covered Taxes Amount is equal to the GloBE Income or Loss for a jurisdiction multiplied by the Minimum Rate[1171].

The purpose of Article 4.1.5. GloBE Model Rules and Article 21(5) GloBE-Directive is anything but obvious and can only be grasped by means of an example.

Assume a CE is subject to a CIT of 15% and in Y1 receives an income of 100 and expenses of 200. Within the income of 100, there is a dividend of 60 received from a 'Short-term Portfolio Shareholdings' that is exempted under domestic law but which is not excluded from the GloBE base due to the fact that the respective dividend does not qualify as 'Excluded Dividend'[1172] under Article 3.2.(b) GloBE Model Rules and Article 16(2)(b) GloBE-Directive.[1173] The comparison of the local tax base and the GloBE base can be seen in Table 7.[1174]

1169. *See GloBE Commentary on Article 4, supra* note 884, para. 4c.
1170. *See Ibid.*
1171. Article 4.1.5. *GloBE Model Rules* and correspondingly, using a slightly different wording, Art. 21(5) GloBE-Directive (2022/2523).
1172. For an example with respect to dividends that are actually excluded, *see* Example 4.1.5 – 4 *GloBE Examples*, at 37–38.

Table 7 The Basic Situation of Article 4.1.5. GloBE Model Rules and Article 21(5) GloBE-Directive: Domestic Losses Exceeding 'GloBE Loss'

	Domestic Tax Base	*GloBE Income or Loss*
Income	40	100
Expenses	-200	-200
Loss	-160	-100
Deferred Tax Asset (15%)	24	(Adopted from financial accounts) 24
Adjusted Covered Taxes	-24	

As can be seen, the loss under domestic law exceeds the 'GloBE Loss'. For accounting purposes, however, the domestic tax base will be relevant with respect to the calculation of the deferred tax asset, which amounts to 24. However, from GloBE's perspective, the deferred tax asset amounts to 24 as well as GloBE adopts the values as reported in the financial statements[1175] but would, without the permanent difference, amount to only 15. So how do Article 4.4. GloBE Model Rules and Article 22 GloBE-Directive handle this issue when the 'Total Deferred Tax Adjustment Amount' is computed? The answer is clear: the financial accounts show the deferred tax asset computed from the domestic tax loss, which is 24. This is because the permanent difference, in this case, arises due to domestic law and not because GloBE excludes a specific item of income which would lead to an exclusion from the 'Total Deferred Tax Adjustment Amount' under Article 4.4.1.(a) GloBE Model Rules and Article 21(5)(a) GloBE-Directive.

However, if GloBE would '*simply allow* [...] *a Constituent Entity to use its local tax loss as the starting point for determining its Total Deferred Tax Adjustment Amount under Article 4.4.* [this]*would undermine the integrity of the GloBE Rules by effectively allowing the Constituent Entity to substitute the (more generous) local tax rules for those agreed under* [...] *GloBE*'.[1176] In this example, GloBE would permit to record a deferred tax asset of 24 in this case, and the respective deferred tax asset could be used in subsequent years to increase the 'Covered Taxes' by 24, although 9 (difference between 24 and 15) of the deferred tax assets are attributable to a permanent difference. Finally, the income of 60 excluded under domestic law would generate a deferred tax asset although the respective income is to be included within GloBE's tax base and would, thus, distort the ETR: if the respective CE, in Y2, receives income of 160, both under domestic law, the domestic tax base would be 0. For this reason, the CE would pay taxes of 0. The GloBE Income would amount to 160. For the purposes of GloBE, the 'Covered Taxes' would, however, include a deferred tax expense of 24, resulting in an ETR of 15% ([24]/160) and finally, the permanent difference that arose

1173. The facts of the example are inspired by Austrian tax law: According to s. 10(1)(5) and 10(1)(6) of the Austrian CIT Act, also dividends from 'Short-term Portfolio Shareholdings' (less than 10% and less than one year) are exempt from Austrian CIT.
1174. Also *see* in particular Example 4.1.5 – 1 in *GloBE Examples*, at 35–36.
1175. *See* s. 4.3.4.5.2.
1176. *See GloBE Commentary on Article 4 GloBE Model Rules (2022)*, *supra* note 884, para. 20.

in Y1 prevents the generation of 'Top-up Tax'. But why is this problematic? Finally, the ETR equals the nominal tax rate. This picture, however, is deceptive: from a multi-period perspective, the following picture emerges (*see* Table 8).

Table 8 What if Article 4.1.5. GloBE Model Rules and Article 21(5) GloBE-Directive Did Not Exist? The Purpose of Article 4.1.5. GloBE Model Rules and Article 21(5) GloBE-Directive

	Domestic Tax Base	*GloBE Income or Loss*
Loss Y1	-160	-100
Income Y2	160	160
Total Income Y1 + Y2	**0**	**60**
Minimum Rate (%)	15	15
Tax paid	0	0
Adjusted Covered Tax in Y2		(Deferred tax expense) 24
GloBE Income in Y2		160
ETR in Y2 (%)		15
Tax to be paid to exceed Minimum Rate		9
'Top-up Tax' not levied		9

As can be seen, the multi-period perspective reveals that the deferred tax asset with respect to the permanent difference caused by the dividend provides shelter for included income of 60 that is exempt under domestic law. From a multi-period perspective, an amount of 60 of the 'MNE Group's' 'GloBE Income' remains untaxed, leading to tax savings of 9 that would have become effective.

For this reason, Article 4.1.5. GloBE Model Rules and Article 21(5) GloBE-Directive solve this issue by levying a 'Top-up Tax' at the amount of the difference between 'Adjusted Covered Taxes' that are less than zero and less than the so-called Expected Adjusted Covered Taxes Amount, which, according to the last sentences of Article 4.1.5. GloBE Model Rules (second half of the first sentence in Article 21[5] GloBE-Directive) is '*equal to the GloBE Income or Loss for a jurisdiction multiplied by the Minimum Rate*'.[1177] Applied to the above example, the provision would be applicable in Y1 and would give rise to 'Additional Current Top-up Tax' (*see* in detail section 4.4.2.6.) according to Article 5.4. GloBE Model Rules and Article 29(3) GloBE-Directive: the 'Adjusted Covered Taxes' are -24 and are, thus, less than zero. Furthermore, the 'Adjusted Covered Taxes' are less than the 'Expected Adjusted Covered Taxes Amount' that is -15 ('GloBE Loss' -100 x 15%). As a result, according to Article 4.1.5. GloBE Model Rules and Article 21(5) GloBE-Directive, a 'Top-up Tax' of 9 would be due. The positive effect of the deferred tax asset in subsequent years has

1177. Article 4.1.5. *GloBE Model Rules* and correspondingly, using a slightly different wording, Art. 21(5) GloBE-Directive (2022/2523).

thus been corrected: if, in Y2, the deferred tax asset reverses, the CE can increase its amount of 'Covered Tax' by an amount of 24, resulting in an ETR of 15% ([24]/160).

One could now very well question the policy behind such a complex adjustment: is the collection of 'Top-up Tax' in a loss situation appropriate? And is the situation addressed in Article 4.1.5. GloBE Model Rules and Article 21(5) GloBE-Directive a likely scenario? At least the latter question can be affirmed. In fact, there are various reasons that may give rise to domestic losses exceeding 'GloBE Losses'. One could, for example, think of any tax exemptions under domestic laws or specific incentives like 'super deductions' or other kinds of premature tax amortizations.[1178] Whether the collection of a 'Top-up Tax' in a loss situation is appropriate is a different story and will be critically assessed in section 4.5.3. The Commentary states in this respect that another option '*would have been to require the Constituent Entity to make an adjustment to the amount of deferred tax asset in these cases to align it with GloBE outcomes. However, this would have required developing an alternative deferred tax accounting methodology for addressing these specific cases as well as mechanisms for tracking and tracing such differences over time, thereby undermining the compliance and administration benefits of relying on deferred tax accounting to address timing differences*'.[1179] This statement is not at all convincing. GloBE could have solved the issue by simply requiring reducing the deferred tax asset in line with the adjustments provided for in Article 4.4.2. GloBE-Directive and Article 22(5) and (4) GloBE-Directive in the year in which domestic loss exceeds the 'Expected Adjusted Covered Taxes Amount'. Among the various adjustments required by Article 4.4. GloBE Model Rules and Article 22 GloBE-Directive, it is difficult to see in which way the collection of 'Top-up Tax' benefits compliance and administration. Furthermore, it must be noted that Article 4.1.5. GloBE Model Rules and Article 21(5) GloBE-Directive give rise to 'Additional Current Top-up Tax' irrespective of the nominal tax rate applied in the respective jurisdiction and that also the SBIE cannot prevent its collection, as 'Additional Current Top-up Tax' is added to the 'Top-up Tax' liability also in a loss situation.[1180]

In the meanwhile, the issue has been addressed by the OECD within its GloBE Administrative Guidance February 2023.[1181] The OECD has developed a special administrative procedure to '*avoid*'[1182] the outcome of Article 4.1.5. GloBE Model Rules: the IF Members are encouraged to grant a so-called *Carry-forward of Excess Negative Tax Expense*. The 'Excess Negative Tax Expense' equals the amount of 'Top-up Tax' that would be due pursuant to Article 4.1.5. GloBE Model Rules. Consequently, '[i]*n each subsequent Fiscal Year in which the MNE Group has positive GloBE Income and Adjusted Covered Taxes for the jurisdiction, the MNE Group shall decrease (but not below zero) the aggregate Adjusted Covered Taxes by the remaining*

1178. *See GloBE Commentary on Article 4, supra* note 884, para. 19.
1179. *See Ibid.*, para. 20.
1180. Also sceptical in that regard, *see* Florian Brugger et al., *Globale Mindestbesteuerung: Ermittlung des GloBE-Steueraufwands*, 97 SWK, *supra* note 1099, at 666–667.
1181. *GloBE Administrative Guidance February 2023*, at 49–54.
1182. *See* the newly added para. 21.4 in the Commentary on Art. 4 GloBE Model Rules implemented in the course of the *Ibid.*, at 51.

balance of the Excess Negative Tax Expense Carry-forward'.[1183] The 'Excess Negative Tax Expense administrative procedure' is designed as an annual election.[1184] Its operation is demonstrated in an additional example added to the OECD's Example Catalogue.[1185] Eventually, if implemented, it can avoid the outcomes of Article 4.1.5. GloBE Model Rules obliging to pay 'Additional Current Top-up Tax' in loss situations.

Although the new procedure undoubtedly seems welcome from a practical and a tax policy point of view, the OECD's subsequent addition is problematic: it is strange that such a fundamental addition that openly contradicts the text of the GloBE Model Rules is clarified in a simple addition to the Commentary. Would the actual implementation of this administrative procedure not have required an adjustment of Article 4.1.5 GloBE Model Rules? For the EU, there is even a problem with the rule of law: the GloBE Administrative Guidances 2023 must remain irrelevant for the Member States, as they were only published in February and July 2023, respectively, after the GloBE-Directive was adopted. Even if the recitals of the GloBE-Directive explicitly allow using the relevant OECD materials with respect to its interpretation,[1186] it is clear that one cannot interpret a directive by using a soft-law document that did not even exist when it was adopted.[1187] Furthermore, it is obvious that the proposed procedure is inconsistent with the wording of Article 21(5) GloBE-Directive and recital 24 explicitly only allows to use of the OECD's materials '*as a source of illustration and interpretation* [...] *to the extent that those sources are consistent with this Directive and Union law*'.[1188] Thus, under the author's opinion, the Member States cannot adopt the suggestions made in the GloBE Administrative Guidance released in February 2023 without either amending or violating the GloBE-Directive.

Irrespective of these rule of law concerns, there is a different intriguing question with respect to Article 4.1.5. GloBE Model Rules and Article 21(5) GloBE-Directive: why does GloBE address this issue only if there is no 'Net GloBE Income' within a specific jurisdiction? Indeed, the effect addressed by Article 4.1.5. GloBE Model Rules and Article 21(5) GloBE-Directive does not occur if there is 'Net GloBE Income' in a specific jurisdiction, even if the domestic tax base was a loss. The deferred tax asset generated in such a situation would reduce the amount of 'Covered Taxes' below zero and would require collecting the respective 'Top-up Tax'. Thus, the collection of the 'Top-up Tax' would be prevented in the absence of an overall 'GloBE Loss'. Rather, if there is 'Net GloBE Income', it is tested against the taxes paid in the jurisdiction. This can be illustrated by the following example: assume a CE is subject to CIT of 15% and in Y1 receives income of 300 and expenses of 200. Within the income of 100, there is a dividend of 160 received from a 'Short-term Portfolio Shareholdings' that is exempted under domestic law but included within the GloBE base. The comparison of the local tax base and the GloBE base shows the following picture (*see* Table 9).

1183. *See* para. 21.5 *Ibid.*, at 52.
1184. *See* para. 21.7 *Ibid.*
1185. *See* Example 4.1.5 – 5 *Ibid.*, at 53–54.
1186. Already *see* s. 4.1.
1187. *See* recital 24 GloBE-Directive (2022/2523).
1188. Recital 24 *Ibid.*

Table 9 Operation of Article 4.1.5. GloBE Model Rules and Article 21(5) GloBE-Directive

	Domestic Tax Base	*GloBE Income or Loss*
Income	40	300
Expenses	–200	–200
Loss	–160	100
Deferred Tax Asset (15%)	24	0
Adjusted Covered Taxes		–24
ETR (%)		–24
'Top-up Tax'		39

As there is 'GloBE Income', 'Top-up Tax' arises at an amount of 39. This is due to the fact that the amount of 'Covered Taxes' is negative: according to financial accounting rules, the CE records a deferred tax asset that reduces the amount of 'Adjusted Covered Tax' below zero. So finally, the ETR is -24%, leading to a 'Jurisdictional Top-up Tax'[1189] of 39% (15%-[-24%]). If, in Y2, the same CE receives a profit of 160, the domestic tax base would be zero, and the GloBE base would be 160. However, there would not be any 'Top-up Tax' in Y2 because the deferred tax asset of 24 now reverses and increases the amount of 'Covered Taxes' to 24, resulting in an ETR of 15% (24/160). Since GloBE takes into account the tax reduction resulting from the deferred tax asset and 'Top-up Tax' can be levied on the basis of a positive 'Net GloBE Income', there is no need for a provision similar to Article 4.1.5. GloBE Model Rules and Article 21(5) GloBE-Directive if there is 'Net GloBE Income' within a jurisdiction.

The examples discussed within this section are based on the premise that there was only one CE per jurisdiction. However, the term 'Net GloBE Income' ('net qualifying income'), as defined in Article 5.1.2. GloBE Model Rules and Article 26(2) GloBE-Directive, is the positive aggregated amount of the 'GloBE Income' minus 'GloBE Losses' of all CEs located in the same jurisdiction. The above examples should, therefore, not obscure the fact that also Article 4.1.5. GloBE Model Rules and Article 21(5) GloBE-Directive are to be applied jurisdiction-wise: for this reason, if there is more than one CE in a jurisdiction, both provisions apply if the aggregated 'GloBE Income or Loss' of all CEs 'located' in that jurisdiction is zero or negative. Also, the 'Adjusted Covered Taxes' and the 'Expected Adjusted Covered Taxes Amount' of the respective CEs need to be aggregated. Thus, if separate CEs receive a profit in a 'Fiscal Year' in which there is no 'Net GloBE Income' in a jurisdiction, the taxes paid by the profitable CEs can indeed mitigate the effects of Article 4.1.5. GloBE Model Rules and Article 21(5) GloBE-Directive. The taxes paid by those profitable CEs, of course, increase the 'Adjusted Covered Taxes' for purposes of Article 4.1.5. GloBE Model Rules and Article 21(5) GloBE-Directive and might reduce the difference between the negative 'Adjusted Covered Taxes' and the 'Expected Adjusted Covered Taxes Amount'. The example catalogue published by the OECD provides two examples in

1189. *See* Art. 5.2.3. *GloBE Model Rules* and Art. 27(3) GloBE-Directive (2022/2523).

that regard;[1190] However, apart from the aggregation of 'GloBE Income or Losses' and 'Adjusted Covered Taxes', the operation of Article 4.1.5. GloBE Model Rules and Article 21(5) GloBE-Directive do not differ from the examples discussed above.

Finally, in the case that there is more than one CE of the same 'MNE Group' 'located' in a specific jurisdiction, there remains the issue as to which of the CEs the 'Top-up Tax' arising pursuant to Article 4.1.5. GloBE Model Rules and Article 21(5) GloBE-Directive is to be assigned to. Eventually, this is relevant with respect to the application of the IIR and the UTPR. This issue is specifically addressed within the rules on the computation of 'Additional Current Top-up Tax' ('Additional Top-up Tax') in Article 5.4.3. GloBE Model Rules and Article 29(3) GloBE-Directive. Accordingly, the respective amount of 'Top-up Tax', which is to be considered as 'Additional Current Top-up Tax', is allocated only to those CEs that record *'an* [amount of] *Adjusted Covered Taxes* [...] *that is less than zero and less than the GloBE Income or Loss of such Constituent Entity multiplied by the Minimum Rate* [the latter equals the CEs 'Expected Adjusted Covered Taxes Amount' according to Article 4.1.5. GloBE Model Rules and Article 21(5) GloBE-Directive]'.[1191] If this again applies to multiple CEs 'located' in the same jurisdiction, both Article 5.4.3. GloBE Model Rules and Article 29(3) GloBE-Directive provide for a formula according to which the allocation among those CEs is made on a pro rata basis upon the difference between the 'GloBE Income or Loss' multiplied by the 'Minimum Rate' and the 'Adjusted Covered Taxes' of the respective CEs.[1192] For further details with respect to the computation, *see* section 4.4.2.6.2. and for the computation and allocation of 'Additional Current Top-up Tax' ('Additional Top-up Tax') arising due to Article 4.1.5. GloBE Model Rules and Article 21(5) GloBE-Directive, *see* sections 4.4.2.6.2 and 4.4.2.7.

4.3.4.8 Allocation of Covered Taxes Between 'Constituent Entities'

4.3.4.8.1 Principles of Tax Allocation

Jurisdictional blending requires that every source of income and every amount of tax paid is allocated to a specific jurisdiction. As has already been discussed in detail, however, reliance on financial statements does not support this jurisdictional perspective. Rather, the values for the numerator and denominator of the ETR fraction are determined on the level of every CE. Finally, both the 'GloBE Income or Loss' as well as the 'Adjusted Covered Taxes' are aggregated on a jurisdictional level. To ensure that every income is correctly allocated to the jurisdiction for which the ETR is to be determined, Article 3.4. and 3.5. GloBE Model Rules as well as Articles 18 and 19 GloBE-Directive how income received by an 'MNE Group' is allocated among its CEs.

1190. *See* the Examples 4.1.5 – 2 and 3 in *GloBE Examples*, at 36–37.

1191. *See* the second sentence of Art. 4.1.5. *GloBE Model Rules* and the corresponding last sentence of Art. 29(3) GloBE-Directive (2022/2523).

1192. For further details on the operation of Art. 5.4.3. GloBE Model Rules and Art. 29(3) GloBE-Directive, *see GloBE Commentary on Article 5 GloBE Model Rules (2022)*, *supra* note 474, paras 69–72.

These rules have already been discussed in sections 4.3.3.5 and 4.3.3.6. Complementary, Article 4.3. GloBE Model Rules and Article 24 GloBE-Directive provide corresponding rules to allocate 'Covered Taxes' among the different CEs of an MNE Group.

However, the necessity for separate rules for allocating taxes is not as obvious as it is with respect to income allocation: one could argue that every amount of 'Covered Tax' paid should be assigned to the jurisdiction that levied the tax. As the Commentary aptly notes: '*In many cases, Covered Taxes will be paid by the Constituent Entity with respect to its own income and to a tax authority in the jurisdiction in which it is located and no allocation is required*'.[1193] International tax law, however, is not that simple. There are various examples which reveal that borders between taxing jurisdictions might become blurred. In a cross-border tax case, there might be more than one jurisdiction that seeks to tax the same source of income. However, even if more than one state taxes the same income, the respective amount of income is still allocated to a single jurisdiction. In such a case, it is all but obvious to which jurisdiction the respective amount of taxes should be allocated for the purpose of ETR computation. Furthermore, it is common practice in international tax law that the foreign recipient's tax is regularly withheld by the paying entity to ensure proper tax collection. To which CE is such a withholding tax allocated? Shall it be included in the ETR of the payor or the recipient? Furthermore, jurisdictions might apply CFC Regimes which tax the income of an entity at the level of its shareholder. Therefore, the question of which taxes are allocated to which CE is a very fundamental one and all but trivial.

In principle, GloBE's answer to the allocation of 'Covered Taxes' is that every amount of tax is '*generally allocated to the Constituent Entity, including a Stateless Constituent Entity, that includes the corresponding income in the computation of its GloBE Income or Loss and then are taken into account in the ETR computation for the jurisdiction in which the Entity is located*'.[1194] This can be described as GloBE's basic principle with respect to tax allocation and can be deduced from GloBE's concept of 'location' and Article 4.1.1. GloBE Model Rules (Article 21[1] GloBE-Directive), according to which the amount of 'Covered Taxes' is to be calculated from the current tax expenses accrued in a CEs financial account. Consequently, for the purposes of GloBE, it does not matter which jurisdiction levies a tax or which CE collects it. Rather, GloBE poses the question of which income the respective amount of 'Covered Tax' was levied and allocates the tax to the CE that received the underlying income. If, e.g., a CE 'located' in jurisdiction A pays a royalty to a CE 'located' in jurisdiction B and the CE located in jurisdiction A is obliged to collect a withholding tax, the tax is allocated to the CE that received the underlying income: finally, the CE-recipient of the royalty 'located' in country B includes '*the corresponding income*'[1195] in its 'GloBE Income or Loss'. For this reason, the withholding tax with respect to the royalty is a tax collected by country A but still increases the amount of 'Adjusted Covered Taxes' in country B. Abstracted from this example, it can be stated that in the system of GloBE, in principle, any withholding tax is allocated to the recipient of the income on which the tax was levied.

1193. *See GloBE Commentary on Article 4 GloBE Model Rules (2022)*, *supra* note 884, para. 42.
1194. *See Ibid.*, para. 41.
1195. *See Ibid.*

As an interim conclusion, one can thus note that GloBE, as a rule, allocates every tax to the CE that includes the respective income in its financial accounts. In this way, GloBE ensures that the numerator of the ETR fraction includes all taxes levied on the income included in the denominator, irrespective of how or where the taxes had been levied. GloBE, therefore, measures the ETR of an 'MNE Group' in relation to income allocated to this jurisdiction rather than the tax levied by that jurisdiction.

Article 4.3. GloBE Model Rules and Article 24 GloBE-Directive, however, provide for exceptions or at least amendments to this allocation principle with respect to five specific cross-border taxes and require reallocation of 'Adjusted Covered Taxes' among CEs:[1196] These include taxes with respect to (i) PEs,[1197] (ii) 'Tax Transparent Entities',[1198] (iii) taxes levied in the course of CFC regimes,[1199] (iv) 'Hybrid Entities'[1200] and (v) taxes on dividends and other distributions,[1201] each of which a separate subsection is devoted below.

4.3.4.8.2 Allocation of Taxes to a Permanent Establishment

The first exception to the basic principle of tax allocation is enshrined in Article 4.3.2.(a) GloBE Model Rules and Article 24(1) GloBE-Directive, according to which '*the amount of any Covered Taxes included in the financial accounts of a Constituent Entity with respect to GloBE Income or Loss of a Permanent Establishment is allocated to the Permanent Establishment*'.[1202] Both provisions are counterparts to the specific allocation rule for PE income provided for in Article 3.4. GloBE Model Rules and Article 18 GloBE-Directive within the 'Covered Tax' determination.

Both the purpose and the basic operation of tax allocation with respect to PEs are simple: the purpose of Article 4.3.2.(a) GloBE Model Rules and Article 24(1) GloBE-Directive is to reallocate 'Covered Taxes' levied by the residence state of the 'Main Entity' to the respective PE. Otherwise, GloBE would underestimate the ETR with respect to PEs that are subject to low taxation at source: if local tax law of the 'Main Entity' includes foreign PE income and taxes at the domestic tax level above the 'Minimum Rate', it would be inappropriate to ignore the residence state tax on the foreign PEs income. For this reason, Article 4.3.2.(a) GloBE Model Rules and Article 24(1) GloBE-Directive allocate the amount of residence state tax on the PEs income (reduced by any foreign tax credit) to the foreign PE qualifying as a separate CE. While

1196. *See* explicitly Art. 4.3.1. *GloBE Model Rules*, which clarifies that the provisions provided for in Art. 4.3.2. GloBE Model Rules only apply with respect to those five situations.
1197. Article 4.3.2.(a) and Art. 4.3.4. *Ibid.* as well as Art. 24(1) and Art. 24(7) GloBE-Directive (2022/2523).
1198. Article 4.3.2.(b) *GloBE Model Rules* and Art. 24(2) GloBE-Directive (2022/2523).
1199. Article 4.3.2.(c) and 4.3.3. *GloBE Model Rules* as well as Art. 24(3) and Art. 24(6) GloBE-Directive (2022/2523).
1200. Article 4.3.2.(d) *GloBE Model Rules* and Art. 24(4) GloBE-Directive (2022/2523).
1201. Article 4.3.2.(e) *GloBE Model Rules* and Art. 24(5) GloBE-Directive (2022/2523).
1202. Article 4.3.2.(a) *GloBE Model Rules* and, using a slightly different wording, *see* Art. 24(1) GloBE-Directive (2022/2523).

the respective amount of tax is included in the amount of 'Adjusted Covered Taxes' of the PE, the corresponding amount is removed from that of the 'Main Entity'.[1203]

Pursuant to the Commentary, three steps are needed to finally determine the amount of 'Adjusted Covered Taxes' attributable to a PE:

- **Step 1 – determine amount of PE income included in 'Main Entity's' local taxable income:** According to Article 3.4. GloBE Model Rules and Article 18 GloBE-Directive the income or loss reported in the financial statements need to be split between the 'Main Entity' and its foreign PE(s). One could, thus, be tempted to assume that CEs could rely on this income allocation. Nevertheless, to finally determine the amount of taxes allocable to the PE, the amount of PE income '*included in the local taxable income is the relevant figure for measuring how much local tax was paid in respect of the PE's income*'.[1204] This is an implicit reference to domestic law or tax treaty treatment of the PE income or loss: if the PE income is exempted at the level of the 'Main Entity', e.g., due to a tax treaty or unilateral relief provided by that jurisdiction, there is no income included in the 'Main Entity's' local taxable income and no need for reallocation. If, however, the 'Main Entity' is either provided for a foreign tax credit on the PE income (irrespective of whether due to a tax treaty or domestic law) or does not receive any relief at all (e.g., because no tax treaty is applicable and domestic law does not provide for unilateral relief), the respective income would very well be included and a reallocation of the amount of 'Covered Tax' would indeed be necessary.
- **Step 2 – determine the 'Main Entity's' tax liability arising from the inclusion of PE income:** Once the amount of PE income that had been included in the local tax base is determined, the taxes paid with respect to this income need to be calculated. In most cases, this will require calculating the total tax liability of the 'Main Entity' before any foreign tax credit is granted to finally determine the amount of domestic tax attributable to the PE's income. This is unproblematic if both the PE and the 'Main Entity' receive profits. If, however, the total taxable income or loss of the 'Main Entity' is below the PE's income included in the local tax base, all 'Covered Taxes' need to be attributed to the PE.[1205] In this respect, the Commentary notes that '*domestic losses and losses of other PEs allowed in the Main Entity's taxable income computation under a credit method are first used against domestic income and then applied to PE income inclusions*'.[1206] This will not be much of an issue if there is no total taxable income because, in most cases, there will not be much of a tax.
- **Step 3 – determine any tax credit allowed with respect to taxes levied in the jurisdiction where the 'Main Entity' is located on the income attributable to the PE:** Finally, when the 'Main Entity's' tax liability with respect to the income attributable to the respective PE is determined, any tax credit provided

1203. *See GloBE Commentary on Article 4 GloBE Model Rules (2022), supra* note 884, para. 46.
1204. *See Ibid.*, para. 47.
1205. *See Ibid.*, para. 48.
1206. *See Ibid.*

by the residence state of the main entity needs to be subtracted from the tax liability attributable to the PE income. This is to make sure that the 'Adjusted Covered Taxes' is only increased with respect to the taxes that are actually paid in the residence state.[1207] Any credit limitations applied by the residence state of the entity, of course, might increase the amount of 'Covered Tax' that may be reallocated to the PE.[1208]

Assume a CE is 'located' in jurisdiction A and receives income of 200, of which 100 are attributable to a PE in jurisdiction B. Jurisdiction A levies a CIT at a rate of 25% on worldwide corporate income. Jurisdiction B taxes resident and non-resident entities at a rate of 10%. Between both states, a tax treaty is in force that provides for credit methods with respect to business income in line with Article 23B OECD MC. Assume both CEs are the only CEs within their jurisdictions. In this case, without any specific allocation rules, the ETR in jurisdiction B would equal its nominal tax rate of 10% because the PE income of 100 is taxed at a rate of 10%. However, from a cross-border perspective, the corporation pays 25 of taxes with respect to the PE's income: additionally, to taxes of 10 levied in the PE jurisdiction B, the corresponding income is also included within the domestic tax base of jurisdiction A and is fully taxed at a rate of 25%, but only receives a credit for the tax levied in jurisdiction B. In this example, jurisdiction A would levy an amount of 15 (25 – 10) with respect to the PE's income. In total, the PE income of 100 is subject to a tax of 25 (jurisdiction A 15 + jurisdiction B 10). If Article 4.3.2.(a) GloBE Model Rules and Article 24(1) GloBE-Directive did not exist, GloBE would nevertheless require collecting a 'Top-up Tax' of 5 with respect to the PE in jurisdiction B. However, pursuant to Article 4.3.2.(a) GloBE Model Rules and Article 24(1) GloBE-Directive, the amount of tax levied in jurisdiction A, which is 15 (Step 1, determine included PE income = 100, Step 2, determine tax levied in residence state with respect to PE income = 25, Step 3, determine credit allowed in residence state = 10), is to be reallocated from the 'Main Entity' to the PE. The ETR in jurisdiction B would then be 25%, and the imposition of a 'Top-up Tax' would be excluded. In return, the 15 in 'Adjusted Covered Taxes' need to be excluded from the 'Main Entities' financial statements. The ETR of jurisdiction A would, however, also amount to 25% because the income of the 'Main Entity' alone (100) is taxed at a rate of 25% anyway.[1209]

Although this approach might seem simple at first glance, the tax allocation with respect to PEs can reveal complex ramifications: assume a CE located in jurisdiction A (nominal CIT of 20%) receives income of 200, of which 100 is attributable to a PE in jurisdiction B (nominal CIT of 30%) and another 100 is attributable to a PE in jurisdiction C (nominal CIT of 0%). Furthermore, assume jurisdiction A provides a worldwide limitation ('cross-crediting') with regard to foreign tax credits. In this case, jurisdiction B would levy a tax of 30, and jurisdiction C would not levy any tax. Jurisdiction A would tax 200 at a rate of 20% which is 40; however, it would provide

1207. *See Ibid.*, para. 49.
1208. *See Ibid.*, para. 51.
1209. A similar example is provided for in *Ibid.*, para. 50.

a credit of 30 (jurisdiction A would not permit a refund with respect to excess taxes in jurisdiction B, however, if the credit is calculated on a worldwide approach there is not excess credit due to the low-taxed foreign income of jurisdiction C) leaving 10 of tax for reallocation. Which amount of tax levied by jurisdiction A may be allocated to jurisdiction C to mitigate or even nullify potential 'Top-up Tax' with respect to jurisdiction C? Could the excess credit from jurisdiction B, in addition to reducing tax liability in jurisdiction A, also be used to reduce 'Top-up Tax' liability in jurisdiction C?

Eventually, one could take the extreme position that with respect to the income attributable to the low-taxed PE in jurisdiction C, jurisdiction A did levy a tax of 20% but simply gave a refund for excess tax credits from PE income in jurisdiction B to allocate 'Covered Taxes' of 20 to the low-taxed PE in jurisdiction C. The Commentary notes in this respect that '[w]*here cross-crediting is allowed, the Taxes paid in respect of an inclusion should be determined by subtracting the credit allowed for Taxes paid by the particular PE, and then further subtracting an appropriate amount of excess creditable Taxes paid by other PEs from the pre-credit tax liability of the PE* [...] [to] *ensure that the amount of the Main Entity's Covered Taxes allocated to PEs does not exceed the amount of Taxes actually arising on the related income inclusions*'.[1210] Transferred to the above example, the Commentary seems to assume that the fictional amount of 20 (100 multiplied by the nominal rate of 20%) levied for the 100 income attributable to the low-taxed PE in jurisdiction C should first be reduced by any taxes paid in jurisdiction C, which is 0 in this example but should then be further reduced by '*subtracting an appropriate amount of excess creditable Taxes paid by other PEs*'.[1211] So, should the amount allocable to the PE in jurisdiction C pursuant to Article 4.3.2.(a) GloBE Model Rules and Article 24(1) GloBE-Directive be reduced by the amount of 10 because the credit from jurisdiction B reduces tax liability in jurisdiction A? As can be seen, it is by no means clear how to allocate residence state 'Covered Taxes' levied on income attributable to PEs in different jurisdictions. It is therefore hardly surprising that the OECD, under the pretext that IF member countries' practices differ in this regard, explicitly acknowledges in the Commentary that further clarification is needed and promises to address the issue within the 'GloBE Implementation Framework'.[1212]

A very special tax allocation rule for PEs is further established in Article 4.3.4. GloBE Model Rules and Article 24(7) GloBE-Directive in situations in which PE losses were treated as an expense of the 'Main Entity' pursuant to Article 3.4.5. GloBE Model Rules and Article 18(5) GloBE-Directive. It is evident that, in this case, it would be odd to allocate any 'Adjusted Covered Taxes' (in this case, only a deferred tax asset is conceivable) with respect to such losses to the PE. For this reason, any such taxes remain at the level of the 'Main Entity'. The deferred tax asset stays at the 'Main Entity' and may be used in subsequent 'Fiscal Years' to increase the amount of 'Covered Taxes'.[1213]

1210. *See Ibid.*, para. 52.
1211. *See Ibid.*
1212. *See Ibid.*, para. 54.
1213. In detail on the operation of Art. 4.3.4. *GloBE Model Rules* and Art. 24(7) GloBE-Directive (2022/2523), *see GloBE Commentary on Article 4*, *supra* note 884, paras 64–66.

4.3.4.8.3 *Allocation of Taxes with Respect to 'Tax Transparent Entities'*

'Tax Transparent Entities' (within GloBE that are 'Flow-through Entities'),[1214] by their very nature, usually *'are not subject to CIT in the jurisdiction where they are created'*.[1215] So why is there an issue with respect to allocation of taxes? First, 'Tax Transparent Entities' are usually considered PEs under tax treaties and domestic laws. If any income of such vehicles is attributable to a PE, it is taxed as a PE of the respective partner. So, if a foreign CE owns a participation in a partnership in a foreign jurisdiction, the latter taxes the CE like a non-resident corporation with respect to its PE-income. However, what if a 'Tax Transparent Entity' does not give rise to a PE for the partner? In this case, it is unlikely that the partnership is subject to any tax. Nevertheless, it is not ruled out that any taxes are *'imposed at the sub-national level or local level on Tax Transparent Entities without causing them to be considered a tax resident of that jurisdiction'*.[1216] But how are taxes of 'Tax Transparent Entities' with respect to its PEs and with respect to income not attributable to a PE allocated within the MNE Group?

As this is the case with respect to income allocation,[1217] also the allocation of taxes is a tricky issue with respect to 'Tax Transparent Entities' ('Flow-through Entities'). Technically, both Article 4.3.2.(b) GloBE Model Rules and Article 24(2) GloBE-Directive only state with respect to 'Tax Transparent Entities' that any amount of 'Covered Taxes' included in its financial accounts with respect to 'GloBE Income or Loss' are to be *'allocated to a Constituent-Entity-owner pursuant to Article 3.5.1(b)* [equivalent to Article 19(4) GloBE-Directive] *is allocated to the Constituent Entity-owner'*.[1218] The lack of further rules in Article 4.3. GloBE Model Rules and Article 24 GloBE-Directive should not obscure the fact that the allocation of taxes for 'Tax Transparent Entities', as discussed in detail on income allocation, requires a five-step process, which is performed in parallel with the income allocation:

- **Step 1 – Separation of taxes attributable to non-Group shareholders:** First, the taxes included in the financial statements of the 'Tax Transparent Entity' (separate CE), which are attributable to non-Group partners, is to be separated from the amount of 'Adjusted Covered Taxes'. Finally, an MNE Group's ETR in a specific jurisdiction shall only include taxes paid by the Group itself.
- **Step 2 – Identification of CE-owners for the purpose of allocating group's share of 'Covered Taxes':** The second step requires determining the different CE-owners of the 'Tax Transparent Entity'. The allocation of taxes is finally to be performed separately for each CE-owner according to its 'Ownership Interest'.
- **Step 3 – Allocation of taxes to PEs of the 'Tax Transparent Entity':** In a third step, every tax attributable to a PE according to Article 4.3.2.(a) GloBE Model

1214. Article 10.2.1.(a) *GloBE Model Rules* and Art. 3(12) GloBE-Directive (2022/2523). On the definition of 'Flow-through Entity', *see* s. 4.2.4.4.2.
1215. *See GloBE Commentary on Article 4, supra* note 884, para. 55.
1216. *See Ibid.*
1217. *See* s. 4.3.3.6.
1218. Article 4.3.2.(b) *GloBE Model Rules* and Art. 24(2) GloBE-Directive (2022/2523).

Rules and Article 24(1) GloBE-Directive is to be allocated to the PE. Consequently, those provisions take precedence over Article 4.3.2.(b) GloBE Model Rules and Article 24(2) GloBE-Directive.[1219] Every amount of 'Covered Taxes' that is attributable to PE income is, thus, excluded from the amount of 'Covered Taxes' of the 'Tax Transparent Entity'.

- **Step 4 – Allocation of taxes to the CE-owners of the 'Tax Transparent Entity':** Any remaining taxes are allocated to the CE-owners (partners of the 'Tax Transparent Entity') pursuant to Article 4.3.2.(b) GloBE Model Rules and Article 24(2) GloBE-Directive. This is in line with Article 3.5.1(b) GloBE Model Rules and Article 19(4) GloBE-Directive requiring that any income of a 'Flow-through Entity' (including 'Tax Transparent Entities') that is not allocable to a PE is to be assigned to its CE-owners.[1220]
- **Step 5 – Residual amount of 'Covered Taxes' remains at the 'Tax Transparent Entity' that is a 'Reverse Hybrid Entity':** Only in two situations is it conceivable that, after the allocation of taxes first to PEs and second to PE-owners, an amount of 'Adjusted Covered Taxes' remains at the level of the 'Tax Transparent Entity'. This is the case with respect to 'Tax Transparent Entities' that are UPE of the 'MNE Group' and 'Reverse Hybrid Entities' that are transparent in the jurisdiction where they have been created but are considered opaque in the state where its CE-owner is 'located'. In the case of transparent UPEs, however, there will not remain any tax in most cases because Article 7.1. GloBE Model Rules (Article 38 GloBE-Directive) permits calculating the UPEs ETR based on those taxes levied at the level of its shareholders. For this reason, any 'GloBE Income' for a 'Fiscal Year' is to be *'reduced by the amount of GloBE Income attributable to each Ownership Interest'*,[1221] pursuant to Article 7.1.1. GloBE Model Rules (reflected in Article 38[1] GloBE-Directive). Correspondingly, the remaining 'Covered Taxes' are to be reduced proportionally pursuant to Article 7.1.3. GloBE Model Rules and Article 38(4) GloBE-Directive as well. For this reason, any remaining tax will be eliminated by Article 7.1.3. GloBE Model Rules and Article 38(4) GloBE-Directive anyway. Finally, however, the taxes of a 'Reverse Hybrid Entity' (to be distinguished from 'Hybrid Entities')[1222] that can neither be assigned to PEs nor to its CE-owners remain at this entity. If the 'Reverse Hybrid Entity' is subject to an IIR in the jurisdiction where it was created, the respective 'Adjusted Covered Taxes' is finally included within the ETR computation of that jurisdiction. Otherwise, the Reverse Hybrid Entity' is considered stateless, and the ETR is to be calculated on an entity basis.[1223]

1219. *See GloBE Commentary on Article 4, supra* note 884, paras 53 and 56.
1220. *See Ibid.*, para. 56.
1221. Article 7.1.1. *GloBE Model Rules* and similar Art. 38(1) GloBE-Directive (2022/2523).
1222. *See* the separate definitions of 'Hybrid Entity' in Art. 10.2.5. and 'Reverse Hybrid Entity' in Art. 10.2.1.(b) *GloBE Model Rules*. For the former, a separate allocation rule is provided for in Art. 4.3.2.(d) *Ibid.* and Art. 24(4) GloBE-Directive (2022/2523), which will be discussed in s. 4.3.4.8.5.
1223. In detail on the location of 'Flow-through Entities', *see* s. 4.2.4.4.2.

As can be seen, the allocation of taxes with respect to 'Tax Transparent Entities' is aligned with the allocation of income according to the rules provided for in Article 3.5. GloBE Model Rules and Article 19 GloBE-Directive.[1224] Any 'Covered Taxes' included within the financial statements of the 'Tax Transparent Entities' (if a transparent vehicle is not obliged to prepare separate statements, it regularly does not qualify as 'Entity' and is not considered a separate CE)[1225] need to first be assigned to PEs of the respective entity. Any remaining amount of tax is allocated to the CE-owners of the respective entity, pursuant to Article 4.3.2.(b) GloBE Model Rules and Article 24(2) GloBE-Directive. Only in the rare case of 'Reverse Hybrid Entities', the situation might occur that an amount of tax remains at the entity itself.

4.3.4.8.4 Taxes Levied on CFC Profits

It is evident that CFC regimes disrupt the jurisdictional allocation of income and taxes. Finally, CFC regimes are characterized by taxing income of a foreign-controlled entity at the level of the parent entity. If a CE-owner, thus, is subject to tax with respect to income of its CFC, the respective tax is paid for income that GloBE assigns to the CFC jurisdiction. The underlying problem with respect to tax allocation is therefore comparable with the issue of tax allocation with respect to PEs:[1226] The residence state of a CE-owner taxes income that is part of the 'GloBE Income' of a foreign CE. To correct this flaw caused by CFC regimes, pursuant to Article 4.3.2.(c) GloBE Model Rules (Article 24[3] GloBE-Directive), '*any Covered Taxes included in the financial accounts of* [a CEs] *direct or indirect Constituent Entity-owners under a Controlled Foreign Company Tax Regime on their share of the Controlled Foreign Company's income are allocated to the Constituent Entity*'.[1227] Therefore, any taxes levied on the CE-owners' share of income received from a CE-subsidiary is to be allocated to the latter. The OECD, therefore, aptly refers to Article 4.3.2.(c) GloBE Model Rules as CFC '*push down*'[1228].

For the purpose of this provision, the term 'Controlled Foreign Company Tax Regime' is separately defined in Article 10.1. GloBE Model Rules (reflected in Article 3[17] GloBE-Directive) as '*a set of tax rules (other than an IIR) under which a direct or indirect shareholder of a foreign entity (the controlled foreign company or CFC) is subject to current taxation on its share or all of the income earned by the CFC, irrespective of whether that income is distributed currently to the shareholder or not*'[1229].[1230] The definition of 'Controlled Foreign Company Tax Regime' (in the following 'CFC regime')

1224. In detail on these provisions, *see* s. 4.3.3.6.
1225. On this issue, *see* s. 4.2.4.1.1.
1226. *See* already s. 4.3.4.8.2.
1227. Article 4.3.2.(c) *GloBE Model Rules* and correspondingly Art. 24(3) GloBE-Directive (2022/2523).
1228. *See, i.a., GloBE Commentary on Article 4 GloBE Model Rules (2022), supra* note 884, para. 62.
1229. Article 10.1. *GloBE Model Rules,* at 54 and correspondingly Art. 3(17) GloBE-Directive (2022/2523).
1230. On the definition of 'Controlled Foreign Company Tax Regime' within the GloBE Model Rules in literature, *see,* e.g., Mindy Herzfeld, *More on GLOBE Ordering: CFC Rules,* 106 Tax Notes Intl. 604 (2 May 2022).

is further explained in the Commentary;[1231] however, it seems, despite BEPS Action 3,[1232] that there is no common understanding of what a CFC regime really is. Nevertheless, if one tries to roughly describe the characteristics of a CFC regime, one would argue that CFC rules are generally applied with respect to foreign fiscally opaque entities[1233] or to exempted foreign PEs[1234] if the residence state of the respective entity or the PE state does not impose CIT or does impose CIT that is significantly below that of the residence state. With respect to CFC regimes that apply to PEs, there is the question of whether the allocation rules for PEs or Article 4.3.2.(c) GloBE Model Rules and Article 24(3) GloBE-Directive should apply to the respective income. The Commentary seems to assume that the latter provisions prevail over the allocation rules for taxes on PE income as provided in Article 4.3.2.(a) GloBE Model Rules and Article 24(1) GloBE-Directive.[1235]

Interestingly, the definition of 'CFC regime' explicitly excludes the IIR,[1236] although it has been pointed out in the literature that it might be arbitrary to distinguish CFC regimes from the IIR[1237] (on the difficult distinction of CFC regimes and the IIR and the possible relevance of this distinction, *see* section 4.4.2.8.2.). The reason for this is obvious: if it would be permissible to allocate an IIR levied by the jurisdiction where the CE-owner is 'located' to the subsidiary CE, this '*would create circularity issues*'.[1238] Finally, an IIR attempts to collect 'Top-up Tax' with respect to 'Excess Income' arising in the CFCs jurisdiction and the 'Top-up Tax' has already been calculated, including any taxes levied by the subsidiary CEs (CFC) jurisdiction and any taxes allocated to it by means of Article 4.3.2.(c) GloBE Model Rules and Article 24(3) GloBE-Directive. Technically, the addition '*other than an IIR*'[1239] as can be found in Article 10.1. GloBE Model Rules would not have been needed due to the fact that Article 4.2.2. GloBE Model Rules excludes IIR, UTPR and QDMTT from the definition of 'Covered Taxes' anyway.[1240] So any taxes levied by an IIR could not be allocated pursuant to Article 4.3.2.(c) GloBE Model Rules and Article 24(3) GloBE-Directive, because both provisions only permit to reallocate 'Covered Taxes'. It is, thus, less of a surprise that this clarification is missing in Article 3(17) GloBE-Directive.

The allocation of taxes arising through CFC regimes to the controlled CEs under Article 4.3.2.(c) GloBE Model Rules and Article 24(3) GloBE-Directive is, however, limited by Article 4.3.3. GloBE Model Rules and Article 24(6) GloBE-Directive. Pursuant to these provisions, any 'Covered Taxes' allocated under Article 4.3.2.(c) GloBE

1231. *See GloBE Commentary on Article 10 GloBE Model Rules (2022)*, *supra* note 280, paras 5–8.
1232. OECD/G20, *Designing Effective Controlled Foreign Company Rules, Action 3 – 2015 Final Report* (OECD 5 Oct. 2015), https://www.oecd.org/ctp/designing-effective-controlled-foreign-company-rules-action-3-2015-final-report-9789264241152-en.htm (last visited 29 Oct. 2022).
1233. *See GloBE Commentary on Article 10*, *supra* note 280, para. 7.
1234. *See Ibid.*, para. 5.
1235. *See* the last sentence of *ibid.*
1236. *See Ibid.*, para. 8.
1237. Mindy Herzfeld, *More on GLOBE Ordering: CFC Rules*, 106 Tax Notes Intl., *supra* note 1230, at 604.
1238. *See GloBE Commentary on Article 4 GloBE Model Rules (2022)*, *supra* note 884, para. 45.
1239. Article 10.1. *GloBE Model Rules*, at 54.
1240. On the definition of 'Covered Taxes', *see* already s. 4.3.4.2.

Model Rules and Article 24(3) GloBE-Directive may not exceed an amount lesser of (i) those 'Covered Taxes' allocated in respect of 'Passive Income' and (ii) the 'Top-up Tax Percentage' for the CE which is considered as CFC, *'determined without regard to the Covered Taxes incurred with respect to such Passive Income by the CE-owner'*,[1241] multiplied by the 'Passive Income'[1242] includable under the 'CFC regime'. According to the Commentary, the limitation is needed to *'maintain the integrity of the jurisdictional blending rules in relation to mobile income'*.[1243]

The purpose of this limitation is best illustrated by means of an example.[1244] Assume CE1 is 'located' in jurisdiction A, subject to tax at a nominal rate of 25%. It holds an 80% participation in CE2, which is 'located' in jurisdiction B and is subject to tax at a nominal rate of 10%. Jurisdiction A applies a 'CFC regime' obliging resident corporations to include passive income within its tax base if the CFC is subject to a nominal tax rate of less than half of the domestic tax rate. Further, assume that in the 'Fiscal Year' at issue, CE1 did not receive any income, and CE2 did receive income of 200, of which 100 are considered as passive income under the domestic CFC regime applied by jurisdiction A. The facts are further illustrated below (*see* Table 10).

Table 10 Example with Respect to Taxes Levied in the Course of CFC Regimes

	CE1 (Jurisdiction A)	*CE2 (Jurisdiction B)*
Income	**0**	**200**
active income	0	100
passive income	0	100
CFC income inclusion (80%)	**80**	**0**
Domestic Tax Base	**80**	**200**
active income	0	100
passive income	80	100
Total Domestic Tax	**12**	**20**
active income	0	10
passive income	20	10
foreign tax credit for inclusion (80%)	-8	–
	Potential pre-tax allocation 'Top-up Tax'	**10**[1245]

1241. *See* Art. 4.3.3.(b) *GloBE Model Rules* and, identical in content, the last sentence of the second subparagraph of Art. 24(6) GloBE-Directive (2022/2523).

1242. The definition of 'Passive Income' provides for an exhaustive list of items of income that shall be considered as 'Passive Income', *see* Art. 10.1. *GloBE Model Rules*, at 63. The GloBE-Directive provides for the exact same list directly within the fourth subparagraph of Art. 24(6) GloBE-Directive (2022/2523).

1243. *See GloBE Commentary on Article 4*, *supra* note 884, para. 62.

1244. Also *see* Example 4.3.3. – 1 in *GloBE Examples*, at 38–39.

1245. As the 'Top-up Tax' is calculated including 'GloBE Income' and 'Adjusted Covered Taxes' that could be allocated to non-Group shareholders, the minority-shareholder's share has not been excluded. Whether CE1 would be obliged to collect the 'Top-up Tax' attributable to those shareholders is a different question, on this *see* in detail s. 4.4.2.8.

As can be seen in the table, without any tax allocated, 'Top-up Tax' would arise, although the respective passive income had been taxed in jurisdiction A. If the amount of CFC tax in jurisdiction A is allocated to CE2 pursuant to Article 4.3.2.(c) GloBE Model Rules and Article 24(3) GloBE-Directive (ignoring Article 4.3.3. GloBE Model Rules and Article 24[6] GloBE-Directive), the following picture arises (*see* Table 11).

Table 11 Computation of CFC Tax 'Push-Down' Ignoring the Limitations Provided in Article 4.3.3. GloBE Model Rules and Article 24(6) GloBE-Directive

	CE1 (Jurisdiction A)	*CE2 (Jurisdiction B)*
GloBE Income	0	200
Covered Taxes	12	20
Reallocation	–12	+ 12
Total Adjusted Covered Taxes	0	32
ETR (%)	–	**16**
'Top-up Tax'		**0**

What does the example reveal? As can be seen in the table above, jurisdiction A's tax exceeding the minimum rate does not only increase the amount of 'Covered Taxes' with respect to the passive income of CE2 but also provides shelter for other parts of the income that has not been included in jurisdiction A's tax base. In other words: '*Without the rule of Art 4.3.3.* [Art 24(6) GloBE-Directive], *an MNE Group could shift mobile income from high-tax jurisdictions to Low-Tax Jurisdictions to reduce overall tax liability (including Top-up Tax liability) in the MNE Group.*'[1246]

To properly consider this instance, the limitations provided in Article 4.3.3. GloBE Model Rules and Article 24(6) GloBE-Directive kick in: CE2 may only be allocated an amount of tax that does not exceed the 'Top-up Tax Percentage' of CE2 with respect to the passive income multiplied by the amount of CE2's passive income includible under jurisdiction A's CFC regime. In the example above, the 'Top-up Tax Percentage' of CE2 with respect to passive income would amount to 5% (15% – [10/100]). The passive income includable in CE1's tax base amounts to 80, so the maximum amount of tax that may be '*pushed down*' from CE1 to CE2 amounts to 4 (80 x 5%). The final result, as accepted by GloBE, is illustrated in Table 12.

Table 12 Computation of CFC Tax 'Push-Down' Considering the Limitations Provided in Article 4.3.3. GloBE Model Rules and Article 24(6) GloBE-Directive

	CE1 (Jurisdiction A)	*CE2 (Jurisdiction B)*
GloBE Income	0	200
Covered Taxes	12	20
Reallocation	–4	+ 4

1246. *See GloBE Commentary on Article 4*, *supra* note 884, para. 62.

	CE1 (Jurisdiction A)	CE2 (Jurisdiction B)
Total Adjusted Covered Taxes	8	24
ETR (%)	-	**12**
'Top-up Tax Percentage' (%)		[15% – 12%] **3**
'Top-up Tax'		[200 × 3%] **6**

As a result, the 'Adjusted Covered Taxes' of CE2 have only been increased to the extent that the passive income included within the local tax base of CE1 (80%) is taxed at the 'Minimum Rate' of 15%. The taxes levied by jurisdiction A did neither level up the taxes paid with respect to 20% of passive income that had not been included within the tax base of CE1 nor with respect to active income that had not been subject to the CFC regime applied by jurisdiction A. In this example, CE2 would be allocated a 'Top-up Tax' of 6 (200 x [15% – 12%]), of which CE1 would most probably collect at least 4.8 (6 x 80%) by means of the IIR.[1247] The amount of CFC taxes that could not be allocated to CE2[1248] remains within the amount of 'Adjusted Covered Taxes' of CE1.[1249]

As has been seen, the allocation of CFC taxes is a comparatively simple issue. Any taxes levied at a parent entity are finally to be located to the jurisdiction where its subsidiary is 'located'. In its GloBE Administrative Guidance February 2023, the OECD took note that things become '*more complex, however, when the CFC tax arises under a Blended CFC Tax Regime. A Blended CFC Tax Regime is one in which the tax charge under the CFC Tax Regime is computed based on a blend of income, losses and/ or creditable taxes of multiple CFCs whose Ownership Interests are held by a Constituent Entity-owner (or multiple Constituent Entity-owners that file a single tax return)*'.[1250] The clarifications and announced changes to the Commentary, in particular, address the US GILTI regime that works similarly to a common CFC regime but applies a global blending approach. If a global blending approach is applied, it is questionable which amount of CFC tax is to be allocated to which jurisdiction. The GloBE Administrative Guidance February 2023 included seven additional subparagraphs to paragraph 58 of the GloBE Commentary on Article 4 GloBE Model Rules and will add two examples to the GloBE Example Catalogue[1251] that specifically address the allocation of CFC taxes with respect to 'Blended CFC Tax Regimes'. The additional materials provide for a simplified allocation method that can be applied for all 'Fiscal Years' beginning before 31 December 2025 '*but not including a Fiscal Year that ends after 30 June 2027*'.[1252] The newly added paras 58.1 to 58.7 of the GloBE Commentary on Article 4 GloBE Model Rules simply provide for a formula that divides the 'Allocable Blended CFC Tax' among

1247. In detail on the collection of the 'Top-up Tax', *see* s. 4.4.2.8.
1248. *See* the last sentence of Art. 4.3.3. *GloBE Model Rules* and the third subparagraph of Art. 24(6) GloBE-Directive (2022/2523).
1249. *See GloBE Commentary on Article 4, supra* note 884, para. 63.
1250. *See* para. 2 *GloBE Administrative Guidance February 2023,* at 67.
1251. *GloBE Examples.*
1252. *See* para. 58.3 *GloBE Commentary on Article 4, supra* note 884 pursuant to the *GloBE Administrative Guidance February 2023,* at 68.

the low-tax jurisdictions where the CFCs of the respective 'MNE Group's' CEs are 'located' pursuant to their proportionate share of income (so-called Blended CFC Allocation Key) whose income had been taxed by way of the 'Blended CFC Tax Regime'. However, an allocation is only made insofar as the respective CFC is 'located' in a 'Low-tax Jurisdiction' (jurisdiction in which the ETR is below 15%).[1253] The formula also allocates CFC taxes to CFCs that do not qualify as CEs. Pursuant to the newly added paragraph 58.7 of the GloBE Commentary on Article 4 GloBE Model Rules, this is necessary to '*ensure such tax is properly excluded from Covered Taxes for GloBE purposes*'[1254] because otherwise, this would include taxes of non-group members into the ETR of the respective CFC's jurisdiction and would, thus, overestimate the ETR. It is interesting to note that a 'CFC regime' only qualifies as a 'Blended CFC Tax Regimes' if it applies a tax rate below 15%. This limitation makes it clear that the simplified mechanism will hardly be applicable to any CFC regime other than USA's GILTI regime, as the latter applies a relatively low tax rate of 13.125%.

4.3.4.8.5 Tax Allocation with Respect to Hybrid Entities

Very similar to the allocation rule for CFC taxes, Article 4.3.2.(d) GloBE Model Rules and Article 24(4) GloBE-Directive provide for a separate allocation rule for taxes levied at the CE-owner with respect to income of a 'Hybrid Entity'. Why is the problem comparable to that of CFC tax allocation? The term 'Hybrid Entity' is defined in Article 10.2.5. GloBE Model Rules and the second sentence of Article 24(4) GloBE-Directive. It means an entity that is treated as a taxable person in the jurisdiction where it had been created, whereas it is treated fiscally transparent in the jurisdiction of its CE-owner (with a 'Reverse Hybrid Entity' which is a 'Flow-through Entity' from the perspective of GloBE, it's the other way round). In any case, taxes levied on the CE-owners with respect to income of 'Hybrid Entities' reveal the same issues as CFC taxes due to the fact that also, in these situations, the residence state of the CE-owners includes its share of income within the local tax base because it simply treats the entity as being fiscally transparent. However, from the perspective of GloBE, the respective income is still allocated to the jurisdiction where the 'Hybrid Entity' is considered a tax resident (this is because a 'Hybrid Entity' is not considered a 'Flow-through Entity')[1255].[1256] Article 4.3.2.(d) GloBE Model Rules and Article 24(4) GloBE-Directive, thus, require to reallocate taxes levied at the CE-owner to the 'Hybrid Entity'. The limitations of Article 4.3.3. GloBE Model Rules and Article 24(6) GloBE-Directive, however, also apply with respect to 'Hybrid Entities'.[1257] Consequently, reference can be made to section 4.3.4.8.4. regarding the operation of this pushdown.

1253. *See* the newly added Examples 4.3.2-1 and 4.3.2-2 *GloBE Administrative Guidance February 2023*, at 69–70.
1254. *See* para. 58.7 *GloBE Commentary on Article 4*, *supra* note 884 pursuant to the *GloBE Administrative Guidance February 2023*, at 69.
1255. *See* Art. 10.2.1. *GloBE Model Rules* and Art. 3(12) GloBE-Directive (2022/2523).
1256. Article 10.3.1.(a) *GloBE Model Rules* and Art. 4(1) GloBE-Directive (2022/2523).
1257. *See GloBE Commentary on Article 4, supra* note 884, para. 59.

4.3.4.8.6 Allocation of Taxes on Dividends and Other Distributions

The last allocation rule enshrined in Article 4.3.2.(e) GloBE Model Rules and Article 24(5) GloBE-Directive address taxes on dividends and distributions of CEs to its CE-owners, which are usually included within the financial statements of the CE-owner but, for the purposes of GloBE, need to be reallocated to the distributing CE. Article 4.3.2.(e) GloBE Model Rules and Article 24(5) GloBE-Directive, thus, only apply with respect to dividends paid within CEs of the same 'MNE Group'.[1258] According to the Commentary, this rule applies to '*withholding taxes and net basis taxes incurred by direct Constituent Entity-owners on distributions*'.[1259] In its GloBE Administrative Guidance February 2023, the OECD has clarified that the allocation rule of Article 4.3.2.(e) GloBE Model Rules also applies with respect to deemed distributions.[1260]

The allocation rules of Article 4.3.2.(e) GloBE Model Rules and Article 24(5) GloBE-Directive seem to be odd at first glance: jurisdictions levy withholding taxes on dividends to tax the recipient rather than the distributing entity, and as has been discussed in section 4.3.4.8.1., any withholding taxes are usually included in the amount of 'Adjusted Covered Taxes' of the CE-recipient. What is the reason for reallocating taxes on dividends and other distributions to the distributing CE?

Already within the Pillar Two Blueprint argued that '[i]*deally, covered taxes paid with respect to distributions of a Constituent Entity's income, including net basis taxes and withholding taxes, should be assigned to the tax jurisdiction of the Constituent Entity that earned the underlying income. However, tracking and tracing distributions through the ownership chain would be extremely complex and burdensome. Accordingly, such taxes should be assigned to the jurisdiction of the Constituent Entity that distributed the dividend that triggered the tax liability*'.[1261] Nearly the same wording is found in the Commentary.[1262] It, thus, seems that both Article 4.3.2.(e) GloBE Model Rules and Article 24(5) GloBE-Directive serve the purpose of simplification. However, this does not seem entirely convincing: withholding taxes are usually recorded in the financial statements of the income recipient anyway. It is difficult to see why it would be easier to reallocate them to the distributing CE.

However, there might be systematic reasons for allocating withholding taxes on dividends or other distribution taxes to the distributing CE: many IF Member States, as has already been discussed in detail,[1263] exempt dividend income at the level of the recipient to avoid economic double taxation of distributed profits. GloBE, for this reason, excludes most dividends from the 'GloBE Income or Loss'.[1264] Correspondingly, however, any taxes on the respective 'Excluded Dividends' would also be excluded from the amount of 'Covered Taxes' in Article 4.1.3.(a) GloBE Model Rules

1258. *See Ibid.*, para. 60.
1259. *See Ibid.*
1260. *See* the newly added paras 60.1 and 60.2 in the *GloBE Commentary on Article 4*, *supra* note 884 by the *GloBE Administrative Guidance February 2023*, at 48.
1261. *Tax Challenges Arising from Digitalisation – Report on Pillar Two Blueprint*, para. 281.
1262. *See GloBE Commentary on Article 4*, *supra* note 884, para. 61.
1263. *See* s. 4.3.3.3.2.
1264. Article 3.2.(b) *GloBE Model Rules* and Art. 16(2)(b) GloBE-Directive (2022/2523).

and Article 21(3)(a) GloBE-Directive at the level of the CE receiving the dividend. Any taxes on dividends, including withholding taxes, would be excluded from the amount of 'Adjusted Covered Taxes' as well. As a result, any taxes with respect to dividends would neither be recognized at the level of the distributing CE nor at the level of the CE receiving the distribution. By allocating such taxes from the CE to its CE-subsidiary, the respective taxes are at least included in the ETR of the jurisdiction where the distributing CE is 'located'.

4.3.4.9 Post-Filing Adjustments and Tax Rate Changes

The tax liability, once determined, may turn out to be incorrect in subsequent 'Fiscal Years' for a variety of reasons: for example, domestic tax liability may increase or reduce due to tax litigation, financial accounting errors from previous years may come to light, or a jurisdiction might subsequently decide to change its domestic tax rate leading to an incorrect assumption with regard to deferred tax expenses.[1265] However, such subsequent adjustments must also be taken into account for GloBE purposes. Finally, '*if the final tax liability in a jurisdiction had been correctly determined when the GloBE Information Return was filed, the shareholder may have computed a different ETR and possibly paid more or less Top-up Tax and may have established a larger or smaller deferred tax liability or asset in that Fiscal Year*'.[1266] For this reason, both the GloBE Model Rules as well as the GloBE-Directive provide for a set of rules in Article 4.6. GloBE Model Rules and Article 25 GloBE-Directive to handle '*Post-filing Adjustments and Tax Rate Changes*'[1267].

However, the critical issue of considering subsequent adjustments to 'Covered Taxes' is not so much whether or how they should be considered, but more importantly, in which 'Fiscal Year' such amendments should be recorded: should GloBE require to tediously recalculate the ETR and 'Top-up Tax' determined for a previous 'Fiscal Year' subsequently, or should the amendment simply be reflected in the amount of 'Adjusted Covered Taxes' in the current 'Fiscal Year'? Both, Article 4.6.1. GloBE Model Rules and Article 25(1) GloBE-Directive in this respect distinguish increases and decreases of 'Covered Taxes for a previous 'Fiscal Year':

- **If the tax liability with respect to 'Covered Taxes' increases for a previous 'Fiscal Year'**, the respective adjustment is, pursuant to the first sentences of Article 4.6.1. GloBE Model Rules and Article 25(1) GloBE-Directive, to be recorded as an increase of adjusted 'Covered Taxes' of the current 'Fiscal Year'. The Commentary notes in this respect that '[w]*hile treating such post-filing adjustments to a tax liability in the current year is not as accurate as recalculating the GloBE tax liability or potential GloBE tax liability with respect to the relevant Fiscal Years, it significantly simplifies the computation of the*

1265. Also *see GloBE Commentary on Article 4*, *supra* note 884, para. 119.
1266. *See Ibid*.
1267. *See* the titles of Art. 4.6. *GloBE Model Rules* and Art. 25 GloBE-Directive (2022/2523).

Top-up Tax under GloBE Rules'.[1268] This simplification makes perfect sense: if a subsequent adjustment or increase of the applicable tax rate leads to an increase in 'Covered Taxes' of a previous 'Fiscal Year', there is no risk that 'Top-up Tax' is avoided. Rather, an increase in 'Covered Taxes' would potentially reduce any amount of 'Top-up Tax' levied in a previous 'Fiscal Year'. However, the simplification comes with the drawback that excess 'Top-up Taxes' levied in previous years cannot be refunded.[1269]

- **If the liability with respect to 'Covered Taxes' decreases for a previous 'Fiscal Year'**, however, the respective second sentences of Article 4.6.1. GloBE Model Rules and Article 25(1) GloBE-Directive require re-computation of the ETR and the 'Top-up Tax' for the previous 'Fiscal Year(s)'. This is because otherwise, jurisdictions and 'MNE Groups' could deliberately provoke a subsequent reduction in 'Covered Taxes' (e.g., by granting subsequent tax cuts or by deliberately increasing tax liability to challenge them in subsequent 'Fiscal Years'). The recalculation is to be made pursuant to Article 5.4.1. GloBE Model Rules and Article 29 GloBE-Directive: if the recalculation for a previous 'Fiscal Year' results in a 'Top-up Tax' liability or increases the amount of 'Top-up Tax' due in that previous 'Fiscal Year', the respective increase in 'Top-up Tax' is levied as 'Additional Current Top-up Tax' (within the GloBE-Directive 'additional top-up tax') in the current 'Fiscal Year', as the 'Additional Current Top-up Tax' is to be added to the amount of 'Jurisdictional Top-up Tax' pursuant to Article 5.2.3. GloBE Model Rules and Article 26(3) GloBE-Directive. However, because a subsequent re-computation of the ETR and 'Top-up Tax' is a cumbersome task, both Article 4.6.1. GloBE Model Rules and Article 25(1) GloBE-Directive allow for an 'Annual Election' to treat immaterial decreases in 'Covered Taxes', which is a decrease of less than EUR 1 million in 'Adjusted Covered Taxes' for the jurisdiction at issue, as a reduction in 'Covered Taxes' for the current 'Fiscal Year'. According to the Commentary, '[t]*he immateriality of an adjustment is determined for each Fiscal Year by reference to the aggregate increase or decrease in Covered Taxes for each Fiscal Year*'.[1270] The immateriality threshold, therefore, relates to the previous 'Fiscal Year' in question. If, e.g., in year Y5, a reduction in 'Covered Taxes' occurs with respect to both year Y2 and year Y3, the EUR 1 million limit is tested separately for each of the two years rather than aggregating the adjustments required in both years.

In a nutshell, the content of Article 4.6.1. GloBE Model Rules and Article 25(1) GloBE-Directive can be summarized as follows: (i) Subsequent increases of 'Adjusted Covered Taxes' are always corrected in the current 'Fiscal Year'. (ii) If a previous adjustment or tax rate change leads to a reduction in 'Covered Taxes' of a previous 'Fiscal Year', GloBE requires to recalculate the 'Top-up Tax' for that year. (iii) If the

1268. *See GloBE Commentary on Article 4*, *supra* note 884, para. 120.
1269. *See Ibid.*
1270. *See Ibid.*, para. 121.

decrease, however, is less than EUR 1 million for the respective previous year, an 'MNE Group' may elect not to recalculate the previous 'Fiscal Year' but to merely reduce the 'Adjusted Covered Taxes' of the current fiscal year.

If an error stems from prior periods, Article 3.2.(h) GloBE Model Rules and Article 15(2)(h) GloBE-Directive make sure that any income or loss included in the financial statements of the current 'Fiscal Year' are excluded from the 'GloBE Income or Loss'. Those provisions are, thus, the counterparts of Article 4.6.1. GloBE Model Rules and Article 25(1) GloBE-Directive within GloBE's base determination. As a result, any changes of 'Covered Taxes' for previous years corrected in the current 'Fiscal Year' are not reflected in the denominator of the ETR fraction. This is because otherwise, the intended effects of including the post-filing adjustment or tax rate change in the numerator of the ETR fraction would be reversed. Article 3.2.(h) GloBE Model Rules and Article 15(2)(h) GloBE-Directive do not apply if recalculation is required. In this case, the adjustment is not made in the current 'Fiscal Year' anyway. For this reason, both rules do not apply with respect to material decreases in 'Covered Taxes'.[1271] In detail in Article 3.2.(h) GloBE Model Rules and Article 15(2)(h) GloBE-Directive *see* section 4.3.3.3.2.

The Commentary also mentions national loss carry-back regimes as a regular application of Article 4.6.1 GloBE Model Rules (Article 25[1] GloBE-Directive):[1272] If a jurisdiction allows to subsequently reduce the tax liability of previous years by deducting subsequently incurred losses, this necessarily requires the recalculation of the respective 'Fiscal Year', unless the decrease in 'Covered Tax' is immaterial. In this case, any credit provided for taxes levied with respect to previous years, of course, reduces the amount of 'Covered Taxes' in this previous year. However, at the same time, a deferred tax liability is generated for the loss carried back under domestic law of that jurisdiction.[1273] The operation of Article 4.6.1. GloBE Model Rules and Article 25(1) GloBE-Directive can easily be demonstrated by means of an example: assume a CE in Y1 receives an income of 100 and is subject to tax at a rate of 25. In the following year Y2, it incurs a loss of 100, which may be carried back under domestic tax law leading to a tax refund of 25 in Y2. In this case, Article 4.6.1. GloBE Model Rules and Article 24(1) GloBE-Directive require recalculation of Y1 in Y2, which is performed as follows: the amount of 'Covered Taxes' in Y1 was 25 and is now reduced by 25. However, at the same time, a deferred tax expense is generated because the loss incurred in Y2 reduces the tax base in Y1. Pursuant to Article 4.4.1. GloBE Model Rules and Article 21(2) GloBE Model Rules any deferred tax expenses need to be recast at the 'Minimum Rate'. For this reason, the deferred tax expense generated amounts to 15. The recalculation, thus, results in an ETR of 15% ([25-25 + 15]/100) and no 'Top-up Tax' is due in this case.[1274]

1271. *See Ibid.*, paras 122–123 and *GloBE Commentary on Article 3 GloBE Model Rules (2022), supra* note 507, paras 79–81.
1272. *See GloBE Commentary on Article 4, supra* note 884, para. 124.
1273. *See Ibid.*, para. 125
1274. A similar example is provided for in *Ibid.*, para. 126.

If a jurisdiction decides to lower its domestic tax rate below the 'Minimum Rate', such a tax policy decision necessarily might also influence the amount of 'Adjusted Covered Taxes' calculated for previous 'Fiscal Years': finally, corporations have to account for deferred tax expenses and if the tax rate is subsequently reduced, any deferred tax expenses might reduce as well. For this reason, Article 4.6.2. GloBE Model Rules and Article 25(2) GloBE-Directive clarify that recalculation is also required with respect to previous 'Fiscal Years' in such situation.[1275] Recalculation is, however, not necessary if the tax reduction does not lead to an applicable tax rate of 15% or above since any deferred taxes taken into consideration by GloBE are recast at the minimum rate if a jurisdiction's nominal tax rate is above 15%. Thus, Article 4.6.2. GloBE Model Rules and Article 25(2) GloBE-Directive are only applicable if the reduction in tax results in a nominal tax rate below 15%. Assume in Y1 a CE 'located' in jurisdiction A is subject to tax at a rate of 20%, received 'GloBE Income' of 100. Under domestic law, the CE was granted a 'super deduction' for a specific asset valued at 100 and, thus, in Y1, accounted for a GloBE deferred tax liability of 15. In Y1, no 'Top-up Tax' was due because the ETR was 15% (15/100). In Y2, jurisdiction A decides to reduce its tax rate to 10%. Now, it is obvious that the deferred tax liability generated in Y1 needs to be corrected pursuant to Article 4.6.2. GloBE Model Rules and Article 25(2) GloBE-Directive requiring recalculation of Y1. Since, in this case, only a deferred tax asset of 10 may be generated in Y1, the ETR would amount to 10 (10/100), resulting in an 'Additional Current Top-up Tax' of 5 to be added to the 'Jurisdictional Top-up Tax' calculated in Y2.[1276]

The reverse scenario is addressed in Article 4.6.3. GloBE Model Rules and Article 25(3) GloBE-Directive: GloBE might create an incentive for jurisdictions to raise their corporate tax rates. If a jurisdiction decides to raise its domestic tax rate to or above the 'Minimum Rate', any increase of the deferred tax expenses may be considered, in line with Article 4.6.1 GloBE Model Rules and Article 25(1) GloBE-Directive, as an adjustment to the 'Covered Taxes' for a previous year, when the deferred tax expense is finally paid.[1277] Assume in Y1 a CE 'located' in jurisdiction A is subject to tax at a rate of 10%, received 'GloBE Income' of 100. Under domestic law, the CE was granted a 'super deduction' for a specific asset valued at 100 and, thus, in Y1, accounted for a GloBE deferred tax liability of 10. In Y2, the CE again receives 'GloBE Income' of 100, but jurisdiction A decides to increase its tax rate to 20%, and the deferred tax liability reverses because the tax is finally paid. Financial accounting rules, thus, require eliminating the respective tax liability. Accordingly, in Y2, the 'Covered Taxes' would amount to 10 because the tax of 20 would be reduced by the reversing tax liability of 10. However, as jurisdiction A increased its tax rate, the deferred tax liability in Y1 should have been 15 (100 x 15% [deferred tax expenses may only be recorded up to the 'Minimum Rate'][1278]). For this reason, Article 4.6.3. GloBE Model Rules and Article 25(3) GloBE-Directive permit to increase the amount of 'Covered Taxes' with respect to

1275. *See Ibid.*, para. 128.
1276. Also *see* the example provided for in *Ibid.*, para. 129.
1277. *See Ibid.*, para. 130.
1278. Article 4.4.1. *GloBE Model Rules* and Art. 22(2) GloBE-Directive (2022/2523).

the deferred tax liability that, wrongly, had not been considered in Y1, increasing the ETR in Y2 to 15% ([20-10 + 5]/100).

In general, Article 4.1.3.(e) GloBE Model Rules and Article 21(3)(e) GloBE-Directive do not allow including tax liabilities in the amount of 'Adjusted Covered Taxes' that are not expected to be paid within three years.[1279] Nevertheless, it can happen that a tax liability had been included but finally is not paid within those three years. For this reason, Article 4.6.4. GloBE Model Rules and Article 24(4) GloBE-Directive also require recalculation if any amount had once been accrued as current tax expense but finally has not been paid in the fourth subsequent year. Consequently, Article 4.6.4. GloBE Model Rules and Article 25(4) GloBE-Directive force CEs to recompute their ETR and 'Top-up Tax' in the fourth subsequent year if the tax liability, once recorded, has not yet been paid. Both provisions explicitly do not require recalculation if the respective amount of tax does not exceed EUR 1 million. Consequently, Article 4.6.4. GloBE Model Rules and Article 25(4) GloBE-Directive force MNE Groups to annually test whether every tax liability accounted for in the fourth preceding year had already been paid.[1280]

4.4 COMPUTATION AND CHARGING OF THE 'TOP-UP TAX'

4.4.1 The 'Top-up Tax' Computation: Linking the Jurisdictional ETR and the Final Minimum Tax Liability

While the previous sections were dedicated to the ETR fraction and, in particular, to the calculation of both its numerator[1281] and denominator,[1282] this section is devoted to the final computation of the 'Top-up Tax'. It has already been revealed in section 4.3.2.2.1. that the ETR computation is a part of the 'Top-up Tax' computation. One could, thus, argue that it is artificial to split the ETR computation, including the determination of the 'GloBE Income or Loss' (within the GloBE-Directive 'qualifying income or loss') and the amount of 'Adjusted Covered Taxes' from the computation of the 'Top-up Tax'. However, both the GloBE Model Rules as well as the GloBE-Directive devote separate chapters to the determination of 'GloBE Income or Loss' (Article 3 GloBE Model Rules and Chapter III GloBE-Directive) and the amount of 'Adjusted Covered Taxes' (Article 4 GloBE Model Rules and Chapter IV GloBE-Directive). But what then is the 'Top-up Tax', and why does it make sense to discuss it separately from the ETR fraction and its determinants?

The 'Top-up Tax' finally is the amount of tax that is to be collected from the members of an 'MNE Group' to achieve the minimum tax level of 15%: it is the result of the comparison of the actual tax burden of an 'MNE Group' within a specific jurisdiction and the minimum tax level.[1283] In principle, the 'Top-up Tax' is the amount

1279. *See* in detail s. 4.3.4.4.4.
1280. Also *see GloBE Commentary on Article 4, supra* note 884, paras 132–133.
1281. *See* s. 4.3.4.
1282. *See* s. 4.3.3.
1283. On this fundamental element of every minimum tax regime, *see* s. 4.3.1.

of 'Net GloBE Income' received in a specific jurisdiction multiplied by the difference between the minimum tax rate and the lower ETR as determined after the adjustments have been made to the 'GloBE Income or Loss' and the amount of 'Adjusted Covered Taxes' that have been discussed extensively in the previous sections. Thus, the computation of the 'Top-up Tax' is at the heart of GloBE and a prerequisite for the application of the GloBE Rules.[1284] The 'Top-up Tax' computation can be described as the process of determining the final minimum tax burden of an 'MNE Group' within a specific jurisdiction. The ETR, as discussed in section 4.3, is merely an element of the 'Top-up Tax' calculation. The starting point for the computation of the 'Top-up Tax' is the 'GloBE Income or Loss' as well as the amount of 'Adjusted Covered Taxes'. The determination of both elements, thus, is a prerequisite for the final 'Top-up Tax' computation. Only if both elements are determined the 'Top-up Tax' can be calculated and allocated among the 'MNE Group's' CEs in a fixed order of mathematical operations and tax mechanisms. Thus, the calculation of the 'Top-up Tax' assumes that both the 'GloBE Income or Loss' and the 'Adjusted Covered Taxes' have already been calculated in advance, which is why the actual calculation of the relevant element of the ETR fraction, although overall part of the 'Top-up Tax' calculation, has already been discussed in the previous sections, while the following sections will specifically focus on the 'Top-up Tax' and will regularly refer to the conclusions drawn above.

As will be seen, this fixed order of operations can be divided into eight steps. This 'eight-step approach' has already been developed by *Kofler* and the author of this thesis in the course of a published article titled *'Computation of the Effective Tax Rate and the 'Top-up Tax''*.[1285] The following sections are based on this publication, reflecting but also developing the findings found there. At the end of each section, the relevant passage of the paper is cited. Table 13 is intended to provide an overview of this eight-step approach. Finally, a separate section is devoted to each of those steps.

Table 13 The 'Eight-Step Approach' for the Computation of the ETR and the 'Top-Up Tax'

Eight-Step Approach for the Computation of the ETR and the 'Top-Up Tax'				
Step	*Process*	*Model Rules*[1286]	*GloBE-Directive*[1287]	*Section*
1	**Determination of CEs and their location** within an MNE Group	Article 5.1.1.	Article 26(1)	Section 4.4.2.1.
2	**Aggregation of GloBE Income or Losses and Adjusted Covered Taxes** of CEs (determined in Step 1) in the same jurisdiction	Articles 5.1.1 and 5.1.2.	Articles 26(1) and (2)	section 4.4.2.2.

1284. Also *see GloBE Commentary on Article 5 GloBE Model Rules (2022), supra* note 474, para. 2.
1285. V. Bendlinger & G. Kofler, *Computation of the Effective Tax Rate and the 'Top-up Tax', in Pillar 2 Global Minimum Tax, supra* note 305.
1286. *GloBE Model Rules.*
1287. GloBE-Directive (2022/2523).

Eight-Step Approach for the Computation of the ETR and the 'Top-Up Tax'

Step	*Process*	*Model Rules*[1286]	*GloBE-Directive*[1287]	*Section*
3	**ETR calculation and Identification of Low-Tax Jurisdictions** (ETR < 15%)	Article 5.1.1.	Article 26(1)	section 4.4.2.3.
4	**Computation of 'Top-up Tax' Percentage** for each low tax jurisdiction	Article 5.2.1.	Articles 27(1) and (2)	section 4.4.2.4.
5	**Calculating Excess Profit** for each low tax jurisdiction by subtracting SBIE	Articles 5.2.2. and 5.3.	Articles 27(4) and 28	section 4.4.2.5.
6	**Calculating Jurisdictional 'Top-up Tax'** by multiplying 'Top-up Tax' percentage (Step 4) by excess profit (Step 5) per low tax jurisdiction	Article 5.2.3.	Article 27(3)	section 4.4.2.6.
7	**Allocate 'Top-up Taxes' to the CEs** resident in Low-Tax Jurisdiction in proportion to income	Article 5.2.4.	Article 27(5)	section 4.4.2.7.
8	**Charging of 'Top-up Tax' by applying IIR or UTPR**	Article 2	Articles 5 to 14	section 4.4.2.8.

4.4.2 Computation and Charging of 'Top-up Tax' as an Eight-Step Procedure

4.4.2.1 Step 1: Determination of CEs and Their 'Location'

According to Article 5.1.1. GloBE Model Rules (reflected in Article 26[1] GloBE-Directive) the 'Effective Tax Rate of the MNE Group for a jurisdiction is equal to the sum of the 'Adjusted Covered Taxes *of each Constituent Entity located in the jurisdiction* divided by the Net GloBE Income of the jurisdiction for each Fiscal Year'[1288] (emphasis added). Thus, this provision basically statutes the mode of calculating ETR and jurisdictional blending in general. For these purposes, however, it must first be determined which CEs belong to the taxable 'MNE Group' at all and in which jurisdiction they are located.

Consequently, the first step of the 'Top-up Tax' calculation is closely related to the scope of GloBE: first of all, it is necessary to check whether there is an 'MNE Group' that is covered by GloBE at all (e.g., revenue of at least EUR 750 million,[1289] cross-border element,[1290] not an excluded entity[1291]). Issues of scope are addressed in

1288. Article 5.1.1. *GloBE Model Rules*. Also *see* Art. 26(1) GloBE-Directive (2022/2523): '*The effective tax rate of an MNE group or of a large-scale domestic group shall be computed, for each fiscal year and for each jurisdiction* […]'.
1289. Article 1.1.1. *GloBE Model Rules*. Also *see* Art. 2(1) GloBE-Directive (2022/2523).
1290. Article 1.2.1. *GloBE Model Rules*. Deviating from this, according to Art. 2(1) GloBE-Directive (2022/2523) also '*large-scale domestic groups*' are covered.

section 4.2. and shall not be discussed further here. However, the actual connection of the 'Top-up Tax' calculation to the scope under Article 1 GloBE Model Rules is the fact that the computation of the 'Top-up Tax' necessarily requires in the first step to determine which CEs are even part of the 'MNE Group' at issue. Here, GloBE focuses on the scope of the consolidation requirement under the UPE's 'Acceptable Financial Accounting Standard': according to Article 1.2.2. GloBE Model Rules a Group is '*a collection of Entities that are related through ownership or control such that the assets, liabilities, income, expenses and cash flows of those Entities*' are either (i) included in the consolidated financial statements of the UPE or (ii) are excluded from the consolidated financial statements of the UPE solely on size or materiality grounds, or on the grounds that the respective entity is held for sale.[1292]

Once the entities included in the consolidated financial statements of the UPE (in consideration of the exceptions just mentioned[1293]) have been determined, the next step is to determine the PEs of all entities within the 'MNE Group'. According to Article 1.3.1. of the GloBE Model Rules and Article 3(2)(b) GloBE-Directive, these are considered stand-alone CEs and shall '*be treated separate from the Main Entity and any other Permanent Establishment of that Main Entity*'.[1294] This artificial splitting of legal entities is a consequence of jurisdictional blending (*see* in particular sections 4.2.4.1.2. and 4.3.2.3.): if the UPE or one of its consolidated entities operates in different tax jurisdictions, the corresponding profits must be allocated to the jurisdiction that has the right to tax or actually taxes the respective profits under its domestic law. Consequently, for GloBE purposes, a separate PE definition (in detail on the PE definition, *see* section 4.2.4.1.2.) is provided in Article 10 GloBE Model Rules and Article 3(13) GloBE-Directive, according to which a '*GloBE PE*' exists if a certain place of business is situated in a jurisdiction and the respective place of business (i) *is subject to a tax treaty* with a provision similar to Article 7 OECD MC, (ii) in the case, there is no applicable tax treaty, *is taxed by a jurisdiction under its domestic law*, (iii) in the case, a jurisdiction does not levy CIT, *would be treated as a PE under the OECD MC* or (iv) in other cases, operates outside the jurisdiction where the main entity is located and the *respective jurisdiction exempts the income attributable to the place of business* ('*Stateless Entity*'). '*GloBE Income or Loss*' and '*Adjusted Covered Taxes*' must, therefore, also be allocated between the Main Entities and the 'GloBE PEs'. For this purpose, Articles 3.4. and 4.3. GloBE Model Rules, as well as Articles 18 and 24(1) GloBE-Directive, provide corresponding regulations.[1295]

As a first conclusion for the 'Top-up Tax' computation, it can thus be stated that the consolidated financial statements determine the scope of the 'MNE Group' and thus the income and tax amounts subject to the GloBE Rules. The first step of the 'Top-up Tax' calculation starts here and requires first the splitting of the 'Consolidated Financial Statements' into individual CEs, which, however, are not to be determined according

1291. Article 1.4. *GloBE Model Rules*. Also *see* Art. 2(3) GloBE-Directive (2022/2523).
1292. Article 1.2.2.(a) and (b) *GloBE Model Rules*. Also *see* Art. 3(3) GloBE-Directive (2022/2523).
1293. Article 1.2.2.(b) *GloBE Model Rules*.
1294. Article 1.3.2. *Ibid*. Also *see* Art. 3(2)(b) GloBE-Directive (2022/2523).
1295. On the allocation of 'GloBE Income or Loss' between a 'Main Entity' and a PE, *see* s. 4.3.3.5. On the allocation of 'Adjusted Covered Taxes', *see* s. 4.3.4.8.2.

to corporate or civil law principles, but according to tax principles: the corresponding assets are to be allocated to the individual CEs. Their income is to be calculated on the basis of the financial statements prepared for the 'Consolidated Financial Statements'. PEs are to be recognized as separate CEs, and the financial statement of the respective legal entity must be split into the Main Entity and the actual GloBE PE for purposes of income and tax determination.

In line with the separation of the 'Consolidated Financial Statements' into individual CEs, jurisdictional blending requires determining which jurisdiction a CE is assigned to in the first place. In this context, GloBE uses the term 'location', which is to be strictly distinguished from tax residency.[1296] Although GloBE's concept of 'location' heavily relies on the concept of tax residency, it also contains provisions for CEs that are considered taxable entities for the purposes of GloBE but cannot establish tax residency in accordance with international tax practice: Article 10.3. GloBE Model Rules and Article 4 GloBE-Directive provide detailed provisions with regard to the 'location' of CEs. Fiscally non-transparent entities are generally considered to be located where they are resident for tax purposes (e.g., place of effective management, place of creation or similar).[1297] If the tax residency cannot be determined, GloBE fictitiously assumes the location of the CE in the jurisdiction in which it was created.[1298] Significantly more complex rules apply to 'Flow-through Entities' (fiscally transparent entities), which are also considered located where they have been created, provided that such entities are a UPE or a Parent Entity, which must apply the IIR.[1299] In all other cases, 'Flow-through Entities' are deemed to be a 'Stateless Entity'[1300].[1301] As will become clear, this status is associated with significant disadvantages within the framework of GloBE. Regarding the location of PEs representing CEs, Article 10.3.3. GloBE Model Rules and Article 4(3) GloBE-Directive provide a number of differentiated rules determining a PE's location. In this respect, GloBE refers to the provisions of the applicable tax treaties and, in the case of non-treaty relations, on domestic tax laws. Thus, a PE's 'location' is considered to be where the PE may be taxed according to a tax treaty or is taxed according to domestic tax laws. Special rules apply when a jurisdiction either does not levy corporate tax at all or unilaterally waives taxation of PE income. With respect to the former, the PE is deemed to be located in the jurisdiction in which the PE would be taxed under Article 7 OECD MC.[1302] In the latter case, the PE would also qualify as a 'Stateless Entity'.[1303]

1296. Already *see* s. 4.2.4.4.1.
1297. Article 10.3.1.(a) *GloBE Model Rules*. Also *see* Art. 4(1) GloBE-Directive (2022/2523).
1298. Article 10.3.1.(b) *GloBE Model Rules*. Also *see* the second sentence of Art. 4(1) GloBE-Directive (2022/2523).
1299. Article 10.3.2.(a) *GloBE Model Rules*. Also *see* Art. 4(2) GloBE-Directive (2022/2523).
1300. The term '*Stateless Entity*' is defined in Art. 10.1. *GloBE Model Rules*. The GloBE-Directive does not contain a separate definition for such entities. Rather the term 'low-taxed constituent entity' includes 'stateless constituent entities', *see* Art. 3(19)(b) GloBE-Directive (2022/2523).
1301. Article 10.3.2.(b) *GloBE Model Rules*. Also *see* Art. 4(2) GloBE-Directive (2022/2523). In detail on those provisions, *see* s. 4.2.4.4.4.
1302. Paragraph (c) of the PE definition in Art. 10.1. and Art. 10.3.3.(d) *GloBE Model Rules*. Also *see* the third subparagraph of Art. 4(3) GloBE-Directive.
1303. Article 10.3.3.(d) *ibid.*, and the fourth subparagraph of Art. 4(3) GloBE-Directive (2022/2523).

For dual resident CEs, special rules apply, which are primarily based on residency under the applicable tax treaty.[1304] If there is no tax treaty according to which tax residency of the CE could be determined, Article 10.3.4 GloBE Model Rules and Article 4(4) and 4(5) GloBE-Directive provide for separate tie-breaker rules: first, the CE is deemed to be resident where it has paid the higher amount of 'Covered Taxes'.[1305] If the location still cannot be determined, the higher amount of the 'Substance-based Income Exclusion' (SBIE) is decisive,[1306] and if this also does not lead to a result, the CE is to be considered as a 'Stateless Entity'.[1307] Admittedly, the latter scenario is extremely unlikely and probably only conceivable in the case of letterbox companies neither being covered by a tax treaty nor being subject to any corporate tax at all.[1308] Further details on the 'location' of entities are discussed in section 4.2.4.4.[1309]

4.4.2.2 Step 2: Aggregation of GloBE Income and Losses and Adjusted Covered Taxes per Jurisdiction

Once the CEs within the 'MNE Group' have been separated and their individual 'location' has been determined, the actual jurisdictional blending is to be performed in Step 2: the 'GloBE Income or Loss' and the 'Adjusted Covered Taxes' allocated to the CEs in the course of the first step are to be aggregated for each jurisdiction individually. Beginning with Step 2, the remaining seven-step process must be conducted for all jurisdictions in which the respective 'MNE Group' owns at least one CE. However, there are also exceptions to jurisdictional blending: as will be seen, in certain situations, the calculation is detached from jurisdictional blending, and a separate jurisdiction is assumed for certain types of CEs.

In respect of Step 2, once again, reference should be made to the wording of Article 5.1.1. GloBE Model Rules (reflected in Article 26[1] GloBE-Directive), which states that '*the Effective Tax Rate of the MNE Group for a jurisdiction is equal to the sum of the Adjusted Covered Taxes of each Constituent Entity located in the jurisdiction divided by the Net GloBE income*'. While Article 5.1.1 GloBE Model Rules refers only to the 'sum of Adjusted Covered Taxes', the country-specific sum of 'GloBE Income' is referred to as 'Net GloBE Income' (within the GloBE-Directive 'Net qualifying income or loss'), which is a separate term within the framework of GloBE. The calculation of this 'Net GloBE Income' per jurisdiction is finally addressed in Article 5.1.2. GloBE

1304. Article 10.3.4.(a) *GloBE Model Rules*. Also *see* Art. 4(4) GloBE-Directive (2022/2523).
1305. Article 10.3.4.(b)(i) *GloBE Model Rules* and the first and second subparagraphs of Art. 4(5) GloBE-Directive (2022/2523).
1306. Article 10.3.4.(b)(ii) *GloBE Model Rules*. Also *see* the third subparagraph of Art. 4(5) GloBE-Directive (2022/2523).
1307. Article 10.3.4.(b)(iii) *GloBE Model Rules*. Also *see* the fourth subparagraph of Art. 4(5) GloBE-Directive (2022/2523).
1308. The same conclusion has already been drawn at s. 4.2.4.4.4.
1309. This section is based on V. Bendlinger & G. Kofler, *Computation of the Effective Tax Rate and the 'Top-up Tax'*, in *Pillar 2 Global Minimum Tax, supra* note 305, at 11–13.

Model Rules (reflected in Article 26[2] GloBE-Directive) and accordingly is defined as the *'positive amount, computed in accordance with the following formula'* (*see* Figure 2).

Figure 2 Formula According to Article 5.1.2. GloBE Model Rules (Also See Article 26[2] GloBE-Directive Proposal, However, Using Slightly Different Terminology)

Net GloBE Income (of a jurisdiction, see Art 5.1.2.[a] and [b]) = GloBE Income of all CEs (within the same jurisdiction) – GloBE Losses of all CEs (within the same jurisdiction)

The 'Net GloBE Income' can only be a positive amount. If the 'GloBE Losses in a jurisdiction predominate, no 'Top-up Tax' can be calculated for the respective jurisdiction.[1310] However, this does not necessarily exclude the possibility of incurring 'Top-up Tax' for this jurisdiction: if a recalculation of the ETR for past years becomes necessary, an 'Additional Current Top-up Tax' (within the GloBE-Directive 'Additional top-up tax') may be due according to Article 5.4. GloBE Model Rules and Article 29 GloBE-Directive. Such an 'Additional Current Top-up Tax' could also occur in case of a 'GloBE Loss' within a specific jurisdiction. This case is specifically addressed in Article 4.1.5 GloBE Model Rules and Article 21(5) GloBE-Directive (in detail on these provisions, see already section 4.3.4.7.) and would require moving forward with Step 6.

The calculations of the 'sum of Adjusted Covered Taxes' and the 'Net GloBE Income' pursuant to Article 5.1.1. GloBE Model Rules and Article 26(1) GloBE-Directive are independent of the charging provisions of the IIR and UTPR. Hence, it is irrelevant to which CE of a 'MNE Group' the 'Top-up Tax' is allocated: as the GloBE Commentary states, '*the ETR of a jurisdiction is not computed solely by reference to the Constituent Entities owned*'[1311] by a respective parent entity, but '[r]*ather the ETR is computed by reference to all the Constituent Entities of the MNE Group located in that jurisdiction*'.[1312] Even if the 'Top-up Tax' incurred in a particular jurisdiction is allocated to different CEs (e.g., 'Intermediate Parent Entities'[1313] or 'Partially Owned Parent Entities'[1314] – in the following IPEs and POPEs), e.g., by applying the IIR, this does not change the jurisdictional aggregation of the 'GloBE Income or Loss' and the 'Adjusted Covered Taxes' of an 'MNE Group' within the same jurisdiction. Rather, it will be seen that ultimately, for the final charging of the 'Top-up Tax' in Step 8, an allocation of the calculated 'Jurisdictional Top-up Tax' to the individual CEs must take place in the preceding Step 7.

1310. *See GloBE Commentary on Article 5 GloBE Model Rules (2022)*, *supra* note 474, para. 11.
1311. *See Ibid.*, para. 4.
1312. *Ibid.*
1313. Article 2.1.2. *GloBE Model Rules* and Art. 6 GloBE-Directive (2022/2523).
1314. Article 2.1.4. *GloBE Model Rules* and Art. 8 GloBE-Directive (2022/2523).

However, there are exceptions to jurisdictional blending. These exceptions have already been discussed in detail within section 4.3.2.2.3., which is why the following enumeration is intended to only briefly sum up those exceptions:

- **Investment Entities**[1315] **and Insurance Investment Entities:**[1316] According to Article 5.1.3. GloBE Model Rules (reflected in Article 26[3] GloBE-Directive) the '*Adjusted Covered Taxes and GloBE Income or Loss of Constituent Entities that are Investment Entities are excluded from the determination of the Effective Tax Rate in Art 5.1.1. and the determination of Net GloBE Income in Art 5.1.2.*'. 'Investment Entities' are therefore excluded from the jurisdictional perspective of the ETR calculation,[1317] and furthermore, the ETR is only calculated with respect to the allocable share of the controlling entities.[1318] For this purpose, the income and taxes of all 'Investment Entities' within the same jurisdiction are aggregated. Article 7.4. GloBE Model Rules and Article 41 GloBE-Directive provide for a separate set of rules on how the ETR for 'Investment Entities' is to be calculated. Once again, it should be emphasized in this respect that Article 7.4. GloBE Model Rules and Article 41 GloBE-Directive are not applicable regarding 'Investment Entities' that are tax transparent or subject to an election under Article 7.5. or Article 7.6 GloBE Model Rules (Articles 42 and 43 GloBE-Directive). In view of these options and due to the fact that most tax jurisdictions generally treat CIVs as transparent, the provisions of Article 7.4. GloBE Model Rules and Article 41 GloBE-Directive are likely to be applied only in very exceptional cases (in detail, see already section 4.3.2.2.3.).
- **Minority-Owned Constituent Entities:** According to Article 5.6.1 GloBE Model Rules (reflected in Article 31[2] GloBE-Directive), the '*computation of the Effective Tax Rate and the Top-up Tax for a jurisdiction [...] with respect to members of a Minority-Owned Subgroup shall apply as if they were a separate group. The Adjusted Covered Taxes and GloBE Income or Loss of members of a*

1315. The term 'Investment Entity' is defined in Art. 10 GloBE Model Rules and Art. 3(30) GloBE-Directive. 'Investment Entities' are 'Investment Funds' and 'Real Estate Investment Vehicles' and corresponding Sub-Entities, provided that they hold assets almost exclusively or derive their income from 'Excluded Dividends' or 'Excluded Equity Gains' in accordance with Art. 3.2.1.(b) and (c) GloBE Model Rules. The terms 'Investment Fund' and 'Real Estate Investment Vehicle' are themselves defined separately. For example, a seven-linked chain of requirements is provided for the term 'Investment Fund', *see GloBE Model Rules*, at 58–59. *See* the corresponding definitions provided for in Art. 3(30) to (32) GloBE-Directive (2022/2523).
1316. 'Insurance Investment Entity' is defined as an entity that would meet the definition 'Investment Fund' or 'Real Estate Investment Vehicle', but is established in relation to liabilities under an insurance or annuity contract and is subject to regulation of insurance companies in its location, *see GloBE Model Rules*, at 58. The GloBE-Directive contains a definition of 'insurance investment entity' in Art. 42(1) GloBE-Directive (2022/2523).
1317. Also *see GloBE Commentary on Article 7 GloBE Model Rules (2022)*, *supra* note 335, para. 80.
1318. Both 'Adjusted Covered Taxes' as well as 'GloBE Income' are allocated according to the MNEs Group's allocable share of the 'Investment Entity', *see* Art. 7.4.2. to 7.4.5. *GloBE Model Rules* and Art. 41(2) to 41(5) GloBE-Directive (2022/2523). Accordingly, also SBIE is to be reduced to the Allocable Share, *see* Art. 7.4.6. *GloBE Model Rules* and the last subparagraph of Art. 41(4) GloBE-Directive (2022/2523). On these issues, *see* s. 4.4.2.5.

Minority-Owned Subgroup are excluded from the determination of the remainder of the MNE Group'.[1319] The term 'Minority-Owned Subgroup' is defined in this context as 'Minority-Owned Parent Entity' (in the following MOPE) and its 'Minority-Owned Subsidiaries'. A MOPE thereby is a CE where the UPE has a direct or indirect Ownership Interest in that entity of 30% ('Minority-Owned Constituent Entity' in the following MOCE) or less and which holds, directly or indirectly, the controlling interests of other MOCEs. If more than one 'Parent Entity' meets the MOCE definition, only the highest-level entity constitutes a MOPE.[1320] The special provisions of Article 5.6. GloBE Model Rules (also *see* Article 31 GloBE-Directive) thus apply when certain CEs are consolidated by UPE even though the capital share of the UPE is 30% or less (MOPEs and/or MOCEs). The special feature of the ETR calculation with respect to MOPEs lies in the fact that all CEs of an 'MNE Group' controlled by the same MOPE form a subgroup of their own within the 'MNE Group', for which the ETR is to be determined on a jurisdictional basis separately from the remaining 'MNE Group'. In the case of a single MOCE different from an '*Investment Entity*'[1321] in a jurisdiction that is not part of a '*Minority-Owned Subgroup*' and does not hold controlling interests in other MOCEs, Article 5.6.2. GloBE Model Rules and Article 31(3) GloBE-Directive provide a special provision according to which the ETR shall be calculated on an entity basis.

- **Stateless Entities:** A further exception to jurisdictional blending is directly stated in the last sentence of Article 5.1.1 GloBE Model Rules as well as in Article 26(4) GloBE-Directive, according to which '*each Stateless Constituent Entity shall be treated as a single Constituent Entity located in a separate jurisdiction*'.[1322] Since a '*Stateless Entity*' cannot be assigned to a jurisdiction, the ETR and the Top-up Tax are calculated at entity level (explicitly, *see* Article 27[7] GloBE-Directive). For non-transparent vehicles, Article 10.3.1 GloBE Model Rules and Article 4(1) GloBE-Directive presume a specific location, which is either tax residency or the jurisdiction in which it was created. Such entities can, therefore, only be considered stateless if they are dual-located entities according to Article 10.3.4(b)(iii) GloBE Model Rules or the fourth subparagraph of Article 4(5) GloBE-Directive, where the GloBE tie-breaking rules fail to determine a specific place of location.[1323] Rather, 'Stateless

1319. Article 5.1.6. *GloBE Model Rules.*
1320. *See GloBE Commentary on Article 5 GloBE Model Rules (2022), supra* note 474, para. 100.
1321. Article 5.6.2. *GloBE Model Rules* and Art. 31(3) GloBE-Directive (2022/2523). are not applicable to minority-owned '*Investment Entities*'. Rather, Art. 7.4. *GloBE Model Rules* and Art. 41 GloBE-Directive (2022/2523) take priority over Art. 5.6.2. *GloBE Model Rules* and Art. 31(3) GloBE-Directive (2022/2523), *see GloBE Commentary on Article 5, supra* note 474, para. 107.
1322. Last sentence of Art. 5.1.1. *GloBE Model Rules*. *See* the similar provision provided for in Art. 26(4) GloBE-Directive (2022/2523).
1323. Also *see* the definition of 'Stateless Entity' in Art. 10.1. *GloBE Model Rules*. The GloBE-Directive, includes the term 'stateless constituent entities' within the definition for LTCEs in Art. 3(19) GloBE-Directive (2022/2523).

Entities' can only arise with respect to 'Flow-through Entities',[1324] PEs[1325] and 'dual-located Entities'[1326] (in detail, already *see* section 4.2.4.4.4.).

Although the Commentary only explicitly mentions those three exceptions to jurisdictional blending,[1327] one could argue that also 'Joint Ventures' (Article 6.4. GloBE Model Rules and Article 36 GloBE-Directive) are an exception to jurisdictional blending because the ETR with respect to 'Joint Ventures' and 'JV Subsidiaries' shall be determined *'as if they were Constituent Entities of a separate MNE Group and as if the Joint Venture was the Ultimate Parent Entity of that Group'*.[1328] However, in deviation of the cases of 'Investment Entities', MOCEs or 'Stateless Entities', 'Joint Ventures' form a separate 'MNE Group' and are not considered as a part of any 'MNE Group'. 'Investment Entities', MOCEs or 'Stateless Entities' are very well part of an 'MNE Group' but need to be separated from different CEs 'located' in the same jurisdiction within the same 'MNE Group' for the purpose of the purposes of ETR and 'Top-up Tax' computation. For this reason, the case of 'Joint Ventures' is not a case of an exception to the jurisdictional blending approach, but rather is a special regime within GloBE fictitiously considering 'Joint Ventures' as separate MNE Groups for the purposes of GloBE (in detail *see* sections 4.2.4.1.3. and 4.3.2.2.3.).

In summary, the following can be stated for the second step: the 'Adjusted Covered Taxes' and the GloBE Income and Losses ('Net GloBE Income') of all CEs located in the same jurisdiction are to be aggregated that do neither qualify as 'Investment Entities', MOCEs nor 'Stateless Entities'. 'Joint Ventures' and their 'JV Subsidiaries' need to be removed from the 'MNE Group' already in advance during Step 1 because they do not qualify as CEs but rather form a separate 'MNE Group'. As a result, both necessary determinants for jurisdictional ETR computation need to be available for proceeding with Step 2. For the CEs qualifying either as 'Investment Entities', MOCEs or 'Stateless Entities', special rules apply: a separate sub-calculation is to be made for all CEs which qualify as 'Investment Entities'. For these purposes, all 'Investment Entities' are aggregated in one jurisdiction, with 'Adjusted Covered Taxes' and 'GloBE Income' included only in respect of the profit share held in the 'Investment Entity'. For CEs in which 30% or less of the shares are held (MOPEs and MOCEs) but which are nevertheless consolidated within the financial statements of the UPE, a separate jurisdictional sub-calculation is necessary. However, in deviation from the 'Investment Entity' exception, there is no reduction neither of 'Adjusted Covered Taxes' nor 'GloBE Income or Losses' to the allocable shares held in such entities. Due to the 'Investment Entity' and MOCE exceptions, an 'MNE Group' may be forced to proceed with multiple jurisdictional blends for a single country. Furthermore, 'Stateless Entities' are to be treated as being located in separate jurisdictions. Consequently, as of Step 2, 'MNE

1324. Article 10.3.2.(b) *GloBE Model Rules* and Art. 4(2) GloBE-Directive (2022/2523).
1325. *See* para. (d) of the PE definition in Art. 10.1. and Art. 10.3.3.(d) *GloBE Model Rules* and Art. 3(13)(d) and the fourth subparagraph of Art. 4(3) GloBE-Directive (2022/2523).
1326. Article 10.3.4.(b)(iii) *GloBE Model Rules* and the fourth subparagraph of Art. 4(5) GloBE-Directive (2022/2523).
1327. *See GloBE Commentary on Article 5 GloBE Model Rules (2022), supra* note 474, paras 5–9.
1328. Article 6.4.1.(a) *GloBE Model Rules* and Art. 36(3) GloBE-Directive (2022/2523).

Groups' must perform the following procedure for each jurisdiction in which they own consolidated CEs at least once. For every jurisdiction in which an 'Investment Entity' or a MOCE is 'located' beside a regular CE, an additional sub-calculation is necessary. In addition, 'Stateless Entities' also require a separate sub-calculation.[1329]

4.4.2.3 Step 3: ETR Calculation and Identification of Low Tax Jurisdictions

Once the 'Adjusted Covered Taxes' and 'GloBE Income' totals are calculated for each jurisdiction and necessary sub-calculation ('Investment Entities',[1330] MOCEs[1331] and 'Stateless Entities'[1332]) in Step 2, the actual calculation of the ETR according to Article 5.1.1. GloBE Model Rules and Article 26(1) GloBE-Directive can be performed (*see* Figure 3).

Figure 3 Computation of the ETR According to Article 5.1.1. GloBE Model Rules (Also See Article 26(1) GloBE-Directive Using Slightly Different Terminology)

$$\text{Effective Tax Rate per jurisdiction} = \frac{\text{Sum of Adjusted Covered Taxes}}{\text{Net GloBE Income}}$$

The same formula can be found for the sub-calculation for *'Investment Entities'* in Article 7.4.2 GloBE Model Rules and Article 41(2) GloBE-Directive (ETR calculated only with respect to the allocable share, *see* section 4.4.2.2.). With respect to the separate computation of the ETR for 'Investment Entities', MOCEs and 'Stateless Entities', the GloBE-Directive is clearer than the GloBE Model Rules. Article 27(1) GloBE-Directive states that 'the MNE group or large-scale domestic group shall compute the top-up tax separately for each of its constituent entities that have qualifying income *included in the computation of the net qualifying income of that jurisdiction*' (emphasis added). This implies that the 'net qualifying income' does not necessarily include the income of all CEs of an 'MNE Group' that are 'located' within the same jurisdiction. Rather, 'Investment Entities', MOCEs and 'Stateless Entities' are not included in the 'net qualifying income' of a jurisdiction because their ETR and 'Top-up Tax' are to be calculated separately.

In any case, the formula requires that the respective 'Sum of the Adjusted Covered Taxes' ('adjusted covered taxes of the constituent entities in the jurisdiction' in the GloBE-Directive) is to be divided by the 'Net GloBE Income' ('net qualifying income' in the GloBE-Directive) calculated for each jurisdiction and additional sub-calculation. As explained above, 'Net GloBE Income' can only be an amount

1329. This section is based on V. Bendlinger & G. Kofler, *Computation of the Effective Tax Rate and the 'Top-up Tax'*, in *Pillar 2 Global Minimum Tax, supra* note 305, at 13–17.

1330. *See* the distinct rules for ETR computation of 'Investment Entities' in Art. 7.4. *GloBE Model Rules* and Art. 41 GloBE-Directive (2022/2523).

1331. The rules for MOCEs directly refer to 'Chapters 3 to 7', which is why Art. 5.1.1. is to be applied with regard to MOCEs as well, *see* Art. 5.6. *GloBE Model Rules*. Also *see* Art. 31(2) GloBE-Directive (2022/2523).

1332. Last sentence of Art. 5.1.1. *GloBE Model Rules*. and Art. 26(4) GloBE-Directive (2022/2523).

greater than zero ('Net GloBE Income [...] is the positive amount, if any';[1333] in Article 26[1] GloBE-Directive, this is clarified directly in the denominator of the ETR fraction by only referring to 'net qualifying income' excluding 'net qualifying losses'). The denominator of the fraction can, therefore, neither be zero nor negative. Consequently, the result of the division is a positive percentage. This, however, does not necessarily mean that the ETR can only be positive. Rather, the ETR can be negative as well if the 'Sum of Adjusted Covered Taxes' is negative (in other words, if the taxpayer receives benefits within a specific jurisdiction without paying 'Covered Taxes' in the respective 'Fiscal Year'). In this case, the 'Top-up Tax Percentage' could exceed 15%.[1334]

If the ETR is equal to or exceeds 15%, the 'Top-up Tax' calculation procedure ends. In such a case, there is no 'Top-up Tax' for the respective jurisdiction or the relevant sub-calculation, and the calculation procedure ends at this point. Only in the case of an 'Additional Current Top-up Tax', i.e., due to a necessary correction of past periods, a 'Top-up Tax' could be incurred. In this case, the procedure would move on to Step 6 (*see* section 4.4.2.6.). However, if the calculated ETR for the jurisdiction or the sub-calculation results in a percentage that is below 15%, a 'Low-Tax Jurisdiction'[1335] and thus 'Low-Taxed Constituent Entities'[1336] (in the following LTCEs) are at issue. The procedure for calculating the 'Top-up Tax' must then be continued. So, in the second step, the 'Low-tax Jurisdictions' are identified and sorted out for further application of GloBE.[1337]

4.4.2.4 Step 4: Computation of the 'Top-up Tax' Percentage

Step 4 is the actual comparison of the ETRs below the minimum tax rate with the minimum tax level. According to Article 5.2.1. GloBE Model Rules, the *'Top-up Tax Percentage' 'shall be the positive percentage point difference* [...] *computed in accordance with the following formula'* (*see* Figure 4).

Figure 4 Computation of the Top-up Tax Percentage According to Article 5.2.1. GloBE Model Rules (For 'Investment Entities' Article 7.4.5. GloBE Model Rules) and Article 27(2) GloBE-Directive (For 'Investment Entities' Article 41[4] GloBE-Directive)

Top-up Tax Percentage = Minimum Rate - Effective Tax Rate

1333. Article 5.1.2. *GloBE Model Rules.*
1334. The OECD has explicitly clarified that '[t]*he "Top-up Tax Percentage" for a jurisdiction can in some circumstances exceed the Minimum Rate*', *see* para. 15.1 *GloBE Commentary on Article 5 GloBE Model Rules (2022)*, *supra* note 474 added in the course of the *GloBE Administrative Guidance February 2023*, at 52–53.
1335. According to Art. 10.1. GloBE Model Rules a *'Low-Tax Jurisdiction'* is a *'jurisdiction where the MNE Group has Net GloBE Income and is subject to an Effective Tax Rate (as determined under Chapter 5) in that period that is lower than the Minimum Rate'*. *See* the corresponding definition provided for in Art. 3(35) GloBE-Directive (2022/2523).
1336. *See* the definition of *'Low-Taxed Constituent Entities'* in Art. 10.1. *GloBE Model Rules*. *See* the corresponding definition provided for in Art. 3(19) GloBE-Directive (2022/2523).
1337. This section is based on V. Bendlinger & Georg Kofler, *Computation of the Effective Tax Rate and the 'Top-up Tax'*, *in Pillar 2 Global Minimum Tax*, *supra* note 305, at 17.

The reference to the '*positive percentage point difference*' clarifies that the '*Top-up Tax Percentage*' is to be calculated only if the ETR falls below 15%. Otherwise, the respective jurisdiction would not qualify as a *'Low-Tax Jurisdiction'* (*see* section 4.4.2.3.).

In any case, the computation of the *'Top-up Tax'* requires that the ETR is deducted from the minimum tax rate. The *'Top-up Tax Percentage'* is, therefore, the difference between the politically desired tax burden of 15% and the actual tax burden achieved by an 'MNE Group' in a jurisdiction. If the amount of 'Adjusted Covered Taxes' is negative (e.g., if tax refunds exceed tax payments within a 'Fiscal Year'), the ETR might be negative and is to be added to the 'Minimum Rate' of 15%, so that '[t]*he 'Top-up Tax Percentage' for a jurisdiction can in some circumstances exceed the Minimum Rate*'.[1338] With respect to 'Investment Entities', MOCEs and 'Stateless Entities', the respective sub-calculations[1339] are based on the same principles.[1340]

4.4.2.5 Step 5: Excess Profits: The Substance-Based Income Exclusion

With the 'Top-up Tax Percentage' and the 'Net GloBE Income' already calculated in Step 2, it would actually already be possible, at least theoretically, to calculate the amount of 'Top-up Tax' for a specific jurisdiction (*see* Step 6 in section 4.4.2.6.). However, the 'Substance-based Income Exclusion' (in the following SBIE) provided in Article 5.3. GloBE Model Rules and Article 28 GloBE-Directive require an intermediate step: the SBIE in GloBE's system works like a tax-free amount, which is to be deducted from the GloBE base. Technically, the deduction of the SBIE is regulated in Article 5.3. GloBE Model Rules (also *see* Article 28 GloBE-Directive): '*The Net GloBE Income for the jurisdiction shall be reduced by the Substance-based Income Exclusion for the jurisdiction to determine the Excess Profit for purposes of computing the Top-up Tax under Article 5.2.*' In Article 5.2.2. GloBE Model Rules and Article 27(4) GloBE-Directive, this procedure is then put in a formula (*see* Figure 5).

Figure 5 Computation of the Excess Profit According to Article 5.2.2. GloBE Model Rules and Article 27(4) GloBE-Directive

Excess Profit (per jurisdiction) = Net GloBE Income – Substance-based Income Exclusion

This approach anticipates that only those profits in excess of the SBIE will be subject to the 'Top-up Tax' ('Excess Profit'). If the SBIE, which is also calculated on a

1338. *See* para. 15.1 *GloBE Commentary on Article 5, supra* note 474 added in the course of the *GloBE Administrative Guidance February 2023*, at 52–53.

1339. While for MOCEs and 'Stateless Constituent Entities' Art. 5.2.1 GloBE Model Rules applies (*see* Art. 5.6. and 5.1.1. GloBE Model Rules), for *'Investment Entities'* a specific, but nevertheless equivalent rule is provided for in Art. 7.4.5. *GloBE Model Rules*. The same legislative technique is used in Arts 26(4), 31(2) and 41(4) GloBE-Directive (2022/2523).

1340. This section is based on V. Bendlinger & G. Kofler, *supra* note 305, at 18.

jurisdictional basis,[1341] exceeds the 'Net GloBE Income' of a jurisdiction, no 'Top-up Tax' is due, even if the ETR falls below 15%. Thus, it is also stated in Article 5.2.2. GloBE Model Rules and Article 27(4) GloBE-Directive that the 'Excess Profit' can only be a 'positive amount'. The Commentary has now also clarified that the SBIE in excess of 'Net GloBE Income' cannot be carried forward into future periods.[1342]

In any case, technically, the SBIE works like a tax-free amount and consists of two components: both components, the payroll as well as the tangible asset carve-out, are calculated on the basis of a fixed percentage of the underlying SBIE base:

- The base for the payroll carve-out is computed from the '*Eligible Payroll Costs of Eligible Employees that perform activities for the MNE Group in such jurisdiction*'.[1343] 'Eligible Payroll Costs' is defined in Article 10.1. GloBE Model Rules as well as Article 28(1)(a) GloBE-Directive and covers all employee compensation expenditures, including, e.g., salaries, wages, personal benefits and social security contributions. 'Eligible Employees' are all full and part-time employees of a CE, including independent contractors.[1344]
- The tangible asset carve-out is computed from the carrying value[1345] of 'Eligible Tangible Assets' located in a jurisdiction which include property, plant and equipment, natural resources, lessee's rights for the use of tangible assets and licenses for the use of immovable property or exploitation of natural resources. The computation '*shall be based on the average of the carrying value [...] at the beginning and ending of the* [year] *as recorded for the purpose of preparing the Consolidated Financial Statements*'[1346] at the entity level. By basing the calculation on the carrying value, the annual SBIE is reduced by scheduled and unscheduled depreciation. The SBIE generated by an asset, therefore, decreases over the useful life of a tangible asset.[1347] The carrying values of property that are held for sale, lease or investment, especially including land or buildings, are specifically excluded from the tangible asset carve-out.[1348]

1341. *See* Art. 5.3.1. and 5.3.2. *GloBE Model Rules*. Also *see* Art. 28(3) and (4) GloBE-Directive (2022/2523).
1342. *See GloBE Commentary on Article 5, supra* note 474, para. 27.
1343. Article 5.3.3. *GloBE Model Rules*. Correspondingly, *see* Art. 28(3) GloBE-Directive (2022/2523).
1344. *See* 'Eligible Payroll Costs' of 'Eligible Employees', Art. 10.1. *GloBE Model Rules* and Art. 28(1)(a) GloBE-Directive (2022/2523). Especially the GloBE Administrative Guidance released in July 2023 brought some significant clarifications on both terms. Since then, the Commentary includes some paragraphs on employees that are working from different states, see *GloBE Administrative Guidance July 2023*, at 44-45.
1345. In the Blueprint, it was once proposed to calculate the tangible asset carve-out from the amount of depreciation, *see Tax Challenges Arising from Digitalisation – Report on Pillar Two Blueprint*, para. 342 et seq.
1346. Article 5.3.5. *GloBE Model Rules*. Correspondingly, *see* Art. 28(5) GloBE-Directive (2022/2523).
1347. Also taking note of this fact, *see* E. Eberhartinger & G. Winkler, *Pillar Two and the Accounting Standards*, 51 Intertax, *supra* note 281, at 151.
1348. Article 5.3.4. *GloBE Model Rules* and Art. 28(4)(b) GloBE-Directive (2022/2523).

Both components specifically exclude payroll costs and carrying values of tangible assets respectively connected to 'International Shipping Income', due to the fact that such income is excluded from the 'GloBE Income'.[1349] Furthermore, special rules apply for PEs and 'Flow-Through Entities': Article 5.3.6. and 5.3.7. GloBE Model Rules (correspondingly Article 28[6] and [7] GloBE-Directive) provide specific location rules to determine to which CEs of an 'MNE Group' the 'Eligible Payroll Costs' and 'Eligible Tangible Assets' are attributed.

The fixed percentage for both components amounts to 5% of the payroll costs and 5% of the carrying values of the tangible assets. However, Article 9.2. GloBE Model Rules and Article 48 GloBE-Directive provide a specific ten-year transitional arrangement for the calculation of the SBIE: at the start of GloBE's applicability in 2023, the payroll carve-out is expected to be 10%, and the tangible asset carve-out 8%. In each of the following five years, i.e., until 2028, the percentages are to decrease by a constant 0.2 percentage points. In the following five years, the percentage is to be reduced constantly to 5% in each case. From 2033, both the payroll carve-out and the tangible asset carve-out will be exactly 5%.[1350]

According to Article 5.3.2. GloBE Model Rules (reflected in Article 28[2] and [9] GloBE-Directive), the SBIE '*amount for a jurisdiction is the sum of the payroll carve-out and the tangible asset carve-out for each Constituent Entity, except for Constituent Entities that are Investment Entities, in that jurisdiction*'.[1351] As in the actual ETR calculation, the SBIE is first calculated on an entity basis. The jurisdictional aggregation of the SBIE amounts is only performed for the purpose of calculating the 'Excess Profits'. The addition in Article 5.3.2. GloBE Model Rules and Article 28(9) GloBE-Directive it is held that 'Investment Entities' are not included in the sum of the payroll carve-out, and the tangible asset carve-out of a jurisdiction is connected to the specific regime for those entities: as already examined in respect with the second step (*see* section 4.4.2.2.), 'Investment Entities' are to be treated as a separate jurisdiction and thus require a sub-calculation also with respect to the calculation of the 'Excess Profit'. Consequently, the SBIE for '*Investment Entities*', according to Article 7.4.5. GloBE Model Rules and Article 41(4) GloBE-Directive must also be calculated separately and only on the basis of the allocable shares of the 'MNE Group' in the 'Investment Entity'. If there is more than one 'Investment Entity' in the same jurisdiction, their SBIE amounts are to be combined.[1352]

The 'Excess Profit' for 'Minority-Owned Subgroups', individual MOCEs and 'Stateless Entities' is to be computed in a similar way: they are each to be treated as a separate jurisdiction, and consequently, in the case of a 'Minority-Owned Subgroup',

1349. *See* Article 3.3. *GloBE Model Rules* and Art. 17 GloBE-Directive (2022/2523). In detail on the shipping income exclusion, *see* s. 4.3.3.4.
1350. *See* the tables provided for in Art. 9.2. *GloBE Model Rules* and Art. 48 GloBE-Directive (2022/2523).
1351. Article 5.3.2. *GloBE Model Rules*.
1352. *See* the last sentence of Art. 7.4.5 *Ibid.* and the third sentence of Art. 41(4) GloBE-Directive (2022/2523).

the SBIE is to be calculated as if it were a separate 'MNE Group'[1353] and for individual MOCEs[1354] and 'Stateless Entities'[1355] the SBIE is to be calculated for the single entity. The SBIE amounts of these structures are, therefore, to be excluded from the calculation of the 'Excess Profit' for the remaining CEs in a given jurisdiction, as set forth in Article 5.3.2 GloBE Model Rules and Article 28(9) GloBE-Directive, which, however, only specifically addresses 'Investment Entities'.

The SBIE is arguably one of the most controversial components of Pillar Two: the Commentary argues that the policy rationale behind the SBIE '*is to exclude a fixed return for substantive activities within a jurisdiction from the application of the GloBE Rules.* [...] *Conceptually, excluding a fixed return from substantive activities focuses GloBE on 'excess income', such as intangible-related income, which is most susceptible to BEPS risks*'.[1356] A similar justification is put forward in Recital 14 of the GloBE-Directive: '*To ensure a proportionate approach, this Directive should take into consideration certain specific situations in which BEPS risks are reduced. Therefore, this Directive should include a substance-based income exclusion based on the costs associated with employees and the value of tangible assets in a given jurisdiction. That exclusion would resolve, to a certain extent, situations where an MNE group or a large-scale domestic group carries out economic activities which require material presence in a low-taxed jurisdiction, as in such case BEPS practices would be unlikely to flourish.*'[1357] The reference to the principle of proportionality is obviously an implicit note of the *Cadbury-Schweppes* doctrine of the ECJ,[1358] which assumes that CFC legislation is not in line with the fundamental freedoms if the CFC regime does not provide for a 'substance escape' from the unfavourable consequence of taxing a CFCs profit in the residence state of a parent entity. This note in the recitals is also relevant from the perspective of EU competence because, without the existence of the SBIE, one could argue that the GloBE-Directive fails to positively affect the establishment or functioning of the internal market (in detail on the EU's competence and the adoption of the GloBE-Directive, *see* section 6.1.2.).

The tax policy behind the SBIE has already been discussed at length: in literature, it is argued that the SBIE undermines the initial purpose of GloBE to set a minimum level of corporate tax: by covering only 'Excess Profits', only part of the global profit of MNE Groups is subject to the minimum tax. The SBIE allows tax jurisdictions to keep or even reduce nominal CIT rates significantly below the minimum tax rate, even down to 0%, as long as the respective income does not exceed the SBIE for that jurisdiction. GloBE, therefore, does not create a real incentive for 'Low-Tax Jurisdictions' to introduce corporate taxes or to increase their corporate income tax level even for

1353. This results from Art. 5.6.1. *GloBE Model Rules*. Also *see* Art. 31(2) GloBE-Directive (2022/2523).
1354. *See* Art. 5.6.2. *GloBE Model Rules*. Also *see* Art. 31(3) GloBE-Directive (2022/2523).
1355. *See* last sentence of Art. 5.1.1. *GloBE Model Rules*. *See* explicitly Art. 28(8) GloBE-Directive (2022/2523).
1356. *See GloBE Commentary on Article 5 GloBE Model Rules (2022)*, *supra* note 474, para. 25.
1357. *See* recital 14 GloBE-Directive (2022/2523).
1358. Case C-196/04, *Cadbury Schweppes plc and Cadbury Schweppes Overseas Ltd v. Commissioners of Inland Revenue*.

in-scope 'MNE Groups'. Rather, Devereux, Vella & Wardell-Burrus have proven that the SBIE, in combination with the 'Qualified Domestic Top-up Tax' (QDMTT), even creates incentives for countries to keep or even decrease their domestic CIT tax level far below 15%.[1359] This raises the legitimate question of what purpose remains for GloBE in its current form (on the question of purpose, *see* section 4.5.8.): apparently, GloBE intends to ensure that 'Excess Profits' are subject to a minimum tax rate of 15%. From a tax policy perspective, this leads to an odd result: the higher the return on payroll and tangible assets, the more likely it is to be captured by the minimum tax. Thus, one could argue that the SBIE, as currently designed, rewards inefficient investments over more efficient ones.[1360]

4.4.2.6 Step 6: Calculating the Jurisdictional 'Top-up Tax'

4.4.2.6.1 Overview

Once the 'Top-up Tax' and the 'Excess Profits' for a jurisdiction and the corresponding sub-calculations have been computed, the so-called Jurisdictional Top-up Tax can be calculated in Step 6. In this respect, Article 5.2.3. GloBE Model Rules and Article 27(3) GloBE-Directive provide for the following formula (*see* Figure 6).

Figure 6 Computation of the Jurisdictional Top-up Tax According to Article 5.2.3. GloBE Model Rules and Article 27(3) GloBE-Directive

$$\text{Jurisdictional Top-up Tax} = (\text{Top-up Tax Percentage} \times \text{Excess Profit}) + \text{Additional Current Top-up Tax} - \text{Qualified Domestic Top-up Tax}$$

Thus, in the first part of the formula, the 'Top-up Tax Percentage' and the 'Excess Profits' of a jurisdiction or sub-calculation are multiplied. Consequently, the 'Jurisdictional Top-up Tax' is the amount of tax that still needs to be paid by a particular 'MNE Group' in the jurisdiction at issue to reach the minimum tax level of 15% on its 'Excess Profits'.

Again, in the case of the 'Jurisdictional Top-up Tax', Article 5.2.3. GloBE Model Rules and Article 27(3) GloBE-Directive also clarify that the amount can only be positive. Rather, if a loss is incurred in a jurisdiction, there is usually no 'Top-up Tax': as already mentioned, the computation process would end at Step 2 (already *see* section 4.4.2.2.) in this case, due to the fact that the 'Net GloBE Income' is defined as a positive amount.[1361] However, in the second part of the formula provided in Article

1359. Extensively on the effects of the SBIE, *see* M. Devereux et al., *Pillar 2: Rule Order, Incentives, and Tax Competition*, SSRN 9 (14 Jan. 2022), https://papers.ssrn.com/sol3/papers.cfm?abstract_id=4009002.

1360. This section is based on V. Bendlinger & Georg Kofler, *Computation of the Effective Tax Rate and the 'Top-up Tax', in Pillar 2 Global Minimum Tax, supra* note 305, at 18–20.

1361. Article 5.1.2. *GloBE Model Rules*. Also *see* Art. 26(1) GloBE-Directive (2022/2523) stating that the computation of the ETR (step 2) requires 'net qualifying income' (synonym of GloBE-Directive for 'Net GloBE Income').

5.2.3. GloBE Model Rules and Article 27(3) GloBE-Directive the 'Additional Current Top-up Tax' (within the GloBE-Directive 'Additional Top-up Tax', both in the following ACTT) is to be added to the result of the multiplication of 'Top-up Tax Percentage' and the 'Excess Profits'. Therefore, it can be seen from the formula alone that the ACTT can lead to a positive 'Jurisdictional Top-up Tax' if the 'Top-up Tax Percentage' or the 'Excess Profits' result in a value of zero. Thus, a 'Jurisdictional Top-up Tax' may occur even if the ETR is 15% or even exceeds 15% or no 'Excess Profits' have been realized due to a loss or if the SBIE exceeds profits in a given jurisdiction.[1362]

4.4.2.6.2 Additional (Current) Top-up Tax

ACTT occurs from the necessary retroactive recalculation of the ETR and the 'Top-up Tax' for previous 'Fiscal Years': the subsequent roll-up of past periods may result in a 'Top-up Tax' that can only be levied in subsequent 'Fiscal Years'. Instead of requiring an amendment of past years, the OECD decided to collect such ACTT in the year in which the retroactive adjustment is made: '*To avoid complexity and administrative burden of requiring an amended GloBE Information Return and additional separate payment of Top-up Tax, the Additional Top-up Tax is instead charged to the Fiscal Year in which the recalculation is performed.*'[1363] The common *modus operandi* for the calculation of ACTT is defined in Article 5.4. GloBE Model Rules and Article 29 GloBE-Directive, respectively. The provisions essentially refer to the calculation of the 'Top-up Tax' according to Articles 5.1. to 5.3. GloBE Model Rules and Articles 26 to 28 GloBE-Directive, respectively. Furthermore, Article 5.4.2. GloBE Model Rules and Article 29(2) GloBE-Directive ensure that the ACTT can also be levied if there is no positive '*GloBE Income*' at all in the relevant jurisdiction: '*If the jurisdiction does not have Net GloBE Income for the current Fiscal Year, the GloBE Income of each Constituent Entity [...] shall be equal to the result of the Top-up Tax allocated to such Entity under Articles 5.2.4 and 5.2.5 divided by the Minimum Rate*'.[1364] Thus, in the case of a 'Net GloBE Loss', a positive 'Net GloBE Income' of all CEs in the jurisdiction is assumed, which corresponds exactly to the income that would be necessary at the level of the CEs to levy the 'Top-up Tax' by means of the IIR or UTPR. This ensures that the ACTT can be levied even if no 'Top-up Tax' could actually be calculated at all due to lack of positive 'GloBE Income'.[1365]

In this respect, the GloBE Model Rules name five different provisions, where a re-calculation of the ETR of previous 'Fiscal Years' gives rise to ACTT. Those five provisions are referred to as so-called ETR Adjustment Articles[1366].[1367] Although all of

---

1362. This section is based on V. Bendlinger & Georg Kofler, *supra* note 305, at 21–22.
1363. *See GloBE Commentary on Article 5 GloBE Model Rules (2022), supra* note 474, para. 66.
1364. Article 5.4.2. *GloBE Model Rules*. Using a slightly different wording, *see* Art. 29(2) GloBE-Directive (2022/2523).
1365. *See GloBE Commentary on Article 5, supra* note 474, para. 68. Corresponding rules are provided for in Arts 21(5) and 29(3) GloBE-Directive (2022/2523).
1366. The definition 'ETR Adjustment Article' in Art. 10.1. *GloBE Model Rules*. covers Arts 3.2.6., 4.4.4., 4.6.1., 4.6.4. and 7.3. GloBE Model Rules.
1367. *See GloBE Commentary on Article 5, supra* note 474, para. 65.

the five provisions are also reflected in the GloBE-Directive as well (the latter even implemented an additional situation where ACTT arises due to subsequent recalculation, *see* below),[1368] the term 'ETR Adjustment Article' is not used. Nevertheless, this does not result in any difference in terms of content.

In any case, all of the respective five ETR adjustment situations relate to subsequent amendments either of the 'GloBE Income or Loss' or the 'Adjusted Covered Taxes' and have already been addressed in the course of sections 4.3.3. and 4.3.4. These situations have in common that either an election provided by GloBE or a subsequent event requires a recalculation of the ETR of previous years to mitigate distortive impacts on the ETR computation. In this respect, it is important to mention that errors in the financial statements may not be corrected by the ACTT. In such cases, the Commentary refers to the *'relevant administrative procedures for correcting such errors'*.[1369] Rather, ACTT, pursuant to Articles 5.4.1. and 5.4.2. GloBE Model Rules and Article 29(1) and (2) GloBE-Directive, only occurs in the following events:

- **Election to retroactively spread 'Aggregate Asset Gains'[1370] over up to five years**: According to Article 3.2.6. GloBE Model Rules and Article 16(7) GloBE-Directive an 'MNE Group' can make an election to retroactively spread gains from immovable property (so-called Local Tangible Asset[1371]) over up to five years, *'to mitigate the effect of recoginising the entire gain in a single year'*.[1372] For example, if immovable property located in a jurisdiction is sold at a profit, the respective profit can be allocated retrospectively to the current and the past four years. This requires a subsequent recalculation of the ETR and the 'Top-up Tax'. However, if profits are attributed to a certain period retrospectively, the ETR of this jurisdiction is retrospectively reduced, and an ACTT may arise, which is then levied in the 'Fiscal Year' of the adjustment and added to the regularly calculated 'Top-up Tax' of this 'Fiscal Year' (in detail, *see* section 4.3.3.3.5.).
- **Recapture from former consideration of temporary differences that did not materialize within five years:** Article 4.4. GloBE Model Rules and Article 22 GloBE-Directive enable MNE Groups to address temporary differences by considering deferred tax expenses. In this way, the calculation of the ACTT considers that certain timing differences arise due to differences in accounting and tax law, but these balance out over time and consequently do not justify the imposition of a *'Top-up Tax'*. However, Article 4.4.4 GloBE Model Rules and Article 22(7) GloBE-Directive only accept such deferred tax liabilities if they are actually paid within five years. If it turns out afterwards that the

1368. Also *see* Art. 29(1), referring to Arts 11(3), 16(7), 22(6), 25(1), 25(4) and 40(5) GloBE-Directive (2022/2523).
1369. *See GloBE Commentary on Article 5, supra* note 474, para. 67.
1370. *See* the definition of 'Aggregate Asset Gains' provided for in Art. 10.1. *GloBE Model Rules*. The GloBE-Directive simply refers to *'qualifying income or loss* [...] *arising from the disposal of local tangible assets'*, *see* Art. 16(7) GloBE-Directive (2022/2523).
1371. *See* the definition of 'Local Tangible Asset' provided for in Art. 10.1. *GloBE Model Rules. The* GloBE-Directive (2022/2523) does not separately define the term 'Local Tangible Asset'.
1372. *See GloBE Commentary on Article 3 GloBE Model Rules (2022), supra* note 507, para. 119.

amount of tax has not been paid within those five years, '[t]*he Amount of the Recaptured Deferred Tax Liability [...] shall be treated as a reduction to Covered Taxes in the fifth preceding Fiscal Year and the Effective Tax Rate and Top-up Tax of such Fiscal Year shall be recalculated under the rules of Art 5.4.1*'.[1373] Interestingly, Article 29(1) GloBE-Directive lacks a direct reference to the deferred tax recapture rule in Article 22(7) GloBE-Directive, while only the latter, and vice versa, refers to Article 29(1) GloBE-Directive. In contrast, Article 4.4.4. GloBE Model Rules as the equivalent of Article 22(7) GloBE-Directive is explicitly considered as an 'ETR Adjustment Article'. Rather, Article 29(1) GloBE-Directive instead refers to Article 22(6) GloBE-Directive (permission to recast deferred tax assets attributable to a 'GloBE Loss' recorded below 15% at the 'Minimum Rate', in detail, *see* section 4.3.4.5.2.), whereas Article 5.4.1. GloBE Model Rules does not refer to Article 4.4.3. GloBE Model Rules in detail concerning the obligation to recapture deferred tax liabilities that have not been reversed or paid within five years, *see* section 4.3.4.5.5.
- **Recapture due to Post-filing Adjustments and Tax Rate Changes:** According to Article 4.6.1. GloBE Model Rules and Article 25(1) GloBE-Directive the amount of 'Covered Taxes' for a fiscal year may be subject to subsequent amendments. For example, adjustments may be necessary in the course of tax audits or reviews of tax returns. While increases in the taxes paid for prior fiscal years can be included as ACTT within the year the adjustments are made,[1374] decreases in covered taxes are to be considered by adding ACTT to the amount of 'Jurisdictional Top-up Tax' computed for the respective jurisdiction in the fiscal year at issue.[1375] In detail, *see* section 4.3.4.9.
- **Recapture of non-paid current tax expense:** Pursuant to Article 4.6.4. GloBE Model Rule and Article 25(4) GloBE-Directive recalculation is required in the case of current tax expenses exceeding a *de minimis* threshold of EUR 1 million. that had increased the 'Covered Taxes' of a CE in a previous year, but which, for whatever reason, has not actually been paid within the following three years. In detail, *see* section 4.3.4.9.
- **Recapture for Deemed Distribution Tax for Eligible Distribution Tax Systems**: Article 7.3. GloBE Model Rules and Article 40 GloBE-Directive provide an election with regard to CEs that are subject to an 'Eligible Distribution Tax System'. This concerns, for example, countries that levy CIT only if profits are distributed to shareholders. In these cases, an 'MNE Group' may add an amount of 'Deemed Distribution Tax' to the amount of 'Adjusted

1373. Article 4.4.4. *GloBE Model Rules. See* the corresponding provision in Art. 22(7) GloBE-Directive (2022/2523).
1374. *See GloBE Commentary on Article 4 GloBE Model Rules (2022), supra* note 884, para. 120.
1375. *See Ibid.*, para. 121. At the election of the 'MNE Group', immaterial decreases of 'Adjusted Covered Taxes' not exceeding 1 million determined for the jurisdiction for a fiscal year may also be considered as an '*adjustment to Covered Taxes for the Fiscal Year in which the adjustment is made*', *see* Art. 4.6.1. *GloBE Model Rules*. Also *see* the third subparagraph of Art. 26(1) GloBE-Directive (2022/2523).

Covered Taxes' for the respective fiscal year. For this purpose, a 'Deemed Distribution Tax Recapture Account' is to be established, comparing the deemed tax on the deemed distributions and the actual taxes paid. Finally, Article 7.3.5. GloBE Model Rules (reflected in Article 40[5] GloBE-Directive) states that '[i]*f there is an outstanding balance* [...] *on the last day of the fourth Fiscal Year after the Fiscal Year for which such account was established, the Effective Tax Rate and Top-up Tax* [...] *must be recalculated*'.[1376] Consequently, any deemed tax that has not been paid within five years is to be added to the 'Jurisdictional Top-up Tax' of the fourth preceding year by way of ACTT pursuant to Article 5.4.1. GloBE Model Rules and Article 29(1) GloBE-Directive. See section 4.3.4.2. as well.

As already emphasized, there is no difference between the GloBE Model Rules and the GloBE-Directive with respect to these five retrospective adjustments leading to ACTT. However, in addition to those five situations, the GloBE-Directive adds two other situations that give rise to ACTT, which are not directly reflected within the GloBE Model Rules:

- The first additional case of ACTT in the GloBE-Directive materializes in the fact that Article 29(1) GloBE-Directive additionally refers to Article 11(3) GloBE-Directive that has no equivalent within the GloBE Model Rules: This is due to the fact that Article 11 GloBE-Directive provides for the Member States' election to implement a QDMTT ('Qualified Domestic Minimum Top-up Tax'). Indeed, the GloBE Model Rules provide a definition of QDMTT which defines when a domestic tax system qualifies as a QDMTT for purposes of GloBE; however, the GloBE Model Rules do not provide for specific rules on how such a QDMTT can be implemented. As will be seen in the following (in detail, *see* section 4.4.2.6.3.), the QDMTT reduces the 'Jurisdictional Top-up Tax' and enables 'Low-Tax Jurisdictions' to soak up any 'Top-up Tax' that would otherwise be collected by any other states where CEs of the same 'MNE Group' are 'located'. In any case, Article 11(3) GloBE-Directive states that '[w]*here the amount of qualified domestic top-up tax for a fiscal year has not been paid within the four fiscal years following the fiscal year in which it was due, the amount of qualified domestic top-up tax that was not paid shall be added to the jurisdictional top-up tax computed in accordance with Article 27(3) and shall not be collected by the Member State which made the election pursuant to paragraph 1 of this Article*'.[1377] This provision ensures that neither Member States nor third states can argue to levy a QDMTT without collecting the tax within a five-year period. This prevents tax authorities from evading the minimum tax by introducing a preferential QDMTT that never materializes, e.g., because a country deliberately introduces a statute of limitations in its domestic procedural law, according to which a certain tax amount cannot be

1376. Article 7.3.5. *GloBE Model Rules*.
1377. Article 11(3) GloBE-Directive (2022/2523).

claimed by the tax authorities if it has not been paid within a certain period of time. Article 11(3) GloBE-Directive indeed does allow to shift the tax burden of QDMTT to the fourth subsequent year; however, if the QDMTT is not collected in the fourth subsequent year, the amount of QDMTT that had initially reduced the 'Jurisdictional Top-up Tax' of the fourth preceding year is to be added back to the 'Jurisdictional Top-up Tax' of the fourth subsequent year as an ACTT pursuant to the rules provided for in Article 29(1) and (2) GloBE-Directive.

- Furthermore, Article 29(1) GloBE-Directive contains a reference to Article 22(6) GloBE-Directive, which is the equivalent to Article 4.4.3. GloBE Model Rules. Both provisions have already been discussed in section 4.3.4.5.2. and contain a specific rule that allow the recast of a deferred tax asset in situations where a deferred tax asset has been recorded at a rate lower than the minimum rate to avoid that 'Top-up Tax' occurs, although, from a multi-period perspective, there had not been any 'GloBE Income'. Usually, such a recast reduces the 'Total Deferred Tax Adjustment Amount' in the 'Fiscal Year' in which the respective 'GloBE Loss' occurred. But why then could a recast under Article 4.4.3. GloBE Model Rules and Article 22(6) GloBE-Directive give rise to ACTT due to a subsequent recalculation? In fact, ACTT can only arise if the recast, pursuant to Article 4.4.3. GloBE Model Rules and Article 22(6) GloBE-Directive, is made in a 'Fiscal Year' after the underlying 'GloBE Loss' materialized. Interestingly, the Commentary assumes that, in this case, ACTT would arise under Article 4.1.5. GloBE Model Rules (equivalent to Article 21[5] GloBE-Directive),[1378] which might be the reason why Article 5.4.1. GloBE Model Rules does not refer to Article 4.4.3. GloBE Model Rules, whereas Article 22(6) GloBE-Directive, which is the equivalent of the latter provision, is directly listed in Article 29(1) GloBE-Directive.

In addition to these situations where a re-calculation of the ETR is to be performed subsequently, according to Article 5.4.3. GloBE Model Rules and Article 29(3) GloBE Model Rules ACTT can also arise in the special case of Article 4.1.5. GloBE Model Rules and Article 21(5) GloBE-Directive. Both provisions have been extensively addressed in section 4.3.4.7.: they give rise to ACTT in situations where, due to a permanent difference, the domestic loss exceeds the 'GloBE Loss' in a specific jurisdiction leading to a deferred tax asset (in other words, a future tax benefit). From a multi-period perspective, this would result in an advantage, which is why GloBE requires the collection of the deferred tax asset in question through a fictional ACTT in this particular situation. ACTT arising pursuant to Article 5.4.3. GloBE Model Rules and Article 29(3) GloBE Model Rules, thus, is an exception to the phenomenon of ACTT: in deviation from that ACTT does not arise from a re-calculation of the ETR for previous years but originates in the year where the deferred tax asset is recorded.

So, what can be concluded on the role of the ACTT within GloBE? The ACTT serves as a simplification for the application of the GloBE Rules if adjustments are necessary that relate to specific multi-period issues. If Article 5.4. GloBE Model Rules

1378. *See GloBE Commentary on Article 4, supra* note 884, para. 88.

and Article 29 GloBE-Directive did not exist, any subsequent amendments or elections would require a complete recalculation of previous 'Fiscal Years', and any GloBE-related tax returns would need to be corrected subsequently. By simply allowing the addition of ACTT to the 'Jurisdictional Top-up Tax' of the 'Fiscal Year' at issue instead of requiring resubmission of returns and tedious recalculations of previous 'Fiscal Years', GloBE reduces administrative burdens for 'MNE Groups' that would otherwise arise. However, the application of Article 5.4. GloBE Model Rules and Article 29 GloBE-Directive is all but easy: both provisions are highly complex and can only be read in connection to the underlying 'ETR Adjustment Articles'. From a policy perspective, it has been criticized that ACTT might give rise to 'Top-up Tax' in 'Fiscal Years' in which a 'MNE Group' suffers losses in a specific jurisdiction. Should the minimum tax really kick in when there are no profits to tax? A detailed analysis of the technical peculiarities of the situations that give rise to ACTT, however, has revealed that the adjustments are necessary to avoid loopholes in the system. Nevertheless, as some authors in the literature have already emphasized,[1379] it is indeed odd that an 'MNE Group' might be subject to a minimum tax in loss situations. In this respect, the provisions of Article 5.4.3. GloBE Model Rules and Article 29(3) GloBE-Directive particularly seem harsh because their application can give rise to 'Top-up Tax' even in jurisdictions where the nominal tax rate is well above 15%, but that provide preferential loss regimes. Finally, and even worse: due to the fact that the ACTT increases the 'Jurisdictional Top-up Tax' and Article 5.4.3. GloBE Model Rules and Article 29(3) GloBE-Directive apply in loss situations, 'Top-up Tax' is levied irrespective of any substance of the 'MNE Group' in that specific jurisdiction because the SBIE cannot prevent the collection of 'Top-up Tax' in these cases either.[1380] In the author's opinion, it would be desirable to enable a refund of the 'Top-up Tax' collected due to Article 5.4.3. GloBE Model Rules and Article 29(3) GloBE-Directive, if the 'MNE Group' subsequently can bring evidence that the use of losses did not lead to a shortfall of the 15% 'Minimum Rate' from a multi-period perspective (in detail on the case of ACTT arising pursuant to Article 5.4.3. GloBE Model Rules and Article 29(3) GloBE-Directive, *see* section 4.3.4.7.). Happily, the OECD has, in the meanwhile, addressed the issue with respect to Article 4.1.5. GloBE Model Rules within its GloBE Administrative Guidance February 2023. Whether the clarifications are helpful for EU Member States, as has been discussed in section 4.3.4.7., however, is questionable.

4.4.2.6.3 The 'Qualified Domestic Minimum Top-up Tax' (QDMTT): Eliminating 'Jurisdictional Top-up Tax'

Finally, the last element of the jurisdictional top-up tax calculation is to be discussed. The calculated 'Jurisdictional Top-up Tax' is to be reduced by a QDMTT levied by the source state. Thus, if a QDMTT is levied, the source state can fully levy the 'Top-up Tax' attributed to its jurisdiction itself. Consequently, if the supposed 'Low-tax

1379. *See* F. Brugger et al., *Globale Mindestbesteuerung: Ermittlung des GloBE-Steueraufwands*, 97 SWK, *supra* note 1099, at 666–667.
1380. *See Ibid.*

Jurisdiction' applies a QDMTT, the allocation of the 'Top-up Tax' (Step 7) and the charging of the 'Top-up Tax' (Step 8) is redundant. But what is the QDMTT, and what is its role within the system of GloBE? At this point, the immense importance and the controversial existence of the QDMTT within GloBE's framework require taking a step back.

From the very beginning, a discussion emerged of how 'Low-Tax Jurisdictions' might react to the implementation of GloBE: by implementing a minimum tax, tax jurisdictions intend to level up the tax burden to an agreed minimum level and tax away the benefit granted by any source jurisdiction, if it leads to an ETR below the minimum tax rate. It was obvious that 'Low-Tax Jurisdictions' and tax havens would not simply accept other jurisdictions to tax away profits that would otherwise fall within their taxing jurisdiction. But how could states react to prevent other states from 'taxing away' those profits? The answer is simple: a jurisdiction could either raise its ETR up to 15% (which is a domestic minimum tax to be distinguished from QD-MTT)[1381] or simply implement a tax that only applies to taxpayers ('MNE Groups' with annual revenues equal or exceeding EUR 750 million.) that are within the scope of the minimum tax and is levied exactly in the amount of the minimum tax. Finally, if profits from local sources are taxed elsewhere, regardless of whether or how much they are taxed domestically, why not 'soak up' the foreign minimum tax domestically? This simple principle is concealed behind the rather technical term of the QDMTT.

At the very beginning of GloBE, the minimum tax was discussed under the keywords 'Income Inclusion Rule' (in the following IIR) and 'Undertaxed Payments Rule' (in the meantime 'UTPR' – in the following UTPR), which are, in very simplified terms, two interlocked tax mechanisms that enable jurisdictions to levy the 'Top-up Tax' arising within a different jurisdiction that qualifies as a 'Low-Tax Jurisdiction' under GloBE.[1382] Consequently, both mechanisms relate to the collection of the 'Top-up Tax' and constitute the last of GloBE's eight-step procedure (*see* section 4.4.2.7.). The Pillar Two Blueprint, published in October 2020,[1383] first revealed the technical details and the design of both the IIR and the UTPR. The Blueprint, however, only sparingly addressed possible defence strategies by national legislatures to defend their own fiscal sovereignty but only mentioned that jurisdictions could simply increase taxes to level up the ETR for in-scope 'MNE Groups'[1384].[1385] The OECD took

1381. H. Wardell-Burrus, *Should CFC Regimes Grant a Tax Credit For Qualified Domestic Minimum Top-up Taxes?*, 106 Tax Notes Intl. 1650–1651 (27 Jun. 2022).

1382. *Programme of Work*, at 25 et seq.

1383. *Tax Challenges Arising from Digitalisation – Report on Pillar Two Blueprint.*

1384. *See*, however, para. 491 of the Blueprint, where it was held: '*Jurisdictions that introduced the UTPR may, for a given MNE Group and a given year, be a jurisdiction where an MNE's jurisdictional ETR is below the agreed minimum rate due to the operation of certain tax incentives or other specific features in the tax system that result in the MNE's operations in that jurisdiction being subject to an ETR falling below the agreed minimum rate in a certain period. However, jurisdictions that wish to ensure that they can apply the UTPR in every year could ensure the jurisdictional ETR of every MNE operating in their jurisdictions is at least at the agreed minimum rate by introducing an annual domestic minimum tax on income with the same tax base and tax rate as the GloBE rules. Introducing such a minimum tax on income would make the exclusion ineffective for their jurisdiction*', *see Ibid.*, para. 491. In the following, the Blueprint further adds: '*As explained above, a domestic minimum tax on*

advantage of the then-still current political momentum of BEPS and the obvious benefits of the minimum tax: GloBE was promoted as the instrument to fight the '*race to the bottom*'[1386] and seemed to promise revenue gains[1387] for 'high-tax jurisdictions'. In particular, the latter argument was regularly put forward by the OECD during the COVID pandemic,[1388] when it was known to have heavily affected the budgets of OECD Members. The Blueprint was then heavily criticized that it did not take the interests of developing countries into account. Finally, the IIR as the primary charging rule would give the residence state of the UPE the right to collect the whole revenues of the minimum tax.[1389]

When the GloBE Model Rules and the EU Commission's Draft Directive[1390] were published in December 2021, it came as quite a surprise that both contained a permission for source jurisdictions to implement a QDMTT to levy the 'Top-up Tax' arising within their territory themselves.[1391] Other states that aim to collect a minimum tax by way of the IIR or UTPR must tolerate a QDMTT applied by the source state and must reduce any 'Top-up Tax' arising from the respective QDMTT levied. Interestingly, neither the Blueprint[1392] nor the announcement of the political consensus by the Inclusive Framework in October 2021[1393] had even hinted that GloBE would permit jurisdictions to skim any 'Top-up Tax' on their own; and finally, one could pose the question, which of the promised revenue gains for the western world remains[1394] if tax havens that GloBE was supposed to dry up simply 'soak up' the minimum tax themselves?

---

income, however, could be introduced in the jurisdiction of the UPE for in-scope taxpayers. Such a domestic minimum tax on income would aim at ensuring that the MNE's jurisdictional ETR in the ultimate parent jurisdiction is at least equal to the agreed minimum rate and would prevent the application of the UTPR in other jurisdictions in relation to profits made in the ultimate parent jurisdiction', see Ibid., para. 502.

1385. *See* early elaborations in literature with respect to potential reactions to the implementation of GloBE and on the limited statements of the Blueprint with respect to defensive tax strategies, *see* N. Noked, *Defense of Primary Taxing Rights*, 40 Va. Tax Rev. 352 et seq. and 362 et seq. (2021); N. Noked, *Potential Response to GLOBE: Domestic Minimum Taxes In Countries Affected by the Global Minimum Tax*, 102 Tax Notes Intl. 944 (17 May 2021).
1386. *See* the explicit reference to the '*race of the bottom*' in *Programme of Work*, para. 54.
1387. '*Pillar Two would yield a significant increase in CIT revenues across low, middle and high income economies', see Economic Impact Assessment*, at 10.
1388. *See* the extensive references to the '*two-pillar solution*' in OECD, *Tax and Fiscal Policies after the COVID-19 Crisis* (OECD 14 Oct. 2021), https://read.oecd-ilibrary.org/view/?ref=1112_1112899-o25re5oxnb&title=Tax-and-fiscal-policies-after-the-COVID-19-crisis (last visited 1 Jan. 2023).
1389. With further references to these developments, *see, i.a.*, N. Noked, *The Case for Domestic Minimum Taxes on Multinationals*, 105 Tax Notes Intl. 667–668 (7 Feb. 2022).
1390. COM(2021)823 final.
1391. Also *see* in literature M. Herzfeld, *How Does the Qualified Domestic Minimum Top-up Tax Fit Into Pillar 2?*, 106 Tax Notes Intl. 315–316 (2022); G. Kofler, *Vor allem die Qualified Domestic Minimum Top-up Tax ist ein echter Game Changer*, 6 TPI 162 (2022).
1392. *Tax Challenges Arising from Digitalisation – Report on Pillar Two Blueprint.*
1393. *OECD/G20 Statement 8 October.*
1394. *See,* however, the perspective pointed out by *Wardell-Burrus* who emphasized that even without QDMTT, GloBE would give precedence to the source state to tax the profits within its territory, *see* H. Wardell-Burrus, *Should CFC Regimes Grant a Tax Credit For Qualified Domestic Minimum Top-up Taxes?*, 106 Tax Notes Intl., *supra* note 1381, at 1649.

It is not without reason that the sudden and unexpected[1395] implementation of QDMTT into the technical framework of GloBE has been called both a 'Game Changer'[1396] and a 'Surprising Development'.[1397] There was considerable discussion about why the QDMTT came at such short notice. In any case, the QDMTT may have been a necessary part of the IF's consensus for common GloBE Model Rules, which at that time included more than 135 states.[1398] The QDMTT takes into account the legitimate sovereignty interest of states to collect the minimum tax themselves if it would be collected by another state, even if the promised additional tax revenue for high-tax countries is unlikely to materialize. However, the QDMTT does not change the goal of limiting the '*race to the bottom*': even if the supposed tax havens levy the minimum tax themselves, the minimum tax level to be established by GloBE is ensured, and the incentive to artificially shift profits is significantly reduced, at least up to the minimum tax level. In this respect, one might argue that GloBE is still fully consistent: it establishes a minimum corporate tax level, irrespective of where the minimum tax is paid.[1399]

Despite the fundamental importance of the QDMTT from a tax policy perspective, the technical framework related to the QDMTT is surprisingly brief: pursuant to the formula provided in Article 5.2.3. GloBE Model Rules and Article 27(3) GloBE-Directive, the QDMTT is to be subtracted from the 'Jurisdictional Top-up Tax'. From this, the 'Rule Order' of QDMTT can be derived in relation to IIR and UTPR (GloBE Rules): any QDMTT applies before any other state can levy a 'Top-up Tax' by means of the IIR and UTPR, simply due to the fact that the QDMTT nullifies 'Top-up Tax' arising in the tested jurisdiction. However, QDMTT is to be ignored for computing the 'Adjusted Covered Taxes' of a jurisdiction[1400] to avoid circular effects on the 'Top-up Tax' computation.[1401]

But what is a QDMTT pursuant to Article 5.2.3. GloBE Model Rules and Article 27(3) GloBE-Directive? Article 10.1. GloBE Model Rules defines the term 'Qualified Domestic Minimum Top-up Tax' as follows:

> *Qualified Domestic Minimum Top-up Tax means a minimum tax that is included in the domestic law of a jurisdiction and that:*

1395. *See* M. Devereux et al., *Pillar 2: Rule Order, Incentives, and Tax Competition*, SSRN, *supra* note 1359, at 1.
1396. Georg Kofler, *Vor allem die Qualified Domestic Minimum Top-up Tax ist ein echter Game Changer*, *supra* note 1391, at 162.
1397. *See* N. Noked, *The Case for Domestic Minimum Taxes on Multinationals*, 105 Tax Notes Intl., *supra* note 1389, at 670.
1398. *See* the foreword of the GloBE Model Rules where it is held that '*over 135 Inclusive Framework members, representing more than 95% of global GDP*' joined the two-pillar solution, *see GloBE Model Rules*, at 3.
1399. Also emphasising the fact, that, despite QDMTT, GloBE might still set a floor of 15% of 'Excess Profits', *see*, e.g., Noam Noked, *supra* note 1389, at 667; J. Englisch, *GloBE Rules and Tax Competition*, 50 Intertax, *supra* note 769, at 858.
1400. *See* Art. 4.2.2.(b) *GloBE Model Rules* and Art. 20(2)(b) GloBE-Directive (2022/2523).
1401. *See GloBE Commentary on Article 4 GloBE Model Rules (2022)*, *supra* note 884, para. 45. In literature, also *see* M. Herzfeld, *More on GLOBE Ordering: CFC Rules*, 106 Tax Notes Intl., *supra* note 1230, at 606.

(a) determines the Excess Profits of the Constituent Entities located in the jurisdiction (domestic Excess Profits) in a manner that is equivalent to the GloBE Rules;
(b) operates to increase domestic tax liability with respect to domestic Excess Profits to the Minimum Rate for the jurisdiction and Constituent Entities for a Fiscal Year; and
(c) is implemented and administered in a way that is consistent with the outcomes provided for under the GloBE Rules and the Commentary, provided that such jurisdiction does not provide any benefits that are related to such rules.

A Qualified Domestic Minimum Top-up Tax may compute domestic Excess Profits based on an Acceptable Financial Accounting Standard permitted by the Authorised Accounting Body or an Authorised Financial Accounting Standard adjusted to prevent any Material Competitive Distortions, rather than the financial accounting standard used in the Consolidated Financial Statements.[1402]

Within the GloBE-Directive, a corresponding definition is established in Article 3(28) GloBE-Directive. The differences in the wording between the definition provided for in the GloBE Model Rules and the GloBE-Directive are merely insignificant.

It is a bit surprising that, despite the fundamental importance of the QDMTT definition, as will be seen, the initial passages of the Commentary remained very superficial. The Commentary, however, promises that GloBE Implementation Framework will provide further guidance on the notion of QDMTT and '*will include implementing a process to assist administrations in determining whether a minimum tax is considered*' as QDMTT also emphasizing that such '*determinations*' could be '*made publicly available*'.[1403] Indeed, the OECD kept its promise and, after all, devoted a separate section to the QDMTT definition in its recently published GloBE Administrative Guidance February 2023, according to which paragraph 118 of the GloBE Commentary have been replaced by newly added 53 (!) sub-paragraphs (paragraphs 118.1 to 118.53) which have, in the meanwhile, been supplemented by further detailed provisions in the course of the GloBE Administrative Guidance July 2023.[1404] In any case, it is obvious that the definition provided for in the GloBE Model Rules and the GloBE-Directive is highly indefinite. What is the scope of 'equivalent to the GloBE Rules', and how far may domestic laws deviate from GloBE principles? What does '*increase in domestic tax liability* [...] *to the Minimum Rate*' mean? Can a 'soak-up' tax that does not entirely meet the minimum tax level not qualify as a QDMTT at all? And finally, when is an '*outcome*' not '*consistent*' with the GloBE Rules and the Commentary?

Meanwhile, many of these questions are addressed in the GloBE Administrative Guidance February 2023 and have been implemented in the Commentary. In particular, the question of 'consistency' is explicitly addressed in the GloBE Administrative Guidance February 2023. First of all, '*a minimum tax must follow the architecture of the GloBE rules using mechanisms that are substantially the same as those used to calculate*

1402. Article 10.1. *GloBE Model Rules*, at 64.
1403. *See GloBE Commentary on Article 10 GloBE Model Rules (2022)*, *supra* note 280, para. 118.
1404. *GloBE Administrative Guidance February 2023*, at 98–111 and *GloBE Administrative Guidance July 2023*, at 56-76

the effective tax rate and top-up tax payable under GloBE'.[1405] Thus, the document notes that '[t]*he simplest way to demonstrate* [...] [consistency] *would be for a jurisdiction to mirror all the requirement of the GloBE Rules with only minor changes*'[1406] but that this would '*result in redundant and complex provisions*'[1407] which is why '[s]*ome degree of customisation of a QDMTT in each jurisdiction is to be expected*'.[1408] Furthermore, the GloBE Administrative Guidance February 2023 adds that '[v]*ariations in outcomes between the minimum tax and GloBE Rules will not prevent that tax from being treated as a QDMTT if those variations systemically produce a greater incremental tax liability or do not systematically produce lower tax liability than would be expected under the GloBE Rules and Commentary*'.[1409] The OECD, therefore, clearly assumes that a QDMTT does not have to reflect the entire complexity of the GloBE Model Rules. What is relevant is that the design of the domestic minimum tax is not such that a tax burden below the minimum tax level specified by GloBE can be achieved on a regular basis. However, most importantly, the GloBE Administrative Guidance February 2023 states that '*[t]he Inclusive Framework will develop a multilateral review process in 2023 to assess whether the domestic minimum tax of a jurisdiction and the way it is administered produce outcomes that are sufficiently consistent with those of the GloBE Rules for such minimum tax to be treated as a QDMTT*'.[1410] However, the document does not provide further indication of the nature of such a review process.

With respect to the technical issues of QDMTT implementation, the Commentary on Article 10 GloBE Model Rules first clarifies that the QDMTT reduces the 'Top-up Tax' liability for a jurisdiction and might eliminate any liability with respect to the IIR or the UTPR.[1411] It further notes that QDMTT '*means a tax that applies to Excess Profits of the domestic Constituent Entities and operates to increase domestic tax liability with respect to those profits to the Minimum Rate*'.[1412] This wording could be understood to mean that a domestic minimum tax does not qualify as a QDMTT at all if it does not collect the total amount of 'Top-up Tax' within its territory. However, on the other hand, the Commentary on Article 5 GloBE Model Rules notes that '*tax payable pursuant to a* [QDMTT] *can offset the Top-up Tax (including any Additional Current Top-up Tax calculated for the Fiscal Year) that would have been computed under Article 5.2.3 for the Fiscal Year absent the* [QDMTT]'[1413] and further adds that '*the* [QDMTT] *will in many cases reduce the Top-up Tax to nil under Art 5.2.3*'.[1414] Consequently, one could argue that every euros of 'Top-up Tax' paid may be offset against any 'Top-up Tax' allocated to the jurisdiction in which 'Top-up Tax' arises, and it might be the case that it does not completely reduce the 'Top-up Tax' to nil. Nevertheless, in its GloBE Administrative Guidance February 2023, the OECD notes that a QDMTT '[t]*o be*

1405. *See* para. 7 of Chapter 5 *Ibid.*, at 99.
1406. *See* para. 8 of Chapter 5 *Ibid.*
1407. *See* para. 8 of Chapter 5 *Ibid.*
1408. *See* para. 9 of Chapter 5 *Ibid.*
1409. *See* para. 10 of Chapter 5 *Ibid.*
1410. *See* para. 4 of Chapter 5 *Ibid.*
1411. *See GloBE Commentary on Article 10 GloBE Model Rules (2022)*, *supra* note 280, para. 115.
1412. *See Ibid.*, para. 116.
1413. *See GloBE Commentary on Article 5 GloBE Model Rules (2022)*, *supra* note 474, para. 20.
1414. *See Ibid.*

functionally equivalent, the tax rate applicable under a QDMTT must equal or exceed the Minimum Rate. Otherwise, the tax collected would consistently fall short of the GloBE Top-up Tax'.[1415]

As both, the definition of QDMTT in Article 10 GloBE Model Rules and Article 3(28) GloBE-Directive reveal, the QDMTT does not require the source state to increase its common ETR up to 15%. Rather, jurisdictions can decide to merely 'skim off' the 'Top-up Tax' arising. Finally, GloBE only supposes to tax the 'GloBE Income' exceeding the SBIE.[1416] The jurisdiction implementing QDMTT can, thus, decide to only collect the amount of 'Top-up Tax' that would arise and would be collected by a different jurisdiction pursuant to GloBE. The ETR, including a QDMTT, can thus be below 15% without necessarily triggering IIR or UTPR 'Top-up Tax'. In contrast, a (non-qualified) domestic minimum tax could only prevent the IIR or UTPR if it achieved an ETR exceeding 15%.[1417]

A separate paragraph in the Commentary is devoted to the requirement stated in letter c of the GloBE Model Rules' QDMTT definition (within the GloBE-Directive, the respective element is included in the first sentence of Article 3[28] GloBE-Directive) including a '*prohibition against the implementing jurisdiction providing any collateral or other benefits that are related to such domestic tax*'.[1418] Instead of explaining what '*collateral or other benefits*' might be, the Commentary states that any change in domestic tax laws in the course of implementing QDMTT shall not be considered a prohibited benefit. But what then is such a '*collateral or other benefit*'? It is probably not without reason that the OECD has kept the definition very vague in order to avoid demonstrating options for defensive legislation of 'Low-Tax Jurisdiction'. However, the OECD might have intended to prevent QDMTT designs like a domestic minimum tax that, for example, is refundable after a certain period of time, that is never collected, or that cannot be executed by the tax authorities within a short deadline. The GloBE Administrative Guidance February 2023 adds another paragraph 118.13 to the GloBE Commentary on Article 10 GloBE Model Rules with respect to this issue and promises that the IF will work on further guidance in that respect.[1419]

Furthermore, the Commentary adds that a domestic tax can qualify as a QDMTT also if the taxed profits are determined pursuant to domestic GAAP not qualifying as an 'Acceptable Financial Accounting Standard' if it is adjusted by any 'Material Competitive Distortion' (on the notion of 'Material Competitive Distortion', *see* section 4.2.3.2.).[1420] The issue of accounting standards with respect to the determination of QDMTT income has also been addressed in the GloBE Administrative Guidance

1415. *See* para. 118.38 *GloBE Commentary on Article 10, supra* note 280 pursuant to the *GloBE Administrative Guidance February 2023*, at 107.
1416. On the interplay between the SBIE and the QDMTT, *see* N. Bammens & D. Bettens, *The Potential Impact of Pillar Two on Tax Incentives*, 51 Intertax 166 et seq. (2023) DOI: 10.54648/taxi2023018.
1417. Also *see*, H. Wardell-Burrus, *Should CFC Regimes Grant a Tax Credit For Qualified Domestic Minimum Top-up Taxes?*, 106 Tax Notes Intl., *supra* note 1381, at 1650–1651.
1418. *See GloBE Commentary on Article 10, supra* note 280, para. 115.
1419. *See* para. 118.13 *GloBE Commentary on Article 10, supra* note 280 pursuant to the *GloBE Administrative Guidance February 2023*, at 102.
1420. *See GloBE Commentary on Article 10, supra* note 280, para. 117.

February 2023. Two new paras, 118.14 and 118.15, will be added to the GloBE Commentary on Article 10 GloBE Model Rules that clarify that the definition of QDMTT '*recognises that the local tax authority would likely be more familiar with accounting standards that are permissible in the jurisdiction than one applied by a UPE in another jurisdiction*'.[1421] But even more importantly, the OECD states that the 'Material Competitive Distortion' threshold of EUR 75 million '*should not apply in the context of a QDMTT applicable to a single jurisdiction and that the Inclusive Framework will consider providing further guidance on the determination of a lower threshold to provide for outcomes that are consistent with the GloBE Rules. For example, the Inclusive Framework could consider whether the threshold could be scaled to the jurisdiction based on the relative amount of the MNE Group's revenues in the jurisdiction*'.[1422] This is an interesting side note. The OECD obviously at least implicitly recognizes that deviating accounting rules might be used by jurisdictions to attract foreign direct investment.

What can be anticipated from the both GloBE Administrative Guidances is the fact that technically implementing a QDMTT is not an easy task: from the perspective of tax havens, there are a number of technical issues that have to be taken into consideration to optimize a QDMTT design. Finally, for a QDMTT, it is not necessary to simply raise the nominal CIT rate but rather to take the technical specifics of GloBE, in particular the SBIE, into account.[1423] Furthermore, jurisdictions could decide not to levy QDMTT with respect to that share of 'Top-up Tax' that is attributable to minority shareholders.[1424] If a certain LTCE is 'located' within the territory of a specific jurisdiction that is partially owned by non-Group members, GloBE would, at least in most cases, only oblige collecting a 'Top-up Tax' with respect to the 'Ownership Interest' that is attributable to an MNE Group. Any minority shareholders could, as also the GloBE Administrative Guidance February 2023 confirms, be excluded from the QDMTT.[1425]

In general, an optimized QDMTT will require determining which members of the 'Group' are required to apply either the IIR or the UTPR because the amount of 'Top-up Tax' levied by means of IIR and UTPR can significantly depend on the level where the respective 'Top-up Tax' is levied. If the corporate structure includes IPE or POPEs, the mechanics of the IIR can influence the final 'Top-up Tax' liability. Furthermore, jurisdictions should keep an eye on the exceptions to jurisdictional blending, including 'Investment Entities', MOCEs and 'Stateless Entities'. If such entities are 'located' in a jurisdiction besides other CEs, domestic QDMTT implementation should take care that the QDMTT is levied with respect to the technical specifics that are foreseen in GloBE's

1421. *See* para. 118.14 *GloBE Commentary on Article 10, supra* note 280 pursuant to the *GloBE Administrative Guidance February 2023*, at 102.
1422. *See* para. 118.15 *GloBE Commentary on Article 10, supra* note 280 pursuant to the *GloBE Administrative Guidance February 2023*, at 102–103.
1423. *See* para. 118.36 and para. 118.37 *GloBE Commentary on Article 10, supra* note 280 pursuant to the *GloBE Administrative Guidance February 2023*, at 107.
1424. This issue had been raised by N. Noked, *Defense of Primary Taxing Rights*, 40 Va. Tax Rev., *supra* note 1385, at 359 et seq.; N. Noked, *The Case for Domestic Minimum Taxes on Multinationals*, 105 Tax Notes Intl., *supra* note 1389, at 669–670.
1425. *See* para. 118.10 *GloBE Commentary on Article 10, supra* note 280 pursuant to *GloBE Administrative Guidance February 2023*, at 101.

framework for those entities. In the meantime, both GloBE Administrative Guidances 2023 have also addressed these issues and acknowledge that an optimal QDMTT design requires specific rules for the exceptions to jurisdictional blending,[1426] in particular, including MOCEs[1427] as well as 'Joint Ventures'.[1428] This includes, for example, avoiding that GloBE considers a CE as a 'Stateless Entity': it has been revealed that a PE might qualify as a 'Stateless Constituent Entity' if it is involved in operations conducted outside the jurisdiction where the 'Main Entity' is located provided that such jurisdiction exempts income attributable to such operations. Some jurisdictions provide a territorial tax regime as part of their tax policy to attract foreign investments. In order to avoid such operations from being considered 'stateless' and giving rise to a 'Top-up Tax' levied by different jurisdictions, it can make sense to adjust the QDMTT in a way that it also captures such operations. The GloBE Administrative Guidance February 2023, in this respect, notes that the IF '*considers providing further guidance on the allocation of income to PEs under QDMTT in particular circumstances (for example, in respect of stateless PEs or reversed hybrid entities)*'.[1429] Last but not least, QDMTT design has to take into consideration the SBIE: 'Top-up Tax' only arises with respect to 'Excess Profits'. Like the GloBE Model Rules, an efficient QDMTT design will thus reduce its base by the SBIE aligned with the design of GloBE. Against the background of these technical difficulties, the clarifications provided by the GloBE Administrative Guidance February 2023 are highly welcome, although it is questionable whether they can be used for interpreting Article 3(28) GloBE-Directive.[1430]

The GloBE-Directive provides an election for Member States to implement a 'qualified domestic top-up tax' (in the following, nevertheless, the abbreviation QDMTT is used) '[i]*n order to allow Member States to benefit from the top-up tax revenues collected on the low-taxed constituent entities located in their territory*'.[1431] This is manifested in Article 1(2) GloBE-Directive: '*Member States may elect to apply a qualified domestic top-up tax in accordance with which top-up tax shall be computed and paid on excess profit of all the low-taxed constituent entities located in their jurisdiction pursuant to this directive*'.[1432] Article 11 GloBE-Directive repeats this permission QDMTT but adds certain requirements with respect to the design of its QDMTT implementation: first of all, Article 11(1) GloBE-Directive states that if a Member State decides to implement a QDMTT, '*all low-taxed constituent entities of the MNE group or large-scale domestic group in that Member State shall be subject to that*

1426. *See* para. 118.33 *GloBE Commentary on Article 10, supra* note 280 pursuant to the *GloBE Administrative Guidance February 2023,* at 106. Also see the additional guidance with respect to the consideration of MOCEs, 'Investment Entities', 'Stateless Constituent Entities' and JVs provided in the *GloBE Administrative Guidance July 2023,* at 56, 60 and 63-70.
1427. *See* para. 118.6 *GloBE Commentary on Article 10, supra* note 280 pursuant to the *GloBE Administrative Guidance February 2023,* at 101.
1428. *See* para. 118.7 and para. 118.8 *GloBE Commentary on Article 10, supra* note 280 pursuant to the *GloBE Administrative Guidance February 2023,* at 101.
1429. *See* para. 118.22 *GloBE Commentary on Article 10, supra* note 280 pursuant to the *GloBE Administrative Guidance February 2023,* at 104.
1430. On the interpretative insignificance of the GloBE Administrative Guidances for the GloBE-Directive, *see* s. 4.1.
1431. *See* recital 13 of the GloBE-Directive (2022/2523).
1432. Article 1(2) *Ibid.*

domestic top-up tax for the fiscal year'. The GloBE-Directive thus obliges an 'all-or-nothing' approach: Member States cannot exclude domestic CEs from the QDMTT but must apply the QDMTT equally to all CEs of 'MNE Groups' or 'large-scale domestic groups'. The question of how to deal with domestic LTCEs of UPEs by way of QDMTT has already been discussed in the literature:[1433] The GloBE Model Rules do not oblige applying the IIR with respect to domestic LTCEs, so UPE jurisdictions could decide to keep the ETR of domestic LTCEs of the UPE below 15%. This, however, would trigger UTPR at the level of a different CE, so it was discussed whether jurisdictions should apply the QDMTT as well. In this instance, the GloBE-Directive leaves no option to the Member States: once they decide to elect to apply a QDMTT, it is to be applied to domestic LTCEs as well. Thus, the GloBE-Directive also ensures that the QDMTT design is non-discriminatory and complies with the fundamental freedoms as well as other non-discrimination provisions like Article 24 OECD MC within the Member States' treaty network.

The last sentence of Article 11(1) GloBE-Directive clarifies that it is permitted to apply the QDMTT to domestic 'Excess Profits' determined pursuant to a financial accounting standard that deviates from the accounting standard used by the UPE. Member States may, thus, allow the recalculation of the 'Excess Profits' based on local GAAP due to the fact that all accounting standards of EU Member States fall within the definition of 'Acceptable Financial Accounting Standards'. If the amount of QDMTT of a 'Fiscal Year' had not been paid within the four subsequent years following the respective year, which gave rise to the respective 'Top-up Tax', '*the amount of qualified domestic to-up tax that was not paid shall be added to the jurisdictional top-up tax* [...] *and shall not be collected by the Member State which made the election pursuant to paragraph 2 of this Article*'.[1434]

Article 11(2) GloBE-Directive finally obliges the Member States where the 'Parent Entity' of an 'MNE Group' is 'located' (which potentially applies the IIR) to reduce any amount of 'Top-up Tax' levied at the level of the 'Parent Entity' by the amount of QDMTT due either by itself or by jurisdictions where subsidiaries of the respective domestic 'Parent Entity' are 'located'. According to the second paragraph of Article 11 GloBE-Directive, no 'Top-up Tax' must be computed for the 'Fiscal Year' '*in respect of constituent entities of that MNE Group or large-scale domestic group located in that Member State*'.[1435] This serves as a simplification: an 'MNE Group' can waive the computation of 'Top-up Tax' if a Member State had levied a QDMTT that was calculated pursuant to the financial accounting standards applied by the UPE of the respective Group. However, pursuant to the last sentence of Article 11(2) GloBE-Directive, this may not prevent any ACTT occurring under Article 29 GloBE-Directive, '*where a Member State does not apply a qualified domestic top-up tax to collect any additional top-up tax arising under Art 29*'.[1436]

1433. N. Noked, *Defense of Primary Taxing Rights*, 40 Va. Tax Rev., *supra* note 1385, at 366–367; N. Noked, *The Case for Domestic Minimum Taxes on Multinationals*, 105 Tax Notes Intl., *supra* note 1389, at 670–671.
1434. Article 11(3) GloBE-Directive (2022/2523).
1435. Second subparagraph of Art. 11(2) *Ibid.*
1436. Last sentence of Art. 11(2) *Ibid.*

Pursuant to Article 11(4) GloBE-Directive, Member States '*shall notify the Commission of that election within four months following the adoption of their national laws, regulations and administrative provisions introducing a qualified domestic top-up tax*'.[1437] Pursuant to recital 13 of the GloBE-Directive, the notification of the Commission serves to provide '*tax authorities of other Member States and third-country jurisdictions, as well as MNE groups, with sufficient certainty as regards the applicability of the qualified domestic top-up tax to low-taxed constituent entities in that Member States*'.[1438] The election is valid and may not be revoked for a period of three years but is renewed automatically. Finally, once a Member State decides to implement QDMTT, it may not abolish it until the end of the three-year period. It seems that this provision is intended to bind Member States to their election: Member States should not be allowed to abolish a QDMTT once introduced if the international Pillar Two implementation process stalls. From a tax policy perspective, it is questionable whether this self-restriction of the Member States really makes sense and is desirable for the EU's position within global tax competition.

An interesting discussion has emerged in the literature[1439] about 'CFC regimes' and their relationship to QDMTTs. Specifically, the issue is the rule order between both mechanisms: should 'CFC regimes' credit taxes levied due to a QDMTT as part of foreign tax liability or do CFC regimes apply in advance to the QDMTT? The question is indeed tricky: if the source state and residence state of a CFC that is a CE of an in-scope 'MNE Group' applies a QDMTT, it is clear from both the GloBE Model Rules and the GloBE-Directive, that any CFC taxes levied at the level of a parent entity are to be allocated to the jurisdiction where the CFC is 'located' and increase the ETR of the source jurisdiction.[1440] Consequently, any CFC tax burdens reduce the amount of QDMTT to be levied by this jurisdiction. In principle, it seems that the GloBE Model Rules and the GloBE-Directive give precedence to CFC rules and incentivize 'CFC regimes'. By way of collecting CFC taxes, the CFC tax 'soaks up' the tax that the QDMTT is supposed to levy. However, if 'CFC regimes' allow crediting QDMTT, this would lead to a spiral reduction of CFC and a corresponding iterate increase of the QDMTT: if the residence state of a parent entity credits the QDMTT levied at the level of a CFC, this would necessarily decrease the 'Adjusted Covered Taxes' in the source jurisdiction, leading to an increase in QDMTT. This would again increase the credit for the CFC tax, further reducing 'Covered Taxes' and increasing QDMTT until no CFC tax is left to increase the amount of 'Adjusted Covered Taxes' in the source jurisdiction. In

1437. Article 11(4) *Ibid.*
1438. *See* recital 13 of the *Ibid.*
1439. *See* above all N. Noked, *The Case for Domestic Minimum Taxes on Multinationals*, 105 Tax Notes Intl., *supra* note 1389; L.A. Sheppard, *Pillar 2 and QDMTT*, 105 Tax Notes Intl. 763–764 (14 Feb. 2022); M. Herzfeld, *More on GLOBE Ordering: CFC Rules*, 106 Tax Notes Intl., *supra* note 1230, at 603–607; H. Wardell-Burrus, *Should CFC Regimes Grant a Tax Credit For Qualified Domestic Minimum Top-up Taxes?*, 106 Tax Notes Intl., *supra* note 1381, at 1649 et seq.; M. Herzfeld, *How to Allocate CFC Taxes Under GloBE*, 108 Tax Notes Intl. 1514–1518 (19 Dec. 2022).
1440. Article 4.3.2.(c) *GloBE Model Rules* and Article 24(3) GloBE-Directive (2022/2523).

any case, the GloBE Model Rules do not seem to give any preference to any of the two approaches.[1441]

The question is also relevant for the relation of the GloBE-Directive and the ATAD, obliging the Member States to introduce a 'CFC regime'. Pursuant to Article 8(7) ATAD, the Member State in which the parent entity is resident '*shall allow a deduction of the tax paid by the entity or permanent establishment from the tax liability of the taxpayer in its state of tax residence or location. The deduction shall be calculated in accordance with national law*'.[1442] On the other hand, there is Article 11(1) GloBE-Directive permitting to apply a QDMTT and Article 24(3) GloBE-Directive explicitly stating that '*any covered taxes included in the financial accounts of its direct or indirect constituent entity-owners under a controlled foreign company tax regime, on their share of the controlled foreign company's income*' shall be allocated to the CE that received the underlying income. It seems that EU law, in particular Article 8(7) ATAD, leaves it to the Member States whether a newly introduced tax like a QDMTT is credited against the CFC tax to be levied pursuant to Article 7 ATAD. So, one could argue that the issue of whether QDMTT is to be credited against CFC tax still is an open issue. However, in this respect, one should consider that the EU Commission deliberately did not address the relation between ATAD and the GloBE-Directive, as it explicitly pointed out in the explanatory memorandum of the GloBE-Directive Proposal:

> The implementation of the GloBE Model Rules in the EU could have implications for existing provisions of the Anti-tax Avoidance Directive (ATAD) and specifically for the Controlled Foreign Company (CFC) rules, which could interact with the primary rule of Pillar 2 – the IIR. The Commission has explored how to best accommodate the interaction between the CFC of the ATAD and the IIR, and concluded that it is not necessary to amend the ATAD in this regard. Moreover, it is consistent with the OECD Model Rules to continue the application of the ATAD CFC rule in parallel to the GloBE Model Rules. In practice, ATAD CFC rules will apply first and any additional taxes paid by a parent company under a CFC regime in a given fiscal year will be taken into consideration in the GloBE Model Rules by attributing those to the relevant low-taxed entity for the purpose of computing its jurisdictional effective tax rate.[1443]

The Commission, as the sole body entitled to initiate legal acts of EU law, is obviously of the opinion that CFC rules prevail over the GloBE-Directive, including permission for the Member States to implement a QDMTT. So, one could argue that the EU legislature assumes that QDMTTs are not creditable. However, this conclusion is not entirely correct: it is obvious that GloBE assumes that the ETR computation includes CFC taxes. Rather, the question is whether Member States consider QDMTT to be creditable against the CFC liability, which is, however, left to the domestic law of the Member States pursuant to Article 8(7) GloBE-Directive. If a Member State decides to credit QDMTT against domestic CFC tax liability, the same Member State waives

1441. For an excessive discussion of the problem, *see* Heydon Wardell-Burrus, *supra* note 1381, at 1649 et seq.
1442. Article 8(7) Council directive (EU) 2016/1164 of 12 July 2016 laying down rules against tax avoidance practices that directly affect the functioning of the internal market, OJ (1164).
1443. *See* COM(2021)823 final 2.

revenues to the advantage of the source jurisdiction applying the QDMTT, which evidently is permitted under EU law. If a Member State denies crediting QDMTT, the GloBE-Directive certainly assumes that the CFC tax increases the ETR of the jurisdiction where the CFC is 'located' pursuant to Article 4 GloBE-Directive. One can, thus, conclude that EU law does leave it up to the Member States to decide whether to allow for a credit of QDMTT with respect to CFC taxes or to deny such a credit. Consequently, neither EU law solves the rule order of QDMTT and CFC legislation.[1444]

From a tax policy point of view, the creditability of QDMTTs against CFC taxes is a delicate issue: residence states of parent entities could argue that CFC rules are to be included in the 'Top-up Tax' computation and could deliberately extend their CFC regimes to 'skim off low-taxed profits even before the respective source state can apply its QDMTT.[1445] Source states (residence states of CFCs and LTCEs), on the other hand, could simply calculate their QDMTTs without considering CFC taxes, possibly arguing that it is up to the state applying the CFC regime to credit the QDMTT to avoid double taxation. The issue has been extensively debated by Wardell-Burrus, who convincingly argues that it should be left up to the source jurisdictions to compute the QDMTT by not 'crediting' CFC taxes (not including those taxes in the computation of the 'Adjusted Covered Taxes') and that the best way to address the issue is by way of any kind of multilateral instrument that could also solve arising conflicts with respect to tax treaties.[1446]

In the meanwhile, the OECD has also addressed this issue in the GloBE Administrative Guidance February 2023 and will add the following in paragraph 118.30 of the GloBE Commentary on Article 10 GloBE Model Rules:

> *A QDMTT shall exclude tax paid or incurred by a Constituent Entity-owner under a CFC Tax Regime that is allocable to a domestic Constituent Entity under Article 4.3.2(c) of the GloBE Rules and tax paid or incurred by a Main Entity that is allocable under Article 4.3.2(a) to a Permanent Establishment located in the jurisdiction.* Excluding such CFC and PE taxes allows the QDMTT to operate as a simple calculation and *does not require the complex calculations required in some cases to allocate CFC taxes* under Article 4.3.2(c) to be reported to a jurisdiction that implements a QDMTT. Further, a specific ordering rule is aimed at attributing primary taxing rights to the jurisdiction applying the QDMTT in relation to its Constituent Entities. *If the ordering rule were the opposite, so that CFC taxes or PE taxes were credited under a QDMTT, additional computations would have been required in order to avoid the QDMTT resulting in taxation that is below the Minimum Rate. Specifically, if a QDMTT is creditable against either a CFC tax charge or a PE tax charge imposed by the parent or main entity jurisdiction, any crediting of that CFC tax or PE tax against a QDMTT would make the calculation of the correct amount of QDMTT problematic, due to the interaction of the two crediting mechanisms.* Excluding credits for CFC or PE taxes from QDMTT calculations will ensure that this practical problem does not arise. The Inclusive Framework will monitor the interaction between the QDMTT and CFC Tax

1444. Also *see* s. 6.3.
1445. Also *see* M. Herzfeld, *More on GLOBE Ordering: CFC Rules,* 106 Tax Notes Intl., *supra* note 1230, at 607 concluding that the GloBE Model Rules give priority to CFC regimes over the QDMTT.
1446. H. Wardell-Burrus, *supra* note 1381, at 1649 et seq.

> Regimes and taxable branch regimes to ensure this interaction results in the intended outcomes under the GloBE Rules and may, in the future, consider solutions to address issues if they arise.[1447] (emphasis added)

It seems that the OECD followed the arguments of Wardell-Burrus in this respect. It can therefore be stated that the QDMTT, at least according to the GloBE Administrative Guidance February 2023, overtakes CFC regimes in GloBE's rule ordering. This leaves the question of how double taxation will be avoided if CFC regimes do not take into account any taxes levied by means of the QDMTT. In the author's view, this means that CFC regimes, from a tax policy perspective, ultimately should provide credit for the QDMTT; otherwise, there is a risk of over-taxation through double taxation of low-taxed income, once by the QDMTT and once by a foreign CFC regime. The new paragraph added to the GloBE Commentary on Article 10 GloBE Model Rules, thus, is a solution for the QDMTT but does not entirely solve the issue. Furthermore, the issue arises again of whether the respective clarification in the GloBE Administrative Guidance February 2023 can be used within the EU, as the additional statements made in paragraph 118.30 of the Commentary on Article 10 GloBE Model Rules are not necessarily consistent with Article 3(28) and Article 11 GloBE-Directive. Again, it should be noted that the GloBE Administrative Guidances 2023 were published after the GloBE-Directive was adopted.

4.4.2.7 Step 7: Allocation of the 'Top-up Tax' to 'Constituent Entities'

In Step 7, the '*Jurisdictional Top-up Tax*', if any, is to be allocated to the respective CEs located in the jurisdiction or the CEs within to the same sub-calculation. According to Article 5.2.4. GloBE Model Rules and Article 27(5) GloBE-Directive the 'Top-up Tax of a CE' '*shall be determined for each Constituent Entity of a jurisdiction that has GloBE Income*' by the following formula (*see* Figure 7).

Figure 7 Allocation of Top-up Tax to CEs According to Article 5.2.4. GloBE Model Rules and Article 27(5) GloBE-Directive

$$\textbf{Top-up Tax of a CE} = \textbf{Jurisdictional Top-up Tax} \times \frac{\textbf{GloBE Income of the CE}}{\textbf{Aggregate GloBE Income of all CEs in same jurisdiction}}$$

The formula, thus, multiplies the '*Jurisdictional Top-up Tax*' by the ratio of the positive GloBE Income of the respective CE and the total aggregated positive 'GloBE Income' of all CEs located in the same jurisdiction. Article 5.2.4. GloBE Model Rules and Article 27(5) GloBE-Directive explicitly clarify that 'Top-up Tax', as a rule, can only be allocated to CEs having positive 'GloBE Income'. This has two meanings for the above formula: first, a calculation for CEs with 'GloBE Losses' is ruled out from the outset, and second, also for the purposes of allocation, the loss-making CEs are to be

1447. *See* para. 118.22 *GloBE Commentary on Article 10 GloBE Model Rules (2022)*, *supra* note 280 pursuant to the *GloBE Administrative Guidance February 2023*, at 105.

excluded from the denominator of the above fraction.[1448] The same principles apply to 'Investment Entities' in the same jurisdiction or MOCE within the same 'Minority-Owned Subgroup' and jurisdiction. For individual 'Investment Entities', MOCEs or 'Stateless Entities', however, an allocation is obsolete, especially since the 'Top-up Tax' is to be calculated on an entity basis anyway.

It goes without saying that Article 5.2.4. GloBE Model Rules and Article 27(5) GloBE-Directive cannot be applied in years where an 'MNE Group' suffers a 'GloBE Loss' in a specific jurisdiction. Both provisions only allow allocating 'Top-up Tax' to CEs receiving positive 'GloBE Income' within the 'Fiscal Year' at issue. However, if in the loss-making year a recalculation of previous 'Fiscal Years' is necessary, this might give rise to ACTT leading to a 'Top-up Tax' liability even if there is no 'Net GloBE Income' ('net qualifying income') within this jurisdiction. But how to allocate the 'Top-up Tax' in such situations?

In these situations, the 'Top-up Tax' caused by ACTT is to be allocated pursuant to Article 5.2.5. GloBE Model Rules (reflected in Article 27[6] GloBE-Directive), which states that the 'Top-up Tax' in these cases *'shall be allocated using the formula in Article 5.2.4.* [equivalent to Article 27(5) GloBE-Directive] *based on the GloBE Income of the Constituent Entities in the Fiscal Years for which the recalculations under Article 5.4.1.* [equivalent to Article 29(1) GloBE-Directive] *were performed'*. In other words, both Article 5.2.5. GloBE Model Rules and Article 27(6) GloBE-Directive, for the purposes of the allocation of the 'Top-up Tax' among the CE 'located' in the same jurisdiction, substitute lacking 'Net GloBE Income' by the respective 'GloBE Income or Loss' received in the preceding 'Fiscal Year' for which the recalculation giving rise to ACTT was made. The Commentary notes with respect to this rule that '[w]*here a jurisdiction lacks Net GloBE Income in the current year, it is more appropriate to allocate Additional Current Top-up Tax based on the GloBE Income of the Constituent Entities in the relevant previous years because all of the Top-up Tax was calculated by reference to the Net GloBE Income of those years*'.[1449]

As already discussed in section 4.4.2.6.2., however, ACTT can also arise in 'Fiscal Years' in which there is no 'Net GloBE Income ' ('net qualifying income') even if there is no need to recalculate the ETR of the previous 'Fiscal Years'. If the amount of 'Adjusted Covered Taxes Amount' is negative and exceeds the so-called Expected Adjusted Covered Taxes Amount within a jurisdiction, Article 4.1.5. GloBE Model Rules and Article 21(5) GloBE-Directive oblige collecting 'Top-up Tax' in overall loss situations because otherwise, 'Top-up Tax' could be avoided from a multi-period perspective. For this reason, both Article 5.4.3. GloBE Model Rules and Article 29(3) GloBE-Directive provide for specific allocation rules which are to be applied in Step 7 in these cases[1450] and prevail[1451] over Article 5.2.5. GloBE Model Rules and Article 27(6) GloBE-Directive. The latter rules finally would not be applicable because the 'Top-up Tax' (ACTT) could not be 'referred' to a previous year but is actually rooted in

1448. *See GloBE Commentary on Article 5 GloBE Model Rules (2022)*, *supra* note 474, para. 21.
1449. *See Ibid.*, para. 23.
1450. In detail *see Ibid.*, paras 69–72.
1451. *See Ibid.*, para. 24.

the 'Fiscal Year'. According to Article 5.4.3. GloBE Model Rules and Article 29(3) GloBE-Directive, 'Top-up Tax' arising due to Article 4.1.5. GloBE Model Rules and Article 21(5) GloBE-Directive may only be allocated to CEs that record an amount of 'Adjusted Covered Taxes' that is less than zero and less than the 'GloBE Income or Loss' ('net qualifying income or loss') of the CE multiplied by the 'Minimum Rate'. If more than one CE fulfils these criteria within the same jurisdiction, the allocation is to be made on a pro rata basis according to the following formula (*see* Figure 8).

Figure 8 Specific Allocation Rule of Article 5.4.3. GloBE Model Rules and Article 29(3) GloBE-Directive in Situations Where 'Top-up Tax' Is Due Pursuant to Article 4.1.5. GloBE Model Rules and Article 21(5) GloBE-Directive in the Absence of Positive 'Net GloBE Income' in Specific Jurisdictions

(GloBE Income or Loss × Minimum Rate) – Adjusted Covered Taxes

Taking a broader perspective, one could critically assess why the calculated *'Top-up Tax'* is again to be allocated to the individual CEs located in a jurisdiction if they are first tediously aggregated jurisdiction-wise. Ultimately, the necessity to allocate the computed *'Top-up Tax'* among the CEs located in a jurisdiction demonstrates a flaw of jurisdictional blending: basically, only the actual tax burden is measured at the level of jurisdictions, whereas the determination of the 'GloBE Income or Loss' and the final charging of the 'Top-up Tax' must still take place at the level of a single legal entity, such as the UPE, an 'Intermediate Parent Entity' (IPE) or a 'Partially Owned Parent Entity' (POPE). Even the Commentary implicitly acknowledges this systematic weakness by providing the rationale for the need to again split and allocate the 'Jurisdictional Top-up Tax': *'Although Top-up Tax is computed on a jurisdictional basis, the IIR charging provisions in Chapter 2 are based on the Parent Entity's rights to the profits of specific LTCEs. The allocation of Top-up Tax among LTCEs under Article 5.2.4 facilitates the application of the IIR by Parent Entities other than the UPE.'*[1452] Since the application of the IIR is directly linked to the allocable share of 'Parent Entities', it must be clear which amount of 'Top-up Tax' is to be allocated to which CE. Finally, on the one hand, several parent entities may be obliged to apply the IIR with respect to the same CE and (*see* step eight section 4.4.2.8.), on the other hand, the income of CEs located in the same jurisdiction possibly being owned by completely different Parent Entities must be blended for the purpose of Top-up Tax calculation. The Commentary attempts to obscure the obvious complexity of this calculation: *'If [...] the UPE is applying an IIR and all of the LTCEs are wholly-owned, all of the Top-up Tax computed for the jurisdiction is allocable to the UPE under Chapter 2 and therefore, as a practical matter, the UPE does not need to make the allocation among LTCEs under Article 5.2.4.'*[1453] This statement clearly is a whitewash: as soon as only one of the LTCEs located in the jurisdiction concerned is not wholly owned, and even if this is only a minority share, an allocation of the *'Top-up Tax'* is necessary.

1452. *See Ibid.*, para. 22.
1453. *See Ibid.*

Furthermore, this presupposes that there are also no minority interests in the shareholding chain that shift the application of the IIR to a lower level, e.g., in the case of POPEs. But more on that in the following section.[1454]

4.4.2.8 Step 8: Charging the 'Top-up Tax': The GloBE Rules

4.4.2.8.1 Overview: Mechanisms and Rule Order

If there is a 'Jurisdictional Top-up Tax' (Step 6) that is to be allocated to a CE (Step 7), the IIR and the UTPR (so-called GloBE Rules) come into play: they provide an interlocked[1455] set of mechanisms enabling the collection of the 'Top-up Tax' allocated to a specific LTCE at the level of a different CE 'located' in a different jurisdiction. Thus, the IIR and the UTPR embody the 'diabolic machinery'[1456] of GloBE: if the CIT system of a jurisdiction does not achieve the minimum level of 15% of the 'Excess Profits' determined pursuant to GloBE and if it does not collect the 'Top-up Tax' due by way of a QDMTT, a different jurisdiction may collect the 'Top-up Tax'.

The terms 'Income Inclusion Rules' and 'UTPR' (initially 'Undertaxed Payments Rule'[1457]) are misleading from today's perspective: under GloBE, in contrast to CFC rules, income is not attributed from controlled foreign companies to controlling companies. Rather, the 'GloBE Income', the ETR and the minimum tax level are used to calculate how much additional tax must be levied to raise the tax burden to the minimum level from a jurisdictional perspective. The amount of additional tax per jurisdiction is referred to as the 'Top-up Tax', which is then allocated to a different entity within the same 'MNE Group' by means of the IIR and UTPR. Thus, under the IIR and UTPR, income is not attributed to a controlling entity, but an additional amount of tax is levied at the level of a different entity[1458].[1459] In principle, both the IIR and the UTPR applied in Step 8 only determine at which tier of the 'MNE Group's' structure the 'Top-up Tax' of an LTCE is to be levied. For these purposes, GloBE first tests whether there is a 'Parent Entity'[1460] where the 'Top-up Tax' could be collected. This mechanism is the famous IIR: similar to 'CFC regimes', the respective 'Top-up Tax' is levied at the level of a 'Parent Entity' and, thereby, follows a so-called top-down approach.[1461]

1454. This section is based on V. Bendlinger & G. Kofler, *Computation of the Effective Tax Rate and the 'Top-up Tax'*, in *Pillar 2 Global Minimum Tax*, *supra* note 305, at 23–24.
1455. *See GloBE Commentary on Article 2 GloBE Model Rules (2022)*, *supra* note 238, para. 1.
1456. R. Mason, *A Wrench in GLOBE's Diabolic Machinery*, 107 Tax Notes Intl. 1391–1395 (19 Sep. 2022).
1457. *See, i.a.*, *Tax Challenges Arising from Digitalisation – Report on Pillar Two Blueprint*, at 123. The Commission's directive proposal also originally referred to the UTPR as the 'undertaxed payments rule', *see* Art. 1(b) COM(2021)823 final.
1458. *See* Art. 2.2.1. *GloBE Model Rules*: '*A Constituent Entity* [...] *shall pay a tax in an amount equal to its Allocable Share of the Top-up Tax* [...]'. Also *see* Art. 1(a) GloBE-Directive (2022/2523) according to which the IIR '*collects* [a parent entity's] *allocable share of top-up tax in respect of the low-taxed constituent entities of the group*'.
1459. V. Bendlinger & G. Kofler, *supra* note 305, at 10.
1460. *See* the definition of 'Parent Entity' in Art. 10.1. *GloBE Model Rules*, at 62 and Art. 3(24) GloBE-Directive (2022/2523).
1461. *See GloBE Commentary on Article 2 GloBE Model Rules (2022)*, *supra* note 238, para. 17.

The 'Top-up Tax' is basically levied at the highest level in the 'MNE Group', which is, besides the specific case of 'Excluded Entities' (*see* section 4.2.4.3.), the UPE. However, since the IIR, like common 'CFC regimes', only applies in relation to shares held indirectly or directly (so-called Ownership Interest), the UPE's (indirect) participation in the LTCE could be diluted by minority shareholdings within the corporate chain to reduce the amount of 'Top-up Tax' that could be collected by way of the IIR. For this reason, GloBE provides an exception to the 'top-down approach' for so-called Partially Owned Parent Entities (in the following POPEs) if the 'Ownership Interests' in profits of non-MNE Group members exceed 20%. In this case, the obligation to apply the IIR 'falls' down to the respective POPE. The mechanics of the IIR will be extensively examined in section 4.4.2.8.2.

The IIR, however, fails to materialize in three situations: this might either occur (i) if 'Top-up Tax' is allocated to the UPE that is not subject to an IIR within the jurisdiction it is 'located', if (ii) 'Top-up Tax' is allocated to a different CE that is not the UPE but neither the UPE nor any other 'Parent Entity' are subject to an IIR or (iii) with respect to profits that are attributable to minority-shareholders of the LTCE.[1462] In most of the scenarios just mentioned, the UTPR solves the issue: the UTPR basically is a formulaic mechanism distributing the 'Top-up Tax' remaining after the application of the IIR to all CEs that are subject to a so-called Qualified UTPR within their jurisdiction pursuant to a formula based on certain substance criteria. Put in simpler terms, the remaining 'Top-up Tax' is distributed to all CEs not qualifying as LTCEs based on substance criteria. Those jurisdictions that implemented GloBE accordingly simply 'share the cake' of 'Top-up Tax' revenue, as will be seen in section 4.4.2.8.3.

This sequence of technical mechanisms, often referred to as the 'Rule Order', has been extensively discussed in the literature. It is relevant because it determines which jurisdiction will collect the minimum tax revenue. The sequence can be described as follows: first comes the domestic CIT and/or a QDMTT implemented by the tested jurisdiction. This necessarily includes taxes that are, like CFC taxes,[1463] levied by a different state but allocated to the tested jurisdiction. Pursuant to the GloBE Administrative Guidance February 2023, however, QDMTTs take precedence over 'CFC regimes'.[1464] The GloBE Rules only kick in if the ETR of all CEs 'located' within the tested jurisdiction or of all CEs tested on the basis of a subgroup or on an entity basis ('Investment Entities', MOCEs or 'Stateless Entities' is below 15%. Basically, this is the jurisdiction where a CE is 'located'. Finally, there is only 'Jurisdictional Top-up Tax' if either the source jurisdiction did not collect a QDMTT or its QDMTT fails to skim off the whole 'Top-up Tax'. As a result, and as Noked describes it, the 'Primary Taxing Right' belongs to the source jurisdiction (here, the vagueness of the term 'source' is acknowledged but not further discussed). Second, if there is a remaining amount of 'Jurisdiction Top-up Tax', the IIR tries to collect the pending 'Top-up Tax' at the level of a 'Parent Entity', preferably the UPE. Finally, if, for whatever reason, there is no

1462. On these three UTPR scenarios, *see* V. Bendlinger & G. Kofler, *supra* note 305, at 26–27.
1463. On the difficult interaction of the QDMTT and CFC legislation, *see* s. 4.4.2.6.3.
1464. *See* para. 118.30 in *GloBE Commentary on Article 10 GloBE Model Rules (2022)*, *supra* note 280 as amended by *GloBE Administrative Guidance February 2023*, at 105–106.

'Parent Entity' within the 'MNE Group' at which the remaining 'Top-up Tax' could be collected, the UTPR splits the 'Top-up Tax' revenue pursuant to a formula based on substance criteria. Briefly summarized, first comes the local CIT system (including QDMTT), then the IIR, and lastly, the UTPR. Any remaining 'Top-up Tax' that the UTPR cannot cover or is excluded from its scope is not subject to the global minimum tax (*see* Table 14).

Table 14 Overview of GloBE's Rule Order Pursuant to the Update of the Commentary by Way of the GloBE Administrative Guidance February 2023[1465]

Rule Order of GloBE – Overview
1. Domestic CIT at source ('Adjusted Covered Taxes') (including withholding taxes on dividends pursuant to Article 4.3.2(e) GloBE Model Rules, but excluding all other withholding taxes)
2. QDMTT at source (excluding tax allocated from 'CFC regimes' pursuant to Article 4.3.2(c) GloBE Model Rules)
3. Taxes levied by means of a 'CFC regime' (allocated to source jurisdictions pursuant to Article 4.3.2(c) GloBE Model Rules)
4. IIR collected either in the state where the UPE, IPE or POPE is 'located'
5. UTPR collected by 'UTPR Jurisdictions' in which CEs are 'located'

4.4.2.8.2 Income Inclusion Rule to Collect Pending 'Top-up Tax' at the Level of 'Parent Entities'

The basic principle of the IIR is simple; nevertheless, its technical ramifications are highly complex. Its basic operation can be summarized as follows: if a 'Top-up Tax' arises at the level of the LTCE that has not been collected, i.e., by a QDMTT, the IIR, as a rule, allows the UPE to collect the respective 'Top-up Tax' and if it cannot be collected at the UPE, i.e., because the UPE is an 'Excluded Entity' or it is not subject to a so-called Qualified IIR (in detail on that term below) where it is 'located', the next CE down the ownership chain may collect the pending 'Top-up Tax' (so-called top-down approach).[1466] The complex ramifications arise from the exceptions to this regime: to avoid that minority shareholdings within the ownership chain ('split-ownership structures')[1467] dilute the effects of the IIR, the application of the IIR is, under certain conditions, pushed down to so-called Partially Owned Parent Entities (POPEs).

As already anticipated, the UPE has priority in the application of the IIR: this is manifested in Article 2.1.1. GloBE Model Rules (reflected in Article 1[a] and Article 5[1] GloBE-Directive): '*A Constituent Entity, that is the Ultimate Parent Entity of an MNE Group, [...] that owns (directly or indirectly) an Ownership Interest in a Low-Taxed*

1465. A similar overview is provided by H. Wardell-Burrus, *GloBE Administrative Guidance – The QDMTT and GILTI Allocation*, SSRN 9 (SSRN 2023), https://papers.ssrn.com/sol3/papers.cfm?abstract_id=4347814 (last visited 28 Mar. 2023).
1466. *See GloBE Commentary on Article 2*, *supra* note 238, para. 1.
1467. This term is in particular used in *Ibid.*, paras 3c and 7.

Constituent Entity at any time during the Fiscal Year shall pay a tax in an amount equal to its Allocable Share of the Top-up Tax of that Low-Taxed Constituent Entity for the Fiscal Year.'[1468] From Article 2.1.1. GloBE Model Rules and Article 5(1) GloBE-Directive results the obligation for the UPE of an 'MNE Group' to apply the IIR in relation to its LTCEs and serves as the 'main rule'[1469] for the IIR. Apart from the condition that the corresponding CE is also UPE of the corresponding 'MNE Group', both provisions require that the UPE holds either directly or indirectly an 'Ownership Interest' in an LTCE at any time during the 'Fiscal Year'. The term 'Low-Taxed Constituent Entity' (LTCE) has already been addressed in the course Step 3 of the 'Top-up Tax' computation in section 4.4.2.3.: an LTCE either is a CE that is 'located' in a 'Low-Tax Jurisdiction' (that is, a jurisdiction for which the ETR calculation in Step 3 resulted in an ETR below the 'Minimum Rate')[1470] or a CE that is considered 'stateless' and is subject to an ETR below the 'Minimum Rate'.[1471] If the application of the IIR is performed in Step 8, it is obvious that this requirement is fulfilled. The next requirement of Article 2.1.1. GloBE Model Rules is the possession of a direct or indirect 'Ownership Interest'. This factual characteristic is also unproblematic: the scope of GloBE already presupposes that an 'MNE Group', i.e., a group of CEs, is linked to each other via 'Ownership Interest'. A UPE of an 'MNE Group' of CEs, therefore, always holds an 'Ownership Interest' in an LTCE of the same 'MNE Group'.[1472] This might be the reason for the fact that neither Article 1(a) nor Article 5(1) GloBE-Directive actually appeal to this implicit requirement. Nevertheless, the term 'Ownership Interest' is separately defined in both the GloBE Model Rules and the GloBE-Directive, covering '*any equity interest that carries rights to the profits, capital or reserves of an Entity, including the profits, capital or reserves of a Main Entity's Permanent Establishment's*'.[1473] The definition is, therefore, mainly relevant to PEs. After all, PEs do not qualify as legal entities in their own right but are recorded as individual CEs for GloBE purposes. The fictitious 'Ownership Interest' in a PE is therefore attributed 100% to the main entity. In the case of partnerships, which, as a rule, also qualify as PEs, different 'Ownership Interest' ratios might, of course, occur, even with respect to PEs. But as the Commentary reveals, the amount of 'Ownership Interest' is not relevant for the applicability of Article 2.1.1. GloBE Model Rules (the same is true for Article 5 GloBE-Directive) as such.[1474] Rather, as Article 2.1.1. GloBE Model Rules states that the

---

1468. Article 2.1.1. *GloBE Model Rules*.
1469. *See GloBE Commentary on Article 2, supra* note 238, paras 4 and 11.
1470. *See* the definition of the term 'Low-Tax Jurisdiction' in Art. 10.1. *GloBE Model Rules*, at 60 and Art. 3(35) GloBE-Directive (2022/2523).
1471. *See* the definition of the term 'Low-Taxed Constituent Entity' in Art. 10.1. *GloBE Model Rules*, at 60 and Art. 3(19) GloBE-Directive (2022/2523).
1472. Note, however, that accounting rules may lead to the fact that the same entity is consolidated within the consolidated financial statements of two different UPEs. In this case, an LTCE would be part of two different MNE Groups and either UPE of the two MNE Groups would be obliged to apply the IIR with respect to their 'Allocable Share' of 'Top-up Tax'.
1473. *See* the definition of 'Ownership Interest' in Art. 10.1. *GloBE Model Rules*, at 62 and using nearly the identical wording, *see* Art. 3(23) GloBE-Directive (2022/2523).
1474. *See GloBE Commentary on Article 2, supra* note 238, para. 11.

'Ownership Interest' must be held '*at any time during the Fiscal Year*'. The Commentary, thus, concludes that '[t]*he holding period of the interests during the Fiscal Year is not relevant for the purposes of applying Article 2.1.1. because this is already reflected in the computation of the Top-up Tax in Chapter 5*' as the 'Top-up Tax' already '*takes into account the amount of income reported in the Consolidated Financial Statements*'.[1475] The Commentary further notes that the details set out in Article 6.2. GloBE Model Rules on CEs joining and leaving the Group provide further details in this respect. Both, Article 1(a) and Article 5 GloBE-Directive have refrained from explicitly mentioning the temporal component at all. The question of whether the requirements of IIR are met depends on the size of the group, and also Article 35 GloBE-Directive already prescribes how to deal with CEs acquired or sold during the year for purposes of ETR and 'Top-up Tax' computation. As a result, one could argue that the prerequisites of Article 2.1.1. GloBE Model Rules and Article 5 GloBE-Directive break down to the question of scope already determined during Step 1 and the ETR computation and merely oblige the UPE to apply the IIR with respect to its 'Allocable Share' of 'Top-up Tax'.

Both the GloBE Model Rules as well as the GloBE-Directive each dedicate a separate article to the definition of the term 'Allocable Share' of 'Top-up Tax' with respect to the IIR. Both, Article 2.2. GloBE Model Rules and Article 9 GloBE-Directive provide for a set of rules to determine the proportion of the 'Parent Entity's' share of the 'Top-up Tax' arising at the LTCE that is to be allocated by means of the IIR. In simplified terms, the 'Allocable Share' (Article 2.2.2. GloBE Model Rules and Article 9[2] GloBE-Directive) is the proportion between '*the (a) GloBE Income of the* [LTCE] *for the Fiscal Year, reduced by the amount of such income attributable to Ownership Interests held by other owners, to (b) the GloBE Income of the [LTCE] for the Fiscal Year*'.[1476] Within the GloBE Model Rules, this proportion is referred to as the so-called Inclusion Ratio (*see* Figure 9).

Figure 9 'Allocable Share' ('Inclusion Ratio') Pursuant to Article 2.2.2. GloBE Model Rules and Article 9(2) GloBE-Directive

$$\text{'Allocable Share'} = \frac{\text{GloBE Income of LTCE} - \text{GloBE Income attributable to third parties}}{\text{GloBE Income of LTCE}}$$

The GloBE Income of the LTCE that is attributable to non-group shareholders is to be computed pursuant to a specific mechanism that is provided for in Article 2.2.3. GloBE Model Rules and the second subparagraph of Article 9(2) GloBE-Directive. The rules are rather technical and closely follow accounting rules: even if the UPE does not own 100% of the shares in an LTCE, it would nevertheless have to consolidate 100% of the assets, liabilities, income, and expenses of the respective entity. For this reason, financial accounting standards regularly require accounting for the cumulative equity of minority shareholders (so-called Non-Controlling-Interest in short NCI). This also

1475. *See Ibid.*, para. 13.
1476. Article 2.2.2. *GloBE Model Rules* and Art. 9(2) GloBE-Directive (2022/2523).

requires, for example, that the income and loss be reduced with respect to the amounts attributable to NCI. Otherwise, as the Commentary emphasizes, '*the Consolidated Financial Statements would overstate the portion of the income of the consolidated group*'.[1477] As the Commentary further sums up, the GloBE Rules '*leverage the principles that the UPE applies* [...] *in its Consolidated Financial Statements to determine the share of income of the Financial Accounting Net Income or Loss that belongs to other owners of an LTCE that it does not wholly own*'.[1478] As a result, the 'Allocable Share' of 'Top-up Tax' of the UPE is to be determined mainly pursuant to accounting principles and the NCI recorded in its 'Consolidated Financial Accounts'.

If GloBE would only enable to subject the MNE to an IIR, the IIR could not be applied to any other 'Parent Entity'[1479] of a LTCE below the UPE. Thus, the IIR would fail either (i) if the UPE state did not apply an IIR to the UPE at all or (ii) if the UPE qualified as an 'Excluded Entity' (*see* section 4.2.4.3.). The GloBE Model Rules address both situations in Article 2.1.2. GloBE Model Rules and simply obliges any other so-called Intermediate Parent Entities (IPEs)[1480] that are not the UPE of the MNE Group to apply the IIR. The same rule can be found in the GloBE-Directive, but in contrast to this, both situations in which it is not possible to collect the IIR at the UPE are found in separate articles: Article 6(1) GloBE-Directive obliges an IPE to apply the IIR if the UPE is 'located' in a third country and Article 7(1) GloBE-Directive obliges an IPE to apply the IIR if the UPE is an 'Excluded Entity'. The Commission might have decided to translate Article 2.1.2. GloBE Model Rules into two different articles because, besides the case of an excluded UPE, an IPE 'located' within the Union should only be forced to apply the IIR if its UPE is 'located' in a third jurisdiction. Finally, if the UPE is 'located' within the EU, the respective UPE would be subject to an IIR pursuant to Article 1(a) and Article 5 GloBE-Directive anyway.

In any case, Article 2.1.2. GloBE Model Rules and its counterparts Articles 6(1) and 7(1) GloBE-Directive, thus, manifest the IIRs 'top-down approach': if IIR collection at the level of the UPE is supposed to fail, every other IPE down the ownership chain would in principle be obliged to apply the IIR.[1481] The term IPE covers all CEs (besides the UPE, PEs[1482] and 'Investment Entities'[1483]) which hold an 'Ownership Interest' in at least one other CE of the same 'MNE Group' and do not have more than 20% of the Ownership Interests in its profits held directly or indirectly by persons that are not CEs

1477. *See GloBE Commentary on Article 2*, *supra* note 238, para. 31.
1478. *See Ibid.*, para. 32.
1479. A 'Parent Entity' either is an UPE that is not an 'Excluded Entity' or an IPE or a POPE, *see* Art. 10.1. *GloBE Model Rules*, at 62 and Art. 3(24) GloBE-Directive (2022/2523).
1480. *See* the definition of 'Intermediate Parent Entity', where it is clarified that neither UPEs, POPEs, GloBE PEs nor 'Stateless Entities' can qualify as 'Intermediate Parent Entity', *see* Art. 10.1. *GloBE Model Rules*. Also *see* Art. 3(20) GloBE-Directive (2022/2523).
1481. *See GloBE Commentary on Article 2*, *supra* note 238, paras 5–6.
1482. The reason for excluding PEs from the IPE definition, is a thought of simplification: Pursuant to the Commentary, the OECD intended to avoid 'difficult factual determinations and disputes as to whether' 'Ownership Interest' shall be attributed to a PE or its 'Main Entity', *see Ibid.*, para. 14.
1483. The Commentary justifies the exclusion of 'Investment Entities' by arguing that their '*tax neutrality* [...] *vis-à-vis any minority-interest holders*' should be preserved, *see Ibid.*, In detail on the concept of 'Investment Entities' within GloBE, *see* s. 4.3.2.2.3.

of the 'MNE Group' (the latter entities would qualify as POPEs and are excluded from the definition of IPEs as well, in detail see shortly).[1484] As with regard to UPEs, the IIR only applies with respect to the 'Allocable Share' of 'Top-up Tax' attributable to the IPE. However, entities below the UPE usually are not required to prepare 'Consolidated Financial Statements' and do not account for NCI. For this reason, Article 2.2.3. GloBE Model Rules and the second subparagraph of Article 9(2) GloBE-Directive provide for a set of assumptions to determine the 'Allocable Share' ('Inclusion Ratio') of 'Top-up Tax':[1485] the IPE is assumed to prepare a hypothetical 'Consolidated Financial Statements' pursuant to the accounting standard applied by the UPE, that it held a 'Controlling Interest' in the LTCE and that all 'Ownership Interests' not directly or indirectly held by the IPE were held by persons other than CEs. If the IIR is applied to IPEs, the latter assumption ensures that the IIR is only applied 'downwards' and not with respect to 'Ownership Interest' held by a CE which is not connected to the IPE (e.g., sister entities within the same 'MNE Group', *see* the far right example provided in Figure 11 in this section).

It is obvious that obliging the UPE and every IPE down the ownership chain to apply the IIR would result in a multiple collection of a LTCE's 'Top-up Tax' within the same MNE Group. For this reason, Article 2.1.3. GloBE Model Rules and Article 6(3) as well as Article 7(3) GloBE-Directive again exempt IPEs from the obligation to apply the IIR (pursuant to Article 2.1.3. GloBE Model Rules and Article 6[1] and Article 7[1] GloBE-Directive), if either the UPE[1486] or another IPE owning a 'Controlling Interest'[1487] at a higher tier within the same 'MNE Group' is subject to a so-called Qualified IIR. But what is 'Qualified IIR'?

The question of whether a domestic tax regime qualifies as a 'Qualified IIR' is key for the functioning of GloBE and is not a mere technicality: if a jurisdiction applies a tax regime to its resident UPEs that do not qualify as 'Qualified IIR', any other jurisdiction where an IPE of the same 'MNE Group' is 'located' might collect any 'Top-up Tax' of an LTCE within the same 'MNE Group'. Indeed, this had been a delicate tax policy debate[1488] with respect to the US hosting by far the most 'MNE Groups' being subject to GloBE: the US GILTI regime had been a role model for the whole minimum tax debate but significantly differs in design from the IIR, in particular, due to the fact that it applies a global blending approach. From the very beginning, it was thus questioned whether the US GILTI regime would qualify as a 'Qualified IIR' because if it does not, other 'source' jurisdictions would consider GILTI as a 'CFC regime' and would apply the IIR to its resident IPEs with respect to 'Top-up Tax' arising at LTCEs below the

1484. Article 10.1. *GloBE Model Rules*, at 58 and Art. 3(20) GloBE-Directive (2022/2523). In detail on the IPE definition in the Commentary, *see GloBE Commentary on Article 2, supra* note 238, para. 14.

1485. *See GloBE Commentary on Article 2, supra* note 238, paras 32–36.

1486. Article 2.1.3.(a) *GloBE Model Rules* and Art. 6(3)(a) GloBE-Directive (2022/2523).

1487. Article 2.1.3.(b) *GloBE Model Rules* and Art. 6(3)(b) and Art. 7(3) GloBE-Directive (2022/2523).

1488. *See*, e.g., M. Herzfeld, *More on GLOBE Ordering: CFC Rules*, 106 Tax Notes Intl., *supra* note 1230, at 603–607; H. Wardell-Burrus, *Should CFC Regimes Grant a Tax Credit For Qualified Domestic Minimum Top-up Taxes?*, 106 Tax Notes Intl., *supra* note 1381, at 1655 et seq.; L.A. Sheppard, *Pillar 2 and QDMTT*, 105 Tax Notes Intl., *supra* note 1439, at 760 et seq.

ownership chain despite the fact that the US resident UPE might be subject to a GILTI tax. Pursuant to the GloBE Model Rules, the term 'Qualified IIR' '*means a set of rules equivalent to Article 2.1 to Article 2.3 of the GloBE Rules (including any provisions of the GloBE Rules associated with those articles) that are included in the domestic law of a jurisdiction and that are implemented and administered in a way that is consistent with the outcomes provided for under the GloBE Rules and the Commentary provided that such jurisdiction does not provide any benefits that are related to such rules*'.[1489] The definition is very similar to that of 'QDMTT', which is why the same issues of interpretation addressed in section 4.4.2.6.3. also, arise with respect to the 'Qualified IIR'. A corresponding definition can be found in Article 3(18) GloBE-Directive, differing only in that it necessarily distinguishes between 'Qualified IIR' of Member States and third countries: the standard of '*equivalence*' for another Member State is, of course, the implementation according to the GloBE-Directive itself; with regard to third countries, Article 3(18) GloBE-Directive refers to the '*equivalence*' with the GloBE Model Rules. So, the elephant in the room is the question of how to interpret the term '*equivalence*'.

The EU Commission did not hesitate to make it clear already in the GloBE-Directive Proposal published in December 2021[1490] and now also in the final GloBE-Directive that the US GILTI regime, at least from a European perspective, should not be viewed as a 'Qualified IIR'. The GloBE-Directive devotes a separate Article 52 to the question, under which conditions the domestic law of a third-country jurisdiction '*shall be considered to be equivalent to a qualified IIR set out in Chapter II, and shall not be treated as a controlled foreign company tax regime*'.[1491] It is interesting to note that Article 52(2) GloBE-Directive empowers the EU Commission to adopt delegated acts '*to determine the list of third-country jurisdictions that have implemented a legal framework in their domestic law which is considered to be equivalent to a qualified IIR*'.[1492] Thus, the Commission has a considerable margin of discretion to decide whether a certain tax regime is considered '*equivalent*' and fulfils the requirements for a 'Qualified IIR' preventing IIR liability on EU resident IPEs of 'MNE Groups' headed in third countries.

The conditions include that (i) the jurisdiction enforces that a 'Parent Entity' within an 'MNE Group' computes and pays its allocable share of top-up tax with respect to LTCEs within the same MNE Group,[1493] (ii) it establishes a tax rate of at least 15%,[1494] (iii) it applies a jurisdictional blending approach[1495] and (iv) it provides for relief for any top-up tax levied by an EU Member State.[1496] With these criteria, it is clear that GILTI does not meet the requirements for a 'Qualified IIR' from the EU perspective and taxes collected by GILTI are included as CFC taxes in the LTCE's 'Adjusted Covered

1489. Article 10.1. *GloBE Model Rules*, at 64.
1490. *See* Art. 51 COM(2021)823 final.
1491. Article 52(1) GloBE-Directive (2022/2523).
1492. Article 52(2) *Ibid.*
1493. Article 52(1)(a) *Ibid.*
1494. Article 52(1)(b) *Ibid.*
1495. Article 52(1)(c) *Ibid.*
1496. Article 52(1)(d) *Ibid.*

Taxes'. For the EU, this is even disadvantageous in terms of tax policy, as already discussed extensively in section 4.4.2.8.1., as CFC taxes are included within the ETR computation even before the IIR. From the perspective of GloBE's 'Rule Order', GILTI prevails.[1497] This would be different if GILTI were considered a 'Qualified IIR'. However, on the other hand, if GILTI fails to raise the ETR of a US resident 'MNE Group' within a specific jurisdiction, the EU Member States are not hindered from collecting any 'Top-up Tax' at the level of EU IPEs of the same MNE Group, because, from an EU perspective, the UPE would not be subject to a 'Qualified IIR'. In the meantime, also the GloBE Administrative Guidance February 2023 clearly points out that the US GILTI regime does not qualify as a 'Qualified IIR' but rather as a 'CFC regime'.[1498]

Leaving the path of tax policy considerations back to the technical framework: the notion of 'Qualified IIR' is essential for consistent implementation of the IIR's 'top-down approach'. IPEs should only be subject to the IIR if the latter cannot be applied at the level of the UPE. Consequently, if the UPE or any IPE below is subject to a 'Qualified IIR', a lower IPE should not be subject to an IIR again, which is why Article 2.1.3. GloBE Model Rules and Article 6(3), as well as Article 7(3) GloBE-Directive, nullify the tax liability of the IPE. It should be noted that the IIR only applies to the 'Allocable Share' of 'Top-up Tax', i.e., essentially to the shares actually held by the parent entity (in detail on the concept of 'Allocable Share', *see* below). The IIR, thus, does not collect any 'Top-up Tax' that is allocable to minority shareholders that are not part of the 'MNE Group'. However, this could circumvent the scope of the IIR: assume an 'MNE Group' consists of three different CEs 'located' in three different jurisdictions. The UPE holds 60% of the shares in an intermediate CE, which again holds 60% of the shares in an LTCE, and the 'Top-up Tax' at the level of the LTCE amounts to 100. If we applied the IIR, it is clear that both the UPE and the intermediate CE would qualify as an IPE and would, in principle, be subject to the IIR. The UPE would have to pay 'Top-up Tax' due to the IIR at the amount of 36. The IPE would have to pay a 'Top-up Tax' in the amount of 60; however, its obligation to apply the IIR pursuant to Article 2.1.2. GloBE Model Rules (reflected in Article 6[1] GloBE-Directive) would not materialize because the IPE would be exempt due to Article 2.1.3.(a) GloBE Model Rules (reflected in Article 6[3] GloBE-Directive). In fact, only 36% of the pending 'Top-up Tax' would be levied by means of the IIR.[1499]

To avoid this outcome and to limit tax planning opportunities[1500] with respect to such 'split-ownership structures', GloBE incorporates an '*exception to the top-down approach*'[1501] for so-called Partially Owned Parent Entities (POPEs). POPEs[1502] are

1497. That point has been made by M. Herzfeld, *More on GLOBE Ordering: CFC Rules*, 106 Tax Notes Intl., *supra* note 1230, at 603 et seq.
1498. *See GloBE Administrative Guidance February 2023*, at 67–70.
1499. *See* the example provided for in *GloBE Commentary on Article 2 GloBE Model Rules (2022)*, *supra* note 238, para. 8.
1500. Further on the purpose of the POPE-exception, *see Ibid.*
1501. *See Ibid.*, para. 9.
1502. *See* the definition of 'Partially Owned Parent Entities' in Art. 10.1. *GloBE Model Rules*, at 62 and Art. 3(22) GloBE-Directive (2022/2523).

defined as CEs which hold an 'Ownership Interest' in other CEs of the same 'MNE Group' and have more than 20 % of the 'Ownership Interest' in its profits held directly or indirectly by persons that are not CEs of the 'MNE Group'.[1503] The definition of IPE and POPE are mutually exclusive: although POPEs would, in principle, qualify as IPE, they are explicitly excluded from the IPE definition (POPEs and IPEs, however, share that they are considered as 'Parent Entities').[1504] This is because, in contrast to IPEs, POPEs have priority in the application of the IIR even over the UPE of the 'MNE Group': according to Article 2.1.4. GloBE Model Rules and Article 8(1) GloBE-Directive, they are subject to the IIR like the UPE or an IPE, but differently to the latter, they are not exempt from applying the IIR, even if the UPE or an IPE above the respective POPE in the ownership chain would be subject to the IIR as well.[1505] Rather, the UPE or any other IPE may reduce its 'Top-up Tax' according to Article 2.3.1. GloBE Model Rules and Article 10 GloBE-Directive to avoid multiple charging of 'Top-up Tax' on the same 'Ownership Interest' (so-called IIR Offset Mechanism).[1506] Within a chain of POPEs that are connected by 100% participation, pursuant to Article 2.1.5. GloBE-Directive and Article 8(3) GloBE-Directive, the IIR only applies to the highest POPE in the ownership chain, establishing a kind of 'top-down approach' among POPEs.[1507]

Again, take the example as set out above: an 'MNE Group' consists of three different CEs 'located' in three different jurisdictions. The UPE holds 60% of the shares in an intermediate CE, which again holds 60% of the shares in an LTCE, and the 'Top-up Tax' at the level of the LTCE amounts to 100. Rather than considering the intermediate CE as an IPE, the respective CE would qualify as POPE and would have priority in the application of the IIR and would collect its allocable share 'Top-up Tax', which is 60 in this example. Consequently, the 'Top-up Tax' is also collected with respect to 'Top-up Tax' that would be attributable to minority shareholders of the intermediate CE whose participation in the 'Top-up Tax' would otherwise not be collected. The UPE would, however, still be subject to the IIR and would be obliged to collect an amount of 36 in 'Top-up Tax'. To avoid double and multiple collections of the same 'Top-up Tax', the UPE can claim an 'IIR Offset' pursuant to Article 2.3.1. GloBE Model Rules and Article 10 GloBE-Directive and can credit any 'Top-up Tax' collected at a lower tier 'Parent Entity'. Consequently, in this example, the UPE would receive a credit for the full amount of 60, and the POPE would collect the total amount of 'Top-up Tax' (100) arising at the level of the LTCE.

The following chart gives an example and compares the operation of the IIR with respect to UPEs, IPEs and POPEs (*see* Figure 10).

1503. It follows that all MOPEs are also POPEs. Consequently, in the case of 'Minority-Owned Subgroups', the 'Top-up Tax' is usually levied at the level of the MOPE.
1504. *See* the definition of 'Intermediate Parent Entity' in Art. 10.1. *GloBE Model Rules*. Also *see* Art. 3(20) GloBE-Directive (2022/2523).
1505. Also *see* Art. 7 GloBE-Directive (2022/2523).
1506. In detail on the 'IIR Offset Mechanism', *see GloBE Commentary on Article 2*, *supra* note 238, paras 38–40.
1507. In detail, *see Ibid.*, paras 22–23.

Figure 10 Comparison on the Application of the IIR at the Level of the UPE, an IPE and a POPE

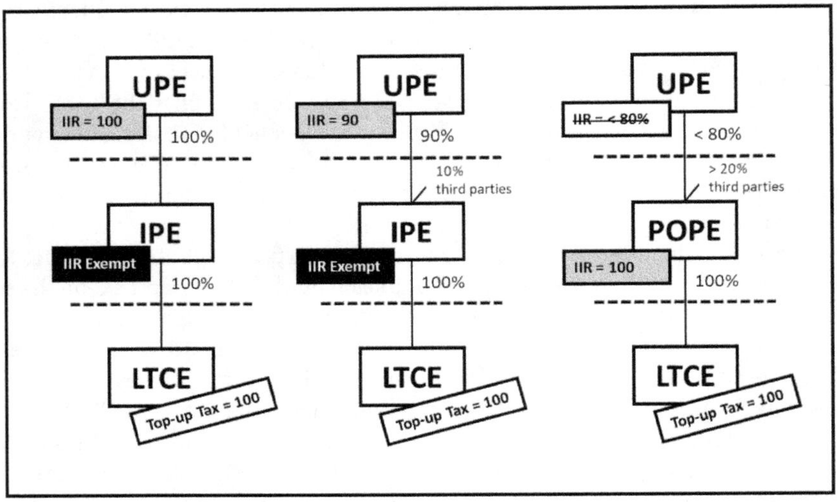

In the corporate structure on the left of Figure 10, the 'MNE Group' consists of 100% participation. The entire 'Top-up Tax' at the level of the LTCE can be allocated by the IIR according to Article 2.1.1 GloBE Model Rules (Article 5[1] GloBE-Directive). The IPE is exempt according to Article 2.1.3 GloBE Model Rules (Article 6[3][a] GloBE-Directive). In the middle structure, the UPE indirectly holds only 90% of LTCE. However, one IPE holds all shares in the LTCE. In the IPE, 10% of the shares are held by shareholders outside the 'MNE Group'. In contrast to the case on the left, one could argue that the obligation to levy the IIR could also become effective to the IPE with respect to the minority shares, for which the 'Top-up Tax' cannot already be levied at the level of the UPE. However, both Article 2.1.3. GloBE Model Rules and Article 6(3)(a) GloBE-Directive state that the obligation of the IPE to apply the IIR shall not become effective if the UPE is subject to a 'Qualified IIR'. For this reason, the 'Top-up Tax' attributable to the minority shareholders would not be collected by the IIR. With regard to the structure on the right, the intermediate CE would, in principle, qualify as IPE but is excluded from the IPE definition due to the fact that it qualifies as a POPE because the UPE only holds less than 80% of the shares in the respective CE. However, as in the other two cases, the POPE holds 100% of the LTCE. Here, the special provisions of Articles 2.1.4. and 2.3. GloBE Model Rules come into play (also *see* Articles 8 and 9[2] GloBE-Directive): according to Article 2.1.4. GloBE Model Rules (Article 8[1] GloBE-Directive), the POPE is obliged to apply the IIR and cannot rely on an exemption under Article 2.1.5. GloBE Model Rules (Article 8[3] GloBE-Directive). The multiple charging of the 'Top-up Tax' at the UPE on the one hand and the POPE on the other is avoided by enabling the UPE to reduce its own allocable share of Top-up

Tax of the LTCE according to Article 2.3.1 GloBE Model Rules (Article 10 GloBE-Directive) through the so-called IIR Offset Mechanism.[1508]

The following chart shall further demonstrate the application of the IIR in the case of 'split-ownership structures' in four different scenarios.

Figure 11 Examples of the Application of the IIR in 'Split-Ownership Structures'

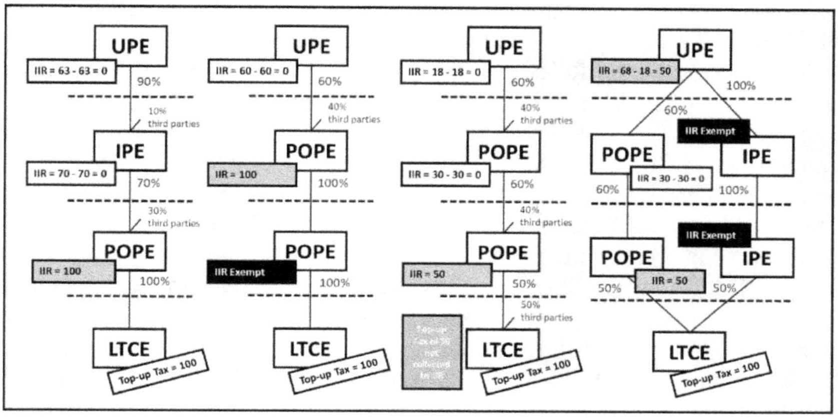

In the first structure on the left, the POPE directly holding an 'Ownership Interest' is subject to the IIR due to Article 2.1.4. GloBE Model Rules or Article 8(1) GloBE-Directive. The UPE and the IPE are subject to the IIR as well, pursuant to Article 2.1.1. and 2.1.2. GloBE Model Rules or Articles 5(1) and 6(1) GloBE-Directive, respectively; however, both the UPE and the IPE will receive an 'IIR Offset' which will fully cover their 'Allocable Share' of 'Top-up Tax'.[1509] The second structure from the left demonstrates the operation of Article 2.1.6 GloBE Model Rules and Article 8(3) GloBE-Directive: although both intermediate CEs would qualify as POPE, only the higher POPE is subject to the IIR because it owns the lower POPE. The UPE would again be subject to 'Top-up Tax' under Article 2.1.1. GloBE Model Rules and Article 5(1) GloBE-Directive, but receives an 'IIR Offset' that fully covers the UPE's 'Allocable Share' of 'Top-up Tax'. In contrast, in the second structure from the right, although the lower tier POPE is held by another POPE, the former does not qualify for an exemption under Article 2.1.6 GloBE Model Rules or Article 8(3) GloBE-Directive, because it is not wholly held by the higher tier POPE. In this case, the IIR is applied to the lower-tier POPE owning an 'Allocable Share' of 'Top-up Tax' of 50.[1510] Both the UPE and the upper-tier POPE are subject to the IIR pursuant to Article 2.1.1. and 2.1.4. GloBE Model

1508. This example is based on V. Bendlinger & G. Kofler, *Computation of the Effective Tax Rate and the 'Top-up Tax'*, in *Pillar 2 Global Minimum Tax, supra* note 305, at 26.
1509. The functioning of the 'IIR Offset' is also demonstrated in Example 2.3.2 – 1 and Example 2.3.2 – 2 *GloBE Examples*, at 13–15.
1510. This is demonstrated in Example 2.1.5 – 2 *Ibid.*, at 9–10.

Rules or Articles 5(1) and 8(1) GloBE-Directive as well but are again eligible to an 'IIR Offset'. The remaining 50 of 'Top-up Tax' are '*attributable to Ownership Interests* [...] *held by*'[1511] non-group shareholders, which is why the IIR will not collect the remaining 50 of 'Top-up Tax'. The structure to the right demonstrates the application of the 'split-ownership rules' in a more complex structure:[1512] the UPE indirectly holds 68% of the 'Ownership Interest' in the LTCE. However, the whole amount of pending 'Top-up Tax' at the LTCE is collected: the UPE holds 18% indirectly via two POPEs. The IIR will finally be collected by the lower-tier POPE as it is not wholly owned by the other POPE. Rather, the higher POPE and the UPE will receive an 'IIR Offset' pursuant to Article 2.3. GloBE Model Rules and Article 10 GloBE-Directive with respect to '*an amount equal to* [their] *portion of [...] Allocable Share of the Top-up Tax that is brought into charge by*'[1513] the POPE below. With respect to the UPE, this is an amount of 18. As can be seen, the lower-tier POPE finally also collects 32 of 'Top-up Tax' that would, from an overall perspective, be attributable to non-group shareholders. In addition to the 18% indirectly held via the two POPEs, the UPE further holds 50% via wholly owned IPEs. While both of the latter would be subject to the IIR pursuant to Article 2.1.2. GloBE Model Rules and Article 6(1) GloBE-Directive, both are exempted from the IIR by way of Article 2.1.3.(a) GloBE Model Rules and Article 6(3)(a) GloBE-Directive, because the UPE is subject to a 'Qualified IIR'. Altogether, the UPE would have to collect an amount of 68 of IIR but can credit an amount of 18 as an 'IIR Offset' with respect to its indirectly held 'Allocable Share' of 'Top-up Tax' that had already been collected by the lower-tier POPE.

From a technical perspective, one can conclude that the application of the IIR might be easy if only wholly owned participations are at issue: in this case, the IIR would, pursuant to Article 2.1.1. GloBE Model Rules and Article 5 GloBE-Directive, only apply to the UPE with respect to all group members. Article 2.2.2. GloBE Model Rules and Article 6(1) GloBE-Directive would, in principle, very well subject any IPEs to the IIR as well. However, these IPEs would be exempt from applying the IIR pursuant to Article 2.1.3.(a) GloBE Model Rules and Article 6(3)(a) GloBE-Directive because the UPE would be subject to a 'Qualified IIR' already. GloBE leads to the same result if any 'Parent Entity' beside the UPE is held to at least 80% by other CEs. In this case, GloBE accepts that 'Top-up Tax' attributable to minority shareholders cannot be collected by means of the IIR. If, however, in between the ownership chain, there is a 'Parent Entity' in which the non-group shareholders' participations exceed 20%, the respective entity qualifies as POPE (instead of an IPE), and the application of the IIR would fall down to the POPE closest to the LTCE within the ownership chain, unless the respective POPE is wholly owned by another POPE that is higher in the ownership chain. As can be seen, the application of the IIR gains significant complexity if minority shareholdings are involved. The complex rules, however, leave loopholes for tax planning: from a

1511. Article 2.2.3. *GloBE Model Rules*. Also *see* Art. 9(2) GloBE-Directive (2022/2523).

1512. Similar examples can be found in the OECD example collection, *see* in particular Example 2.2.3 – 1 and 2.3.2 – 2 *GloBE Examples*, at 10–11 and 14–15.

1513. Article 2.3.2. *GloBE Model Rules*. Using a similar phrasing, *see* Art. 10 GloBE-Directive (2022/2523).

technical perspective, it is advantageous to have participations below 100% but above 80% within the MNE Group because, in this case, any 'Top-up Tax' attributable to minority shareholders would not be collected by means of the IIR.

Pursuant to Article 2.1.6. GloBE Model Rules, the IIR is either to be collected from the UPE, an IPE or a POPE and shall only apply with respect '*to a Low-Taxed Constituent Entity that is not located*' within the same jurisdiction. The GloBE Model Rules, thus, assume that the IIR shall not be applied with respect to domestic LTCEs, even if the LTCE is the UPE itself. The Commentary, thus, recognizes '*that some IF members may wish to extend the application of the IIR domestically in order to avoid discriminating between domestic and foreign*'[1514] CEs and implement a so-called domestic IIR.[1515] This is a silent acknowledgement in particular to the EU, as doubts were raised whether the exclusion of domestic CEs would be in line with the requirements of the fundamental freedoms and indeed, the GloBE-Directive in this respect deviates from the GloBE Model Rules: to avoid any discrimination that might be in tension with the fundamental freedoms or the treaty non-discrimination provision of Article 24 OECD MC, the GloBE-Directive explicitly requires that the IIR is also applied with respect to LTCEs '*that are located in the same Member State*' as the respective 'Parent Entity', irrespective of whether the IIR is applied at the level of a UPE,[1516] an IPE,[1517] an IPE held by an 'Excluded Entity'[1518] or a POPE.[1519] This ensures that the EU Member States do not treat domestic LTCEs differently from foreign LTCEs and serves to assure the GloBE-Directive's compatibility with EU primary law (in detail on this issue, *see* section 6.2.2.1.). Consequently, Articles 6 to 8 GloBE-Directive also force EU resident UPEs, IPEs or POPEs to apply the IIR with respect to themselves. If, e.g., an EU resident UPE is an LTCE, the UPE would collect the 'Top-up Tax' with respect to itself.[1520]

The IIR has regularly been compared to 'CFC regimes'[1521] (also advocated by the OECD),[1522] and indeed, there are definitely common elements: both pursue to increase the tax burdens of profits, and both are levied at the level of a 'Parent Entity'. Nevertheless, one might also find distinctive elements: while 'CFC regimes' regularly level up the tax on specific categories of foreign profits up to the domestic tax level of the parent entity's residence state, the IIR subjects all foreign profits (besides 'International Shipping Income') without distinction but only up to the minimum tax rate. Furthermore, the IIR is not levied on certain kinds of profits but rather collects a 'Top-up Tax', which is not an item of income but rather an amount of tax. Finally, it has been argued that common

1514. *See GloBE Commentary on Article 2 GloBE Model Rules (2022)*, *supra* note 238, para. 24.
1515. On the 'domestic IIR', *see Ibid.*, paras 10 and 24-26.
1516. Article 5(2) GloBE-Directive (2022/2523).
1517. Article 6(2) *Ibid.*
1518. Article 7(2) *Ibid.*
1519. Article 8(2) *Ibid.*
1520. Explicitly, *see* Arts 5(2), 6(2), 7(2) and 8(2) *Ibid.*
1521. *See*, e.g., Kasper Dziurdź, *Income Inclusion Rule Im Vergleich Zur Hinzurechnungsbesteuerung – Funktionsweise, Zweck Und Auswirkungen*, 31 SWI 554-563 (2021); J. Hey, *The 2020 Pillar Two Blueprint: What Can the GloBE Income Inclusion Rule Do That CFC Legislation Can't Do?*, 49 Intertax 7-13 (2021) DOI: 10.54648/taxi2021002; A.P. Dourado, *The Pillar Two Top-Up Taxes: Interplay, Characterization, and Tax Treaties*, 50 Intertax 392-393 (1 May 2022) DOI: 10.54648/taxi2022045.
1522. *Tax Challenges Arising from Digitalisation – Report on Pillar Two Blueprint*, para. 411.

'CFC regimes' usually either apply on an entity basis, whereas the IIR follows jurisdictional blending. One might find further differences and similarities; however, it has been pointed out in literature that the distinction between 'CFC regimes' and the IIR is somewhat arbitrary:[1523] although BEPS Action 3 might have, at least to a certain extent, found a common understanding of what a CFC regime could look like; however, there is a wide variety of CFC regimes even within the EU as even the ATAD allows the EU Member States to choose either of two basic designs.[1524] Jurisdictions might also implement CFC legislation that is applied jurisdiction-wise, which could pose the question of whether such a regime should be considered as an IIR or part of a CFC tax.[1525] But is the distinction between a CFC regime and the IIR really relevant?

Unfortunately for GloBE, this question is too much of an issue: whereas CFC taxes are to be included in the amount of 'Adjusted Covered Taxes' of the jurisdiction where the CFC is resident (or 'located' in the terminology of GloBE), the IIR is excluded from the definition of 'Covered Taxes' (already *see* section 4.3.4.2.). The exclusion of the IIR is, as the Commentary explicitly notes,[1526] necessary to avoid circularity issues with respect to ETR computation. If the IIR was included in the amount of 'Adjusted Covered Taxes', the IIR would iteratively reduce and would literally 'eat up' itself. Consequently, it indeed makes a difference whether a domestic tax scheme is defined as an IIR or a CFC rule; and having the discussion on rule order between CFC and QDMTT in mind (*see* section 4.4.2.6.3.), from a tax policy point of view, a tax regime might be designed so that it either qualifies as an IIR or a CFC regime, which makes a significant difference, given the fact that the latter is to be included within the definition of 'Covered Taxes' and, thus, is applied before the IIR is applied.[1527] This might create an incentive to design a tax scheme that is characterized as a CFC regime under GloBE: assume an 'MNE Group' consists of a wholly owned three-tier structure and the lowest CE is an LTCE so that, in principle, only the UPE state would be permitted to apply the IIR with respect to any 'Top-up Tax' allocable to the LTCE. The residence state of the IPE could simply 'soak-up' the UPE State's IIR revenue by simply applying legislation that is considered a 'CFC regime' under GloBE. The respective tax levied by the IPE state would increase the ETR of the LTCE, reducing the amount that could be levied by the UPE state by way of the IIR.

4.4.2.8.3 UTPR to Collect Remaining 'Top-Up Tax' by Formulary Apportionment to Entities Having 'Substance'

The UTPR's role is to serve '*as a backstop to the IIR*':[1528] if a 'Top-up Tax' remains with a CE that cannot be collected at the level of a 'Parent Entity' within the 'MNE Group' by

1523. M. Herzfeld, *More on GLOBE Ordering: CFC Rules*, 106 Tax Notes Intl., *supra* note 1230, at 604.
1524. Article 7(2) ATAD.
1525. Mindy Herzfeld, *supra* note 1230, at 604.
1526. *See GloBE Commentary on Article 4 GloBE Model Rules (2022)*, *supra* note 884, para. 45.
1527. '*The IIR operates in a way that is similar to a CFC rule in that it subjects a domestic taxpayer to tax on its share of the foreign income of any controlled subsidiary*', *see Tax Challenges Arising from Digitalisation – Report on Pillar Two Blueprint*, para. 411.
1528. *See GloBE Commentary on Article 2 GloBE Model Rules (2022)*, *supra* note 238, para. 1.

way of the IIR, the UTPR enables to collect the remaining 'Top-up Tax' at the level of every other CE of the same 'MNE Group'. The so-called Total UTPR Top-up Tax Amount (within the GloBE-Directive, the 'UTPR top-up tax amount' – in simple terms, the remaining 'Top-up Tax' not collected by IIR) is finally allocated to all CEs that are subject to a 'Qualified UTPR' by a fixed formula.[1529] The actual obligation to apply the UTPR and its definition is laid down in Article 2.4.1. GloBE Model Rules (reflected in Article 1[b] GloBE-Directive): CEs of an 'MNE Group' '*shall be denied a deduction in an amount resulting in those Constituent Entities having an additional cash tax expense to the UTPR Top-up Tax Amount for the Fiscal Year allocated to that jurisdiction*'[1530].[1531] The 'Total UTPR Top-up Tax Amount', according to Article 2.5.1. GloBE Model Rules is equal to the sum of the 'Top-up Tax' calculated for each LTCE (Steps 1 to 7). However, as will be seen, the respective amount is to be reduced (i) either to zero if all of the UPEs 'Allocable Share' of 'Top-up Tax' were subject to an IIR[1532] at the level of another 'Parent Entity' (either the UPE itself, an IPE or a POPE) or, if this is not the case, (ii) to the extent the 'Top-up Tax' has already been collected by an IIR.[1533] As will be seen, in the latter case, the UTPR also enables collecting 'Top-up Tax' that would be, in principle, not attributable to the 'MNE Group' at all. In this scenario, GloBE also subjects shareholders to the minimum tax that would be outside the scope of GloBE. It has been concluded in the literature that there is no scope for the UTPR in intra-EU situations.[1534] As will be shown, this conclusion can only be confirmed at second glance. The GloBE-Directive slightly limits the scope of application of the UTPR compared to the GloBE Model Rules in order to avoid UTPR application in intra-EU situations.

The decisive element of the UTPR is that it does not require any 'Ownership Interest' at all: the mere 'membership' to the 'MNE Group' is sufficient for the applicability of the UTPR. Thus, while the IIR can only be applied by the 'Parent Entity' in relation to its 'Allocable Share' in a low-taxed subsidiary (LTCE in GloBEs terminology), the UTPR allows the tax to be charged within the 'MNE Group' in all conceivable directions: for example, if the UPE itself is low-taxed and not subject to a QDMTT or an IIR where it is 'located', any CE-subsidiary within the 'MNE Group' could also levy 'Top-up Tax' arising in the UPE's jurisdiction. For this reason, the UTPR did receive the status of a 'Reverse CFC Rule', which, however, underestimates the UTPR. Rather, the UTPR is also applicable in every other direction, either to the side or in all other conceivable diagonals of an MNE Group's organizational chart.[1535] However, as will be seen, GloBE limits the excessive scope of the UTPR to a certain extent.

1529. *See* the formula provided in Art. 2.6.1. *GloBE Model Rules*. Also *see* Art. 14(5) GloBE-Directive (2022/2523).
1530. Article 2.4.1. *GloBE Model Rules* and Art. 1(b) GloBE-Directive (2022/2523).
1531. On the technical options, either to deny a deduction or to enforce an 'equivalent adjustment', to implement a UTPR in domestic law, *see GloBE Commentary on Article 2, supra* note 238, para. 44 et seq.
1532. Article 2.5.2. *GloBE Model Rules* and Art. 14(3) GloBE-Directive (2022/2523).
1533. Article 2.5.3. *GloBE Model Rules* and Art. 14(4) GloBE-Directive (2022/2523).
1534. *See*, e.g., A.P. Dourado, *The Pillar Two Top-Up Taxes: Interplay, Characterization, and Tax Treaties*, 50 Intertax, *supra* note 1521, at 391.
1535. *See* already V. Bendlinger & G. Kofler, *Computation of the Effective Tax Rate and the 'Top-up Tax'*, in *Pillar 2 Global Minimum Tax, supra* note 305, at 26–27.

But in which situations could the UTPR come into play? Although not explicitly listed in the GloBE Model Rules, the Commentary or the GloBE-Directive, one can distinguish three 'UTPR situations' that would, at least in principle, lead to the application of the UTPR. In this respect, it is necessary to reiterate that the UTPR in the rule order can only become effective if (i) the CIT of the jurisdiction (including any CFC taxes levied in other jurisdictions) of the LTCE does not reach the ETR of 15 % and does not levy a QDMTT and (ii) the IIR is not able to levy the 'Top-up Tax' of the LTCE either. Finally, all three situations have in common that the pending 'Top-up Tax' could neither be collected by means of QDMTT nor IIR:

- **Situation 1 – The UPE does not apply a 'Qualified IIR' with respect to LTCEs within the MNE Group:** If the UPE is 'located' in a jurisdiction that does not apply a 'Qualified IIR', any pending 'Top-up Tax' of LTCEs 'located' in any other jurisdiction different to the jurisdiction in which the UPE is 'located' could not be collected. This, however, also requires that no other 'Parent Entity' (either an IPE or a POPE) in between the ownership chain is forced to apply the IIR. In this situation, the UTPR, pursuant to Article 2.4.1. GloBE Model Rules and Article 12 GloBE-Directive would kick in and would distribute the uncollected 'Top-up Tax' among all remaining CEs within the 'MNE Group' that are 'located' in a jurisdiction that subjects its CEs to a 'Qualified UTPR'. Since all UPEs, IPEs, and POPEs that are located in the EU are subject to mandatory IIR and also have to apply the IIR with respect to themselves,[1536] this case can only occur from the perspective of the GloBE-Directive if the respective LTCE is 'located' in a third country and if no CE within the EU has 'Ownership Interest' in the respective LTCE.
- **Situation 2 – The UPE itself qualifies as an LTCE:** If the UPE is 'located' in a jurisdiction where the 'MNE Group' does not reach the minimum tax level, there might be no IIR either. Finally, the IIR, at least pursuant to the GloBE Model Rules, does not enable to collect a 'Top-up Tax' from itself, simply due to the fact that no other CE within the 'MNE Group' can have 'Ownership Interest' in the UPE. This is the so-called reverse CFC case that has been mentioned above: in this situation, UTPR distributes the remaining 'Top-up Tax' of the UPE and all CEs 'located' within the UPE's jurisdiction (which qualify as LTCEs at the same time) to any CE-subsidiaries that are subject to a 'Qualified UTPR'. This situation is covered by Article 2.4.1. GloBE Model Rules as well. The GloBE-Directive provides a separate Article 13 GloBE-Directive to cover this situation. Since all UPEs 'located' in the EU are subject to mandatory IIR and have to apply the IIR with respect to themselves,[1537] this case can only occur from the perspective of the GloBE-Directive if the UPE is 'located' in a third country. Furthermore, this situation cannot occur in intra-EU situations, as every UPE 'located' in the EU and does itself qualify as LTCE is subject to an IIR pursuant to Article 5(2) GloBE-Directive.

1536. Explicitly, *see* Arts 5(2), 6(2), 7(2) and 8(2) GloBE-Directive (2022/2523).
1537. Again, *see* Arts 5(2), 6(2), 7(2) and 8(2) *Ibid.*

- **Situation 3 – IIR fails to collect 'Top-up Tax' remaining at the level of minority shareholders:** As set out in section 4.4.2.8.2., the IIR fails to collect 'Top-up Tax' allocated to an LTCE if it is attributable to minority shareholders (also see the third structure shown in Figure 11). Due to the fact that the UTPR does not require any connection via 'Ownership Interest' at all, it, at least in principle, also enables to collect 'Top-up Tax' attributable to minority shareholders. As has been shown in section 4.3., both the 'GloBE Income or Loss' as well as the 'Adjusted Covered Taxes' (the only exception are 'Investment Entities' for which the ETR is determined with respect to the MNE Group's 'Allocable Share' of the 'Investment Entity')[1538] are computed for each individual CE irrespective of its shareholder level.[1539] GloBE, thus, would, pursuant to Article 2.4.1. GloBE Model Rules and either Article 12 or 13 GloBE-Directive,[1540] in principle, also allocate 'Top-up Tax' to the LTCE during Steps 1 to 7 which is not attributable to the 'MNE Group' at all. This is the only situation which would be conceivable to give rise to the UTPR also in intra EU-situations. However, first, both Articles 12 and 13 GloBE-Directive only apply if the UPE is 'located' in a third-country jurisdiction, and second (ii) the low-taxed UPE would be subject to the IIR in its Member State pursuant to Article 5(2) GloBE-Directive. Thus, also the third situation cannot occur in an intra-EU scenario (*see* Figure 12).

Figure 12 The Three UTPR Situations

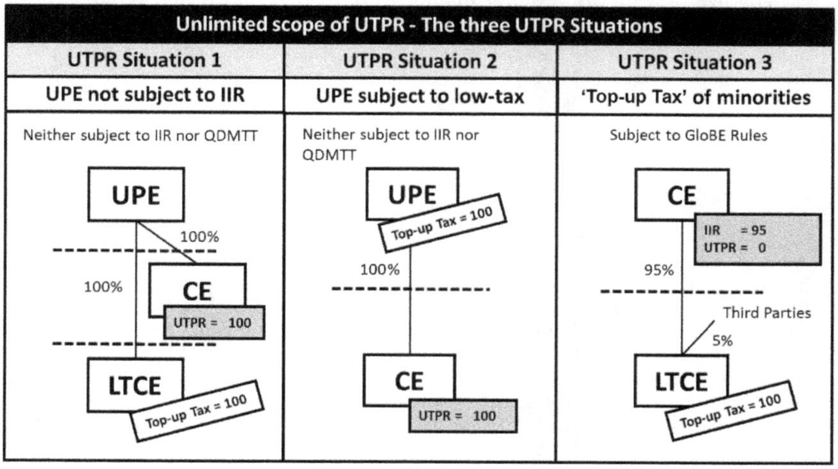

1538. *See* Art. 7.4.2. *GloBE Model Rules* and Art. 41(2) GloBE-Directive (2022/2523).
1539. Explicitly, *see GloBE Commentary on Article 3 GloBE Model Rules (2022)*, *supra* note 507, para. 8.
1540. The third situation can either occur under both Art. 12 or Art. 13 GloBE-Directive. The former applies, if the 'Top-up Tax' did arise with a LTCE that is not 'located' in the UPE jurisdiction, while the latter requires that the respective LTCE is 'located' in the jurisdiction of the UPE (either the UPE itself or a domestic subsidiary of the UPE).

In particular, the third UTPR situation is interesting as it might oblige collecting 'Top-up Tax' attributable to shareholders that would, in principle, not be covered by GloBE. Thus, the following question remains from a tax policy point of view: should GloBE be to the disadvantage of minority shareholders that are not even part of the MNE Group?[1541] In principle, also the Commentary, at several places, besides the exception for applying the IIR to POPEs, seems to at least show a tendency to answer this question in the negative,[1542] and, pursuant to Article 2.5.2. GloBE Model Rules (reflected in Article 14[3] GloBE-Directive), the *'the Top-up Tax calculated for a Low-Taxed Constituent Entity that is otherwise taken into account [...] shall be reduced to zero if all of the UPE's Ownership Interests in such [LTCEs] are held directly or indirectly by one or more Parent Entities that are required to apply a Qualified IIR'*.[1543] Consequently, by reducing the 'Total UTPR Top-up Tax' amount to zero if all 'Ownership Interests' of the UPE have been included in the 'Allocable Share' of 'Top-up Tax' and have been subject to a 'Qualified IIR', there is no room for collecting the UTPR. Thus, although in principle covered by the UTPR, the third situation will, in many cases, not become effective. However, if Article 2.5.2. GloBE Model Rules and Article 14(3) GloBE-Directive do not apply because not all of the UPE's 'Allocable Share' of 'Top-up Tax' of an LTCE, have been collected by POPEs or IPEs, according to Article 2.5.3. GloBE Model Rules and Article 14(4) GloBE-Directive, the 'Total UTPR Tax Amount' '*shall* [only] *be reduced by a Parent Entity's Allocable Share of the Top-up Tax of that [LTCE] that is brought into charge under a Qualified IIR*'.[1544] In this latter case, the UTPR will also force CEs to apply the UTPR with respect to 'Top-up Tax' that is not allocable to the 'MNE Group' at all. The following chart demonstrates an 'MNE Group' structure that would oblige the collection of the minimum tax with respect to minority shareholders.

1541. Sceptical as well, *see* Jefferson VanderWolk, *The UTPR, Treaties, and CFC Rules: A Reply to Avi-Yonah and Schler*, 109 Tax Notes Intl. 187 (9 Jan. 2023); Nathan Boidman, *UTPR's Effect on Outside Shareholders: Another Reason to Oppose?*, 109 Tax Notes Intl. 189 (9 Jan. 2023).

1542. That tendency is reflected, e.g., in *GloBE Commentary on Article 2 GloBE Model Rules (2022)*, *supra* note 238, paras 14 and 52. In particular, para. 52, where it is held that '[a] *UTPR Jurisdiction may therefore provide that the Top-up Tax is allocated first to those Constituent Entities that are wholly-owned or almost wholly-owned by the MNE Group, in order to minimise the extent to which those minority interest holders share the burden of Top-up Tax allocated from LTCEs in which they do not have an economic interest*'. With respect to the computation of the 'GloBE Income' irrespective of the shares held by the 'MNE Group', *see GloBE Commentary on Article 3*, *supra* note 507, para. 8. Furthermore, in particular with respect to 'Investment Entities', the Commentary notes that GloBE '*seeks to ensure that minority investors are not subject to Top-up Tax on their interest in a low-taxed Investment Entity controlled by an MNE Group*', *see GloBE Commentary on Article 7 GloBE Model Rules (2022)*, *supra* note 335, at 74.

1543. Article 2.5.2. *GloBE Model Rules* and Art. 14(3) GloBE-Directive (2022/2523).

1544. Article 2.5.3. *GloBE Model Rules* and Art. 14(4) GloBE-Directive (2022/2523).

Figure 13 UTPR Collecting 'Top-up Tax' Attributable to Non-Group Minority Shareholders

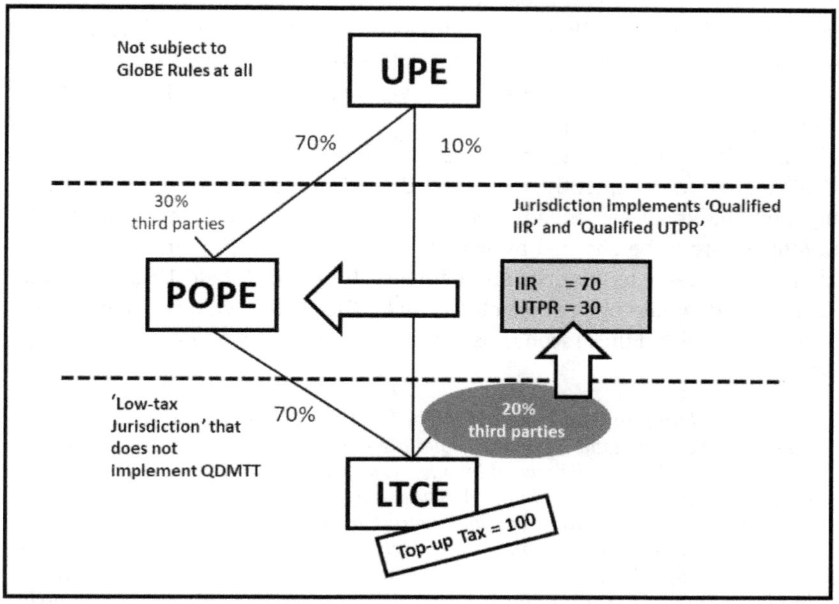

The example in Figure 13 illustrates a situation where a CE is obliged to collect 'Top-up Tax' that is attributable to third-party shareholders:[1545] the UPE is 'located' in a jurisdiction that neither subjects it to a QDMTT nor a 'Qualified IIR' with respect to its 'Allocable Share' of 'Top-up Tax' of the LTCE that would amount to 59 (49% indirect participation via a POPE and 10% held directly). However, since the LTCE is indirectly held via an intermediate 'Parent Entity' in which the UPE holds less than 80%, this POPE is obliged to apply the IIR with respect to its 'Allocable Share' of 'Top-up Tax' pursuant to Article 2.1.4. GloBE Model Rules or Article 8(1) GloBE-Directive. Having applied the IIR, 30 of the 'Top-up Tax' allocated to the LTCE remains. The 'Total UTPR Top-up Tax Amount' pursuant to Article 2.5.1. GloBE Model Rules and Article 14(2) GloBE-Directive '*shall be equal to the sum of the Top-up Tax calculated for each* [LTCE]'.[1546] As LTCE is the only CE within the group that is lowly taxed, the 'Total UTPR Top-up Tax' is 100. However, it is now necessary to examine the extent to which the IIR levied at POPE reduces the 'UTPR Top-up Tax Amount': Article 2.5.2. GloBE Model Rules and Article 14(3) GloBE-Directive would reduce it to zero '*if all of the* [UPE's] *Ownership Interests in such* [LTCE] *are held directly or indirectly by*

1545. A similar example is provided for in the Example catalogue, *see* Example 2.5.3 – 1 in *GloBE Examples*, at 19–20.

1546. Article 2.5.1. *GloBE Model Rules* and Art. 14(2) GloBE-Directive (2022/2523).

one or more Parent Entities that are required to apply a Qualified IIR'.[1547] It is true that the POPE is such a 'Parent Entity' that is subject to a 'Qualified IIR', but not all of the UPE's 'Ownership Interests' are held by the POPE. Rather, 10% of the LTCE is directly held by the UPE, which is not part of the POPE's 'Allocable Share' of 'Top-up Tax' pursuant to Article 2.1.4. GloBE Model Rules or Article 8(1) GloBE-Directive. For this reason, the 'Total UTPR Top-up Tax Amount' pursuant to Article 2.5.1. GloBE Model Rules and Article 14(2) GloBE-Directive may only be reduced '*by* [the] *Parent Entity's Allocable Share of the Top-up Tax of that* [LTCE] *that is brought into charge under a Qualified IIR*'[1548] pursuant to Article 2.5.3. GloBE Model Rules and Article 14(4) GloBE-Directive. Consequently, the 'Total UTPR Top-up Tax Amount' of 100 may be reduced by 70, which has already been collected by the POPE by way of the IIR. The remaining 30 are to be charged by way of the UTPR, including an amount of 20 that would be attributable to minority shareholders. If the POPE held 10% of the shares of the UPE, that 20 would not be collected at all by GloBE. So, what is the justification for collecting the UTPR in these scenarios?[1549] The Commentary notes the following in this respect:

> *It is expected that, in most cases, either the LTCEs will be wholly-owned by another Constituent Entity that is subject to a Qualified IIR (and the UTPR will not apply) or their shares will be wholly-owned by other Constituent Entities that are not subject to an IIR (and the UTPR will apply). There may be situations, however, where an Intermediate Parent Entity owns an interest in an LTCE and applies the IIR in respect of its share of the income of such LTCE under Article 2.1.2, but the application of the IIR in the Intermediate Parent Entity's jurisdiction does not result in all the Top-up Tax attributable to the UPE's Ownership Interests being brought into charge under a Qualified IIR.*[1550]

The Commentary further adds:

> Because Article 2.5.3 reduces the Total UTPR Top-up Tax Amount by the amount of Top-up Tax subject to the IIR (rather than reducing it to zero), it leaves, within the charge to tax, low-taxed income that is beneficially owned by minority shareholders. Unlike the exclusion mechanism under Article 2.5.2, this deduction mechanism under Article 2.5.3 does not allow the MNE Group to limit the total amount of Top-up Tax payable to the allocable share of Top-up Tax that would have been allocated to the UPE if the UPE had been subject to a Qualified IIR with respect of the LTCE. Equally, it does not require a determination of whether a POPE would have been subject to tax under the IIR because of the ownership structure of the MNE Group or the Allocable Share of Top-up Tax that would have been allocated to that POPE. Instead, Article 2.5.3 deducts the tax due under an IIR from the amount of Top-up Tax that is computed on the total amount of income of the LTCE, irrespective of the UPE's Allocable Share of the Top-up Tax due in respect of the LTCE. Applying the UTPR to the total amount of Top-up Tax of an

1547. Article 2.5.2. *GloBE Model Rules* and Art. 14(3) GloBE-Directive (2022/2523).
1548. Article 2.5.3. *GloBE Model Rules* and Art. 14(4) GloBE-Directive (2022/2523).
1549. Sceptically posing the same question, *see* J. VanderWolk, *The UTPR, Treaties, and CFC Rules: A Reply to Avi-Yonah and Schler*, 109 Tax Notes Intl., *supra* note 1541, at 187; N. Boidman, *UTPR's Effect on Outside Shareholders: Another Reason to Oppose?*, 109 Tax Notes Intl., *supra* note 1541, at 189.
1550. *See GloBE Commentary on Article 2 GloBE Model Rules (2022)*, *supra* note 238, para. 77.

> LTCE (i.e., not limited to the UPE's Ownership Interest in the LTCE) simplifies its application. It allows for a greater tax expense than the Top-up Tax that would have been collected under the IIR if it had applied at the UPE level because it is not limited to the UPE's Allocable Share of the Top-up Tax due in respect of LTCE.[1551]

Obviously, the Commentary justifies this approach on the one hand by the argument that this might not be the 'regular' case, in other words, that UTPR would collect the minorities' 'Top-up Tax' only in exceptional cases and on the other hand, that this '*simplifies*' GloBE's application. Both assumptions are neither true nor convincing.[1552] First of all, it might very well be the case that the UPE of an 'MNE Group' that is not subject to GloBE Rules at all within its jurisdiction holds a direct participation in a partially owned LTCE. Furthermore, the fact that it will not apply '*in most cases*', which is, as said, a mere assumption, does not justify deviating from the silent principle that GloBE should only apply to in-scope 'MNE Groups'. Besides this, it is questionable in which way this rule simplifies the application of the UTPR: in any case, an 'MNE Group' will have to provide a detailed chart of its organizational structure, so why is it simpler to include 'Top-up Tax' attributable to non-group shareholders compared to reducing the 'Top-up Tax' with respect to their shares? Furthermore, as will be seen, this situation might trigger very difficult issues with respect to EU law, as it opens up the scope for minorities to invoke the freedom of capital movement: in a situation where the UPE is 'located' in the EU, it would always be subject to an IIR excluding that Article 14(4) GloBE-Directive is applicable and leaves 'Top-up Tax' to collect by means of the UTPR. A third country situation would, thus, always be treated worse than a domestic one (in detail, *see* section 6.2.2.1.3.). Furthermore, one could question whether this situation is in line with the non-discrimination provision of Article 24 OECD MC (in detail, *see* section 5.2.5.).

It is interesting to note that the GloBE-Directive would not oblige the Member States to apply the UTPR with respect to the 'Top-up Tax' attributable to minority shareholders in intra-EU situations. If all group members shown in Figure 13 were resident in the EU, neither Article 12 nor Article 13 GloBE-Directive were applicable with respect to the 20% minority shareholders' 'Allocable Share' of 'Top-up Tax' because both provisions require that the UPE is resident in a third-country jurisdiction. Furthermore, Article 14(3) GloBE-Directive would reduce the 'UTPR Top-up Tax' to zero, as pursuant to Article 5(2) GloBE-Directive, the low-taxed EU UPE has to be subject to the IIR in its Member State anyway. In these scenarios, the GloBE-Directive deviates from the framework of the GloBE Model Rules as the latter would oblige to collect the 'Top-up Tax' attributable to the minority shareholders.

The examples above did assume that only one single CE within the Group was subject to a 'Qualified UTPR'. This leaves two questions: first, which CE is about to collect the 'UTPR Top-up Tax' if more than one single CE is subject to a 'Qualified UTPR' and second, what is a 'Qualified UTPR'? The allocation of the UTPR is key for its

1551. *See Ibid.*, para. 78.
1552. This view is also shared by D. Hohenwarter-Mayr, *Globale Mindeststeuer aus unionsrechtlicher Sicht*, in *Handbuch zur Globalen Steuerreform* 160 (D. Hohenwarter et al., eds, Facultas 2023).

implementation: within an 'MNE Group' having CEs in numerous jurisdictions, every jurisdiction that implements GloBE and in which a CE of the 'MNE Group' is 'located' could potentially collect the 'UTPR Top-up Tax Amount' leaving a high potential for multiple taxations. To solve this issue, Article 2.6. GloBE Model Rules and Article 14(5) to (8) GloBE-Directive provide a formula that distributes the UTPR revenue among jurisdictions. The so-called UTPR Percentage determines a jurisdiction's share of the 'UTPR Top-up Tax Amount' and is to be calculated pursuant to the following formula (*see* Figure 14).

Figure 14 Computation of the 'UTPR Percentage' for the Formulary Apportionment of UTPR Revenue Pursuant to Article 2.6.1. GloBE Model Rules and Article 14(5) GloBE-Directive

$$50 \times \frac{\text{Numbers of Employees in the jurisdiction}}{\text{Numbers of Employees in all UTPR Jurisdictions}} + 50\,\% \times \frac{\text{Total value of Tangible Assets in the jurisdiction}}{\text{Total value of Tangible Assets in all UTPR Jurisdictions}}$$

Thus, the 'UTPR Top-up Tax' is allocated among jurisdictions pursuant to substance criteria.[1553] In this way, GloBE intends to provide '*for a simple transparent allocation key which facilitates the co-ordination among tax jurisdiction*' and aims '*to reduce the risk of allocating Top-up Tax to a jurisdiction that does not have enough capacity to impose the UTPR adjustment*'.[1554] The substance factors of the formula and their computation are further defined in Articles 2.6.1. and 14(5) GloBE-Directive and discussed in the Commentary. Above all, the Commentary emphasizes that the respective data required for UTPR allocation should be available from the CbCR of an 'MNE Group'.[1555] One should emphasize that the formula provided in Article 2.6.1. GloBE Model Rules and Article 14(5) GloBE-Directive does '*not prescribe how the UTPR Top-up Tax is allocated amount the* [CEs]'[1556] 'located' in the same jurisdiction. Rather, it is up to the implementing jurisdiction to allocate its share in the 'UTPR Top-up Tax Amount' among its domestic CEs.

What is decisive for the formula is the fact that it calculates a jurisdiction's share of 'UTPR Top-up Tax' by dividing the respective factors of the jurisdiction by the '*Total value* [either of the Number of Employees or the Tangible Assets] *in all UTPR Jurisdictions*'. A 'UTPR Jurisdiction' is a jurisdiction that has a 'Qualified UTPR' in force.[1557] The definition of 'Qualified UTPR' equals the definition of 'Qualified IIR', which is why reference can be made to the elaborations on the interpretation above in

1553. The computation of the 'UTPR Percentage' is illustrated in Example 2.6.4 – 1 in *GloBE Examples*, at 20–21.
1554. *See GloBE Commentary on Article 2, supra* note 238, para. 81.
1555. *See Ibid.*, paras 82–85.
1556. *See Ibid.*, paras 51 and 65.
1557. *See* the definition of 'UTPR Jurisdiction' in Art. 10.1. *GloBE Model Rules*, at 66. The GloBE-Directive does not separately define the term.

section 4.4.2.8.2. Also, the Commentary on the definition of 'Qualified UTPR' merely repeats the statements made with respect to the 'Qualified IIR' definition.[1558] In any case, to qualify as a 'UTPR jurisdiction', it requires that the jurisdiction implements a measure that is again '*equivalent*' to the UTPR as provided for in the GloBE Model Rules.[1559] This ensures that no UTPR is allocated to a jurisdiction that does not collect the respective UTPR. This argument has been put forward also with respect to UTPR's compatibility with tax treaties: if a jurisdiction does not apply UTPR because it assumes that collecting UTPR was not in line with one or more of its treaties, the respective jurisdiction's share in 'UTPR Top-up Tax' (= 'UTPR Percentage) would simply be distributed among all other 'UTPR Jurisdictions'. Finally, Article 2.6.3. GloBE Model Rules states that if a jurisdiction fails to collect its share of the 'UTPR Top-up Tax', all other jurisdictions should deem its 'UTPR Percentage' to be zero.[1560]

Contrary to the IIR that is very similar to existing 'CFC regimes', the UTPR is the true innovation within GloBE's technical framework. It is not limited with respect to any ownership connections and, in principle, also enables the collection of 'Top-up Tax' that would otherwise be outside the scope of GloBE. However, the UTPR probably is the most challenging element of GloBE: its compatibility with discrimination prohibitions and tax treaties has been intensively debated (*see* in further detail section 5.2.6.3.), and its administrability might be one of the big question marks for the implementation of GloBE. The simple formula to allocate UTPR provided in Article 2.6.1. GloBE Model Rules and Article 14(5) GloBE-Directive belies its complexity and inherent risk of double and multiple taxation.[1561] Jurisdictions could, for example, have different views with respect to the requirements for a 'Qualified UTPR', meaning that single jurisdictions overestimate their 'UTPR Top-up Tax Percentage' and the same amount of 'Top-up Tax' is levied multiple times. They could calculate the underlying factors differently and could disagree with respect to the 'UTPR Top-up Tax Amount'. It is for a good reason that the QDMTT was initially discussed as a measure to avoid UTPR's complexity.[1562] In any case, for an 'MNE Group', it is advisable to avoid the application of the UTPR. The same is true for any jurisdiction hosting low-taxed UPEs: it might even be to the benefit of the UPE to apply QDMTT simply to avoid potential risks of double and multiple taxation because of the UTPR's backstop function.

1558. *GloBE Commentary on Article 10 GloBE Model Rules (2022)*, *supra* note 280, at 139–143.
1559. *See* the definition of 'Qualified UTPR' in Art. 10.1. *GloBE Model Rules*, at 65 and Art. 3(43) GloBE-Directive (2022/2523).
1560. On that argument, *see* Heydon Wardell-Burrus, *Four Questions for UTPR Skeptics*, 108 Tax Notes Intl. 702 (7 Nov. 2022).
1561. In the same vein, *see* R. Goulder, *Confessions of a UTPR Skeptic*, 108 Tax Notes Intl. 907 (14 Nov. 2022).
1562. *See Tax Challenges Arising from Digitalisation – Report on Pillar Two Blueprint*, para. 491: '*Such a domestic minimum tax on income would aim at ensuring that the MNE's jurisdictional ETR in the ultimate parent jurisdiction is at least equal to the agreed minimum rate and would prevent the application of the UTPR in other jurisdictions in relation to profits made in the ultimate parent jurisdiction.*'

4.4.2.8.4 *Transitional Rules for the Initial Phase of an MNE Group and Election to Delay Application of GloBE Rules*

Due to the significant complexity of the UTPR, Article 9.3. GloBE Model Rules suggests that 'MNE Groups' in their initial phase of international activity shall be excluded from UTPR by way of reducing the 'Total UTPR Top-up Tax Amount' in Article 2.5.1. GloBE Model Rules to zero. An 'MNE Group' is within its initial phase if it (i) has CEs in no more than six jurisdictions, and (ii) the sum of the 'Net Book Values' of 'Tangible Assets' of all CEs located in all jurisdictions do not exceed EUR 50 million.[1563] The exception shall not apply later than five years after the 'MNE Group' originally came within the scope of the GloBE Rules.[1564] The GloBE-Directive implements the initial phase exclusion in Article 49 GloBE-Directive, but slightly deviates for technical reasons: first of all, for UPEs 'located' in a Member State, the exclusion according to Article 49(1) GloBE-Directive applies with respect to the IIR as well but only with respect to the obligation to apply the IIR to domestic LTCEs pursuant to Articles 5(2) and 7(2) GloBE-Directive.[1565] If the UPE is located in a third-country jurisdiction, Article 49(2) GloBE-Directive mirrors the provision of Article 9.3.1. GloBE Model Rules and states that the 'Total UTPR Top-up Tax Amount' shall be reduced to zero under the same conditions as set out in Article 9.3. GloBE Model Rules. The 'Initial Phase Exclusion' raises interesting questions regarding the GloBE-Directive's compatibility with primary law, which will be discussed in section 6.2.2.1.4.

In addition to Article 49 GloBE-Directive, Article 50 GloBE-Directive provides an election for those Member States that host less than twelve UPEs of in-scope 'MNE Groups' to delay the application of the IIR and UTPR for six consecutive years beginning from 31 December 2023. The respective Member States that make use of the election must notify the Commission by 31 December 2023 but only need to implement GloBE by 31 December 2029. The provision had been added in the course of negotiations in council and is a concession in particular to the Baltic Member States.[1566] Other Member States, however, are obliged to collect the 'UTPR Top-up Tax' with respect to UPEs 'located' in a jurisdiction that makes use of the election pursuant to Article 50(2) GloBE-Directive. For these purposes, the 'UTPR Percentage' of this jurisdiction is deemed to be zero, so the Member State making use of the election can, for obvious reasons, not participate in the UTPR revenue allocation. However, given the complexity of the UTPR and the resulting disadvantage of MNE Groups being subject to the UTPR, it is very likely that all Member States that make use of the election provided for in Article 50 GloBE-Directive, will also make use of the election to implement a QDMTT pursuant to Article 11 GloBE-Directive leaving no 'Top-up Tax' to collect by way of the UTPR for any other Member States. In any case, the exclusion of

1563. In detail on these requirements, *see GloBE Commentary on Article 9 GloBE Model Rules (2022)*, paras 14–32.
1564. Article 9.3.4. *GloBE Model Rules*.
1565. A reference to Art. 6(2) GloBE-Directive is missing, as the latter provision only applies in situations where the UPE is 'located' in a third – country jurisdiction.
1566. Also *see* A. P. Dourado, *Is There A Need for A Directive on Pillar Two?*, 50 Intertax 522 (1 May 2022) DOI: 10.54648/taxi2022056.

Article 50 GloBE-Directive probably is the only conceivable situation in which UTPR liability could possibly arise also in intra-EU situations.[1567]

4.4.3 *De Minimis* Exception for Jurisdictional 'Top-up Tax' Computation

It needs no further explanation that the computation of the 'Top-up Tax' is a complex procedure. Accordingly, since the beginning of the development of GloBE, there has always been intense discussion in the literature[1568] as well as in the OECD[1569] about possible simplifications[1570] for the practical application of GloBE. However, simplifications always entail that they deviate from the actual set of rules and run the risk of being used to circumvent the actual regulations. Simplifications in the GloBE framework must therefore strike a balance between maintaining effectiveness while simplifying the complex set of rules.

One of these simplifications discussed from the beginning is the so-called *de minimis* exclusion implemented in Article 5.5. GloBE Model Rules and Article 30 GloBE-Directive, which, at the election of the 'Filing Constituent Entity', exempts an 'MNE Group' from computing the 'Top-up Tax' for a specific jurisdiction. Therefore, neither the ETR nor the 'Top-up Tax' need to be calculated for all CEs located in that jurisdiction[1571] and a specific Fiscal Year.[1572] Rather, the 'Top-up Tax' '*for the Constituent Entities located in* [that] *jurisdiction shall be deemed to be zero for a Fiscal Year*'.[1573] According to the Commentary, this exception serves '*to avoid the complexities of a full ETR computation in cases where the amount of any Top Up Tax would not seem to justify the associated compliance and administrative costs*'.[1574]

The requirements for the applicability of the 'De minimis exclusion' are as follows: the election is available if (i) the 'Average GloBE Revenue'[1575] of such jurisdiction is less than EUR 10 million; and (ii) the 'Average GloBE Income or Loss' of such jurisdiction is a loss or less than EUR 1 million. Both conditions require the aggregation of all 'GloBE Revenues'[1576] and 'GloBE Income or Loss'[1577] of all CEs located within a jurisdiction and must be met cumulatively.[1578] If either the revenue is above EUR 10 million or the 'GloBE Income' exceeds EUR 1 million, an 'MNE Group'

1567. Also *see* s. 6.2.2.1.3.
1568. *See*, *i.a.*, T. Velling, *Pillar Two: Simplification is Key (via Passle)*, Passle, https://www.europeantax.blog//post/102gp2a/pillar-two-simplification-is-key (last visited 13 Apr. 2022).
1569. *See*, e.g., the Pillar Two Blueprint where a separate chapter was devoted to possible simplifications, *see Tax Challenges Arising from Digitalisation – Report on Pillar Two Blueprint*, paras 376–409.
1570. Also *see* the recent suggestions provided by C. Döllefeld et al., *Tax Administrative Guidance: A Proposal for Simplifying Pillar Two*, 50 Intertax (2021).
1571. *See GloBE Commentary on Article 5 GloBE Model Rules (2022)*, *supra* note 474, para. 75.
1572. In detail, *see Ibid.*, para. 79.
1573. Article 5.5.1. *GloBE Model Rules.*
1574. *See GloBE Commentary on Article 5*, *supra* note 474, para. 74.
1575. The GloBE-Directive proposal uses the term '*average qualifying revenue*', *see* Art. 30(1) GloBE-Directive (2022/2523).
1576. Article 5.5.3.(a) *GloBE Model Rules*. Also *see* Art. 30(1)(a) GloBE-Directive (2022/2523).
1577. Article 5.5.3.(b) *GloBE Model Rules*. Also *see* Art. 30(1)(b) GloBE-Directive (2022/2523).
1578. *See GloBE Commentary on Article 5*, *supra* note 474, para. 81.

cannot make use of the '*de minimis* exclusion'. The terms 'Average GloBE Revenue' and 'Average GloBE Income or Loss' are defined in Article 5.5.2. GloBE Model Rules. Accordingly, both values shall be calculated using a three-year average of the 'GloBE Revenues' and the 'GloBE Income or Loss', respectively. If there were no CEs in a jurisdiction in the two previous years, however, these years are to be excluded from the calculation.[1579] The Commentary also provides further guidance, e.g., with respect to the calculation of the revenue and income thresholds,[1580] for situations in which the threshold is exceeded due to a subsequent recalculation[1581] and for situations in which the scope of the 'MNE Group' changes over the years due to mergers and similar transactions.[1582]

The 'De minimis exclusion' is not available to 'Stateless Entities' and 'Investment Entities'.[1583] Their income is to be consequently excluded from the de minimis thresholds.[1584] However, according to the Commentary, the 'GloBE Income' of CEs that are part of a 'Minority-Owned Subgroup' are, contrary to the principles GloBE applies elsewhere with respect to such MOCEs, to be included in the thresholds provided for in Article 5.5.1. GloBE Model Rules and Article 30(1) GloBE-Directive.[1585]

In principle, the introduction of a de minimis exception is to be welcomed: the revenue generated by a 'Top-up Tax' for jurisdictions in which only marginal profits are made does not justify the expense of a full 'Top-up Tax' calculation. Nevertheless, this exception is a drop in the ocean: again, a separate side calculation is necessary for each jurisdiction, which also requires the jurisdiction-wise aggregation of revenues. It cannot be ruled out that 'MNE Groups' will waive the application of Article 5.5. GloBE Model Rules and Article 30 GloBE-Directive from the outset. This could be advisable in cases, e.g., where for technical reasons, all data of CEs in a potential de minimis jurisdiction are available, and the ETR of the de minimis jurisdiction is above 15% anyway. This ultimately saves an 'MNE Group' a tedious recalculation if it turns out in a subsequent examination that the de minimis thresholds were exceeded after all. It can, therefore, already be anticipated that much more comprehensive safe harbours will be needed for real relief of administrative burdens.[1586]

4.5 CONCLUSION: EIGHT THESES RESULTING FROM THE TECHNICAL ANALYSIS OF GLOBE

4.5.1 GloBE Is to Be Applied in an Eight-Step Procedure

The computation of the ETR and the 'Top-up Tax' is the core element of GloBE and is the prerequisite for the application of the GloBE Rules (IIR and UTPR). Although the

1579. *See* the last sentence of Art. 5.5.2. *GloBE Model Rules*.
1580. *See GloBE Commentary on Article 5, supra* note 474, paras 88–91.
1581. *See Ibid.*, paras 92–93.
1582. *See Ibid.*, para. 94.
1583. Article 5.5.4. *GloBE Model Rules*. Also *see* Art. 30(5) GloBE-Directive (2022/2523).
1584. *See GloBE Commentary on Article 5, supra* note 474, para. 96.
1585. On CEs being part of *'Minority-Owned Subgroups'*, *see Ibid.*, para. 82.
1586. Gladly, those are under development, *see GloBE Safe Harbours and Penalty Relief*.

steps involved in calculating the 'Top-up Tax' are simple mathematical operations, the technical details and legal ramifications turn out to be extremely complex. In section 4.4., the calculation of the 'Top-up Tax' was described as an eight-step procedure which can be summarized as follows: the calculation of the ETR and the 'Top-up Tax' begins with an analysis of the scope of GloBE (in detail section 4.2.): the starting point is the determination of the group of legal entities being consolidated in the financial statements of the UPE. However, the application first requires the splitting of these legal entities into their main entities and PEs, which are to be specifically qualified as CEs for the purposes of GloBE and their 'location' needs to be determined. Finally, according to Articles 3 and 4 GloBE Model Rules (Chapter III and Chapter IV GloBE-Directive), the amounts of 'Adjusted Covered Tax' and 'GloBE Income or Loss' are to be determined separately for each CE (Step 1).[1587] Once the respective CEs are determined, GloBE requires jurisdiction-wise aggregation, with exceptions for 'Investment Entities', MOCEs and 'Stateless Entities',[1588] of both amounts to receive the 'sum of Adjusted Covered Tax' and the 'Net GloBE Income' (Step 2),[1589] to finally calculate the ETR, which is the ratio between those two elements (Step 3).[1590] The ETR is the main benchmark for the minimum tax level of 15%. Thus, GloBE requires calculating the difference between 15% and the calculated ETR, the result of which is called the 'Top-up Tax Percentage' (Step 4).[1591] Subsequently, the 'Excess Profit' must be calculated, which is the difference between the 'Net GloBE Income' calculated in Step 2 and the SBIE (Step 5).[1592] By multiplying the 'Excess Profit' and 'Top-up Tax Percentage', the 'Jurisdictional Top-up Tax' can be determined. However, this is to be increased by an ACTT[1593] and reduced by the QDMTT[1594] levied in the respective jurisdiction (Step 6).[1595] If a 'Top-up Tax' remains in a jurisdiction or any sub-calculation, the 'Jurisdictional Top-up Tax' must be allocated to all LTCEs (entities located in a 'Low-Tax Jurisdiction') with positive 'GloBE income' located in that jurisdiction (Step 7).[1596] In the final step, the remaining 'Top-up Tax' at the level of the individual LTCEs can be collected from their 'Parent Entities' (UPE, IPE or POPEs) by way of IIR; and if 'Top-up Tax' remains after the application of the IIR, the UTPR will apply, apportioning the remaining tax to all non-low-taxed CEs subject to a 'Qualified UTPR' (Step 8)[1597].[1598]

1587. *See* s. 4.4.2.1.
1588. On these exceptions of jurisdictional blending, *see* s. 4.3.2.2.3.
1589. *See* s. 4.4.2.2.
1590. *See* s. 4.4.2.3.
1591. *See* s. 4.4.2.4.
1592. *See* s. 4.4.2.5.
1593. In detail, *see* s. 4.4.2.6.2.
1594. In detail, *see* s. 4.4.2.6.3.
1595. *See* s. 4.4.2.6.
1596. *See* s. 4.4.2.7.
1597. *See* s. 4.4.2.8.
1598. This section is based on V. Bendlinger & G. Kofler, *Computation of the Effective Tax Rate and the 'Top-up Tax', in Pillar 2 Global Minimum Tax, supra* note 305, at 40. An overview of the Eight-Step Approach is provided for in Table 13.

4.5.2 GloBE Establishes a Minimum Tax on 'Excess Profits'

It is one story to fix a minimum tax rate of 15%, and it is different to fix the base to which the minimum rate is applied.[1599] In principle, the framework of GloBE covers all profits determined pursuant to financial accounting rules, excluding the exception of 'International Shipping Income'. In public media, the OECD's Pillar Two project regularly is promoted as a global minimum tax of 15% for MNE Groups meeting the revenue threshold of EUR 750 million.[1600] This statement, however, gives a distorted picture: the profits subject to GloBE are reduced by the SBIE, including a payroll and a tangible asset component. GloBE only subjects the profits exceeding the SBIE, the so-called Excess Profits, to the minimum tax rate of 15%. Consequently, profits that are covered within a specific amount of SBIE are not subject to a minimum tax, irrespective of how much tax is levied on the underlying profits: if the profits received in a specific jurisdiction do not exceed the SBIE of a specific jurisdiction, there would be no 'Top-up Tax' even if the jurisdiction would not levy corporate tax at all. Neither would 'Top-up Tax' arise if the respective jurisdiction provided for a 'Non-Qualified Refundable Tax Credit' leading to a negative amount of 'Adjusted Covered Taxes'.

One might argue that this is a simple conclusion, but still, it is an important one: the effect of the minimum tax on a specific 'MNE Group' directly depends on the amount of SBIE the respective 'MNE Group' can claim within a specific jurisdiction. The SBIE simply takes a fixed percentage of payroll and so-called Local Tangible Assets that can be set off from the 'GloBE Income' of a specific 'Fiscal Year'. What can be concluded from this design?

The SBIE in its current form reveals some interesting flaws: first of all, the SBIE seems to incentivize less efficient businesses over more efficient ones: the higher the profits compared to payroll and 'Local Tangible Assets' within a specific jurisdiction, the more likely 'GloBE Income' will exceed SBIE that is to be tested against the 'Adjusted Covered Taxes' within the respective jurisdiction. In other words, the higher a business's rate of return on payroll and tangible assets, the more likely it will be subject to a 'Top-up Tax'. Second, SBIE can be used fraudulently by multinational corporations, as can be shown hyperbolically: from a technical point of view, MNE Groups, e.g., could shelter profits from GloBE by employing high-payroll managers in tax havens and providing them with 'Local Tangible Assets' like a sports car that can further increase the SBIE.[1601] The OECD is well aware of this fact and, for example, has explicitly excluded, investment property from the scope of the tangible asset carve-out.[1602] It is true that the SBIE will not protect profits of empty shell entities, but as can

---

1599. Also *see* s. 4.3.2.1.1.

1600. *See*, e.g., the recent headline in *EU Adopts Global Minimum 15% Tax on Multinationals*, France 24, https://www.france24.com/en/europe/20221216-eu-adopts-global-minimum-15-tax-on-multinationals (last visited 4 Jan. 2023).

1601. In the same vein, *see*, e.g., E. Eberhartinger & G. Winkler, *Pillar Two and the Accounting Standards*, 51 Intertax, *supra* note 281, at 151; N. Bammens & D. Bettens, *The Potential Impact of Pillar Two on Tax Incentives*, 51 Intertax, *supra* note 1416, at 164.

1602. *See* the elaborations made in the Commentary in that respect, *see GloBE Commentary on Article 5 GloBE Model Rules (2022)*, *supra* note 474, paras 46–48.

be seen, it still leaves the option to shift payroll and investments in 'Local Tangible Assets' to 'Low-Tax Jurisdictions'. Third, also jurisdictions can indirectly amend their tax policy to impact the SBIE: the payroll component, e.g., includes benefits and remunerations like payments to 'Pension Funds', retirement benefits, social security contributions or any payroll taxes.[1603] By, for example, increasing social security contributions or payroll taxes, the SBIE of 'MNE Groups' doing business in the respective jurisdictions will rise as well, leaving more tax policy leeway to provide for CIT benefits.

It has been pointed out in several places that any exemption from a minimum tax is in tension with the objectives of such a tax. Both the SBIE as well as the 'International Shipping Income Exclusion' constitute such exemptions. Nevertheless, it is understandable that the OECD decided to implement a substance carve-out: in international tax law, it was taken for granted for decades that countries should be free to decide for themselves whether and to what extent to tax corporations, as long as the economic substance of a structure ('substance-over-form' principle) can be demonstrated in a comprehensible manner. Against this background, it is not surprising that the SBIE was a core issue of debate within the IF from the very beginning: traditional 'Low-Tax Jurisdictions' and developing countries insisted on a substance-based carve-out to keep tax policy leeway to attract foreign direct investments by granting corporate tax benefits. Thus, the SBIE is simply part of the compromise of the IF on the famous 'Global Tax Deal'. Nevertheless, as shown, it is clearly in tension with the principle aims of a minimum tax.

4.5.3 GloBE Obliges to Collect 'Top-up Tax' Even in Loss Situations

GloBE, at least pursuant to the OECD's political mantra, aims to establish a minimum tax on profits. However, the case of ACTT has shown (*see* section 4.4.2.6.2.) that 'Top-up Tax' can also arise in a 'Fiscal Year' in which an 'MNE Group' suffers losses within a jurisdiction. But why is there a minimum tax if there are no profits?

As has been revealed, ACTT may arise either (i) if GloBE requires the recalculation of both the ETR and the 'Top-up Tax' (in detail, *see* section 4.4.2.6.2.) pursuant to Article 5.4.1.(a) GloBE Model Rules and Article 29(1) GloBE-Directive or (ii) in the special case of deferred tax assets arising due to a permanent difference in a year in which there is no 'Net GloBE Income' in a specific jurisdiction (in detail *see* section 4.3.4.7.) pursuant to Article 5.4.1.(b) GloBE Model Rules and Article 29(3) GloBE-Directive. In the first kind of scenario, it is obvious that any ACTT arising is due to a 'Top-up Tax' that should have been but had not been levied due to any act or event that only took place subsequently: these events require a complete re-computation of the ETR and the 'Top-up Tax' of a previous 'Fiscal Year'; but instead of requiring the correction of previous tax returns filed by an MNE Group, GloBE, as a simplification, allows the adjustment of the 'Jurisdictional Top-up Tax' in the 'Fiscal Year' in which the recomputation is to be made. In these cases, it is completely consistent to levy the

1603. *See Ibid.*, para. 34.

respective amount of 'Top-up Tax' that had not been levied in the previous 'Fiscal Year'. Finally, in these scenarios, any ACTT can only occur to the extent the subsequent adjustment would have affected the 'Top-up Tax' liability of previous years. Consequently, positive ACTT can only arise if the 'Top-up Tax' of the previous years had been underestimated and if the subsequent increase of 'Top-up Tax' is not covered by the SBIE of the 'Fiscal Year' subject to recomputation.

The special case of Article 4.1.5. GloBE Model Rules and Article 21(5) GloBE-Directive, however, is different. In this case, the cause for ACTT arising pursuant to Article 5.4.1.(b) GloBE Model Rules and Article 29(3) GloBE-Directive is traced within the current year in which the ACTT is to be levied: as a matter of fact, any losses permitted to be carried forward pursuant to domestic tax laws are to be accounted as a deferred tax asset under accounting rules. If, however, due to a permanent difference, the domestic tax loss exceeds the 'GloBE Loss', the recorded deferred tax asset, pursuant to financial accounting rules, exceeds the amount that would have been recorded if the deferred tax asset had to be recognized in line with GloBE. For this reason, Article 4.1.5. GloBE Model Rules and Article 21(5) GloBE-Directive oblige to collect the amount of deferred tax that is attributable to the permanent difference. This measure is odd for several reasons: first, ACTT would arise irrespective of the nominal tax rate of the jurisdiction at issue. GloBE requires recasting any deferred tax assets recorded at a rate exceeding 15% at the minimum rate. So even if the tax rate of the jurisdiction at issue would be far above 15%, 'Top-up Tax' would be due, although the domestic loss in excess to the 'GloBE Loss' would never lead to an ETR below the 15% from a multi-period perspective. Second, in general, Article 4.1.5. GloBE Model Rules and Article 21(5) GloBE-Directive give rise to 'Top-up Tax' before it is even clear that the excess loss can finally be used to reduce domestic tax liability in subsequent years. Rather, the respective ACTT would be levied even if the 'MNE Group' never receives profits again within the tested jurisdiction. The third and most triggering oddity (iii) is the fact that Article 4.1.5. in conjunction with Article 5.4.3. GloBE Model Rules and Articles 21(5) and 29(3) GloBE-Directive give rise to ACTT irrespective of whether there is substance within a specific jurisdiction.[1604] As set out above, the ACTT directly reduces the 'Top-up Tax' liability calculated by multiplying 'Excess Profits' (step 5) by the 'Top-up Tax Percentage' (step 4) of a specific jurisdiction. Consequently, the SBIE cannot provide shelter from any ACTT levied. The provisions are, thus, highly questionable from a tax policy point of view and should be amended in such a way that the respective loss attributable to a permanent difference cannot be used to increase the amount of 'Covered Taxes' in subsequent years but does not give rise to a deferred tax asset in the current 'Fiscal Year'.[1605] According to the current design of Article 4.1.5. GloBE Model Rules and Article 21(5) GloBE-Directive, 'Top-up Tax' might be levied irrespective of whether the loss can really be used in future and irrespective of whether it would be covered under the SBIE within the tested jurisdiction. Although the OECD

1604. *See* in particular Florian Brugger et al., *Globale Mindestbesteuerung: Ermittlung des GloBE-Steueraufwands*, 97 SWK, *supra* note 1099, at 666–667.

1605. Convincingly, *see Ibid.*, at 667.

has addressed the issue within its GloBE Administrative Guidance February 2023,[1606] it is questionable whether the proposed 'administrative procedure' will be implemented by the IF Member States if it obviously conflicts with the wording of Article 4.1.5. GloBE Model Rules. Within the GloBE-Directive, the implementation of the respective procedure would, in the author's opinion, even require an amendment of the GloBE-Directive.[1607]

4.5.4 GloBE Aggregates Taxes and Profits of Entities Located in the Same Jurisdictions

The OECD intensively discussed several blending options and decided to take a jurisdictional approach, and as pointed out in several places above,[1608] the jurisdictional blending approach is first not implemented in a fully consistent manner and, second, has its natural flaws. The GloBE base heavily relies on 'Consolidated Financial Statements', which aim to inform relevant environments of an 'MNE Group' about the financial situation of a whole 'MNE Group' irrespective of how it is structured and where its group entities are tax resident or where they constitute PEs. Rather, the 'Consolidated Financial Statements' combine individual statements of every 'Entity' within a single balance sheet. But isn't it odd to artificially split the 'Consolidated Financial Statements' of an 'MNE Group' into the statement of its individual corporate tax paying entities prepared in advance of consolidation, even requiring a further split of these individual statements into 'Main Entity' and its PEs?

From the author's perspective, one can only affirm this question. The artificial splitting of financial accounts is the source of GloBE's complexity and, as will be seen, its odd relationship with tax treaties (*see* section 5). GloBE requires determining fictitious individual financial statements aligned with the financial accounting standard of the UPE for every single CE (necessarily including PEs and even including CEs that are excluded from consolidation due to materiality thresholds) within the 'MNE Group' simply to be able to aggregate profits jurisdiction-wise. One can doubt whether this is the best option to implement a minimum tax system.[1609]

The crucial point is that jurisdictional blending is not only complicated but can lead to curious results: if a UPE is a mixed holding which has participations in various sub-groups in different business sectors, all CEs located in the same jurisdiction must nevertheless be aggregated for the purposes of the ETR computation. This consequence occurs despite the fact that the various group divisions may have nothing in common at all, apart from the fact that they are included within the same 'Consolidated Financial Statements'. But much worse than that: if the shareholdings of a UPE in the sub-holding entities are below 80%, these sub-holding entities must apply the IIR as POPEs and need to calculate the ETR and 'Top-up Tax' by including entities that do not

1606. *GloBE Administrative Guidance February 2023*, at 49–54.
1607. In detail *see* s. 4.3.4.7.
1608. *See* s. 4.3.2.1.3, s. 4.3.2.2.2. and 4.3.2.2.3.
1609. On a perspective from game-theory, *see* C. W. Sanchirico, *Should a Global Minimum Tax Be Country-by-Country?*, Tax Notes Intl. (25 Apr. 2022).

even form part of their own sub-groups. Indeed, the question arises whether it would not have made more sense to create a regime for POPEs similar to that for 'Minority-Owned Subgroups', which are considered a separate 'MNE Group' for the purposes of ETR and 'Top-up Tax' calculation. Finally, if a POPE is obliged to apply the IIR, it does not even prepare the 'Consolidated Financial Accounts' itself and might not receive the information required to proceed with the jurisdictional blending.

As has been revealed in the previous sections, there are exceptions to jurisdictional blending. These include 'Investment Entities', 'Minority-Owned Constituent Entities' and 'Stateless Entities'. With respect to 'Investment Entities' and 'Minority-Owned Constituent Entities' jurisdictional blending only takes place among 'Investment Entities' and MOCEs (forming so-called Minority-Owned Subgroups) being 'located' within the same jurisdiction. 'Stateless Entities' are to be considered as being 'located' in a separate jurisdiction, leading to the consequence that their ETR and 'Top-up Tax' is always computed on an entity level. The same holds true for single 'Investment Entities' and MOCEs 'located' in a jurisdiction in which no other 'Investment Entities' or 'Minority-Owned Constituent Entity' is 'located'. The policy reasoning behind those schemes and the fact that not all of them are convincing have already been discussed in section 4.3.2.2.3.

4.5.5 GloBE Allows Tax Revenues to Be Collected by Low-Tax Jurisdictions

In contrast to the initial concept of the OECD's 'GloBE-Proposal' that was first presented in the PoW published in May 2019,[1610] the final consensus on the global minimum tax permits every jurisdiction to collect the 'Top-up Tax' arising within its tax sovereignty on its own. In technical terms, GloBE acknowledges so-called soak-up taxes by reducing the 'Jurisdictional Top-up Tax' (step 6). Finally, if there is no 'Jurisdictional Top-up Tax' remaining, there is no need to apply either IIR or UTPR.

As has been revealed in section 4.4.2.6.3., it is thus unlikely that 'high-tax jurisdictions' will, at least directly, gain much of revenues by implementing GloBE. Rather, GloBE creates a strong incentive for jurisdictions, irrespective of whether they are high- or low-tax jurisdictions, to introduce a QDMTT simply to protect domestic tax revenues.[1611] Nevertheless, GloBE for sure reduces the incentive to shift profits to tax havens due to the fact that a minimum tax of 15% on 'Excess Profits' might be collected anyway, irrespective of which state finally collects the respective tax. In this way, despite QDMTT, GloBE might indirectly increase CIT revenues of 'high-tax jurisdictions' because 'MNE Groups' will increasingly baulk at artificial profit shifting via complex and expensive multi-tier corporate structures, including shell entities, as the created tax benefits might be nullified by GloBE anyway. Furthermore, in the long-term, developed countries might regain investments from 'Low-Tax Jurisdictions' simply due to the fact that they provide a better business environment and, due to the

1610. *Programme of Work.*

1611. *See*, e.g., N. Noked, *The Case for Domestic Minimum Taxes on Multinationals*, 105 Tax Notes Intl., *supra* note 1389, at 667.

global minimum tax, the tax advantages provided for in the respective 'Low-Tax Jurisdictions' cannot make up their competitive disadvantage compared to a developed market anymore.[1612] However, shifting payroll and tangible assets to 'Low-Tax Jurisdictions' might give rise to amounts of SBIE that could provide shelter from any 'Top-up Tax' arising. Finally, even for in-scope 'MNE Groups', profit shifting remains attractive if 'Excess Profits' can successfully be reduced, either by the SBIE or tax strategic accounting policy; this concerns the next two theses.

4.5.6 GloBE from an Overall Perspective Might Reduce Tax Competition but Certainly Does Not Put an End to It

The impact of GloBE on global tax competition is probably one of the most discussed topics in the scientific community of international tax law in recent years.[1613] It would, thus, be presumptuous to make a final assessment here. Nevertheless, the technical analysis of GloBE has revealed conclusions that, in the meanwhile, are also undisputed in literature: GloBE certainly tackles harmful tax competition. Once a 'critical mass' of jurisdictions decided to implement Pillar Two, the 'diabolic machinery'[1614] of GloBE starts to work out: if certain 'Excess Profits' are not taxed at the minimum rate, the respective tax is levied elsewhere. But just as certainly as GloBE might harm tax competition, it is beyond doubt that GloBE is not the end of tax competition. This conclusion can be drawn in three respects.

First of all, every tax has its scope, and so does GloBE. GloBE does not pose any limits for jurisdictions to compete by way of tax measures with respect to corporate taxpayers that are, for whatever reason, not within the scope of its framework. Above all, this includes individuals irrespective of any revenue threshold (finally, GloBE only taxes 'Constituent Entities' *'that are members of an MNE Group'*, requiring that an 'Entity' is at issue)[1615] and all MNE Groups that stay below the EUR 750 million. However, also 'Excluded Entities' including 'Governmental Entities', 'International Organisations', 'Non-profit Organisations' as well as 'Pension Funds' are completely outside the scope of GloBE and do not need to provide any evidence that their profits are taxed at any minimum and irrespective of whether their role is similar to an 'MNE Group' or a CE within an 'MNE Group'. However, admittedly, most of the listed organizations do not pose any BEPS risks. This does not hold true for 'Investment Funds' and 'Real Estate Investment Trusts'. However, these only qualify as 'Excluded Entities' if they are the UPE of an 'MNE Group'. Consequently, for the latter group of 'Excluded Entities', the minimum tax kicks in at the level of any participation held by such vehicles, which is why their profits regularly will be subject to the minimum tax at the level of their participation.

1612. On that argument, *see* L. Parada, *Tailoring Developing Country Advice: A Response to Noam Noked*, 105 Tax Notes Intl. 783 (14 Feb. 2022).

1613. *See* in particular J. Becker & J. Englisch, *supra* note 469, at 483 et seq.; J. Englisch, *supra* note 769; M. Devereux et al., *supra* note 1359; M. Devereux et al., *supra* note 774.

1614. This term was prominently used by R. Mason, *A Wrench in GLOBE's Diabolic Machinery*, 107 Tax Notes Intl., *supra* note 1456, at 1391–1395.

1615. In detail on the technical ramifications of the term 'Entity', *see* s. 4.2.3. and 4.2.4.

Second, every tax has its exemptions, and so does GloBE. Nearly every domestic system of corporate income tax provides for certain tax exemptions or specific deductions like free amounts to specifically incentivize acts of corporate taxpayers. Within GloBE, such a deduction is the SBIE, working like a free amount directly deducted from the amount of payroll employed and tangible assets located within the jurisdiction that is tested for the purposes of the minimum tax. Any profit that is covered within the SBIE is exempted from the minimum tax, regardless of the amount at which these profits are actually taxed. The same holds true for 'International Shipping Income' that is exempted from the GloBE base and is excluded from the 'GloBE Income or Loss'. Consequently, any profits that qualify as 'International Shipping Income' are tested against the minimum tax level. Thus, GloBE does not pose any limits to tax competition with respect to profits covered by the SBIE or falling within the definition of 'International Shipping Income'.

Every piece of tax legislation leaves loopholes and does leave leeway for interpretation, and so does GloBE. It is true that GloBE's set of rules is extremely comprehensive and has already closed many conceivable gaps. However, as the technical analysis has also shown, the devil is, as so often, in the details: GloBE exceeds any notion of complexity, and it is well known that complex provisions are necessarily more complex to interpret as well. It is impossible to list all the interpretation problems here, but there is no question that both national tax administrations and 'MNE Groups' will interpret the provisions of GloBE to their advantage as much as possible. For example, those jurisdictions that wish to attract foreign direct investment will subject the SBIE to the broadest possible meaning vis-à-vis other jurisdictions to prevent collection of 'Top-up Tax' by way of IIR and UTPR: take, for example, the term 'Local Tangible Asset' which can be interpreted in many ways; although the Commentary provides some guidance to give the appearance of certainty with respect to its interpretation.[1616] Similar problems are likely to arise with respect to 'Qualified Refundable Tax Credits' enabling jurisdictions to give a tax credit to corporate taxpayers without reducing the amount of 'Adjusted Covered Taxes' within the respective jurisdiction.[1617] However, the question of interpretation arises with almost every provision. Ultimately, tax competition is also possible to the extent that the legal framework leaves room for interpretation or implementation options for the jurisdictions.

Finally, there is an argument that GloBE even promotes tax competition to a certain extent: pursuant to Devereux, Vella & Wardell-Burrus 'Low-Tax Jurisdictions', due to GloBE must give even more tax-related benefits to remain attractive to 'MNE Groups'. Since the SBIE allows for any tax rate with respect to profits that are covered within the amount of SBIE, GloBE might even create an incentive to reduce the nominal CIT rate down to zero.[1618] Evidently, reducing the CIT rate necessarily includes the risk

1616. *See GloBE Commentary on Article 5 GloBE Model Rules (2022)*, *supra* note 474, para. 37 et seq.
1617. In detail, *see* s. 4.3.3.3.3. and 4.3.4.3.4.
1618. M. Devereux et al., *supra* note 1359, at 9. Reaching at a similar conclusion, also *see* N. Bammens & D. Bettens, *The Potential Impact of Pillar Two on Tax Incentives*, 51 Intertax, *supra* note 1416, at 169.

that any profits not covered within the SBIE might be subject to 'Top-up Tax' collected by jurisdictions that implemented GloBE. However, jurisdictions could still implement a QDMTT skimming off the 'Top-up Tax' on those profits that are not covered within the SBIE of an 'MNE Group' within a specific jurisdiction.

4.5.7 GloBE Shifts Tax Competition from Tax Laws to Accounting Standards, At Least to a Certain Extent

Through a consistent reliance on the 'Consolidated Financial Statements', GloBE heavily interacts with financial accounting rules;[1619] and this interaction is still under-researched. In general, it is a novelty that 'MNE Groups' are taxed based on their 'Consolidated Financial Statements'.[1620] The author of this thesis is convinced that it will take years, if not decades, to scientifically reveal the complex interrelationship between accounting rules and GloBE.

It had been extensively discussed in the previous sections[1621] that not only does GloBE's base determination heavily rely on the accounting standard applied by the UPE, rather, what is even more important, also the scope of GloBE is directly connected to the financial accounting standards of the UPE (in detail, *see* section 4.2.3.2.).[1622] Actually, the financial accounting standard applied by the UPE to prepare its 'Consolidated Financial Statements' is significant for the determination of the scope of an 'MNE Group'. Finally, the group of entities consolidated in the financial statements also influences the EUR 750 million threshold, of course. It is, thus, obvious that GloBE could shift competition between tax legislation to competition between accounting legislation. GloBE certainly limits tax policy leeway of tax legislatures but leaves the door open to change accounting rules.

One could argue that jurisdictions can protect their domestic UPEs by providing more generous accounting rules. However, to limit the risk of shifting tax competition to accounting legislation, any 'Consolidated Financial Statements' that are not prepared under an 'Acceptable Financial Accounting Standard' are under the scrutiny of the so-called Material Competitive Distortion Test obliging the alignment of the respective accounts of the 'MNE Group' to IFRS-standards, if the aggregated variation exceeds EUR 75 million. GloBE only expresses uncontrolled confidence in the so-called Acceptable Financial Accounting Standards, including the IFRS, US GAAP, and every other GAAP applied within the EU. Interestingly, 'Acceptable Financial Accounting Standards' are not tested whether their consolidation requirements are consistent with the purpose of GloBE: 'Acceptable Financial Accounting Standards' could be freely adjusted in a way that they only require consolidation at a very high shareholding percentage, that they tend to underestimate profits and that they provide for extensive

1619. For an extensive analysis of this interaction, *see* E. Eberhartinger & G. Winkler, *supra* note 281, at 134–154.
1620. V. Bendlinger, *Minimum Taxation – Ergebnisse der Konsultationen zum GloBE Proposal der OECD*, 32 SWI, *supra* note 187, at 31.
1621. *See* in particular ss 4.2.3.2. and 4.3.3.2
1622. Also emphasizing the direct connection of accounting rules and the scope of GloBE, *see* B. Salehy, *A Global Tax System? Appraising the Model GloBE Rules*, 67 BTR 621 (2022).

elections to adjust accounting policy in a way that is beneficial under the legal framework of GloBE. However, as *Englisch* has pointed out, the QDMTT might mitigate the risk of jurisdictions trying to compete by way of accounting standards.[1623] Changing accounting principles applied to the UPE intend to tackle IIR collection. If, however, source jurisdictions introduce a QDMTT anyway, the UPE's jurisdiction will not profit from providing more generous accounting rules.[1624]

Another interesting and noteworthy point in this regard was made by *Herzfeld*, who pointed out that IFRS is being further developed, in particular, by the IASB, which is a private board that is not subject to control by fiscal authorities.[1625] Also, in this respect, GloBE raises new questions with regard to the interrelationship of tax and accounting rules. Should the decision on basic principles of scope and profit determination for tax purposes be placed in private hands? It is certainly true that private boards like the IASB might have significant influence on accounting rules. However, at least in the EU, the IFRS must be adopted by the EU legislature. Given this fact, the risk that non-government institutions could really influence accounting principles in a way that undermines GloBE can be assumed to be low.

4.5.8 GloBE Reveals Not Only Technical Inconsistencies But Also Lacks Consistent Policy Goals

Indeed, it is the technical implementation of the 'Top-up Tax' that sheds light on the ambit of the global tax deal for a global minimum tax. First of all, it is worth emphasizing that there can be no doubt that the creation of the GloBE Model Rules and the corresponding Commentary, which, in the meanwhile, has reached consensus among more than 140 jurisdictions, is a significant achievement. Nevertheless, GloBE is a political compromise, and it is in the nature of a compromise that it necessarily includes inconsistencies: first, the analysis of Article 5 GloBE Model Rules reveals the technical drawbacks of GloBE and second, apart from these, the analysis of the ETR and 'Top-up Tax' calculation also reveals inconsistencies in tax policy.

To start with the technical inconsistencies, let us first elaborate on the constant change of perspective of the GloBE Model Rules: on the one hand, the scope of an 'MNE Group' for GloBE purposes is determined from the consolidated financial accounts of the UPE presenting the assets and liabilities of all entities within a group, on the other hand, the 'Adjusted Covered Taxes' as well as the 'GloBE Income' are to be determined from the financial accounts of every single CE within the 'MNE Group'. One could already critically assess why the 'Consolidated Financial Statements' are used if they must be artificially split up again into the respective legal entities. Nevertheless, there is certainly an argument for this procedure: after all, a line-by-line consolidation can only be carried out when the individual entities adjust their separate financial statements to the accounting standard of the consolidating 'ultimate' parent. The

1623. Also *see* Eva Eberhartinger & Georg Winkler, *supra* note 281, at 147.
1624. J. Englisch, *GloBE Rules and Tax Competition*, 50 Intertax, *supra* note 769, at 4.
1625. M. Herzfeld, *U.S. Treasury to Congress: Hand Over the Tax Keys, Please*, 102 Tax Notes Intl., paras 1585 et seq. (2021).

individual financial statements thus already exist, which can be used by GloBE to determine the GloBE Income and the 'Adjusted Covered Taxes'. The matter becomes odd, however, if one considers that GloBE's jurisdictional blending approach again requires a jurisdiction-wise aggregation of 'Adjusted Covered Tax' and 'GloBE Income and Loss', and once the jurisdiction-wise ETR and the resulting 'Jurisdictional Top-up Tax' is determined, the application of the GloBE Rules again requires an allocation of the 'Jurisdictional Top-up Tax' to the respective CEs located in a 'Low-Tax Jurisdiction'. To exaggerate, the procedure for the 'Top-up Tax' computation is as follows: GloBE starts from the consolidated financial statement, which is then split into individual legal entities and PEs in order to aggregate Tax as well as Income jurisdiction-wise and finally allocate the resulting 'Top-up Tax' again to individual companies. And still, this is not the end: rather, the pending 'Top-up Tax' of every single LTCE is to be attributed to other legal entities by means of the IIR and the UTPR; and as has been shown, this is no easy task either.[1626]

Last but not least, the tax policy inconsistencies of GloBE resulting from the analysis of its technical framework should be addressed. If one remembers the beginnings of GloBE, the result of the global consensus now promoted by the OECD seems quite strange: while GloBE was once clearly credited with combating harmful tax competition, from today's perspective, one can doubt as to whether GloBE in its current form actually prevents tax competition.[1627] Looking at the consideration of economic substance within GloBE, it becomes clear that the minimum tax level of 15% does not mean that the profits of an 'MNE Group' reported in its 'Consolidated Financial Statements' are actually taxed at 15%. Rather, the SBIE still enables 'MNE Groups' to push the corporate tax rate to well below 15% and, in extreme cases, even to 0%. As a result, tax competition between states is not harmed at all as long as sufficient assets are located, and payroll costs occur in the respective 'Low-Tax Jurisdiction'.[1628]

Furthermore, the implementation of the QDMTT, which enables countries to protect their tax jurisdiction against the IIR and the UTPR, completely changes the perspective. Since the Pillars had initially been launched by OECD in 2019, it has become apparent that Pillar Two developed significantly faster than Pillar One. The reason for the faster progress of Pillar Two and especially GloBE could have been that the large Western industrialized countries, which are usually high-tax countries themselves, were expecting to gain revenue through Pillar Two by simply collecting 'Top-up Tax' arising in low tax jurisdictions, specifically investment hubs, whereas Pillar One, as a mere redistribution of taxation rights, also entailed an obvious risk of losing tax revenues for the western world. The QDMTT, however, has reversed this supposed effect of GloBE. The QDMTT allows 'Low-tax Jurisdictions' (and high-tax countries with low-taxed CEs) to collect the 'Top-up Tax' arising at domestic CEs

1626. *See* s. 4.4.2.8.
1627. Also taking note of the fact that the final design of GloBE is 'not fully aligned with' the 'broad objective' of curbing harmful tax competition, *see* N. Bammens & D. Bettens, *supra* note 1416, at 156 et seq.
1628. Already *see* s. 4.5.6.

themselves. Thus, with the introduction of GloBE, countries have even less incentive to raise taxes since there is the SBIE and even where profits exceed the SBIE, they can simply 'skim off' the arising 'Top-up Tax' through a QDMTT.[1629] Finally, the possibility of introducing a QDMTT may even be an active incentive for tax havens to reduce nominal CIT rates.[1630]

But what, then, is the remaining purpose of GloBE? Is it to establish a minimum tax level for excess profits? Is it the creation of a de facto obligation for tax havens to tax those profits? Or is GloBE intended to create a mere deterrent effect for aggressive tax arrangements, whatever one may understand by that? Which policy rationale remains for this additional layer of administrative burdens to taxpayers? The author's opinion is that the purpose of GloBE is what the technical framework has revealed: GloBE is a minimum tax on 'Excess Profits' and simply reduces the leeway for domestic tax legislatures to introduce a highly preferential CIT-environment for MNE Groups hitting the EUR 750 million threshold. Admittedly, this simple conclusion does not fit the highly complex regulatory framework of GloBE. However, the sheer complexity of GloBE does not change anything in this respect. Politically, GloBE was intended to create a minimum level of tax for large 'MNE Groups'; that GloBE does not consistently pursue this goal is obvious and is, certainly, a different story. The GloBE Model Rules represent a compromise of an IF that, in the meanwhile, includes more than 140 jurisdictions. Finally, as with every compromise, the GloBE Model Rules are as good as the compromise could be; the technical framework of GloBE is a proxy for 140 diverging tax policy interests, necessarily including perspectives of well-known 'Low-Tax Jurisdictions' seeking to attract foreign investments by heavily granting tax benefits to multinationals. Otherwise, the existence of the SBIE (*see* section 4.4.2.5.) or the 'Shipping Income Exclusion: (*see* section 4.3.3.4.) could not be explained: any exception to the minimum tax is necessarily at odds with the actual goal of establishing a minimum tax level. In any case, it is the scope and complexity of the set of rules created by the OECD make it clear that a new era of international tax cooperation against harmful tax competition has dawned. However, the GloBE Model Rules and its Commentary also reveal that GloBE will probably not be the end of this era.[1631]

1629. Comprehensively on tax policy perspective of the SBIE and the QDMTT, *see* M. Devereux et al., *supra* note 1359.
1630. *See*, e.g., N. Bammens & D. Bettens, *supra* note 1416, at 166.
1631. This section is based on V. Bendlinger & G. Kofler, *Computation of the Effective Tax Rate and the 'Top-up Tax'*, in *Pillar 2 Global Minimum Tax*, *supra* note 305, at 41.

CHAPTER 5

The GloBE Model Rules and the GloBE-Directive and Their Relation to Tax Treaties and Other Sources of Public International Law

5.1 OVERVIEW: THE IMPLEMENTATION OF GLOBE AND ITS RELATION TO THE PRE-EXISTING LANDSCAPE OF INTERNATIONAL TAX LAW

Traditionally, international tax law has been based mainly on bilateral tax treaties, which still form the pillars of international tax law. The entire BEPS discussion revolved to a large extent around the comprehensive network of tax treaties around the globe. As in any legal system, a new set of rules must find a place in the fabric of existing law; and of course, this is also true for the global minimum tax. Once implemented, GloBE will co-exist with comprehensive networks of tax treaties among taxing jurisdictions[1632] and for quite some time, it seemed that this might not be an issue: contrary to tax treaties, GloBE does not aim to distribute taxing rights. Thus, the OECD argued that it could not identify any significant conflicts between GloBE and tax treaties. Already the Blueprint concluded, with reference to the 'saving clause' enshrined in Article 1(3) OECD MC, that '[a]*s a general matter, then, tax treaties should not present any obstacle to jurisdictions implementing an IIR and UTPR along the lines envisaged under the GloBE*'[1633].[1634] One could argue that GloBE simply does not care

1632. Also *see* D.G. Noren, *Modifying Bilateral Income Tax Treaties to Accommodate Pillar Two UTPR Rules*, Bloomberg Tax – Tax Management Memorandum 1 (14 Nov. 2022), https://images.mwe.com/Web/MCDERMOTTWILLEMERYLLP/%7B92249201-7ae1-4c77-9dc4-459255e5a7d6%7D_Modifying_Bilateral_Income_Tax_Treaties_to_Accommodate_Pillar_Two_UTPR_Rules_David_Noren.pdf?utm_campaign=MITN%2012.9.22&utm_medium=email&utm_source=Eloqua.

1633. *Tax Challenges Arising from Digitalisation – Report on Pillar Two Blueprint*, para. 680.

about the question of which state may tax what. GloBE's sole purpose, if such a consistent purpose can be defined at all,[1635] is to achieve a minimum level of tax of 15 % levied on 'Excess Profits' of 'MNE Groups' exceeding the EUR 750 million revenue threshold. In principle, according to the designated political goal of GloBE, it does not matter which state ensures the tax level and finally levies the minimum tax. So why could the relation between GloBE and tax treaties raise issues at all?

The GloBE Model Rules themselves contain, as far as can be seen, only one minor reference on potential treaty issues. In Art 10.3.5. GloBE Model Rules it is stated: "*Where* [...] *a dual-located Entity that is a Parent Entity is located in a jurisdiction where it is not subject to a Qualified IIR, then the other jurisdiction can require such Entity to apply its Qualified IIR* unless it is restricted by an applicable Tax Treaty in force" (emphasis added). Although this provision clearly confirms that there may be situations where the application of GloBE may raise treaty issues, it does not add much to the question of whether the GloBE Rules are consistent with tax treaties in general. The provision merely clarifies that, in the case of a dual resident entity, both residence states are in principle entitled to apply the IIR.

Also the GloBE Commentary makes only marginal reference to GloBE's potential treaty conflicts in two separate paragraphs: first, the GloBE Commentary recognizes that '*concerns about the intended application of* [the IIR] *can arise where a Parent Entity jurisdiction, which would otherwise apply the IIR in accordance with the provisions of Article 2* [GloBE Model Rules], *has entered into bilateral Tax Treaties in which it has adopted the exemption method (instead of a credit method) to eliminate double taxation of income arising in the other jurisdiction*'.[1636] In the next sentence, however, the GloBE Commentary addresses this concern with the recommendation to negotiate a possible 'switch-over rule', a change from the exemption to the credit method, in the DTCs, which otherwise apply exemption with respect to business profits. The GloBE SOR, which was once explicitly envisaged in the Blueprint[1637] as a supplement to the IIR, suddenly disappeared in the October Statement of the OECD/G20[1638] for unknown reasons. Apparently, the OECD considers the potential conflicts of the IIR with DTCs caused by the exemption method to be so marginal that it only merited two sentences in the GloBE Commentary to the issue. In its GloBE Administrative Guidance February 2023, the OECD and the IF continue to uphold this maxim: '*Consistent with the intention of the Inclusive Framework, the GloBE Rules (including the IIR and UTPR) are designed so that the imposition of top-up tax in accordance with those rules will be compatible with the provisions of the UN and the Model Tax Convention on Income and*

1634. In detail on the OECD's statements regarding the relation of GloBE and tax treaties in the Blueprint, *see* J. Li, *The Pillar 2 Undertaxed Payments Rule Departs From International Consensus and Tax Treaties*, 174 Tax Notes Intl. 1700 (21 Mar. 2022).
1635. *See* the previous s. 4.5.8.
1636. *See GloBE Commentary on Article 2 GloBE Model Rules (2022)*, *supra* note 238, para. 2.
1637. *Tax Challenges Arising from Digitalisation – Report on Pillar Two Blueprint*, paras 453–456.
1638. *OECD/G20 Statement 8 October*.

on Capital Condensed Version 2017, (the 'OECD Model Tax Convention')'.[1639] However, as has been recently noted in the literature, the statement adds nothing to the debate about whether the GloBE Rules are really in line with tax treaties or not.[1640]

With regard to the UTPR, the OECD's statements in the Blueprint[1641] are, in the meanwhile, outdated, as the design of the former 'Undertaxed Payments Rule' as a deduction limitation for intra-group payments[1642] in the Blueprint has significantly changed to the 'UTPR' as a backstop 'Top-up Tax' collection mechanism in the GloBE Model Rules.[1643] It is curious that the GloBE Commentary does not take a position at all but merely states that the domestic law provisions implementing the UTPR shall be '*coordinated with* [...] *a jurisdiction's international obligations, including those under Tax Treaties*'.[1644] The OECD, therefore, implicitly acknowledges that there may be legitimate doubts about the treaty compatibility of the UTPR but hesitates to identify and solve potential conflicts.

It is not surprising that a lively discussion has emerged in the literature as to whether the OECD has underestimated the potential treaty conflicts caused by GloBE, in particular with respect to the UTPR.[1645] From a historical perspective, tax treaties simply aimed to prevent double taxation by determining which of the two states may tax what. The state having the taxing right could tax, and the other would either be restricted to tax under the treaty or would be obliged to provide relief by way of credit or exemption. But that is all that a DTC can do: tax treaties generally do not restrict either state in its decision as to which events it wishes to tax under domestic law, how it calculates the tax, to whom it attributes the taxable income and at what rate it is levied. The traditional 'taxing right' under a tax treaty, thus, inherently includes the sovereignty to decide not to exercise this right that has been assigned to one of the contracting states ('jurisdiction not to tax').[1646] It is a very recent development of the BEPS project that tax treaties, besides eliminating double taxation, additionally aim to tackle double non-taxation.[1647] Thus, in the treaty models of the OECD and the UN, as

1639. *See* para. 2 of the executive summary of the *GloBE Administrative Guidance February 2023*, at 6.
1640. *See* in that regard, M. Herzfeld, *Who Wins Out in the Latest Pillar 2 Guidance?*, 109 Tax Notes Intl. 824 (13 Feb. 2023).
1641. *Tax Challenges Arising from Digitalisation – Report on Pillar Two Blueprint*, at 123 et seq.
1642. For a detailed examination of the former design of the UTPR, *see* J. Becker & J. Englisch, *supra* note 469, at 507 et seq.
1643. On the current design of the UTPR, *see* already s. 4.4.2.8.3.
1644. *See GloBE Commentary on Article 2 GloBE Model Rules (2022)*, *supra* note 238, para. 47.
1645. *See*, e.g., M. F. De Wilde, *Why Pillar Two Top-Up Taxation Requires Tax Treaty Modification – Kluwer International Tax Blog*, Kluwer International Tax Blog, https://kluwertaxblog.com/2022/01/12/why-pillar-two-top-up-taxation-requires-tax-treaty-modification/ (last visited 22 Jan. 2023); R. Goulder, *Pillar 2 and Tax Treaties: MLI, Where Are Thou?*, 108 Tax Notes Intl. 775 (7 Nov. 2022); J. VanderWolk, *Tax Treaties Pose Problems for the UTPR*, 108 Tax Notes Intl. 29 (3 Oct. 2022); J. VanderWolk, *The UTPR is Inconsistent with the Nexus Requirement of Tax Treaties*, Kluwer International Tax Blog, https://kluwertaxblog.com/2022/10/26/the-utpr-is-inconsistent-with-the-nexus-requirement-of-tax-treaties/ (last visited 22 Jan. 2023).
1646. For a broader perspective, *see* B.F. Liotti, *Limits of International Cooperation: The Concept of 'Jurisdiction Not to Tax' from the BEPS Project to GloBE*, 76 Bull. Intl. Taxn. 63–81 (2022).
1647. However, double non-taxation was not the primary focus of BEPS. Rather, the OECD emphasized that double non-taxation is problematic, if profits are shifted artificially to achieve a situation of double non-taxation, *see Action Plan on Base Erosion and Profit Shifting*,

well as in international DTC practice, certain mechanisms have become established that aim to prevent the use of treaties to achieve a result of double non-taxation and to avoid unintended non-taxation.[1648] However, this does not change the fact that a taxing right under a DTC, unless a specific provision ('subject-to-tax clauses') is agreed upon between the contracting states, also includes the right of the contracting states to waive its taxing right without allowing the other contracting state to tax the respective income. Finally, this right not to tax (or to sovereignly decide at which rate) is the source of potential conflicts between the global minimum tax and tax treaties: if a contracting state applies the IIR or the UTPR to one of its resident CEs of an 'MNE Group' because a CE in the other contracting state is subject to an ETR that is below 15%, one could argue that the former state uses the taxing right the other did not exercise (this is what has been called the 'Use-It-or-Lose-It Principle' of GloBE).[1649] The latter contracting state could, of course, prevent the IIR or the UTPR either by way of increasing domestic ETR or by implementing a QDMTT. But still, the respective state is theoretically deprived of its 'right not to tax' if such a right was granted to the state pursuant to a specific tax treaty.[1650] The sources of potential conflicts arising from the distribution of taxing rights under tax treaties will be examined in section 5.2. The analysis will largely be based on the OECD MC and largely follows its technical structure.

Once it is determined which sources of conflict might occur between GloBE and tax treaties, the question arises of how such conflicts can be solved. In order to get to the bottom of this question, it must first be determined from which legal sphere a conflict with an international agreement such as a tax treaty could arise. From the perspective of international law, the following question occurs: are the GloBE Model Rules to be seen as part of a global consensus (keyword '*common approach*')[1651] establishing something like a source of international law *sui generis*, which de facto obliges IF Member States to implement GloBE or are implementations of the GloBE Model Rules simply to be assigned to the domestic legal sphere of the implementing jurisdiction(s)? The first result would mean that a potential conflict between GloBE and tax treaties would be a conflict between norms within the same legal sphere of public international law that is to be resolved by the methodology of public international law. Contrary, the latter result would indicate that potential conflicts would involve both domestic and international legal spheres and would have to be solved by domestic constitutions. Section 5.3. is devoted to this question.

The implementation of GloBE within the EU by way of a directive raises special issues and adds another layer of complexity to the resolution of normative conflicts: directives oblige the EU's Member States to implement the directive's content into their

---

at 10: '*No or low taxation is not per se a cause of concern, but it becomes so when it is associated with practices that artificially segregate taxable income from the activities that generate it*'. In detail, *see* Liotti, *supra* note 1646, at 69 et seq.

1648. *See* for example Art. 23A(4) OECD MC.

1649. A. Christians & T.D. Magalhaes, *Undertaxed Profits and the Use-It-or-Lose-It Principle,* 108 Tax Notes Intl. 705 et seq. (7 Nov. 2022).

1650. In the same vein, *see* Liotti, *supra* note 1646, at 79.

1651. *OECD/G20 Statement 8 October*, at 3–4.

domestic laws, and if a Member State fails to do so, the Member State is in violation of EU law, and the directive trumps domestic law of the Member States. But is EU law also supreme over tax treaties concluded by the Member States? In particular, from the perspective of third countries, EU law belongs to the domestic legal sphere of the respective Member State. So, what is the relation of the GloBE-Directive to tax treaties of the Member States, and how will the EU's legal order solve the potential normative conflicts identified in section 5.2.? These questions will be addressed in section 5.4.

It is undisputed that tax treaties are by far the most important source of international tax law. Nevertheless, most literature assumes the existence of basic principles of international taxation in the sense of customary international (tax) law. For example, it has become established practice that a person's state of residence should have the primary right to tax his or her income and that corporate profits, for example, should only be taxed in the source state if a PE is established there. In the recent literature, a turbulent debate has been triggered as to whether there is a kind of customary international tax law and to what extent GloBE might conflict with such legal spheres.[1652] This will be examined in more detail in section 5.5., before drawing a conclusion on the relationship between GloBE and international (tax) law in section 5.6.

5.2 POTENTIAL CONFLICTS BETWEEN THE REGULATORY FRAMEWORK OF GLOBE AND EXISTING TAX TREATIES

5.2.1 'Constituent Entities' as Covered Persons under Article 1 OECD MC

Each application of a DTC starts with the question of whether the taxpayer invoking the treaty is a covered person under Article 1 OECD MC. Consequently, a potential conflict

1652. *See*, e.g., J. Li, *The Pillar 2 Undertaxed Payments Rule Departs From International Consensus and Tax Treaties*, 174 Tax Notes Intl., *supra* note 1634, at 1699; S. Picciotto, *UTPR Critics Miss the Point of Tax Treaty Principles*, 108 Tax Notes Intl. 153 (10 Oct. 2022); J. VanderWolk, *The UTPR Disregards the Need for Nexus*, 108 Tax Notes Intl. 545–546 (31 Oct. 2022); H. Wardell-Burrus, *Four Questions for UTPR Skeptics*, 108 Tax Notes Intl. (2023), *supra* note 1560, at 699 et seq.; S. Picciotto, *Justifying the UTPR: Nexus and Economic Connection*, 108 Tax Notes Intl. 667 (7 Nov. 2022); A. Christians & T.D. Magalhaes, *supra* note 1649, at 705–709; J. VanderWolk, *Much Ado About Pillar 2*, 108 Tax Notes Intl. 821–823 (14 Nov. 2022); R.S. Avi-Yonah, *UTPR's Dynamic Connection To Customary International Law*, 108 Tax Notes Intl. 951–952 (21 Nov. 2022); J. VanderWolk, *The UTPR Is Far From Becoming Part of Customary International Tax Law*, 108 Tax Notes Intl. 1069–1070 (28 Nov. 2022); J. Kadet, *Defending the UTPR: Creative Corporate Structuring Can't Hide Real Connections*, 108 Tax Notes Intl. 1072–1073 (28 Nov. 2022); T.D. Magalhaes, *Give Us the Law: Responses and Challenges to UTPR Resisters*, 108 Tax Notes Intl. 1257–1261 (5 Dec. 2022); S. Picciotto, *Rebutting the Logic of UTPR Skeptics*, 108 Tax Notes Intl. 1371 (12 Dec. 2022); N. Boidman, *An Ironic Turn: Skeptic and Supporter Find Some UTPR Common Ground*, 108 Tax Notes Intl. 1533 (19 Dec. 2022); J. VanderWolk, *The UTPR: Taxing Rights Gone Wild*, 108 Tax Notes Intl. 1369–1370 (12 Dec. 2022); H. Wardell-Burrus, *The UTPR as a Rule of Recognition*, 108 Tax Notes Intl. 1528–1529 (19 Dec. 2022); F. Debelva & L. De Broe, *Pillar 2: An Analysis of the IIR and UTPR from an International Customary Law, Tax Treaty and European Union Law Perspective*, 50 Intertax 898–900 (2022) DOI: 10.54648/taxi2022098; R.S. Avi-Yonah, *The UTPR and the Treaties*, 109 Tax Notes Intl. 46 (2 Jan. 2023).

between a tax treaty (for the purposes of this analysis, every reference without specific note relates to the OECD MC 2017) and GloBE can only arise for persons that fall within the personal scope of both legal frameworks. But this is where it gets complicated: the OECD MC covers persons '*who are residents of one or both*'[1653] of the two contracting states, while GloBE covers a bundle of such residents, known as 'MNE Groups'. The OECD MC, however, only recognizes single entities and follows a 'separate entity approach';[1654] an 'MNE Group' can never qualify as a resident person pursuant to Article 1(1) OECD MC[1655] unless domestic law treats such 'MNE Groups' as a separate '*corporate body for tax purposes*' (Article 3[1][b] OECD MC) which is not the case in most tax jurisdictions. Therefore, 'MNE Groups' are non-existent from the perspective of tax treaties; rather, every entity within the 'MNE Group' is considered a separate taxpayer and if the respective taxpayer qualifies as a person that is a resident pursuant to Article 4 OECD MC, the respective entity may invoke the treaty. However, it should not be overlooked that GloBE does not deviate from the 'separate entity approach' in principle:[1656] both the 'GloBE Income' as well as 'Adjusted Covered Taxes' are computed on an entity basis, and the IIR and UTPR are applied to separate CEs. It is true that the scope of GloBE might deviate from the 'separate entity approach' in a certain way; however, this does not mean that GloBE considers the 'MNE Group' as a taxpayer on its own.[1657] The jurisdictional ETR computation does not change this either, since jurisdictional blending only changes the standard of the ETR computation, but not the fact that the minimum tax is ultimately levied at the level of a legal entity or a PE of such a legal entity. Pursuant to GloBE, the respective CEs of an 'MNE Group' are subject to a QDMTT, an IIR or the UTPR and not the 'MNE Group' as such. Isolated literature claims postulating the existence of a 'unitary approach' according to which GloBE taxes the 'Group' as such and not its members can, under the author's opinion, neither be derived from the legal framework of GloBE nor from tax treaties and are, in my opinion, untenable.[1658] Such a view may (or may not) be a desirable future path in tax policy, but it cannot be derived from the existing legal framework.[1659] It is true that GloBE, to a certain extent, as Magalhaes puts it, forms '*a hybrid model that combines elements of*

1653. Article 1(1) OECD MC 2017.
1654. Also *see* D. G. Noren, *supra* note 1632, at 3; L.E. Schoueri, *Some Considerations on the Limitation of Substance-Based Carve-Out in the Income Inclusion Rule of Pillar Two*, 75 Bull. Intl. Taxn. 547 (2021).
1655. Consequently, Picciotto fails to recognize fundamentals of treaty law when he concludes that the separate entity approach '*has no basis in tax treaties*', *see* S. Picciotto, *Justifying the UTPR: Nexus and Economic Connection*, *supra* note 1652, at 667. Convincingly criticizing Picciotto in this respect, *see* J. VanderWolk, *supra* note 1652, at 821; R. Goulder, *supra* note 1561, at 909.
1656. Also *see* R. Goulder, *supra* note 1561, at 908–909.
1657. Convincingly emphasizing this point, *see* Jefferson VanderWolk, *Much Ado About Pillar 2*, *supra* note 1652, at 821.
1658. Nevertheless taking this view, *see* S. Picciotto & J. Kadet, *The Transition to Unitary Taxation*, 108 Tax Notes Intl. 454 (24 Oct. 2022).
1659. In the same vein, *see* N. Boidman, *No Rational Role for the UTPR*, 108 Tax Notes Intl. 287 (17 Oct. 2022), who notes, that he '*agree*[s] *with that thought* [that it is irrational to treat a subsidiary as an independent person], *but it does not support a linkage to the UTPR because that linkage ignores the architecture and its effects in terms of UTPR of current tax systems*'.

the separate-entity and unitary approach'.[1660] However, the links of the IIR and the UTPR to separate entities are too strong to argue that GloBE, only because its scope is defined in a 'unitary' manner by including an 'MNE Group' of entities, would establish such a 'unitary approach'.

So, the question arises as to which CE within the in-scope 'MNE Group' can rely on which DTC and which treaty might be violated by the GloBE Rules or the QDMTT.[1661] From the perspective of an 'MNE Group', the application of the GloBE Rules could potentially conflict with a variety of DTCs. The number of potentially affected DTCs depends on the number of states in which an 'MNE Group' has a CE that is considered a resident for purposes of a DTC and the number of DTCs concluded among each of those states. Consequently, the number of potentially affected DTCs depends on the number of states in which an 'MNE Group' establishes CEs that are considered a resident for purposes of a DTC and the number of DTCs concluded between each of those states. Assume an 'MNE Group' has CEs (each of them legal entities) resident in 50 jurisdictions. If each of these 50 states had concluded DTC with each other, conflicts with 1225 bilateral DTCs could arise for just the one 'MNE Group' at issue. As will become apparent, this is only one of the reasons why the relation between GloBE and DTCs is legally challenging.

In any case, one can already anticipate that it is not possible to draw any general conclusions about whether the IIR and the UTPR are in line with tax treaty law or not from a global perspective. Rather, the (in)compatibility of the IIR and the UTPR with DTCs depends on the individual circumstances of a specific case and the specific structure of the 'MNE Group' at issue: if the IIR is applied at the level of a specific 'Parent Entity' within the Group, it needs to be tested first, whether the respective CE is a resident of the jurisdiction applying the IIR and which treaty might be violated. The same holds true with respect to the UTPR. Whether a specific contracting state violates a treaty by applying a 'Qualified IIR' or a 'Qualified UTPR' needs to be assessed based on the individual DTC. If, e.g., the 'Top-up Tax' allocated to an LTCE is levied at the level of two different 'Parent Entities' within the same 'MNE Group' by way of the IIR, it is quite conceivable that collecting IIR from the first 'Parent Entity' will constitute a violation of a treaty but not for the other 'Parent Entity'. Whether the levying of an IIR or UTPR violates a DTC must therefore be examined at the level of the CE to which they are applied. Figure 15 illustrates the issue.

1660. T.D. Magalhaes, *UTPR Opposition: A Game of Whack-a-Mole*, 108 Tax Notes Intl. 1531–1532 (19 Dec. 2022).

1661. Also posing this question with regard to the compatibility of UTPR with DTCs, *see* H. Wardell-Burrus, *supra* note 1560, at 702.

Figure 15 Tax Treaty Entitlement Pursuant to Article 1 OECD MC – Which Treaties Could Be Violated by the GloBE Rules?

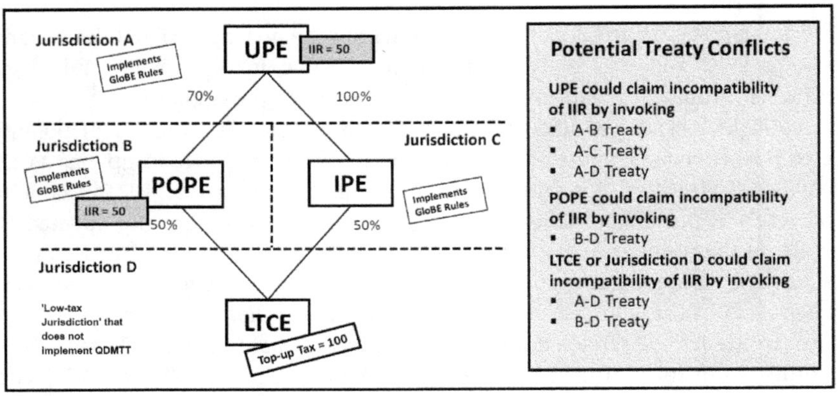

But which CEs are considered covered persons pursuant to Article 1(1) OECD MC? Article 3(1)(a) OECD MC defines the term person as an '*individual, a company and other body of persons*'.[1662] This definition is supplemented by another separate definition of the term company in Article 3(1)(b) OECD MC, including '*any body corporate or any entity that is treated as a body corporate for tax purposes*'.[1663] Thus, it is obvious that not every CE within an 'MNE Group' is entitled to apply a tax treaty. Not every CE is a covered person under Article 1(1) OECD MC and *vice versa*. This is especially true for PEs: as explained in detail above, GloBE adopts the PE definition for purposes of allocating taxes and income to specific jurisdictions and, for this reason, considers PEs as CEs in their own right.[1664] However, from the perspective of the OECD MC, a PE is not a resident person but rather an inseparable part of a non-resident taxpayer. Thus, if the IIR or the UTPR is collected at the level of a PE qualifying as a CE of an 'MNE Group', the respective CE is, as a rule, and besides exceptional cases of the PE non-discrimination provision on Article 24(3) OECD MC in certain triangular situations,[1665] not entitled to invoke a treaty. Also, 'Flow-through Entities' or 'Investment Entities' might qualify as separate CEs but might lack treaty entitlement.[1666] In any case, one can conclude that a normative conflict between GloBE and a DTC is only conceivable if a jurisdiction either applies the GloBE Rules to a treaty-entitled entity that is a CE of an in-scope 'MNE Group' or if it taxes income by way of the QDMTT, IIR or UTPR that is attributable to a treaty entitled taxpayer.

1662. Article 3(1)(a) OECD MC 2017.
1663. Article 3(1)(b) OECD MC 2017.
1664. *See* s. 4.2.4.1.2.
1665. *OECD Model Tax Convention on Income and on Capital: Commentary on Article 24*, para. 69 et seq. (21 Nov. 2017).
1666. On the treaty entitlement of 'Collective Investment Vehicles', *see OECD Model Tax Convention on Income and on Capital: Commentary on Article 1*, para. 23 et seq. (21 Nov. 2017).

5.2.2 'Top-up Tax' as a Covered Tax under Article 2 OECD MC

A normative conflict between DTC and the QDMTT, IIR or UTPR is only conceivable if they are applied to a resident person pursuant to Articles 1 and 4 OECD MC or, arguably if they tax income of such a person. However, in addition to the personal scope of application, the material scope of application of the respective DTC must also be fulfilled. The latter is defined in Article 2 OECD MC and covers '*taxes on income or capital*'. Thus, the question arises whether 'Top-up Tax' levied by way of the IIR and UTPR can be qualified as covered taxes within the meaning of Article 2 OECD MC. If one concludes that taxes levied by way of GloBE are not covered by DTCs, this would mean that there could be no conflict between DTCs and GloBE.[1667]

However, Article 2 OECD MC leaves little doubt that any 'Top-up Tax' levied might be within its ambit: first, it is clear that GloBE imposes a 'tax'. If a contracting state implements the global minimum tax along the lines of the GloBE Model Rules, QDMTT, IIR and UTPR are compulsory payments.[1668] One might argue that the way the 'Top-up Tax' is levied might deviate from common CIT systems; however, Article 2(1) OECD MC makes clear that the '*manner in which* [a tax] *is levied*'[1669] is irrelevant for its qualification as a covered tax. Second, it is also clear that both the IIR and UTPR levy taxes on income. Both collect an amount of tax ('Top-up Tax') on 'Excess Profits' ('GloBE Income' - SBIE). GloBE's base determination also allows for deduction of expenses, which is usually understood as a strong indication for the qualification as an income tax, although the term 'income' does not necessarily have to be associated with a net figure.[1670] Third, pursuant to Article 2(4) OECD MC, '[t]*he Convention shall apply also to any identical or substantially similar taxes that are imposed after the date of signature of the Convention in addition to, or in place of, existing taxes*'.[1671] Indeed, one could question whether GloBE is either '*identical*' or '*substantially similar*' to a common CIT system, as it is only levied if and to the extent that the ETR is below the minimum rate of 15%.[1672] But the same argument could be invoked in favour of '*substantial similarity*' of GloBE to existing income taxes as well. Finally, GloBE levies a tax in the absence of '*sufficient*' domestic taxation and, finally, taxes '*in place of existing taxes*', arguably, in place of non-existing source taxation or source taxation that is simply below an ETR of 15%. But is there any argument at all that taxes collected under GloBE are not covered by DTCs?

1667. This had been claimed by A. Christians & S.E. Shay, *The Consistency of Pillar 2 UTPR With U.S. Bilateral Tax Treaties*, 109 Tax Notes Intl. 454 (2023).
1668. Also *see* A.P. Dourado, *The Pillar Two Top-Up Taxes: Interplay, Characterization, and Tax Treaties*, 50 Intertax (2022), *supra* note 1521, at 395.
1669. Article 2(1) OECD MC 2017.
1670. Extensively on Art. 2(3) OECD MC, *see* M. Klokar, *Chapter 5: The List of Taxes According to Article 2(3) OECD Model Convention 1982 and 2017*, in *Taxes Covered under Article 2 of the OECD Model*, s. 5.2 (G. Kofler et al., eds, 2020).
1671. Article 2(4) OECD MC 2017.
1672. Also *see* De Broe, emphasizing that '*the IIR and UTPR are not typical direct income taxes*', *see* L. De Broe, *Some EU and Tax Treaty Law Considerations on the Draft EU Directive on Global Minimum Taxation for Multinationals in the Union*, 50 Intertax 882 (2022) DOI: 10.54648/taxi2022096.

The strongest argument could be that, in 2022, there is not a single DTC that refers to QDMTT, IIR or UTPR in the typical list of covered taxes (Article 2[3] OECD MC). It is true that the list in Article 2(3) OECD-MC is, according to the Commentary on Article 2 OECD MC, not exhaustive and is of a purely declaratory nature.[1673] Nevertheless, there are still DTCs in force in which the covered taxes article is limited to an exhaustive list of covered taxes. For such DTCs, it would be difficult to argue that the contracting parties intended the 'Top-up Tax' levied by IIR or UTPR to be captured by the treaty.[1674] This is all the more true if such a DTC is concluded subsequently to domestic adoption of GloBE of one of the two contracting states. In this case, one could only see GloBE as being a covered tax by extensively interpreting the separate items of the list of covered taxes. If, for example, the exhaustive list referred to the CIT of both contracting states, one could try to interpret the term 'corporate income tax' in such a way that it would also cover the tax on 'MNE Groups' levied by the global minimum tax. However, if a specific DTC contains an equivalent provision, at least like Article 2(2) OECD MC, it seems almost impossible to see any 'Top-up Tax' levied by GloBE falling outside the ambit of the respective DTC.[1675] Nevertheless, Christians & Shay[1676] have taken a minority view with respect to the question of whether UTPR qualifies as an income tax under Article 2 OECD MC: '*No precedent for the UTPR has been identified so far, nor are we aware of authority that would support the view that the UTPR is identical or substantially similar to any treaty partner's existing covered tax under a U.S. tax treaty*'.[1677] Eventually, the authors conclude that the UTPR is not a tax on profits but rather a sort of 'excise tax'.[1678]

This view, however, is not at all convincing: first of all, the OECD itself considers both IIR and UTPR as covered taxes, as its elaborations on treaty compatibility in the Blueprint[1679] and the Commentary[1680] would otherwise be redundant. Second, which is even more important, neither IIR nor UTPR are the minimum tax as such. Rather, both are collection mechanisms for an amount of 'Top-up Tax' that is to be calculated from an amount of 'GloBE Income' (*see* Step 6 of 'Top-up Tax' computation in section 4.4.2.6.) multiplied by the so-called Jurisdictional Top-up Tax (which is the difference between the minimum rate of 15% and the jurisdictional ETR). Certainly, it can be conceded that the UTPR is a new mechanism to tax profits of other taxpayers, is neither identical nor substantially similar to other mechanisms to collect income taxes, nor one could claim, although this might be a rather weak argument, that '*the UTPR liability is several steps removed from the taxable profit of the related entity*'.[1681] However, this does not change the fact that, as Article 2 OECD MC presupposes, the UTPR imposes a

1673. *OECD Model Tax Convention on Income and on Capital: Commentary on Article 2*, *supra* note 990, para. 6.
1674. For the same conclusion, *see* Klokar, *supra* note 1670, s. 5.5.
1675. Drawing the same conclusion, *see* Luc De Broe, *supra* note 1672, at 882.
1676. A. Christians & S.E. Shay, *supra* note 1667, at 450–451.
1677. *Ibid.*, at 451.
1678. *Ibid.*, at 448–449 and 454.
1679. *Tax Challenges Arising from Digitalisation – Report on Pillar Two Blueprint*, paras 679–696.
1680. *GloBE Commentary on Article 2 GloBE Model Rules (2022)*, *supra* note 238, paras 2 and 47.
1681. This argument has been put forward by, although not directly related to the interpretation of Art. 2 OECD MC, *see* H. Wardell-Burrus, *supra* note 1560, at 701.

tax on income, and already Article 2(1) OECD MC clearly states that the OECD MC '*shall apply* [...] *irrespective of the manner in which* [the income tax is] *levied*'.[1682] However, this need not apply to DTCs that do not contain a provision corresponding to Article 2(1) OECD-MC. In the latter case, IIR and UTPR could only be considered as covered taxes by way of an autonomous interpretation of the respective covered taxes article.

It will be exciting to see to what extent GloBE will be taken into account by international state practice in future DTC negotiations with respect to the covered taxes article. For example, contracting states could explicitly exclude QDMTT, IIR, or UTPR from the definition of covered taxes, as was also done in the GloBE Model Rules.[1683] This could eliminate conflicts between DTCs and GloBE from the outset. Although unlikely, the opposite would also be at least conceivable: contracting states could also agree on explicitly adding QDMTT, IIR and UTPR to the list of covered taxes for the purpose of a tax treaty. In any case, it is obvious that a treaty containing a covered taxes article patterned pursuant to Article 2(1) OECD MC covers the QDMTT, IIR and UTPR. As the OECD, with respect to treaty compatibility, referred to Article 1(3) OECD MC and paragraph 81 of the Commentary on Article 1 OECD MC addressing CFC Regimes,[1684] also the OECD has implicitly confirmed that it considers both the IIR and the UTPR as being covered taxes pursuant to Article 2 OECD MC.[1685] Because if the OECD considered neither IIR nor UTPR to be a covered tax under Article 2 OECD MC, the respective reference would be superfluous.

5.2.3 GloBE and the Distribution of Taxing Rights

5.2.3.1 Basic Considerations on GloBE and the Distribution of Taxing Rights

As it turns out, then, neither the personal nor substantive scope of DTCs prevents a conflict between GloBE and DTCs per se. Any CE that is a resident person can invoke a treaty, provided that the covered taxes article can be interpreted as covering the imposition of a 'Top-up Tax'; and as long as one starts from the OECD MC, it can hardly be argued that this would not be the case. However, fulfilling the ambit of a treaty does not necessarily produce a conflict with GloBE. Once it has been established that there is nothing to prevent the application of a DTC, the distributive rules of Articles 6–8, 10–19 and 21 OECD MC must be used to determine which contracting state (in terms of GloBE which jurisdiction) is entitled to tax the relevant income. A conflict between DTCs and GloBE is therefore only conceivable if, by way of QDMTT, IIR or UTPR, a tax is levied on a resident or, with respect to the QDMTT and UTPR, a PE of a non-resident although the 'Top-up Tax' is attributable to income that, according to the respective

1682. Article 2(1) OECD MC.
1683. Article 4.2.2. *GloBE Model Rules* and Art. 20(2) GloBE-Directive (2022/2523).
1684. *Tax Challenges Arising from Digitalisation – Report on Pillar Two Blueprint*, para. 679 et seq.
1685. Also *see* L. De Broe, *supra* note 1672, at 883.

treaty, '*may be taxed*' in the other contracting state.[1686] But what income does the 'Top-up Tax' actually tax?

From the perspective of DTCs, this question is tricky: first of all, GloBE's 'Top-up Tax' is an amount of tax and not income.[1687] Thus, one cannot simply argue that any 'Top-up Tax' levied is in conflict with the distributive rules. Second, GloBE aggregates the 'Top-up Tax' jurisdiction-wise while tax treaties distribute taxing rights among resident persons. So how can we even analyse how the DTC distribution of taxing rights relates to GloBE? There is probably no way around looking at the GloBE base. Finally, the 'Top-up Tax' is the result of a previous income determination. Its collection, either by way of QDMTT, IIR or UTPR, is the actual exercise of a taxing right that is either permitted or not permitted by the legislative framework of a tax treaty. In order to get to the bottom of the question of the compatibility of GloBE with the distribution of taxing rights according to the OECD MC, the GloBE base determination must be brought into focus.

As already discussed in detail in section 4.3.3., the actual GloBE base determination starts from the individual financial statements of each CE prepared in preparation for consolidation.[1688] Therefore, GloBE primarily assigns the income to the jurisdiction in which the corresponding CE is 'located'. For good reasons, the OECD has not used the DTC term 'resident' for the purposes of GloBE, although the concepts of 'residency' and 'location' are undoubtedly comparable and overlap. The actual distinction of the terms does not even mean that they mean something different; on the contrary, rather, Article 10.3.1 GloBE Model Rules and Article 4(1) GloBE-Directive are based on the same criteria as Articles 1 and 4 OECD MC. In other words, if a legal entity (that is neither a 'Flow-through Entity' nor a PE) is considered a tax resident in a state under that state's domestic law based on its '*place of management, place of creation or similar criteria*',[1689] the same legal entity is a 'resident person' for DTC purposes as well as 'located' for GloBE purposes in that state. Differences between the terms 'residency' and 'location' exist only because, as explained in section 4.2.4.4.1. above, there are CEs that are treated as separate persons by GloBE but are usually not considered as separate persons in DTCs (e.g., PEs, 'Flow-through Entities' or 'Investment Entities'). So basically, both DTCs and GloBE start from the same premise: a legal entity's income is primarily assigned to the jurisdiction where it is considered to be a tax resident under domestic law.

Based on this premise, however, the following question arises: which state may tax which income under the OECD MC of a resident or a PE of a non-resident CE and in which situations does a state that implements GloBE along the lines of the GloBE

1686. The IIR can never be applied at the level of a CE that is a PE because the IIR only applies to UPEs, IPEs or POPEs, none of which a PE can qualify for, *see* Art. 10.1. *GloBE Model Rules*. Also *see* Arts 3(14), 3(20) and 3(22) GloBE-Directive (2022/2523). Also *see* s. 5.2.6.2.

1687. Also *see* Luc De Broe, *supra* note 1672, at 883–884.

1688. *See* Art. 3.1.2. *GloBE Model Rules* and Art. 15(1) GloBE-Directive (2022/2523).

1689. *See* Art. 10.3.1.(a) *GloBE Model Rules*, Art. 4(1) GloBE-Directive (2022/2523) and Art. 4(1) OECD MC 2017 referring to very similar criteria.

Model Rules pose taxes on income that *'may be taxed'* or *'may only be taxed'* in the other state pursuant to a treaty? In principle, the distributive rules of Articles 6, 7, 8, 10 to 12, 13 and 21 OECD MC may be relevant for a resident CE, whereby the distributive rule for business profits in Article 7 OECD MC is by far the most relevant. Thus, the following section will first address the relation of GloBE to Article 7 OECD MC and, in the subsequent section, to other distributive rules that could conceivably be relevant for CEs of an 'MNE Group' will be addressed. For the purpose of keeping a clear structure to the analysis of the relation between GloBE and the distributive rules, the 'saving clause' will deliberately be ignored in the following three sections but will be discussed in depth in section 5.2.6.

5.2.3.2 The GloBE Rules and Their Relation to the Distributive Rule for Business Profits in Article 7 OECD MC

According to Article 7(1) OECD MC 'Business Profits' may only be taxed in the state of residence unless the enterprise has a PE in the other contracting state. In the latter case, the PE state may, pursuant to the second sentence of Article 7(1) OECD MC, tax the profits that are attributable to the PE. However, even if there is a PE in the other state, the residence state may still tax as well but is obliged to either provide for relief of source taxation by way of exempting the PE income (Article 23A[1] OECD MC) or by giving a credit for the PE's tax (Article 23B[1] OECD MC). GloBE takes note of the PE concept in several ways: first of all, PEs are considered as separate CEs. Every legal entity is, thus, for purposes of GloBE, split into the 'Main Entity' and its PEs. Second, the PE definition heavily relies on applicable tax treaties. If a tax treaty is in force, then GloBE explicitly refers to the PE definition of the respective treaty. Thus, the question of whether a PE exists for purposes of GloBE must be determined directly by reference to the applicable DTC. Third, GloBE also allocates income between the 'Main Entity' and a PE along the lines of an applicable treaty. As it is enshrined in Article 3.4.2. GloBE Model Rules (reflected in Article 18[2] GloBE-Directive), the financial account of a PE shall be adjusted *'to reflect only the amount and items of income and expense that are attributable to the Permanent Establishment in accordance with the applicable Tax Treaty'*.[1690] In summary, then: GloBE allocates the 'Business Profits' covered by the minimum tax to that state which has the right to tax those 'Business Profits' according to an applicable DTC. But where, then, is a potential conflict between GloBE and an applicable DTC?

The point is that while GloBE allocates 'Business Profits' to the jurisdiction that may tax the income according to an Article 7 OECD MC equivalent distributive rule, it allows if the source state only taxes below the minimum tax level, the other state, or more other states to impose a 'Top-up Tax' on this respective income (less the SBIE). It is, therefore, in the nature of IIR and UTPR to tax income that, pursuant to a tax

1690. Article 3.4.2. *GloBE Model Rules.*

treaty, may actually be taxed in the other state according to Article 7 OECD-MC, which is the residence state of the LTCE: if the IIR is applied at the level of the UPE or any other CE within the group to collect a 'Top-up Tax' that had been allocated to an LTCE, the respective 'Top-up Tax' is based on income that may, pursuant to Article 7(1) OECD MC only be taxed by the state of residence of the respective LTCE.[1691] As will be seen, it cannot automatically be concluded that this is contrary to the treaty, as Article 1(3) OECD MC states that the treaty does not restrict the contracting states (state of residence of the CE obliged to apply either IIR or UTPR) to tax its residents; nevertheless, the example shows that the GloBE Rules intend to tax income that may in principle be taxed exclusively in the state where the LTCE resides. However, on the other hand, a tax treaty does not restrict contracting states from applying their definition of income. In principle, a state is not restricted to including undistributed profits of lowly taxed subsidiaries into the domestic tax base for resident entities. This is the case with respect to many CFC regimes that simply add the income of a CFC to the tax base of the resident shareholder. For this reason, *Lang* once prominently argued that CFC legislation does not violate tax treaties as undistributed profits of subsidiaries were likely to be covered by the dividend article in Article 10 OECD MC rather than the business profits article in Article 7 OECD MC.[1692] The author of this thesis doubts that this reasoning can be applied with respect to GloBE. Contrary to CFC legislation, even if the operation of the IIR might be comparable to 'CFC regimes', GloBE does not tax undistributed profits because it would, by means of UTPR, also tax profits at the level of a taxable person that would never receive the dividend. Therefore, the IIR cannot be considered in isolation from the UTPR in terms of treaty law as both merely serve as collection mechanisms but do not change anything with respect to the income they intend to tax. In the author's opinion, by applying either IIR or UTPR, a contracting state aims to tax income that is, besides certain exceptions (*see* below in section 5.2.3.3.), to be considered as business profits under Article 7 OECD MC.

If the IIR or UTPR are applied to collect a 'Top-up Tax' that had been allocated to an LTCE that is a PE, different issues might occur: in this case, the PE state may tax. However, the residence state of the 'Main Entity' may tax as well but is obliged to either exempt the income attributable to the PE or credit the source state tax on the PE pursuant to the respective treaties method article. If, for example, the IIR is applied to the 'Main Entity' with respect to income attributable to its low-taxed PE (which is a separate CE), a potential treaty conflict may only arise if the treaty follows the exemption method. This is because if the treaty applies the credit method to PE income,

1691. Also *see*, e.g., J. VanderWolk, *The UTPR Is Flawed: A Response to Prof. Picciotto*, 108 Tax Notes Intl. 285 (17 Oct. 2022); J. VanderWolk, *The UTPR is Inconsistent with the Nexus Requirement of Tax Treaties*, Kluwer International Tax Blog, *supra* note 1645.

1692. Michael Lang, *CFC Regulations and Double Taxation Treaties*, 57 Bull. Intl. Taxn. 55–56 (2003).

the residence state of the 'Main Entity' would be permitted to include the PE's income within its tax base anyway.

However, UTPR might also give rise to the reverse situation where the UTPR is collected at the level of the PE for 'Top-up Tax' arising from 'GloBE Income' of its 'Main Entity' resident in the other contracting state. In this case, a treaty conflict would be inevitable: if the PE state collects the 'Top-up Tax' by means of a UTPR, it collects a tax on income for which the residence state has the exclusive taxing right, irrespective of whether the credit or exemption method is applied in the respective treaty, as the method article is not applicable in the PE state as its taxing right is limited to the PE's income anyway.

Thus, one can conclude that the IIR is obviously at odds (as will be seen in section 5.2.6.2., not necessarily in conflict) with Article 7(1) OECD MC in all situations in which the IIR is applied to a legal entity that is considered a resident person in a contracting state of the jurisdiction in which the CE that is subject to the IIR is 'located'. The only situation in which the IIR does not conflict with Article 7 OECD MC at all is a scenario in which the 'Main Entity' is obliged to apply the IIR to one of its low-taxed PEs, and the credit method is applied. As far as the UTPR is concerned, there are no situations where there is no tension (again, not necessarily in conflict) at all with Article 7 OECD MC: the UTPR is only applied at the level of entities and with respect to items of income that do not qualify as '[p]*rofits of* [the respective] *enterprise*' or profits received by carrying on a '*business in the other Contracting State through* [its] *Permanent Establishment*'. Consequently, UTPR always levies 'Top-up Tax' resulting from income received by a different taxpayer and may only be taxed by the respective LTCE's residence state.

5.2.3.3 *The GloBE Rules and Their Relation to the Distributive Rules of Articles 6, 8, 10 to 12 and 13 OECD MC*

It is true that GloBE will predominantly cover income that is covered by Article 7 OECD MC. Nevertheless, income subject to minimum taxation under GloBE could very well be covered by other distributive rules as well. In principle, Article 6 ('Income from Immovable Property'), Article 8 ('International Shipping and Air Transport'), Articles 10 to 12 ('Dividends', 'Interest' and 'Royalties') as well as Article 13 ('Capital Gains') are conceivable. Furthermore, Article 21 OECD MC could be relevant with respect to third-state income. This section will shortly address each of these distributive rules with respect to their relation to GloBE. In any case, with respect to the IIR and UTPR, the same issues occur as with respect to Article 7 OECD MC. Both IIR and UTPR tax profits are (besides the case of PEs) received by different taxpayers being resident in a state different from that applying the GloBE Rules. As these issues have been addressed in the previous section already, the following part will focus on potential conflicts that might only arise with respect to those specific distributive rules (*see* Figure 16).

Figure 16 Potential Conflicts Between GloBE and Article 6 OECD MC

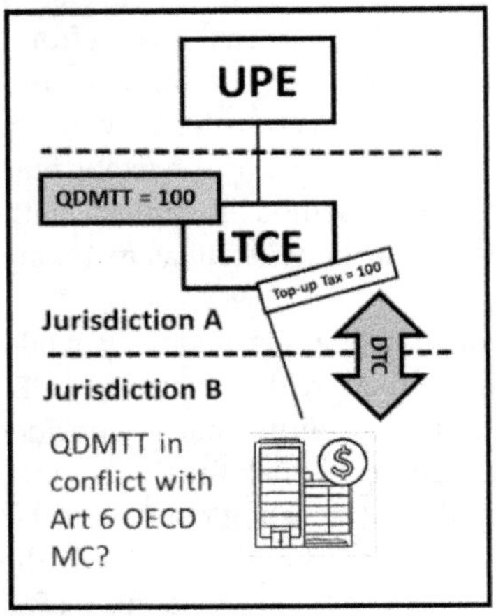

The first distributive rule that comes into consideration besides Article 7 OECD MC is Article 6 OECD MC.[1693] If a resident corporation receives income from 'Immovable Property' that is situated in the other contracting state, the respective income may be taxed in the state where the property is situated. Article 6(1) OECD MC might be of relevance for CEs subject to GloBE due to the fact that, according to Article 6(4) OECD MC, the provision is also applicable '*to the income from immovable property of an enterprise*'.[1694] Contrary to Article 6(1) OECD MC, within GloBE, any income from immovable property will be assigned to the jurisdiction in which the CE owning the 'Immovable Property' is 'located': any income of a CE from 'Immovable Property' situated beyond its residence state will finally be included in its 'Financial Accounting Net Income or Loss' of the CE-owner of the property. The respective income from immovable property will not be allocated to a PE pursuant to Article 3.5.1.(a) GloBE Model Rules (Article 18 GloBE-Directive), because the applicable tax treaty will not attribute the respective income to the PE. GloBE could, thus, conflict with Article 6 OECD MC not only with respect to the IIR and UTPR but also with respect to any QDMTT levied by the residence state of a CE owning 'Immovable Property' in a different state: assume a CE is resident in jurisdiction A. It is subject to an ETR below 15% and owns immovable property situated in state B, and the respective property cannot be allocated to a PE. If jurisdiction A applies a QDMTT to prevent any jurisdiction of the CE's 'Parent Entity' from collecting the 'Top-up Tax' by means of IIR, it levies a tax (QDMTT) on income that may be taxed in B. In this case, even QDMTT might conflict with a DTC's (in the given example, the treaty between A and B) distributive rule for immovable property. Only the 'saving clause' in Article 1(3) OECD

1693. Also considering income from real property in connection with GloBE, *see* L. De Broe, *supra* note 1672, at 885.
1694. Article 6(4) OECD MC 2017.

MC might prevent a treaty conflict in this case. However, if the exemption method is applied with respect to Article 6 OECD MC, the 'saving clause' might also not eliminate the potential conflict between QDMTT and Article 6 OECD MC as the method articles are excluded from its scope. Similar issues might arise with respect to the alienation of 'Immovable Property' pursuant to Articles 13(1) and 13(4) OECD MC.

With respect to income that falls within the ambit of Article 8 OECD MC (or the scope of Article 13[3] OECD MC), such an issue cannot arise. Pursuant to Article 8 OECD MC, the exclusive taxing right is assigned to the residence state of the enterprise irrespective of whether it has a PE in the other contracting state or not and also GloBE, thus, assigns the income to the residence state of the entity receiving income covered by Article 8 OECD MC. Issues might arise with respect to treaties, which include distributive rules for 'International Shipping and Air Transportation' where the enterprise's effective management is decisive (*see* Article 8 OECD MC 2014), as the latter might deviate from the residence of the taxpayer.[1695] In this case, the QDMTT could be in conflict with a treaty as well, as it taxes income at the level of a resident CE although the CE's income, pursuant to a treaty, may only be taxed in the other contracting state. However, one should mention that GloBE explicitly excludes 'International Shipping Income', so any conflicts between GloBE and DTC could only arise with respect to income from 'Air Transportation', which is neither covered by Article 3.3. GloBE Model Rules nor Article 17 GloBE-Directive.

As with Business Profits, GloBE allocates income from dividends, interest, and royalties to the CE-recipient, especially since it is shown in the financial statements of these entities. If such income is attributable to a PE of the 'Main Entity' under an applicable tax treaty, GloBE also attributes the income to the jurisdiction where the PE is 'located'. In these situations, the GloBE base determination, thus, follows the allocation of taxing rights under Articles 10 to 12 OECD MC, as all of these provisions also give precedence to Article 7 OECD MC if the respective income is *'effectively connected'*[1696] with a PE in the other contracting state. All three distributive rules do not pose specific risks for GloBE treaty incompatibility that goes beyond the issues that also arise with respect to Article 7 OECD MC. If either the IIR or the UTPR is applied to collect the 'Top-up Tax' of an LTCE that received either dividends, interest or royalties, the risk of incompatibility arises from the fact that the jurisdiction applying the GloBE Rules does not have the taxing right with respect to this income as the recipient is not a resident of that state. The same holds true for capital gains pursuant to Articles 13(2) and 13(5) OECD MC, both of which grant the residence state the exclusive taxing right for those gains.

1695. *See* on the relation and applicability of the 'saving clause' to Art. 8 OECD MC, *see* G. Kofler, *Some Reflections on the 'Saving Clause'*, 44 Intertax 580 (2016) DOI: 10.54648/taxi2016048.
1696. Articles 10(4), 11(4) and 12(3) OECD MC 2017.

5.2.3.4 *Interim Conclusion on the Relation of GloBE and the Distribution of Taxing Rights under Tax Treaties*

Potential treaty conflicts between GloBE and tax treaties do not arise from the distribution of income among CEs within the 'MNE Group', but from jurisdictions collecting the 'Top-up Tax' with respect to income that 'may be taxed' or 'may only be taxed' in a different state. As has been revealed, there is no conflict between the distributive rules and the GloBE base determination, besides the exceptional cases of Article 6 OECD MC 2017 and Article 8 OECD MC 2014, where the QDMTT might also give rise to treaty issues. Rather, GloBE itself makes use of the PE concept to allocate an 'MNE Group's' income among the individual jurisdictions in which it operates to finally test whether the taxable profits, for which a specific jurisdiction has a right to tax under tax treaties, are subject to an ETR of at least 15%. Thus, a conflict between the GloBE Rules and DTCs might arise due to the fact that the residence state of a CE, by applying the IIR or UTPR, taxes income that is solely taxable within the other contracting state, either because the income taxed is received by a foreign PE of the CE that is subject to the GloBE Rules or because it is received by a different legal entity resident of the other contracting state.

Essentially, then, the question now is whether a DTC does prohibit a contracting state from taxing income that was initially received by a non-resident corporation. It is not without reason that the OECD[1697] and recent literature debates[1698] draw a parallel to the question of whether CFC rules are compatible with DTCs. At its core, the DTC compatibility of GloBE is a question of whether and to what extent the residence state may tax income of another entity at the level of a resident taxpayer. In particular, the 'saving clause' in Article 1(3) OECD MC is regularly invoked, according to which a DTC should not affect the liberty of the residence state to tax its residents. So does the 'saving clause' assure GloBE's treaty compatibility? This question will be addressed in section 5.2.6. First, it must be clarified whether other provisions of the OECD-MA besides the distributive rules, namely Article 9 OECD MC or Article 24 OECD MC, might also conflict with GloBE.

5.2.4 The Relation of GloBE to Article 9 OECD MC

The GloBE Rules impose taxes on profits received by associated enterprises. It is, therefore, not too far-fetched to consider Article 9 OECD MC as a relevant provision whose relationship with the GloBE should also be examined.[1699] The essence of Article 9(1) OECD MC is that contracting states may increase the profits of associated enterprises to the extent that they have not accrued in accordance with the arm's length principle. Article 9(2) OECD MC then forces the other contracting state to make a

1697. *Tax Challenges Arising from Digitalisation – Report on Pillar Two Blueprint*, para. 681.
1698. M. Schler, *UTPR: The CFC Precedent*, 109 Tax Notes Intl. 27 (2 Jan. 2023).
1699. Also *see* R. Szudoczky, *Does the Implementation of Pillar Two Require Changes to Tax Treaties?*, 33 SWI 150 (2023).

corresponding adjustment to avoid economic double taxation.[1700] Some voices in literature did identify a parallel of the adjustments made pursuant to Article 9 OECD MC to the IIR and the UTPR: GloBE raises the tax base of another associated entity and collects it there, by way of IIR or UTPR, and as they adjust the base beyond the arm's-length-principle, they could potentially be seen as a violation of Article 9 OECD MC.[1701]

This theory has been refuted in the literature with convincing arguments. First of all, in the Blueprint, the OECD noted that the UTPR is not in conflict with Article 9 OECD MC as it is '*recognised,* [...] *that once the profits have been allocated in accordance with the arm's length principle, how they are taxed is a matter determined by the domestic law of each country*'[1702].[1703] In general, a conflict of GloBE with Article 9 OECD MC is excluded: Article 9(1) OECD MC is only applicable if a certain transaction between affiliated enterprises is not accrued at arm's-length. However, the GloBE Model Rules and the GloBE-Directive themselves require recording any transactions between CEs in accordance with the arm's-length-principle. This principle is found in Article 3.2.3. GloBE Model Rules and Article 16(4) GloBE-Directive (in detail on these provisions, *see* section 4.3.3.3.4.). Even before the 'Top-up Tax' is levied by way of IIR or UTPR, every transaction in the group (with specific exceptions within a jurisdiction)[1704] must be mandatorily adjusted. Neither the IIR nor the UTPR can therefore be applied in non-arm's-length situations. Furthermore, both the IIR and UTPR, if seen as adjustments at all, adjust the profits beyond the arm's-length-principle. Consequently, Article 9 OECD MC does in no way conflict with the regulatory framework of GloBE.[1705]

Another view in the literature, that of Picciotto, even goes so far as to try to justify the compatibility of the UTPR with tax treaties by interpreting Article 9 OECD-MC as permission to arbitrarily increase the tax base of taxpayers: after all, the provision '*underpins the broad right* [...] *for the state to adjust the accounts of a subsidiary to restore any profits that have been shifted due to the existence of common ownership and control*'.[1706] However, Picciotto's thesis is not at all convincing and was immediately met with rejection.[1707] Article 9 OECD MC simply permits to adjust individual accounts with respect to transactions between affiliates that had not been recorded at arm's-length. This has nothing to do with GloBE. Rather, GloBE adopts the arm's-length principle for the purpose of jurisdictional ETR calculation. Consequently, there is no

1700. *OECD Model Tax Convention on Income and on Capital: Commentary on Article 9*, para. 5 (21 Nov. 2017).
1701. Taking such potential conflicts into consideration, *see* V. Chand et al., *Tax Treaty Obstacles in Implementing the Pillar Two Global Minimum Tax Rules and a Possible Solution for Eliminating the Various Challenges*, 14 WTJ 12–13 (2022) DOI: 10.2139/ssrn.3967198.
1702. *Tax Challenges Arising from Digitalisation – Report on Pillar Two Blueprint*, para. 689.
1703. Also referring to the respective sentence, *see* R. Szudoczky, *supra* note 1699, at 150.
1704. *See* s. 4.3.3.3.4.
1705. *See* already J. Becker & J. Englisch, *supra* note 469, at 521; Vikram Chand et al., *supra* note 1701, at 14; R. Szudoczky, *supra* note 1699, at 150.
1706. S. Picciotto, *supra* note 1652, at 153.
1707. J. VanderWolk, *supra* note 1691, at 285.

conflict for GloBE arising from Article 9 OECD MC, nor can its DTC compatibility be based on this provision.

5.2.5 The Relation of GloBE to Non-Discrimination Pursuant to Article 24 OECD MC

Tax treaties undoubtedly focus on distributing taxing rights and, as a rule, do not limit contracting states with respect to the way they tax residents and non-residents. The design of a tax is the sole responsibility of the domestic law of the contracting states. However, there are certain provisions in the OECD MC that go beyond the distribution of taxing rights. One of these provisions is Article 24 OECD-MA containing five different prohibitions of tax discrimination, which force contracting states to eliminate discriminating tax provisions in their domestic law in specific situations. The reason for the limited scope of Article 24 OECD MC is aptly summed up in the Commentary: '*All tax systems incorporate legitimate distinctions [...]. The non-discrimination provisions of the Article seek to balance the need to prevent unjustified discrimination with the need to take account of these legitimate distinctions*'.[1708] The Commentary, thus, adds that '*the Article should not be unduly extended to cover so-called indirect' discrimination.*[1709] The core statements of the Commentary are, therefore, straightforward: national legislatures are free to treat certain situations differently. However, in certain limited situations, which are explicitly addressed in Article 24 OECD MC, the contracting states may not make such a distinction and are obliged to treat the taxpayer in the same way as in purely domestic situations. The special feature of Article 24 OECD-MA is that it is also applicable to taxes that are not mentioned in Article 2 OECD-MA,[1710] and that even the 'saving clause' does not protect the residence state from its effect.[1711] The non-discrimination provisions in the DTC are, therefore, of an absolute character.

It is obvious that discriminatory elements may be inherent in the system of GloBE: take, for example, the IIR. The IIR only applies to a 'Parent Entity' if it has a low-taxed subsidiary. If a comparable 'Parent Entity' has a subsidiary that is taxed at an ETR of at least 15%, it would not be obliged to collect the IIR. It is in the nature of a minimum tax regime that it distinguishes between a tax level that is perceived to be too low and a fixed minimum tax level. Consequently, it is not surprising that the OECD, particularly in the Pillar Two Blueprint,[1712] as well as the literature on the global minimum tax,[1713] addressed the discriminatory elements of GloBE very early on. Nevertheless, not every discrimination is prohibited; on the contrary: each provision

1708. *OECD Model Tax Convention on Income and on Capital: Commentary on Article 24*, *supra* note 1665, para. 1.
1709. *Ibid.*
1710. Article 24(6) OECD MC.
1711. Also *see*, e.g., A. Christians & S.E. Shay, *supra* note 1667, at 451–452.
1712. *See*, e.g., the elaborations of the OECD in the Blueprint with respect to the compatibility of the former design of the UTPR and Art. 24 OECD MC, *see Tax Challenges Arising from Digitalisation – Report on Pillar Two Blueprint*, at 690–696.
1713. *See* for example the pioneering work of Englisch & Becker with respect to the compatibility of the Blueprint's UTPR design and Art. 24(4) OECD MC, *see* J. Becker & J. Englisch, *supra* note 469, at 521–524.

has its scope, and the same applies to the prohibitions of discrimination in Article 24 OECD MC. Furthermore, the elaborations of the OECD in the Pillar Two Blueprint are outdated with respect to the UTPR, as the design of the UTPR in the GloBE Model Rules has significantly evolved since then. Nevertheless, this does not mean that the IIR and UTPR, as incorporated in the GloBE Model Rules, could not conceivably be in conflict with Article 24 OECD MC. In particular, the two prohibitions of discrimination in paragraphs 3 and 5 could conceivably be relevant and will be briefly discussed below.

Pursuant to Article 24(3) OECD MC, '[t]*he taxation on a permanent establishment which an enterprise of a Contracting State has in the other Contracting State shall not be less favourably levied in that other State than the taxation levied on enterprises of that other State carrying on the same activities*'. So the essence of Article 24(3) OECD MC can be summarized as follows: if a non-resident taxpayer has a PE in the other state, the source state must tax the non-resident – in respect of its PE in the same way as a resident taxpayer involved in the same business. The addressee of Article 24(3) OECD MC, therefore, is the source state, i.e., the state in which the PE is established. Article 24(3) OECD MC requires a comparison between the tax burden of a non-resident on its PE income and the tax burden of a resident subsidiary of the non-resident enterprise. So, are there situations where the GloBE Rules discriminate against PEs of non-residents? The answer is no. The IIR is not applicable to PEs. So, there is no situation conceivable which would leave a PE in a worse situation than a resident entity that qualifies as a CE. On the contrary, the UTPR also applies to PEs. A jurisdiction could indeed collect a part of the 'Total UTPR Top-up Tax' even if there is not a single resident CE, but only a PE that is a CE of the 'MNE Group' within its jurisdiction. However, this would not be discriminatory either because a fictitious resident entity that qualified as a CE of the same 'MNE Group' would be obliged to collect the UTPR as well. The GloBE rules therefore do not conflict with the PE non-discrimination provision in Article 24(3) OECD MC.

According to Article 24(5) OECD MC '[e]*nterprises of a Contracting State, the capital of which is wholly or partly owned or controlled, directly or indirectly, by one or more residents of the other Contracting State to a resident of the other Contracting State shall, for the purpose of determining the taxable profits of such enterprise, be deductible under the same conditions as if they had been contracted to a resident in the first-mentioned State*'.[1714] Under Article 24(5) OECD MC, the prohibited discriminatory element is the fact that the shareholders of corporate taxpayers are non-residents. The provision could be relevant for the UTPR, as GloBE requires a shareholder connection among all group members within the same 'MNE Group' and, pursuant to Article 2.3.1. GloBE Model Rules and the second sentences of Articles 12 and 13 GloBE-Directive, the UTPR can be implemented in a way that the CEs subject to the UTPR might be denied a deduction leading to an additional cash tax expense in the amount of the 'UTPR Top-up Tax'. So, the question is whether the UTPR denies a deduction solely because '*the capital of which is wholly or partly owned or controlled, directly or indirectly, by one or more residents of the other Contracting State*'.[1715] More abstractly, does a state

1714. Article 24(5) OECD MC.
1715. Article 24(5) OECD MC.

discriminate by applying the UTPR to resident entities because it is held by non-resident CEs? The question is not easy to answer. If the CE subject to the UTPR were held by a resident CE, the former CE would not necessarily be subject to the UTPR: consider, for example, a situation with a UPE that is resident abroad but not subject to IIR there. In this case (*see* Figure 17), the UTPR would apply to the domestic CE. If the same UPE were a resident of the same contracting state, the UPE would apply the IIR, and the same resident CE would not be subject to the UTPR. Would this situation be a prohibited discrimination under Article 24(5) OECD MC?

Figure 17 Is the UTPR Potentially in Conflict with Article 24(5) of the Treaty Between Jurisdiction A and B (Following Article 24[5] OECD MC)?

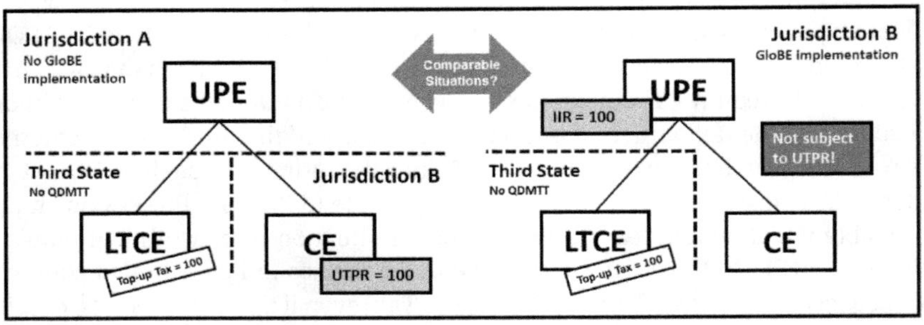

Given the fact that Article 24 OECD MC in general, according to the Commentary, only prohibits direct discrimination,[1716] one can doubt whether, in this situation, the UTPR violates Article 24(5) OECD MC and whether the situation of a CE being held by a domestic UPE being subject to an IIR is comparable to the scenario where the same CE is held by a foreign UPE not being subject to GloBE Rules at all. Pursuant to Christians & Shay, there is no violation of Article 24(5) OECD MC because the discrimination '*would not arise from the fact of foreign ownership or control but would result from the fact that the foreign owner is not in a pillar 2 country*'.[1717] Indeed, if one assumes that jurisdictions implement the UTPR along the pattern of the GloBE Model Rules, the UTPR does not lead to a prohibited discrimination under Article 24(5) OECD MC. It seems that the discriminatory element in the situation above is not the fact that the CE is held by a resident in the other contracting state[1718] but rather the fact that the 'Top-up Tax' remained uncollected if the UPE was resident in a jurisdiction that does not treat the UPE in the same way as domestic law treats domestic UPEs: if the UPE is resident in the same state as the UTPR taxpayer, the UTPR, in principle, also applies to the domestic CE, however, its 'UTPR Top-up Tax' can be reduced by the IIR levied at the level of the UPE according to Article 2.5.2. GloBE Model Rules and Article 14(3)

1716. Sentence four of *OECD Model Tax Convention on Income and on Capital: Commentary on Article 24*, *supra* note 1665, para. 1.
1717. A. Christians & S.E. Shay, *supra* note 1667, at 452.
1718. Also *see* V. Chand et al., *supra* note 1701, at 31.

GloBE-Directive. The foreign shareholding as such is not decisive in this respect. Thus, one might assume that the UTPR gives rise to 'indirect' discrimination, which is not within the scope of Article 24(5) OECD MC. As a result, one can conclude that the GloBE Rules are unlikely to be seen as violating Article 24 OECD MC. Neither IIR nor UTPR discriminates against PEs, and also Article 24(5) OECD MC does not pose a problem to the UTPR.

5.2.6 Does the 'Saving Clause' Assure GloBE's Treaty Compatibility?

5.2.6.1 The Nature and Scope of the 'Saving Clause'

According to Article 1(3) OECD MC, the '*Convention shall not affect the taxation, by a Contracting State, of its residents except with respect to the benefits granted under paragraph 3 of Article 7, paragraph 2 of Article 9 and Articles 19, 10, 23 [A] [B], 24, 25 and 28*'.[1719] The provision was included in the OECD MC in the course of the 2017 update as a reaction to the OECD's BEPS Action 6 report[1720] on preventing the abuse of tax treaties, which recommended implementing the 'saving clause' into the OECD MC.[1721] Apart from the US, which has a long tradition of using the provision as a tax policy tool (every US tax treaty currently in force contains some sort of a 'saving clause'),[1722] the provision has not yet become firmly established in the international DTC network.[1723] The vast majority of global DTCs do not contain a provision equivalent to Article 1(3) OECD MC. However, the inclusion in the OECD MC and Article 15 Multilateral Instrument (MLI) is likely to result in the 'saving clause' being increasingly scattered in the global DTC network in the long term.[1724]

The purpose and the operation of the 'saving clause' are simple: the provision intends to preserve the taxing right of the residence state that won the tiebreaker in Article 4 OECD MC,[1725] even if one of the distributive rules granted an exclusive taxing right to the source state. It clarifies that a tax treaty should primarily restrict taxation of non-residents in the source state but should not simply turn off taxation in the state of residence. Consequently, the operation of a 'saving clause' is also closely related to the distributive rules. First, one has to examine the treaty and whether the distributive rule at issue grants the source state an exclusive taxing right on income received by a

1719. Article 1(3) OECD MC.
1720. OECD/G20, *Preventing the Granting of Treaty Benefits in Inappropriate Circumstances, Action 6: 2015 Final Report*, para. 61 et seq. (OECD 5 Oct. 2015), https://www.oecd.org/ctp/designing-effective-controlled-foreign-company-rules-action-3-2015-final-report-9789264241152-en.htm (last visited 29 Oct. 2022).
1721. In detail on BEPS Action 6 and the discussions on including the 'saving clause' into the OECD MC, *see* L. De Broe & J. Luts, *BEPS Action 6: Tax Treaty Abuse*, 43 Intertax 137 et seq. (2015) DOI: 10.54648/taxi2015011.
1722. Allison Christians & S. E. Shay, *supra* note 1667, at 449.
1723. Also *see* De Broe & Luts, *supra* note 1721, at 138.
1724. For further reference, *see* G. Kofler, *supra* note 1695, at 574.
1725. The Commentary on Art. 1 OECD MC explicitly notes that, in the case of a taxpayer qualifying as a resident under the domestic law of both states, the 'saving clause' may only be invoked by the contracting state which 'won' the tie-breaker, *see OECD Model Tax Convention on Income and on Capital: Commentary on Article 1*, *supra* note 1666, para. 21.

resident person. If this is the case, the 'saving clause' trumps the respective distributive rule and the residence state remains entitled to tax the respective income.[1726] So what does this mean for the GloBE Rules, more specifically, the IIR and the UTPR?

As already mentioned, the OECD already stated in the Blueprint at the very beginning of its elaborations under the title 'Treaty compatibility' that '[t]*he common starting point for an analysis of the compatibility of the IIR and UTPR with existing tax treaty obligations is the general principle that, with limited exceptions, tax treaties are not intended to restrict a jurisdiction's right to tax its own residents*'[1727] and immediately concludes that '[a]*s a general matter, then, tax treaties should not present obstacles to jurisdictions implementing an IIR and UTPR along the lines envisaged under the GloBE*'.[1728] Thus, in the Blueprint, the OECD assumed that the 'saving clause' could eliminate almost any potential conflict of the IIR and the UTPR with existing treaties; and it also tacitly assumed that this was a 'general principle' of tax treaties, suggesting that this 'principle' would prevent treaty conflicts even if tax treaties did not contain a 'saving clause' at all. As has already been pointed out in section 5.2.1., there is almost no further comment with respect to potential conflicts between GloBE and treaty law, so it seems that the OECD still relies on the 'saving clause' to argue GloBE's compatibility with existing treaty obligations of the IF Member States.

However, contrary to what some authors[1729] and arguably the OECD seem to believe, the existence of a 'saving clause' in a DTC does not mean that the resident State can do whatever it wants to its resident taxpayers.[1730] Like any legal provision, 'saving clauses' whether based on Article 1(3) OECD MC or Article 1(4) and (5) US MC, have their scope and, thus, also have their limits and do not establish a blanket approval of taxation of the residence state. Most importantly for GloBE, the 'saving clause' neither turns off the residence state's obligation to grant relief from double taxation pursuant to the method article nor does it affect the applicability of the non-discrimination provision of tax treaties, like the ones provided for in Article 24 OECD MC. Furthermore, especially with respect to the UTPR, it has been questioned in the literature whether the 'saving clause' could really preserve the taxing right on profits that have been received by an affiliate without control or any other ownership connection ('nexus' problem). The following sections will, thus, examine whether the 'saving clause' is the panacea for every potential treaty issue arising from the application of the IIR and the UTPR. Since both mechanisms work differently, at least from a technical point of view, their treaty compatibility is tested separately from each other.

1726. In detail, *see* Georg Kofler, *Some Reflections on the 'Saving Clause'*, *supra* note 1695, at 574 et seq.
1727. *Tax Challenges Arising from Digitalisation – Report on Pillar Two Blueprint*, para. 679.
1728. *Ibid.*
1729. *See*, e.g., H. Wardell-Burrus, *supra* note 1560, at 700 stating that a '*black letter interpretation* [of the saving clause'] *would suggest that the treaty does not prevent a contracting state form taxing its own residents on whatever basis it chooses*'.
1730. In the same vein, *see* R. Goulder, *supra* note 1561, at 908.

5.2.6.2 *(In)compatibility of 'Top-up Tax' Imposed by Means of the IIR with the OECD MC*

In order to analyse the treaty compatibility of the IIR, it is first necessary to recall how the mechanism works: the IIR is applied at the level of a 'Parent Entity' to level up the tax on income received by CEs 'located' in a 'Low-taxed Jurisdiction' to the 'Minimum Rate' of 15%. From a tax treaty perspective, the parent entity and its foreign CE-subsidiaries are separate resident persons. The income of the CE-subsidiaries may, according to Article 7(1) OECD MC, be taxed in their residence state unless the respective CE-subsidiaries have PEs in the 'Parent Entities' residence state. If the IIR now collects a tax that is based on the CE-subsidiaries income at the level of the 'Parent Entity', one could argue that the IIR taxes profits of the CE-subsidiary that is not a resident of the state which collects the IIR. The 'Parent Entity', however, is a separate resident person, and its residence state could again claim that it may also tax pursuant to Article 7(1) OECD MC because it taxes a different resident. In essence, this question is identical to the long-running debate on whether CFC regimes are compatible with tax treaties. As already explained, the IIR and 'CFC regimes' are by no means identical, and the term 'CFC regime' itself is difficult to grasp, especially since such tax mechanisms are used in domestic laws in various forms, and there is no common definition (at least outside the GloBE-Directive) of what CFC legislation is. Nevertheless, the underlying treaty issues are at least similar:[1731] Do contracting states violate a treaty if they tax residents with respect to fictitious income that equals the profits of a controlled subsidiary?

In principle, as *Kofler*[1732] points out, there are two different legal positions with respect to the answer to this question: first (i) it was[1733] and sometimes still is argued[1734] that Articles 7(1) and 10(5) OECD MC[1735] would restrict to tax income initially received by a non-resident subsidiary or second (ii), that neither of the provisions does restrict the residence state to tax its resident corporations, even if it

1731. However, several authors argue that there are reasons to negate the comparability of the IIR and CFC legislation with respect to their treaty compatibility, *see* R. Szudoczky, *supra* note 1699, at 151.

1732. G. Kofler, *Some Reflections on the 'Saving Clause'*, 44 Intertax, *supra* note 1695, at 582–583.

1733. *See* the famous decision of the French Conseil d'État, FR: Conseil d'État, 28 June 2002, No. 232276, *Société Schneider Electric.* Klaus Vogel Commentary For further reference on the opinion that CFC legislation might violate Arts 7(1) and 10(5) OECD MC, despite holding a different opinion, *see Ibid.*, at 583.

1734. *See*, e.g., Schoueri, who argues that the IIR is not an anti-abuse rule and, thus, if a treaty does not contain a 'saving clause', conflicts with tax treaties, *see* L.E. Schoueri, *supra* note 1654, at 547–548. Also *see* the observation of Switzerland on *OECD Model Tax Convention on Income and on Capital: Commentary on Article 1, supra* note 1666, para. 81, where it is stated that '*controlled foreign corporation legislation may, depending on the relevant concept, be contrary to the spirit of Article 7*', *see Ibid.*, para. 110

1735. *See*, however, the Commentary, which explicitly rejects that Art. 10(5) OECD MC could prevent the residence state from applying CFC rules, *see OECD Model Tax Convention on Income and on Capital: Commentary on Article 10*, para. 37 (21 Nov. 2017).

taxes, by means of legal fiction, undistributed income of a controlled entity.[1736] The Commentary on the OECD MC 1992 first included a paragraph with respect to treaty compatibility of CFC regimes, which stated that it was '*not easy to reconcile [...] divergent opinions*'[1737] but added that '*the view of a wide majority* [is] *that such rules and the underlying principles, do not have to be confirmed in the text of the convention to be applicable*'.[1738] In the meanwhile, the Commentary on Article 1 OECD MC 2017 states that CFC legislation '*results in a State taxing its own residents, paragraph 3 of Article 1 confirms that it does not conflict with tax conventions. The same conclusion must be reached in the case of conventions that do not include a provision similar to paragraph 3 of Article 1*'.[1739] The Commentary, thus, applies the 'saving clause' but, beyond that, argues that it is declaratory anyway, as even those treaties not containing a 'saving clause' should not stand in the way of CFC legislation. While it is not convincing that the 'saving clause' is considered a principle even applying to treaties that do not contain such a provision,[1740] it is difficult to argue that the IIR violates a treaty that includes the 'saving clause'. From a historical perspective, the 'saving clause' is not a blanket permission for the residence state to tax its residents but was intended to allow the residence state to apply CFC legislation to its resident corporations. The first predecessor of the 'saving clause', first negotiated into a DTC between Sweden and the USA in 1939, can be traced back to a preferential tax scheme of Sweden that its treaty partner intended to turn off by sort of CFC rules.[1741] Therefore, it cannot be denied that one of the main purposes of the 'saving clause' is to permit the residence state to tax its residents irrespective of whether one argues that the underlying income could be attributed to a different taxpayer.[1742] It is therefore not surprising that, in the Blueprint, the OECD referred both to the 'saving clause' in Article 1(3) OECD-MA[1743] and to paragraph 81 of the Commentary on Article 1 OECD-MA 2017[1744] to manifest the compatibility of the IIR with treaty law.

Nevertheless, some authors argue that the OECD's position regarding treaty compatibility would not be tenable because, contrary to CFC legislation, the IIR does not tackle abuse but rather aims to curb tax competition.[1745] The IIR would also apply in the absence of abusive arrangements and, thus, could not '*justify lifting the corporate*

1736. *See*, e.g., Lang, who argues that income that is taxed by way of CFC legislation is covered by the dividend article, giving the residence state the right to tax the respective income, *see* M. Lang, *supra* note 1692, at 55–56.
1737. *OECD Model Tax Convention on Income and on Capital: Commentary on Article 1*, para. 24 (1 Sep. 1992).
1738. *Ibid.*
1739. *OECD Model 2017: Commentary on Article 1*, *supra* note 1666, para. 81.
1740. As Szudoczky points out, the '*saving clause can hardly be considered a general principle of international law (neither a longstanding one given that it was inserted in the OECD MC in 2017 as a result of Action 6 of the BEPS project)*', *see* R. Szudoczky, *supra* note 1699, at 151.
1741. For a detailed examination of the issue, *see* G. Kofler, *supra* note 1695, at 582.
1742. In the same vein, *see Ibid.*, at 584.
1743. *Tax Challenges Arising from Digitalisation – Report on Pillar Two Blueprint*, paras 679–680.
1744. *Ibid.*, para. 682.
1745. L.E. Schoueri, *supra* note 1654, at 547; M. F. De Wilde, *supra* note 1645; R. Szudoczky, *supra* note 1699, at 151; P.G.L. Schoueri & R.A. Galendi, *CFCs and Tax Treaties: Historical Elements for the IIR Debate*, 51 Intertax (2023) forthcoming.

veil'.[1746] Furthermore, it is argued that the IIR merely presupposes ownership, whereas CFC legislation usually requires control over the respective CFC.[1747] The author of this thesis is sceptical with respect to both arguments: first of all, CFC legislation is not necessarily limited to cases of abuse. Many CFC regimes also apply in situations that are not necessarily considered abusive. Furthermore, it cannot be denied that also the IIR, at least in a broad sense, tackles abuse[1748] and could be considered an anti-abuse provision, as the very term abuse is indefinable in itself. Thus, it is difficult to see in which way the purpose of CFC legislation deviates from the IIR, as both rules intend to level up the ETR of subsidiary profits at the level of a parent entity up the ownership chain. Second, it is difficult to see why control should make a difference. Admittedly, one could argue that only the entity having control over the other could decide whether a distribution is made or not.[1749] However, even if the IIR can be applied at the level of a non-controlling 'Parent Entity', the IIR requires that the LTCE and its 'Parent Entity', the latter being subject to the IIR, are at least under common 'control'; otherwise they would not be included within the same 'Consolidated Financial Statements' and not be covered within the same 'MNE Group'. It is obvious that one cannot deny that even a minority shareholder will sooner or later receive the profits of its participation, which is why, in the author's opinion, the fact that IIR is not limited to situations of 'control' does not make any difference with respect to the treaty compatibility of the IIR. Finally, as shown, the historical purpose of the 'saving clause' is to allow the residence state to tax subsidiary profits. How, then, should one argue that the IIR would be incompatible with a treaty containing a 'saving clause'? Nevertheless, even if a treaty contains a 'saving clause', it cannot be concluded that the IIR is generally in line with the treaty obligations of a contracting state for two reasons: first, the 'saving clause', whether designed pursuant to Article 1(3) OECD MC or Article 1(4) and (5) US MC, does not exempt the residence state from applying the method article. Second (ii), the 'saving clause' only justifies the taxation of residents, but not of non-residents. Thus, these two issues still need to be discussed.

First, the exception of the application of the method article for the purposes of the 'saving clause' should be examined. The 'saving clause' states that the residence state may tax, irrespective of the distributive rule applied with respect to a certain item of income. However, as the method article is excluded, the residence state has to grant relief for any taxes paid in the other state pursuant to Article 23A or 23B OECD MC. Prior to the OECD MC 2017, this left the question open as to whether and if affirmative, to which extent the residence state has to eliminate double taxation: finally, if the residence state of the shareholder taxes income by way of a CFC regime, providing an exemption or credit would mean, that the shareholder's residence state would either

1746. F. Debelva & L. De Broe, *supra* note 1652, at 902.
1747. R. Goulder, *supra* note 1645, at 777; R. Szudoczky, *supra* note 1699, at 151.
1748. Also *see* Wardell-Burrus, also arguing with respect to the UTPR that it '*is (at least in part) an anti-avoidance rule*', *see* H. Wardell-Burrus, *supra* note 1560, at 701.
1749. *Ibid.*

exempt income or credit tax of the CFC which is a different taxpayer. The OECD finally addressed this issue by adding a parenthetical to the first paragraphs of Article 23A and 23B OECD MC, stating that the residence state may refrain from providing relief '*to the extent* [the relevant distributive rules] *allow taxation by that other State solely because the income is also income derived by a resident of that State*'. Consequently, under the OECD MC 2017, if the residence state of the shareholder applies its CFC regime, it must neither exempt the income received nor credit the taxes paid by the CFC resident in the other contracting state. Conversely, the parenthetical in Articles 23A and 23B OECD MC would not exempt the residence state from providing relief if the income is attributable to a PE of the shareholding entity. Whether the shareholding entity being subject to CFC legislation within its residence state has a PE in the other state is, pursuant to the prevailing opinion in literature, tested by a so-called look-through approach: it is to be determined whether the shareholding entity would have a PE if its CFC did not exist, which also excludes consideration of Article 5(7) OECD MC.[1750]

These findings can be largely transferred to the IIR. The residence state of the 'Parent Entity' may apply the IIR pursuant to Articles 7(1) and 1(3) OECD MC and only must provide for a relief if the 'Parent Entity' had a PE in the other state if the CE-subsidiary did not constitute a resident person. However, contrary to CFC legislation, the IIR itself already provides for relief of taxes paid in the other contracting state, as the ETR is deducted from the 'minimum rate'. The IIR inherently already contains the actual credit mechanism. Thus, if a DTC provides for the credit method for 'business profits', the IIR does not conflict with the DTC. The situation is different in the case of DTCs that apply the exemption method to PE income. In this case, neither Article 1(3) OECD MC nor the parentheses in Article 23A OECD MC can prevent a conflict between the IIR and the respective treaty. The OECD is well aware of this issue, as the GloBE Commentary on Article 2 notes: '*However, concerns about the intended application of* [the IIR] *can arise where a Parent Entity jurisdiction, which would otherwise apply the IIR in accordance with the provisions of Article 2* [GloBE Model Rules], *has entered into bilateral Tax Treaties in which it has adopted the exemption method (instead of a credit method) to eliminate double taxation of income arising in the other jurisdiction. In this case, a switch-over rule in a Tax Treaty could facilitate the application of the IIR by the jurisdiction of residence of the Parent Entity to tax the income arising in the other jurisdiction*'.[1751] As can be seen, the 'saving clause' certainly 'saves' the IIR with respect to treaties applying the credit method but might be in conflict with treaties applying the exemption method. However, also in the latter case, the IIR may be applied if the parentheses in Article 23A OECD MC comes into play: if the CE-subsidiary lacks substance, it is unlikely that it can, under a 'look-through approach', be considered as a PE of the 'Parent Entity' leading to the consequence, that the obligation to exempt would be eliminated (*see* Figure 18).

1750. *See* M. Lang, *supra* note 1692, at 55.
1751. *See GloBE Commentary on Article 2 GloBE Model Rules (2022)*, *supra* note 238, para. 2.

Figure 18 Treaty Conflict Caused by Application of IIR to Partnerships

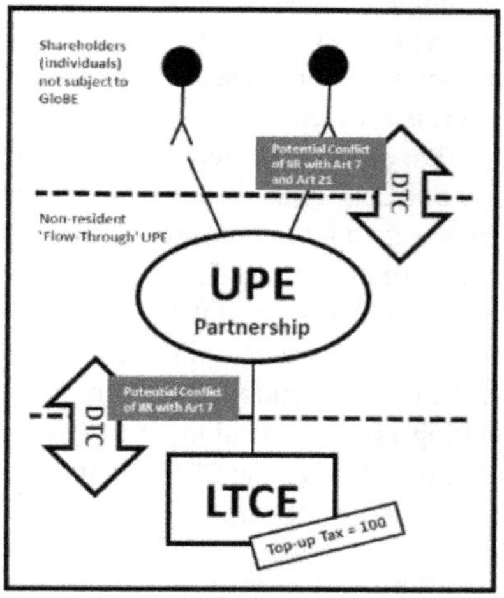

Besides the case of exempted PEs, the 'saving clause' could not prevent conflicts if the IIR were applied to non-residents. As the IIR only applies to 'Parent Entities' that are either a non-excluded UPE, an IPE or a POPE, none of which a PE can qualify for, the IIR can, as a rule, only be applied with respect to persons that would qualify as a resident person under a tax treaty of the state applying the IIR. However, there are scenarios with partnerships (within the terminology of GloBE so-called Flow-through Entities) to which the IIR is applied and where the 'saving clause', due to a lack of a resident person, is not applicable to eliminate a treaty conflict: according to Article 10.3.2.(a) GloBE Model Rules (Article 4(2) GloBE-Directive) a 'Flow-through Entity' is considered 'located' and, thus, is subject to the IIR, either (i) if the 'Flow-through Entity' is the UPE of the 'MNE Group' or (ii) if the jurisdiction in which it was created decides to apply the IIR.[1752] From a treaty perspective, both situations give rise to the same issue: if the shareholder of the partnership (the 'Flow-through Entity') is resident and entitled to a treaty between its state of residence and the state applying the IIR to the partnership, the latter state might violate Article 7(1) OECD MC as it would not be entitled to tax the business profits of non-resident shareholders unless the partnership constitutes a PE of those shareholders. Furthermore, if the IIR was applied with respect to an LTCE resident in a third state, pursuant to the treaty between the residence state of the shareholders and the state applying the IIR to the partnership, the LTCE's income would be covered by Article 21 OECD MC granting the exclusive taxing right to the shareholder's residence state. Besides this, the state applying the IIR to the partnership may also violate the treaty concluded with the residence state of the LTCE if the LTCE constitutes a PE for its 'Parent Entity' if the LTCE as a separate taxpayer was ignored.

1752. *See* ss 4.2.4.4.2. and 4.3.3.6.

For the IIR, the conclusion can be drawn that the 'saving clause' can avoid most of the conceivable conflicts to tax treaties. However, even the 'saving clause' is not capable of resolving all conflicts and is, therefore, not a panacea for the IIR. Treaty issues might arise with respect to treaty-exempt PEs as well as in cases where the IIR is applied to non-resident persons as, in these cases, the 'saving clause' fails to apply. The latter scenario, however, is only conceivable in rare situations in which the IIR is collected from partnerships that are not entitled to a treaty. In any case, one should not underestimate the diversity of existing tax treaties. Most of the treaties in force do not contain a 'saving clause'. It is true that the Commentary on Article 1 OECD MC assumes that also, with respect to these treaties, the residence state should not be restricted from taxing its residents. Nevertheless, this cannot be generalized, especially since each DTC must be interpreted on its own merits, and it cannot be ruled out that a restriction of the state of residence was indeed intended. Furthermore, if a DTC provides for a tax sparring clause or a matching credit provision, it can neither be ruled out that the residence state of a parent entity violates the DTC if it applies the IIR with respect to an LTCE's income without granting a notional tax credit.[1753]

5.2.6.3 (In)compatibility of 'Top-up Tax' Imposed by Means of the UTPR with the OECD MC

As has been shown, the existence of a 'saving clause' in a DTC is a strong argument for the compatibility of the IIR with the respective treaty, even though the 'saving clause' is not a 'panacea' to solve all conflicts with DTC. The question of whether and to what extent the 'saving clause' can ensure the compatibility of the UTPR is, however, much more complex. In this respect, it should be emphasized once again that the explanations in the Blueprint[1754] on the compatibility of the UTPR have lost their value in solving the issue. In the Blueprint, the UTPR (at that time, thus, explicitly named the 'Undertaxed *Payments* Rule') was still conceived as a specific deduction restriction for intra-group payments. Such a restriction would be much easier to justify with the 'saving clause' than the current design of the UT*P*R as the former simply would implement a denial of deduction solely influencing the resident entity's tax base while the current UTPR design intends to tax profits of a different resident at the level of a very different taxpayer.

It has already been revealed in section 4.4.2.8.3. that the UTPR, in its current design, does neither require control nor any other ownership connection to an affiliate entity at all, nor is it related to any intra-group payments. The mere membership within the same 'MNE Group' is sufficient to fulfil the scope of the UTPR, allowing to tax income at the level of a taxpayer that has no connection to the income's recipient at all. In the literature, the question of treaty compatibility of GloBE has strongly focused on

1753. Aitor Navarro, *Jurisdiction Not to Tax, Tax Sparing Clauses and the Income Inclusion Rule of the OECD Pillar 2 (GloBE) Proposal: The Demise of a Policy Instrument of Developing Countries?*, Copenhagen Business School Law Research Paper Series 23 (2020).

1754. *Tax Challenges Arising from Digitalisation – Report on Pillar Two Blueprint*, at 679–680 and 684 et seq.

the UTPR. Opinions in the literature are deeply divided, which has led to the term 'UTPR supporters'[1755] being coined for those in favour of UTPR's treaty compatibility and the term 'UTPR sceptics'[1756] for those against it.[1757] In the meanwhile, the discussion on treaty compatibility of the UTPR has even reached a political level: in December 2022, the Republican Party published an open letter to the US Congress where it is assumed that the UTPR is in violation of tax treaties despite all US treaties containing a 'saving clause'.[1758]

In the end, the debate can be reduced to the question of whether tax treaties require a minimum nexus to a certain income or whether the 'saving clause' leaves any freedom to the residence state. Whether it makes sense to group legal views remains to be seen. In any case, the distinction between both positions, which will be adopted for the purposes of this section, is also in no way intended to conceal the fact that differences of opinion also exist among both the group of 'UTPR supporters' and the 'UTPR sceptics'.

'UTPR supporters' mainly argue that the difference between the UTPR, IIR and CFC legislation is insignificant and claim that if CFC legislation is considered as

1755. Among the so-called UTPR Supporters, *see* A. Christians & S.E. Shay, *The Consistency of Pillar 2 UTPR With U.S. Bilateral Tax Treaties*, 109 Tax Notes Intl., *supra* note 1667, at 445 et seq.; J. Kadet, *Defending the UTPR: Creative Corporate Structuring Can't Hide Real Connections*, *supra* note 1652, at 1072 et seq.; T.D. Magalhaes, *Give Us the Law: Responses and Challenges to UTPR Resisters*, 108 Tax Notes Intl., *supra* note 1652, at 1257 et seq.; S. Picciotto, *Rebutting the Logic of UTPR Skeptics*, 108 Tax Notes Intl., *supra* note 1652, at 1371; T.D. Magalhaes, *UTPR Opposition: A Game of Whack-a-Mole*, 108 Tax Notes Intl., *supra* note 1660, at 1531 et seq.; A. Christians & T. Diniz Magalhaes, *Undertaxed Profits and the Use-It-or-Lose-It Principle*, 108 Tax Notes Intl., *supra* note 1649, at 705 et seq.; S. Picciotto, *Justifying the UTPR: Nexus and Economic Connection*, 108 Tax Notes Intl., *supra* note 1652, at 667; S. Picciotto, *UTPR Critics Miss the Point of Tax Treaty Principles*, 108 Tax Notes Intl., *supra* note 1652, at 153.

1756. Identifying themselves as so-called UTPR Sceptics, *see* Maarten Floris De Wilde, *Why Pillar Two Top-Up Taxation Requires Tax Treaty Modification – Kluwer International Tax Blog*, Kluwer International Tax Blog, *supra* note 1645; Jefferson VanderWolk, *The UTPR is Inconsistent with the Nexus Requirement of Tax Treaties*, Kluwer International Tax Blog, *supra* note 1645; J. VanderWolk, *The UTPR Disregards the Need for Nexus*, 108 Tax Notes Intl., *supra* note 1652, at 545 et seq.; R. Goulder, *Pillar 2 and Tax Treaties: MLI, Where Are Thou?*, 108 Tax Notes Intl., *supra* note 1645, at 775 et seq.; J. VanderWolk, *Much Ado About Pillar 2*, 108 Tax Notes Intl., *supra* note 1652, at 821 et seq.; R. Goulder, *Confessions of a UTPR Skeptic*, 108 Tax Notes Intl., *supra* note 1561, at 907 et seq.; J. VanderWolk, *The UTPR Is Far From Becoming Part of Customary International Tax Law*, 108 Tax Notes Intl., *supra* note 1652, at 1069 et seq.; J. VanderWolk, *The UTPR: Taxing Rights Gone Wild*, 108 Tax Notes Intl., *supra* note 1652, at 1369 et seq.; J. VanderWolk, *The UTPR Is Flawed: A Response to Prof. Picciotto*, 108 Tax Notes Intl., *supra* note 1691; J. VanderWolk, *Tax Treaties Pose Problems for the UTPR*, 108 Tax Notes Intl., *supra* note 1645; N. Boidman, *UTPR's Effect on Outside Shareholders: Another Reason to Oppose?*, 109 Tax Notes Intl., *supra* note 1541, at 189 et seq.; J. VanderWolk, *The UTPR, Treaties, and CFC Rules: A Reply to Avi-Yonah and Schler*, 109 Tax Notes Intl., *supra* note 1541, at 187 et seq.; A. Nikolakakis & Jinyan Li, *UTPR: Unprecedented (and Unprincipled?) Tax Policy Response*, 109 Tax Notes Intl. 743–751 (2023).

1757. On the invention of this group classification, *see* Heydon Wardell-Burrus, *Four Questions for UTPR Skeptics*, 108 Tax Notes Intl., *supra* note 1560, at 699.

1758. *Letter of Kevin Brady and Jim Risch to the Congress of the United States, Washington, DC 20515* (14 Dec. 2022), https://waysandmeans.house.gov/wp-content/uploads/2022/12/sfc-sfrc-wm-r_letter_to_secretary_yellen-1.pdf.

compatible with tax treaties, the UTPR should be considered compatible as well.[1759] This is an obvious argument: true, one might counter that the UTPR requires neither control nor ownership interest of the entity to which it is applied, but UTPR, as the IIR, still simply taxes income of an affiliate entity within the same 'MNE Group'. Also, CFC legislation and the IIR tax the income of different taxpayers resident in different jurisdictions.[1760] Why should the UTPR be in breach of a treaty if CFC regimes apparently are not? Finally, 'UTPR supporters' heavily rely on the 'saving clause' and argue that there are no limits for the residence state to tax their residents anyway, besides those cases where the UTPR is applied to local PEs of non-resident CEs.[1761] Some even take the position that '[t]*he UTPR is not a tax on income, nor is it likely to be characterized as in lieu of a tax on income*',[1762] probably due to the fact '*the UTPR liability is several steps removed from the taxable profit of the related entity*'.[1763] While the latter argument is hardly convincing, the questionable distinction between CFC regimes or IIR on the one hand and UTPR on the other and the strong wording of the 'saving clause' are quite noteworthy arguments.

Also, among the so-called UTPR sceptics, a broad facet of opinions is represented. The extreme position is that one cannot transfer the justification of CFC regimes to the GloBE Rules simply because the latter do not aim to tackle abuse (already on that argument with respect to the IIR, *see* section 5.2.6.2.). These authors regularly argue that both the IIR and, in particular, the UTPR are incompatible with Articles 7(1) and 10(5) OECD MC.[1764] As already explained, there are significant counter-arguments to this argumentation, especially since it can hardly be denied that the UTPR can also be assumed to have an anti-abuse function in the broadest sense.[1765] To distinguish the UTPR from CFC regimes in this sense is therefore hardly tenable. The predominant group of 'UTPR sceptics', however, focuses, first, on the technical differences between UTPR and CFC regimes as well as the IIR, respectively and, second, question whether states can really justify the application of the UTPR by invoking the 'saving clause'. Both arguments are obviously closely related. CFC regimes are commonly justified by the 'saving clause'. Anyone who wants to dispute the compatibility of the UTPR with tax treaties must be able to identify a significant difference between the former and CFC regimes, apart from the argument for abuse just mentioned, and most 'UTPR supporters' state that ownership interest or control alone is not sufficient to distinguish UTPR

1759. *See*, e.g., T. D. Magalhaes, *supra* note 1652, at 1258. For a good summary of this position, *see* H. Wardell-Burrus, *supra* note 1560, at 701.
1760. A minority of authors also supports a 'unitary approach' and assumes that GloBE is taxing a single 'MNE Group' anyway, which is why, under this position, GloBE would tax a single taxpayer anyway, *see* in particular Sol Picciotto, *supra* note 1652, at 667 et seq.; S. Picciotto & J. Kadet, *supra* note 1658, at 453 et seq. The author of this thesis rejects this position, already *see* s. 5.2.1.
1761. A. Christians & S. E Shay, *supra* note 1667, at 449.
1762. *See Ibid.*, at 454. The correctness of this conclusion can, however, be doubted for several obvious reasons, *see* already s. 5.2.2.
1763. H. Wardell-Burrus, *supra* note 1560, at 701.
1764. *See* in example, L.E. Schoueri, *supra* note 1654, at 547; R. Szudoczky, *supra* note 1699, at 151 et seq.
1765. H. Wardell-Burrus, *supra* note 1560, at 701.

from the IIR or CFC legislation.[1766] Why should it make a difference if an entity's profit is taxed at the level of one of its shareholders or at any other entity?

'UTPR sceptics' mostly argue that tax treaties (or at least customary international law, *see* section 5.5.) require a 'nexus' between the income and the taxing jurisdiction and that either ownership interest or control could make the difference and that UTPR would tax 'extraterritorial' income that might lack any connection to the respective jurisdiction collecting the UTPR.[1767] This is because the shareholder at least owns parts of the underlying entity as well as its property and can, thus, regularly also influence whether the income is finally distributed.[1768] Thus, one could argue that both the IIR and CFC regimes indeed tax the income of a different taxpayer, but in principle, only because this income will sooner or later stream to the parent entity anyway. Accordingly, the IIR and CFCs regime merely anticipate a notional distribution of the actual. There are certainly some objections to this view. First of all, tax treaties, at least the OECD MC, neither explicitly state anything about nexus besides the residence-principle enshrined in Article 4 OECD MC, nor do they explicitly define the term 'income'. Second, it is far from clear how far such a 'nexus' should extend under tax treaties, if it exists at all. Tax treaties simply distribute the taxing rights for 'income' among contracting states without defining the notion of 'income'. The term 'income' as used in a treaty is the sum of the distributive rules and domestic tax bases for taxes covered under Article 2 OECD MC. Thus, contracting states are, in principle, free to define their domestic corporate income tax bases. So why should the residence state be limited to providing a fictitious concept of income within its domestic laws, which includes income of a different taxpayer within the taxable income of a resident entity, even if the latter is not directly related to the resident entity?

In the author's view, this is where the real discussion about the compatibility of the UTPR with the treaties begins. Just because the OECD MC does not explicitly define the term income, this does not mean that each of the two states can expand the concept of income under income law as they wish. The OECD MC applies to resident persons (Articles 1 and 4 OECD MC) subject to a covered tax in either the source or the residence state (Article 2 OECD MC), and whether a state may tax according to the treaty is to be decided by the distributive rule. Of course, the problem is that the UTPR intends to tax the income of a taxpayer at the level of a different person, and it already follows from Article 1 OECD MC that the treaty applies to each individual person. However, in deviation from CFC regimes or the IIR, under UTPR, an implementing jurisdiction fictitiously includes 'income' within the tax base of a resident entity that the resident entity would never conceivably receive on its own. Worse still, the relevant jurisdiction would not tax the relevant income if the resident entity was not part of an 'MNE Group' falling within the scope of GloBE. As De Broe convincingly argues, one could question whether a contracting state taxing exterritorial income by way of including such income into the domestic tax base really interprets its '*tax*

1766. *See* in particular S. Picciotto, *supra* note 1652, at 667; T.D. Magalhaes, *supra* note 1652, at 1258.
1767. *See*, e.g., R. Goulder, *supra* note 1561, at 908.
1768. H. Wardell-Burrus, *supra* note 1560, at 701.

treaties in good faith (as required by Article 31 VCLT)'.[1769] In the author's opinion, ownership interests indeed make the difference between CFC legislation and the IIR on the one side and the UTPR on the other. Article 10(1) OECD MC, in principle, allows the residence state to tax dividends distributed by corporations resident in the other contracting state. It is, therefore, not far-fetched to allow the state of residence of a parent entity to also tax the dividends that have not yet been distributed[1770] (in the author's opinion, it makes no difference whether controlling shares or only minority shares are held). It can be derived from a shareholder relationship that the shareholder has an interest in the assets of the company held and either receives profits distributed or benefits from the profits of the company held by way of an increase in the value of the shares. How the residence state then taxes its resident corporation on its holding is up to it, at least if the residence state taxes in accordance with its treaty obligations.

The UTPR, however, is different. The UTPR enables the residence state of a corporation to tax income which is in no way related to the corresponding entity besides the fact that they are consolidated within the same 'Consolidate Financial Statements'. Even if one were to consider the 'MNE Group' as a separate 'unitary' tax subject (which is, under the author's opinion, explicitly rejected by Articles 1, 3 and 4 OECD MC),[1771] the income of a 'sibling' entity, for example, would never end up with the UTPR entity but with the UPE.[1772]

In the author's opinion, it can therefore be deduced from the OECD MC's system that the levying of 'income' from another taxpayer is not permissible in the absence of any ownership interest and that the UTPR is, therefore, not compatible with tax treaties. This awareness brings us back to the 'saving clause': the texting of a legal provision is the beginning of its interpretation and not its end. It is true that the wording of the 'saving clause' indeed would suppose that a tax treaty does not pose any limits to the state of residence. Nevertheless, a teleological and historical interpretation, at least with respect to Article 1(3) OECD MC shows that, as de Wilde aptly points out, it cannot have been intended to enable the residence state '*to subject any taxable group entity to corporate tax on effectively the worldwide profits* [...], *on any arbitrarily founded taxable basis or* [...] – *without any restriction under the tax treaties concluded*'.[1773] Indeed, interpreting the 'saving clause' in a way that would permit profits of another person to be taxed without any substantial connection would, as de Wilde emphasizes, render tax treaties meaningless[1774] and would equal an *ad absurdum* interpretation[1775] of tax treaties. In my opinion, this result could not be supported in an autonomous interpretation of a DTC.

1769. L. De Broe, *supra* note 1672, at 884.
1770. *See* on that perspective, M. Lang, *supra* note 1692, at 55 et seq.
1771. Completely convincing in that respect, *see* J. VanderWolk, *supra* note 1652, at 821.
1772. On this argument, also *see* J. VanderWolk, *supra* note 1652, at 1369–1370.
1773. M. F. De Wilde, *Why Pillar Two Top-Up Taxation Requires Tax Treaty Modification – Kluwer International Tax Blog*, Kluwer International Tax Blog, *supra* note 1645.
1774. In the same vein, and also with reference to de Wilde, *see* R. Szudoczky, *supra* note 1699, at 152.
1775. M. F. De Wilde, *supra* note 1645.

Furthermore, even if one takes the common view of 'UTPR supporters' conflicts might occur that cannot be solved by the 'saving clause': the latter applies neither to non-residents nor does it eliminate the residence state's obligation to apply the method articles. As PEs do qualify as separate CEs and UTPR subjects all CEs to the 'UTPR Top-up Tax', there can be no doubt that UTPR violates Article 7 OECD MC if it is applied to a local PE, irrespective of whether the individual treaty contains a 'saving clause' or not.[1776] In any case, the UTPR is also in conflict with a tax treaty if the exemption method is applied for income covered by a distributive rule equivalent to Article 7 OECD MC in the respective treaty between the state applying the UTPR and the residence state of the LTCE. The 'saving clause' does not release the residence states from their obligation to exempt the foreign PE income according to Article 23A OECD MC. For this reason, the UTPR would obviously conflict with the treaty.[1777]

However, despite all these arguments that could swing the pendulum in favour of the 'UTPR sceptics', there is one factual argument in favour of the 'UTPR supporters': even if a jurisdiction that implemented a 'Qualified UTPR' assumed to be restricted by a treaty and waived the collection of its share of the 'Total UTPR Top-up Tax', its piece of the '*UTPR cake*' would be divided among all other UTPR jurisdictions anyway pursuant to Article 2.6.3. GloBE Model Rules and Article 14(8) GloBE-Directive. So why should jurisdictions care about potential conflicts between the UTPR and tax treaties at all, in particular, if it is implemented by a so-called critical mass of implementing jurisdictions?[1778]

It is true that from a tax policy perspective, it might be unwise for a jurisdiction to not collect its 'UTPR percentage' (a jurisdiction's share of the 'UTPR Top-up Tax' amount);[1779] this is not an argument to ignore existing treaties.[1780] Jurisdictions implementing a 'Qualified UTPR', under the rule of law, cannot simply justify a breach of an international agreement such as a tax treaty by arguing that any other state would collect the tax instead. From the perspective of an implementing jurisdiction, a normative conflict between domestic GloBE implementation and a tax treaty is a highly delicate matter. This does not mean that a state could not decide to 'override' a tax treaty by domestic law without, e.g., violating its constitution. However, from a legal point of view, any treaty override can lead to a breach of the *pacta sunt servanda* principle under Article 26 VCLT and might be, at least diplomatically, unwise. For this reason, the next sections are dedicated to the question of how conflicts between domestic and the EU's GloBE implementation and tax treaties are to be resolved.

1776. Even declared 'UTPR supporters' do not deny potential treaty conflicts in these situations, *see* A. Christians & S. E Shay, *supra* note 1667, at 449; R.S. Avi-Yonah, *supra* note 1652, at 46. Also on this issue, *see* A. Nikolakakis & J. Li, *supra* note 1756, at 746.
1777. Also *see* on that argument, L. De Broe, *supra* note 1672, at 885.
1778. In this vein, *see* H. Wardell-Burrus, *supra* note 1560, at 702.
1779. In detail on this technicality, *see* s. 4.4.2.8.3.
1780. In the same vein, *see* A. Nikolakakis & J. Li, *supra* note 1756, at 751.

5.3 RESOLVING NORMATIVE CONFLICTS BETWEEN GLOBE AND TAX TREATIES FROM THE PERSPECTIVE OF PUBLIC INTERNATIONAL AND DOMESTIC LAW

The above analysis has revealed that the co-existence of the GloBE Rules IIR and UTPR, as well as QDMTT with existing DTCs, will give rise to numerous potential conflicts between DTC and GloBE. This raises the question of how such conflicts are going to be solved. Such an analysis first requires determining which sources of law might be in conflict. The question is simple with regard to DTCs: DTCs are international agreements and, thus, are sources of public international law. The legal status of GloBE or Pillar Two, whatever synonym is used for the global minimum tax, is not so clear from an international law perspective, at least if one takes into account the material published by the OECD on the political consensus on the pillars. In particular, the October Statement of 2021 took the following note on the rule status of GloBE:

> *The GloBE rules will have the status of a common approach.*
> *This means that IF members*:
>
> - *are not required to adopt the GloBE rules*, but, *if they choose to do so*, they will *implement and administer the rules in a way that is consistent with the outcomes provided for under Pillar Two*, including in light of model rules and guidance agreed to by the IF;
> - accept the application of the GloBE rules applied by other IF members including agreement as to rule order and the application of any agreed safe harbours.[1781] (emphasis added)

It is obvious that the 'common approach' neither poses any binding obligations to IF Member States nor to other states, and, consequently, neither the GloBE Model Rules nor the Commentary are sources of public international law. It is not surprising that the OECD is trying to give the IF a kind of binding cloak. In its GloBE Administrative Guidance February 2023, the OECD once renewed the claim to consider the 'common approach' as a binding commitment and even states that '[t]*he common approach also means that Inclusive Framework members accept the application of the GloBE rules applied by other members, including agreements as to rule order and the application of any agreed safe harbours*'.[1782] The latter statement is especially problematic from a rule of law point of view: the OECD is by no means a legislative body, nor is it competent for creating any source of binding international law.

One cannot deny the fact that, from a legal point of view, there are no legal obligations under public international law for IF Member States, even if they 'choose' to implement GloBE.[1783] In fact, the OECD is trying to give the GloBE materials a kind of binding character under the guise of a 'common approach'. Nevertheless, the so-called common approach is nothing but a vague political commitment of support for

1781. *OECD/G20 Statement 8 October*, at 3.
1782. *See* para. 1 of the executive summary of the *GloBE Administrative Guidance February 2023*, at 6.
1783. In the same vein, *see* V. Bendlinger, *supra* note 258, at 3.

the OECD's work on the two-pillar approach.[1784] The GloBE Model Rules are, thus, far from becoming a part of an international agreement or any other source of public international law, such as customary international law.[1785] In the literature, however, it is not ruled out that this could change in the future - if GloBE actually becomes commonplace internationally.[1786] If GloBE were indeed a source of international law, the general rules of conflict resolution, in particular *lex specialis* and *lex posterior derogat legi priori*, would have to be applied to resolve conflicts between the GloBE and DTC frameworks. This would have immense consequences for the implementation of GloBE: GloBE would, in almost every situation, trump existing DTC due to the *lex posterior* principle.[1787] Only in the scenario that a DTC is concluded after national implementation of GloBE, which would nevertheless be in conflict with GloBE, would the DTC prevail over GloBE. *Lex specialis* would probably, not be applicable in most situations as the GloBE Model Rules and tax treaties do not necessarily completely overlap. The author, however, is of the conviction that the global consensus, the so-called common approach on GloBE, is far from these hypothetical scenarios.

Under these conditions, any implementation of GloBE must be attributed to the domestic legal spheres of the implementing jurisdiction from the perspective of public international law. Any conflicts arising from domestic law with tax treaties concluded by that jurisdiction is, thus, a matter of domestic constitutional law. It is the national constitutional order that determines how domestic law relates to existing obligations under international law. In those states where treaty overrides are constitutionally permissible, there are, therefore, no obstacles for the legislature to implement GloBE and violate any treaty obligations.[1788] It will therefore depend on the position of the treaty partner whether such a violation will be tolerated: if both contracting states of a tax treaty implement GloBE along the lines of the 'common approach', it is unlikely that any of the contracting states will invoke a treaty violation. Conversely, a national GloBE implementation may become an issue if the contracting state of an implementing jurisdiction actually objects to the conflict. In the latter scenario, however, a treaty override can lead to diplomatic disputes, provided that the state implementing GloBE does not waive the application of the GloBE Rules to comply with the treaty.

Within the EU, the GloBE-Directive may raise particularly sensitive issues in relation to the resolution of normative conflicts: if a Member State applies the GloBE Rules, although conflicting with one of its tax treaties in force, the respective Member State might face a dilemma. On the one hand, it is forced to implement and effectuate the GloBE Rules as the GloBE-Directive is binding as to the result to be achieved[1789] and, furthermore, is supreme to the Member States' domestic law. On the other hand,

1784. In the same vein, *see Ibid.*
1785. *See*, e.g., J. VanderWolk, *supra* note 1652, at 1069–1070.
1786. R.S. Avi-Yonah, *supra* note 1652, at 951–952; F. Debelva & L. De Broe, *supra* note 1652, at 904.
1787. Also *see* Debelva & De Broe concluding that '[t]*he application of either of those rules would lead to the result that all incompatibilities between the Pillar 2 framework and the nexus rule would be resolved in favour of the Pillar 2 rules, and no alleged incompatibility would remain*', *see* F. Debelva & L. De Broe, *supra* note 1652, at 903.
1788. Also *see* J. Li, *supra* note 1634, at 1702.
1789. Article 288(3) TFEU.

there might be a tax treaty limiting the Member State's tax jurisdiction. How to solve conflicts between the GloBE-Directive and tax treaties concluded by its Member States, in particular to those that have already been concluded at the time the GloBE-Directive was enacted? These questions will be explored in the following sections.

5.4 RESOLVING NORMATIVE CONFLICTS BETWEEN THE GLOBE-DIRECTIVE AND TAX TREATIES OF THE MEMBER STATES

5.4.1 Overview

The relation of the GloBE-Directive to DTCs of the Member States is not a Pillar Two specific issue. Rather, the GloBE-Directive raises the much more fundamental question of how newly created secondary law relates to the existing tax treaty framework of the Member States in general. The relationship between bilateral DTCs and EU law is extremely complex and has already been the subject of extensive research on several occasions.[1790] The discussion is, thus, highly controversial and, due to the successful enactment of the GloBE-Directive, gains renewed relevance. At this point, it is necessary to take a step back.

As has been revealed in section 5.2., the GloBE-Directive is likely to give rise to numerous treaty conflicts and might require extensive adjustments to the existing tax treaty network (*see* the discussed GloBE MLI or MLC)[1791] of the Member States, which consists of an estimated amount of more than 1600 mostly bilateral tax treaties among each other and with third countries. Thus, the GloBE-Directive's relationship to existing DTCs concluded by the Member States must be clarified. Can EU law oblige Member States to amend their DTCs with other Member States or with third states and, in the most extreme case, even oblige the states to suspend them?

Neither public international law[1792] nor EU law[1793] provide for a general prohibition of double taxation.[1794] Nevertheless, according to the literature and case law of

1790. *See, i.a.*, T. Scherer, *Doppelbesteuerung und Europäisches Gemeinschaftsrecht* (C.H.Beck 1995); W. Gassner et al., *Doppelbesteuerungsabkommen und EU Recht* (Linde 1995); P. Pistone, *The Impact of Community Law on Tax Treaties* (Kluwer 2002); G. Kofler, *Doppelbesteuerungsabkommen und Europäisches Gemeinschaftsrecht* (Linde 2007); J. Dombrowsky, *Die Einwirkungen des Unionsrechts auf Doppelbesteuerungsabkommen* (Duncker & Humblot 2019).

1791. Comprehensively, *see* s. 6.1.3.2.

1792. Public international law hardly sets any limits to the tax sovereignty of states. According to *Douma*, customary international law allows jurisdictions to tax nationals and residents on their worldwide income and non-residents with regard to the sources of income received in a jurisdiction's territory, in detail S. Douma, *The Three Ds of Direct Tax Jurisdiction: Disparity, Discrimination and Double Taxation*, 46 Eur. Taxn. 523 (2006); G. Kofler & R. Mason, *Kerckhaert & Morres: A European 'Switch in Time?'*, in *Is the European Court of Justice Taking a New Approach?* 176 (S. von Thiel ed., 2007); G. Kofler, *supra* note 1790, at 133.

1793. Case C-513/04, *Mark Kerckhaert, Bernadette Morres v. Belgische Staat*, para. 22; Case C-298/05, *Columbus Container Services BVBA & Co. v. Finanzamt Bielefeld-Innenstadt*, para. 45; Case C-67/08, *Margarete Block v. Finanzamt Kaufbeuern*, para. 30.

1794. J. Dombrowsky, *supra* note 1790, at 27.

the ECJ, the avoidance of double taxation is one of the objectives of the Union.[1795] This is not altered by the fact that Article 293 of the EEC Treaty, which expressly held that Member States shall conclude DTCs among each other,[1796] was not incorporated into the Treaty of Lisbon.[1797] From a legal perspective, however, nothing can be gained from the mere objective of the EU. Therefore, some authors convincingly state that neither the existence nor the deletion of Article 293 EEC Treaty had much legal impact.[1798] Nevertheless, it is inherent and thus undisputed that juridical double taxation works against the ideal[1799] of a complete internal market.[1800] For this reason, *Kemmeren* prominently stated that DTCs and EU treaties '*are natural friends, because*

1795. Case C-336/96, *Mr and Mrs R. Gilly v. Directeur des services fiscaux du Bas-Rhin*, para. 16; were the Court states: '*the abolition of double taxation within the Community is thus included among the objectives of the Treaty*', for further reference *see* E. Kemmeren, *Double Tax Conventions on Income and Capital and the EU: Past, Present and Future*, 21 EC Tax Review 168 (2012).
1796. Article 293 EEC Treaty (Art. 220 EC Treaty of Rome) explicitly laid down that '*Member States shall, so far as is necessary, enter into negotiations with each other with a view to securing for the benefit of their nationals*: ... [second indent] – *the abolition of double taxation to ist own nationals*'. However, the Court emphasized that Art. 293 EEC Treaty was not directly applicable and that no obligation of the Member States to abolish all double taxation could be derived from that provision, *see* Case C-336/96, *Mr and Mrs Gilly* paras 14–17 and 30. In detail to the history and purpose of Art. 293 EEC treaty, its predecessor (Art. 220 EEC treaty) and its abolition, *see* E. Kemmeren, *supra* note 1795, at 160–161 and 168; for further reference on Art. 293 EC and its abolition in the course of the Lisbon Treaty, *see* G. Kofler, *EU Power to Tax: Competences in the Area of Direct Taxation, in Research Handbook on European Union Taxation Law* 17 in particular n. 42 (C. Panayi et al., eds, Edward Elgar Publishing 2020).
1797. According to *Kemmeren*, the objective of avoiding double taxation can even be understood more broadly after the repeal of Art. 293 EEC Treaty, E. Kemmeren, *After Repeal of Article 293 EC Treaty under the Lisbon Treaty: The EU Objective of Eliminating Double Taxation Can Be Applied More Widely*, 17 EC Tax Review 156 et seq. (2008) DOI: 10.54648/ecta2008068; *see also* E. Kemmeren, *supra* note 1795, at 161.
1798. L. Hinnekens, *The Uneasy Case and Fate of Article 293 Second Indent EC*, 37 Intertax (2009) DOI: 10.54648/taxi2009061; M. Lang, *Treaty Override und Gemeinschaftsrecht*, in *Reden zum Andenken an Klaus Vogel* 74 (Moris Lehner ed., C.H.Beck 2010); K. Daxkobler & E. Huisman, *Levy & Sebbag: The ECJ Has Once Again Been Asked To Deliver Its Opinion on Juridical Double Taxation in the Internal Market*, 53 Eur. Taxn. 404 (2013); J. Snell, *Free Movement of Capital: Evolution as a Non-Linear Process, in the Evolution of EU Law* 593 in particular n. 93 (Oxford 4th ed.); P.J. Wattel, *Taxation in the Internal Market*, in *Research Handbook of the EU's Internal Market* 327 (Panos Koutrakos & Jukka Snell eds, Edward Elgar Publishing 2017).
1799. Or as *Wattel* smugly states: '*it is difficult to think of better ways to thwart cross-border economic activity than to double tax it*', *see* P.J. Wattel, *supra* note 1798, at 326.
1800. *See* already U. Anschütz, *Harmonization of Direct Taxes in the European Economic Community*, 13 Harv. Int'l. Law J. 6 (1972); and L. Hinnekens, *Compatibility of Bilateral Tax Treaties with European Community Law. The Rules*, 3 EC Tax Review 158 (1994) DOI: 10.54648/ecta 1994027. Also the Commission stressed that '*double taxation is a major obstacle to cross-border activity and investment within the EU*', *see* European Commission, *Communication from the Commission to the Council, the European Parliament and the European Economic and Social Committee – Co-Ordinating Member States' Direct Tax Systems in the Internal Market* 5 (19 Dec. 2006). In detail on the Commission's position, also *see* G. Kofler & R. Mason, *Kerckhaert & Morres: A European 'Switch in Time?'*, in *Is the European Court of Justice taking a new approach?*, *supra* note 1792, at 218–219; G. Kofler, *Doppelbesteuerungsabkommen und Europäisches Gemeinschaftsrecht*, *supra* note 1790, at 27; J. Klabbers, *Treaty Conflict and the European Union* 208 (Cambridge 2009).

they pursue mutual objectives'.[1801] However, the Commission once stressed the fact that the purpose of DTCs and EU treaties is not quite identical: while DTCs essentially distribute taxing rights, the EU treaties seek to realize a single market without internal borders.[1802] These complex interrelationships between these legal spheres have prompted the Commission to comment on their relationship on several occasions since the European Community was established.[1803] Ambitiously, both the introduction of an EU Model[1804] and a multilateral '*EU DTC*'[1805] have been proposed and discussed several times; however, the success of such harmonization measures failed to materialize.

1801. E. Kemmeren, *Principle of Origin in Tax Conventions: A Rethinking of Models* 246 (Dongen 2001); also referring to *Kemmeren, see* G. Kofler, *supra* note 1790, at 131; again emphasizing that '*DTC's and the TFEU have common goals*', *see* E. Kemmeren, *supra* note 1795, at 157.
1802. *See* European Commission, *EC Law and Tax Treaties*, para. 3 (9.6.2005); G. Kofler, *supra* note 1790, at 133; sceptical on the commission's statement, *see* E. Kemmeren, *supra* note 1795, at 165–166.
1803. As early as 1962, the so-called *Neumark*-Report dealt with the possible harmonization of direct taxes within the European Community, *see* EC Commission, *Rapport Du Comitee Fiscal et Financier* (1962). The Committee concluded that the bilateral DTCs of the then Member States should be replaced by a multilateral agreement as soon as possible. The *Neumark*-Committee's call for a multilateral tax treaty was also echoed and supported in a report published in 1966 on the establishment of a common capital market (so-called *de Segré*-report), were it was stated that '*the ideal way of eliminating the remaining cases of double taxation between Member States would undoubtedly be by conclusion of a multilateral convention among them. This course is in fact now under consideration, with the OECD model used as basis*', *see* EC Commission, *The Development of a European Capital Market* 296 (1966). Finally, in 1968, a draft for an EC multilateral DTC was actually presented, based heavily on the OECD Model 1963, but never came to negotiation, *see* EC Commission, *Vorentwurf zu einem Europäischen Doppelbesteuerungsabkommen, Dok 11.414/XIV/68-D* (1.7.1968). The discrepancies between national tax systems were too great, which is why the Community henceforth focused on harmonizing national tax systems and thus did not pursue the project of a multilateral DTC any further, *see EC Law and Tax Treaties*, para. 13 – n. 44. In 1992, the relationship between DTCs and EC law was put back on the agenda of the Community by the so-called *Ruding*-Report. The *Ruding*-Report finally stressed the Member States to '*not only conclude bilateral income tax treaties where none exist between them, but also to complete those where their coverage is limited*', *see* EC Commission, *Report of the Committee of Independent Experts on Company Taxation* 206 (1992). The focus was therefore on completing the bilateral DTC network among the Member States, although there have been again isolated calls for a multilateral tax agreement, *see* EC Economic and Social Committee, *Opinion on Direct and Indirect Taxation, 19 Mar. 1996, No C 82/49*, 59 (1996).; for further reference, *see* G. Kofler, *supra* note 1790, at 142. In 2005 the EC Commission finally produced a working document on the relationship between EC law and DTCs. The Commission finally concluded that '[w]*ithout denying the indisputable advantages that a directive, a multilateral treaty, or other alternatives could offer, it seems that a model treaty – at least as a first stage – would be the easiest solution to apply*', *see EC Law and Tax Treaties*, para. 59. In detail with further reference on the discussion about DTCs within the EU and the commission's initiatives, *see* G. Kofler, *supra* note 1790, at 134–150; in detail also E. Kemmeren, *supra* note 1795, at 157–166.
1804. Providing for a comprehensive and sophisticated draft, *see* P. Pistone, *The Impact of Community Law on Tax Treaties*, *supra* note 1790, at 235–323; for an overview, *see* P. Pistone, *An EU Model Tax Convention*, 11 EC Tax Review 129 et seq. (2002) DOI: 10.54648/5092579.
1805. For comprehensive analysis of a possible multilateral convention among the Member States, *see* M. Lang, *The Concept of a Multilateral Tax Treaty, in Multilateral Tax Treaties – New Developments in International Tax Law* 187–196 (Helmut Loukota et al., eds, Kluwer Law International 1998). The same book also contains a draft of such a treaty on the basis of the

It is important to emphasize that the EU does not have all-encompassing competence in the area of direct taxation (in detail, *see* section 6.1.). The CJEU regularly notes that the conclusion of DTCs, due to a lack of harmonization in the field of direct taxation, falls within the competence of the Member States,[1806] which are '*therefore at liberty to conclude bilateral double-taxation treaties*'.[1807] Moreover, the Court has stated that the reciprocal nature of a DTC may preclude the existence of discrimination on the basis of nationality:[1808] In the famous '*D*' case, the Dutch tax authorities refused to allow a German resident to claim a certain tax allowance on capital tax due in the Netherlands. While the DTC between Germany and the Netherlands applicable to the taxpayer did not contain any provisions to this effect, the DTC between Belgium and the Netherlands obliged the Netherlands to grant the tax allowance to Belgian citizens based on the DTC between Belgium and the Netherlands. The German taxpayer claimed a violation of the free movement of capital because he was at a disadvantage compared to Belgian residents, who could rely on the advantageous Dutch-Belgian DTC. The Court, however, held that the fact that the allowance is only granted to Belgian residents '*is an inherent consequence*' of the reciprocal nature of bilateral DTCs. The CJEU thus rejected a most-favoured-nation treatment[1809] prescribed by the fundamental freedoms with respect to tax treaties.[1810]

These considerations should, however, not obscure the fact that it is also settled case law that '*although direct taxation is a matter for the Member States, they must nevertheless exercise their taxation powers consistently with Community law*'.[1811] This is all the truer if a future EU legal act regulates how certain taxation powers are to be exercised. Within its scope, the GloBE-Directive prescribes to the Member States how their taxing powers have to be exercised to reach a minimum level of tax and therefore

OECD MC, *see* M. Lang et al., *Draft for a Multilateral Tax Treaty, in Multilateral Tax Treaties – New Developments in International Tax Law* (Michael Lang et al., eds, Kluwer Law International 1998).

1806. *See*, i.e., Case C-336/96, *Mr and Mrs Gilly* paras 30–31.

1807. Case C-307/97, *Compagnie des Saint-Gobain v. Finanzamt Aachen-Innenstadt*, para. 54.

1808. J. Klabbers, *supra* note 1800, at 207.

1809. For an extensive analysis of the question, whether EU law provides a Most-Favored-Nation Treatment with regard to DTCs, before the ECJs decision in the D case, *see* G. Kofler, *Most-Favored-Nation Treatment in Direct Taxation: Does EC Law Provide for Community MFN in Bilateral Double Taxation Treaties?*, 5 Houston Business and Tax Law Journal 1–89 (2005), examining the same issue regarding bilateral investment treaties (BITs), *see* A. Dimopoulos, *The Validity and Applicability of International Investment Agreements Between EU Member States under EU and International Law*, 48 Common Market Law Review 81–82 (2011) DOI: 10.54648/cola2011004.

1810. For detailed analysis of this case in literature, *see*, i.e., S. Douma, *The Three Ds of Direct Tax Jurisdiction: Disparity, Discrimination and Double Taxation*, 46 Eur. Taxn., *supra* note 1792, at 528; G. Kofler, *'Dancing with Mr D': The ECJ's Denial of Most-Favoured-Nation Treatment in the 'D' Case*, 45 Eur. Taxn. 530–540 (2005); R. Schütze, *EC Law and International Agreements of the Member States – An Ambivalent Relationship?*, 9 Cambridge Yearbook of European Legal Studies 423–425 (2007); R. Schütze, *Foreign Affairs and the EU Constitution – Selected Essays* 153–155 (Cambridge 2014).

1811. Case C-307/97, *Saint-Gobain*, para. 57; first though Case C-279/93, *Finanzamt Köln-Altstadt v. Roland Schumacker*, para. 21; also *see* Case C-513/04, *Kerckhaert Morres*, para. 15; also Case C-35/98, *Staatssecretaris von Financiën v. B.G.M Verkooijen*, para. 32; in literature *see*, i.e., Sjoerd Douma, *supra* note 1792, at 522.

possibly overrides existing tax treaties concluded by them. Once again, it should be borne in mind that this is not a specific problem of tax treaties. Tax treaties are sources of public international law.[1812] The question of the interaction between the GloBE-Directive and tax treaty law therefore mirrors the much more fundamental question of the relationship between EU law and international treaties concluded by the Member States.[1813]

5.4.2 EU Law, Its Supremacy and Treaties Concluded by the Member States: A Clash of Legal Orders

In contrast to international treaties concluded by the Union itself, which are binding pursuant to Article 216(2) TFEU,[1814] the EU is, in principle, not bound by international treaties concluded by its Member States.[1815] While treaties concluded by the EU become part of its autonomous legal order, treaties concluded by Member States fall, at least under an EU law perspective, within the legal sphere of the Member States' domestic law,[1816] regardless of whether the respective Member State's constitution follows a monistic or dualistic approach. From the perspective of international law, the Member States themselves are therefore bound by the international treaties (such as tax treaties) they have concluded among themselves or with third states.[1817] In the case of a potential conflict of norms between EU law and international treaties concluded by

1812. *See*, i.e., G. Kofler, *supra* note 1790, at 269; G. Kofler, *Einleitung, in Doppelbesteuerungsabkommen*, para. 10 (D. Aigner et al., eds, Linde 2nd ed. 2018); J. Dombrowsky, *supra* note 1790, at 31.

1813. C. Panayi, *The Effect of Community Law on Pre-Accession Tax Treaties*, 16 EC Tax Review 121 (2007).

1814. In detail on Art. 216 TFEU and on the question, whether the EU has competence to conclude treaties in the field of GloBE, *see* s. 6.1.3.

1815. However, in its famous decision on the *International Fruit Company* case, the ECJ ruled, that the European Community is bound to GATT, although it was not a party of the agreement, *see*, Joined Cases C-21 to 24/72, *International Fruit Company NV v. Produktschap voor Groeenten en Fruit*, paras 14–18; *see* P. Craig & G. De Búrca, *EU Law – Text, Cases and Materials* 391–392 (Oxford 7th ed. 2020); for further reference *see* R. Schütze, *EC Law and International Agreements of the Member States—An Ambivalent Relationship?*, *supra* note 1810, at 394 and 396 et seq.

1816. For example, in the *Vandewehge-Case,* the CJEU stated that it did not have jurisdiction to interpret a bilateral treaty between Belgium and Germany '*which bind* [them] *outside the framework of Community law*'. *See* Case C-130/73, *Magdalena Vandeweghe and others v. Berufsgenossenschaft für die chemische Industrie*, para. 2. However, such jurisdiction of the CJEU may be established under Art. 273 TFEU, if the dispute is submitted to it under a special agreement between the parties. Such a special agreement is not uncommon in tax treaties between the Member States. Thus, Art. 25(5) of the German-Austrian DTC designates the ECJ to rule on interpretation disputes between the contracting states. In detail with further reference on the extraneous status of treaties concluded by the Member States within the EU's legal order, see, *see* H.G. Schermers, *Community Law and International Law*, 12 Common Market Law Review 81–82 (1975); P. Manzini, *The Priority of Pre-Existing Treaties of EC Member States within the Framework of International Law*, 12 EJIL 787 (2001) DOI: 10.1093/ejil/12.4.781; A. Rosas, *The Status in EU Law of International Agreements Concluded by EU Member States*, 34 Fordham International Law Review 1311–1114 (2011).

1817. *See* P. Craig & G. de Búrca, *supra* note 1815, at 389–390.

the Member States, the question arises whether there is a hierarchy between both legal orders.[1818]

The hierarchy between community law and the legal systems of the Member States was crucial to the creation of the EC in 1958.[1819] The implementation of a common market required a legal instrument that could give precedence to EC law over national law of the Member States. However, since the Community was established by the Treaties of Rome, which were sources of international law,[1820] it was difficult to justify this precedence with constitutional arguments: especially in legal systems that recognize international law only by an act of transposition (dualistic states), it would have been possible for national parliaments to overrule the treaties by subsequent adoption of legal acts.[1821] However, the EEC Treaty did not contain a specific provision expressly establishing the supremacy of Community law over the domestic law of the Member States,[1822] nor did it contain a specific rule declaring that the EEC Treaty was directly applicable and that its provisions could be invoked before domestic Courts.[1823] Thus, it was up to the CJEU to define the EEC Treaty's relation to the domestic law of the Member States.

The Court did so in its famous *Van Gend & Loos* decision, in which it declared that the '*Community constitutes a new legal order of international law for the benefit of which the states have limited their sovereign rights*'.[1824] The Court ruled that today's Article 18 TFEU was directly applicable to individuals and thus could be invoked by them before national Courts.[1825] Thereby the CJEU clearly distinguished the legal system of the Community from 'ordinary' public international law and declared its independence.[1826] However, it did not clarify whether Member States could override the treaties through subsequent national legislation. This question was finally brought before the CJEU in *Costa v. ENEL*, in which the Court further argued that the EC '[b]*y contrast with ordinary international treaties, [...] has created its own legal system which,... became an integral part of the legal systems of the Member States and which their Courts are bound to apply*'.[1827] Finally, the Court concluded that '*the law stemming from the Treaty, an independent source of law, could not, because of its special and original nature, be overridden by domestic legal provisions, however framed,*

1818. K.M. Meessen, *The Application of Rules of Public International Law within Community Law*, 13 Common Market Law Review 485 (1976) DOI: 10.54648/cola1976031.
1819. In detail on the history of Art. 351 TFEU, *see* V. Bendlinger, *Chapter 351 – Article 351 TFEU on Prior Agreements of the Member States*, in *Smit & Herzog on The Law of the European Union*, s. § 351.02 (Peter E Herzog et al., eds, LexisNexis 2022).
1820. Karl Matthias Meessen, *supra* note 1818, at 15; R. Schütze, *EC Law and International Agreements of the Member States – An Ambivalent Relationship?*, *supra* note 1810, at 387; Jan Klabbers, *Treaty Conflict and the European Union*, *supra* note 1800.
1821. R. Schütze, *EC Law and International Agreements of the Member States – An Ambivalent Relationship?*, *supra* note 1810, at 387.
1822. P.Craig & G. de Búrca, *supra* note 1815, at 304; R. Schütze, *European Union Law* 195 (Oxford 3rd ed. 2021).
1823. P. Craig & G. de Búrca, *supra* note 1815, at 218; R. Schütze, *supra* note 1822, at 152
1824. Case C-26/62, *Van Gend & Loos* at 12; R. Schütze, *supra* note 1810, at 387; also in detail to this judgement, *see* R. Schütze, *supra* note 1822, at 153.
1825. Paul Craig & Gráinne de Búrca, *supra* note 1815, at 218 et seq.
1826. R. Schütze, *supra* note 1822, at 153.
1827. Case C-6/64, *Costa v. ENEL* at 593; R. Schütze, *supra* note 1810, at 387.

without being deprived of its character as Community law and without the legal basis of the Community itself being called into question. The transfer by the states from their domestic legal system to the Community legal system of the rights and obligations arising under the Treaty carries with it a permanent limitation of their sovereign rights, against which a subsequent unilateral act incompatible with the concept of the Community cannot prevail'.[1828] These words finally laid the foundation for comprehensive CJEU case law on the EU law's supremacy over the Member States' domestic law.[1829]

Although the relationship between Union law and pre-existing international law was of no less relevance to the Union legal order, it took much longer for the CJEU to address this relationship. *Schütze*[1830] sums up the reason for this hesitant development: in the founding period of the EC, the main issue for the establishment of a new Union legal order was the relationship to the existing network of international treaties between the six founding Member States. However, with respect to existing treaties concluded among the Member States, the *lex posterior* principle, which at that point in time had already been an acknowledged rule of public international law,[1831] secured the priority of Union law over pre-existing treaties among Member States.[1832] Thus, the Rome Treaty could simply override those by means of international law. Nevertheless, neither the proclaimed '*autonomy*' of the EC's legal order nor *lex posterior* could justify the supremacy of EC law over treaties concluded by the Member States after the Treaty of Rome[1833] entered into force or change the fact that the Member States were still bound to pre-existing treaties concluded with third states.[1834] Since the EU's legal order is itself '*an offspring of international law*',[1835] the reasoning of a superiority of EU law over public international law, therefore, contains, as *Klabbers* notes, a certain irony: the supremacy of EU law over public international law means that '*the one actor above the law would itself be a creation of that law*'.[1836] From this perspective, public international law would prevail over EU law simply due to the fact that the EU legal order itself is created on the basis of public international law.[1837]

When the EC came into existence in 1958, according to the rules of public international law, it was not possible to simply override existing international treaties of the Member States with third countries.[1838] Moreover, it was not in the Community's interest to do so: requiring Member States to break treaties with third countries would

1828. Case C-6/64, *Costa v. ENEL* at 594.
1829. P. Craig & G. de Búrca, *supra* note 1815, at 304–316.
1830. R. Schütze, *supra* note 1810, at 390.
1831. *Ibid.*, at 389–390 in particular n. 15.
1832. The *lex posterior* principle is also codified in Art. 30(3) VCLT: '*When all the parties to the earlier treaty are parties also to the later treaty but the earlier treaty is not terminated or suspended in operation under article 59, the earlier treaty applies only to the extent that its provisions are compatible with those of the later treaty*'.
1833. In detail, *see* R. Schütze, *supra* note 1810, at 390.
1834. *Ibid.*, at 389–390.
1835. J. Klabbers, *supra* note 1800, at 231.
1836. *Ibid.*, at 17; R. Schütze, *supra* note 1810, at 438.
1837. In further detail on these arguments *see also*, *Meesseen* who, however, rejects the superiority of public international law, *see* K.M. Meessen, *supra* note 1818, at 497–500. *See also* R. Schütze, *supra* note 1810, at 47 et seq.; V. Bendlinger, *supra* note 1819, s. § 351.02.
1838. *See also* P. Pistone, *supra* note 1790, at 83; J. Klabbers, *supra* note 1800, at 117.

have gone at the cost of the Community's acceptance and would have harmed its establishment. Article 234 of the Treaty of Rome therefore stated that the '*rights and obligations arising from agreements concluded before the entry into force of this Treaty between one or more Member States on the one hand, and one or more third countries on the other, shall not be affected by the provisions of this Treaty*'. Almost the same wording can be found in today's Article 351 TFEU, which is the only provision within the constitutional framework of the EU explicitly dealing with the relationship between international treaties of the Member States and EU law.[1839] When examining the question of whether the GloBE-Directive obliges the Member States to amend their tax treaty network, there is no way around Article 351 TFEU.

5.4.3 Suspension/Subordination of Supremacy for Pre-existing Treaties under Article 351 TFEU

5.4.3.1 Telos and Purpose of Article 351 TFEU

The current wording of Article 351(1) TFEU reads as follows: '*Rights and obligations arising from agreements concluded before 1 January 1958 or, for acceding States, before the date of their accession, between one or more Member States on the one hand, and one or more third countries on the other, shall not be affected by the provisions of the Treaties*'. The norm is regarded as a primary law recognition of *pacta sunt servanda* codified in Article 26 VCLT.[1840] Through Article 351(1) TFEU, EU law recedes in favour of a treaty that already existed before 1 January 1958 or the respective Member State's subsequent accession to protect Member States from violations of public international law in case of a normative conflict.[1841] Pursuant to Article 351(1) TFEU, Union law should not prevent Member States from fulfilling their obligations vis-à-vis third countries. The provision is, therefore, also an expression of the '*obligation of loyalty between the Community and the Member States*'[1842] under Article 4(3) TEU.[1843]

According to the CJEU, the purpose of Article 351 TFEU '*is to make clear, in accordance with the principles of international law, that application of the Treaty does not affect the commitment of the Member State concerned to respect the rights of non-member countries under an earlier agreement and to comply with its corresponding*

1839. P. Pistone, *supra* note 1790, at 86; J. Klabbers, *supra* note 1800, at 10; J.P. Terhechte, *Art. 351 TFEU, the Principle of Loyalty and the Future Role of the Member States' Bilateral Investment Treaties*, in *International Investment Law and EU Law* 84 (Marc Bungenberg et al., eds, Springer 2011); C. De Pietro, *Tax Treaty Override and the Need for Coordination between Legal Systems: Safeguarding the Effectiveness of International Law*, 7 WTJ 92 (2015).

1840. J. P. Terhechte, *supra* note 1839, at 83; P. Koutrakos, *EU International Relations Law* 321 (Hart Publishing 2015); J. Kokott, *Art 351 – Verhältnis Zu Früheren Verträgen, in EUV/AEUV*, para. 1 (R. Streinz ed., C.H.Beck 3rd ed. 2018); S. Lorenzmeier, *Art. 351, in Das Recht der Europäischen Union*, para. 2 (E. Grabitz et al., eds, C.H.Beck 72nd ed. 2019).

1841. Case C-124/95, *The Queen ex parte Centro-Com Srl and H. M. Treasury and The Bank of England*, para. 56.

1842. Case C-188/07, *Commune de Mesquer v. Total France SA and Total International Ltd*, para. 101; in detail to the relationship of Art. 351(2) TFEU and the principle of loyalty under Art. 4(3) TEU, *see* J. P. Terhechte, *supra* note 1839, at 87.

1843. S. Lorenzmeier, *supra* note 1840, paras 3 and 77.

obligations'.[1844] In subsequent decisions, the CJEU also explicitly refers to Article 30(4)(b) VCLT: '[T]*he purpose of the first paragraph of* [Art 351] *of the Treaty is to make it clear, in accordance with the principles of international law (see, in that connection, Article 30(4)(b) of the 1969 Vienna Convention on the Law of Treaties), that application of the EC Treaty is not to affect the duty of the Member State concerned to respect the rights of third countries under a prior agreement and to perform its obligations thereunder'*.[1845] Article 30(4)(b) VCLT states that a posterior treaty cannot affect the rights and obligations of a state derived from an anterior treaty of the same subject matter if it is not a party to the posterior treaty. This provision thus clarifies that the *lex posterior* principle codified in Article 30(3) VCLT cannot become decisive for third parties. This is also in line with the *res inter alios acta* or *pacta tertiis* principle in Article 34 VCLT, according to which an agreement cannot affect the rights or obligations of non-contracting parties.[1846] Article 351 TFEU is, in this respect, a mere recognition of these principles of (customary) international law.[1847] The provision secures that the Treaties are in conformity with international law (*'principle of conformity/commitment of international law' – 'völkerrechtskonforme/völkerrechtsfreundliche Integration'*).[1848]

5.4.3.2 Scope of Article 351 TFEU

Article 351 TFEU is to be understood as a rule of conflict:[1849] In the event of a normative conflict between EU law and an international treaty concluded between Member States and third states, EU law shall step back if the relevant international treaty was concluded before 1 January 1958 or before the accession of the respective Member

1844. Case C-158/91, *Jean-Claude Levy*, para. 12; Case C-324/93, *The Queen and Secretary of State for the Home Department, ex parte Evans Medical Ltd and Macfarlan Smith Ltd*, para. 27; Case C-124/95, *Centro-Com Srl*, para. 56.
1845. Case C-62/98, *Commission of the European Communities v. Portuguese Republic*, para. 44; Case C-84/98, *Commission of the European Communities v. Portuguese Republic*, para. 53; Case T-315/01, *Yassin Abdullah Kadi v. Council of the European Union and Commission of the European Communities*, para. 186.
1846. R. Schütze, *supra* note 1810, at 389–390 and 407; C. Panayi, *supra* note 1813, at 122; J. W. Van Rossem, *Interaction Between EU Law and International Law in the Light of Intertanko and Kadi: The Dilemma of Norms Binding the Member States but Not the Community, in Netherlands Yearbook of International law – 2009*, 198 (I. F. Dekker & E. Hey eds, Springer 2010).
1847. C. Panayi, *supra* note 1813, at 122; G. Kofler, *supra* note 1790, at 423; S. Lorenzmeier, *supra* note 1840, para. 3; J. Kokott, *supra* note 1840, para. 1; P. Koutrakos, *supra* note 1840, at 321; R. Geiger, *Article 351 [Former Agreements of the Member States]*, in *European Union Treaties* (R. Geiger et al., eds, C.H.Beck 2015).
1848. P. Pistone, *supra* note 1790, at 83; with further detail on an international law perspective, *see* J. Klabbers, *supra* note 1800, at 116–117; J. P. Terhechte, *supra* note 1839, at 83. Also in detail on the telos and purpose of Art. 351 TFEU, *see* V. Bendlinger, *supra* note 1819, s. § 351.02.
1849. *See, i.a.*, T. Scherer, *supra* note 1790, at 48; J. Klabbers, *Moribund on the Fourth of July? The Court of Justice on Prior Agreements of the Member States*, 26 European Law Review 187–197 (2001); E. Vranes, *Die EU-Außenkompetenzen im Schnittpunkt von Europarecht, Völkerrecht und nationalem Recht*, 133 Juristische Blätter 18–19 (2011); K.V. Papp, *Solving Conflicts with International Investment Treaty Law from an EU Law Perspective: Article 351 TFEU Revisited*, 42 Legal Issues of Economic Integration 327 (2015) DOI: 10.54648/leie2015021; S. Lorenzmeier, *supra* note 1840, para. 2; V. Bendlinger, *supra* note 1819, s. § 351.04[2].

State. In other words, Article 351(1) TFEU establishes the primacy of an anterior treaty concluded with at least one-third state over EU law. Article 351(1) TFEU is therefore often understood as a 'suspension of EU law's supremacy'.[1850] *Argumentum e contrario*, Article 351(1) TFEU thus implicitly declares supremacy of EU law over international treaties between Member States and third countries concluded after 1 January 1958 or after the respective Member State's accession, as well as over treaties concluded solely between Member States (*inter se* treaties). In the latter case of so-called *inter se* treaties, EU law even prevails if the respective agreement at issue was concluded before 1 January 1958 or before the respective Member State's accession.[1851] Treaties concluded after 1 January 1958 or after the accession of the respective Member States are not covered by Article 351 TFEU at all, regardless of whether they are concluded between Member States or with third countries.[1852]

The material scope of Article 351(1) TFEU is, in principle, unrestricted and therefore applies to every kind of international treaty to which at least one Member State and at least one-third state is a party.[1853] This interpretation has been explicitly confirmed by the CJEU on several occasions, i.e., in the *Burgoa*-Case, in which the Court held that '[Art 351 TFEU] *is of general scope and it applies to any international agreement, irrespective of subject matter, which is capable of affecting the application of the Treaty*'.[1854] Article 351 TFEU is therefore indisputably also applicable to DTCs.[1855]

1850. R. Schütze, *supra* note 1810, at 391.

1851. This reading is confirmed by the CJEU, which held that Art. 351 TFEU '*is not concerned with agreements concluded solely between Member States*', *see* Case C-235/87, *Annunziata Matteucci v. Commissariat general aux relations internationals of the Communauté française of Belgium*, para. 21; *see also* explicitly Case C-478/07, *Budějovický Budvar, národní podnik v. Rudolf Ammersin GmbH* 98–99; with further reference on case law, *see* A. Rosas, *supra* note 1816, at 1319 in particular n. 66; C. Panayi, *supra* note 1813, at 122; K. Von Papp, *supra* note 1849, at 328; S. Lorenzmeier, *supra* note 1840, para. 9; J. Klabbers, *supra* note 1800, at 205; P. Koutrakos, *supra* note 1840, at 322; A. Dimopoulos, *supra* note 1809, at 70; V. Bendlinger, *supra* note 1819, s. § 351.04[3][a].

1852. A. Rosas, *supra* note 1816, at 1322; K. Von Papp, *supra* note 1849, at 330; J. Kokott, *supra* note 1840, paras 2–4.

1853. K. Stöger, *Art. 351, in Kommentar zu EUV und AEUV*, para. 7 (T. Jäger & K. Stöger eds, Manz 2019).

1854. Explicitly, *see* Case C-812/79, *Attorney General v. Juan C. Burgoa*, para. 6; confirmed, i.e., in Case C-158/91, *Levy*, para. 11; Case C-62/98, *Commission v. Portugal*, para. 43; Case C-466/98, *Commission of the European Communities v. United Kingdom of Great Britain and Northern Ireland*, para. 23. With further reference on CJEU case law, *see* P. Manzini, *The Priority of Pre-Existing Treaties of EC Member States within the Framework of International Law*, 12 EJIL, *supra* note 1816, at 123; G. Kofler, *Doppelbesteuerungsabkommen und Europäisches Gemeinschaftsrecht*, *supra* note 1790, at 423; C. Panayi, *supra* note 1813; Panos Koutrakos, *supra* note 1840, at 322; V. Bendlinger, *supra* note 1819, s. § 351.04[3][a].

1855. F. Vanistendael, *The Limits to the New Community Tax Order*, 31 Common Market Law Review 300 (1994); T. Scherer, *supra* note 1790, at 48–54; M. Lang, *Die Bindung der Doppelbesteuerungsabkommen an die Grundfreiheiten des EU-Rechts*, in *Doppelbesteuerungsabkommen und EU-Recht* 30 (Wolfgang Gassner et al., eds, Linde 1996); G. Kofler, *European Taxation Under an 'Open Sky': LoB Clauses in Tax Treaties Between the US and EU Member States*, Tax Notes Intl. 64 (2004); *EC Law and Tax Treaties*, para. 16; K. Vogel et al., *Tax Treaties between Member States and Third States: 'reciprocity' in Bilateral Tax Treaties and Non-Discrimination in EC Law*, 15 EC Tax Review 83 (2006). C. Panayi, *supra* note 1813, at 121–132; G. Kofler, *supra* note 1790, at 423; J.C. Guerra, *Limitation on Benefits Clauses and EU Law*, 51 Eur. Taxn. 94 (2011); C. Marchgraber, *Cross-Border Tax Arbitrage, the*

The temporal scope of Article 351 TFEU raises a controversial question of interpretation in literature, namely whether the time of the formal signing of the respective treaty or its entry into force is relevant for its application. According to a literal interpretation, the '*conclusion*' of the respective agreement should be relevant.[1856] However, contrary to the wording of the provision *Manzini*, among others,[1857] argues that only treaties in force would give rise to '*rights and obligations*' and Article 351(1) TFEU could only be invoked for treaties which came into force before 1 January 1958 or the respective Member State's accession.[1858] The predominant and more convincing counter-opinion considers the ratification of the respective agreement as relevant. This view can be based not only on the wording but also on arguments of international law: according to Article 14 VCLT, international treaties become binding upon ratification. In addition, according to Article 18 VCLT, contracting states are obliged '*not to defeat the object and purpose of a treaty before its entry into force*'.[1859] With respect to tax treaties, one can refer to the provision of Article 31(2) OECD MC 2017, stating that the DTC '*shall enter into force upon the exchange of instruments of ratification*'. The date on which the DTC becomes effective can be determined separately, according to the OECD MC 2017. In any case, in the event of a conflict between EU law and a DTC, the ratification of the DTC is the decisive point in time to determine whether or not the relevant DTC is protected by Article 351(1) TFEU.

Of far greater relevance, in particular for DTCs,[1860] however, is the question of whether a later amendment of an anterior treaty affects the applicability of Article 351(1) TFEU. Can Member States still rely on Article 351 TFEU if an anterior treaty was (partially) renegotiated or amended? The CJEU answered the question in the negative: a Member State may not invoke Article 351(1) TFEU if the new treaty '*entails new and*

Parent-Subsidiary Directive (2011/96) and Double Tax Treaty Law, 70 Bull. Intl. Taxn. 123–132 (2016); L. De Broe, *Can Tax Treaties Confer State Aid?*, 26 EC Tax Review 228 (2017) DOI: 10.54648/ecta2017025; H. Vermeulen, *Comments on Professor Yariv Brauner's Lecture 'The True Nature of Tax Treaties'*, 74 Bull. Intl. Taxn. 51 (2020); A. Garcia Prats et al, *EU Report Subject 1 – Reconstructing the Treaty Network, in cahier de droit fiscal international* 62–63 (International Fiscal Association 2020); V. Bendlinger, *supra* note 1819, s. § 351.0 4[3][a].

1856. K. Stöger, *supra* note 1853, para. 14.

1857. *See*, i.e., T. Scherer, *supra* note 1790, at 51–52.

1858. *Manzini* thereby refers to para. 7 of Case C-812/79, *Burgoa*, in which the Court considered the applicability of today's Art. 351 TFEU and held that '*the London Fisheries Convention came into force on 15 March 1966. It had been signed and ratified by both States on dates prior to that of Ireland's accession to the Community*'; P. Manzini, *supra* note 1816, at 785; approving, *see* J. Kokott, *Art. 351 – Verhältnis Zu Früheren Verträgen, in EUV/AEUV*, *supra* note 1840, para. 1. But as *Stöger* convincingly points out, in para. 7 of Case C-812/79, *Burgoa* the Court only examined the applicability of Art. 351 TFEU in general terms and did not take a clear position on the question of whether it is the conclusion or the entry into force that is decisive; *see* K. Stöger, *supra* note 1853, para. 14. For further reference on this discussion, *see Stöger, see Ibid.*, at 427.

1859. Comprehensively on this issue, *see* G. Kofler, *supra* note 1790, at 427–430.

1860. International tax treaty practice shows that DTCs are occasionally renegotiated and adjusted.

significant international commitments'[1861] or gives *'rise to new rights and obligations'*.[1862] The ECJ further clarified that even provisions, which were incorporated identically or were only subject to minor changes, lose their status as anterior treaties if they were *'confirmed during renegotiation'*.[1863] According to the CJEU, Member States are *'prevented not only from contracting new international commitments but also from maintaining such commitments in force if they infringe Community law'*.[1864] A renegotiation of an anterior agreement thus most likely excludes the applicability of Article 351(1) TFEU[1865] and, moreover, obliges Member States to eliminate existing incompatibilities with Union law resulting from previously existing provisions of the anterior treaty.[1866] Even if the respective provision remains untouched during the negotiation of amendments, Member States might, thus, lose the privilege to rely on Article 351(1) TFEU.

Particularly with regard to DTCs, the following question comes up: where is the threshold of a *'renegotiation'* which leads to *'new and significant international commitments'*, or does every amendment preclude the application of Article 351(1) TFEU? According to *Kofler*, it must be examined whether the provisions contrary to EU law were *'confirmed'* in the partial renegotiation of the respective tax treaty.[1867] If the respective provision conflicting with EU law is confirmed during the treaty negotiations, the respective Member State, pursuant to the above-mentioned case law, may not rely on Article 351(1) TFEU anymore if they did not try to eliminate the incompatibility.[1868] This result is implicitly related to Article 351(2) TFEU, which calls on Member States to *'take all appropriate steps'* to eliminate existing incompatibilities with agreements within the meaning of paragraph 1 (*see* below).[1869] When Member States renegotiate an anterior DTC with a third country, they must eliminate existing conflicts with Union law.[1870] However, after having analysed the case law on Article 351(1) TFEU cited above, it can be concluded that renegotiated treaties can hardly be considered anterior treaties. Pursuant to the CJEU's settled case law, the objection of Article 351(1) TFEU will probably only be effective when it comes to minor technical adjustments.[1871] Even if such small adjustments were to exist, one could still object

1861. Case C-475/98, *Commission of the European Communities v. Republic of Austria (Open Skies)*; for further reference, *see* K. Stöger, *supra* note 1853, para. 15; C. Panayi, *supra* note 1813, at 125.
1862. Case C-466/98, *Commission v. Portugal*, para. 29.
1863. Case C-475/98, *Commission v. Austria (Open Skies)*, para. 49.
1864. *Ibid.*
1865. For a detailed and critical discussion of the rationale in the ECJs *Open Skies* judgements, *see* J. Klabbers, *supra* note 1800, at 134–135 and 198–199.
1866. G. Kofler, *supra* note 1790, at 428.
1867. *Ibid.*
1868. However, sceptical P. Pistone, *supra* note 1790, at 88, who argues that *'substantial treaty issues should* [not] *be left with no legal protection from the perspective of Community law'*.
1869. G. Kofler, *supra* note 1790, at 428.
1870. In detail, *see* s. 5.4.3.4.
1871. J. Klabbers, *Treaty Conflict and the European Union*, *supra* note 1800, at 198.

that, according to Article 351(2) TFEU, the Member State would be obliged to establish a situation compatible with Union law in the course of the adjustment anyway.[1872]

5.4.3.3 *Effect and Reach of Supremacy's Suspension According to Article 351(1) TFEU*

The application of Article 351(1) TFEU is, as shown above, limited to third-country agreements ratified before the establishment of the Community or before the respective Member State's accession. However, the CJEU further limited the scope of Article 351(1) TFEU when it held that '*the terms "rights and obligations" in* [Art 351 TFEU] *refer, as regards the "rights", to the rights of third countries and, as regards the "obligations", to the obligations of Member States*'.[1873] Thus, according to the CJEU, a Member State may only invoke Article 351(1) TFEU in order to comply with an obligation towards a third country. This also presupposes the existence of obligations '*whose performance may still be required by third countries*' according to the rules of public international law.[1874] With regard to rights provided by a third country agreement to the Member State, the respective Member State remains bound by EU law and cannot invoke the objection[1875] of Article 351(1) TFEU. Therefore, the Court also states that if '*an international agreement allows, but does not require, a Member State to adopt a measure which appears to be contrary to Community law, the Member State must refrain from adopting such a measure*'.[1876] According to the CJEU's decision in *Luksan v. Petrus*, this expressly also applies '*when, because of a development in European Union law, a legislative measure adopted by a Member State in accordance with the power offered by an earlier international agreement appears contrary to European Union law*'.[1877] Article 351 TFEU is, therefore, not to be seen as a general suspension of EU law's supremacy, even if a respective treaty falls within its scope: rather, Union law merely gives way to a specific international treaty obligation of the respective Member State.[1878] Thus, if an obligation from an anterior treaty with a third

1872. In detail to the Member States' obligation to renegotiate or even terminate international treaties that violate EU law, *see* s. 5.4.3.4.
1873. Case C-10/61, *Commission of the European Economic Community v. Government of the Italian Republic* 10 et seq.; for further reference, *see*, i.e., G. Kofler, *supra* note 1790, at 423 in particular n. 803; R. Schütze, *supra* note 1822, at 199; and S. Lorenzmeier, *supra* note 1840, para. 14.
1874. Joined Cases C-364/95 and 365/95, *T. Port GmbH & Co. and Hauptzollamt Hamburg-Jonas*, para. 60; *see* G. Kofler, *supra* note 1790, at 425 in particular n. 816; R. Schütze, *supra* note 1810, at 393; S. Lorenzmeier, *supra* note 1840, para. 20.
1875. G. Kofler, *supra* note 1790, at 424.
1876. Case C-324/93, *Evans Medical Ltd and Macfarlan Smith Ltd*, para. 32; confirmed, i.e., in Case C-124/95, *Centro-Com Srl*, para. 60; and Case C-277/10, *Martin Luksan v. Petrus van der Let*, para. 62; *see also* J. Kokott, *Art. 351 – Verhältnis Zu Früheren Verträgen, in EUV/AEUV*, *supra* note 1840, para. 9.
1877. Case C-277/10, *Luksan v. Petrus*, para. 63; *see also* J. Kokott, *supra* note 1840, para. 9; S. Lorenzmeier, *supra* note 1840, para. 26; The same statement may be understood as a recognition of an analogous application of Art. 351 TFEU of the CJEU, if an posterior agreement initially complied with Union law, but only became incompatible due to the adoption of a secondary act of the Union. Again on this issue, *see* s. 5.4.3.5.
1878. Panos Koutrakos, *supra* note 1840, at 322.

country can be fulfilled in conformity with Union law, the respective Member State must not rely on Article 351(1) TFEU.[1879] Accordingly, a Member State cannot invoke Article 351 TFEU to its advantage and may only leave EU law unapplied if this is necessary to avoid a breach of international law.[1880] This interpretation is a favourable one for the EU; however, it is also convincing: Article 351(1) TFEU aims to avoid normative conflicts between third-country agreements and EU law. If a third-country agreement grants a right to a Member State, it is up to the Member State to make use of its right, and if the Member State can waive its right to avoid a normative conflict, the suspension of supremacy pursuant to Article 351(1) TFEU should not be granted. With respect to an obligation towards a third country, however, normative conflicts cannot be avoided. However, it should be emphasized in this respect that Article 351 TFEU, on the other hand, in no way obliges Member States to satisfy their obligations under public international law. Rather, Article 351(1) TFEU only permits to leave EU law unapplied if it would force the Member State to violate an obligation towards a third country.

Thus, if a Member State has an obligation towards a third country based on an anterior agreement, the respective agreement '*shall not be affected by the provisions of the Treaties*'. Even if Article 351(1) TFEU only mentions '*treaties*', this *argumentum maiore ad minus* must also apply to secondary law. Anterior treaties, therefore, also remain unaffected by any legal acts of EU law[1881] as far as third-country rights are concerned. However, the Union, as such, is not bound by agreements within the meaning of Article 351(1) TFEU. The provision solely permits the Member States to leave EU law unapplied with respect to their own treaties.[1882] However, in *Burgoa*, the Court made clear that '*although the first paragraph of* [Art 351] *makes mention only of the obligations of the Member States, it would not achieve its purpose if it did not imply a duty on the part of the institutions of the Community not to impede the performance of the obligations of Member States which stems from a prior agreement. However, that duty of the Community institutions is directed only to permitting the Member State concerned to perform its obligations under the prior agreement and does not bind the Community as regards the non-member country in question*'.[1883] The Union, thus, is even free to adopt secondary legislation contrary to anterior treaties of the Member States. In this case, however, the Member States remain shielded from infringement proceedings since the Commission and other EU institutions are prevented from enforcing such secondary legislation.[1884] For the GloBE-Directive, this means that Article 351(1) TFEU, as such, did not prohibit the adoption of the GloBE-Directive even if it might conflict with some treaties of the Member States. Article 351(1) TFEU does not limit the secondary legislature in any way. However, the institutions of the EU

1879. G. Kofler, *supra* note 1790, at 426.
1880. P. Pistone, *supra* note 1790, at 88; P. Koutrakos, *supra* note 1840, at 323.
1881. P. Pistone, *supra* note 1790, at 86; G. Kofler, *supra* note 1790, at 424; A. Rosas, *supra* note 1816, at 1321; J. Kokott, *supra* note 1840, para. 9.
1882. R. Schütze, *supra* note 1810, at 394.
1883. Case C-812/79, *Burgoa*, para. 9; in detail R. Schütze, *supra* note 1810, at 394; J. Kokott, *supra* note 1840, para. 21.
1884. S. Lorenzmeier, *Art. 351, in Das Recht der Europäischen Union*, *supra* note 1840, para. 22.

cannot enforce a violation of the GloBE-Directive, if a Member State applies the provisions of a DTC covered by Article 351(1) TFEU to meet an obligation granted to a third state in the respective DTC. In this context, it should also be mentioned that the Member States are still under an obligation to remedy incompatibilities with anterior third-country agreements according to Article 351(2) TFEU, as will be seen shortly.[1885]

An interesting discussion concerns the question of whether only states or also individuals can invoke rights granted to them by a posterior treaty.[1886] This question is of particular relevance to the area of DTC in general, and in particular with respect to the GloBE-Directive: can a taxpayer directly rely on a posterior DTC if it is more favourable than conflicting EU law, e.g., the GloBE-Directive? The CJEU also answered this question in *Burgoa*: '*Since the purpose of the first paragraph of* [Art 351 TFEU] *is to remove any obstacle to the performance of agreements previously concluded with non-member countries* [...] *it cannot have the effect altering the nature of the rights which may not flow from such agreements. From that it follows that that provision does not have the effect of conferring upon individuals who rely upon an agreement concluded prior to the entry into force of the Treaty or, as the case may be, the accession of the Member State concerned, rights which the national Courts of the Member States must uphold. Nor does it adversely affect the rights which individuals may derive from such an agreement.*'[1887] The Court thus expresses that Article 351 TFEU itself cannot convey rights on individuals, or as *Von Papp* puts it: '*Art 351 does only reach as far as the protection provided by the anterior treaty.*'[1888] The legal effect of an agreement thus depends exclusively on the constitutional law of the respective Member State and the legal character of the respective treaty. If a particular international treaty grants certain rights to individuals and if it is directly applicable under domestic law, those individuals may rely on the anterior treaty before the domestic Courts. National Courts can then ignore Union law which contradicts the anterior third country agreement, and, thus, avoid a normative conflict. From the perspective of tax treaty law, it can be concluded that an individual may rely on rights provided by an anterior DTC with a third country under Article 351(1) TFEU if it is directly applicable under the domestic constitutional law of the respective Member State.[1889] The prerequisite, however, is that the Member State would breach an obligation under international law by applying Union law. Thus, the author's opinion is; that a legal entity subject to the GloBE-Directive could indeed invoke Article 351(1) TFEU if a jurisdiction, by applying the IIR or the UTPR, violated a right given to a third state under a pre-existing tax treaty.

1885. J. Kokott, *supra* note 1840, para. 21; in detail *see* s. 5.4.3.4.

1886. At a glance, *see* K. Von Papp, *supra* note 1849, at 341–343; S. Lorenzmeier, *supra* note 1840, para. 16.

1887. Case C-812/79, *Burgoa*, para. 10. also confirmed in Case C-62/98, *Commission v. Portugal*, para. 44; also referring to this issue, *see* Jan Klabbers, *Treaty Conflict and the European Union*, *supra* note 1800, at 193–194.

1888. Konstanze Von Papp, *supra* note 1849, at 332–333.

1889. Also from the perspective of Bilateral Investment Treaties (BITs), *see Ibid.*, at 333–334; also affirmative to an possible application of Art. 351 TFEU to individuals, if a certain treaty provides for individual rights, *see* S. Lorenzmeier, *supra* note 1840, para. 16; the opposite opinion, however, is represented by J. Kokott, *supra* note 1840, para. 11.

One should note here that neither the narrow wording of Article 351 TFEU nor its even narrower interpretation by the CJEU are surprising from a policy point of view. Ultimately, it would be contrary to the ideal of the Community if the Member States could circumvent the EU legal order by concluding treaties among themselves or exempt themselves from their EU law obligations to other Member States by concluding treaties with third states.[1890] However, the strict line of the CJEU has been strongly criticized in literature for good reasons, especially by advocates of public international law, who complain that the Court's strict approach weakens the EU's credibility.[1891] *Klabbers* finally concludes that Article 351 TFEU '*is more about balancing Community law with international law than that it affords outright protection to international commitments*'.[1892]

5.4.3.4 Obligation to Eliminate Incompatibilities under Article 351(2) TFEU

As shown above, Article 351(1) TFEU has an extremely limited scope of application. But in addition, even if it applies and may be invoked, Article 351(2) TFEU sets limits to the suspension of Union law: '*To the extent that such agreements are not compatible with the Treaties, the Member State or States concerned shall take all appropriate steps to eliminate the incompatibilities established. Member States shall, where necessary, assist each other to this end and shall, where appropriate, adopt a common attitude.*' Article 351(2) TFEU obviously entails a certain contradiction with Article 351(1) TFEU and is thus, as *Meessen* explicitly points out, in tension[1893] with Article 351(1) TFEU: on the one hand '[t]*he Community takes notice of the continuous existence of the treaty commitments of its Member States*', but '*urges their adaptation to its own needs*' on the other.[1894] This tension soon led to a discussion of the scope of the second paragraph of Article 351 TFEU. How far does the obligation of the Member States to eliminate existing incompatibilities extend? What exactly is meant by '*all appropriate steps*'? Are Member States under certain circumstances even obliged to denounce an anterior treaty, and if so, when would such a treaty have to be denounced?

The question of whether Union law can force Member States to denounce international treaties was addressed by the Court for the first time between 1998 and 2000 when the Commission initiated a series of infringement proceedings against various Member States for violations of Regulation 4055/86[1895] stipulating rules to apply the freedom to provide services to maritime transport between Member States

1890. *See also* J. W. Van Rossem, *supra* note 1846, at 200; A. Rosas, *supra* note 1816, at 1319; a different view, however, is taken by *Lorenzmeier*, who argues that Art. 351(1) and (2) TFEU are legally independent, *see* S. Lorenzmeier, *supra* note 1840, para. 28.
1891. *See*, i.e., J.W. Van Rossem, *supra* note 1846, at 225–226; and *Von Papp*, who argues for reconsidering the Courts narrow understanding of Art. 351 TFEU according the so far case law, *see* K. Von Papp, *supra* note 1849, at 355–356.
1892. J. Klabbers, *supra* note 1800, at 148.
1893. Also *see* P. Manzini, *supra* note 1816, at 788; and Konstanze Von Papp, *supra* note 1849, at 333–334.
1894. K.M. Meessen, *supra* note 1818, at 490; J. Kokott, *supra* note 1840, paras 2–4.
1895. Council Regulation (EEC) No 4055/86, of 22 December 1986 applying the principle of freedom to provide services to maritime transport between Member States and third countries, OJ (1).

and third countries:[1896] Articles 3 and 4 of Regulation 4055/86, which entered into force on 1 January 1987, provided for existing bilateral cargo-sharing agreements with third countries to be phased out or adjusted to comply with the so-called UN Code of Conduct for Liner Conferences within a certain time-limit.[1897] However, some Member States failed to amend or terminate their treaties in time. One of the Court's most famous decisions in this series of cases was *Commission v. Belgium*, which concerned an agreement between Zaire (today's Democratic Republic of the Congo) and Belgium, which was concluded before Regulation 4055/86 entered into force, but after Belgium's accession to the EC.[1898] It contained a provision according to which 40% of the cargo was reserved for Belgian traders, while traders from other Member States were excluded from providing such services, which resulted in a violation of Regulation 4055/86 (1986/1).[1899] The Belgian government argued that it had indeed tried to renegotiate the agreement but that this had not been successful due to political developments in Zaire and that it had not been on duty to denounce the agreement.[1900] The Court, however, remained unimpressed and held that '[t]*he existence of a difficult political situation in a third State which is a contracting party, as in the present case, cannot justify a failure to fulfil obligations. If a Member State encounters difficulties which make it impossible to adjust an agreement, it must denounce the agreement*'.[1901]

Although the respective agreement between Zaire and Belgium was concluded after Belgium's accession to the EC and did not fall within the scope of Article 351 TFEU, the case had significant influence on the *Commission v. Portugal*[1902] cases, in which the Court had to decide on similar agreements now within the scope of Article 351 TFEU and finally gave its second paragraph some shape.[1903] Contrary to Belgium, Portugal had already concluded several cargo-sharing agreements before its accession to the EU. The Portuguese government, therefore, invoked Article 351 TFEU, argued that it could not be forced to breach its obligations via third countries[1904] and did not even deny that the respective agreements were in conflict[1905] with Regulation 4055/86.[1906] Rather, it was stressed that although Article 351(2) TFEU provides for an

1896. *See, i.a.*, the Courts landmark decision in Joined Cases C-176/97 and 177/97, *Commission of the European Communities v. Kingdom of Belgium and Grand Duchy of Luxembourg.*
1897. For further detail, *see* Jan Klabbers, *supra* note 1800, at 188–189.
1898. For this reason Art. 351 TFEU was not at issue. Also *see* V. Bendlinger, *supra* note 1819, s. § 351.05[2].
1899. Case C-170/98, *Commission of the European Communities v. Kingdom of Belgium*; *see* P. Koutrakos, *supra* note 1840, at 325.
1900. Case C-170/98, *Commission v. Belgium*, paras 37 and 41.
1901. *Ibid.*, para. 42.
1902. Case C-62/98, *Commission v. Portugal*; Case C-84/98, *Commission v. Portugal.*
1903. Also in detail on the *Commission v. Portugal cases, see*, i.e., C. Hillion, *Case C-62/98 Commission of the European Communities v. Portugal, and Case C-84/98 Commission of the European Communities v. Portugal*, 38 Common Market Law Review 1269–1283 (2001); R. Schütze, *supra* note 1810, at 393–394; J. Klabbers, *supra* note 1800, at 137–139 and 187–197; R. Schütze, *supra* note 1810, at 107.
1904. Case C-62/98, *Commission v. Portugal*, para. 24; Case C-84/98, *Commission v. Portugal*, para. 30.
1905. Panos Koutrakos, *supra* note 1840, at 326.
1906. Case C-62/98, *Commission v. Portugal*, para. 21; Case C-84/98, *Commission v. Portugal*, para. 26; *Klabbers* thus argued that the objection of Art. 351 TFEU had brought the Court to a

obligation to take '*all appropriate steps*' to remedy incompatibilities with Union law, a termination of an agreement in this sense would not constitute an '*appropriate step*'[1907] and would be '*a disproportionate disregard of foreign-policy interests of the Portuguese Republic as compared with the Community interest*'.[1908] Moreover, with regard to the agreements with Angola and Yugoslavia, the Portuguese government additionally argued that the political situation in those countries prevented a renegotiation of the respective agreements.[1909] Not surprisingly, the Court relied on its decision in *Commission v. Belgium* and repeated that a political situation in a third state could not '*justify a continuing failure on the part of a Member State to fulfil its obligations under the treaty*'[1910] and that '*in so far as denunciation is possible under international law, it is incumbent on the Member State concerned to denounce*'[1911] a respective agreement. Since the relevant treaties explicitly mentioned their possible denunciation '*so that denunciation by the Portuguese Republic would not encroach upon the rights*'[1912] of the other contracting states, according to the CJEU, there was nothing to prevent an obligation to denounce the agreements.[1913] Finally, the Court applied the respective provisions of Regulation 4055/86 and added that they had not been affected by Article 351 TFEU. With regard to Article 351(2) TFEU, the Court furthermore held that '[i]*f a Member State encounters difficulties which make adjustment of an agreement impossible, an obligation to denounce that agreement cannot therefore be excluded*'[1914].[1915]

The scope of Article 351(2) TFEU was further shaped in 2009 when the ECJ had to rule on several bilateral investment treaties (BITs), which Austria, Finland and Sweden had each concluded with several third countries.[1916] The agreements contained clauses under which each party guaranteed to the investors of the other party the free transfer, in freely convertible currency, of payments connected with an investment. The Commission considered that these provisions were incompatible with Union law since they prevent possible restrictions adopted by the Council on the free

dilemma: The Court could not avoid addressing the legal character of Art. 351 TFEU and its relation to Regulation No 4055/86. With interesting thoughts on the relation between the *Commission v. Belgium* and *Commission v. Portugal* cases, *see* J. Klabbers, *supra* note 1800, at 194–195.

1907. Case C-62/98, *Commission v. Portugal*, para. 25; Case C-84/98, *Commission v. Portugal*, para. 31.
1908. Case C-62/98, *Commission v. Portugal*, paras 40 and 50; Case C-84/98, *Commission v. Portugal*, paras 37, 49 and 59.
1909. Further on the arguments stressed by the Portuguese government, *see* P. Koutrakos, *supra* note 1840, at 326.
1910. Case C-62/98, *Commission v. Portugal*, para. 39; Case C-84/98, *Commission v. Portugal*, para. 48.
1911. Case C-62/98, *Commission v. Portugal*, paras 34 and 48; Case C-84/98, *Commission v. Portugal*, paras 40 and 57.
1912. Case C-62/98, *Commission v. Portugal*, para. 46; Case C-84/98, *Commission v. Portugal*, para. 55.
1913. *See also* P. Manzini, *supra* note 1816, at 791.
1914. Case C-62/98, *Commission v. Portugal*, paras 48–49; Case C-84/98, *Commission v. Portugal*, paras 57–58.
1915. In detail also on the Portugal cases, *see* V. Bendlinger, *supra* note 1819, s. § 351.05[2].
1916. Case C-205/06, *Commission of the European Communities v. Republic of Austria*; Case C-249/06, *Commission of the European Communities v. Kingdom of Sweden*; Case C-118/07, *Commission of the European Communities v. Republic of Finland*.

movement of capital under today's Articles 64, 66 and 67 TFEU. More precisely, it argued that the respective Member States had failed to comply with their obligation under today's Article 351(2) TFEU to amend or denounce those agreements.[1917] The interesting issue of these cases is the fact that the Commission did not invoke an actual incompatibility with Union law but only a hypothetical one.[1918] Several national governments of the Member States thus argued that the question of '*incompatibility*' with EU law did not arise at all, and the respective agreements at issue did not even fall within the scope of application of Article 351 TFEU.[1919] However, this also left the Court unimpressed. The ECJ finally argued that the effectiveness of the powers of the Council provided by EU law required potential measures to be '*applied immediately with regard to the* [third] *States to which they relate*'.[1920] The Court finally found that Austria, Sweden and Finland, '*by not having taken appropriate steps to eliminate incompatibilities,* [...] *failed to fulfil* [their] *obligations under the second paragraph of* [Art 351 TFEU]'[1921].

The Court's extensive interpretation[1922] of Article 351(2) TFEU obviously limits the scope of its first paragraph.[1923] Against the background of the already narrow interpretation of its second paragraph, the question arises as to which scope of application of Article 351(1) TFEU remains at all.[1924] The CJEU seems to defend the supremacy of EU law at all costs and seems to give higher weight to the obligation of the Member States to eliminate any incompatibilities of anterior treaties with Union law than to the interest of the Member States to comply with their obligations under international law towards third countries. Consequently, Article 351(1) TFEU seems to be mostly relevant for new Member States: after their accession, they may invoke Article 351(1) TFEU to fulfil obligations towards third countries arising from anterior treaties. However, the protection of pre-accession treaties is only of a temporary nature. The respective Member State must amend the agreement as soon as possible and, if renegotiations fail, is even obliged to denounce the respective agreement as far as this is permissible under international law.[1925] The one question that still remains is

1917. Case C-249/06, *Commission v. Sweden*, paras 3 et seq.; Case C-205/06, *Commission v. Austria*, paras 3 et seq.; Case C-118/07, *Commission v. Finland*, paras 33 et seq.; In detail to these cases, *see*, *i.a.*, Jörg Philipp Terhechte, *supra* note 1839, at 85–86; E. Vranes, *supra* note 1849, at 18–19.

1918. Jörg Philipp Terhechte, *supra* note 1839, at 85.

1919. In detail on this and related arguments brought up by the Member States, *see* Case C-249/06, *Commission v. Sweden*, paras 18–20; Case C-205/06, *Commission v. Austria* at 18–21; Case C-118/07, *Commission v. Finland*, para. 16.

1920. Case C-249/06, *Commission v. Sweden*, paras 37–38; Case C-205/06, *Commission v. Austria*, paras 36–37; Case C-118/07, *Commission v. Finland*, paras 30–31.

1921. Case C-249/06, *Commission v. Sweden*, para. 45; Case C-205/06, *Commission v. Austria* at 45; Case C-118/07, *Commission v. Finland*, para. 50.

1922. Also *see* C. Hillion, *Case C-62/98 Commission of the European Communities v. Portugal, and Case C-84/98 Commission of the European Communities v. Portugal*, 38 Common Market Law Review, *supra* note 1903, at 1282–1283.

1923. K. Von Papp, *supra* note 1849, at 336 in particular n. 50. Also *see* V. Bendlinger, *supra* note 1819, s. § 351.05[1] and [2].

1924. *See* Konstanze Von Papp, *supra* note 1849, at 356, who argues, that the broad reading of Art. 351(2) TFEU by the ECJ makes '*its first paragraph redundant*'.

1925. *Ibid.*, at 336.

simply at what point of time the obligation to denounce an anterior treaty materializes. Considering the fact that Article 351(2) TFEU does not provide any guidance in this respect and that the CJEU tends to interpret the provision very broadly, Member States are well advised to amend or denounce their anterior treaties as soon as possible.[1926]

5.4.3.5 *Mutatis Mutandis* Application of Article 351 TFEU on Subsequently Adopted Secondary Law?

The question as to how the GloBE-Directive may affect existing DTCs of the Member States seems to be clear with regard to *inter se* DTCs and anterior DTCs with third states covered by Article 351 TFEU. While *inter se* DTCs are never protected by Article 351(1) TFEU, anterior treaties are protected by Article 351(1) TFEU; the Member State invoking Article 351(1) TFEU, however, is obliged to eliminate the incompatibility as soon as possible. However, the question of whether the *principle of conformity /commitment of international law*, which is subject to Article 351 TFEU, also applies if a treaty concluded by a Member State becomes incompatible with EU law due to the subsequent adoption of a legal act of secondary law has not yet been addressed so far.

First of all, one could question whether Article 351 TFEU applies with respect to secondary law at all. Finally, Article 351 TFEU only states that treaties of the Member States 'shall not be affected by the provisions of the *Treaties*'[1927] (emphasis added). Thus, one could argue that Article 351(1) TFEU is not at issue if the respective treaty conflicts with secondary law. However, it had already been mentioned earlier that one can derive from an *argumentum maiore ad minus* that Article 351(1) TFEU equally applies with respect to secondary law.[1928] Indeed it would be odd to suspend supremacy with respect to primary law but enforce supremacy in the case of secondary law. After all, this would turn the hierarchy of norms of the EU legal order upside down. For this reason, Article 351(1) TFEU also applies when a treaty is compatible with primary law but conflicts with an act of secondary law. But what if the secondary legislation in question was adopted after the Member State joined the EU? Can a Member State invoke Article 351(1) TFEU with respect to a treaty that had been concluded after its accession to the EU but before the treaty came into conflict with EU secondary law? Finally, this is precisely the question that arises with regard to the relation of DTCs and the GloBE-Directive: what happens to DTCs concluded by the Member States with third countries after accession to the EU but before December 2022, when the GloBE-Directive had finally been enacted? Does the GloBE-Directive's supremacy apply to such conventions without restrictions?

So if one takes Article 351 TFEU literally, there is little doubt that this is the case: Article 351(1) TFEU explicitly requires that the protected agreement must be either

1926. Drawing a similar conclusion on the relationship between Art. 351 TFEU's first and second paragraph, *see* Jan Klabbers, *supra* note 1800, at 147–148. In detail, also *see* V. Bendlinger, *supra* note 1819, s. § 351.05.
1927. Article 351(1) TFEU.
1928. P. Pistone, *supra* note 1790, at 424; A. Rosas, *supra* note 1816, at 1321; J. Kokott, *supra* note 1840, para. 9.

'*concluded before 1 January 1958*' or '*before the* [Member States'] *date of* [subsequent] *accession*' to the EU. Given the fact that the GloBE-Directive was published in the EU's Official Journal on 22 December 2022, the wording of Article 351(1) TFEU suggests that any DTC concluded between a Member State and a third country before 22 December 2022 but after its accession to the EU is not covered by Article 351(1) TFEU.

Nevertheless, the wording is not the limit of interpretation but the point at which it begins. Indeed there is a long-standing discussion in the literature on the question of whether Article 351 TFEU should be applied by extension or analogy (*mutatis mutandis*) in the case of subsequently adopted legal acts of primary or secondary EU law.[1929] The analogous application of Article 351 TFEU on subsequently adopted EU law was already discussed in the middle of the 1960s of the 20th century, at a time when there was hardly any case law on today's Article 351 TFEU.[1930] One oft-quoted passage from *Churchill* and *Foster*,[1931] in particular, gets to the heart of the problem:

> 'Because of the evolutionary nature of the Community, the state of Community law in the future is not easy to predict. A Member State may conclude a treaty relating to a particular subject matter years before the community develops a comprehensive policy in the same subject area and before the development of such a policy could have been foreseen.'[1932] Finally, the authors concluded that 'it would seem desirable for Community law to develop some sort of duty on the Community institutions analogous to that under Article [351] so that the Community may help prevent individual Member States from being faced with conflicting treaty obligations'.[1933]

Convincing arguments are presented in predominant literature in favour of a *mutatis mutandis* application of Article 351(1) TFEU in the case of subsequently adopted legal acts of the EU. Among the proponents of an analogous applicability of Article 351 (1) TFEU is Advocate General *Kokott*, who addressed this issue in her opinion on the *Total France SA* case: '*A mutatis mutandis application of the first paragraph of* [Art 351 TFEU] *[...] is conceivable where an international obligation on*

1929. For the state of opinion *see*, i.e., J.H.F. Van Panhuys, *Conflicts Between the Law of the European Communities and Other Rules of International Law*, 3 Common Market Law Review 434 (1966) DOI: 10.54648/cola1966031; K.M. Meessen, *supra* note 1818, at 491; R. Churchill & N. G. Foster, *European Community Law and Prioer Treaty Obligations of Member States: The Spanish Fishermen's Cases*, 36 International and Comparative Law Quarterly 519–520 and 523 (1987) DOI: 10.1093/iclqaj/36.3.504; P. Manzini, *supra* note 1816, at 786–787; R. Schütze, *supra* note 1810, at 435–436; J. P.Terhechte, *supra* note 1839, at 84; Konstanze Von Papp, *supra* note 1849, at 329 in particular n. 15; J. Kokott, *supra* note 1840, para. 6; K. Stöger, *supra* note 1853, paras 17–20; S. Lorenzmeier, *supra* note 1840, paras 24–27; A. Garcia Prats et al, *supra* note 1855, at 61; V. Bendlinger, *supra* note 1819, s. § 351.04[3][d].
1930. *See* in particular *Van Panhuys*, who had already stated in 1966: '*In appropriate cases, for instance, there would be every reason to apply Article 234 of the E.E.C. Treaty by extension or analogy, e.g., in the case of conflicts between an agreement entered into by a Member State and a non-Member State after the entry into force of the E.E.C. Treaty on the one hand, and rules of 'secondary law', such as a 'Regulation', enacted subsequently to such an agreement on the other (provided always that the agreement is not per se incompatible with the Treaty)*'; *see* Van Panhuys, *supra* note 1929, at 434.
1931. Churchill & Foster, *supra* note 1929, at 523; also explicitly referring to the same sections, *see* R. Schütze, *supra* note 1810, at 435.
1932. Churchill & Foster, *supra* note 1929, at 523.
1933. *Ibid.*

the part of a Member State conflicts with a subsequently agreed measure of secondary law.'[1934] Proponents in literature argue, above all, that the full application of EU law supremacy would deprive the Member States of their competence to conclude treaties: international treaties could not be concluded without risking a conflict with Union law at a later stage.[1935] However, most of these proponents further argue that analogous application of Article 351 (1) TFEU should only be permitted if a certain shift of competence to the Union or the release of EU law was not foreseeable at the time when the affected treaty was concluded.[1936] *Kokott*, although not in her capacity as Advocate General, agrees with this view but further elaborates that this will rarely be the case with regard to the '*dynamic development of European integration*'.[1937]

The opposing view is first and foremost advocated by *Manzini*, who relies on a literal interpretation of Article 351(1) TFEU and states that, according to the ECJ's *Kramer* decision, the Member States are obliged to not hinder the Union's exercise of competences.[1938] This view, however, is not convincing. The undisputed purpose of Article 351 TFEU is the recognition of the obligations of Member States under international law towards third countries, which are not bound by Union law by virtue of the legal principle *res inter alios acta*.[1939] Agreements that had already existed before the founding of the Union or before the accession of the respective Member State were to be protected. It could not have been intended not to apply the same rules to subsequently adopted EU law if the amendment or development of EU law had not been foreseeable for the Member States.[1940]

Interestingly, the ECJ has not addressed this issue explicitly for a long time. A first statement on a possible analogous application can be found in the Court's decision in the *Luksan v. Petrus* case, where the ECJ held that its case law[1941] '*must also be applicable mutatis mutandis when, because of a development in European Union law, a legislative measure adopted by a Member State in accordance with the power offered by an earlier international agreement appears contrary to European Union law*'.[1942] Indeed, the ECJ, therefore, seems to allow an analogous application of Article 351 TFEU in the case of incompatibilities arising from the subsequently adopted EU law.[1943]

1934. Case C-188/07, *Total France*, para. 95.
1935. To this argument among others, K.M. Meessen, *supra* note 1818, at 491; Churchill & Foster, *supra* note 1929, at 519–520 and 523; R. Schütze, *supra* note 1810, at 436; S. Lorenzmeier, *supra* note 1840, para. 24; K. Stöger, *supra* note 1853, para. 18. Also favouring an application of Art. 351(1) TFEU, in particular with regard to the ATAD, P. Arginelli, *The ATAD and Third Countries, in The External Tax Strategy of the EU in a Post-BEPS Environment* 218 (Adolfo Martín Jiménez ed., IBFD 2019); V. Bendlinger, *supra* note 1819, s. § 351.04[3][d].
1936. For further reference on this and related opinions, *see* R. Schütze, *supra* note 1810, at 436; J. Kokott, *supra* note 1840, para. 6; S. Lorenzmeier, *supra* note 1840, para. 24.
1937. Translation by the author. *See* J. Kokott, *supra* note 1840, para. 6; similar K. Stöger, *supra* note 1853, para. 18.
1938. P. Manzini, *supra* note 1816, at 786; referring to Joined Cases C-3/76, 4/76, 6/76, *Cornelius Kramer, Hendirk van den Berg, Bennootschap onder Firma Kramer en Bais*, para. 44.
1939. On the telos and purpose of Art. 351 TFEU, *see* s. 5.4.3.1.
1940. With further arguments, *see* S. Lorenzmeier, *supra* note 1840, para. 24.
1941. Explicitly referring to Case C-324/93, *Evans Medical Ltd and Macfarlan Smith Ltd* and Case C-124/95, *Centro-Com Srl*, *see* Case C-277/10, *Luksan v. Petrus*, paras 61–62.
1942. Case C-277/10, *Luksan v. Petrus*, para. 63.
1943. Arguing for this understanding, *see* S. Lorenzmeier, *supra* note 1840, para. 26.

However, the above-mentioned statement in the *Luksan v. Petrus* case should not be overestimated in this respect. In fact, the ECJ only affirmed an analogous application of its case law in order to state in its following sentence that '*the Member State concerned cannot rely on that agreement in order to exempt itself from the obligations that have arisen subsequently from European Union law*'.[1944] An analogous application of Article 351 TFEU in favour of the Member States has not yet been affirmed by the ECJ at times,[1945] and the above analysis has shown that the Court seems to be less than generous with regard to potential Union law incompatibilities caused by treaties concluded by the Member States. Apart from this, it must also be emphasized that an analogous application of Article 351(1) TFEU also entails a supplementary analogous applicability of its second paragraph.[1946] Even if Member States could invoke Article 351 TFEU by analogy in the case of subsequently enacted EU law, they remain obliged to take '*all appropriate measures*' to eliminate the incompatibilities pursuant to Article 351(2) TFEU.

If the above is applied to the legal problem of the relationship between the GloBE-Directive and the DTCs of the Member States, there seem to be valid arguments in favour of a *mutatis mutandis* application of Article 351(1) TFEU to tax treaties, which had been concluded after the respective Member States accession to the EU, but before the GloBE-Directive had been enacted in December 2022. Accordingly, with regard to obligations arising from third-country DTCs, it would be conceivable that Member States could object to leaving the GloBE-Directive unapplied in the case of a conflict arising with such a DTC. However, it should also be emphasized that an analogous applicability of Article 351 TFEU can only be considered, according to the predominant view held in literature, if a shift in competence or the adoption of a respective legal act had not been '*foreseeable*'. It is certainly debatable at which point the enactment of the GloBE-Directive had been '*foreseeable*' for the Member States. Rather, one should emphasize that the plans to harmonize corporate tax law as well as tax treaty law already go back a long way. One could even ask: what is still predictable at all in the international tax policy landscape? In the author's opinion, the adoption of the GloBE-Directive was 'foreseeable' by 22 December *2021* (!) at the latest, when the Commission published its Proposal[1947] for the GloBE-Directive. Given that the Commission had already announced its intention to implement Pillar Two by means of a Directive, it is even conceivable that the adoption was '*foreseeable*' at an earlier date.[1948] However, given that the detailed architecture of GloBE was not known before December 2021, it is reasonable to consider 22 December 2021 as the date when the adoption of the GloBE-Directive was '*foreseeable*'.

In any case, apart from the fact that the adoption of the GloBE-Directive was 'foreseeable', an analogous application of Article 351(1) TFEU might not be a panacea

1944. Case C-277/10, *Luksan v. Petrus*, para. 63.
1945. In detail on the wide misunderstanding that *Luksan v. Petrus* confirmed the *mutatis mutandis* applicability of Art. 351 TFEU, *see* V. Bendlinger, *supra* note 1819, s. § 351.04[3][d].
1946. Likewise K. Stöger, *Art 351, in Kommentar zu EUV und AEUV, supra* note 1853, para. 20.
1947. COM(2021)823 final.
1948. European Commission, *Communication from the Commission to the European Parliament and the Council – Business Taxation for the 21st Century, supra* note 196, at 8.

to avoid potential normative conflicts: finally, an analogous application of the first paragraph would not eliminate the obligation under the second paragraph to eliminate any incompatibilities resulting from a third country DTC.

5.4.4 Interim Conclusion

As it turns out, the question of whether the GloBE-Directive can oblige the Member States to adapt their DTC network can only be answered on the basis of the principle of supremacy of EU law on the one hand and Article 351 TFEU on the other. With regard to the resolution of normative conflicts between the GloBE-Directive and existing or future bilateral DTCs concluded by the Member States, four different categories of treaties have to be distinguished:[1949]

- **Inter-se DTCs:** The GloBE-Directive overrides existing *inter-se* DTCs already based on the legal principle *lex posterior derogat legi priori*. The supremacy of EU law becomes fully effective with regard to these DTCs.[1950]
- **DTCs between Member States and third countries concluded after enactment of the GloBE-Directive:** Furthermore, the GloBE-Directive requires Member States to (re)negotiate DTCs with third countries concluded during negotiations or after its entry into force. If, after its entry into force, a DTC between a Member State and a third country is concluded, which contravenes the provisions of the GloBE-Directive, EU law does not give way to a third country DTC. The Member State is then bound by both EU law and the respective DTC. Supremacy cannot be applied because the third country is not bound by EU law; however, the supremacy of the GloBE-Directive prevents the Member State from applying the respective DTC within its domestic law. Thus, in the case of a conflict between a treaty of a Member State concluded after the enactment of the GloBE-Directive, the latter prevails.
- **DTCs between Member States and third countries concluded before accession of the respective Member State:** If a certain DTC between a Member State and a third country has already been concluded prior to 1.1.1958 or prior to the accession of the respective Member State, the Member State may invoke Article 351 TFEU.[1951] The respective Member State may leave the respective provisions of the GloBE-Directive in conflict with the DTC unapplied, provided that this is necessary to fulfil an obligation towards a third country. However, under Article 351(2) TFEU, this protection is only granted temporarily. The Member States remain obliged to resolve the incompatibility, and, as the case law shows, the CJEU hardly seems to accept any excuses for a lack of ambition in this regard.[1952]

1949. For an overview of the legal effects of Art. 351 TFEU, see the table provided in Valentin Bendlinger, *supra* note 1819, s. § 351.07[1].
1950. Section 5.4.2.
1951. Section 5.4.3.2.
1952. Section 5.4.3.4.

- **DTCs between Member States and third countries concluded after Member State's accession, but before enactment of the GloBE-Directive was 'foreseeable':** For DTCs concluded after the accession of the respective Member State, but before the creation process of the GloBE-Directive started, the respective Member State could invoke Article 351 TFEU by analogy and may, under the same conditions, leave EU law unapplied. It has been pointed out that a *mutatis mutandis* application of Article 351(1) TFEU is conceivable for all treaties that had been concluded before 22 December 2021, when the Commission published its Proposal for the GloBE-Directive. However, whether the CJEU allows such a *mutatis mutandis* application of Article 351 TFEU, however, remains open. Anyway, the benefit of such an analogous application must not be overestimated, especially since Article 351(2) TFEU would also have to be observed in these cases.[1953]

Table 15 reflects the different categories.

Table 15 The Resolution of Conflicts Between the GloBE-Directive and DTCs Concluded by the Member States in a Nutshell

Resolving Conflicts Between the GloBE-Directive and DTCs Concluded by EU Member States		
DTC	*Concluded Between Member State(s) and Third Country*	*Concluded Among Member States (Inter-Se Treaties)*
Treaty concluded before Member States' accession	DTC prevails over GloBE-Directive pursuant to Article 351(1) TFEU, but obligation to eliminate incompatibilities under paragraph 2	GloBE-Directive prevails (EU law forces treaty override, obligations derived from DTC remain under public international law)
Treaty concluded after Member States' accession but before GloBE-Directive was proposed by the Commission (22 December 2021)	DTC prevails over GloBE-Directive due to *mutatis mutandis* applicability of Article 351(1) TFEU, but obligation to eliminate incompatibilities under paragraph 2	
Treaty concluded after GloBE-Directive was proposed by the Commission (22 December 2021)	GloBE-Directive prevails (EU law forces treaty override, obligations derived from DTC remain under public international law)	

This simple distinction into categories should not obscure the fact that Article 351 TFEU, despite the existence of comprehensive jurisprudence, still raises many questions of interpretation. Above all, the relationship of its first to its second paragraph has

1953. Section 5.4.3.5.

not been conclusively clarified due to the casuistic case law of the CJEU. As has been shown, the CJEU seems to have a very broad understanding of the obligation of Member States to eliminate any incompatibilities. In any case, the GloBE-Directive puts Member States in a dilemma: with regard to third-country DTCs, the Member States are obliged to take all appropriate steps to eliminate incompatibilities with EU law and may even have to terminate them, *ultima ratio*, if renegotiation is not possible for whatever reason. It should be borne in mind, however, that the termination of DTCs cannot be in the interest of the Union either since double taxation is, without doubt, the most serious obstacle to cross-border business activity and to the functioning of the internal market. The GloBE-Directive, therefore, faces the challenge of, on the one hand, preserving the existing DTC network between Member States and third countries while, on the other hand, remaining faithful to its purpose and implementing an effective minimum taxation system. An alignment of the GloBE-Directive with the DTC network of Member States seems inevitable and will require a balancing act. Nevertheless, it is interesting that the GloBE-Directive leaves the issue of DTCs unaddressed. Similar to the above-cited Articles 3 and 4 of Regulation 4055/86,[1954] the GloBE-Directive could have explicitly provided for an obligation to amend or denounce treaties with third states. It would even have been conceivable that the GloBE-Directive had explicitly extended the principles laid down in Article 351 AEUV, as the EU legislature did in Article 28 of Regulation 864/2007 (Rome II),[1955] were it is stated that the '*regulation shall not prejudice the application of international conventions to which one or more Member States are parties at the time when this Regulation is adopted*'.[1956] Admittedly, this would have, to some degree, undermined the purpose of GloBE, which is to set up a global minimum tax level.

It should, however, be emphasized that Article 351 TFEU in no way obliges Member States to satisfy their obligations under public international law.[1957] So once the Member States implement the GloBE-Directive into their domestic laws and the domestic law is in conflict with a DTC, it is a question of domestic constitutional law whether domestic law is permitted to override the DTC. Article 351 TFEU has no effect on the domestic implementation of the GloBE-Directive within the Member States. Rather, Article 351(1) TFEU only allows certain provisions of the GloBE-Directive not to be applied if the Member State would otherwise be forced to breach an obligation towards a third country.

In any case, the GloBE-Directive leaves open questions with regard to its relation to DTCs and as has been revealed in the previous sections, conflicts between GloBE and DTCs cannot be excluded.[1958] This is, of course, highly unsatisfactory: normative conflicts are problematic for any legal system because they place those affected by the conflicting rules in a position of uncertainty. Once again, it is clear that the EU would

1954. Regulation No 4055/86.
1955. Regulation 864/2007/EC of the European Parliament and of the Council of 11 July 2007 on the law applicable to non-contractual obligations (Rome II), OJ (40).
1956. *See Schütze*, who calls this example a '*legislative extension*' of Art. 351 TFEU, *see* R. Schütze, *supra* note 1810, at 437.
1957. Also *see* Daniela Hohenwarter-Mayr, *supra* note 1552, at 144.
1958. *See* s. 5.2.

also benefit if the treaty issues of Pillar Two could be resolved through a multilateral agreement. However, this will be discussed in detail in section 5.6.

5.5 ARE THERE POTENTIAL CONFLICTS BETWEEN GloBE AND CUSTOMARY INTERNATIONAL (TAX) LAW?: UTPR AND THE 'NEXUS' DEBATE

Does international law pose limits to states with respect to income taxes? Is there something else besides tax treaties in the sphere of international tax law? It is a longstanding discussion whether there is a kind of legal sphere with respect to income taxes that goes beyond tax treaties.[1959] Specifically, the question is how far the tax sovereignty of states extends: will the UK tax a distribution paid by an Australian taxpayer made to its US shareholder at the level of a UK resident taxpayer?[1960] Some years ago, tax lawyers would have answered this question in the negative without a doubt; and indeed, the idea of taxing extraterritorial income seems strange. Nevertheless, it is also the legal tradition of various states to tax the worldwide income of nationals. Under US tax law, income earned by a US citizen resident in Germany and earned in Austria would also be taxable in the US. So, is there something that could prevent states from taxing a corporate entity on extraterritorial income, like a 'national' resident in a different state receiving third-state income? One might argue that there is still a connection to a 'national'.

The UTPR takes the issue of taxation of extraterritorial income to the extreme. It allows jurisdictions to tax income that has no connection to the territory of the respective jurisdiction at all. It is therefore not surprising that the question of whether the UTPR is precluded by a superior sphere of law, namely customary international (tax) law (in the following Customary International Law (CIL)), has gained momentum.[1961] Some argue that CIL indeed poses limits to tax jurisdictions. It has been attested, for example, that it is in accordance with CIL for a state to tax its residents on their worldwide income.[1962] Recently, it has been stated that CIL also requires a certain kind of 'nexus' or a 'genuine link' between a jurisdiction's territory and taxable income,[1963] which would undoubtedly bring the UTPR into conflict with CIL.[1964] Others opine that, on the contrary, it is a part of CIL to allow jurisdictions to tax income that is not taxed anywhere else. In particular, Christians & Magalhães take the latter position and argue that there is such a 'Use-It-Or-Lose-It-Principle' which, under their view, could be seen as a blank permission to tax jurisdictions to tax whatever they

1959. Also *see* R. Szudoczky, *supra* note 1699, at 145.
1960. *See* the apt example of Goulder: '*It's not proper to tax Peter on Paul's profits, notwithstanding that Peter happens to be a resident for tax purposes*', R. Goulder, *supra* note 1561, at 908.
1961. H. Wardell-Burrus, *supra* note 1560, at 699–700; R.S. Avi-Yonah, *supra* note 1652, at 951–952; J. VanderWolk, *supra* note 1652, at 1069–1070; F. Debelva & L. De Broe, *supra* note 1652, at 898 et seq.; T.D. Magalhaes, *supra* note 1652, at 1257–1261; M. Lennard, *Customary International Law and Tax – The Fog of Law*, 109 Tax Notes Intl. 601–608 (30 Jan. 2023) DOI: 10.37733/tkjt.2023.8.1.; R. Szudoczky, *supra* note 1699, at 145 et seq.
1962. Filip Debelva & Luc De Broe, *supra* note 1652, at 898.
1963. *Ibid.*, at 898 and 905.
1964. *See* in particular J. VanderWolk, *supra* note 1652, at 1369–1370.

intend to tax.[1965] What remains from these deviating positions is a simple question: is there a source of CIL with respect to income taxes?

In any case, these questions must be strictly separated from the sphere of tax treaties;[1966] and the author of this thesis is sceptical about the existence of a source of public international law in direct tax matters other than tax treaties. Only a few principles have become so well established in the past that they are accorded CIL status by governments, national authorities and courts.[1967] One can question whether such principles exist at all in international tax law.[1968] Indeed, one is tempted to question the legality of the UTPR: is it really permissible to tax a local entity in respect of a royalty payment made by one group member to another group member which is resident in a different country and has no connection with the shareholders? Nevertheless, it is difficult to define sources of law other than tax treaties that would prohibit such tax legislation.[1969] On the contrary, this approach is confronted with many doubtful questions: isn't it basically up to each jurisdiction to define the term 'income' itself? Why should national legislatures, outside the scope of tax treaties, be restricted in their right to define their tax base? And even then, if one were to recognize a 'nexus' as a necessity of tax jurisdiction, what would be the scope of this 'nexus'?[1970]

A final answer to these questions is beyond the scope of this thesis, and the author is fully aware that he cannot answer them conclusively. In general, one can doubt whether they can be answered conclusively at all. Fortunately, however, they are only theoretical: as the recent literature also recognizes, CIL is mutable, and once a 'critical mass' of jurisdictions[1971] has decided to implement GloBE, GloBE itself could be granted CIL status[1972] in the future.[1973] And even if the CIL 'nexus' were then still in

1965. A. Christians & T. Diniz Magalhaes, *supra* note 1649, at 705–710.
1966. Also *see* H. Wardell-Burrus, *supra* note 1560, at 699; R. Goulder, *supra* note 1561, at 908; R. Szudoczky, *supra* note 1699, at 145.
1967. On potential 'standards' or 'principles' that have been considered as CIL in literature, *see* T.D. Magalhaes, *supra* note 1652, at 1259–1260.
1968. M. Lennard, *supra* note 1961, at 602. In a similar vein, *see* Tarcisio Diniz Magalhaes, *supra* note 1652, at 1257–1261.
1969. In a similar vein on the 'nexus' requirement, *see* C. Brokelind, *Direct Taxation and the Future of EU Harmonization: Lessons from Past Experiences, in Tax Nexus and Jurisdiction in International and EU Law* 187 (E. Traversa ed., IBFD 2022).
1970. Also sceptical, *see* R. Szudoczky, *supra* note 1699, at 147. Also *see* Kokott, who argues that there is a 'new concept' of territoriality meaning 'that states can exercise jurisdiction without justification, whereas extraterritorial jurisdiction *is not excluded*, but requires justification' (emphasis added), *see* J. Kokott, *Public International Law and Taxation: Nexus and Territoriality, in Tax Nexus and Jurisdiction in International and EU Law* 17 (E. Traversa ed., IBFD 2022). The question of what such a 'justification' could be, however, remains open.
1971. *See* in that respect, Heydon Wardell-Burrus, *The UTPR as a Rule of Recognition*, 108 Tax Notes Intl., *supra* note 1652, at 1527–1529.
1972. Affirmative with respect to the UTPR's status of CIL, *see* in particular Reuven S Avi-Yonah, *supra* note 1652, at 951–952.
1973. On that argument, *see* R. Szudoczky, *supra* note 1699, at 147. Also *see* VanderWolk, agreeing that CIL can change over time, but arguing that UTPR is 'far from' receiving CIL status, *see* Jefferson VanderWolk, *supra* note 1652, at 1069–1070. In general posing the idea that the 'OECD's Inclusive Framework process [could] express a custom', *see* Cécile Brokelind, *supra* note 1969, at 192.

place, the question is, who would sanction the breach of the CIL 'nexus' if most states do support the global minimum tax?

5.6 CONCLUSION: DOES GloBE IMPLEMENTATION REQUIRE A MULTILATERAL AGREEMENT?

International tax law, that is, tax treaties and probably nothing beyond,[1974] poses limits to the implementation of the global minimum tax. While the extent to which conflicts between GloBE and DTCs can occur is debatable, even the proponents of the 'saving clause' admit that conflicts are by no means excluded. As argued in this thesis, the potential for normative conflicts between GloBE and DTCs is significantly greater than initially expected by the OECD. The 'saving clause' is not a panacea to justify the IIR, and it can be doubted whether it can be invoked with respect to the UTPR at all. In addition, the IIR and UTPR also apply in situations outside the scope of the 'saving clause'. This is the case, for example, when they are applied to non-resident corporations, e.g., if the IIR is applied to partnerships or the UTPR is to be paid by a CE that is a PE. Furthermore, the 'saving clause' fails if a certain treaty applies the exemption method with respect to PE income; and apart from that, the vast majority of global tax treaties do not contain a 'saving clause' at all. One might argue that it is likely that implementing jurisdictions will implement a QDMTT, and both IIR and UTPR will be rare phenomena. However, as has been shown, also the QDMTT might give rise to treaty issues, in particular with respect to Article 6 OECD MC, if the exemption method is applied to such income.[1975]

Given the enormous potential for normative conflicts, the question arises as to how conflicts between GloBE and DTCs can be resolved. In principle, conflict resolution between GloBE and tax treaties works equivalently with respect to a conflict between domestic and tax treaty law. The GloBE Model Rules are not a source of public international law; rather, jurisdictions implement GloBE into their domestic law. The question of whether domestic GloBE implementation must give way to a tax treaty is, therefore, a question of domestic constitutional law.[1976]

However, for EU Member States, any conflicts between their domestic GloBE implementation and DTC might give rise to sophisticated multiple-tier conflicts: EU Member States are forced to implement the GloBE-Directive, which is superior to domestic law and arguably also superior to DTCs. Normative conflicts between EU law and international agreements of the Member States, including tax treaties, are governed by Article 351 TFEU. Pursuant to this provision, international agreements between a Member State and a third state prevail over EU law if the respective agreement had been concluded before the Member State acceded the EU. As has been revealed, the provision can be applied *mutatis mutandis* to secondary law and might

1974. As has been revealed, there can be doubts as to whether CIL exists at all, *see* s. 5.5.
1975. *See* s. 5.2.3.3.
1976. *See* s. 5.3.

protect any treaties that had been concluded before the enactment of the GloBE-Directive could have been 'foreseen' by the Member States.[1977] As the EU institutions soon committed to the Commission's plans to implement the two-pillar solution by a directive, one could argue that Article 351 TFEU cannot be invoked with respect to treaties that have been concluded after the Commission has published its draft proposal for the GloBE-Directive on 22 December 2021. In any case, Article 351 TFEU only provides protection for a limited period of time: pursuant to Article 351(2) TFEU, the Member States are obliged to eliminate any incompatibilities arising from their third state agreements in due course. However, Article 351(2) TFEU does not specify a fixed deadline. In a reverse conclusion from Article 351(1) TFEU, it can be derived that the GloBE-Directive is, in any case, superior to DTCs concluded among Member States, even if the respective treaty was concluded before the enactment of the GloBE-Directive or even before the Member States joined the Union.[1978] However, Article 351(1) TFEU does not oblige Member States to fulfil their treaty obligations. Rather, if Member States implement the GloBE-Directive into their domestic laws, it is a question of constitutional law whether the domestic GloBE laws prevail over treaties. Article 351(1) TFEU only permits Member States to deviate from the GloBE-Directive if it would force the Member States to breach a treaty obligation towards a third country.

As can be seen, from a legal point of view, every conflict between GloBE and DTCs might give rise to complex issues of conflict resolution and might end in a dilemma of clashing legal spheres. It is, therefore, somewhat surprising that the OECD does not seem to be pushing for a multilateral treaty to make Pillar Two a binding source of public international law (MLC or GloBE MLI). Many authors quite rightly call for a multilateral agreement to avoid normative conflicts between GloBE and DTC from the outset.[1979] One can only agree with this call. Indeed, it is to be hoped that the complex framework of GloBE will be moulded into a multilateral legal framework, which could also probably include mechanisms for dispute resolution and safe harbours. Again, however, such an agreement would give rise to various new legal questions. From the perspective of the EU, the question arises of whether the Member States or the EU itself should conclude such an agreement.[1980] This and many other questions will be addressed in the following section, which will deal with the role of the GloBE-Directive within the EU's legal order.

1977. *See* ss 5.4.3.5. and 5.4.4.
1978. *See* s. 5.4.
1979. *See* J. Becker & J. Englisch, *supra* note 469, at 524; J. Li, *supra* note 1634, at 1703; D.G. Noren, *supra* note 1632, at 8; R. Goulder, *supra* note 1645, at 775–778; M. F. De Wilde, *supra* note 1645, s. 2.3; R. Goulder, *supra* note 1645, at 775; J. VanderWolk, *supra* note 1652, at 823; L. De Broe, *supra* note 1672, at 885; F. Debelva & L. De Broe, *supra* note 1652, at 905–906; A. Tomassini & M. De Rosa, *Uncertainties Hold Back Achievement of OECD Pillar 2 Goals*, 51 Intertax 190 (2023).
1980. On this issue, *see* s. 6.1.3.

CHAPTER 6

The GloBE-Directive Within the EU's Legal Order

6.1 THE GloBE-DIRECTIVE WITHIN THE EU'S CONSTITUTIONAL FRAMEWORK: THE DIVISION OF COMPETENCE BETWEEN THE EU AND DOMESTIC TAX LEGISLATURES

6.1.1 Implementation of GloBE Via a Legal Act of Secondary Law

Even before the OECD published its Blueprints on both Pillars, the European Parliament as well as the Commission expressed their support for the work at the OECD level and announced its intention to introduce a set of rules for setting up a system of minimum corporate taxation even if the OECD failed to reach a consensus.[1981] Finally, on 18 Mai 2021, the Commission released a communication entitled '*Business Taxation for the 21st Century*' (also referred to as BEFIT – '*Business in Europe: Framework for Income Taxation*') and announced its intention to implement Pillar Two by means of a directive.[1982] The Commission thus held '*in order to ensure its consistent application within the EU and compatibility with EU law, the principal method for implementing Pillar 2 will be an EU Directive that will reflect the OECD Model Rules with the necessary adjustments*'.[1983] When the OECD finally published the long-awaited GloBE Model Rules[1984] on 20 December 2021, the Commission's reaction was not long in coming: on 22 December 2021, the Commission finally published a 70-page proposal for the

1981. *See* European Parliament, *Motion for a Resolution – European Parliament Resolution of Fair Taxation in a Digitalised and Globalised Economy: BEPS 2.0, B9-0238/2019, supra* note 189, para. 39. Also *see* the tax agenda provided by the Commission in 2020, even before the Blueprints were published, *COM(2020) 312 Final*, at 1–2. Already *see* s. 3.4.
1982. European Commission, *Communication from the Commission to the European Parliament and the Council – Business Taxation for the 21st Century supra* note 196, 8.
1983. *Ibid.*
1984. *GloBE Model Rules.*

GloBE-Directive based on Article 115 TFEU. Exactly one year later, the GloBE-Directive was published in the EU's Official Journal and has become a part of the EU's legal order. As has been revealed, the GloBE-Directive strongly follows the GloBE Model Rules. The explanatory memorandum of the proposal already stated: '*The Directive reflects the global OECD agreement, with some necessary adjustments, to guarantee conformity with EU law*'.[1985] The content of today's GloBE-Directive could hardly have been summed up more aptly in one sentence.

As with any piece of secondary legislation, numerous constitutional questions naturally arise with respect to the GloBE-Directive. However, the issuance of the GloBE-Directive is particularly explosive in several respects: first, the directive concerns direct taxation, which is an area of law that is politically extremely sensitive from the outset. Some even argue that direct taxes are one of the few areas left where Member States can autonomously adopt economic and social policies, something they have stubbornly tried to defend in the past.[1986] Second, the GloBE-Directive provides, for the first time, in addition to harmonizing the corporate tax base, an effective minimum corporate tax level. Thus, the GloBE-Directive goes far beyond the few legislative acts that have been successfully adopted by the EU in the field of direct taxes and even surpasses the Commission's failed legislative initiatives in this area,[1987] some of which were already described as ambitious.[1988] Third, the GloBE initiative also goes beyond a mere Union-wide discussion. The GloBE Model Rules are a global, albeit merely political,[1989] agreement of over more than 140 countries, collectively representing 95 % of global GDP.[1990] In order to enable a coordinated implementation of GloBE, the OECD – not without reason – is even discussing the development of its own multilateral convention.[1991] Implementation within the Union is, thus, only one piece of the puzzle in a global network of new tax rules.

The constitutional issues raised by the GloBE-Directive, therefore, involve multiple dimensions: the first dimension relates to the division of competence between the Union and the Member States to adopt legislative acts internally. To what extent does the Union have legislative powers under the Treaties, to what extent can it exercise them, and had the Union exceeded those powers by enacting the GloBE-Directive and finally, is Article 115 TFEU the correct legal basis for the GloBE-Directive or would there have been alternative provisions available? The second dimension relates to the division of competence to conclude legally binding treaties under public international law regarding third states. Which legislature is competent to conclude a GloBE MLC? Is it the Union's or the Member State's task to conclude such a convention, and what role does the GloBE-Directive play in this respect?

The following chapter will address these questions. As will be seen, the dimensions just addressed are interrelated. For this reason, the following structure appears to

1985. In detail on these developments, *see* V. Bendlinger, *supra* note 258, at 13–14.
1986. Also for a broad perspective, *see* P.J. Wattel, *supra* note 1798, at 323.
1987. V. Bendlinger, *supra* note 258, at 14–16.
1988. *See*, i.e., P.J. Wattel, *supra* note 1798, at 330.
1989. V. Bendlinger, *supra* note 258, at 3–4.
1990. *GloBE Model Rules*, at 3.
1991. *OECD/G20 Statement 8 October*, at 7.

be the most appropriate: first, the internal competence of the Union to issue the GloBE-Directive will be discussed (section 6.1.2.). Then, it will be examined to what extent this internal competence allows the Union to act externally (section 6.1.3.).

6.1.2 The EUs Legal Competence to Implement GloBE Via a Legal Act of Secondary Law

6.1.2.1 Overview

Since the EU is not a sovereign state, it can only legislate if the Member States have transferred their legislative powers to the Union.[1992] Consequently, Article 4(1) and the last sentence of Article 5(2) TEU state that '*competences not conferred upon the Union in the Treaties remain within the Member States*'. According to this *Principle of Conferral*, as it is expressly designated by Article 5(2) TEU, the EU '*shall act only within the limits of the competences conferred upon it by the Member States in the Treaties, to attain the objectives set out there*'.[1993] Any legislative act adopted by the EU must therefore be based on, and must also be covered by the material scope of a particular competence provided for in the Treaties.[1994] If a legal act is based on an incorrect legal basis or is not based on a specific competence at all, the CJEU may according to Article 263 TFEU be called upon an action of judicial review '*to declare the act concerned to be void*'[1995] due to a '*lack of competence*',[1996] if a Member State objects within two months after enactment of the respective legal act[1997].[1998] In fact, a single action for annulment of the GloBE-Directive has been brought before the General Court (docket number T-143/23, *VF v. Council*) within the time limit of Article 263 TFEU, which, among other arguments, brings a '*lack of competence*' into the race as a possible primary law infringement of the GloBE-Directive.[1999] The chances of success of this action for annulment, however, are likely to be limited (*see* section 6.2.1.1.).

But even if the deadline for a procedure of judicial review has now expired and thus precludes future actions for annulment, '*the validity* [...] *of acts of the institutions, bodies, offices or agencies of the Union*'[2000] can also be subject of a preliminary rulings pursuant to Article 267(1)(b) TFEU (in detail on both procedures and their relation, *see* section 6.2.1.1.). The question of the EU competence of a secondary act is therefore, at

1992. *See*, *i.a.*, R. Schütze, *EU Competences: Existence and Exercise*, in *The Oxford Handbook of European Union Law* 76 (A. Arnull & D. Chalmers eds, Oxford 2015); P. Conconi et al., *EU Trade Agreements: To Mix or Not to Mix, that is the Question* 1 (May 2020), http://respect.eui.eu/wp-content/uploads/sites/6/2020/05/Mixity.pdf (last visited 21 Jul. 2021); G. Kofler, *supra* note 1796, at 11.
1993. P. Craig & G. de Búrca, *EU Law – Text, Cases and Materials*, *supra* note 1815, at 103.
1994. R. Schütze, *EU Competences: Existence and Exercise*, *supra* note 1992, at 75.
1995. Article 264(1) TFEU.
1996. Article 263(2) TFEU.
1997. Article 263(6) TFEU.
1998. R. Schütze, *supra* note 1822, at 360–361; G. Kofler, *supra* note 1796, at 16 in particular n. 36.
1999. *See* the case pending before the Court of First Instance under reference number T-143/23, *VF v. Council*. Details of the case are available at https://eur-lex.europa.eu/legal-content/EN/TXT/PDF/?uri=CELEX:62023TN0143 (accessed 7 Jul. 2023).
2000. Article 267(1)(b) TFEU.

least theoretically, remains relevant for eternity. As will become clear, however, the CJEU has been more than reluctant to declare legal acts of secondary law to be void.

In any case, as *Schütze*[2001] points out that the definition of the *Principle of Conferral* in Article 5(2) TFEU is ambiguous in two respects: on the one hand, conferred legislative powers to the Union do not exclude all regulatory competence of the Member States. Most of the EU's competences provided for in the TFEU are shared competences. According to Article 2(2) TFEU this means, that the Member States may still '*exercise their competence to the extent that the Union has not exercised its competence*'. According to Article 4(2)(a) TFEU, these shared competences also include the area of the '*internal market*', which is of particular relevance for the field of taxes, as will be shown shortly. On the other hand, the Union's regulatory competence is not entirely excluded even in areas not explicitly conferred to it by the Treaties. Indeed, EU legislation has in the past extended its competences to such matters that were not explicitly conferred to it by the treaties by the use of very vague and broad competences like Article 114, 115 or 352 TFEU and their predecessors ('general competences')[2002] as well as by means of teleological interpretation[2003] of TFEU provisions.[2004] This is particularly evident in the area of direct taxation, which (even) according to the CJEU, as a rule, explicitly fall outside the Union's sphere of competence,[2005] but where legal acts have nevertheless been adopted on the basis of Article 115 TFEU.[2006] It should be noted here that the CJEU in general leaves a wide leeway to the Union legislature, when it comes to the interpretation of the Union's competences.[2007] In fact, the CJEU[2008] has so far only once declared a decided legal act to be void because it was not covered by the legal competence provided for by today's Article 114 TFEU on which it was based.[2009] Nevertheless, it should not be overlooked that the *Principle of Conferral*

2001. R. Schütze, *supra* note 1992, at 76–77.
2002. *See* R. Schütze, *supra* note 1822, at 230–233.
2003. Comprehensively on the teleological interpretation of competence provisions, *see* R. Schütze, *supra* note 1992, at 229; R. Schütze, *supra* note 1822.
2004. Comprehensively on the *Principle of Conferral, see* R. Schütze, *supra* note 1992, at 76–77.
2005. Even though the Court has always additionally emphasized that the Member States must nevertheless exercise their taxation powers '*consistently with Community law*', *see, i.a.*, Case C-279/93, *Schumacker*, para. 21; Case C-391/97, *Frans Gschwind and Finanzamt Aachen-Außenstadt*, para. 20; Case C-35/98, *Verkooijen*, para. 32; Case C-385/00, *F.W.L. de Groot v. Staatssecretaris van Financiën*, para. 75; Case C-376/03, *D. v. Inspecteur van de Belastingdienst/Particulieren/Ondernemingen buitenland te Heerlen*, para. 36.
2006. *See* already s. 6.1.2.2.2.
2007. *See, i.a.*, P. Craig & G. de Búrca, *supra* note 1815, at 105.
2008. *See* Case C-376/98, *Germany v. Parliament and Council (Tobacco Advertising)*, in which the court decided to annul Directive 98/43/EC on the prohibition of tobacco advertising. The directive had been based on the predecessor of Art. 114 TFEU (former Art. 100a in the Treaty of Maastricht). The Court, however, mainly accepted the arguments put forward by the German government that Art. 114 TFEU did not provide for a sufficient legal basis for the subject matter of this directive. Although the Court conceded that certain forms of advertising and sponsorship of tobacco products '*could have been adopted on the basis of Article* [114 TFEU]', it held, that '*amendments are a matter for Community legislature*' and declared the entire directive null and void, *see Ibid.*, para. 117. Referring to this judgement, *see, i.a.*, R. Schütze, *supra* note 1992, at 78 in particular n. 12; P. Craig & G. de Búrca, *supra* note 1815, at 105. In detail to the ramifications of the *Tobacco Advertising* case, *see* s. 6.1.2.2.3.
2009. Nevertheless, it is emphasized in literature, that the Court's decision in Case C-376/98, *Tobacco Advertising* remained the exception to the rule. The CJEU tends to be more than

according to Article 5(1) and (2) TFEU set limits to an extensive interpretation of the Union's competences. These limits must be determined interpretatively for each legal act on the basis of the respective competence provided for in the EU Treaties.[2010] The following chapters therefore examine where these limits could lie in the competence of Article 115 TFEU and in further consequence, whether the GloBE-Directive[2011] exceeds these limits and whether an alternative provision in the Treaties could have provided for a Union competence to implement GloBE.

In addition to the *Principle of Conferral*, Article 5 TFEU also sets out two further constitutional barriers for the Union legislature: while the *Principle of Conferral* limits the existence of the Union's competences, the *Principles of Subsidiarity* and *Proportionality* constitute barriers to the exercise of the Union's competence.[2012] Both principles are closely linked together and intend to protect federal interests of the Member States from extensive encroachment into their legal spheres by the Union legislature:[2013] According to the *Principle of Subsidiarity* defined in Article 5(3) TFEU the Union in areas of shared competence shall act '*only if and in so far as the objectives of the proposed action cannot be sufficiently achieved by the Member States*' and according to the *Principle of Proportionality* defined in Article 5(4) TFEU the Union's '*action shall not exceed what is necessary to achieve the objectives of the Treaties*'. Since the GloBE-Directive must also comply with these constitutional principles, it is also necessary to elaborate on these principles in detail. However, since the question of *Subsidiarity* and *Proportionality* can only arise if a competence exists in the first place, these constitutional limits will finally be discussed after the possible legal base for the implementation of GloBE in section 6.1.2.5.

6.1.2.2 General Considerations on the Union's Competence for Harmonization in the Area of Direct Taxation

6.1.2.2.1 Taxes and the EUs Internal Market Competences

Taxes have always been seen as a fundamental pillar of state sovereignty.[2014] Consequently the harmonization of taxes has been and still is a major point of political

generous in its interpretation of Union competences. For further reference, *see* P. Craig & G. de Búrca, *supra* note 1815, at 105; R. Schütze, *supra* note 1992, at 78.

2010. *See also* R. Barents, *The Internal Market Unlimited: Some Observations on the Legal Basis of Community Legislation*, 30 Common Market Law Review 88 (1993) DOI: 10.54648/cola1993 005.
2011. GloBE-Directive (2022/2523).
2012. *See, i.a.*, Joined Cases C-376/98 and C-74/99, *Germany v. Parliament and Council (Tobacco Advertising)*, para. 131; Udo di Fabio, *Some Remarks on the Allocation of Competences between the European Union and Its Member States*, 39 Common Market Law Review 1294 (2002) DOI: 10.54648/5109944; R. Schütze, *supra* note 1992, at 76.
2013. Comprehensively, *see* P. Craig & G. de Búrca, *supra* note 1815, at 126–134; and R. Schütze, *supra* note 1992, at 94 et seq.
2014. See, e.g., B.H. Ter Kuile, *Legal Aspects of Fiscal Sovereignty within the Internal Market*, 19 Intertax 503–509 (1991) DOI: 10.54648/taxi1991080; di Fabio, *supra* note 2012, at 1294–1295 and 1297; S. Kingston, *The Boundaries of Sovereignty: The ECJ's Controversial Role Applying Internal Market Law to Direct Tax Measures*, in *Cambridge Yearbook of European Legal Studies*

contention in the process of European integration. However, in order to create a functioning internal market, at least the harmonization of indirect taxes seemed inevitable to the founding fathers of the EEC treaties:[2015] Taxes on cross-border supplies of goods and services through indirect taxes such as Value-Added Tax (VAT) or excise duties directly impact the price of goods and services and thus '*may create an immediate obstacle to the free movement of goods and the free supply of services*'.[2016] Since the establishment of the EU the treaties therefore provide for a competence for the Council, '*acting unanimously in accordance with a special legislative procedure* [...], [to] *adopt provisions for the harmonization of legislation concerning turnover taxes, excise duties and other form of indirect taxation to the extent that such harmonization is necessary to ensure the establishment and the functioning of the internal market*'[2017].[2018] Today, almost the same wording can be found in Article 113 TFEU.[2019] This provision, as well as its predecessors serve as a legal basis, e.g., for the VAT-Directive[2020] or the Directive 2008/118/EC on excise duties.[2021]

Unlike in the area of indirect taxes, Member States have always been reluctant to agree upon quite ambitious harmonization efforts by the Commission[2022] in the field of

287–290 (2007); N. Braun Binder, *Rechtsangleichung in der EU im Bereich der direkten Steuern* 71 (Mohr Siebeck 2017); G. Kofler, *supra* note 1796, at 12; with regard to DTCs J. Klabbers, *Treaty Conflict and the European Union, supra* note 1800, at 207–208.

2015. Alex Easson, *Harmonization of Direct Taxation in the European Community: From Neumark to Ruding*, 40 Can. Tax J. 602 (1992); R. Schütze, *supra* note 1822, at 573.
2016. These words where found by the commission in 2001, when it published a Communication on the tax policy of the EU at that time, *see* EC Commission, *Tax Policy in the European Union – Priorities for the Years Ahead*, s. 2.4. (10 Oct. 2001), https://eur-lex.europa.eu/legal-content/EN/TXT/PDF/?uri = CELEX:52001DC0260&from = EN; referring to this communication, *see* P. Craig & G. de Búrca, *supra* note 1815, at 692.
2017. *See* former Art. 99 EEC Treaty.
2018. R. Schütze, *supra* note 1822, at 572–573.
2019. In detail to the history of Art. 113 TFEU, *see* C. Seiler, *Art. 113 [Harmonisierung der indirekten Steuern], in Das Recht der Europäischen Union*, paras 1–3 (E. Grabitz et al., eds, C.H.Beck 2016); and R. Schütze, *supra* note 1822, at 572.
2020. Council Directive 2006/112/EC of 28 Nov. 2006 on the common system of value added tax, OJ (1).
2021. Council Directive (EC) No 2008/118 of 16 December 2008 concerning the general arrangements for excise duty and repealing Directive 92/12/EEC, OJ (12).
2022. Thus, reference should be made at this point to numerous failed proposals for directives by the Commission. *See, i.a.*, Proposal for a Council Directive concerning the harmonization of systems of company taxation and of withholding taxes on dividends, COM(75) 392 final; Proposal for a Council Directive on the application to collective investment institutions of the Proposal for a Council Directive on the application to collective investment institutions of the Council Directive concerning the harmonization of systems of company taxation and of withholding taxes on dividends, COM(78) 340 final (1978), 380; Proposal for a council directive concerning the harmonization of income taxation provisions with respect to freedom of movement for workers within the community, COM(79) 737 withdrawn on 9 Sep. 1992; Proposal for a Council Directive on the harmonization of the laws of the Member States relating to tax arrangements for the carry-over of losses of undertakings, COM(84) 404 final withdrawn on 4 Jan. 1997 OJ C2/6; Proposal for a council directive for the taking into account by enterprises of the losses of their permanent establishments and subsidiaries situated in other Member States, COM(90) 595 final withdrawn on 21 Dec. 2001, *see* COM(2001)763 final/2, p. 24. For an comprehensive overview of failed initiatives of the Commission to harmonize direct taxes, *see* G. Kofler, *supra* note 1796, at 13–14.

direct taxation.[2023] Due to the facts that, at first, Article 113 TFEU only explicitly covers indirect taxes and, second, other competences like Article 114(2) TFEU specifically exclude taxes from their scope, it is common ground that the EU treaties do not provide for a specific competence of the EU in direct tax matters.[2024] Rather, it could also be argued that direct taxes are entirely excluded from the Union's regulatory competence because, unlike indirect taxes, they are not explicitly addressed by the Treaties.[2025] Nevertheless, direct taxes do not fall completely outside the regulatory competence of the Union legislature. Indeed, Article 115 TFEU empowers the council with a special legislative procedure to unanimously '*issue directives for the approximation of such laws, regulations or administrative provisions of the Member States as directly affect the establishment or functioning of the internal market*'. The provision and its predecessors have been described in the literature as '*quite simply unlimited*'.[2026] Already in the late 1960s, *Paul Leulex* stated on the provision that its requirement of unanimity '*is easily explained by the unlimited scope ratione materiae of this provision of the Treaty, which applies, [...], to matters which may be entirely outside the competence of the Community*' (translation by the author).[2027] It is not without reason that Article 115 TFEU and

2023. A. C. May Zaidan, *The External Tax Treaty Making Powers of the Member States: Defining Limits and Obligations under the Current European Legal Order*, 41 Intertax 274 (2013) DOI: 10.54648/taxi2013024; N. Braun Binder, *Rechtsangleichung in der EU im Bereich der direkten Steuern, supra* note 2014, at 141; Martijn Nouwen, *The Market Distortion Provisions of Articles 116–117 TFEU: An Alternative Route to Qualified Majority Voting in Tax Matters?*, 49 Intertax 14 (2021) DOI: 10.54648/taxi2021003; M. Scherleitner, *Should the EU Implement a Minimum Corporate Taxation Directive?* 5 (2021), https://papers.ssrn.com/abstract=3697903 (last visited 13 Jul. 2021).
2024. *See, i.a.*, B.H. Ter Kuile, *Legal Aspects of Fiscal Sovereignty within the Internal Market*, 19 Intertax, *supra* note 2014, at 507; A. Easson, *supra* note 2015, at 603; S. Elwes, *The Internal Market versus the Right of Member States to Levy Direct Tax – A Clash of Fundamental Principles*, 41 Intertax 15 (2007) DOI: 10.54648/taxi2013002; S. Kingston, *supra* note 2014, at 289; C. Seiler, *supra* note 2019, para. 52; N. Braun Binder, *supra* note 2014, at 34; G. Bizioli, *An EU Policy for the Future of International Tax Law, in EU Tax Law and Policy in the 21st Century* 240 (W. Haslehner et al., eds, Wolters Kluwer 2017); W. Haslehner, *Chapter 3: EU-US Relations in the Field of Direct Taxes from the EU Perspective: A BEPS-Induced Transformation?*, in *The Implementation of Anti-BEPS Rules in the EU: A Comprehensive Study*, s. 3.2. (Pasquale Pistone & D. Weber eds, IBFD 2018); A. Langer, *Die Grenzen des Country-by-Country Reportings* 149 (LexisNexis 2019); D.W. Blum & A. Langer, *At a Crossroads: Mandatory Disclosure under DAC-6 and EU Primary Law – Part*, 59 Eur. Taxn. 284 (2019); G. Kofler, *EU Power to Tax: Competences in the Area of Direct Taxation, supra* note 1796, at 12; R.A. Achleitner & V. Bendlinger, *GloBE (Pillar Two) – Kompetenzrechtliche Erwägungen zur Umsetzung eines Mindestbesteuerungssystems innerhalb der Europäischen Union*, 2 Digitax 2–3 (2021).
2025. For further evidence on this possible line of reasoning, but rejecting this argument, *see* G. Kofler, *EU Power to Tax: Competences in the Area of Direct Taxation, supra* note 1796, at 12 in particular n. 13; G. Kofler, *Entwicklungslinien und Zukunftsfragen des Europäischen Steuerrechts, in 100 Jahre Steuerrechtsprechung in Deutschland 1918–2018 – Festschrift für den Bundesfinanzhof Band I* 701–702 (K.-D. Drüen et al., eds, Otto Schmidt 2018); Also to this argument, *see* H.M.A.L. Hamaekers, *The EC on the Brink of Full Corporate Tax Harmonization?*, 32 Eur. Taxn. 102 (1992).
2026. *See* R. Schütze, *Limits to the Union's 'Internal Market' Competence(s): Constitutional Comparisons*, in *The Question of Competence in the European Union* 224 (Loic Azoulai ed., Oxford 2014); R. Schütze, *supra* note 1822, at 559.
2027. *See* P. Leleux, *Le rapprochement des législation dans la Communauté économique européenne*, 4 Cahiers de droit européen 138 (1968): '*En revanche, cette règle de l'unanimité n'est pas*

its predecessors have served as the legal basis for all harmonization acts[2028] in the field of direct taxation without exception.[2029] However, in particular, the unanimity principle required by Article 115 TFEU has proved to be a major obstacle to past harmonization attempts by the European Commission.[2030] It is, therefore, not surprising that even the Commission has, on several occasions, openly discussed not only the abolition of the unanimity principle but also the choice of an alternative legal basis for the adoption of legal acts in the field of direct taxation.[2031]

One should mention here, however, that even the suitability of Article 115 TFEU as a legal basis for harmonization in the tax area is far from undisputed. Already in the

toujours exigée dans le cas des dispositions spécifiques. Cette exigence s'explique aisément en raison même du champ d'application ratione materiae illimité de cette disposition du traité, qui s'applique, nous l'avons déjà relevé, à des matières qui peuvent être tout à fait en dehors de la compétence de la Communauté'. Also referring to Leleux, *see* R. Schütze, *supra* note 1822, at 559.

2028. See, e.g., Council Directive 2003/49/EC of 3 Jun. 2003 on a common system for taxation applicable to interest and royalty payments made between associated companies of different Member States, OJ (49); Council Directive 2011/96/EU of 30 Nov. 2011 on the common system of taxation applicable in the case of parent companies and subsidiaries of different Member States, OJ (96); Merger Directive; Council Directive 2011/16/EU of 15 Feb. 2011 on administrative cooperation in the field of taxation and repealing Directive 77/799/EEC, OJ (1).
2029. N. Braun Binder, *supra* note 2014, at 141.
2030. Already in 1997, the Economic and Social Committee held that '[t]*he requirement for unanimity in the Council on tax decisions is clearly a barrier to progress on taxation and the requirements of the internal market*', *see* Opinion of the Economic and Social Committee on Taxation in the European Union – Report on the development of tax systems, OJ 40; also *see* S. Elwes, *The Internal Market versus the Right of Member States to Levy Direct Tax – A Clash of Fundamental Principles*, 41 Intertax, *supra* note 2024, at 18; Nadja Braun Binder, *supra* note 2014, at 141; W. Schön, *Facilitating Entry by Facilitating Exit: New Paths in EU Tax Legislation*, 46 Intertax 339 (2018) DOI: 10.54648/taxi2018033; R.A. Achleitner & V. Bendlinger, *supra* note 2024, at 9.
2031. Recently the Commission, e.g., held, that '*the question is no longer whether there is a need to move away from unanimity in taxation, but rather how and when to do it*', *see* European Commission, *Communication from the Commission to the European Parliament, the European Council and the Council – Towards a More Efficient and Democratic Decision Making in the EU Tax Policy*, COM(2019) 8 final 11 (15 Jan. 2019). These ambitions are also reflected in the political guidelines of the Commission headed by Ursula von der Leyen: '*I will make use of the clauses in the Treaties that allow proposals on taxation to be adopted by co-decision and decided by qualified majority voting in the Council*', *see* Ursula von der Leyen, *A Union that Strives for More – My Agenda for Europe – Political Guidelines for the next European Commission 2019–2024*, 12 (2019). In the meantime, the Commission has concretized its plans and held that it will '*explore how to make full use of the provisions of the Treaty on the functioning of the EU (TFEU) that allow proposals on taxation to be adopted by ordinary legislative procedure, including Art. 116 TFEU*', *see COM(2020) 312 Final*, at 2. The use of today's Art. 116 TFEU in direct tax matters had already been proposed by the Economic and Social Committee in 1997 (former Art. 101 Treaty of Maastricht at that time), *see* Opinion C 296/37 – Report on the development of tax systems 40. In detail on Art. 116 TFEU, *see* s. 6.1.2.4. For further considerations on alternative competences and other solutions to circumvent unanimity in the field of direct taxation, *see* M. Nouwen, *The Market Distortion Provisions of Articles 116–117 TFEU: An Alternative Route to Qualified Majority Voting in Tax Matters?*, 49 Intertax, *supra* note 2023, at 14 et seq.; J. Englisch, *Article 116 TFEU – The Nuclear Option for Qualified Majority Tax Harmonization?*, 29 EC Tax Review 58–61 (2020); Wolfgang Schön, *supra* note 2030, at 339–341; G. Bizioli, *Taking EU Fundamental Freedoms Seriously: Does the Anti-Tax Avoidance Directive Take Precedence over the Single Market?*, 26 EC Tax Review 167–175 (2017); R. Szudoczky & D. Weber, *Constitutional Foundations: EU Tax Competences; Legal Basis for Tax Integration; Sources and Enactment of EU Tax Law*, *in*

case of the ATAD,[2032] which was enacted in 2016 and is based on Article 115 TFEU as well, doubts were expressed in the literature as to whether the avoidance of tax abuse complies with Article 115 TFEU's requirement of *'directly affecting the establishment or functioning of the internal market'*.[2033] At latest the Commission's announcement of a GloBE-Directive[2034] and the corresponding GloBE-Directive Proposal published on 22 December 2021[2035] which had been based on Article 115 TFEU has thus breathed new life into the discussion on the Union's regulatory competence in the area of direct taxation.[2036] The following section is therefore dedicated to the questions, of whether the GloBE-Directive was correctly based on Article 115 TFEU and whether alternative competences could have been chosen for an implementation of GloBE within the EU. To this end, it will be necessary to take a general look at the Union's regulatory powers in the area of direct taxation.

6.1.2.2.2 The Framework of Internal Market Competences in a Historical Context

As already emphasized, the *'Internal Market'* (Article 26 TFEU) is, pursuant to Article 4(2)(a) TFEU, a shared competence. The Member States thus retain their legislative powers in those areas, in which the Union does not exercise its competences conferred to it by the treaties. Title VII chapter 3 of the TFEU is entitled *'approximation of laws'* and contains those competences that enable the Union to create the internal market (so-called *'internal market competences'*).[2037] This section of the TFEU is introduced by the general regulatory competence of Article 114 TFEU which allows the European Parliament and the Council *'save where otherwise provided in the Treaties* [...] *for the achievement of the objectives set out in Art 26'* TFEU to *'adopt measures* [...] *which have as their object the establishment and functioning of the internal market'* in an ordinary legislative procedure by qualified majority. This extremely general formulation covers almost all conceivable policy areas.[2038] Although *'save where otherwise provided in the Treaties'* could imply that a legislative measure could not be adopted on the basis of

---

Terra/Wattel – European Tax Law 21–22 (P.J. Wattel et al., eds, Wolters Kluwer 7th ed. 2019); P. Craig & G. de Búrca, *supra* note 1815, at 693; R. A. Achleitner & V. Bendlinger, *supra* note 2024, at 9 in particular n. 100.

2032. ATAD (2016/1164).

2033. Comprehensively on the question, whether Art. 115 TFEU provides for a sufficient legal basis for the ATAD, *i.a.*, A. de Graaf & K.-J. Visser, *ATA Directive: Some Observations Regarding Formal Aspects*, 25 EC Tax Review 201 and 204 et seq. (2016) DOI: 10.54648/ecta2016021; Gianluigi Bizioli, *supra* note 2031, at 167–174; N. Braun Binder, *supra* note 2014, at 92–94; Wolfgang Schön, *supra* note 2030, at 340; with further reference on literature and further thoughts on the legal basis of the ATAD, *see* G. Kofler, *supra* note 1796, at 24–25.

2034. *See* European Commission, *Communication from the Commission to the European Parliament and the Council – Business Taxation for the 21st Century*, *supra* note 196, at 8.

2035. COM(2021)823 final.

2036. *See*, *i.a.*, R. A. Achleitner & V. Bendlinger, *supra* note 2024, at 2–13.

2037. R. Schütze, *supra* note 1822, at 558.

2038. *See*, *i.a.*, Barents who notes that *'the scope of the Community's power to harmonize national legislations has become so vast, that one may very well take the position that this provision can no longer be seen as the attribution of a specific power, but that it amount to a general authorization for the Community to legislate in nearly all the areas which directly or indirectly concern the internal market'*, R. Barents, *supra* note 2010, at 87–88.

Article 114 TFEU if a more specific competence of the Union is provided for in the Treaties,[2039] the CJEU has accepted the use of Article 114 TFEU as a distinct legal basis, since legal acts in the field of the internal market might pursue multiple goals.[2040]

The only substantial limit to the vague scope of Article 114 TFEU is defined by its second paragraph, which explicitly carves out three politically sensitive policy areas, in particular including '*fiscal provisions*'.[2041] These areas, however, might still be covered by the competence of Article 115 TFEU, which in addition to Article 114 TFEU, also contains a general competence for the Council to '*issue directives for the approximation of such laws, regulations or administrative provision of the Member States as directly affect the establishment or functioning of the internal market*'.[2042]

The co-existence of two almost identical bases of general competence can only be explained by their historical context: at one time, the internal market competences consisted only of the predecessors of today's Article 115 (Article 100 EEC Treaty) and Article 116 TFEU (Article 101 EEC Treaty).[2043] Article 115 TFEU served as the key provision[2044] within the internal market competences and required unanimity, whereas Article 116 TFEU was also to allow qualified majority voting where differences in laws, regulations or administrative action '*is distorting the conditions of competition in the internal market*'. Article 116 TFEU should provide a competence for the Union to eliminate such distortions, meant are particularly serious ones, as will be shown,[2045] as quickly as possible, without being bound to an unanimity requirement. Due to the complex interpretation of its wording, however, Article 116 TFEU was soon denied any practical applicability in the literature.[2046] These assumptions ultimately proved to be accurate.[2047] Rather, the predecessors of Article 115 TFEU served as the primary competence for the harmonization of laws in the internal market.

2039. Further on this issue, *see* P. Craig & G. de Búrca, *supra* note 1815, at 650.
2040. *See, i.a.*, Case C-300/89, *Commission of the European Communities and European Parliament v. Council of the European Communities (Directive 89/428/EC Titanium Dioxide)*, para. 11, in which the court annulled a directive adopted unanimously by the council based on a specific competence in the field of environmental law because the regulated matter concerned the internal market and according to the ECJ, today's Art. 114 TFEU would have been the proper legal basis. In detail this judgement, *see* R. Barents, *supra* note 2010, at 94–96. For further reference, *see* R. Schütze, *supra* note 1822, at 567.
2041. G. Kofler, *EU Power to Tax: Competences in the Area of Direct Taxation, in Research Handbook on European Union Taxation Law, supra* note 1796, at 11; R. Schütze, *supra* note 1822, at 568; C. Tietje, *Art. 114 [Beschlussfassung; einzelstaatliche Regelungen; Schutzklausel], in Das Recht der Europäischen Union*, para. 88 (E. Grabitz et al., eds, C.H. Beck 2016).
2042. Article 115 TFEU.
2043. S. Strohmayr, *Kompetenzkollisionen zwischen europäischem und nationalem Recht* 141 (Nomos 2006); R. Schütze, *supra* note 1822, at 559.
2044. For further reference, *see* C. Tietje, *Art. 115 [Richtlinien zur Angleichung von Rechtsvorschriften für den Binnenmarkt], in Das Recht der Europäischen Union*, para. 1 (E. Grabitz et al., eds, C.H.Beck 2018).
2045. *See* s. 6.1.2.4.2.
2046. *See, i.a.*, U. Everling, *Zur Funktion der Rechtsangleichung in der Europäischen Gemeinschaft – Vom Abbau der Verzerrungen zur Schaffung des Binnenmarktes, in Du droit international au droit de l'integration – Liber Amicorum Pierre Pescatore* 231–232 (F. Capotorti et al., eds, Nomos 1987), who stated that Arts 116 and 117 TFEU are '*unlikely to be reasonably applied*' (translation by the author).
2047. In detail to Art. 116 TFEU, *see* s. 6.1.2.4.

With the growing number of Member States, the unanimity principle emerged as an outdated obstacle to European integration as early as the mid-1970s.[2048] Finally, with the Single European Act coming into effect on 1 July 1987, Article 100a EEC Treaty, the ancestor of today's Article 114 TFEU, became part of the Treaties,[2049] leaving hardly any scope for the provision of today's Article 115 TFEU.[2050] Since direct taxes are explicitly excluded from the scope of Article 114 TFEU, whereas the other areas named in Article 114(2) TFEU ('*free movement of persons*' and '*rights and interests of employed persons*') are meanwhile specifically addressed in other provision of the TFEU,[2051] it is regularly assumed in the literature that the area of direct taxes could be the last remaining scope of Article 115 TFEU beside Article 114 TFEU.[2052] The current role of Article 115 TFEU as a supplementary catch-all[2053] provision, as well as its extensive scope, imply its procedural peculiarities:[2054] first, legal acts based on Article 115 TFEU can only be issued in the form of directives, which naturally leave leeways to domestic legislatures.[2055] Second, Article 115 TFEU requires unanimity within the Council, while the European Parliament and the Economic and Social Committee are only consulted. Each individual Member State can, thus, prevent the adoption of a directive on the basis of Article 115 TFEU.[2056]

6.1.2.2.3 The Elusive Scope of Article 115 TFEU

Indeed, the material scope of Article 115 TFEU is difficult to grasp. Where are the boundaries of '*establishment or functioning of the internal market*', what are the characteristics of a '*direct affect*' with it, and above all, where are the material limits of Article 115 TFEU?[2057] Some even argue that there are none,[2058] others that there are a

---

2048. P. Craig & G. de Búrca, *supra* note 1815, at 649. Also *see* S. Weatherhill, *The Competence to Harmonise and Its Limits, in Research Handbook of the EU's Internal Market* (Panos Koutrakos & Jukka Snell eds, Edward Elgar Publishing 2017).
2049. Fundamental to the implementation of Art. 100a EEC Treaty in the course of the Single European Act, *see* Ulrich Everling, *supra* note 2046, at 239 et seq.
2050. For further reference on the historical development of Art. 114 TFEU, *see* C. Tietje, *supra* note 2041, paras 8-16.
2051. *Ibid.*, para. 92 et seq.; C. Tietje, *supra* note 2044, para. 1.
2052. Explicitly and providing for further reference in German literature, *see* D.-E. Kahn & D. Eisenhut, *Art. 115 [National Law with Immediate Effect on the Internal Market; Approximation of Laws], in European Union Treaties*, para. 2 (R. Geiger et al., eds, C.H.Beck 2015); C. Tietje, *supra* note 2044, para. 1; providing for a list of legal acts based on former Art. 94 EC Treaty, *see* S. Strohmayr, *supra* note 2043, at 142-in particular n. 633.
2053. C. Tietje, *supra* note 2044, para. 2; R.A. Achleitner & V. Bendlinger, *GloBE (Pillar Two) – Kompetenzrechtliche Erwägungen zur Umsetzung eines Mindestbesteuerungssystems innerhalb der Europäischen Union*, 2 digitax, *supra* note 2024, at 3.
2054. *See* already P. Leleux, *supra* note 2027, at 559; R. Schütze, *supra* note 1822, at 559.
2055. Article 288(3) TFEU.
2056. *See* G. Kofler, *supra* note 1796, at 19.
2057. The same questions were asked by Leleux as early as 1968, *see* P. Leleux, *supra* note 2027, at 139–144.
2058. *Ibid.*, at 138, *see* already n. 2025.

few[2059] and still others conclude that they cannot be determined by legal methods of interpretation but that there is only the political limit of unanimity.[2060]

In addition to the already very vague scope, the interpretation of Article 115 TFEU is further complicated by the fact that, despite its once fundamental role in the Treaty of Rome, there is, in contrast to Article 114 TFEU, almost[2061] no case law on the provision and its predecessors.[2062] The prevailing view, notwithstanding marginal textual differences,[2063] however, argues that the vast case law on Article 114(1) TFEU may, in principle, be transferred *mutatis mutandis* for the interpretation of Article 115 TFEU.[2064] Since both provisions share their purpose and are, as already pointed out above, historically closely intertwined, this view is convincing: both Articles 114 and 115 TFEU are intended to enable the Union to achieve its objective of '*establishing and ensuring the functioning of the internal market*' according to Article 26 TFEU and Article 3(3) TEU by harmonizing divergent Member State legislation.[2065] The fact that both provisions provide for an almost all-encompassing competence of the Union for the internal market is not due to the intention of creating different sets of competences but to the political agreement to move away from unanimity. The case law on Article

2059. Stephen Weatherhill, *supra* note 2048, at 94.
2060. *See, i.a.*, U. Anschütz, *supra* note 1800, at 4–5. In this direction also Case C-122/15, *C*, para. 52: '*The number of areas of law capable of directly affecting the internal market is incalculably large. Moreover, the determination of whether or not such an effect is present will to a large extent fall within the discretion of the legislature alone. At a procedural level, however, the substantive scope of the competence in matters affecting the internal market as provided for in Article* [115 TFEU] *is limited by the requirement of unanimity within the Council.*'
2061. Among the few decisions that touch at least briefly on the scope of Art. 115 TFEU, *see, i.a.*, Case C-91/79, *Commission v. Italian Republic*, para. 8, in which the court held, that it is not ruled out, that environmental provisions may be based on Art. 115. Furthermore, *see* Case C-193/80, *Commission v. Italian Republic*, para. 17.
2062. C. Tietje, *supra* note 2044, para. 7.
2063. While Art. 114 TFEU allows the adoption of legal acts '*which have as their object the establishment and functioning of the internal market*', Art. 115 concerns the harmonization of domestic legislation '*as directly affect the establishment or functioning of the internal market*'. Textually, the provisions thus differ in the '*direct effect*' required under Art. 115 TFEU which could lead to the assumption that the scope of Art. 115 TFEU is narrower compared to Art. 114 TFEU. However, as R. Schütze, *supra* note 1822, at 565–566, points out, the ECJ seems to regularly impute this prerequisite to Art. 114 TFEU as well, *see, i.a.*, Case C-210/03, *The Queen, on the application of: Swedish Match AB and Swedish Match UK Ltd v. Secretary of State for Health*, para. 29, where the court explicitly referred to a required '*direct effect on the functioning of the internal market*'. Using the same phrase, *see, i.a.*, Case C-58/08, *The Queen on the application of Vodafone Ltd, Telefónica O2 Europe plc, T-Mobile International AG, Orange Personal Communications Services Ltd v. Secretary of State for Business, Enterprise and Regulatory Reform*, para. 32. The CJEU therefore also seems to assume an approximately identical understanding of both provisions, despite their slight textual differences.
2064. *See, i.a.*, A. Schrauwen, *Sources of EU Law for Integration in Direct and Indirect Taxation, in Traditional and Alternative Routes to European Tax Integration*, s. 1.2. (IBFD 2010); C. Tietje, *supra* note 2044, paras 7–8; I. Lazarov & S. Govind, *Carpet-Bombing Tax Avoidance in Europe: Examining the Validity of the ATAD Under EU Law*, 47 Intertax 860 (2019) DOI: 10.54648/taxi2019086; G. Kofler, *supra* note 1796, at 20 in particular n. 61.
2065. GA Fennelly, therefore, when examining the scope of Art. 114 TFEU, concluded in his Opinion on Tobacco Advertising that '*the scope of competence under* [Art 114 TFEU] *is defined exclusively by reference to its stated objective, rather than its material subject-matter*', Joined Cases C-376/98 and C-74/99, *Tobacco Advertising* at 62.

114 TFEU can therefore be, in principle, transferred to the interpretation of the scope of Article 115 TFEU without hesitation.

The CJEU has always given the EU institutions extremely generous leeway in interpreting the EU's competences. This is especially true for the frequently used internal market competences. For example, as early as the 1970s, the ECJ held that a '*direct affect*' within the meaning of today's Article 115 TFEU, without further elaborating on its scope, can already exist if different regulations of the Member States are '*likely to distort or harm the functioning of the Common Market*'[2066].[2067] Even purely potential influences on the internal market have thus been considered sufficient for the existence of a harmonization competence of the Union. In *Spain v. Council*, the Court even went a step further and affirmed a '*direct affect*' (referring to Article 114 TFEU) even if future but not yet existing legislative measures of the Member States could create obstacles to the internal market.[2068] A legal act can therefore be based on Article 115 TFEU (or Article 114 TFEU) in order '*to prevent the heterogeneous development of national laws leading to further disparities which would be likely to create obstacles to*' the fundamental freedoms.[2069] For a lawful application of Article 115 TFEU (or Article 114 TFEU), it is therefore essential that there are likely to be obstacles to the fundamental freedoms and that the measures under Union law are designed to prevent them.[2070]

The assumption that there are no limits at all for the EU legislature within the framework of the internal market competences was finally rejected by the CJEU in its famous *Tobacco Advertising* judgement.[2071] The subject of this dispute was a directive on the prohibition of advertisement and sponsorship of tobacco products issued on the basis of the predecessor of Article 114 TFEU, which was successfully challenged by Germany in a procedure of judicial review. Until today, this case contributes to the interpretation of Articles 114 and 115 TFEU and gives at least a rudimentary contour to the phrase '*establishment and functioning of the internal market*'. The decision's awareness is due to the fact that the CJEU, for the first time and the only time to date,[2072] considered a certain legal act of secondary Union legislature as being not covered by the material scope of the internal market competence it was based on. The CJEU held that only such measures may be based on today's Article 114 TFEU, which actually '*improve the conditions for the establishment and functioning of the internal market*'[2073] and finally acknowledged that the ambit of the Union's harmonization

2066. Case C-33/76, *Rewe-Zentralfinanz eG and Rewe-Zentral AG v. Landwirtschaftskammer für das Saarland*, para. 5.
2067. R.A. Achleitner & V. Bendlinger, *supra* note 2024, at 3.
2068. Case C-350/92, *Kingdom of Spain v. Council of the European Union*; for further reference and the relevance of this judgement, *see* R. Schütze, *supra* note 1822, at 562–563.
2069. Case C-350/92, *Spain v. Council*, para. 35.
2070. Also referring to *Spain v. Council* (C-350/92) *see, i.a.*, Case C-491/01, *British American Tobacco (Investments) Ltd and Imperial Tobacco Ltd*; with further reference to other judgements, *see* Case C-380/03, *Germany v. European Parliament and Council of the European Union (Tobacco Adverdising II)*, para. 38. On the possible preventive use of the internal market competences, *see* S. Weatherhill, *supra* note 2048, at 90.
2071. Case C-376/98, *Tobacco Advertising*.
2072. *See also* R. Schütze, *supra* note 1992.
2073. Case C-376/98, *Tobacco Advertising*, para. 83.

competence is not unlimited,[2074] since this would undermine the *Principle of Conferral* laid down in Article 5 TEU.[2075] As a result, the ECJ in *Tobacco Advertising* defined two alternative conditions for the existence of a direct effect on the '*establishment and functioning of the internal market*':[2076] Either there is an obstacle to the fundamental freedoms,[2077] or there is a distortion of competition that a certain legislative measure is intended to eliminate.[2078] With regard to the scale of these requirements, the court held that neither '*a mere finding of disparities between national rules*' nor an '*abstract risk*' are sufficient to evidence a competence of the Union.[2079] So far, the CJEU still regularly refers to its *Tobacco Advertising* decision.[2080] Nevertheless, the ECJ has not annulled any measures based on Article 114 or 115 TFEU due to a lack of competence since then and has indeed remained very generous in the interpretation of the internal market competences.[2081]

6.1.2.2.4 Article 115 TFEU and Harmonization of Direct Taxation in a Post-BEPS Context

Although certain guidelines can be derived from the case law on Articles 114 and 115 TFEU, the contours for a deeper harmonization in direct tax law remain blurred and have hardly been developed despite extensive discussion[2082] in the literature.[2083] In any case, it is undisputed that mere differences in direct tax systems cannot, in principle, themselves conflict with the internal market.[2084] Thus, a complete harmonization of direct taxes on the basis of Article 115 TFEU seems not to be possible at the current

2074. Also in detail to the limits laid out this judgement, *see* R. Szudoczky, *Is the CCCTB Proposal in Line with the Principle of Subsidiarity?: Negative Opinions Submitted by National Parliaments in the 'Yellow Card Procedure', in CCCTB: Selected Issues* 112 (D. Weber ed., Wolters Kluwer 2012); S. Weatherhill, *supra* note 2048, at 93; R. Schütze, *supra* note 1822, at 564.
2075. Case C-376/98, *Tobacco Advertising*, para. 83.
2076. For further discussion on these prerequisites established by the ECJ, *see*, *i.a.*, R. Schütze, *supra* note 1822, at 565–566; G. Kofler, *supra* note 1796, at 20.
2077. Case C-376/98, *Tobacco Advertising*, paras 96 et seq.
2078. *Ibid.*, paras 106 et seq.
2079. *Ibid.*, para. 84.
2080. *See*, *i.a.*, Case C-545/17, *Mariusz Pawlak v. Prezes Kasy Rolniczego Ubezpieczenia Społecznego*, para. 30; Case C-547/14, *Philip Morris Brands SARL and others v. Secretary of State for Health*, paras 58, 82 and 131; Case C-491/01, *British American Tobacco*, para. 60; Case C-58/08, *Vodafone Ltd and others*, para. 32; Case C-380/03, *Tobacco Advertising II* at 37.
2081. Further on the developments, *see* R. Schütze, *supra* note 1822, at 565–567. Also *see* with respect to GloBE, D. Hohenwarter-Mayr, *supra* note 1552, at 131.
2082. *See* only an exemplary and not conclusive selection of authors, i.e., U. Anschütz, *supra* note 1800, at 3 et seq.; B.H. Ter Kuile, *supra* note 2014; A. Easson, *supra* note 2015; S. Kingston, *supra* note 2014, at 288 et seq.; A. Schrauwen, *supra* note 2064, s. 1.1.; C. Seiler, *supra* note 2019, para. 50 et seq.; Nadja Braun Binder, *supra* note 2014; Werner Haslehner, *supra* note 2024, at 3.2.
2083. Reaching the same conclusion, C. Brokelind, *The Anti-Tax Avoidance Directive under Scrutiny: A Matter of Competence?, in Liber Amicorum Bertil Wiman* 47 and 55 (J. Monsenego & J. Bjuvberg eds, Wolters Kluwer 2019); and G. Kofler, *supra* note 1796, at 20.
2084. *See* already in the early 1970s, also providing for further reference Ulrich Anschütz, *supra* note 1800, at 6.

stage of European integration.[2085] Nevertheless, tax policy developments over the past decade show that direct taxes have long since ceased to be a purely domestic issue. Recent developments on the OECD level and the much-acclaimed BEPS Project have shown that taxation is not going to become but already is a global matter of issue. The EU is therefore trying to establish itself as a global player in the international tax landscape, and consequently, tax policy is high on the Commission's agenda. Solely within the term of the Commission led by *Jean-Claude Juncker* between 2014 and 2019, 26 legislative proposals on tax issues have been put forward;[2086] and also, the current Commission headed by *Ursula von der Leyen* has again confirmed its intention to press ahead with tax harmonization[2087] and ultimately made good on that promise by, among other initiatives, proposing the successfully adopted GloBE-Directive. It is therefore not surprising that the discussion on the Union's competences for the harmonization of direct taxes, which has been going on since the founding of the Union,[2088] gains renewed relevance with each measure proposed or enacted: every legal act of the Union must be based on a specific legal basis and, in the case of Article 115 TFEU, it must be shown that there is a direct effect on the establishment or functioning of the internal market.[2089] Thus, nearly each of the Commission's harmonization initiatives or even successful enactments of directives in the field of direct taxes in the last decade has again evoked the question of whether Article 115 TFEU provides for a sufficient legal basis for the respective measures;[2090] and, indeed a lively discussion already developed before the GloBE-Directive Proposal was released, whether GloBE might be implemented on the basis of Article 115 TFEU as well.[2091] In particular, the fact that the tax policy of the Union, certainly increasingly motivated by the OECD BEPS Project,[2092] recently tends to focus strongly on combating tax abuse has led to doubts as to whether such acts contribute to the establishment or functioning of the internal market: at the centre of this discussion are primarily the ATAD (ATAD I[2093] and ATAD II[2094]) and the DAC 6[2095] which, unlike the corporate tax directives issued in

2085. Werner Haslehner, *supra* note 2024, at 3.2.; G. Kofler, *supra* note 1796, at 21.
2086. European Parliament, *European Parliament Resolution of 26 March 2019 on Financial Crimes, Tax Evasion and Tax Avoidance*, 2018/2121(INI), para. 3 (26 Mar. 2019), https://eur-lex.europa.eu/legal-content/EN/TXT/PDF/?uri=CELEX:52019IP0240&rid=7 (last visited 28 Jul. 2021); for further details, *see* Moritz Scherleitner, *Should the EU Implement a Minimum Corporate Taxation Directive?*, *supra* note 2023, s. 1.3.
2087. *See*, *A Union that Strives for More – My Agenda for Europe – Political Guidelines for the next European Commission 2019–2024*, at 12 and 20.
2088. *See* the already ambitious proposals for harmonization of taxes within the Union of the committee of experts led by *Fritz Neumark* in the early 1960s, *see The EEC Reports on Tax Harmonization (Neumark Report 1962), Translation H. Thurston* (IBFD 1963).
2089. *See also* D.W. Blum & A. Langer, *supra* note 2024, at 285.
2090. For a comprehensive overview, *see* G. Kofler, *supra* note 1796, at 20–26.
2091. R.A. Achleitner & V. Bendlinger, *supra* note 2024, at 2–13; L. De Broe & M. Massant, *Are the OECD/G20 Pillar Two GloBE-Rules Compliant with the Fundamental Freedoms?*, 30 EC Tax Review 94 (2021) DOI: 10.54648/ecta2021011; J. Englisch, *Designing a Harmonized EU-GloBE in Compliance with Fundamental Freedoms*, 30 EC Tax Review 136 (2021) DOI: 10.54648/ecta2021015; Moritz Scherleitner, *supra* note 2023, s. 3.1.
2092. Also *see* Daniel W. Blum & Andreas Langer, *supra* note 2024, at 282.
2093. ATAD.
2094. Council directive (EU) 2017/952 of 29 May 2017 amending Directive (EU) 2016/1164 as regards hybrid mismatches with third countries, OJ (952).

pre-BEPS times,[2096] do less to reduce obstacles to the fundamental freedoms but rather create burdensome tax mechanisms and reporting obligations for taxpayers.[2097] Thus, one might argue that such measures do not '*improve the conditions for the establishment and functioning of the internal market*' as initially laid down in the ECJ's *Tobacco Advertising* judgement.[2098] Nevertheless, the recourse to Article 115 TFEU to enact measures against tax abuse is not a post-BEPS development. As *Kofler*[2099] points out, already the preamble to the 1977 directive on mutual assistance held that '*practices of tax evasion and tax avoidance extending across the frontiers of Member States lead to budget losses and violations of the principle of fair taxation and are liable to bring about distortions of capital movements and of conditions of competition; whereas they therefore affect the operation of the common market*'.[2100]

In the course of the BEPS project, this second view of the internal market was taken up again by the Commission, to manifest the competence of the Union to adopt various measures proposed by the OECD. This could not be more evident than in Recital 2 of the ATAD (2016/1164), where it is held, that the functioning of the internal market requires '*action to discourage tax avoidance practices and ensure fair and effective taxation*', that only '*a common framework could prevent a fragmentation of the market*' and that ATAD '*would* [finally] *provide legal certainty to taxpayers*'.[2101] Nevertheless, these considerations present a one-sided picture, which is why all of these arguments have also been countered by well-founded reasons and Article 115 TFEU as a sufficient legal basis for the ATAD has indeed be questioned:[2102] Many authors have pointed out, that (i) the recourse to a fair and effective tax system (whatever this is meant to be) was merely a tax policy diction and would not be suitable as a legal argument for a sufficient competence of the Union,[2103] that (ii) the content of the ATAD went beyond BEPS,[2104] that (iii) some measures like the interest barrier (Article 4 ATAD) or the GAAR (Article 6 ATAD) go beyond the regulatory scope

2095. Council directive (EU) 2018/822 of 25 May 2018 amending Directive 2011/16/EU as regards mandatory automatic exchange of information in the field of taxation in relation to reportable cross-border arrangements, OJ (822) 822.
2096. Parent Subsidiary Directive; Merger Directive; Interest and Royalty Directive.
2097. Also *see* A. de Graaf & K.-J. Visser, *supra* note 2033, at 203; C. Staringer, *Die Anti-Tax-Avoidance-Richtlinie: Gesamtwürdigung Aus Steuerpolitischer Sicht, in Die Anti-Tax-Avoidance-Richtlinie* 11–12 (Michael Lang et al., eds, Linde 2017); D. W. Blum & A. Langer, *supra* note 2024, at 286; G. Kofler, *supra* note 1796, at 23.
2098. Case C-376/98, *Tobacco Advertising*, para. 83; Case C-547/14, *Philip Morris*, para. 131.
2099. G. Kofler, *supra* note 1796, at 15 and 22.
2100. Council directive of 19 December 1977 concerning mutual assistance by the competent authorities of the Member States in the field of direct taxation, OJ (799).
2101. Recital 2 of the ATAD; also emphasizing this recital, *see* G. Bizioli, *supra* note 2031, at 169; *supra* note 2083, at 48; and G. Kofler, *supra* note 1796, at 24.
2102. Comprehensively G. Kofler, *supra* note 1796, at 24–25; and W. Haslehner, *The General Scope of the ATAD and Its Position in the EU Legal Order, in A Guide to the ATAD* 38–47 (Werner Haslehner et al., eds, Edward Elgar Publishing 2020).
2103. C. Staringer, *supra* note 2097, at 8–10; Werner Haslehner, *supra* note 2024, at 3.3.2.; W. Haslehner, *supra* note 2102, para. 2.19.
2104. In this direction A. P. Dourado, *The EU Anti Tax Avoidance Package: Moving Ahead of BEPS?*, 44 Intertax 442 (2016) DOI: 10.54648/taxi2016036; Gianluigi Bizioli, *supra* note 2031, at 172; I. Lazarov & S. Govind, *supra* note 2064, at 860.

of the internal market, since they also relate to purely domestic situations[2105] and that (iv) the ATAD is merely a minimum standard (Article 3 ATAD) and, thus, allows Member States to apply stricter rules and does not even avoid, but actually promotes fragmentation.[2106] In addition, the ATAD has also been accused of creating new potentials of occurring double taxation, which is obviously contrary to the ideal of the internal market.[2107] Consequently, doubts have also arisen as to whether the ATAD can be of any benefit at all to the legal certainty of taxpayers.[2108] All of these arguments in favour as well as against the existence of a direct effect on the establishment and functioning of the internal market as presupposed by Article 115 TFEU can probably also be invoked with respect to the GloBE-Directive and, thus, will be discussed in more detail below.

6.1.2.3 *Article 115 TFEU as a Sufficient Legal Basis for the GloBE-Directive?*

6.1.2.3.1 *Methodological Caveats to the Examination of the EU's Competence to Implement GloBE*

When discussing competence-related issues of the GloBE-Directive, there is no way around a reference back to the discussion on the legal basis of the ATAD for a number of reasons[2109]:

- First, like ATAD,[2110] the GloBE-Directive is strongly influenced by legislative patterns provided by the OECD.[2111] The Commission made no secret of the fact that the set of rules is strongly based on the GloBE Model Rules. This had already been pointed out in the Explanatory Memorandum of the GloBE-Directive Proposal: '*The Directive reflects the global OECD agreement, with some necessary adjustments, to guarantee conformity with EU law.*'[2112] Furthermore, also in the final GloBE-Directive, a direct reference to the GloBE

2105. C. Staringer, *supra* note 2097, at 11; Ivan Lazarov & Sriram Govind, *supra* note 2064, at 853.
2106. *See, i.a.*, Ana Paula Dourado, *supra* note 2104, at 442; Gianluigi Bizioli, *supra* note 2031, at 171–172; C. Staringer, *supra* note 2097, at 13–14; Werner Haslehner, *supra* note 2024, at 3.3.2.; Ivan Lazarov & Sriram Govind, *supra* note 2064, at 860; W. Haslehner, *supra* note 2102, para. 2.18; Alexander Rust, *Controlled Foreign Company Rule (Articles 7 and 8 ATAD), in A Guide to the ATAD*, para. 7.51 to 7.53 and 7.61 (Werner Haslehner et al., eds, Edward Elgar Publishing 2020).
2107. *See, i.a.*, G. Kofler, *supra* note 1796, at 25.
2108. C. Staringer, *supra* note 2097, at 14.
2109. R.A. Achleitner & V. Bendlinger, *supra* note 2024, at 6.
2110. The strong alignment of the ATAD with the Reports published by the OECD in the course of the BEPS Project is particularly evident in the recitals of both ATAD I and ATAD II. *See, i.a.*, Recital 1-3 of the ATAD and Recital 1-2, 5,7 and 28 of the ATAD II. Of particular note is Recital 28 of ATAD II (2017/952), which even calls on Member States to '*use the applicable explanations and examples in the OECD BEPS report on Action 2 as a source of illustration or interpretation to the extent that they are consistent with the provisions of this Directive and with Union law*'.
2111. *See* R. A. Achleitner & V. Bendlinger, *supra* note 2024, at 5; and also M. Scherleitner, *Should the EU Implement a Minimum Corporate Taxation Directive?*, *supra* note 2023, s. 3.2.
2112. COM(2021)823 final 1

Model Rules is found in recital 6, where the directive emphasizes that it intends to implement GloBE '*as close as possible to the global agreement*' and again notes that the '*Directive closely follows the content and structure of the OECD Model Rules*'.[2113]

- Second, the GloBE-Directive and the ATAD have, in fact, a similar regulatory subject matter.[2114] The ATAD obliges Member States to implement six fiscal instruments, including in particular CFC Rules (Articles 7 and 8 ATAD), which have some commonalities with the GloBE IIR as enshrined in Article 1(a) and Articles 5 to 8 GloBE-Directive.[2115] In addition, one can also find similarities between the policy rationale of the UTPR (as laid down in Article 1(b) and Article 11 et seq. GloBE-Directive Proposal) and certain other mechanisms of the ATAD, e.g., the interest barrier (Article 4 ATAD) as well as the hybrid mismatch rules (Article 9 ATAD);[2116] although, admittedly, the UTPR pursuant to Articles 12 to 14 GloBE-Directive clearly distinguishes from the measures adopted by the ATAD.
- Third, as can already be concluded from the previous argument, both the objectives and purposes of the GloBE-Directive and those of ATAD are at least comparable, though not identical. The OECD documents referring to GloBE regularly state that Pillar Two should address the '*remaining BEPS issues*'.[2117] Nevertheless, GloBE goes much further and is ultimately intended to curb tax competition.[2118]
- Fourth, since the ATAD was also successfully based on Article 115 TFEU, it is not surprising that the Commission, as will be seen shortly, has used similar competence-related arguments with regard to the GloBE-Directive as it did with regard to the ATAD.

Nevertheless, one should (again) emphasize here that the density of the harmonization measures taken by the GloBE-Directive goes far beyond the mechanism implemented by way of the ATAD. The measures implemented by means of the GloBE-Directive are much more detailed, and, most importantly, the GloBE has its own objectives beyond simply combating tax avoidance.[2119] The following section will therefore focus on the question of whether and how the GloBE-Directive contributes to the establishment or functioning of the internal market as required by Article 115 TFEU, taking into account the arguments already put forward in the academic discourse on the ATAD. It will then be discussed whether the Commission correctly

2113. Recital 6 GloBE-Directive (2022/2523).
2114. Also *see* the explanatory note in COM(2021)823 final 2, where the Commission refers to the overlap of Arts 7 and 8 of ATAD.
2115. Explicitly, *see Tax Challenges Arising from Digitalisation – Report on Pillar Two Blueprint*, para. 411; among many others in literature, *see* Johanna Hey, *supra* note 1521, at 7–13.
2116. R. A. Achleitner & V. Bendlinger, *supra* note 2024, at 6.
2117. The phrase can be found, i.e., in the foreword and Executive Summary of the Blueprint, *see Tax Challenges Arising from Digitalisation – Report on Pillar Two Blueprint*, at 3 and 10.
2118. *See*, *i.a.*, J. Hey, *supra* note 1521, at 7–8. In detail to the spongy purpose and policy rationale of GloBE, *see* s. 4.5.8.
2119. To these arguments R. A. Achleitner & V. Bendlinger, *supra* note 2024, at 6.

used Article 115 TFEU to adopt the GloBE-Directive. It should be emphasized that the considerations of competence-related lines of argumentation discussed here neither claim to be exhaustive nor can they always be clearly distinguished from one another and are very political. The following classification of arguments is based on the existing case law of the ECJ and the existing discourse in the literature, in particular, with regard to ATAD.

6.1.2.3.2 Prevention of Fragmentation of the Internal Market

As the CJEU has already stated in its decision in *Spain v. Council*, the prevention of heterogeneous legislation by the Member States may justify recourse to the internal market competences if such disparities are likely to create obstacles to the fundamental freedoms or distort competition.[2120] The same competence-related argument has been used by the ATAD[2121] and is also brought forward in the GloBE-Directive with respect to the implementation of GloBE, where it is held that '[i]*n a Union of closely integrated economies, it is crucial that the global minimum tax reform be implemented in a sufficiently coherent and coordinated fashion. Considering the scale, detail and technicalities of those new international tax rules, only a common Union framework would prevent a fragmentation of the internal market in the implementation of them*'.[2122] The GloBE-Directive, thus, implicitly assumes that tax policy developments at the OECD level might suggest an uncoordinated approach by Member States which could directly affect the internal market.[2123] It should be borne in mind, however, that mere disparities in tax jurisdictions are, according to the CJEU, not sufficient to establish a direct effect on the establishment or functioning of the internal market presupposed by Article 115 TFEU. The disparities to be feared must constitute a likely obstacle to the internal market,[2124] and the respective directive must '*be designed to prevent them*'.[2125] The goal of avoiding legal fragmentation as a legitimate objective for the internal market is also widely accepted in literature.[2126] So could preventing fragmentation be a valid competence-related argument for enacting a GloBE-Directive?

This is, without doubt, a valid argument put forward by the GloBE-Directive. Most of the Member States are willing to push ahead with global tax reform. A lack of initiative of the Union would have tempted Member States to implement the GloBE rules unilaterally. This finally also proved to be true: at a time when it appeared that the Council would not reach unanimity on the GloBE-Directive, some Member States even

2120. Case C-350/92, *Spain v. Council*, paras 32 and 35.
2121. *See* recital 2 of ATAD, where it is held that „*only a common framework could prevent a fragmentation of the market and put an end to currently existing mismatches and market distortions*'.
2122. Recital 4 GloBE-Directive (2022/2523).
2123. Already before the GloBE-Directive was initiated, *see* P. K. Schmidt, *A General Income Inclusion Rule as a Tool for Improving the International Tax Regime – Challenges Arising from EU Primary Law*, 48 Intertax 992 (2020) DOI: 10.54648/taxi2020100; R. A. Achleitner & V. Bendlinger, *supra* note 2024, at 8.
2124. *See* Case C-376/98, *Tobacco Advertising*, paras 32–33; Case C-58/08, *Vodafone Ltd and others*.
2125. Case C-58/08, *Vodafone Ltd and others*, para. 33.
2126. *See, i.a.*, C. Staringer, *supra* note 2097, at 14.

publicly announced that they would adopt GloBE in the absence of an EU-wide implementation,[2127] and, finally, the set of rules proposed by the OECD has no binding legal character.[2128] It therefore appears that the GloBE-Directive can indeed avoid disparities that were likely to emerge in the absence of a legislative act of the EU.

Nevertheless, this line of reasoning is not compelling: while the IF Member States are not to be obliged to actually implement GloBE, there is agreement that '*if they choose to do so, they will implement and administer the rules in a way that is consistent with the outcomes provided for under Pillar Two, including in light of model rules and guidance agreed to by the IF*'.[2129] Since, as of November, all EU Member States except Cyprus belong to the Inclusive Framework,[2130] one might wonder whether the OECD's GloBE project is not already taking sufficient precautions against the threat of legal fragmentation.[2131] Furthermore, it has already been argued in the context of ATAD that not every legal act might contribute to defragmentation, but even could have the opposite effect: it is inherent in a directive that it, as Article 288(3) TFEU states, '*shall leave to the national authorities the choice of form and methods*'. In this respect, a supposed harmonization, as it was also argued for the CFC provisions in Articles 7 and 8 ATAD, which even provide for options, for example,[2132] could rather cause a fragmentation of law than prevent it. Thus, it is doubted whether ATAD promoted defragmentation, all the more due to the fact that ATAD only sets a minimum standard.[2133]

In contrast, the GloBE-Directive is much more compact and conclusive. The GloBE-Directive is extremely sparing with options left to the Member States,[2134] and it seems that the GloBE-Directive, contrary to the ATAD, is not intended to set a minimum standard but to exhaustively implement GloBE. While Article 3 ATAD clarifies that the ATAD is not intended to prevent Member States from taking more stringent measures,[2135] there is no indication within the Commission's proposal that the GloBE-Directive should be implemented only as a minimum standard. According to

2127. *See* the *Joint Statement by France, Germany, Italy, Netherlands and Spain*, *supra* note 223, where it was held: '*At the June 2022 Ecofin, 26 out of 27 EU member states expressed their willingness to implement this important step towards tax justice, and our first goal remains to gather a consensus. Should unanimity not be reached in the next weeks, our governments are fully determined to follow through on our commitment. We stand ready to implement the global minimum effective taxation in 2023 and by any possible legal means. We are also fully committed to complete the work on the better reallocation of taxing rights from huge global multinationals' profits with the objective of signing a multilateral convention by mid-2023.*'

2128. V. Bendlinger, *supra* note 258, at 3–4.

2129. *OECD/G20 Statement 8 October*, at 3.

2130. OECD/G20, *Members of the OECD/G20 Inclusive Framework on BEPS* (Nov. 2021), https://www.oecd.org/tax/beps/inclusive-framework-on-beps-composition.pdf (last visited 9 Dec. 2021).

2131. This argument is of course closely linked to the '*principles of subsidiarity and proportionality*'. *See* s. 6.1.2.5.

2132. On that specific argument, *see, i.a.*, C. Staringer, *supra* note 2097, at 14.

2133. Regarding this argument in the context of the ATAD, *see* I. Lazarov & S. Govind, *supra* note 2064, at 860; G. Kofler, *supra* note 1796, at 25; W. Haslehner, *supra* note 2102, at 40.

2134. See, however, the election to apply a 'qualified domestic top-up tax' in Art. 11 GloBE-Directive (2022/2523).

2135. In detail on the ATAD's character as a minimum standard, *see* W. Haslehner, *supra* note 2102, at 35–38.

Article 2(1) GloBE-Directive, the directive '*shall apply to* [...] *MNE group or large-scale domestic group which has an annual revenue of EUR 750 000 000*'. This, of course, raises the question of whether Member States are free to apply the rules to groups of companies with lower revenues. Does this supposedly mean that Member States are free to provide for a lower threshold?

Indeed, the GloBE-Directive does not prohibit that the Member States apply the GloBE Rules also for 'MNE Groups' outside of its scope. However, this does not mean that GloBE would be a minimum standard. Rather, within the scope of the GloBE-Directive, there is hardly any leeway for Member States to implement the global minimum tax, and contrary to the ATAD,[2136] as the GloBE-Directive does not include '*explicit options for any down- or upward derogations*'.[2137] Rather, the GloBE-Directive contains detailed and binding rules on the GloBE base,[2138] the computation of the 'Adjusted Covered Tax',[2139] and finally also contains detailed rules on the calculation of the 'Top-up Tax' liability[2140] and the collection of the respective tax liability.[2141] It even includes details on the 'Filing obligations'[2142] of the taxpayer, just to give another example. With regard to all these regulations, the GloBE-Directive leaves no room for manoeuvre to the Member States' legislature. Finally, the GloBE-Directive obliges the Member States to collect the minimum tax at a rate of 15% on the tax base to be calculated pursuant to its Chapter III. Not levying the minimum tax would be a violation of the GloBE-Directive. In contrast, the ATAD does not specify whether Member States must levy a tax on corporate profits at all,[2143] nor how the tax base of a CIT is to be calculated. Only if Member States levy a tax on corporate profits they have to apply individual mechanisms, such as CFC rules, pursuant to Articles 7 and 8 ATAD. As has been pointed out, pursuant to Article 3 ATAD, Member States are explicitly allowed to implement even stricter rules. As a matter of fact, one can, thus, assume that the GloBE-Directive, contrary to the ATAD, establishes exhaustive harmonization in the field of Pillar Two.[2144]

As already mentioned, ATAD has been accused of not achieving its self-promoted goal of avoiding fragmentation[2145] from the outset and, as it establishes a mere minimum standard that could not achieve defragmentation at all. With regard to the GloBE-Directive, this objection would not be valid, at least as long as the GloBE-Directive is not interpreted as a minimum standard but as an exhaustive harmonization, and there is much to believe that the GloBE-Directive rather achieves exhaustive

2136. *See* Art. 3 ATAD.
2137. G. Kofler & A. Schnitger, *Does the 'Initial Phase Relief' Make the EU's Pillar Two Directive Invalid?*, 63 Eur. Taxn. 5 (2023) DOI: 10.2139/ssrn.4392892.
2138. Articles 15 to 19 GloBE-Directive (2022/2523).
2139. Articles 20 to 25 *Ibid.*
2140. Articles 26 to 31 *Ibid.*
2141. Articles 1 and 5 to 14. *Ibid.*
2142. Article 44. *Ibid.*
2143. In this vein, *see*, in particular, M. Caziero & I. Lazarov, *The Substantive Scope of the Anti-Tax-Avoidance Directive: The Remaining Leeway for National Tax Sovereignty*, 58 Common Market Law Review 1789 (2021) DOI: 10.54648/cola2021112.
2144. Drawing the same conclusion, *see* G. Kofler & A. Schnitger, *supra* note 2137, at 189.
2145. *See* recital 2 ATAD.

harmonization. The GloBE-Directive ensures, on the one hand, that GloBE is implemented consistently and, on the other hand, that GloBE is implemented by the Member States without exception. Consequently, the GloBE-Directive can justifiably rely on the competence-related argument of avoiding fragmentation of the internal market.[2146]

6.1.2.3.3 *Ensuring Compatibility with Fundamental Freedoms by a Common Framework*

The Commission already made clear in the Explanatory Statement of the GloBE-Directive Proposal that the aim of the proposal is to implement GloBE '*with some necessary adjustments, to guarantee conformity with EU law*'.[2147] This intention is now enshrined in the recitals of the GloBE-Directive, where it is held that the directive is '*designed to be compatible with the fundamental freedoms guaranteed by the Treaty*'.[2148] This phrase also finds a predecessor in the ATAD, which in its recitals equally refers to the need for a '*common line*' in order to implement the envisaged measures in compatibility with EU law.[2149] The reference to conformity with Union law and, in particular, compatibility with the fundamental freedoms is of particular importance for the justification of a competence based on Article 115 TFEU requiring a direct effect on the '*establishment or functioning of the internal market*' and is of course closely related to the fragmentation argument discussed above: the internal market, as defined in Article 26(2) TFEU, is inseparable from the fundamental freedoms.[2150] Infringements of fundamental freedoms are, therefore, inevitably against the very intention of the internal market. A directive that implements content that potentially conflicts with fundamental freedoms must therefore accept the reproach that it does not contribute to the establishment or functioning of the internal market but rather actually works against it.[2151] However, the Union legislature admittedly has a wide margin of manoeuvre in this respect, as has already been shown and will again be discussed with respect to the GloBE-Directive's compatibility with the substantive requirements of primary law in section 6.2. Nevertheless, the ECJ has already confirmed that harmonization is not an end in itself and that there are also limits to the legislative freedom of the Union legislature.[2152] But does the GloBE-Directive exceed these limits?

Even before the announced implementation of GloBE, there were intensive discussions on how to implement the IIR and UTPR in conformity with Union law. After the Pillar Two Blueprint was published in October 2020, well-founded concerns were expressed in the literature as to whether the measures proposed there could

2146. In the same vein, *see* M. Scherleitner, *supra* note 2023, at 12.
2147. COM(2021)823 final.
2148. Third sentence of Recital 4 GloBE-Directive Proposal (2021).
2149. Last sentence of Recital 2 ATAD.
2150. *See, i.a.*, C. Tietje, *supra* note 2041, paras 81 and 104.
2151. V. Bendlinger, *supra* note 258, at 14.
2152. Case C-376/98, *Tobacco Advertising*.

actually be implemented in conformity with EU law without adjustments:[2153] the imposition of a 'top-up tax' on low-taxed profits limited to the cross-border context is obviously discriminatory and as the CJEU has also stated, not least in its famous *Cadbury Schweppes* decision, neither low taxation abroad[2154] nor a blanket suspicion of abuse can justify discrimination against the freedom of establishment,[2155] because such a restriction would not meet proportionality.[2156] The relationship of the IIR and UTPR to fundamental freedoms will be examined below.[2157] However, it does not require a more in-depth investigation to state that the top-up tax to be levied by the IIR or the UTPR according to the GloBE Model Rules could not simply be adopted by the EU legislature without adjustments: according to Article 1.1.1. of the GloBE Model Rules, minimum taxation should apply to MNE Groups, which according to Article 1.2.1. of the GloBE Model Rules is any Group that includes at least one Entity or PE that is not located in the same jurisdiction in which the Ultimate Parent Entity is a resident. Furthermore, pursuant to Article 2.1.6. GloBE Model Rules, the IIR would only be applied with respect to non-resident CEs. Consequently, purely domestic situations will not lead to a 'Top-up Tax' liability pursuant to the GloBE Model Rules. The extension of GloBE to 'large-scale domestic groups' pursuant to Article 2(1) GloBE-Directive and to domestic CEs pursuant to Articles 5(2), 6(2), 7(2) and 8(2) GloBE-Directive solve these issues by simply including domestic situations within the scope of the directive, which are the '*necessary adjustment*[s]'[2158] the Commission referred to within the Explanatory Memorandum of the initial proposal.

This shows a clear difference in the competence-related argumentation in connection with the ATAD: the ATAD tries to reach compatibility of its CFC rules with the fundamental freedoms by implementation of a substance-based carve-out. Thus, Article 7(1)(a) ATAD implicitly admits its discriminatory character but relies on a ground of justification to discriminate. With respect to the GloBE-Directive, a different approach was taken: the IIR and UTPR should be applied non-discriminatory, which is why concerns about the EU's legal competence to enact a GloBE-Directive find less fertile ground than in the case of the ATAD; but even if one assumes that the GloBE-Directive has discriminatory content, the GloBE-Directive also provides for a substance-based income exclusion in Article 28 GloBE-Directive that might safeguard the GloBE-Directive's compatibility with primary law, although one can doubt whether

2153. *See* previously to the directive proposal, *i.a.*, J. Becker & J. Englisch, *supra* note 469, at 524 et seq.; P.K. Schmidt, *supra* note 2123, at 983 et seq.; L. De Broe & M. Massant, *supra* note 2091, at 86 et seq.; C. Brokelind, *An Overview of Legal Issues Arising from the Implementation in the European Union of the OECD's Pillar One and Pillar Two Blueprint*, 75 Bull. Intl. Taxn. 216 et seq. (2021); J. Englisch, *supra* note 2091, at 136 et seq.; J.F.P. Nogueira, *GloBE and EU Law: Assessing the Compatibility of the OECD's Pillar II Initiative on a Minimum Effective Tax Rate with EU Law and Implementing It within the Internal Market*, 12 WTJ 469 et seq. (2020); J.F.P. Nogueira & Alessandro Turina, *Pillar Two and EU Law, in Global Minimum Taxation?* 283 et seq. (IBFD 2021).

2154. Case C-196/04, *Cadbury Schweppes*, para. 49 and the case law cited therein.

2155. *Ibid.*, paras 55 et seq.

2156. *Ibid.*, paras 60 et seq.

2157. *See* s. 6.2.2.1.

2158. *See* COM(2021)823 final 1.

the current design of the SBIE is in line with the CJEU's *Cadbury Schweppes* jurisprudence.[2159] Nevertheless, the GloBE-Directive, at least in my opinion, fulfils its ambition[2160] and serves to avoid incompatibilities with fundamental freedoms.[2161]

6.1.2.3.4 Legal Certainty by a Common Framework

The Pillar Two Blueprint of October 2020 already refers in several places to the need to provide taxpayers with legal certainty in the implementation of GloBE.[2162] The empty phrase '*legal certainty*' is certainly more of a political dictum than a valid legal argument for or against a regulatory competence of the Union. One may well ask to what extent '*legal certainty*' can influence the functioning of the internal market as presupposed by Article 115 TFEU. Nevertheless, the phrase is found in the preamble of the ATAD, which, after mentioning various arguments relevant in the context of competence, states that '*national implementing measures which follow a common line across the Union would provide taxpayers with legal certainty in that those measures would be compatible with Union law*'[2163] and also in the GloBE-Directive the reference to '*legal certainty*' is chewed again in the recitals: 'Moreover, a common framework [...] would provide taxpayers with *legal certainty* when implementing the rules'[2164] (emphasis added).

Legal certainty means that a person subject to the law can rely on compliance with the law, that it can, without doubt, make out its content and can anticipate the law's execution by the legal authorities. Legal certainty in the legal sense is therefore expressed in the rule of law. *Kelsen* already describes legal certainty as an ideal that can only be '*approximately realised*' in the abundance of legal norms due to the fact that law is subject to interpretation, and each provision could be interpreted in various different ways. Thus, according to *Kelsen*, there is not just one '*correct*' way to interpret a norm. Finally, *Kelsen* concludes that the one correct interpretation of law is merely a '*fiction that case law uses to maintain the ideal of legal certainty*' (translation by the author).[2165]

If one transfers this doctrine to the underlying legal problem, it can be stated that the internal market is also based on law and requires its observance. Thus, anyone who invokes legal certainty in the context of Article 115 TFEU must invoke the fact that the

2159. On the design of the SBIE in light of EU law, *see* L. De Broe, *supra* note 1672, at 878–879.
2160. Recital 4 GloBE-Directive (2022/2523).
2161. In detail on potential conflicts between the IIR and the UTPR and the fundamental freedoms, *see* s. 6.2.2.
2162. Among numerous references throughout the report, the phrase '*tax certainty*' is found in Chapter 10 on the implementation of GloBE, where explicit reference is made to 'to effective co-ordination and tax certainty', *see Tax Challenges Arising from Digitalisation – Report on Pillar Two Blueprint*, para. 668.
2163. Recital 2 ATAD.
2164. Last sentence of recital 4 GloBE-Directive (2022/2523), but also *see* recital 26.
2165. '*Rechtswissenschaftliche Interpretation muss auf das sorgfältigste die Fiktion vermeiden, daß eine Rechtsnorm stets nur eine, die "richtige" Deutung zulässt. Das ist eine Fiktion, deren sich die traditionelle Jurisprudenz zur Aufrechterhaltung des Ideals der Rechtssicherheit bedient. Angesichts der Vieldeutigkeit der meisten Rechtsnormen ist dieses Ideal nur annäherungsweise realisierbar*', *see* H. Kelsen, *supra* note 32, at 366–367.

law as it stands is not being observed '*correctly*'. Thus, if legal certainty is put forward as a competence-related argument in tax matters, it must be claimed, while strictly maintaining the fiction that there is only one '*correct*' interpretation of law, that (i) the authorities do not enforce tax laws correctly and/or that (ii) taxpayers do not comply with tax laws. In the broadest sense, it could then be argued that a certain legal act of the Union contributes to the functioning of the internal market because it potentially eliminates differences in interpretation and in enforcement or improves compliance of law among the Member States. Then one could assume that there might be an obstacle to the internal market that could be eliminated by harmonization.

It must be admitted, though, that uniform interpretation and application of the law can be a legitimate goal of harmonization and can undoubtedly contribute to the establishment or functioning of the internal market. Nevertheless, as mentioned above, the CJEU requires a certain intensity for there to be an obstacle to the internal market. In any case, abstract risks of distortions are not sufficient to justify an effect on the functioning of the internal market.[2166] In my opinion, this case law makes it clear that indirect and far-fetched connections with the internal market, like this, is the case with the '*legal certainty*' argument, are in no way sufficient to justify competence under Article 115 TFEU. The invocation of legal certainty, rather, is an empty phrase or, as *Kelsen* puts it, an '*ideal*' that may have political significance.[2167] Nevertheless, from a legal point of view, nothing can be gained from it neither for nor against the existence of the Union's competence. Thus, the references to legal certainty in recitals 4 and 26 of the GloBE-Directive do not contribute to a lawful issuance of the GloBE-Directive.

6.1.2.3.5 Ensure Fair and Effective Taxation

The reference to the '*fairness*' or '*effectiveness*' of taxation has also become part of the classic canon of tax policy argumentation. Such a reference to fairness can also be found in the cover statement of the Pillar Two Blueprint[2168] and is also mentioned in the preamble of the ATAD, which refers to the need to '*restore trust in the fairness of tax systems*'[2169] and to '*ensure fair and effective taxation*';[2170] also in order to underpin Union's competence. Unsurprisingly, also the recitals of the GloBE-Directive recur to '*fairness*' as well as '*effectiveness*' in various places: recital 2 of the proposal refers to the OECD developments '*to ensure that MNEs pay a fair share of tax wherever they operate*',[2171] while recital 3 emphasizes that '*it is essential that Member States effectively*

2166. Case C-58/08, *Vodafone Ltd and others*, para. 32.
2167. The same is true of Kelsen, who explicitly states that the fiction of one single '*correct*' interpretation of law may be politically advantageous, *see* Hans Kelsen, *supra* note 32, at 367.
2168. 'A consensus-based solution comprised of two pillars [...] can not only play an important role to ensure *fairness and equity* in our tax systems and fortify the international tax framework in the face of new and changing business models; it can also help put government finances back on a sustainable footing' (emphasis added), *see Tax Challenges Arising from Digitalisation – Report on Pillar Two Blueprint*, at 10.
2169. Recital 1 of the ATAD.
2170. Recital 2 of the *Ibid.*
2171. Recital 2 GloBE-Directive (2022/2523).

implement their commitment to achieve a global minimum level of taxation'.[2172] Furthermore, also recital 11 refers to the concept of '*fairness*' as it is the goal '*of the global minimum tax reform* [to achieve] [...] *fair tax competition amongst jurisdictions*'.[2173] Finally, recital 25 states that the Member States need to implement penalties to ensure proper enforcement of the global minimum tax as this would be necessary for the '*effectiveness and fairness of the global tax reform*'.[2174] First of all, it should be noted that '*fairness*' and '*effectiveness*' are independent arguments. They are, therefore, to be examined separately.

The term '*fairness*' is inherently connected to the concept of '*justice*'.[2175] The demand for fair taxation is thus a demand for just taxation. As *Staringer* cogently notes, in the context of the Union's authority to enact the ATAD, the question of the meaning of justice is, if at all, difficult to grasp from a legal perspective. The question of the meaning of justice was ultimately pursued not only by *Kelsen* but also by important philosophers from antiquity.[2176] In his monograph entitled '*What is Justice?*' (in German 'Was ist Gerechtigkeit?') published in 1953, *Kelsen* admits on the last page to be aware that he has not answered the question of what justice means, but that he is not alone in having failed on this issue and that even the great philosophers of antiquity failed in the defining the concept of '*justice*'.[2177] In the meantime, *Kelsen's* words have not lost any of their relevance. In any case, the feat of providing a satisfying definition of justice has not been achieved in the preamble of the ATAD either, which merely invokes fairness without reasoning, and, also with regard to GloBE, it is questionable whether the Commission succeeded in proving that the current framework of corporate tax lacks justice when issuing the GloBE-Directive. In general, the question arises whether GloBE can contribute at all to more '*justice*' or '*fairness*', whatever is to be understood under both concepts. In this context, one could, for example, ask the question whether it is 'just' (or 'fair') that an 'MNE-Group' generating less than EUR 750 million in sales is likely not to be affected by GloBE while 'MNE Groups' above this threshold will be. Similar questions arise in all components of scope or possible carve-outs of GloBE, and it is obvious that there can be no right answer to any of these questions.

As a matter of fact, the terms '*fairness*' and '*justice*' are political mantras without legal character. Nevertheless, these ideas are not alien to many legal systems and find certain expressions in the Union's legal order. From the perspective of the rule of law, the concept of '*fairness*' or '*justice*' is implied in the principle of equality, which is strongly settled within the EU's legal order: according to Article 20 Charter of

2172. Recital 3 *Ibid.*
2173. Recital 11 *Ibid.*
2174. Recital 25 *Ibid.*
2175. Also *see* C. Staringer, *supra* note 2097, at 8–10.
2176. Comprehensively, *see* the references provided by *ibid.*, at 8–9.
2177. '*Was ist Gerechtigkeit? Nun, an ihrem Ende, bin ich mir wohl bewußt, diese Frage nicht beantwortet zu haben. Meine Entschuldigung ist, daß ich in dieser Hinsicht in bester Gesellschaft bin. Es wäre mehr als anmaßend, meine Leser glauben zu machen, mir könnte gelingen, was die größten Denker verfehlt haben*', H. Kelsen, *Was ist Gerechtigkeit?* 43 (Franz Deuticke 1953).

Fundamental Rights of the European Union (CFR),[2178] everyone is equal before the law. The CFR is part of primary law[2179] and binds[2180] the Union legislature.[2181] When discussing the use of Article 115 TFEU, one could indeed argue that there is undoubtedly a link between equality and the internal market. This is already evident in the fundamental freedoms, which explicitly prohibit different treatment of cross-border situations. Thus, if it is possible to actually prove unequal treatment or blatant distortions of competition brought about by different tax systems, it would not be inconceivable to prove sort of an equality argument, like the creation of a 'level playing field',[2182] for the existence of at least an improvement of the conditions for the functioning of the internal market by the adoption of a GloBE-Directive.[2183] Could one then justify the use of Article 115 TFEU by the Council to adopt the GloBE-Directive on the grounds that such a Directive is improving the functioning of the internal market by establishing '*equality*'?

Such an argument can only be successful if there are objective reasons and if there is evidence which supports action. However, evidence in that regard proves to be extremely difficult.[2184] Indeed, there are empirical analyses of the impacts of BEPS[2185] and resulting welfare losses as well as on the possible impact of Pillar Two,[2186] but with wide ranges, natural caveats, and only a few directly related to the EU.[2187] Thus, it is hardly possible to actually evidence that an implementation of GloBE through a directive could create a 'more' 'level playing field' or that a GloBE-Directive would achieve more equality within the internal market. In addition, reference should again be made to the case law of the ECJ, according to which mere indirect influences like findings of disparities between domestic rules or abstract risks of infringements of

2178. *See* the latest consolidated version, Charter of Fundamental Rights of the European Union, OJ (391–407).
2179. Article 6(1) TEU.
2180. According to Art. 51(1) CFR, the Charter is addressed to the institutions of the EU.
2181. Comprehensively on the complex relation of primary and secondary law, *see* R. Szudoczky, *supra* note 260, at 93 et seq.
2182. Also *see* Bizioli and Reimer who also *see* the '*common denominator*' of current existing direct tax harmonization in '*the adjustment of single national tax territories to one "level playing field"*', *see* G. Bizioli & E. Reimer, *Equality, Ability to Pay and Neutrality, in Research Handbook on European Union Taxation Law* 73 (C. Panayi et al., eds, Edward Elgar Publishing 2020).
2183. Finally, according to the case law, the invocation of Art. 115 TFEU is only possible if the respective measures adopted '*improve the conditions for the establishment or functioning of the internal market*', *see, i.a.*, Case C-491/01, *British American Tobacco*, para. 60; Case C-58/08, *Vodafone Ltd and others*, para. 32.
2184. On the lack of sufficient empirical evidence for the 'unfairness' of current corporate tax laws, *see* comprehensively C. Staringer, *supra* note 2097, at 9–10.
2185. OECD/G20, *Base Erosion and Profit Shifting Project: Measuring and Monitoring BEPS, Action 11: 2015 Final Report* (OECD 5 Oct. 2015), https://www.oecd-ilibrary.org/docserver/9789264241343-en.pdf?expires=1639170582&id=id&accname=ocid177428&checksum=7A07A98101DE9DF951A3E8F601D7FBFC (last visited 10 Dec. 2021).
2186. *Economic Impact Assessment*.
2187. For a comprehensive study on the impact of BEPS on the EU, *see, i.a.*, M. T. Álvarez-Martínez et al., *How Large is the Corporate Tax Base Erosion and Profit Shifting? A General Equilibrium Approach*, Economic Systems Research (24 Feb. 2021). For comprehensive reference on empirical studies on BEPS relating to minimum taxation, *see* J. Becker & J. Englisch, *supra* note 469, at 485–486.

Union law or inappreciable distortions do not justify a reliance on internal market competences.[2188] For these reasons, in the author's opinion, the *'fairness'* debate is not helpful to the question of Union competence. Rather, it blocks the view of much more promising and viable legal arguments, like the prevention of legal fragmentation or ensuring compatibility with EU law. The potential impact of *'equality'* again, as is the case with regard to *'legal certainty'*, is not sufficient to justify a perceptible obstacle to the internal market, which needs to be removed. The claim of *'fairness'* cannot contribute anything to the discussion on whether the Union has competence to enact a GloBE-Directive or not.[2189]

Reference to the *'effectiveness of taxation'* also comes with similar complexities. What is the content of *'effectiveness'*? Does the term refer to the effectiveness of the tax in an economic context or to the effectiveness of the collection of tax? If one takes the former perspective, one could argue that taxes do not contribute to the internal market by their very nature; on the contrary, they rather create obstacles to it and are always associated with deadweight losses from a macroeconomic perspective.[2190] However, the latter perspective of effectiveness is also not a promising argument in favour of a Union's competence: effective collection of income taxes, whatever this is supposed to mean, only benefits the Member States[2191] and does not contribute to the *'establishment or functioning'* of the internal market as required by Article 115 TFEU. In this respect, the appeal to the *'effectiveness of taxation'* also seems not to be a useful argument for the discussion of EU competence regarding the GloBE-Directive.

6.1.2.3.6 Tackling Tax Avoidance, Tax Abuse and Aggressive Tax Planning

Preventing tax avoidance and abuse is closely related to tax *'fairness'* and was probably the main motive for the enactment of ATAD. However, while ATAD is strongly committed to fighting tax avoidance, abuse, and aggressive tax planning,[2192] references to those concepts in the Pillar Two Blueprint do exist, but infrequently.[2193] This is remarkable in that the BEPS discussion to date has constantly emphasized the need to tackle avoidance, abuse and aggressive tax planning. However, the missing link is simply explained by the fact that GloBE goes far beyond these political claims: the introduction of a global minimum tax system simply makes the use of artificial arrangements and aggressive tax planning unattractive. Even if it were possible to shift profits earned in high-tax countries and traditional market states to low-tax jurisdictions, the respective profits would probably be captured by the GloBE Rules and

2188. *See, i.a.*, Case C-376/98, *Tobacco Advertising*, paras 84 and 106; Case C-380/03, *Tobacco Advertising II*, para. 37; Case C-58/08, *Vodafone Ltd and others*, para. 32.
2189. In the same direction and very convincing, *see* C. Staringer, *supra* note 2097, at 9–10.
2190. In the same vein, *see* R. Ismer, *Abuse of Law as a General Principle of European Union (Tax) Law, in A Guide to the ATAD* 84 (Werner Haslehner et al., eds, Edward Elgar Publishing 2020).
2191. *See, i.a.*, W. Haslehner, *supra* note 2102, at 40.
2192. Recitals 2 and 3 of the ATAD.
2193. It is true that the search terms 'avoidance', 'abuse' and 'tax planning' can be found. A general reference in connection to the purpose of GloBE, however, is completely absent, *see Tax Challenges Arising from Digitalisation – Report on Pillar Two Blueprint*.

channelled up to at least the minimum tax rate. The incentive for avoidance, abuse and aggressive tax planning is, thus, limited at least to a certain minimum.[2194] Although the fight against tax avoidance, abuse and aggressive tax planning is not a direct objective of GloBE, these concepts are undoubtedly inherent in the global minimum tax initiative, and also the GloBE-Directive refers to them at least indirectly in the recitals: '*While it is necessary to ensure that tax avoidance practices are discouraged, adverse impacts on smaller MNEs in the internal market should be avoided.*'[2195] Thus, the Commission sees the objective of the GloBE initiative as being the prevention of tax avoidance. At the same time, the revenue threshold of EUR 750 million is justified by stating that small companies should not be additionally burdened. This statement also contains, admittedly only implicitly, that there is a lower risk of tax avoidance below this threshold. Evidence for this is lacking, as expected.

There is widespread agreement that it is difficult to capture concepts like tax avoidance, abuse, or aggressive tax planning[2196] by legal methodology and the rule of law.[2197] None of the terms has a uniform meaning, and each of them depends on subjective views. Nevertheless, the preamble of the ATAD tries to leave no doubt that all three terms are directly related to the internal market:[2198] First of all, it is stipulated that '[i]*t is essential for the good functioning of the internal market, as a minimum, Member States* [...] *take action to discourage tax avoidance practices and ensure fair and effective taxation*'.[2199] Only in the next recital, probably in order to lend weight to the matter, the ATAD emphasizes the necessity '*to lay down rules in order to strengthen a level of protection against aggressive tax planning in the internal market*'.[2200] When comparing these statements to the definition of the internal market in Article 26 TFEU and, in particular, its second paragraph, which is clearly tied to fundamental freedoms,[2201] it is difficult to see a connection between the internal market and tax avoidance, abuse and tax planning, respectively.[2202] The only way to include avoidance, abuse and tax planning in the traditional internal market would be to prove that there would be a significant disruption of the internal market in terms of distortion of competition: in the internal market, the 'faithful' taxpayer should in no way be placed in a worse position than the 'unfaithful' one. This reasoning has also been adopted by recital 7 of the GloBE-Directive when it demands that '*adverse impacts on smaller MNEs*' caused by anti-avoidance measures '*should be avoided*'.[2203] This again reveals

2194. Although GloBE does not put an end to tax competition, *see* s. 4.5.6.
2195. Recital 7 GloBE-Directive (2022/2523).
2196. On the conceptual vagueness of 'aggressive tax planning', *see* Michael Lang, '*Aggressive Steuerplanung' – eine Analyse der Empfehlung der Europäischen Kommission*, 2 SWI 13, 62 et seq. (2013).
2197. C. Staringer, *supra* note 2097, at 14.
2198. Also *see* Gianluigi Bizioli, *supra* note 2031, at 169.
2199. Recital 2 ATAD.
2200. Recital 3 *Ibid.*
2201. J. Englisch, *Wettbewerbsgleichheit im grenzüberschreitenden Handel* 220 (Mohr Siebeck 2008); C. Tietje, *supra* note 2041, para. 82; Gianluigi Bizioli, *supra* note 2031, at 171; R.A. Achleitner & V. Bendlinger, *supra* note 2024, at 3; V. Bendlinger, *supra* note 258, at 14.
2202. Also *see* C. Staringer, *supra* note 2097, at 11–12; comprehensively also W. Haslehner, *supra* note 2102, at 40.
2203. Recital 7 GloBE-Directive (2022/2523).

the obvious connection to the discussion of tax fairness previously mentioned: the '*small*' and '*well-behaved*' taxpayer should be excluded from the global minimum tax.

Even sceptical voices have conceded that such a competition-distorting component of avoidance or abuse could conceivably create the presupposed link to the internal market to lawfully apply Article 115 TFEU.[2204] However, when is there a distortion of competition that might '*directly affect*' the internal market as required by Article 115 TFEU? It is difficult to provide evidence in that respect. If one aimed to bring evidence for a distortion, this would require specific empirical data, which is difficult to collect and has not yet been provided to a sufficient extent, neither in the course of the adoption of ATAD nor with regard to the GloBE-Directive. Nevertheless, it is questionable whether the EU legislature is required to provide any evidence of such a '*direct affect*' at all. Rather, AG Kokott concluded with respect to the '*direct affect*' criterion that '*the determination of whether or not such an effect is present will to a large extent fall within the discretion of the legislature alone.*[2205] So can the EU legislature simply refer to concepts like tax avoidance, abuse and aggressive tax planning without providing arguments in that regard?

Based on a traditional understanding of the internal market in terms of fundamental freedoms, it seems difficult to reconcile the policy objectives of combating tax avoidance, abuse, or aggressive tax planning with the objectives of the internal market. Nevertheless, the legal concept of the EU's internal market seems to have moved away from this traditional concept of liberalization based on fundamental freedoms. In the literature, two main reasons are given for this shift:[2206] first, although the legislative bodies of the EU are also bound by fundamental freedoms, they are free to refine the scope of application of the internal market to a certain extent through secondary legislation.[2207] Eventually, it has been shown in the past that the CJEU is much more lenient in examining the compatibility of EU legal acts with primary law than in the case of national legal acts.[2208] The Union legislature, therefore, has, albeit limited, leeway to reshape the internal market.[2209] Second, the ECJ has postulated that it is not permissible to abusively invoke EU law,[2210] that prohibition of abuse is a general

---

2204. C. Staringer, *supra* note 2097, at 9–10.
2205. Case C-122/15, *C*, para. 52.
2206. *See* W. Haslehner, *supra* note 2102, at 40.
2207. *Ibid.*
2208. The ECJ, e.g., notes that legal acts of the EU '*are in principle presumed to be lawful and accordingly produce legal effects, even if they tainted by irregularities, until such time as they are annulled of withdrawn*', *see* Case C-137/92 P, *Commission v. BASF and others*, op. 48. Also *see* Case C-245/92 P, *Chemie Linz GmbH v. Commission*, para. 93; Case C-475/01, *Commission v. Hellenic Republic (Excise duty on alcohol)*, para. 18.
2209. W. Haslehner, *supra* note 2102, at 40. In detail, *see* s. 6.2.1.2.
2210. *See* the landmark decisions Case C-33/74, *Johannes Henricus Maria van Binsbergen v. Bestuur van de Bedijfsvereniging voor de Metallnijverheid*, paras 10–13 in which the ECJ denied the application of the freedom to provide services to a Dutch lawyer, who solely became resident of Belgium to escape Dutch professional law and Case C-110/99, *Emsland-Stärke GmbH v. Hauptzollamt Hamburg-Jonas*, paras 46 et seq. where the court denied relief in the context of export of agricultural products.

principle of Union law, which is also relevant for VAT[2211] and which has primary law character;[2212] and finally, the court further held that this general principle must also be observed in the field of direct taxation[2213].[2214] Consequently, the implementation of anti-abuse rules by secondary legislation would be a mere realization of the objectives of Union law and, thus, also of the internal market. Consequently, the GloBE-Directive could claim to strengthen the internal market against tax avoidance, abuse and aggressive tax planning.

For good reason, the revised view of the internal market has been criticized, and some argue that it is unconvincing.[2215] The original telos of the internal market is, as already stated, inevitably linked to the fundamental freedoms,[2216] which undoubtedly also bind the EU's legislative bodies.[2217] It is problematic to place barely tangible concepts, such as the avoidance of abuse, as an overriding principle above the primary law concept of the internal market.[2218] If the abolition of tax avoidance or aggressive tax planning is to be considered as a competence-related argument for the GloBE-Directive, an attempt should rather be made to demonstrate the actual positive impact of the GloBE-Directive on the internal market. In any case, the author is of the opinion that general references to tax avoidance, abuse and aggressive tax planning should not be considered valid arguments for the existence of an EU competence under Article 115 TFEU, neither for the GloBE-Directive nor any other legal act enacted by the EU.

2211. *See* the ECJ's decision in *Halifax*, where it was held that the '*principle of abusive practices also applies to the sphere of VAT*', *see* Case C-255/02, *Halifax plx v. Commissioners of Customs & Excise*, para. 70.

2212. Finally, *see* the ECJ's decision in *Cussens*, in which the Court finally addresses the legal character of the general principle of prohibition of (tax) abuse with regard to VAT: '*It is thus apparent that that principle is not of the same nature as the rights and advantages to which it applies. The principle that abusive practices are prohibited* [...] *thus displays the general, comprehensive character which is naturally inherent in the general principles of EU law*', *see* Case C-251/16, *Edward Cussens and others v. T.G. Brosnan*, paras 30–31.

2213. *See* the famous decisions in *Danish Beneficial Ownership Cases*, where the Court rejected that taxpayers can rely on the Parent Subsidiary Directive and the Interest and Royalty Directive in an abusive manner, *see* Joined Cases Joined Cases C-116/16 and C-117/16, *Skatteministeriet v. T Danmark*, paras 68 et seq. and; Joined Cases Joined Cases C-115/16, C-118/16, C-119/16 C-299/16, *N Luxembourg 1 v. Skatteministeriet*, paras 95 et seq..

2214. In detail and comprehensively on the abuse of law as a general principle of EU law in the context of direct taxation and the ATAD, *see* I. Lazarov & S. Govind, *supra* note 2064, at 857–859; Roland Ismer, *supra* note 2190, at 66–85 and W. Haslehner, *supra* note 2102, at 40.

2215. Gianluigi Bizioli, *supra* note 2031, at 169 et seq. Also critical with regard to abuse as a general principle of EU law, *see* Roland Ismer, *supra* note 2190, at 84. However, there are also very notable dissenting voices, *see, i.a.*, Joachim Englisch, *supra* note 2091, at 136; W. Haslehner, *supra* note 2102, at 40.

2216. Article 26(2) TFEU, on this perspective of the internal market, *see* Gianluigi Bizioli, *supra* note 2031, at 171; C. Tietje, *supra* note 2041, para. 82; R.A. Achleitner & V. Bendlinger, *supra* note 2024, at 3; V. Bendlinger, *supra* note 258, at 14.

2217. R. Szudoczky, *supra* note 260, at 93 et seq.; L. De Broe & M. Massant, *supra* note 2091, at 94–95.

2218. Also very sceptical, *see, i.a.*, A.M. Jiménez, *Towards a Homogeneous Theory of Abuse in EU (Direct) Tax Law*, 66 Bull. Intl. Taxn. 291–292 (2012); D. Leczykiewicz, *Prohibition of Abusive Practices as a 'General Principle' of EU Law*, 56 Common Market Law Review 741 (2019) DOI: 10.54648/cola2019053. For further reference on the state of the literature and criticism, *see* Roland Ismer, *supra* note 2190, at 67–68.

6.1.2.3.7 *Setting a Limit to Tax Competition by Establishing a Minimum Tax Rate*

Finally, one argument remains to be discussed when it comes to the use of internal market competence with regard to minimum taxation. Recital 2 of the GloBE-Directive refers to GloBE's aim '*to put a floor on competition over corporate tax rates through the establishment of a global minimum level of taxation. By removing a substantial part of the advantages of shifting profits to jurisdictions with no or very low taxation, the global minimum tax reform will level the playing field for businesses worldwide and allow jurisdictions to better protect their bases*'.[2219] Recital 5 then relates these goals specifically to the Union, where it states: '*It is necessary to lay down rules in order to establish an efficient and coherent framework for the global minimum level of taxation at Union level*'.[2220] This obviously raises interesting questions, whether the setting of a minimum tax level itself could be seen as a contribution to the functioning of the internal market as required by Article 115 TFEU. Can the GloBE-Directive eliminate distortions of competition by targeting low taxation and does the GloBE-Directive create the 'level playing field' that the internal market is striving for?

Comparing the GloBE-Directive with past ambitious harmonization initiatives of the Commission with regard to taxation, such as the Common Consolidated Corporate Tax Base (CCCTB), GloBE clearly outshines previous legislative visions of the Commission: for the first time, the EU succeeded in adopting a legal act in the area of direct taxation that contains a minimum corporate tax rate and, in addition, a uniform basis for the determination of taxable profits.[2221] The former, in particular, is remarkable in that the Commission has regularly[2222] emphasized in the past that the choice of tax rate is an essential sovereign interest of the Member States and that the Member States should not be taken their sovereignty to choose the level of corporate tax they levy.[2223]

2219. Recital 2 GloBE-Directive (2022/2523).
2220. Recital 5 *Ibid.*
2221. V. Bendlinger, *supra* note 258, at 19.
2222. This does not mean, however, that the setting of a minimum tax rate under EU law in the area of corporate income tax has not already been considered: for example, the Ruding Committee noted in 1992 that '*wide differences in tax regimes*' remain within the Community and that '[s]*ome of these differences distort the functioning of the internal market both for goods and for capital, and it is unlikely they will be reduced significantly through independent action by Member States*', *see Report of the Committee of Independent Experts on Company Taxation (Ruding Report)* 13 (1992). Finally, the Committee recommended the Community to set '*a minimum level for the statutory corporation tax rate*' *ibid.*, at 202. For further reference on these developments, *see* G. Kofler, *supra* note 1796, at 22.
2223. With that in mind, *see* the Commission's very clear statement in a communication from 2001 with regard to the CCTB: '*Under all approaches Member States would retain the right to set company tax rates which the quantitative analysis found was the most important factor in determining the effective tax rate. This essential sphere of national competence in the area of company taxation would – intentionally – remain untouched and Member States would be left with the autonomy to adjust the most important element for tax revenues. The introduction of single or common tax base could lead to some Member States adapting their tax rates to reflect changes in the tax base, but this would be for each Member State to decide*', *see* European Commission, *Communication from the Commission to the Council, the European Parliament and the Economic and Social Committee – Towards and Internal Market without Tax Obstacles*, COM(2001) 582 final 17 (23 Oct. 2001). Notably, also with respect to the revised CCCTB, the Commission stated in its proportionality considerations that the proposed directive should

Nevertheless, two things need to be put into perspective here: first, the sovereignty to choose the tax rate is not completely taken away from the Member States. Rather, Member States are free – even under the GloBE-Directive – to tax at a rate above 15%.[2224] Second, a minimum tax rate established by EU law is not an entirely new development. Both the VAT-Directive[2225] and the Energy and Electricity Tax Directive[2226] provide for minimum tax rates. Both directives are based on Article 113 TFEU, which is, as well as Article 115 TFEU, an internal market competence and requires '*establishment and the functioning of the internal market and to avoid distortion of competition*'.[2227] The substantive scope of Articles 113 and 115 TFEU, thus, differs only in the fact that the latter does not explicitly address distortions of competition. Nevertheless, doctrine[2228] assumes that the definition of the internal market according to Article 26(2) TFEU, which defines the ambit of Articles 114 and 115 TFEU, necessarily also includes competition aspects,[2229] which is why there is no difference in the content of the substantive scopes of Articles 113 and 115 TFEU. In any case, the competence of the Union to set minimum tax rates in the VAT-Directive or the Energy and Electricity Tax Directive based on Article 113 TFEU, as far as can be seen, has not been questioned so far. Consequently, it cannot be disputed that the minimum tax rates of both directives were obviously considered necessary for the establishment or functioning of the internal market or for the avoidance of distortions of competition, at least if one considers the VAT-Directive to be covered by the legal competence of Article 113 TFEU. Since there is no substantive difference between Articles 113 and 115 TFEU, one could argue that also with regard to the GloBE-Directive that had been based on Article 115 TFEU, there should be no competence-related concerns about setting a minimum corporate tax rate.

Nevertheless, this can be countered by the fact that direct and indirect taxes affect the internal market in different ways. This is already evident from the fact that the TFEU only addresses the latter explicitly in Article 113 TFEU, while direct taxes are not

---

'*not affect Member States' right to set their own corporate tax rates*', *see* Proposal for a Council Directive on a Common Consolidated Tax Base, COM(2016) 685 final 5; in detail and providing for further reference, *see* G. Kofler, *supra* note 1796, at 22.

2224. R.A. Achleitner & V. Bendlinger, *supra* note 2024, at 8.

2225. According to Art. 97 VAT-Directive, the standard rate of VAT may not be less than 15%, while according to Art. 99 VAT-Directive may not be less than 5%.

2226. *See* Annex I, Table A of the Council Directive 2003/96/EC of 27 October 2003 restructuring the Community framework for the taxation of energy products and electricity, OJ (51).

2227. Article 113 TFEU.

2228. According to Art. 3(1) letter b TFEU, the EU shall have exclusive competence to establish the competition rules necessary for the functioning of the internal market. In the doctrine, it is systematically deduced from this that the internal market necessarily also covers competition. On the systematic derivation of the competition component of the internal market, *see* J. Bast, *Art. 26 AEUV [Auftrag zur Gestaltung des Binnenmarkts], in Das Recht der Europäischen Union*, para. 12 (E. Grabitz et al., eds, C.H.Beck 2018); from the perspective of the internal market competences C. Tietje, *supra* note 2041, para. 81.

2229. *See, i.a.*, Case C-58/08, *Vodafone Ltd and others*, para. 76 where the court held: '*In this respect, it must be pointed out that the Community legislature, wishing to maintain competition* [...], *has* [...] *introduced a common approach, in order in particular to contribute to the smooth functioning of the internal market, allowing those operators to act within a single coherent regulatory framework*'.

mentioned at all and can only be subject to harmonization due to the catch-all provision of Article 115 TFEU; and if one considers the actual objective of the GloBE-Directive, namely '*to put a floor on competition over corporate tax rates*',[2230] the question arises, in view of the previous case law of the CJEU on the fundamental freedoms in the field of direct taxes, whether low taxation is at all detrimental to the internal market: in settled case law the court has regularly rejected Member State's appeals to argue that infringements of the fundamental freedoms could be justified by the fact that certain income is taxed at a low level and domestic tax revenue is reduced.[2231] As already explained in detail, the internal market, according to Article 26(2) TFEU, initially only explicitly refers to fundamental freedoms and only implicitly also covers competition aspects.[2232] The fundamental freedoms still remain the primary focus of the internal market competence of Articles 114 and 115 TFEU.[2233] Thus, if one ties the internal market to fundamental freedoms, there is much to suggest that low taxation does not harm the internal market but that measures to address low taxation, as the ECJ has held several times,[2234] indeed might do so; and even if considering that also competition is part of the internal market concept: in light of the cited case law, it seems that the Court put more weight to the fundamental freedoms than to the possible justification of an infringement of the fundamental freedom, because a Member State tried to protect its own tax level. Moreover, it could be argued that limiting tax competition is detrimental to the internal market because a minimum tax level necessarily leads to welfare losses.[2235] For these reasons, it can be questioned whether a minimum level of corporate income tax contributes to the internal market.

However, there are two objections to this view: first, many authors argue that solely tying the internal market to fundamental freedoms is a one-sided perspective.[2236] From a competition perspective, one might indeed invoke that a minimum tax level creates a 'level-playing field': a minimum level of corporate tax does not leave any loopholes for profit shifting to reduce the corporate tax burden and might reduce deadweight losses from a macroeconomic perspective.[2237] Second, even if one still relies on the narrow internal market concept along the fundamental freedoms, GA *Kokott*, in her Opinion in *Allianzgi Fonds*, argues that '*the fight against tax evasion has also become a high priority for the European legislature*'[2238] and notes that '[f]*inally, the second pillar of measures recommended by the OECD to combat tax avoidance also shows that combating tax evasion is to be regarded as one of the overriding reasons in*

2230. Recital 2 GloBE-Directive (2022/2523).
2231. Case C-270/83, *Commission of the European Communities v. French Republic (Avoir Fiscal)*, para. 21; Case C-294/97, *Eurowings Luftverkehrs AG v. Finanzamt Dortmund-Unna*, paras 44–45; Case C-422/01, *Försäkringsaktiebolaget Skandia Ola Ramstedt and Riksskatteverket*, paras 52–53; Case C-196/04, *Cadbury Schweppes*, para. 49.
2232. C. Tietje, *supra* note 2041, at 181.
2233. *Ibid.*, para. 82.
2234. Case C-196/04, *Cadbury Schweppes*.
2235. *See English*, who, however, rejects this argument, *see* J. Englisch, *supra* note 2091, at 136.
2236. C. Tietje, *supra* note 2041, at 181. In the same vein, Joachim Englisch, *supra* note 2091, at 136.
2237. In detail with further reference to the economic perspective of a minimum taxation regime, *see* M. Scherleitner, *supra* note 2023, at 20.
2238. Case C-545/19, *Allianzgi-Fonds Aevn v. Autoridade Tributária e Aduaneira*, para. 95.

the public interest'.[2239] The court did not pick up this line of argument. Nevertheless, one could counter the line of reasoning above that, despite conceivable tensions between GloBE and fundamental freedoms,[2240] any infringements of the freedoms by a system of global minimum taxation could be justified by reasons of public interest. Of course, one can doubt whether this is convincing. However, GA Kokott's opinion shows that there are possible ways to argue that low taxation works against the objectives of the internal market and that limiting tax competition among Member States benefits the internal market. Therefore, in my opinion, setting a minimum tax level is a viable argument that the GloBE-Directive is correctly based on Article 115 TFEU.

6.1.2.3.8 Interim Conclusion

As has been shown, the limits of Article 115 TFEU are not so much of a legal but of a political nature: the requirement of a '*direct effect*' on the '*establishment or functioning of the internal market*' remains vague and its interpretation takes legal methodology to its limits. Already in the founding phase of the Union, it was recognized that hardly any substantive barriers could be identified from Article 115 TFEU's predecessor.[2241] The legislative barrier of the Union rather is the requirement of unanimity voting in council and the limitation to the legislative instrument of directives, which by their very nature leave leeways to domestic legislatures.[2242] Nevertheless, the CJEU has made it clear that harmonization cannot be a self-fulfilling purpose. Rather, the Union legislature must demonstrate that the respective legal act promotes a positive impact on the internal market objective.[2243]

In light of this case law, it makes sense to compare the GloBE-Directive to the ATAD, which had been heavily criticized for not being covered by the EU's legislative competence. The Union's competence to enact the ATAD was very openly questioned for several reasons[2244] and some of the elements of the GloBE-Directive are at least comparable to those of ATAD. It is therefore reasonable to conclude that the considerations in literature made with regard to the ATAD should also be discussed with regard to the EU's competence to issue the GloBE-Directive, and as has been shown, the Commission's proposal also brought into play very similar competence-related arguments as the ATAD:[2245] Both, the GloBE-Directive as well as ATAD try to emphasize that they promote '*fairness*', '*effectiveness*',[2246] '*legal certainty*'[2247] and, last

2239. *Ibid.*, para. 96.
2240. Section 6.2.2.1.
2241. P. Leleux, *supra* note 2027, at 138.
2242. Article 288(3) TFEU.
2243. Case C-376/98, *Tobacco Advertising*, para. 83.
2244. Section 6.1.2.2.4.
2245. Section 6.1.2.3.1.
2246. Section 6.1.2.3.5.
2247. Section 6.1.2.3.4.

but not least, that they tackle '*tax avoidance*', '*tax abuse*' and '*aggressive tax planning*'.[2248] Anyway, none of these political phrases can justify the EU's competence to adopt the GloBE-Directive. It is nearly impossible to prove that these factors would '*likely create obstacles*'[2249] to the internal market and that the GloBE-Directive is '*designed to prevent them*'.[2250] Consequently, these phrases have no legal relevance at all.

Nevertheless, it has become apparent that there are indeed good arguments to believe that the EU was competent to enact the GloBE-Directive and that the competence of the Union to issue the GloBE-Directive probably is easier to argue than was the case with the ATAD for several reasons:

- A key objective of harmonization is to avoid fragmentation, which is, thus, a legitimate goal for the realization of the internal market. Although the ATAD attempted to rely on the avoidance of fragmentation through divergent implementations of the OECD BEPS measures by the Member States, the literature regularly raised the justified objection that the ATAD could not achieve this goal at all because the ATAD is a mere minimum standard and thus even promotes fragmentation.[2251] However, unlike the ATAD, the GloBE-Directive is not subject to this objection due to the fact that the GloBE-Directive is not supposed to set a minimum standard: on the contrary, it is intended that the GloBE-Directive achieves exhaustive harmonization. Consequently, it is reasonable to believe that the GloBE-Directive can legitimately be based on the fact that it '*prevent*[s] *fragmentation of the internal market*'[2252].[2253]
- While the ATAD has created obvious tensions with the fundamental freedoms, the GloBE-Directive deliberately tries to carefully avoid frictions with the fundamental freedoms in the GloBE-Directive. According to the GloBE-Directive, the GloBE Rules also apply to purely domestic situations.[2254] Neither the IIR nor the UTPR are therefore applied in an obviously discriminatory way. Thus, the GloBE-Directive largely (although not entirely, as will be seen in section 6.2.2.1.) frees itself from accusations of working against the '*functioning of the internal market*' required by Article 115 TFEU. In this respect, it is convincing when the GloBE-Directive refers to its goal to achieve '*a common framework, designed to be compatible with the fundamental freedoms*'.[2255] Since the GloBE Model Rules intentionally do not cover purely domestic situations, the GloBE-Directive contributes to the functioning of the internal

2248. Section 6.1.2.3.6.
2249. *See, i.a.*, Case C-350/92, *Spain v. Council*, para. 35.
2250. *See, i.a.*, Case C-376/98, *Tobacco Advertising*, para. 86; Case C-58/08, *Vodafone Ltd and others*, para. 33.
2251. *See, i.a.*, A.P. Dourado, *supra* note 2104, at 442; G. Bizioli, *supra* note 2031, at 171–172; C. Staringer, *supra* note 2097, at 13–14; Werner Haslehner, *supra* note 2024, at 3.3.2.; I. Lazarov & S. Govind, *supra* note 2064, at 860; W. Haslehner, *supra* note 2102, para. 2.18; Alexander Rust, *supra* note 2106, para. 7.51 to 7.53 and 7.61.
2252. Recital 4 GloBE-Directive (2022/2523).
2253. Section 6.1.2.3.2.
2254. Articles 2(1), 5(2), 6(2), 7(2) and 8(2) GloBE-Directive (2022/2523).
2255. Recital 4 *Ibid.*

market by providing preventive protection against possible infringements of EU law by domestic implementation of GloBE by the Member States.[2256]

- Moreover, the GloBE-Directive has another competence-related argument at its disposal on which ATAD could not rely: the GloBE-Directive establishes a uniform minimum corporate income tax rate throughout the EU. Now, one can skeptically object that low taxation has never been accepted by the ECJ as a justification for infringements of fundamental freedoms[2257] and that tax competition between states is conducive and its abolition is *e contrario* detrimental to the internal market objective. However, one can counter that the GloBE-Directive carefully avoids tensions with the fundamental freedom and even if there are discriminatory elements in it, there is, at least according to GA Kokott, the argument that the avoidance of tax evasion could have the character of a justification for overriding reasons in the public interest.[2258] With regard to the tax competition argument within the internal market it can be contested that the GloBE-Directive does not completely abolish tax competition between Member States but only limits it to 15% on 'Excess Profits'.[2259] One could even argue that the establishment of a minimum tax rate is beneficial for the internal market, because market distortions due to different rates are completely eliminated by the GloBE-Directive. This is all the more convincing, since minimum tax rates are not alien to the EU's legal sphere. Both, the VAT-Directive[2260] as well as the Energy and Electricity Tax Directive[2261] are legal acts which have been based on the internal market competence of Article 113 TFEU, without having been subject to critics being not covered by EU's legislative competence. Since Articles 113 and 115 TFEU share the same substantive scope, there is much to suggest that the Union legislature is competent to implement a minimum corporate tax rate.[2262]

Accordingly, the GloBE-Directive has, in my opinion, appropriately been based on Article 115 TFEU. However, irrespective of the fact that the GloBE-Directive had successfully been based on Article 115 TFEU, there is the interesting question, whether GloBE could have been based on different provisions and if there would have been an alternative to unanimity voting. Furthermore, possible alternatives to unanimity voting might still be relevant for GloBE if the EU needs to adopt related legal acts in the future. When it comes to direct taxation, there already is a longstanding discussion whether Article 116 TFEU could be an option for comprehensive tax harmonization. This raises the interesting question, whether the GloBE-Directive could have been based on Article 116 TFEU and whether the latter provision could be used for future legislative acts in the field of GloBE.

2256. Section 6.1.2.3.3.
2257. Case C-270/83, *Avoir Fiscal*, para. 21; Case C-294/97, *Eurowings*, paras 44–45; Case C-422/01, *Skandia*, paras 52–53; Case C-196/04, *Cadbury Schweppes*, para. 49.
2258. Case C-545/19, *Allianzgi-Fonds* at 95–96.
2259. *See* already s. 4.5.
2260. VAT-Directive (2006/112/EC).
2261. Energy and Electricity Tax Directive (2003/96/EC).
2262. Section 6.1.2.3.7.

6.1.2.4 *Article 116 TFEU: Could the Union Have Based the GloBE-Directive on Article 116 TFEU?*

6.1.2.4.1 *The Shadowy Existence of Article 116 TFEU and Its Consideration as a Potential 'Nuclear Option' for Future Direct Tax Harmonization*

Since the unanimity requirement of Article 115 TFEU has regularly proved to be a hurdle to the harmonization of direct taxes in the past, it is not surprising that the Commission has considered possible viable alternative legal basis provided by the Treaties. As early as 1997, the EC Economic and Social Committee brought Article 116 TFEU into play as a conceivable basis to enact directives by qualified majority and recommended that the Commission '*should act as soon as possible under*' now Article 116 TFEU.[2263] According to Article 116(1) TFEU, the Commission shall consult a Member State where it '*finds that a difference between the provisions laid down by law, regulation or administrative action in Member States is distorting the conditions of competition in the internal market and that the resultant distortion needs to be eliminated*'. In its second paragraph Article 116 TFEU eventually states that '[i]*f such consultation does not result in an agreement eliminating the distortion in question, the European, Parliament and the Council, acting in accordance with the ordinary legislative procedure, shall issue the necessary directives. Any other appropriate measures provided for in the Treaties may be adopted*'.

The founding treaties already contained, in addition to now Article 115 TFEU, a provision corresponding to today's Article 116 TFEU.[2264] Already its predecessors had always been 'hidden' directly behind what is now Article 115 TFEU and led a shadowy existence beside the other internal market competences. Although the provision finally found its way into the Lisbon Treaty, the Commission only once in 1967 unsuccessfully submitted a proposal for a directive which should be based on Article 116 TFEU.[2265] However, not a single piece of legislation had been finally enacted on the basis of this

2263. *See* Opinion of the Economic and Social Committee on 'Taxation in the European Union—Report on the development of tax systems, OJ s. 3.2.5.; where the Committee held that '[t]*he requirement for unanimity in the council on tax decisions is clearly a barrier to the progress on taxation and the requirements of the internal market*'. Finally the Committee expressed its opinion that the Commission with Art. 101 EC Treaty, now Art. 116 TFEU, had '*the instruments at its disposal*' and recommended its use to the Commission. *See* already n. 2029 in s. 6.1.2.2.1.

2264. C. D. Classen, *Art. 116 (ex-Artikel 96 EGV) [Beseitigung vorhandener Verzerrungen], in Europäisches Unionsrecht*, para. 1 (H. Groeben et al., eds, Nomos 7th ed. 2015).

2265. Commission of the European Coal and Steel Community, the European Economic Community and the European Atomic Energy Community, *First General Report on the Activities of the Communities 1967*, 99 (12 Feb. 1968), where it is held that the Commission submitted a proposal for a directive based on now Art. 116 TFEU on 13 Jun. 1967, since the Commission had addressed a recommendation to Germany concerning a change of domestic turnover-tax law, which had been ignored by Germany. Also *see* P. Collins & M. Hutchings, *Articles 101 and 102 of the EEC Treaty: Completing the Internal Market*, 11 European Law Review 195 (1986); also providing for further reference, *see* M. Nouwen, *supra* note 2023, at 22.

provision.[2266] This also explains why the CJEU never had the opportunity to comprehensively comment on its interpretation.[2267] As early as the mid-1980s, *Everling* already predicted it would be unlikely that the Commission would ever make use of Article 116 TFEU and identified the reasons for the provision's lack of practicability:[2268] Article 116 TFEU is highly open to interpretation[2269] and over all invites non-consenting Member States to challenge an act based on this provision to bring an action for judicial review according to Article 263 TFEU by invoking a lack of its applicability.[2270] Another reason given by the literature for the sparse practical significance of Article 116 TFEU is its factual proximity to the State Aid rules;[2271] and indeed, Article 108 TFEU provides for a much simpler procedure to address national tax related or other monetary related laws, regulations or administrative actions causing distortions of competition,[2272] although the CJEU already emphasized that the Treaty *'makes a clear distinction'* between both instruments.[2273] In any case, the essential difference between State Aid and the market distortion provisions in Articles 116 and 117 TFEU is that the latter do not require the distortion to be selective.[2274]

2266. *See, i.a.*, Claus Dieter Classen, *supra* note 2264, para. 3; C. Tietje, *Art. 116 [Beseitigung vorhandener Verzerrungen]*, in *Das Recht der Europäischen Union*, para. 2 (E. Grabitz et al., eds, C.H. Beck 2018). For further reference, *see* RA. Achleitner & V. Bendlinger, *supra* note 2024, at 10.

2267. Statements of the jurisprudence on Art. 116 TFEU are extremely scarce, nevertheless *see* Case C-6/64, *Costa v. ENEL* at 595; and Case C-6/64, *Flamanio Costa v. ENEL* 608–609. Furthermore the CJEU once held that '*Articles 92 to 102* [today Arts 107 to 117 TFEU] *of the Treaty provide for detailed rules for the abolition of generic distortions resulting from differences between the tax and social security systems of the different Member States whilst taking account of structural difficulties in certain sectors of industry*', *see* Case C-173/73, *Italian Republic v. Commission of the European Communities (Family allowances in the textile industry)*, para. 17. The ECJ has thus *'co-addressed'* the predecessor of Art. 116 TFEU. Also *see* Martijn Nouwen, *supra* note 2023, at 19.

2268. U. Everling, *supra* note 2046, at 231–232. Approvingly also R. Schütze, *supra* note 1822, at 559 (in particular n. 7), who refers to Art. 116 TFEU as a *'practical oblivion'*.

2269. Also *see* M. Hofstätter, *Who is Competent to Issue Measures for the Elimination of Double Taxation within the Community?, in Tax Treaty Law and EC Law* 35 (M. Lang et al., eds, Linde 2007); R. A.Achleitner & V. Bendlinger, *supra* note 2024, at 10; C. D. Classen, *supra* note 2264, para. 3.

2270. On this argument, *see* R. A. Achleitner & V. Bendlinger, *supra* note 2024, at 12. In the same vein J. Englisch, *supra* note 2031, at 61.

2271. On the relation of the prohibition of Arts 107 and 116 TFEU, also with regard to taxes, *see* A. Bartosch, *Die Selektivität der Selektivität – Wie ist es um die Gestaltungsfreiräume der Mitgliedstaaten in der Wirtschaftsförderung bestellt?*, 26 EuZW 101 (2015).

2272. *See, i.a.*, C. D. Classen, *supra* note 2264, paras 33–34; J. Englisch, *supra* note 2031, at 61.

2273. Case C-174/02, *Streekgewest Westelijk Noord-Brabant v. Staatssecretaris van Financiën*, para. 24; Case T-151/11, *Telefónica de España, SA and Telefónica Móviles España, SA v. European Commission*, para. 98. The relationship between Arts 107 et seq TFEU and Arts 116 and 117 TFEU has also been commented in detail by AG *Geelhoed* in his opinion on the *GIL Insurance* case: AG *Gellhoed* considered that a strict distinction must be made between a tax, i.e., an additional burden, and state aid. According to this view distortions caused by taxes should only be addressed, by now Arts 116 and 117 TFEU and precisely not by the prohibition of state aid according to now Arts 107 and 108 TFEU, *see* Case C-308/01, *GIL Insurance Ltd and Others v. Commissioners of Customs & Excise*, para. 77; in detail, also *see* Bartosch, *supra* note 2271, at 101; and R. A. Achleitner & V. Bendlinger, *supra* note 2024, at 12.

2274. M. Nouwen, *The Market Distortion Provisions of Articles 116–117 TFEU: An Alternative Route to Qualified Majority Voting in Tax Matters?*, 49 Intertax, *supra* note 2023, at 25.

Anyway, there is already a long-standing scholarly debate as to whether Article 116 TFEU could be used as a legal basis for the harmonization of taxes in general and direct taxes in particular.[2275] Recent initiatives by the Union institutions have also contributed to a resurrection of the discussion of Article 116 TFEU as an appropriate harmonization basis for direct taxes: in its Communication published on 15 January 2019, the Commission under former President *Jean-Claude Juncker* explicitly expressed to consider Article 116 TFEU as an alternative legal basis for harmonization of taxes by qualified majority voting in the future.[2276] Accompanied by various parliamentary questions and proposals to bring Article 116 TFEU to life for tax harmonization,[2277] this

2275. On the possible suitability of Art. 116 TFEU and its predecessors for the harmonisation of direct taxes, *see, i.a.*, P. Collins & M. Hutchings, *Articles 101 and 102 of the EEC Treaty: Completing the Internal Market*, 11 European Law Review, *supra* note 2265, at 191–199; K. Vogel, *Harmonisierung des Internationalen Steuerrechts in Europa als Alternative zur Harmonisierung des (materiellen) Körperschaftsteuerrechts*, 70 StuW 383–384 (1993); L. Hinnekens, *Compatibility of Bilateral Tax Treaties with European Community Law. The Rules*, 3 EC Tax Review, *supra* note 1800, at 155; Johanna Hey, *Harmonisierung Der Unternehmensbesteuerung in Europa* 81–84 (Otto Schmidt 1997); S. Alber, *European Community Tax Law and Its Development in Light of the Recent Case Law of the European Court of Justice*, 22 Fordham Int'l L. J. 768 (1999); Pasquale Pistone, *The Impact of Community Law on Tax Treaties*, *supra* note 1790, at 59; Matthias Hofstätter, *Who is Competent to Issue Measures for the Elimination of Double Taxation within the Community?*, *in Tax Treaty Law and EC Law*, *supra* note 2269, at 35–36 and 53–55; G. Kofler, *Doppelbesteuerungsabkommen und Europäisches Gemeinschaftsrecht*, *supra* note 1790, at 32 (in particular n. 10) and 300; Franz Leidenmühler, *Art. 116 AEUV*, *in EUV/AEUV*, para. 16 (T. Jäger & K. Stöger eds, Manz 1 Oct. 2018); D.S. Smit, *The Influence of EU Tax Law on the EU Member States' External Relations*, in *EU Tax Law and Policy in the 21st Century* 222 (Werner Haslehner et al., eds, Wolters Kluwer 2017); P.J. Wattel, *Taxation in the Internal Market*, *in Research Handbook of the EU's Internal Market*, *supra* note 1798, at 328–329; G. Kofler, *Entwicklungslinien und Zukunftsfragen des Europäischen Steuerrechts*, *in 100 Jahre Steuerrechtsprechung in Deutschland 1918–2018 – Festschrift für den Bundesfinanzhof Band I*, *supra* note 2025; J. Braunecker, *Digitalsteuer: Endlich angemessene Steuern für Google, Apple, Facebook und Co. in der EU?*, 29 EuZW 629; R. Szudoczky & D. Weber, *Constitutional Foundations: EU Tax Competences; Legal Basis for Tax Integration;Sources and Enactment of EU Tax Law*, *in Terra/Wattel – European Tax Law*, *supra* note 2031, at 21–22; J. Becker & D. Fehling, *Art. 116 AEUV Im Recht Der Direkten Steuern – Rechtliche Und Steuerpolitische Einordnung*, 29 IStR 813–821 (2020); Maria Gesina Marquardsen, *Einstimmigkeit in Steuerfragen – Reformbedarf?* 9–11 (IFST 2020); G. Kofler, *EU Power to Tax: Competences in the Area of Direct Taxation*, *in Research Handbook on European Union Taxation Law*, *supra* note 1796, at 17; Joachim Englisch, *supra* note 2031, at 58–61; P.K. Schmidt, *A General Income Inclusion Rule as a Tool for Improving the International Tax Regime – Challenges Arising from EU Primary Law*, 48 Intertax, *supra* note 2123, at 992; Martijn Nouwen, *supra* note 2023, at 14–28; R. A. Achleitner & V. Bendlinger, *supra* note 2024, at 11 et seq.

2276. *See COM(2019) 8 Final*, at 9, where the Commission held '*Article 116 TFEU has not been used so far, although the Commission is ready to employ it should the specific necessity arise*'.

2277. *See, i.a.*, European Parliament, *Motion for a Resolution – European Parliament Resolution of Fair Taxation in a Digitalised and Globalised Economy: BEPS 2.0, B9-0238/2019*, *supra* note 189, para. 42 in which the European Parliament '[c]*alls on the Commission to explore the possibility of avoiding a legal base requiring unanimity in the Council*'. Also *see* European Parliament Recommendation following the enquiry on money laundering, tax avoidance and tax evasion, OJ para. 187, in which the European Parliament explicitly requests the Commission make use of Art. 116 TFEU with regard to money laundering, tax avoidance and tax evasion. Also recalling on the procedure laid down in Art. 116 TFEU, *see* Opinion of the European Committee of the Regions – Towards a more efficient and democratic decision making in EU tax policy, OJ para. 2; European Parliament resolution of 21 Jan. 2021 on

political intention was once again confirmed by the Commission headed by *Ursula von der Leyen* in mid-2020.[2278] With the planned implementation of the OECD Pillars, this discussion has also again gained momentum in the scholarly debate around corporate tax harmonization within the EU.[2279] Would Article 116 TFEU have been a suitable basis for a GloBE-Directive and might it be an option for future legal acts or amendments of the directive? To properly answer this question, it is necessary to take a closer look at the scope of Article 116 TFEU.

6.1.2.4.2 The Scope of Article 116 TFEU: What Is a 'Distortion' and When Is There a 'Need' for Its Elimination?

Without question it is difficult to establish what might constitute a '*distortion of the conditions of competition in the internal market*' which '*needs to be eliminated*' and when such a distortion is caused by '*provisions laid down by law, regulation or administrative action in Member States*'[2280].[2281] In the past, attempts were often made to derive the scope of Article 116 TFEU by its historical context: the provision's origin goes back to the *Spaak*-Report[2282] published in 1956, which should form the basis for the later Rome Treaty of 1957. The report discussed how a common market within the Member States of the European Coal and Steel Community could be established.[2283] Thus, the report devoted a separate section to 'distortions', drawing a distinction between 'general' and 'specific' ones.[2284] Accordingly, a general distortion exists if it is the result of different cost levels, i.e., due to direct or indirect taxes and social security contributions. In this context, the Committee around *Paul-Henri Spaak* argued that such distortions could not be regulated by legislative harmonization but rather by exchange rate adjustments.[2285] In contrast, according to the *Spaak*-Report, only

reforming the EU list of tax havens, OJ para. 10. For further reference Martijn Nouwen, *supra* note 2023, at 15 (in particular n. 7).

2278. *See COM(2020) 312 Final*, at 2, where the Commission again announced that '*it will explore how to make full use of the provisions of the* [TFEU] [...] *including Article 116 TFEU*'.

2279. *See, i.a.*, R. A. Achleitner & V. Bendlinger, *supra* note 2024, at 9–12; M. Scherleitner, *supra* note 2023, at 32.

2280. Article 116 TFEU.

2281. Among others, *see, i.a.*, U. Everling, *supra* note 2046, at 231–232; J. Hey, *supra* note 2275, at 81; C. D. Classen, *supra* note 2264, para. 3.

2282. Comité Intergouvernemental créé par la conférence de messine, *Rapport des chefs de délégation aux ministres des affaires etrangères* (21 Apr. 1956). The report was only published in French, however, there is an unofficial translation of main parts of the document, *see* Comité Intergouvernemental créé par la conférence de messine, *The Brussels Report on The General Common Market* (June 1956), http://aei.pitt.edu/995/1/Spaak_report.pdf (last visited 27 Nov. 2021).

2283. For an overview of the background and the significance of the *Spaak*-Report, *see, i.a.*, R. Schütze, *European Union Law*, *supra* note 1822, at 12.

2284. *See Spaak-Report*, at 60 et seq., drawing a distinction between '*distorsion générale*' and '*distorsion particulière*'. In detail, also *see* Claus Dieter Classen, *supra* note 2264, paras 14–15.

2285. *Spaak-Report*, at 60. Where it is held that '*the differences between the burdens borne by different economies, for example of public expenditure or social security schemes, do not in themselves distort the conditions of distort, by themselves, the conditions of competition, being normally compensated by the normally offset by the general conditions of trade, in particular the exchange rate*' (translation by the author).

'specific' distortions should be eliminated within the common market by means of approximation of laws.[2286] What is to be understood under an 'specific' distortion was finally addressed by the Commission in several responses to questions of the European Parliament in the 1980s until the early 1990s.[2287] Along the lines of the *Spaak*-Report, the Commission held that such distortions occur, when: '*(a) an industry or part of an industry bears an additional burden – or enjoys an extra advantage – as compared with the average of the economy of the State to which it belongs*' and[2288] when '*(b) no similar burden or advantage occurs in a similar industry or part of an industry in one or more of the other Member States*'[2289].[2290] Thus, based on this understanding, a distortion according to Article 116 TFEU could only occur in the case of very specific benefits or burdens created '*by law, regulation or administrative action*' within a specific Member State, while, moreover, no such benefits or burdens exist in any other Member State.[2291]

The prevailing, and, in the author's opinion, also convincing view in the literature considers this understanding to be antiquated for a number of reasons:[2292] First, there is nothing in the wording of Article 116 TFEU that indicates a distinction between two kinds of 'distortions'. Rather, Article 116 TFEU seems to cover all kinds of possible distortions, irrespective of whether they are of a 'general' or 'specific' manner.[2293] Moreover, this distinction is in itself highly open to interpretation. Second, there is also nothing to suggest that it is a prerequisite of Article 116 TFEU, like held in the *Spaak*-Report and confirmed by the Commission in early times that a distortion occurs also within a specific Member State '*as compared with the average of the economy*' of that State. The wording of Article 116 TFEU certainly also seems to cover distortions which only occur between Member States, but not within a single Member

2286. *See Ibid.*, at 61, where the Committee notes that '[t]*he deliberate and concerted action that is necessary for the functioning of the common market appears to be much more limited to correct or eliminate the effect of specific distortions which favour or disadvantage certain branches of industry*' (translation by the author).
2287. Specifically with respect to tax matters, *see*, *i.a.*, Answer given by Mr Thorn on behalf of the Commission (26 Jul. 1983) to the written question No 2226/80 by Mr Hemmo Muntingh (S – NL) to the Commission of the European Communities (6 Mar. 1981), at p. 2, OJ C 257/1 (1983).Providing for further reference from a tax perspective, *see* M. Nouwen, *supra* note 2023, at 18 (in particular n. 42).
2288. The English version of the document, however, uses the phrase 'or when'. But as *Englisch* correctly recognizes, all other language versions use 'and when'. It must therefore be assumed that the Commission assumed a cumulative connection of both elements and that the 'or when' is a mistake in translation, *see* J. Englisch, *supra* note 2031, at 59.
2289. Supplementary answer given by Mr Thorn on behalf of the Commission (26 July 1983) to the written question No 2226/80 by Mr Hemmo Muntingh (S – NL) to the Commission of the European Communities (6 Mar. 1981), at p. 2, OJ C 257/1 (1983). For further references on the Commissions position on Art. 116 TFEU in the 1980s and 1990s, *see* Martijn Nouwen, *supra* note 2023, at 18.
2290. In detail on the Commission's position on now Art. 116 TFEU in early times, *see* K. Vogel, *supra* note 2275, at 383–384; Joachim Englisch, *supra* note 2031, at 59.
2291. Comprehensively, *see* C. D. Classen, *supra* note 2264, para. 15.
2292. In detail *Ibid.*, para. 20; J. Englisch, *supra* note 2031, at 59; M. Nouwen, *supra* note 2023, at 18.
2293. In the same vein J. Hey, *supra* note 2275, at 83; C. D. Classen, *supra* note 2264, para. 19.

State.[2294] Third, at least within the Euro zone, it is no longer possible to combat 'general' distortions by adjusting exchange rates and even within the Member States not part of the Euro zone, the option to adjust exchange rates is very limited.[2295] For these reasons, many authors argue for a less restrictive interpretation of Article 116 TFEU;[2296] and also the above-cited initiatives by the Commission indicate that the Commission itself may also have rejected this outdated understanding.[2297] But what then is the scope of Article 116 TFEU?

Not only the wording of Article 116 TFEU but also the systemic context of the internal market competences in Article 113 to 116 TFEU show that the scope of Article 116 TFEU must be narrower compared the ambit(s) of Article 113, 114 and 115 TFEU.[2298] The character of a 'distortion' must undoubtedly be more severe than an '[e]*ffect on the establishment or functioning of the internal market*' as required by Article 115 TFEU, for example.[2299] Nevertheless, Article 116 TFEU is neither *lex specialis*[2300] compared to the other internal market competences nor does it supersede

2294. J. Englisch, *supra* note 2031, at 59.
2295. Comprehensively on this argument, *see Ibid.*
2296. *Ibid.*, at 59 et seq.
2297. However, in 2019 the former Commissioner Pierre Moscovici held that '*Article 116 TFEU is not a possible legal basis for proposals on tax harmonisation, such as the common consolidated corporate tax base (CCCTB) and the DST*', *see* European Commission, Answer given by Mr Moscovici on behalf of the European Commission, E-001797/2019 from 27 June 2019, available at https://www.europarl.europa.eu/doceo/document/E-8-2019-001797-ASW_EN.pdf (accessed 4 Dec. 2021).In a similar manner, *see* European Commission, *Follow up to the European Parliament Non-Legislative Resolution on the European Parliament Report on Financial Crimes, Tax Evasion and Tax Avoidance (TAX3 Report)*, 2018/2121 (INI), paras 66 and 426 (Mar. 2019), https://www.politico.eu/wp-content/uploads/2019/08/A8-0170-2019-EN.pdf?utm_source = POLITICO.EU&utm_campaign = 8eb14ec3bc-EMAIL_CAMPAIGN_2019_08_05_05_36&utm_medium = email&utm_term = 0_10959edeb5-8eb14ec3bc-190490293 (last visited 4 Dec. 2021), where the Commission also stated that '*Article 116 TFEU is not the appropriate means to employ*' for the adoption of the CCTB.
2298. Claus Dieter Classen, *supra* note 2264, para. 21; and C. Tietje, *Art. 116 [Beseitigung vorhandener Verzerrungen], in Das Recht der Europäischen Union, supra* note 2266, para. 15, who argues that the provision's narrow scope is an additional indicator for its practical insignificance.
2299. In the same vein, *see* N. Braun Binder, *supra* note 2014, at 62; M. Nouwen, *supra* note 2023, at 19.
2300. The application of the *lex specialis* rule always requires a normative conflict. This is not the case between Arts 113 to 115 TFEU compared to Art. 116 TFEU. Also denying a competition between Arts 114 and 116 TFEU, *see* Stefan Korte, *Art. 114 (Ex-Art. 95 EGV) [Beschlussfassung; Einzelstaatliche Regelungen; Schutzklausel], in EUV/AEUV*, para. 172 (Christian Calliess & Matthias Ruffert eds, C.H. Beck 6th ed. 2022). Rather, if the prerequisites of Art. 116 TFEU are met, the Commission could also simply initiate a proposal for a legal act based on Arts 113 to 115 TFEU. This may already be deduced from the second sentence of Art. 116(2) TFEU. Also *see* D.-E. Kahn & D. Eisenhut, *Article 116 [Provisions Distorting Competition], in European Union Treaties*, para. 7 (R. Geiger et al., eds, C.H.Beck 2015). The relationship of Art. 116 TFEU to the other internal competences is therefore not a case of application of *lex specialis*. In the same vein *see* S. Korte, *Art. 116 (Ex-Art. 96 EGV) [Reaktion Auf Wettbewerbsverfälschende Vorschriften]*, in *EUV/AEUV*, para. 20 (Christian Calliess & Matthias Ruffert eds, C.H.Beck 6th ed. 2022); N. Braun Binder, *supra* note 2014, at 65. However, the opposing view is wrongly taken by *Nouwen*, who assumes that Art. 116 TFEU indeed constitutes *lex specialis* compared to Arts 113 to 115 TFEU, *see* M. Nouwen, *supra* note 2023, at 15 et seq.

those.[2301] This is made clear above all by the last sentence of Article 116(2) TFEU, according to which '[a]*ny other appropriate measures provided for in the Treaties may be adopted*'.[2302] Already from this regulatory system of the internal market competences, it can be deduced, as also confirmed by the comprehensive analysis of the literature, that Article 116 TFEU presupposes a particularly serious distortion, which must be eliminated in a fast-track procedure. The provision itself makes this clear by stating that the distortion at issue '*needs to be eliminated*' and that the Parliament and the Council '*shall issue the necessary directives*'.[2303] This is also reflected in the procedural peculiarities of Article 116 TFEU: the adoption of a directive is only possible if the Commission has first unsuccessfully consulted the relevant Member State(s) on the elimination of the distortion in question. Thus, the adoption of a directive on the basis of Article 116 TFEU is only permitted, if the respective Member States insist on their national laws, regulations or administrative practices at issue. Only if this is the case, Article 116 TFEU allows the adoption of a directive by qualified majority vote, precisely also against the vote of the Member State(s) causing the distortion.[2304] The procedure of Article 116 TFEU therefore has a certain 'urgent'' character.[2305] Thus, the distortion involved must be so damaging to the internal market that deferral cannot be tolerated and that the distortions as a prerequisite '*needs to be eliminated*'.[2306] From this texting it can also be deduced that indirect distortions or distortions of a merely potential nature cannot fulfil the prerequisites of Article 116 TFEU. For potential distortions this already results from the fact that these are specifically covered by Article 117 TFEU.[2307] Thus, the respective distortion must exist at the time of the adoption of a directive, it must also be observable, have a certain intensity and its elimination must finally be inevitable.[2308] However, the fact that it is up to the Commission, to decide whether a procedure according to Article 116 TFEU is put in place at the first hand, indicates that the Commission also has some leeway with regard to its application and interpretation.[2309]

2301. *See, i.a.*, J. Hey, *supra* note 2275, at 83; C. D. Classen, *supra* note 2264, para. 8; D.-E. Kahn & D. Eisenhut, *supra* note 2300, para. 3; N. Braun Binder, *supra* note 2014, at 65.
2302. C. Tietje, *supra* note 2266, para. 20.
2303. Claus Dieter Classen, *supra* note 2264, para. 26.
2304. This, however, does not mean that a directive according to Art. 116 TFEU could merely be addressed to the Member State causing the distortion at issue. However, the prevailing opinion in literature argues that this is not the case. In detail, *see* J. Englisch, *supra* note 2031, at 60.
2305. C. Tietje, *supra* note 2266, paras 11 and 19.
2306. Some authors therefore even go so far as to understand Art. 116 TFEU in such a way that it even obliges the Commission to act if all conditions are met, *see, i.a.*, C. D. Classen, *supra* note 2264, paras 29 and 32.
2307. Case C-6/64, *Costa v. ENEL* at 608; C. D. Classen, *supra* note 2264, para. 10; C. Tietje, *supra* note 2266, para. 6; J. Englisch, *supra* note 2031, at 58–59.
2308. At a glance, *see* N. Braun Binder, *supra* note 2014, at 63.
2309. Stefan Korte, *supra* note 2300, para. 11; C. Tietje, *supra* note 2266, para. 14; C. D. Classen, *supra* note 2264, para. 25.

6.1.2.4.3 *Would Article 116 TFEU Have Been a Sufficient Legal Basis for the GloBE-Directive and Might It Be a Suitable Option for Future Initiatives?*

The majority of the literature assumes that Article 116 TFEU, at least in principle, can also be used as a legal basis for harmonization in the area of direct taxation, provided that its strict requirements are met.[2310] Indeed, also the ECJ seems to confirm this view.[2311] Accordingly, a directive to implement GloBE may well be based on Article 116 TFEU, provided that '*a difference between the provisions laid down by law, regulation or administrative action in Member States is distorting the conditions of competition in the internal market and that the resultant distortion needs to be eliminated*'. Moreover, the issuance of a directive on the basis of Article 116 TFEU according to its second paragraph is only possible if the Commission unsuccessfully consulted the respective Member State causing the distortion.

The first set of requirements is, thus, that the tax laws of one or more Member States cause a 'distortion of competition' within the internal market. As shown above, this distortion must already exist at the time of the Commission's action and may not be of a merely potential nature. If the Commission were to use Article 116 TFEU as a legal basis for a GloBE-Directive, the question is which '*provisions laid down by*' the Member states lead to '*distortions*' which '*need to be eliminated*' and which might be eliminated by the adoption of the GloBE-Directive? Already the first element of this question leads to tricky ramifications: what kind of '*provisions laid down by*' tax laws might cause distortions which Article 116 TFEU intends to address and are solved by GloBE? Could one argue that the different tax laws might constitute '*provisions*' which cause distortions? Are these the different corporate tax levels in the Member States that make a '*race-to-the-bottom*' possible in the first place and, thus, cause a distortion that the GloBE-Directive could at least mitigate? Or does Article 116 TFEU require that specific provisions and measures in domestic tax laws cause a distortion of competition within the internal market?

As the analysis of the scope of Article 116 TFEU has shown, only the latter interpretation is tenable. It is settled case law that direct tax law falls within the

2310. *See, i.a.*, N. Braun Binder, *supra* note 2014, at 213; J. Englisch, *supra* note 2031, at 58. *See*, however, *Gröpl* who argues that Art. 116 TFEU is no longer applicable to direct taxation since the adoption of the Single European Act, although the provision, according to its origin, should very well also be applicable with respect to tax matters, *see* C. Gröpl, *J. Steuerrecht*, in *Handbuch des EU-Wirtschaftsrechts*, para. 61 (M.A. Dauses & M. Ludwig eds, C.H.Beck 53rd ed. 2021). Also sceptical whether Art. 116 TFEU is applicable with regard to direct taxes, *see* H. Schaumburg, *Kapitel 11 – Steuergesetzgebungskompetenz der Union*, in *Europäisches Steuerrecht*, para. 11.39 (H. Schaumburg & Joachim Englisch eds, Otto Schmidt 2nd ed. 2019). Nevertheless, the ECJ has in the meanwhile clarified, that Art. 116 TFEU undoubtedly also covers tax provisions, *see* Case T-151/11, *Telefónica de España*, para. 98.

2311. *See* Case C-174/02, *Streekgewest*, para. 24, where the Court noted that now Arts 116 and 117 TFEU concern '*distortions which arise from differences between the laws, regulations or administrative provisions of the Member States and, in particular, their tax provisions*'. This decision has also been confirmed in post-Lisbon times, *see* Case T-151/11, *Telefónica de España*, para. 98.

competence of the Member States.[2312] This in particular applies, as the Commission has also emphasized on several occasions,[2313] to the level of the selected tax rates chosen by the Member States.[2314] Furthermore, in *Eurowings*[2315] the CJEU confirmed that the use of a lower tax rate in a different Member State is a right to be protected within the internal market.[2316] These objections, admittedly, do not necessarily hold true with respect to the adoption of minimum tax rates,[2317] which are not entirely alien to the EU legal order.[2318] However, the prevailing and also convincing view in literature holds that tax competition in itself may indeed cause indirect distortion, but does not violate the Treaties.[2319] In order to invoke Article 116 TFEU to implement a system of minimum taxation, it is therefore not sufficient to base a distortion merely on the lack of harmonization of national tax systems or on different tax levels below a certain minimum.[2320] As *Hey*[2321] convincingly concludes, Article 116(2) TFEU can only provide for a legal basis for a directive to adopt very '*selective*' adjustments to the national corporate tax systems of the Member States. Apart from that, even if one rejects a restrictive interpretation along the lines of the *Spaak*-Report, it is not sufficient to consider such indirect distortions caused by a broad domestic legal framework to fulfil the requirements of Article 116 TFEU. Rather, Article 116 TFEU presupposes that specific provisions of domestic law trigger a certain, not merely indirect or potential and, moreover, serious distortion of competition within the internal market. A mere reference to distorting effects in connection with broad grounds like tax avoidance, the

2312. *See* the ECJ's well-known phrases '[...] *direct taxation does not as such fall within the purview of the Community*', from Case C-279/93, *Schumacker*, para. 21, as well as '[...] *direct taxation falls within the competence of Member States* [...]', *see, i.a.*, Case C-80/94, *G. H. E. J. Wielockx v. Inspecteuer der Directe Belasting*, para. 16; Case C-35/98, *Verkooijen*, para. 32; Case C-315/02, *Anneliese Lenz v. Finanzlandesdirektion für Tirol*, para. 19; Case C-513/04, *Kerckhaert Morres*, para. 15.

2313. Thus, also in the course of the discussion on the CCTB, the Commission has regularly emphasized that the choice of corporate tax rate should be left to the Member States, *see COM(2001) 582 Final*, at 17; 2016 Proposal CCTB 5. In detail on the issue of competence with regard to tax rates, *see, i.a.*, G. Kofler, *EU Power to Tax: Competences in the Area of Direct Taxation, in Research Handbook on European Union Taxation Law*, *supra* note 1796, at 22; R. A. Achleitner & V. Bendlinger, *supra* note 2024, at 7–8.

2314. G. Kofler, *supra* note 1796, at 22; R. A. Achleitner & V. Bendlinger, *supra* note 2024, at 7. In detail on the issue of harmonized tax rates, *see* s. 6.1.2.3.7.

2315. '*Any tax advantage resulting for providers of services from the low taxation to which they are subject in the Member State in which they are established cannot be used by another Member State to justify less favourable treatment in tax matters given to recipients of services established in the latter State*', *see* Case C-294/97, *Eurowings*, para. 44.

2316. In this vein, also *see* Philipp Genschel et al., *Speeding up, down the Hill: How the EU Shapes Corporate Tax Competition in the Single Market* 15–16, https://www.econstor.eu/bitstream/10419/27910/1/600427145.PDF (last visited 29 Mar. 2023).

2317. G. Kofler, *supra* note 1796, at 22; R. A. Achleitner & V. Bendlinger, *supra* note 2024, at 7–8.

2318. *See, i.a.*, Art. 97 VAT-Directive and Annex I Table A of Energy and Electricity Tax Directive.

2319. For further reference, *see* J. Kokott, *Das Steuerrecht der Europäischen Union*, paras 162 and 191 (C.H.Beck 2018).

2320. First and foremost M. Nouwen, *supra* note 2023, at 24, who notes '*When a market distortion is too generic in nature, for example, when it is caused by (very) low statutory corporate tax rates, the resulting tax disparity would appear to be too unspecific to be addressed under the market distortion rules and can only be remedied on the legal basis of Article 115 TFEU*'. Holding a similar position, *see* K. Vogel, *supra* note 2275, at 384.

2321. J. Hey, *supra* note 2275, at 84.

abolition of tax competition or fragmentation of laws can, in my opinion, not be qualified as a *'distortion'* within the meaning of Article 116 TFEU.[2322] But what provisions of domestic law could create such a distortion that could be eliminated by the GloBE-Directive?

One could think here, for example, of national tax incentives, such as patent boxes and other beneficial tax regimes,[2323] which make it possible to reduce the income tax burden substantially.[2324] In this case, it would be conceivable, also in the historical context of Article 116 TFEU, to assume such a significant distortion, which could be eliminated by the GloBE-Directive. At this point, however, the second set of requirements of Article 116 TFEU come into play: even if one argues, that a patent-box-regime or any other beneficial tax regime might cause a 'distortion' as required by Article 116 TFEU, however, the question arises as to whether this is a distortion that *'needs to be eliminated'* according to Article 116(1) TFEU and whether the GloBE-Directive is a *'necessary directive'* as required by Article 116(2) TFEU. It is interesting that Article 116 TFEU directly requires that a directive based thereon to be *'necessary'*. Although this wording could be seen as a mere confirmation of the *Principle of Subsidiarity* in Article 5(3) TFEU which will also be addressed below,[2325] there is much to suggest that a legal act can only be based on Article 116 TFEU to the extent that the legal act is necessary to eliminate the distortion. Thus, staying with the example of a patent-box-regime, the introduction of a Union-wide minimum taxation along the lines of GloBE would probably not be *'necessary'* to eliminate the distortion caused by these *'provisions'*. Rather, a directive in this example could only be based on Article 116 TFEU to the extent that it achieves the elimination of the patent-box regime. If the scope of Article 116 TFEU would not be limited to the *'necessary'*, the respective procedures provided for in Article 113 or 115 TFEU, both requiring unanimity, could simply be circumvented by first identifying a specific distortion, which would then open the scope of Article 116 TFEU to harmonize a much broader area of law by qualified majority.[2326] This is, in the author's opinion, also confirmed by the last sentence of Article 116(2) TFEU, according to which the Commission may also use any other appropriate legal basis to adopt a measure to eliminate the distortion:[2327] If any measure is implemented via a directive,

2322. Also *see* M. Nouwen, *supra* note 2023, at 24.
2323. *Nouwen* also discusses the applicability of Art. 116 TFEU in the context of the planned introduction of a special *Group interest box regime* in the Netherlands in 2007. According to *Nouwen*, the regime should be designed in such a way as to circumvent selectivity under state aid rules and also the Commission agreed that this regime did not violate EU's state aid provisions. Indeed, the question whether the *Dutch Group interest box regime* could have been tackled by the Commission by the proceedings in Arts 116 and 117 TFEU was initially raised by the Dutch government, however, the Commission has not taken any action. The author finally concludes, that it is at least conceivable that the Commission could combat such regimes in the future by using the market distortion rules under Arts 116 and 117 TFEU, *see Ibid.*, at 25 et seq.
2324. *See* the Recommendation of the European Parliament, which in its para. 10 advises the Commission to make use of the procedure laid down in Art. 116 TFEU, while also referring, *i.a.*, to patent box regimes, *see* Recommendation OJ C 369/132 paras 53 and 57.
2325. On the *Principle of Subsidiarity*, *see* s. 6.1.2.5.
2326. A similar position is also held by M. Nouwen, *supra* note 2023, at 24.
2327. D.-E. Kahn & D. Eisenhut, *supra* note 2300, para. 3.

which goes beyond the scope of Article 116 TFEU, the Commission should base the directive on the respective Treaty provision different from Article 116 TFEU. Thus, it is unlikely that the GloBE-Directive could have been based on Article 116. Finally, the GloBE-Directive as adopted, goes far beyond the elimination of qualified distortions as presupposed by Article 116 TFEU.

Nonetheless, things could be different if Member States decide to move forward with the implementation of global tax deal beyond the pattern of the GloBE Model Rules. In general, as *Englisch* describes, Member States could intentionally introduce distortive laws in order to allow the Commission to act on the basis of Article 116 TFEU if one or more Member States are of the opinion that a Union-wide extension or amendment of GloBE would be desirable.[2328] The Commission could then consult the relevant Member States, which finally deliberately refuse to drop their national rules in order to help the legislative procedure under Article 116 TFEU to become applicable. Thus, artificial distortions caused by national provisions could be created by Member States, and if those distortions also '*need to be eliminated*', it could indeed be argued that a directive is '*necessary*' to tackle these. But even then, one could counter that the need relates precisely only to the elimination of this distortion caused by the respective Member State. Non-consenting Member States could, thus, argue that any measure based on Article 116 TFEU could simply have required the respective Member States, causing the distortions to abolish its laws. In any case, the idea that individual Member States could intentionally open the scope of application of Article 116 TFEU is, admittedly, fascinating. However, it would then still depend to a large extent on the Commission to pick up on the distortion and ultimately take the initiative for a directive. Finally, also the political limits posed by Article 116 TFEU would still remain, and the risk of an action of judicial review by non-consenting Member States would be considerable.

As a result, the previously asked question of whether Article 116 TFEU could have been a suitable basis for the GloBE-Directive or future extensions or amendments of the global tax deal must, therefore, be denied for the reasons just put forward. Even if the Commission and the Member States undoubtedly have considerable leeway in interpreting the term '*distortion*' in Article 116 TFEU,[2329] the provision's wording and context form its limits; and the adoption of GloBE-related legal acts based on this provision would likely exceed this limit. However, it would also be inadvisable to base a legal act on Article 116 TFEU from a political perspective: as has been shown, legal methods of interpretation are pushed to their limits by the extremely vague scope of Article 116 TFEU. Article 116 TFEU's advantage of a qualified majority decision could therefore be detrimental: as raised at the outset, it is very likely that outvoted Member States would challenge the choice of legal basis and invoke that the act based on Article 116 TFEU is invalid.[2330] Since the ECJ has never directly commented on Article 116 TFEU or its predecessors, there is also no indication of how the Court might interpret

2328. Comprehensively, *see* J. Englisch, *supra* note 2031, at 16.
2329. Stefan Korte, *supra* note 2300, para. 11; C. Tietje, *supra* note 2266, para. 14; C. D. Classen, *supra* note 2264, para. 25.
2330. Drawing the same conclusion, *see* R. A. Achleitner & V. Bendlinger, *supra* note 2024, at 13.

the provision from a current perspective. Furthermore, *Nouwen* adds another perspective: the qualified majority could also become a stumbling block, as Member States that agree in principle could be reluctant to approve a directive on the basis of Article 116 TFEU for fear of themselves becoming the subject of a further procedure under Article 116 TFEU at some point in the future.[2331] For these reasons, there is much to suggest that future initiatives in the direct tax area should not be based on Article 116 TFEU.

6.1.2.5 *The Principles of Subsidiarity and Proportionality as Obstacles for the GloBE-Directive?*

The preceding sections have now addressed the question of whether the Union adopted the GloBE-Directive in accordance with the *Principle of Conferral*. As already explained in detail, Article 115 TFEU has been correctly chosen as the legal basis for the GloBE-Directive,[2332] and Article 116 TFEU, although unlikely, would not have been completely precluded.[2333] However, this is not the end of the story. The Treaties also impose constitutional limits on the Union in terms of whether and to what extent it may actually '*use*' an existing competence conferred on it by the Treaties: according to the second sentence of Article 5(1) TEU, the Union may only make '*use*' of a competence conferred on it if its action complies with the requirements of the *Principle of Subsidiarity*'[2334] and *Proportionality*,[2335] Both principles are intended to serve as constitutional guardians of the legislative autonomy of the Member States and give the CJEU jurisdiction to rule on compliance with these principles.[2336]

Since the Lisbon Treaties, special rules for the application of the *Principles of Subsidiarity* and *Proportionality* are laid down in Protocol Nr 2 of the TFEU. Article 5 of Protocol Nr 2 of the TFEU requires draft legislative acts to be '*justified with regard to the principles of subsidiarity and proportionality*' and should '*contain a detailed statement making it possible to appraise compliance*' with those principles. The Commission has fulfilled this obligation in the GloBE-Directive Proposal and accordingly addresses these issues in the Explanatory Memorandum.[2337] Furthermore, the Commission additionally published a Commission Staff Working Document,[2338] which deepened the subsidiarity and proportionality considerations with regard to the GloBE-Directive. A detailed analysis of the arguments put forward by the Commission first requires a look at the theoretical understanding of *Subsidiarity* and *Proportionality* and the corresponding case law of the CJEU.

2331. M. Nouwen, *supra* note 2023, at 26.
2332. *See* already s. 6.1.2.3.
2333. *See* already s. 6.1.2.4.
2334. Article 5(3) TEU.
2335. Article 5(4) TEU.
2336. *See* Art. 263 TFEU. In detail on the Courts jurisdiction with regard to the principle of subsidiarity, *see* P. Craig, *The Lisbon Treaty – Law, Politics, and Treaty Reform* 185 (Oxford 2010).
2337. GloBE-Directive (2022/2523) 2–3.
2338. Commission Staff Working Document - Subsidiarity Grid accompanying the document Proposal for a Council Directive on ensuring a global minimum level of taxation for multinational groups in the EU, SWD (2021) 580 final.

The first point to be discussed is, therefore, the *Principle of Subsidiarity* which is defined in Article 5(3) TFEU as follows: '*Under the principle of subsidiarity, in areas which do not fall within its exclusive competence, the Union shall act only if and in so far as the objectives of the proposed action cannot be sufficiently achieved by the Member States, either at central level or at regional and local level, but can rather, by reason of the scale or effects of the proposed action, be better achieved at Union level.*' Consequently, *Subsidiarity* contains both a negative and a positive component, with both components mutually influencing each other: on the one hand, (i) the Union shall act if the Member States could not sufficiently achieve the targeted objectives on their own (*national insufficiency test*), and (ii) on the other hand, shall not act, where the Member States could do better alone (*comparative efficiency test*).[2339] *Subsidiarity*[2340] is, however, not an invention of the Union legal order but was rather adopted from political theory:[2341] originally, the term subsidiarity originates from the military field and refers to a reserve force that is to go into battle only when it turns out that the troops fighting at the front cannot achieve victory on their own.[2342] In political theory, the term was thus adopted to express that a certain community should act in its unified strength but without abolishing the diversity of its Members.[2343] This understanding also indicates the purpose of the subsidiarity principle under the current constitutional framework of the EU: the Maastricht Treaty codified the already previously recognized unwritten principle[2344] to reflect the desire of Member States to preserve their legislative autonomy vis-à-vis the Union. The *Principle of Subsidiarity* should, thus, become, as *Schütze* describes, '*a political and judicial safeguard of federalism*'.[2345] Nevertheless, the role of *Subsidiarity* has fallen far short of expectations,[2346] not least because of the generous case law of the CJEU, which was supposed to give the Union institutions a wide margin of discretion:[2347] The Court held on the principle of subsidiarity that '[o]*nce the Council has found that it is necessary* [...] *to harmonise the conditions*' in a certain area of law, '*achievement of that objective* [meant is the objective of the

2339. R. Schütze, *supra* note 1992, at 90.
2340. The term is derived from the Latin word '*subsidium*' which could be translated roughly as '*assistance from the background*', *see* Christian Calliess, *Subsidiaritäts- und Solidaritätsprinzip in der Europäischen Union* 25 (Nomos 2nd ed. 1999); also *see* R. Schütze, *supra* note 1822, at 257.
2341. Comprehensively on the history and the theoretical development of 'subsidiarity', *see* C. Calliess, *supra* note 2340, at 25 et seq.
2342. *Ibid.*, at 25.
2343. *See Ibid.*; R. Schütze, *supra* note 1992, at 90.
2344. Before the Maastricht Treaty, However, the existence and legal character of the principle of subsidiarity was quite controversial. In detail D. Cass, *The Word that Saves Maastricht? The Principle of Subsidiarity and the Division of Powers within the European Community*, 29 Common Market Law Review 1112 et seq. (1992) DOI: 10.54648/cola1992064; C. Calliess, *supra* note 2340, at 35 et seq.
2345. *See* the headings of R. Schütze, *supra* note 1822, at 258–265; R. Schütze, *supra* note 1992, at 91 et seq.
2346. For a comprehensive analysis, *see* N. Bernard, *The Future of European Economic Law in the Light of the Principle of Subsidiarity*, 33 Common Market Law Review 664–666 (1996) DOI: 10.54648/cola1996038.
2347. *See, i.a.*, Case C-377/98, *Kingdom of the Netherlands v. European Parliament and Council (Directive on legal protection of biotechnical inventions)*, para. 32; Case C-491/01, *British American Tobacco*, paras 180–185.

respective legal act[2348]] *necessarily presupposes* [EU]-*wide action*'.[2349] The CJEU, therefore, interprets *Subsidiarity* in a tautological way:[2350] If the Union legislature intends to harmonize an area of law, Union-wide action is required, and, thus, the Union could better achieve harmonization than the individual Member States. Thus, the mere will of an EU institution to harmonize a particular area of law seems sufficient to meet the requirements of *Subsidiarity*. In view of this case law, it is not surprising that, although many Member States' governments severally tried to invoke the plea of *Subsidiarity*:[2351] to date, not a single appeal has been successful.[2352] For this reason, the *Principle of Subsidiary* in the literature has been accused of actually being a '*subsidiary principle of EU law*'.[2353] Its lax application by the CJEU and the EU's institutions has always been subject to extensive political and scholarly debate.[2354]

In contrast to *Subsidiarity*, *Proportionality* is not a question of whether the Union or, better, the Member States legislate but whether the Union's legislation does not go beyond what is necessary to achieve the objectives of a given legislative act. According to Article 5(4) TFEU, '*the content and form of Union action shall not exceed what is necessary to achieve the objectives of the Treaties*'. The *Proportionality* test, therefore, already implicitly presupposes compliance with *Subsidiarity*. It is inherent that both principles are closely related, and a clear demarcation is sometimes difficult.[2355] Not least in *British American Tobacco*,[2356] the CJEU examined the intensity of a Union act under subsidiarity, which then raises the question of what scope for *Proportionality* remains at all, even though the CJEU has made a clear distinction in other cases.[2357] But

2348. This also becomes clear from subsequent case law of the ECJ, *see, i.a.*, Case C-377/98, *Netherlands v. European Parliament (Directive on legal protection of biotechnical inventions)*, para. 32, where the Court made the following statement: '*The objective by the directive [...] could not be achieved by action taken by the Member States alone*'.
2349. Case C-84/94, *United Kingdom v. Council (working time directive)*, para. 47.
2350. *See* R. Schütze, *EU Competences: Existence and Exercise*, *supra* note 1992, at 92; R. Schütze, *supra* note 1822, at 263.
2351. *See, i.a.*, Case C-58/08, *Vodafone Ltd and others*; Case C-491/01, *British American Tobacco*; Case C-377/98, *Netherlands v. European Parliament (Directive on legal protection of biotechnical inventions)*; Case C-84/94, *United Kingdom v. Council (working time directive)*.
2352. R. Szudoczky, *supra* note 260, at 101.
2353. *See* R. Schütze, *supra* note 1992, at 91; R. Schütze, *supra* note 1822, at 258.
2354. Fundamental to the concept of *Subsidiarity* under the Maastricht Treaty, *see, i.a.*, D. Cass, *supra* note 2344, at 1107–1136; G.A. Berman, *Taking Subsidiarity Seriously: Federalism in the European Community and the United States*, 94 Col. L. Rev. 331–456 (1994); N. Bernard, *supra* note 2346, at 633–666; G. Davies, *Subsidiarity: The Wrong Idea, in the Wrong Place, at the Wrong Time*, 43 Common Market Law Review 63–84 (2006) DOI: 10.54648/cola2005083; X. Groussot & Sanja Bogojevic, *Subsidiarity as a Procedural Safeguard of Federalism*, in *The Question of Competence in the European Union* 234–252 (Loic Azoulai ed., Oxford 2014). The selection of literature listed here is, of course, by no means exhaustive.
2355. Also *see Schütze*, who convincingly notes that '*the "whether" and "how" of the specific action are inherently linked together*', *see* R. Schütze, *supra* note 1822, at 265. In the same vein W. Haslehner, *supra* note 2102, at 41.
2356. In para. 184 of the judgement, the Court notes that '*the intensity of the action undertaken by the [EU] in this instance was also in keeping with the requirements of the principle of subsidiarity in that* [...] *it did not go beyond what was necessary to achieve the objective pursued*'. Consequently, the Court examined proportionality as part of subsidiarity, *see* Case C-491/01, *British American Tobacco* at 184.
2357. The ECJ clearly tested both principles separately, *i.a.*, in Case C-58/08, *Vodafone Ltd and others* at 51 et seq. and 72 et seq.; Joined Cases C-154/04 and C-155/04, *Alliance for Natural*

anyway, the clear distinction between the *Subsidiarity* and the *Proportionality*-test is rather theoretical: the CJEU is also extremely generous with regard to *Proportionality* and only assumes an infringement if a legal act is '*manifestly inappropriate in terms of the objective which the competent institution is seeking to pursue*'.[2358] Furthermore, the Court adds that '*the criterion to be applied is not whether the measure adopted by the legislature was the only one or the best one possible but whether it was manifestly inappropriate*'[2359].[2360] Thus, the CJEU applies a similarly low standard of review to the *Proportionality*-test as it does with respect to *Subsidiarity*.[2361]

Finally, the question arises whether the GloBE-Directive meets the requirements of *Subsidiarity* and *Proportionality*. Since the GloBE-Directive is based on Article 115 TFEU, which is a shared competence pursuant to Article 4(2)(a) TFEU,[2362] there can be no doubt that the GloBE-Directive must comply with the requirements of *Subsidiarity*.[2363] If one considers the regulatory content of the GloBE-Directive, the Commission submitted good reasons for such a set of rules to be better implemented throughout the Union: the objective of GloBE is to implement a global system of minimum taxation, and, therefore, the objective of the GloBE-Directive is undoubtedly to implement such a system across the Union under a common framework. Thus, the Commission convincingly stated that '[t]*he nature of the subject requires a common initiative across the internal market*'.[2364] Furthermore, the Commission put forward that the GloBE rules require a coordinated[2365] application, that the rules primarily apply in cross-border situations,[2366] and that compatibility with the fundamental freedoms needs to be secured.[2367] The number of arguments provided by the Commission in the GloBE-Directive Proposal is certainly far from exhaustive and might indeed be challenged: the objective of the GloBE-Directive is the implementation of a coordinated system of global minimum taxation along the lines of the OECD Model Rules.[2368] However, all Member States, besides Cyprus, are Members of the IF as well, and the IF plans to find a '*common approach*'. None of the IF Member States is obliged to implement GloBE, but

Health and Nutri-Link Ltd, paras 99 et seq. and 108 et seq.; Case C-491/01, *British American Tobacco*, paras 112 et seq and 173 et seq.

2358. Case C-189/01, *Jippes*, para. 82.
2359. *Ibid.*, para. 83.
2360. Also *see* Case C-491/01, *British American Tobacco*, para. 123; Joined Cases C-154/04 and C-155/04, *Alliance for Natural Health*, para. 52; Case C-58/08, *Vodafone Ltd and others*, para. 52.
2361. R. Schütze, *European Union Law*, *supra* note 1822, at 264.
2362. Already *see* s. 6.1.2.1. and 6.1.2.2.2. Also *see* L.. De Broe & M Massant, *supra* note 2091, at 94.
2363. Explicitly with regard to Art. 114 TFEU, *see* Case C-491/01, *British American Tobacco*, para. 179; Case C-58/08, *Vodafone Ltd and others*, para. 75. However, this case law is likely to apply equally to Art. 115 TFEU, *see* G. Kofler, *supra* note 1796, at 28. Also *see* C. Calliess, *supra* note 2340, at 129–130. Although there is no case law on the *Subsidiarity Principle* with respect to Art. 116 TFEU, the prevailing opinion in the literature is that subsidiarity is also relevant for Art. 116 TFEU, *see* R. A. Achleitner & V. Bendlinger, *supra* note 2024, at 11. However, the conditions of the *Subsidiarity Principle* will always be met, *see* below.
2364. *See* COM(2021)823 final 2.
2365. *Ibid.*
2366. *Ibid.*
2367. *Ibid.*
2368. *See* Recital 6 GloBE-Directive (2022/2523).

if an IF Member State decides to do so, there is, at least, a certain political obligation to align the domestic implementation of GloBE with the OECD Model Rules.[2369] One could therefore argue that the objectives of the GloBE-Directive could have been achieved by domestic legislation of the Member States as well and that the IF already had reached a certain degree of harmonization of GloBE.[2370] So does the GloBE-Directive meet the national sufficiency test of Article 5(3) TFEU?

Indeed, this is a valid argument to state that the GloBE-Directive might not meet the *Subsidiarity Principle*, which is why the Commission explicitly addressed this issue in the Explanatory Memorandum in the GloBE-Directive Proposal: '[T]*he OECD Model Rules are 'a common approach', so it should be important to have one set of uniform rules and a common minimum level of protection in the internal market*'.[2371] This reasoning is obviously circular: the OECD Model Rules obviously constitute a '*set of uniform rules*', and the '*common approach*' could indeed be seen as a kind of legal alignment. Since the CJEU itself follows the same kind of circulation, when the Court states that the mere motive of harmonization is sufficient to meet the *Subsidiarity* requirement, there can be no doubt that the Court would accept this argument.[2372] On the other hand, if one reads the Commission's considerations in an overall context, the Commission did indeed present good arguments that could mitigate the concerns just described without having to rely on a tautology: first, one can still argue that OECD materials are only soft law and presumably leave room for implementation. Second, within the Union, there is a need to ensure compatibility with the fundamental freedoms, and as already analysed with regard to Article 115 TFEU, this indeed is a valid point to state that the EU can better achieves this goal than the Member States if they would implement GloBE unilaterally. In addition, a further argument can be gained from the overall context: even if the Member States would implement GloBE strongly in line with the OECD Model Rules, there still might be the risk of double or multiple taxation of profits, e.g., if one Member State does not recognize the GloBE Rules of another Member State. In general, the Model Rules can by no means exclude conflicts of qualification. A uniform framework ensures, at least within the Union, that this framework is uniformly applied and, in the event of a dispute, uniformly interpreted by the CJEU.

Besides these substantive arguments, also the modalities of the aforementioned competence provisions must be taken into account when examining *Subsidiarity*: since the Commission based the GloBE-Directive on Article 115 TFEU, it should be borne in mind that it had been adopted by unanimous decision of the Council. Consequently, none of the states will be able to successfully argue that the respective directive goes beyond what would have been necessary and that the objectives could have been better achieved at the level of the Member States since every Member State has voted for the adoption of the GloBE-Directive. Which Member State would have agreed to a

2369. *OECD/G20 Statement 8 October*, at 3.
2370. On this argument, also *see* s. 6.1.2.3.2.
2371. *See* COM(2021)823 final 2.
2372. In the same vein, *see* L. De Broe & M. Massant, *supra* note 2091, at 95–96.

directive if it had been convinced that the objectives of this legal act would have been better achieved by domestic legislation?

For good reasons, it is thus argued that if the requirements of Article 115 TFEU are met, the subsidiarity principle is also satisfied.[2373] This consideration would not have applied if the GloBE-Directive were based on Article 116 TFEU, which provides for a qualified majority decision. Nevertheless, the subsidiarity principle would also likely take a back seat in the case of Article 116 TFEU: pursuant to Article 116(2) TFEU, a legal act may only be based on Article 116 TFEU if the consultation by the Commission to eliminate the distortion unilaterally was not successful.[2374] In the case of Article 116 TFEU, too, there is, therefore, much to suggest that the requirements of *Subsidiarity* are already met if Article 116 TFEU is applied correctly.

With regard to *Proportionality*, the Commission, as with *Subsidiarity*, has also been very brief. The Commission put forward only two arguments with regard to *Proportionality*: first, the Commission argued that only large-scale taxpayers of a group turnover with at least EUR 750 million are subject to the GloBE rules. Second, it is submitted that the measures implemented by the GloBE-Directive do not go beyond OECD's GloBE Model Rules, with the exception of measures to ensure compatibility with EU law. Of course, there are counter-arguments to be raised: first of all, it is questionable whether the benchmark for *Proportionality* is the number of covered entities. Rather the question could also be whether the rules for 'MNE Groups' covered by a minimum tax are proportionate. Depending on how broadly one applies the *Proportionality*-test, one would probably arrive at completely different results. With regard to compatibility with EU law, it could also be argued that the GloBE-Directive cannot create any added value in this respect because the Member States would, in any case, be directly bound by the fundamental freedoms to implement GloBE in conformity with EU law. Why should the primary law obligation to guarantee fundamental freedoms not be sufficient in itself? Again, these objections are purely theoretical. As has been shown, in view of the case law of the CJEU to date, the GloBE-Directive could only be accused of violating the *Principle of Proportionality* if it was '*manifestly inappropriate*' for implementing a system of minimum taxation.[2375] However, there can be no doubt that the GloBE-Directive in its current form would pass this test under

2373. Also *see* C.D. Classen, *Art. 115 (ex-Artikel 94 EGV) [Rechtsangleichung; Richtlinien], in Europäisches Unionsrecht*, para. 24 (H. Groeben et al., eds, Nomos 7th ed. 2015); A. Langer, *supra* note 2024, at 182; Stefan Korte, *Art. 115 (Ex-Art. 94 EGV) [Richtlinien Zur Angleichung von Rechtsvorschriften Für Den Binnenmarkt], in EUV/AEUV*, para. 20 (Christian Calliess & Matthias Ruffert eds, C.H.Beck 6th ed. 2022); M. Schröder, *Art. 115 – Richtlinien zur Angleichung gewisser Vorschriften, in EUV/AEUV*, para. 17 (R Streinz ed., C.H.Beck 3rd ed. 2018). *See*, however, *Calliess*, who states that subsidiarity is not automatically inherent in today's Art. 115 TFEU, *see* C. Calliess, *supra* note 2340, at 35–36.

2374. J. Englisch, *supra* note 2031, at 60; R. A. Achleitner & V. Bendlinger, *supra* note 2024, at 11; Stefan Korte, *supra* note 2300, para. 16.

2375. *See* Case C-491/01, *British American Tobacco*, para. 123; Joined Cases C-154/04 and C-155/04, *Alliance for Natural Health*, para. 52; Case C-58/08, *Vodafone Ltd and others*, para. 52. Concluding the same, *see* J. Englisch, *Designing a Harmonized EU-GloBE in Compliance with Fundamental Freedoms*, 30 EC Tax Review, *supra* note 2091, at 136; and L. De Broe & M. Massant, *supra* note 2091, at 96–98, who conclude that the proportionality requirement could be secured primarily with a substance-based carve-out.

the scrutiny of the CJEU. As a result, it is very unlikely that any Member State could successfully invoke that the GloBE-Directive violates the *Principle of Proportionality*.

For all these reasons, the likelihood that the CJEU would declare the GloBE-Directive void due to a violation of the *Principles of Subsidiarity* and *Proportionality* is vanishingly small. Nevertheless, the Commission is, of course, obliged[2376] to base its choice on objective criteria[2377] for each legal act proposed, whether and on what grounds Union action complies with the *Principles of Subsidiarity* and *Proportionality*;[2378] and the Commission has probably explained this sufficiently. In any case, the Commission has done well to base the GloBE-Directive on valid arguments regarding *Subsidiarity* and *Proportionality* from a political standpoint:[2379] Especially in the highly sensitive area of tax law, which touches the core of Member States' sovereignty, the Commission needed to convince the Member States that Union-wide harmonization can better achieve the objective of a global minimum tax than domestic legislation.[2380] In my opinion, the GloBE-Directive meets the requirement set by the CJEU with regard to the *Principles of Subsidiarity* and *Proportionality*.

6.1.2.6 The 'Passerelle Clause' of Article 48(7) TEU: Alternative Approach to Enact or Amend Tax Related Legal Acts by Qualified Majority?

The discussion on *Subsidiarity* and *Proportionality* has already revealed that there are fewer legal than political hurdles in the way of issuing the GloBE-Directive. As has been shown, the internal market competences set almost no substantive limits for the Union legislature.[2381] In contrast, the substantive limits of Article 116 TFEU are likely to be too high to base GloBE-related legal acts on this provision.[2382] After all, once again, the question arises whether the political hurdle of unanimity required by Article 115 TFEU could be overcome. The *Juncker* Commission had once brought up the use of Article

2376. Article 5 Protocol (No 2) on the application of the principles of subsidiarity and proportionality, OJ C 115/206 (2008). In detail on the Protocol No 2 and its content, *see* P. Craig, *supra* note 2336, at 185; G. Kofler, *supra* note 1796, at 30–31.
2377. Case C-58/08, *Vodafone Ltd and others* at 53.
2378. Even if the degree of control by the ECJ in this respect is low, *see* Case C-233/94, *Germany v. European Parliament and Council (Deposit Guarantee Scheme)*, paras 22–29. In detail on the obligation to provide for evidence with regard to the *Principle of Subsidiarity*, *see* R. Schütze, *European Union Law*, *supra* note 1822, at 262.
2379. In general, it is argued that *Subsidiarity* and *Proportionality* should be understood less as a legal hurdle than as a political one, *see*, *i.a.*, G. Davies, *supra* note 2354, at 80; J. Hey, *supra* note 2275, at 99; M. Valta, *Verfassungs- und Abkommensrechtsfragen des Richtlinienentwurfs für eine Steuer auf digitale Dienstleistungen*, 27 IStR 769 (2018).
2380. It is not without reason that comprehensive considerations on the *Subsidiarity Principle* as well as on *Proportionality* can be found in almost all directive preambles in the field of direct tax law, comprehensively and providing for a table listing reasoned opinions and votes by national parliaments with regard to existing directives in direct tax law, *see* G. Kofler, *supra* note 1796, at 31–34.
2381. *See* already s. 6.1.2.2.
2382. *See* already s. 6.1.2.4.3.

48(7) TEU (so-called *Passerelle clause*) for tax matters in 2019 to enable further harmonization of direct taxes.[2383]

According to the second subparagraph of Article 48(7) TEU, the European Council may adopt '*a decision allowing for the adoption of such acts in accordance with the ordinary legislative procedure*', where the TFEU '*provides for legislative acts to be adopted by the Council in accordance with a special legislative procedure*'. Indeed, Article 115 TFEU prescribes just such a special procedure. A legislative act based on Article 115 TFEU could therefore be the subject of proceedings under Article 48(7) TEU. However, according to the third and fourth subparagraphs of Article 48(7) TFEU, the European Council can only adopt such a decision by unanimity after notification of national parliaments. Each national parliament may express concerns, and if a single national parliament does so within a deadline of six months, a decision may not be adopted.[2384] The supposed alternative to unanimity, thus, itself requires unanimity. For this reason, Article 48(7) TEU is unlikely to be a promising instrument for positive integration in the area of direct taxation,[2385] at least from a short-term perspective.[2386] If the Council struggles to unanimously adopt legal acts in the field of direct tax law, as this was the case with respect to the GloBE-Directive,[2387] it is unlikely that both the European Council and the national parliaments could unanimously give their permission to switch to qualified majority voting in the Council. Probably for this reason, contrary to Article 116 TFEU, the '*Passerelle clause*' was no longer considered by the *von der Leyen* Commission in its action plan for tax harmonization even before the GloBE-Directive Proposal had been released[2388].[2389]

6.1.2.7 Interim Conclusion

A new legislative act of the EU in a politically sensitive area, like direct taxation, necessarily raises the question of the Union's competence to enact such a legal act. Consequently, the adoption of the GloBE-Directive establishing a minimum level of corporate tax needs to be tested with regard to Union competence. Since the Union is

2383. '*The most practical way to move from unanimity to qualified majority voting in taxation would be to use the 'Passerelle' clauses in the Treaties. These would allow for a more structured way of moving away from unanimity than the options outlined above*', *see COM(2019) 8 Final*, at 9–10. Finally the Commission directly refers to Art. 48(7) TEU. For a comprehensive analysis of the Commission's communication, *see*, *i.a.*, A.P. Dourado, *The Commission Proposal to Replace Unanimity with a Qualified Majority in the Case of Tax Matters*, 47 Intertax 341–344 (2019) DOI: 10.54648/taxi2019033.
2384. *See* the third subparagraph of Art. 48(7) TEU.
2385. Also sceptical, *see* M. G. Marquardsen, *supra* note 2275, at 34.
2386. For a broader perspective on the '*Passerelle clause*' as a way out of unanimity in tax matters, *see* W. Schön, *supra* note 2030, at 339–341. Thus, *Schön* suggests that qualified majority voting should not be permitted for the enactment but for the subsequent amendment of directives, so that a subsequent adaptation of secondary legislation would be possible, since, after all, the amendment of secondary legislation based on Art. 115 TFEU also requires unanimity. Also referring to Schön in this context, *see* M.G. Marquardsen, *supra* note 2275, at 44–45; R. A. Achleitner & V. Bendlinger, *supra* note 2024, at 9.
2387. *See* s. 3.4.
2388. COM(2020) 312 Final, at 2.
2389. R. A.Achleitner & V. Bendlinger, *supra* note 2024, at 9.

not a sovereign state, it can – according to the *Principle of Conferral* laid down in the first sentence of Article 5(1) TFEU only act '*within the limits of competences conferred upon it by the Member States*'. These limits are defined within the TFEU, which states in which fields of law the EU may adopt legal acts. If a certain area of law is not mentioned within the Treaties, the competence to rule in this field necessarily remains upon the Member States.

Since direct taxes are, contrary to indirect taxes, not explicitly addressed in the Treaties, only the general internal market competences or the residual competence of Article 352 TFEU come into consideration. Since Article 352 TFEU is only available if treaties do not provide the necessary powers, only the internal market competences of Articles 114 to 116 TFEU conceivably provide for the EU's competence to enact legal acts in the field of direct tax law. However, Article 114(2) TFEU explicitly excludes taxes from its scope, which is why only Articles 115 and 116 TFEU remained as conceivable legal basis for the GloBE-Directive. Finally, Article 115 TFEU has served as a legal basis for the GloBE-Directive.

The internal market competences evidently serve the internal market objective as laid down in Article 3(3) TEU. Consequently, the scope of the internal market competences is defined by the definition of the internal market in Article 26 TFEU, which in turn is defined by the fundamental freedoms (Article 26[2] TFEU). Although not explicitly mentioned in Article 26(2) TFEU, the internal market also covers competition. The consequence of this systematic relation between the internal market definition and the internal market competences is obvious: a legal act based on an internal market competence must promote the internal market, which means that it must effectuate the fundamental freedoms or must contribute to the creation or maintenance of a 'level-playing field' within this internal market. Nevertheless, fundamental freedoms remain the main focus of the internal market.[2390]

It goes without further consideration that the internal market concept is a very vague one.[2391] It is, thus, not surprising that legal methodology struggles to define the scope of Article 115 TFEU, which requires '*a direct affect*' on the '*establishment or the functioning*' of the internal market. It is difficult to imagine areas of law that could not affect the internal market at all. As has been shown, the ECJ only once declared a legal act based on an internal market competence void because the Union legislature failed to evidence a contribution to the internal market objective.[2392] However, it has become clear that Article 115 TFEU hardly provides for any material limits, but to a political one, which is the required unanimity voting in Council.[2393]

Nevertheless, there was the adoption of ATAD, which, in 2016, finally raised the question of how far tax harmonization within the internal market can go. Since ATAD poses new burdens to cross-border taxpayers and cross-border tax squarely falls within the scope of fundamental freedoms, it is not surprising that it was questioned whether ATAD could promote the internal market as required by Article 115 TFEU. Since not a

2390. *See* s. 6.1.2.2.2.
2391. *See* s. 6.1.2.2.3.
2392. Case C-376/98, *Tobacco Advertising*.
2393. Section 6.1.2.2.

single Member State brought ATAD to judicial review within the two-month deadline of Article 263(6) TFEU, the competence-related questions with regard to ATAD might still be relevant, as the question of ATAD's validity could still be invoked in the course of Article 267 TFEU, however, remain theoretical ones. The ATAD, thus, confirmed that the Union legislature faces almost only political hurdles. However, the discussion on EU competence is awakening to a new life with the enactment of the GloBE-Directive, which is, at least with respect to competence-related questions, comparable with ATAD in several respects.[2394] Accordingly, the question has been raised whether the EU correctly used Article 115 TFEU to adopt the GloBE-Directive and whether Article 116 TFEU could have served as an alternative basis to avoid the unanimity principle enshrined in Article 115 TFEU.

As has been argued, there are good reasons to believe that the GloBE-Directive has correctly been based on Article 115 TFEU and is, in any case, 'safer' than the ATAD in this respect for three reasons: first, the GloBE-Directive clearly tries to avoid frictions with the fundamental freedoms, by explicitly extending the framework set out in the GloBE Model Rules to purely domestic situations. Second, the GloBE-Directive clearly avoids fragmentation by setting not only a minimum standard but exhaustive harmonization. Third, there is much to suggest that setting a minimum level of tax in itself contributes to the '*functioning of the internal market*'[2395].[2396]

The Commission has based the GloBE-Directive on Article 115 TFEU; nevertheless, the question was raised whether Article 116 TFEU could have served as a legal basis to implement GloBE within the EU. As has been shown, Article 116 TFEU is not an appropriate legal basis because of its high material burdens: Article 116 TFEU requires a legal act to eliminate severe distortions of the internal market.[2397] However, it is impossible to evidence that different levels of tax cause such distortions. Consequently, Article 116 TFEU could not have served as an alternative to the unanimity principle. Rather, the Commission did well not to consider Article 116 TFEU, especially since the likelihood of a successful challenge by outvoted Member States would have been considerable, and the qualified majority decision would probably not have helped a GloBE-Directive to succeed if the Council failed to achieve unanimous consent.[2398]

The same applies to the '*Passerelle clause*' of Article 48(7) TEU, which was brought into play as an alternative way to overcome unanimity. It is true that Article 48(7) TEU allows a decision to adopt legal acts in an ordinary legislative procedure, even if the TFEU only permits the adoption of such an act in a special legislative procedure. The catch, however, is that such a decision requires the approval of national parliaments of all (!) Member States. The supposed alternative to unanimity, thus, itself requires unanimity.[2399] For this reason, the Commission had no other option but to accept the political hurdle of unanimity and to choose Article 115 TFEU as the only existing competence for establishing a system of corporate minimum taxation

2394. *See* s. 6.1.2.3.1.
2395. Article 115 TFEU.
2396. *See* s. 6.1.2.3.
2397. *See* s. 6.1.2.4.2.
2398. *See* s. 6.1.2.4.3.
2399. *See* s. 6.1.2.6.

within the EU along the lines of the global tax deal defined in the OECD's GloBE Model Rules. Finally, with the successful adoption of the GloBE-Directive, the EU has shown that the unanimity hurdle is not insurmountable.

The existence of a competence under the *Principle of Conferral*, however, does not yet mean that the Union may exercise this competence: according to the second sentence of Article 5(1) TFEU, '[t]*he use of Union competences are governed by the principles of subsidiarity and proportionality*', which are defined in Article 5(3) and 5(4) TFEU. Both principles intend to 'safeguard' federalism within the Union. Nevertheless, as has been shown, the case law of the CJEU has reduced both principles to toothless instruments, living a shadow existence within the division of competence between EU and its Member States: regarding *Subsidiarity*, the CJEU held, that '[o]*nce the Council has found that it is necessary* [...] *to harmonise the conditions*' in a certain area of law, '*achievement of that objective necessarily presupposes* [EU]-*wide action*'.[2400] Transposed to the GloBE-Directive, this means that the adoption of the GloBE-Directive can be justified by the fact that the Council decided to implement a system of minimum taxation along the lines of the GloBE Model Rules. Admittedly, this reasoning is a tautology. Nevertheless, one has to face the fact that the CJEU has not once overturned a legal act as being contrary to *Subsidiarity*. The CJEU takes a similar line with regard to the *Proportionality*-test. The CJEU only sees the *Principle of Proportionality* to be violated if the respective legal act is '*manifestly inappropriate in terms of the objective which the competent institution is seeking to pursue*'.[2401] It goes without saying that the GloBE-Directive passes this test. As a result, it has been shown that the GloBE-Directive meets the requirements of *Subsidiarity* and *Proportionality* set by the CJEU.[2402]

6.1.3 External Competence of the EU to Implement GloBE Via International Agreements

6.1.3.1 Overview

Although the Union is not a sovereign state, it nevertheless has legal personality according to Article 47 TFEU, is a subject of public international law[2403] and may, according to Article 216(1) TFEU, also conclude international treaties with third states,[2404] which '*are binding upon the institutions of the Union and on its Member States*'.[2405] Like with its internal competences, however, the Union can only do so within the powers conferred on it by the Treaties.[2406] However, the TFEU does not

2400. *See* Case C-84/94, *United Kingdom v. Council (working time directive)*, para. 47.
2401. *See* Case C-189/01, *Jippes*, para. 82.
2402. Section 6.1.2.5.
2403. P. Craig & G. de Búrca, *supra* note 1815, at 359.
2404. *Ibid.*; W. Haslehner, *supra* note 2102, para. 2.27; G. Kofler, *supra* note 1796, at 35.
2405. Article 216(2) TFEU. Comprehensively, G. Kofler, *supra* note 1796, at 34–38.
2406. Article 5(2) TEU. In detail on the *Principle of Conferral* with regard to external competences, *see* S. Vöneky & B Beylage-Haarmann, *Art. 216 [Vertragsschlusskompetenz], in Das Recht der Europäischen Union*, paras 1–5 (E. Grabitz et al., eds, C.H.Beck 2016).

provide for an explicit external competence with respect to direct taxation.[2407] Nevertheless, this is not the end of the story. The legal framework governing external competences is characterized by significant complexity[2408] and seems to follow entirely own principles:[2409] Already in its famous and not less fundamental decision of *ERTA* in 1971, at a time when the Treaties only provided for a few explicit external competences, the CJEU held that an external competence of the Union '*arises not only from an express conferment by the Treaty* [...] *but may equally flow from other provisions of the Treaty and from measures adopted, within the framework of those provisions, by the Community institutions*'.[2410] The Court thus found that the Treaties provide, besides explicit external competences, also implied external powers of the EU legislature. In terms of the scope of these competences, the Court further held that '*the system of internal Community measures may not* [...] *be separated from that of external relations*'.[2411] Finally, the CJEU concluded that if the Union had already taken legislative measures internally, Member States are precluded from concluding international agreements, which '*may affect those rules or alter their scope*'.[2412] This still-relevant, although in the meantime, codified '*ERTA*-doctrine' had two dimensions:[2413] first, in terms of the scope of the EU's external competence, the EU Treaties contain implied external powers, which, however, depend on the existence and exercise[2414] of the EU's internal competences.[2415] Second, in terms of its effects, such competence might take the Member State's powers to conclude treaties in areas of law where the Union has

2407. However, it is argued in literature, that there might be external competence with regard to the freedom of capital movement in Art. 64(2) TFEU, which could by applied also in the area of direct taxation. *See* D. S. Smit, *The Influence of EU Tax Law on the EU Member States' External Relations, in EU Tax Law and Policy in the 21st Century, supra* note 2275, at 225. In detail, *see* s. 6.1.3.3.1. in particular *supra* note 2573. On the lacking explicit external competence in the area of direct taxation in pre-Lisbon times, *see* P. Pistone, *General Report*, in *The EU and Third Countries: Direct Taxation* 53 (Michael Lang & Pasquale Pistone eds, Linde 2007); R. Lyal, *Note on the External Competence of the European Community in Tax Matters – the Example of the Agreement with Switzerland on the Taxation of Savings*, in *The EU and Third Countries: Direct Taxation* 67 (Michael Lang & Pasquale Pistone eds, Linde 2007).

2408. P. Craig, *supra* note 2336, at 162; P. Koutrakos, *supra* note 1840, at 129; P. Craig & G. de Búrca, *supra* note 1815, at 109.

2409. A. Arena, *Exercise of EU Competences and Pre-Emption of Member States' Powers in the Internal and the External Sphere: Towards 'Grand Unification'?*, 35 Yearbook of European Law, para. 98 (2016); in the same vein S. Strohmayr, *supra* note 2043, at 28; G. Kofler, *supra* note 1796, at 37.

2410. Case C-22/70, *Commission of the European Communities v. Council of the European Communities – European Agreement on Road Transport (ERTA)*, para. 16.

2411. *Ibid.*, para. 19.

2412. *Ibid.*, para. 22.

2413. Comprehensively on *ERTA* and its post-Lisbon impacts, *see, i.a.*, M. Chamon, *Implied Exclusive Powers in the ECJ's Post-Lisbon Jurisprudence: The Continued Development of the ERTA Doctrine*, 55 Common Market Law Review 1101–1142 (2018) DOI: 10.54648/cola2018 094; A. Rosas, *EU External Relations: Exclusive Competence Revisited*, 38 Fordham International Law Review 1084 et seq. (2015).

2414. *See* W. Haslehner, *supra* note 2024, at 3.2. and 3.5.

2415. Sometimes referred to as the '*principle of parallelism of internal and external powers*', *see, i.a.*, P. Craig & G. de Búrca, *supra* note 1815, at 353 and 362. Comprehensively on the relationship between internal and external competence, *see, i.a.*, M. Cremona, *External Relations and External Competence of the European Union, in The Evolution of EU Law* 431–438 (Oxford 3rd ed. 2021).

exercised its internal competence conferred upon it in the Treaties.[2416] In other words, the respective implied powers could be of an exclusive nature.

Many other decisions followed, which shaped and further extended the Union's external competences.[2417] The Lisbon Treaty finally tried to codify the sophisticated case law of the CJEU on the Union's power to conclude treaties in Articles 3(2) and 216 TFEU.[2418] The corresponding procedural rules are provided for in Article 218 TFEU. However, as will be seen shortly, codification has done little to clear the thicket of the Union's external competences.[2419]

The Union's external competence is of particular relevance when it comes to the implementation of GloBE within the EU. GloBE is not a solely intra-European project, and the GloBE-Directive certainly not only concerns intra-European issues: on the contrary, it is one of the major aims of GloBE to establish a global minimum level of taxation. Implementing GloBE along the lines of the GloBE Model Rules primarily affects third-country matters and this with regard to two complementary respects: first, the IIR is intended to ensure that profits earned in third countries by 'MNE Groups' resident within the EU are taxed at a minimum level (inbound minimum taxation). Second, the UTPR, which is a subsidiary of the IIR, also safeguards that outbound payments are taxed at this minimum tax level (outbound minimum taxation). Necessarily, the GloBE-Directive, therefore, not only affects EU-MNEs but, in particular, such 'MNE Groups' which exclusively reside in third states. An effective implementation of those rules, however, also requires an effective coordination of the proposed measures not only among the Member States but also in relation to third states. At times, three different kinds of international agreements related to GloBE have been discussed in this context:

- **Multilateral GloBE Convention (GloBE MLC):** Already in the Pillar Two Blueprint,[2420] the OECD considered that a GloBE MLC in co-existence with the existing global tax treaty network would be desirable. Moreover, also the OECD's Statement in October 2021 teased that '*IF members will consider the merits and possible content of a multilateral convention in order to further ensure co-ordination and consistent implementation of the GloBE rules.*'[2421]
- **Competent Authority Agreements relating to exchange of GloBE information:** In addition, there will also be a '*GloBE Implementation Framework*',

2416. M. Chamon, *supra* note 2413, at 1105–116.
2417. *See, i.a.*, Joined Cases C-3/76, 4/76, 6/76, *Kramer*; *Opinion 1/76 (Draft Agreement establishing a European laying-up fund for inland waterway vessels)* 76; *Opinion 1/94 (WTO)*; *Opinion 2/91 (ILO Convention)* 91; *Opinion 2/92 (OECD)* 92; *Opinion 1/03 (Lugano Convention)*.
2418. I. Govaere, *'Setting the International Scene': EU External Competence and Procedures Post-Lisbon Revisited in the Light of Opinion 1/13*, 52 Common Market Law Review 1278 (2015); G. Kofler, *supra* note 1796, at 35–37; P. Craig & G. de Búrca, *supra* note 1815, at 363.
2419. This view is shared by many authors, *see, i.a.*, P. Koutrakos, *supra* note 1840, at 76, 127 and 129; C. Heber, *Die Kompetenzverteilung im Rahmen der Austrittsverhandlungen nach Art. 50 EUV unter besonderer Berücksichtigung bestehenden Sekundärrechts*, 52 EuR 595 and 604 (2017); I. Govaere, *supra* note 2418, at 1305–1306; M. Klamert, *The Principle of Loyalty in EU Law* 157 and 159 (Oxford 2014).
2420. *Tax Challenges Arising from Digitalisation – Report on Pillar Two Blueprint*, paras 705–708.
2421. *OECD/G20 Statement 8 October*, at 7.

which is intended to ensure procedural coordination for the application of GloBE[2422] and will probably also require agreements under international law. This concerns, in particular, so-called *Qualifying Competent Authority Agreements* on automatic exchange for GloBE-related information among countries[2423] or on simplified reporting obligations.[2424]

- **GloBE Multilateral Instrument (GloBE MLI):** For the treaty-based rules of GloBE (STTR and SOR), a multilateral agreement modelled on the MLI is planned to implement those rules within the comprehensive tax treaty networks among the IF Member States (hereinafter GloBE MLI).[2425] Furthermore, at least in the literature, it has been pointed out that a GloBE MLI might be useful to address potential treaty conflicts between DTCs and GloBE.[2426]

In the following sections, the agreements just listed are collectively referred to as 'GloBE-related agreements'. However, this should not obscure the fact that, at the current stand of this thesis, there is no information available in which form and whether such agreements will be concluded and that these agreements not only differ significantly in their content but also in their role within GloBE's conceptual framework. In any case, it is obvious that a global implementation of GloBE requires multidimensional interrelationships under international law, which admittedly also affects the implementation of GloBE within the EU. The Commission is also aware of these complex ramifications of the GloBE-Directive and potential future GloBE-related agreements and has even explicitly addressed certain kinds of GloBE-related conventions in Article 55 of the GloBE-Directive, according to which the EU '*may conclude agreements with third country jurisdictions* [...] *for simplifying*' certain reporting procedures.

Anyway, the question of the EU's external competence, therefore, arises in several respects: what is the role of the EU in the development process of international agreements related to GloBE? Can the EU be a party to such conventions, or could the EU even conclude GloBE-related agreements on behalf of the Member States? In light of the *ERTA*-doctrine, the possible implementation of a GloBE-Directive also plays a significant role: what impact does the GloBE-Directive take on the Union's external competence in the area of direct taxation? Does the GloBE-Directive establish the EU's competence to conclude GloBE-related agreements, and if so, could such a competence, according to Article 3(2) TFEU, even be an exclusive one? And in further consequence, what does the GloBE-Directive mean for the Member States' competence to conclude bilateral DTCs? The following sections shall be devoted to these questions. However, before these questions can finally be answered, a look at the sophisticated framework of external competences in the TEU and TFEU seems inevitable.

2422. Article 8.1.4. of the *GloBE Model Rules* and the corresponding definition in Chapter 10 of the GloBE Model Rules.
2423. *Ibid.*, at 65.
2424. *See* Art. 55 GloBE-Directive (2022/2523).
2425. *OECD/G20 Statement 8 October*, at 7.
2426. Already *see* s. 5.6.

6.1.3.2 *The Thicket of the Union's External Competences*

6.1.3.2.1 *Article 216 TFEU: The Existence of Union's Competence to Conclude International Treaties*

The conditions under which the Union may conclude international treaties are laid down in Article 216(1) TFEU, which states that the '*Union may conclude an agreement with one or more third countries or international organisations where the Treaties so provide or where the conclusion of an agreement is necessary in order to achieve, within the framework of the Union's policies, one of the objectives referred to in the Treaties, or is provided for in a legally binding Union act or is likely to affect common rules or alter their scope*'. The provision of Article 216 TFEU does not provide the Union with a legal basis per se.[2427] Rather, Article 216 TFEU defines in which cases an external competence of the EU might occur.[2428] For this purpose, Article 216(1) TFEU lists four alternative sources of competence, each of which is essentially based on the pre-Lisbon case law of the CJEU.[2429] Accordingly, the Union may conclude an international treaty, where (i) '*the treaties so provide*', (ii) '*the conclusion is necessary in order to achieve [...] one of the objectives referred to in the Treaties*', or (iii) '*is provided for in a legally binding Union act*' or (iv) '*is likely to affect common rules or alter their scope*'. The first limb is merely a reference to the *Principle of Conferral*[2430] and lacks a separate scope.[2431] The substantive content of Article 216(1) TFEU rather consists of a list of three different situations in which the Treaties provide for implied external powers.[2432]

According to the second limb of Article 216(1) TFEU, the Union has a treaty-making power if this is necessary to achieve the objectives of the Treaties. The provision can thus be understood as a reference to the objectives of the Union set out in Article 3 TEU,[2433] has its roots in the ECJ decision in *Kramer* and was explicitly developed in the CJEU's *Opinion 1/76*:[2434] In *Kramer*, the Court held that the EU had the power to conclude international treaties even in the case, where an internal competence had not yet been exercised, due to the fact, that the respective internal

2427. *See* the statement of GA *Kokott* in her Opinion on *UK v. Council*: '*Article 216(1) TFEU must not be confused with a general conferral of powers on the Union institutions for external action. On the contrary, an external competence can only ever be inferred from that rule in conjunction with the provisions of the Treaties, objectives of the Union, legal acts and rules of Union law mentioned in it*', *see United Kingdom of Great Britain and Northern Ireland v. Council of the European Union* 102. In detail on this issue, *see, i.a.*, M. Cremona, *EU External Competence – Rationales for Exclusivity, in The Division of Competences between the EU and the Member states* 135–136 (Sacha Garben & Inge Govaere eds, Hart Publishing 2017); S. Vöneky & B Beylage-Haarmann, *supra* note 2406, para. 19.
2428. S. Vöneky & B Beylage-Haarmann, *supra* note 2406, para. 5; Marcus Klamert, *Zur Pragmatik der Kompetenzverteilung in der EU*, in *Europarecht und Rechtstheorie* 144 (G. Herzig et al., eds, Verlag Österreich 2017).
2429. G. Kofler, *supra* note 1796, at 35–36.
2430. Article 5(1) and (2) TEU; also *see Ibid.*, at 35.
2431. Concluding the same, C. Heber, *supra* note 2419, at 604.
2432. R. Schütze, *supra* note 1822, at 278; M. Cremona, *supra* note 2415, at 437.
2433. S. Vöneky & B Beylage-Haarmann, *supra* note 2406, para. 9.
2434. Marise Cremona, *supra* note 2415, at 437.

competence, in the case of *Kramer* that was fishery, could only effectively be implemented by also including non-Member States.[2435] The CJEU, therefore, already indirectly appealed to the implicit objectives of the Treaties: the Member States could already be pre-empted from concluding corresponding treaties if the Union has not yet exercised its internal competences.[2436] In even clearer words, the CJEU in *Opinion 1/76* states that '[although] *the internal Community measures are only adopted when the international agreement is concluded and made enforceable* [...] *the power to bind the Community vis-à-vis third countries nevertheless flows by implication from the provisions of the Treaty creating the internal power and in so far as the participation of the Community in the international agreement is* [...] *necessary for the attainment of one of the objectives of the Community*'.[2437] The second limb of Article 216(1) TFEU leans heavily on this wording.[2438] What is different, however, is the fact that the provision only refers to '*objectives referred to in the Treaties*', whereas *Opinion 1/76*, along the lines of the conditions set out in *ERTA*,[2439] requires an internal competence for the existence of an external competence. The wording of Article 216(1) TFEU could, therefore, also be understood as if an external competence of the EU could be derived directly from the objectives mentioned in the Treaties.[2440] However, this understanding would lead to the odd result that the EU's external competences would be much more comprehensive than its internal ones and would probably not be compatible with the *Principle of Conferral*.[2441] In the light of the pre-Lisbon jurisprudence on implied external competences, this interpretation is hardly tenable and, thus, has met with justified criticism in the literature.[2442] For these reasons, the prevailing view is that Article 3 TEU only sets out the objectives of the Union in the abstract, whereas the specific objectives, which the second limb of Article 216(1) TFEU refers to, are to be derived from the specific competences provided for in the Treaties.[2443] It also seems that the CJEU has clarified by now that the second limb is precisely not to be understood as a vague reference to the Union's objectives.[2444] An appeal on the

2435. Joined Cases C-3/76, 4/76, 6/76, *Kramer*, paras 30–33.
2436. Extensively on *Kramer* and *Opinion 1/76* line of case law, *see* E. Stein, *External Relation of the European Community: Structure and Process, in Collected Courses of the Academy of European Law* 147 (European University Institute 1990); P.E. Herzog, *Treaty-Making Power of the European Community Thirty Years (Approximately) after the ERTA Case – And Where Does This Leave the United States*, 30 Syracuse J. Int'l. L. 209–210 (2003); G. V. Puig & C. Darcis, *The Development of European Union Implied External Competence: The Court of Justice and Opinion 1/03, in Anuario Espanol de Derecho Internacional* 513–514 (2009) DOI: 10.15581/010.25.28336; extensively also Panos Koutrakos, *EU International Relations Law, supra* note 1840; M. Cremona, *supra* note 2427, at 134.
2437. *Opinion 1/76 (inland waterways)*, para. 4.
2438. P. Koutrakos, *supra* note 1840, at 126; S. Vöneky & B Beylage-Haarmann, *supra* note 2406, para. 8.
2439. Case C-22/70, *ERTA*, paras 16–22.
2440. R. Schütze, *supra* note 1822, at 278–279; P. Koutrakos, *supra* note 1840, at 126.
2441. Article 5(1) and 5(2) TEU. In detail on the *Principle of Conferral*, *see* already s. 6.1.2.1.
2442. *See* i.a P. Koutrakos, *supra* note 1840, at 126. For further reference, also *see* S. Vöneky & B Beylage-Haarmann, *supra* note 2406, para. 9; C. Heber, *supra* note 2419, at 604.
2443. S. Vöneky & B Beylage-Haarmann, *supra* note 2406, para. 10; C. Heber, *supra* note 2419, at 605.
2444. *See* the following statement in Opinion 1/13: '*In particular, whenever EU law creates for those institutions powers within its internal system for the purpose of attaining a specific objective,*

Treaties' objectives according to the second limb of Article 216(1) TFEU, therefore, also presupposes the existence of an internal competence as was already the case under previous case law. The question of when the conclusion of an international treaty is 'necessary' has finally been addressed by the ECJ in *Opinion 2/15*. The Court held that '*the conclusion of international agreements which contribute*' to the achievement of the Treaties' objectives '*may be classified as necessary*'.[2445] Thus, it seems that the mere '*contribution*' to the objectives of an internal competence is sufficient for the establishment of an external competence of the EU. Where the limit of a 'contribution' lies, however, remains unclear. In any case, the essence of the first limb of Article 216(1) TFEU is simply that the adoption of an internal legal act is not required for the establishment of an external competence if a competence exists internally and a treaty to be concluded by the Union could '*contribute*' to the objectives ('*objectives referred to in the Treaties*') of the respective internal competence.[2446]

The third limb of Article 216(1) TFEU grants the EU an external competence when this is '*provided for in a legally binding Union act*'. The interpretation of this alternative compared to the second limb seems comparatively simple: the legal acts of the Union are listed in Article 288 TFEU,[2447] and if the Member States agree on the adoption of a legal act of secondary law, they are free to confer on the Union the competence to conclude agreements with third countries. But is it really up to the secondary legislature to simply extend its external competences by enacting legal acts and redefine the division of powers between the Union and the Member States contrary to the constitutional framework provided by the Treaties? The doctrine is unanimous that such an interpretation is not sustainable in light of the *Principle of Conferral*.[2448] Many argue that the third limb is the result of a legalistic mistake and that it codifies jurisprudence that does not deal with the existence of an external competence but with its nature (exclusive or shared);[2449] indeed, a look into ECJ's *Opinion 1/94* strongly supports this view. In its conclusions, the Court holds that '[w]*henever the Community has included in its internal legislative acts provisions relating to the treatment of nationals of non-member countries or expressly conferred on its institutions powers to negotiate with non-member countries, it acquires exclusive external competence in the spheres covered by those acts*'.[2450] Obviously, *Opinion 1/94* describes the situation that

---

the EU has authority to undertake international commitments necessary for the attainment of that objective even in the absence of an express provision to that effect [...]. *The last-mentioned possibility is also referred to in Article 216(1) TFEU*', *see Opinion 1/13 (Hague Convention)*, para. 67.

2445. *Opinion 2/15 (Free Trade Agreement Singapore)*, para. 240.

2446. *See* M. Cremona, *supra* note 2415, at 437–438. In a similar manner, *see* C. Heber, *supra* note 2419, at 604–605.

2447. S. Vöneky & B. Beylage-Haarmann, *supra* note 2406, para. 12.

2448. P. Koutrakos, *supra* note 1840, at 127; S. Vöneky & B. Beylage-Haarmann, *supra* note 2406, para. 12; C. Heber, *supra* note 2419, at 605.

2449. *See* the remarks of *Schütze*, who assumes that the third limb '*is likely* [...] *the result of a fundamental confusion within the minds of those drafting*' Art. 216 TFEU, *see* R. Schütze, *supra* note 1822, at 279; also sceptical on the scope of the third limb of Art. 216(1) TFEU, *see* C. Heber, *supra* note 2419, at 605.

2450. *Opinion 1/94 (WTO)*, para. 95. Also *see Opinion 2/92*, para. 33.

the third limb of Article 216(1) TFEU intends to address.[2451] It seems that the drafters of the Lisbon Treaty wanted to address situations in which a legal act of secondary law explicitly empowers the Union to bind the Member States under public international law. In the above-cited paragraph of *Opinion 1/94*, however, the ECJ did not discuss the existence of a Union competence but merely elaborated on the question of whether such a competence was exclusive. Rather, it seems that the Court silently assumed the existence of an external competence of the Union since the question of exclusivity already presupposes the existence of such competence. Like the first limb, the third limb thus lacks scope:[2452] a legal act of secondary law cannot confer external competence on the Union.[2453] Rather, external competence can be derived from the existence of an internal competence, which is conferred to the Union. This already follows from the fact that Article 216(1) TFEU is not a basis for competence per se but only lists situations in which external competence can be derived implicitly from the treaties. As a result, the phrase '*provided for in a legally binding Union act*' is misplaced in Article 216(1) TFEU. Rather, the respective phrase should be ignored for the purposes of Article 216(1) TFEU. The phrase, however, is correctly implemented in Article 3(2) TFEU:[2454] although an express authorization of the Union to conclude international treaties by a legal act of secondary law does not in itself establish the existence of an external competence of the EU, it may influence its nature (*see* in detail section 6.1.3.2.2.).

Finally, according to the fourth and last limb of Article 216(1) TFEU, the Union also has external competence when a conclusion of an international agreement '*is likely to affect common rules or alter their scope*'. The fourth limb of Article 216(1) TFEU consequently codifies the *ERTA*-doctrine, according to which the existence of internal secondary law, enacted on the basis of an internal competence, leads to the establishment of an external competence in the regulatory matter of the corresponding secondary legislation.[2455] The wording mirrors the wording used by the CJEU in *ERTA*[2456] and is furthermore used in Article 3(2) TFEU nearly in the same way.[2457] However, while the fourth limb of Article 216(1) TFEU requires that an international treaty '*is likely to affect*' common rules, the third limb of Article 3(2) TFEU requires that it '*may affect*' these.[2458] This naturally raised the question of whether both provisions are to be interpreted in the same way, and indeed, this question has, at least for some

2451. Panos Koutrakos, *supra* note 1840, at 127–128.
2452. *See also Heber*, who concludes that the existence of an external competence thus is to be determined on the other limbs of Art. 216(1) TFEU, *see* C. Heber, *supra* note 2419, at 605.
2453. S. Vöneky & B Beylage-Haarmann, *supra* note 2406, para. 12.
2454. Also *Heber* notes, that the third limb should not be mentioned in Art. 216(1) TFEU, but in Art. 3(2) TFEU, *see* C. Heber, *supra* note 2419, at 606.
2455. P. Koutrakos, *supra* note 1840, at 127; C. Heber, *supra* note 2419, at 605–606; S. Vöneky & B Beylage-Haarmann, *supra* note 2406, paras 15–17.
2456. *See* Case C-22/70, *ERTA*, para. 22.
2457. *Opinion 1/13 (Hague)*, para. 67; Case C-66/13, *Green Network SpA v. Autorità per l'energia elettriica e il gas*, para. 26.
2458. In detail on this linguistic fuzziness, *see* P. Koutrakos, *supra* note 1840, at 128; P. Eeckhout, *EU External Relations Law* 113 (Oxford EU Law Library 2nd ed. 2011).

time, not been conclusively settled.[2459] Nevertheless, it seems that the CJEU has indeed affirmed that the fourth limb of Article 216(1) TFEU and the third limb of Article 3(2) TFEU are closely related and must therefore be interpreted correspondingly.[2460] Thus the textual difference between both provisions is insignificant. As a result, any competence occurring on the basis of the fourth limb of Article 216(1) TFEU is also necessarily an exclusive one (in detail, *see* section 6.1.3.2.2.).[2461] However, in relation to the fourth limb, one could again question which scope remains beside the second one (*'objectives referred to in the treaties'*): the enactment of secondary law requires an internal competence provided for in the Treaties, and if an international agreement *'is likely to affect'* this secondary law, one could at the same time argue, that a competence of the Union would, thus, be necessary in order to achieve the objectives of the Treaties.[2462] Irrespective of the extent to which the scopes of the individual alternatives overlap, the interpretation of the phrase *'affect common rules or alter their scope'* is difficult to grasp. When does an international agreement concluded by a Member State *'affect'* common rule *'or alter their scope'*? At first, it is worth mentioning that little importance is attached to the term *'alter their scope'* because every change of scope is probably also accompanied by an *'affect'* on the corresponding provisions.[2463] The essential normative content is, therefore, to be drawn from the interpretation of the term *'affect'*. Again, this term cannot be interpreted in isolation from the basis of Article 216(1) TFEU, but only with regard to pre-Lisbon case law and in awareness of the fact that some of this case law did not always clearly distinguish between the existence and nature of external competences.[2464] The essential key points for the interpretation of the term *'affect'* were summarized by the CJEU in its *Opinion 1/03*, where the Court

2459. *See* I. Govaere, *supra* note 2418, at 1289–1291, who points that an identical interpretation *'would seem to be at odds with Opinion 2/91'* because the ECJ clearly distinguished between the existence and the nature of external competence, *see Opinion 2/91 (ILO)*, para. 13.

2460. This becomes particularly clear in Opinion 2/15, were the Court first refers to the fourth limb of Art. 216(1) TFEU and at once holds that '[u]*nder Article 3(2) TFEU, the competence of the European Union to conclude such an agreement is exclusive*', *see Opinion 2/15 (Singapore)*, paras 171–172. The same opinion was already held by A.G. Sharpston: '*Showing that the conclusion of an international agreement 'may affect common rules or alter their scope' automatically satisfies the conditions of the fourth ground under Article 216(1) TFEU and the third ground under Article 3(2) TFEU*', *see Opinion 2/15 (Free Trade Agreement Singapore)*, para. 70. In a similar manner, *see* Case C-600/14, *Federal Republic of Germany v. Council of the European Union (COTIF)*, para. 49. In detail providing for further reference, *see* Marise Cremona, *External Relations and External Competence of the European Union, in The Evolution of EU Law*, *supra* note 2415, at 460; M. Chamon, *supra* note 2413, at 1123.

2461. *See, i.a.*, P. Eeckhout, *supra* note 2458, at 113; S. Vöneky & B. Beylage-Haarmann, *supra* note 2406, para. 17; G. Kofler, *supra* note 1796, at 44; A.C.M. Zaidan, *supra* note 2023, at 278.

2462. R. Schütze, *supra* note 1822, at 279 in particular n. 52.

2463. *See, i.a.*, S. Vöneky & B. Beylage-Haarmann, *supra* note 2406, at 15. The focus of the literature has very soon shifted to the interpretation of the term *'affect'*, *see, i.a.*, M. Chamon, *supra* note 2413, at 1113–1116.

2464. *See, i.a.*, Case C-22/70, *ERTA* at 17–22. Also *see* Koutrakos, who concludes that the fourth limb of Art. 216(1) TFEU *'is what the Court has viewed as the foundation of the Union's exclusive competence'*, *see* P. Koutrakos, *supra* note 1840, at 127; and M. Chamon, *supra* note 2413, at 105; also emphasizing the relevance of pre-Lisbon case law for the interpretation of Art. 3(2) TFEU, *see* M. Klamert, *supra* note 2419, at 150.

finally concludes that the effectiveness of Community law is to be preserved.[2465] Whether an international agreement affects Union law is accordingly to be assessed '*based not only on the scope of the rules in question but also on their nature and content*'.[2466] Furthermore, the Court also emphasizes that '[i]*t is also necessary to take into account not only the current state of Community law in the area in question but also its future development, insofar as that is foreseeable at the time of that analysis*'.[2467] An '*affect*' on Union law may, therefore, also be of a mere potential nature. An existing conflict of norms is, therefore, not a prerequisite for the fourth limb of Article 216(1) TFEU[2468] since the future development of existing Union law could potentially cause such a conflict.[2469] The mere overlapping of the scope of an international treaty and existing legal acts of the EU may, thus, establish an '*affect*' on Union law.[2470] Furthermore, the CJEU assumes an '*affect*' if a certain area of law is harmonized exhaustively[2471] and if a certain legal act provides for rules addressed to nationals of non-member countries[2472].[2473] However, there is no '*affect*' on common rules if EU law, as well as the international agreement, merely lay down minimum standards:[2474] in these cases, there is no conceivable risk of normative conflicts[2475] which might affect EU law.[2476] Finally, it appears that the fourth limb of Article 216(1) TFEU aims to avoid the normative conflicts of international agreements and EU law, irrespective of whether they eventually occur and even in situations where there is no conflict at all.[2477] One should again emphasize that the fourth limb of Article 216(1) TFEU should

2465. *Opinion 1/03 (Lugano)*, paras 125–131 (in particular para. 128). In detail on the effectiveness argument, also *see* Merijn Chamon, *supra* note 2413, at 1113.
2466. *Opinion 1/03 (Lugano)*, para. 126.
2467. *Ibid.* The ECJ derives this from Opinion 2/91, *see Opinion 2/91 (ILO)*, para. 25. More recently, *see* Case C-66/13, *Green Network*, para. 61.
2468. This can be deduced above all from Opinion 2/91, *see Opinion 2/91 (ILO)*, paras 25–26. Also *see* S. Vöneky & B. Beylage-Haarmann, *supra* note 2406, para. 18.
2469. A. Arena, *supra* note 2409, at 69; S. Vöneky & B. Beylage-Haarmann, *supra* note 2406, para. 18.
2470. Extensively, *see* A. Arena, *supra* note 2409, at 73–79; Merijn Chamon, *supra* note 2413, at 1118–1119; also *see* S. Vöneky & B. Beylage-Haarmann, *supra* note 2406, para. 18; A. Rosas, *supra* note 2413, at 1085–1086; G. Kofler, *supra* note 1796, at 45.
2471. *Opinion 1/94 (WTO)*, para. 96; *Opinion 1/03 (Lugano)*, para. 122.
2472. *Opinion 1/94 (WTO)*, para. 95.
2473. At this point one should, once more, point out that the ECJ does not elaborate on these criteria in the passages just quoted in relation to the existence of the competence, but in relation to its exclusivity. Extensively, *see* C. Heber, *supra* note 2419, at 601–603; also *see* S. Vöneky & B. Beylage-Haarmann, *supra* note 2406, para. 18.
2474. *Opinion 2/91 (ILO)*, para. 18; *Opinion 1/03 (Lugano)*, para. 123; Case C-459/03, *Commission of the European Communities v. United Kingdom of Great Britain and Northern Ireland (Mox Plant)*, paras 104–105.
2475. However, normative conflicts may very well arise if the minimum standards of secondary law and an international agreement are set in different directions. Such a situation occurs, i.e., in the relationship of the ATAD to DTCs: while the ATAD obliges the Member States to apply certain minimum tax burdens, DTCs often require contracting states to waive tax collection in certain situations, *see* G. Kofler, *supra* note 1796, at 45-in particular n. 232; W. Haslehner, *supra* note 2024, at 3.5.
2476. Extensively, *see* A. Arena, *supra* note 2409, at 85–88; also *see* P. Eeckhout, *supra* note 2458, at 86; M. Chamon, *supra* note 2413, at 1116; A. Rosas, *supra* note 2413, at 1084.
2477. *Opinion 2/91 (ILO)*, paras 25–26; Case C-66/13, *Green Network*, para. 32; Case C-114/12, *European Commission v. Council of the European Union (Broadcasting Convention)*, para. 71.

not be misunderstood in the sense that it would not require the existence of an internal competence. Rather, every internal legal act must be based on an internal competence. Consequently, also according to the last limb of Article 216(1) TFEU, an external competence is not conceivable if there is no internal competence conferred to the Union in the Treaties. Conversely, this does not mean that the mere existence of an internal competence can automatically establish an implied external competence.[2478]

An analysis of Article 216(1) TFEU has thus shown that, in addition to the competences explicitly provided for in the Treaties, the Union may have external competence in three alternative situations. There is not always a clear distinction between the scope of those different situations. With regard to the second limb of Article 216(1) TFEU (*'provided for in a legally binding Union act'*), it can be stated that there is no scope remaining with respect to the other limbs and that this term is misplaced in Article 216(1) TFEU, but better fits into Article 3(2) TFEU. As a result of the interpretation just made in this section, external competence of the Union *exists* if (i) such competence is explicitly provided for in the Treaties (primary law), (ii) if the conclusion of an agreement by the Union at least '*contributes*' to the objectives deduced from one of the internal competences of the Union, or (iii) if the conclusion of agreements by the Member States are likely to affect common rules or alter their scope. If at least one of these conditions is met, the Union has external legislative competence for the respective *ratione materiae*. But what is the impact of the Union's external competence? To what extent can Member States still enter into obligations under public international law? Or to put it in another way, what is the *nature* of the Union's external competence?

6.1.3.2.2 Article 3(2) TFEU: The Nature of Union's External Competence

The question of the nature of an EU competence can only arise when it is established that such a competence exists.[2479] For this reason, the Lisbon Treaty also distinguishes between the *existence* and *nature* of external competences: while Article 216(1) TFEU contains the requirement of the competences' *existence*, Article 3(2) TFEU rules on the question of whether it is exclusive.[2480] If there is a competence under Article 216(1) TFEU but if such competence is not exclusive according to Article 3(2) TFEU, the respective external competence is, consequently, shared.[2481] In this respect, it is worth mentioning that neither Article 216(1) TFEU nor Article 3(2) TFEU determine whether a non-exclusive external competence in post-Lisbon times might occur at all. This indeed has fueled doubts as to whether shared external competences really exist within

2478. M. Cremona, *supra* note 2427, at 141.

2479. P. Craig & G. de Búrca, *supra* note 1815, at 371; M. Nettesheim, *Art. 3 [Ausschließliche Zuständigkeiten], in Das Recht der Europäischen Union*, para. 21 (E. Grabitz et al., eds, C.H.Beck 2016).

2480. Case C-600/14, *Germany v. Council (COTIF)*, para. 46. Already in pre-Lisbon times, *see Opinion 2/91 (ILO)*, para. 13; *Opinion 1/03 (Lugano)*, paras 114–115. On the system of implied external competence established by the Lisbon-Treaty, comprehensively P. Craig, *supra* note 2336, at 399–400.

2481. M. Klamert, *The Principle of Loyalty in EU Law*, *supra* note 2419, at 158.

the legal framework of the Treaties.[2482] However, despite the similar wording, as will be shown, the CJEU has clarified that the scope of Article 3(2) TFEU is narrower compared to that of Article 216(1) TFEU. Thus, not every external competence of the Union is necessarily an exclusive one.[2483]

According to Article 3(2) TFEU, the Union's external competence shall be exclusive if (i) *'its conclusion is provided for in a legislative act of the Union'*, or (ii) *'it is necessary to enable the Union to exercise its internal competence'*, or (iii) in so far as *'conclusion may affect common rules or alter their scope'*. Consequently, Article 3(2) TFEU establishes three situations in which exclusivity occurs.[2484] The textual connection to Article 216(1) TFEU is obvious, and the substantive connection cannot be denied either. Nevertheless, cross-references are missing;[2485] the wording is similar but not entirely identical,[2486] and consequently, their scopes are not entirely congruent.[2487] Undoubtedly, there is a close link between Articles 216(1) and 3(2) TFEU, which raises many questions that have not been fully clarified despite extensive discussion in the literature;[2488] and not without reason, the provisions were accused of being a *'textual fiasco'*[2489] and *'patently flawed'*.[2490] The reason for the odd relationship of Articles 3(2) and 216(1) TFEU might be the fact that both codify pre-Lisbon case law of the CJEU, which did itself not always clearly distinguish between the *existence* and *nature* of a competence.[2491] Already in its decision in *ERTA*, the CJEU did not distinguish between the *existence* and the exclusive *nature* but merely held that if *'the Union adopts provisions laying down common rules* [...] *Member States no longer have the right, acting individually or even collectively, to undertake obligations with third countries which affect those rules'*[2492].[2493] Thus, *Chamon* aptly sums up that the codification of

2482. In detail on this discussion, *see* P. Craig, *supra* note 2336, at 167; M. Klamert, *supra* note 2419, at 157–159.
2483. Case C-600/14, *Germany v. Council (COTIF)*, para. 51.
2484. I. Govaere, *supra* note 2418, at 1288–1289; M. Cremona, *supra* note 2427, at 145; M. Chamon, *supra* note 2413, at 1122; J. Bauerschmidt, *Die Rechtsperson Der Europäischen Union Im Wandel* 235 (Mohr Siebeck 2018).
2485. P. Koutrakos, *supra* note 1840, at 128; M. Chamon, *supra* note 2413, at 1121–1122.
2486. P. Eeckhout, *supra* note 2458, at 112–113 and 123; R. Schütze, *supra* note 1810, at 318; P. Koutrakos, *supra* note 1840, at 128; M. Nettesheim, *supra* note 2479, para. 20.
2487. Thus, the ECJ in Case C-600/14, *Germany v. Council (COTIF)*, para. 50 also explicitly states that *'it is clear from a comparison of the respective wording of Article 216(1) TFEU and Article 3(2) TFEU that the situations in which the Union has an external competence, in accordance with the former provision, are not limited to the various scenarios set out in the latter provision, where the Union has exclusive external competence'*. Also on the fact that the scope of both provisions is not identical, *see* C. Heber, *supra* note 2419, at 606.
2488. Only *see* a selection of the numerous examples from the literature, in R. Schütze, *supra* note 1810, at 318 and 340; I Govaere, *supra* note 2418, at 1288–1291; P. Koutrakos, *supra* note 1840, at 128; Marise Cremona, *supra* note 2427, at 133–150; C. Heber, *supra* note 2419, at 606 et seq.; M. Chamon, *supra* note 2413, at 1121 et seq.; M. Cremona, *supra* note 2415, at 460; R. Schütze, *supra* note 1822, at 309–310.
2489. *See* R. Schütze, *supra* note 1822, at 310.
2490. M. Klamert, *supra* note 2419, at 150.
2491. As *Craig & De Búrca* put it, the ECJ in its early case law *'tied the very existence of implied powers to their exclusive nature'*, *see* P. Craig & G. de Búrca, *supra* note 1815, at 364.
2492. Case C-22/70, *ERTA*, para. 17.
2493. M. Cremona, *supra* note 2427, at 143–144; M. Chamon, *supra* note 2413, at 1105–1106; M. Cremona, *supra* note 2415, at 460.

the *ERTA*-doctrine is '*as good as it could be*', due to the fact that '*ERTA is a complex judge-made doctrine which does not lend itself to a perfect codification in one or two lines*'.[2494] In the meantime, however, the CJEU has somewhat clarified that the *existence* of an external competence very well is to be distinguished from its *nature*.[2495] Moreover, the CJEU has now also clearly neglected that every treaty-making competence provided by Article 216(1) TFEU entails an exclusive competence of the Union pursuant to Article 3(2) TFEU.[2496]

According to the first limb of Article 3(2) TFEU, the external competence of the Union is exclusive, provided that this is foreseen '*in a legislative act of the Union*'. The similarity with the third limb of Article 216(1) TFEU can hardly be overlooked, where it says that the Union has explicit implied external powers, when this is provided for '*in a legally binding Union act*'.[2497] Again, the parallelism of Articles 216(1) and 3(2) TFEU, which has already been denounced several times (and which is probably caused by *Opinion 1/94*, mixing existence and exclusivity),[2498] raises the question of whether this is a deliberate differentiation; and again, the prevailing view argues, that this is not the case.[2499] However, as already pointed out, the third limb of Article 216(1) TFEU lacks of scope because secondary legislation can never confer competences[2500] and therefore cannot authorize the EU to conclude international agreements.[2501] Secondary law can only do so if the corresponding regulatory area and, thus, the corresponding objectives of internal competence on which the act is based on make it 'necessary' to take external action.[2502] However, the fact that the relevant internal competence may textually only allow for intra-Union harmonization, because the '*only objective expressly mentioned* [...] *is the attainment of those* [objectives] *for nationals of the Member States of the Community*', does not preclude the Union '*from using the powers*

2494. M. Chamon, *supra* note 2413, at 1140–1141. Already in the same vein *see* P. Craig, *supra* note 2336, at 162.
2495. *See* the ECJ's decision in *Germany v. Council* where the ECJ notes that '*it follows from the Court's settled case-law that a distinction must be made between whether the Union has an external competence and whether any such competence is exclusive or shared*', *see* Case C-600/14, *Germany v. Council (COTIF)*, para. 46.
2496. '*It follows that* [...] *the European Union may have an external competence that falls outside the situations laid down in Article 3(2) TFEU*', *see Ibid.*, paras 50–51. In further detail on this case law and the long-awaited distinction between existence and nature of external competence, *see* M. Cremona, *supra* note 2415, at 457–458.
2497. In detail on the textual differences, S. Vöneky & B. Beylage-Haarmann, *supra* note 2406, para. 13. Also *see* C. Heber, *supra* note 2419, at 606.
2498. *See* in particular *Opinion 1/94 (WTO)* at 95. Also *see* P. Koutrakos, *supra* note 1840, at 109; M. Nettesheim, *supra* note 2479, para. 22. In detail on the respective paragraph of Opinion 1/94, also *see* s. 6.1.3.2.1.
2499. S. Vöneky & B. Beylage-Haarmann, *supra* note 2406, para. 14.
2500. In detail, *see* R. Schütze, *supra* note 1810, at 274. This already follows from the principles of conferral and subsidiarity and becomes in particular evident in Art. 5(2) TFEU where it is held that '*the Union shall act only within the limits of the competences conferred upon it by the Member States in the Treaties to attain the objectives set out therein*' (emphasis added). Already Art. 5(2) TFEU excludes a redistribution of competences outside the framework of primary law.
2501. Comprehensively and also critical on the constitutional perspective of a possible extension of Union competences by the enactment of secondary law, *see* R. Schütze, *supra* note 1822, at 286–287. Also *see* M. Klamert, *supra* note 2419, at 153.
2502. C. Heber, *supra* note 2419, at 607.

conferred on them in that field in order to specify the treatment which is to be accorded to nationals of non-member countries'.[2503] In this case, the existence of the competence is necessarily already derived from the second limb of Article 216(1) TFEU (*'necessary in order to achieve ... one of the objectives referred to in the Treaties'*).[2504] Only with this understanding the first limb of Article 3(2) TFEU fits into the normative complex of external competences: if a legal act of secondary law (which was correctly based on an internal competence) authorizes the Union to enter into international agreements within its material scope, because this is necessary to achieve the objectives of the corresponding (internal) Union competence on which the legal act was based,[2505] the external competence becomes exclusive under the first limb of Article 3(2) TFEU. In effect, this means that the Member States are excluded from concluding international agreements within the scope of the specific legal act empowering the Union to conclude a treaty in the respective area. Again, this is only true to the extent that the relevant legal act *'contributes'* to the objectives of the Union,[2506] since otherwise external competence of the Union could not arise at all.

The second situation addressed in Article 3(2) TFEU also raises complex issues of interpretation. According to the second limb, the external competence of the Union is to be exclusive when this *'is necessary to enable the Union to exercise its internal competence'*. The essential normative contribution of the second limb in Article 3(2) TFEU in the overall system of external competences is the fact that an external competence can be exclusive even if the Union has, at least before the conclusion of an international agreement, not yet exercised its internal competence in line with the *Opinion 1/76 doctrine*, but where the conclusion of an international agreement is *'necessary'* to do so. The situation described in the second limb of Article 3(2) TFEU, thus, finds its equivalent in the second limb of Article 216 TFEU, where, however, reference is made to the necessity *'in order to achieve* [...] *one of the objectives referred to in the Treaties'*.[2507] Although the textual differences are considerable, there is a significant similarity regarding its interpretation:[2508] As already pointed out, the second limb of Article 216(1) TFEU is not to be understood as a mere general reference to the objectives of the Union (Article 3 TEU) against the background of *Opinion 1/76*,[2509] but as a reference to the objectives of the respective internal competence.[2510] If one assumes this understanding, there seems to be no difference in content between the

2503. *Opinion 1/94 (WTO)*, para. 90. Extensively, *see* C. Heber, *supra* note 2419, at 606–607.
2504. In detail on the interpretation of the second limb of Art. 216(1) TFEU, *see* s. 6.1.3.2.1.
2505. In other words, the external competences' existence can be based on the second limb of Art. 216(1) TFEU.
2506. *Opinion 2/15 (Singapore)*, para. 240.
2507. Also the curious relationship between the respective second limbs of Arts 216(1) and 3(2) TFEU, *see* M. Cremona, *supra* note 2415, at 460.
2508. R. Schütze, *supra* note 1822, at 284–285. Similar P. Koutrakos, *supra* note 1840, at 128.
2509. *Opinion 1/76 (inland waterways)*, para. 4.
2510. *See* M. Klamert, *supra* note 2419, at 155, who convincingly notes that the exclusivity in the case of the second limb of Art. 3(2) TFEU is based on the fact, that the exclusivity *'is already to some degree 'built into' a certain Treaty norm, the objectives of which cannot be realized in the external sphere unless an international agreement is concluded by the Union alone'*.

second limbs of Article 216(1) TFEU and Article 3(2) TFEU, respectively. Consequently, any external competence resulting from the second situation mentioned in Article 216(1) TFEU would be an exclusive external competence; and since the respective last limbs of Articles 3(2) and 216(1) TFEU ('*affect common rules or alter their scope*') are indeed worded almost identically, this would mean that there would be no conceivable situation at all in which the Union would only have a shared external competence.[2511] Nevertheless, the CJEU has affirmed the existence of shared external competences also in the post-Lisbon era. In *Germany v. Council*, the CJEU clarified that the EU indeed '*may have an external competence that falls outside the situations laid down in Article 3(2) TFEU*'.[2512] But where is the interpretative difference between the second alternatives in Articles 3(2) and 216(1) TFEU? The difference in scope between the two provisions becomes most readily apparent in the ECJ's *Opinion 2/15*, where the Court had to deal with the question of whether the Union was competent to conclude a Free Trade Agreement with Singapore and, if so, whether the Union's competence could even be exclusive. Among other things, the exclusivity for the area of so-called non-direct investment was at issue. The CJEU thus examined each individual limb of Article 3(2) TFEU separately and quite soon concluded that an exclusive competence of the Union could neither be derived from the first nor the third limb of Article 3(2) TFEU.[2513] Finally, the CJEU reached the question of whether the regulation of non-direct investment was '*necessary to exercise its internal competence*' according to the second limb of Article 3(2) TFEU. The CJEU ultimately answered this question in the negative[2514] but expressly held that '[o]*n the other hand, the conclusion by the European Union of an international agreement relating to such investments may prove 'necessary in order to achieve, within the framework of the Union's policies, one of the objectives referred to in the Treaties', within the meaning of Article 216(1) TFEU*'[2515] to finally conclude that the Union had a shared competence. Finally, the Court held that the conclusion of international agreements '*which contribute to the establishment of free movement on a reciprocal basis may be classified as necessary*' according to the second limb of Article 216(1) TFEU.[2516] The CJEU has thus clarified that the respective second limbs of Articles 216(1) and 3(2) TFEU are precisely not congruent and at least indicated the distinction between existence and nature of competence with respect to the term '*necessity*': the Court already seems to assume the *existence* of competence under the second limb of Article 216(1) TFEU if an international agreement '*contributes*' to the achievement of '*one of the objectives referred to in the treaties*'. However,

2511. *See Cremona*, who concluded on the draft provisions of the Draft for the 'Treaty Establishing a constitution for Europe', which have been adopted identically in Arts 216(1) and 3(2) TFEU, that such an interpretation would suggest '*that implied shared competence would disappear*', *see* M. Cremona, *A Constitutional Basis for Effective External Action? An Assessment of the Provisions on EU External Action in the Constitutional Treaty*, EUI Working Papers (Law No. 2006/30) 10 (European University Institute 2006). Also referring to Cremona, *see* R. Schütze, *supra* note 1822, at 285-in particular n. 76.
2512. Case C-600/14, *Germany v. Council (COTIF)*, para. 51.
2513. *Opinion 2/15 (Singapore)*, paras 235–236.
2514. *Ibid.*, paras 237–238.
2515. *Ibid.*, para. 239.
2516. *Ibid.*, para. 240. *See* already s. 6.1.3.2.1.

the mere '*contribution*' is not considered sufficient to justify exclusivity if the respective agreement is not '*necessary to enable the Union to exercise its internal competence*' according to the second limb of Article 3(2) TFEU.[2517] *Cremona*, therefore, rightly states that the second limb of Article 216(1) TFEU '*emerged as a distinct basis for (non-exclusive)* [external] *competence*'.[2518] However, it remains unclear when exactly such a necessity presupposed by Article 3(2) TFEU might occur. Nevertheless, some guidance on the interpretation of the second limb of Article 3(2) TFEU can probably be derived from pre-Lisbon case law on the exclusive *nature* of external competence. The CJEU has affirmed exclusivity, i.e., '*where the conclusion of an international agreement is necessary in order to achieve Treaty objectives which cannot be attained by the adoption of autonomous rules*'[2519] and where the treatment '*of nationals of the Member States is inextricably linked to the treatment* [...] *to nationals of non-member countries*'[2520].[2521]

Finally, the *ERTA*-doctrine is also directly anchored in Article 3(2) TFEU.[2522] According to the third limb of Article 3(2) TFEU, the Union has external competence '*in so far as its conclusion may affect common rules or alter their scope*' (regularly discussed as '*subsequent exclusivity*').[2523] As already explained above, the CJEU in *Germany v. Council* and *Opinion 2/15* clarified that this term is to be interpreted in the same way as the fourth limb of Article 216(1) TFEU: if an international agreement affects existing legal acts of the Union or changes their scope, the competence established is necessarily exclusive.[2524] With regard to the interpretation of the '*affect*', reference is therefore made to the above.[2525] However, with regard to the third limb of Article 3(2) TFEU, there is an interesting textual issue brought up by *Schütze*, which is worth mentioning.[2526] On the one hand, the essence of the decision in the *ERTA* case is that '*the Member States cannot, outside the framework of the Community institutions, assume obligations which might affect* [common] *rules or alter their scope*'.[2527] On the other hand, the last limb of Article 3(2) TFEU does not refer to treaties concluded by the Member States but merely to the Union's competence to conclude such a treaty.

2517. In the same vein, *see* C. Heber, *supra* note 2419, at 608.
2518. M. Cremona, *supra* note 2415, at 460.
2519. *See, i.a.*, *Opinion 2/92*, para. 32. *See* already *Opinion 1/94 (WTO)*, para. 85.
2520. *See, i.a.*, Case C-476/98, *Commission of the European Communities v. Federal Republic of Germany (Open Skies)*, para. 87. *See* already *Opinion 1/94 (WTO)*, para. 86.
2521. On this line of case law, *see* R. Schütze, *supra* note 1822, at 284, who also criticizes that these '*restrictive definitions*' are not reflected in the wording of Art. 3(2) TFEU.
2522. P. Koutrakos, *supra* note 1840, at 128; M. Cremona, *supra* note 2427, at 53; M. Cremona, *supra* note 2415, at 438.
2523. *See, i.a.*, R. Schütze, *Classifying EU Competences: German Constitutional Lessons?, in The Division of Competences between the EU and the Member states* 52 (Sacha Garben & Inge Govaere eds, Hart Publishing 2017); A. Arena, *supra* note 2409, at 84.
2524. The wording of the EU Court of Justice leaves no room for doubt in this respect: the Court emphasizes that '*that the scenario in which the conclusion of an agreement is liable to affect common rules or to alter their scope* [is] *a scenario where the Union competence is, under Article 3(2) TFEU, exclusive*', *see* Case C-600/14, *Germany v. Council (COTIF)*. Also *see Opinion 2/15 (Singapore)*, paras 171–172. For further reference also *see supra* note 2458.
2525. *See* s. 6.1.3.2.1.
2526. R. Schütze, *supra* note 1822, at 285.
2527. Case C-22/70, *ERTA*, para. 22.

Consequently, the question has been justifiably raised in the literature as to whether this differentiation was made deliberately and whether the last limb of Article 3(2) TFEU was to be interpreted differently from the original *ERTA*-doctrine.[2528] In the meantime, however, the CJEU has expressly emphasized that the third limb of Article 3(2) TFEU is to be interpreted on the basis of *ERTA* and that the *ERTA*-doctrine should also continue to have significance for the question of exclusivity.[2529]

As a result, the following findings can be made with regard to Article 3(2) TFEU: the first situation addressed in Article 3(2) TFEU assigns exclusive competence to the Union when this is expressed in secondary law. In these cases, however, the external competence is still derived from the internal competence in the Treaties. The second situation in Article 3(2) TFEU refers to the *Opinion 1/76*-doctrine, according to which exclusive external competence might even occur in situations where internal competence had not yet been exercised.[2530] It seems that the second limb has 'emerged'[2531] as the only situation where shared external competence might occur, due to the fact, that the CJEU considers a mere '*contribution*' to the objectives provided for in the Treaties as necessary to attain the objective of the Treaties according to the second limb of Article 216(1) TFEU,[2532] while it assumes that a mere '*contribution*' is not enough to be considered as '*necessary to enable the Union to exercise its internal competence*'.[2533] Non-exclusive external competences thus may arise from the case law of the CJEU through different interpretations of the second limbs of Articles 216(1) and 3(2) TFEU. The third and final situation codifies the *ERTA*-doctrine and is, according to the CJEU, to be strictly interpreted along the lines of the fourth limb provided for in Article 216 TFEU.[2534]

After looking at Articles 216(1) and 3(2) TFEU, there still is the question the effects of which are associated with an external competence of the Union. In which way are the Member States preempted from acting on the international plane? What effects does an exclusive competence have on the sovereignty of the Member States to conclude international agreements? And above all, what are the effects in the case of non-exclusive external competence, and who is competent for agreements which possibly contain both exclusive and non-exclusive competences?

6.1.3.2.3 The 'Creeping' Exclusivity and the 'Pre-emptive' Effects of International Agreements in Areas of Shared External Competence

The system of external competences differs significantly from the Union's competences in the internal sphere. Nevertheless, as the CJEU had already stated in *ERTA*, '*the*

2528. *See Schütze* who notes that the '*third alternative in Article 3(2) – strangely – breaks the link between a Member State agreement and internal European law*', *see* R. Schütze, *supra* note 1822, at 285.
2529. Case C-114/12, *Broadcasting Convention*, para. 68.
2530. *Opinion 1/76 (inland waterways)*, paras 1-4.
2531. M. Cremona, *supra* note 2415, at 460.
2532. *Opinion 2/15 (Singapore)*, paras 239–240.
2533. *Ibid.*, para. 237.
2534. Case C-114/12, *Broadcasting Convention*, para. 68.

system of internal Community measures may not [...] *be separated from that of external relations*'.[2535] As just shown, this principle is likely to continue to apply even after the codification of implicit external competences in Article 216(1) TFEU. Also, implied external competences require at least the existence of an internal competence,[2536] even if the Union does not necessarily have to have already exercised the competence conferred to it in the internal sphere.[2537] Nevertheless, although external action of the Union is also tied to the *existence* of internal competences and depends to a certain extent on the exercise of these internal competences (*see* shortly), there is, at least with regard to the nature of external competence – no complete parallelism of internal and external competence (no '*in foro interno, in foro externo*').[2538] This becomes particularly evident with regard to the nature of external competences under Article 3(2) TFEU: Article 3(2) TFEU is not limited to the internal exclusive competences listed in its first paragraph. Rather, the competences listed in Article 3(1) TFEU by themselves are of an exclusive *nature* also in the external sphere.[2539] From this fact alone, it is evident that internally shared competence, according to Article 3(2) TFEU, can thus be exclusive with respect to the external sphere.[2540] But what does this mean for the division of competences between the EU and its Member States?

In particular, the last situations mentioned in Articles 216(1) and 3(2) TFEU, respectively ('*affect common rules or alter their scope*'), make it clear that both the *existence* and possible exclusive *nature* of external competence seem to be linked to the exercise of internal competence. In other words, the scope and *nature* of external competence seems to depend on the existence or adoption of internal legal acts by the Union legislature. However, this would also mean that the division of external legislative powers between the Union and the Member States is not fixed from the outset:[2541] the more exhaustive the harmonization in the internal sphere, the more comprehensive the Union's competences in external relations. But can the existence of external powers really depend on the exercise of internal ones?

Once again, one must not fall into the temptation of confusing the *existence* prescribed by Article 216(1) TFEU with the *nature* of external competence prescribed by Article 3(2) TFEU: internal legislation itself is always based on internal competence. The mere enactment of secondary legislation can never confer treaty-making powers to

2535. Case C-22/70, *ERTA*, para. 19.
2536. Also *see Opinion 1/13 (Hague)*, para. 67. *See* already s. 6.1.3.2.1.
2537. Joined Cases C-3/76, 4/76, 6/76, *Kramer*, paras 30–33; *Opinion 1/76 (inland waterways)*, para. 4.
2538. *See, i.a.*, G. Kofler, *supra* note 1790, at 319. Also *see* Cremona who concludes that '*the link between internal and external competence is still strong*' but also notes that exclusivity is '*based on the adoption of legislation requiring external unity to safeguard this internal acquis*', *see* M. Cremona, *EU External Relations: Unity and Conferral of Powers*, *in The Question of Competence in the European Union* 85 (Loic Azoulai ed., Oxford 2014).
2539. *See* M.Cremona, *supra* note 2427, at 144.
2540. In the same vein, *see* R. Schütze, *supra* note 2523, at 52–53; R. Schütze, *supra* note 1822, at 282. Similar, *see* M. Cremona, *supra* note 2427, at 134 and 144–145.
2541. M. Chamon, *supra* note 2413, at 1126; R. Schütze, *supra* note 1822, at 286.

the Union without the *existence* of internal powers within the respective policy area.[2542] The last limb of Article 216(1) TFEU merely clarifies that the exercise of implied external powers – in other words, powers that are not explicitly provided for in the Treaty – may, in principle, only occur if the Union legislature has exercised its internal competence. Only in one exceptional case can the Union obtain external implicit competence without having exercised its competence: according to the second limb of Article 216(1) TFEU, the Union may exercise implicit external competence even though internal competence has not yet been exercised if '*the conclusion of an agreement is necessary in order to achieve, within the framework of the Union's policies, one of the objectives*' which, however, also in these cases can be derived from an internal competence.[2543] With regard to its *existence*, it is indeed correct to assume that the external powers of the Union are parallel to the internal ones ('*doctrine of parallel powers*').[2544]

However, according to the last limb of Article 3(2) TFEU, the adoption of internal legal acts can impact the *nature* of external competence ('*subsequent exclusivity*'). The EU acquires exclusive competences in external relations by enactment of secondary legislation in a certain policy area, and the more rules are adopted internally, the more the national legislature will be pre-empted from entering commitments under public international law (*ERTA*-effect).[2545] The nature of legislative powers is thus not conclusively predetermined but can be extended in the EU's favour by adoption of secondary law.[2546] This phenomenon is commonly referred to as '*competence creep*'[2547] or, better, '*subsequent exclusivity*' and has been the subject of controversial debate since the doctrine of implied external powers was created by the CJEU in *ERTA*.[2548] It was argued that the possible gain of exclusive external competences by the adoption of secondary law would leave it to secondary law to define the separation of powers laid down in primary law. Many thus argued that this would be untenable due to the principle of subsidiarity of Article 5(3) TFEU.[2549] Nevertheless, at least with regard to exclusivity, the case law of the CJEU and also the wording of Article 3(2) TFEU leave no room for doubt in this respect.[2550] The fact that the balance of external powers between the EU and its Member States is not fixed finally raises the question of the degree to which Member States are excluded from concluding international agreements

2542. For this reason, *Schütze* correctly notes that the identification of '*the area of exclusivity formed by secondary law as an exclusive competence wrongly suggests that the policy field delineated could be used as a legal basis itself*', *see* R. Schütze, *supra* note 1810, at 274.
2543. In further detail *see* s. 6.1.3.2.1.
2544. M. Klamert, *supra* note 2419, at 149; J. Bauerschmidt, *supra* note 2484, at 239; R. Schütze, *supra* note 1822, at 279-in particular n. 52; R. Schütze, *supra* note 1810, at 284.
2545. R. Schütze, *supra* note 1822, at 285; A. Arena, *supra* note 2409, at 104.
2546. R. Schütze, *supra* note 1822, at 285–286; J. Bauerschmidt, *supra* note 2484, at 239.
2547. For further discussion of this phenomenon with regard to the division of powers within the EU, *see* K. Bradley, *The Exclusive Competences of the European Union: Some Random Jottings*, in *The Division of Competences between the EU and the Member states* 185–186 (Sacha Garben & Inge Govaere eds, Hart Publishing 2017).
2548. R. Schütze, *supra* note 1822, at 286–287.
2549. Extensively C. Calliess, *supra* note 2340, at 95; R. Schütze, *supra* note 1810, at 274–275 and 319; R. Schütze, *supra* note 1822, at 287.
2550. Case C-114/12, *Broadcasting Convention*, para. 73.

if the Union had adopted internal legislation. To what extent are Member States 'pre-empted' from acting on the international plane? To which extent does the exercise of shared competence pre-empt the Member States from concluding international agreements? And finally, who may conclude a treaty which contains both exclusive and shared matters of Union competence?

In order to answer these questions, it is first necessary to take a closer look at the effects of an exclusive external competence and the doctrine of community 'pre-emption' in external relations.[2551] If an exclusive competence exists according to Article 3(2) TFEU or arises through the subsequent adoption of internal legal acts of the Union, the national legislatures are deprived of any competence to conclude international treaties in the specific area of exclusive competence.[2552] The mere conclusion of an international agreement in the respective scope of the external competence by the Member State leads to a violation of primary law.[2553] Whether a conflict of norms arises is therefore irrelevant if an exclusive competence exists; rather, its mere existence excludes domestic action in the external sphere.[2554]

The situation is, however, different with regard to shared external competences. In this case, legislative action by the Member States is not 'excluded' from the outset. Rather, at least if one takes into account the internal competences and the provision of Article 2(2) TFEU, it should be left to the Member States to continue to enter into obligations under international law as long as the Union has not exercised its external competence.[2555] As the CJEU in its pre-Lisbon case law put it, the '*Member States are accordingly entitled to enter into commitments themselves vis-à-vis non-Member States, either collectively or individually, or even jointly with the Community*'.[2556] Consequently, both the Union and the Member States may conclude a corresponding international agreement, either alone or jointly. Past experience shows that international treaties are regularly concluded as '*mixed agreements*' in the context of EU law because there might not occur disputes with regard to competence and because Member States are still recognized as distinct parties.[2557] If a certain international agreement concerns both competences of the Union and those of the Member States,

2551. R. Schütze, *supra* note 1810, at 271.
2552. *See* Art. 2(1) TFEU. *See* M. Nettesheim, *Art. 2 [Ausschließliche Zuständigkeiten], in Das Recht der Europäischen Union*, para. 18 (E Grabitz et al., eds, C.H.Beck 2016). In general to the effect of exclusive competences, *see* R. Schütze, *Supremacy without Pre-Emption? The Very Slowly Emergent Doctrine of Community Pre-Emption*, Common Market Law Review 1023 and 1037 (2006) DOI: 10.54648/cola2006051. In particular to Art. 3(2) TFEU, *see* J. Bauerschmidt, *supra* note 2484, at 236.
2553. M. Klamert & N. Maydell, *Rechtfragen der impliziten Außenkompetenz der EG illustriert am Beispiel der Dienstleistungsrichlinie und der Minimum Platform on Investment*, 42 EuR 589; R. Schütze, *supra* note 1810, at 270–271.
2554. R. Schütze, *supra* note 1810, at 270–271.
2555. See, however, *Cremona* who notes that the relation of the codification of the *ERTA*-effect in Art. 3(2) TFEU '*to Article 2(2) TFEU is far from clear*', *see* M. Cremona, *supra* note 2538, at 72; similar M. Cremona, *supra* note 2427, at 145. Also drawing a parallel with Art. 2(2) TFEU, *see* M. Klamert, *supra* note 2419, at 149 et seq.
2556. Case C-316/91, *European Parliament v. Council of the European Union (Lomé Convention)*, para. 26.
2557. In general on the phenomenon of mixed agreements, *see* M. Cremona, *supra* note 2415, at 461 et seq.; R. Schütze, *supra* note 1822, at 302.

there is no choice but to conclude the agreement as a mixed agreement (*'obligatory mixity'*).[2558] Nevertheless, shared competences, in principle, do not preclude the EU from acting alone.[2559] However, irrespective of the question of whether the Union exercises a shared competence alone or jointly with the Member States, the question arises to what extent the Union's exercise of external powers 'pre-empts' the ability of Member States to enter into commitments themselves.

This question can only be answered on the basis of the so-called doctrine of *'pre-emption'*.[2560] This doctrine, which originated in US law,[2561] seeks to explain the extent to which legislative action by one legislative body precludes action by another and has found its way into the European legal order, first into the doctrine of internal competences and later into the external sphere of the Union. The legislative phenomenon of *'pre-emption'*[2562] thus attempts to describe to which degree the EU legislature can occupy a particular policy area in order to prevent or restrict external action by the Member States and has received remarkable attention in the discussion on external competence.[2563] The literature distinguishes between three types of *'pre-emption'*, which describe the density of the displacement of national law by EU law:[2564] The first and most comprehensive manifestation of *'pre-emption'* is the so-called *field pre-emption*. In these cases, a certain policy area is occupied by Union law to such an extent that the national legislatures are left with no regulatory leeway at all in this *'field of law'*. With regard to *'field pre-emption'*, it is not of relevance whether there is a normative conflict; the legislation by the Union is exhaustive in such a way that there is simply no room for manoeuvre left for the national legislatures. On the other hand, the mildest form of *'pre-emption'* is *'rule-preemption'*, which requires a specific normative conflict between a provision of Union law and one of national law. As long as national law does not cause such a conflict, national legislatures are free in their regulatory leeway. In between lies the concept of *'obstacle pre-emption'*, which in principle requires normative conflict, but on a more abstract level. In the case of *'obstacle pre-emption'*, the Court also considers such national regulations to be displaced that conflict with the objectives or the functioning of Union law. It is obvious that the boundaries between the different types of *'pre-emption'* are blurred. Thus, the extent to which the regulatory density of Union law excludes the ability of Member

---

2558. G. Kofler, *supra* note 1796, at 37.
2559. Comprehensively and also providing for examples, *see* M. Cremona, *supra* note 2538, at 78–80; R. Schütze, *supra* note 1822, at 303; G. Kofler, *supra* note 1796, at 37.
2560. Extensively on the doctrine of *'pre-emption'*, *see* A. Arena, *supra* note 2409, at 28–105; R. Schütze, *supra* note 1822, at 213; C. Calliess, *supra* note 2340, at 91 et seq.
2561. To the origins of *'pre-emption'* and its understanding in US constitutional law, *see* R. Schütze, *supra* note 2552, at 1037–1038; A. Arena, *supra* note 2409, at 35–36.
2562. R. Schütze, *supra* note 1810, at 272.
2563. Extensively with further reference, *see* A. Arena, *supra* note 2409, at 64 et seq.; also *see* M. Klamert, *supra* note 2538, at 72–73; P. Craig & G. de Búrca, *supra* note 1815, at 364; M. Cremona, *supra* note 2415, at 453–456.
2564. Comprehensively J. Bauerschmidt, *supra* note 2484, at 237–239; R. Schütze, *supra* note 1822, at 213–216.

States to conclude international treaties must be determined in relation to the respective regulatory matter. For the conclusion of GloBE-related agreements, such a determination is attempted in the following sections.[2565]

Against the background of the exclusive external competence of the Union, which has been examined in detail above, the question arises as to how the exclusivity of an external competence differs from the concept of '*field pre-emption*'. In both situations, the internal legislative power of the Union precludes the legislative action of the Member States. The oddity lies above all in the fact that an exhaustive density of legislation in the internal sphere leads to '*field pre-emption*', whereas according to the third limb of Article 3(2) TFEU, such exhaustive exercise of internal competence might lead to the gain of an exclusive competence in the external sphere. Nevertheless, *Schütze,* in particular, pleads for a strict distinction between exclusivity of Union competences from '*pre-emption*' in the external sphere. Exclusivity is a constitutional instrument which precludes any legislative action of the Member States,[2566] while '*pre-emption*' solely is a legislative phenomenon arising from exhaustive regulation of the superior legislative body.[2567] Based on constitutional critics on to the aforementioned '*competence creep*',[2568] *Schütze* argues that the doctrine of pre-emption would '*enhance the clarity of legal argumentation*' in the external sphere and that it would align the '*constitutional principles applied in the internal and external hemisphere of the European legal order*'.[2569] Although convincing, admittedly, this dogmatic discourse is mainly theoretical: both exclusivity according to Article 3(2) TFEU and the theoretical concept of '*field pre-emption*' in the external sphere arise from the enactment of exhaustive internal legislation and preclude the Member States to take action within the respective area.[2570] Apart from this, the exclusivity of external competences is now explicitly enshrined in the Treaties through Article 3(2) TFEU and also the CJEU does not seem to reinterpret the provision.

As a result, it should be noted that the internal competence sphere differs significantly from the external one. Nevertheless, the Union's external competence to act undoubtedly also requires the existence of an internal competence, which in turn does not mean that the mere existence of an internal competence can automatically establish an implied external one.[2571] However, the nature of external competence depends significantly on the perception of internal competence by the Union legislature. The following sections will now examine whether and in what form the Union has external competences with regard to minimum taxation: might the EU conclude GloBE-related international agreements in the future?

2565. Section 6.1.3.3.
2566. The mere enactment of a legal act within the scope of exclusive competence would lead to a violation of primary law.
2567. R. Schütze, *supra* note 1810, at 275.
2568. *Ibid.*, at 274–277.
2569. *Ibid.*, at 286.
2570. Also *see* M. Cremona, *supra* note 2538, at 85.
2571. M. Cremona, *supra* note 2427, at 141.

6.1.3.3 Does the EU Have Power to Conclude GloBE-Related International Agreements?

6.1.3.3.1 General Discussion on the Union's External Competence in Direct Taxation

Taxation does not end at the borders of the EU. It is therefore not surprising that the EU is increasingly trying to establish itself as a global actor in the evolving international tax policy[2572] and with the steadily increasing attempts to harmonize direct tax law internally, the Commission soon tried to explore the possibilities the Union might have to conclude tax related international agreements.[2573] In fact the Union has already successfully acceded to international agreements in the field of direct taxation with some EU neighboring countries, albeit admittedly only in the very limited area of taxation of interest savings.[2574] Of course, this does not change the fact that the Union's legal competence to rule on direct tax matters in the external sphere so far is very limited. As in the internal sphere, the Treaties do not provide for a comprehensive, if any, explicit external competence of the EU in tax matters;[2575] and as already discussed above, only a few directives have so far been issued in the area of direct taxation on the

2572. *See* G. Kofler, *supra* note 1796, at 11.

2573. As early as the early 1980s, the Commission tried – ultimately in vain – to bring the *ERTA*-doctrine into play for a multilateral agreement on the exchange of information, *see* Recommendation for a council decision authorizing the Commission to negotiate a multilateral convention on administrative assistance in tax matters within the Council of Europe, COM(83)685 final withdrawn on 29 Apr. 1988. The ambitions ultimately failed due to the resistance of the Member States, for details *see* G. Kofler, *supra* note 1796, at 38-in particular, *see* n. 191.

2574. *See* Agreement between the European Community and the Principality of Andorra providing for measures equivalent to those laid down in Council Directive 2003/48/EC on taxation of savings income in the form of interest payments – Memorandum of Understanding, OJ (33); Agreement between the European Community and the Principality of Liechtenstein providing for measures equivalent to those laid down in Council Directive 2003/48/EC on taxation of savings income in the form of interest payments – Memorandum of Understanding, OJ (84); Agreement between the European Community and the Republic of San Marino providing for measures equivalent to those laid down in Council Directive 2003/48/EC on taxation of savings income in the form of interest payments, OJ (33); Agreement between the European Community and the Swiss Confederation providing for measures equivalent to those laid down in Council Directive 2003/48/EC on taxation of savings income in the form of interest payments –Memorandum of Understanding, OJ (30).

2575. Nevertheless, it is argued that, at least with respect to the free movement of capital, there is an explicit external competence that could possibly also be applied to adopt legal acts in the field of corporate taxes. According to Art. 64(2) TFEU the Council, acting in accordance with the ordinary legislative procedure, may adopt measures '*on the movement of capital to or from third countries involving direct investment – including investment in real estate – establishment, the provision of financial services and the admission of the movement of capital to or from third countries*'. Similarly, under the same conditions, the Council may according to Art. 64(3) TFEU also adopt such measures '*which constitute a step backwards in Union law as regard the liberalization of the movement of capital to or from third states*'. Until now, no legal acts have yet been based on these provisions. However, this does not mean that tax law would actually be excluded from the scope of Art. 64(2) and (3) TFEU, *see* D. S. Smit, *supra* note 2275, at 225.

basis of the residual internal market competence of Article 115 TFEU.[2576] Nevertheless, the question was soon raised and extensively discussed in the literature whether enacted secondary law in the direct tax area could trigger an implied external competence under the *ERTA*-principle and to what extent Union law could interfere with the freedom of Member States to conclude DTCs with third countries.[2577] This discussion has again gained momentum with regard to the Commission's recent initiatives in the direct tax area, i.e., the adoption of ATAD,[2578] the proposals for a CCCTB[2579] (now BEFIT[2580]) or a significant digital presence.[2581] One could very well argue that the actual adoption of these legal acts could limit or would have limited the Member States' ability to conclude international agreements such as DTCs in those fields and that their adoption could provide the Union with external competence under the *ERTA*-doctrine in the future. In view of the GloBE-Directive, these questions gain further relevance. To what extent does the GloBE-Directive affect the external powers of the Member States to conclude GloBE-related treaties or bilateral tax treaties? Admittedly, this first requires a look at the current state of harmonization in the area of direct taxation, which might be affected by future GloBE-related international agreements as proposed by the OECD[2582] and addressed by Article 55 GloBE-Directive.

6.1.3.3.2 The Scope of Secondary Law in Direct Tax Matters Before the GloBE-Directive Was Adopted

Indeed there is no doubt, that the adoption of harmonization measures based on the internal market competences such as Article 115 TFEU might also impact the Union's scope of external power and its nature.[2583] In examining whether and to what extent the Union has external options for action in the implementation of GloBE, there is thus no way around the *ERTA*-doctrine,[2584] codified in the last limbs of Articles 216(1) and 3(2) TFEU. In order to determine whether an external competence of the Union to implement GloBE via an international agreement exists at all it is first necessary to examine existing secondary legislation in this area before the GloBE-Directive was enacted and to explore, whether future international agreements are '*likely to affect common rules or alter their scope*' according to the last limb of Article 216(1) TFEU.

2576. Comprehensively, *see* 6.1.2.
2577. *See, i.a.*, H.M.A.L. Hamaekers, *Corporate Tax Policy and Competence of the European Community: An EC Tax Convention with Non-Member States*, 30 Eur. Taxn. 358–361; L. Hinnekens, *supra* note 1800, at 156–157; J.F. Avery Jones, *Flows of Capital between the EU and Third Countries and the Consequences of Disharmony in European International Tax Law*, 7 EC Tax Review 102 (1998); K. Vogel et al., *supra* note 1855, at 89–90. More recently, *see, i.a.*, A.C.M. Zaidan, *supra* note 2023, at 274–293.
2578. *See, i.a.*, W. Haslehner, *supra* note 2102, at 44–47.
2579. 2016 Proposal CCTB.
2580. European Commission, *Communication from the Commission to the European Parliament and the Council – Business Taxation for the 21st Century*, *supra* note 196.
2581. COM(2018) 147 final.
2582. *See, i.a.*, *Tax Challenges Arising from Digitalisation – Report on Pillar Two Blueprint*, paras 21–22, 39, 677–678, 697, 705–708, 715.
2583. Explicitly, *see* A. Arena, *supra* note 2409, at 92.
2584. Case C-22/70, *ERTA*.

Could the EU have established external competence in the field of GloBE even if the GloBE-Directive had not been adopted?

Again, it should be emphasized that at times no details are known about the conclusion of GloBE-related agreements yet. The considerations made here are therefore of a theoretical nature and can certainly not provide a conclusive answer. Rather, the following examination aims to identify possible lines of argument for and against the existence of external competence of the Union in the context of GloBE along the lines of the ECJ's jurisprudence already examined in section 6.1.3.2 and the GloBE-Directive as proposed by the Commission.

According to the CJEU, an (exclusive) external competence is established under the *ERTA*-doctrine when '*there is a risk that common Community rules might be adversely affected by international commitments* [...] *when those commitments fall within the scope of those rules*'.[2585] It is therefore necessary to examine the actual scope of the current stand of direct tax harmonization. Excluding directives merely relating to procedural aspects of direct taxation,[2586] secondary legislation in the area of corporate taxation includes the Parent-Subsidiary Directive (PSD),[2587] the Interest and Royalties Directive (IRD),[2588] the Merger Directive[2589] (corporate tax directives) and the ATAD.[2590]

With regard to the corporate tax directives, there are good reasons to believe that implicit external competences cannot be derived from these with respect to the implementation of GloBE: Although there may be certain technical overlaps in scope between GloBE and the corporate tax directives,[2591] these directives probably do not establish external competence of the Union under the *ERTA*-doctrine[2592] for future legal acts in the area of GloBE, as they only regulate very specific and, moreover, only internal matters[2593].[2594] But even if one takes the view that such external competence can be derived from the corporate tax directives,[2595] the possible area of conflict of a

2585. Case C-114/12, *Broadcasting Convention*, para. 68; Case C-66/13, *Green Network*, para. 29.
2586. Directive on Administrative Cooperation and Council Directive 2010/24/EU of 16 March 2010 concerning mutual assistance for the recovery of claims relating to taxes, duties and other measures, OJ (1).
2587. Parent Subsidiary Directive (2011/96/EU).
2588. Interest and Royalty Directive (2003/49/EU).
2589. Merger Directive (2009/133/EU).
2590. ATAD (2016/1164).
2591. Comprehensively on the relation of Pillar Two and the existing EU legislation, *see* João F. P. Nogueira, *supra* note 2153, at 490–492.
2592. *See, i.a.*, J.F. Avery Jones, *supra* note 2577, at 102. Also sceptical, *see* K. Vogel et al., *supra* note 1855, at 89–90.
2593. Explicitly, *see* J.F. Avery Jones, *supra* note 2577, at 102. However, recent literature counters this view by arguing that the harmonization of laws under Art. 115 TFEU may not be effective if internal harmonization does not cover situations vis-à-vis third countries, *see, i.a.*, A.C.M. Zaidan, *supra* note 2023, at 284.
2594. Comprehensively and providing for further reference on the question whether the corporate tax directives establish an external competence of the Union, *see* G. Kofler, *supra* note 1796, at 43–44.
2595. Some authors have even argued that the Union might have an exclusive competence in the area of the corporate tax directives under the *ERTA*-principle, *see* first and foremost Hamaekers who concludes that the '*Member States are no longer free to agree on clauses in new bilateral or multilateral tax treaties with third countries which deviate contents of the*

GloBE-related agreements with these directives would be very limited. It would be far-fetched to claim that the corporate tax directives would in any way exclude or '*pre-empt*' Member States from concluding such conventions.

With regard to ATAD and an external competence according to the *ERTA*-doctrine, one might come to a similar conclusion. Indeed, at first glance, there are strong reasons to believe that the ATAD might not establish external competence in the field of GloBE under the *ERTA*-doctrine either: One has to note that the ATAD only prescribes minimum standards. According to Article 3 ATAD, the rules of the ATAD '*shall not preclude the application of domestic or agreements-based provisions aimed at safeguarding a higher level of protection for domestic corporate tax bases*'. Two arguments against the applicability of the *ERTA*-doctrine might be derived from this formulation: First, the introduction of stricter taxation measures, like GloBE surely intends to implement, is not prevented by the ATAD.[2596] Therefore, if a GloBE-related agreement would also only contain minimum standards, there would be no '*effect on common rules*' according to the settled case law of the CJEU originally developed in the court's *Opinion 2/91* on the *ILO convention*.[2597] Second, it could be argued that the EU has explicitly renounced the exercise of any external competences due to the reference to '*agreement-based provisions*'. Finally, the most promising argument against the applicability of the *ERTA*-doctrine comes into play: the measures proposed in the GloBE Model Rules are only to be applied after national abuse rules as laid down by the ATAD and implemented by the Member States.[2598] Thus, for example, taxes levied under CFC schemes are considered covered taxes for the purposes of GloBE.[2599] Accordingly, the tax mechanisms of GloBE only become effective if an 'MNE Group' achieves, in the end, despite the application of the ATAD, a tax burden below the minimum tax rate.

Nevertheless, these arguments can be countered by the post-Lisbon case law of the CJEU. It is true that an 'affect' in the sense of the last limbs of Articles 216(1) and 3(2) TFEU, according to the Court – as already pointed out above – requires '*a risk that common Community rules might be adversely affected by international commitments* [...] *when those commitments fall within the scope of those rules*'.[2600] Nevertheless, the CJEU regularly adds to that statement (i) that an effect on common rules '*does not presuppose* [...] *that both rules coincide fully*',[2601] (ii) an affect might also occur where

Parent-Subsidiary Directive', *see* H.M.A.L. Hamaekers, *supra* note 2577, at 358–361. agreeing with Hamaekers C.M. Harris, *The European Community's Parent-Subsidiary Directive*, 9 Fla. J. Int'l L. 141–143 (1994); also *see* A. de Graaf, *Avoidance of International Double Taxation: Community or Jount Policy?*, 7 EC Tax Review 266–267 (1998) DOI: 10.54648/ecta1998040. Assuming at least a shared competence, *see* A. C. M. Zaidan, *supra* note 2023, at 287.

2596. Comprehensively on this issue, *see* W. Haslehner, *supra* note 2102, at 35–38.

2597. *Opinion 2/91 (ILO)*, para. 18; *Opinion 1/03 (Lugano)*, para. 123.

2598. J.F.P. Nogueira, *supra* note 2153, at 490.

2599. Explicitly *see Tax Challenges Arising from Digitalisation – Report on Pillar Two Blueprint*, para. 145.

2600. Case C-114/12, *Broadcasting Convention*, para. 68; Case C-66/13, *Green Network*, para. 29; *Opinion 2/15 (Singapore)*, para. 180.

2601. *Opinion 1/03 (Lugano)*, para. 126; Case C-114/12, *Broadcasting Convention*, para. 69; Case C-66/13, *Green Network*, para. 30; *Opinion 2/15 (Singapore)*, para. 181.

'*an area* [is] *already largely covered by* [community] *rules*',[2602] and (iii) that Member States are precluded from entering into commitments, '*even if there is no possible contradiction between those commitments and the common community rules*'.[2603] Finally, the Court has noted that an affect to common rules is not only to be assessed '*on the scope of the rules in question but also on their nature and content*'[2604] but also on the '*foreseeable future development*[s]' of the respective provisions of secondary law.[2605]

Thus, taking the arguments just made against implied competence established by the ATAD in the light of this case law, the following conclusions may be countered: even though the ATAD should apply before GloBE (at least with respect to the IIR and UTPR),[2606] this does not preclude the establishment of an external competence of the Union, since neither a coincidence nor a contradiction is presupposed for an affection of common rules according to the cited case law.[2607] Rather, it could be stated that the nature and content of a GloBE-related agreement and existing rules laid down by the ATAD could be relevant. With regard to the minimum standard as clarified in Article 3 ATAD one should emphasize, that the '*ILO exception*' according to *Opinion 2/91* regarding minimum standards only applies if both, EU secondary law and the international agreement, lay down minimum standards in the same direction.[2608] GloBE and related future treaties do not necessarily provide a '*higher level of protection*' than the ATAD. The following example should be mentioned here: while the IIR is applied on a jurisdictional level, the ATADs CFC rule laid down in Articles 7 and 8 ATAD is to be applied on an entity level. It could very well be the case that individual companies fall under the regulations of Articles 7 and 8 ATAD by virtue of low-taxed individual companies, whereas the IIR does not apply because the tax burden of a 'MNE Group' in this state as a whole is above the minimum tax rate. This example shows, that if one or more Member States reach an agreement with one or more third countries on the coordinated implementation of an IIR along the lines of GloBE, this does not mean that this agreement guarantees a '*higher level of protection*' than the ATAD. Apart from that, it is by no means clear what is meant by a '*higher level of protection*' in the sense of Article 3 ATAD.[2609] Consequently, the argument that Article

2602. *Opinion 2/91 (ILO)*, para. 25; Case C-114/12, *Broadcasting Convention*, para. 70; Case C-66/13, *Green Network*, para. 31.
2603. *Opinion 2/91 (ILO)* at 25–26; Case C-114/12, *Broadcasting Convention*, para. 71; Case C-66/13, *Green Network*, para. 32.
2604. *Opinion 2/91 (ILO)*, para. 25; Case C-114/12, *Broadcasting Convention*, para. 50; Case C-66/13, *Green Network*, para. 33.
2605. Case C-66/13, *Green Network*, para. 33.
2606. Indeed, pursuant to the OECD, QDMTT should apply before 'CFC regimes', *see* s. 4.4.2.8.1.
2607. *See, i.a.*, Case C-114/12, *Broadcasting Convention*, paras 69 and 71; Case C-66/13, *Green Network*, paras 30 and 32.
2608. *Opinion 2/91 (ILO)*, para. 18. This is clearly summarized by the ECJ, especially in its *Opinion 1/03*, where it notes on *Opinion 2/91* that '*the Court did not find that the Community had exclusive competence where, because both the Community provisions and those of an international convention laid down minimum standards, there was nothing to prevent the full application of Community law by the Member States*', *see Opinion 1/03 (Lugano)*, para. 123.
2609. Providing for a comprehensive analysis and also addressing the open issues on Art. 3 ATAD, *see* W. Haslehner, *supra* note 2102, at 36.

3 ATAD could be understood as a waiver of the Union to invoke the existence of an *ERTA* competence is also not convincing. Such a waiver could again only be objected to in relation to the higher level of protection. In the interim result, the existence of an external competence established by the ATAD is neither excluded nor yet proven. Rather, the case law requires a comprehensive analysis of the respective international commitment with the subject matter of the secondary law. Since such international GloBE-commitments do not exist yet and it is far but certain whether there will ever be such commitments, this analysis can only be carried out based on the ATAD for the time being.

If one compares the personal scope of ATAD to the expectable scope of a future GloBE MLC along the lines of the GloBE Model Rules, it is clear that nearly all entities of an 'MNE Group' which are covered by the scope of such a GloBE MLC are certainly also subject to the rules laid down by the ATAD. The ATAD has no general *de minimis* limits and only provides for very explicit carve-outs with respect to individual measures.[2610] Furthermore, the ATAD clearly covers corporations resident in third states.[2611] According to Article 1(1) ATAD, the directive '*applies to all taxpayers that are subject to corporate tax in one or more Member States, including permanent establishments in one or more Member States of entities resident for tax purposes in a third country*'. Consequently, the ambits of GloBE and the ATAD overlap with respect to all CEs resident within the EU and all non-resident CEs that have a PE within the EU.[2612] The only requirement for the personal scope pursuant to the ATAD is tax subjectivity to corporate tax in at least one Member State.[2613] ATAD therefore rules on the '*treatment of nationals of non-member countries*' by also addressing non-Member State entities, which according to the ECJ's line of reasoning developed in *Opinion 1/94 (WTO)*, might give rise to exclusive external competence of the Union.[2614] Accordingly, the subjective scope of GloBE-related agreements is likely to overlap with ATAD.

Furthermore, strong overlaps in the material scope of a GloBE MLC are likely as well: first and foremost, once again, the undeniable similarity between the IIR and the CFC rules should be mentioned here.[2615] Both concepts intend, at least in principle, to tax non-distributed profits of controlled foreign companies at the level of parent entities. Of course, there are three major conceptual differences: first (i), the IIR allocates 'Top-up Tax', which is an amount of tax liability, while the ATAD's CFC rule allocates profits. Furthermore, while (ii) the IIR applies only to the ultimate parent

2610. For example, the ATAD allows exceptions to be introduced for financial undertakings under the interest barrier and the CFC rules; however, there are no general exemptions for specific industries or companies.
2611. Comprehensively on the external dimension of ATAD, *see* W. Haslehner, *supra* note 2102, at 34 and 44–47.
2612. Comprehensively on Art. 1 ATAD and its interpretation, *see* M. Caziero & I. Lazarov, *supra* note 2143, at 1789 et seq.
2613. W. Haslehner, *supra* note 2102, at 34.
2614. On this requirement of external competence, *see Opinion 1/94 (WTO)*, para. 95; *Opinion 2/92*, para. 33; *Opinion 1/03 (Lugano)*, para. 122.
2615. *See* only the explanation of the IIR in the Blueprint, where it is stated that '[t]*he IIR operates in a way that is similar to a CFC rule*', *see Tax Challenges Arising from Digitalisation – Report on Pillar Two Blueprint*, para. 411.

entity on a jurisdictional basis,[2616] Articles 7 and 8 ATAD apply to any individual entity or permanent establishment within EU borders.[2617] In addition, (iii) the IIR imposes a top-up tax equal to the difference between the effective tax burden and the minimum tax rate,[2618] whereas the ATAD requires taxation at the full rate of the state of residence if the effective tax burden in the source state is less than half.[2619] Furthermore, (iv) the IIR applies to all low-taxed profits of a foreign entity which is beneficially owned by a group within the scope of GloBE,[2620] whereas Article 7(2) ATAD gives Member States the choice of recognizing either income from passive sources only[2621] or income from 'non-genuine arrangements'[2622] and therefore only covers certain types of income.[2623]

Nevertheless, despite all these conceptual differences, an overlapping scope, at least with regard to passive income and income from non-genuine activities, cannot be denied. Finally, as has been shown, the rule order between 'CFC regimes' and QDMTT is not quite clear. 'CFC regimes', thus, do interact with the QDMTT, and the latter might indeed 'affect' Articles 7 and 8 ATAD. For income that is included in the tax base of an entity pursuant to Articles 7 and 8 ATAD, therefore, it could well be argued that an exclusive external competence might arise under the last limbs of Article 216(1) TFEU and Article 3(2) TFEU. Only with regard to purely active income and income from genuine activities, an overlapping scope of application between Articles 7 and 8 ATAD and the IIR can be excluded in any case. A GloBE-related agreement providing for an IIR only for active or genuine activities is unlikely to 'affect' the rules of ATAD. If one argues that an external competence can be derived from the ATAD under the *ERTA*-principles, one would therefore have to admit that a GloBE MLC would have to be concluded obligatory as a mixed agreement if the IIR were to be applied indiscriminately to all income as currently proposed by OECD.

With respect to the treaty-based STTR, there are only indirect linkages with existing measures that have already been implemented by ATAD. One could argue that the STTR partly operates in a similar manner as Articles 9 and 9a ATAD dealing with hybrid mismatches. This is especially true for the cases regulated in Article 9(2) ATAD, where deduction is provided in one state, while the respective payment is not included in the tax base of the other state ('deduction non-inclusion').[2624] In these cases, the

2616. *Ibid.*, para. 413.
2617. *See* Art. 7(1) ATAD where it is stated, that the 'Member State of a taxpayer shall *treat an entity, or a permanent establishment* [...] as a controlled foreign company [...]' (emphasis added).
2618. *Tax Challenges Arising from Digitalisation – Report on Pillar Two Blueprint*, para. 410 et seq.
2619. Article 7(1)(b) ATAD.
2620. The IIR does not distinguish between any types of income, *see Tax Challenges Arising from Digitalisation – Report on Pillar Two Blueprint*, para. 410 et seq.
2621. *See* the list of income categories provided for in Art. 7(2)(a) ATAD.
2622. According to Art. 7(2)(b) ATAD an arrangement is considered as '*as non-genuine to the extent that the entity or permanent establishment would not own the assets or would not have undertaken the risks which generate all, or part of, its income if it were not controlled by a company where the significant people functions, which are relevant to those assets and risks, are carried out and are instrumental in generating the controlled company's income*'.
2623. However, it should be noted that according to Art. 3 ATAD, the Member States are free to adopt stricter rules and to include other income as well, in detail on the two options, *see* A. Rust, *supra* note 2106, at 191–194.
2624. Compare only the definition of the STTR in the Blueprint, which states that the STTR should '*provide jurisdictions with a right to 'tax back' up to the agreed minimum rate where other*

ATAD first prescribes that the deduction should be denied in the payer's state, and if deduction is not denied there, the corresponding payment should be taxed in the state of the recipient of the income stream. In a similar vein, the STTR simply allows the source state to levy tax on such payments made to a recipient in a different state, although the respective tax treaty provides the taxing right of the residence state of the recipient. Thus, it can be assumed that Article 9(2) of ATAD and the future STTR might point in similar directions, although the parallels are not nearly as pronounced as with Articles 7 and 8 of ATAD and the IIR. Thus, it is also conceivable that the ATAD, at least indirectly, could have an impact on the external powers of Member States for the proposed GloBE MLI.

In light of these considerations, it is conceivable that the content of future GloBE-related agreements, e.g., a GloBE MLC as well as a GloBE MLI, will fall within the subjective and material scope of ATAD. It should also be emphasized here that the '*nature*' of ATAD and GloBE probably share some similarities, since both GloBE and ATAD pursue comparable, although clearly not identical, purposes: both want to contribute to a '*fairer*' and '*more effective*' tax system,[2625] whatever that means,[2626] and both want to combat BEPS[2627] and aggressive tax planning, at least in the widest sense.[2628] Certainly, GloBE's political rationales go beyond these political platitudes.[2629] However, if the CJEU assesses the question of competence on the basis of the 'nature and content' of EU law and an international agreement,[2630] there is much to suggest that ATAD's and GloBE's intentions point in the same direction.

As a result, it can be stated that the spillovers of ATAD into the external sphere of the Union in the regulatory area of GloBE should not be underestimated. It cannot be ruled out that the CJEU would affirm the *existence* of an exclusive external competence of the EU to conclude GloBE-related agreements, at least with regard to the IIR and sources of passive income, on the basis of the ATAD and in the light of its complex *ERTA*-jurisprudence codified in the last limbs of Articles 216(1) and 3(2) TFEU. Nevertheless, there are also good reasons against exclusive competence based on the ATAD since the GloBE rules consider taxes paid due to ATAD as 'Covered Tax'. However, if it is argued that an exclusive competence might not arise, there is still the question of whether and to which extent ATAD might, nevertheless, 'pre-empt' the

---

jurisdictions have not exercised their primary taxing rights', *see Tax Challenges Arising from Digitalisation – Report on Pillar Two Blueprint*, para. 566.

2625. *See* Recitals 1 and 2 of the ATAD and the Cover Statement of the October Blueprint, which, however, mentions the terms 'fair' and 'more efficient' with regard to Pillar I, *see Tax Challenges Arising from Digitalisation – Report on Pillar Two Blueprint*, at 11. There can nevertheless be no doubt that the same policy rationale also applies to Pillar Two.

2626. With comprehensive and convincing criticism of the political justification concepts of '*fairness*' and '*effectiveness*' mentioned here, *see* C. Staringer, *supra* note 2097, at 7 et seq.

2627. *See* Recitals 1–4 of the ATAD and the Cover Statement of the October Blueprint, according to which Pillar Two should be dedicated to the '*remaining base erosion and profit shifting (BEPS) challenges* [...]', *see Tax Challenges Arising from Digitalisation – Report on Pillar Two Blueprint*, at 11.

2628. Recital 3 of the ATAD.

2629. Extensively on the policy rational of GloBE, *see* already s. 4.5.8.

2630. *Opinion 2/91 (ILO)*, para. 25; Case C-114/12, *Broadcasting Convention*, para. 50; Case C-66/13, *Green Network*, para. 33.

Member States' ability to conclude international agreements in the area of GloBE. From my point of view, only '*field pre-emption*' can definitely be ruled out because there can be no doubt that direct tax law has not been exhaustively harmonized. It remains open, however, whether the external influence of ATAD only precludes Member States from implementing provisions which are in conflict with the provision of ATAD ('*rule pre-emption*') or whether ATAD also precludes Member States from acting against its goals ('*obstacle pre-emption*').[2631] However, since ATAD and GloBE probably have a strong common interest, possible future GloBE-related agreements are unlikely to work against ATAD's goals. Apart from that, the considerations just made have lost some of their relevance as the EU succeeded in adopting the GloBE-Directive, which, as has been revealed, exhaustively harmonizes the implementation of GloBE.[2632] As will be seen, this could make a huge difference with regard to the EU's external competence, at least with regard to a future GloBE MLC. The following section is therefore devoted to the question of how the GloBE-Directive influences the external competence of the EU in the field of Pillar Two. Does the GloBE-Directive provide the EU with an exclusive external power to conclude GloBE-related agreements under the *ERTA*-doctrine?

6.1.3.3.3 *The Effects of the GloBE-Directive on the External Competence of the Union*

As has been shown, it cannot be ruled out that the ATAD alone could trigger an *ERTA*-effect with regard to international agreements to be concluded in the future for the implementation of GloBE and might, at least with respect to passive income or income from non-genuine arrangements, establish an exclusive external competence according to the last limbs of Articles 216(1) and 3(2) TFEU. Consequently, this must apply all the more for the GloBE-Directive. Now that the GloBE-Directive has successfully been adopted, the legally exciting question remains to what extent the GloBE-Directive affects the external sphere of the Union under the *ERTA*-doctrine? Once again, it is necessary to refer to the case law of the ECJ, according to which '*any competence, especially exclusive competence, must have its basis in conclusions drawn from a comprehensive and detailed analysis of the relationship between the international agreement envisaged and the Community law in force*'.[2633] However, the content of any GloBE-related agreements is not yet known at this point in time. Thus, one can, of course, only speculate about their content and whether there will be any GloBE-related agreements concluded at all.

Nevertheless, there are some conclusions to draw from the GloBE-Directive and the suggested agreements in the GloBE Model Rules. As explained at the outset,[2634] several completely different groups of international agreements are currently planned in connection with GloBE: first, OECD discussed the release of a GloBE MLC; second, it is planned to implement a network on bi- and/or multilateral agreements for

2631. In the same vein, *see* W. Haslehner, *supra* note 2102, at 44.
2632. *See* in detail s. 6.1.2.3.2.
2633. *Opinion 1/13 (Hague)* at 13; Case C-66/13, *Green Network*, para. 33.
2634. Section 6.1.3.1.

automatic exchange of GloBE-related information and third, OECD plans to implement the treaty-based provisions STTR and SOR via a GloBE MLI. Of course, an analysis of the external competence brought about by the GloBE-Directive must be carried out separately for each kind of agreement(s) just mentioned.

First, the GloBE MLC within the framework of the IF is to be discussed. The content of such an agreement would presumably concern the substantive component of GloBE and, above all, would transform the '*common approach*' referred to by the OECD into a binding obligation under international law: IF Member States should not be required to adopt the GloBE rules, but, if they choose to do so, they should implement and administer the rules in a way that is consistent with the GloBE Model Rules.[2635] Such an agreement would probably cast this '*common approach*' into binding international law for IF Member States and would oblige IF Member States to implement GloBE along the lines of the GloBE Model Rules.[2636] Based on this premise, it would be clear that such a GloBE MLC would effectuate a competence under the last limb of Article 216(1) TFEU: such a convention would affect the scope of the GloBE-Directive by coordinating the application of the IIR and the UTPR in relation with third states. However, the IIR and the UTPR are exhaustively harmonized by the GloBE-Directive. Consequently, the external competence in unison would be exclusive according to Article 3(2) TFEU because the GloBE-Directive is not a mere minimum standard. Consequently, there would also be no room for the above-mentioned '*ILO exception*', even if the GloBE MLC were established as a minimum standard.[2637] In my opinion, such a GloBE MLC would have to be concluded by the EU itself by virtue of exclusive external competence. Consequently, the Member States could only become party to such an agreement if the Union expressly waived to exercise its exclusive external competence.

The second sort of agreements are proposed in the GloBE Model Rules (so-called *Qualifying Competent Authority Agreement*) and intend to implement a network of bi- or multilateral agreements on exchange of annual GloBE-related information returns. Since the GloBE tax assessment is explicitly addressed in Article 44 GloBE-Directive, the solution with respect to such agreements would be identical to that of the GloBE MLC: such agreements concluded with third states would necessarily be covered by the last limbs of Article 216(1) TFEU and Article 3(2) TFEU respectively, because such agreements would certainly directly affect the procedural rules laid down by the GloBE-Directive in Article 44 GloBE-Directive. What is different, however, is the fact that Article 55 GloBE-Directive explicitly allows the Union to '*conclude agreements with third-country jurisdictions whose legal frameworks have been assessed as equivalent to a qualified IIR in accordance with Article 52, with a view to arranging a framework for simplifying the reporting procedures laid down in Article 44(6)*'. Article 44(6) of the GloBE-Directive allows for a simplification of GloBE tax returns of an 'MNE Group' if a CE is located in a Member State, but the PE is located in a third country jurisdiction. Of course, in the case of simplification granted to third country 'MNE Groups', Member

2635. *OECD/G20 Statement 8 October*, at 3.
2636. V. Bendlinger, *supra* note 258, at 4.
2637. *Opinion 2/91 (ILO)*, para. 18; *Opinion 1/03 (Lugano)*, para. 123.

States have an increased interest in exchanging information with the respective third country where the UPE of this 'MNE Group' is established. Article 55 GloBE-Directive is obviously intended to be an enabling basis for such so-called *Qualifying Competent Authority Agreements*. For the existence of an external competence of the Union, there is consequently a competing case of the third limb but also of the fourth limb of Article 216(1) TFEU. Here the redundancy of the third limb in Article 216 TFEU becomes clear: it would not have been necessary to mention the competence to conclude such '*bilateral agreements on simplified reporting obligations*' in Article 54 of the GloBE-Directive, because such agreements would have an effect on the GloBE-Directive according to the last limb of Article 216(1) TFEU anyway. With regard to the nature of this external competence, Article 55 GloBE-Directive in itself is the source for exclusivity: finally, according to the first limb of Article 3(2) TFEU, the Union has exclusive external competence if the conclusion of an agreement is explicitly provided for in a secondary act. However, exclusivity, in this case, would certainly also arise from the last limb of Article 3(2) TFEU because such agreements would 'affect' the GloBE-Directive. The fact that the GloBE-Directive explicitly refers only to '*bilateral agreements on simplified reporting obligations*' is, therefore, of no relevance at all from the perspective of competence: even without this reference, the Union would have exclusive external competence for such agreements. Consequently, it can neither be derived from Article 5 GloBE-Directive that the Union would not have competence for all agreements not mentioned therein nor that it would waive its competence to conclude other GloBE-related agreements. Article 55 GloBE-Directive only emphasizes that the EU can conclude such agreements on its own.

The last type of GloBE-related agreement to be addressed is the GloBE MLI. Here, however, the position is different from that of the other agreements just addressed: the GloBE MLI governs content that the GloBE-Directive consciously does not address. The STTR (and the SOR) is not contained in the GloBE-Directive.[2638] It is thus much more difficult to determine whether the GloBE-Directive could give rise to external competence with respect to a GloBE MLI. It is questionable whether the STTR '*affects*' the GloBE-Directive or '*alters its scope*'. In any case, the STTR is planned to be applied '*before*' GloBE. Taxes levied due to the application of the STTR will be considered as a covered tax within the GloBE regime. With respect to the SOR, one should note that the IIR also applies with respect to PEs that are exempt under tax treaties. Thus, with respect to the SOR, one might argue that a GloBE MLI including the SOR '*affects*' the GloBE-Directive. But might that be enough to establish exclusive external competence based on Articles 216(1) and 3(2) TFEU? As has been pointed out above, one could argue that the GloBE MLI could affect CFC rules of ATAD, at least to a certain extent.[2639] Consequently, one could argue that the same would have to apply to the STTR enshrined in an international treaty such as DTC. In my opinion, however, this

2638. *See* the Explanatory Memorandum: „*The Subject to Tax Rule (STTR) is a treaty-based rule* [...] *However since this will be for jurisdictions to implement individually, there will be no EU action in relation to the STTR and this proposal does not concern the STTR*', *see* COM(2021)823 final 5.

2639. Section 6.1.3.3.2.

connection would be too far-fetched. CFC rules are obviously not identical, but at least comparable to the IIR. However, the STTR functions entirely differently from the IIR and UTPR and is not comparable to these mechanisms. For this reason, the author believes that the GloBE-Directive would probably not be 'affected' by a GloBE MLI, at least with respect to the STTR. On the contrary, there might be an argument for an exclusive external competence of the EU with respect to a GloBE MLI with respect to the SOR. In any case, whether the EU has (exclusive) external competence to conclude such a GloBE MLI would have to be examined in light of the content of such an agreement.

Regardless of the final design of the GloBE-Directive, the conceivable '*creep*'[2640] of external competence through the adoption of a GloBE-Directive is considerable: as was also widely discussed after the adoption of the ATAD[2641] or also on the CCTB-Proposals,[2642] the adoption of a GloBE-Directive certainly leads to a shift of powers in favour of the Union – not only in terms of a GloBE MLC but probably also with respect to GloBE-related agreements on exchange of information.[2643] Conversely, the impact of the GloBE-Directive on the external competence to conclude a GloBE MLI might be limited.

In any case, Member States have always been reluctant to give away powers, especially when fiscal interests are at stake and even with an exclusive external competence of the Union, there might be a procedural barrier to the enactment of a future GloBE-related agreement: the Union can only enter into international commitments in accordance with the procedure set out in Article 218 TFEU. According to Article 218(2) TFEU, the Council – in principle acting by qualified majority according to the first sentence of Article 218(8) TFEU – has to '*authorise the opening of negotiations, adopt negotiating directives, authorise the signing of agreements and conclude them*'. Nevertheless, Article 218(8) TFEU prescribes that the Council can only act unanimously '*when the agreement covers a field for which unanimity is required for the adoption of a Union act*'. Since the GloBE-Directive[2644] has been based on Article 115 TFEU, unanimity in the Council is also required for the conclusion of international agreements in the area of direct tax law – even if an exclusive external competence of the Union exists.[2645] The conclusion of a future GloBE MLC or other GloBE-related agreements, like agreements for automatic exchange of information or the GloBE MLI, is, thus, subject from the outset to the same political hurdles as the adoption of the GloBE-Directive itself. Nevertheless, it remains to be considered that the actual adoption of the GloBE-Directive might give rise to exclusive competence of the EU pursuant to the last limbs of Articles 216(1) and 3(2) TFEU. This precludes Member

2640. G. Kofler, *supra* note 1796, at 48–49.
2641. ATAD.
2642. 2016 Proposal CCTB; and Proposal for a Council Directive on a Common Consolidated Tax Base (CCTB), COM(2011) 121 final.
2643. Extensively on the question, whether the Union could obtain competence to conclude DTCs, *see, i.a.*, G. Kofler, *supra* note 1790, at 341–358; W. Haslehner, *supra* note 2024, at 3.5.2.; G. Kofler, *supra* note 1796, at 47–48.
2644. *See* already s. 6.1.2.
2645. Extensively on this issue from a direct tax perspective, *see* A.C.M. Zaidan, *supra* note 2023, at 292.

States from entering into a GloBE MLC or other GloBE-related agreements even if the adoption of such agreements concluded by the EU were to fail.[2646] Thus, if the Council does not authorize the conclusion of the treaty, individual Member States cannot become parties to such a treaty on their own, as exclusive competence precludes the Member States from taking any legislative action. This, in turn, could force Member States to agree on the conclusion of a GloBE-related agreement by the EU in the course of a procedure under Article 218 TFEU.

6.1.3.3.4 External Competence Without or Outside the Scope of the GloBE-Directive: Is GloBE 'Necessary to Attain One of the Objectives Referred to in the Treaties'?

Last but not least, there remains a scenario to be dealt with in connection with a possible external competence of the Union in the context of GloBE. According to the second limb of Article 216(1) TFEU, codifying the principle developed by the ECJ in *Opinion 1/76*[2647] and *Kramer*,[2648] an (exclusive) external competence of the Union may occur even if no internal legislation has been adopted, but the conclusion of an agreement is '*necessary to attain one of the objectives referred to in the treaties*'. Consequently, the question arises whether GloBE is necessary to achieve one of the Union's goals and whether an exclusive external competence could arise even if the GloBE-Directive did not exist or if the EU planned to conclude a treaty related to Pillar Two that is outside the scope of the GloBE-Directive. Could the EU also gain exclusive external competence under the second limb of Article 3(2) TFEU if the GloBE-Directive did not exist or with respect to issues of Pillar Two that are not directly regulated by the GloBE-Directive?

When thinking about the Union's objectives, there is certainly no way around Article 3 TEU and therein, the objective to establish the internal market in Article 3(3) TEU could be considered an objective GloBE might be related to. According to this provision, the Union shall, i.e., '*establish an internal market*', '*work for the sustainable development of Europe based on balanced economic growth and price stability*' and '*a highly competitive social market economy*'. However, as already pointed out previously, the second limb of Article 216(1) TFEU is, according to the CJEU, precisely not to be interpreted as a vague reference to the Union's objectives listed in Article 3 TEU but rather needs a basis in a specific legal competence provided for in the treaties.[2649] Finally, the respective international agreement must at least '*contribute*' to the objectives of the Treaties.[2650] Therefore, once more, reference is to be made to Article 115 TFEU, which probably is the only appropriate legal basis for harmonization in the area

2646. On the effects of exclusive external competence, *see* already s. 6.1.3.2.3.
2647. *Opinion 1/76 (inland waterways)* at 76.
2648. Joined Cases C-3/76, 4/76, 6/76, *Kramer*.
2649. S. Vöneky & B. Beylage-Haarmann, *supra* note 2406, para. 10; C. Heber, *supra* note 2419, at 605.
2650. *Opinion 2/15 (Singapore)*, para. 240.

of direct taxation.[2651] Indeed, by referring to a '*direct affect* [on] *the establishment or functioning of the internal market*', Article 115 TFEU is inherently related to the objectives set out in Article 3(3) TEU. So the question is: is GloBE necessary to establish the internal market or affect its functioning?

As already examined with regard to the internal competence of the Union to implement GloBE,[2652] this question can hardly be answered conclusively by using legal methodology. If one understands the internal market purely in the light of fundamental freedoms, one will tend to reject the necessity requirement, and if one takes the perspective of the internal market as a level playing field, one could easily find arguments to affirm it. However, it is a matter of fact that the CJEU has so far set hardly any limits to the interpretation of the internal market competences and,[2653] especially with regard to Article 115 TFEU, the unanimity requirement, which according to Article 218(8) TFEU would also have to be taken into account with respect to international commitments of the EU, seems to be the only considerable obstacle of the EU secondary legislature. Nevertheless, it is difficult to determine to what extent the implementation of a minimum taxation regime is '*necessary*'[2654] for the establishment of the internal market, as required by the second limb of Article 216(1) TFEU, since one could as well argue that a minimum taxation might even harm the establishment and the functioning of the internal market.[2655]

Since the very existence of an external competence under the second limb of Article 216(1) TFEU is on shaky ground, it is all the more difficult to establish the exclusivity of such a competence. As the CJEU pointed out in *Opinion 2/15*, it might be the case that an external competence might be classified as necessary according to the second limb of Article 216(1) TFEU if it '*contributes*' to the objectives of the treaty, while such an agreement is not '*necessary*' to enable the Union to exercise its competence.[2656] From this point of view, there is much to suggest that a GloBE-related treaty could not be based on the second limb of Article 216(1) TFEU if the GloBE-Directive had not been adopted or with respect to issues that are outside the scope of the GloBE-Directive. Finally, there are even less arguments that the exclusivity of such a competence under the second limb of Article 3(2) TFEU could be successfully argued.

6.1.3.4 Interim Conclusion

EU primary law does not provide for an explicit internal competence for the harmonization of corporate tax law for the EU and likewise does not provide for any external competence in that field of law.[2657] Nevertheless, the Treaties, according to Article

2651. Section 6.1.2.7.
2652. *See* already s. 6.1.2.3.
2653. Comprehensively on the ECJ's jurisprudence with regard to the internal market competences, *see* 6.1.2.2.3.
2654. To be understood as '*contribute*', according to the ECJ, *see* again *Opinion 2/15 (Singapore)*, para. 240.
2655. *See* on this argument, s. 6.1.2.3.7.
2656. *Opinion 2/15 (Singapore)*, paras 237–242.
2657. *See, i.a.*, R. Lyal, *supra* note 2407, at 67.

216(1) TFEU, also provide for implied external powers of the EU, which according to Article 3(2) TFEU may, in certain situations, even become exclusive (subsequent exclusivity). An implied external competence of the Union may arise according to the second and fourth limbs of Article 216(1) TFEU:[2658] The Union has external competence to conclude international agreements if the conclusion of such an agreement might *'affect common rules or alter their scope'* or if the conclusion of such an agreement by the Union *'is necessary to achieve* [...] *one of the objectives referred to in the treaties'*. The fourth limb of Article 216(1) TFEU is a codification of the *ERTA*-doctrine,[2659] according to which the Union becomes competent to conclude international agreements if secondary law might be affected by a certain international agreement. Given the fact that the GloBE-Directive has been adopted and exhaustively harmonizes the field of GloBE, there is much to suggest that GloBE-related agreements might 'affect' the GloBE-Directive pursuant to the *ERTA*-doctrine. However, whether this is the case finally depends on the content of the respective GloBE-related agreement at issue, and it is neither known whether such agreements will be concluded nor what content such agreements might have. As pointed out, with regard to GloBE, three types of such GloBE-related agreements have been under discussion:

- first, the OECD discussed the release of a **GloBE MLC;**
- second, it is planned to implement a network of bi- and/or multilateral agreements for automatic exchange of GloBE-related information (**'Qualified Competent Authority Agreements'**); and
- third, the OECD plans to implement the treaty-based provisions STTR and SOR via a **GloBE MLI**.

As has been shown, the adoption of the GloBE-Directive makes a huge difference with regard to the EU's external competence. In this respect, it was first discussed whether the EU would have gained (exclusive) external competence to conclude GloBE-related agreements if the GloBE-Directive had not been adopted. As the examination has revealed, the subject matter of GloBE-related agreements is unlikely to establish an *'affect'* on the corporate tax directives[2660] but could indeed establish an *'affect'* on the ATAD. There is a significant overlap between the IIR and the CFC Rules provided for in Articles 7 and 8 ATAD, although the mechanisms are clearly different. Furthermore, the STTR also finds comparable provisions in Article 9 ATAD. Nevertheless, there are also many arguments against an effect on the ATAD: the measures provided for in the ATAD are applied before GloBE, and also Article 3 ATAD could be understood as a waiver of external competence due to its reference to 'agreement-based provisions'. Thus, there are also good reasons to believe that GloBE-related agreements will not 'affect' the ATAD. Nevertheless, it is clear from settled case law that an 'effect on common rules' does not require a normative conflict, but may already

2658. Both the first and third limb in Art. 216(1) TFEU lack normative content, *see* 6.1.3.2.1.
2659. Case C-22/70, *ERTA*.
2660. Interest and Royalty Directive (2003/49/EC); Merger Directive (2009/133/EC); Parent Subsidiary Directive (2011/96/EC).

occur, if the international agreement falls within the scope of secondary legislation.[2661] It should be mentioned here, however, that a final assessment ultimately depends on the content of such GloBE-related agreements. In any case, it cannot be excluded that the ATAD alone gives rise to an external competence of the EU to conclude a GloBE MLC or a GloBE MLI. This applies in particular to Articles 7 and 8 ATAD in relation to IIR, which is a possible content of a future GloBE MLC insofar as passive income is concerned.[2662] As has been shown, even if the GloBE-Directive had not been enacted, there would have been some arguments in favour of an EU external competence to conclude GloBE-related agreements.

Finally, the adoption of the GloBE-Directive is a true game changer for the Union's external competence in the field of corporate taxation under the *ERTA*-doctrine.[2663] By adopting GloBE-Directive, the EU gained exclusive external competence to conclude the GloBE MLC or *'Competent Authority Agreements'* relating to GloBE pursuant to Articles 216(1) and 3(2) TFEU. Admittedly, this, of course, highly depends on the actual content of such agreements. Given the scope and high density of harmonization achieved by the GloBE-Directive, however, it is almost inconceivable that a GloBE MLC or any other GloBE-related procedural agreements would not affect the GloBE-Directive under the *ERTA*-doctrine. As has been shown, things might only be different with regard to the GloBE MLI: the GloBE-Directive would probably not be affected by the GloBE MLI with regard to the STTR. Rather, as has been argued, the ATAD might be affected by the adoption of the SOR by means of a GloBE MLI.[2664] This is because the IIR also applies with respect to PEs exempt under tax treaties, and the SOR might, therefore, make a difference with respect to the application of the IIR. Thus, the GloBE-Directive might be affected by a GloBE MLI if it aimed to implement the SOR.

The GloBE-Directive only explicitly addresses GloBE-related agreements on the exchange of information for simplified GloBE tax assessments in its Article 55 GloBE-Directive and emphasizes that such agreements may be concluded by the EU itself. However, this does not mean that the EU could not be involved with respect to other GloBE-related agreements. Rather, pursuant to the *ERTA*-doctrine, the GloBE-Directive gives rise to the exclusive competence of the EU, in particular with regard to a future GloBE MLC but conceivably also with respect to other GloBE-related agreements. One can, therefore, conclude that the GloBE-Directive precludes Member States from taking any international commitments related to issues laid down in the GloBE-Directive.[2665] This, of course, will also raise the interesting question of whether the GloBE-Directive will impact the Member States' ability to conclude DTCs insofar as certain provisions of the GloBE-Directive might be *'affected'*.[2666]

2661. *Opinion 2/91 (ILO)*, paras 25–26; Case C-66/13, *Green Network*, para. 32; Case C-114/12, *Broadcasting Convention*, para. 71. In detail, *see* s. 6.1.3.2.1.
2662. *See* s. 6.1.3.3.2.
2663. *See* s. 6.1.3.3.3.
2664. *See* s. 6.1.3.3.2.
2665. *See* s. 6.1.3.3.3.
2666. On the interrelation of GloBE and DTC, *see* already s. 5.

6.2 THE GLOBE-DIRECTIVE AND ITS RELATION TO PRIMARY LAW

6.2.1 General Considerations on the Relation of Primary and Secondary EU Law

6.2.1.1 An Introductory Note on the Relation of Secondary to Primary EU Law and the Enforcement of Primary Law Incompatibilities of Secondary Law

As has been concluded in section 6.1.2.7., there are good arguments to believe that the GloBE-Directive had correctly been based on the internal market competence of Article 115 TFEU and that the Union has probably not exceeded its competence by adopting GloBE by means of a directive. However, the existence of an EU competence does not in itself mean that primary law only poses *formal* or *procedural* limits to the EU legislature: Primary law can also impose *substantive* limits on the secondary legislature. This applies above all to fundamental rights pursuant to the ECHR or the CFR.[2667] But also, the EU Treaties themselves contain substantive provisions that can pose potential barriers for the EU legislature. In the case of the GloBE-Directive, these are, above all, the TFEU's provisions on the internal market, especially the fundamental freedoms, and the relationship between GloBE and state aid has already been discussed in the literature. Both issues will be addressed in section 6.2.2.; and as will be seen in section 6.2.2.1., the GloBE-Directive very well forces Member States to levy 'Top-up Tax' in situations that might be seen as conflicting with the fundamental freedoms. However, first there is the question of whether and how the limits posed by primary law could finally be enforced. Eventually, the question of primary law compatibility with secondary law would be moot if there were no possibility of challenging a legal act of secondary law that is in conflict with primary law.

The EU's system to review the legality of legislative acts is complex and twofold: while Article 263 TFEU provides for a distinct mechanism that enables Member States and EU institutions,[2668] as well as natural or legal persons that can bring evidence of direct and individual concern[2669] to *directly* challenge the legality of '*acts*' at the CJEU, the validity of legal acts may also be brought to the Court *indirectly* via a preliminary ruling pursuant to Article 267(1)(b) TFEU.[2670] The combination of Articles 263 and 267 TFEU, as the Court has emphasized, forms a '*complete system of legal remedies and procedures to permit the Court of Justice to review the legality of measures adopted by the institutions*'[2671] necessarily including legal acts of secondary law. However, as will be seen shortly, there are considerable reasons to question the '*completeness*' of the EU's system of judicial review.

2667. For some reflections on the relation of the GloBE-Directive to the fundamental rights, *see* D. Hohenwarter-Mayr, *supra* note 1552, at 147 et seq.
2668. Article 263(2) and (3) TFEU.
2669. Article 263(4) TFEU.
2670. On the distinction of direct and indirect judicial review, *see* P. Craig & G. de Búrca, *supra* note 1815, at 540 et seq.
2671. Case C-294/83, *Les Verts*, para. 23.

Pursuant to the first sentence of Article 263(1) TFEU, the '*Court of Justice of the European Union shall review the legality of legislative acts, of acts of the Council, of the Commission and of the European Central Bank, other than recommendations and opinions, and of acts of the European Parliament and of the European Council intended to produce legal effects vis-à-vis third parties*'.[2672] Therefore, Article 263 TFEU is the primary mechanism of judicial review within the EU and provides the CJEU with jurisdiction to '*declare the act concerned to be void*'.[2673] Finally, Article 263(2) TFEU lists the grounds on which judicial review can be claimed, including 'grounds of lack of competence, infringement of an essential procedural requirement, *infringement of the Treaties* or of any rule of law relating to their application, or misuse of powers'[2674] (emphasis added). For the purposes of this section, judicial review on the grounds of '*infringement of the Treaties*' is of particular interest. Does Article 263 TFEU enable the CJEU to strike down certain provisions of the GloBE-Directive if they are found to violate the fundamental freedoms?

In principle, Article 263(2) TFEU gives the answer: if a legislative act of the EU is found to violate the Treaties (including the fundamental freedoms), the Court has jurisdiction to declare the whole act or certain provisions void. At first glance, therefore, it appears that Article 263 TFEU is a powerful instrument of judicial review, but this is a distorted picture, as the procedure is subject to rigid limitations: first of all, pursuant to Article 263(6) TFEU, an action for judicial review is only permissible if it is '*instituted within two months of the publication of the measure* [...]'. For the GloBE-Directive, which was published in the Official Journal of the EU on 22 December 2022, the deadline was 22 February 2023, which has already passed at the time of this thesis had been submitted. Second, Article 263 TFEU distinguishes between three different types of applicants.[2675] Only Member States, the European Parliament, the Council, and the Commission, essentially without further preconditions (so-called privileged applicants), may initiate a procedure under Article 263 TFEU. While paragraph 3 still lists special legal standing for other so-called semi-privileged applicants, Article 263(4) TFEU regulates the legal standing of all other natural and legal persons ('non-privileged applicants'): '*Any natural or legal person may, under the conditions laid down in the first and second paragraphs, institute proceedings against an act addressed to that person or which is of direct and individual concern to them, and against a regulatory act which is of direct concern to them and does not entail implementing measures*'.[2676] The scope of Article 263(4) TFEU and its predecessors have long been highly controversial. In its famous *Plaumann*-decision,[2677] the Court, much to the displeasure of the literature,[2678] severely weakened the standing of private parties for action for judicial review when it imposed high burdens on so-called non-privileged applicants in terms

2672. Article 263(1) TFEU.
2673. Article 264(1) TFEU.
2674. Article 263(2) TFEU.
2675. R. Schütze, *supra* note 1822, at 367.
2676. Article 263(4) TFEU.
2677. Case C-25/62, *Plaumann & Co v. Commission*.
2678. For further reference to literature, *see* R. Schütze, *supra* note 1822, at 370.

of proving an '*individual concern*'.[2679] With the Treaty of Lisbon, former Article 230(4) EC Treaty was rewritten in Article 263(4) TFEU and supposedly liberalized compared to its predecessor. While Article 230(4) EC Treaty once only allowed to proceed against decisions, Article 263(4) TFEU allows 'any natural or legal person' to proceed against '*regulatory acts*', supposedly now without the strict requirement of proofing '*individual concern*'. However, what are '*regulatory acts*' and what distinguished the term of '*legislative acts*' used in Article 263(1) TFEU? In *Iniut*, the CJEU finally concluded that the term 'regulatory act' 'must be understood as covering all acts of general application *apart from legislative acts*'[2680] (emphasis added). This leads to the consequence that both individuals nor legal entities can still only bring an action for judicial review against a legislative act like the GloBE-Directive, if they if they can prove not only '*direct*' but also '*individual concern*'. The narrow interpretation of the 'individual concern' requirement therefore makes the hurdle for '*non-privileged applicants*' particularly high.[2681]

As a result, the Article 263 TFEU procedure for the GloBE-Directive was not a real threat in the first place: first, the GloBE-Directive was adopted in a special legislative procedure under Article 115 TFEU, which requires unanimity. It was, therefore, unlikely from the outset that a 'privileged applicant' such as a Member State would have challenged the GloBE-Directive, especially in view of the short deadline of Article 263(6) TFEU.

Other claimants, i.e., affected 'MNE Groups' or individual CEs, faced the hurdles of the '*direct*' and '*individual concern*' requirements. However, one multinational group has succeeded in bringing an action for annulment before the Court of First Instance, which is currently pending under case number T-143/23 (*VF v. Council*). The following information is known at the time of going to press:

> 'By application notified to the Council on 4 April 2023, the Applicant has brought an action before the General Court, on the basis of Article 263 TFEU, seeking the annulment of Council Directive (EU) 2022/2523 of 14 December 2022 on ensuring a global minimum level of taxation for multinational enterprise groups and large-scale domestic groups in the Union, in so far as: Article 17 excludes from its scope income from a shipping activity covered by Member States' tonnage tax regimes authorized under State aid rules, other than "international shipping income" and "qualified ancillary international shipping income". Article 17 applies only if "the constituent entity demonstrates that the strategic or commercial management of all ships concerned is effectively carried on from within the jurisdiction where the constituent entity is located". The Directive does not lay

2679. This has become known as the so-called Plaumann-test: persons other than those to whom a decision is addressed may only claim to be individually concerned if that decision affects them by reason of certain attributes which are peculiar to them or by reason of circumstances in which they are differentiated from all other persons and by virtue of these factors distinguishes them individually just as in the case of the person addressed', *see* Case C-25/62, *Plaumann* at 107. In detail on the 'Plaumann-Test' and its ongoing significance, *see* R. Schütze, *supra* note 1822, at 370 et seq.; P. Craig & G. de Búrca, *supra* note 1815, at 548 et seq.
2680. Case T-18/10, *Inuit v. Parliament and Council*, para. 56.
2681. In detail on the complex procedural framework and the evolvement of Art. 263 TFEU; *see* R. Schütze, *supra* note 1822, at 371 et seq.

down transitional measures for taxpayers that made substantial investments relying on a national tonnage tax regime.'[2682]

In support of its application, the applicant relies on (i) a possible breach of the general principle of equal treatment, (ii) a breach of the general principle of proportionality (on the one hand because the GloBE-Directive goes beyond what is necessary and on the other because it extends GloBE to domestic situations), (iii) a breach of the protection of legitimate expectations and legal certainty and, finally, the applicant claims that the GloBE-Directive (iv) infringes Articles 115 and 107 TFEU.[2683] Most of these claims have already been rejected in previous sections[2684] or will be refuted in the further course of this section.[2685] Only the violation of the general principle of equal treatment and legitimate expectations will not be dealt with in this book, as fundamental rights are beyond the scope of this analysis. Reference is made to recent literature on these issues.[2686] In general, however, it can be expected that neither the principle of equal treatment nor the protection of legitimate expectations will lead the Court to annul Article 17 GloBE-Directive, let alone the entire GloBE-Directive. Nevertheless, the outcome of the case remains to be seen.

Apart from this case, no other action for annulment under Article 263 TFEU appears to have been brought, and now that the time limit of Article 263(6) TFEU has also expired, such an action can no longer be brought. But is the GloBE-Directive, apart from the case of *VF v. Council*, immune from any allegation of infringement of primary law? Has the GloBE-Directive already achieved absolute validity?

In fact, the GloBE-Directive is now immune from future actions of direct judicial review under Article 263 TFEU, unless an act based on it[2687] is challenged in the future and 'incidentally' challenges the GloBE-Directive under Article 277 TFEU. This, however, is a very unlikely scenario. Nevertheless, legislative acts can be *indirectly* reviewed under Article 267(1)(b) TFEU as the Court has jurisdiction to give preliminary rulings on '*the validity* [...] *of acts of the institutions, bodies, offices or agencies of the Union*'.[2688] In contrast to Article 263 TFEU, preliminary rulings '*can be brought against any Union act* [...], *on any grounds* [...], *by anyone* [...] *at any time*',[2689] leading the Court to the already anticipated conclusion that the TFEU, considering the combination of Articles 263 and 267 TFEU, provided for a '*complete system of legal remedies and procedures*'[2690] of judicial review. However, there are significant drawbacks to challenging the 'validity' of a legal act under Article 267 TFEU procedure: first, a

2682. Council of the European Union, *Information Note From the Legal Service to the Permanent Representative Committee (Part 2) – Doc. 08476/23* 1 (24 Apr. 2023).
2683. *Ibid.*, at 2.
2684. Regarding Art. 115 TFEU, *see* s. 6.1.2.3. and on proportionality, *see* s. 6.1.2.5.
2685. Regarding Art. 107 TFEU, *see* s. 6.2.2.2.
2686. *See*, e.g., D. Hohenwarter-Mayr, *supra* note 1552, at 147–155.
2687. E.g. a delegated act under Art. 52(2) and Art. 53 GloBE-Directive is adopted on the basis of the GloBE-Directive, where an applicant could invoke the so-called 'plea of illegality' pursuant to Art. 277 TFEU which allows to challenge an EU act irrespective of the time limit set out in Art. 263(6) TFEU.
2688. Article 267(1)(b) TFEU.
2689. R. Schütze, *supra* note 1822, at 378.
2690. Case C-294/83, *Les Verts*, para. 23.

preliminary ruling can only be initiated by domestic courts. Thus, challenging a legal act via a preliminary ruling presupposes the existing implementation of the measure in the domestic law of the Member State. Furthermore, the applicant does not have a subjective 'right' that the validity of the EU's legal act is actually tested by the CJEU but rather has to 'convince' the domestic Court to initiate a preliminary ruling.[2691] Second, the applicant must be in violation of EU law, because otherwise there would be no chance to challenge a specific provision before the domestic Court. Third, as will be seen, the Court is very generous to the EU legislature when it comes to standard of review of secondary law against substantive rules of primary law – in particular, when it comes to *indirect* actions of judicial review.

Finally, as has been revealed, it turns out to be difficult for legal entities being subject to GloBE to challenge the 'validity' of the GloBE-Directive on the ground of Treaty infringements, e.g., infringements of the fundamental freedoms (or a lack of competence, *see* section 6.1.). Nevertheless, the fact that the existence of a conflict between a provision of a secondary law and primary law is not merely theoretical and is also actually taken up by the CJEU has once again been demonstrated by the proceedings of the ECJ in the *Orde van Vlaamse*[2692] case. The Court held, in a preliminary ruling, that a provision in the DAC6[2693] was invalid because it was incompatible with the CFR. Legal acts of EU corporate tax law are therefore not immune to violations of primary law; and neither is the GloBE-Directive. However, unlike domestic legislatures, which are subject to rigorous scrutiny in relation to compliance with primary law, the CJEU has consistently granted the EU secondary legislature a 'broad discretion' in interpreting the substantive limits of the Treaties. What is meant by 'broad discretion' will be discussed in the following sections.

6.2.1.2 The Standard of Review of Substantive Primary Law Incompatibilities: The Secondary Legislature's 'Broad Discretion'

Like any other constitutional framework, EU law has an established hierarchy of norms.[2694] The constitutional foundations of the EU are what is known as primary law including first and foremost the EU Treaties, the CFR, the ECHR, and general principles of EU law;[2695] the norms adopted on the basis of primary law are secondary law, which is subordinate to the requirements of primary law. If a normative conflict between primary and secondary law occurs, the CJEU has jurisdiction, as has been revealed in the previous section, to declare the respective act of secondary law or individual provisions of the respective acts void.[2696] But what is the standard of review with respect to the *substantive* primary law compatibility of secondary law? Does primary

2691. R. Schütze, *supra* note 1822, at 378.
2692. Case C-694/20, *Orde van Vlaamse Balies*.
2693. DAC6.
2694. Also on the hierarchy of norms within the EU from the perspective of tax law, *see* W. Haslehner, *supra* note 2102, at 48 et seq.
2695. In detail on the hierarchy of norms within the EU, *see* P. Craig & G. de Búrca, *supra* note 1815, at 136 et seq.; R. Szudoczky, *supra* note 260, at 93–94.
2696. R. Szudoczky, *supra* note 260, at 94.

law pose the same limits to the secondary legislature as it does to the Member States' domestic legislature or do the Treaties allow the EU legislature to move the EU's framework by secondary law if the Member States agree to do so?

Although, from a legal point of view, there can be no doubt that a legal understanding of the EU's constitutional order requires a strict hierarchy between primary and secondary law. To put it differently: from a legal perspective, secondary law must always be in line with the primary law and the way the CJEU interprets primary law. However, the CJEU's statements on the relationship between primary and secondary EU law speak a different language. As Szudoczky aptly puts it, the Court clearly '[avoids] *the need to annul or invalidate secondary law on the ground of incompatibility with primary law*'.[2697] This is all the truer, if not the *procedural* compatibility of secondary law is tested, but secondary law's *substantive* compatibility with primary law is at issue.

In fact, the Court grants the secondary legislature a '*broad discretion*'[2698] in the interpretation of primary law when it comes to the creation and compatibility of secondary law. It grants significantly more leeway to the secondary legislature than it would grant to national legislatures of the Member States to comply with the *substantive* limits of primary law. If one starts from the fundamental freedoms, which, as will be shown, could well be seen as a substantive primary law hurdle for the GloBE-Directive, it must be noted that the CJEU has hardly ever declared a secondary act to be void because it found a violation of the fundamental freedoms, whereas the fundamental freedoms have become significant legislative barriers for domestic legislatures. In fact, there are very few cases in which the CJEU has found a violation of fundamental freedoms by secondary EU legislation. However, such cases do exist: in *Ramel*, for example, the CJEU declared a regulation invalid because it violated the free movement of goods.[2699] Other cases concern legislative acts in the field of social security law.[2700] However, all these cases in which the ECJ has annulled a legal act of secondary law on the grounds of incompatibility with the fundamental freedoms have in common that they concerned situations in which individual Member States were granted the right to derogate from a general rule. The legal acts concerned were therefore particularly problematic because they supported a fragmentation of the internal market.[2701] However, the CJEU has not yet found any legal act to be contrary to fundamental freedoms if the secondary act introduced a measure restricting the fundamental freedoms for the entire internal market.

In principle, when it comes to the fundamental freedoms, the CJEU at least with regard to the scope of the fundamental freedoms applies the same standards to secondary law as it does to domestic law of the Member States: the EU's as well as

2697. *Ibid.*, at 95.
2698. See, e.g., Case C-203/12, *Billerud Karlsborg AB*, para. 35; Case C-390/15, *RPO*, para. 54; Case C-620/18, *Hungary v. Parliament and Council*, para. 112.
2699. Joined Cases Joined Cases 80 and 81/77, *SARL Les fils de Henri Ramel v. Receveur des douanes*; Joined Cases Joined Cases C-363/93, C-407/93, C-408/93 C-409/93 C-410/93 C-411/93, *René Lancry SA*.
2700. Case C-41/84, *Pinna*; Case C-20/85, *Roviello*.
2701. R. Szudoczky, *supra* note 260, at 103–104.

Member States' legislation do in principle fall within the scope of the fundamental freedoms, if the measure is either discriminatory or non-discriminatory but imposes a restriction. However, the standard of review of secondary law and national law of the Member States differs with regard to possible grounds for justification and, above all, the proportionality test. With regard to justification, the CJEU grants the secondary legislature recourse to grounds of justification that are not open to domestic legislatures.[2702] In relation to secondary legislation, the CJEU has accepted e.g., grounds of justification such as 'promote completion of the internal market'[2703] or the prevention of disturbance in the market,[2704] which a Member State could never invoke to justify a discriminatory or a restrictive measure.[2705] Furthermore, the CJEU is far more generous to the EU legislature, when it comes to the *Proportionality*-test. Contrary to domestic measures, the CJEU only declares secondary law to be in violation with the *Principle of Proportionality*, if the legal act of secondary law is '*manifestly inappropriate in terms of the objective which the competent institution is seeking to pursue*'[2706].[2707] Furthermore the Court adds that '*the criterion to be applied is not whether the measure adopted by the legislature was the only one or the best one possible but whether it was manifestly inappropriate*'[2708].[2709] In detail on the CJEU's jurisprudence on the *Principle of Proportionality*, *see* section 6.1.2.5.

In summary, it can be stated that the CJEU hardly outlaws any substantive primary law barriers in the secondary legislature. On the contrary, the CJEU seems to accept that the Member States can also withdraw the fundamental freedoms to a certain extent, if the procedural provisions of the Treaties are complied with.[2710] As a result, it can be concluded in advance that it is indeed unlikely that the CJEU will annul the GloBE-Directive, even if there is evidence of certain tensions between GloBE and the fundamental freedoms. This raises the question of the extent to which the national transposition laws of the Member States are protected by the GloBE-Directive from review against the fundamental freedoms.

2702. *Ibid.*, at 104.
2703. Case C-114/96, *René Kieffer and Romain Thill.*
2704. Case C-233/94, *Germany v. Parliament (Deposit Guarantee Scheme)*, para. 57.
2705. In detail for further reference, *see* R. Szudoczky, *supra* note 260, at 104.
2706. Case C-189/01, *Jippes*, para. 82.
2707. R. Szudoczky, *supra* note 260, at 105.
2708. Case C-189/01, *Jippes*, para. 83.
2709. Also *see* Case C-491/01, *British American Tobacco*, para. 123; Joined Cases C-154/04 and C-155/04, *Alliance for Natural Health*, para. 52; Case C-58/08, *Vodafone Ltd and others*, para. 52.
2710. Also *see* the conclusion of J. Hey before the GloBE-Directive had been adopted, arguing that the '*fundamental freedoms will take a back seat if Member States unanimously agree to an EU legislative measure*', *see* J. Hey, *Chapter 17: Global Minimum Taxation (GloBE): What Is It About and What Could Be a European Answer?*, in *Thinker, Teacher, Traveler: Reimagining International Tax Essays in Honor of H. David Rosenbloom*, s. 17.4.4. (Georg Kofler et al., eds, IBFD 2021).

6.2.1.3 *The 'Shielding-Effect' of Secondary Law: The GloBE-Directive Protecting Domestic Laws from Primary Law Violations*

As both, primary and secondary law, trump domestic laws of the Member States pursuant to the doctrine of supremacy, any domestic laws that simply transform a valid act of secondary law, are automatically in line with primary law. At first glance, this conclusion seems redundant: it is obvious that, if the superior norm is compatible with the ultimate norm, the subordinate norm is necessarily also in line with the ultimate norm. However, given the different standards of review applied by the ECJ with respect to the primary law compatibility of secondary law, compared to the rigorous scrutiny of domestic law, a phenomenon occurs that in literature has been described as '*shielding-effect*' of secondary law: if the EU's secondary legislature makes use of the '*broad discretion*' awarded by the CJEU, directives have the ability to '*shield*' domestic legal provisions from the strict scrutiny that the CJEU would apply if the respective directive did not exist. In the words of the CJEU, '[i]*t should be borne in mind that, in a field which has been exhaustively harmonised at Community level, a national measure must be assessed in the light of the provisions of that harmonising measure and not of primary law*'[2711].[2712]

Given the fact that the GloBE-Directive very closely follows the detailed pattern of the GloBE Model Rules and leaves little options for the Member States, one can assume that the GloBE-Directive achieves '*exhaustiveness*'.[2713] For the implementation of Pillar Two by the Member States, this means, that domestic law that simply transforms the content of the GloBE-Directive does not infringe the fundamental freedoms, if the domestic law is applied to a situation that is actually covered by the directive and the directive does not leave discretion to the Member State. If the same domestic rule is applied to a situation that is not covered by the directive,[2714] for example if the respective rule is applied to an entity that is not part of an 'MNE Group' exceeding the EUR 750 million threshold, or that is within the scope of the directive but the latter leaves discretion or different options[2715] to the Member State, the same domestic rule could very well infringe the fundamental freedoms. The GloBE-Directive, thus, '*shields*' or '*immunizes*'[2716] domestic law from possible infringements of the fundamental freedoms as long as the domestic rule is applied to situations that are within the

2711. Case C-210/03, *Swedish Match*, para. 81 and the case law cited there.
2712. In the same vein, *see* Case C-569/07, *HSBC*, para. 26., where the court held: '*where a matter is harmonised at Community level, national measures relating thereto must be assessed in the light of the provisions of that harmonising measure and not of those of the EC Treaty*'.
2713. Also *see* A. Schnitger, *Vereinbarkeit der Vorschläge zur Einführung von GloBE-Regelungen mit den Grundfreiheiten des AEUV*, 31 IStR 742 (2022). In detail on the exhaustive character of the GloBE-Directive, *see* s. 6.1.2.3.7.
2714. As the court regularly notes: the fact that a certain situation is not covered by a measure of secondary law '*does not of itself mean that the Member States are entitled to impose measures that contravene the freedoms of movement guaranteed by the EC Treaty*', *see* Case C-379/05, *Amurta*, para. 24; Case C-303/07, *Aberdeen Property Fininvest Alpha OY*, para. 28; Case C-446/04, *Test Claimants in the FII Group Litigation v. Commissioners of Inland Revenue*, para. 54.
2715. See, e.g., Case C-168/01, *Bosal Holding BV*, para. 26.
2716. In this vein, *see* A. Schnitger, *supra* note 2713, at 742.

scope of the GloBE-Directive or as long as the domestic rule does not go beyond the cases regulated by secondary law. Eventually, if the domestic rule merely transforms secondary law, the domestic rule is only tested against secondary law but not against primary law.[2717]

6.2.2 Potential Conflicts Between the GloBE-Directive and the TFEU

6.2.2.1 The Relation of the GloBE-Directive and the Fundamental Freedoms

6.2.2.1.1 Some Preliminary Remarks on the Relation of GloBE and the Fundamental Freedoms

Given the abundance of CJEU case law on cross-border taxation and fundamental freedoms, the compatibility of GloBE implementation with fundamental freedoms has been examined in the literature from the very beginning of the minimum tax debate.[2718] In particular, the *Cadbury Schweppes* doctrine developed by the CJEU[2719] was often seen as a possible hurdle for national GloBE implementations. It is not without reason that the Commission in the GloBE-Directive Proposal held in the Explanatory Memorandum that the directive was supposed to *'reflect the OECD Model Rules with the necessary adjustments'*[2720] in order to comply with the fundamental freedoms. Within the final directive, in particular, recital 6 of the GloBE-Directive addresses the issue of compliance with the fundamental freedoms:

> It is necessary to implement the OECD Model Rules agreed by the Member States in a way that remains as close as possible to the global agreement, in order to ensure that the rules implemented by the Member States pursuant to this Directive are qualified within the meaning of the OECD Model Rules. This Directive closely

---

2717. In further detail on the relation between primary, secondary and domestic law, *see* R. Szudoczky, *supra* note 260, at 114–117. Specifically with respect to the GloBE-Directive, *see* D. Hohenwarter-Mayr, *supra* note 1552, at 156.

2718. J. Becker & J. Englisch, *supra* note 469, at 524–528; D.W. Blum, *The Proposal for a Global Minimum Tax: Comeback of Residence Taxation in the Digital Era?: Comment on Can GILTI + BEAT = GloBE?*, 47 Intertax 521–522 (2019); J.F.P. Nogueira, *supra* note 2153, at 465–498; P.K. Schmidt, *supra* note 2123, at 983–997; J. F. P. Nogueira & A. Turina, *supra* note 2153, at 283–313; J. Hey, *supra* note 2710, s. 17.1. et seq.; C. Brokelind, *supra* note 2153, at 212–219; A.P. Dourado, *supra* note 1566, at 521–526; J. Englisch, *supra* note 2091, at 136–142; L. De Broe & M. Massant, *supra* note 2091, at 86–98; J. Englisch, *Effective Minimum Tax Implementation by the EU: Which Alternatives?*, Kluwer International Tax Blog, https://kluwertaxblog.com/2021/10/25/effective-minimum-tax-implementation-by-the-eu-which-alternatives/ (last visited 12 Mar. 2023); J. Englisch, *Non-Harmonized Implementation of a GloBE Minimum Tax: How EU Member States Could Proceed*, 30 EC Tax Review 207–219 (2021) DOI: 10.54648/ecta2021022; L. De Broe, *supra* note 1672, at 874–887; F. Debelva & L. De Broe, *supra* note 1652, at 898–905; A.P. Dourado, *Pillar Two from the Perspective of the European Union*, 67 BTR 573–600 (2022); W. Haslehner, *Is There A Need for a Directive on Pillar 2? A Few Normative Comments*, 50 Intertax 527–530 (2022) DOI: 10.54648/taxi2022057; A. Schnitger, *supra* note 2713.

2719. Case C-196/04, *Cadbury Schweppes*.

2720. European Commission, *Communication from the Commission to the European Parliament and the Council – Business Taxation for the 21st Century*, *supra* note 196, at 8.

> follows the content and structure of the OECD Model Rules. To ensure compatibility with primary Union law, and in particular with the principle of freedom of establishment, the rules of this Directive should apply to entities resident in a Member State as well as to non-resident entities of a parent entity located in that Member State. This Directive should also apply to large-scale purely domestic groups. In that way, the legal framework would be designed to avoid any risk of discrimination between cross-border and domestic situations. All entities located in a Member State that is low-taxed, including the parent entity that applies the IIR, should be subject to the top-up tax. Equally, constituent entities of the same parent entity that are located in another Member State that is low-taxed should be subject to the top-up tax.[2721]

In the meantime, the discussion around the compatibility of GloBE with the fundamental freedoms has lost some steam, mainly due to two reasons: first, the EU finally succeeded in adopting GloBE by means of a legal act of secondary law. Second, the GloBE-Directive explicitly also applies GloBE to 'large-scale domestic groups' and extends the IIR to domestic LTCEs. As already revealed in the previous sections, the EU legislature as a broad discretion with respect to the interpretation of substantive limits set by primary law and, indeed, the Commission has put some efforts to design the GloBE-Directive in a non-discriminatory way. The EU has therefore taken comprehensive precautions against potential accusations of incompatibility with fundamental freedoms.[2722] This does not mean, however, that there are not individual conflicts or areas of tension between the GloBE-Directive and fundamental freedoms. The following sections are therefore devoted to the questions of whether the GloBE Rules, as implemented in the GloBE-Directive, are in line with the fundamental freedoms.

6.2.2.1.2 The IIR and the Fundamental Freedoms

Under Article 1.2.1. GloBE Model Rules, the term MNE Group requires that a Group either includes '*at least one Entity or Permanent Establishment that is not located in the jurisdiction of the Ultimate Parent Entity*'. For this reason, it is obvious that the GloBE Model Rules assume that the IIR as well as the UTPR should neither be applied to domestic groups nor to domestic LTCEs. As a consequence, the GloBE Model Rules treat foreign companies less-favorable than domestic ones.[2723] It was, thus, evident already from the very beginning that the implementation of GloBE either by Member States or by way of a legislative act of the EU would require modification to comply with the fundamental freedoms and the CJEU's jurisprudence in direct tax matters in that respect.[2724] Technically, these modifications can be found on the one hand in Article 2 GloBE-Directive, which includes 'large-scale domestic groups' in the scope of the directive, and Articles 5(2), 6(2), 7(2) and 8(2) GloBE-Directive which oblige the

2721. Recital 6 GloBE-Directive (2022/2523).
2722. Already *see* s. 6.1.2.3.3.
2723. J. F. P. Nogueira & A. Turina, *supra* note 2153, at 289; J. Englisch, *supra* note 2718, at 2.
2724. *See* above all Case C-196/04, *Cadbury Schweppes*.

Member States to subject domestic UPEs to the IIR with respect to their own and to their domestic CEs. From a purely technical point of view, the GloBE-Directive, therefore, does not distinguish between a domestic and a cross-border situation with regard to IIR. In doing so, the Commission followed recommendations made in the literature even before the final draft of the GloBE Model Rules was published to eliminate potential conflicts with the fundamental freedoms from the outset by simply extending the application of the IIR to domestic situations.[2725] However, does the extension to domestic situations really protect the GloBE-Directive from infringements of primary law?

It can be anticipated that, most likely, this question can be answered in the affirmative. Nevertheless, a supposedly neutral regulation can *de facto* discriminate,[2726] and even non-discriminatory restrictions can violate fundamental freedoms. It is obvious that, e.g., the inclusion of 'large-scale domestic groups' is merely a formalistic requirement, and it is not a secret that such groups hardly exist. Accordingly, a violation of fundamental freedoms cannot be excluded from the outset.

First of all, there is the question of which freedom needs to be tested at all. With regard to the IIR, only the freedom of establishment[2727] is at stake.[2728] This is because the IIR only applies to CEs controlled by another CE. The CJEU has held that it is not the amount of ownership interest held that decides whether the freedom of establishment is applicable, but rather whether '*a definite influence on the decisions of the company* [is] *concerned*'.[2729] In this respect, pursuant to more recent case law, the '*intention to influence the management and control of the undertaking*'[2730] is decisive for the scope of the freedom of establishment. In fact, it is nearly inconceivable that the IIR could be applied in situations where there is no 'control' and could be tested against the freedom of capital movement. The IIR can only be applied with respect to 'Ownership Interest' in a different CE that is consolidated within the same financial statement as the 'Parent Entity' that is obliged to apply the IIR. Even if the consolidated financial accounting standard applied by the UPE requires consolidation below a participation of 50%, usually, the financial accounting standard requires consolidation because the respective UPE has 'de facto' control over the underlying entity. Consolidation without control is inconceivable. As the freedom of establishment is not applicable in situations including third countries, the application of the IIR seems to be unproblematic if it is applied with respect to LTCEs 'located' in third countries.[2731]

The question now is whether the GloBE-Directive leads to a factual or indirect discrimination in breach of the freedom of establishment, as the extension to

2725. J. Becker & J. Englisch, *supra* note 469, at 526; P.K. Schmidt, *supra* note 2123, at 993–994; J. Englisch, *supra* note 2718, at 211 et seq.
2726. J. Englisch, *supra* note 2718, at 3.
2727. Article 49 TFEU.
2728. J. Hey, *supra* note 2710, s. 17.4.4.; J. Englisch, *supra* note 2718, at 2; J. Englisch, *supra* note 2718, at 209 et seq.; A. P. Dourado, *supra* note 2718, at 585; A. Schnitger, *supra* note 2713, at 742.
2729. Case C-35/11, *Test Claimants (FII Group Litigation II)*, para. 91.
2730. Case C-464/16, *SECIL*, para. 40.
2731. Also *see* D. W. Blum, *supra* note 2718, at 521.

'large-scale domestic groups' and domestic CE-subsidiaries might be seen as merely formalistic; and in fact, this is not a new question. Rather, it has been intensively discussed in the past whether Member States could avoid frictions of domestic CFC legislation with the fundamental freedoms by simply extending the application of CFC rules to domestic low-taxed subsidiaries. While some have argued that the equalization of the domestic situation necessarily eliminates any prohibited discrimination,[2732] others have opposed that such a simple extension is not sufficient in order to comply with the discrimination prohibitions of fundamental freedoms.[2733] Indeed, the case law of the CJEU has always held that the freedoms also prohibit covert discrimination,[2734] which could feed the assumption that a mere formal extension of the IIR could well be in tension with the freedom of establishment. However, more recent jurisprudence shows that the Court is reluctant to determine factual discrimination in tax matters. With respect to the IIR, many scholars refer to the CJEU's statements with regard to progressive turnover taxes, where the Court held that although the progressive tax scale might lead to '[t]*he fact that the greater part of such a special tax is borne by* [...] *persons of other Member States*',[2735] this does '*not, inherently, create any discrimination*'[2736].[2737] Although it is not clear whether this case law can directly be transferred to the Pillar Two implementation, as the CJEU, on the other hand, recognized a discrimination of a similar rule in *Hervis*,[2738] e.g., Kofler & Schnitger point out that the EUR 75 million threshold is found in several legislative initiatives of the Commission and that the CJEU might take into account that the Commission indeed tried to implement the GloBE Model Rules as non-discriminatory as possible.[2739] For good reasons, many others also conclude that the EU indeed avoided a prohibited discrimination under the freedom of establishment by way of extending the application of the IIR to purely domestic situations.[2740]

However, even if one were to conclude that the IIR results in prohibited discrimination, such discrimination could be justified, and again it should be

2732. Taking that position, *see* in particular A. Rust, *CFC Legislation and EC Law*, 36 Intertax 498 (2008) DOI: 10.54648/taxi2008072. For further reference on this position, *see* J. Englisch, *supra* note 2718, at 213.
2733. Sceptical with regard to the extension of the IIR to domestic situations, *see* Michael P Devereux et al., *The OECD Global Anti-Base Erosion ('GloBE') Proposal*, Oxford University Centre for Business Taxation 50–51 (2020), https://oxfordtax.sbs.ox.ac.uk/files/oecdglobepropo salreportpdf (last visited 15 Mar. 2023). In a similar vein, *see* P. K. Schmidt, *supra* note 2123, at 12 and 31. Again for further references, *see* J. Englisch, *supra* note 2718, at 214.
2734. In the area of tax, see, e.g., Case C-98/14, *Berlington Hungary Tanácsadó és Szolgáltató kft*, para. 38; Case C-385/12, *Hervis Sport- és Divatkereskedelmi Kft.*, para. 39. For further reference, *see* J. Englisch, *supra* note 2718, at 214.
2735. Case C-75/18, *Vodafone Magyarország Mobil Távközlési Zrt.*, para. 52.
2736. *Ibid.*, para. 54.
2737. Also referring to this case law, *see* J. Englisch, *supra* note 2718, at 214.
2738. Case C-385/12, *Hervis*.
2739. G. Kofler & A. Schnitger, *supra* note 2137, at 189 et seq.
2740. *See* J.F.P. Nogueira, *supra* note 2153, at 479; J. Englisch, *supra* note 2718, at 215–216; J. F. P. Nogueira & A. Turina, *supra* note 2153, at 306–309; J. Englisch, *supra* note 2718, at 3; L. De Broe, *supra* note 1672, at 877–878; A.P. Dourado, *supra* note 1566, at 526; A. P. Dourado, *supra* note 2718, at 585–586 and 599; Georg Kofler & A. Schnitger, *supra* note 2137, at 189 et seq.

emphasized that the CJEU is generally very generous to the secondary legislature, also with regard to justifications (*see* section 6.2.1.2.). Particularly interesting for the GloBE-Directive is a statement of AG Kokott in the *Allianzgi Fonds* case:

> Finally, the second pillar of measures recommended by the OECD to combat tax avoidance also shows that combating tax evasion is to be regarded as one of the overriding reasons in the public interest. In the foreword to its most recent report on the consultation process on its recommendations to combat tax avoidance, the OECD underlined that a minimum level of taxation contributes to ensuring fairness and equity between tax systems, providing a stable tax architecture for new business models, and guaranteeing government finances, thereby emphasising its particular importance for the general public.[2741]

AG Kokott thus introduces the 'fight against tax evasion' and apparently also the 'avoidance of non- or low taxation' as possible new grounds of justification for restrictions of fundamental freedoms. This would, however, be in stark contrast to the previous case law of the CJEU and the EFTA-Court in cases like *Cadbury Schweppes*,[2742] *Olsen*[2743] and *X GmbH*[2744] as well as *Royal Bank of Scotland*,[2745] *Eurowings*[2746] or *Lexel*[2747].[2748] In the author's opinion, there is much to suggest that the 'fight against tax evasion' or 'avoidance of non- or low taxation' are not sufficient to justify violations against fundamental freedoms. It should also be pointed out in this respect that the CJEU, in its final decision on the *Allianzgi Fonds* case,[2749] ultimately did not take up the considerations put forward by AG Kokott on those 'new' grounds of justification.[2750] Nevertheless, given the fact that the CJEU leaves a wide leeway to the EU legislature, it is very likely that the CJEU would accept similar justifications if it had to decide on the validity of the GloBE-Directive. Furthermore, there is the 'manifestly inappropriate' test applied by the CJEU with respect to the substantive primary law compatibility of secondary law; and there is much to suggest that the IIR as designed in the GloBE-Directive would pass that test.

6.2.2.1.3 The UTPR and the Fundamental Freedoms

The relationship of the UTPR with the freedoms is a different story. The UTPR, as a rule, will not be applied within the EU pursuant to Articles 12 and 13 GloBE-Directive as every UPE, IPE, or POPE 'located' within the EU is subject to the IIR. Indeed, there

2741. Case C-545/19, *Allianzgi-Fonds*, para. 96.
2742. Case C-196/04, *Cadbury Schweppes*.
2743. Joined Cases E-3/12 and E-20/13, *Fred. Olsen and Others v. the Norwegian State*.
2744. Case C-135/17, *X GmbH v. Finanzamt Stuttgart*.
2745. Case C-311/97, *Royal Bank of Scotland plc*.
2746. Case C-294/97, *Eurowings*.
2747. Case C-484/19, *Lexel AB v. Skatteverket*.
2748. Also referring to this case law, *see* G. Kofler & A. Schnitger, *supra* note 2137, at 190.
2749. Case C-545/19, *Allianzgi-Fonds Aevn v. Autoridade Tributária e Aduaneira*.
2750. Also *see* on AG Kokott's statement with respect to these potential grounds of justification, V. Bendlinger, *Die Besteuerung von österreichischen Portfoliodividenden ausländischer Investmentvehikel – Nimmt die Quellensteuerrückerstattungssaga bald ein Ende?*, 34 ecolex 16 (2023).

is the exceptional situation of Article 50 GloBE-Directive, according to which small Member States are allowed to delay the application of the IIR and the UTPR leading to the consequence that the UTPR might also be applied by different Member States in intra-EU situations.[2751] Nevertheless, this is an exceptional case. In principle, within the EU, there is no need to apply the IIR, as any 'Top-up Tax' not collected by means of a QDMTT is already 'skimmed off' by way of the IIR. In general, the UTPR is, therefore, only relevant with respect to third-country situations that are not protected by the freedom of establishment. The second issue is that the UTPR is applied to CEs that do not have direct 'control' over the entity whose income the UTPR intends to tax. So, the entity that is obliged to apply the UTPR has no '*definite influence on the decisions of the company concerned*'.[2752] Rather, the CE being obliged to apply the UTPR and the LTCE is only under 'common control' of the same UPE.[2753] So what does this mean from the perspective of fundamental freedoms?

Given the fact that the UTPR, ignoring the very tiny and timely limited exception of Article 50(2) GloBE-Directive, only applies either (i) with respect to the income of a low-taxed UPE 'located' in a third state or (ii) with respect to a low-taxed CE 'located' in a third country that is neither directly held by an EU CE nor is taxed by way of an IIR, there is the question whether the UTPR could be in conflict with the fundamental freedoms at all. If one assumes that only the freedom of establishment could be invoked as the UTPR only applies within an 'MNE Group' under 'common control', the UTPR could not be infringing upon the freedoms as it merely applies in third-country situations. However, given the fact that the UTPR, e.g., also applies to PEs of third-country CEs within the EU, there might be situations where the UTPR charges 'Top-up Tax' with respect to a CE 'located' in a third country that has already exercised its freedom of establishment. Consequently, there might be certain (but limited) scenarios in which the freedom of establishment could pose a problem for the UTPR, although it is mostly applied in third-country situations.

Nevertheless, as already anticipated, one could argue that the UTPR never applies in a 'control' situation. While it is true that the application of the UTPR requires that the LTCE and the CE taxed by way of the UTPR are consolidated within the same financial statements and thus under the 'common control' of the same UPE, it could nevertheless be argued that the CE subject to the UTPR has no control over the LTCE whose 'Top-up Tax' the UTPR is supposed to collect. So, the entity that is taxed by way of the UTPR could invoke that it is taxed on the income of a taxpayer which it does not 'control' and that it is not restricted in its freedom of establishment but rather in its freedom of capital movement. In turn, however, it can be countered that in the absence of direct participation by the UTPR taxpayer, there is also a lack of investment; the latter, however, is necessary for the scope of application of the freedom of capital

2751. Article 50(2) GloBE-Directive (2022/2523).
2752. Case C-35/11, *FII Group Litigation II*, para. 91.
2753. Also taking note of this issue, *see* A. Schnitger, *supra* note 2713, at 746.

movement. Thus, it seems, at first glance, that the UTPR mainly concerns situations that could only fall within the scope of the freedom of establishment. However, since the UTPR is almost always applied in third-country cases, it is difficult to find situations in which the UTPR could potentially be in conflict with the freedom of establishment. Nevertheless, as will be shown, there are. But in which way could the UTPR be discriminatory at all?

In principle, one could argue that the UTPR is discriminatorily applied in every situation, as in a purely intra-EU or domestic situation, the UTPR could never come into effect. Rather, the 'Top-up Tax' within 'large-scale domestic groups' of domestic UPEs and their domestic LTCEs is collected by way of the IIR, which leaves no 'Top-up Tax' to collect for the UTPR. In a domestic situation at the level of the UPE, IPE or POPE, which had to apply the IIR while, if the UTPR is applicable, a domestic CE would have to apply the UTPR with respect to its parent or other non-directly related CEs. But can the IIR compensate for the lack of a UTPR in domestic scenarios?

In the light of the CJEU's case law, in particular *Cadbury Schweppes*, this is not the case.[2754] However, it could be argued that the discrimination by way of the UTPR could be justified under a 'coherence' argument: the less favourable treatment of the UTPR taxpayer could be compensated by the fact that no domestic CE is subject to the IIR in those cases. Given the fact, however, that IIR and the UTPR apply at the level of different entities, it is unlikely that a 'coherence' argument could justify the restriction. Nevertheless, it is unlikely that the CJEU would strike down the GloBE-Directive for that reason, as the Court might accept unconventional grounds of justifications for the secondary legislature, as pointed out in sections 6.2.1.2 and 6.2.2.1.2 and would probably not see a prohibited discrimination of the fundamental freedoms (if they are territorially applicable at all). Furthermore, it is likely that the Court would see this issue to be covered within the 'broad discretion' of the secondary legislature and would not find the GloBE-Directive's rules with respect to the UTPR to be 'manifestly inappropriate'.

However, a much more drastic discrimination arises in the special case of Article 14(4) GloBE-Directive. Usually, the 'UTPR Top-up Tax Amount' is reduced to zero if all of the UPE's 'Ownership Interests' in an LTCE are subject to a 'Qualified IIR'. However, if the 'Qualified IIR' does not collect the 'Top-up Tax' with respect to all 'Ownership Interests' held by the MNE Group, the UTPR, as already pointed out in section 4.4.2.8.3 (in particular Figure 13), collects the 'Top-up Tax' also with respect to ownership interests of non-group shareholders. In these situations, the UTPR collects more of the 'Top-up Tax' than would ever be collected under the IIR. Figure 19 aims to demonstrate the issue.

2754. Case C-196/04, *Cadbury Schweppes*, para. 45.

Figure 19 Discrimination Caused by Article 14(4) GloBE-Directive?

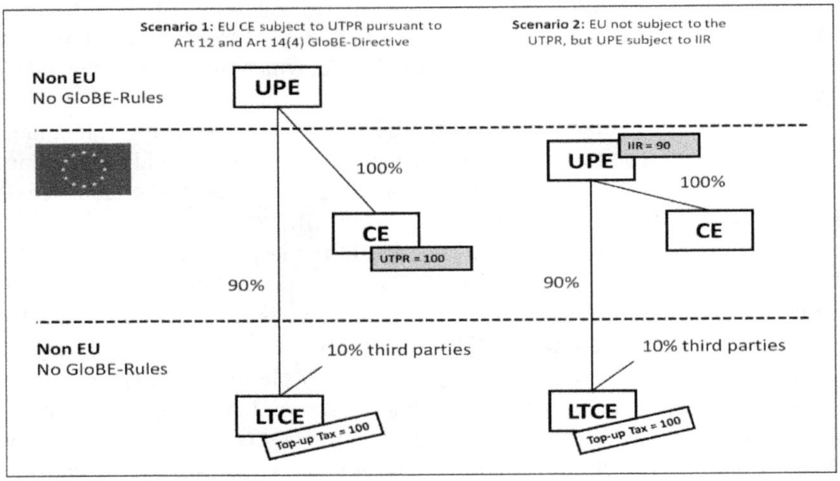

The figure above shows two scenarios: the first scenario shows an MNE structure in which an EU CE is obliged to apply the UTPR, whereas, in the second scenario, the UPE is 'located' within the EU and applies the IIR with respect to 'Top-up Tax' arising in an LTCE 'located' in a third state. In the first scenario, the UPE is 'located' in a third country and is not subject to a 'Qualified IIR' there. In this situation, the EU CE is obliged to apply the UTPR with respect to the 'Top-up Tax' of its sibling, notably without directly having ownership interest in the LTCE. Due to the fact that there is no IIR in the state of the UPE in the first scenario, the CE is obliged to collect the total amount of 100 of the 'Top-up Tax' irrespective of the MNE Group's share in the LTCE. The UTPR, thus, collects an amount of 10 that is, in principle, attributable to non-group shareholders. In the second scenario, where the UPE is located within the EU, the IIR would apply, but only with respect to 90% of the 'Top-up Tax' pending at the LTCE. The remaining 10% would not be collected, as the 'UTPR Top-up Tax Amount' would be zero pursuant to Article 14(3) GloBE-Directive. To put the issue in a nutshell: Article 14(4) GloBE-Directive collects an amount of tax that would never be collected in an intra-EU or a purely domestic situation. Given the fact that the UTPR cannot apply within the EU, 'Top-up Tax' attributable to non-group shareholders would never be collected in an intra-EU or domestic situation. Might this be an issue under the fundamental freedoms?

Indeed, the case of Article 14(4) GloBE-Directive is a tricky problem that has already gained some attention in the literature.[2755] Does it lead to a discrimination, and if yes, who is discriminated? Is it the EU CE, the whole 'MNE Group', or is it the minority shareholders of LTCE?

2755. A. P. Dourado, *supra* note 1566, at 526; P. Dourado, *supra* note 2718, at 591–592.

It is particularly interesting to look at the non-group minority shareholders. They do not have control over the LTCE and simply hold an investment, so they would therefore fall squarely within the scope of the freedom of capital movement.[2756] From this point of view, the UTPR would indeed be endangered because the territorial scope of the freedom of capital movement also extends to third countries. However, from a technical viewpoint, the minority shareholders do not suffer from the UTPR, as it is charged at the level of a different taxpayer. As a consequence, it is not the minority shareholders that might be discriminated against, but rather the UTPR taxpayer (the EU CE). The EU CE again is part of the 'MNE Group', which feeds the argument that the reason for applying the UTPR is 'common control' of the EU CE and the LTCE, which means that the situation is not covered by the freedom of capital movement, but rather the freedom of establishment is at stake; and as third states are involved, the situation above would not infringe the freedom of establishment. Also, with regard to Article 14(4) GloBE-Directive, it can thus be concluded that the provision probably does not establish a case of prohibited discrimination, even if the additional inclusion of top-up tax on non-group shareholders seems strange; and even if one argued that it is a prohibited discrimination under the freedoms, Article 14(4) GloBE-Directive would, most likely, pass the CJEU's 'manifestly inappropriate' test. For this reason, it is unlikely that the CJEU would find Article 14(4) GloBE-Directive incompatible with primary law.

6.2.2.1.4 Does the 'Initial Phase Relief' Pursuant to Article 49 GloBE-Directive Make a Difference with Respect to the GloBE-Directive's Compatibility with the Fundamental Freedoms?

Pursuant to Article 49(1) GloBE-Directive, Member States have to exempt 'MNE Groups' in their 'initial phase of international activity' (CEs in no more than six Member States and tangible assets in all other jurisdictions than the so-called reference jurisdiction[2757] do not exceed EUR 50 million) as well as 'large-scale domestic groups' from the IIR with respect to domestic CEs and the UPE itself for a limited period of five years. Furthermore, in line with the provisions of Article 9.3 GloBE Model Rules, the application of the UTPR is also generally suspended for 'MNE Groups' under Article 49(2) GloBE-Directive also to a limited period of time of five years. In detail on Article 49 GloBE-Directive and its role model Article 9.3. GloBE Model Rules, *see* already section 4.4.2.8.4.

Recently, the so-called initial phase relief under Article 49 GloBE-Directive has received considerable attention in the literature with respect to the substantive primary law compatibility of the GloBE-Directive.[2758] In fact, Article 49 GloBE-Directive exempts domestic UPEs (or the highest entity that is not an 'Excluded Entity) from their obligation to apply the IIR with respect to themselves and their domestic CEs pursuant to Article 5(2) GloBE-Directive (if the UPE is an 'Excluded Entity', Article 7[2]

2756. A. P. Dourado, *supra* note 1566, at 526; A. P. Dourado, *supra* note 2718, at 591.
2757. *See* the definition in Article 49(3) GloBE-Directive (2022/2523).
2758. L. De Broe, *supra* note 1672, at 877; G. Kofler & A. Schnitger, *supra* note 2137, at 189 et seq.

GloBE-Directive), while the obligation to apply the IIR in relation to foreign CEs under Article 5(1) GloBE-Directive remains in place. Could the discrimination of the cross-border situations brought about by Article 49(1) GloBE-Directive constitute a violation of fundamental freedoms and render the GloBE-Directive invalid?

First of all, it is relevant to note that Article 49 GloBE-Directive could only be seen as problematic in intra-EU situations. As has been pointed out above, the IIR only applies in 'control' situations (*see* section 6.2.2.1.2.). Thus, Article 49(1) GloBE-Directive could only be tested against the freedom of establishment, which is only applicable within the EU. The UTPR exemption pursuant to Article 49(2) GloBE-Directive is unproblematic, as it only applies in third-country situations, as, in principle, every UPE 'located' in the EU is obliged to apply the IIR anyway (besides the exception of Member States electing for a delayed application of the IIR and the UTPR under Article 50 GloBE-Directive, *see* Article 50[2] GloBE-Directive). As a consequence, Article 49(1) GloBE-Directive leads to a discrimination if the UPE is forced to apply the IIR with respect to a CE 'located' in a different Member State, while it can refrain from applying the IIR with respect to its own 'Top-up Tax' or 'Top-up Tax' arising in a CE-subsidiary 'located' within the same Member State. Furthermore, one could argue that Article 49(1) GloBE-Directive discriminates against 'MNE Groups' that are not eligible for the 'initial phase relief'. Could this strike down the GloBE-Directive?

All discussants who have dealt with this question doubt that Article 49 GloBE-Directive could pose a risk of invalidity.[2759] As has been pointed out above, the CJEU leaves 'broad discretion'[2760] to the secondary legislature and only sanctions substantive conflicts with primary law if the secondary legislation causes a 'manifest error',[2761] and one can doubt whether the 'initial phase relief' can be considered as such a 'manifest error'. Furthermore, *Kofler & Schnitger*[2762] convincingly emphasize that Article 49 GloBE-Directive grants the benefit only for a limited period of time and that the CJEU seems to be very generous if the EU legislature adopts measures 'in stages or gradually'[2763].[2764] In addition, the authors argue that the blame could be on the Member States because the discrimination caused by the 'initial phase relief' could be prevented if the Member State implemented a QDMTT that is applied to domestic UPEs and their domestic CE-subsidiaries. There are, therefore, many arguments against the GloBE-Directive being in conflict with primary law due to the provision of Article 49(1) GloBE-Directive.[2765]

2759. L. De Broe, *supra* note 1672, at 877–878; G. Kofler & A. Schnitger, *supra* note 2137, at 196.
2760. *See*, e.g., Case C-203/12, *Billerud Karlsborg AB*, para. 35; Case C-390/15, *RPO*, para. 54; Case C-620/18, *Hungary v. Parliament and Council*, para. 112. Already *see* s. 6.2.1.2.
2761. Case C-491/01, *British American Tobacco*, para. 123; Case C-203/12, *Billerud Karlsborg AB*, para. 35.
2762. G. Kofler & A. Schnitger, *supra* note 2137, at 189 et seq.
2763. Case C-247/08, *Gaz de France*, para. 52.
2764. G. Kofler & A. Schnitger, *supra* note 2137, at 196.
2765. For an in debt discussion of the issue, *see Ibid.*

6.2.2.2 *GloBE and the Prohibition of State Aid*

Besides the fundamental freedoms, also the prohibition of state aid enshrined in Article 107(1) TFEU could conceivably pose a *substantive* limit of primary law to the secondary legislature in tax matters.[2766] With regard to GloBE, the EUR 750 million threshold is particularly eye-catching in terms of the prohibition of state aid: is it not a selective advantage if a certain group of taxpayers above a certain turnover threshold is covered by a tax, while the group below the threshold is not subject to the same tax at all? The compatibility of progressive turnover taxes with the prohibition of state aid under Article 107(1) TFEU has already been the subject of proceedings before the CJEU, and the Court had no concerns in this respect.[2767] It could therefore be doubted from the outset that the EUR 750 million threshold could be problematic from the point of view of state aid law.

Much more decisive, however, is that Article 107(1) TFEU explicitly prohibits only aid granted by Member States, but not aid granted by the Union itself.[2768] Pursuant to Article 107(1) TFEU, '[s]*ave as otherwise provided in the Treaties, any aid granted by a Member State* [...] *shall,* [...] *be incompatible with the internal market*'.[2769] For this reason, state aid is not an issue with respect to the implementation of Pillar Two within the EU due to the fact that any aid would be imputable to the EU and not to the Member States.[2770] Given the fact that the GloBE-Directive is a legal act of the Union and does make a distinction between in-scope and out-of-scope taxpayers, domestic laws that merely implement the GloBE-Directive do not infringe the prohibition of state aid. Only if a Member State would cover situations beyond those regulated by the GloBE-Directive, it is conceivable that a national provision in connection with GloBE would violate the staid aid rules. If a Member State would, e.g., lower the turnover threshold to EUR 375 million, one could argue that the Member State infringes Article 107(1) TFEU by collecting 'Top-up Tax' of 'MNE Groups' or domestic Groups that exceed the EUR 375 million threshold while it does not with respect to all below that threshold. In view of the CJEU's recent case law,[2771] however, it is questionable whether a violation of the prohibition of state aid could be argued from the example just mentioned.[2772]

2766. R. Szudoczky, *supra* note 260, at 96.
2767. Case C-562/19 P, *Commission v. Hungary*; Case C-596/19 P, *Commission v. Poland*.
2768. R. Szudoczky, *supra* note 260, at 96.
2769. Article 107(1) TFEU.
2770. *See* Case T-351/02, *Deutsche Bahn AG*, paras 101–102 where the General Court held: '*In transposing* [EU law] *in national law, Member States are only implementing Community provisions in accordance with their obligations stemming from the Treaty. Therefore, the provision at issue is not imputable to the German State, but in actual fact stems from an act of the Community legislature*'. A similar position was taken in a Commission Notice on the notion of state aid: '*A measure is not imputable to a Member State if the Member State is under an obligation to implement it under Union law without any discretion. In that case, the measure stems from an act of the Union legislature and is not imputable to the State*', *see* European Commission Notice on the notion of State aid as referred to in Art. 107(1) of the Treaty on the Functioning of the European Union, OJ para. 44.
2771. Case C-562/19 P, *Commission v. Hungary*; Case C-596/19 P, *Commission v. Poland*.
2772. In the same vein, *see* D. Hohenwarter-Mayr, *supra* note 1552, at 145–146.

6.2.3 Interim Conclusions on the Primary Law Compatibility of the GloBE-Directive

Primary law does not only pose procedural limits to the secondary legislature but rather also requires that secondary law complies with *substantive* requirements of primary law. The previous sections have examined GloBE-Directive's compliance with primary law from a *substantive* viewpoint. It has been shown that primary law compatibility is an issue of validity: if the GloBE-Directive did not comply with primary law, the GloBE-Directive could be subject to judicial review by the CJEU in the course of procedures pursuant to Article 263 or Article 267 TFEU. As the deadline for a *direct* judicial review under Article 263(4) TFEU has already passed on 22 February 2023, the CJEU could only be forced to scrutinize the GloBE-Directive's validity if a domestic court brought the issue to the court via a preliminary ruling pursuant to Article 267 TFEU.[2773] However, it has been shown that the CJEU grants the secondary legislature 'broad discretion' when it comes to *substantive* limits of primary law. Furthermore, the CJEU only penalizes *substantive* primary law incompatibilities if the legal act at issue is 'manifestly inappropriate'.[2774]

As the GloBE-Directive seems to establish 'exhaustive' harmonization,[2775] it unfolds a 'shielding effect' towards domestic legislation implementing GloBE, as the 'exhaustiveness' of the directive prevents that domestic law is tested against primary law. Rather, in this case, the harmonization measure itself must be tested against primary law. Domestic law in the context of Pillar Two, therefore, only has to be scrutinized against primary law if it regulates cases that go beyond the scope of the GloBE-Directive or if the latter leaves discretion to the Member States. Given the fact that the secondary legislature has 'broad discretion' when adopting harmonization measures, the GloBE-Directive can go beyond the limits that primary law would pose to domestic legislatures if the directive had not been adopted.[2776]

Section 6.2.2. has shown that while the GloBE-Directive does indeed contain elements that could be considered indirect discrimination,[2777] it has also been revealed that these discriminatory elements are most likely not prohibited under the fundamental freedoms. Given the fact that the CJEU has been very reluctant to strike down indirect discrimination in the matter of tax law, it can be assumed that the court would not find the GloBE-Directive to infringe the fundamental freedoms; and even if one assumed that the discriminatory elements of the GloBE-Directive did constitute restrictions, the court would probably find the restrictions justified.[2778] Furthermore, all the said discriminatory elements would most likely pass the 'manifestly inappropriate' test applied by the CJEU with regard to primary law. Furthermore, it has been pointed out that the prohibition of state aid pursuant to Article 107 TFEU does not pose a risk for the

2773. *See* s. 6.2.1.1.
2774. *See* s. 6.2.1.2.
2775. *See* s. 6.1.2.3.2.
2776. *See* s. 6.2.1.3.
2777. *See* s. 6.2.2.1.3 and 6.2.2.1.4.
2778. *See* in particular s. 6.2.2.1.2.

GloBE-Directive, as the latter provision only prohibits aid granted by the Member States but does not address aid granted by the Union itself.[2779]

6.3 THE GLOBE-DIRECTIVE AND ITS RELATION TO OTHER LEGAL ACTS OF SECONDARY LAW ON CORPORATE TAXATION WITHIN THE EU

While the previous sections have dealt with the question of how the GloBE-Directive relates to primary EU law, the GloBE-Directive's relation to secondary legislation in the field of corporate income tax still is to be addressed. How does the new GloBE-Directive fit into the EU's so far only hesitantly harmonized corporate tax law?

In this respect, it is first necessary to emphasize that the relation between different legal acts is not a question of a hierarchy of norms.[2780] Rather, if conflicts between two legal acts of secondary law do exist, the common legal conflict resolution and prevention mechanisms, e.g., *lex posterior* or *lex specialis,* come into play. However, these mechanisms are only relevant if there are conflicting rules. So, the question is: are there conflicts between the GloBE-Directive and other legal acts of secondary law in the field of direct taxation? It is obvious that there is no conclusive answer to that question. An answer to this question requires an analysis of the respective legal acts. This section will deal abstractly with the relationship of GloBE to existing directives in the field of corporate income tax.

When thinking about EU corporate taxation, the first legal acts to look at are the so-called corporate tax directives, which include the PSD, the IRD as well as the Merger Directive. As has already been discussed in section 6.1.2.2.4., all three directives, in principle, aim to eliminate tax obstacles in the internal market. Both the PSD and the IRD primarily intend to avoid economic double taxation by eliminating withholding taxes on dividends and interest as well as royalties, respectively. Thus, their co-existence with the GloBE-Directive does not lead to any conflicts. The PSD and the IRD indeed indirectly influence the ETR of 'MNE Groups' because withholding taxes would, in principle, increase the 'Adjusted Covered Taxes' in the case of dividends, those of the subsidiary distributing the profits and in the case of interest and royalties those of the recipient of the interest or royalties' payment. However, both the PSD and the IRD only prevent source taxation to solely allow the residence state of the recipient to tax the dividend, interest, or royalty in specific situations. Furthermore, all dividends covered by the PSD (participation above 10%) are 'excluded dividends' under Article 16(2)(b) GloBE-Directive. As a consequence, the PSD does not even indirectly influence the ETR of an 'MNE Group' in either jurisdiction. The IRD prevents source taxation of interest and royalty payments between connected enterprises with a participation of at least 25%. Both interest and royalties are included in the GloBE base; however, both will be regularly taxed in the residence state of the recipient anyway. As a consequence, there is no significant interaction between the PSD and the IRD.

2779. *See* s. 6.2.2.2.
2780. J. F.P. Nogueira, *supra* note 2153, at 489.

The Merger Directive also does not lead to significant issues with respect to the GloBE-Directive. The Merger Directive enables companies to merge into a different jurisdiction without being obliged to tax hidden reserves. The transfer of assets and liabilities in the course of reorganizations is addressed in Article 35(3) GloBE-Directive (and Article 16[2][e] GloBE-Directive) that allows to exclude any gains or losses arising from a disposal from the computation of the 'qualifying income or loss'.[2781] As a consequence, the ETR computation is thus, adjusted for untaxed hidden reserves or hidden charges. For this reason, also the Merger Directive is not in tension with the GloBE-Directive.

Much more interesting, however, is the relation of the GloBE-Directive to the ATAD. In particular, the ATAD's provisions on CFC rules overlap with those of the GloBE-Directive.[2782] CEs that are part of an in-scope 'MNE Group' are, in principle, subject to both the ATAD and the GloBE-Directive. But which rule prevails? What is the rule order between ATAD and the GloBE-Directive? At first glance, one would assume that the relation is simple: the ATAD obliges Member States to implement and maintain certain rules that might influence and regularly increase the domestic CIT base, and pursuant to GloBE, the domestic CIT is first in GloBE's rule order.[2783] This is, e.g., true for the interest barrier: if a certain part of interest payments is not deductible under Article 4 ATAD, the domestic CIT system will deny deduction, and the GloBE ETR will certainly increase. Thus, in principle, the mechanism of the ATAD is applied before GloBE, and the GloBE base already takes into account the base adjustments required by the ATAD. Things become awkward with respect to the CFC rules in Articles 7 and 8 ATAD. Their relation to GloBE has already been discussed in several places in this thesis.[2784] It has been pointed out that CFC rules apply before the IIR and the UTPR. The latter (IIR and UTPR) already take into account the taxes levied by means of CFC rules. However, according to Article 10 GloBE-Directive, allowing the Member States to implement a QDMTT changes the picture, as the rule order between CFC rules and the QDMTT had not been settled when the GloBE-Directive had been adopted.[2785] Only recently, the IF has taken position in the GloBE Administrative Guidance February 2023 published in February 2023 that the QDMTT should prevail over CFC rules[2786] and obviously assumes that the latter should credit the QDMTT. However, the GloBE Administrative Guidance February 2023 cannot be invoked with regard to the interpretation of the GloBE-Directive and the ATAD first, as it is mere 'soft law' and not of a legally binding nature and second, even though the recitals of the GloBE-Directive suggest an interpretation along the lines of the OECD consensus,[2787] the GloBE-Directive had been adopted before the GloBE Administrative Guidance February 2023

2781. In detail, *see* already s. 4.3.3.3.2.
2782. Already *see* s. 6.1.3.3.2.
2783. In the same vein, *see* J. F. P. Nogueira, *supra* note 2153, at 490.
2784. In detail on the rule order between CFC taxes and the QDMTT, *see* s. 4.4.2.6.3. In general on the rule order between QDMTT, IIR and UTPR, *see* s. 4.4.2.8.1. On the overlap of the ATAD and the GloBE-Directive in general, *see* s. 6.1.3.3.2.
2785. In detail on the issue, *see* s. 4.4.2.6.3.
2786. *GloBE Administrative Guidance February 2023*, para. 118.30.
2787. *See* Recital 24 GloBE-Directive (2022/2523).

had been published.[2788] So the settled rule order, as proposed in the GloBE Administrative Guidance February 2023, does not solve the issue from the EU's perspective. So is there a normative conflict between the ATAD and the GloBE-Directive that could be solved either by *lex specialis* or *lex posterior*?

In fact, neither of these conflict resolution mechanisms is applicable as the relation of Articles 7 and 8 ATAD to the GloBE-Directive is not a normative conflict at all. Both rules simply awkwardly co-exist next to each other without being in conflict. Articles 7 and 8 ATAD, as well as QDMTT, IIR and UTPR, can be applied without violating each other. Thus, the relation of the ATAD's CFC rules and the GloBE-Directive is not a legal but a tax policy issue. Does it make sense to force MNE Groups to apply both rules at the same time? Doesn't it harm the internal market if there is a risk that EU CEs might be forced to apply CFC legislation, although the CFC might be subject to a QDMTT on the same profits in a different state (be it a Member State or a third country)?

There is no doubt that the co-existence of CFC legislation and GloBE is problematic from a tax policy point of view. It seems that the Commission underestimated the issue when it held in the Executive Summary of the GloBE-Directive Proposal that it deliberately did not address the relation between the ATAD's CFC rule and the GloBE-Directive.[2789] In the author's opinion, it needs further elaboration on whether it still makes sense to apply CFC legislation to entities being part of an 'MNE Group' that is subject to GloBE. It is true that Articles 7 and 8 ATAD oblige to level up the tax on a CFC's profits to the domestic tax level, while the GloBE-Directive only obliges to level up to the minimum tax level of 15%, and there are further significant differences between the EU's CFC rule and the mechanism applied by GloBE. Nevertheless, both mechanisms point in similar directions, and their interaction contains the potential of double taxation that should, from a policy perspective, be avoided.

6.4 INTERIM CONCLUSION: WHAT IS THE IMPACT OF THE GloBE-DIRECTIVE ON THE EU'S LEGAL (TAX) ORDER?

The previous section was devoted to the implementation of GloBE within the EU's legal order. The examination has shown that, despite doubts as to whether Article 115 TFEU is actually suitable as a comprehensive harmonization competence in the field of direct

2788. On the interpretation of the GloBE-Directive, *see* s. 4.1.
2789. *'The implementation of the GloBE Model Rules in the EU could have implications for existing provisions of the Anti-tax Avoidance Directive (ATAD) and specifically for the Controlled Foreign Company (CFC) rules, which could interact with the primary rule of Pillar 2 – the IIR. The Commission has explored how to best accommodate the interaction between the CFC of the ATAD and the IIR, and concluded that it is not necessary to amend the ATAD in this regard. Moreover, it is consistent with the OECD Model Rules to continue the application of the ATAD CFC rule in parallel to the GloBE Model Rules. In practice, ATAD CFC rules will apply first and any additional taxes paid by a parent company under a CFC regime in a given fiscal year will be taken into consideration in the GloBE Model Rules by attributing those to the relevant low-taxed entity for the purpose of computing its jurisdictional effective tax rate'*, *see* COM(2021)823 final 2. Already *see* s. 4.4.2.6.3.

taxation, the EU has probably not exceeded its competence by issuing the GloBE-Directive. It has been argued that there are good reasons to believe that the GloBE-Directive has correctly been based on Article 115 TFEU and is in any case 'safer' than the ATAD in this respect as the GloBE-Directive clearly tries to avoid frictions with the fundamental freedoms, by explicitly covering domestic situations. Furthermore, the GloBE-Directive clearly avoids fragmentation by setting not only a minimum standard but exhaustive harmonization.[2790] Furthermore, it was considered whether Article 116 TFEU or the '*Passerelle clause*' of Article 48(7) TEU could have enabled the GloBE-Directive to be adopted by a qualified majority. However, neither Article 116 TFEU nor the '*Passerelle clause*' of Article 48(7) TEU would have been viable options. However, as the Council did unanimously agree to adopt the GloBE-Directive on the basis of Article 115 TFEU, the question of alternative paths is no longer relevant for the GloBE-Directive anyway.[2791]

Now that the GloBE-Directive has been successfully adopted, however, the discussion on the GloBE-Directive's influence on the EU's external competence moves into the focus of the Pillar Two discussion. The analysis of Article 216 TFEU[2792] and Article 3(2) TFEU,[2793] as well as related case law, has revealed that within the scope of the GloBE-Directive, the EU might have gained exclusive external competence ('creeping exclusivity').[2794] The GloBE-Directive thus leads to a significant shift of regulatory competence from national tax legislatures to the Union: Future GloBE-related international agreements concluded in connection with Pillar Two will henceforth fall within the exclusive competence of the Union. Any international agreements must therefore be negotiated by the EU Commission and no longer by the Member States. Although the GloBE-Directive is unlikely to have a direct impact on the ability of Member States to conclude DTCs, the GloBE-Directive, like almost every piece of Union legislation in the field of direct taxation, reduces the external room for manoeuvre of Member States' legislature with regard to the conclusion of tax treaties.[2795]

The successful adoption of the GloBE-Directive also opened the question of whether the GloBE-Directive is in line with the substantive requirements of primary law. Given the hierarchy of norms within the EU's legal order, secondary law, in principle, is bound to the *substantive* limits of primary law, as is the domestic law of the Member States. However, it has been shown that it is unlikely that the CJEU would cast doubt on the validity of the GloBE-Directive in proceedings under Article 267 TFEU (judicial review under Article 263 TFEU no longer even comes into question due to the fact that the two-month deadline pursuant to Article 263[6] TFEU for the GloBE-Directive has already passed).[2796] First of all, the CJEU, in the case of exhaustive harmonization, which can be assumed from the GloBE-Directive, only tests secondary

2790. *See* s. 6.1.2.3.8. On the exhaustive nature of the GloBE-Directive, also *see* D. Hohenwarter-Mayr, *supra* note 1552, at 155.
2791. *See* s. 6.1.2.7.
2792. *See* s. 6.1.3.2.1.
2793. *See* s. 6.1.3.2.2.
2794. *See* s. 6.1.3.2.3.
2795. *See* s. 6.1.3.4.
2796. *See* s. 6.2.1.2.

law against primary law but not domestic implementation of the GloBE-Directive.[2797] Second, the CJEU leaves 'broad discretion' to the EU legislature and only declares legal acts of secondary law void if they turn out to be 'manifestly inappropriate'.[2798] The examination has shown that any tensions between the fundamental freedoms and the final architecture of the GloBE-Directive are unlikely to lead to the GloBE-Directive's invalidity. Although tensions between GloBE and fundamental freedoms may exist, the GloBE-Directive passes the 'manifestly inappropriate' test.[2799] With regard to the prohibition of state aid, according to Article 107 TFEU, it was stated that this prohibition is not binding for the EU legislature and is, therefore, not relevant to the GloBE-Directive.[2800]

Finally, the GloBE-Directive's compatibility with existing secondary law in the field of direct taxation has been examined. It turned out that the corporate tax directives (PSD, IRD and Merger-Directive) are not in conflict with GloBE but only very indirectly influence the ETR computation. In principle, the same holds true with respect to the ATAD: the ATAD is likely to increase domestic tax bases and, therefore, indirectly influences the ETR computation for 'MNE Groups' operating within the EU. However, as pointed out, from a policy perspective, the co-existence of the EU's CFC regime enshrined in Articles 7 and 8 ATAD leads to awkward interactions between Member States making use of their election to implement a QDMTT. It has been argued that, from a policy perspective, the EU should consider amending or even abolishing Articles 7 and 8 ATAD with respect to 'MNE Group' that fall within the scope of GloBE, as the co-existence of both measures might lead to potentials of double-taxation.[2801]

Following the comprehensive EU law analysis of the GloBE-Directive, the much broader question arises as to what impact the GloBE-Directive might have on future EU tax policy as a whole. Will there ever be a comprehensively harmonized corporate tax law in the EU? Will the EU ever be able to agree on a multilateral internal DTC and will the EU ever negotiate DTCs with third countries for all its Member States?

Only one decade ago, these questions would have been described as utopian. The decision on national tax bases and the choice of tax rate were considered to be at the core of Member States' sovereignty. It is not without reason that the CCCTB also failed due to the sovereignty interests of the Member States. In the author's view, the unanimous decision of the Council to finally adopt the GloBE-Directive is likely to massively change the EU's tax landscape in this respect. The GloBE-Directive has achieved harmonization of a uniform tax base and a fixed minimum tax rate. It, thus, obliges Member States to tax certain groups of companies and even fixes a minimum tax rate which is to be applied mandatorily among all Member States. So, what might be the impact of the GloBE-Directive on the EU's legal (tax) order?

Of course, one can only speculate about this question. However, it cannot be denied that the project of a common CIT base within the EU has become much more

2797. *See* s. 6.2.1.3.
2798. *See* s. 6.2.1.2.
2799. *See* s. 6.2.2.1.
2800. *See* s. 6.2.2.2.
2801. *See* s. 6.3.

likely as a result of the successful adoption of GloBE-Directive. Given the fact that GloBE already foresees a common base for a minimum tax, the Commission might use the preparatory work of the OECD for its renewal of the CCCTB, the so-called BEFIT-Proposal,[2802] which is to be expected in the near future. Thus, the GloBE-Directive could prove to be a booster for the Commission's BEFIT project.[2803] In any case, there can be no doubt that the Commission will further use the political momentum to build on the consensus for GloBE and to push ahead with tax harmonization. The recent directive proposals for DEBRA[2804] and 'Unshell',[2805] as well as the initiative for comprehensive harmonization of withholding taxes,[2806] also point in this direction. In addition, it is unlikely that the GloBE-Directive is the last legal act adopted by the EU in the field of Pillar Two. It is to be expected that the EU will also have to take action in areas such as the administration of GloBE or possible future multilateral agreements.

In any case, it remains to be seen to what extent the GloBE-Directive will influence future EU tax law for the positive or negative. Finally, the GloBE-Directive might also bring the EU into a new dilemma: the unanimous decision of the Council to adopt the GloBE-Directive is a significant achievement. On the other hand, any change to the framework now also requires a unanimous decision in the Council. If the global implementation of Pillar Two does not develop as expected (*see*, e.g., the GloBE Administrative Guidance February 2023 that brought some surprising changes), the EU could find itself in a stalemate. How will the EU be able to implement a framework that is still under construction? The unanimity requirement in tax harmonization could, thus, continue to be a challenge for the global minimum tax and its implementation within the EU.

2802. European Commission, *Communication from the Commission to the European Parliament and the Council – Business Taxation for the 21st Century*, *supra* note 196.
2803. In the same vein, *see* J. Hey, *supra* note 2710, s. 17.1. and 17.5. Also on the possible future interaction of the GloBE-Directive and BEFIT, *see* E. Eberhartinger & G. Winkler, *supra* note 281, at 154.
2804. Proposal for a Council Directive on laying down rules on a debt-equity bias reduction allowance and on limiting the deductibility of interest for corporate income tax purposes, COM(2022) 216 final.
2805. Proposal for a Council Directive laying down rules to prevent the misuse of shell entities for tax purposes and amending Directive 2011/16/EU, COM(2021) 565 final.
2806. European Commission, *Inception Impact Assessment – New EU System for the Avoidance of Double Taxation and Prevention of Tax Abuse in the Field of Withholding Taxes*, Ref. Ares(2021)5900310 (28 Sep. 2021).

Chapter 7
Conclusions

Born out of the intention to address the tax challenges of the Digital Economy,[2807] the OECD has designed a comprehensive framework for a global minimum tax in less than four years, which is now supported by more than 140 IF Member States. The OECD GloBE project thus eclipses all previous multinational initiatives in the field of international tax law. Anyone who claimed a decade ago that there would be a global consensus on a 15% minimum tax for multinationals by 2021 would probably have been labelled an out-of-touch visionary. Anyone who then claimed that the EU would succeed in translating this consensus – including a common tax base and a common minimum tax rate – into a binding directive by unanimous decision in the Council by December 2022 would probably have been called a dreamer. With the release of the GloBE Model Rules by the OECD and the simultaneous release of a proposal for a GloBE-Directive by the EU Commission in December 2021,[2808] global minimum taxation has become a hard reality, both for the covered taxpayers as well as for domestic legislatures and tax administrations. The complexity and level of detail of the final framework are unprecedented, even for international tax law, which is not exactly known for being straightforward.

The technical base for GloBE is its rules on the scope.[2809] In very simplified terms, GloBE applies to 'MNE Groups' whose turnover exceeds EUR 750 million. An 'MNE Group' at least consists of a UPE and either a single subsidiary that qualifies as an 'Entity' or a single PE in a different state.[2810] To avoid discrimination issues, the GloBE-Directive extends its scope to 'large-scale domestic groups'.[2811] The scope of the 'MNE Group' (or 'large-scale domestic groups') is derived from the 'Consolidated Financial Statement'.[2812] The size of an 'MNE Group' is, therefore, directly related to

2807. *See* s. 3.
2808. *See* s. 3.4.
2809. *See* s. 4.2.
2810. *See* s. 4.2.1.
2811. *See* s. 4.2.2.
2812. *See* s. 4.2.3.

the consolidation rules of the accounting standard applied by the UPE of the 'MNE Group'. Particular importance is attached to the so-called Acceptable Financial Accounting Standards. These include, first and foremost, IFRS, US GAAP and all national GAAPs applied in the EU and are accepted for determining the GloBE Income. 'Acceptable Financial Accounting Standards' are not subject to any further control. If an 'MNE Group' applies a different accounting standard that is not listed as an 'Acceptable Financial Accounting Standard', there is a so-called Material Competitive Distortion test, according to which only a certain deviation of the statement from IFRS is tolerated as a benchmark.[2813] If the UPE of the 'MNE Group' does not prepare any 'Consolidated Financial Statements' at all, IFRS must be applied. GloBE, thus, implicitly engages in 'IFRS enforcement'.[2814]

Within the framework of GloBE, the term 'Constituent Entity' is of paramount importance.[2815] The term 'Constituent Entity' defines the requirements necessary for membership in an 'MNE Group'. CEs can be predominantly legal entities that have legal personality.[2816] The decisive element is an entity's inclusion within the 'Consolidated Financial Statements' of the UPE. However, the PEs of such entities are considered separate CEs.[2817] The separate recording of PEs as CEs is a necessity of jurisdictional blending: GloBE requires splitting the profits reported in the 'Consolidated Financial Statements' into jurisdictions to enable jurisdiction-wise computation of the ETR. For this reason, both elements of the ETR computation, the 'Adjusted Covered Taxes' in the numerator as well as the 'GloBE Income or Loss' in the denominator of the ETR fraction, are determined on the basis of every individual CE. The starting point for the ETR computation is the individual financial statements of every CE prepared for consolidation within the 'Consolidated Financial Statements' of the UPE. Those individual statements of a legal entity need to be split again between the 'Main Entity' and its foreign PEs. By treating PEs and 'Main Entity' as separate CEs, GloBE enables to meticulously allocate both the income[2818] and the taxes paid[2819] to a specific jurisdiction or – in the absence of territorial connecting factors – to a fictitious jurisdiction ('stateless CEs'). For certain types of CEs (MOCEs, 'Investment Entities' and 'Stateless Entities', GloBE establishes exceptions from jurisdictional blending. Furthermore, special rules apply with respect to 'Joint Ventures'.[2820]

The territorial linkage of CEs to a specific jurisdiction is established with the concept of 'location'. The 'location' of an entity is closely linked to the concept of resident persons under Articles 1 and 4 OECD MC but goes beyond. As the term also includes PEs and consequently also transparent entities, the term 'location' is not equal

2813. *See* s. 4.2.3.2.
2814. *See* s. 4.2.3.2.
2815. *See* s. 4.2.4.1.
2816. *See* s. 4.2.4.1.1.
2817. *See* s. 4.2.4.1.2.
2818. *See* s. 4.3.3.5. and 4.3.3.6.
2819. *See* s. 4.3.4.8.
2820. *See* s. 4.2.4.1.3. and 4.3.2.2.3.

to 'residency'. The concept of 'location' is undoubtedly one of the main pillars of GloBE's technical framework.[2821]

The 'heart' of GloBE is the ETR computation, which includes both the determination of the Adjusted Covered Taxes' and the 'GloBE Income or Loss'. By dividing the aggregated values of both elements, GloBE determines the ETR that is to be compared with the minimum tax level of 15%. This comparison is the basic element of every minimum tax; and, thus, also for GloBE.[2822]

One of the most complex parts of GloBE is its rules on base determination. In principle, the 'GloBE Income or Loss' is determined on the basis of individual financial statements as prepared for consolidation in the financial accounting standard of the UPE. Given the fact that domestic tax bases highly deviate globally, the OECD made deliberate policy choices to make adjustments to the accounting base.[2823] GloBE, thus, excludes common permanent differences between domestic tax systems and accounting rules from the GloBE base.[2824] Furthermore, a bunch of elections to the base computation are provided to 'MNE Groups'.[2825] In addition, GloBE explicitly requires that transactions between CEs are recorded in line with the 'Arm's Length Principle'. The latter is a necessity for the exact allocation of the 'GloBE Income' to the individual jurisdictions.[2826]

Of similar complexity is the computation of the 'Adjusted Covered Taxes', which determines the nominator of the ETR fraction. The 'Adjusted Covered Tax' computation also starts from individual financial statements of every CE. The calculation is based on the current tax expense reported in those statements, again subject to several adjustments. Most importantly, every tax on items of income that are excluded from the 'GloBE Income or Loss' need to be removed from the amount of 'Adjusted Covered Taxes' to avoid that the ETR computation will be distorted. Those adjustments are either made by additions or reductions to the 'Covered Taxes'. The 'Adjusted Covered Tax' computation is of particular importance for the recognition of temporary differences between domestic tax bases and accounting income. For this purpose, GloBE uses a deferred tax mechanism which enables to balance temporary effects over several periods. Also, with respect to deferred taxes, GloBE heavily relies on financial statements but requires extensive adjustments. Based on the deferred taxes reported in the financial statements, the so-called Total Deferred Tax Adjustment Amount is to be calculated, which ultimately either increases or decreases the 'Adjusted Covered Taxes'. In this respect, it is important to emphasize that GloBE requires recapturing deferred tax liabilities if the respective liability does not materialize within five years.

The deferred tax mechanism also enables GloBE to take into account corporate losses: if there is a loss in a specific jurisdiction for a specific 'Fiscal Year' for which domestic tax systems will grant a carry-forward, GloBE takes care that in the subsequent years the ETR is not underestimated. If a CE receives a loss in a specific year, it

2821. *See* s. 4.2.4.4.
2822. *See* s. 4.3.1. and 4.3.2.
2823. *See* s. 4.3.3.3.1.
2824. *See* s. 4.3.3.3.2.
2825. *See* s. 4.3.3.3.5.
2826. *See* s. 4.3.3.3.4.

will account for a deferred tax asset that will reduce its 'Adjusted Covered Tax' in the loss-year. This, however, will regularly not lead to a 'Top-up Tax'. However, in subsequent years, when a CE can use the losses due to a carry-forward, there would be a risk that the ETR would be underestimated. In this case, GloBE would permit to use the deferred tax asset recorded to increase the 'Adjusted Covered Tax' of the subsequent year. Consequently, in general, GloBE will not pose any additional tax burdens in loss situations. However, if the domestic loss exceeds the 'GloBE Loss', Article 4.1.5. GloBE Model Rules obliges to collect a 'Top-up Tax' in the amount that is attributable to the permanent difference between domestic tax law and the GloBE base. As a consequence, GloBE might levy a 'Top-up Tax' even in overall loss situations. It has been pointed out that this is not comprehensible from a tax policy point of view.[2827] The GloBE Administrative Guidance February 2023 took note of the issue and amends the Commentary to provide for a special administrative procedure to mitigate the effects of Article 4.1.5. GloBE Model Rules. However, this proposed procedure is not reflected in the GloBE Model Rules, and it is questionable whether the procedure could be applied by EU Member States as Article 21(5) GloBE-Directive reflects Article 4.1.5. GloBE Model Rules and the procedure proposed in the GloBE Administrative Guidance February 2023 is in evident conflict with the text of Article 21(5) GloBE-Directive.[2828] Furthermore, the GloBE Administrative Guidance February 2023 has been released after the GloBE-Directive had been adopted, which is why the amendments made in the Commentary cannot readily be used to interpret the GloBE-Directive.[2829]

The 'Top-up Tax' is a synonym for the actual minimum tax liability. It has been pointed out, that the determination of the 'Top-up Tax' is an eight-step procedure.[2830] It starts with the determination and 'location' of the single CEs of the 'MNE Group' (Step 1).[2831] If the 'GloBE Group Chart' is painted, both the 'GloBE Income or Losses' and the 'Adjusted Covered Taxes' determined on a CE-basis need to be aggregated jurisdiction wise. For CEs that underlie an exception for jurisdictional blending, a separate aggregation is necessary (Step 2).[2832] Based on the blended values of 'Adjusted Covered Taxes' and the 'GloBE Income or Losses' the ETR is computed (Step 3).[2833] The ETR is finally subtracted from the 'Minimum Rate' of 15%. This results in the so-called Top-up Tax Percentage. If the 'Adjusted Covered Taxes' are negative, the ETR can fall below 0% and might give rise to a 'Top-up Tax Percentage' exceeding the 'Minimum Rate' of 15% (Step 4).[2834] Once the 'Top-up Tax Percentage' is determined, the SBIE needs to be subtracted from the 'Net GloBE Income', the latter being the aggregated value of 'GloBE Income or Losses' of all CEs located within the same jurisdiction. The result of this subtraction is the so-called Excess Profits, which are the

2827. *See* s. 4.5.3.
2828. *See* s. 4.3.4.7 and 4.5.3.
2829. On the interpretation of the GloBE-Directive, *see* s. 4.1.
2830. *See* s. 4.4.1.
2831. *See* s. 4.4.2.1.
2832. *See* s. 4.4.2.2.
2833. *See* s. 4.4.2.3.
2834. *See* s. 4.4.2.4.

basis for the 'Top-up Tax' calculation (Step 5).[2835] Finally, the 'Excess Profits' from Step 5 are multiplied by the 'Top-up Tax Percentage from Step 4, which is the 'Jurisdictional Top-up Tax' or in other words, the actual minimum tax that should be collected under GloBE. The 'Jurisdictional Top-up Tax' increases for any 'Additional Current Top-up Tax'[2836] and can be reduced down to zero, if the respective jurisdiction collects a QDMTT (Step 6).[2837] If this is not the case, the 'Jurisdictional Top-up Tax' is to be allocated among all CEs 'located' within the same jurisdiction (Step 7);[2838] and once this has been done, in the eighth and last step, the charging provisions of the IIR and the UTPR are to be applied (Step 8).[2839] Finally, it should be noted that the simplicity of the individual mathematical operations should not obscure the high complexity of the rules and their application.[2840]

The charging provisions of the IIR and the UTPR are highly complex as well. The IIR, as a rule applies to the UPE and only if the UPE is not subject to a 'Qualified IIR', the next highest entity, the so-called IPE, within the 'MNE Group' is subject to the IIR. If the UPE has less than 80% of 'Ownership Interest', the IIR 'falls down' to the respective POPE. The IIR, thus, only applies with respect to UPEs, IPEs or POPEs. The IIR cannot be collected at the level of the PEs. The IIR focuses directly on 'Ownership Interest' and, thus, only collects the amount of 'Top-up Tax' that is allocable to shares held by the 'MNE Group'.[2841] Within the EU, the GloBE-Directive ensures that – if the UPE is 'located' in a third state and not subject to a 'Qualified IIR' – the highest entity within a 'MNE Group' that is 'located' in the EU is subject to the IIR with respect to itself, its domestic CEs and its 'Ownership Interest' in LTCEs in different jurisdictions.

The UTPR is a 'backstop' to the IIR. It is not bound to the existence of 'Ownership Interest' at all. It applies in three situations:[2842] First (i), it can collect 'Top-up Tax' of any other group member that is not 'located' in the jurisdiction of the UPE at the level of any other group member. Second (ii), it can collect 'Top-up Tax' pending at the UPE and any other CE 'located' in the jurisdiction of the UPE that is neither collected by a 'Qualified IIR' or a QDMTT in its jurisdiction and third (iii) it can collect 'Top-up Tax' that is attributable to non-group shareholders.[2843] The latter scenario also collects 'Top-up Tax' attributable to non-group shareholders, however, gladly the third of those three 'UTPR situation' is restricted to specific cases. Contrary to the IIR, the UTPR can also be applied to PEs. If several CEs within the same group are subject to a 'Qualified UTPR' in their jurisdiction, GloBE distributes the UTPR revenue among those jurisdictions pursuant to a formula that is fixed on certain substance criteria. The UTPR contains potentials for double and multiple taxation.[2844] In general, for both the IIR and the UTPR it can be stated that they work fine if only 100% participations are at issue.

2835. *See* s. 4.4.2.5.
2836. *See* s. 4.4.2.6.2.
2837. *See* s. 4.4.2.6.
2838. *See* s. 4.4.2.7.
2839. *See* s. 4.4.2.8.
2840. *See* s. 4.5.1.
2841. On the architecture of the IIR, *see* s. 4.4.2.8.2.
2842. In detail, *see* s. 4.4.2.8.3. In particular, *see* s..
2843. *See* s. 4.4.2.8.3. In particular *see* Figure 12.
2844. On the architecture of the UTPR, *see* s. 4.4.2.8.3.

As soon as minority shareholdings are involved, the application of the GloBE Rules becomes extremely complex even in the simplest group structures. Various inconsistencies were also identified in this respect.[2845]

One of the weaknesses of GloBE's conceptual framework identified within this thesis is the concept of jurisdictional blending. First of all, jurisdictional blending is difficult to reconcile with 'Consolidated Financial Statements'. The purpose of 'Consolidated Financial Statements' is to give a financial picture of an 'MNE Group's' worldwide business activity. Jurisdictional blending forces GloBE to artificially split the 'Consolidated Financial Statements' into single entities and their PEs, to finally aggregate taxes and income of the CEs jurisdiction-wise.[2846] Strangely enough, however, an allocation of the 'Jurisdictional Top-up Tax' to individual CEs becomes necessary (Step 7 of the eight-step procedure) before the IIR and the UTPR can be applied. Although there are good policy arguments in favour of jurisdictional blending too, the latter causes a lot of complex ramifications that could have been avoided by either entity or worldwide blending.[2847] Furthermore, jurisdictional blending can lead to unintended effects in many ways: within 'MNE Group' conglomerates that are concerned with several industries, GloBE's jurisdictional perspective can lead to odd results. 'MNE Groups' might be forced to blend income and taxes among CEs located in the same jurisdiction although they have nothing to do with each other from an operational and business viewpoint. Any GloBE elections must be exercised equally for all CEs 'located' within the same jurisdiction. In extreme situations, a POPE may have to apply the IIR to the blended income of one of its subsidiaries with a CE from a completely different group strand.[2848]

An additional result of the technical analysis is the manifold linkage between GloBE with accounting rules. It is often overlooked that not only GloBE's base directly relies on accounting rules, but that the scope of the global minimum tax is directly linked to the scope of consolidation rules set out by accounting standards. Accounting rules, thus, not only set the rules for computing the ETR but even define the size of the 'MNE Group' that is subject to GloBE. Consequently, accounting rules have a very direct influence on the application of GloBE. For this reason, it has been concluded that GloBE might lead to a shift from tax competition to a competition of preferential accounting standards in the future. However, it was also shown that GloBE has taken certain precautions, for example with the 'Material Competitive Distortion' test.[2849] It has been revealed that it might be problematic that independent accounting boards such as the IASB will gain influence on the tax base of the global minimum tax.[2850]

The technical analysis has not only revealed technical but also policy inconsistencies.[2851] First of all, contrary to what the OECD and EU seem to promote in public, GloBE is not a minimum tax of 15%. It is a minimum tax of 15% on 'Excess Profits' as

2845. For example, the different treatment of IPEs and POPEs, *see* s. 4.4.2.8.2.
2846. *See* s. 4.3.2.3.
2847. *See* s. 4.3.2.3.
2848. *See* s. 4.5.4.
2849. *See* s. 4.5.7.
2850. *See* s. 4.5.7.
2851. *See* s. 4.5.8.

the basis for the global minimum tax may be reduced by the SBIE.[2852] The design of the SBIE is strange in many ways: it is a simplistic formula to assess the existence of 'substance' in a specific jurisdiction by simply multiplying the carrying values of tangible assets and payroll costs in that jurisdiction by a fixed percentage. By adding up both components, the SBIE works like a free amount from the minimum tax: if the domestic profits do not exceed the SBIE, there is no minimum tax irrespective of the domestic tax level. Furthermore, the design of the SBIE also leads to odd incentives: it is vulnerable to abuse, as tangible assets can easily be shifted among jurisdictions and also the amount of payroll can deliberately be shifted among jurisdictions to prevent the collection of 'Top-up Tax'. Similar objections exist with respect to the exclusion of shipping income, which is questionable from a tax policy point of view.[2853]

The SBIE (like the shipping income exclusion) also heavily influences the impact of GloBE on tax competition. The OECD has always emphasized that Pillar Two aims to curb tax competition. However, as has been pointed out, the SBIE limits GloBE's impact on tax competition. Due to the design of the SBIE, jurisdictions can offer nominal tax rates far below the minimum rate even down to zero, as long as domestic profits do not exceed the SBIE. This has led to the conclusion that GloBE to a certain extent might reduce tax competition, but it certainly does not end jurisdictions competing for direct investments via their CIT systems. Rather, there are arguments that GloBE might even promote tax competition for tax havens.[2854]

Besides the SBIE, also the QDMTT[2855] has a significant influence on GloBE's impact on tax competition. The QDMTT allows jurisdictions to 'skim off' 'Top-up Tax' arising within their territory on their own and is, thus, a concession to national tax sovereignty. Contrary to what had been promoted in advance to the global tax deal, the QDMTT will lead to most of GloBE's tax revenues accruing to low-tax jurisdictions. A jurisdiction can prevent profits of domestic headed 'MNE Groups' or domestic CEs of such 'MNE Groups' being taxed by way of the IIR or the UTPR in a different jurisdiction. This might also create incentives to abolish domestic CIT systems and replace it with a QDMTT that only applies to in-scope 'MNE Groups' having CEs in the respective jurisdiction. Consequently, the implementation of GloBE does not necessarily mean that countries will increase their nominal CIT rates.[2856]

The overall architecture of the GloBE Model Rules leaves the question what the purpose of GloBE could be.[2857] As a matter of fact, the SBIE and the QDMTT, to a certain extent, jeopardize the character of a minimum tax. It has been argued that the purpose of GloBE seems to be to simply reduce the leeway for domestic tax legislatures to introduce a highly preferential CIT-environment for 'MNE Groups' hitting the EUR 750 million threshold. In any case, GloBE does not follow a consistent policy goal but rather is the result of a compromise among more than 140 IF Member States. Conceptually, however, this leaves the question, whether GloBE is a step forward in

2852. *See* s. 4.5.2.
2853. *See* s. 4.3.3.4.
2854. *See* s. 4.5.6.
2855. *See* s. 4.4.2.6.3.
2856. *See* s. 4.5.5.
2857. *See* s. 4.5.8.

the international tax discussion. Would there be a need for a minimum tax if the international tax system's architecture would correspond to the social ideal (whatever such an ideal could be)? In any case, it is odd to introduce a minimum tax because it simply compares the ETR with a minimum that is supposed to be 'fair' or 'adequate'. If the tax system were considered to be either 'fair' or 'adequate', no one would argue that such a comparison is necessary. In any case, the complex framework of GloBE will have to justify itself over time, as it is questionable whether the tax revenues generated by GloBE will ever compensate for the administrative burden on both 'MNE Groups' and tax administrations.

The fifth section of this thesis was dedicated to the relation of the GloBE Model Rules and the GloBE-Directive to international tax law, including tax treaties and customary international (tax) law. The analysis of GloBE's treaty compatibility has shown that it is difficult to generalize the impact of GloBE on tax treaties. Within an 'MNE Group', every single CE that is subject to the GloBE Rules could be entitled to several treaties under Articles 1 and 4 OECD MC. It has been demonstrated that GloBE, contrary to some beliefs in literature, confirms a separate entity approach. Any taxes levied by way of QDMTT, IIR or UTPR are taxes paid by a specific CE, whose treaty entitlement needs to be tested individually. While the IIR only in exceptional cases applies to 'non-residents' (e.g., fiscally transparent entities), the UTPR also applies with respect to PEs. For this reason, when testing whether the collection of 'Top-up Tax' is in conflict with a treaty, also the way of its collection can matter for the treaty analysis. In any case, the treaty entitlement of the respective taxpaying CE is to be tested first.[2858] It has been pointed out that any 'Top-up Tax', whether collected by way of the QDMTT, IIR or UTPR, is undoubtedly to be qualified as covered tax within the meaning of Article 2 OECD MC.[2859]

Since GloBE relies heavily on the applicable DTCs for the jurisdictional allocation of profits to individual tax jurisdictions, there are no direct conflicts between GloBE and the distributive rules. In particular via its autonomous PE definition which is directly connected to the applicable tax treaty, GloBE ensures a treaty-compliant allocation of profits to the individual jurisdictions.[2860] However, the allocation of profits within GloBE can be at odds with the distributive rules of Articles 6 and 8 OECD MC, according to which the taxing right is assigned to a specific jurisdiction in deviation from the PE principle.[2861] It has been shown that the QDMTT might be in conflict with Article 6 OECD MC. If a treaty-entitled entity receives income in another state under Article 6 OECD MC, this income is allocated to the state of residence in the GloBE system, but under the OECD MC the income may be taxed in the other state. The state of residence might then apply the QDMTT to profits that this state is not allowed to tax pursuant to a treaty. However, at least if the credit method is applied with respect to income falling under Article 6 OECD MC, the 'saving clause' under Article 1(3) OECD MC might

2858. *See* s. 5.2.1.
2859. *See* s. 5.2.2.
2860. *See* s. 5.2.3.2.
2861. *See* s. 5.2.3.3. and 5.2.3.4.

eliminate the conflict. If Article 6 OECD MC falls within the exemption method, a conflict would arise even if the treaty contained a 'saving clause'.[2862]

Article 9 OECD MC and Article 24 OECD MC do not give rise to any significant potential for normative conflicts. With respect to Article 9 OECD MC one can note that GloBE explicitly adopts the 'Arm's Length Principle', so it is difficult to argue that a conflict might arise anyway.[2863] With regard to Article 24 OECD MC, a conflict cannot be ruled out *a priori*, but conflicts are unlikely. The PE non-discrimination provision of Article 24(3) OECD MC is no risk to GloBE, as there are no situations in which PEs are treated worse than domestic corporations. The IIR cannot apply to PEs and the UTPR applies to PEs in the same way as to resident corporations. With respect to the UTPR, a conflict with Article 24(5) OECD MC is at least conceivable. However, a prohibited discrimination is unlikely also in this case, due to the narrow scope of Article 24(5) OECD MC.[2864]

Potential conflicts between GloBE and tax treaties, however, do not result from GloBE's allocation of profits among the jurisdictions an 'MNE Group' is operating but rather from the collection of 'Top-up Tax' arising within those jurisdictions by a group member being a resident in a different country. Both the IIR and the UTPR might force residents (in some cases also non-residents) to collect tax with respect to profits of a different taxpayer. In order to justify both GloBE Rules, not only the OECD recourses to the 'saving clause' in Article 1(3) OECD MC. Nevertheless, it has been shown that the 'saving clause' is not a panacea to avoid potential conflicts between tax treaties and GloBE. Every provision has its scope, and so does the 'saving clause'. For example, the 'saving clause' cannot be applied if the GloBE Rules apply to non-residents or the method article obliges the state of residence to grant relief. Above all, however, the 'saving clause' is not yet so widespread in the international DTC network that it could actually safeguard the DTC compliant application of the GloBE Rules in general.[2865]

With respect to the IIR, many potential conflicts with treaties are indeed solved by the 'saving clause'. As the IIR only applies with respect to UPEs, IPEs or POPEs and not to PEs, the IIR is mainly applied to persons that qualify as residents. Only in exceptional cases the IIR is also applied to partnerships that do not qualify as residents. In such cases, the IIR might be in conflict with tax treaties. Another argument in favour of the IIR's compliance with tax treaties is the fact that it shows many structural similarities to CFC legislation. The 'saving clause's' history is clearly connected to the emergence of CFC legislation and, among other things, clearly aims to permit CFC rules. As CFC rules seem to be accepted from the perspective of tax treaties, it is difficult to generally argue that the IIR is not permissible under treaties. The opposing view in literature that the justification for CFC legislation cannot be transferred to the IIR, as the latter aims to curb tax competition and not abuse, is not entirely convincing. GloBE, at least in the broadest sense, also aims to tackle abuse. As a consequence, there is much to suggest that the IIR is in line with tax treaties, as long as it is applied to resident

2862. *See* s. 5.2.3.3.
2863. *See* s. 5.2.4.
2864. *See* s. 5.2.5.
2865. *See* s. 5.2.6.1.

persons with respect to income of a different legal person. If a CE, however, is subject to the IIR with respect to one of its exempt PEs, it is clear that the IIR violates against the treaty. As the 'saving clause' does not eliminate the residence state's obligation to apply the method article, Article 1(3) OECD MC cannot be invoked to avoid a treaty conflict.[2866]

However, there are serious concerns about the compatibility of the UTPR with tax treaties. First of all, the UTPR can also be charged with respect to PEs. In this case, the 'saving clause' cannot apply and the source state collects taxes on income of a resident in a different contracting state. Thus, even those who generally argue that the UTPR would be in line with tax treaties (so-called UTPR supporters), admit that the UTPR conflicts with treaties if it is charged on PEs. It has been argued, however, that it is questionable whether the UTPR can be justified under the 'saving clause' at all. If it were permissible for contracting states to simply include the income of different group members (despite a lack of control or other forms of participation) within the domestic tax base, tax treaties would lose their legitimacy. If one would interpret tax treaties in such a way, any contracting state could make a mockery of the distribution of taxing rights under the treaty by reshaping the domestic tax base (e.g., by simply adding income of a different taxpayer to the base of a resident corporation). Article 1(3) OECD MC cannot be interpreted in such a way. For this reason, there is much to suggest that the UTPR is not compatible with tax treaties, even if treaties contain a 'saving clause'.[2867]

Ultimately, however, the question arises as to how an emerging conflict between GloBE and tax treaties can be resolved. Since GloBE is to be implemented by national laws, the question of the relationship between GloBE and tax treaties is ultimately a question of national constitutional law. If national constitutional law allows a treaty to override, the national legal system will give priority to GloBE, either due to the *lex specialis* or *lex posterior* principle. If, however, national constitutional law gives precedence to international agreements, the tax treaty would trump domestic GloBE implementation.[2868]

Within the EU, things are significantly more complex. As EU law can override domestic laws, the question arises in which way the GloBE-Directive can override tax treaties. It has been pointed out that the relation of EU law and international agreements concluded by the Member States is governed by Article 351(1) TFEU.[2869] Accordingly, EU law steps back if a treaty between a Member State and a third state was already concluded before the respective Member State's accession to the EU (anterior treaty). From a reverse conclusion from Article 351(1) TFEU one can, thus, conclude that EU law prevails over any treaty concluded between Member States and over treaties concluded between Member States and third states concluded after the respective Member State's accession to the EU. However, there are good arguments to suggest that Article 351(1) TFEU can be applied *mutatis mutandis* with respect to

2866. *See* s. 5.2.6.2.
2867. *See* s. 5.2.6.3.
2868. *See* s. 5.3.
2869. *See* s. 5.4.

treaties which were concluded after the accession of the respective Member State but had been compatible with EU law before the adoption of the GloBE-Directive had been 'foreseeable' (as has been shown, the adoption of the GloBE-Directive was 'foreseeable' from 22 December 2021, when the GloBE-Directive Proposal was published by the Commission).[2870] However, even if a treaty between a Member State and a third state is protected by Article 351(1) TFEU, the Member States are under an obligation to eliminate the incompatibility under Article 351(2) TFEU as soon as possible. *Ultima ratio*, the Member States are even obliged to terminate the respective DTC after some time.[2871]

It has been argued, that the OECD's silence with respect to the (in)compatibility of the IIR and UTPR with tax treaties is a bit surprising. Many authors convincingly call for a multilateral agreement to avoid normative conflicts between GloBE and DTC from the outset. This thesis agrees with this demand.[2872]

The division of competence between the Member States and the EU is defined by the *Principle of Conferral* in Article 5 TEU, according to which the EU may only legislate if the Treaties grant the Union the competence to do so.[2873] Traditionally, the EU has no comprehensive harmonization competences in direct tax law, but can only rely on the residual internal market competence of Article 115 TFEU. Pursuant to this provision, the EU may '*issue directives for the approximation of such laws, regulations or administrative provisions of the Member States as directly affect the establishment or functioning of the internal market*'. Although elements of the GloBE-Directive can be seen as being in tension with the concept of the internal market as enshrined in Article 26 TFEU, the GloBE-Directive most likely had correctly been based on Article 115 TFEU.[2874]

For the future, the GloBE-Directive's influence on the EU's power to conclude international agreements might be of significant importance. Pursuant to the EU Treaties and settled case law of the CJEU, the EU might gain exclusive external competence pursuant to Article 3(2) TFEU depending on the density of EU harmonization in a specific field.[2875] Given the fact the GloBE-Directive exhaustively harmonizes the implementation of a minimum tax,[2876] it is likely that the EU, by adopting the GloBE-Directive, gained exclusive external competence in the field of Pillar Two. For this reason, the conclusion of future GloBE-related agreements[2877] most likely falls within the exclusive competence of the EU. Although the GloBE-Directive only slightly touches tax treaties, the GloBE-Directive leads to a loss of competence ('competence creep') for the Member States in favour of the EU that should not be underestimated.[2878]

2870. *See* s. 5.4.3.5.
2871. *See* s. 5.4.3.4.
2872. *See* s. 5.6.
2873. *See* s. 6.1.2.1.
2874. *See* s. 6.1.2.3.8.
2875. *See* s. 6.1.3.
2876. *See* s. 6.1.2.3.2.
2877. *See* s. 6.1.3.1.
2878. *See* s. 6.1.3.4.

Since the EU's legal order is also determined by a hierarchy of norms, the GloBE-Directive must also comply with the substantive requirements of EU law. Among these substantive requirements are above all the fundamental freedoms that define the EU's internal market. As has been shown, with regard to some of the mechanisms provided for in the GloBE-Directive, there are certainly some tensions with the fundamental freedoms.[2879] Nevertheless, the validity of the GloBE-Directive is most likely assured: in the case of exhaustive harmonization, which is true with regard to the GloBE-Directive, the CJEU only tests whether the secondary legislation is in line with primary law and does not question the compatibility of domestic law with primary law anymore ('shielding effect of secondary law').[2880] However, the CJEU grants a 'broad discretion' to the EU legislature with respect to interpreting the *substantive* limits of primary law.[2881] Furthermore, the CJEU only declares secondary law for void if it fails a so-called manifestly inappropriate test.[2882] Given the fact that the Commission took particular attention to avoid frictions with the fundamental freedoms as far as possible,[2883] it is almost inconceivable that the GloBE-Directive would fail the 'manifestly inappropriate' test.[2884] Most likely, the GloBE-Directive is valid under primary law.

The relationship of the GloBE-Directive to existing secondary law only gives rise to problems with respect to Articles 7 and 8 ATAD, although there are no 'hard' normative conflicts between the GloBE-Directive and the EU CFC rules. However, the odd co-existence of both mechanisms can lead to double-taxation, as the rule order between the QDMTT and CFC legislation is now addressed by OECD soft law, but is not regulated under EU law.[2885] Under the opinion of the author, this problem should be addressed in some way by the EU legislature. In general, it is doubtful whether the co-existence of a CFC regime and GloBE makes sense from a tax policy perspective.[2886]

So, what can be concluded for the global minimum tax and its implementation within the EU? The speed at which GloBE has been developed is as breathtaking as it is frightening. In just four years, a framework has been developed to ensure that all activities of 'MNE Groups' are taxed at a minimum rate of 15 % on 'Excess Profits' using a common tax base based on accounting profits. Now that it is time to transpose the complex framework into national law, GloBE's framework poses major challenges for taxpayers, domestic legislatures, and national tax administrations alike. The tight timetable has left its mark: although the publication of the GloBE Model Rules and the adoption of the GloBE-Directive are significant achievements, the newly created system is not flawless. As the technical analysis and examination of GloBE's relationship with tax treaty and EU law has shown, GloBE is not yet fully balanced. The rushed nature of GloBE's development is demonstrated by the fact that fundamental issues

2879. *See* s. 6.2.2.1.
2880. *See* s. 6.2.1.3.
2881. *See* s. 6.2.1.2.
2882. *See* s. 6.2.1.2.
2883. *See* s. 6.2.2.1.
2884. *See* s. 6.2.3.
2885. *See* s. 4.4.2.6.3.
2886. *See* s. 6.3.

such as the order of rules between QDMTT and CFC had to be clarified by GloBE Administrative Guidance February 2023. It is particularly worrying that this clarification took place after the GloBE-Directive had already been adopted. In addition, GloBE leaves many open questions of interpretation and complex technical and fiscal inconsistencies that, in the author's view, should have been examined in greater depth before the implementation phase.

In any case, one should not be tempted to believe that the minimum tax debate will soon come to an end. Rather, national implementation is likely to be a new starting point for the discussion around the 'global tax deal', and GloBE is certainly not the end of the discussion on its architecture. The OECD's Pillar One on the redistribution of taxing rights or the EU's BEFIT project are still to come, and the conclusion of MLCs may also be on the agenda in the near future, to name just some examples of future tax initiatives that could build on the Pillar Two consensus. At the very beginning of this thesis, reference was made to a wave of multilateralism in the international tax landscape that initiated the OECD's GloBE/Pillar Two project. At the end of this thesis it can, thus, be anticipated that this wave of multilateralism is unlikely to be broken.

Bibliography

Journal Articles, Book Contributions and Monographs

H.E. Abrams & R.L. Doernberg, *How Electronic Commerce Works*, 14 Tax Notes Intl. 1573 (1997).

R.A. Achleitner, *Die sekundärrechtliche Ausformung der Grundfreiheiten des Binnenmarktes*, in *Autoritäres vs Liberales Europa* (M. Kopetzki et al., eds, Jan Sramek 2019).

R.A. Achleitner & V. Bendlinger, *GloBE (Pillar Two) – Kompetenzrechtliche Erwägungen zur Umsetzung eines Mindestbesteuerungssystems innerhalb der Europäischen Union*, 2 digitax 1 (2021).

R. Adhikari, *Tax Policy and Administration in Asian Countries: A Review of Key Issues and Options*, 56 Bull. Intl. Taxn. 2 (2002), IBFD Journals.

S. Alber, *European Community Tax Law and Its Development in Light of the Recent Case Law of the European Court of Justice*, 22 Fordham Int'l L. J. 3 (1999).

J. Allenbach-Ammann, *Orbán Backs Down: EU Agrees on Ukraine Aid and Minimum Tax*, Www.Euractiv.Com (13 December 2022), available at https://www.euractiv.com/section/economy-jobs/news/orban-backs-down-eu-agrees-on-ukraine-aid-and-minimum-tax/ (accessed 6 February 2023).

M.T. Álvarez-Martínez et al., *How Large Is the Corporate Tax Base Erosion and Profit Shifting? A General Equilibrium Approach*, 24 February 2021 Economic Systems Research 1–32, available at 10.1080/09535314.2020.1865882.

L. Anker-Sørensen, *Financial Engineering as an Alternative Veil for the Corporate Group*, 13 European Company Law 5 (1 October 2016), available at 10.54648/EUCL2016023.

U. Anschütz, *Harmonization of Direct Taxes in the European Economic Community*, 13 Harv. Int'l. Law J. 1 (1972).

P.R. Anthony, *Electronic Commerce and Transfer Pricing*, 12 Asia-Pac. Tax Bull. 2 (2006), IBFD Journals.

A. Arena, *Exercise of EU Competences and Pre-Emption of Member States' Powers in the Internal and the External Sphere: Towards 'Grand Unification'?*, 35 Yearbook of European Law 1 (2016).

P. Arginelli, *The ATAD and Third Countries*, in *The External Tax Strategy of the EU in a Post-BEPS Environment* (A.M. Jiménez ed., IBFD 2019).

B.J. Arnold, *Tax Treaties and Tax Avoidance: The 2003 Revisions to the Commentary to the OECD Model*, 58 Bull. Intl. Taxn. 6 (2004), IBFD Journals.

B.J. Arnold, *The 2008 Update of the OECD Model: An Introduction*, 63 Bull. Intl. Taxn. 5 (2009), IBFD Journals.

B.J. Arnold, *Threshold Requirements for Taxing Business Profits under Tax Treaties*, 57 Bull. Intl. Taxn. 10 (2003), IBFD Journals.

H.J. Ault, W. Schön & S.E. Shay, *OECD Base Erosion and Profit Shifting: A Roadmap for Reform*, 68 Bull. Intl. Taxn. 6–7 (2014), IBFD Journals.

J.F. Avery Jones, *2008 OECD Model: Place of Effective Management – What One Can Learn from the History*, 63 Bull. Intl. Taxn. 5–6 (2009), IBFD Journals.

J.F. Avery Jones, *Flows of Capital Between the EU and Third Countries and the Consequences of Disharmony in European International Tax Law*, 7 EC Tax Review 2 (1998).

J.F. Avery Jones, *Place of Effective Management as a Residence Tie-Breaker*, 59 Bull. Intl. Taxn. 1 (2005), IBFD Journals.

R.S. Avi-Yonah, *The UTPR and the Treaties*, 109 Tax Notes Intl. 45–49 (2 Jan. 2023).

R.S. Avi-Yonah, *UTPR's Dynamic Connection to Customary International Law*, 108 Tax Notes Intl. 951–952 (21 Nov. 2022).

P. Baker & R. Collier, *2008 OECD Model: Changes to the Commentary on Article 7 and the Attribution of Profits to Permanent Establishments*, 63 Bull. Intl. Taxn. 5 (2009), IBFD Journals.

A.J. Bakker, *Attribution of Profit to a Permanent Establishment of a Global Trading Company*, 11 ITPJ 11–12 (2004), IBFD Journals.

N. Bammens & D. Bettens, *The Potential Impact of Pillar Two on Tax Incentives*, 51 Intertax 2 (2023).

R. Barents, *The Internal Market Unlimited: Some Observations on the Legal Basis of Community Legislation*, 30 Common Market Law Review 1 (1993).

E. Barret, *Aspects of the 2010 Update Other than Those Relating to Article 7 of the OECD Model Tax Convention*, 65 Bull. Intl. Taxn. 1 (2011), IBFD Journals.

A. Bartosch, *Die Selektivität der Selektivität – Wie ist es um die Gestaltungsfreiräume der Mitgliedstaaten in der Wirtschaftsförderung bestellt?*, 26 EuZW 3 (2015).

J. Bast, *Art 26 AEUV [Auftrag zur Gestaltung des Binnenmarkts]*, in *Das Recht der Europäischen Union* (E. Grabitz, M. Hilf & M. Nettesheim eds, C.H.Beck 2018).

J. Bauerschmidt, *Die Rechtsperson Der Europäischen Union Im Wandel* (Mohr Siebeck 2018).

J. Becker & J. Englisch, *International Effective Minimum Taxation – The GLOBE Proposal*, 11 WTJ 4 (2019), IBFD Journals.

J. Becker & D. Fehling, *Art. 116 AEUV Im Recht Der Direkten Steuern – Rechtliche Und Steuerpolitische Einordnung*, 29 IStR 21 (2020).

S. Bendlinger, *Betriebsstätten im Rahmen der globalen Mindestbesteuerung*, 33 SWI 1 (2023).

S. Bendlinger, *Internet und E-Commerce im internationalen Steuerrecht*, 9 SWI 7 (1999).

V. Bendlinger, *Chapter 351 – Article 351 TFEU on Prior Agreements of the Member States*, in *Smit & Herzog on The Law of the European Union* (P.E. Herzog, C. Campbell & G. Zagel eds, LexisNexis 2022).

V. Bendlinger, *Die Besteuerung der Digital Economy – Eine kritische Würdigung*, 3 StAW 3 (2018).

V. Bendlinger, *Die Besteuerung von österreichischen Portfoliodividenden ausländischer Investmentvehikel – Nimmt die Quellensteuerrückerstattungssaga bald ein Ende?*, 34 ecolex 1 (2023).

V. Bendlinger, *Die OECD Model Rules für ein globales Mindestbesteuerungsregime*, 32 SWI 1 (2022).

V. Bendlinger, *Minimum Taxation – Ergebnisse der Konsultationen zum GloBE Proposal der OECD*, 32 SWI 1 (2020).

V. Bendlinger & G. Kofler, *Computation of the Effective Tax Rate and the 'Top-up Tax'*, in *Pillar 2 Global Minimum Tax* (W. Haslehner et al., eds, 2022).

M. Bennett, *The Attribution of Profits to Permanent Establishments: The 2008 Commentary on Art. 7 of the OECD Model Convention*, 48 Eur. Taxn. 9 (2008), IBFD Journals.

G.A. Berman, *Taking Subsidiarity Seriously: Federalism in the European Community and the United States*, 94 Col. L. Rev. 2 (1994).

N. Bernard, *The Future of European Economic Law in the Light of the Principle of Subsidiarity*, 33 Common Market Law Review 4 (1996).

G. Bizioli, *An EU Policy for the Future of International Tax Law*, in *EU Tax Law and Policy in the 21st Century* (W. Haslehner, G. Kofler & Rust, Alexander eds, Wolters Kluwer 2017).

G. Bizioli, *Taking EU Fundamental Freedoms Seriously: Does the Anti-Tax Avoidance Directive Take Precedence over the Single Market?*, 26 EC Tax Review 3 (2017).

G. Bizioli, *The Evolution of the Concept of the Place of Management in Italian Case Law and Legislation: Interaction with Tax Treaties and EC Law*, 48 Eur. Taxn. 10 (2008), IBFD Journals.

G. Bizioli & E. Reimer, *Equality, Ability to Pay and Neutrality*, in *Research Handbook on European Union Taxation Law* (C. Panayi, W. Haslehner & E. Traversa eds, Edward Elgar Publishing 2020).

D.W. Blum, *The Proposal for a Global Minimum Tax: Comeback of Residence Taxation in the Digital Era?: Comment on Can GILTI + BEAT = GloBE?*, 47 Intertax 5 (2019).

D.W. Blum & A. Langer, *At a Crossroads: Mandatory Disclosure under DAC-6 and EU Primary Law – Part*, 59 Eur. Taxn. 6 (2019), IBFD Journals.

N. Boidman, *An Ironic Turn: Skeptic and Supporter Find Some UTPR Common Ground*, 108 Tax Notes Intl. 1533 (19 December 2022).

N. Boidman, *No Rational Role for the UTPR*, 108 Tax Notes Intl. 287 (17 October 2022).

N. Boidman, *UTPR's Effect on Outside Shareholders: Another Reason to Oppose?*, 109 Tax Notes Intl. 189 (9 January 2023).

P.J. Bourgeois & L. Blanchette, *Income_taxes.ca.Com: The Internet, Electronic, Commerce, and Taxes – Some Reflections: Part 1*, 45 Can. Tax J. 5 (1997).

P.J. Bourgeois & L. Blanchette, *Income_taxes.ca.Com: The Internet, Electronic, Commerce, and Taxes – Some Reflections: Part 2*, 45 Can. Tax J. 6 (1997).

K. Bradley, *The Exclusive Competences of the European Union: Some Random Jottings*, in *The Division of Competences between the EU and the Member States* (S. Garben & I. Govaere eds, Hart Publishing 2017).

N. Braun Binder, *Rechtsangleichung in der EU im Bereich der direkten Steuern* (Mohr Siebeck 2017).

J. Braunecker, *Digitalsteuer: Endlich angemessene Steuern für Google, Apple, Facebook und Co. in der EU?*, 29 EuZW 15.

C. Brokelind, *An Overview of Legal Issues Arising from the Implementation in the European Union of the OECD's Pillar One and Pillar Two Blueprint*, 75 Bull. Intl. Taxn. 5 (2021), IBFD Journals.

C. Brokelind, *Direct Taxation and the Future of EU Harmonization: Lessons from Past Experiences*, in *Tax Nexus and Jurisdiction in International and EU Law* (E. Traversa ed., IBFD 2022).

C. Brokelind, *Royalty Payments: Unresolved Issues in the Interest and Royalties Directive*, 44 Eur. Taxn. 5 (2004), IBFD Journals.

C. Brokelind, *The Anti-Tax Avoidance Directive under Scrutiny: A Matter of Competence?*, in *International Taxation in a Changing Landscape – Liber Amicorum in Honour of Bertil Wiman* (J. Monsenego & J. Bjuvberg eds, Wolters Kluwer 2019).

W. Brugger, *Concretization of Law and Statutory Interpretation*, 11 Tul. Eur. & Civ. Law. F. 207–250 (1996).

F. Brugger, M. Melcher & N. Wosak, *Globale Mindestbesteuerung: Ermittlung des GloBE-Einkommens*, 97 SWK 13/14 (2022).

F. Brugger, M. Melcher & N. Wosak, *Globale Mindestbesteuerung: Ermittlung des GloBE-Steueraufwands*, 97 SWK 15 (2022).

M. Butler et al., *Taxation of Global E-Commerce*, 6 Asia-Pac. Tax Bull. 7 (2000), IBFD Journals.

C. Calliess, *Subsidiaritäts- und Solidaritätsprinzip in der Europäischen Union* (2nd ed., Nomos 1999).

A. Caridi, *Proposed Changes to the OECD Commentary on Article 5: Part I – The Physical PE Notion*, 43 Eur. Taxn. 1 (2003), IBFD Journals.

D. Cass, *The Word that Saves Maastricht? The Principle of Subsidiarity and the Division of Powers within the European Community*, 29 Common Market Law Review 6 (1992).

M. Caziero & I. Lazarov, *The Substantive Scope of the Anti-Tax-Avoidance Directive: The Remaining Leeway for National Tax Sovereignty*, 58 Common Market Law Review 6 (2021).

M. Chamon, *Implied Exclusive Powers in the ECJ's Post-Lisbon Jurisprudence: The Continued Development of the ERTA Doctrine*, 55 Common Market Law Review 4 (2018).

V. Chand, A. Turina & K. Romanovska, *Tax Treaty Obstacles in Implementing the Pillar Two Global Minimum Tax Rules and a Possible Solution for Eliminating the Various Challenges*, 14 WTJ 1 (2022).

A. Christians & T.D. Magalhaes, *Undertaxed Profits and the Use-It-or-Lose-It Principle*, 108 Tax Notes Intl. 705–710 (7 November 2022).

A. Christians & S.E. Shay, *The Consistency of Pillar 2 UTPR with U.S. Bilateral Tax Treaties*, 109 Tax Notes Intl. 445–454 (2023).

R. Churchill & N.G. Foster, *European Community Law and Prioer Treaty Obligations of Member States: The Spanish Fishermen's Cases*, 36 International and Comparative Law Quarterly 3 (1987).

C.D. Classen, *Art 115 (ex-Artikel 94 EGV) [Rechtsangleichung; Richtlinien]*, in *Europäisches Unionsrecht* (H. Groeben, J. Schwarze & A. Hatje eds, 7th ed., Nomos 2015).

C.D. Classen, *Art 116 (ex-Artikel 96 EGV) [Beseitigung vorhandener Verzerrungen]*, in *Europäisches Unionsrecht* (H. Groeben, J. Schwarze & A. Hatje eds, 7th ed., Nomos 2015).

P. Collins & M. Hutchings, *Articles 101 and 102 of the EEC Treaty: Completing the Internal Market*, 11 European Law Review 3 (1986).

P. Conconi, C. Herghelegiu & L. Puccio, *EU Trade Agreements: To Mix or Not to Mix, that is the Question*, May 2020, available at http://respect.eui.eu/wp-content/uploads/sites/6/2020/05/Mixity.pdf (accessed 21 July 2021).

P. Craig, *The Lisbon Treaty – Law, Politics, and Treaty Reform* (Oxford 2010).

P. Craig & G. de Búrca, *EU Law – Text, Cases and Materials* (7th ed., Oxford 2020).

M. Cremona, *A Constitutional Basis for Effective External Action? An Assessment of the Provisions on EU External Action in the Constitutional Treaty*, 2006 EUI Working Papers (Law No. 2006/30).

M. Cremona, *EU External Competence – Rationales for Exclusivity*, in *The Division of Competences Between the EU and the Member States* (S. Garben & I. Govaere eds, Hart Publishing 2017).

M. Cremona, *EU External Relations: Unity and Conferral of Powers*, in *The Question of Competence in the European Union* (L. Azoulai ed., Oxford 2014).

M. Cremona, *External Relations and External Competence of the European Union*, in *The Evolution of EU Law* (3rd ed., Oxford 2021).

H. van Dam et al., *Taxing the Digitalized Economy: Key Takeaways from the OECD Public Consultation on the Pillar One and Pillar Two Blueprints*, 28 ITPJ 3 (2017), IBFD Journals.

G. Davies, *Subsidiarity: The Wrong Idea, in the Wrong Place, at the Wrong Time*, 43 Common Market Law Review 1 (2006).

K. Daxkobler & E. Huisman, *Levy & Sebbag: The ECJ Has Once Again Been Asked To Deliver Its Opinion on Juridical Double Taxation in the Internal Market*, 53 Eur. Taxn. 8 (2013).

L. De Broe, *Can Tax Treaties Confer State Aid?*, 26 EC Tax Review 5 (2017).

L. De Broe, *Some EU and Tax Treaty Law Considerations on the Draft EU Directive on Global Minimum Taxation for Multinationals in the Union*, 50 Intertax 12 (2022).

L. De Broe & J. Luts, *BEPS Action 6: Tax Treaty Abuse*, 43 Intertax 2 (2015).

L. De Broe & M. Massant, *Are the OECD/G20 Pillar Two GloBE-Rules Compliant with the Fundamental Freedoms?*, 30 EC Tax Review 3 (2021).

C. De Pietro, *Tax Treaty Override and the Need for Coordination Between Legal Systems: Safeguarding the Effectiveness of International Law*, 7 WTJ 1 (2015), IBFD Journals.

M.F. De Wilde, *Why Pillar Two Top-Up Taxation Requires Tax Treaty Modification – Kluwer International Tax Blog*, Kluwer International Tax Blog (12 January 2022), available at https://kluwertaxblog.com/2022/01/12/why-pillar-two-top-up-taxation-requires-tax-treaty-modification/ (accessed 22 January 2023).

F. Debelva & L. De Broe, *Pillar 2: An Analysis of the IIR and UTPR from an International Customary Law, Tax Treaty and European Union Law Perspective*, 50 Intertax 12 (2022).

M.P. Devereux et al., *The OECD Global Anti-Base Erosion ('GloBE') Proposal*, 2020 Oxford University Centre for Business Taxation, available at https://oxfordtax.sbs.ox.ac.uk/files/oecdglobeproposalreportpdf (accessed 15 March 2023).

M. Devereux, J. Vella & H. Wardell-Burrus, *Pillar 2: Rule Order, Incentives, and Tax Competition*, 14 January 2022 SSRN, available at https://papers.ssrn.com/sol3/papers.cfm?abstract_id=4009002.

M. Devereux, J. Vella & H. Wardell-Burrus, *Pillar 2's Impact on Tax Competition*, 26 August 2022 SSRN, available at https://papers.ssrn.com/sol3/papers.cfm?abstract_id=4203395.

A. Dimopoulos, *The Validity and Applicability of International Investment Agreements between EU Member States under EU and International Law*, 48 Common Market Law Review 1 (2011).

R.L. Doernberg, *Electronic Commerce and International Tax Sharing*, 16 Tax Notes Intl. 1013–1022 (1998).

R.L. Doernberg & L. Hinnekens, *Electronic Commerce and International Taxation* (Kluwer Law International 1999).

C. Döllefeld et al., *Tax Administrative Guidance: A Proposal for Simplifying Pillar Two*, 50 Intertax 3 (2021).

J. Dombrowsky, *Die Einwirkungen des Unionsrechts auf Doppelbesteuerungsabkommen* (Duncker & Humblot 2019).

S. Douma, *The Three Ds of Direct Tax Jurisdiction: Disparity, Discrimination and Double Taxation*, 46 Eur. Taxn. 11 (2006), IBFD Journals.

A.P. Dourado, *Is There A Need for A Directive on Pillar Two?*, 50 Intertax Issue 6/7 (1 May 2022), available at 10.54648/TAXI2022056.

A.P. Dourado, *Pillar Two from the Perspective of the European Union*, 67 BTR 5 (2022).

A.P. Dourado, *The Commission Proposal to Replace Unanimity with a Qualified Majority in the Case of Tax Matters*, 47 Intertax 4 (2019).

A.P. Dourado, *The EU Anti Tax Avoidance Package: Moving Ahead of BEPS?*, 44 Intertax 6–7 (2016).

A.P. Dourado, *The Pillar Two Top-Up Taxes: Interplay, Characterization, and Tax Treaties*, 50 Intertax Issue 5 (1 May 2022), available at 10.54648/TAXI2022045.

J. Drucker, *Google 2.4% Rate Shows How $60 Billion Is Lost to Tax Loopholes*, 21 October 2010 Bloomberg.Com, available at https://www.bloomberg.com/news/articles/2010-10-21/google-2-4-rate-shows-how-60-billion-u-s-revenue-lost-to-tax-loopholes (accessed 9 July 2021).

R.S.J. Dwarkasing, *The Concept of Associated Enterprises*, 41 Intertax 8–9.

K. Dziurdź, *Income Inclusion Rule Im Vergleich Zur Hinzurechnungsbesteuerung – Funktionsweise, Zweck Und Auswirkungen*, 31 SWI 11 (2021).

A. Easson, *Harmonization of Direct Taxation in the European Community: From Neumark to Ruding*, 40 Can. Tax J. 3 (1992).

E. Eberhartinger & G. Winkler, *Pillar Two and the Accounting Standards*, 51 Intertax 2 (2023).

P. Eeckhout, *EU External Relations Law* (2nd ed., Oxford EU Law Library 2011).

S. Elwes, *The Internal Market versus the Right of Member States to Levy Direct Tax – A Clash of Fundamental Principles*, 41 Intertax 1 (2007).

F. Engelen, *Interpretation of Tax Treaties under International Law* (IBFD 2004).

J. Englisch, *Article 116 TFEU – The Nuclear Option for Qualified Majority Tax Harmonization?*, 29 EC Tax Review 2 (2020).

J. Englisch, *Designing a Harmonized EU-GloBE in Compliance with Fundamental Freedoms*, 30 EC Tax Review 3 (2021).

J. Englisch, *Effective Minimum Tax Implementation by the EU: Which Alternatives?*, Kluwer International Tax Blog (25 October 2021), available at https://kluwertaxblog.com/2021/10/25/effective-minimum-tax-implementation-by-the-eu-which-alternatives/ (accessed 12 March 2023).

J. Englisch, *GloBE Rules and Tax Competition*, 50 Intertax 12 (2022).

J. Englisch, *Non-Harmonized Implementation of a GloBE Minimum Tax: How EU Member States Could Proceed*, 30 EC Tax Review 5–6 (2021).

J. Englisch, *Wettbewerbsgleichheit im grenzüberschreitenden Handel* (Mohr Siebeck 2008).

U. Everling, *Zur Funktion der Rechtsangleichung in der Europäischen Gemeinschaft – Vom Abbau der Verzerrungen zur Schaffung des Binnenmarktes*, in *Du droit international au droit de l'integration – Liber Amicorum Pierre Pescatore* (F. Capotorti et al., eds, Nomos 1987).

U. di Fabio, *Some Remarks on the Allocation of Competences between the European Union and Its Member States*, 39 Common Market Law Review 6 (2002).

D. Fehling & M. Valta, *Aktionpunkt 1: Besteuerung der digitalen Wirtschaft*, in *BEPS-Handbuch* (G. Kofler & A. Schnitger eds, C.H.Beck 2019).

P. Fernandez, G. Heij & D.J. Pope, *Tax Policy and Electronic Commerce*, 56 Bull. Intl. Taxn. 1 (2002), IBFD Journals.

M. van Financiën, *Netherlands Launches Online Consultation on Draft Bill for the Proposed Minimum Tax Rate Act 2024 – News Item – Government.Nl* (24 October 2022), available at 10/24/netherlands-launches-online-consultation-on-draft-bill-for-the-proposed-minimum-tax-rate-act-2024 (accessed 9 February 2023).

D.L. Forst, *The Continuing Vitality of Source-Based Taxation in the Electronic Age*, 15 Tax Notes Intl. 1455 (1997).

A. Garcia Prats et al., *EU Report Subject 1 – Reconstructing the Treaty Network*, in *Cahier de Droit Fiscal International* vol. 105/A (International Fiscal Association 2020).

W. Gassner, *Interpretation und Anwendung der Steuergesetze: kritische Analyse der wirtschaftlichen Betrachtungsweise des Steuerrechts* (Orac 1972).

W. Gassner, M. Lang & E. Lechner, *Doppelbesteuerungsabkommen und EU Recht* (Linde 1995).

R. Geiger, *Article 351 [Former Agreements of the Member States]*, in *European Union Treaties* (R. Geiger, D.-E. Kahn & M. Kotzur eds, C.H.Beck 2015).

P. Genschel, A. Kemmerling & E. Seils, *Speeding up, down the Hill: How the EU Shapes Corporate Tax Competition in the Single Market*, available at https://www.econstor.eu/bitstream/10419/27910/1/600427145.PDF (accessed 29 March 2023).

M. Geurts, *How to Tax Electronic Commerce Transactions?*, 26 Intertax 10 (1998).

R. Goulder, *Confessions of a UTPR Skeptic*, 108 Tax Notes Intl. 907–910 (14 November 2022).

R. Goulder, *Pillar 2 and Tax Treaties: MLI, Where Are Thou?*, 108 Tax Notes Intl. 775–778 (7 November 2022).

I. Govaere, *'Setting the International Scene': EU External Competence and Procedures Post-Lisbon Revisited in the Light of Opinion 1/13*, 52 Common Market Law Review 5 (2015).

I. Govaere & G. Sacha, *Introduction: The Interface between EU and International Law*, in *The Interface Between EU and International Law* (I. Govaere & G. Sacha eds, Hart Publishing 2019).

A. de Graaf, *Avoidance of International Double Taxation: Community or Jount Policy?*, 7 EC Tax Review 4 (1998).

A. de Graaf & K.-J. Visser, *ATA Directive: Some Observations Regarding Formal Aspects*, 25 EC Tax Review 4 (2016).

C. Gröpl, *J. Steuerrecht*, in *Handbuch des EU-Wirtschaftsrechts* vol. I (M.A. Dauses & M. Ludwig eds, 53rd ed., C.H.Beck 2021).

X. Groussot & S. Bogojevic, *Subsidiarity as a Procedural Safeguard of Federalism*, in *The Question of Competence in the European Union* (L. Azoulai ed., Oxford 2014).

H. Grubert & R. Altshuler, *Fixing the System: An Analysis of Alternative Proposals for the Reform of International Tax*, 66 Nat. Tax J. 3.

J.C. Guerra, *Limitation on Benefits Clauses and EU Law*, 51 Eur. Taxn. 2–3 (2011), IBFD Journals.

H.M.A.L. Hamaekers, *Corporate Tax Policy and Competence of the European Community: An EC Tax Convention with Non-Member States*, 30 Eur. Taxn.

H.M.A.L. Hamaekers, *The EC on the Brink of Full Corporate Tax Harmonization?*, 32 Eur. Taxn. 4–5 (1992), IBFD Journals.

C.M. Harris, *The European Community's Parent-Subsidiary Directive*, 9 Fla. J. Int'l L. 1 (1994).

W. Haslehner, *Chapter 3: EU-US Relations in the Field of Direct Taxes from the EU Perspective: A BEPS-Induced Transformation?*, in *The Implementation of Anti-BEPS Rules in the EU: A Comprehensive Study* (P. Pistone & D. Weber eds, IBFD 2018).

W. Haslehner, *Is There a Need for a Directive on Pillar 2? A Few Normative Comments*, 50 Intertax 6–7 (2022).

W. Haslehner, *The General Scope of the ATAD and Its Position in the EU Legal Order*, in *A Guide to the Anti-Tax-Avoidance-Directive* (W. Haslehner et al., eds, Edward Elgar Publishing 2020).

C. Heber, *Die Kompetenzverteilung im Rahmen der Austrittsverhandlungen nach Art. 50 EUV unter besonderer Berücksichtigung bestehenden Sekundärrechts*, 52 EuR 5 (2017).

A.G. Heredia, *Software Royalties in Tax Treaties: Should Copyright Rights Be Reconsidered in the OECD Commentary on Article 12?*, 59 Bull. Intl. Taxn. 6 (2005), IBFD Journals.

M. Herzfeld, *How Does the Qualified Domestic Minimum Top-up Tax Fit Into Pillar 2?*, 106 Tax Notes Intl. 315–319 (2022).

M. Herzfeld, *How to Allocate CFC Taxes under GloBE*, 108 Tax Notes Intl. 1512–1518 (19 December 2022).

M. Herzfeld, *How to Think About How the US Congress Thinks About International Tax Reforms*, 67 BTR 5 (2022).

M. Herzfeld, *More on GLOBE Ordering: CFC Rules*, 106 Tax Notes Intl. 603–607 (2 May 2022).

M. Herzfeld, *U.S. Treasury to Congress: Hand Over the Tax Keys, Please*, 102 Tax Notes Intl. 1585–1589 (2021).

M. Herzfeld, *Who Wins Out in the Latest Pillar 2 Guidance?*, 109 Tax Notes Intl. 821–825 (13 February 2023).

P.E. Herzog, *Treaty-Making Power of the European Community Thirty Years (Approximately) after the ERTA Case – And Where Does This Leave the United States*, 30 Syracuse J. Int'l. L. 2 (2003).

J. Hey, *Chapter 17: Global Minimum Taxation (GloBE): What Is It About and What Could Be a European Answer?*, in *Thinker, Teacher, Traveler: Reimagining International Tax Essays in Honor of H. David Rosenbloom* (G. Kofler, R. Mason & Rust, Alexander eds, IBFD 2021).

J. Hey, *Harmonisierung Der Unternehmensbesteuerung in Europa* (Otto Schmidt 1997).

J. Hey, *The 2020 Pillar Two Blueprint: What Can the GloBE Income Inclusion Rule Do That CFC Legislation Can't Do?*, 49 Intertax 1 (2021).

C. Hillion, *Case C-62/98 Commission of the European Communities v. Portugal, and Case C-84/98 Commission of the European Communities v. Portugal*, 38 Common Market Law Review 5 (2001).

L. Hinnekens, *Compatibility of Bilateral Tax Treaties with European Community Law. The Rules*, 3 EC Tax Review 4 (1994).

L. Hinnekens, *Income Taxation of Electronic Commerce and Other Cross-Border Business Coordinated by the OECD Also Involves the European Community*, 41 Eur. Taxn. 9 (2001), IBFD Journals.

L. Hinnekens, *International Taxation of Electronic Commerce: An Emerging Framework*, 27 Intertax 12 (1999).

L. Hinnekens, *Looking for an Appropriate Jurisdictional Framework for Source-State Taxation of International Electronic Commerce in the Twenty-First Century*, 26 Intertax 6–7 (1998).

L. Hinnekens, *New Age International Taxation in the Digital Economy of the Global Society*, 25 Intertax 4 (1997).

L. Hinnekens, *The Challenges of Applying VAT and Income Tax Territoriality Concepts and Rules to International Electronic Commerce*, 26 Intertax 2 (1998).

L. Hinnekens, *The Uneasy Case and Fate of Article 293 Second Indent EC*, 37 Intertax 11 (2009).

M. Hofstätter, *Who is Competent to Issue Measures for the Elimination of Double Taxation within the Community?*, in *Tax Treaty Law and EC Law* (M. Lang, J. Schuch & C. Staringer eds, Linde 2007).

D. Hohenwarter-Mayr, *Globale Mindeststeueraus unionsrechtlicher Sicht*, in *Handbuch zur Globalen Steuerreform* (D. Hohenwarter et al., eds, Facultas 2023).

K. Holmes, *The Concept of Income: A Multi-Disciplinary Analysis* (IBFD 2001).

T. Hutchinson & N. Duncan, *Defining and Describing What We Do: Doctrinal Legal Research*, 17 Dea. L. Rev. 1 (2012).

R. Ismer, *Abuse of Law as a General Principle of European Union (Tax) Law*, in *A Guide to the Anti-Tax-Avoidance-Directive* (W. Haslehner et al., eds, Edward Elgar Publishing 2020).

A.M. Jiménez, *Towards a Homogeneous Theory of Abuse in EU (Direct) Tax Law*, 66 Bull. Intl. Taxn. 4/5 (2012), IBFD Journals.

J. Kadet, *Defending the UTPR: Creative Corporate Structuring Can't Hide Real Connections*, 108 Tax Notes Intl. 1072–1073 (28 November 2022).

D.-E. Kahn & D. Eisenhut, *Article 115 [National Law with Immediate Effect on the Internal Market; Approximation of Laws]*, in *European Union Treaties* (R. Geiger, D.-E. Kahn & M. Kotzur eds, C.H.Beck 2015).

D.-E. Kahn & D. Eisenhut, *Article 116 [Provisions Distorting Competition]*, in *European Union Treaties* (R. Geiger, D.-E. Kahn & M. Kotzur eds, C.H.Beck 2015).

H. Kelsen, *Reine Rechtslehre – 5. Neudruck der 2. Auflage aus 1960* (Verlag Österreich 2020).

H. Kelsen, *Was ist Gerechtigkeit?* (Franz Deuticke 1953).

H. Kelsen, *What Is the Pure Theory of Law?*, 34 Tul. Law Rev. 2 (1959–1960).

E. Kemmeren, *After Repeal of Article 293 EC Treaty under the Lisbon Treaty: The EU Objective of Eliminating Double Taxation Can Be Applied More Widely*, 17 EC Tax Review 4 (2008).

E. Kemmeren, *Double Tax Conventions on Income and Capital and the EU: Past, Present and Future*, 21 EC Tax Review 3 (2012).

E. Kemmeren, *Principle of Origin in Tax Conventions: A Rethinking of Models* (Dongen 2001).

S. Kingston, *The Boundaries of Sovereignty: The ECJ's Controversial Role Applying Internal Market Law to Direct Tax Measures*, in *Cambridge Yearbook of European Legal Studies* (2007).

J. Klabbers, *Moribund on the Fourth of July? The Court of Justice on Prior Agreements of the Member States*, 26 European Law Review 2 (2001).

J. Klabbers, *Treaty Conflict and the European Union* (Cambridge 2009).

M. Klamert, *The Principle of Loyalty in EU Law* (Oxford 2014).

M. Klamert, *Zur Pragmatik der Kompetenzverteilung in der EU*, in *Europarecht und Rechtstheorie* (G. Herzig et al., eds, Verlag Österreich 2017).

M. Klamert & N. Maydell, *Rechtfragen der impliziten Außenkompetenz der EG illustriert am Beispiel der Dienstleistungsrichlinie und der Minimum Platform on Investment*, 42 EuR 4.

E.D. Kleinbard, *The Lessons of Stateless Income*, 11 Fla. Tax Review 9 (2011).

M. Klokar, *Chapter 5: The List of Taxes According to Article 2(3) OECD Model Convention 1982 and 2017*, in *Taxes Covered under Article 2 of the OECD Model* vol. 19 (G. Kofler et al., eds, WU - Tax Law and Policy Series, 2020).

G. Kofler, *'Dancing with Mr D': The ECJ's Denial of Most-Favoured-Nation Treatment in the 'D' Case*, 45 Eur. Taxn. 12 (2005), IBFD Journals.

G. Kofler, *Doppelbesteuerungsabkommen und Europäisches Gemeinschaftsrecht* (Linde 2007).

G. Kofler, *Einleitung*, in *Doppelbesteuerungsabkommen* (D. Aigner, G. Kofler & M. Tumpel eds, 2nd ed., Linde 2018).

G. Kofler, *Entwicklungslinien und Zukunftsfragen des Europäischen Steuerrechts*, in *100 Jahre Steuerrechtsprechung in Deutschland 1918–2018 – Festschrift für den Bundesfinanzhof Band I* (K.-D. Drüen, J. Hey & R. Mellinghoff eds, Otto Schmidt 2018).

G. Kofler, *EU Power to Tax: Competences in the Area of Direct Taxation*, in *Research Handbook on European Union Taxation Law* (C. Panayi, W. Haslehner & E. Traversa eds, Edward Elgar Publishing 2020).

G.W. Kofler, *European Taxation Under an 'Open Sky': LoB Clauses in Tax Treaties Between the U.S. and EU Member States*, 2004 Tax Notes Intl. 45–89.

G. Kofler, *Most-Favored-Nation Treatment in Direct Taxation: Does EC Law Provide for Community MFN in Bilateral Double Taxation Treaties?*, 5 Houston Business and Tax Law Journal 1 (2005).

G. Kofler, *Some Reflections on the 'Saving Clause'*, 44 Intertax 8/9 (2016).

G. Kofler, *Vor allem die Qualified Domestic Minimum Top-up Tax ist ein echter Game Changer*, 6 TPI 5 (2022).

G. Kofler & R. Mason, *Kerckhaert & Morres: A European 'Switch in Time?'*, in *Is the European Court of Justice Taking a New Approach?* (S. von Thiel ed., 2007).

G. Kofler, G. Mayr & C. Schlager, *Taxation of the Digital Economy: A Pragmatic Approach to Short-Term Measures*, 58 Eur. Taxn. 4 (2018).

G. Kofler, G. Mayr & C. Schlager, *Taxation of the Digital Economy: 'Quick Fixes' or Long-Term Solution?*, 59 Eur. Taxn. 12 (2017).

G. Kofler & A. Schnitger, *Does the 'Initial Phase Relief' Make the EU's Pillar Two Directive Invalid?*, Eur. Taxn. forthcoming (2023).

J. Kokott, *Art 351 – Verhältnis Zu Früheren Verträgen*, in *EUV/AEUV* (R. Streinz ed., 3rd ed., C.H.Beck 2018).

J. Kokott, *Das Steuerrecht der Europäischen Union* (C.H. Beck 2018).

J. Kokott, *Public International Law and Taxation: Nexus and Territoriality*, in *Tax Nexus and Jurisdiction in International and EU Law* (E. Traversa ed., IBFD 2022).

S. Korte, *Art. 114 (Ex-Art. 95 EGV) [Beschlussfassung; Einzelstaatliche Regelungen; Schutzklausel]*, in *EUV/AEUV – Das Verfassungsrecht Der Europäischen Union*

Mit Europäischer Grundrechtecharta (C. Calliess & M. Ruffert eds, 6th ed., C.H.Beck 2022).

S. Korte, *Art. 115 (Ex-Art. 94 EGV) [Richtlinien Zur Angleichung von Rechtsvorschriften Für Den Binnenmarkt]*, in *EUV/AEUV – Das Verfassungsrecht Der Europäischen Union Mit Europäischer Grundrechtecharta* (C. Calliess & M. Ruffert eds, 6th ed., C.H.Beck 2022).

S. Korte, *Art. 116 (Ex-Art. 96 EGV) [Reaktion Auf Wettbewerbsverfälschende Vorschriften]*, in *EUV/AEUV – Das Verfassungsrecht Der Europäischen Union Mit Europäischer Grundrechtecharta* (C. Calliess & M. Ruffert eds, 6th ed., C.H.Beck 2022).

P. Koutrakos, *EU International Relations Law* (Hart Publishing 2015).

R. Krever, *Electronic Commerce and Taxation – A Summary of the Emerging Issues*, 6 Asia-Pac. Tax Bull. 6 (2000), IBFD Journals.

M. Lambooij, A. Sinyor & V. Chew, *Recent OECD Initiatives With E-Commerce Taxation*, 22 Tax Notes Intl. 17 (2001).

M. Lang, *'Aggressive Steuerplanung' – eine Analyse der Empfehlung der Europäischen Kommission*, 2 SWI 13 (2013).

M. Lang, *CFC Regulations and Double Taxation Treaties*, 57 Bull. Intl. Taxn. 2 (2003).

M. Lang, *Die Bindung der Doppelbesteuerungsabkommen an die Grundfreiheiten des EU-Rechts*, in *Doppelbesteuerungsabkommen und EU-Recht* (W. Gassner, M. Lang & E. Lechner eds, Linde 1996).

M. Lang et al., *Draft for a Multilateral Tax Treaty*, in *Multilateral Tax Treaties – New Developments in International Tax Law* (M. Lang et al., eds, Kluwer Law International 1998).

M. Lang, *The Concept of a Multilateral Tax Treaty*, in *Multilateral Tax Treaties – New Developments in International Tax Law* (H. Loukota et al., eds, Kluwer Law International 1998).

M. Lang, *Treaty Override und Gemeinschaftsrecht*, in *Reden zum Andenken an Klaus Vogel* (M. Lehner ed., C.H.Beck 2010).

A. Langer, *Die Grenzen des Country-by-Country Reportings* (Schriften zum österr. Abgabenrecht No. 81, LexisNexis 2019).

C. Lau & A. Halkyard, *From E-Commerce to E-Business Taxation*, 9 Asia-Pac. Tax Bull. 1 (2003), IBFD Journals.

I. Lazarov & S. Govind, *Carpet-Bombing Tax Avoidance in Europe: Examining the Validity of the ATAD under EU Law*, 47 Intertax 10 (2019).

D. Leczykiewicz, *Prohibition of Abusive Practices as a 'General Principle' of EU Law*, 56 Common Market Law Review 3 (2019).

F. Leidenmühler, *Art 116 AEUV*, in *EUV/AEUV* (T. Jäger & K. Stöger eds, Manz 1 Oct. 2018).

S. Leitner-Hanetseder & D. Schausberger, *Änderung der Einbezugskriterien gem. IFRS 10*, 6 IRZ 9 (2011).

I. Lejeune et al., *Does Cyber-Commerce Necessitate a Revision of International Tax Concepts? – Part I*, 38 Eur. Taxn. 1 (1998), IBFD Journals.

I. Lejeune et al., *Does Cyber-Commerce Necessitate a Revision of International Tax Concepts? – Part II*, 38 Eur. Taxn. 2 (1998), IBFD Journals.

P. Leleux, *Le rapprochement des législation dans la Communauté économique européenne*, 4 Cahiers de droit européen 2 (1968).

K. Lenaerts & J.A. Gutiérrez-Fons, *To Say What the Law of the EU Is: Methods of Interpretation and the European Court of Justice*, 2012 European University Institute, available at https://cadmus.eui.eu/bitstream/handle/1814/28339/AEL_2013_09_DL.pdf?sequence=1&isAllowed=y (accessed 28 September 2021).

M. Lennard, *Customary International Law and Tax – The Fog of Law*, 109 Tax Notes Intl. 601–608 (30 January 2023).

U. von der Leyen, *A Union that Strives for More – My Agenda for Europe – Political Guidelines for the next European Commission 2019–2024* (2019).

J. Li, *The Pillar 2 Undertaxed Payments Rule Departs From International Consensus and Tax Treaties*, 174 Tax Notes Intl. 1695–1703 (21 March 2022).

B.F. Liotti, *Limits of International Cooperation: The Concept of 'Jurisdiction Not to Tax' from the BEPS Project to GloBE*, 76 Bull. Intl. Taxn. 2 (2022).

S.-O. Lodin, *International Tax Issues in a Rapidly Changing World*, 55 Bull. Intl. Taxn. 1 (2001), IBFD Journals.

S.-O. Lodin, *What Ought To Be Taxed and What Can Be Taxed: A New International Dilemma*, 54 Bull. Intl. Taxn. 5 (2000), IBFD Journals.

S. Lorenzmeier, *Art. 351*, in *Das Recht der Europäischen Union* (E. Grabitz, M. Hilf & M. Nettesheim eds, 72nd ed., C.H.Beck 2019).

R. Lyal, *Note on the External Competence of the European Community in Tax Matters – the Example of the Agreement with Switzerland on the Taxation of Savings*, in *The EU and Third Countries: Direct Taxation* (M. Lang & P. Pistone eds, Linde 2007).

M.P. Maduro, *Interpreting of European Law: Judicial Adjudication in a Context of Constitutional Pluralism*, 1 European Journal of Legal Studies 2 (2007).

T.D. Magalhaes, *Give Us the Law: Responses and Challenges to UTPR Resisters*, 108 Tax Notes Intl. 1257–1261 (5 December 2022).

T.D. Magalhaes, *UTPR Opposition: A Game of Whack-a-Mole*, 108 Tax Notes Intl. 1531–1532 (19 December 2022).

K. Maier, *Investitionsanreize im Spannungsfeld der Bilanzierungsvorschriften von IAS 12 und IAS 20 Zuwendungen*, 2017 PWC - IFRS Aktuell 2–4, available at https://www.pwc.at/de/newsletter/ifrs/2017/ifrs-newsletter-2017-06.pdf.

P. Manzini, *The Priority of Pre-Existing Treaties of EC Member States within the Framework of International Law*, 12 EJIL 4 (2001).

C. Marchgraber, *Cross-Border Tax Arbitrage, the Parent-Subsidiary Directive (2011/96) and Double Tax Treaty Law*, 70 Bull. Intl. Taxn. 3 (2016), IBFD Journals.

M.G. Marquardsen, *Einstimmigkeit in Steuerfragen – Reformbedarf?* (IFST-Schrift No. 534, IFST 2020).

A. Martin Jimenez, *The 2003 Revision of the OECD Commentaries on the Improper Use of Tax Treaties: A Case for the Declining Effect of the OECD Commentaries?*, 58 Bull. Intl. Taxn. 1 (2004), IBFD Journals.

R. Mason, *A Wrench in GLOBE's Diabolic Machinery*, 107 Tax Notes Intl. 1391–1395 (19 September 2022).

G. Mayr & C. Schlager, *Digitale Geschäftsmodelle und Betriebsstättenkonzept*, in *Digitalisierung im Konzernsteuerrecht* (S. Kirchmayr et al., eds, Linde 2018).

C.E. McLure, *Globalization, Tax Rules and National Sovereignty*, 55 Bull. Intl. Taxn. 8 (2001), IBFD Journals.

K.M. Meessen, *The Application of Rules of Public International Law within Community Law*, 13 Common Market Law Review 4 (1976).

M. Mitterlehner, *Die Digital Economy im internationalen Steuerrecht*, in *Die österreichischen DBA nach BEPS – SWI-Spezial* (S. Bendlinger et al., eds, Linde 2018).

A. Navarro, *Jurisdiction Not to Tax, Tax Sparing Clauses and the Income Inclusion Rule of the OECD Pillar 2 (GloBE) Proposal: The Demise of a Policy Instrument of Developing Countries?*, 2020 Copenhagen Business School Law Research Paper Series.

M. Nettesheim, *Art. 2 [Ausschließliche Zuständigkeiten]*, in *Das Recht der Europäischen Union* vol. 60th (E. Grabitz, M. Hilf & M. Nettesheim eds, C.H.Beck 2016).

M. Nettesheim, *Art. 3 [Ausschließliche Zuständigkeiten]*, in *Das Recht Der Europäischen Union* vol. 60th (E. Grabitz, M. Hilf & M. Nettesheim eds, C.H.Beck 2016).

A. Nikolakakis & J. Li, *UTPR: Unprecedented (and Unprincipled?) Tax Policy Response*, 109 Tax Notes Intl. 743–751 (2023).

J.F.P. Nogueira, *GloBE and EU Law: Assessing the Compatibility of the OECD's Pillar II Initiative on a Minimum Effective Tax Rate with EU Law and Implementing It within the Internal Market*, 12 WTJ 3 (2020), IBFD Journals.

J.F.P. Nogueira & A. Turina, *Pillar Two and EU Law*, in *Global Minimum Taxation? – An Analysis of the Global Anti-Base Erosion Initiative* (IBFD 2021), IBFD Books.

N. Noked, *Defense of Primary Taxing Rights*, 40 Va. Tax Rev. 2 (2021).

N. Noked, *Potential Response to GLOBE: Domestic Minimum Taxes In Countries Affected by the Global Minimum Tax*, 102 Tax Notes Intl. 943–947 (17 May 2021).

N. Noked, *The Case for Domestic Minimum Taxes on Multinationals*, 105 Tax Notes Intl. 667–674 (7 Feb. 2022).

C. Noonan & V. Plekhanova, *Compliance Challenges of the BEPS Two-Pillar Solution*, 67 BTR 5 (2022).

D.G. Noren, *Modifying Bilateral Income Tax Treaties to Accommodate Pillar Two UTPR Rules*, 14 Nov. 2022 Bloomberg Tax – Tax Management Memorandum, available at https://images.mwe.com/Web/MCDERMOTTWILLEMERYLLP/%7B92249201-7ae1-4c77-9dc4-459255e5a7d6%7D_Modifying_Bilateral_Income_Tax_Treaties_to_Accommodate_Pillar_Two_UTPR_Rules_David_Noren.pdf?utm_campaign=MITN%2012.9.22&utm_medium=email&utm_source=Eloqua.

M. Nouwen, *The Market Distortion Provisions of Articles 116–117 TFEU: An Alternative Route to Qualified Majority Voting in Tax Matters?*, 49 Intertax 1 (2021).

X. Oberson & L. Piaget, *Electronic Commerce and Taxation: A Swiss Perspective*, 52 Bull. Intl. Taxn. 12 (1998), IBFD Journals.

J. Owens, *Progress Report: Taxation and Electronic Commerce*, 39 Eur. Taxn. 11 (1999), IBFD Journals.

J. Owens, *Taxation and E-Commerce: Progress Report*, 29 Intertax 1 (2000).

C. Panayi, *The Effect of Community Law on Pre-Accession Tax Treaties*, 16 EC Tax Review 3 (2007).

L. Parada, *Tailoring Developing Country Advice: A Response to Noam Noked*, 105 Tax Notes Intl. 783–784 (14 February 2022).

S. Picciotto, *Justifying the UTPR: Nexus and Economic Connection*, 108 Tax Notes Intl. 667 (7 November 2022).

S. Picciotto, *Rebutting the Logic of UTPR Skeptics*, 108 Tax Notes Intl. 1371 (12 December 2022).

S. Picciotto, *UTPR Critics Miss the Point of Tax Treaty Principles*, 108 Tax Notes Intl. 153 (10 October 2022).

S. Picciotto & J. Kadet, *The Transition to Unitary Taxation*, 108 Tax Notes Intl. 453–461 (24 October 2022).

H. Pijl, *Interpretation of Article 7 of the OECD Model, Permanent Establishment Financing and Other Dealings*, 65 Bull. Intl. Taxn. 6 (2011), IBFD Journals.

H. Pijl, *The Concept of Permanent Establishment and the Proposed Changes to the OECD Commentary with Special Reference to Dutch Case Law*, 56 Bull. Intl. Taxn. 11 (2002), IBFD Journals.

R. Pinkernell, *Ein Musterfall zur internationalen Steuerminimierung durch US-Konzerne*, 89 StuW 4 (2012).

R. Pinkernell, *Internationale Steuergestaltung im Electronic Commerce* (IFST-Schrift No. 494, IFST 2014).

P. Pistone, *An EU Model Tax Convention*, 11 EC Tax Review 3 (2002).

P. Pistone, *General Report*, in *The EU and Third Countries: Direct Taxation* (M. Lang & P. Pistone eds, Linde 2007).

P. Pistone, *The Impact of Community Law on Tax Treaties* (Kluwer 2002).

R. Portner, *Ertragsteuerliche Aspekte des E-Commerce* (IFST-Schrift No. 390, IFST 2001).

J.P. Powers, *International Tax Issues in Cyberspace: Taxation of Cross-Border Electronic Commerce*, 25 Intertax 4 (1997).

A. Rosas, *EU External Relations: Exclusive Competence Revisited*, 38 Fordham International Law Review 4 (2015).

A. Rosas, *The Status in EU Law of International Agreements Concluded by EU Member States*, 34 Fordham International Law Review 5 (2011).

R. Russo, *The 2005 OECD Model Convention and Commentary: An Overview*, 45 Eur. Taxn. 2 (2005), IBFD Journals.

R. Russo, *The 2008 OECD Model: An Overview*, 48 Eur. Taxn. 9 (2008), IBFD Journals.

A. Rust, *CFC Legislation and EC Law*, 36 Intertax 11 (2008).

A. Rust, *Controlled Foreign Company Rule (Articles 7 and 8 ATAD)*, in *A Guide to the Anti-Tax-Avoidance Directive* (W. Haslehner et al., eds, Edward Elgar Publishing 2020).

B. Salehy, *A Global Tax System? Appraising the Model GloBE Rules*, 67 BTR 5 (2022).

C.W. Sanchirico, *Should a Global Minimum Tax Be Country-by-Country?*, 25 April 2022 Tax Notes Intl. 485–494.

H. Schaumburg, *Kapitel 11 – Steuergesetzgebungskompetenz der Union*, in *Europäisches Steuerrecht* (H. Schaumburg & J. Englisch eds, 2nd ed., Otto Schmidt 2019).

T. Scherer, *Doppelbesteuerung und Europäisches Gemeinschaftsrecht* (C.H.Beck 1995).

M. Scherleitner, *Should the EU Implement a Minimum Corporate Taxation Directive?*, 2021, available at 10.2139/ssrn.3697903 (accessed 13 July 2021).

H.G. Schermers, *Community Law and International Law*, 12 Common Market Law Review 1 (1975).

W. Schickli, *Characterization of E-Commerce Revenue – The Final OECD Report Revealed*, 22 Tax Notes Intl. 14 (2001).

M. Schler, *UTPR: The CFC Precedent*, 109 Tax Notes Intl. 27 (2 January 2023).

P.K. Schmidt, *A General Income Inclusion Rule as a Tool for Improving the International Tax Regime – Challenges Arising from EU Primary Law*, 48 Intertax 11 (2020).

A. Schnitger, *Vereinbarkeit der Vorschläge zur Einführung von GloBE-Regelungen mit den Grundfreiheiten des AEUV*, 31 IStR 20 (2022).

W. Schön, *Facilitating Entry by Facilitating Exit: New Paths in EU Tax Legislation*, 46 Intertax 4 (2018).

W. Schön, *Ten Questions About Why and How to Tax the Digitalized Economy*, 72 Bull. Intl. Taxn. 4/5 (2018).

L.E. Schoueri, *Some Considerations on the Limitation of Substance-Based Carve-Out in the Income Inclusion Rule of Pillar Two*, 75 Bull. Intl. Taxn. 11/12 (2021), IBFD Journals.

P.G. Lindenberg Schoueri & R.A. Galendi, CFC*s and Tax Treaties: Historical Elements for the IIR Debate*, 51 Intertax (2023) forthcoming.

A. Schrauwen, *Sources of EU Law for Integration in Direct and Indirect Taxation*, in *Traditional and Alternative Routes to European Tax Integration* (IBFD 2010).

M. Schröder, *Art 115 – Richtlinien zur Angleichung gewisser Vorschriften*, in *EUV/AEUV* (R. Streinz ed., 3rd ed., C.H.Beck 2018).

R. Schütze, *Classifying EU Competences: German Constitutional Lessons?*, in *The Division of Competences Between the EU and the Member States* (S. Garben & I. Govaere eds, Hart Publishing 2017).

R. Schütze, *EC Law and International Agreements of the Member States: An Ambivalent Relationship?*, 9 Cambridge Yearbook of European Legal Studies 387–440 (2007).

R. Schütze, *EU Competences: Existence and Exercise*, in *The Oxford Handbook of European Union Law* (A. Arnull & D. Chalmers eds, Oxford 2015), available at 10.1093/oxfordhb/9780199672646.013.44 (accessed 19 July 2021).

R. Schütze, *European Union Law* (3rd ed., Oxford 2021).

R. Schütze, *Foreign Affairs and the EU Constitution – Selected Essays* (Cambridge 2014).

R. Schütze, *Limits to the Union's 'Internal Market' Competence(s): Constitutional Comparisons*, in *The Question of Competence in the European Union* (L. Azoulai ed., Oxford 2014).

R. Schütze, *Supremacy without Pre-Emption? The Very Slowly Emergent Doctrine of Community Pre-Emption*, 2006 Common Market Law Review 1023–1048.

J.S. Schwarz, *Transfer Pricing and Electronic Commerce*, 53 Bull. Intl. Taxn. 7 (1999), IBFD Journals.

C. Seiler, *Art 113 [Harmonisierung der indirekten Steuern]*, in *Das Recht der Europäischen Union* (E. Grabitz, M. Hilf & M. Nettesheim eds, C.H.Beck 2016).

D. Shaviro, *What Are Minimum Taxes, and Why Might One Favor or Disfavor Them?*, 40 Va. Tax Rev. 2 (2021).

S.E. Shay, J.C. Fleming & R.J. Peroni, *Designing a 21st Century Corporate Tax – An Advance U.S. Minimum Tax on Foreign Income and Other Measures to Protect the Base*, 17 Fla. Tax Review 9 (2015).

L.A. Sheppard, *Pillar 2 and QDMTT*, 105 Tax Notes Intl. 759–764 (14 February 2022).

D.S. Smit, *The Influence of EU Tax Law on the EU Member States' External Relations*, in *EU Tax Law and Policy in the 21st Century* vol. 55 (W. Haslehner, G. Kofler & A. Rust eds, EUCOTAX Series on European Taxation, Wolters Kluwer 2017).

J. Snell, *Free Movement of Capital: Evolution as a Non-Linear Process*, in *The Evolution of EU Law* (4th ed., Oxford).

G.D. Sprague & O.A. Schindler, *Another Step Towards Uniformity – Relative Consensus of the OECD TAG on Income Characterization of E-Commerce Transactions*, 30 Tax Mgt. Int'l. J. 6.

C. Staringer, *Die Anti-Tax-Avoidance-Richtlinie: Gesamtwürdigung Aus Steuerpolitischer Sicht*, in *Die Anti-Tax-Avoidance-Richtlinie* (M. Lang et al., eds, Linde 2017).

E. Stein, *External Relation of the European Community: Structure and Process*, in *Collected Courses of the Academy of European Law* vol. 1 (European University Institute 1990).

K. Stöger, *Art 351*, in *Kommentar zu EUV und AEUV* (T. Jäger & K. Stöger eds, Manz 2019).

S. Strohmayr, *Kompetenzkollisionen zwischen europäischem und nationalem Recht* (Nomos 2006).

G. Strunk, *Grenzüberschreitende Geschäftsaktivität durch das Internet als weißer Fleck der Besteuerung*, 6 IStR 9 (1997).

R. Szudoczky, *Does the Implementation of Pillar Two Require Changes to Tax Treaties?*, 33 SWI 2 (2023).

R. Szudoczky, *Is the CCCTB Proposal in Line with the Principle of Subsidiarity?: Negative Opinions Submitted by National Parliaments in the 'Yellow Card Procedure'*, in *CCCTB: Selected Issues* (D. Weber ed., EUCOTAX Series on European Taxation No. 35, Wolters Kluwer 2012).

R. Szudoczky, *The Relationship Between Primary, Secondary and National Law*, in *Research Handbook on European Union Taxation Law* (C. Panayi, W. Haslehner & E. Traversa eds, Edward Elgar Publishing 2020).

R. Szudoczky & D. Weber, *Constitutional Foundations: EU Tax Competences; Legal Basis for Tax Integration; Sources and Enactment of EU Tax Law*, in *Terra/Wattel – European Tax Law* vol. I (P.J. Wattel, O. Marres & H. Vermeulen eds, 7th ed., Wolters Kluwer 2019).

N. Tadmore, *Source Taxation of Cross-Border Intellectual Supplies – Concepts, History and Evolution into the Digital Age*, 61 Bull. Intl. Taxn. 1 (2007), IBFD Journals.

B.H. Ter Kuile, *Legal Aspects of Fiscal Sovereignty within the Internal Market*, 19 Intertax 11 (1991).

J.P. Terhechte, *Art. 351 TFEU, the Principle of Loyalty and the Future Role of the Member States' Bilateral Investment Treaties*, in *International Investment Law and EU Law* (M. Bungenberg, J. Griebel & S. Hindelang eds, Springer 2011) (accessed 7 July 2021).

C. Tietje, *Art 114 [Beschlussfassung; einzelstaatliche Regelungen; Schutzklausel]*, in *Das Recht der Europäischen Union* (E. Grabitz, M. Hilf & M. Nettesheim eds, C.H.Beck 2016).

C. Tietje, *Art 115 [Richtlinien zur Angleichung von Rechtsvorschriften für den Binnenmarkt], in Das Recht der Europäischen Union* (E. Grabitz, M. Hilf & M. Nettesheim eds, C.H.Beck 2018).

C. Tietje, *Art 116 [Beseitigung vorhandener Verzerrungen]*, in *Das Recht der Europäischen Union* (E. Grabitz, M. Hilf & M. Nettesheim eds, C.H.Beck 2018).

D.R. Tillinghast, *The Impact of the Internet on the Taxation of International Transactions*, 50 Bull. Intl. Taxn. 11–12 (1996), IBFD Journals.

A. Tomassini & M. De Rosa, *Uncertainties Hold Back Achievement of OECD Pillar 2 Goals*, 51 Intertax 2 (2023).

A. Uricchio, *Some Thoughts for E-Reforming the Tax System: Beyond the Bit Tax*, 34 Intertax 12 (2006).

US Department of the Treasury, *Selected Tax Policy Implications of Global Electronic Commerce* (1996), available at https://www.treasury.gov/resource-center/tax-policy/Documents/Report-Global-Electronic-Commerce-1996.pdf (accessed 9 July 2021).

M. Valta, *Verfassungs- und Abkommensrechtsfragen des Richtlinienentwurfs für eine Steuer auf digitale Dienstleistungen*, 27 IStR 19 (2018).

J.H.F. Van Panhuys, *Conflicts Between the Law of the European Communities and Other Rules of International Law*, 3 Common Market Law Review 4 (1966).

J.W. Van Rossem, *Interaction Between EU Law and International Law in the Light of Intertanko and Kadi: The Dilemma of Norms Binding the Member States but Not the Community*, in *Netherlands Yearbook of International Law – 2009* vol. 40 (I.F. Dekker & E. Hey eds, Springer 2010).

J. VanderWolk, *Much Ado About Pillar 2*, 108 Tax Notes Intl. 821–823 (14 November 2022).

J. VanderWolk, *Tax Treaties Pose Problems for the UTPR*, 108 Tax Notes Intl. 29 (3 October 2022).

J. VanderWolk, *The UTPR Disregards the Need for Nexus*, 108 Tax Notes Intl. 545–546 (31 October 2022).

J. VanderWolk, *The UTPR Is Far From Becoming Part of Customary International Tax Law*, 108 Tax Notes Intl. 1069–1070 (28 November 2022).

J. VanderWolk, *The UTPR Is Flawed: A Response to Prof. Picciotto*, 108 Tax Notes Intl. 285 (17 October 2022).

J. VanderWolk, *The UTPR is Inconsistent with the Nexus Requirement of Tax Treaties*, Kluwer International Tax Blog (26 October 2022), available at https://kluwertaxblog.com/2022/10/26/the-utpr-is-inconsistent-with-the-nexus-requirement-of-tax-treaties/ (accessed 22 January 2023).

J. VanderWolk, *The UTPR: Taxing Rights Gone Wild*, 108 Tax Notes Intl. 1369–1370 (12 December 2022).

J. VanderWolk, *The UTPR, Treaties, and CFC Rules: A Reply to Avi-Yonah and Schler*, 109 Tax Notes Intl. 187 (9 January 2023).

F. Vanistendael, *The Limits to the New Community Tax Order*, 31 Common Market Law Review 2 (1994).

P.G. Végh, *Facing the Challenges of Electronic Commerce (Direct Taxation)*, 41 Eur. Taxn. 4 (2001), IBFD Journals.

J. Vella, *The Two Pillar Solution One Year On*, 67 BTR 5 (2022).

T. Velling, *Pillar Two: Simplification Is Key (via Passle)*, Passle, available at https://www.europeantax.blog//post/102gp2a/pillar-two-simplification-is-key (accessed 13 April 2022).

H. Vermeulen, *Comments on Professor Yariv Brauner's Lecture 'The True Nature of Tax Treaties'*, 74 Bull. Intl. Taxn. 1 (2020).

G. Villalta Puig & C. Darcis, *The Development of European Union Implied External Competence: The Court of Justice and Opinion 1/03*, in *Anuario Espanol de Derecho Internacional* vol. 25 (2009).

K. Vogel, *Harmonisierung des Internationalen Steuerrechts in Europa als Alternative zur Harmonisierung des (materiellen) Körperschaftsteuerrechts*, 70 StuW 4 (1993).

K. Vogel, D. Gutmann & A.P. Dourado, *Tax Treaties Between Member States and Third States: 'Reciprocity' in Bilateral Tax Treaties and Non-Discrimination in EC Law*, 15 EC Tax Review 2 (2006).

K. Von Papp, *Solving Conflicts with International Investment Treaty Law from an EU Law Perspective: Article 351 TFEU Revisited*, 42 Legal Issues of Economic Integration 4 (2015).

S. Vöneky & B. Beylage-Haarmann, *Art. 216 [Vertragsschlusskompetenz]*, in *Das Recht Der Europäischen Union* vol. 60th (E. Grabitz, M. Hilf & M. Nettesheim eds, C.H.Beck 2016).

E. Vranes, *Die EU-Außenkompetenzen im Schnittpunkt von Europarecht, Völkerrecht und nationalem Recht*, 133 Juristische Blätter 1 (2011).

H. Wardell-Burrus, *Four Questions for UTPR Skeptics*, 108 Tax Notes Intl. 699–703 (7 November 2022).

H. Wardell-Burrus, *GloBE Administrative Guidance – The QDMTT and GILTI Allocation*, 2023 SSRN, available at https://papers.ssrn.com/sol3/papers.cfm?abstract_id=4347814 (accessed 28 March 2023).

H. Wardell-Burrus, *Should CFC Regimes Grant a Tax Credit For Qualified Domestic Minimum Top-up Taxes?*, 106 Tax Notes Intl. 1649–1658 (27 June 2022).

H. Wardell-Burrus, *The UTPR as a Rule of Recognition*, 108 Tax Notes Intl. 1527–1529 (19 December 2022).

P.J. Wattel, *Taxation in the Internal Market*, in *Research Handbook of the EU's Internal Market* (P. Koutrakos & J. Snell eds, Edward Elgar Publishing 2017).

S. Weatherhill, *The Competence to Harmonise and Its Limits*, in *Research Handbook of the EU's Internal Market* (P. Koutrakos & J. Snell eds, Edward Elgar Publishing 2017).

R. Weninger, *http://www.e-commerce.xy/no-tax/anonymous?! Verändert der elektronische Geschäftsverkehr die Besteuerung?*, 73 SWK 17 (1998).

A. Wintsch, *Attribution of Profits to Permanent Establishments: The 2008 Article 7 versus the 2010 Article 7 of the OECD Model Tax Convention*, 71 Bull. Intl. Taxn. 9–10 (2017), IBFD Journals.

A. Zachová, *Czech EU Presidency Aims for 15% Corporate Tax Deal by End of October*, Www.Euractiv.Com (18 July 2022), available at https://www.euractiv.com/section/politics/short_news/czech-eu-presidency-aims-for-15-corporate-tax-deal-by-end-of-october/ (accessed 6 February 2023).

A.C.M. Zaidan, *The External Tax Treaty Making Powers of the Member States: Defining Limits and Obligations under the Current European Legal Order*, 41 Intertax 5 (2013).

OECD Reports and Policy Notes

OECD/G20 Base Erosion and Profit Shifting Project, *Tax Challenges Arising from Digitalisation – Administrative Guidance on the Global Anti-Base Erosion Model Rules (Pillar Two)* (OECD 17 July 2023), https://www.oecd.org/tax/beps/administrative-guidance-global-anti-base-erosion-rules-pillar-two-july-2023.pdf (last visited 26 Aug. 2023).

OECD, *Public Consultation Document – Pillar Two – GloBE Information Return* (20 December 2022), available at https://www.oecd.org/tax/beps/public-consultation-document-pillar-two-globe-information-return.pdf (accessed 6 February 2023).

OECD/G20 Base Erosion and Profit Shifting Project, *Safe Harbours and Penalty Relief: Global Anti-Base Erosion Rules (Pillar Two)* (15 December 2022), available at https://www.oecd.org/tax/beps/safe-harbours-and-penalty-relief-global-anti-base-erosion-rules-pillar-two.pdf (accessed 6 February 2023).

OECD, *Members of the OECD/G20 Inclusive Framework on BEPS (Updated: December 2022)* (1 December 2022), available at https://www.oecd.org/tax/beps/inclusive-framework-on-beps-composition.pdf (accessed 25 March 2023).

OECD, *Tax Incentives and the Global Minimum Corporate Tax: Reconsidering Tax Incentives after the GloBE Rules* (6 October 2022), available at 10.1787/25d30b96-en (accessed 9 February 2023).

OECD/G20 Inclusive Framework on BEPS, *Tax Challenges Arising from Digitalisation –Global Anti-Base Erosion Examples (Pillar Two)* (14 March 2022), available at https://www.oecd.org/tax/beps/tax-challenges-arising-from-the-digitalisation-of-the-economy-global-anti-base-erosion-model-rules-pillar-two-commentary.pdf (accessed 22 March 2022) [hereinafter *GloBE Examples* (2022)].

OECD/G20 Inclusive Framework on BEPS, *Tax Challenges Arising from Digitalisation – The Global Anti-Base Erosion Model Rules (Pillar Two)* (20 December 2021), available at https://www.oecd.org/tax/beps/tax-challenges-arising-from-the-digitalisation-of-the-economy-global-anti-base-erosion-model-rules-pillar-two.pdf (accessed 22 March 2022) [hereinafter *GloBE Model Rules* (2021)].

OECD/G20, *Members of the OECD/G20 Inclusive Framework on BEPS*, November 2021, available at https://www.oecd.org/tax/beps/inclusive-framework-on-beps-composition.pdf (accessed 9 December 2021).

OECD, *Tax and Fiscal Policies after the COVID-19 Crisis* (14 October 2021), available at 10.1787/abb4c3d1-en (accessed 1 January 2023).

OECD, *Tax Challenges Arising from Digitalisation – Economic Impact Assessment* (14 October 2020), available at 10.1787/abb4c3d1-en (accessed 10 December 2021).

OECD, *Corporate Tax Statistics: Third Edition* (29 July 2021), available at https://www.oecd.org/tax/tax-policy/corporate-tax-statistics-third-edition.pdf (accessed 9 June 2022).

OECD/G20 Inclusive Framework on BEPS, *Statement on a Two-Pillar Solution to Address the Tax Challenges Arising From the Digitalisation of the Economy – 8 October 2021* (8 October 2021), available at https://www.oecd.org/tax/beps/statement-on-a-two-pillar-solution-to-address-the-tax-challenges-arising-from-the-digitalisation-of-the-economy-october-2021.pdf [hereinafter *OECD/G20 Statement 8 October* (2021)].

OECD/G20 Inclusive Framework on BEPS, *Statement on a Two-Pillar Solution to Address the Tax Challenges Arising From the Digitalisation of the Economy – 1 July 2021* (1 July 2021).

OECD/G20 Inclusive Framework on BEPS, *Tax Challenges Arising from Digitalisation – Report on Pillar One Blueprint* (14 October 2020), available at 10.1787/abb4c3d1-en (accessed 12 July 2021) [hereinafter *Tax Challenges Arising from Digitalisation – Report on Pillar Two Blueprint* (2020)].

OECD/G20 Inclusive Framework on BEPS, *Tax Challenges Arising from Digitalisation – Report on Pillar Two Blueprint* (14 October 2020), available at 10.1787/abb4c3d1-en (accessed 12 July 2021) [hereinafter *Tax Challenges Arising from Digitalisation – Report on Pillar Two Blueprint* (2020)].

OECD/G20 Inclusive Framework on BEPS, *Public Consultation Document – Global Anti-Base Erosion Proposal ('GloBE') – Pillar Two 8 November 2019 – 2 December 2019* (8 November 2019), available at https://www.oecd.org/tax/beps/public-consultation-document-global-anti-base-erosion-proposal-pillar-two.pdf.pdf [hereinafter *Public Consultation Pillar Two 2019* (2019)].

OECD/G20 Inclusive Framework on BEPS, *Programme of Work to Develop a Consensus Solution to the Tax Challenges Arising from the Digitalisation of the Economy* (29 May 2019), available at https://www.oecd.org/tax/beps/programme-of-work-to-develop-a-consensus-solution-to-the-tax-challenges-arising-from-the-digitalisation-of-the-economy.pdf [hereinafter *Programme of Work* (2019)].

OECD/G20 Base Erosion and Profit Shifting Project, *Addressing the Tax Challenges of the Digitalisation of the Economy – Policy Note – As Approved by the Inclusive Framework on BEPS on 23 January 2019* (23 January 2019), available at https://www.oecd.org/tax/beps/policy-note-beps-inclusive-framework-addressing-tax-challenges-digitalisation.pdf (accessed 30 March 2023).

OECD, *Tax Challenges Arising from Digitalisation – Interim Report 2018: Inclusive Framework on BEPS* (16 March 2018), available at 10.1787/9789264293083-en (accessed 3 February 2023).

OECD/G20, *Preventing the Granting of Treaty Benefits in Inappropriate Circumstances, Action 6: 2015 Final Report* (5 October 2015), available at 10.1787/abb4c3d1-en (accessed 29 October 2022) [hereinafter *BEPS Action 6: 2015 Final Report* (2015)].

OECD/G20, *Transfer Pricing Documentation and Country-by-Country Reporting, Action 13: 2015 Final Report* (5 October 2015), available at 10.1787/abb4c3d1-en (accessed 23 May 2022) [hereinafter *BEPS Action 13: 2015 Final Report* (2015)].

OECD/G20, *Base Erosion and Profit Shifting Project: Measuring and Monitoring BEPS, Action 11: 2015 Final Report* (5 October 2015), available at 10.1787/abb4c3d1-en (accessed 10 December 2021) [hereinafter *BEPS Action 11: 2015 Final Report* (2015)].

OECD/G20, *Designing Effective Controlled Foreign Company Rules, Action 3 – 2015 Final Report* (5 October 2015), available at 10.1787/abb4c3d1-en (accessed 29 October 2022) [hereinafter *BEPS Action 3: 2015 Final Report* (2015)].

OECD, *Addressing the Tax Challenges of the Digital Economy, Action 1 – 2015 Final Report* (5 October 2015), available at 10.1787/9789264241046-en (accessed 3 February 2023).

OECD, *Report on the Attribution of Profits to Permanent Establishments* (22 July 2010), available at https://www.oecd.org/ctp/transfer-pricing/45689524.pdf (accessed 9 July 2021).

OECD, *Report on the Attribution of Profits to Permanent Establishments* (17 July 2008), available at https://www.oecd.org/tax/transfer-pricing/41031455.pdf (accessed 9 July 2021).

OECD, *Draft Contents of the 2008 Update to the Model Tax Convention* (2008), available at https://www.oecd.org/tax/treaties/40489100.pdf (accessed 9 July 2021).

OECD, *Report on the Attribution of Profits to Permanent Establishments, Parts I (General Considerations), II (Banks) and III (Global Trading)* (2006), available at https://www.oecd.org/tax/transfer-pricing/37861293.pdf (accessed 9 July 2021).

OECD Technical Advisory Group on Treaty Characterization of Electronic Commerce Payments, *Are the Current Treaty Rules for Taxing Business Profits Appropriate for E-Commerce?* (2005), available at http://www.oecd.org/ctp/treaties/35869032.pdf (accessed 9 July 2021).

OECD, *Discussion Draft on the Attribution of Profits to Permanent Establishment – Part I (General Consideration)* (2 August 2004), available at https://www.oecd.org/ctp/transfer-pricing/33637685.pdf (accessed 9 July 2021).

OECD, *Discussion Draft 27 May 2003 – Place of Effective Management Concept: Suggestions for Changes to the OECD Model Tax Convention*, available at https://www.oecd.org/tax/treaties/2956428.pdf (accessed 9 July 2021).

OECD, *Action Plan on Base Erosion and Profit Shifting* (19 July 2013), available at https://www.oecd.org/ctp/BEPSActionPlan.pdf (accessed 23 March 2023).

OECD, *Addressing Base Erosion and Profit Shifting* (12 February 2013), available at https://read.oecd-ilibrary.org/taxation/addressing-base-erosion-and-profit-shifting_9789264192744-en (accessed 3 February 2023).

OECD, *Implementation of the Ottawa Taxation Framework Conditions – The 2003 Report* (2003), available at https://www.oecd.org/tax/administration/20499630.pdf (accessed 9 July 2021).

OECD Technical Advisory Group on Monitoring the Application of Existing Treaty Norms for the Taxation of Business Profits, *The Impact of the Communications Revolution on the Application of 'Place of Effective Management' as a Tie Breaker Rule – February 2001* (2001), available at http://www.oecd.org/tax/treaties/1923328.pdf (accessed 9 July 2021).

OECD Technical Advisory Group on Treaty Characterization of Electronic Commerce Payments, *Tax Treaty Characterization Issues Arising from E-Commerce, Report to Working Party No. 1 of the OECD Committee on Fiscal Affairs* (2001), available at http://www.oecd.org/tax/consumption/1923396.pdf (accessed 9 July 2021).

OECD, *Taxation and Electronic Commerce: Implementing the Ottawa Taxation Framework Conditions* (2001), available at https://www.oecd.org/tax/consumption/Taxation%20and%20eCommerce%202001.pdf (accessed 9 July 2021).

OECD Committee on Fiscal Affairs, *Electronic Commerce: Taxation Framework Conditions* (1998), available at https://www.oecd.org/ctp/consumption/1923256.pdf (accessed 9 July 2021).

OECD, *The Tax Treatment of Software* (1992), available at https://www.oecd-ilibrary.org/docserver/690f0e4a-en.pdf?expires=1625867446&id=id&accname=ocid177428&checksum=94DB83A48D3E1C1119B5830F2DC61307 (accessed 9 July 2021).

Table of Cases

ECJ, EGC and EFTA-Court

BE: ECJ, 8 December 2022, Case C-694/20, *Orde van Vlaamse Balies*, ECLI: EU:C:2022:963, 475

HU: ECJ, 16 March 2021, Case C-562/19 P, *Commission v. Hungary*, ECLI: EU:C:2021:201, 489

PL: ECJ, 16 March 2021, Case C-596/19 P, *Commission v. Poland*, ECLI:EU:C:2021:202, 489

SE: ECJ, 20 January 2021, Case C-484/19, *Lexel AB v. Skatteverket*, ECLI:EU:C:2021:34, 483

HU: ECJ, 8 December 2020, Case C-620/18, *Hungary v. Parliament and Council*, ECLI:EU:C:2020:1001, 476, 488

HU: ECJ, 3 March 2020, Case C-75/18, *Vodafone Magyarország Mobil Távközlési Zrt.*, ECLI:EU:C:2020:139, 482

PL: ECJ, 27 March 2019, Case C-545/17, *Mariusz Pawlak v. Prezes Kasy Rolniczego Ubezpieczenia Społecznego*, ECLI:EU:C:2019:260, 388

DE: ECJ, 26 February 2019, Case C-135/17, *X GmbH v. Finanzamt Stuttgart*, ECLI: EU:C:2019:136, 483

DK: ECJ, 26 February 2019, Case Joined Cases C-117/16 and C-117/16, *Skatteministeriet v. T Danmark*, ECLI:EU:C:2019:135, 405

DK: ECJ, 26 February 2019, Case Joined Cases C-115/16, C-118/16, C-119/16 C-299/16, *N Luxembourg 1 v. Skatteministeriet*, ECLI:EU:C:2019:134, 405

DE: ECJ, 5 December 2017, Case C-600/14, *Federal Republic of Germany v. Council of the European Union (COTIF)*, ECLI:EU:C:2017:935, 441, 443–445, 447, 448

IR: ECJ, 22 November 2017, Case C-251/16, *Edward Cussens and others v. T.G. Brosnan*, ECLI:EU:C:2017:881, 405

EU: ECJ, 16 May 2017, *Opinion 2/15 (Free Trade Agreement Singapore)*, ECLI: EU:C:2017:376, 439, 441, 446–449, 458, 467, 468

PL: ECJ, 7 March 2017, Case C-390/15, *RPO*, ECLI:EU:C:2017:174, 476, 488

PT: ECJ, 24 November 2016, Case C-464/16, *SECIL*, ECLI:EU:C:2016:896, 481

UK: ECJ, 10 December 2002, Case C-491/01, *British American Tobacco (Investments) Ltd and Imperial Tobacco Ltd*, ECLI:EU:C:2002:741, 387, 388, 401, 424–426, 428, 477, 488

UK: ECJ, 5 November 2002, Case C-466/98, *Commission of the European Communities v. United Kingdom of Great Britain and Northern Ireland*, ECLI:EU:C:2002:624, 353

AT: ECJ, 5 November 2002, Case C-475/98, *Commission of the European Communities v. Republic of Austria (Open Skies)*, ECLI:EU:C:2002:630, 355,

DE: ECJ, 5 November 2002, Case C-476/98, *Commission of the European Communities v. Federal Republic of Germany (Open Skies)*, ECLI:EU:C:2002:631, 448

NL: ECJ, 9 October 2001, Case C-377/98, *Kingdom of the Netherlands v. European Parliament and Council (Directive on legal protection of biotechnical inventions)*, ECLI:EU:C:2001:523, 424

NL: ECJ, 12 July 2001, Case C-189/01, *Jippes*, ECLI:EU:C:2001:420, 426, 433, 477

DE: ECJ, 14 December 2000, Case C-110/99, *Emsland-Stärke GmbH v. Hauptzollamt Hamburg-Jonas*, ECLI:EU:C:2000:695, 404

DE: ECJ, 5 October 2000, Case C-376/98, *Germany v. Parliament and Council (Tobacco Advertising)*, ECLI:EU:C:2000:544, 378, 379, 387, 388, 390, 402, 409, 410

PT: ECJ, 4 July 2000, Case C-62/98, *Commission of the European Communities v. Portuguese Republic*, ECLI:EU:C:2000:358, 352, 353, 358, 360-362

PT: ECJ, 4 July 2000, Case C-84/98, *Commission of the European Communities v. Portuguese Republic*, ECLI:EU:C:2000:359, 352, 360-362

NL: ECJ, 6 June 2000, Case C-35/98, *Staatssecretaris von Financiën v. B.G.M Verkooijen*, ECLI:EU:C:2000:294, 347, 378, 420

DE: ECJ, 26 October 1999, Case C-294/97, *Eurowings Luftverkehrs AG v. Finanzamt Dortmund-Unna*, ECLI:EU:C:1999:524, 408, 411, 420, 483

DE: ECJ, 21 September 1999, Case C-307/97, *Compagnie des Saint-Gobain v. Finanzamt Aachen-Innenstadt*, ECLI:EU:C:1999:438, 347

BE: ECJ, 14 September 1999, Case C-170/98, *Commission of the European Communities v. Kingdom of Belgium*, ECLI:EU:C:1999:411, 360

DE: ECJ, 14 September 1999, Case C-391/97, *Frans Gschwind and Finanzamt Aachen-Außenstadt*, ECLI:EU:C:1999:409, 378

EU: ECJ, 8 July 1999, Case C-245/92 P, *Chemie Linz GmbH v. Commission*, ECLI:EU:C:1999:363, 404

GE: ECJ, 29 April 1999, Case C-311/97, *Royal Bank of Scotland plc*, ECLI:EU:C:1999:216, 483

BE/LU: ECJ, 11 June 1998, Case C-176/97 and 177/97, *Commission of the European Communities v. Kingdom of Belgium and Grand Duchy of Luxembourg*, ECLI:EU:C:1998:285, 360

FR: ECJ, 12 May 1998, Case C-336/96, *Mr and Mrs Robert Gilly v. Directeur des services fiscaux du Bas-Rhin*, ECLI:EU:C:1998:221, 345, 347

DE: ECJ, 10 March 1998, Case C-364/95 and 365/95, *T. Port GmbH & Co. and Hauptzollamt Hamburg-Jonas*, ECLI:EU:C:1998:95, 356

LU: ECJ, 25 June 1997, Case C-114/96, *René Kieffer and Romain Thill*, ECLI:EU:C:1997:316, 477

Advocate General Opinions

Table of Treaties and Models

Table of EU Official Documents and Reports of EU Institutions

EC Commission, *Report of the Committee of Independent Experts on Company Taxation (Ruding Report)* (1992), 406

EC Commission, *Report of the Committee of Independent Experts on Company Taxation* (1992), 346

EC Commission, *Tax Policy in the European Union – Priorities for the Years Ahead*, Communication from the Commission to the Council, the European Parliament and the Economic and Social Committee (10 October 2001), COM(2001) 260 final, available at https://eur-lex.europa.eu/legal-content/EN/TXT/PDF/?uri=CELEX:52001DC0260&from=EN (accessed 30 March 2023), 380

EC Commission, *The Development of a European Capital Market* (1966), 346

EC Commission, *The EEC Reports on Tax Harmonization (Neumark Report 1962), Translation H. Thurston* (IBFD 1963), 389

EC Commission, *Vorentwurf zu einem Europäischen Doppelbesteuerungsabkommen, Dok 11.414/XIV/68-D* (1.7.1968), 346

EC Economic and Social Committee, *Opinion on Direct and Indirect Taxation, 19. March 1996, No C 82/49* (1996), 346

European Commission, *Communication from the Commission to European Parliament and the Council – An Action Plan for Fair and Simple Taxation Supporting the Recovery Strategy*, COM(2020) 312 final (15 July 2020), 28

European Commission, *Communication from the Commission to the Council, the European Parliament and the Economic and Social Committee – Towards and Internal Market without Tax Obstacles*, COM(2001) 582 final (23 October 2001), 406

European Commission, *Communication from the Commission to the Council, the European Parliament and the European Economic and Social Committee – Co-Ordinating Member States' Direct Tax Systems in the Internal Market* (19 December 2006), COM(2006) 823 final, available at 10.1163/2210-7975_HRD-4679-0058 (accessed 2 February 2022), 345

European Commission, *Communication from the Commission to the European Parliament and the Council – Business Taxation for the 21st Century* (18 May 2021), COM(2021) 251 final, available at 10.1163/2210-7975_HRD-4679-0058 (accessed 30 March 2023), 29, 366, 375, 383, 456, 479, 496

European Commission, *Communication from the Commission to the European Parliament, the European Council and the Council – Towards a More Efficient and Democratic Decision Making in the EU Tax Policy*, COM(2019) 8 final (15 January 2019), 382

European Commission, *EC Law and Tax Treaties* (9.6.2005), DOC(05)23306, 346

European Commission, *Follow up to the European Parliament Non-Legislative Resolution on the European Parliament Report on Financial Crimes, Tax Evasion and Tax Avoidance (TAX3 Report)*, 2018/2121 (INI) (March 2019), available at https://www.politico.eu/wp-content/uploads/2019/08/A8-0170-2019-EN.pdf?utm_source=POLITICO.EU&utm_campaign=8eb14ec3bc-EMAIL_CAMPAIGN_2019_08_05_05_36&utm_medium=email&utm_term=0_10959edeb5-8eb14ec3bc-190490293 (accessed 4 December 2021) [hereinafter *Follow up to the European Parliament (TAX3 Report)* (2019)], 417

European Commission, *Inception Impact Assessment – New EU System for the Avoidance of Double Taxation and Prevention of Tax Abuse in the Field of Withholding Taxes*, Ref. Ares(2021)5900310 (28 September 2021), 496

European Commission, *Report of the Commission Expert Group on Taxation of the Digital Economy* (28 May 2014), available at https://www.diplomacy.edu/wp-content/uploads/2021/10/COMMISSION-EXPERT-GROUP-ON-TAXATION-OF-THE-DIGITAL.pdf (accessed 30 March 2023), 23

European Council, *Press Release 12 December 2022 – International Taxation: Council Reaches Agreement on a Minimum Level of Taxation for Largest Corporations* (12 December 2022), available at https://www.consilium.europa.eu/en/press/press-releases/2022/12/12/international-taxation-council-reaches-agreement-on-a-minimum-level-of-taxation-for-largest-corporations/ (accessed 6 February 2023), 32

Council of the European Union, *Information Note From the Legal Service to the Permanent Representative Committee (Part 2) – Doc. 08476/23* (24 April 2023), 474

European Parliament Recommendation following the inquiry on money laundering, tax avoidance and tax evasion, OJ C 369/132 (2017), 421

European Parliament, *European Parliament Resolution of 26 March 2019 on Financial Crimes, Tax Evasion and Tax Avoidance*, 2018/2121(INI) (26 March 2019), available at https://eur-lex.europa.eu/legal-content/EN/TXT/PDF/?uri=CELEX:52019IP0240&rid=7 (accessed 28 July 2021), 389

European Parliament, *Motion for a Resolution – European Parliament Resolution of Fair Taxation in a Digitalised and Globalised Economy: BEPS 2.0, B9-0238/2019* (12 December 2019), available at https://www.europarl.europa.eu/doceo/document/B-9-2019-0238_EN.pdf (accessed 27 January 2022), 28, 375, 414

Note from the Council Presidency to the Permanent Representatives Committee/Council, 2018/0073(CNS) 7420/18 FISC 151 ECOFIN 277 DIGIT 48 IA 78 (2019), 24

Note from the Permanent Representatives Committee (Part 2) to Council on the Directive on ensuring a global minimum level of taxation for multinational groups in the Union, 2021/0433(CNS) 6976/22, FISC 62/ECOFIN 200, 31

Note from the Presidency to Council on the Council Directive ensuring a global minimum level of taxation for multinational enterprise groups and large-scale domestic groups in the Union, 2021/0433(COD) 15349/22, FISC 241/ECOFIN 1251 (2022) (accessed 5 February 2023), 32

Opinion of the Economic and Social Committee on Taxation in the European Union – Report on the development of tax systems, OJ C 296/37 (1997) (accessed 8 July 2021), 382

Opinion of the European Committee of the Regions – Towards a more efficient and democratic decision making in EU tax policy, OJ C 404/6 (2019), 414

Opinion of the European Economic and Social Committee on COM(2018) 147 final and COM(2018) 148 final, 2018/0072(CNS) FISC 325 ECOFIN 767 (2018), 24

Index

Q

R

S

www.ingramcontent.com/pod-product-compliance
Lightning Source LLC
Chambersburg PA
CBHW071235230926
51849CB00001B/106
* 9 7 8 9 4 0 3 5 3 2 8 7 5 *